Andrew Carnegie

Andrew Carnegie

ANDREW

CARNEGIE

Joseph Frazier Wall

UNIVERSITY OF PITTSBURGH PRESS

Published by the University of Pittsburgh Press, Pittsburgh, Pa., 15260
Copyright © 1970 by Oxford University Press
Copyright © 1989 by the University of Pittsburgh Press
All rights reserved
Baker and Taylor International, London
Manufactured in the United States of America

Library of Congress Cataloging-in-Publication Data

Wall, Joseph Frazier.
  Andrew Carnegie / Joseph Frazier Wall.
    p. cm.
  Originally published: New York: Oxford University Press, 1970.
  Bibliography: p.
  Includes index.
  ISBN 0-8229-3828-6
  ISBN 0-8229-5904-6 (pbk.)
  1. Carnegie, Andrew, 1835–1919. 2. United States—Biography.
3. Philanthropists—United States—Biography. 4. Industrialists—United States—
Biography. 5. Steel industry and trade—United States. I.Title.
CT275.C3W33 1989
973.8'092'4—dc19
[B]   88-38160
                                                 CIP

FOR ALLAN NEVINS

Teacher, Mentor, and Friend

Contents

CONTENTS

Preface to the Second Edition

In the acknowledgments to the first edition of this biography, published by Oxford University Press in October 1970, I wrote, "A preface . . . traditionally serves as an introduction of the reader to the book, and as such it seems to this author to be quite unnecessary. A book, particularly a biography, should introduce itself. Here is a man and here is his life, as seen by his biographer. Meet him within the pages of the text, and depending upon the skill and understanding of the biographer, no special introduction to the subject outside of the text is needed." This was a sentiment with which I felt that the reader, struggling merely to hold this massive tome, would surely agree.

Except for a disavowal of its implied sexism, I still hold to the above statement. Once again, however, I find myself observing the conventions of the publishing world by offering to the overly assiduous consumer of the printed word a preface for this new edition. The only valid reason for so doing is to call attention to the fact that in the intervening two decades since this book's initial publication, a few additional studies of Andrew Carnegie have appeared which merit the attention of the reader interested in this subject. These works include most notably Harold C. Livesay's short but excellent evaluation of Carnegie's business career, *Andrew Carnegie and the Rise of Big Business* (Boston: Little, Brown, 1975); George Swetnam's highly eulogistic study of Carnegie as a writer and orator, *Andrew Carnegie,* in Twayne's United States Authors Series (Boston: Twayne, 1980); and Margaret Ann Farrah's insightful doctoral dissertation, "Andrew Carnegie: A Psychohistorical Sketch" (Pittsburgh: Carnegie Mellon University, 1982). In addition, I have written, at the request of Andrew Carnegie's daughter, Margaret Carnegie Miller, and with the support of the Carnegie Corporation of New York, a short history of the Carnegie estate in Scotland, *Skibo* (New York: Oxford University Press, 1984), which deals in the last two chapters with the story of the Carnegie family after Andrew's death in 1919.

Each of these monographs would have been quite useful in providing depth as well as breadth to my presentation had these works been available to me at the time I wrote this biography. It is, however, the decision of both Frederick A. Hetzel, director of the University of Pittsburgh Press, and me to republish *Andrew Carnegie* just as it originally appeared, with no additions, no deletions, and no corrections. There are certainly changes that could have been made, but the basic theme of this book—Carnegie's continuing attempt to reconcile the entrepreneurial success and the paramountcy within the American plutocracy which he achieved as an adult with the egalitarian and radical Scottish Chartist ideals of his childhood, an attempt which provides the main tension and complexity to his life—remains a sound thesis, I am convinced. I am quite willing to say once again, "Here is Andrew Carnegie, and here is his life, as seen by this biographer."

Joseph Frazier Wall

Grinnell College
September 1988

Acknowledgments

A preface, like a dust jacket, is part of the publisher's form. It traditionally serves as an introduction of the reader to the book, and, as such, it seems to this author quite unnecessary. A book, particularly a biography, should introduce itself. Here is a man and here is his life, as seen by his biographer. Meet him within the pages of the text, and, depending upon the skill and understanding of the biographer, no special introduction to the subject outside of the text is needed.

But a preface also fulfills another and quite necessary purpose. It permits the author, who has pursued a particular topic for many months, and in this instance many long years, to acknowledge those who have helped him in his pursuit. Being an iconoclast by nature, I should like to reverse the form by elevating what is usually a postscript to first position, by thanking my wife, Beatrice Mills Wall, for her assistance in every function basic to the making of a book: critic, editor, typist, indexer, and fellow traveler down whatever road my research took me.

And these roads were many, long, and seldom dull. Some of the people who made the journey possible and pleasant are:

Margaret Carnegie Miller, Andrew Carnegie's only child, who most graciously encouraged me in this undertaking. When I first met her at her home in New York and announced that I wished to write a biography of her father, her response, characteristically, was, "I hope that you will write an honest biography of my father and tell his life as it was." This I have tried to do to the degree that any man can depict another man, with all of his complexities, his weaknesses, and strengths.

John Gardner, then president of the Carnegie Corporation of New York, and Florence Anderson, Secretary, who gave generously of their time and interest in this project. Miss Anderson even accompanied me to Hoboken, New Jersey, to the garret of the Home Trust Company office building, where, in the heat of that dusty attic, we sorted through the papers of Robert Franks, Andrew Carnegie's business secretary.

J. W. Ormiston, executive secretary of the Carnegie Dunfermline Trust, who gave to me the "freedom of the city" of the Auld Grey Toon. For his generous help, I can never adequately express my appreciation.

Professor George S. Shepperson of the University of Edinburgh, who during my year as a Fulbright research scholar in Scotland, became a close friend and colleague in our mutual interest in American and Scottish history. And also to J. R. Peddie of the Carnegie Dunfermline Trust for the Universities of Scotland and David Lowe of the Carnegie United Kingdom Trust, who made accessible important materials on Carnegie foundations.

The librarians in the manuscript divisions of the New York Public Library and the Library of Congress where the major collections of Andrew Carnegie's papers are housed.

Mr. L. L. Lewis and Miss Louise Bowman of the Law Department of the United States Steel Corporation in Pittsburgh, who gave me free access to the exceedingly important collection of letter books and business files of Andrew Carnegie during his earliest ventures into business. These papers had not previously been made available to any scholar outside of the United States Steel Corporation, and they proved to be absolutely essential to this biography.

My colleagues at Grinnell College and the several generations of Grinnell College students who not only endured but encouraged this project.

My children, Ane, Joel, and Julie, who also endured—through

long years and many travels, and were willing to live with Andrew Carnegie, like Banquo's ghost, at the dinner table. My daughter Ane, in particular, engaged in research assistance when I needed it most.

Sheldon Meyer, Leona Capeless, and Caroline Taylor of Oxford University Press, who read, edited, and corrected this manuscript.

Finally, Allan Nevins, to whom this book is dedicated, who first suggested this biography to me.

I have provided no bibliography other than the bibliographical information given in the notes. Andrew Carnegie, to the delight of any biographer, was a prolific writer, and an absentee employer, who insisted upon full written reports and complete Board minutes of his companies' operations. To the degree that any man leaves a record of his life in the written word, Andrew Carnegie did.

J. F. W.

Grinnell, Iowa
1 June 1970

PART I

THE
CHARTER
1835 - 1853

"My childhood's desire was, to get to be a man and kill a king."
Carnegie to W. T. Stead, 1897.

*

"Death to Privilege."
Motto on the escutcheon designed by Carnegie as the family coat of arms.

*

"We have the Charter."
Carnegie to George Lauder, 1853.

CHAPTER I

Prologue
Dunfermline 1835

Twenty years after the Napoleonic War, and Britain, once fearful but now proud in her isolation, stood alone as the dominant power in the world. Watchdog of the seven seas, workshop foreman of the world, welder of empires, her position appeared invulnerable. Already historically minded Europeans were comparing their century to that one other period in human history when concentrated power had brought order and security to turbulent civilization—the second century after Christ—and, either in pride or in envy, were calling their age *Pax Britannica*.

It was a peace, however, that had been won only after a protracted struggle that had involved all of Europe and much of the rest of the world. Moreover, the fact that the shopkeeper should eventually have defeated the laurel-crowned Emperor could only mean that any historical comparison with Rome would be inaccurate. For power was now manifest in a new form, and it had been the old Roman imperial dream that had been defeated at Waterloo, defeated by new forces that had yet to create their myths and symbols of glory. The smoke of factories had proved more potent than the smoke of artillery, however brilliantly employed, and Caesar, it was believed, was forever dead.

3

But if the Emperor Napoleon had been defeated on that June day in Belgium, it could not be forgotten that he was a self-crowned Emperor who had once been a corporal, and that he had risen to power not through dynastic inheritance, but through disruptive revolution. Caesarism might be sent in chains to Saint Helena, but that revolutionary force which had been its progenitor was not so easily exiled. Legitimacy and established order were easy words to say at Vienna, but along the waterfronts in Naples and the factory rows in Manchester there were those other words—liberty, equality, and fraternity—that could not be completely erased. The very forces that had first created and then defeated Napoleon were still alive, and neither Wellington nor Metternich, after using these forces, could now succeed in turning them back.

The ruling Establishment in Britain during these twenty years since Waterloo had found its own position becoming ever less secure. It was cruel irony that Britain, so triumphant in India, must be so fearful at home. Expecting gratitude from the people for saving their homes from invasion, the ruling class had found only sullen suspicion and distrust. In response to that proud boast of Wellington, that Waterloo had been won on the playing fields of Eton, the working people posed the hard question, "And what has been won for us on the battle field of Waterloo?" and then gave their own bitter, mocking answer: "Peterloo!"

The two parties of the Establishment, the Whigs and the Tories, had tried both repression and reform: shooting down workers in peaceful assembly at the St. Peter's Field Meeting in Manchester (the Peterloo Massacre) and granting the first change in Parliamentary representation since the reign of Charles II. This policy of vacillation had failed. It had neither allayed the fears of the classes nor reduced the demands of the masses. In 1819, the poet Robert Southey, while touring northern Britain, wrote in his journal, "There is at this time a considerable ferment in the country." And in the following year, a Mr. Macqueen of Lanarkshire, writing to the Duke of Hamilton in a more frantic if less sympathetic tone, warned, "The actual force ready to attack us consists of *many thousands*. Look at this and say if there is no danger in the country." [1]

4

Thirteen years later, following the Great Reform Act of 1832, the Duke of Wellington wrote in despair to Stanhope, "We are going, but I think it will be gradually. There will be no catastrophe; we are not equal to one. . . . [I would] do anything to quit this unfortunate and unhappy country." [2]

Nor could the monarchy be relied upon as a symbol of national loyalty and unity. During the long period of the Regency, while George III lived out the last thirty years of his reign in madness, and especially during the succeeding reigns of his two sons, George IV and William IV, the Hanoverian family had achieved the seemingly impossible by making itself both scandalous and dull at the same time. The romance of nationalism lay not with the gouty German Georges, but rather with the departed dreams of the Stuart pretenders or with the anticipated hopes of the Paine republicans.

Britain, in this year of 1835, presented itself as a curious paradox of power and impotency, of imperial grandeur without an imperium, of the greatest accumulated wealth in history and the worst slums in Christendom. Nowhere else was agriculture so heavily subsidized, yet one would have to search out the meanest hovels in Galicia or Sicily to find such rural poverty as existed in the Highland *bothies* of Scotland.[3] As Charles Dickens would write of another period, but in so doing aptly describe his own, "It was the best of times, it was the worst of times, it was the age of wisdom, it was the age of foolishness . . . it was the spring of hope, it was the winter of despair, we had everything before us, we had nothing before us, we were all going direct to Heaven, we were all going direct the other way . . ."

But why the hope and why the despair? With her immense wealth, her great power, what more could Britain hope for? And by the same measure, how could any Briton, however lowly his station, despair? Did not the knowledge that the sun never set on his Empire add savor enough to his porridge; knowing the rich source, did he not find the smoke-filled air sweet to breathe; was he not the most privileged, the freest man in all Europe, just because he was a Briton? Had not the House of Lords and the King —against their better judgment—yielded to the demands of the people and granted that which the people said was all they ever wanted, the Great Reform Act of 1832? Why then this continuing tension? These were the anxious questions that the men in Whitehall, in Apsley House, in Downing Street would ask, but could not answer.

There were no easy answers to these questions, for although the symptoms of unrest were the same throughout Britain, the causes were quite different. There was the Highland cotter, driven from his miserable black house in Sutherland to an even more abject and surer starvation in the city; there was the underpaid collier, only recently freed from serfdom, pushing mole-like through ever deeper and narrower veins of coal in Wales or Fife; there were the underemployed factory worker and his overemployed child, beseeching the cotton textile mill of Manchester or the pottery factory of Stoke for their crumbs of existence; there was the Irish peasant, whose sharp hunger for land was whetted by frustrated nationalism; and, most dangerous of all, there was the skilled handcraftsman, the weaver or cobbler, threatened by the factory machine that sought to take away not only his livelihood but also his pride. A curious assortment, this opposition to the Establishment. Its numbers could be counted in the millions and could be found from John o' Groats land in the far north to Lands End in Cornwall. These were the members of the "Disestablishment," and in 1835 their hopes and their despairs were forces to be reckoned with by those who had once so naïvely thought that the defeat of Napoleon would mean the end to all danger and strife.

Public disorder, to be sure, was not a peculiarity of this postwar period. The eighteenth century had not been a period of tranquillity, but the English nobleman or Scottish laird, who of necessity had hired bodyguards to protect his sedan chair when he ventured out into the streets in broad daylight, and who had carefully planned his dinner parties for three o'clock in the afternoon so that his guests might be safely home before nightfall, had feared only robbery or personal abuse. When there were instances of general public disorder, as the Calico and the Turnpike Riots in the early decades of the eighteenth century, they were spontaneous, and limited to specific and immediate objectives.[4] Even the great Meal Riots, so widespread throughout Britain in the 1760's and 1770's that they represented real threats to public order, had lacked any kind of organization and had raised no basic political issues.

But the French Revolution had changed all this. It had given dissatisfaction a rallying cry, and, by example, it had showed that any order, however ancient, could be changed. The fall of the Bastille in Paris on 14 July 1789 had evoked a popular response in Britain which the Establishment had not anticipated. Robert Burns spoke for the people when he wrote:

> Heard ye o' the Tree o' France,
>   And wat ye what's the name o't?
> Around it a' the patriots dance—
>   Weel Europe kens the fame o't!
> It stands where ance the Bastille stood—
>   A prison built by kings, man,
> When Superstition's hellish brood
>   Kept France in leading-strings, man.
>
>   .   .   .
>
> I'd give the shoon frae aff my feet,
>   To taste the fruit o't here, man;
> And blythe we'll sing, and herald the day
>   That gives us liberty, man.

Burns's readers had heard of the Tree of Liberty, and they were already busily planting its seedlings throughout Britain. The Society of the Friends of the People, originally formed in London in April 1792 by Richard Sheridan, the Earl of Lauderdale, and other moderate Whigs to offset the more Radical groups such as the London Corresponding Society, became itself more Radical as local chapters were formed in northern England and Scotland. Tom Paine's *Rights of Man* was widely distributed and read by the chapters throughout Britain—and, as a hero of two revolutions, Paine had a great impact upon the British. In Aberdeen, the sailors, with a cry of "Liberty, Equality and no King," went on strike, and throughout Scotland, Henry Dundas, Home Secretary in the Pitt ministry and virtual dictator of Scotland, was burned in effigy.[5]

The excesses of the Reign of Terror in France and the government's appeal to national patriotism in time of war did much to bank the fires of radicalism when Britain prepared for a death struggle with the revolutionary French armies.[6] Even Robert Burns put on a uniform and served in the Home Guards, and radicalism throughout Britain seemed to be effectively stamped out. Dundas's power was more oppressive than ever, and repression was the answer to all suggestions of reform. But the fires were only banked; they still smouldered. And, finally, they broke out in the great conflagration of 1832.

Whatever the various depressed groups in Britain might ultimately seek in the way of remedial action—repeal of the Poor Law, repeal of the Corn Laws, land reform, or even the impossible hope of turning back to handcraft industry—they could all unite under the banner of political democracy.

It is a mistaken notion that men who are hungry have no political interests and are concerned only with filling their bellies. The great revolutions of the nineteenth and twentieth centuries show that men will almost invariably seek political panaceas for economic ills. This faith in political change is our inheritance from the French Revolution, and all of us, Americans, Chinese, Russians, and Congolese, are its legatees. The depressed classes in Britain in 1835 were no exception. With threats of revolution they had got the Reform Act of 1832, but as an amelioration of their condition it had proved to be a cruel illusion. It had only broadened the base of the Establishment, had added recruits to the oppressors. Now, in this late autumn of 1835, Britain was waiting in hope and fear for the next great popular demonstration for political reform.

Nowhere in all Britain was hope for reform more apparent than in the ancient town of Dunfermline, the largest parish in the county of Fife, Scotland. Located some fourteen miles northwest of Edinburgh and three miles from the Firth of Forth, Dunfermline took pride in being the first capital of an united Scotland under Malcolm Canmore and his pious wife Margaret, when Edwines-burgh was only a minor fortification, built to protect Scotland from the threat of English invasions from the south. Here in the Glen, beside the crooked Lyne burn which was to give Dunfermline its name, Malcolm, following his victory over Macbeth, had built his castle tower, and his wife had built her first church. Here too their even more pious son, David I, "a sair sanct for the Crown," began the construction of the great Abbey, which was to serve as the Scottish counterpart of Westminster Abbey, as a burial place for Scottish royalty. By the nineteenth century, close to the ravine through which the burn flowed, there stood only a single wall, like a badly constructed stage flat. It was all that remained of the royal palace of Scotland. The unhappy Mary Stuart once held court in this palace, and her equally ill-fated grandson, Charles I, was born here, in a room where the aperture of the fireplace still could be seen like a punctured hole in the flat wall.

The proudest relic of the past, however, was the tomb of Robert the Bruce, which was found in 1818, when workmen were excavating for the foundations of the new church Abbey that was to connect with the nave of the old Norman Abbey of King David's reign. The skeleton was still wrapped in its shroud of gold and linen threads. After scholars had verified it as the remains of the heroic Bruce, it was placed in a lead coffin filled with melted pitch and reburied behind the pulpit of the new church. To commemorate for all time this most auspicious discovery, the design for the great central tower of the church was changed so that it would be topped on its four sides with letters four feet high, spelling out the words: KING ROBERT THE BRUCE.[7] So the two Abbeys stand together today, sharing a common back wall, but separated in time by 800 years: the one a handsome preservation of Scottish Norman architecture at its best; the other a remarkable illustration of the false pretense of latter-day Gothic perpendicular, its bizarre lettered tower a permanent testimonial to the decline in architectural taste and style over the millennium from the age of William of Normandy to the time of William of Hanover.

If the people of Dunfermline took pride in the glories of their remote past, they were more concerned with the problems associated with their more immediate situation. For Dunfermline, in the first decades of the nineteenth century, had become essentially a one-industry town. To be sure, the coal mines immediately north of the town, around the small community of Townhill, and the better agricultural lands south of Dunfermline, where oats, barley, potatoes, and some wheat were grown, were important to the economic life of the community. But linen weaving dominated all other economic activities in the burgh. In this year of 1835, the burgh of Dunfermline had a population of approximately 11,500 people.[8] Of this number, 5044 persons—men, women, and children—nearly half of the total population, were

9

employed in the linen weaving industry.[9] These figures would indicate, even by a conservative estimate, that at least two-thirds of the persons in the community were directly dependent upon this single industry of weaving for their subsistence.

The first historical record of weaving in Dunfermline annals is the notation of 10 January 1491, that six weavers appeared in the magistrate's court on the charge of being "strubblers," or disturbers of the peace,[10] an appropriate introduction into history of a craft which would so notably and so frequently be guilty of the same charge in the centuries that lay ahead.

The earliest weaving of linen in Dunfermline was primarily of coarse material—ticks, checks, and huck-a-buck, used for mattress and pillow casings as well as work clothes. In the summer months, however, when there were many more hours of daylight, the better weavers would also produce finer linen or diapers for tablecloths.[11] The union of Scotland and England in 1707, which had opened up the entire English Empire to Scottish commerce, served as an impetus to the development of the linen trade throughout Scotland, but the greatest boost to Dunfermline weaving came after 1718, with the introduction of damask cloth weaving. A young weaver named James Blake, hearing stories of the wonderful new cloth of fine linen woven in many beautiful designs by a secret process known only to the weavers of neighboring Drumscheugh, was determined to bring the process to the weavers of his native Dunfermline. The legend among all Scottish weavers is that Blake, posing as a village idiot, wandered into Drumscheugh, and by his idle babbling and vacant smiles gave so convincing a performance that he threw the damask weavers completely off guard. He was permitted to wander freely among the looms, where his quick mind made mental note of every detail of the complicated machinery. Hurrying back to Dunfermline, he made drawings of what he had seen, and soon he had a loom—the first successful damask loom in operation in that city.[12] From that time on, Dunfermline monopolized the damask weaving trade of Scotland and the world. By 1835, of the 3517 looms in Dunfermline, 2249 were for the weaving of damask and the remainder for diapers, worsted warps, and bed-quilts.[13]

Many and wonderful were the designs that could be produced on these damask looms: thistles, unicorns rampant, roses, and even portraits. In 1734, that same James Blake wove for the Friendly Society of Weavers its craft guild flag, a large silk damask ensign with a different pattern on either side. On one side, surrounded by a design of trees, weaving shuttles, swords, and other decorative symbols, was the weavers' ensign: a boar's head with a shuttle in its mouth and the weaver's motto "Trust with Truth." On the other side was a lion rampant, encircled by a border of Scottish thistles, with a crown and St. Andrew's cross at the top, and the appropriately bold words *"Nemo me impune lacessit."* This flag served as the weavers' colors, and it was carried proudly at the head of all parades in Dunfermline for over a century.[14] It was Henry Meldrum, however, who became the great hero of his craft: in 1808, after many attempts, he succeeded in weaving a seamless shirt, the ancient ambition of all handloom weavers.[15]

This pride in artistry is indicative of the damask weavers' attitude toward their craft. They would always regard themselves in the same occupational class as goldsmiths, jewelers, and cabinet-makers. They had nothing in common with and little sympathy for the blackened and uneducated coal miners of neighboring Townhill and Muircockhall. Nor had they any desire to become mere slaves of a machine, as were the cotton weavers of Lanarkshire and Manchester. They were a guild, a profession, and they jealously guarded their ancient prerogative.

Linen weaving in Scotland, however, had always felt itself pressed by other textiles, particularly wool. Although woolen goods were not directly competitive with linen, Scotland had long resented the favored treatment that wool had been given in England. One of the great fears among the linen weavers concerning union with England at the beginning of the eighteenth century had been that in a united country English woolen interests would dictate to the Scottish linen industry. So great was this distrust of wool that, in spite of the advantages of the free market the union of the two kingdoms would provide, the people of Dunfermline instructed their Parliamentary delegate, Sir Peter Halkett, to vote against union—to which instructions Sir Peter cheerfully assented and then just as cheerfully ignored when the final vote was taken.[16] Although the fears of the linen weavers did not materialize and the linen industry prospered in the years after the union

11

as never before, the linen weavers remained apprehensive. As the industry grew and the flax growers of Scotland could no longer begin to meet the demands of the ever-increasing number of looms for more thread, the weavers sought direct government action to protect their source of raw material. In 1790, the Scottish economist, John Naismith, served as their spokesman when he attacked the Scottish writer, James Anderson, for favoring wool over linen. "Fashion may, on occasion, run against linen for a time," Naismith wrote, but, he added, "its long approved excellence for the service of the body, the bed, and the table, will always render it so acceptable and even so necessary for many purposes that scarce any will find it convenient to dispense totally with the use of it." He urged direct subsidies to farmers that would be high enough to encourage them to put some of the land now used for sheep-grazing into the growing of flax.[17]

By the time of Naismith's writing, however, wool and linen were finding themselves more and more in an unaccustomed alliance against a new threat in the textile industry—cotton. Before the 1700's, cotton, like silk, had been a luxury fabric, and not a direct competitor of either of the two basic textiles of Britain. But in the eighteenth century there had come that remarkable series of inventions affecting the spinning and weaving of cotton which historians would label the beginning of the Industrial Revolution. Within a generation, calico and gingham had become the dress of Cinderella—not when she went to the royal ball, but when she sat by the kitchen fire. Cotton sheeting, cotton table cloths, and cotton shirting rolled off the great power looms of Britain in a never-ending stream. By the 1830's the cotton hand-loom weavers of Paisley and Glasgow had either given up their special craft and accepted the machine, or, more likely, they sat home in sullen unemployment while their wives and children trooped off to the mills. A Parliamentary report in 1835 revealed what had happened to the weavers' wages with the coming of the machine. In 1804, the average weekly wage of the cotton hand-loom weaver in Glasgow was twenty shillings. By 1834, it had dropped to five shillings sixpence. In more descriptive language, the report pictured the workers of Glasgow as dressed in rags, and unable to attend church for lack of suitable clothing. Instead, "they take skulking walks in the country on a Sunday." [18]

It is not surprising that the linen weavers of Dunfermline

should feel they were caught between the two stones of a grinding mill. They could hardly hope to compete with the low prices for cotton unless the linen industry became industrialized, but industrialization of their trade could only mean the end of their craft. Many aspects of their trade had already been industrialized, to be sure. Once all of the linen threads used in weaving had been produced by hand spinning wheel within the district itself. Now, virtually all of the thread was imported, produced by the great powered spinning factories in Belfast, Leeds, and Preston. The fly shuttle, a simple device that made it possible for one man to work the loom, instead of three, had been invented in 1778 by John Wilson, a Dunfermline weaver, and the weavers themselves had paid honor to and quickly accepted it. More recently, a new loom had been invented by a French straw hat manufacturer in Lyons, Joseph Jacquard. Alexander Robertson had already introduced its use in Dunfermline, and it threatened to revolutionize the weaving of damask by making it possible for any weaver to produce designs more complicated and intricate than any ever dreamed of by James Blake.[19] With these inventions, it was illogical for the damask handloom weaver to deny that the next step in changing the industry would be the introduction of the power loom. Actually the first power loom for damask had already been built in the county of Fife at Kircaldy in 1821, and although it had not been a great success, the damask handloom weavers were deluding themselves if they thought it would not eventually be perfected.[20]

But in Dunfermline in 1835, there was still a little time for delusions, and the handloom weavers hoarded this time. They wanted to believe that their eighteen shillings a week would continue unaffected by the five shillings sixpence pay of the cotton weavers. They still had their pride in artistry, their belief in community, and their sense of continuity with the past. Shutting their eyes to the realities of economics, they waited for the political panacea that would solve these vexing problems and preserve their ancient and honorable craft. So they cursed the stupid old king and his more stupid ministers sitting in far-off, alien London, talked of Corn Law repeal, and dreamed

> That sense and Worth o'er a' the earth
> Shall bear the gree an' a' that!

13

For a' that an' a' that,
It's comin' yet for a' that,
That man to man the world o'er
Shall brithers be for a' that.

And all the while the busy looms kept clacking out the fine damask linen with its beautiful designs. This was the weavers' reality—their world.

CHAPTER II

The Inheritance

1740-1835

The *Dunfermline Almanack and Register for 1835* duly recorded that on Wednesday, 25 November 1835, the sun rose at 7:52 a.m. and set at 3:40 p.m. But the few persons who ventured outside on that miserably cold and wet day would have had to take the *Almanack*'s word that the sun rose or set at all, for precious little light managed to get through the rain and mist that fell all day on the "Auld Grey Toon." [1]

Those fortunate few who had sevenpence, and could afford to buy *The Scotsman,* Edinburgh's leading newspaper, which made its semi-weekly appearance on that day, would have noted that the major news item was the death of the popular poet, James Hogg, "the Ettrick Shepherd." "It is our melancholy duty to announce the death of James Hogg, the most distinguished peasant that Scotland has ever produced, with the single exception of his great prototype, Burns. . . . His 'Queen's Wake' alone will carry his name to the latest posterity." His funeral would be held on Friday, the 27th, at his residence on the banks of the Yarrow.

Two other items of literary interest were a brief review of the seventh volume of Boswell's *Life of Johnson,* and a notice of the English publication of *Democracy in America,* written by an un-

15

known young French writer, M. de Focqueville (the correct spelling of his name was still unknown to *The Scotsman*). "We recommend this as the very best on the subject of America we have ever met with." As the Scots had considerable interest both in America and in democracy, it was an appropriate book for *The Scotsman* to review.

On the subject of top interest, the weather, *The Scotsman* had sensational news to report. One of the worst gales in the memory of man had hit Aberdeen and Petershead four days before, perhaps the cause of the bad weather the Lowlands region was now having. Also "a dreadful accident" was reported: on the other side of Scotland, near Greenock, a dam had burst, flooding the entire village of Cartsdyke.[2] November gave promise of a stormy winter ahead.

The bad weather kept trade at the monthly fair to a minimum and most of the farmers and merchants were only too willing to close their stalls early and start for home before it was entirely dark. The weavers, too, had had a poor day because of the darkness. Those ambitious enough to work after the evening meal might, if they could afford it, make use of the single jet gas flame permitted them. Dunfermline had had gas lighting since 1828, but its use was carefully rationed by the local gas company. A weaver might have one flame near his loom, turned not more than three inches high, to be used only at specified hours—from 6 a.m. to sunrise, and from sunset until 10 p.m. Few weavers could afford the cost of eight shillings sixpence for the use of this service, and generally those who had to work after sunset used the same primitive lighting that they used in their living quarters: crusies, the small two-wicked lamps fed with foul-smelling fish oil, or tallow candles.[3] On this night, most of the weavers were happy to retire early, hoping to find in their beds a little of the warmth they had sorely missed all day.

By eight o'clock nearly all the weavers' cottages were dark, and outside, the rainswept streets, lacking even the light from the quarter moon, were dark and nearly deserted. Only the four dials of the town hall clock, lighted by gas for the first time this past year, like four cloud-misted moons cast their dim lights over the town.[4]

But at the corner of Moodie Street and Priory Lane, in the

low one-and-a-half story cottage that was the home and workshop
of the weaver William Carnegie, the lights would continue to
burn until late that night. All day, in spite of the rain, there had
been much traffic up to the front street door, and anxious inquiries made. The loom, usually so busy, had been quiet since early
morning. The weaver's wife, Margaret, had for hours been in
labor with her first child, who was finally safely delivered. Her
girlhood friend, Ailie Ferguson Henderson, who had served as
midwife, hurried down the steep narrow steps to tell the man,
waiting in near darkness by his loom, that he had just become the
father of a fine, healthy son.[5]

Now, in the evening hours, the family and a few close friends,
as was the Scottish custom, would gather in the single small attic
room that served as the Carnegie living quarters. They would
congratulate the mother, who was lying propped up in the small
bunk bed, for even though she was small of stature, the bed was
too short for her to lie full length upon it. They would beam at
the small baby lying by her side and approve of his being named
Andrew, for in Scotland the first son is usually named after the
paternal grandfather. They would comment upon his unusually
large head—"Morrison brains," Uncle Tom Morrison would say.
Then they would partake of the small cakes and the caudle,
which the thoughtful Ailie "Fargie" had provided, and sip the
whisky which William would proudly but carefully measure out
into the single glass that must serve the entire company.[6]

It was also the custom in the Lowlands for the visitors to
bring on a birth-night small gifts for the baby and the mother.
Except for Seaton Lauder, Margaret's oldest sister, whose husband
owned a grocer's shop on High Street, most of these callers could
have afforded to bring very little. A bit of ribbon, perhaps, a
horn spoon, or a piece of fine linen or a hand-me-down baby
dress. But however meager the tangible gifts might be, the two
families, the Carnegies and the Morrisons, now gathered together
to celebrate this birth, were giving to the child a rich inheritance.

There was first of all, the gift of his surname, a not unusual
name in Scotland, belonging in common to peasant and nobleman, to the Carnegies of Pattiemuir, the child's direct ancestors,
and to the Earls of Northesk and Southesk, holders of vast estates,
to whom he could claim no direct relationship. Carnegie was orig-

17

inally a Celtic place name, derived from the Gaelic words *caither
an eige,* "fort at the gap." The first appearance in history of Carnegie as a family name is on a charter, issued by David II in 1350,
from which the Earl of Southesk traced his lineage.[7]

The earliest direct ancestor of that name to whom the infant
Andrew could lay direct claim was his great-grandfather, James
Carnegie, who appeared in the little village of Pattiemuir, three
miles south of Dunfermline, sometime during the 1760's. Nothing
was known of his past, and his romantically inclined descendants
liked to think that he was perhaps a grandson of Sir James Carnegie, the fifth Earl of Southesk, who, having fought on the side of
James Stuart, the Old Pretender, in the rebellion of 1715, had
died in exile in France in 1729. It was possible that Sir James's
son had also taken up the cause of the Stuarts, and having fought
in vain for Bonnie Prince Charlie in 1745, had sought exile in
the remote Highlands, raising his children to respect the secret of
their past. At any rate, James Carnegie never spoke of his childhood or his parents. He seemed content to settle down in Pattiemuir, to become a weaver like most of his neighbors, and to
marry a local girl, Charlotte Walker. The only bit of evidence
pointing to a more romantic and noble past was based on an incident that occurred in 1770, when James, active in the Meal Riots
of that year, was imprisoned for seditious activity. While in
prison he was visited by a mysterious lady, who spoke earnestly to
him, and then, upon leaving him, gave him a jeweled snuff box
with the initials J.C. and the date 1712 on the cover.[8] James
never explained either the visit or the gift, and the family had
only the small snuff box upon which to build their legends.

That James had tried his hand at weaving before arriving in
Pattiemuir is doubtful, but in this small community he became a
good weaver and was sufficiently prosperous to feed and clothe a
large family. His oldest son, Andrew, was probably born about
the time that James was sent to prison. He, too, took up his father's trade of weaving and eventually took over his father's loom.

In the late eighteenth century in such small communities as
Pattiemuir, the weavers were still entirely independent of any outside mercantile controls. As weavers had been doing since the
Middle Ages, a Pattiemuir weaver, upon the completion of a web,
would strap the finished piece upon his back and set off to find a

market for his product. Because the roads were bad and there was always the danger of robbery, two or three weavers usually traveled together to the larger towns in the area. But Andrew, who feared no living man, and who always sought adventure in life, would go off alone, trudging the roads to Stirling, Perth, or Edinburgh, and singing loudly the many ballads and songs that he knew.

It was perhaps on one of these selling trips that Andrew first met Elizabeth Thom, the daughter of a wealthy ship owner in the neighboring port of Limekilns. Thereafter Andrew's journeys to Edinburgh by way of Limekilns must have become more frequent, for his suit prospered. The proud Captain Thom, however, had no desire to have his daughter and heiress marry an impecunious weaver, and he threatened her with the loss of her patrimony should she carry out her plans to marry the Pattiemuir weaver. But Elizabeth was no timid young lady, and family lore would relate how she stood up boldly to her father and said, " 'Tis better to marry for love and work for siller than to marry for siller and work for love." With this declaration of independence she went off to Pattiemuir as Andrew's bride.

Elizabeth got what she had sought—much love, many children, and precious little siller. She had no regrets, not even when her father gave to each of her three sisters a ship from his fleet for their marriage dowry. She did, however, belatedly seek a reconciliation with her family. When the Thoms intimated that if she and Andrew would name their next child after someone on their side of the family, they would be pleased to resume their relationship again, Elizabeth readily assented and promised that the next child if a boy would be named after her father, and if a girl, after one of her sisters. The child was a girl, and on baptismal day, the proud Thom family gathered in the small Limekilns Secessionist Church for the reconciliation. But Andrew Carnegie had his sense of pride and dignity too, and when the Reverend Mr. Hadden asked for the child's name Andrew spoke out sharply, "She is to be called Ann for my aunt of the same name." The Thoms indignantly left the church, and no further communication between the Thoms and the Carnegies was ever attempted.[9]

Such bitterness was unusual in Andrew Carnegie's relations with his fellowmen. He had a lively curiosity and a great love for life that was contagious. Pattiemuir depended upon him for its intellectual stimulation and its good times. It was he who began and was the leader of the famous "College" of Pattiemuir. In a long, narrow, single-roomed cottage in the center of the village, the weavers and farmers of Pattiemuir would gather almost nightly for informal seminars which Andrew, as the self-appointed "Professor," would lead. "The discussions never lagged, even though radicalism was the sentiment common to all. The participants, well fortified with malt whisky, were equal to any topic—theological, philosophical, political, or economic that might be presented." [10] The community had, almost in a body, supported the Erskine Secessionist movement from the Established Church of Scotland, and had long had a tradition of Radical political thought, as evidenced by James Carnegie's participation in the Meal Riots. Andrew accepted his father's theological and political doctrines, and if his work at the loom suffered from his avocational interests in a way James's had never done, he was not overly concerned. With a Micawber-like faith that the future could take care of itself, Andrew attended political rallies, country dances, and kirk sessions, and participated with a vigor and enthusiasm that his contemporaries never forgot. One old man in Pattiemuir told Andrew's grandson many years later, "Eh, mon. I ha'e seen the day when your grandfaither and I could ha'e hallooed ony reasonable man oot o' his jidgment." [11] Whether dressing up in a costume and mask and going out with the children on Hogmanay Night, or at the age of sixty-five dancing the liveliest steps of the country dances at his son's wedding, Andrew was so exuberant that some of his more sober neighbors would always refer to him as that "daft callant Andra Carnegie."

"Daft Andra" could not welcome his small grandson with a silver drinking cup or a handsome sum of money, but he did welcome him with boisterous good humor. Years later this grandson would acknowledge his inheritance from his grandfather by writing: "I think my optimistic nature, my ability to shed trouble and to laugh through life, making 'all my ducks swans,' as friends say I do, must have been inherited from this delightful old masquerading grandfather whose name I am proud to bear." [12]

As William Carnegie's family had been skilled weavers for three generations, Margaret's family, the Morrisons, had been shoemakers for at least the same length of time. But, unless one is willing to give credence to antique snuff boxes, the Morrisons belonged to a higher social class than the Carnegies. The Clan Morrison is probably of Scandinavian origin, coming into Scotland during the great Norse migrations of the ninth and tenth centuries, when the Northmen conquered and populated the Shetlands, Orkneys, the Western Isles, and the most northern part of the mainland of Scotland, which is still today called Sutherland, being the southernmost county of the Norse conquest. The Morrisons were first to be found on the island of Lewis, in the far northwest, where for generations they carried on a clan feud with the MacLeods. When the Clan MacKenzie acquired the island of Lewis in 1610, over the claims of both the Morrisons and the MacLeods, many of the Morrisons began moving southward into Perthshire and adjacent counties. John Morrison, Margaret Morrison's earliest direct ancestor of whom there is positive record, was born around 1740. He established himself in Edinburgh as a prosperous leather merchant. His two sons, Thomas and Robert, were given a good education for that day, and Thomas, Margaret's father, later took over his father's leather business in Edinburgh. He married Ann Hodge, the daughter of a well-to-do Edinburgh merchant. The Morrisons appeared to be well-established in Scotland's capital city. Margaret's oldest sister and brother, Seaton and Tom, Jr., could remember living in a fine house in Edinburgh and having their own ponies to ride.[13] But Thomas made some unwise speculative investments, and before his fourth child, Margaret, was born he had lost his father's business and his wife's inheritance. The unfortunate results of his speculations left the family with a tradition of shunning stock market ventures.[14]

After this financial loss, the Morrisons moved to Dunfermline, where Thomas, having as a young man learned the cobblers' trade in his father's leather shop, became a leading shoemaker in the town. In a celebrated article, "Heddekashun and Handication," which he later wrote for William Cobbett's *Political Register* and which Cobbett called "the best communication I ever received in my life for the *Register*," Morrison concluded, "Blessed be God, I learned in my youth to make and mend shoes: the awls were my resource and they have not failed me." [15]

Whether Thomas Morrison had had Radical leanings prior to

his financial losses is not known, but it was soon apparent after his arrival in Dunfermline that radicalism in eastern Scotland had found a new and powerful voice. Accepting the political leadership of those Radicals who, since the days of the Friends of the People in the 1790's, had planned land confiscation and still dreamed of a new and more Glorious Revolution for Britain, Thomas Morrison remolded Dunfermline radicalism into his own design. Having little patience for such ephemeral dreams as the dividing into equal shares of Pittencrieff estate, the largest single landholding in Dunfermline, and entirely out of sympathy with the dreams of violent, bloody revolution, Morrison proposed for his group of Radicals a program of political action and non-violent resistance that would serve as a basis for the later Chartist movement in east Scotland. Although his large family made great demands upon his time and limited resources, particularly after the death of his wife in 1814, Morrison was always ready to travel the roads of Fife, speaking at political rallies, heckling the supporters of the Establishment, and drumming up enthusiasm for reform among the working classes. His pen was as facile as his tongue, and his Edinburgh education served him in a way that his father might not have approved.[16]

By the late 1820's, Morrison had organized the skilled craftsmen of Dunfermline into "The Political Union," which had as its motto, "Knowledge, Union, Fraternization," and as its rallying principle, "Agitation is the order of the day—the night of monastic ignorance is passed." [17] Having kept in close contact with Cobbett and other English Radicals, Morrison and his followers were ready for the great political agitation that led to the Reform Act of 1832.

It is difficult for us today, in light of the many political changes that have occurred in Britain in the past 130 years, to understand the hysteria surrounding this first great political reform of the 1830's. Those who opposed it did so with pictures of Buckingham Palace in flames and tumbrils loaded with their human cargo rolling toward a guillotine in Trafalgar Square. Those who fought for it did so with promises of victorious cotters reclaiming their land from the sheep, happy craftsmen whistling at their work, and well-fed children trooping off to public schools. It was this vision of the promised land that Tom Morrison, like a latter-day Moses on Mount Pisgah, showed to the children of Dunfermline.

The liberally inclined Scottish statesman, Henry Cockburn, Solicitor General in the ministry of Earl Grey, gave in his journal a vivid picture of Scotland in those months. On 14 November 1831, after the defeat of the Reform bill in the House of Lords, he wrote, "The whole country is still in a most excited and uncomfortable state, but disgraced by no violence. Political unions have been very generally formed. The Edinburgh one . . . held a meeting of about 4000 to 8000 upon Arthur's Seat." And again, on 26 April 1832, "There was another Reform meeting held here on the 24th—the greatest that ever took place in Edinburgh. . . . The Trades assembled in the Meadows, and walked there with banners and music, and when the whole were convocated some calculated there were 20,000, and others 60,000 present." [18] Undoubtedly there were members of Dunfermline's Political Union, headed by Morrison, in that gathering. On 8 May, Dunfermline held its own Great Reform Procession: 400 persons marched and the whole town turned out to watch.[19] Two weeks later, Cockburn, again writing in his journal, described the mood of the country, "What a fortnight the last has been! . . . But for the restraint of the Whigs, who everywhere put themselves at the head of the people, revolution would unquestionably have broken out. . . . I never before actually felt the immediate presence of a great popular crisis. I advise nobody to create it. The fearful part of it was the absence of riot. There was nothing to distract the attention, or to break the terrible silence—nothing but grave looks. . . ." [20]

On 7 June 1832, after the Tories' desperate efforts to form a ministry had failed and the distraught William IV had agreed to the Whigs' demands that he create new peers if it should seem necessary in order to ensure the successful passage of the bill, the House of Lords yielded to the inevitable and the Reform bill became law. Two months later the Act was extended to include Scotland, and the jubilant Cockburn wrote, "The regeneration of Scotland is now secured! Our Reform Bill has become law. . . . The Tory party, as such, is extinguished. . . . In a few years the Whigs will be the Tories, and the Radicals the Whigs." [21]

On 10 August, the Liberals and Radicals of eastern Scotland

gathered on the Bruntsfield Links in Edinburgh to celebrate the victory. The weavers of Dunfermline were there, proudly carrying James Blake's silken ensign, and, in all, 15,000 workers paraded, while the huge crowd, in a burst of newly found patriotism, sang *God Save the King* and *Rule Britannia*—as well as *Scots Wha' Hae Wi' Wallace Bled*.[22]

It was a glorious day, but for the ultra-Radicals, including Morrison, who were present for the celebration, the Reform Act was but the first step in their program which would call for universal suffrage and equal representation in Parliament. These men were eager to bury the old Tory party and to fulfill Cockburn's prophecy of converting the Whigs into Tories and themselves into the second party of the nation.

On that day, although it still lacked a name and a point-by-point program of action, Chartism was born. Paradoxically, at the same time, although neither Radical, Liberal, nor Conservative had the vision to see it, Chartism was killed. Radical leaders such as Morrison might cheer Whig Reform as the first step to universal suffrage, and the Tory Establishment might curse the Whigs for having opened the door to mobocracy, but both extremes were blind to their real heroes and villains. The Tories should have been passing resolutions praising the moderate Whig leadership of Grey and Russell, which had by its action delayed political democracy in Britain for two generations. And in the tumultuous weeks just passed, the Radicals, instead of burning the Duke of Wellington in effigy, might better have placed their hopes in his Bourbon-like attempts to stop the hands of time. Had the Duke insisted upon his original plan of seizing power and ruling the country by military force in that dangerous spring of 1832, nothing—certainly not his small army, consisting of soldiers of doubtful loyalty to the older order—could have prevented the immediate realization of the Radicals' political hopes. Britain would have had a genuine political revolution, carried on by a spontaneous and overwhelming majority.[23] Instead, the great crowds gathered that summer throughout Britain to cheer the Whigs, the King, and the quarter-loaf of reform that had been given. They were unwittingly cheering the counterrevolution to a revolution that had never occurred. They dispersed in a glow of patriotic satisfaction, and never again could they be so easily assembled, however diligently the Chartists might work. There would be protest meetings and petitions and even violence in the next fifteen years, but the effective alliance between the Liberal middle class and the Radical working class had been broken. It would not be realized again until the twentieth century. Britain would inch forward, not explode, into political democracy.

With the possible exception of a few astute Whig leaders, no one in Britain realized what had been won or lost in those June days of 1832. Certainly Thomas Morrison did not. He was at once busy preparing his country for a continuation of the revolution that he regarded as barely begun. The Political Union of Dunfermline changed its name to The Dunfermline Universal Sufferage [sic] Association, with the stated purpose of working peacefully for political democracy "so long as . . . Reasonable hopes can be entertained of carrying our Charter by such means." [24]

Morrison also notified his larger public outside of Dunfermline—by means of the newspaper columns in the *Glasgow Free Press*—that he was at work writing what he hoped would be an important document for the cause. "The inalienable rights of the Poor to support from the land rents, will be shown in a Lecture, to be delivered soon, and afterwards published,—On the Rights of Land; in which the claims of the Land Lords will be repelled, and the rights of the community established on principles of Justice and Utility. Published and sold by Thos. Morrison, Senior. Maygate, Dunfermline." [25]

This essay which Morrison promised his readers may have been delivered in a public lecture, but there is no record that it was ever published. The original manuscript, neatly written in Morrison's precise hand, still exists, a most literate and flamboyantly provocative statement of pre-Chartist thought.

Morrison began his essay by stating that "the rights, as they are called, of Land Lords are of four kinds: and I hope to shew that each and all of them are *wrong:* the titles being founded in usurpation and maintained in justice." The four claims to land rights which he summarily dismissed were: (1) the right of squattage, or first possession; (2) the right of conquest; (3) the right of inheritance, which he found the most damnable of all; and (4) the right of purchase.

Going beyond Thomas Spence's early proposals for land reform, and anticipating by some fifty years Henry George's arguments, Morrison's solution to the land problem was the immediate nationalization of all land, with the income earned above the amount actually acquired by the exertion of labor to be returned to the state for the benefit of all. "Our rule is *Each shall possess; all shall enjoy;* Our principle, *universal and equal right;* and our 'law of the land' shall be *Every man a lord; every woman a lady; and every child an heir.* Call you this robbery? It is *justice* strict and impartial." [26] He criticized Bentham for not going far enough in his statement of the greatest happiness to the greatest number, preferring instead the doctrine of the greatest happiness of all, but he saved his harshest indictment for the "accursed Malthusians."

Morrison concluded his essay with a bitter denunciation of wealth and privilege: "Behold the condition of those who have made the poor to be poor, and remember that wealth is only one element of happiness; that virtue is rarely its companion, that without virtue wealth ceases to be a cause of happiness, nay becomes a positive increment of misery." He quoted Robert Burns on Poosie Nancy and her girls and then mocked the titled ladies of the realm, the Marchioness of Connyngham and the Countess of Jerseys, who performed the same function in society, only at a higher price.[27] Finally he condemned what he called

The little aristocracies of Grocerdom! and Grazierdom, of Manufacturedom and Merchantdom—the Knobocracy—the tyranny of the rising middle class and their unhappiness and fear—fear lest they may slip and have to work. . . . As for the working men the most numerous and meritorious class, ask them if they have happiness in this Bentham world. . . . They will answer Happiness! We scarcely know what it is. Our growth has been stunted in childhood; our corporeal frames are wasted in manhood; our minds are paralyzed and stultified, from scanty, coarse food, with constant wearisome incessant toil. We have no time to be good, no leisure to be wise. . . . Perhaps some little piecer walking more than twenty miles a day with motion continuous as that of the rollers which he feeds, inattentive to your question will ask you "When shall we have the ten-hour bill?" and you will stave the child off with a monody over the miseries of the blacks, a lamentation for their *slavery* and an exortation [sic] to thankfulness for its white skin and blessed *freedom* and you will give it a preachment of piety and a dissertation on political economy and the principles of "free-trade"—of free trade in the bones, muscles and sinews of factory children. I will reply for the child. . . . Curse your hypocracy [sic]; blast your economy.[28]

Toward this stricture against wealth Thomas Morrison's grandson would at a much later date express himself, somewhat laconically: "My Grandfather Morrison's book and his essay. A great man for his day. Andrew Carnegie, N.Y. Dec. 2, 1903."

In October 1832, Morrison's friend and political associate, William Cobbett, came to Dunfermline on his tour of Scotland and Wales. An epidemic of cholera, which had struck England earlier in the year, was now widespread in southern Scotland, but in spite of the danger of infection a large crowd gathered to hear Cobbett "harrangue them," as he himself expressed it, "on the necessity of driving out at the door . . . any candidate, who, offering himself as their representative, should have the audacity to tell them that it was beneath him to pledge himself to do that which they wanted him to do for them." After the lecture, Cobbett met with Morrison and his political group, "the intelligent and zealous men of Dunfermline," and together they planned their future campaigns.[29] Significantly, neither Morrison nor Cobbett saw universal suffrage and equal representation as ends in themselves, but only as means to the ends of general economic and social reforms. This was a distinction many later Chartists were to forget.

It may have been at this meeting with Cobbett that Morrison got the inspiration for starting a Radical newspaper in Dunfermline, for it was soon after this that he began serious preparations for his journalistic venture. The paper was to be called *The Precursor;* it was to be published monthly and was to sell for twopence a copy. Morrison had hopes of becoming the journalistic voice of radicalism throughout eastern Scotland, and he announced that *The Precursor* would "be devoted to the interests of the Tradesmen and Mechanics in particular." The first issue, a four-page paper, carrying no advertising, was published in Dunfermline, and appeared in January 1833. Unfortunately no copies

27

of this first issue are known to exist now, but apparently it was considered so inflammatory as to be almost seditious. No printer in Dunfermline would handle the copy for the second issue. Morrison, undaunted, walked to Edinburgh with his copy and there found a Radical printer who would publish it for him.[30] The second issue appeared as scheduled, on Friday, 1 February 1833.[31] Its tone was justifiably triumphant over the fact that it had appeared at all, but its tone was more moderate than that expressed in his essay on "The Rights of Land." Morrison denied that his paper could be described as advocating "levelling principles."

> We say,—honour to wisdom and worth, comfort and independence to industry and frugality; the accidents of birth we regard not, titles and orders we despise; and *mere wealth* we will not worship. If this is "levelling," we plead guilty to the charge; but if we are represented as enemies to all distinction in society and as desirous . . . of making an equal division of property without regard to the respective merits of the producers and just rights of the holders; we despise the charge, and the ignorant or wicked beings who prefer it, too much to descend to a refutation.[32]

This statement was something of a retreat for the man who in his earlier essay had praised "the Christian and Owenian economy of having '*All things in common.*'"[33] But it was not enough of a retreat to silence critics or to give it a wider circulation. After one more issue, *The Precursor* quietly expired.

Old Tom Morrison was not defeated by the failure of his paper. He continued writing for any journal that would print his words, and he could still strike terror in the hearts of his political opponents. For all of his grand visions of total reform, Morrison was a realist and something of a gradualist. Small skirmishes were as important for total victory as great battles, and he would expend as much energy in a local Parliamentary contest as he did in working for a nationwide general strike. During these years the representative in Parliament for the Stirling district, which included Dunfermline, was the young Tory nobleman, Lord Dalmeny. This unfortunate young man not only had to suffer the indignity of constant heckling by Morrison and his son, Tom, Jr., whenever he had to appear on the public platform in his district; he also had to put up with the many lengthy communiqués from the Dunfermline cobbler even when he was far away in London. Whenever Lord Dalmeny opened a letter that began, "I will offer you a short advice and a little instruction," he knew without looking at the signature the identity of his correspondent. During the 1834 campaign Lord Dalmeny received the following communication from Morrison:

My advice to you is—Remain at Home; you will not succeed: at least, I hope you will not succeed . . . for your success would be injurious to the public weal, and disgraceful to the constituency which should again elect you. For,

1st, You are a Lord. The interests of Lords and Commoners are not identical; they are different, nay opposite; . . . and as a question respecting the construction of the House of Lords and perhaps another,—namely whether there shall be any Lords at all will be tried in next parliament, to send you to it as our representative would be like the sheep choosing the wolf to regulate their policy. . . .

2dly, You are too young for a Legislator. You want information; you want experience; you want judgment. . . . Tarry, my Lord, at Dalmeny Park till your beard be grown. . . .

3rdly, I doubt whether Nature ever intended you for a legislator. Your recitation in Maygate Chapel . . . defective in grammar, wretched in composition, clumsy and ambiguous in style, and unmeaning as to idea or sentiment, with other circumstances which from delicacy to your lordship [!] I avoid mentioning, all tend to convince me that you have not the talents necessary for a representative of the people. . . .

Now, my Lord, . . . if you want to learn the art [of being a legislator], I will tell you how to acquire it, that is, if you have the capacity. First, you must read and study, reason and reflect. Then you must mix in society with the people of all grades, and every condition of life. Of the higher aristocracy you know enough, perhaps too much, already: try next the second order; and go downwards . . . till you come to the "Hop and Raisin" sort. Next make yourself acquainted with the producing part of the community, with those who till the land, build the houses, make the clothes—who in short, support you in luxury and themselves in life: . . . follow the track of my apprentice master

[Cobbett] through Ireland: see what he has seen, and so minutely and pathetically described—the same cabin inhabited by the ass, the pig, the father, the mother, the children; and this and vast deal more misery, in one of the most fertile countries in the world—could your Lordship see all this and then go to Parliament and vote for a coercion Bill?

. . . Should your Lordship think, as you probably will, that I have not written in a style sufficiently respectful, I assure you I do not wish to give unnecessary pain; but I have a duty to perform to my townsmen and countrymen, which must not be compromised. You may hear from me again.[34]

Lord Dalmeny could be sure that he would hear from Morrison again—many times. His faithful correspondent could be almost as irritating when, on rare occasions, he wrote to praise an action of Lord Dalmeny as when he wrote in condemnation. Maddeningly patronizing in tone, like a teacher attempting to coach a feebleminded child, Morrison would write:

Your vote for continuance of the malt tax was very bad, but you have made an atonement by supporting the resolution of Lord John Russell. It is for this, My Lord, I enrol your name among the names of Cobbett, O'Connel [sic] and all the O's.
. . . It is for this, I offer you the right hand of fellowship as a Radical-brother. Oh, how much is involved in this resolution!
. . . The resolutionists, many of them, may not see this . . . but a thinking "Cobler" [sic], as I am, can anticipate without alarm, and predict without fear. A Cobler can afford to be honest, when a Knight or a Lord cannot.[35]

Morrison's letters remain as the best refutation of his own argument that the tyranny of the upper classes had suppressed freedom of speech in Britain. One can imagine with what personal pleasure Lord Dalmeny would later accept the family's hereditary title of the Earl of Rosebery and retire from the House of Commons into the nonelective and relatively safe sanctuary of the House of Lords, where he might escape the weekly communiqués of his verbose constituent.

Both the Carnegie and Morrison families were strongly opposed to the Established Church of Scotland. The Carnegies had early departed from the Church of Scotland and had joined the Erskine Secessionist movement, not so much in opposition to Calvinistic theology as because of a dispute over church polity. The Morrisons, as might be expected, had gone further in their revolt from orthodox Presbyterianism. They had seceded even from the Secession, for their dispute involved ideology as well as church government. Thomas Morrison had led his family into communion with the small group of Baptists of Dunfermline. Since the local Baptist Church was too small and too poor to attract a regularly ordained minister to its service, Morrison found time, in spite of his numerous political activities, to serve the congregation as its lay minister for many years.[36]

But in spite of their disavowal of Calvinism, Tom Morrison and his children were more deeply imbued with its ethos than they knew. If they regarded such tenets of the faith as infant damnation and predestination as being savagely primitive, fatalistic, and cruel, they nevertheless displayed in their own personalities those traits of character that had made possible the theological doctrines they had discarded. For them, ethics was the simple process of selecting white from black. There were no confusing shadings of shadow and light to camouflage the moral issue, and like all true Calvinists the Morrisons had supreme confidence in their own unerring moral right. They also had the same kind of terrible energy that had enabled John Knox to pull down the Cathedrals of Scotland and the Puritans of Massachusetts to push back the wilderness. Tom Morrison's grandson best expressed this compulsive drive when as a young man he wrote of himself (and in so doing, of his maternal ancestors), "Whatever I engage in I must push inordinately." And, in spite of their professions of democratic faith and their denial of selective salvation, the Morrisons, because of their belief in their own righteousness, must have displayed that same arrogance of spiritual pride that comes to the Calvinist who knows of his own pre-election. Grandfather Morrison was indeed "a great man for his day," but he could not have proved to be a very comfortable neighbor.

Each of the relatives gathered in the Carnegie home on that November evening would prove to have an influence upon the child whose birth they were celebrating. There was Seaton Morri-

31

son's husband, George Lauder, a romantic lover of Scottish history; Tom Morrison, Jr., florid in face and loud in voice, thumping his huge walking stick on the floor to emphasize his every word, a passionate Radical, the only man in Dunfermline who could out-halloo his father; and Margaret's younger twin sisters, Kitty Hogan and Annie Aitkin, who would soon leave with their husbands for the United States. And of course, there were the child's parents: William, the sixth child of Andrew Carnegie, born on 19 June 1804, and Margaret, six years Will's junior to the very day.

It was always difficult for strangers to believe that the quiet, shy William could be the son of the irrepressible Andrew. William had none of his father's boisterous high spirits. His favorite recreations had always been solitary ones: reading—"an awfu' boy for books," the neighbors had said—and long walks by himself along the country roads of Pattiemuir. Above all, as a boy William had wanted to be a weaver, like his father and grandfather. He became a better weaver than either, though it served him little.

William had been the first of the Carnegies to move from Pattiemuir to Dunfermline. With the changes in the weaving industry it was no longer possible for an ambitious young weaver to be entirely independent, to make and sell his own webs as his ancestors had done. Weaving was becoming a centralized and specialized trade, each town in Scotland developing its own particular linen product. The center for the damask trade was Dunfermline, and William wanted to be a damask weaver. As a child, he had been fascinated by the intricate designs his father could weave. William saw the loom as a great and wonderfully empty canvas which a man could fill with his own dreams of beauty. But damask weavers now must depend upon the so-called manufacturers, actually entrepreneurial wholesalers, who furnished the hand-loom weavers with their spindles of thread, or "pirns," provided the large bleaching fields for the weavers to use in common, and did the dyeing and finishing of the completed webs. In return, the manufacturers set the prices for the weavers and then marketed the finished products throughout the world. No damask weaver in the 1820's could hope to make a satisfactory living independent of the manufacturers. He needed their facilities even more than the manufacturers needed him.

Realizing this, William left Pattiemuir sometime around the year 1830. In Dunfermline he rented half of a duplex cottage, at the corner of Moodie Street and Priory Lane. It provided ample accommodations for a young bachelor. Here he had a large room on the first floor for his loom and a smaller, low-ceilinged attic room above for living. From the first, William's skill as a weaver was recognized by the manufacturers of the city, and he began to prosper.

It must have been difficult, however, for this shy young man who had lived his entire life in the small village of Pattiemuir to make friends in what was to him a very large city. It is easy to imagine how pleased and flattered he must have been to be noticed by his neighbors, the influential Morrison family, who lived just up the street at Maygate. The Morrisons invited him into their home, shared their meals with him, and soon accepted him as one of the family. Although rarely saying much himself, William was fascinated with the lively political arguments of Old Tom Morrison and his equally vocal son. He shared their political views and was greatly impressed by the visits of their many political friends, including the great William Cobbett himself.

In time, however, the political activities of Tom Morrison became less important to William than the feminine charms of his daughter, Margaret. Like all of the Morrisons, Margaret was as dark of coloring as William Carnegie was fair. Her black hair and eyes gave beauty to a face that might otherwise have seemed plain and masculine in appearance, for Margaret had the strong jaw and determined chin of Tom Morrison. Although she always quietly deferred to her father, a more perceptive observer than William might have sensed the great strength of will and determination that Margaret possessed. Intensely loyal to those whom she loved, and fiercely possessive of all that she could call her own, Margaret could on occasion display a ruthless determination that William would never understand.

William's courtship of Margaret prospered with the blessings of both their families. In December 1834 they were married, and they moved into the half-cottage that served as William's workshop and home.[37] Margaret proved a good wife, hard-working, frugal, and neat, as devoted to the interests of her husband as she had been to those of her father.

They made an interesting study in contrasts, this quiet unassuming weaver, who, sitting at the loom, could move his small hands and feet so deftly, making a reality of the beauty he felt within himself, and his hard-working, outspoken young wife, who knew the necessity of being strong in order to survive. Yet William, in spite of his shyness, could on occasions show a courage, a dedication to his convictions, that would be impressive even to the Morrisons. It was as painful for him as it was pleasurable to his father-in-law to speak out in public, yet when he felt a matter of principle was involved, he did speak.

Now, as William looked at his newborn son, he must have felt more strongly than ever before the compelling necessity for being courageous, for working for the kind of world which the Morrisons and their friends assured him could be achieved, where his son could become a craftsman like him and have pride in his own skill. It must have been this realization that gave William the courage to make the most dramatic speech of his life. On the Sunday following his son's birth, William, as was his custom, attended the local Secessionist Presbyterian Church, where the minister, quite fortuitously, if inappropriately, had chosen for his morning sermon the subject of infant damnation. As the minister began to speak, eloquently and with all of the vivid imagery favored by Scottish Calvinists, on the tortures of infants damned for their sins to eternal Hell-fire by a wrathful God, William felt an anger rising within him that he had never known before, anger toward the minister for preaching this dreadful doctrine and even more anger toward the congregation who could accept these pronouncements as calmly and complacently as if the minister had been speaking of the unpleasantness of a northeast rain squall. Rising up from his seat, unaware of the astonished stares of the rest of the congregation, and with a voice choked with emotion, William made his public declaration. "If that be your religion and that your God, I shall seek a better religion and a nobler God." [38] With those words William Carnegie left the Calvinist Church. He never returned.

Thomas Morrison had once written, in a different context to be sure, that "the accidents of birth we regard not." But the accidents of birth can never be disregarded. The child Andrew Carnegie, born on a stormy November day in 1835 in the town of Dunfermline, Scotland, to a weaver and the daughter of a cobbler, had "by the accidents of birth" become heir to all that these people were and to all that they believed in. It was a richly endowed inheritance. Many times in later years it would even prove to be an embarrassment, and there would be those who would say that the birthright had been sold for a mess of pottage. But birthrights of this kind can never be sold, and the boy would be as bound by his inheritance as any young lord of Britain who, willingly or not, had to accept a title and an inherited seat in the House of Lords. Andrew Carnegie's origin would prove basic to all that was to follow.

CHAPTER III

Dunfermline Childhood

1835-1848

The year 1836 was one of relative prosperity for the handloom weavers of Dunfermline. Although prices paid by the manufacturers per spindle were reduced—again—that year, from three shillings twopence to two shillings nine and a quarter pence, trade was still brisk. Weavers who wanted employment at these reduced prices could find it, and, if he worked longer hours, a man could make a satisfactory living.[1] The heavy demand for damask cloth encouraged many of the master weavers to expand their operations by purchasing more looms and taking on additional apprentices.

William Carnegie, whose finished webs were eagerly sought by the manufacturers of the town, was a participant in this expansion. He used his savings to purchase three additional looms, but more space was needed for them than was available in the small half-cottage on Moodie Street, which was capable of accommodating only two looms, at best. On Edgar Street he found a house with room on the ground floor for four looms; and on the second floor, reached by an outside stone staircase, there was a much more commodious apartment than the single room that had been the Carnegies' home on Moodie Street.

The child Andrew's earliest memories were of this Edgar Street house, which faced the pleasant little green square known as Reid's Park. He had been a healthy, happy baby, unafflicted by the usual infant complaints of colic. From the first, he had had a voracious appetite, and at the age of one would be finished with his oatmeal porridge, which he would scoop up with two spoons, one held tightly in each hand, before his mother was ready to serve his father. One of his first demands, "Mair, mair!" delighted his parents and always brought the desired result.[2]

The small boy's first hero was his father. The earliest insistent sound in his consciousness would have been the repetitive clatter of the looms in the large room directly below. The sound of a loom in operation, although noisy, is not disagreeable. It has none of the harshness of metal striking on metal, nor the monotonous pattern of the carpenter's or the cobbler's hammer. There is a pattern of sound, but it is broken in its rhythm, rich in variety, and curiously pleasing to the ear even in its dissonance. Andrew was happy when his mother would carefully lead him down the steep outside steps and into the loom shop. His father would beckon him over to stand close by the bench at the loom, and the child, silenced by the clatter about him, would watch in awe as his father's feet danced lightly on the treadles, while, at the same time, his hands worked the driver stick and the batten. The bodily movements required of the weaver are as complex and rapid as those the organist performs. Even more fascinating is the wonder of the emerging patterned cloth of the web that slowly rolls up on itself before one's eyes. Andrew never tired of watching this phenomenon of his father's skill, and his earliest ambition, which both he and his father confidently expected to be realized, was to become a weaver.[3]

These visits to his father could not be as frequent or as long as the child would have liked. The shop was a busy place, and with one loom to run and three looms to supervise, his father could not be expected to give Andrew much of his time. Even when the looms were silent, and the small boy would wait expectantly by the door leading to the outside stairs, his father might not appear for a very long time. Will Carnegie, like most of his friends, would use his precious moments of relaxation to read a newspaper that he and several of the neighboring weavers would buy in common, or to discuss the latest political news with his apprentices, or sometimes to read from a book that he might have rented from the Tradesman's Subscription Library, which his own uncle had helped to found.[4]

With his mother busy at household tasks, the young child, like all children, had to find his own amusement. In a home where there are few toys, a child must make his own, with pieces of paper, box covers, and bits of string, letting his imagination fill in the outlines of a world of his own creation. John Kirk, a neighbor boy, who on occasion stayed with Andrew when Margaret Carnegie had to leave the house on an errand, many years later would remember, with perhaps greater verisimilitude because of its symbolic significance than with verity to the actual event, seeing the small Andrew sitting on the floor, playing with the pennies from his mother's cash box. "The ploy he seemed to like best," John Kirk would recall, "was tae get haud o' as mony pennies as he could, build them up on the tap o' each ither, an' then knock them o'er wi' his haund." [5]

When Andrew was four, in January 1840, William and Margaret had a second child, a daughter, whom they named Ann. She was a delicate baby, frequently ill, and Margaret had even less time to give to her son. It was then Andrew found that without help he could open the door that led to the stairs and to the world outside, and soon all of Dunfermline became his to explore. In the next few years he was to find in this town "the wonder of all the gay world," from his uncle's grocery store on High Street, to the old Abbey at the top of the hill, to the forbidding gates of Pittencrieff and the Glen. Andrew would have been too young in the summer of 1837 to have seen from the heights of Dunfermline the great fires that were lighted in Edinburgh to celebrate the ascension to the throne of the young Queen Victoria, and to mark the beginning of a new era for Britain and the world. But now as a young boy, four years later, he could stand at the top of High Street, and on one of those rare days when the haze lifted and the air would be as clear as a fogged glass wiped clean, he could see far to the south, past the village of Pattiemuir to the streak of water that was the Firth of Forth, and beyond that to the chimney tops of Edinburgh.

It would probably not have occurred to the boy to wish, even

38

to himself, that he might visit that distant city. The wide horizon that lay around him was but a painted backdrop for the only world that he knew or for the present wanted, the streets of Dunfermline. At a much later date, after he had seen a great part of the world, he would write, with a self-conscious sophistication: "What Benares is to the Hindoo, Mecca to the Mohammedan, Jerusalem to the Christian, all that Dunfermline is to me." [6] But now, knowing of nothing else, he would need no such words to express his joy in exploration, in discovery, and in making all that he saw and heard his own personal possession: the many loom shops, so much like his father's and yet, because they belonged to strangers, so alien; the fish market; the drapers; the leather shop of Uncle Tom; and beyond the city streets, the green Elgin bleaching fields, where, on those days when there was no linen whitening in the sun, a boy could swing on the high wooden bars until the sky and ground blurred dizzily into one. [7]

Each season had its own attractions. In the early spring there would be, at the foot of Moodie Street, Mr. Chicken's Circus Royal, at which place, "Brilliantly illuminated with gas," Mr. Chicken promised, in an advertisement in the Dunfermline *Journal,* he would "have the honour of introducing his far-famed white mare, Beda, or the Omrah's Treasure!" If, as was usually the case, one did not have the sixpence for admission, one could stand by the back entrance to catch a glimpse of the accomplished —if inappropriately named—Mr. Chicken, dressed as "La Sylphide," or gaze with envy at the precocious Master Chicken, "the Infant Equestrian," as he prepared to "ride his Daring Act of Equestrianism!" [8]

In summer there would still be occasional tent preaching on the outskirts of the town—the "Holy Fair" vividly described by Burns a half-century before. But these religious spectacles were becoming rarer each year. Both the Established Church and the Seceders frowned upon such religious enthusiasms, and the newly formed Dunfermline Temperance Society, perhaps overly influenced by the Bard's poetic account, openly attacked such gatherings. [9] There were also the purely secular, if less exciting, monthly trade fairs, where one could wander among the stalls and occasionally be rewarded with an apple or a "sweetie."

The best time of all was in midwinter, when there came the

day that all Scottish children dreamed of for the whole year. Scotland scorned Christmas as a Papish holiday, but on New Year's Eve the best parts of all holidays were combined into one glorious Hogmanay Night. For weeks, children would plan their costumes and masks and prepare skits to act out when they made their rounds. Then, on the last night of the old year, the looms would be silenced early, the table would be set for guests, and around five-thirty in the evening, the father, bringing his apprentices with him, would appear for supper. The steaming haggis would be served, to the cheers of the men, and if the trade had been good that year, each apprentice would find beside his plate a piece of silver.

If you were only six or seven on this wonderful night, you would hardly be able to eat the good food in anticipation of the excitement that lay ahead. At last your father would be finished eating and would excuse you from the table, and you would dash into the bedroom to put on your costume, and if you had no mask, to blacken your face with lamp soot. Then down the stone steps you would race, nearly tripping over your trailing costume, and on the corner, under the feeble gas street light, you would meet your bizarrely dressed friends. The weather would never be bad enough to keep you from your appointed rounds, knocking on doors and shouting:

> Rise up, guid wife, an' shake your feathers
> Dinna think that we are beggars
> We are bairns come oot to play
> So let us have our hogmanay.

The door would open, you would act out a carefully rehearsed and wildly staged presentation of the encounter between Norval and Glenalvon, and then you would be rewarded with your "hogmanay," a small three-cornered biscuit.

Even after you had exhausted the neighborhood's supply of biscuits and you could hear your name being called from an upstairs window, the excitement of the evening was not yet over. You might have to go to bed, but certainly not to sleep, for now the adults would sally forth, carrying long, blazing flambeaux, and the streets would be bright with light and loud with laughter. The Abbey bells would toll midnight and then you would listen expectantly for the first visitors of the New Year, the first-footers, to knock on your door, and to be welcomed with a glass of whisky and a biscuit. It was considered a fortunate omen for the New Year if the first caller was dark, and for this reason the Morrisons were particularly favored by their neighbors on Hogmanay. So you would lie in bed, waiting and hoping that the first sounds you would hear at the door after the Abbey bell had ceased ringing would be the heavy thump of a walking stick and the booming voice of Uncle Tom. Then you would sleep, content to know that you would have good luck for all the coming year.[10]

Andrew could find the pleasures of cosmopolitan variety in the streets of Dunfermline, even when there was no Circus Royal with its allurements, and Hogmanay was only a distant dream of the past and of the future. There were always the traveling beggars, daft Archie and Frank Weir, strange men who would for a penny tell wonderful tales of lands that only they in their idiocy or prophetic vision would ever see.[11] And there was the illiterate Fifeshire poetess, who would stroll the streets of Dunfermline, selling for tuppence broadsides of her ballads that her neighbors had written down for her, and advertising her wares by singing, in her curiously plaintive voice, her latest songs, "On the Gallant Sailors," or "On an Accident at the Brig o' Allan." [12]

It is important to a child in his early years that he acquire a sense of the continuity of time, for it is only in the realization that the verb "to live" has past, present, and future tenses that he can successfully establish his own identity, his own place in the complex world of which he finds himself a part.

All three tenses are necessary to a child, and that child is fortunate who can find a balance of past, present, and future and relate this to himself. Andrew Carnegie was to find this balance in Dunfermline, and each of those who could best teach him the meaning of time was to leave a mark upon the boy and add complexity to his character.

It would have been difficult for any child living in Dunfermline who evinced any curiosity at all about the monuments that surrounded him to have failed to acquire a sense of the past. In Uncle George Lauder, Andrew was to find the teacher best quali-

41

fied to satisfy his curiosity and give dramatic meaning to history. Lauder, who had married Margaret Morrison's oldest sister, Seaton, was a lonely man after the early death of his wife. He had much more time to give to his own small son, George, Jr., and to his inquisitive nephew, than did Andrew's own father. Here in his grocer's shop, when business was slow, Lauder would talk history by the hour to the two little boys. Andrew Carnegie would always remember those sessions:

> My uncle possessed an extraordinary gift of dealing with children and taught us many things. Among others I remember how he taught us British history by imagining each of the monarchs in a certain place upon the walls of the room performing the act for which he was well known. Thus for me King John sits to this day above the mantelpiece signing the Magna Charta, and Queen Victoria is in the back of the door with her children upon her knees. . . . In the list of the monarchs which I learned the grand republican [Oliver Cromwell] appeared writing his message to the Pope of Rome, informing His Holiness that "if he did not cease persecuting the Protestants the thunder of Great Britain's cannon would be heard in the Vatican." It is needless to say that the estimate we formed of Cromwell was that he was worth them "a' thegither." It was from my uncle I learned all that I know of the early history of Scotland—of Wallace and Bruce and Burns, of Blind Harry's history of Scott, of Ramsey, Tannahill, Hogg, and Fergusson. I can truly say in the words of Burns that there was then and there created in me a vein of Scottish prejudice (or patriotism) which will cease to exist only with life. Wallace, of course, was our hero. Everything heroic centered in him.[13]

It was Uncle Lauder who patiently rehearsed the two boys, Dod and Naig, as they called each other, in their skits for Hogmanay, on the encounters of Norval and Glenalvon, Roderick Dhu and James Fitz-James. It was Uncle Lauder who was always ready to reinforce their Scottish patriotism should it be subjected to critical doubts. Once Andrew came heartbroken to his uncle to report that he had been told in school that England was much larger than Scotland. "Not at all, Naig," Lauder reassured him. "If Scotland were rolled out flat as England, Scotland would be

the larger, but would you have the Highlands rolled down?"
Again, he was ready with a quick response when the boy asked
him about England's larger population: "Yes, Naig, seven to
one, but there were more than that odds against us at Bannockburn." [14]

Andrew had little personal contact with Scotland's religious
history from which he might draw knowledge of the past. There
was the Abbey, of course, which dominated the landscape and was
therefore a part of every Dunfermline child's life, but the religious mysteries of Scottish Presbyterianism had no meaning for
the boy. Although Dunfermline was to be the storm center of another great schism within the Established Presbyterian Church in
1843, the Morrisons and Carnegies, delighted as they were by the
attacks upon the Establishment, took no active role in furthering
the Free Kirk movement. Margaret Morrison Carnegie had given
up interest in any organized religious group, even the Baptist
Church of her father. She preferred keeping to her own devices
and counsel on the Sabbath, although she did own and would on
occasion read from a book of sermons by the American Unitarian,
William Channing.

Andrew's father, having so dramatically broken with Calvinism following the birth of his son, searched and finally found religious solace among the small group of Swedenborgians who met
in Dunfermline. Here was "the nobler God" for which he had
been looking—the God of love, not of wrath, of salvation and
peace, not of damnation and torture. Although he was not successful in persuading his wife to join him in the New Jerusalem
of the Swedish philosopher, he did insist upon taking his young
son to that church. It was here, in the bleak little building which
the Swedenborgians rented for their service, that the small boy
had his first understanding of aesthetics. He would later recall
one Sunday morning when, being bored by the minister's long
discourse in metaphysical abstractions, he stared up at the window behind the pulpit and noticed for the first time that this window, unlike the others in the church, had a narrow border, not
more than three inches wide, of small square pieces of blue and
red glass. As the sunlight came through these bits of colored glass
it threw a checkered pattern of color on the floor beneath. The
boy was deeply moved by the sight, and his eyes filled with

tears.[15] This curious introduction to the aesthetic was all he ever gained from his father's efforts to give him a religious education.

It was his mother who served as instructor for his understanding of the practical realities of the present. It was she who handled the family finances, hoarded the precious pennies, and tended the family garden. With a tough resiliency that her husband lacked, she accepted life for what it was, a competitive struggle for existence. Although in sympathy with the Radical causes of her brother and her husband, she expected no millennium on this earth nor any Paradise in the next. She knew that her daily bread would never be given; it had to be bought in the marketplace with money earned by hard labor. All this she taught her son, and Andrew learned his lesson well.

On occasion, too well. Andrew never forgot his embarrassment on his first day at school, when the master called on each child to stand up and say a proverb from the Bible. When it came Andrew's turn, he stood up proudly and repeated from his mother's personal catechism: "Take care of your pence, the pound will take care of themselves." Then in bewildered fright he took his seat as the master glared and his schoolmates giggled.[16]

In time, many of the tasks that Margaret had had to perform —filling the waterbuckets in the morning, or getting the pirns of linen yarn from the spinning mills—could be delegated to her energetic son. He would proudly march off to the mill, carrying his father's great stovepipe "lum" hat, and a short time later would as proudly deliver the pirns to his father's loomshop.[17]

The early morning trips to the city wells were not quite so pleasant, however. Public water facilities in Dunfermline were inadequate for the growing population, and there was always keen competition to be at the head of the water line in the morning. Otherwise there might be an hour's wait before one could fill his water cans. Andrew quickly learned that a water-line protocol existed, which he considered unfair: at night the women of the neighborhood would place old buckets in line before the pump to make reservations in the morning line. The boy took his proper place in line for the first several mornings, but when he saw day after day women arriving much later than he and moving far ahead of him in line, his patience gave out. The following morning he simply kicked the waiting buckets aside and walked to the head of the line. His fellow water-bearers scolded at him, but he got his water first. It is small wonder that many of the women of the neighborhood regarded the Carnegie boy as "an awfu' laddie." [18]

The boy also learned that if one cannot always push others aside in order to get what one wants, there are other ways to reach the same goal. One day William Carnegie brought home a pair of rabbits as a gift for Andrew. Margaret Carnegie was not so pleased as her young son, however, and immediately she raised questions about feeding what inevitably would be a whole family of rabbits. She pointed out that they had no greens in their garden to waste. The boy pleaded for his pets and was finally granted permission to keep them, providing he would find his own sources for their food. When the not unexpected additions to the family occurred, Andrew was ready with their provender, for he had promised each boy in the neighborhood that one rabbit would be named after him if that boy would feed his namesake.[19] The well-fed rabbits of course remained Andrew's possessions. The education of Andrew Carnegie was progressing well, and much of it was to be self-taught.

His formal education, however, did not begin until he was eight years old. When he was five, the age at which most Scottish children began their schooling, he had protested against attending, and his indulgent parents promised that he need not go to school until he himself should ask to do so. Over the next few years William and Margaret began to regret their rash promise, as the boy, thoroughly enjoying his free life, showed no interest in school. Finally, they asked Robert Martin, the schoolmaster of the neighboring Lancastrian School on Rolland Street, if he would perhaps be willing on a Saturday afternoon to take the boy on a long hike and speak to him of the advantages and pleasures of school. The schoolmaster must have been a persuasive salesman, for to the delight of his parents Andrew asked the next day if he might attend Mr. Martin's school.[20]

The Rolland Street School was the least expensive school in Dunfermline, being based on the Lancastrian Method of education, in which the older children, after receiving their instruction from the schoolmaster, would listen to and correct the recitation of the younger children in the same classroom. This method made it possible for a single schoolteacher to accommodate many children at a very low fee for each child, and it was a practical if ineffective way of providing education for those families throughout Britain who could not afford to pay more than a few pence a week in fees. Both the teacher and the children paid a high price in nervous strain by this method, however, and discipline was necessarily harsh. Mr. Martin's school was no exception. He had under his charge from 150 to 180 children in a single large room, and it is not surprising that he had to depend heavily upon the "tawse," the leather whip, in order to maintain discipline. With several groups reciting at once, the room must have frequently resembled Bedlam, and Andrew had been wise to postpone schooling for as long as he did.

After his initial error on the Biblical proverbs, however, the boy seemed to thrive in this confusion. Here was the most rugged kind of competition, for one had to be either very good or very bad to catch the attention of the schoolmaster, and Andrew, who felt he must push as "inordinately" here as he did in the water line, soon proved to Mr. Martin that he was very good. Very quickly the other children labeled him as "Snuffy Martin's pet," and although Andrew bitterly resented the epithet, he kept on pushing.[21]

Although Robert Martin was a dour Calvinist, he had much the same outlook on life and held to the same philosophy as Margaret Carnegie. Life was a stern taskmaster and gave its rewards only to those who worked for them. "Ye hae na been put into this world to enjoy yoursel', but to do yair duty" was a favorite axiom of schoolmaster Martin. The first penny Andrew ever earned from someone outside his own family was one he received from Mr. Martin, when he recited, with flawless accuracy and with the proper emotion, Robert Burns's poem, "Man was Made to Mourn":

> A few seem favourites of Fate,
>   In Pleasure's lap carest;
> Yet, think not all the rich and great,
>   Are likewise truly blest.
> But Oh! what crouds in ev'ry land,
>   All wretched and forlorn,
> Thro' weary life this lesson learn,
>   That Man was made to mourn!

It was Mr. Martin's favorite poem, but, however well he might recite it, it was not Andrew's. He did not really believe that man, by some kind of ineluctable fate, was made to mourn.[22] He believed that beyond the harsh realities of the present there lay a possible future, one which schoolmaster Martin could not imagine and which Andrew's mother did not believe in. The romantic past of crumbling castle walls behind the locked gates of Pittencrieff might be inaccessible to him, the harsh present of brawling water lines might be his morning ordeal, but the future promised to him by his father, grandfather, and uncle lay clear and open before him, uncontaminated by practical doubts or despair.

It was a simple dream that he was taught to cherish above all other dreams for the future. It promised no individual glory, no great material wealth. Nevertheless it was deceptively simple, for it did offer itself as a panacea to all of society's ills. "Political equality—that is all we ask," these dreamers of the good life said, "and then everything else will follow: the prosperous yeoman, the respected artisan, the happy child. Give us the Charter, and we can then take care of ourselves." In these first years of the Victorian Age, all the rationalism of the Enlightenment, the wild enthusiasms of the French Revolution, and the grim despair of industrialism had become blended and distilled into a simple solution. Never before had political democracy been so easily and so simply defined as it was in the six demands of the proposed People's Charter: universal manhood suffrage, the secret ballot, annual elections of Parliament, equal electoral districts, the removal of all property qualifications for election to Parliament, and salary payments to members of Parliament large enough to permit persons without independent means to serve.

Written by a committee consisting of William Lovett, Francis Place, and the Radical M.P. from Bath, J. A. Roebuck, the People's Charter was first published by the London Working Men's Association 8 May 1838 and made public at the great Glasgow rally later in the month. All of the economic misery of the past thirty years, all of the frustration of the social reformers from Spence to Owen, and all of the political disillusionment that had followed the Reform Act of 1832 lay behind its composition. But the spontaneous approval that the publication of the Charter evoked from the lower classes throughout Britain tended to obscure the diversity of opinion that existed among the Charter's supporters. The very concreteness and simplicity of its demands gave a false illusion of uniformity to this movement which historians have since labeled Chartism. From the very beginning there was no consensus among the so-called Chartists, and, depending upon the section in which they lived or their occupational group, they differed among themselves about both the methods that should be employed to achieve the Charter and the economic goals that lay beyond the establishment of political democracy. As the noted British historian of Chartism, Asa Briggs, has observed, "The Charter was a symbol of unity, but it concealed as much as it proclaimed—the diversity of local social pressures, the variety of local leaderships, the relative sense of urgency among different groups." [23] Chartism was never a single movement, but rather a combination of local reforming groups that were only superficially united by a single proclamation, and it was localism that was to contribute in great part to the eventual defeat of the Charter itself.

The most apparent initial division among the supporters of the Charter occurred over the methods to be employed in forcing the Establishment to accept the six points of political reform. There were those who felt that the Reform Act of 1832 was in the final instance passed only by the threat of revolution. Because the demands now were so much greater than those of six years before, they felt that threats alone would no longer be enough. Actual revolt would probably prove necessary. These Chartists, led by Fergus O'Connor, sought action, immediate and direct. In opposition to these "physical-force" men were those who called themselves Constitutionalists, or moral persuasionists. They believed that physical action could lead only to violent reaction, and that reform in Britain had never been and would never be achieved behind the barricades of disorder, but only before the bar of constitutional order. So the methodological lines were drawn, and the Chartists as individuals and in groups gave their allegiance to one side or the other.

In Scotland, and particularly in the eastern section, which had not received the heavy influx of unskilled labor from Ireland, the moral persuasionists were the stronger of the two groups. Several factors contributed to the superior strength of this Constitutionalist group. Depressed as the linen weaving trade was after 1838, general economic conditions in eastern Scotland were not as bad as they were in England or in the Paisley-Glasgow cotton textile area. In addition, although many men were unemployed, the hated English Poor Law of 1834 did not apply to Scotland, so that there were no workhouses to serve as visible symbols of the tyranny of the Establishment. Moreover, memories of 1745 were still strong among the Scots, and they, whose grandfathers had faced English soldiers, were more realistic in their evaluation of the efficacy of a civilian revolt against government troops than were their English counterparts. Finally, the Constitutionalists in Scotland had initially stronger and more effective leadership, with such men as John Fraser, Abram Duncan, and the Reverend Patrick Brewster, than did the physical-force men, whose leader, Dr. John Taylor, was more interested in supervising the movement in England than he was in directing Chartism in his native Glasgow.[24]

A more serious, if less apparent, difference of opinion dividing the Chartists was the question of what purpose the Charter served. Assuming that the six points for political democracy should be achieved, what should the people do with such a victory? The answers to this question indicated a much more varied and complex division among the Chartists than the relatively simple division over the question of method. Some Chartists saw the Charter as only the first step in a social and economic revolution that would redistribute all wealth and create the ancient dream of the Levellers—a true commonwealth, in which all wealth would be held in common. Others would pursue the land reforms of Spence or the industrial democracy of Owen. For some, a democratic Parliament meant the realization of a particular social reform: equal rights for women, or the abolition of slavery throughout the world, or the national prohibition of alcoholic beverages, or free compulsory education for all children. But to many, perhaps to the majority, the Charter had become an end in itself. For them, political democracy meant equality of opportunity, and they sought no other goal than the ending of the rule of the Establishment in the House of Commons. These differences over goals never became sharply defined during the decade of struggle for the Charter. If they had, they might somehow have been resolved. As it was, it would seem that, had the Chartists suddenly succeeded, by force or otherwise, in obtaining government sanction for their national petition, they would have been unable to take immediate advantage of their victory by presenting a program of action to the people. The Establishment did not need to divide in order to conquer. Division was built into the Chartist movement, and could be ignored only if one did not ask questions about ultimate goals.

Among the artisans and unskilled workers within the Chartist movement in Dunfermline the same divisions existed as elsewhere in the nation. The People's Charter was supported by nearly all of the working classes, but the occupational groups openly differed over methods to be employed and individuals differed over goals. The depressed miners and the unemployed crofters who had drifted into town from the outlying farms and the more remote Highlands were impatient with the gradualism of the Constitutionalists. These men had nothing left to lose, and they had less fear of the possibility of sharp pain from a cracked head than fear of the certainty of dull pain from an empty belly. Fraser's program, as enunciated in his paper, the *Edinburgh Monthly Democrat,* advocating massive, passive resistance, had little appeal, especially in contrast with O'Connor's program of bold, direct, militant action.

The skilled artisans of the town, however, and the handloom weavers in particular, wanted no sweeping economic revolution. Their hopes centered upon the conservation of an old order, and they accepted the promise of the Charter not for what it might destroy but rather for what it might protect. Because the weavers made up the great majority of the workers of the city, the attitude of this group was decisive in determining the nature of the Chartist movement in Dunfermline and throughout most of southeastern Scotland. Like other skilled artisans, the carpenter, cobbler, or goldsmith, the weaver by nature was highly individualistic and private-property-minded. He had little sympathy for the trades-union movement, which was growing increasingly strong among the cotton textile workers in western Scotland, and he was openly contemptuous of the even more extreme socialistic schemes of many of the Chartist leaders. Yet, at the same time, the handloom weaver was more dependent upon co-operation than most of his fellow artisans. Long before he had become dependent upon the manufacturer for his supply of thread, as well as for bleaching, dyeing, and marketing facilities, the weaver, by technical developments within his craft, had been forced to accept the communal sharing of tools, and this limited the individual pursuit of his trade and made him dependent upon co-operative organization. With the development of damask weaving early in the eighteenth century, the weaver had to meet precise standards of size and fineness in the weaving of a web that had not been required of the weavers of coarse linen fabric. To achieve these standards, the weaver had to make use of nifflers, or eveners—wood pen reeds used in beaming to spread the web evenly. Nifflers came in various assortments of widths and degrees of fineness, and each niffler had to be precisely constructed with mathematical exactness for a web of a particular size requiring a certain pattern of divided threads, or "pins." As a weaver had to have available a large assortment of nifflers in order to be prepared for whatever weaving order he might receive, early in the history of damask weaving it had become necessary for weavers to combine and purchase a sufficient quantity of nifflers to serve the entire weaving community.[25]

Thus, throughout the damask weaving centers of Scotland, there developed niffler societies, to which the individual weaver paid an annual assessment based upon the number of looms he owned and from which he was free to borrow nifflers to meet his daily requirements. The niffler house from the first was more than a tool stockroom to the weaver, however. Here he came daily to get his supplies, and here he met his fellow weavers both morning and evening. He would sit for a time in the large, gloomy room, with the great wooden framework, stowed with nifflers, hanging overhead, smoke a pipe, and discuss the state of the trade, the political issues of the day, and the prospects for reform with his fellow craftsmen. In effect, the weavers had a trades-union, however much they might deny that their highly skilled and individualistic craft could or should be organized. Born out of the practical necessity of tool-sharing, the niffler societies gave the weaving craft a cohesive unity lacking in the other highly

51

skilled trades. This may explain in part why, when the need for concerted action arose, as it did with the advent of Chartism, the weavers, organized in these societies, were able to assume a position of leadership in north Britain over that of any other skilled craft.[26]

In Dunfermline there were three niffler societies to meet the needs of the numerous weavers throughout the city: one in Woodhead Street, another in Queen Anne Street, and a third in the Nethertown. Although the records kept by these societies were meager, and few have been preserved, those records extant indicate that the societies during the Chartist period elected as officers those men who were conspicuously active in the Chartist movement. William Carnegie belonged to the Nethertown Society, and in the years 1844 to 1846 he served as its president.[27]

It was to be expected that William Carnegie and the Morrisons, long active in Radical politics, would take up the Chartist cause as soon as it was launched at the Glasgow rally. Old Tom Morrison, still pursuing his dreams of land reform, had died while on a lecture tour in England in 1837, and so missed all the excitement engendered by the Chartist movement, which he would have most certainly enjoyed. Convinced to his last day that reform was imminent, his final letter to his children, written as he lay ill in Bradford, Yorkshire, was of his success in getting his message to the people. "I took more money out of Dewsbury than ever I took out of any town," he wrote with satisfaction.[28]

His son and namesake took up the Chartist cause with all the enthusiasm the elder Morrison would have showed had he lived. Supported by the weavers, Tom, Jr., made Dunfermline a center for Chartist activity in Fife and hospitably received Chartist leaders from all over Britain.[29]

Many of the Chartist leaders Morrison welcomed were physical-force men, but they were unable to convert their host or most of his Dunfermline followers from Fraser's Constitutionalism. Both Morrison and Will Carnegie worked closely with Fraser in the early months of the Chartist movement. In the first issue of Fraser's *Edinburgh Monthly Democrat*, on 7 July 1838, there appeared the following letter from Carnegie, with Fraser's introduction and heading: [30]

SPLENDID TRIUMPH OF DEMOCRACY IN THE WESTERN DISTRICT OF FIFE

We have been highly gratified with the following intelligence from Dunfermline. Who that has the soul of a man within him cannot read it without feelings of exultation and brightening hopes for the redemption of his country! Men of Dunfermline, fervidly do we thank you. Your great strength will give spirit and life to many that are dead, and courage to many that are weak in heart. Men of Edinburgh and Mid-Lothian, see what those patriots have done. Go ye and do likewise!—

"To the Editor of the Democrat.

"Sir,—the Working Men's Association of Dunfermline, at a meeting of their Committee, held last night, (July the 1st) for the purpose of despatching our petition, found it contained 6,106 signatures, which trebles the number appended to this petition above any ever sent from Dunfermline.

"The work goes on gloriously here. Some of our friends have gone to the surrounding towns and villages, and I am happy to state they were most enthusiastically received, and their labours crowned with the most cheering success. The Association is very strong in number, still increasing, and every man is nobly doing his duty. Indeed, we flatter ourselves, were all the country as the 'Western district of Fife,' the advocates of misrule and corruption would soon have to give place to a better order of things; but

" 'It's comin' yet for a' that,' &c. Will Carnegie."

As the months dragged on, the better order of things seemed a precious long time in coming, and the Chartists were becoming painfully aware of the divisions within their own ranks. While the moral-force men might congratulate themselves upon their legal correctness and their concern for public order, their program of gradualism, of evolutionary democracy, and of enlightenment through public education was not winning many new converts. To the hungry, hopes for the future were a poor substitute for bread. In the 1840's, as the economic depression worsened, Fraser's program appeared more and more illusory and utopian. Unemployment increased throughout northern Britain, and the roads were filled with people moving from town to town in a vain search for work and a desperate desire to stay out of the work-houses. William Thom, poet laureate of the unemployed weavers, in *Rhymes and Recollections of a Hand-Loom Weaver,* published in London in 1845, described the plight of the unemployed weaver, tramping the roads of north Scotland with his family, sleeping in sheds, and playing the flute to earn a few pence to feed his children. The old nursery rhyme of "little Tommy Tucker sings for his supper" had taken on a cruel reality.[31] With handloom weavers in Dumfries and Aberdeen receiving only one web a week to weave and being paid four shillings for that web, begging had become more profitable than weaving.[32]

In the summer of 1842, after the second national petition sent to Parliament for the enactment of the Charter had been rejected by the House of Commons, and by a larger majority than the first petition in 1839, the factory workers of north England and then Scotland, in a spontaneous outbreak of strikes, attempted to take direct measures to alleviate their grievous situation. Because their method of attack involved pulling out the plugs from the factory boilers, thus extinguishing the fires and stopping the engines, their strikes were labeled as Plug-Plot riots. The forces of law and order saw in them a revival of the old Luddite movement of the early days of industrialism. But these strikes, unlike the Luddite attacks, were no savage acts of sabotage against the hated machine. These strikes were purposeful attempts to force the Establishment to pass remedial legislation.[33]

With the spread of the strikes into Scotland, the moral-force men were embarrassed by the linking of the riots with Chartism. Morrison became convinced that the movement could not be ignored, however, and when the miners of neighboring Clackmannan went out on strike in late August, Morrison and William Fleming quickly organized a Cessation-from-Labour Committee. They hoped to spearhead a peaceful general strike throughout Great Britain. Resolutions were printed and sent to every town in Scotland and England where organized Chartist or Working Men's Associations were known to exist. It was Morrison's hope that, by assuming leadership of a hitherto unorganized and sporadic movement in this manner, the moral-force men would be able to strengthen their own position within Chartism and at the same time prevent the riots from getting out of control.

The response in Dunfermline to the call for a general strike was nearly unanimous compliance. Hopes ran high in the first few days that Dunfermline's action would serve as a pattern for all of Britain. The hundreds of looms in the city were silent; the neighboring coal mines and even the retail shops were deserted. One old man, as he put up wooden shutters across his store front, spoke for all the workers of Dunfermline when he said to a neighbor, "Thae shutters'll no come aff till we gain the Charter, the hale Charter, an' naething but the Charter!" [34]

Unfortunately for the Chartists, the depressed economic conditions throughout the industrial areas of Britain were not conducive to the success of a general strike movement. Men might riot and temporarily leave their jobs, but at a time when there were thousands of unemployed, easily available to be used as strikebreakers, any general strike was doomed, and so was Morrison's program. After a week he had to admit that his committee had had favorable response only from neighboring Tillicoultry and Airdrie in Lanarkshire. Two days later government troops arrived in Clackmannan to put down the miners' riots and the striking citizens of Tillicoultry, and a special company of soldiers and constables arrived in Dunfermline. Morrison, Fleming, and Andrew Henderson, president of the local Chartist Association, were arrested and all their papers and letters in the committee room seized. [35] The old man's shutters came down and the strikers returned to work, without the Charter or any part of the Charter.

One of the first vivid memories of Andrew Carnegie's childhood was his being awakened by a tap on the window near the outside staircase. He saw his father hurry to the door, and then he heard an unfamiliar voice saying that Tom Morrison had just been arrested for seditious activity against the Queen's Government. The next morning the boy heard the full story from his parents. A week earlier Uncle Tom had avoided arrest when a meeting of the strikers at Torryburn on the border between the counties of Fife and Perth was interrupted by the approach of the Sheriff and his deputies. Before the officers could arrive, Morrison had marched his Chartist band in orderly process across the narrow bridge over the stream that divided the two counties. The frustrated Sheriff, having no authority to make an arrest in Perth, had had to let the meeting continue undisturbed. Morrison had become a hero to the strikers, but now, a week later, he, Fleming, and Henderson, returning after midnight from a meeting held in Kirkcaldy, had been arrested on the streets of Dunfermline and were now behind bars in the Dunfermline gaol.[36]

The next morning Andrew must have seen the hastily printed broadsides that were being circulated throughout the town by a committee formed to raise a subscription for the defense of Henderson and Morrison.[37] He even may have heard the whispered plans of the strikers, impatient with the slowness of judicial procedure, to rescue Morrison from the gaol that evening—by force if necessary.

Tom Morrison, because of his boisterous behavior, had a reputation for being far more radical than he actually was. Since the death of his father he had been the most noted heckler at public meetings in all Fifeshire. With his black, bushy hair, and his face reddened by an incipient case of St. Anthony's fire, he gave the appearance of a wild man.[38] His raucous "Hear, Hear" and the strange cuckoo song he would bray forth to show disagreement with a speaker made him conspicuous even at Dunfermline political meetings, never noted for their decorous proceedings. The Conservative Dunfermline *Journal* had frequently commented on his behavior. "The manner in which he heckles the speaker is most disgusting and the low contemptible sneer with which it is frequently accompanied, and with which he can laugh at the most sacred emotions of the human heart, too often characterises his public conduct, and renders it an abomination to every well-regulated mind." [39]

Morrison, however, had always believed in barking, not in biting. On that second night after his arrest, when the crowd did gather to free their hero, he gave full testimony to his moral-force convictions. Angry and wild as his florid face must have appeared, gazing out at his rescuers from behind the bars, he himself was calm and reasonable. He asked those in the crowd who supported him and believed in his principles to drop whatever weapons they were carrying and to fold their arms. The men complied. "Now depart in peace," he said. And they did.[40] The people of Dunfermline voted their approval of Morrison by electing him "Bailie," or town councilman, at the next election.[41]

It would not be surprising that a young boy, growing up in

Dunfermline in these years of Chartist agitation, would find the events of his own day infinitely more exciting than the historic legends taught in school or in his Uncle Lauder's grocer's shop. Listening to his father speaking to a crowd at the Pends on the glories of Chartism, or watching his Uncle Morrison, carrying his great walking cane like a scepter before him, move with majestic aloofness down the streets of Dunfermline, gave to heroism a vitality that the old legends could never convey.

If Andrew found the Chartist leaders of Dunfermline heroic, he was as properly contemptuous of royalty as a young Chartist should be. His mother, for some inexplicable reason, took him and his cousin Dod to Edinburgh to see the young Queen, who was on her first visit to Scotland. He would later remember that, when the Queen appeared, Dod whispered to him, "She's not sae tall as your mither."

"And her dress is nae sae braw," Andrew replied.[42]

The Queen might well have been grateful that the boy's criticism on this occasion was restricted to her costume, for a potential regicide in knee pants stood in the crowd before her. His father and uncle might be moral-force men, but Andrew's attitude toward the Establishment was more sanguinary. "As a child I could have slain king, duke, or lord, and considered their deaths a service to the state and hence an heroic act." [43]

The Chartists oversimplified the economic and social ills of Britain in the mid-nineteenth century. They had too easily accepted the political democracy defined by the six points of the People's Charter as the panacea. As the struggle between the Establishment and the disestablished continued throughout the decade of the 1840's, it became a war, and, as in all wars, its objective became simply victory. What kind of post-Chartist world should be created out of this victory was a question seldom asked and almost never answered. Andrew Carnegie, as a boy, listening to this talk of the Charter, came to believe there was a magical power in the Charter itself. He dreamed of a world in which his father would march to Parliament over the slain body of privilege. Andrew had become a rebel with a cause but without an understanding of effect. He saw means synonymous with end, and this confusion was to persist with him always.

As the fight for the Charter continued, it should have become apparent to its leaders that the dream of victory was an illusion and that it was time to seek more practical measures of economic relief. Some Chartists in these years did desert the cause, and they turned to fight for an end to agricultural subsidies. But the true Chartist regarded the Anti-Corn Law League as a diversionary tactic, inspired by the Establishment to weaken the cause of political democracy. The marches, the strikes, the petitions, must continue, and if economic conditions became worse, prospects for attaining the Charter would become brighter.

Economic conditions did become worse. Unemployment grew at an alarming rate, and now, for the first time, even the master weavers knew what hunger was. And with hunger came disease and death. Ebenezer Henderson, faithful chronicler of Dunfermline, reported that in 1841 the number of deaths in the city totaled 513, the largest number ever recorded in the burgh for one year. Among those who died was Andrew's young sister Ann. Her short life seems to have made no impression upon the boy, for he was never to mention her name in his later writings about his family or his childhood.

In 1843, the third and last child of Margaret and William was born, a boy, named Tom after his maternal grandfather and uncle. Soon thereafter, William was forced to dismiss one of his apprentices and to sell one of his four looms. The second and third looms soon followed, and now, no longer needing or able to afford the commodious quarters on Edgar Street, the Carnegies moved back to another small cottage on Moodie Street, not far from the house in which William and Margaret had begun their married life ten years before. Again they lived in a single upstairs room, as William's one remaining loom occupied the ground floor space. Even this one loom was frequently idle, and Margaret, in order to supplement the family's dwindling income, opened a small shop in the front part of the loom room, selling a few staple supplies—flour, salt, cabbages, leeks, and potatoes— along with snuff for the men and candy for the children of the neighborhood. She persuaded Tom Morrison, whose time was increasingly devoted to political activities and civic duties, to let her assist him in his cobbling. In the evenings, after her shop was closed, she would stitch shoes on consignment from her brother.[44]

Andrew would later recall,

Shortly after this I began to learn what poverty meant. Dreadful days came when my father took the last of his webs to the great manufacturer, and I saw my mother anxiously await- ing his return to know whether a new web was to be obtained or that a period of idleness was upon us. It was burnt into my heart then that my father, though neither "abject, mean, nor vile," as Burns has it, had nevertheless to

> "Beg a brother of the earth
> To give him leave to toil."

And then and there came the resolve that I would cure that when I got to be a man. We were not, however, reduced to any- thing like poverty compared with many of our neighbors. I do not know to what lengths of privation my mother would not have gone that she might see her two boys wearing large white collars, and trimly dressed.[45]

Protected by proud and self-sacrificing parents, Andrew may not have known in these years what real poverty was, but he was taught early the consequences of political dissent. It was fine to be the son of a hero, to be able to say to the other boys attending a mass meeting for reform that that man up there speaking was your father, but for such distinction there was a price to be paid. Andrew, who loved the sound of the great Abbey bell that tolled each evening at sundown, must have wondered what it would be like to walk with one's parents through those great doors to church on a Sunday morning. As a child of "seceders even from the Secession," he was not to know.

There were other gates barred to him that he resented much more. From his upstairs window on Moodie Street he could look out upon the rolling greens of Pittencrieff, the largest estate in Dunfermline. Behind its great stone walls lay not only the most beautiful park in all Fife, but also, near the deep Glen, the his- toric ruins of Scotland, Malcolm's Tower, and the remaining walls of the monastery and palace. The Hunt family, owners of the estate, carefully guarded their purchased treasures from the rabble of the town. Only once a year, in May, would the great iron gates swing open and all Dunfermline be invited in to view the ruins, to walk the neatly graveled paths and admire the ex- travagantly planted gardens. All Dunfermline but for a few notable exceptions: old Tom Morrison and all his descendants. Following a bitter political altercation between James Hunt and Morrison, the Hunt family ruled that neither Morrison nor any of his family should ever again set foot upon Pittencrieff ground.[46] The Morrisons were too proud ever to attempt a test of this ban. For a small boy, however, who must stand outside and wait for his friends to return with marvelous stories of seeing peacocks with tails outspread, or of climbing the ancient mound of Malcolm's Tower, such an interdiction must have been heartbreaking. Nevertheless, this annual act of personal sacrifice made all that his family believed in appear even more heroic to the boy. Andrew knew that he would never change his politics in order to gain admission to that forbidden green garden. Instead, he vowed that someday he would push open those gates and would himself hold a great meeting in the sacred park of Pittencrieff.

CHAPTER IV

The Flitting 1848

In the year 1845, the youthful and ambitious Conservative M.P. for Shrewsbury, Benjamin Disraeli, published his second novel, *Sybil, or the Two Nations*. Still suspect within his own party for having voted for the national petition of the Chartists in 1839, Disraeli with his novel did little to allay these suspicions. Woven into the conventional melodrama of his story was a biting criticism of a society which had in effect become two nations, one of wealth and the other of poverty. One literary critic caustically commented that Disraeli and his Young England movement "can imagine only two modes of amalgamating the Two Nations— killing off the poor, or making them rich." [1]

For the Irish peasants, who were in that year beginning to feel the first devastating effects of the potato blight, for the cotton textile men of Lanarkshire, who had been replaced by child labor, and for the handloom weavers of Fife, who were being replaced by power looms, there was little prospect of being made rich. But there was the very real possibility that, by one means or another, by workhouse or potato famine, they would be killed off. The moral suasionists still spoke hopefully of achieving the Charter by constitutional means, but it was hard to feel hopeful. There had been too many failures, too many national petitions voted down by Parliament, too many peaceful "cessations from labor" broken by government troops and the use of easily obtained "black leg" strikebreakers. Class consciousness, an awareness of the existence of two nations separated by an unbridgeable chasm, was growing in Britain. The workers, skilled and unskilled alike, would now agree with Friedrich Engels, who, observing the English scene in 1844, wrote,

> It is too late for a peaceful solution. The classes are divided more and more sharply, the spirit of resistance penetrates the workers, the bitterness intensifies, the guerilla skirmishes become concentrated in more important battles, and soon a slight impulse will suffice to set the avalanche in motion. Then, indeed, will the war-cry resound through the land: "War to the palaces, peace to the cottages!"—but then it will be too late for the rich to beware.[2]

Even in Dunfermline, among the handloom weavers, those aristocrats of labor who had always been a source of strength for the moral-force Chartists, there was an increasing impatience with gradualism. Spontaneous mob action was becoming ever more frequent in 1844 and 1845. Weavers, borrowing the disguise used by their children on Hogmanay Night, their faces blackened with soot, attacked and burned a small power-loom mill that had been established in the town in 1843. The Nethertown Weicht, an ancient drum reputedly once the property of the revolutionary Friends of the People Society, was brought out of its carefully guarded hiding place, and its deep boom was the signal for the weavers to attack. One weaver carried a banner with the slogan, "May Tories' hides become drumheads to beat republicans to arms." [3] To Tom Morrison and Will Carnegie, lying in their beds listening in the night, the distant muffled beat of the Weicht must have sounded like a funeral drum roll to their hopes of peaceful reform.

There was to be a brief flurry of new hope when, in 1846, under the ministry of Robert Peel, the hated Corn Laws, the protective tariffs on grains, were substantially reduced. As elsewhere in Britain, the workers of Dunfermline demonstrated their enthusiasm for "Peel and Repeal" by holding on 3 July "a grand procession and mammoth celebration on the Pends." Again the Nethertown Weicht was brought out of hiding, this time to celebrate this signal victory over the old order. Bonfires were lighted and joyous festivities lasted far into the night.[4]

This victory proved as illusory as the Great Reform Act of 1832. With good grain harvests that year, and with the increased importation of wheat from America, bread prices were substantially reduced—but so also were wages throughout Britain. The table of prices set by the manufacturers of Dunfermline for damask linen was further reduced, from two shillings three-eighths pence per web to one shilling tenpence, and the weaver was happy to have a commission even at these prices.[5]

By 1847, it must have been apparent to all but the most naïve Constitutionalists that those Chartists who had from the first opposed the Anti-Corn Law League had been right. An alliance between the moderate Chartists and the League had been attempted at Manchester in 1842, but it had been an unnatural alliance, and it did not survive the year. It was unnatural because there could be no basic agreement between the middle class entrepreneurs, who sought the repeal of the Corn Laws as part of a pronounced policy of laissez-faire, and the working proletariat, who needed more, not less, government regulation. The weaver from Bolton who testified before the Parliamentary Select Committee on the Handloom Weavers' Petitions in 1834 had seen the basic issue more clearly than many of the Chartist leaders. When asked if repeal of the Corn Laws would benefit the weavers, he had at once replied, "not one farthing excepting a law was to take place that was to secure the present wages we have. . . . [I]f we could live upon a shilling a day, the system would take care we did not get [only] 9 d. to live upon; that is my idea, and all those I associate with." [6] It was precisely that kind of "system," however, that Cobden, Bright, and the Manchester Liberals, who were leaders of the Anti-Corn Law League, would most zealously oppose.

When free trade in agricultural products failed to bring an improvement in working conditions throughout Britain, the already waning influence of the moral-force Chartists was further weakened. O'Connor and his followers were only too eager to point out the error of the Constitutionalists in not looking beyond the Charter and the repeal of the Corn Laws to a more substantial program of planned social welfare. The moral-force men had confused means with ends. They had foolishly allied themselves with Manchester Liberalism in the vain hope that free trade meant a free society, and they had been betrayed by their allies. Old Tom Morrison had tried to warn his sons, and all of the moral suasionists, that free trade was a cruel delusion. As he wrote in 1832:

> . . . you will stave the child off with . . . a dissertation on political economy and the principles of "free-trade"—of free trade in the bones, muscles and sinews of factory children. . . . I will reply for the child. . . . Curse your hypocracy [sic]; blast your economy.

The winter of 1847–48 brought the worst weather in the memory of the oldest Dunfermline citizen. The strong gales that swept in from the North Sea intensified the misery of unemployment. And 600 weavers were out of work. If it had not been for the railway construction underway south of town, the lines in front of the charity soup kitchen would have been longer than they were.

During the previous summer, a large steam-power weaving factory had begun operations on Pitmuir Street. While 400 weavers had felt themselves fortunate to find employment there, the many hundreds of handloom weavers saw in this Pitmuir Street factory a symbol of their defeat. This was no small power loom that a mob could destroy in a night of rioting. This was the Machine, come at last to the linen industry. The gray smoke that poured out of the factory's chimneys to float over the town was the pennant of victory of the Machine over the Weaver, and everyone knew it. All during that dreadful winter there was no relief from the cold or from the despair. It was as if the town itself were dying. There were no funds in the city treasury for lighting the streets, but there was little need for the gas lamps at night, for people with no food for supper went to bed early to forget their cold and their hunger. Shutters covered the fronts of the loom shops. Their former occupants were grateful for an occasional day's work in the coal mines, happy, for a few pence, to join the once-despised coalies and to crawl naked like moles through the narrow underground seams.[7] Even so, Dunfermline was better off than Ireland and western Scotland, where over 300,000 people had died of starvation as a direct result of the potato blight. Reports of typhus and cholera following in the wake of the famine gave little reason to hope that eastern Scotland would escape the consequences of the blight.

It was during this winter that Will Carnegie came back from one of his many fruitless visits to the manufacturers and quietly announced to his son, waiting at the door to welcome him, "Andra, I can get nae mair work." [8] Will Carnegie had often come back home during these last few years with no web assignments for that week, but this time the manufacturers could give him no assurance that there would ever again be an order for him to fill. The day of the handloom weaver was over.

It must have been at that time that Margaret Carnegie, who, with her little shop, had been for many months the chief provider, took over as the real head of the family. If she had ever subscribed to the millennial dreams of her brother and husband, she had long ago given them up. It is true that she had rejected most of the tenets of orthodox Scottish Calvinism, but sin and evil had remained realities for her. Society was not going to be remade by a paper Charter nor human nature changed by Parliamentary decree. She could have told Tom and Will that all of their talk of moral persuasion would not put one farthing in their pockets or change one vote in Parliament. The men who had power and wealth—the two words were synonyms for her—owed their position not to goodness of character but to their own or their ancestors' ruthless determination to have and to hold. While Will had been signing petitions and attending Chartist rallies, she had been out early in the mornings, finding the cheapest and freshest vegetables available to sell in her shop, or staying up late at night stitching shoes by cruisie light. She had fought the Establishment not with words but in the only way she knew, by accepting its values, which could only be measured in pence, shillings, and pounds. If she had not been willing to haggle with the turnip farmer over a penny's difference in price or to count out carefully the small bits of candy to be sold in paper pokes, her children would have been queuing in the soup lines along with most of her neighbor's children. Since the time they had had to sell the extra looms and move back to Moodie Street, it had been she who had kept food on the table and Andrew in school. Her husband, still seeking employment for a skill that had no future, may not have realized this, but her son Andrew did. He was to write,

> My father did not recognize the impending revolution, and was struggling under the old system. His looms sank greatly in value, and it became necessary for that power which never failed in any emergency—my mother—to step forward and endeavor to repair the family fortune.[9]

Now that there was never again to be an order for his loom to fill, Will Carnegie could no longer fail to recognize the revolution that had taken place. He could seek work at the factory, or crawl on his belly in the coal mines, and Margaret could go on with her shopkeeping and shoe-stitching, and perhaps they could continue to subsist, as others were doing. For Margaret Carnegie, however, mere survival under the system was not enough. There was another alternative, one that she had been considering for nearly a decade, which was to emigrate as some of her friends and relatives had done. Her younger sisters, Annie and Kitty, had gone with their husbands to Pennsylvania in 1840. At first they sent back reports which were not encouraging. Annie had written in October 1840:

> My dear Margaret things being in such an unsettled condition in this country at present, it would be the height of folly to advise you . . . to venture out at this season at any rate, as it is very difficult for one to get employment of any kind, and more particularly weaving which is scarcely carried on here at all. . . . The thought therefore that William may be idle &c renders us all very uneasy but if affairs were once settled again I would not hesitate to recommend you to come, as it is easy to get into situations here of different sorts, although you may know at all of the work to be done, the people here stick at nothing. Just set to, and drive on the best way you can; many of them will be at two or three different occupations in a very short time.

Andrew Aitkin had added a note, addressed to his brother-in-law George Lauder, saying, "I wish I had taken your advice & not come to America this soon—the banking system has made sad havoc here—business is at a stand here." He also warned that although wages were fairly good for those who had work, prices were also very high. "A shave costs 6 cents—hair cutting 21 so you see the Barbers are well paid." [10]

Two years later, Annie was still discouraging any emigration plans Margaret might have. "I would not advise any person to come out at present who can get a lively hood at home, as trade is very dull here, indeed many who are both able & willing to work find it impossible to get employment." [11] But two years after that, she was encouraging such a move:

> Business here is much better now, as most individuals can find employment although some are out of a job yet, & the wages are considerably reduced. . . . This country's far better for the working man than the old one, & there is room enough & to spare, notwithstanding the thousands that flock into her borders. As for myself, I like it much better than at home, for in fact you seem to breathe a freer atmosphere here; but as Andw. Hoggan says no wonder them women like it, for they are so much thought of in this country. Indeed you would be surprised to see how kind men are to their wifes; they seem so anxious to let them have an easy life although they toil very late themselves. [12]

Margaret and Will Carnegie read these letters over many times and often discussed the possibility of emigrating. For Will it had always been just talk, even though his children had often heard him, down in the loom shop, singing the popular tune of the day:

> To the West, to the West, to the land of the free,
> Where the mighty Missouri rolls down to the sea;
> Where a man is a man even though he must toil
> And the poorest may gather the fruits of the soil. [13]

However brightly America might gleam in the reports of his fellow Chartists, who regarded it as a model for Britain, [14] and however strongly his emigrant relatives might urge him to follow their example, Will could not really imagine leaving Dunfermline, to give up the only thing he knew how to do well, to admit that Chartist reform was an impossible dream.

The winter of 1847, however, convinced Margaret that there was no other alternative but to migrate. Will might sit staring at his empty loom, waiting for an order that he had been told would never come. He might even find day work at the mill. But what of their sons? What of their plans to train their sons for a craft that now no longer existed? Should they now become factory hands or, worse yet, coalies?

Margaret, as always, could face a reality that Will Carnegie would try to ignore. It was she who made the final decision to move, she who arranged the public auction—the roup—to sell their furniture, she who urged Will on to find a buyer for his one remaining loom. And so the plans were made—as they were being made in so many other households in Britain in that dark winter—for the "flitting"—that curiously flippant term the Scots used for emigration, perhaps hoping that by its very insouciance one could disguise the anguish that emigration imposed upon those who left and those who stayed behind.

It was while the Carnegies were making their plans in the early spring of 1848 that, suddenly, all of Europe seemed to explode into revolution. Ironically enough, the Charter never seemed closer to being realized than at that moment, when Will Carnegie was preparing to abandon the fight. The revolution began in France, toppling the bourgeois order of Louis Philippe, then swept across Italy, Germany, and into Austria itself, forcing the proud Metternich to flee in disguise, assuming the shamefully plebeian name of "Mr. Smith." For a brief moment it must have seemed as if the millennium could be achieved, that old systems could be destroyed—by nothing more than a sharp push from the people.

With the moral-force men now thoroughly discredited, Fergus O'Connor and Jones had nothing more original to propose than that the Chartists should reassemble on 10 April and march as a body to Parliament to present a third national petition to the House of Commons. This would be no ordinary petition, however; this would be a monster petition of over five million names, which O'Connor assured the Convention had already been obtained. This time Parliament could not ignore the thundering voice of the people.

All Britain waited in fear or hope for this most curious of all revolutions, a scheduled rebellion, publicly announced a week in advance. Only the British could have planned such a revolution, or taken it seriously. But the British people did take it seriously, and so did the government. Will Carnegie in distant Dunfermline must have stopped the energetic moving preparations of his wife for a moment, at least, to await the latest news from London. Indeed, all Britain seemed to be waiting for the announcement that would conclude the story of Chartism in one way or another.

The day of revolution was bright and fair, an early warm spring day designed by nature for boating or country walks, not for the storming of a Bastille. When O'Connor arrived at the Convention Hall in Fitzroy Square, the crowds had already begun to assemble—but not the 150,000 Chartists that had been expected to carry the petition in triumph to Parliament. Even a generous estimate of the Chartists assembled on Kensington Common could not make the number larger than 23,000. The Chartists were outnumbered by constables and curious spectators by at least ten to one. Quite suddenly, all of the fire seemed to have gone out of the physical-force leaders, and, over the angry protests of some of their followers, O'Connor agreed with the police that the Chartists who had assembled should not accompany their leaders to Parliament with the petition. The monster petition, containing its much-publicized list of 5,700,000 names, was reverently placed in a four-wheel cab, like a marquise being driven to Court, while the selected leaders rode ahead in a twenty-foot van bearing the stirring motto, "Liberty is worth living for and worth dying for." In this manner was the final hope of the Chartists delivered over to Parliament.[15]

The Chartists had expected the House to be so impressed with the bulk of the petition that it would neglect an inspection of its contents. In this, as in so much else, they were mistaken. The House appointed a large committee of tellers, and the lists were examined with the careful scrutiny customarily given to the returns from a general election. After three days the committee reported that the lists contained precisely 1,975,496 names, some of them of doubtful authenticity, as, for example, Victoria Rex, the Duke of Wellington, Sir Robert Peel, and Mr. Punch (not to mention certain obscene names "which your committee will not hazard offending the House by repeating").[16] This time the House did not even bother to vote on the national petition. With the report of the tellers completed, the petition was simply laughed out of Parliament, and the laughter of London reached to the farthest corners of Britain. The petition had truly become a monster, a side-show freak, to be exposed to the raillery of the populace. Laughter proved to be the most effective weapon of all against this latest unhappy attempt at organized rebellion.

To the million or so people who had signed the last Chartist petition, and to the many other millions who had hoped for the quick millennium, this April had indeed been the cruelest of months. Certainly there was nothing now on the immediate horizon to delay further Will Carnegie's packing. Never again in Dunfermline could he know that tranquillity that comes to the man who is master of his own craft and has provided a future for his heir. The roup crier disposed of their household goods, and Will Carnegie at last disposed of his loom for little more than the value of the wood that was in it. The spring of 1848 was a bad season for the seller, and the sale of all of these possessions brought only a fraction of what had once been paid for the loom alone. When these funds were all counted up, along with the pence and shillings that Margaret Carnegie had managed to save even during the leanest years, the Carnegies were still several pounds short of even a conservative estimate of their transportation costs to Pennsylvania. Only a loan of twenty pounds from the ever faithful Ailie Ferguson Henderson, who had served Margaret as midwife at the births of the Carnegie children, finally made the venture possible.

Tom Morrison, undaunted by the recent events in London, and busily engaged this spring in holding pro-French republican rallies at the old Dunfermline Relief Church,[17] had from the first regarded his sister's proposed flitting as idiotic, and he warned Ailie against her generous loan. He would not aid the migrants by so much as a penny, and with his usual bluntness he accused his brother-in-law of deserting the good fight at its most critical moment. George Lauder, who also looked with disfavor upon the

70

Carnegies' planned departure, was more helpful. It was he who made the arrangements for the least expensive bookings he could obtain, reservations on a small 800-ton sailing ship, the *Wiscasset,* a former whaling vessel, which was scheduled to depart from the Broomielaw of Glasgow on 17 May.[18]

Having disposed of all their household effects, the Carnegies spent their last night in Dunfermline with the Andrew Ritchie family, who were their next-door neighbors on Moodie Street.[19] On this last evening in Dunfermline, while Margaret was busy with the final packing of the absolute essentials, Will sat alone on a borrowed chair in the empty room that had once been his loom shop. His older sister, Charlotte Drysdale, would always remember coming by that evening to say goodby and finding her brother sitting alone in the empty cottage, with his head in his hands. "His attitude was verra sad." When Charlotte held out her hand and said, "I've two pound ten to give ye," Will was overcome with emotion. "If ever I've anything," he promised her, "I'll mind ye." [20]

Will Carnegie, however, spoke with no assurance that he would ever again have anything. He might wish that he had his wife's spirit and determination and could reply to his critics with the same conviction that she had had in quoting an old Scottish proverb to her brother: "I'll make a spoon or spoil the horn." [21] But Will Carnegie at forty-three was a tired and defeated man. The horn had already been spoiled for him, and he did not feel equal to the task of carving another.

As for the children, Tom, not yet five, was too young to realize what was happening, but Andrew during these past weeks had shared all of his mother's excitement and none of his father's doubts. He had been something of a hero in Mr. Martin's classroom, and the other children had treated him with a certain deference that they had never before shown to "Snuffy Martin's pet." He had made Cousin Dod envious with his highly embellished tales of what life in America would be like.

The rail omnibus for Charlestown, on the Firth of Forth, some five miles from Dunfermline, left each morning at six o'clock. Long before that the Carnegies were at the station, ready to depart. From the number of people who would later remember having assisted the Carnegies in their flitting, it would appear as if half of Dunfermline was also there to bid them farewell. Andrew would remember only Uncle Lauder, who would accompany them to Charlestown where they would board the steamer that would take them to Glasgow.

It was only after they had taken their seats in the omnibus that Andrew came to a realization of what this departure meant. "I remember that I stood with tearful eyes looking out of the window until Dunfermline vanished from view, the last structure to fade being the grand and sacred old Abbey . . . [with] the talismanic letters on the Abbey tower—'King Robert the Bruce.' " [22]

At Charlestown harbor the Carnegies were to take a small launch out into the Firth, where they would board a canal steamer out from Edinburgh, bound for Glasgow via the Forth and the Clyde Canal. As Margaret and Will were saying goodby to George Lauder before getting into the launch, Andrew "rushed to Uncle Lauder and clung round his neck, crying out, 'I cannot leave you! I cannot leave you!' " A sailor from the launch had to pull the boy away from his uncle and place him in the launch beside his parents.[23]

Still, Andrew, like his mother, was not "made to mourn." His tears were dried before they had boarded the steamer that would take them through the Canal to Glasgow, the first small part of their four-thousand-mile voyage, all by water, to Allegheny, Pennsylvania. Already, Andrew was farther away from Dunfermline than he had ever been before, and, although the countryside along the Canal was much the same as that around Dunfermline, he looked at the turnip fields, the low stone walls, and the small cottages with the eager eyes of a foreign traveler.

The canal boat took its passengers directly to the Broomielaw on the Clyde, the dismally dirty harborside of Glasgow. The canal trip had taken the entire day, and as the *Wiscasset* was scheduled to sail the next morning, the Carnegies saw no more of the city. Along with many other passengers, they were herded aboard the ship and assigned their bunks. On the morning of 17 May, the *Wiscasset* beat down the Clyde and, with the outgoing tide, moved out into the Atlantic Ocean.

For the crew of the *Wiscasset* this was but one more trip by one small sailing vessel taking human cargo to New York. There were many such ships and many such trips across the Atlantic in this year of 1848, which would set a new record for the number of British emigrants to the United States—188,233 in all.[24] But for each individual passenger on the ship, this voyage, so often considered, so long prepared for, was to mark the great division in his life, the moment in time from which, ever afterwards, one would count the years either before or after sailing. And the passengers, crowded into their bunks, accepted without complaint the inadequate quarters and the miserable food. Like most of their countrymen who would leave Britain in this year, they had been driven out by poverty and were now sustained only by hope. Each would have the same story to tell and each would tell it in the same words: No work, not even for a good weaver . . . a sister in New York (or Pennsylvania, or Ohio) . . . jobs, they say, for someone willing to work . . . with luck and the good Lord willing, we'll make it. Old phrases, worn smooth with the saying, but words that must be spoken and must be listened to, for like a familiar litany there was solace in their very repetition. With these words and the hope that lay behind them, perhaps one could pass safely through this "brutal filter" that was the sea-passage to America.

For the boy Andrew Carnegie, however, this trip was not an ordeal, to be stoically endured. From the first moment he had felt the ship running before the tide and had seen the great square-rigged sails fill with wind overhead, he had suddenly felt alive in a way he had never felt before. In the days ahead, in rough seas or long swells, most of the passengers might lie miserably ill in their bunks or sit abjectly on the deck. But the boy never was to know a sick moment at sea. There was a sense of power here that he loved, of man using nature because he could ride with it. He marveled at the sailors' skill as they instinctively took advantage of every wind or met the roll of any sea.

Within twenty-four hours of sailing, of all of the many passengers crowded on board the small tow-haired boy was the one person that every sailor knew. Andrew's curiosity was unlimited: he wanted to know every detail of the rigging; how the bowline, the stevedore, and the reef knots were tied; how the sextant was used; how to plot the ship's position. The crew delighted in such an eager and apt pupil. Because the ship was undermanned, the passengers were frequently asked to help out. It was little Andrew who carried the messages of the boatswain or the ship's stewards to the passengers' quarters, giving orders to his fellow passengers and loving every minute of it. Again he had made himself the pet of those in authority. His bustling, officious industry had its own sweet reward. On Sundays, when the rest of the passengers were obliged to eat the same coarse fare that they were given on every other day of the week, the boy was "invited by the sailors to participate . . . in the delicacy of the sailors' mess, plum duff. I left the ship with sincere regret." [25] Undoubtedly, Andrew was the only passenger aboard who held to that sentiment.

On the fiftieth day out from the Broomielaw, the *Wiscasset* dropped anchor off Castle Garden in New York Harbor. From the ship's rail the eager passengers could see the lower end of Manhattan and, beyond, the green forests and open farmland of Long Island and the Bronx. Here at last lay the focal point of all their hopes, and without elaborate formalities they pushed ashore into the bewildering confusion that was New York. Except for his brief visit to Edinburgh to see the Queen, it was Andrew's first introduction to metropolitan life. He would remember how "the bustle and excitement of it overwhelmed me," and for once he was willing to stay as close to his parents' side as his five-year-old brother.[26]

The Carnegies knew no one in New York except a former weaver from Dunfermline named Sloane, whose wife, Euphemia Douglas, had been one of Margaret's girlhood friends. The Sloanes received them hospitably, but the Carnegies were eager to get on to their relatives in Pittsburgh. Seeking information from the Immigrant Society, Will Carnegie was advised that the best way to get to Pittsburgh from New York was to go by the roundabout route, on the Erie Canal, Lake Erie, and the Ohio and Erie Canal. There were no railroad connections to Pittsburgh, and while it was true that there was a quicker way, by an elaborately complicated system of stage coaches, canals, and inclined-plane railcars that one could take from Philadelphia to Pittsburgh, this route was not recommended. The immigration agents pointed out that the fare on the Philadelphia-Pittsburgh line was six cents a mile, while one could negotiate with various canal boat agents and probably secure passage for each adult at less than two cents a mile. Will and Margaret Carnegie, counting over their precious, meager funds, hastily decided upon the Erie Canal route, and they booked passage on the night steamer up the Hudson to Albany, where they could get a canal boat to Buffalo.

It is doubtful that the Carnegies realized how long a boat trip they had agreed to. They could not have had a very clear concept of the size of the country, and the New York agents, instructed to push the advantages of the Erie Canal route, would certainly not have emphasized that the trip would take over three weeks.

Once again the Carnegies found themselves aboard a ship, heading north up the Hudson River on a hot night early in July 1848. In the morning they would be in Albany, with no time to inspect the capital city of New York, for they must be early at the great wharf on the canal basin to negotiate the next stage of the journey.

Carrying their badly scuffed traveling bags, the Carnegies would be quickly spotted as likely customers by the many boat agents that clustered around the wharf, and soon they would be surrounded by eager men vying for their patronage. Out of the confusion, Will and Margaret would learn that there were two kinds of passenger transportation available—the packet-boats, which provided meals and sleeping quarters and had an average speed of about three miles an hour, and the line-boats, which provided no meals and only the most primitive sleeping accommodations and averaged about one and a half miles an hour. As most of the packet-boats charged three cents a mile for adults and the line-boats only one and a half cents, the Carnegies, like most immigrants traveling west, undoubtedly took a line-boat up the Canal.[27]

And so they crept slowly westward. Averaging 36 miles a day, it would take 10 days to cover the 364 miles of canal between Albany and Buffalo. Horace Greeley has given an account of his trip on a canal line-boat. It must have been typical:

> I made the journey by way of the Erie Canal, on those line-boats whose "one and a half a mile, mile and a half an hour" so many yet remember. Railroads as yet were not. The days passed slowly yet smoothly on those arks, being enlivened by various sedentary games. But the nights were tedious beyond any sleeping-car experience. At daybreak you were routed out of the

shabby shelf-like berth, and driven on deck to swallow fog, while the cabin was cleared of its beds and made ready for breakfast. I say nothing about "the good old times"; but if anyone would recall the good old line-boats, I object.[28]

For Will and Margaret Carnegie, the ten-day trip must have made even the *Wiscasset* seem luxurious: ten days without taking off one's clothes at night, sleeping on a narrow shelf in a hot room with no ventilation, Margaret with Tom in the women's quarters, Will and Andrew in the men's; waiting for meals until the canal boat docked at some little village or until some vendor jumped on board the boat with sandwiches and lukewarm tea at exorbitant prices. But for a boy of twelve, the canal boat, like the *Wiscasset,* was high adventure. A single horse slowly pulled the boat down the Canal, and the passengers could sit on the top deck— the roof of the passengers' quarters below—and watch the countryside in as leisurely a fashion as if they were taking a Sunday afternoon walk in the country: the narrow green valley of the Mohawk; the numerous little villages of two or three houses in a clearing; and the few larger towns, Palmyra, Utica, and Syracuse, unable to conceal their raw newness with the strange, inappropriate aliases they had borrowed from a long-dead culture. When the boat passed under one of the many low stone bridges, the warning cry from the helmsman, "Low bridge!" would force most of the passengers on the top deck to bend double, but a small boy could stand up straight and touch the rough underside of the bridge and feel himself suddenly to be a giant, ten feet tall.[29]

A canal ride had a strange dreamlike quality to it that made it different from any other mode of travel, by land or by sea, for it was an incongruous hybrid of the two. To move so slowly and endlessly onward upon a still-water channel, and at the same time be so close to land that one could talk to strangers standing on the tow path, gave the traveler a unique perspective. The deep, tunnel-like cuttings through which the boat would be drawn; the hot moonlight nights when sleep was impossible in the cabin and one could sit on the top deck and look into the lighted windows and open doors of houses along the path; and above all, the exciting moment when the boat would enter a lock, heavy doors

76

would close behind it, and, the water rushing in, the boat would suddenly be lifted, as a child might lift his toy from a basin, and one could look back at the canal far below—all of these moments would be forever after vivid in the traveler's mind. Andrew would "look back upon my three weeks as a passenger upon the canal-boat with unalloyed pleasure." [30]

At Buffalo, those canal boat passengers going farther west transferred to a lake steamer, which took them more than half-way down this great inland sea to the town of Cleveland, the rapidly growing lake port city on the south central shore. Again, there was no opportunity to see more of the city than the busy wharf, where hundreds of immigrants were arriving weekly on their way to western Pennsylvania, the Ohio River, and points west. And again the weary immigrants were surrounded with eager canal boat agents bidding for their business. The Carnegies were to take a canal boat down the Ohio and Erie Canal to the village of Akron, where they could get another boat that would take them eastward again to Beaver, Pennsylvania. Akron, a boisterous, commercial village, filled with saloons and cheap boarding houses, existed only for the canal trade, but there was little here to induce even the most exhausted traveler to delay his trip.[31] The Carnegies gratefully took the first canal boat going eastward to the headwaters of the Ohio.

It must have seemed to the Carnegies, traveling almost constantly for ten weeks, that this hegira would never end. Now as they headed bewilderingly back to the east, after having come so far westward, their travels seemed to take on a circular movement that might well go on forever. The very size of this land must have added to the unreality of the nearly three weeks of traveling up great rivers, through hundreds of miles of canals, and across a lake larger than the Black Sea—and yet they had been in only three of the thirty states that made up the American Union. Andrew at least could be consoled by the fact that this country need never be rolled out flat so that it might compare favorably in size with England.

The canal agent had assured the Carnegies that when they reached the village of Beaver, Pennsylvania, on the Ohio River, they could immediately board a river steamer that would take them directly to Pittsburgh and the end of their travels. But when the canal boat arrived at the pier in Beaver, there was no steamer waiting for them, and there would be none until the following morning. With little money left, not enough for a room, even if they could have found one in the small village, the Carnegies had to spend the night on the wharf. It was a hot, clear night, so they needed no protection from the weather, but they suffered indescribable agony from their first serious encounter with the American mosquito. A multitude of these insects emerged from the swampish backwaters of the river and descended upon them from dusk on throughout the night. Andrew was to remember this night as being the one disagreeable experience of the entire journey. "My mother suffered so severely that in the morning she could hardly see. We were all frightful sights, but I do not remember that even the stinging misery of that night kept me from sleeping soundly. I could always sleep, never knowing 'horrid night, the child of hell.' " [32]

In the morning, the Carnegies boarded the paddle-wheeler from Cincinnati, which made a stop at Beaver on its way to Pittsburgh. As they ascended the river it could no longer, by any generous stretch of poetic license, be called the beautiful Ohio. Long before the steamer turned the last bend a passenger could tell by a glance at the dark, muddy-green water below that he was approaching a city. But even the river could not prepare him for the smoke-begrimed town at the junction of the Allegheny and Monongahela rivers. European travelers were already calling Pittsburgh the dirtiest and ugliest city in America, and for the Carnegies, remembering how contemptuously the people of Dunfermline referred to Edinburgh as "Auld Reekie," Pittsburgh was further evidence of how everything in America was on a much greater scale. No Edinburgher or even Glaswegian could know what true reek was until he had visited Pittsburgh.

The downtown section of the city had been nearly destroyed by fire only three years earlier, yet the new wooden and brick buildings, hastily constructed as replacements, had already become so thoroughly darkened with grime that it was impossible to separate them from the older buildings. The narrow streets were filled with wagons, dray carts, and carriages. Everywhere there seemed to be a desperate, almost frenetic busyness, frightening to any visitor. Significantly, there were no parks in all of Pittsburgh. Apparently the townspeople had no time for leisure and no confidence that in this atmosphere green grass and flowers could survive.

In spite of the general confusion, the Carnegies obtained directions and found transportation across the river to the suburb of Allegheny, where Margaret's two sisters lived. There they were given a joyous welcome, and the long flitting was at last over.

Annie Aitkin, whose husband Andrew had recently died, lived with her twin sister Kitty and Kitty's husband, Thomas Hogan, in a frame house on Rebecca Street. That house belonged to Thomas's brother, Andrew, but Annie still owned the small house she and her husband had bought on the back end of the Hogan lot. She had rented this to Andrew Hogan, a weaver by trade, but there were two small rooms unoccupied on the second floor, and she offered these rooms to the Carnegies rent-free until they should get established.

It was into this small, dark, frame house, facing out on a muddy back alley, that the Carnegies moved during their first week in Pittsburgh. Now nearly penniless after their long voyage, they were, of course, most grateful to sister Annie for her generous offer, but they found in this first week of life in America that poverty here was more squalid and depressing than they had ever thought it could be. In Scotland the poor were at least blessed in having lumber so scarce a commodity that their houses, no matter how modest, must be built of stone. Dunfermline cottages had a style and honesty in construction, for they were built by masons who took pride in their work and built homes to last for generations. In America, only the rich could have houses of brick or stone, and the poor must live in flimsy, jerry-built wooden structures that appeared to be constructed as haphazardly as a crudely designed tree house built by a child. Unfortunately, these "temporary" packing-box structures were lived in generation after generation—unless, as frequently happened, the buildings were swept away by a cleansing fire.

Like so many immigrants, the Carnegies had held hopes that were too high, had had these hopes magnified during long weeks of anticipation as they traveled the great distances of sea and land, and now they must accept the reality of two rooms at 336½ Rebecca Street in Allegheny—better known as Slabtown, Pa. If Margaret Carnegie thought that she had indeed "spoilt the horn," she was too proud to say it—and Will was too kind.

CHAPTER V

The Charter Acquired

1848-1855

Popular reading material in Great Britain in the decades of the 1830's and 1840's had presented the United States as a land of rich opportunity. Prospective emigrants had sought in these writings a confirmation of their hopes and dreams, and most readers were quite prepared psychologically to accept even the most extravagant statements in these pages as literal truths. One of the most widely read of these propaganda pieces had been S. H. Collins's *The Emigrants Guide to and Description of the United States of America.* Regarding opportunities for skilled artisans in the American Republic, Collins had written:

> Industrious men need never lack employment in America. Laborers, carpenters, masons, bricklayers, stonecutters, blacksmiths, turners, weavers, curriers, shoemakers, and tailors, and all useful mechanics generally, are always sure of work and good wages.[1]

If, as is quite possible, the Carnegies had read this guide before coming to America, they might well have wondered during these first hard months in Pittsburgh just what kind of weaving

Mr. Collins had had in mind. Certainly not handloom weaving, for Will Carnegie quickly discovered that his craft had become as much of an anachronism here in America as it was in Scotland. When the Carnegies moved into the two upstairs rooms of the small house on Rebecca Street, Andrew Hogan, who had been using the first floor for a loom shop, had just given up the struggle of trying to make a living by weaving. He offered his loom to Carnegie for a small annual rental and, having no other immediate prospects for employment, Will accepted. Once again the clatter of a loom could be heard in the Carnegie household, but Will was no longer weaving fine damask cloth with patterns of intricate beauty. On this small, primitive loom he could produce only the same kind of cloth that his grandfather and father had woven in Pattiemuir, checkered tablecloths and coarse ticking. His marketing facilities were equally primitive. There were no manufacturers here to furnish orders and buy his finished products. His son would remember that when Will had woven several tablecloths, he would, like old Andrew Carnegie a half-century before, be "compelled to market them himself, selling from door to door. The returns were meager in the extreme." [2]

For this reason, Margaret too was forced to return to the vocational skill that she had thought she had given up forever when she left Scotland. In their Rebecca Street neighborhood there was a cobbler named Henry Phipps. Margaret went to him, as she had gone to her brother Tom in Dunfermline, and persuaded Phipps to give her take-out work of binding shoes. So once again she sat up late at night stitching shoe leather. Now it was the five-year-old Tom's job, as it had once been Andrew's, to sit beside her in the evening, threading needles and waxing thread.

It would have been difficult even for Margaret to say how they had improved their present condition or their prospects for the future by flitting. All that they had fled from in Scotland—poverty, toil, despair for the future—had been found again, in more squalid surroundings, here in America. It was as if their burdens had been inadvertently packed along with their few worn pieces of clothing and transported across the Atlantic with them.

Only for the boy Andrew had the move to America marked a decisive change in status and in his immediate future. Now nearly thirteen, the boy had a tacit understanding with his parents that his school days were over and that he must expect to find work to help in the support of the family. He had had five years of schooling under Mr. Martin's somewhat remote tutelage. He could read, write, and cipher, knew a little Latin, and could recite a few poems. In accordance with the standards of the day, in both Scotland and America, he had all of the basic educational essentials and a few unnecessary frills. He must now put these skills and his wits to work.

For Andrew, this change came as no hardship. Undismayed by the blackness of his immediate environment, the boy had in great abundance the self-confidence of youth. The twelve formative years of his childhood had given Andrew certain basic convictions that were to determine his attitude toward this new land to which he had been brought.

The Carnegies, like the thousands of other Scottish, Irish, and German refugees in this year of 1848, had left a pre-Marxian Europe in which liberalism was still generally defined in political rather than in economic terms. The older emigrants, like Will Carnegie, had fought for reform in Edinburgh, Glasgow, Dublin, and Frankfurt on the assumption that the achievement of political democracy in their native land would be all that was necessary to preserve the old economic order to which they were committed and under which they had once flourished. Since these efforts for political reform had failed, they had turned to America, which had always been held up to them as a model society. Now, in America, they discovered that political democracy was not enough to guarantee the handloom weaver, the shoemaker, the lace maker, or the small farmer a decent living. Disillusioned, these older men lost the last shred of hope and adjusted as best they could to an alien and hostile society.

To young men from Europe, imbued with the same tenets as their fathers, but as yet uncommitted to a particular skill or craft, America presented quite a different face. In an America of Jacksonian Democracy, they had found, they believed, the realization of liberalism. One can say that this migration at this particular moment caused in boys like Andrew Carnegie and young men like Carl Schurz a kind of arrested development, and they would look no further into the meaning of liberalism.

Long indoctrinated in Chartism, the boy Andrew, with the naïveté of childhood, had reduced this simple creed of political democracy until it had become for him a slogan, "Death to all privilege." By "privilege" he meant a royal crown, a duke's carriage, a bishop's church. He had never been taught to look beyond these obvious symbols of established power to its many other forms. As a precocious child too often in the company of his elders, he had learned too much and at the same time too little of the world. Now, finding himself in a land where he was unfettered by special privilege of birth, church, or ballot, the boy felt free and at ease with his world, even in the slums of Slabtown. Here was a country in which any career was open to him and there could be no limits imposed upon his ambition.

This confidence in himself had also been carefully nurtured by the special kind of privilege that he had enjoyed throughout his childhood. In spite of the harshness of his world, he had always been peculiarly protected from it—in part by an overly solicitous mother and an indulgent father and in part by his own personal charm, combined with an aggressive nature. He had seen pinched hunger in the faces of his playmates in Dunfermline; he had heard weavers, friends of his father, march by, carrying with them heavy pikes to smash factory machines; he had been transported in little better than steerage quarters across the Atlantic; and he now lived in the slums of a back alley of Pittsburgh—not the usual record of special privilege, certainly. But in all of these experiences he had been more an observer than a participant. There had always been for him the bowl of hot porridge on the table, the clean collar in the dresser drawer, the plum duff with the sailors on Sundays. The protective shield of personal privilege that he enjoyed in childhood distorted his observation and warped his later recollections of his early environment, so that as a man he would actually extol the virtues of poverty. Writing, for example, to young people in the midst of a great depression in 1896, he could say:

It is because I know how sweet and happy and pure the home of honest poverty is . . . that I sympathize with the rich man's boy. . . . It seems, nowadays, a matter of universal desire that poverty should be abolished. We should be quite willing to abolish

luxury, but to abolish honest, industrious, self-denying poverty
would be to destroy the soil upon which mankind produces the
virtues which enable our race to reach a still higher civilization
than it now possesses.[3]

Only someone who was naïvely ignorant of the full meaning of
poverty could write these words with such obvious self-righteous-
ness. Carnegie was closer to revealing his own actual experience
with poverty when he wrote in his autobiography, "We were not
reduced to anything like poverty compared with our neighbors. I
do not know to what lengths of privation my mother would not
have gone . . . to keep us in comfort and 'respectable.' " [4]

There is a story told of Andrew as a young child in Dunfermline which may be apocryphal but is, nevertheless, illustrative of
parental sacrifice for him and of his own complacent acceptance
of it. On a Sunday afternoon, when he was six or seven years old,
he and his father had gone for a long walk in the country. On the
return trip, the boy, being tired, climbed upon his father's back.
After carrying his son for nearly three miles, Will Carnegie suggested, when they came to a steep hill near their home, that he
was a bit tired and that Andrew might like to walk the rest of the
way.

"Ah, father," murmured the boy, holding on tighter than before, "never you mind. Patience and perseverance makes the man,
you know."

Evidently his father had a sense of humor, for, shaking with
laughter, Will carried the boy the rest of the way home.[5] If the
story is true, it is probably also true that Andrew never understood his father's laughter. For him, it would always be commendable to try to bolster the spirits of the downtrodden with little
homilies of moral uplift as he rode along.

By the age of twelve, Andrew Carnegie had been a witness to
or was conversant with some of the great historic forces of his
time: Chartism, political revolutions, industrialization, the mass
migration of peoples, urban poverty. As a child will naturally do,
he had personalized all of these movements in terms of his own
experience. History for him in effect had become egocentric. At
the same time, having been shielded from the full impact of these
forces, he failed to develop a sense of empathy with those victim-

ized by history. His basic attitudes, developed in childhood, did not change with maturity, and he would continue to view all later events in terms of personal experience and, paradoxically, personal detachment. Poverty would always remain for him honest, sweet, and pure, because that was what it had been for him in the Carnegie household; democracy would mean only the absence of titled nobility, because that was what his Uncle Tom had taught him; the opportunity for advancement would always be available to everyone, because that was what he had found in the crowded classroom of the Rolland Street School, on board the overburdened *Wiscasset,* and in the teeming alleys of Slabtown. Those had been his experiences, and he would never quite realize that there could be any other. "I congratulate poor young men upon being born to that ancient and honorable degree which renders it necessary that they should devote themselves to hard work," he would tell the graduates of the Curry Commercial College of Pittsburgh in 1885. "The partner's sons will not trouble you much, but look out that some boys poorer than yourselves, whose parents cannot afford to give them the advantages of a course in this institute, advantages which should give you a decided lead in the race—look out that such boys do not challenge you at the post and pass you at the grandstand. Look out for the boy who has to plunge into work direct from the common school and who begins by sweeping out the office. He is the probable dark horse that you had better watch." [6] It was quite unnecessary for Carnegie to add that he was referring to a particular dark horse who by the time he made that speech had already proved dramatically how fast and far he could run.

There had been no Curry Commercial College or any other training school for Andrew as he prepared to become a wage-earner in the late summer of 1848 in Allegheny, Pennsylvania. But there was still Margaret Carnegie, zealously protecting him and trying to see that he had the inside lane in any race. When Andrew Hogan pointed out that there was good money in selling and suggested that the boy might be started out on this career by being given a basket of odds and ends to peddle along the wharves of the city, all of Margaret Carnegie's protective instincts flared up. Andrew later wrote that he had never known until that moment what was meant by an enraged woman. . . . My mother was sewing at the moment, but she sprang to her feet with outstretched hands and shook them in his face.

"What! my son a peddlar and go among rough men upon the wharves! I would rather throw him into the Allegheny River. Leave me!" she cried, pointing to the door, and Mr. Hogan went.

She stood a tragic queen. The next moment she had broken down, but only for a few moments did tears fall and sobs come. Then she took her two boys in her arms and told us not to mind her foolishness. There were many things in the world for us to do and we could be useful men, honored and respected, if we always did what was right . . . we were taught that idleness was disgraceful; but the suggested occupation was somewhat vagrant in character and not entirely respectable in her eyes. Better death. Yes, mother would have taken her two boys, one under each arm, and perished with them rather than they should mingle with low companions in their extreme youth.[7]

This incident made an impression upon the twelve-year-old boy which he was never to forget. His mother's dramatic gesture toward the unfortunate Andrew Hogan, who had only tried to be helpful, was always to be for the boy a vivid picture of renunciation of all that was "low, mean . . . and coarse. . . . Tom and I could not help growing up respectable characters, having such a mother. . . ."[8] What one would find among the "rough men upon the wharves" the boy at this moment could only half guess, but he had been as thoroughly impressed by his mother's outburst as any Scottish child had ever been frightened of the fiends of Hell by the thundering voice of a Presbyterian divine.

There still remained unresolved the question of employment for the boy. Among the Scottish immigrants of Allegheny there was a close bond of community spirit, however, and the Carnegies learned that jobs were available at the nearby cotton textile mills, owned and operated by Mr. Blackstock, a respectable Scotsman who gave preferment in hiring to recent Scottish immigrants. Andrew could have a job as bobbin boy at $1.20 a week, and there would be a job available for Will Carnegie as well. It was as satisfactory an arrangement as Margaret could wish for under the circumstances. The work would be hard and monotonous, the hours long and the pay meager, but it was honest employment under respectable management, and Will would be there to watch over his son. Will Carnegie agreed to give up his handloom, and to accept what he had left Dunfermline to avoid, factory work in a textile mill.

He and Andrew would arise early and be at the factory each morning before it was daylight and, with only a short break for lunch, work until after dark. "The hours hung heavily upon me," Andrew would recall, "and in the work itself I took no pleasure." But he liked the regular pay and felt that he was making his proper contribution to the family's welfare. "I was now a helper of the family, a breadwinner, and no longer a total charge upon my parents. . . . I was going to make our tiny craft skim." [9]

When another manufacturer in Allegheny, John Hay, whose family had been known to the Morrisons back in Dunfermline, offered young Andrew a job in his bobbin factory at $2.00 a week, Andrew accepted the offer. Will, who found factory work even more irksome than his son did, no longer felt his protective presence necessary, and he gratefully returned to his own little loom on Rebecca Street to weave the tablecloths for which there were so few customers.

The boy was for the first time on his own—in a very literal sense. In Mr. Hay's factory he was stationed in what proved to be solitary confinement in the cellar of the factory, where he was to run the steam engine and fire the boiler. It was a frightening responsibility. As thoroughly indoctrinated as Andrew was against all machines, he approached the boiler and engine as a fearful St. George facing his first dragon.

> It was too much for me. I found myself night after night, sitting up in bed trying the steam gauges, fearing at one time that the steam was too low and that the workers above would complain that they had not power enough, and at another time that the steam was too high and that the boiler might burst. [10]

There was one mitigating element in the job, and Andrew, who had a fastidious nature, was thankful for it. "The firing of the boiler was all right, for fortunately we did not use coal, but the refuse wooden chips, and I always liked to work in chips. . . ." [11]

His mother might also be thankful that this work separated him from possible contact with coarse and undesirable companions. In fact, it kept him isolated from all personal contact with other workers in the factory. He was a lonely and frightened boy, but still "my hopes were high, and I looked every day for some change to take place. What it was to be, I knew not, but that it would come I felt certain if I kept on." [12]

He kept on, and the change came. John Hay, needing a clerk one day to make out some bills, asked Andrew to show him a sample of his penmanship. Hay was pleased with the boy's bold, open style and gave him the job of making out his weekly statements as well as taking care of his correspondence. The boy sensed that the protective feeling he seemed to arouse in others was in evidence here also—"dear old man, I believe he was moved by good feeling toward the white-haired boy, for he had a kind heart and was Scotch and wished to relieve me from the engine." [13]

Hay was also a businessman, however, and there was not enough clerical work for Andrew to earn his $2.00 a week. As a supplementary job, the boy was given the task of dipping the newly made bobbins in a preservative oil. Again he was put in a room alone to perform this task, and he was to remember it as being the most loathsome job he ever had to perform. "Not all the resolution I could muster, nor all the indignation I felt at my own weakness, prevented my stomach from behaving in a most perverse way. I never succeeded in overcoming the nausea produced by the smell of oil. . . . But if I had to lose breakfast or dinner, I had all the better appetite for supper, and the allotted work was done. A real disciple of Wallace or Bruce could not give up; he would die first." [14]

But he would not die until he had tried by the use of his wits to get out of his torment. Hating the dirtiness of coal and the smell of oil, the boy was learning that to survive in an industrial society he must develop skills that would remove him from the crude basic realities of a mechanized order. Sitting on the high stool before the clean ledger book, with its neat orderly columns of figures, was for Andrew as pleasant as bending over the oil vats was repugnant. If he could make himself an indispensable occupant of that high stool, he might never again have to go down into the vat room. Since Mr. Hay still kept his books in single entry, Andrew saw an opportunity to become a full-time accountant by learning the double-entry system of bookkeeping and convincing his employer of its merits. During the winter of 1848–49, Andrew persuaded several of his young friends in the neighborhood, John Phipps, Thomas Miller, and William Crowley, to go with him into Pittsburgh two or three nights a week to learn double-entry bookkeeping from an accountant named Williams. Andrew had always been very quick at ciphering. He liked the precise logic of mathematics, and the double-entry system of accounting gave to him an almost aesthetic satisfaction in its symmetrical balancing of numbers.

Andrew, however, never had the opportunity to revolutionize Hay's accounts. A new door opened up, confirming the boy's faith in the magical wonder of the world. One evening, early in the spring of 1849, when he had returned from work, his Uncle Thomas Hogan came over from next door to say that he had been playing a game of draughts with an old friend, David Brooks, who was manager of a Pittsburgh telegraph office. Brooks had said that he was looking for another messenger boy and wondered if Hogan knew of any bright young lad who might be interested. When Hogan had mentioned his nephew, Brooks had said that if the boy were interested he should come down to the telegraph office for an interview. "Upon such trifles," Andrew later wrote, "do the most momentous consequences hang. A word, a look, an accent may affect the destiny not only of individuals, but of nations. He is a bold man who calls anything a trifle. . . . The young should remember that upon trifles the best gifts of the gods often hang." [15]

A family council was at once held. The boy was "wild with delight" at the proposal, but Will Carnegie was not so enthusiastic. He felt that Andrew had no chance for the job and that the interview would result only in the loss of a day's wages, for if Brooks was paying $2.50 per week, as Hogan reported, he obviously had in mind a much older and more experienced boy. This time it was Will who felt protective toward his son. He was not at all sure that he liked the idea of Andrew running around the streets of downtown Pittsburgh unsupervised and unprotected at any hour of the day or night. Surprisingly, Margaret, on this occasion, did not raise similar objections. She knew Mr. Brooks and was sure that he would be diligent in watching out for his youthful employees, who were, she was informed, nice young men who would make fine companions for their son, most of them being Scottish immigrant children. Moreover, the additional 50¢ a week would be a most welcome addition to the family income. As was usually the case, at the end of the discussion Will yielded to his wife and son and agreed that Andrew should at least be allowed to apply for the position.

The next morning, dressed in his one good suit of clothes, Andrew, accompanied by his father, walked the two miles to the O'Reilly telegraph office at the corner of Third and Wood streets in downtown Pittsburgh.[16] When they arrived at the street door, Andrew asked his father to wait for him outside. Confident of his own success, the boy was afraid that his father's diffidence might jeopardize his chances.

The interview was brief. Brooks carefully scrutinized the boy, who was small for his age, then abruptly asked when he could start work. Andrew was prepared for this question and answered without hesitation that he was ready to begin right then. The other messenger boy in the office was called in and told to show Andrew around the office and give him some instruction on what his duties would be. So exhilarated was Andrew by Brooks's quick acceptance of him, and so eager was he to learn about his new job, that some time passed before he remembered his father, still waiting for him on the street. Andrew dashed out, said that it was all right, he had the job, and that his father could go home and tell his mother the good news.

In later years Carnegie would remember,

> What a change an entrance to a telegraph office was to me then. My "Good Fairy" found me in a cellar firing a boiler and a little steam engine, and carried me into the bright and sunny office surrounded with newspapers, pencils, pens and paper, and ringing in the ears, the miraculous tick, tick, tick of the tamed lightning and doing the work of a man. I was the happiest boy alive, carried from darkness to light.[17]

But Andrew was not one to depend on his "Good Fairy" to keep him in the light. Fearful during the first few days that he might make some error or appear too young and inexperienced for the job after all, the boy zealously learned every trick that would make him the most efficient messenger obtainable. He would lie awake at night now, not in nightmare fear of the steam gauges, but trying to remember the names of every business establishment on every street in downtown Pittsburgh, and then trying to recall the faces and names of those men to whom he had already delivered a message. It proved to be an invaluable memory exercise, not only for the delivery of telegrams, but for later associations in the business world.[18]

There were two telegraph lines that had their terminal facilities in Pittsburgh. The O'Reilly Telegraph Company handled all messages received from the East Coast over the Eastern Telegraph Line, while the rival company, located in the basement of the St. Charles Hotel, received all telegrams coming into Pittsburgh from points west.[19] O'Reilly's was the busier of the two companies, and it soon became necessary to employ additional messengers to handle the incoming business. Another Scottish boy from Allegheny, David McCargo, was added to the force, and it was Andrew's proud task to show him around the office and instruct him in his duties. When still another messenger was needed, Andrew was asked to make a recommendation and without hesitation he proposed Robert Pitcairn, his closest friend on Rebecca Street. Pitcairn got the job. The telegraph messenger service in Pittsburgh was rapidly becoming a Scottish monopoly, and the three boys, Andy, Davy, and Bob, swelled with their own importance, felt that the entire communication system between Pittsburgh and the East Coast was dependent upon their fast-moving legs.

Andrew soon knew the narrow back ways of Pittsburgh better than he had ever known the streets of Dunfermline. At night and in the murky gloom that passed as daylight in Pittsburgh, he could without delay deliver a message to any address in town. His greatest pride was to be able to recognize on the street a man for whom he had a message and to deliver it on the spot. This usually meant a tip and, at the least, the opportunity to introduce himself to the customer. One could never tell when such an introduction might be important.

Special dividends for a messenger boy ranged from apples and pastries to the opportunity of learning an amazing amount of confidential information about the business life of the community. No other employment could have given Andrew such a feeling of importance, and he loved it.

Another special dividend was the privilege of delivering a telegram to the old Pittsburgh Theater, where the messenger could wheedle permission to slip up into the balcony to see part of the performance. It was here that Andrew first became acquainted with the plays of Shakespeare, the magic of which could make even Burns seem secondary.

An extra charge of ten cents was made for a telegram delivered beyond a certain limit in downtown Pittsburgh, and the messenger boy was allowed to keep the charge. There was, of course, keen competition for the privilege of delivering "dime messages," and quarrels frequently arose among the boys as to whose turn it was. Andrew, after six months in the office, regarded himself as dean of the messengers, and he came forth with the solution. After delivering such a message a boy would not keep the dime for himself but would put it in a "pool." The sum thus collected would be divided equally among all the boys at the end of the month. "Peace and good humor reigned ever afterwards. This pooling of extra earnings," Carnegie would hastily go on to explain, "not being intended to create artificial prices was really cooperation. It was my first essay in financial organization." [20]

Andrew took his unofficial deanship seriously, and the other boys, particularly the newest members of the force, Henry Oliver and Will Morland, must have found him overbearing and officious. He was as ready to safeguard the morals of his colleagues as his mother had been to protect his. Most of the other boys, not knowing his family background, thought him a fundamentalist in religion. Although his parents had denied the Presbyterian dogma, they had held to the morality of John Knox and had carefully schooled their son in it. Andrew would leave the office with an ostentatious display of disapproval whenever any of the other boys told a story that might be considered even faintly salacious. Even when he tried to unbend and indulge in what he considered wholesome fun, his associates found him awkward in this unaccustomed role. One of his friends in the office wrote him many years later, "The whole trend of your mind seemed to be towards big things. Indeed, I recall that your efforts to do the pranks of the average boy struck me at the time as being almost grotesque. You would not follow the fashions in dress, because, I supposed, you believed it to be the evidence of a little mind." [21] Andrew had contempt for those weak enough to indulge in the use of tobacco or intoxicants, and he even frowned upon an excessive consumption of sweets. He often found it necessary to reprimand Bob Pitcairn about this bad habit. Bob, as well as some of the other boys, would frequently run up a bill at the confectioner's shop. When Bob, hoping to win sympathy, confided in Andrew that he "had live things in his stomach that gnawed his insides until fed upon sweets," Andrew's response was to request the confectioner not to extend credit to the boys on the security of future earnings from the "dime message" pool. The treasurer of the pool—Andrew—"would not be responsible for any debts contracted by the too hungry and greedy boys." [22]

Andrew's superiors, at least, appreciated his scrupulous attention to duty. John P. Glass, manager of the front office, who was in charge of the delivery of messages, depended more and more upon Andrew to handle some of the routine administrative details of the office. Andrew now received the messages from the operating room and assigned them to the other boys for delivery. He was sensitive enough to perceive that the other messengers resented his authority, his penurious habits, and his officious meddling in their affairs, but, although he might have liked to have been popular among his associates, he was much more concerned with his relationship to his superiors.

One Saturday evening, when the boys lined up for their monthly pay, Mr. Glass waved Andrew aside and paid all the other boys. For one sickening moment, the boy felt that he had somehow fallen into disgrace and was going to be discharged. When the other messengers had bolted out of the office with whoops of joy at having another month's pay in hand, Glass took Andrew behind the counter and counted out not the usual $11.25, but $13.50. He told Andrew that his services were worth that much more to the company and hereafter this sum would be his monthly pay. Andrew dashed home and turned over to his mother the usual amount, but he kept the extra $2.25 in his pocket. He wanted to savor a little longer in private the pleasure of this bonus. Only after he was in bed that night with his brother Tom did he share the good news. As Andrew later remembered, he told his seven-year-old brother that this was only the beginning. Someday they would go into business together. They would have a large firm. Andrew was vague as to its nature, but he was sure it would carry the imposing sign, "Carnegie Brothers." They would all be rich and ride in their own carriage through the streets of Pittsburgh. At Sunday breakfast he proudly presented the extra pay to his parents, who were even more impressed than Tom had been. Praise from his mother was particularly gratifying, for he always valued her approval above all others.[23]

This raise in pay, which Andrew regarded as a promotion, was but the first step in the fulfillment of Andrew's hopes for his immediate future. All the messengers were required to be at work each morning an hour before opening time to sweep out the office and clean up from the day before. For the other boys it was the least attractive part of their duties, but for Andrew it was a golden opportunity. While the others dallied over their tasks, and Bob Pitcairn made an elaborate ceremony of putting a bandana handkerchief over his shirt front to keep it from becoming dusty,[24] Andrew would race through his chores and dash into the operating room to study and play with the telegraph instruments. Soon he was sending practice messages to other boys in offices along the line and receiving answers. Early one morning, when a special call came through from Philadelphia, Andrew had the temerity to respond that, although there was no regular operator on duty, he would take the message if it was sent slowly. He got the message and delivered it. When Brooks arrived, instead of scolding his overly eager messenger, he praised him for his initiative.

Boldness had paid off. Soon Andrew was relieving the regular operators when they wanted to take a break. It was easy to make the transition from messenger to regular operator, for, as Andrew expressed it, "we were blessed at this time with a rather indolent operator." [25] Indolence soon gave way to ambition.

The Carnegies, after three years in Pennsylvania, were at last realizing some of the material benefits that Margaret Carnegie had promised in proposing emigration to America. Andrew, as operator, was now making what seemed to them to be a munificent sum: $20 a month. Margaret, in addition to her nighttime cobbling, was helping out in Sister Annie's grocery store. Tom was doing well in school and looking forward to joining his brother in the telegraph office. The £20 debt to Ailie Henderson had been paid in full, and Margaret was hopeful that they could soon move from the upstairs rooms on the alley into a house of their own.

Only Will Carnegie had failed to find the fulfillment that America had promised. Andrew, to be sure, wrote encouraging notes about his father to the family in Dunfermline: "Father has been working a linnen [sic] web for a lady these two weeks past & has got along first rate with it, he also is working some linnen cloths for himself he thinks he can make more on them than on cotton ones." Andrew further reported that his father was just the same as when they left—which was true, but not as Andrew meant it, for Will remained the same defeated and disillusioned man that had left Dunfermline. "I think he would still build rabbit houses for us yet &c- it pleased him greatly to hear of his letter being read at a meeting in the park. I think that will be an inducement to write again." [26]

In spite of these little notes of cheer, both Andrew and his mother would have had to have been most unperceptive not to see how removed from, if not insignificant to, their present and future plans Will had become. He continued to sit at his loom weaving or to go for several days to towns further down the Ohio River, trying to sell what he had woven. What he was able to bring to the family treasury was less than what Margaret made in her part-time work. Andrew had become, under his mother's tutelage and encouragement, the main support of the family, and they all knew it. Will was no longer much interested even in politics. The reports received from Scotland clearly indicated that Chartism as such was a dead issue. Although Tom Morrison continued working hopefully for a new order, it was apparent even to him that reform would have to be achieved by other means than petitions for universal suffrage. Clippings sent to them of letters in the Dunfermline *Journal* pointed up the wretched condition of those few remaining handloom weavers who had obstinately tried to continue in their craft:

A year ago it was expected that returning spring would dispel the dark clouds of adversity that hung over us; but spring has come and gone, and summer too is fast receding from us, while the prospect remains dark and cheerless as ever.

This letter concluded that the ratepayers must "put up money to remove the unemployed to some more hospitable region." [27]

The one bright political note from Dunfermline in these years was Tom Morrison's celebrated victory in 1850 over his old enemy, James Hunt. After one of their periodic public quarrels, the Laird of Pittencrieff had rashly written a letter to the editor of the Dunfermline *Advertiser* in which he called Morrison "a bully, an infidel, and a horrible and gastly [sic] character." Following publication of this letter Morrison had brought suit for defamation of character in the Court of Sessions and had not only won damages of 50 guineas and costs from Hunt, but a court order requiring Hunt to print a public apology and retraction of his charges in the same paper. It was a personal and family triumph over the hated Hunts, and the Carnegies celebrated Tom's victory in far-off Allegheny. [28]

Will Carnegie's general apathy in regard to political events both in Scotland and America widened the gulf separating him from his son. Andrew, the young Chartist émigré, had left neither his hopes nor his interest buried in Dunfermline. He had arrived in an America that was intoxicated with the heady wine of Manifest Destiny and had just completed its drive to the Pacific by conquering a neighboring republic and taking half of that nation's territory. Like all good Chartists, the boy was a militant pacifist, but he could hardly escape the excitement of being a young man in Young America. He could even find justification for military aggrandizement in the stated mission of America: to carry its democratic ideals, by force if necessary, to the entire continent and eventually to the world. It was difficult for Andrew to understand his father's indifference to this mission. The boy filled his own letters to Cousin Dod and Uncle Lauder with extravagant praise for his new nation.

Andrew's Scottish relatives, reading these letters, were hardly given a true picture of America in this period, for their American correspondent was highly selective in his choice of material. He wrote in detail of the number of miles of railroad track being laid, of telegraph wires being extended, of temperance reform bills in Maine, of the abolition of flogging in the Navy. But of those events which were to make this decade perhaps the most tragic in the history of the Republic—the repeal of the Missouri Compromise, the passage of a more stringent Fugitive Slave Law, the weak and vacillating men who occupied the White House, Bleeding Kansas, John Brown, Dred Scott—there is little mention. What this young transplanted Chartist stressed were the American constitutional forms, which he considered ideal, and in emphasizing form he tended to ignore function. He did of course admit the existence of that evil snake, slavery, in this republican Eden, but he was sanguine in his prediction that here Adam in all his purity would scotch the serpent. For Andrew, "America was promises," promises of growth, opportunity, and mission accomplished.

In discussing the approaching presidential election of 1852, he wrote to his Uncle Lauder:

> You would laugh to see how low they [the politicians] have to bow to their soverigns [sic] the People. The 2 most prominent candidates I am sorry to say are warriors one Gen[1] Scott Com-in-Chief U.S.A. he is a whig; the Whigs here go for Protection against foreign labor are in favor of a National Bank & are conservative. The Democrats go for Free Trade and no Chartered Bank. I take great interest in politics here and think when I am a man I would like to dabble a little in them. I would be a democrat or rather a free-soil-Democrat, free soilers got that name from their hatred of Slavery and slave labor. Slavery I hope will soon be abolished in the Country. . . . There is much excitement here upon the subject of Temperance. The State of Maine passed a law prohibiting the manufacture or sale except for medical purposes of all intoxicating liquors several states have passed similar laws and of course the Rum sellers are trying all they can to protect their right to sell what they please. That is a step in advance of you at any rate.

Even his father, Andrew reported, although "he does not take very much interest in politics here," had become excited over the proposed Homestead Bill then pending in Congress.

Father said this morning to be sure and tell you that the greatest Reform of the Age has just taken place here, it is a law recently passed the House of Representatives granting 160 acres
of unoccupied land to every man that will cultivate it and when
he dies his children get the land . . . the Law has not yet come
into operation but will come soon, send out your poor tax ridden honest men and they will soon get a home here. . . . Land
reform has really excited him he is in great glee about it.[29]

Unfortunately, the great land reform act did not "come soon
into operation." It was defeated in the Senate by Southern votes.
But if this failure of land reform deepened Will Carnegie's pessimism, it left his son's faith in the future of America untouched.
When Uncle Lauder, still playing pedagogue to Dod and Naig,
suggested an exchange of letters between the two, in which each
boy would defend the political structure of the country in which
he lived, Andrew entered into the project with enthusiasm. In a
series of letters, he carefully explained just how the government
of the United States operated. First he gave a brief history of the
founding of the Republic and sent Dod a copy of the American
Constitution with the taunting note:

Bye the bye, either send me your boasted British one or lets
know what you understand by it. I have no doubt but what
you will be surprised at its (i.e. the American constitution) simplicity and won't believe that such a Nation as this composed of
25,000,000 from all ends of the earth can be governed by such
an insignificant looking document as that but thats because you
have been brought up to think a Constitution should have
something *mysterious* about it as it is the case with your own—
a thing to be talked about but never seen. Our Con. was made
by the People and can be altered amended or done away with
by them whenever thay see fit.[30]

According to his intention, Andrew next wrote:

In my last letter I promised to tell you how we were governed. Your Monarchial statesman if informed that we succeeded in *preserving order (that bugbear of the middle classes)*
would at once conclude that the dominant race kept the others

98

in absolute subjection denied them all civil rights. . . . But how erroneous his idea would be for our government is founded upon justice and our creed is that the will of the People is the *source* & their happiness the end of all legitimate "Government." Such a government needs none of the wretched props necessary to the existence of despotisms—Our army consists of a few thousand men employed in protecting our frontiers from Indian depredations. . . . We have perfect political Equality. . . . It is strange that with your immense Army and police system you cannot keep the Peace. . . . Here they [newly arrived immigrants] find no Royal Family (increasing with fearful rapidity) to squander their hard made earnings—no aristocracy to support—No established Church with its enormous sinecures. . . . they find the various reforms which they struggled for at home in successful operation here. . . . We have all your good traits which are many with few or none of your bad ones which I must say are neither few nor far between. . . . We have the Charter which you have been fighting for for years as the Panacea for all Britian's [sic] woes, the bulwark of the people. . . . But we are not at a standstill we have only commenced the great work of reform.

. . . But the best proof of the superiority of our system is seen in the general prosperity & progress of its citizens. . . . We have now in the National Treasury nearly 22,000,000$ Our debt is being paid off as fast as it becomes due. . . . Our public Lands of almost unlimited extent are becoming settled with an enterprising people. . . . Pauperism is almost unknown. . . . Everything around us is motion—mind is freed from superstitious reverence for old customs, unawed by gorgeous and unmeaning shows & forms. . . . But you may reply, Government has little or nothing to do with this state of affairs—Why then I would ask the contrast between the U. States & the Canadas. They were settled by the same people, at the same time—under the same Government—& look at the difference—Where is her Rail Roads Telegraphs & Canals? . . . We have given to the world a Washington, a Franklin, a Fulton, a Morse—What has Canada ever produced—Ah Dod "There's something rotten in Denmark" How can you account for this—Is it not a fair sample of our respective systems. The one exhibits the vigor of manhood, the other the lassitude of old age. . . . the one is "old England" the other "young America"—that's where the secret lies.[31]

99

When Dod, in defense of Britain, replied that at least there was no Negro slavery within the British Empire, he touched on a very sore point. Andrew did his best to meet this criticism:

> Allow me to say that I am an enthusiastic & ultra abolitionist, admit and deplore the great evils that necessarily flow in the wake of slavery feel as keenly the great wrong perpetrated upon the African as you can do. It is the greatest evil in the world and I promise you that whatever influence I may acquire shall be used to overthrow it. In short I am a Republican and believe in our Noble declaration "That all men are born free and equal." You must not think then that I want to smooth it over & give you the bright side, for I hope I shall never be found upholding palliating oppression in any shape or form.

But, he continued, Britain was responsible for introducing slavery and the slave trade in the first place, and the Third Congress of the United States had abolished the slave trade. "Pennsylvania our own noble state abolished Slavery in 1798. N York did the same these two are the greatest states in the Union, containing more than a fifth of the total population." He pointed out to his cousin that slavery was a state question and each state was properly jealous of its own rights.

> Indeed, I consider that doctrine one of the main pillars of our Republic. It would be impossible for a country as extensive as this is, to be properly governed by a Central Government. . . . And so if Mississippi holds slaves, what have we to do with it? What can we do to prevent it? . . . We are all abolitionists in the North, Uncle Tom's Cabin is lauded to the skies, read in every parlor, taught in some Sunday Schools & played in our theatres. . . . That a way will be opened by which they [the Southern states] can cast off this only blot on our glorious Republic is the earnest prayer of an overwhelming majority of the people. . . . Slavery is sectional, Liberty alone is National.[32]

If faults could be found in the consistency of Andrew's arguments, none certainly could be found in his patriotism.

These letters reveal how easily Andrew had been assimilated into the American society, how quickly Scotland had become "you" and the United States had become "I." He was even losing the last traces of his Scottish accent within a few years after his arrival in Pittsburgh. In one of his letters to the Lauders, he told of the visit to their home of an old Dunfermline neighbor, James Sloan. "I was glad to hear him say that Dod and I looked very much alike far more so than when I was in Scotland. We are also about the same height He was laughing at me a few days ago because I could not say sow crae as broad as he says it. I tried it over and over but could not do it." [33] "Sow crae" being a shibboleth for true Scottish dialect, Andrew could no longer pass the test. His naturalization was complete.

He continued to feel nostalgia for Scotland, to be sure. In one letter he told of hearing Jenny Lind at the Pittsburgh Theater as one of his perquisites of being a telegraph operator. "She is the strangest woman I ever heard of, when I heard her I thought Oh if she could only sing some Scotch songs if she could give us 'Auld Lang Syne' I would have been better pleased than with all the others put together." [34] And in another letter:

> Although I cannot say sow crae just as broad as I once could I can read about Wallace, Bruce and Burns with as much enthusiasm as ever and feel proud of having been a son of old Calodonia [sic], and I like to tell people when they ask, "Are you native born?" "No sir, I am a scotchman," and I feel as proud as I am sure as ever Romans did when it was their boast to say, "I am a Roman citizen." [35]

He frequently expressed the hope that "I will see Dunfermline again for I can easily manage to save as much money if I behave well." [36] And at a much later date he would write that "during my first fourteen years of absence [from Dunfermline] my thought was almost daily as it was that morning [of departure], 'When shall I see you again?' " [37]

But these were only expressions of a sentimental attachment to the past, which Andrew readily admitted in no way altered his allegiance to his new home. He wrote his uncle, "Although I sometimes think I would like to be back in Dunfermline working at the Loom it's very likely I would have been a poor weaver all my days, but here, I can surely do something better than that if I don't it will be my own fault, for anyone can get along in this country." [38]

For Andrew, the significant phrase was "anyone can get along in this country." The boy had always felt that compelling Faustian drive to be "someone," not just "anyone," to do more than simply "get along." The inappetence for achievement of his associates, whether in the Dunfermline classroom or in the Pittsburgh telegraph office, had always been for him both inexplicable and, at the same time, wonderfully useful. He could believe in competition because he had so far in his life found that he was competing only with himself. It was the standards he had imposed upon himself, not pressure from others, that had made the competition rugged.

His rapid rise from messenger boy to operator within a year and a half had been gratifying, but hardly satisfying. As operator, he would now set up new rules for his game of solitaire. Andrew heard rumors that there were some operators in the country who were quick enough to receive a message directly by ear without having to go through the complicated process of translating the printed tape upon which the received message had been recorded. His fellow operators scoffed at the veracity of such reports, but for Andrew a standard had been established which he must meet. Tom David, one of the operators in the other telegraph company, would always remember the day when Andrew stopped by to pick up some messages coming in from the West to be relayed to the East Coast. "The instruments were ticking—I can see your eyes sparkle as they did when you exclaimed exultingly—'Tom, I can read nearly every word of that.' " [39]

Soon Andrew was taking all messages he received by ear. He became a celebrity, not only among the other operators, but also among the local businessmen, who, at the invitation of J. D. Reid, general superintendent of the telegraph company, would stop in to the O'Reilly office to watch the young boy perform. Andrew's salary was increased to $25.00 a month, but, of greater importance to the boy, these businessmen were learning his name and were asking for him personally to send out their more important messages.

The extra time he gained by this method of receiving could also be put to good advantage. At this time, all foreign news for the Pittsburgh press was received by wire from Cape Race. One operator was responsible for receiving these news items, and since Andrew preferred this branch of the office routine,

> it was soon tacitly assigned to me. The lines in those days worked poorly, and during a storm much had to be guessed at. My guessing powers were said to be phenomenal, and it was my favorite diversion to fill up gaps instead of interrupting the sender and spending minutes over a lost word or two. This was not a dangerous practice in regard to foreign news, for if any undue liberties were taken by the bold operator, they were not of a character likely to bring him into serious trouble.[40]

Not dangerous, perhaps, to the "bold operator" who was willing to take a chance—and Andrew was always willing to take a chance—but the effect of such a practice upon the trustworthiness of the news submitted to the press was quite a different matter. How much of what appeared in the Pittsburgh papers was an accurate transmission of foreign news dispatches, and how much was the product of the "phenomenal guessing powers" of a sixteen-year-old boy, no one in the city but Andrew could say. To the traditional meaning of the phrase "free press" Andrew had added that other definition of "free," as given in the dictionary: "not held to strict form, hence not literal or exact, as, a free translation."

This telegraphic duty on the Cape Race line led quite naturally to another assignment which Andrew alone had the time and interest to accept. All of the newspaper offices in Pittsburgh had hired one man to serve as a central agency for overseas press dispatches received in the telegraph office. He in turn offered Andrew $1.00 a day to make duplicate copies for the papers.

This job gave him an additional income of $30.00 a month, which enabled the Carnegies to buy the house his mother wanted.[41] It was the one belonging to Andrew Hogan, located on the same lot as the little alley loom shop where the Carnegies had been living since they arrived in Allegheny. Sister Kitty and her husband, Tom, along with Sister Annie, who had been living in the house, had decided to move to East Liverpool, Ohio, where Margaret's second brother, William, lived. Hogan had hoped to sell the house for $700, but a bad flood on the Allegheny River had caused some water damage in the house. When he could get no better offer, Hogan agreed to sell it to the Carnegies for $550. "Mother says that rents are so very high," Andrew wrote to the Lauders, "that tradesmen pay about 6 & 8 dolls. per. mo. for houses with 4 rooms—so we concluded to risk a little & bought it . . . we have two years to pay it in." [42]

With each passing month, Andrew was running faster in the race he had set for himself. How far away the goal was he did not know, nor what the prize would be, but he was running as if the finish line were already in sight. More and more responsibility was being given to him by his supervisors, Glass and Reid. When there was a temporary vacancy in the small branch office at Greensburgh, some thirty miles away, it was Andrew who was sent down to be the sole operator for two weeks, until the regular operator should return.[43] The following spring, a flood on the Ohio destroyed all telegraphic communication between Steubenville and Wheeling. Andrew was sent to the Steubenville office to take Eastern business coming in by wire from Pittsburgh and send the dispatches by boat down the river to Wheeling, where they could be relayed on to the West. For over a week, until the lines along the Ohio could be repaired, the Steubenville office, with Andrew in charge, was responsible for keeping the telegraphic communications open to and from the entire Ohio River valley. He wrote to his Uncle Lauder, "I enjoyed myself first rate." [44]

One evening, when he took some dispatches down to the regularly scheduled passenger boat headed downriver for Wheeling and Cincinnati, Andrew met his father on board. Will Carnegie was traveling to Cincinnati, hoping to sell a few tablecloths he had woven. The river, still at high water stage, was dangerous to travel upon, and the boat was already several hours late in its run from Pittsburgh. It was a raw spring night. Andrew was shocked to discover that his father did not have the money for cabin passage and was prepared to spend the night on the open deck. Suddenly, the contrast in their situations became painfully apparent to both: the sixteen-year-old boy, already acting the part of a business executive, charged with an important assignment and thoroughly enjoying his responsibility; the father, defeated and yet unable to surrender to his defeat, continuing on in his profitless selling trips because there was nothing else to do. Andrew's response, as he would later remember it, was characteristic of him: "There was comfort [to me] in saying, 'Well, father, it will not be long before mother and you shall ride in your carriage.' "

And Will Carnegie's response was equally characteristic.

> He . . . grasped my hand with a look I often see and can never forget . . . "Andra, I am proud of you." The voice trembled and he seemed ashamed of himself for saying so much. The tear had to be wiped from his eye, I fondly noticed, as he bade me good-night and told me to run back to my office. Those words rang in my ear and warmed my heart for years and years. We understood each other. How reserved the Scot is! Where he feels most he expresses least. Quite right. They are holy depths which it is sacrilege to disturb. Silence is more eloquent than words.[45]

Carnegie was right. Silence can be more eloquent than words. For all of the eloquence of his own words in recalling this scene, it is doubtful if he ever did understand his father or ever did realize that there could be both pain and pride for the man in this encounter with his son. The boy had been shocked to find his father traveling on the open deck of the river boat, like a homeless peddler, and had been properly concerned for his father's physical welfare. But that there could be any other emotional response except fatherly pride to his own eager promise that someday *he* would provide a carriage for his father to ride in required an insight that Andrew would never have. Not knowing failure himself, Carnegie would always be insensitive to the feelings of those who had failed.

Andrew returned to the telegraph office in Pittsburgh after his assignments in Greensburgh and Steubenville "surrounded with something like a halo, so far as the other boys were concerned."[46] "I still continue to like my business," he wrote the Lauders, "and intend to continue at it. I have very easy times, and I may say I have no master. . . ."[47]

Andrew was careful to put even his free time to good use. It would be remembered in later years in Pittsburgh that the parents of a certain Miss Lou Atherton paid Andrew 25¢ on several occasions to serve as an escort for their daughter to take her to evening parties and to return her safely home. How this rather delicate arrangement was negotiated the legend-makers of Pittsburgh unfortunately do not relate, nor is there on record any indication of how Miss Atherton may have felt about utilizing the services of a professional escort.[48] If the story is true, however, one can be certain that young Andrew considered the arrangement as being simply another task, however pleasant, by which he might supplement the family income.

For recreation, he organized a debating society, which met in the Phipps's cobbler shop to debate such issues as "Should the judiciary be elected by the people?" Here he and his friends, John Phipps, Tom Miller, and Bob Pitcairn, would argue long and vehemently. Tom Miller would remember that Andy once spoke for an hour and a half without interruption on the elective judiciary issue. "Of course, you took the affirmative," Miller recalled,[49] for to most of his youthful associates Andrew was still the wild Chartist Radical.

Andrew was a voracious reader. Having been introduced to Shakespeare in the Pittsburgh Theater, he was eager to read all of the plays, and committed great sections to memory as easily as he had memorized the poetry of Robert Burns for Mr. Martin's benefit.

His continuing debate by correspondence with Cousin Dod required of him a thorough knowledge of American history and government. The great difficulty was in obtaining books. He had quickly exhausted the few books in the possession of his friends in Allegheny, and it was with delight that he read in the local press that a certain Colonel James Anderson of Allegheny would open his personal library of 400 volumes each Saturday afternoon to any young working boy who wished to borrow a book for the following week. In the Carnegie Birthplace Memorial Building in Dunfermline today, in a glass showcase, are some of the books Andrew borrowed as a boy from the Anderson library. The selection is impressive in its variety, if not in its quality of literary excellence: J. Bron, *History and Present Condition of St. Domingo;* Mrs. Hofland, *Reflection;* J. W. Revere, *Tour of Duty in California;* Mrs. Somerville, *Connection of the Physical Sciences;* Mrs. Steele, *Heroines of Sacred History;* and Anonymous, *Confessions of a Reformed Inebriate.*[50]

106

Although not displayed in this collection, there were other works of greater merit which Andrew's letters indicate that he borrowed from Colonel Anderson. His favorite volumes were George Bancroft's *History of the United States,* particularly valuable to the boy in his correspondence with the Lauders; the collections of essays by Macaulay and Lamb; and Prescott's *Conquest of Mexico.*[51] For Andrew, Colonel Anderson "opened to me the intellectual wealth of the world . . . I revelled week after week in books." [52]

So successful had this modest experiment in a free library been that Anderson decided to expand it by adding several hundred volumes and moving the collection to a building of its own. "The Mechanics' and Apprentices' Library" became Allegheny's first public library, with an annual subscription fee of $2.00, but free of charge to all apprentices. When Andrew appeared at the new library, he found that with expansion had come a bureaucratic order he had not encountered in the hospitable home of Colonel Anderson. The librarian in charge informed him that, inasmuch as he was not an apprentice, but a salaried telegraphic operator, he must pay the regular subscription fee. Although this was not an unreasonable request, the boy protested, claiming that in his opinion Colonel Anderson's intention had been to continue the free library privileges to all those who had held them before. Receiving no satisfaction from the librarian, who was bound by the letter of the bequest, Andrew decided to take his case to the public rather than accept this ruling as final. Shortly thereafter, there appeared in the Pittsburgh *Dispatch* the following letter: [53]

Allegheny, May 9th, 1853

Mr. Editor:

Believing that you take a deep interest in whatever tends to elevate, instruct and improve the youth of this county, I am induced to call your attention to the following. You will remember that some time ago Mr. Anderson (a gentleman of this city) bequested a large sum of money to establish and support a Library for working boys and apprentices residing here. It has been in successful operation for over a year, scattering precious seeds among us, and although fallen "by the wayside and in

stony places," not a few have found good ground. Every working boy has been freely admitted only requiring his parents or
guardian to become surety. But its means of doing good have
recently been greatly circumscribed by new directors who refuse
to allow any boy *who is not learning a trade and bound* for a
stated time to become a member. I rather think that the new
directors have misunderstood the generous donor's *intentions*.
It can hardly be thought that he meant to exclude boys employed in stores merely because they are not bound.

> A Working Boy
> though not bound.

The following week there appeared another letter to the editor, signed "X.Y.Z." This letter, presumably from the librarian,
pointed out that the terms of Colonel Anderson's gift specifically
designated apprentices as the only persons who should have free
access to the library. To this letter, "Working Boy" replied, on 17
May, that although "apprentice" may have been used in the wording of the bequest, as a frequent user of that library he was confident that Colonel Anderson had never intended to exclude any
working boys from the free use of his library.

Three days later, on the editorial page of the *Dispatch,* there
appeared a short notice: "A 'Working Boy' will confer a favor by
calling at our office." [54]

The Working Boy lost no time in calling at the *Dispatch* office. There he was informed that Colonel Anderson's attention
had been called to the recent exchange of letters and he had graciously restated the terms of his gift to the city in order to grant
free library privileges to all working boys under a certain age,
whether bound as apprentices or not. Andrew's triumph was complete. [55]

It was also his first literary success, and for Andrew nothing
else that he had known in the way of recognition by others had
been quite as exhilarating as this experience of seeing his own
words in print. It fed his vanity and at the same time increased
his appetite for more such food. At that moment a journalistic
ambition was born which he would spend the remainder of his
life attempting to satisfy.

That the leading newspaper of Pittsburgh should publish his

letter, and that by these letters, he, "A Working Boy," could effect a change in municipal policy, were evidence enough for Andrew of the power of the individual in a democracy. His letters to the Lauders from this moment on became, even more than before, testimonials on behalf of the American nation. "The great error in your country is that things are just upside down," he wrote to Dod not long after his triumph over the library bureaucracy. "You look to your officials to govern you instead of you governing them. . . ." [56] And again,

> We believe that we have a great mission to fulfill with our independence a new light dawned upon the world. The momentous question whether man was capable of self government was to be decided our govt was an experiment & with the cause of human progress was for a time to sink or swim. It was & is still the great hope of Reformers throughout the world.[57]

Here was the realized Utopia of a young Scot's Chartist dreams. Only in a land where "we have the charter" would a prosperous young man have to fight for the same privileges enjoyed by "the working boy who was bound." This, to Andrew, was the wonder and the glory of America. It would remain his most basic creed, and never in the years ahead would he have reason to doubt it.

PART II

THE
CONTRACT
1853 - 1901

"Man must have an idol—the amassing of wealth is one of the worst species of idolitary—no idol more debasing than the worship of money."
Personal Memorandum, December 1868.

*

"My opinion is that if we give our laborers one dollar a day, we will be treating them very liberally."
Carnegie to W. P. Shinn, December 1876.

*

"Do not be fastidious; take what the gods offer."
Lecture delivered at Cornell University, January 1896.

*

"Mr. Carnegie, I want to congratulate you on being the richest man in the world!"
J. P. Morgan to Carnegie, February 1901.

CHAPTER VI

Mr. Scott's Andy

1853-1859

On 10 December 1852, the stockholders of the Pennsylvania Railroad Company received an announcement from the management which was of considerable interest to them, to the state of Pennsylvania, and, more especially, to the city of Pittsburgh. On this date, the management of the company declared they had officially opened "to trade and travel" a continuous single-track railroad between Philadelphia and Pittsburgh, the first all-rail line to connect the headwaters of the Ohio with the Atlantic seaboard.[1] This announcement was somewhat misleading, in that it implied uninterrupted rail service; in actual practice, until 1854 the old state-owned inclined plane tracks would still be used in going through the mountains. Nevertheless, Pittsburgh was connected directly by rail with the East Coast. No longer was the city an isolated community, dependent upon a circuitous route of canals, lakes, and rivers through Ohio and New York for the movement of goods and people from and to the East. Pittsburgh could at last be what she claimed to be, the Gateway to the West.

No business concern in Pittsburgh welcomed this development more heartily than did the O'Reilly Telegraph Office, for the office of the Western Division of the Pennsylvania Railroad would be an important customer. Young Carnegie, as the quickest and most efficient operator in the telegraph office, could expect that the opening of this new railroad would be of particular significance to him, but he could not foresee at this moment just how significant. Thomas A. Scott, the newly appointed superintendent for the Western Division of the line, was a constant caller in the operator's room, and within the first week he had singled out young Carnegie as his operator.

Carnegie, as always, bloomed under this special recognition. He did not object to the extra demands upon his time, and he was fascinated with the idea that by tapping his telegraphic key he could transfer freight up through mountain passes, order locomotives to wait on sidings, and move people toward their destinations. Such dispatches were far more interesting than the usual business orders or routine personal messages. Most of all, he liked the daily contacts with Thomas Scott. He was flattered that Scott would ask for him by name, and he knew from the first meeting that here was "an extraordinary man, . . . one to whom the term 'genius' in his department may be safely applied." [2]

Thomas Scott was an impressive figure. Born in Franklin County in eastern Pennsylvania in 1823, he had been largely self-supporting since the age of ten, when his father had died leaving eleven children for his widow to support. At seventeen Scott became a clerk for his brother-in-law, James Patton, collector of tolls for the state-owned system of roads and canals. In 1850 he became a station agent for the Pennsylvania Railroad at Duncansville, which was at that time the western terminal point for the railroad. When the line was opened to Pittsburgh, two years later, Scott was promoted to third assistant superintendent, in charge of the Western Division of the company, from Altoona to Pittsburgh. The offices of the Western Division were in Pittsburgh, so Scott moved there.[3] He was not yet thirty.

Scott was a handsome man, and, in spite of being largely self-educated, he was cultured and refined. He was also gentle and affable, with great warmth and charm of personality. This was all to the good, for he had been placed in a difficult situation. There was in the city considerable hostility toward the Pennsylvania Railroad. Businessmen blamed the company for having obtained an exclusive charter from the state which had prevented the Baltimore & Ohio line from entering Pittsburgh at an earlier date. Pittsburgh had thus been kept in its isolated position until, after many false starts, the Pennsylvania had finally succeeded in opening a line into the city.[4] Scott met this animosity with understanding and tact, and he won considerable community support for his company. Company policy helped him in this, for in 1852 passenger rates had been reduced to two and a half cents a mile, making them highly competitive with canal and river boat fares.[5] Most effective in winning the respect of business was the Pennsylvania's concern, in spite of its monopolistic position in Pittsburgh, to give fast and efficient service. A single-track operation eastward to Altoona, which included transferring to the inclined plane tracks through the mountains, presented many problems in maintaining good service, but Scott met these with a quiet efficiency that was particularly impressive to shippers accustomed to the poor service of other transportation facilities.

It is not surprising that the young telegraph operator in O'Reilly's office would look upon Scott as a hero. From the first Scott had been attracted to young Carnegie. He liked the boy's quickness, and was amused by his bustling efficiency and cheerfulness. Like others before and after him, Scott soon had a protective, almost paternal feeling toward Andrew. He called him "my boy, Andy."

Within a few weeks after his arrival in Pittsburgh, Scott realized the necessity of having his own telegraph operator and an open line direct to Altoona and points east. He could not afford the time to make frequent trips to the telegraph office. Upon receiving approval from the president of the railroad, J. Edgar Thomson, of the unprecedented request for his own telegraph facilities, Scott, with characteristic energy, immediately went to work on it. The necessary equipment was purchased, and arrangements were made with the telegraph company for direct service. The only thing lacking was an operator, and here, too, Scott knew exactly what he wanted.

Andrew Carnegie, talking with one of Scott's clerks one day, was surprised to hear that Scott had been making inquiries as to whether "my boy, Andy" might be lured away from his job at O'Reilly's to be Scott's personal operator. As Carnegie would recall the incident in his autobiography, the clerk said that he had told Scott the boy was O'Reilly's chief operator in Pittsburgh and would not leave his present position. Not at all pleased with this summary disposition of his own future, Carnegie would recall that he told the clerk with sharpness, "Not so fast. Scott can have me. I want to get out of a mere office life. Please go and tell him so." [6]

Some of Carnegie's fellow operators would later be convinced in their own minds that Carnegie was curiously reluctant to accept Scott's offer when it was formally made, and that they had persuaded him that his prospects would be better with the railroad. Tom David, in particular, would write his former colleague in 1903, "I remember very clearly the circumstances of your going to the Penna. R. R. It took some persuation [sic] on the part of John P. Glass to convince you that it offered better opportunities. I saw Mr. Glass having an earnest talk, and to my question, 'What is the matter with Andy,' he intimated that you did not like to make a change." [7]

This account is clearly at variance with Carnegie's recollection of his conversation with Scott's clerk. If Carnegie showed any hesitation in leaving, he probably did so only to see how high the telegraph company's superintendent, J. D. Reid, would go in offering a salary increase to retain his services. Reid went as high as $33 a month. Scott had offered $35, but Carnegie did not need this extra inducement to be convinced that the opportunities for advancement in the railroad business were far greater than in the telegraph office. His own eagerness to accept Scott's offer was plainly expressed in a letter he wrote to the Lauders soon after he had made the change:

> I have some news to tell you. I left my old place in the telegraph office and am now in the employ of the Pennsylvania Railroad Co., one of (if not the first of) the three leading roads from our Atlantic cities to the Great West. It forms a continuous line from Philadelphia to Pittsburgh & here connects with Western roads & the Ohio River. Mr. Scott he's the supt. of it with whom I became acquainted while in the office by often talking for him on business by telegraph, offered me 35 dollars per month to take charge of their Telegraph office which the Co. has in this City for its own exclusive use—& also to assist

him in writing and auditing accounts which I accepted. The Teleg. Co. would have increased my salary to $400 per year if I had remained there but we all thought that the new situation held out better prospects for the future—I resigned my station on the first of February & have been employed at my new place since that time. I am liking it far better than the old one— instead of having to stay every other night till 10 or 11 o'clock, I am done every night at 6, which is a great advantage, and am not so much confined. Although I thought my old berth a very good one for the present, Still for the future, I felt it did not hold out great inducements—I must always have been an employee—& the highest station I could reasonably expect to at- tain to was Manager of an office with 7 or 8 hundred a year and I had begun to think that if another situation would turn up which would be better for the future, I would accept it even though the salary was less than at present when Mr. Scott (without my application) offered me my present berth—he is having an office fixed up for his own use and I am to be along with him in it & help him—I have met with very few men that I like so well in this Country—& I am sure we will agree very well. There is not much telegraphing to do, but it is neces- sary for them to have an office—The line runs along side of the RRoad & as there is only one track laid yet—the time the different trains pass stations must be known.[8]

So young Carnegie on 1 February 1853 entered into a new occupation which, with careful deliberation, he had judged to be "better for the future." The wages were higher, the hours shorter, and the opportunity for advancement far greater. There were, however, some disadvantages for a young man who had hitherto kept himself remarkably well-insulated from some of the basic realities of life.

I had now stepped into the open world, and the change at first was far from agreeable. I had just reached my eighteenth birth- day [he had actually only recently become seventeen] and I do not see how it could be possible for any boy to arrive at that age much freer from a knowledge of anything but what was pure and good. . . . I knew nothing of the base and vile. For- tunately I had always been brought into contact with good people.

117

Now for the first time young Carnegie knew what his mother had meant when she had harshly accused Andrew Hogan of wanting her boy to associate with the "rough men of the wharves." The railroads had brought into their service much the same class of men that had previously served the river boats. Although Carnegie's normal duties as telegraph operator had no direct connection with the operating crews, his position in the front office of the Pittsburgh railroad yard, as well as the errands he ran for Scott, brought him into daily contact with these men.

> This was a different world, indeed, from that to which I had been accustomed. I was not happy about it. I ate, necessarily, of the fruit of the tree of knowledge of good and evil for the first time. . . . I passed through this phase of my life detesting what was foreign to my nature and my early education.

Always for Carnegie, though, there was a refuge from the vulgar, "there were still the sweet and pure surroundings of home, where nothing coarse or wicked ever entered," and to this he held fast.

Characteristically, Carnegie, much as he disliked this experience at the time, would later feel that he had drawn from it certain lessons of value. "This experience with coarse men was probably beneficial because it gave me a 'scunner' [disgust] to use a Scotism, at chewing or smoking tobacco, also at swearing or the use of improper language, which fortunately remained with me through life." [9]

Emotionally, however, this experience was probably not beneficial. Carnegie's introduction to what he chose to call "the fruit of the tree of knowledge" had come too abruptly and too late, and had been presented in too coarse a manner for one whose innocence at the age of seventeen surprised even himself. It would appear from his own account that this was Carnegie's first acquaintance with the most basic facts of sex, and his teachers—"those rough characters from the river," as Carnegie called them—were hardly sensitive to the kind of instruction that would have benefited Andrew. It would not be strange if from this introduction Carnegie would regard the sexual experience as being something coarse and vulgar, like swearing or chewing tobacco. His disgust for and rejection of all that he observed and learned from these men, causing him to turn too readily to the "sweet and pure surroundings of home," offer an explanation for his later development. It was not easy for Carnegie to overcome the effect of his first acquaintance with the unsheltered life, for from it he learned rudely and belatedly what should have been part of the normal education of an adolescent boy.

In these weeks of adjustment to his new occupation, Carnegie paid frequent visits to his old friends at the telegraph office, but to them he gave no hint of his disturbing experiences. In fact, he presented himself as a worldly young railroad executive, to be envied and emulated, if possible.[10] He even persuaded his two closest friends, Dave McCargo and Bob Pitcairn, to join him as employees of the Pennsylvania Railroad Company. After Scott obtained his own private office, which Carnegie shared, life became much more pleasant for Andrew. He could now look back on his first associations with the railroad section hands with more charity.

> I do not wish to suggest that the men of whom I have spoken were really degraded or bad characters. Railroading was new, and many rough characters were attracted to it from the river service. But many of the men were fine young fellows who have lived to be highly respectable citizens and to occupy responsible positions. And I must say that one and all of them were most kind to me.[11]

As Scott's personal telegraph operator and private secretary, Carnegie quickly learned the basic elements of railroading. He found that the railroad business and telegraphy had the same advantages, for, quite fortuitously, he had been successively engaged in communications and transportation, the two business activities best designed to provide a liberal education in the whole general area of business. He made good use of those advantages. Just as there had never been a dispatch to send or a message to receive which had not contained some information that was interesting and might prove useful, so now there was no such thing as an unimportant shipment of cargo. Each bill of lading told him something about the sender and the receiver and gave him a means to judge the strength and weakness of the firm, and each customer who called at the office gave him a further opportunity to evaluate the management of that concern. Few men in Pittsburgh could have had a broader knowledge of the total business activity of the city than this eighteen-year-old boy.

At the time Carnegie joined the railroad, in the winter of 1853, construction was already well advanced toward the completion of the laying of a double track through the mountains, which would permit the company to dispense with the use of the old state-owned, inclined plane Portage Railroad between Hollidaysburg and Johnstown, across the Allegheny divide. In preparation for the opening of this final link in the Pennsylvania Railroad system, the small village of Altoona, just north of Hollidaysburg, had already been selected by the officials of the company to be the main center for railroad shops, yards, and offices between Pittsburgh and Philadelphia. Into this mountain hamlet by the spring of 1853 were pouring hundreds of German, Scottish, and Irish immigrants, seeking employment as yard workers and section hands, and the town, only four years before a valley farm belonging to Archibald Wright, had lost forever its mountain isolation.[12]

One of Carnegie's first assignments in his new job was to go to the Altoona company offices to pick up the monthly payroll for the employees in the Pittsburgh area. It was his first long railroad trip, a hundred miles from Pittsburgh, and over one of the most unusual railroad lines in the country. A passenger going east from Pittsburgh at this time would travel over the Pennsylvania line as far as Johnstown, but there his car would be transferred to the Portage Line, which consisted of a series of inclined planes and intervening levels which raised the individual cars to the summit of the mountain divide, 1172 feet above Johnstown. Then, by another series of five inclined planes and levels, the car would descend to Hollidaysburg, 1399 feet below. Over a decade earlier, Charles Dickens had written a vivid description of travel on the Portage:

> Occasionally the rails were laid upon the extreme verge of a giddy precipice; and looking from the carriage window, the traveler gazes sheer down, without a stone or scrap of fence between, into the mountain depths below. . . . It was very pretty

travelling thus at a rapid pace along the heights of the mountains in a keen wind, to look down into a valley full of light
and softness; catching glimpses, through the treetops, of scattered cabins; . . . men in their shirtsleeves, looking in at their
un-finished houses, planning out tomorrow's work; and we riding onward, high above them, like a whirlwind. It was amusing, too, when we had dined, and rattled down a steep pass,
having no other moving power than the weight of the carriages
themselves, to see the engine, released long after us, come buzz-
ing down alone, like a great insect, its back of green and gold
so shiny in the sun.[13]

Young Carnegie's trip over the Portage must have been even
more exciting than that of Dickens, for as a railroad employee he
scorned the ordinary passenger coach. He insisted upon riding in
the front cab of the engine, alongside the engineer and fireman,
which, as he said, "made the journey a remarkable one to me."

Arriving in Altoona, Carnegie went to the office of the general superintendent of the Pennsylvania, Herman Lombaert,
Thomas Scott's immediate superior. For here, working in Lombaert's office, was Carnegie's closest friend, Bob Pitcairn. Scott
had told Carnegie about Mr. Lombaert's stern, unbending nature, and the strict discipline he demanded from his employees, a
report that Bob Pitcairn confirmed in detail. Both Pitcairn and
Carnegie consequently were surprised that afternoon when Lombaert came into the outer office where the two boys were talking
and invited Carnegie to his home for tea. Lombaert's introduction of Carnegie to his wife was, "This is Mr. Scott's 'Andy.' "
Carnegie glowed with pleasure. His name had already become
known in the higher echelons of the Pennsylvania system.[14]

The next morning, Carnegie, with the payrolls and checks
wrapped in a bundle and placed under his waistcoat, caught a
ride on the locomotive that went to Hollidaysburg, where the
train for Pittsburgh was made up for the ride over the Portage
Line. So interested was he in talking with the crew and in climbing around in the cab of the engine to inspect the various controls
that it was not until the locomotive was approaching Hollidaysburg that Carnegie, reaching perfunctorily inside his jacket to
make sure the package was secure, discovered to his horror that
the payroll was missing. Knowing that this loss would mean the

end of his career with the Pennsylvania, he begged the engineer to back up the locomotive, in the desperate hope that the bundle might be spotted along the track. The engineer obliged, and as the locomotive backed slowly along the track, Carnegie, nearly suffocating with fear, scrutinized every foot of the right-of-way. As the engine backed across a bridge over a wide mountain stream, Carnegie saw the package lying on the farther bank, within a foot of the water. He jumped off the locomotive, dashed down the embankment, and clutched the bundle to him.

It was long after the event that I ventured to tell the story. Suppose that package had fallen just a few feet farther away and been swept down by the stream, how many years of faithful service would it have required upon my part to wipe out the effect of that one piece of carelessness! I could no longer have enjoyed the confidence of those whose confidence was essential to success had fortune not favored me. I have never since believed in being too hard on a young man, even if he does commit a dreadful mistake or two; and I have always tried in judging such to remember the difference it would have made in my own career but for an accident which restored to me that lost package at the edge of the stream a few miles from Hollidaysburg. I could go straight to the very spot to-day, and often as I passed over that line afterwards I never failed to see that light-brown package lying upon the bank. It seemed to be calling; "All right, my boy! the good gods were with you, but don't do it again!" [15]

Carnegie was correct about the good gods being with him. They almost always were. Not so applicable to his career as he appears to have believed is the other moral he drew from the story, for, unfortunately, he did not show the tolerance to error in others that he claimed he acquired as a part of the lesson learned from this experience. Only a few months after this incident of the lost payroll bundle (and, incidentally, only a few pages further on in his autobiography), he was given an opportunity to exhibit this spirit of forbearance, and he failed the test. Scott had to be out of town for a week, and he left his young assistant in charge of the office. During Scott's absence, an accident occurred which was attributable to the negligence of the ballast crew. Without waiting for Scott's return, Carnegie immediately held what he called "a court-martial," investigated the cause of the accident, and summarily dismissed one man and suspended two others from their duties for a month without pay. For Carnegie,

> that this accident should occur was gall and wormwood to me. . . . Mr. Scott after his return, of course was advised of the accident, and proposed to investigate and deal with the matter. I felt I had gone too far, but having taken the step, I informed him that all had been settled. . . . Some of these [men] appealed to Mr. Scott for a reopening of the case, but this I never could have agreed to, had it been pressed. More by look I think than by word Mr. Scott understood my feelings upon this delicate point and acquiesced. It is probable he was afraid I had been too severe and very likely he was correct. . . . I had felt qualms of conscience about my action in this, my first court. A new judge is apt to stand so straight as really to lean a little backward.[16]

Scott may have been disturbed by these martinet tendencies in his young assistant, but he was probably not entirely surprised. There had already been several incidents to make Scott realize that Andrew was more than an efficient and pleasant clerk.

One morning Scott had received a telegram from Colonel Niles A. Stokes, chief counsel for the Pennsylvania Railroad, asking him to find out who had written the unsigned letter published in the *Pittsburgh Journal* that morning. The letter had strongly defended the railroad against criticism still being directed against it by some of the businessmen in the city. Stokes wished to thank the author for this support. When Carnegie gave the telegram to Scott, he quietly informed him that, although the editor of the *Journal* would not be able to tell him who the author was—for the letter had been sent anonymously—he, Carnegie, could, for the simple reason that he himself was the author. "[Scott] seemed incredulous," Carnegie remembered, and "his incredulous look did not pass me unnoticed. The pen was getting to be a weapon with me." Shortly afterwards, young Carnegie was invited to Greensburgh to spend a Sunday with Colonel Stokes.

The visit was one of the bright spots in my life. Henceforth we were great friends. The grandeur of Mr. Stokes's home impressed me, but the one feature of it that eclipsed all else was a marble mantel in his library. In the center of the arch, carved in the marble, was an open book with this inscription:

> He that cannot reason is a fool,
> He that will not a bigot,
> He that dare not a slave.

These noble words thrilled me. I said to myself, "Someday, someday, I'll have a library and these words shall grace the mantel as here." And so they do. . . .[17]

The goal was still far distant, but Carnegie now knew what some of the prizes might be.

Another incident, of greater importance in helping Scott to understand the true capabilities of his assistant, occurred on a day when Scott was prevented by other business from appearing in his office at the usual time. Carnegie, alone in the office, received a message from Altoona that a serious accident on the Eastern Division line had delayed the westbound passenger train and that the eastbound passenger train was proceeding only by having a flagman stationed at every curve. None of the freight trains could move in either direction. Carnegie made an effort to locate Scott and, when he failed to find him, decided to take matters in his own hands. He knew, he felt, exactly what kind of orders Scott would send out. Why wait for Scott? Why not send the orders right away, with the familiar "T.A.S." signature attached? It was a repetition of the incident of the early morning telegraph he had dared take when he was only a messenger boy in O'Reilly's office. Much more was at stake here, of course, and the wrong order could tie up the whole line for hours or lead to even more serious consequences. Even so, Carnegie, without much hesitation, plunged in. At the moment of decision, the quotation that came to him (at least as he later remembered it) is as revealing of his character as the action he took. " 'Death or Westminster Abbey' flashed across my mind." With this, the orders were sent, orders that started every locomotive and moved each train to its proper station.

When Scott, who heard of the accident nearly an hour later, came rushing into the office to send out the necessary orders, his young assistant calmly reported, "Mr. Scott, I could not find you anywhere and I gave these orders in your name early this morning."

Carnegie showed him the dispatches sent, gave him the position of every train on the line, and the answers received from the conductors and the stations which the various trains had passed.

> All was right. He looked in my face for a second. I scarcely dared look in his. I did not know what was going to happen. He did not say one word, but again looked carefully over all that had taken place. Still he said nothing. After a little he moved away from my desk to his own, and that was the end of it. He was afraid to approve what I had done, yet he had not censured me. . . . So it stood, but I noticed that he came in regularly and in good time for some mornings after that.[18]

With any other employer, Carnegie might well have been dismissed for this presumptuous act, but Scott, being the kind of man he was, easy-going and generous in recognizing talent in others, was more pleased than disturbed. Carnegie was informed by the supervisor of the freight department, a man named Franciscus, that on the evening after this incident Scott was bragging to him of what "that little white-haired Scotch devil of mine did."

Carnegie had been momentarily abashed by his own presumption and Scott's silence in regard to it, and had made up his mind not to take such a precipitate course of action again. When he realized that Scott had been telling the story to his associates as a proud father might boast of the latest exploit of his offspring, his self-confidence was quickly restored. "This satisfied me. Of course I had my cue for the next occasion, and went boldly in. From that date it was very seldom that Mr. Scott gave a train order." [19] This last statement is surely an exaggeration, but not because of any timidity on Carnegie's part.

Even the great J. Edgar Thomson, president of the Pennsylvania Railroad Company, heard of Carnegie's exploit, and when he was next in Pittsburgh he made a point of putting his head into the telegraph room. He looked at Carnegie solemnly and said, "So you are Scott's Andy."

Taken all together, it is quite a record that Carnegie presents of his activities in his first few months with the railroad company —a well-publicized record, that had already brought an invitation to tea from the general superintendent, a Sunday at the country home of the general counsel for the company, and personal recognition from Thomson himself. As Carnegie with complacency summed up his career at this point, "The battle of life is already half won by the young man who is brought personally in contact with high officials; and the great aim of every boy should be to do something beyond the sphere of his duties—something which attracts the attention of those over him." [20]

There are critics who claim that during these early years with the Pennsylvania Carnegie was receiving much more in the way of tangible rewards than the satisfaction of becoming personally known to the chief officers of the company. It has been suggested that in this rapidly developing industrial area, where production far outran freight car capacity, this mercenary young man had taken advantage of his position to satisfy his personal ambitions by conferring preferential treatment to certain shippers willing to purchase his favor.[21] Neither available evidence nor any realistic appraisal of the transportation business, however, substantiates these charges. There is no indication that Carnegie at this time had any surplus earnings above that of his monthly paycheck. Indeed, when the first opportunity came his way for an investment in stock, he had to borrow money to raise the necessary funds. Considering the importance of freight traffic to the company and the necessity always of first satisfying the demands of the larger shippers in the area, one can be fairly certain that a small bribe to an office clerk, no matter how highly that clerk might regard his own importance, could hardly have obtained preferential treatment for an individual shipper. Carnegie was undoubtedly correct in his own evaluation of the personal advantages he was receiving as "Mr. Scott's Andy." He was attracting the attention of the chief officers in the company, and, more important for his future, he was becoming known to the important business leaders in the area. For the moment, this was all he could expect. The financial rewards would surely follow.

During these early years with the Pennsylvania Railroad, in spite of Andrew's salary of $35 a month, which seemed a handsome sum, the Carnegies continued to live as penuriously as before. Will worked at his loom, and Margaret at her nighttime cobbling and Saturday clerking, to help pay for the Rebecca Street house within the two-year period allowed by the contract. The Carnegies would then be out of debt, and to attain this status no temporary sacrifice could be too great.

Will Carnegie's contribution to the family income became less each month. He tried his hand at weaving nearly every day, but he was no longer physically able to make the exhausting trips by boat down the river to find a market for his goods. Friends and neighbors purchased an occasional tablecloth or piece of yard goods, but most of what he now wove he had to store away on shelves in the loom shop. His only outside interest was the small Swedenborgian church in the neighborhood. He and his sister-in-law, Annie Aitkin, were the church's main supporters, and although Margaret refused to participate, Will took his two sons, Andrew and Tom, with him to church. They both enjoyed singing in the choir and the companionship of the few other young people in the congregation, but neither would agree to accepting membership in the church. Will did not demand this, and although Auntie Aitkin was more outspoken in her conviction that her nephews should become members, she was thankful that at least they were not accepting the doctrines of any other faith. When another nephew, Leander, the son of her brother in Ohio, came to Pittsburgh for a visit and proudly announced that he had become a Baptist, she roundly berated him. He protested, asking her why she was so harsh with him and not with Andrew, who refused to belong to any church. Her reply was quick and decisive, "Andy! Oh! Andy, he's naked, but you are clothed in rags." [22]

Will Carnegie might not be able to convince his sons that they should join his church but Andrew succeeded in persuading his father to give political allegiance to the United States. Will Carnegie, having lost all interest in politics, had showed no inclination to become a naturalized citizen when he became eligible. It was only after much prodding from his son that he appeared before the clerk of the Court of General Sessions for Allegheny County on 20 November 1854 and formally filed his declaration of intention to be a citizen.[23] For Andrew, this declaration of intent was tantamount to the act of naturalization itself, and he assumed that, as he himself was a minor at the time, this action of his father had also made *him* an American citizen. He apparently did not understand that by law the person seeking naturalization had to wait two years after filing a declaration of intention before taking the oath of allegiance and receiving certification of naturalization. It would not be until many years later that the charge would be made by some of his political critics that Carnegie was not a citizen of the United States, inasmuch as his father had not completed the naturalization process prior to his death. But by that time no government official or court was prepared to gainsay Carnegie's claim to the rights of citizenship which he had long exercised, and Carnegie simply ignored the charge, however technically correct it was.[24]

By the spring of 1855, Will Carnegie was unwilling and unable to continue even the pretense of being a weaver. He wove his last piece of cloth and then took to his bed. There followed long months of illness that the physician could neither diagnose nor cure. On 2 October 1855, Will Carnegie died. He was fifty-one years old. The comment of his son, written many years later, might appropriately serve as his epitaph: "My father was one of the most lovable of men . . . not much of a man of the world, but a man all over for heaven." [25]

Will Carnegie's death did not mean that there would be an added burden for his widow and children to bear in the management of the household. Margaret would be what she had long been in fact, the head of the family, and Andrew would continue to be its chief financial support. Twelve-year-old Tom could stay in school and complete his high school education. Will had for so long been on the periphery of the family circle that his death could not seriously affect the general routine, but a softening influence within the family had been lost which Margaret could not provide. It was a loss which perhaps only the boy Tom could fully appreciate.

Will's death did not bring Margaret Carnegie and her elder son any closer than they had been before. Their relationship was already fixed and would remain so for as long as Margaret should live. Carnegie would continue to look to his mother for guidance and support in each undertaking, and she would not only give what was expected of her, but she would demand the right to give it. Some commentators have suggested that at this time Carnegie made a definite promise to his mother that he would never marry as long as she lived,[26] but it is doubtful if any such formal pledge was ever made. It was not necessary.

Filial devotion, however, did not keep Carnegie from having an active social life in the community. By nature gregarious, he thoroughly enjoyed the company of young people of both sexes. His quick wit, good humor, and talent as a raconteur made him a lively companion. There were ice-skating parties, play-reading sessions, and weekly choir practices, and, first in his affections, the debating society. He and his closest friends, John Phipps, Tom Miller, William Crowley, and Dave McCargo, continued to meet regularly in the back of Phipps's cobbler shop to debate the major political issues of the day. Carnegie was still regarded as the most radical of the group—an abolitionist in slavery, a Jacksonian Democrat in politics, and a skeptic in religion. Although there was general agreement among his companions on most of these issues, it was Carnegie who took the most extreme positions.

Most of his friends had a more orthodox religious background than Carnegie. As a young boy he had been the envy of his friends—and the scandal of their parents—because of his Sunday morning practice of ice-skating on the river, which was not only permitted but actively encouraged by his mother. She took a particular pleasure in flouting the strict Sabbatarian code of her Calvinist neighbors.[27] Carnegie had readily accepted his mother's religious skepticism, resisting even the gentle Swedenborgian faith of his father, but now, badly outnumbered in his circle of Scottish friends, he had been persuaded to attend the social activities at one of the Presbyterian churches in Pittsburgh. The minister, the Reverend Mr. McMillan, was a strict Calvinist, whose sermons Carnegie scrupulously avoided. But Mrs. McMillan was a charming woman, "a born leader of the young," and all the boys, including Carnegie, looked forward eagerly to the weekly evening discussion meetings at her home. One Sunday morning, Tom Miller, a Methodist, made the mistake of attending McMillan's church, and he was appalled to hear for the first time the doctrines of predestination and infant damnation. After the services, young Miller could not help blurting out to the surprised pastor, "Mr. McMillan, if your idea were correct, your God would be a perfect devil."

This blunt pronouncement created a crisis within the group of young men who heretofore had found the best topics for debate in the area of politics. Was Miller right, and if they should agree that he was, would this mean that they should be forever excluded from Mrs. McMillan's company? For several weeks they debated this issue. From the first Miller had a strong ally in Carnegie, and gradually a consensus was reached which, for Phipps, McCargo and Crowley, meant a surrender of the Calvinist faith in which they had been raised. "A forgiving God would be the noblest work of man," was the axiom they all agreed upon, and intoxicated with their concept that God is created in man's own best image, they were prepared to accept even the sacrifice of losing Mrs. McMillan's company in order to hold fast to their newly won freedom from dogma.

> We accepted as proven that each stage of civilization creates its own God, and that as man ascends and becomes better his conception of the Unknown likewise improves. Thereafter we became less theological, but I am sure more truly religious. The crisis passed. Happily we were not excluded from Mrs. McMillan's society. It was a notable day, however, when we resolved to stand by Miller's statement, even if it involved banishment and worse. We young men were getting to be pretty wild boys about theology, although more truly reverent about religion.[28]

The trans-Atlantic debates with Cousin Dod had continued, and during the mid 1850's their liveliest topic was the Crimean War. Dod accused the United States, the self-proclaimed champion of liberty, of not coming forward as Britain had done for the defense of Turkish national freedom against the imperialistic designs of the Russian Czar. "Oh! Dod! that's capital," was Carnegie's derisive answer, and he continued:

> Great Britian [sic] come forward? Why she has brought upon herself the contempt of honest men throughout the world for her course on this very question. . . . Indeed, I have been boiling at your cowardly ministry all along and now to hear you

come out eulogizing their course is too bad. If you will read Kossuth's letter to the citizens of Glasgow or Mr. Urquhart's speech at Paisley I don't think you could hurra for the firm stand your govt has taken or praise the manner in which she has come forward. . . . But this is not to be surprised at for looking to the past course of Britian I have still to learn that she ever did the cause of Liberty on the continent much service or even been found on the right side. I see her stand idly by & look on Hungary, Italy & Poland crushed without coming forward or even remonstrating against it or did she defend the most sacred right of nations,—Self Government.[29]

When Dod responded with an attack upon the recent Kansas-Nebraska Act, which had repealed the Missouri Compromise, Carnegie agreed that his cousin's criticism was justified. "You cannot hate the measure more than I do but the people cannot be held responsible for it. . . . Well, the President degraded his high office by using his influence & he succeeded in getting a majority of 13 out of 200 votes." As for those Northern representatives that voted for it, "their political warrants are signed and will surely be executed. The just indignation of an insulted & betrayed people is consigning them to infamy. Yes Sir." [30] This young Free-Soil Democrat was ready to move, along with many of his elders, into any new party that would hasten the execution of these Northern "dough faces." He watched with interest the spontaneous multiple formation of the Republican party in several of the Midwestern states in the spring and summer of 1854. By the time the first great national meeting of the Republican party was held, in Pittsburgh on George Washington's birthday in 1856, young Carnegie, although still too young to vote, considered himself an active member. He had written several antislavery editorials, had sent them to Horace Greeley's *Tribune,* and had had the pleasure of seeing one of them published. This literary success had prompted him to form a "New York Weekly Tribune Club" among the railroad employees, whose purpose was to meet and discuss Greeley's latest editorial comments on the Free-Soil movement.[31]

Up to this point Carnegie had found no difficulty in reconciling his Radical heritage with his materialistic ambitions. He was not aware that there could be any other gulf than the geographic one between his old world in Dunfermline and his new world in

Pittsburgh. America, as he had written Dod, was simply the realization of the hopes of Chartist Scotland. He continued to think of himself as a young Radical, and could still write to Dod, "wealth is always conservative and dreads innovation & you know monied power has ruled your country so far but that there's a better time coming when you will follow the example of your daughter in that respect who can doubt." [32] These are words that his father and his grandfather might well have written, and young Carnegie saw no conflict between their ideals and his own. The newly organized Republican party stood for free soil and free land, and if it did not also stand for free trade, still it was liberal enough for Carnegie's wholehearted support. Wealth remained for him the old Conservative enemy, but he continued to identify it with the landed gentry of Britain. Here in America, he had to admit to Dod in his more candid moments, this privileged landed aristocracy showed an even more cruel face than it did in Britain. Here the symbol of authority was not the scepter, but the overseer's whip; and behind the classical façade of the white portico lay the black slave quarters of oppression. Fortunately, however, in America such naked power had been isolated in one geographic section, as he explained to Dod.

As Carnegie's childhood indoctrination in Chartism had blurred his insight into the causes of social distress, so also was slavery to blind him to social realities. Once for him radicalism had been equated with universal suffrage. Now it was equated with the abolition of slavery, an even more undemanding definition than that which the Scottish moral persuasionists had held. It is always comforting to have the devil properly identified, with tail and horns, and carefully segregated as to residence, and it is easy to think that you are on the side of the angels if you believe that you are living in Heaven. This ambitious young American from Chartist Scotland could breathe the free—if smoky—air of Pittsburgh, avidly read Mrs. Stowe's shocking revelations of life in the South, cheer for free enterprise and Frémont, and proudly call himself a Radical. Slavery had so simplified social ethics in America that not until the Civil War was over and the slaves were freed would it be necessary for him to redefine radicalism.

In the spring of 1856 Carnegie took a significant step forward in the new world of capitalism in which he would eventually find himself a leading citizen. Thomas Scott, always interested in helping his young assistant, mentioned to Carnegie that there was an unusual opportunity available to purchase a few shares of Adams Express stock, a blue chip stock that was not sold on the open market. A certain William Reynolds had recently died, leaving as part of his estate ten shares of Adams Express Company stock. His widow had sold these shares to a Mrs. Ann Patrick for $600. But Mrs. Patrick, after having the stock for less than a month, suddenly had an immediate. needed for cash, and she told Scott that she would sell the shares for what she had paid for them.[33] Scott said that he himself owned several shares of Adams Express and there was no sounder investment possible. Would Andy like to buy these ten shares?

Carnegie would indeed, but, unfortunately, after having made the final payments on their home, and, more recently, having had the medical and funeral expenses of his father to pay, he did not have even $50 in savings with which to make an investment. The account which Carnegie was later to give in his autobiography of this opportunity, and how he was able to accept it —an account which has been dutifully repeated by all of his biographers [34]—is that his mother left immediately for East Liverpool, Ohio, where, through the good offices of her brother, she was able to obtain the necessary funds by mortgaging their home. The evidence in Carnegie's personal papers does not substantiate this romantic story, however. In the packet of papers and letters regarding this transaction, which Carnegie carefully preserved, there is an IOU note, dated Pittsburgh, 17 May 1856, in which Carnegie promises to pay to the order of Thomas A. Scott within six months $610 for value received. Written across the face of this IOU is the notation, "Paid by cash, deposited in M&M Bank to credit. T. A. Scott, Nov. 1st." [35] Quite clearly, Scott himself advanced the money so that Carnegie could take advantage of Mrs. Patrick's offer.

On the first of November, in order to meet Scott's note, it was necessary for Carnegie to seek a new source of credit, for by that date he had been able to save only $200 of the $610 he owed. At that time he borrowed, at a considerably higher rate of interest, $400 from a certain George Smith, "for which we hereby agree to pay him interest at the rate of eight per cent per annum as long as it is held by me. It being understood that I have the privilege of retaining the principal longer than one year if required, but not for a shorter period." For collateral Carnegie offered the ten shares of Adams Express stock, which Smith was to hold until the principal and interest should be paid.[36]

Carnegie made one payment of $100 plus interest on this loan in November 1857.[37] It was not until the spring of 1858, after having made other investments with savings he might have used to pay off this loan, that Carnegie turned to his mother for help. It was then, while in East Liverpool visiting her brother and helping out as a nurse to a neighbor family, that she arranged for a mortgage on their home in Allegheny in order to secure the necessary funds to pay off the Smith loan.[38]

This rather complicated transaction that lay behind Carnegie's first investment shows a remarkable talent, particularly in one so young and inexperienced in finance, for juggling notes to keep his credit rating high. Within one month after he had secured the first loan from Scott and had the ten precious shares transferred to his name, Carnegie knew that the rewards of capitalism more than compensated for the risks taken. When he came to work one morning in June 1856, he found a large white envelope, addressed to "Andrew Carnegie, Esquire," lying upon his desk. He liked the title, however much it might smack of the old hated privileged gentry, but he liked even more what he found inside the envelope—a check for $10 from the Adams Express Company. "I shall remember that check as long as I live, and that John Hancock signature of 'J. C. Babcock, Cashier.' It gave me the first penny of revenue from capital—something that I had not worked for with the sweat of my brow. 'Eureka!' I cried. 'Here's the goose that lays the golden eggs.' "[39]

The next Sunday, when he proudly showed the check to his friends assembled for their weekly meeting, these young Liberals had a new topic for discussion that proved more interesting than questions concerning an elective judiciary or the relativity of God. "The effect produced upon my companions was overwhelming. None of them had imagined such an investment possible. . . . How money could make money, how, without any attention from me, this mysterious golden visitor should come, led to much speculation upon the part of the young fellows, and I was for the first time hailed as a 'capitalist.' You see, I was beginning to serve my apprenticeship as a business man in a satisfactory manner." [40] The gulf between his two worlds was beginning to widen, whether he was aware of it or not.

In the late fall of 1856, Scott was promoted to the position formerly held by Herman Lombaert. As general superintendent for the Pennsylvania, he would have to move to the central line offices in Altoona. Carnegie, of course, was to go with him as secretary for the Altoona office, at a salary of $50 a month. Scott's young wife had recently died, and, since he had to find a home in Altoona and a housekeeper to care for his two young children, he decided to leave his family in Pittsburgh under the care of his niece, Rebecca Stewart. As Margaret Carnegie also found it necessary to stay in Allegheny until she could find someone to rent their house, Scott and his assistant shared a room in a bleak railway hotel near the main shops. Carnegie liked to think that by this time his companionship was indispensable to Scott's peace of mind. "He seemed anxious always," Carnegie would later write, "to have me near him." [41]

Neither man was at first very happy with his new assignment. Scott was a lonely man, still grieving over the loss of his wife, and he made little effort to make friends in Altoona. Carnegie had no other companion except Scott during these first long weeks in Altoona, and he missed his friends and family back in Allegheny. Moreover, a serious labor situation confronted the new superintendent and his assistant immediately upon their arrival. There had been sporadic strikes among the freight-train men throughout the line that winter, and there was now more serious talk of a strike among the maintenance men in the main shops in Altoona.

One evening, as Carnegie was walking back to the hotel from the main office, he became aware of the fact that someone was following him. In the shadow of one of the buildings, the man caught up with him and, according to Carnegie's later memory, said that, as Carnegie had once done a favor for him in helping him to get a job as blacksmith in the Altoona railroad yard, he now wanted to return the favor and "tell you something for your own good." The man then informed Carnegie that papers were being circulated among the shop men in Altoona, calling for a pledge to strike on the following Monday morning. Carnegie's informant gave the names of the leaders of the movement and

135

promised him a list of all who had signed the petitions. With this valuable information in hand, Carnegie hurried back to the hotel and gave his news to Scott. The following morning Scott posted notices in all the shops, giving the names of the strike leaders and those who had signed the pledges, and announcing that these men were summarily dismissed from their jobs and that they should call at the central office to receive their final wages. As Carnegie wrote, "Consternation followed and the threatened strike was broken." [42]

It had been only eight years since the Carnegies had left Scotland, but young Carnegie had come a long way from his life in Chartist Scotland, where the most hated name had been that of the company or government spy. Carnegie was to draw quite a different moral from this incident than the one Grandfather Morrison would have seen.

> I have had many incidents, such as that of the blacksmith, in my life. Slight attentions or a kind word to the humble often bring back a reward as great as it is unlooked for. No kind action is ever lost. . . . I am indebted to these trifles for some of the happiest attentions and the most pleasing incidents of my life. And there is this about such actions: they are disinterested, and the reward is sweet in proportion to the humbleness of the individual whom you have obliged. It counts many times more to do a kindness to a poor working-man than to a millionaire, who may be able some day to repay the favor. How true Wordsworth's lines:
>
> > That best portion of a good man's life—
> > His little, nameless, unremembered acts
> > Of kindness and of love.[43]

In the spring of 1857 Scott and Carnegie were reunited with their families, and both men then found Altoona a more attractive place. The choice of Archibald Wright's narrow valley farm for the central shops and office of the Pennsylvania Railroad in the state was a curious one, for already, in less than five years, the railroad buildings covered most of the flat land of the valley floor. This meant that Altoona's residential streets had to be built on the slopes around the valley until they could be extended no further and ended as cul-de-sacs against the sheer cliffs of the surrounding mountains. The valley reverberated with the incessant sounds of whistles and bells, chugging engines, cars being coupled, and the hammering of metal in the maintenance shops. To the visitor, it was sheer bedlam. But surrounding it all was the beauty of the mountains, and on the higher slopes, where the better houses were located, the air was fresh and clean. To the Carnegies, long accustomed to the polluted air of Pittsburgh, it was as if they were really breathing for the first time since they had arrived in Pennsylvania.

Here Carnegie had his first opportunity to take up horseback riding, and he was immediately an enthusiastic rider. In any other physical activity he was not particularly daring. He hated violent personal contact of any sort, and by wit and discretion he had been able to avoid the usual fisticuffs of boyhood, even in the crowded schoolyard on Rolland Street. Later on, his fellow messengers in Pittsburgh had teased him for avoiding the one duty that he detested, climbing telegraph poles to assist the linemen in making repairs on broken lines.[44] But on horseback, he seemed a different person. Just as on the *Wiscasset,* there seemed to come to him on a horse a wonderful feeling of power—power straining to be unleashed, but power that could be controlled. Soon he was riding the fastest horses available, his favorite being a high-spirited stallion named Dash. In Carnegie, the horse had a rider who could fully appreciate his name.[45]

On warm summer Sundays, Carnegie would often ride far out of Altoona, up steep roads a thousand feet higher than the town, where the air was as cool and fresh as it was in the open fields outside Dunfermline. He occasionally saw some of his old friends, Miller and McCargo and Pitcairn, who came to town on business, but he made few close friends of his own age in Altoona, and this was perhaps the loneliest period of his life.

Scott's niece, Rebecca Stewart, had come to Altoona with Scott's children to supervise their care and to serve as Scott's hostess. Rebecca was only a few years older than Carnegie, and both being separated from their friends in Pittsburgh, they welcomed each other's company. Undoubtedly there was talk among the railroad officials and their wives of a possible romance, but if Rebecca had any such ideas, certainly Carnegie did not. He would later write of this relationship:

> She played the part of elder sister to me to perfection. . . .
> We were much together, often driving in the afternoons
> through the woods. She was not much beyond my own age, but
> always seemed a great deal older. Certainly she was more ma-
> ture and quite capable of playing the elder sister's part. It was
> to her I looked up in those days as the perfect lady.[46]

Tom Miller would recall that, on one of his visits to Altoona, he and Carnegie were invited to Scott's home for dinner. When Rebecca left the table briefly to attend to the next course, Carnegie hastily took up a cream pitcher and said, "Real silver, Tom!" [47] An elder sister, the perfect lady—particularly a lady who used real silver—these apparently were the qualities that Carnegie enjoyed in female companionship at this time, not romance.

An opportunity was soon to present itself to Carnegie which would eventually enable him to have real silver upon his own table. Burton Hendrick did not exaggerate when he wrote in his biography of Carnegie that Carnegie's investment in the Woodruff Sleeping Car Company was "more than a nest-egg; it was the start of the Carnegie fortune." Carnegie himself readily admitted that "the first considerable sum I ever made was from this source. . . . Blessed be the man who invented sleep." [48]

Again, there is little agreement between Carnegie's own account of how he became involved with Woodruff and his sleeping cars and the other, more convincing evidence available in his papers. Carnegie, in his book, *Triumphant Democracy,* wrote that one day, when he was sitting on the end seat of the rear car of a passenger train, he was approached by another passenger:

> . . . a tall, spare, farmer-looking kind of man . . . wished me to
> look at an invention he had made. With that he drew from a
> green bag (as if it were for lawyers' briefs) a small model of a
> sleeping berth for railway cars. He had not spoken a minute,

before, like a flash, the whole range of discovery burst upon me. "Yes," I said, "that is something which this continent must have."

Carnegie promised Woodruff that he would speak to Scott about the matter as soon as he returned to Altoona from this business trip to Ohio.

> I could not get that blessed sleeping-car out of my head. Upon my return I laid it before Mr. Scott, declaring that it was one of the inventions of the age. He remarked: "You are enthusiastic, young man, but you may ask the inventor to come and let me see it." I did so, and arrangements were made to build two trial cars, and run them on the Pennsylvania Railroad. I was offered an interest in the venture, which, of course, I gladly accepted. . . . A triumphant success was scored. And thus came sleeping-cars into the world.[49]

It is a typical Carnegie story, replete with all the stock situations of popular melodrama: the shy, unworldly inventor, the crude, hand-made model, the chance meeting with the bold young business executive, who in a flashing moment of truth recognizes genius when he sees it. There is even the mysterious green bag, in which the stranger carries his invention. It is all too pat and too familiar, but those commentators upon Carnegie's life who have dealt with this incident have accepted his story in every detail. The only person to question it publicly was the inventor of the sleeping car, Theodore Woodruff.

In 1886, soon after the publication of *Triumphant Democracy,* in which Carnegie's account of his meeting with Woodruff appeared in print for the first time, Woodruff wrote to his alleged discoverer:

> Your arrogance spurred you up to make the statements recorded in your book, which is misleading and so far from the true facts of the case and so damaging to your friend of old as to merit his rebuke. You must have known before you ever saw me that there were many sleeping cars furnished with my patent seats and couches running upon a number of railways, viz: B.E. & C. R.R., N.Y.C. R.R., M.C. R.R., C. and G. R.R.,

O. and M. R.R., C.C. and C. R.R., M.S. and N. I. R.R., together with my sample sleeping car. In the aggregate there were twenty-one sleeping cars running before my application had been made for the right to place them on the Pennsylvania Railroad.

Now I will relate to you what transpired in connection with the introduction of sleeping cars upon the Penn. R. R. Firstly, I met J. Edgar Thomson . . . at the Monongahela House in Pittsburgh, and gave him a letter of introduction from the then President of the O. and M. Rr. Co. (I cannot recall his name). Mr. Thomson read the letter and requested me to give it to Mr. Scott, who was then the general superintendent of the road, and was then in Pittsburgh. I asked Mr. Thomson if he would call at the depot and see my sample car, which was standing there. He responded that his engagements were such that he could not then go to the depot, and that he was to take the early morning train to Philadelphia. Thinking, perhaps, that he might have time to drop in the car in the morning before the train left, I resolved to give him an opportunity to see the car, and accordingly had the interior properly arranged for inspection with the car doors left open. It so happened that Mr. Thomson's industrious habits led him to inspect the said sleeping car, though it appeared to not have any attendant, and yet the porter was in the car when Mr. Thomson and one other gentleman came in, inspected and commented on its merits, which was overheard by the said porter. In the meantime I had seen Mr. Scott and on the following evening Mr. Scott and myself sat upon the same car seat and concluded an arrangement for the operation of my patent sleeping cars upon the Pennsylvania Railroad before we reached Altoona. One of the conditions of the said agreement was that a certain specified interest therein should be held for another person, and represented (as the talk ran) by a boy then in the superintendent's office at Altoona; and that four cars should be immediately constructed under my direction as the agent of the patent company.

When we came to consummate the agreement in a written form, I learned that the boy alluded to was "Andie Carnegie." A contract was entered into with Murphy and Allison, of Philadelphia, for the construction of four sleeping cars, which were built and placed upon the Pennsylvania Rail R. Their rank in numerical order was Nos. 22, 23, 24 and 25, the model of which was a full sized car of the finest construction . . . and a little too big for the said green bag in use for lawyers' briefs, to which you allude in that fine spun recollection of events.[50]

Failing to get a public acknowledgment from Carnegie of this reinterpretation of the incident as Carnegie had related it in his book, Woodruff then had the letter published in the *Philadelphia Sunday News* later that same year. Because of the importance Carnegie's initial investment in the sleeping-car business had for his later career, Woodruff's account must be seriously examined.

Certainly Woodruff is correct in stating that his patented invention had progressed far beyond the green-bag model stage when he made his first overture to the Pennsylvania Railroad. Woodruff had conceived the idea for a sleeping car as early as the 1830's, when the first night passenger trains began scheduled runs. Most railroads at that time did have a crude arrangement of bunks available in a single car for those few hardy individuals who wished to stretch out, fully dressed, on wooden benches that had no bedding. Woodruff, however, envisioned building a coach whose seats at night could be converted into regular beds, with mattresses, pillows, and clean linen. As a master car builder for the Terre Haute and Alton Railroad in Alton, Illinois, he continued during the next two decades to work on models and sketches, and on 2 December 1856 he received his first two patents for what he called a railway-car seat and couch. With limited capital obtained from friends, he was able to order the construction of the first sleeping car from the T. W. Watson Company of Springfield, Massachusetts, early in 1857, and by the end of that year he had persuaded the New York Central to permit him to put his car, at his own expense, upon the night express train from New York to Albany. The following year, he had introduced a few more such cars upon several rail lines in the East and Midwest.[51]

When he first brought his invention to the Pennsylvania Railroad Company in 1858 Woodruff, then, was not an undiscovered and untried inventor. It seems highly probable that he would open these important negotiations directly with the president of the company, as he said he did, for Thomson had undoubtedly heard of the introduction of his sleeping car on the

141

rival New York Central. Quite properly, Thomson would refer the matter to Scott, whose approval as general superintendent of the line would be essential to the introduction of a sleeping car. But it would also be characteristic of Thomson to investigate the matter himself, as Woodruff stated he did, and to be receptive to this innovation, as he was to many others during his years as president of the company. The actual contract between Woodruff and the Pennsylvania Railroad Company was signed on 15 September 1858.[52]

There remains the interesting question of how and under whose auspices Carnegie obtained an interest in the company. Carnegie claimed that in grateful recognition for his having brought the model of the invention to the attention of Scott, Woodruff voluntarily offered Carnegie one-eighth interest in the company. Woodruff gave quite a different account, and unfortunately there appears to be no concrete evidence to substantiate or refute either man's statement. Carnegie's claim, however, is dependent upon his having been Woodruff's "discoverer," a claim that has no substantial merit, whereas Woodruff's statement that he was told by Scott at the time the contract was negotiated that a "certain specified interest should be held for another person," who was later identified as "Andie Carnegie," is entirely consistent with Scott's many previous favors given to his young assistant. In this connection, it is of interest that in his reply to Woodruff's letter in 1886 Carnegie did not deny a single detail of the account as related by Woodruff. He avoided the entire argument, and only wrote:

> Your letter surprises me. Your error lies in the supposition that I intended to write a history on the "rise and progress of sleeping cars." I only mention them incidentally. . . . It is impossible to enter into details in one volume, which aims to give a history of the country as a whole. Please take the will for the deed.[53]

Under whatever circumstances he may have obtained his one-eighth interest, the fact remains that by 1859 Carnegie had what would later prove to be an exceedingly valuable interest in the Woodruff Sleeping Car Company. He was permitted to pay for this interest, as he later remembered it, on a monthly installment basis. When the first monthly installment of $217.50 came due, Carnegie did not have the necessary cash on hand. Rather than repeat the complicated operation that he had followed in financing his investment in the Adams Express stock, Carnegie this time felt confident enough of his reputation to apply directly to a local banker for the funds. "I explained the matter to him, and I remember that he put his great arm (he was six feet three or four) around me, saying, 'Why, of course I will lend it. You are all right, Andy.' And here I made my first note, and actually got a banker to take it. A proud moment that in a young man's career!" [54]

This loan was the only one he had to have in order to pay for his interest in Woodruff's company. Thereafter each monthly dividend from the company was more than adequate to pay for the installment due for his interest in the company. Within two years this initial investment of $217.50, which was the only amount he contributed directly from an outside source to the company, was returning to him an annual income of nearly $5000—over three times his yearly salary from the Pennsylvania Railroad Company. Carnegie had reason to rejoice in being "Mr. Scott's Andy."

In the early fall of 1859 there was general talk in the offices of the Pennsylvania that Scott was slated for promotion to the office of vice presidency of the company. Carnegie, who was certainly privy to such talk, was naturally concerned about what effect Scott's promotion would have on his future. Would he be asked to go with Scott to the general office in Philadelphia, or, more likely, would he now have to serve a new superior? "To part with Mr. Scott was hard enough," Carnegie thought, "to serve a new official in his place I did not believe possible. The sun rose and set upon his head so far as I was concerned. The thought of my promotion, except through him, never entered my mind." [55]

Surely Carnegie was being too modest. Ambitious as he was, he must have often dreamed of promotion, and he knew precisely the position he would like to have. When Scott returned from a trip to Philadelphia, where he had talked to J. Edgar Thomson, he asked Carnegie to come to his home to see him. There he told his assistant that the expected promotion to the vice presidency had been confirmed, and Enoch Lewis, superintendent of the Eastern Division, would succeed him as general superintendent. There remained the question of Carnegie's future with the company. Scott came directly to the point. "Now about yourself. Do you think you could manage the Pittsburgh Division?"

Carnegie's response to this question is in itself indicative of how seriously he had entertained this particular promotion. He was somewhat offended that Scott should even ask the question, for "I was at an age when I thought I could manage anything." Then he realized that Scott's question was perhaps a rhetorical one, which indeed it was. The only way Carnegie could have further surprised his employer would have been to say no. But Carnegie's "model then was Lord John Russell, of whom it was said he would take the command of the Channel Fleet tomorrow. . . . I told Mr. Scott I thought I could."

When Scott mentioned the question of salary, Carnegie was almost indifferent. "Salary, what do I care for salary? I do not want the salary; I want the position." When Scott persisted and suggested that Carnegie should have what he himself had received in the same position, $1500 a year, Carnegie replied, "Oh please, don't speak to me of money." For Carnegie the important thing was that "I was to have a department to myself, and instead of signing 'T.A.S.', orders between Pittsburgh and Altoona would now be signed 'A.C.' That was glory enough for me." [56] Carnegie might have added that salary had become relatively insignificant to a young man who had discovered the wonderful egg-laying potential of the capitalistic goose.

Nevertheless, Carnegie's salary was arranged as Scott had proposed it. On 21 November 1859, Thomas Scott sent out General Order No. 10 to all employees of the Western Division, that "On and after December 1st, 1859, the Western Division, from Pittsburgh to Conemaugh, including the Indiana Branch, will be under the superintendence of Andrew Carnegie, whose title will be Superintendent of the Western Division. His office will be at Pittsburgh. Employees of the Company . . . will be under his charge." [57] At twenty-four, Carnegie was on his own. He was no longer "Mr. Scott's Andy."

CHAPTER VII

War and
Profits of War
1860-1865

In December 1859, the Carnegies returned to Pittsburgh—but not to Slabtown. Margaret Carnegie's nights of cobbling were over forever. While in Altoona, Andrew had even persuaded her to hire a servant girl. As people who had servants did not live on Rebecca Street, Margaret sold her house—the house that only a year and a half before she had had to mortgage in order to pay off her son's loan for the Adams Express shares. The Carnegies rented a much larger house on Hancock Street, in the center of Pittsburgh, near the Pennsylvania Railroad Station.

Their three years in Altoona, where they had had clean mountain air to breathe and a green yard in which flowers would grow, had made them forget what Pittsburgh was, particularly in the early winter when the fog hung over the two river valleys and the smoke did not lift more than fifty feet above the ground. "Any accurate description of Pittsburgh at that time," Carnegie wrote, "would be set down as a piece of the grossest exaggeration. The smoke permeated and penetrated everything. If you placed your hand on the balustrade of the stair it came away black; if you washed face and hands they were as dirty as ever in an hour. The soot gathered in the hair and irritated the skin, and for a time after our return from the mountain atmosphere of Altoona, life was more or less miserable." [1] Pittsburgh still had no parks, and there were few green things hardy enough to survive in this industrial jungle through which the sun seldom penetrated. A corps of servant girls could not have kept their Hancock Street house clean. But, though Margaret longed for a clean house, she longed even more for a garden where flowers would grow as they had in Dunfermline and Altoona.

David Stewart, Rebecca Stewart's brother, was freight agent for the Pennsylvania Railroad in Pittsburgh at this time, and upon hearing Carnegie complain about having to live in the city, Stewart suggested that the Carnegies might be interested in a house next door to his own, in the outlying residential district of Homewood. This suburb, some fifteen miles northeast of Pittsburgh in the East Liberty valley, had once been part of a large estate owned by Judge William Wilkins, who still lived in his mansion in the center of the suburb. One look at the two-story frame house, surrounded by Norway spruce, green lawns, and flower beds, was enough to convince Carnegie and his mother, and they purchased the house at once. [2]

The move to Homewood opened an entirely new world to Carnegie. In addition to the Stewarts, who lived next door, Carnegie became acquainted with the Vandevort family, whose two sons, Benjamin and John, soon became his close friends. These families introduced him to other socially prominent people, both in Homewood and in Pittsburgh, particularly the William Colemans and the Addison family. One resident of Homewood needed no introduction. Tom Miller, back in Pittsburgh as a railroad official, had also purchased a home there, and he was a welcome link to Carnegie's old days on Rebecca Street.

Judge Wilkins, now in his eightieth year, ruled over Homewood like a feudal baron, and his home, into which Carnegie was soon introduced, was the formal social center for the community. To meet Wilkins, for Carnegie, "was touching history itself," for the Judge's political career extended back over most of the history of the Republic. Originally a Federalist, he had later been appointed a Federal Judge for western Pennsylvania by President John Quincy Adams, and then in 1828 he had deserted the party of Adams to become an ardent Jacksonian Democrat. After serving as Jackson's minister to Russia in the 1830's, and as Secretary of War in Tyler's cabinet in the 1840's, he had retired from politics in the 1850's and had returned to Pittsburgh, where he purchased the large estate he called Homewood. Wilkins's wife, Mathilda Dallas Wilkins, came from an even more illustrious family, for she was the daughter of Alexander Dallas, Madison's Secretary of the Treasury, and sister of George Dallas, Vice President of the United States during Polk's administration.[3] One can picture young Carnegie, the avid reader of Bancroft, sitting in that great long drawing room, and listening in awe as Judge Wilkins would casually remark, "As President Jackson once said to me," or "As I told the Duke of Wellington what the Czar had said."

Carnegie was never so overawed as to suppress his own opinions on current topics. Judge and Mrs. Wilkins had remained staunch Democrats, and Mrs. Wilkins, in particular, was pro-Southern in sympathy during these years when the country was drifting toward sectional war. Carnegie would recall one incident in which he, as an abolitionist, could not keep a respectful silence. Mrs. Wilkins was complaining that the Negroes in the North were becoming so forward that there would soon be no place that would not be open to them. " 'Is it not disgraceful,' she said. 'Negroes admitted to West Point.' "

" 'Oh, Mrs. Wilkins,' Carnegie replied, 'there is something even worse than that. I understand that some of them have been admitted to heaven!'

"There was a silence that could be felt. Then dear Mrs. Wilkins said gravely:

" 'That is a different matter, Mr. Carnegie.' "[4]

He was still the young Radical—and he thoroughly enjoyed playing the role. He had, of course, by now outgrown the old debating society in the back of Phipps's cobbler shop. John Phipps was dead, killed tragically at the age of eighteen in a fall from a horse. Henry Phipps, Jr., who was several years younger, belonged to Tom Carnegie's group of friends, so the Carnegies still kept in touch with their Allegheny friends, but Carnegie and Tom Miller, along with John Vandevort, had formed a new inner circle, which they called the Original Six. Miller, Carnegie, and William Crowley—the three who had studied double-entry bookkeeping together—had also been asked to become members of the Webster Literary Club, a group of young men who met weekly to read from and discuss the great literary masterpieces of the English language, particularly the works of Shakespeare.

During the short time since its founding in September 1854, the club had led a somewhat nomadic existence. Meeting during the first two years in the Quarter Sessions room of the county court house, by the time Carnegie joined it the club had moved from various members' homes to the Presbyterian Church, and had at last found quarters in the Sons of Temperance Hall, on the second floor above the old O'Reilly Telegraph Office. The constitution of the club forbade discussions of topics either of a partisan political or of a sectarian religious nature. The years 1859 and 1860, however, were not years in which young men could avoid topics of a partisan political nature, as the nation, under the inept leadership of President Buchanan, stumbled toward Civil War. Certainly such a proscription could not force Carnegie into silence, and so "a gentlemen's agreement" was reached whereby the by-laws would be suspended and there would be an open meeting in which any topic might be discussed. "They dispensed with the reading of the Bard," as the members enthusiastically entered into a free-for-all discussion on the topic "Resolved: That the Democratic Party is no longer deserving of the confidence reposed in it in the past." Although the records do not indicate it, one can be sure that Carnegie was not backward in arguing the case for the affirmative. The minutes do show that "The debate continued until after midnight; when, a state of disorder existing, the President felt called upon to exercise his constitutional prerogative and peremptorily declared the club adjourned." [5]

As superintendent of the Western Division, Carnegie was a hard taskmaster. He was well aware of the fact that he owed his appointment to this responsible position directly to Scott, and that President Thomson must have had misgivings about entrusting the Western Division to a twenty-four-year-old youth. Carnegie had to justify Scott's faith in him and prove himself to Thomson in the first few weeks. But most of all, he had to prove himself to himself. It was a bad winter, the worst in many years. The line west from Altoona to Pittsburgh, through the most difficult terrain that any railroad in the country had to traverse at that time, had been hastily and poorly constructed. Over a great part of the line the track could not be laid directly upon a level road bed, but had to be laid upon blocks of stone, with cast-iron chairs holding the rails. Cold weather, with frequent thawing and freezing, caused breaks in the cast iron, and on a single night there might be as many as forty-seven breaks along the line in the mountain areas.

As a superintendent who was overly sensitive about his position, Carnegie would not delegate any authority in times of emergency. There was to be no "Mr. Scott's Andy" for him. He would go out in all kinds of weather, work for twenty-four hours without a rest, and expect his men to do the same. He would later recall that

> at one time for eight days, I was constantly upon the line, day and night, at one wreck or obstruction after another. I was probably the most inconsiderate superintendent that ever was entrusted with the management of a great property, for, never knowing fatigue myself, being kept up by a sense of responsibility probably, I overworked the men and was not careful enough in considering the limits of human endurance. I have always been able to sleep at any time. Snatches of half an hour at intervals during the night in a dirty freight car were sufficient.[6]

Tom Miller would confirm this devotion to duty, recalling one evening at the Webster Literary Club when Carnegie was in the midst of presenting his side of the topic under discussion. A message was received for "you to go to 26 St. 2 miles or more and no st. cars, and snow quite deep and falling,—but there was a wreck at Derry, and you buttoned your great coat on, and were off in a burst of glory as if going to see your best girl—!" [7]

Nor could personal friendship make any special claims on Carnegie's favor in his dealing with his subordinates. George Alexander, an old friend from the Rebecca Street days, whom Carnegie took on as a conductor on the Altoona passenger run, would remember one Sunday when he, Carnegie, and Carnegie's mother went to visit the Forrester family, who lived along the Pittsburgh, Fort Wayne and Chicago Railroad line, several miles west of Allegheny.

> The day was as beautiful as could be, and I well remember that we had to wade through dust up to our shoe tops for about a mile and one half to get from the station to the house. We had a delightful time until about 10 o'clock when there came up a terrible wind and rain storm. It simply poured. I was a passenger conductor at that time and my train left the depot at two o'clock A.M. I knew there was no train for me to get to Pittsburgh on, and I did not fancy much the idea of having to get there for that train, so I approached the Supt. (A.C.) and asked him how about my getting to town to take out my train. He replied, "Well, George, you know that train goes out at two o'clock and it can't go very well without a conductor." That is all the satisfaction I got and there was nothing left me but to foot it through all the storm and I arrived at the depot just in time to get on the train, soaked to the skin.[8]

Carnegie, as superintendent, no longer felt any of his earlier squeamishness over associating with railroad crews. He could now sleep in dirty freight cars, be out with section hands and maintenance men in all weather, eat their coarse food, and dress in the same rough clothing. The difference now was that he could associate with them not as their equals but as their employer. He was not expected to be a part of their rough horseplay and could be deaf and blind to their crudities of language and manners. Only rarely did his youthful appearance and shortness of stature—he was only five feet three inches tall—put him in an embarrassing position. One such occasion took place soon after he had taken over the Western Division. A serious accident occurred, and several freight cars were derailed. Carnegie, as usual, was quickly on the scene, giving orders to lay a temporary track around the wreck so that traffic could be kept moving while the main line was being cleared. He tried to be everywhere at once, and in his hopping about he frequently got in the way of the men who were carrying the rails to be laid. Finally a big burly Irishman grabbed him up off the ground and set him down to one side. "Get out of my way, you brat of a boy. You're eternally in the way of the men who are trying to do their job." [9] Later, Carnegie greatly enjoyed telling the story, particularly in describing the look on the Irishman's face when one of the other men informed him that he had just accosted the superintendent. At the moment, however, Carnegie may not have been amused, for it was shortly after this incident that he began to grow a thin fringe of beard (rather like Horace Greeley's), which framed his otherwise clean-shaven face, and, if anything, accentuated his boyish countenance.

For Carnegie the important thing always in the successful management of the line was to keep the traffic flowing, whatever the cost either to men or material. He would lay track around wrecks, or, if that was impossible, he would without hesitation burn the wrecked freight cars that were blocking the right-of-way. Scott, when he was superintendent of the Western Division, had been astonished at this proposal when Carnegie had first suggested it to him, but it soon became standard procedure, and it paid off in maintaining the Pennsylvania's reputation for quick service.[10] Carnegie had a special telegraph line installed between his home and the Pittsburgh station so that he could be in constant communication with the line throughout the division day and night, and he needed no operator to take messages for him.[11]

Carnegie did not fear the charge of nepotism, providing those relatives whom he hired performed their tasks satisfactorily and expected no special privileges. One of his first appointments after accepting the position of superintendent was that of his brother as his personal secretary. Tom, who was now sixteen, had finished two years of high school in Altoona and had learned telegraphy in the railroad office there, under Carnegie's instruction. He proved to be most valuable in this job, for he could take any message by wire if Carnegie was not available, and, unlike his older brother, was never so impetuous and personally ambitious as to take authority without permission. Quiet and reserved in manner, he was absolutely discreet in all matters, personal and official, and Carnegie could trust him implicitly.

Carnegie surprised and shocked some of the old-time railroad men by appointing his cousin, Maria Hogan, as telegraph operator in the freight department. She was the first woman operator in the country, and eventually she was to train many other women for the same occupation. Carnegie's old friend, David McCargo, was made general superintendent of the telegraph department, and with this appointment Carnegie had the important area of communications under the supervision of a man in whom he had the highest trust. For Carnegie, the proper organization of personnel was imperative to the successful operation of a business.[12]

Carnegie moved easily between his business life and his social life with no apparent problems in adjusting to their differing demands and values. To his associates he appeared equally at home in Judge Wilkins's formal drawing room, attending musicales, playing charades, and discussing English philosophy, and in the Pittsburgh freight yards of the Pennsylvania, consigning cars, ordering new equipment, and checking on crews. He himself was more aware of his deficiencies in the drawing room than he was of his errors in the freight yards, and as he became conscious of making mistakes in speaking in both grammar and pronunciation, his pride was touched as it had not been before. Instead of retreating in embarrassment, he advanced on the citadels of culture in the same spirit of aggressive determination with which he would approach a freight car mix-up on the main line. He returned to night school, not as before, for lessons in double-entry bookkeeping, but for instruction in French and elocution.[13]

The kind of education he now sought, however, could better be found in association with those who had the cultural attributes that he so desperately wanted. In this acquisition of culture by association he was assisted immeasurably by his friendship with the Addison family of Pittsburgh. Mrs. Addison, whose late husband had been one of the leading physicians of Pittsburgh, was originally from Edinburgh, where she had been raised in an environment of wealth and refinement. As a young girl she had been privately tutored by Thomas Carlyle, and in provincial America she had insisted upon high standards of education for her children. Her three daughters were sent abroad for their education and in their own home were encouraged to develop an interest in literature and the arts by their parents' example.

152

Mrs. Addison, upon meeting Carnegie at one of Judge Wilkins's musicals, took an immediate interest in him, because, Carnegie thought, of "the wee drop of Scotch bluid atween us." Soon he was a frequent visitor in the Addison home. The eldest daughter, Leila, took as her special project the education of this interesting young railroad executive, who was so unlike any other young man she had met. "She was my best friend," Carnegie would later write, "because she was my severest critic." She did not hesitate to correct any error in his speech; she taught him how to read scores and listen appreciatively to music; and she gave a direction to his reading, where before he had simply read anything available. It is not surprising that he would "record with grateful feelings the immense advantage which that acquaintance brought to me." On her part, Leila Addison thoroughly enjoyed her role as a female Pygmalion, attempting to create a new kind of Galatea out of a Slabtown immigrant boy.[14]

Carnegie's speech and grammar improved, as did his manners, under this tutelage, but he quite rightly never confused wrappings with content, and he firmly maintained his own personality, which had always been his soundest capital. He was too much a Morrison to do otherwise. He also knew that older men might often be amused and even condescending toward him, but they did not ignore him or have to ask a second time for his name.

In being so uncompromisingly himself, Carnegie frequently was indebted to others for their forbearance in accepting with good humor his brash assaults upon their convictions. He would later recall a Sunday afternoon spent at Greensburgh, in the home of Niles Stokes, soon after South Carolina had seceded from the Union. Carnegie "was all aflame for the flag," while Stokes, a conservative Democrat, argued that the North had no constitutional right to use force to return a sovereign state to the Union. Unable to restrain himself during the course of the discussion, Carnegie, with the same impetuosity that had flavored his debates in Phipps's cobbler shop, burst out, "Mr. Stokes, we shall be hanging men like you in less than six weeks." Stokes laughed heartily at this preposterous outburst from his young subordinate and shouted to his wife in the next room, "Nancy, Nancy, listen to this young Scotch devil. He says they will be hanging men like me in less than six weeks." [15]

Surely there were others whom Carnegie must have encountered in these months prior to the Civil War who did not accept Carnegie's outspoken Republicanism with either the mild patience of Mrs. Wilkins or the good humor of Niles Stokes. Whatever counterattacks there may have been, they were neither then nor later of any great concern to Carnegie. He felt that both history and morality were on his side, and if it should take a hangman's noose to convince his opponents, so be it. The affirmative case for the proposition of the bankruptcy in leadership of the Democratic party, which he had argued so vociferously before the Webster Literary Club, was being proven every day, he felt, by each event that threatened the continuation of the Union.

An avowed Republican since the formation of the party in 1854, Carnegie cast his first presidential vote for Lincoln in 1860. How comforting it was for this young Chartist Liberal and enthusiastic capitalist to find within the Republican party both the Radical idealism of Dunfermline and the business opportunism of America. It was a new party for a new era, a party with no place for the old planter aristocracy, which Carnegie had identified with the hated Tory aristocracy of Britain. This new party had found a new kind of leader, a one-time rail-splitter, river man and storekeeper, a self-educated lawyer, a man of the people, who could in words with the stately cadence of the Bible express the inarticulated aspirations of the people, their hunger for dignity and possessions, their commitment to the Charter. One did not need to compromise either ideals or ambition to support Lincoln —a phenomenon rare indeed in politics.

In the weeks following the election of Lincoln and prior to his inauguration, Carnegie vociferously argued for force to bring the seceding states back into the Union. Although a professed pacifist, he was not for the peace-at-any-price policy of many of his business associates and friends in Pittsburgh. He was sorely disappointed in his former idol, Horace Greeley, whose editorial advice to the nation, to let "the erring sisters go in peace," he totally rejected. Carnegie's new hero was Edwin M. Stanton, the Pittsburgh lawyer to whom Carnegie, as messenger boy, had often delivered telegrams. Stanton, brought into the moribund Buchanan administration as Attorney General in December 1860, joined forces with Joseph Holt, the newly appointed Secretary of War. Together they persuaded Secretary of State Jeremiah Black, who as Stanton's predecessor in the Attorney General's office had counseled Buchanan that he had no constitutional power to use force to protect Federal property, to change his opinion. Stanton, Holt, and Black then convinced the unhappy and vacillating Buchanan that he should stand firm on Fort Sumter, Stanton announcing publicly that "its surrender by the Government would be a crime equal to that of Arnold, and that all who participated should be hung like André."

This was the kind of declaration that the passionate Unionists had been waiting to hear from the Buchanan administration. Carnegie would later say that, for the pressure Stanton brought to bear upon Buchanan in 1861, he was "destined to live in American history as one whose service to the republic in her darkest hour rank in value with those of the foremost early fathers: Franklin, Hamilton, Adams, Jefferson, Jackson, and Lincoln. No lower place can be assigned him than in that circle." [16] Stanton's subsequent career as Secretary of War in the Lincoln and Johnson administrations but corroborated for Carnegie his high estimate of Stanton the patriot in 1861.

By the time of Lincoln's inauguration in March 1861, Carnegie was convinced that war could no longer be avoided. Lincoln, however, seemed to have nothing more to offer than a continuation of Buchanan's policy. An overt military act apparently was needed to stir the new administration into action, and staunch Unionists like Carnegie fervently hoped that the South would be rash enough to commit such an act. At last Lincoln, after one month of hesitation and delay, did send a supply ship south for the relief of Major Robert Anderson's troops at Fort Sumter. First, however, he informed Governor Francis Pickens of South Carolina, with a diplomatic correctness that seemed to exceed even the finicality of Buchanan, that he was sending food and needed supplies only, and that there would be no attempts to "throw in men, arms, or ammunition." The decision for war now rested with the Confederacy. As a divided nation waited tensely, the little *Harriet Lane* sailed southward during the second week of April. And Jefferson Davis made his fateful decision. The South *would* be rash enough to commit the irrevocable act that the extreme patriots on both sides so ardently desired. In the last darkness of the early morning, on 12 April, a single shell from Fort Johnson on James Island burst brightly over the Union fort in the bay. The war had begun.

The first news of the attack on Fort Sumter reached Pittsburgh about ten o'clock on the evening of the same day. Within minutes men had gathered "upon street corners discussing the all-absorbing topic of the hour." At the Pittsburgh Theater a large audience had assembled after the evening's performance had concluded, and the latest dispatches were read to them by a newspaper editor. "These elicited the wildest enthusiasm, the reader being interrupted by repeated bursts of applause. . . . At the close [of the reading], a patriotic individual arose in the audience, exclaiming, 'I'm a Democrat! But three cheers for Major Anderson!' " [17]

Carnegie would never forget his train ride from Homewood to his Pittsburgh office the following morning.

> That morning the cars resembled a disturbed bee hive. Men could not sit still or control themselves. One of the leading Democrats who had the previous evening assured me that the people would never approve the use of force against their southern brethren, nor would he, came forward greatly excited, and I am sorry to say, some of his words were unquotable. "What's wrong with you," I asked. "Didn't I tell you last night what the Secessionist intended?" In less than a week I saw my friend one morning drilling to be ready as captain of a company to revenge that unpardonable crime. So with others of like views the night before. Stanton was right: the Union was stronger than all its foes.[18]

Pittsburgh was like all Northern cities in those last two weeks of April. Even before Lincoln's call on 15 April to the governors of all loyal states to furnish 75,000 militia men for ninety days to put down the "unlawful combination" of the seceded states, men throughout the North were seeking to enlist. In Pittsburgh, where the city militia companies had already organized, there were more than enough men enlisted to meet the initial quota.

Volunteer companies from the outlying areas of western Pennsylvania had begun to converge on Pittsburgh. These men were without supplies or funds, and the city had to take emergency action in these first feverish days of war to take care of the recruits. The fair grounds east of the city near the Allegheny River were hastily converted into a military camp, and a citizens' committee, headed by Judge Wilkins, who had so recently decried the Black Republican agitation, called on Governor Andrew Curtin for permission to make these temporary quarters a permanent camp under the direction of the military department of the state.[19]

The war that Carnegie had so often predicted and had so eagerly awaited was at last an actuality. Its reality could be found in the downtown streets, clogged by mule teams pulling supplies and munitions down to the wharves on the river; in the fresh pine barracks out at the fair grounds, now proudly named Camp Wilkins; on the bewildered but excited faces of young farm boys, arriving daily by foot and horseback from Greensburgh, Beaver Falls, and Kittanning; and, more soberingly, on the dispatch boards outside the newspaper offices, announcing the surrender of Fort Sumter and the secession of Virginia. Carnegie must have seen all of these manifestations of war, felt the excitement, and pondered what his own role should be. He did not have long to debate whether he should himself enlist. The decision was made for him.

Within ten days after Fort Sumter fell to the Confederates, Secretary of War Simon Cameron asked Thomas Scott to leave his position with the Pennsylvania Railroad and to come to Washington as an official in the War Department, primarily to keep the Northern Central Railroad from Harrisburg to Baltimore open for the movement of men and supplies from the North into the nation's capital. Scott replied that he was then serving on the staff of Governor Andrew Curtin in Harrisburg, but he added that he was confident a "positive order" from Cameron would secure his release.[20]

Curtin was one of the few Northern governors who not only had foreseen the very real possibilities of conflict but also had made definite preparations for that conflict by calling up militia for the defense of the state. With some reluctance, he released Scott from his staff. The Pennsylvania Railroad also gave its vice president a temporary leave of absence to serve his country. Scott hurried south from Philadelphia on the Cumberland Valley Railroad, by way of Hagerstown, Maryland, and thence by carriage to Washington.[21]

In Washington, Scott found the situation to be a truly desperate one. In spite of the enthusiasm in the North for the war, the Union was ill-prepared for the conflict. Men in Boston, New York, Philadelphia, and Pittsburgh might be enlisting by the thousands to put down the traitorous rebels, but there was a strong possibility that before the antique machinery of state recruitment could begin to function, the nation's capital, already nearly isolated, would have been lost to the Rebel forces. On 19 April, the Sixth Massachusetts regiment, the first fully organized state regiment to be sent south after the fall of Fort Sumter, while en route from Boston to Washington had been attacked by pro-Southern men in Baltimore. Although the Sixth Massachusetts did reach Washington late in the afternoon of that day, the mobs in Baltimore, completely out of hand, tore up the railroad tracks in the city and threatened to ambush any other Union troops who attempted to go through the city. Governor Thomas Hicks of Maryland, frightened by the mob's ferocity, assured the people of Baltimore that he had telegraphed President Lincoln to "send no more troops here." Going further than this pronouncement of defiance, Hicks then encouraged Police Marshal George P. Kane to destroy all railroad bridges north of Baltimore. Kane, an active Secessionist, was only too pleased to oblige, and on 20 April the four key bridges to the north of the city were destroyed.

Scott arrived in Washington only to find that Maryland mobs, in connivance with the state government, had already destroyed the main line of communication that Secretary Cameron had charged him with keeping open. Despair and panic were the dominant moods of the city. Hundreds were preparing to leave before the expected arrival of Rebel forces from Virginia, important government archives were being packed to send out of the city—no one could say by what means—and Lincoln himself, waiting anxiously for some news of the Seventh New York, reported to be on its way south via Philadelphia, cried in anguish, "Why don't they come? Why don't they come?"[22]

Before leaving Philadelphia for Washington, Scott had made

his staff plans, and the first name that had occurred to him was that of his former assistant, Andrew Carnegie. Carnegie accepted the summons with alacrity. Arriving in Philadelphia on 20 April, Carnegie, with a small corps of hand-picked railroad men, received the news that Baltimore was still in the hands of the Secessionist mobs and that his only hope of reaching Washington was to take a train to Perryville, Maryland, on the Chesapeake, and then go by boat down the bay to Annapolis. Carnegie and his railway crew took this route, only to find that the short line from Annapolis to Annapolis Junction, where a connection was made with the Baltimore & Ohio main line into Washington, had been largely torn up by Secessionist sympathizers. In Annapolis itself there were some coach and freight cars, but apparently no locomotive to pull them. With General Ben Butler and his 800 militiamen of the Eighth Massachusetts already in Annapolis, and with the New York Seventh expected momentarily, it was imperative to open the Annapolis short line as quickly as possible in order to move these troops into Washington where they were so desperately needed.

Under the supervision of Carnegie's railroad crew, Butler's troops at once began the task of repairing the line into Annapolis Junction. At the same time, quite fortuitously, a partially dismantled locomotive was found in a railroad shed, and this was quickly put into operable condition. By the time the New York Seventh arrived in Annapolis by troop ship the railroad was ready. In the early morning hours of Thursday, 25 April, the hastily improvised train was ready for its first run into Washington. With General Butler and his staff in the first coach, and the Massachusetts Eighth taking up most of the remaining available space in the coaches and freight cars, the New York Seventh was obliged to march the ten miles to Annapolis Junction, where additional cars and a heavier engine could be obtained to transport them on into Washington. Carnegie rode in the cab of the locomotive with the engineer and fireman, keeping a watch for obstructions on the track. When these were spotted, they were hastily removed by the troops. At Annapolis Junction additional car space was provided for all the weary troops of the New York Seventh, and the train then proceeded on toward Washington. Near the outskirts of the District of Columbia, Carnegie, still riding in the engine cab, saw that the telegraph lines between two low poles along the railroad right-of-way had been pulled to the ground and pinned down with stakes. By grounding the wires, the rebels had cut telegraphic communication. Stopping the train, Carnegie jumped down to remove the stakes and release the wires. In his excitement and haste, he foolishly leaned over the wires and pulled the stakes up toward him. The wires, suddenly released, struck him full in the face, cutting a gash across his cheek and forehead. Undaunted, Carnegie climbed back into the cab and gave the signal for the train to move on. With blood streaming down his face, Carnegie could sense the full drama of bringing the first troops into Washington since it had been isolated by the Secessionist mobs in Baltimore. It was for him the high, exultant moment of the war, and he would ever afterward boast that he was the first man to be wounded in defense of the nation's capital.[23]

As the troop train pulled into the Washington station, shouts from the Sixth Massachusetts on Capitol hill could be heard in wildly happy greeting. Butler's men and the Seventh New York troops climbed down from the train and were quickly assembled for their march up Pennsylvania Avenue.

The effect of this troop arrival upon the morale of Washington was instantaneous. No longer was the capital cut off from the North, and a smiling Lincoln, standing upon the White House porch to greet the troops, had the answer to his anguished plea of two days before. Carnegie's pride in his own role in opening up lines of communication with the North is understandable. Now the North could send those men who had so impatiently waited to move out from New York, Boston, Philadelphia, and Pittsburgh—the colorful Zouaves of New York City, the Connecticut Yankees, and the Pennsylvania farmers. Washington was quite suddenly filled with troops, and its citizens, in their newfound security, could once again talk scornfully of the traitorous rebels, whose total defeat now appeared imminent.[24]

Carnegie, on his arrival in Washington, reported to Thomas Scott and received his assignment. Under Scott's supervision, he was to organize the railroads and telegraphic communications south into Virginia. The Union's ultimate objective was Richmond, for already that unfortunate cry of "On to Richmond," which the suddenly militaristic Greeley had coined and the other

160

Northern papers had quickly picked up, had become the dominant slogan of the war. Washington, so recently in peril itself, had accepted this journalistic war objective as the basic strategy to defeat the enemy. Richmond had no real military significance and should never have been made the chief objective of the war, but the journalists and politicians were to make of it the very symbol of the Confederacy—a symbol that was to be so thoroughly accepted by both sides as to make its defense or capture absolutely basic to the termination of the war. The South would eventually be defeated in Vicksburg and Chattanooga and Atlanta, but she could never recognize that defeat so long as the Stars and Bars remained on the state-house mast in Richmond. It was a tragically costly objective for both sides, and thousands of men would die in four long years of brutal, fruitless fighting before that symbol could be smashed.

But in these first bright spring days of May 1861, the ninety miles between Washington and Richmond were still measured by crows' wings and not by soldiers' boots. The distance seemed short and the objective close at hand. The North appeared to have all the men needed to crush this "unlawful combination"—if only she had the trains available to carry them south to Richmond. These trains Carnegie was determined to provide. For to Carnegie, too, Richmond had become a symbol—a very personal symbol for all that he had been taught to hate since those days of Chartism in Dunfermline: the special privilege of the old aristocracy, the enslavement of men, and the tyranny of inherited wealth. Carnegie, with characteristic energy, threw himself into the task of delivering the force necessary to smash this citadel.

His first need being telegraph operators, he sent out an urgent request to David McCargo for the best operators he had on the Pennsylvania line. McCargo sent David Strouse, Samuel Brown, Richard O'Brien, and David Homer Bates, the first of a large number who were to compose the United States Military Telegraphers Corps.[25]

These telegraphers arrived in Washington on 2 May, and by that time Carnegie was hard at work in preparation for a railroad connection between the Baltimore & Ohio line in Washington and the line in Virginia as soon as the army should open operations across the river. The B. & O. line was extended from its terminal depot, just north of the Capitol building, southwest along Maryland Avenue to the Potomac. Here the old road bridge, Long Bridge, had to be rebuilt so that it could accommodate the movement of troops and heavy supply trains. Day and night Carnegie drove his railroad foremen and crew to finish the bridge job, and within seven days the bridge was ready for use. On 24 May, when the Union forces under Brigadier General Irvin McDowell pushed into Virginia, it was across the reconstructed Long Bridge that they moved. As soon as Alexandria had fallen to the Federal troops, Carnegie established his headquarters there, where connection could be made between the extended B. & O. line and the Orange & Alexandria Railroad, which ran south through Manassas Junction into the very heart of the Old Dominion.[26]

Telegraphic communication was as vital to an advancing army as the railroad, and here, too, Carnegie pushed his newly recruited operators and linemen hard in order to complete the job south into Virginia. Stations were established at Alexandria, Burke Station, and Fairfax so that there could be instantaneous communication between the central headquarters in Washington and the advance listening posts across the Potomac in Virginia. It was apparent to all that some kind of showdown between the Rebel and Union forces would take place by mid-summer, somewhere between the two rival capitals. Scott and Carnegie were determined that the Northern troops should not be lacking in either transportation or communication facilities between the battlefront and Washington whenever that confrontation should take place.

Mounting public pressure in both North and South was forcing an engagement before the military on either side felt itself ready for decisive battle. The journalists' cry of "On to Richmond" was now being echoed by the summer patriots everywhere throughout the North: in the banks and saloons, in railroad cars, in government offices, and in the White House itself. General McDowell, who, four days after the capture of Alexandria, had been appointed commander of the Department of Northeastern Virginia, had a field army estimated at 25,000 men by the end of June, and Washington felt it was high time it was being used in the field.

It is easy for the street-corner general to confuse mere numbers with an army, and McDowell's large collection of men was just that—it was not an army. Allan Nevins has written that "it is difficult to describe the levies assembled under McDowell except in terms of a rabble. The peasants who milled about Wat Tyler with clubs and pitchforks were little inferior in equipment and training." Green young farm boys and department store clerks had not received, during their two months of service, even the most rudimentary training in military procedure. There were so many accidents among the troops in the handling of firearms that one Senator seriously suggested that all troops be deprived of their revolvers.[27]

Nor had the various service branches of the army worked to prepare and equip this army of invasion with anything like the diligence that Thomas Scott and Carnegie had shown in providing railroad and telegraphic facilities for the advance. Lieutenant General Winfield Scott, the highest ranking military officer in the army, veteran of the War of 1812 and the Mexican War, was senile at seventy-five. He had opposed the appointment of McDowell as Commander of the Virginia department and did all that he could to thwart McDowell's plans for the invasion of Virginia. McDowell had virtually no staff, and his intelligence service was nonexistent. Provisions were lacking, and although Carnegie had provided the track, the Quartermaster General, Montgomery C. Meigs, refused to provide the necessary baggage cars to carry food supplies and tents.[28] McDowell knew that his army was not ready to go anywhere, but by the first week of July the mounting pressures for action could no longer be ignored. On 16 July the army headed south into Virginia.

The objective was Manassas Junction, some thirty miles westsouthwest of Washington, a small village, but an important railroad junction between the Orange & Alexandria Railroad and the Manassas Gap Railroad, which ran due west to Winchester and the Shenandoah Valley, both held by Rebel forces. This was to be the first war in which the control of railroad lines was crucial, and to a great extent railroads determined the strategy of battle. Manassas was the logical first point of encounter between the North and South on Virginia soil.

General Pierre Beauregard, commander of the Confederate

forces, realizing the strategic importance of this railroad town, had moved his 22,000 troops up to Manassas early in July, and there they awaited the enemy. McDowell's army left its encampment near Alexandria on the afternoon of 16 July, moving almost due west along the Warrenton turnpike. So undisciplined and untrained was this army that it took two and a half days to march the twenty miles to Centreville, some ten miles north of Manassas. There the army encamped to gather its force for the attack upon the Confederates, who had spread out in a cordon defense over a distance of ten miles along a small tributary of the Potomac River—Bull Run.

Carnegie had headed out of Alexandria shortly after the army and had set up advanced telegraph operations at Burke Station and Fairfax on the Orange & Alexandria Railroad, about ten miles northeast of Manassas. An elaborate courier system was established by which messengers on horseback could bring dispatches directly from the battlefield to Fairfax for relay by wire back to Washington. The first couriers began to arrive with their dispatches early on that hot Sunday morning of 21 July, as the main body of McDowell's troops moved south and west, down from the line established south of Centreville, crossing Bull Run at Sudley Springs, and turning the Confederate left flank along its scattered defense line facing Bull Run. The first dispatches that Carnegie sent to Washington contained only good news. As late as two o'clock in the afternoon Washington was being informed that McDowell's strategy had worked and that the encounter at Bull Run had been a smashing victory for the North. Lincoln was so reassured by the news he was receiving that he left the telegraph room to go for a ride, and General Scott retired for his customary mid-afternoon nap.

But on Henry House Hill, just south of Stone Bridge across Bull Run, a different story was being enacted from the one that the initial dispatches had so confidently predicted. The Confederate forces, pushed back from Sudley Springs ford and Stone Bridge, had, at the suggestion of Brigadier General Thomas Jackson, rallied their forces at the top of the Henry House Hill. McDowell had thought that General Joseph Johnston's fresh troops were miles away in Winchester, effectively checked by the Union General Robert Patterson. But, because of Patterson's ineptness and lack of intelligence information, Johnston and his troops had been able to leave Winchester by train, and on the evening of 20 July they arrived to reinforce Beauregard. These 12,000 additional troops now proved to be the decisive element in the afternoon battle. Jackson's brigade, on the crest of the hill, remained "standing like a stonewall" as other sections of the Confederate line threatened to bolt under the rapidly advancing Union troops. Then Edmund Kirby-Smith's brigade, which had arrived on the train from Winchester only a few hours before, was thrown into the fight, and the Confederate line stiffened and held. The advancing Union troops, hitting this reinforced line, hesitated for a moment and then fell back. The raw, untrained troops lacked the discipline for a holding action. Nervous energy and fear could carry them forward, but it could not hold them in place. When they could no longer move forward, the same propelling fear would drive them back. Then fear would quickly turn into panic, and what had begun as an orderly retreat for regrouping suddenly became a choking, lung-bursting rout. The men dropped their guns, their haversacks, their coats. And they ran. The mounted officers, most of them as inexperienced as their men, were seized by the same terrible emotion. Spurring their horses on, they soon outran their men in retreat. Down the Warrenton turnpike the army fled, seeking only the Potomac and the sanctuary of Washington that lay beyond that protecting moat.

The Confederates were as unnerved in their sudden success as the Union forces were by retreat. Had they pursued this fugitive army, which had so quickly reverted to its true status of being but a rabble, they could have easily swept back into Alexandria and perhaps into Washington itself. But the Confederates, exhausted by the fighting and the searing heat of the day, were in no mood for an advance. When Jefferson Davis visited the battlefield late that afternoon, soon after the Union rout, both Johnston and Beauregard counseled against taking the offensive. So the opportunity for a morale-crushing drive on Washington was lost. The Confederates stayed in Manassas while the Union forces fled back to the Potomac. Neither Washington nor Richmond would be invaded this summer, and, for the first time, each side began to have some concept of what crossing those ninety miles would mean in terms of human suffering.[29]

All that hot Sunday Carnegie and his crew of telegraph operators and railroad men had been at their various stations between Alexandria and Fairfax, sending messages and putting the most seriously wounded men, brought in on wagons from the battle, onto trains to take them to the hospitals in Washington. The first inkling Carnegie had that something might be going wrong at Bull Run was in mid-afternoon, when the couriers failed to appear with dispatches for relay. Then the first panicky troops could be seen rushing up the road from Bull Run, and Carnegie knew with dreadful certainty that his earlier messages promising a Union victory had become grievously outdated. His operator at Fairfax had time to send only one final dispatch to Washington, "our army is retreating," before the full flood of the rout swept down upon him. From that moment on, Carnegie and his crew had to devote all their energies to keeping the trains running back to Alexandria, filled with those wounded who could not make it on foot.

The Union troops fully expected the Confederate forces to pursue them back into Alexandria, and by nightfall Carnegie decided the advance stations at Fairfax and Burke Station must be closed before they were captured by the Rebels. The remaining wounded men were placed in the boxcars and Carnegie and his crew took the last train back to Alexandria. He was there early the next morning to see the exhausted, defeated Union troops straggle across Long Bridge back into Washington. It had taken McDowell's army two and a half days to march out from Washington to Centreville, but less than fifteen hours to return from Bull Run.[30]

The first encounter had been made, and if the South was understandably exultant over the result, the North for the first time realized that this would be no simple summer exercise against an "unlawful combination" of individual rebels. Old General Scott's absurdly gloomy prediction in May, that this would be a three-year war, had taken on a terrible Cassandra-like ring of truth. Lincoln's initial request for 75,000 men for a three-month period of service was now seen by all to be pathetically inadequate. Carnegie, on that black Monday morning after the rout, sent the following dispatch back to the Pittsburgh *Chronicle:*

166

After our forces had full possession of the Bull Run batteries last night, Gen. Johnson [sic] with twenty thousand men came up and forced them to retire. Our forces are now forming at Alexandria, and will attack the enemy again shortly.[31]

It was a brave message, but at the very moment he was sending it Carnegie could look out of his station window in Alexandria and see the last of the Union forces trudging across Long Bridge into Washington. There was no regrouping in Alexandria, and it would take a great deal of training and the infusion of new blood before the Union army would be ready to "attack the enemy again." Carnegie was more realistic in his evaluation of the situation when he wrote to a friend four days later:

Depend upon it, the recent defeat is a blessing in disguise. We shall now begin in earnest. Knowing our foes, the necessary means will be applied to ensure their overthrow. . . . What might have been half work, a mere scotching of the snake, will now be thorough & complete. You shall at no distant time be able to proclaim in New Orleans that God has made all men free and equal and that slavery is the sum of all villanies [sic].

Alexandrians are now getting used to the utterance of some strange sentiments. We wanted a gang of laborers the other day. Sam Barr, one of our best boys from Pgh, was delegated to organize it—the first question—boys are you all free?—Yes all but one—Why ain't you free? "Case Massa owns me Sar"—Why don't you go and tell him you now owns yourself & if he say you don't—show him you do by knocking him down—you can't work with Free Negroes unless you do—That gave the Colored population something to think over.

I am delighted with my occupation here—hard work, but how gratifying to lie down at night & think By George you are of some use in sustaining a great cause & making the path clearer for those who come hereafter as well as maintaining the position that humanity has, after laborious efforts, succeeded in reaching.[32]

Carnegie had been working hard, the hardest physical labor of his life. Above all, he hated the heat that covered the Potomac valley that summer like an all-enveloping shroud, stifling and inescapable. Soon after Bull Run, while working out on the line supervising the repair of a railroad bridge, he suffered a mild sunstroke and had to return to Washington for several days' rest. This minor affliction proved to be a permanent disability, and ever afterwards he was to be particularly sensitive to heat.[33]

Although apparently recovered after a few days, Carnegie dreaded going out on the line in Virginia again, and he was delighted when Thomas Scott, who had been formally appointed Assistant Secretary of War in August, asked him to stay in Washington as his assistant in charge of railroads and telegraph service. His office, next to Scott's in the War Department building, was the center for all incoming dispatches from the field. President Lincoln was a frequent visitor, half-sitting, half-leaning against Carnegie's desk, waiting for a reply to some dispatch, and all the while talking to whoever had the time to listen. Carnegie would remember him as "one of the most homely men I ever saw when his features were in repose," but mostly he would remember Lincoln talking, for "when excited or telling a story, intellect shone through his eyes and illuminated his face to a degree which I have seldom or never seen in any other. . . . I have often regretted that I did not note down carefully at the time some of his curious sayings, for he said even common things in an original way. I never met a great man who so thoroughly made himself one with all men as Mr. Lincoln." [34]

But if Lincoln won Carnegie's approval, there were few other men in the administration who did. He was appalled by his first impression of General Winfield Scott: "He was being helped by two men across the pavement from his office into his carriage . . . an old, decrepit man, paralyzed not only in body, but in mind; and it was upon this noble relic of the past that the organization of the forces of the Republic depended." General Scott's staff, Carnegie believed, was no better: they "were seemingly one and all martinets who had passed the age of usefulness. Days would elapse before a decision could be obtained upon matters which required prompt action. There was scarcely a young active officer at the head of any important department—at least I cannot recall one. Long years of peace had fossilized the service." [35]

Carnegie could not fail to compare the lassitude and inefficiency he found in Washington with the methods of private business he had known in Pittsburgh. His Washington experience was not one likely to impress him with governmental operations. After the failure at Bull Run, the whole country seemed to be waiting for some kind of positive action. Carnegie, like so many others, was at first delighted with the news of the appointment of General McClellan as Commander of the newly organized Union forces within the week after Bull Run. This appointment gave promise of quick decisive action against the Rebels. McClellan, arriving in Washington on 6 July, fresh from his well-advertised successes in minor engagements in West Virginia, was not one to underestimate his own abilities. He particularly liked being told that he was now "where Napoleon had stood after Arcola." [36] The young Napoleon from out of the West—and in his conceit he failed to note the symbolic significance of his traveling to the East—to Alexandria.

The Northern states had responded to Bull Run with a new burst of patriotism; thousands of men eagerly signed up under the new Military Act of 1861 for a three-year term of service, and states had little difficulty meeting their quotas in this first summer of the war. There was much confusion and inefficiency in this recruitment. The individual states were responsible for raising their own troops, with the result that there was no over-all co-ordinated national military organization. Regular army men were in a small minority, and high command positions in each state went to the amateurs—ambitious politicians and home-town heroes, who tried to make up with enthusiasm and brash aggressiveness their lack of even the most basic fundamentals of military expertise.

Nor did the governors of the several states have effective control of the military organization within their own states. Single individuals were permitted to recruit and, in effect, raise their own private companies to go off to war. Whole communities would be drained of available manpower without any authorization from either the state or Federal government. One of the private armies so haphazardly formed in these first months of war was the home guard of Pennsylvania railroad men, organized in Pittsburgh by John B. Dailey and Captain William Mills. These men notified

Carnegie that they were naming their company after him, and Carnegie, who had never before had anything named for him, was inordinately proud of this honor. He wrote to Dailey and Mills,

> Although temporarily separated it is still a matter of congratulations that we are all permitted to take some part in the noble effort now going forward for the preservation of the Republic and the overthrow of her enemies, nor is your share in this good work less important because performed at home. If ever called into active service I feel well assured the same skill, courage and energy, the same prompt performance of duty which have hitherto characterized those composing your command in their operations upon the "Great Western" will continue to distinguish them upon the field of battle. Please tend to all my sincere acknowledgements for the compliment bestowed and believe me with best wishes for their & your future welfare & prosperity.[37]

Carnegie may have been highly complimented by this private military enterprise upon the part of his former subordinates, but for Governor Andrew Curtin, who was trying to bring some kind of order out of the military chaos within his state, such individual activities were anything but helpful to the national war effort.

Nevertheless, the men were recruited, equipped in one fashion or another, and transported to Washington. They came by the hundreds of thousands, and soon the hills surrounding the Capital were white with their tents. McClellan had his army. It was hoped that he would soon make use of it.

It was, however, a curiously hesitant and cautious Napoleon who had come out of the West to save the nation. He spoke boldly of crushing the rebellion "at one blow," of terminating the war "in a single campaign." And this was the kind of talk that the North desperately wanted to hear in the weeks after Bull Run. First, though, he needed time—time to organize this vast, inchoate citizens' army into a thoroughly trained, equipped, and disciplined fighting force; time to complete the great peripheral defenses of Washington; time to select the most advantageous place and moment for the blow.

The long summer days ended, and all through the exceptionally warm and bright autumn of 1861, McClellan continued his preparations, and still showed no sign of being ready for actual combat.[38]

The truth is that McClellan was not a Napoleon, but rather a Frederick I of Prussia, who loved organization far more than he did battle. No detail was too insignificant for McClellan; he gave each his full attention and interest. Supplies, transportation, communications, and, above all, personnel, were to him the essence of militarism. He took McDowell's primitive, almost nonexistent staff and reorganized it into a resplendent administration that could dazzle even the sophisticated European noblemen who came over to observe.

Carnegie was to be a none too reluctant victim of this reorganization. Never having felt completely well since his sunstroke in July, Carnegie was in constant discomfort in Washington and fearful that in his weakened condition he might contract typhoid, which had reached epidemic proportions in the camps around the city. He used McClellan's reorganization plan as an excuse to approach Thomas Scott with the suggestion that he might be of more service to the cause back in Pittsburgh, in his old job as supervisor of the Western Division of the Pennsylvania. Scott gave his reluctant consent, and Carnegie returned to Pittsburgh in early September.[39]

Carnegie found Pittsburgh to be a busy, prosperous city, its iron products in great demand by the army and its trains filled with produce and manufactured goods for the Eastern markets. Carnegie threw himself into his old familiar routine with great enthusiasm. After the weeks of waiting for something to happen in Washington, it was a relief to be again giving orders that he knew would be carried out with a minimum of delay, to see trains moving and men working with an energy that he had not seen in Washington. Soon he was writing sharp, pointed notes to Enoch Lewis, general superintendent of the line, suggesting that double tracks be laid from Altoona to Pittsburgh to accommodate the increased traffic, that telegraph stations be kept open all night, and that additional property be acquired west of the city for the building of more sidings and freight yards.[40]

These letters to Lewis, written soon after his return to Pittsburgh, reveal the basic philosophy that was to underlie Carnegie's business methods throughout his life: reduce prices by reducing cost. He argued strenuously for a five-cent reduction of passenger fares to the outlying suburbs of Swissvale, Braddock, and Brinton, to meet the competition of the newly opened Pittsburgh and Connellsville Railroad, and at the same time he urged that the working hours for trainmen be increased from ten to twelve or thirteen per day, thus making unnecessary a change of crews at Conemaugh, between Altoona and Pittsburgh.

> The whole question revolves itself into this—Can train men perform 12 to 12½ hours service per day coupled with occasional Sunday runs and such delays as are incident to a first class, well managed Double Track Rail Road? . . . From personal knowledge of what has been done for years past on this Division I have no hesitation in answering decidedly in the affirmative. . . . When it is remembered that the amount of Manual Labor required from Train Men is very small twelve or thirteen hours of mere exposure will not be considered excessive—I do not regard 13 hours Train service as being more exhaustive than ten hours manual labor—We have never found the efficiency of the force impaired by the amount of service required from the crews referred to.[41]

Drive and expand, reduce costs and increase profits—these were his maxims, and they were appropriate to the times.

Pittsburgh was a pushing, driving city, eager to profit from the war and from the general industrial expansion of the day. But there was a special feverish activity in Pittsburgh in these months after Carnegie returned from Washington that had nothing to do with the war or railroads or iron manufacturing, but which gave the city the excitement of San Francisco in 1849. Oil had been discovered, or, rather, had been suddenly made available in prodigious quantities, by well-drilling some ninety miles north of Pittsburgh, along Oil Creek, a small tributary of the Allegheny River.

The existence of oil in that region had been known by the first pioneer farmers, who had skimmed the oil off the surface of the water with blankets. Like the Seneca Indians before them, they had valued it for its alleged medicinal properties. It took many hours of dipping and blanket-wringing to fill a small keg with Seneca oil, but for those who had the time and patience to do so there was a handsome reward—$15 to $18 for a single keg.

In 1847, a more enterprising entrepreneur, Samuel Kier, the owner and operator of canal boats in Pittsburgh, attempted to commercialize this rock oil, or petroleum, on a much larger scale. His father, in digging salt wells at Tarentum, Pennsylvania, on the Allegheny a few miles north of Pittsburgh, had come upon oil, which he had regarded only as a nuisance. Young Kier, however, collected the oil and brought it into Pittsburgh to bottle it. He then sent agents in gaudily painted little medicine carts throughout western Pennsylvania and Ohio to peddle this "Natural Remedy" as a cure for ailments afflicting either man or beast. The "remedy" sold well at $2 a bottle, but even so, oil production from the Tarentum salt wells far exceeded the market.

Seeking another use for this apparently abundant supply of petroleum, Kier consulted a chemist in Philadelphia, who suggested that it would make an excellent illuminant, providing its crudities could be refined out through distillation, and the disagreeable smoky odor removed.[42]

Whale oil, then the chief fuel for lamps, was becoming almost prohibitively expensive at $2.50 a gallon, and the world needed an illuminant that would be clean, safe, and inexpensive. Petroleum gave promise of being that long-sought-after product, and Kier set up the first refinery in America for what he called "carbon oil," a one-gallon still on 7th Avenue in Pittsburgh. Selling the oil at $1.50 a gallon, he found a market so eager for his product that within a year he built an enlarged refinery in Lawrenceville, a suburb of Pittsburgh, and was able to sell all that he could produce.

The distillation of an illuminant oil from bituminous coal or shale rock was an old process in England, dating at least as far back as 1604, when a patent was granted to three men for a method of extracting "oyle out of a sort of stone." In 1846 a Canadian doctor, Abraham Gisner, had distilled a clear oil from the coal on Prince Edward Island. He had named the oil kerosene, from the Greek *keros,* meaning wax.[43] Kier, however, was the first to refine petroleum, a much less difficult process, and word of his success in making a satisfactory illuminant quickly spread throughout the East.

In the early 1850's, Francis Beattie Brewer, a young physician, was practicing in Titusville, Pennsylvania, a remote village on Oil Creek. Brewer was the son of a farmer, and the family farm lay about two miles south of Titusville. In 1853, young Brewer went east to visit his college, Dartmouth, and he took along a sample of the petroleum from his father's farm. He showed the sample to Dr. Dixi Crosby and Professor O. P. Hubbard of the geology department, and after analyzing it, they pronounced it to be an excellent grade of petroleum, highly suitable for refining into an illuminant. Another Darmouth alumnus, George H. Bissell, who visited Crosby a few weeks later, became excited about the commercial possibilities of this find, and he and his New York law partner, Jonathan G. Eveleth, bought the Brewer farm in November 1854. They in turn persuaded a group of New Haven businessmen, headed by James M. Townsend, to invest in a company to be called the Pennsylvania Rock Oil Company. It was reorganized as the Seneca Oil Company under the direction of Townsend in 1858, and the company hired a former railroad man, Edwin L. Drake, to go out to Titusville as general agent, to drill for oil.

At the old Brewer farm Drake built an engine house, erected a derrick, and drove an iron pipe down 32 feet through sand and clay to bedrock. The drilling tools were placed inside the pipe, and by the middle of August 1859 Drake was ready to begin drilling. After two weeks of drilling with his primitive tools, Drake had cut down through the rock to a depth of 69½ feet. Then, on Saturday, 27 August, just as the men were quitting for the day, the drill slipped down through a crevice in the rock. On Sunday the men did not work, but one of them, "Uncle Billy" Smith, an old hand at salt-well drilling, inspected the well and found oil floating on top of the water in the pipe, only a few feet under the derrick floor. Drake had proved that petroleum, like water, could be drilled for, and within two days he was pumping up oil at the rate of ten barrels a day. A great new industry was born, and the first oil rush was on. [44]

Men came to Oil Creek as they had come to the American River in California ten years before, but not, this time, with picks and washing pans. They came with drills and dowsing sticks, trampling over the poor hard-scrabble farms along Oil Creek and bidding feverishly for the right to buy or lease what had been some of the poorest farmland in the state. This first oil fever had struck western Pennsylvania in the winter of 1859, about the time Carnegie had returned to Pittsburgh from Altoona. He had remained quite indifferent to what he regarded as a temporary speculative craze, and although there must have been ample opportunities for him to make an investment in these first well-drillings, he had refused to become involved.

In the fall of 1861, however, there was a great change—both in the scale of the Titusville operations and in the kind of men who were interested in the development of the oil fields. The newer fields at the lower end of Oil Creek were producing in quantities that made Drake's first well appear as primitive and inefficient as the blanket-wringing operations of the Seneca Indians. The Little and Merrick well, on the John Buchanan farm, opened in April 1861, was flowing at the rate of 3000 barrels a day, while the Empire well, on the McElhenny farm, opened in September 1861, gushed forth 4000 barrels a day. This was production on a mass scale, and some of the most conservative and careful businessmen in Pittsburgh were now showing an interest in the development.[45]

One of Carnegie's neighbors in Homewood, William Coleman, an iron manufacturer whom Carnegie respected above almost any other businessman in the city, was the man who persuaded Carnegie to invest in the oil fields of Titusville. Coleman and his associates had formed the Columbia Oil Company, which had on option to buy the Storey farm for $40,000. This farm was ideally situated, on the west branch of Oil Creek—at that time believed to be the only oil reservoir in the area—five miles north of the junction of the creek with the Allegheny River. Carnegie wanted to see the farm before investing in it, so in the late fall of 1861 he and Coleman made the long, difficult trip up the Allegheny to the oil fields.

Oil Creek flows through what was then one of the most isolated parts of western Pennsylvania. There were no railroads into Titusville and the surrounding oil farms. Coleman and Carnegie took a steamboat up the Allegheny to the mouth of Oil Creek, where a boom town, Oil City, had already sprung up, and from there a wagon carried them over rough dirt roads to the wells beyond. Carnegie had never before experienced anything like this. Rough shanties sufficed for houses, and crude derricks rose all around like strange leviathans, spouting not water but a black, foul-smelling liquid more precious than gold. Oil was everywhere, soaking back into the ground from which it had come, giving a strangely beautiful irridescent sheen to the mud puddles along the road, floating thick and heavy on the creek itself, and covering everyone's clothing and skin so that a man felt he could never scrub himself clean again. It was a raucous, wild scene, which no one who had not visited the mining camps of the Far West could possibly have been prepared for. What surprised Carnegie, however, was that, in spite of the feverish activity and the desperate competition for land and equipment, "good humor prevailed everywhere. It was a vast picnic, full of amusing incidents. Everybody was in high glee; fortunes were supposedly within reach; everything was booming. On the tops of the derricks floated flags on which strange mottoes were displayed. I remember looking down toward the river and seeing two men working their treadles boring for oil upon the banks of the stream, and inscribed upon their flag was 'Hell or China.' They were going down, no matter how far." [46]

One need not fear malaria in this region, where every puddle wore a sheen of oil, but no man could walk along the banks of Oil Creek and not be infected with the fever for oil. Carnegie was a quick victim. On the long ride back to Pittsburgh, he completed his arrangements with Coleman to take an interest in the Columbia Oil Company for the purchase of the Storey farm. The company was organized with an initial capital of $200,000, but the $100 shares were sold to the initial investors at $10 a share. Carnegie, using his dividends from the Woodruff Sleeping Car Company, purchased over 1000 shares in the company, and considering the amount of capital involved, it proved to be one of the most spectacularly profitable investments he was ever to make. The company got into full operation the following year, and although the yield was not as abundant as that of the Empire well, it did produce over 2000 barrels a day. During the first year of production, the Columbia Oil Company passed four dividends, giving a return of 160 per cent upon the investment. Carnegie, who had invested a little over $11,000 in the venture, realized a return of $17,868.67 in this first year alone.[47]

176

Even so, there were problems. With no railroad close to the Oil Creek fields, the oil had to be taken out by wagon teams or, during the relatively short period of high water, floated down Oil Creek to the Allegheny in flatboats. Barrels and other containers were at a high premium. But most serious of all, this sudden flood of oil upon the world market quickly reduced the price of petroleum from $5 a barrel down to 10¢ a barrel. The world at last had a cheap illuminant, but the mass production of it ruined the small investors who had dug small wells along the upper banks of Oil Creek.[48]

Coleman and Carnegie believed that this underground reservoir of oil would be quickly exhausted by the great gushing wells. Then, they shrewdly figured, the price of petroleum would rise again and, at the same time, there would not be the intense competition for containers and wagon space to ship the crude oil out of the fields to the refineries. They were able to convince the other shareholders of the soundness of this argument, and, consequently, the Columbia Oil Company ordered the excavation of a hole sufficiently large to hold 100,000 barrels of crude oil. No attempt was made to line the hole to prevent seepage; it was to be simply a vast pond of oil, with the loss from seepage to be made good from the daily production of the wells. Coleman confidently predicted that all the wells in the area would soon go dry, and then the price of petroleum would go back up, even up to $10 a barrel. They would have a million-dollar pond on their land, needing only to be drained.

But the months passed, and the wells showed no signs of being exhausted. On the contrary, new wells were being opened up along the small tributaries of Oil Creek, along Benninghoff, Pioneer, and Cherrytree runs. The amount of waste through seepage in the Storey farm pool was far greater than Coleman and Carnegie had anticipated, and after several months of loss, running into thousands of barrels, the reservoir plan was abandoned.[49] In October 1862, a branch railroad was built into Titusville from Corry, Pennsylvania, to the north, and the transportation problem was considerably eased. The Columbia Oil Company finally realized that the price of petroleum was going to remain low, and that profits would come only to those concerns which could most efficiently produce the crude oil in mass bulk.

177

One way to achieve this efficiency would be to hire and maintain the best labor force available in the region. This policy would cost money, for it was hard to attract and harder still to keep good drillers and roustabouts at a time when every man with a hundred dollars' worth of tools and a divining rod had the dream of striking it rich on his own. The Columbia Oil Company decided to spend the money necessary to keep good workers, not only by paying higher wages, but also by building adequate housing for the men and their families, by providing the best machine shops in the region, and even by establishing a library (which may have been Carnegie's first contribution to library building) and encouraging the formation of the Columbia Cornet Band, the only musical organization in the oil fields. Soon the Storey farm had the reputation of being the best-managed—and also the best-paying—field in the area.[50] Coleman's failure to secure a million-dollar pool of oil was more than compensated for by this new policy of efficient mass production. In one year alone, the returns in dividends to the stockholders in the Columbia Oil Company was over $1,000,000. In all, the men who had invested $40,000 in the Storey farm were to take out over $5,000,000. Carnegie, for once, was guilty of an understatement in his autobiography: "This forty-thousand-dollar investment proved for us the best of all so far. The revenues from it came at a most opportune time."[51] At the age of twenty-six, Carnegie was well on his way toward his first million.

During these first months back in Pittsburgh, Carnegie had driven himself hard, as had always been his custom. The heavy freight and passenger traffic occasioned by the war had meant long hours out on the line in all kinds of weather. His several trips up to Oil Creek to supervise operations on the Storey farm had been anything but comfortable. Bad food, inadequate protection from the elements, irregular hours—all these took a heavy toll upon his constitution, for he had never fully recovered from his illness in Washington the previous summer. By early spring, he was seriously ill for the first time in his life, and the doctor strongly advised him to take several months' rest if he did not wish his health permanently impaired.

In May 1862 Carnegie applied to president Thomson for a three-month leave of absence, and it was granted. It was Carne-

gie's first vacation since the morning, fourteen years before, when
he had reported for work with his father at Blackstock's textile
mill, and he knew precisely what he would do. On the day he received word that a leave would be granted him, he was in Altoona. He at once sat down and dashed off a letter to Cousin
Dod:

> Ten minutes since I received glorious news—the dream of a
> dozen years is at last on the very threshold of realization—*Yes,
> I am to visit* Scotland, see and talk with you all again!—Uncles,
> Aunts and Cousins, my schoolfellows and companions of my
> childhood—all are to be greeted again. . . . I shall once more
> wander through Woodmill Braes, see Torry and Pitreavie, Lime-
> kilns, the Rumbling Well and a hundred other spots that have
> haunted me for years till Dunfermline and its neighborhood has
> grown to be a kind of "Promised Land" to me. . . . The exuber-
> ance of my joy I find is tempered by a deep feeling of thankful-
> ness for the privilege vouchsafed—it seems so much in advance
> of my deserts. I hope I may be enabled to make good use of the
> blessing.
> . . . Surely Aunt Charlotte will be to the fore when I arrive.
> . . . I do not know certainly whether Mother will accompany
> me. . . . But I am almost sure she will. . . . We will make a
> bee line for Dunfermline won't turn my head to look at any-
> thing until I see Bruce's monument. I remember that was the
> last thing I saw of Dunfermline and I cried bitterly when it
> could be seen no more—intend to remain in Dunfermline until
> I'm glutted with all it can give and then will take a run over
> the continent as far as the Rhine perhaps. Can't you go along?
> . . . But of this more when we meet—four weeks and I'm
> afloat, six and I'm in "Dumfarline Town"—Whew, that's enough
> to make one jolly isn't it—I confess I'm clean daft about
> it. . . .[52]

Margaret Carnegie, of course, went along. Nothing could have
kept her from this triumphal return to Dunfermline. She would
meet her brother and the others who had called her daft for leaving, and in all her finery show that she "had made the spoon"
after all, and it was a spoon not of horn but of gold. Carnegie's
old friend and neighbor, Thomas Miller, now an executive with
the Pittsburgh, Fort Wayne and Chicago Railway and a silent

partner in the prosperous iron forging company of Kloman and Company, agreed to go along with them. The Carnegies and Miller sailed on the *Aetna* on 28 June 1862. Traveling first class on the prize passenger steamship of the Inman Line, the Carnegies could hardly have failed to compare their return voyage with their steerage trip out fourteen years before. The old *Wiscasset* had taken seven weeks to cross the Atlantic; the *Aetna* took but two to reach Liverpool.[53]

The train that took them north to Scotland seemed to move as slowly as the *Wiscasset*, so eager were Carnegie and his mother to reach Dunfermline. At last they crossed the border, and on the bare, bleak Cheviot Hills they saw bright yellow bushes in full bloom. Margaret Carnegie, with tears running down her cheeks, cried, "Oh! there's the broom, the broom!" Then the River Tweed, the high smoke pots on top of the Edinburgh closes, the ferry across the Firth of Forth, and ahead of them the tower of the Abbey. Carnegie and his mother were both quite overcome with emotion.

The Morrisons and the Carnegies were at the station to meet them: Uncle Tom, now the Bailie Morrison, as loud of voice and florid of face as ever, Uncle Lauder and Cousin Dod, and Aunt Charlotte Drysdale to the fore, as Carnegie had predicted. They were all duly impressed with their American relatives, with their dress and luggage and general air of prosperity, just as Margaret had hoped they would be. Aunt Charlotte, perhaps remembering that last night the Carnegies had spent in Dunfermline, when she had come over to the empty cottage on Moodie Street to give her brother Will the last two pounds ten in her purse, now, as she embraced her nephew, burst out, "How fine you are. Oh, you will just be coming back here some day and keep a shop in the High Street." She could imagine nothing finer than that, but her nephew could hardly refrain from smiling at her innocence. Already his annual income was undoubtedly greater than the combined profits of all the merchants on High Street.[54]

The narrowness of his aunt's vision, Carnegie quickly realized, was appropriate to the limited dimensions of her small world. Walking up Guildhall Street to High Street, where he would stay with Uncle Lauder in his rooms above the store, Carnegie looked in amazement around him. Everything was the same, no new buildings, nothing torn down or replaced. Yet all was changed. He knew for the first time the cruel truth of not being able to go home again. It was not that the home had changed, but that he had. Everything he as a child had believed imposing and grand now shrank before his adult eyes to miniature proportions. Arriving at Uncle Lauder's store, Carnegie exclaimed, "You are all here; everything is just as I left it, but you are now all playing with toys." In his walks through the town and down to the seashore, Carnegie found only "a city of the Lilliputians. I could almost touch the eaves of the house in which I was born. . . . The rocks at the seashore, among which I had gathered wilks [whelks] seemed to have vanished, and a tame flat shoal remained. The schoolhouse, around which had centered many of my schoolboy recollections––my only Alma Mater—and the playground, upon which mimic battles had been fought and races run, had shrunk into ridiculously small dimensions. The fine residences, Broomhall, Fordell, and especially the conservatories at Donibristle, fell one after the other into the petty and insignificant. . . . Everything was there in miniature." Only the Abbey and the Glen were as he had remembered them, grand and glorious, and in no way disappointing.[55]

The old friends and political associates of his family he found to be equally disappointing in their provincial outlook. They were still agitating for universal suffrage and against special privilege, to be sure, but only to preserve what they had once had, not to advance their status. They wanted the old days of the handloom weaver to return and, like Aunt Charlotte, their ambition did not extend beyond High Street. They refused to see that the smoking chimneys of St. Leonard's textile mill, which they still hated even though they might beg at the gates for a job, were the nineteenth century in microcosm. Carnegie could no longer understand why they should fight industry; they should capture and control it, as he fully intended to do. Even Dod was strangely lacking in ambition—without any of the wonderful visions of great wealth which to Carnegie and his friends in Pittsburgh were as real as the mystic sight of religious ecstasy was to a medieval saint. Carnegie spent long hours talking with Dod, trying to make him see what America was and what he intended to make of it, but he was not at all sure that Dod understood.[56] It must have been then that Carnegie for the first time suspected that Dunfermline and America were two worlds, and that he could not, as he had always before assumed, have them both. America was not just Dunfermline with the Charter. It was Brobdingnag—a land impossible for the Lilliputians to comprehend.

Carnegie had not expected to find himself an alien in his native land, and he certainly did not expect that his friends and relatives would treat him as such. He felt that at least in politics he and they would still be in accord, and he was shocked to find that most of his old Radical associates, the men who had stood with his father and grandfather at political rallies to heckle Lord Dalmeny or had marched in Chartist parades, were now pro-Southern in their attitudes toward the American Civil War. That these former Chartists would be on the side of the planter aristocracy and special privilege, and against the American democracy, now locked in mortal combat to preserve and extend the basic Charter as expressed in the Declaration of Independence, was as incomprehensible to Carnegie as it was shocking.

The Dunfermline *Journal,* since the outbreak of the conflict in America, had been openly pro-Confederate, giving much space to Southern victories at Bull Run and in the peninsular campaigns and jeering editorially at Lincoln, "a President who does not know his own mind." But this did not particularly surprise Carnegie.[57] The *Journal* had always been a reactionary paper, the political enemy of his grandfather, uncle, and father. But to have such Radical labor papers as the *Reynolds News* and the *British Miner*, as well as the Glasgow *Sentinel,* the journal of the Glasgow Trades Council, openly advocating British intervention on the side of the Confederacy seemed to Carnegie a betrayal of everything these journals had advocated in the past.[58] He could not understand them or his Dunfermline friends, including his Uncle Tom Morrison, with whom he tried to argue. The argument only ended, as was usual in any discussion with the Bailie, in a shouting match that Carnegie had no chance of winning.

Carnegie could understand why the British people should be upset over the *Trent* Affair, in which an overzealous United States Navy captain had forcibly taken as prisoners two Confederate agents, James Mason and John Slidell, off a British steamer on the high seas. He himself had been shocked by this incident and had written a strong letter to the Pittsburgh *Daily Post* condemning Captain Charles Wilkes and urging the Lincoln administration to release the two Southerners.[59] But this unhappy incident had occurred over eight months before, and furthermore, Lincoln, after some hesitation, had yielded to British public opinion and had permitted Mason and Slidell to continue on their mission to Europe.

The antipathy that Carnegie discovered in Scotland toward the Union cause could not be attributed to any single such incident. It was much more fundamental and complex. Like Carnegie before his visit to Dunfermline, most Americans of that time believed, as do most today, that the overwhelming majority of the common people of Britain were solidly on the side of the Federal Union from the outbreak of the American Civil War, and that it was only the Establishment, the Tories and the rich Whig merchants, who flirted dangerously and outrageously with the Confederacy. One of the most cherished events of the war for the American people was the brave resolution of support sent to Lincoln by the unemployed workers of Birmingham and Manchester, and Lincoln's moving reply. That there was an important ideological bond between the workers in Britain and the Lincoln government, particularly after the issuance of the Emancipation Proclamation, cannot be denied, but that this class response was universal throughout Britain should not be assumed.

In Scotland especially, the hostility among the Radicals throughout the war toward the Union cause was a very real fact. There was, of course, first of all, an economic basis to this hostility. The unemployed cotton textile workers of Glasgow and Paisley could and did blame their hunger on the Union blockade. Long indoctrinated in free trade principles, they feared that the victory of the Northern Republicans over the Southern, free trade Democrats would simply institutionalize the blockade in the form of a high protective tariff. As the United States represented a major portion of the export trade in textiles, they foresaw no relief even after the war was over. The linen and jute workers of eastern Scotland might have been expected, on the other hand, to have supported the Northern blockade, inasmuch as the demand for their products would increase as the cotton trade was restricted. This was true in such towns as Dundee, Dysart, and Tayport, where the demand of the American Army for canvas tarpaulin, rope, and coarse linen fabrics did much to revive a depressed industry. In Dunfermline, however, which had always been the center for the luxury goods of the linen trade, damask tablecloths and fine linen sheeting, the war had had an adverse effect.[60] Carnegie had arrived back in Dunfermline in the midst of the worst economic depression since the hungry 'forties. "Groups of listless and hopeless looking men are to be seen daily at the Cross and the Canon," the Edinburgh *Scotsman* reported during the first winter of the war.[61] By the summer of 1862, several private charity groups had been formed to give food to the unemployed, and the soup lines, so familiar to Carnegie's childhood, could again be seen on the streets of Dunfermline.

Scottish attitudes toward the Civil War cannot be explained wholly in terms of economics, however, for the English cotton textile workers were enduring the same hardships. To a great extent the pro-Southern sympathies of the Scottish workers must be understood as an emotional response based on the romantic history of Scotland. If there is truth in Mark Twain's half-facetious remark that Sir Walter Scott was responsible for the American Civil War, because by his novels he gave to the Southern planter the romanticized ideal of feudalism, then it may also be argued that, ironically, the South had been exporting that romance back to Scotland along with its cotton. The old cause, lost so long ago at Culloden, could be lived again vicariously at Bull Run, Fredericksburg, and Chancellorsville, for it was easy enough for the romance-starved Highlander to identify the dashing young cavaliers of Carolina with the clansmen of Bonnie Prince Charles. The very names of Charleston, the James River, and Carolina evoked memories of the Stuart past.

If the Highlander was attracted to the Southern cause for reasons of the past, the Radicals of the Lowlands tended to be as emotional in his hostility toward the North because of the present. There were many labor leaders who thought that the agitation for Negro emancipation was but a red herring to distract the reform movement from its true goal of industrial reform. These men suspected a conspiracy between the abolitionists and the industrial magnates, and their suspicions seemed to be confirmed by the leadership they observed within the American Republican party. Carnegie might have had a better understanding of this attitude had he read his grandfather's essay on *The Rights of Land,* written twenty-five years earlier, in which old Tom Morrison had made the bitter comment: "Perhaps some little piecer . . . will ask you 'When shall we have the ten-hour bill?' And you will stave the child off with a monody over the miseries of the blacks, a lamentation for their *slavery* and an exortation [sic] to thankfulness for its white skin and blessed *freedom. . . .*" [62] A Scottish weaver, William Thomson, had written on slavery as he had seen it on the Southern plantations, and he compared it favorably with the conditions he had experienced in Scottish factories. Thomson's works were widely read, and they led such labor leaders as Alexander Campbell and George Troup to state unequivocally that the war was "not a war for or against slavery. It is a war against independence, against trade—for centralization, pride and vanity. . . ." [63]

Harriet Beecher Stowe, one of the few American abolitionists who visited Scotland, and certainly the best known, also unwittingly contributed to this anti-Northern sentiment. On a visit to Scotland in 1853 she was lionized by the hated Duchess of Sutherland, who was infamous among the Scottish working classes for having cleared her vast Highland estates of tenant farmers so that she might use the land for the raising of sheep. The displaced crofters had drifted to the cities, where they made the name of the Duchess a hated word in the tenement districts. It was bad enough for Mrs. Stowe's Scottish reputation that she should receive the Duchess's seal of approval at a levee at Stafford House on 8 May 1853, but Mrs. Stowe added insult to injury when, upon her return to America, she wrote *Sunny Memories of Foreign Lands,* in which she praised the Duchess for having, by her land policy, given to the world "an almost sublime instance of the benevolent employment of superior wealth and power in shortening the struggles of advancing civilization." This comment was enough to turn the stomachs of many ardent Scottish abolitionists. Highlander Donald McLeod, who had been a staunch supporter of Mrs. Stowe, rushed into print with a pamphlet entitled "Gloomy memories in the Highlands . . . : or, a faithful picture of the extirpation of the Celtic Race. . . ." Many Scottish reformers were inclined to agree with McLeod when he wrote that Harriet Beecher Stowe's account of Scottish clearances, which she had obtained secondhand from James Loch, the Duchess's factor, was enough to cast doubt upon all of the evidence against slavery that she had presented in *Uncle Tom's Cabin*.[64]

Whether for reasons of economic hardship, a romantic indentification with the South, or Radical cynicism—reasons of which he undoubtedly had little understanding—Carnegie found almost no support for his pro-Northern position in his native town. His Uncle Lauder was one of the very few prominent men on his side in discussions of the Civil War. Carnegie would never forget that his uncle gave tangible evidence of the strength of his convictions by asking Carnegie to purchase Federal bonds for him. "At the darkest hour of the conflict, when gold was worth nearly three times the value of currency, this staunch friend of the Republic remitted me a considerable sum of money, saying: 'Invest this for me as you think best, but if you put it in United States bonds it will add to my pleasure, for then I can feel that in her hour of danger I have never lost faith in the Republic.'" It eventually proved to be a most profitable faith, Lauder getting back in gold double his investment, and for Carnegie it was proof that "faith in the triumph of Democracy" has very tangible rewards.[65]

Aside from this support from Uncle Lauder, Carnegie had found little to cheer him on this first visit back to Dunfermline. On top of his other disappointments, Carnegie became seriously ill and had to cancel his plans for a tour of Britain and western Europe. In his eagerness to escape the heat of an American summer he had forgotten how damp and cold Scotland could be in July. Tramping around the countryside in the rain, he caught what seemed to be a cold, but which quickly developed into pneumonia. For six weeks he lay in the front upstairs bedroom of his uncle's flat on High Street. "Scottish medicine," he wrote, "was as stern as Scottish theology, and I was bled." With the bleeding he grew weaker, and for a time his life was in danger. Only after he had escaped the ministrations of the local doctors and his numerous aunts by taking a room in a lodge on Loch Leven did he begin to recover.[66] As soon as he was strong enough, he and his mother sailed for America. This time he did not weep upon leaving Scotland, for he knew now where his home was.

In the spring of 1863, the Union cause was not going well. After the bloody battles at Fredericksburg and Chancellorsville, the Army of the Potomac was no closer to Richmond than McDowell's troops had been on that hot July day two years earlier, when they had marched south to Manassas. Rumors were strong in western Pennsylvania that Lee was ready to invade the state, and the people of Pittsburgh were convinced that their key city would be the object of the Confederate attack. Carnegie must have remembered the gloomy predictions of his Scottish friends, who had repeatedly advised Carnegie that the best thing Lincoln could do would be to sue for peace and try to get the most advantageous boundary line he could for his diminished United States. Nevertheless Carnegie's faith never wavered: "You will see by the newspapers," he wrote Dod in June 1863, "that Pittgh. is busy fortifying—6800 men (volunteers) have been at work all week, we will not quit until the City is surrounded by formidable works and then we are secure from Rebel raids—the last one so far is a perfect fizzle and it now looks as if Lee will make no serious advance. I hope all our friends are by this time convinced that the Govt. has not exhausted its resources. We have today in Penna. over 30,000 volunteers armed and equipped. . . . I have orders from Maj. Genl. Brooks to refuse to bring more men in—he has too many now. Of course I am as certain as ever that the Govt. is to emerge triumphant—& slavery to go down. . . . If this is not the fight of Freedom, that principle never before required defence & Bannockburn was a farce—for the question is essentially one of national existence—wait a little longer." [67] Within two weeks, Lee did come into Pennsylvania—and was turned back at Gettysburg. Although the war was to last for nearly two more years before Richmond would fall and the last Confederate army surrender, the North was never again to be threatened.

For Carnegie, who had never doubted the conclusion, the war receded into the background as he became more and more engrossed in his own business affairs. These affairs were becoming more complex—and more profitable—with each passing month. With increasing dividends from his investments in the Woodruff Sleeping Car Company, now reorganized as the Central Transportation Company with Carnegie holding a controlling interest, and the Columbia Oil Company, Carnegie had ample funds and credit to invest in other enterprises that attracted his attention. His trip to Scotland with Thomas Miller had brought the two men into a closer friendship than they had known since the days of the Webster Literary Club. Miller, a restless, eager young capitalist, had many irons in the fire and was eager to have Carnegie as a partner. Together they invested in the Pennsylvania Oil Company, the Western Union Telegraph Company, and the Iron City Forge, and helped in the formation of the Third National Bank of Pittsburgh.[68]

William Coleman, too, continued to promote oil ventures that attracted Carnegie's interest. In the early spring of 1864, Coleman and he took a long and difficult trip by rail and horseback to the Duck Creek oil fields in south central Ohio, where a particular quality of oil, well-suited for lubricating purposes, had been discovered. So great was Coleman's and Carnegie's enthusiasm for oil at this point that without a very thorough investigation they bought the Brick House farm on the spot. It was one of the few investments that Carnegie made during this period that did not prove profitable, and it was this experience that eventually soured him on the entire oil business.[69]

There were other investments during these war years too: in the newly opened Pit Hole oil wells east of Oil Creek; the Lochiel Iron Company in Harrisburg; the East Sandy Oil Company; the Pittsburg Manufacturing Company; the Freedom Iron Company; and a venture with Robert Pitcairn in forming the Neptune Company to dig coal out of the Monongahela River bed, this last proving to be a complete failure.[70]

The most important investment that Carnegie made during this period, in view of his future interests, was in the Piper and Shiffler Company, organized in Pittsburgh for the manufacturing and erection of iron and wooden bridges. Carnegie had first met John Piper, an engineer in charge of bridge building for the Pennsylvania Railroad, in Altoona, in 1858. From the first the two men struck up a close friendship—for Piper liked any man who could appreciate a good horse. Horses and bridges were Piper's two passions in life, and he was a master in the handling of both. Carnegie had worked with Piper again in the spring of 1861 on rebuilding Long Bridge across the Potomac. Upon returning to Pittsburgh, he had suggested to Piper that he and his partner, Aaron Shiffler, should form an independent company for the erection of bridges, particularly railroad bridges, which Carnegie promised would be a booming business in the postwar years. The company was formed in February 1862 and Carnegie received a one-fifth interest for $1250.[71]

At the end of 1863, to comply with the recently enacted Federal income tax, Carnegie made out a statement of his income for that year. It is a revealing document, not only in showing that at the age of twenty-eight he had come close to his goal of an annual income of $50,000, but also in showing the diversity of his investments. By far the largest single return for that year had come from the Columbia Oil Company, which, including the sale of forty shares of stock in the company at a profit of $3600, had contributed a total of over $21,000 to his income. Next in importance was the Piper and Shiffler Company, which, in the first year of operation, had returned $7500. The Central Transportation Company paid him over $5000 in dividends, and even the old faithful Adams Express Company, with whom he had begun his capitalistic ventures, had contributed $1440. His total income for the year was $42,260.67.[72] It was a phenomenal record, for in terms of interest upon principal it came close to representing the income of a millionaire. Only two years before, William Fahnestock, the wealthiest man in Pittsburgh, had retired from business. He had been bought out by his partners for what had seemed an enormous sum, $174,000. Young Carnegie's income tax statement for 1863 showed that in this one year alone he had received almost a quarter of what represented the lifetime accumulated capital of Fahnestock. When a friend dropped into Carnegie's railroad office one morning that winter and asked how he was getting along, Carnegie answered, "Oh, Tom, I'm rich. I'm rich!"[73] It had happened so suddenly that Carnegie himself was bewildered and awed.

One of the minor items that he duly listed on his income tax statement was his yearly salary from the Pennsylvania Railroad, which came to $2400. An insignificant amount compared to his many other returns, it represented a considerable amount of Carnegie's time and energy, which he increasingly resented having to give. His only reason for continuing as an employee of the railroad was that he regarded it as his contribution to the war effort. He vowed to himself, however, that he would resign as soon as the war was over.

The war dragged on, but except for the daily reminders from the movement of troop trains and military supplies, it became more and more unreal to Carnegie. He did meet Ulysses S. Grant when the General came through Pittsburgh on his way to Washington to assume command of the Army of the Potomac, and as they talked at dinner about Grant's plans for victory in the East, Alexandria and Bull Run became for Carnegie realities once again.[74] But for Carnegie, as for most Northerners engaged in their own demanding business affairs, the war had become a kind of dreadful, perpetual nightmare of slaughter and destruction, somewhere far off to the south, that apparently no amount of men or supplies could end.

Then quite unexpectedly—and absurdly, as it seemed to him —in the summer of 1864 Carnegie was drafted for military service. He was twenty-eight and unmarried—certainly a qualified draftee. But somehow this possibility had not occurred to him. Under the terms of the Conscription Act of 1863, he could avoid service by paying $300 to the Federal government or by finding an alternate to go in his place. Carnegie felt entirely justified in not going into the service. Although technically not in the army, had he not already given military service and been wounded in the defense of his country? Was he not now in a critical job, more needed in Pittsburgh than on the field of battle? These were questions for which there were easy answers. Perhaps believing it was more patriotic, Carnegie insisted upon furnishing a substitute rather than taking the easier alternative of paying money. A Pittsburgh draft agent, H. M. Butler, was approached. He was one of many who were making a good living by furnishing substitutes for those who could afford them. Butler got Carnegie his substitute, John Lindew, a recent immigrant from Ireland. Substitutes came high for men like Carnegie, and the fee Butler demanded and received for his services was $850. Carnegie thus obtained a certificate of non-liability for the draft, good for three years.[75]

In the fall and winter of 1864–65, the South was cut and divided into the last pieces of resistance, and slowly bled to death in the process. Atlanta fell. Sherman marched through Georgia to the sea and then turned north, rolling up the war as a West Point instructor might roll up a wall map. In late March, Grant stood before Richmond, and the long-sought prize was at last at hand. The duration could now be counted in days and hours.

On 28 March 1865, Carnegie, as his last official act as superintendent of the Pittsburgh Division of the Pennsylvania Railroad, sent out a brief note to all officers and employees of his Division:

> Gentlemen: I cannot allow my connection with you to cease without some expression of the deep regret felt at parting. Twelve years of pleasant association have served to inspire feelings of personal regard for those who have so faithfully labored with me in the service of the Company. The coming change is painful only as I reflect that in consequence thereof, I am not to be in the future, as in the past, intimately associated with you . . . who have become my personal friends. . . . Thanking you most sincerely for . . . your most zealous efforts made at all times to meet my wishes, . . . I bid you all Farewell.[76]

The war was over. Carnegie was eager to meet the future head on. "I am determined," he had earlier written to Dod, "to expand as my means do," [77] and his means were expanding in a most spectacular way.

CHAPTER VIII

Many Eggs,
Many Baskets
1865-1874

Carnegie's formal farewell to the men of the Pittsburgh Division had a tone of final, total separation from the Pennsylvania Railroad which his later career was to prove false. For only in the sense of being a salaried officer of the company had Carnegie separated himself from the Pennsylvania, and his life was inextricably involved with railroading as long as he remained active in business.

This continuing involvement could hardly be avoided by a man whose main interests in 1865 were in sleeping cars, bridge building, and telegraphy. In a larger sense, all American business was related to and dependent upon railroading, for this industry was to be the motif for America's post-Civil-War industrial expansion. The building of the great transcontinental lines has been justly celebrated as symbolizing American enterprise in this second half of the nineteenth century—a tying together of a great continent so recently torn apart by Civil War. The driving of the final spike at Promontory Point, Utah, in May 1869, seemed to

Americans everywhere the appropriate epilogue to a drama that had begun at Charleston and had ended at Appomattox. This last spike binding together the Central and Union Pacific may have been made of gold, but the thousands upon thousands of other spikes preceding it along the way had been made of iron. They in turn had held down rails made of iron upon which the iron wheels would roll.

The transcontinental roads were but a small portion of the total mileage of track that was being laid in these years—lines binding state to state, county to county, and village to farm. The potential market for iron in its many forms was obvious, and Pittsburgh was very conscious of it. The railroad, however, was more than just a direct consumer, demanding more and more rails, wheels, axles, and engines. As these tracks were pushed out into the empty prairies, far ahead of the farming frontier, the railroad companies, by necessity, were forced to provide their own customers. They had to bring the land-hungry farmers of Ohio, Michigan, and Illinois out into Iowa, Nebraska, and the Dakotas; and because there were not enough migrant American farmers to fill this vast expanse, the railroads sent agents to Europe, to Norwegian villages and Rhineland estates, to lure to these prairies the peasants of Europe.

And so the farmers came. They came by the thousands, to a land that had few trees and almost no stone. They needed many things that the railroads would have to bring: lumber for barns, cribs, and houses; wire for fencing; heavy plows to turn up the tough, matted prairie grass; coffee and salt; cloth and firearms. The railroads created a vast interior market, and the whole economy of the nation was affected by this creation. No enterprise was as basic to our economic growth as this single development in transportation.

Recent historical interpretation has tended to de-emphasize the economic significance of the Civil War at the same time that it has given a new emphasis to the moral issues involved in that conflict. Certainly the view of Charles Beard and other economic determinists, that the Civil War should be regarded as "the second American Revolution—the industrial revolution," is too simple and convenient a periodization, one that cannot be substantiated by available data on economic development and growth. Studies of economic statistics for the period show that the Civil War if anything had the effect of retarding the economy in such basic areas as the manufacturing of textiles, railroad construction, and agricultural production. Without the intense sectional rivalry that finally culminated in war, a transcontinental railroad would undoubtedly have been completed ten years earlier than it was. What was true for railroads was true also for the development of such enterprises as oil refining, iron manufacturing, and commercial agriculture, enterprises that we have long regarded as being peculiar to America's postwar industrial growth. In all these areas, rapid expansion was well under way before the first guns were fired at Fort Sumter, and this expansion, to a large extent, was temporarily checked by the very magnitude of the civil conflict.[1]

But however useful this most recent revisionist interpretation may be as a needed corrective to an understanding of the Civil War itself, it is still evident that the regressive impact of the Civil War was only temporary, and that, by checking industrial expansion, the war was at the same time building up behind the battle-fields a vast reservoir of demand for the exploitation of resources that would spill out in a flood when the dam of war was removed. Nor should it be forgotten that it was during the Civil War that Congress, through legislative action, was to provide the smooth channels through which this flood could easily flow in the post-war period. The Lincoln administration must be judged as one of the most significant in our history, with or without the Civil War, for its legislative measures—among them the Homestead Act; the Railroad Act, granting Federal subsidization to a transcontinental line; the Morrill high protective tariff; and the National Bank Act—marked as radical a departure from the previous administrative policies of a Southern, agrarian-dominated government as the New Deal would, at a later date, mark a break from the business-oriented government of the 1920's.

More important than the economic changes, although more difficult to analyze, is the change in national character that the triumph of Northern Republicanism ensured. The concept of *Zeitgeist*, born of romantic German historicism, is a dangerously elusive term which many historians would like to ignore as being too mystical and unscientific to be worthy of notice. It cannot be denied, however, that each historical period has a character peculiar to itself which is identifiable to even the most casual observer. At any given time in history certain cultural assumptions, values, and traditions are established and prevail, and these characteristics are quite inappropriate to any other time. The German term remains as useful shorthand for describing this historical phenomenon. Because of the difficulty in analyzing the essential quality of *Zeitgeist,* the poet, with his economy of words and subjective sensitivity, is often more successful in its delineation than is the historian, who seeks causal rationality and literal accuracy. So Stephen Vincent Benét, in his great epic poem of the Civil War, could sum up the end of an epoch in these few lines:

> Bury the bygone South . . .
> Bury the unmachined, the planters' pride,
> The courtesy and the bitter arrogance. . . .
> And with these things, bury the purple dream
> Of the America we have not been, . . .
> The pastoral rebellion of the earth
> Against machines, against the Age of Steam,
> The Hamiltonian extremes against the Franklin mean, . . .[2]

It was more than the purple dream of the South that had been buried at Appomattox, however. The old order, the old dreams, both purple and brown, had been broken, North as well as South, in Concord, Massachusetts, as well as in Charleston, South Carolina. The records of the past were being written over with the accounts of new heroes, and only poets and historians would attempt to read the erasures on the palimpsest. Young men like Andrew Carnegie, tormented by ambition, abandoned their earlier dreams of a career in journalism or politics, and looked now to business to satisfy the craving of their egos. Webster, Clay, Greeley, and Raymond had been buried in history along with John Brown and Jefferson Davis. That popular debate topic which the Webster Literary Club had undoubtedly once soberly argued, "Resolved: That the pen is mightier than the sword," had become an academic issue, for money was more powerful than either and could easily purchase the services of both. The center of power had shifted, and talent, energy, ambition, and greed, always responsive to such movements, quickly followed.

No one had predicted this, but quite suddenly here was President Grant to replace President Lincoln, and Ben Wade and Oliver Morton were now speaking in the forum where Calhoun and Webster had but lately prevailed. The Republican party, having achieved power with a felicitous combination of idealism and practicality, had spent its ideals along with the nation's treasure in war, and its opportunism, like its wartime greenbacks, no longer had specie backing.

It is a false generalization, however, to say that disillusionment follows naturally upon the back of war and that all postwar periods in American history have been marked by cynicism and the lack of morality. It would seem more accurate to say that war, by setting its mark too low, tends to make the ideal too easily obtainable. After achieving his simplified objective, triumphant Ulysses returns home satisfied. It is not disillusionment that corrupts in a postwar world; it is complacency. Having freed the slave and preserved the Union, the Republican party leaders sincerely believed that they had built up an unlimited reservoir of grace from which future indulgences could be drawn in perpetuity. Only a few men such as Wendell Phillips—and, in his own way, Thaddeus Stevens—saw the war as unfinished and held out new objectives to be reached. These unsatisfied idealists asked embarrassing questions about what kind of freedom the Blacks had been granted, and they demanded more for the Union than its simple preservation. But these were isolated men, who had become anachronisms standing in the way of economic progress and sectional reconciliation. "Let us have peace," said President Grant in his only memorable political utterance, and the nation agreed. The war was over, and although the Republicans still found it politically expedient to wave the bloody shirt quadrennially, this was accepted as a formal ritual of commemoration, like the lighting of fireworks on the Fourth of July. The day of the Radical and the Fire-eater was over. Politics belonged to the Blaines, the Garfields, and the Clevelands; and power belonged to the iron-makers, the railroad builders, and the oil refiners. This was the *Zeitgeist,* and Carnegie would understand it well.

Carnegie was in rapport with his age, but he was not at all certain, as he surveyed the business world of 1865, in which realm he would seek to wield a scepter of power. At a later date one of his favorite maxims for business success would be "Put all your eggs in one basket, and then watch that basket." It was an inverted aphorism that not only pleased his sense of the humorous but also contained, he was convinced, a hard core of common sense. (It also amused Mark Twain, who borrowed it—much to Carnegie's delight.) In 1865, Carnegie had not as yet discovered this formula for success. Indeed, it may be said—to pursue this nidatory metaphor further—that the ten years from 1865 to 1875 mark the cowbird period of Carnegie's career, years in which he was busy depositing eggs in many different kinds of nests. For a cowbird, he proved an unusually solicitous guardian of these clutches, and it was a mark of his genius that he could keep careful watch over so many nests, any one of which could have provided him with a full-time career.

There were, first of all, his continuing interests in his first capitalistic ventures. Of these early interests, only that in oil failed to excite his ambition for expansion and larger investment. He still held a sizable amount of stock in the Columbia Oil Company, and as late as 1868 these shares were returning an annual dividend of $2000. Rewarding as the Storey farm venture had been, however, Carnegie had never felt any enthusiasm for oil as a product, for he had never forgotten his early distaste for it in the vat room of the bobbin factory. Even a little oil was cloying and penetrating in its sticky dirtiness. With effort, it could be scrubbed away, but its stench could never be forgotten.[3]

By 1865, Carnegie had come to dislike oil as a business also. He remembered how he and William Coleman in 1862 had stood at the edge of their pond of oil on the Storey farm and watched as their hoarded wealth seeped slowly back into the ground from which it had come. Ironmaking might be noisy and dirty, and the heat from the furnaces as searing as Hell itself, but iron had a reality and a permanency which the evanescent oil could never have. The red ore could be piled up and left until it was needed. It did not spew itself forth with insane extravagance over the countryside, and it could be converted by fire into something more solid and durable than quickly spent power or light. Carnegie's ventures into oil outside of the Storey farm enterprise, such as Duck Creek in Ohio and the East Sandy and Wirt oil companies in Pennsylvania, had proved unprofitable and further dampened any interest he might have had in pursuing this particular line of endeavor. Writing from Europe to his brother Tom in 1865, Carnegie urged him not to invest heavily in the Pit Hole wells. "Your announcement about Pitt [sic] Hole is taken with much allowance. It seems very large and promises big things, but, my boy, we have been in Duck Creek and are sobered. Sell out for cash by all means, and at once. . . ." A few weeks later he wrote, "You do not mention Pit hole. Sell out if you can there at a good figure. Oil has seen its best days." [4]

Carnegie, to be sure, would give to oil the credit for providing him with his first substantial start in business, but he was never to have any regret for leaving a business that he regarded as being too highly speculative for his taste.[5] He strongly advised his closest friends to do the same.[6] The considerable respect with which Carnegie would later regard John D. Rockefeller was due to the admiration Carnegie could feel toward a man who had brought order out of a business that he himself had found to be so chaotic as to be beyond remedy.

It was natural, of course, for Carnegie to be attracted to the iron business. One could not live in Pittsburgh and be as closely associated with railroads as he had been without seeing the potentiality that ironmaking had for the future development of the country. But in 1865 Carnegie was much more interested in using iron for the fabrication of finished products than he was in the actual process of making iron. With his customary optimistic expansiveness, he could clearly foresee the vast transcontinental network of railroads that would be built in the immediate future, and he was shrewd enough to realize which of his varied investments would be most important to that development.

Before railroads could cross this great imperial domain, rivers would have to be bridged—and the men who built and controlled the bridges could have a powerful voice in the affairs of the railroads themselves. The days of the old wooden bridges, so vulnerable to both fire and flood, were clearly over. It took no necromancer's crystal ball to see that the beams that would in the near future span the Ohio, the Mississippi, and the wide Missouri would be made of iron. Moreover, railroads everywhere—along the crowded tracks of the East and on the empty grasslands and deserts of the West—had to depend upon telegraph wire for the instantaneous communication now vital to their operations. Finally, if the railroads were to have more than the freight business to make returns upon their heavy bonded indebtedness, they must be prepared to offer sleeping facilities to those hardy passengers who would travel the great distances between Chicago or St. Louis and California.

It was then, in this immediate postwar period, as the nation eagerly awaited the moment when the last spike of gold would be driven to complete a transcontinental railroad, that Carnegie turned with renewed interest to those activities in which he had already invested much time and money: sleeping cars, telegraphy, and bridge building.

The first of these interests, both in point of time and in returns received, was the Central Transportation Company, which Carnegie had organized in 1862 as a successor to the original partnership of T. T. Woodruff and Company. Woodruff's many talents as an inventor unfortunately did not extend to financial organization, and once Woodruff had secured the franchise to place his sleeping cars on the Pennsylvania line, he was in desperate need of capital for the construction of additional cars to meet the growing demand for sleeping accommodations. Moreover, several rival companies, among them the Gates Sleeping Car Company and the Knight Cars, were being formed as competitors to Woodruff, and many were copying features of Woodruff's berths in violation of his patent rights.[7] Carnegie, convinced that only a strong organization could save the Woodruff Company, had persuaded Woodruff and his brother, Jonah Woodruff, to reorganize as a stock company in order to gain the necessary capital and to be prepared to carry the patent fight into the courts if necessary.

Woodruff had long since discovered that the one-eighth interest that he had granted to an unknown party at Thomas Scott's request had proved to be the proverbial camel's nose inside the tent. With the formation of the Central Transportation Company the camel moved inside, and Woodruff found himself occupying a very small corner of the tent. Carnegie brought with him several

199

men of capital from Pittsburgh and Philadelphia: Springer Harbaugh, John Childs, L. B. Franciscus, and even the potential rival, William Knight of the Knight Cars. The most valuable allies Carnegie had were his former employers, J. Edgar Thomson and Thomas Scott, who as president and vice president of the Pennsylvania Railroad Company were in a position to guarantee an expansion of the use of the Woodruff sleeping cars on the Pennsylvania line. Thomson and Scott, sensitive to the possible charges of impropriety in having a personal interest in an independent sleeping-car company under contract with the Pennsylvania Railroad, hid their substantial investments by having Thomson's stock registered in the name of his personal secretary, R. D. Barclay, and having Scott's stock held by "his boy, Andy." With a majority of the stock in his name, Carnegie was able to take over the direction of Central Transportation Company and push for the extension of the Woodruff cars on other railroads.

Carnegie urged Woodruff and his brother Jonah to be constantly alert to the improvement of their basic patents and to push aggressively for the introduction of their cars on new lines. The company needed this kind of prodding, for Woodruff had already lost the first contract he had made, that with the New York Central, to the Wagner Palace Sleeping Car Company, in which Cornelius Vanderbilt held a secret interest similar to that held by Thomson and Scott in the Central Transportation Company.[8] Remembering his own arduous trip up to the oil fields of northwestern Pennsylvania a decade before, Carnegie successfully pushed Jonah Woodruff into acquiring the franchise on the newly opened Allegheny Valley Railroad, which ran to the oil fields.[9]

The real prize, as all of the various sleeping-car companies knew, would be the franchise for cars on the Union Pacific. Whoever held the right to place his cars upon the first transcontinental line would be in a position to dominate the industry. Carnegie had been acutely aware of this almost from the moment that the Pacific Railroad Act had passed Congress in 1862. It had been mainly for this prize that he had brought about the reorganization of the Woodruff Company, and with it as an enticement, he had lured both Scott and Thomson as well as Knight and the others into the company. However preoccupied he might be with his other interests, he never lost sight of the Union Pacific franchise, and even while in Europe he would write Scott urging him to use his influence to secure the contract.[10]

A new rival, George Mortimer Pullman, had by this time appeared on the scene, however, and this man gave promise of providing very keen competition indeed to the Central Transportation Company. Pullman's early career closely resembled that of Woodruff's. Like Woodruff, Pullman was born in upstate New York, had early left his father's home with very little formal education, and had become a skilled craftsman in cabinetmaking. Although he did not have Woodruff's creative inventive genius, Pullman did have all those qualities of character, so lacking in Woodruff, which are essential for a successful career in business enterprise. He was forceful, aggressive, confident of his own abilities, quick to seize upon the moment of opportunity, and, above all, highly ambitious. In 1855, Pullman left Albion, New York, for Chicago.[11]

With a little capital, Pullman was ready to turn his entrepreneurial talents to a field that had for some years stirred his imagination. As a young man in upstate New York he had ridden in Woodruff's first sleeping cars on the New York Central. He had been intrigued with Woodruff's basic concept of turning day coaches into sleeping compartments, and he was convinced that by using this basic design he could provide more comfortable sleeping accommodations than those in Woodruff's first cars.

In Chicago Pullman had drawn sketches and made several crude models of sleeping-car berths from Woodruff's design as he remembered it. In 1858 he obtained a contract with the Chicago and Alton Railroad Company to remodel two of their day coaches into sleeping cars. These cars cost Pullman between $1000 and $2000. They were rather crude affairs, for Pullman was not then, and was never himself to become, a gifted mechanical inventor. In this first experiment he achieved only an approximation of Woodruff's earliest cars, without any of the refinements of design which Woodruff had in the meantime developed. The conductor on this first Pullman car, J. L. Barnes, later described the initial night run, made from Bloomington, Illinois, to Chicago, on 1 September 1859:

> All the passengers were from Bloomington and there were no
> women on the car that night. The people of Bloomington, little

reckoning that history was being made in their midst, did not come down to the station to see the Pullman car's first trip. There was no crowd, and the car, lighted by candles moved away in solitary grandeur, if such it might be called. . . . I remember on the first night I had to compel the passengers to take their boots off before they got into the berths. They wanted to keep them on—seemed afraid to take them off. . . .

The first Pullman car was a primitive thing. Beside being lighted with candles it was heated by a stove at each end of the car. There were no carpets on the floor, and the interior of the car was arranged in this way: There were four upper and four lower berths. The backs of the seats were hinged and to make up the lower berth the porter merely dropped the back of the seat until it was level with the seat itself. Upon this he placed a mattress and blanket. There were no sheets. The upper berth was suspended from the ceiling of the car by ropes and pulleys attached to each of the four corners of the berth. The upper berths were constructed with iron rods running from the floor of the car to the roof, and during the day the berth was pulled up until it hugged the ceiling. . . . We used curtains in front and between all the berths. In the daytime one of the sections was used to store all the mattresses in. . . . There was a very small toilet room in each end, only large enough for one person at a time. The wash basin was made of tin. The water for the wash basin came from the drinking can which had a faucet so that people could get a drink.[12]

These first Pullman cars were not a success, and by the end of 1859, the restless Pullman, discouraged by his failure, had left Chicago to seek a quicker fortune with the "fifty-niners" in the gold fields of Colorado. There he did not waste his time with pick and placer pan. He opened a general store where, with inflated prices, he was more sure of obtaining gold than out along the mountain streams. By 1863 he had accumulated nearly $20,000 and was ready to return once again to Chicago for another try at producing a successful sleeping car.

This time, however, it would be no crudely converted day coach in which he would invest his money and time. He would start with the wheel trucks and build a wholly new car, larger than any railroad car before produced. Without permission—or shame—he openly copied Woodruff's designs for the hinged upper berth, replacing his own earlier design of a berth suspended by ropes from the ceiling. But if he was dependent upon Woodruff and other inventors for his basic design, he himself would contribute what these other pioneers in the field had not thought important—a lavishness of decoration and an elegance that would make of his cars, as he loudly proclaimed, rolling palaces. As one historian has said, Pullman's only "real invention was railroad comfort." [13] Pullman invited the leading citizens of Chicago and several newspapermen to ride as his guests on the trial run of this car, which he had proudly named "Pioneer." The resulting newspaper feature stories were effusive in describing "the elegant window curtains, looped in heavy folds," the "French plate-bearers suspended from the walls," the "beautiful chandeliers," and "the ceiling painted with chaste and elaborate design on a delicately tinged azure ground." The interior painting of the car alone was reported to have cost over $500. It was truly a palace on wheels, the newspapers assured their readers.[14]

In the late spring of 1865, Pullman obtained the reluctant permission of the Michigan Central to try his car out on its night run to Detroit at his own expense. He was not discouraged by the railroad officials' gloomy predictions that no one would pay an extra $2 for a sleeping berth in his car, and the first week's operation proved Pullman right.

Every cent that Pullman could spare was put back into the expansion of the company. In 1867, with much fanfare, the Pullman Palace Car Company was incorporated. With forty-eight of his rolling palaces in operation on the Michigan Central, the Burlington, and the Great Western Railroad of Canada, Pullman was already a familiar name throughout the North and West. The following year he was able to break the monopoly of the Wagner Sleeping Car Company and place seven of his cars on the New York Central. With this invasion of the Eastern lines, he had become a direct and formidable competitor of Carnegie's Central Transportation Company. Carnegie needed no second sight to know that Pullman would be his major opponent in the struggle for the all-important franchise on the Union Pacific line.

Pullman was the kind of competitor Carnegie could both understand and appreciate. Here was no impractical, unaggressive inventor such as Carnegie had had to deal with in Woodruff.

Here was a man who knew the full value of publicity, of self-advertising: a man who gave the public what they wanted in the way of ostentatious luxury, and who was not overly scrupulous about such legal niceties as patent rights and corporation franchises. In short, here was a man who, in Carnegie's opinion, could not be beaten in any open competition for the Union Pacific franchise. "He was, indeed," as Carnegie said, "a lion in the path."

The Central Transportation Company had some powerful weapons in its arsenal, to be sure, including Woodruff's patents, which Pullman had been rather free with in developing his own cars. Carnegie was convinced that these patents would be upheld by the courts—but legal battles, particularly in patent right cases, could be costly and protracted. In the meantime, Pullman might well grab off the Union Pacific prize, and any later court-assessed damages against him would be quite insignificant compared with this victory.

More important, however, Carnegie had behind him the Pennsylvania Railroad Company, and the personal interest of Thomson and Scott. If Pullman was seeking a monopoly in this field, he would need the Pennsylvania, and in any event, he would need the kind of capital which Thomson, Scott, and Carnegie could command.

The Union Pacific Company called a meeting in New York early in 1867, at which representatives of the several sleeping-car companies were given the opportunity to present their proposals for placing their cars upon the transcontinental line. There Carnegie had an opportunity to size up this aggressive competitor from Chicago. He saw Pullman's strength—but he was also able to assess the palace-maker's weakness.

The evening after the first day's session, Carnegie managed to meet Pullman on the main staircase of the St. Nicholas Hotel, where they were both staying. In his autobiography, Carnegie told of this planned encounter:

> "Good evening, Mr. Pullman! Here we are together, and are we not making a nice couple of fools of ourselves?" He was not disposed to admit anything and said:
> "What do you mean?"
> I explained the situation to him. We were destroying by our rival propositions the very advantages we desired to obtain.

"Well," he said, "what do you propose to do about it?"

"Unite," I said. "Make a joint proposition to the Union Pacific, your party and mine, and organize a company."

"What would you call it?" he asked.

"The Pullman Palace Car Company," I replied.

This suited him exactly; and it suited me equally well.

"Come into my room and talk it over," said the great sleeping-car man.[15]

Carnegie could fully appreciate Pullman's vanity, and he knew how to capitalize on it. The naming of rabbits, as Carnegie had discovered back in Dunfermline, could always bring dividends.

The merger was not as easily accomplished as Carnegie implies in this story, however. Some of the other directors in Carnegie's own company quite understandably looked with a jaundiced eye upon his efforts to form an alliance with Pullman. They were not at all convinced that so quick a surrender was justified under the circumstances. They felt that the Central Transportation Company had the means to wage a successful fight against this intruder from the West, and it took all of Carnegie's arts of persuasion to cajole them into letting him continue his negotiations with Pullman to form a joint company for the purpose of obtaining the franchise from the Union Pacific.

Pullman, too, proved difficult; he was suspicious of Carnegie's efforts and motives, and at first quite uncompromising in his demand that he and his company be given the majority interest in the proposed merger. Carnegie finally had to threaten immediate court action on patent rights in order to bring Pullman into line. On 29 May 1867, Carnegie wrote Pullman:

I spent Sunday and part of Monday among our friends in Philad. & saw Messrs. Knight, Childs & Franciscus [directors in the Central Transportation Company].

I found them determined that the next proposition should come from you. They had made several, now if you had anything to offer they would consider it.—Harding advises them that an injunction be asked for at once with a view to compel you, or the Railway Co. to give bonds to secure the judgment which they feel certain of obtaining. Whiting recently wrote to

Mr. Knight a friendly letter assuring him that he never had a plainer case &c, &c, & that judgment would be had within the present year, & so on. Messrs. Knight & Franciscus agreed with me that were you & they to combine, a company with one million capital could be made & the stock made par . . . & further, that by judicious management, its life could be perpetuated beyond the term of ordinary patents. . . . It is a sore point with them that while they have made propositions to you, that none has ever been made to them. It strikes me they should forgo all past patent fees from you & give you such a proportion in the patent company as would represent the fees upon the interests held by you in Sleeping Cars. In other words, they to make all your personal [interest] free of patent fees provided the interests held by companies with whom you contract are made to contribute to the Company ten per cent upon the gross receipts. Something of this kind should be concluded between you. Mr. Childs is the fighting one of the party, although none of them entertain a doubt of the result of the suit.[16]

Under this threat of court action, Pullman yielded. In June 1867, Carnegie wrote to Pullman that the latter's proposals were satisfactory to the directors of the Central Transportation Company. "We now will be able to arrange matters to our liking," he confidently concluded.[17] Hastily Carnegie drew up a contract to present to the directors of the Union Pacific, which was in the form of a personal agreement between Pullman and himself as parties of the first part and the Union Pacific Railroad Company as the party of the second part, whereby Pullman and Carnegie agreed to furnish sleeping cars for the line, and would "keep up the upholstery, bedding clean, and furnish one porter per car." The Union Pacific in return agreed "at its own expense to furnish fuel for the stoves and lights and keep the cars in good running order." [18]

Simple enough as far as it went, this contract was used by the Union Pacific directors as a basis for demanding more than just the service which Pullman and Carnegie jointly promised to provide. They demanded a controlling share of the stock in any company that would be organized to provide sleeping cars for the transcontinental line. So Carnegie was forced to serve as an intermediary for still another party, and with the adroitness of a juggler he kept Pullman, his own Central Transportation Company, and the directors of the Union Pacific moving smoothly in unison. It was no easy task, but in this kind of operation Carnegie was at his best, catching and tossing up into the air each ball in proper sequence, until November 1867, when, after several turns, he at last had a contract to which all parties would agree. There would be a new company, properly named the Pullman Pacific Car Company, with a capital stock of $500,000 in 5000 shares of $100 each. Of these shares, 2600 would go to Oliver Ames in trust for the stockholders of the Union Pacific, 1200 shares would go to Pullman, and 1200 shares to Carnegie and his associates (meaning Scott), on the condition that Carnegie should "cause to be assigned to said company all patents now owned by the Central Transportation Company" for the stated price of $20,000.[19]

Even then there were delays. Before the major stockholders of the Central Transportation Company would agree to the stated price for their company's patent rights, they demanded from Carnegie the right to purchase some of his interest in the projected Pullman Pacific Car Company. Carnegie did not hesitate to let Pullman know of his self-sacrifice in order to secure the contract. "Our C.T. patentees," he wrote in March 1868, "deem the price far below its value & I have had to augment it considerably out of my own stock, but I am always willing to share with associates & do not regret having given away a portion to make all satisfactory."[20] His generosity in this matter, to be sure, had its own reward, for he charged his associates $45 a share for stock in the company which he and Pullman had issued to themselves at $25 a share. The nearly 100 per cent profit he made on this transaction was more than adequate to meet the payments of the first installment of $10 a share on his total subscription of 1200 shares in the company. Once again, Carnegie had given a demonstration of how to invest in a business without having to furnish any capital of one's own.[21]

Pullman caused trouble, too, by his reluctance to pay the $20,000 that had been agreed upon as the price for the Central Transportation Company's patent rights. In May 1868, six months after the final contract had been agreed to, Carnegie wrote Pullman's secretary, C. W. Angell, asking him when the Central Transportation Company could expect payment.[22] There was no answer. In February 1869, somewhat desperately, Carnegie wrote to Pullman:

> I am with my partner Mr. Scott responsible to the patentees of the Central Transportation Co. for $20,000 being placed in the hands of a trustee by your Co. The Central Transportation patentees notify me they now wish this matter closed. Please let me hear how you propose to arrange it. As I have no interest in either partner, and am responsible for the whole matter to each of you, having been the agent in making the arrangement, I would agree to act as said trustee giving of course any security required. Hope you will have no objection to my doing so.[23]

Apparently Pullman did have an objection, for Carnegie's offer was not accepted. The matter continued to drag on without settlement. Pullman, feverishly building cars in preparation for the opening of the transcontinental lines, wanted all the working capital he could obtain, and he had no intention at that time of paying out money for patent fees until forced to do so by a more imperious command than that which Carnegie could give. Instead, it was Carnegie who was forced to make payments to Pullman on the stock to which he had subscribed, and at a much earlier date than he had anticipated. In March 1869, Carnegie sent Pullman $6400, one-half of the second installment due on his stock. "It is difficult to imagine," Carnegie wrote, "how you require so much money *all at once,* or indeed how we can judiciously put $400,000 into Cars to equip 1200 miles of line through the desert—I fear your anticipations of business upon it are not to be realized. However you know better than I. I only hope your estimates are correct." [24] For once, Carnegie had encountered a man whose expansive optimism exceeded his own.

But by the time the transcontinental line was officially opened, in May 1869, Carnegie had become as optimistic as Pullman in counting future dividends on stock—so optimistic, in fact, that he foresaw the possible necessity of concealing these profits by overcapitalization. Writing to Charles Angell, he expressed the hope that Pullman would decide "to double capital at the start, and pay what he can upon it; better 6% upon double than 12% on actual cost, as with the inevitable increase of business, there is danger that extraordinary dividends will attract too much attention, while the fact that the capital was originally doubled will very soon be lost sight of, even if it is ever known by the public at large. Please suggest this to Mr. P. and let me have his views." [25]

Pullman, as always, kept his own counsel, and did not rush to embrace Carnegie's proposal. It was not until November 1871 that he acted upon Carnegie's advice and issued new bonds in the Pullman Pacific Car Company at a rate of two for one in exchange for stock shares.[26] In the meantime, Carnegie devised another ploy in dealing with the wily Pullman. He gave renewed attention to his own company, the Central Transportation Company, in order to make it attractive enough to excite further Pullman's interest in its operations. This was not difficult to do, for although the company had been virtually squeezed out of the Union Pacific negotiations, it continued to hold a predominant position among the sleeping-car companies in the East, particularly because of its franchises with the Pennsylvania and the Southern lines. For the year September 1868 through August 1869, its books showed net earnings of $256,095.45; or 17.8 per cent on invested capital, and Carnegie confidently predicted dividends of 20 per cent for the following year.[27] As this profit was nearly two-thirds again as great as that of the Pullman Pacific Car Company, it is not surprising that Carnegie found Pullman amenable to his suggestion of a further consolidation of interests. Delicate negotiations between the two companies were once again renewed, and on 1 January 1870 directors of the Central Transportation Company settled upon a contract whereby the company agreed to lease in perpetuity to the Pullman Palace Car Company "its entire business, including cars, patents, contracts with railroad companies, etc., in consideration of which the Pullman Palace Car Company agrees to pay in perpetuity, an annual net rental of $264,000, and divide same in quarterly installments among the stockholders of the Central Transportation Company in proportion to their holdings." [28] Carnegie's work in consolidating the sleeping-car business was now nearly complete. He could write with some confidence to J. Edgar Thomson, "I wish to put myself on the record as advising you to arrange for a large interest in the Pullman Co. as suggested by Mr. Pullman at our recent interview. . . . I should know Mr. Pullman by this time & his mode of conducting business. You can rely upon him, & upon the satis-factory condition of his enterprise & I am as sure as I can be of anything that you will scarcely number, among all your strategic investments, one which will be regarded hereafter with more favor than that I now take the responsibility of recommending." [29]

By 1872, Carnegie's many other business interests prevented him from giving as much attention to the sleeping-car business as he would have liked. Even so, he was still active enough in nego-tiating contracts with various railroad lines to bring a word of warning from Pullman that he was not being careful enough in negotiating these contracts. "As a Sleeping Car Company," Pull-man wrote to his energetic associate,

> we furnish to railways, valuable equipment to be used by them in the transaction of their ordinary business. . . . The speciali-ties pertaining to our department (the upholstery and bedding) we take care of—but in all other respects, the cars after being put into service, belong to the roads, in so far as the question of maintenance is concerned. And it should also be noted that our contracts do not contemplate such a thing as the wearing out or destruction of a car. After having been accepted by a Company and put into service on its line of road, that Company must by proper renewals and repairs, from time to time, keep the equip-ment always in the same state of efficiency—to be returned to us at the expiration of the agreement.

Pullman concluded with the admonition that Carnegie "keep all of this in mind whenever conferences are held with railroad managers." [30] Apparently Carnegie, who was at the same time ne-gotiating with railroad managers on many other matters—bridges, rails, telegraph franchises, and the sale of securities—was too prone to use the sleeping-car contract as a leader item to pro-mote his other interests. It was therefore with no great regret that by 1874 Pullman was to lose the services of Carnegie as a negotiator of these contracts. Carnegie, however, kept a very siza-ble investment in the Pullman Palace Car Company for many years, and the dividends from that investment helped to provide surplus capital for his expanding steel interests.[31] Carnegie also found the Pullman stock useful in paying off old debts to friends, whose past services he was not inclined to forget. He was happy to obtain 150 shares of Pullman stock, at a special discount price, for his former teacher of rhetoric and manners, Leila Addison, and her family. It was very pleasant to repay old favors in such a materially satisfying way.[32]

For the Central Transportation Company, which Carnegie had delivered over to Pullman in 1870, the outcome was not quite so felicitous. Although Carnegie continued to serve as vice president of the company after it had leased its facilities to Pullman, he had little further concern in aggressively supporting its interest. When in 1877 the then acting president of the company, J. F. Cottringer, went to court to seek a release from the contract in perpetuity with Pullman, on the ground that Pullman had not lived up to the agreement in paying the rental for the Southern Car franchise, Carnegie made no effort to aid the suit.[33] Although Cottringer won his suit in court and the lease was broken, it was a hollow victory. Pullman now so dominated the field that no independent company could hope to compete. Carnegie, who had been anonymously selling his stock in the Central Transportation Company through an independent broker since 1875, sold his last ninety-four shares in the company in 1884, and shortly thereafter the company liquidated all of its equipment and other assets and paid off the remaining shareholders at $30 per share.[34]

Most of the major shareholders in the company had fared well in these transactions, for they, like Carnegie, had long ago seen the inevitable outcome and had exchanged their stock for Pullman stock. The smaller investors, however, including the man who had first had the dream of a practical sleeping car, did not share in the profits resulting from these manipulations. T. T. Woodruff, after having been forced out of the sleeping-car business in 1872, had turned his active mind to other fields and had experimented with a new process for the manufacture of indigo and a coffee hulling machine. These experiments had failed, and he had gone through bankruptcy in 1875.[35] By the time his old company was dissolved in 1884, Woodruff had been almost entirely forgotten. Then Carnegie paid his tribute to Woodruff in his highly imaginative account of the introduction of the sleeping car on the Pennsylvania line, and Woodruff's rejoinder stirred Carnegie's conscience. In 1891 Carnegie placed Woodruff on his personal pension list for $200 a month. One year later, when, ironically, Woodruff was struck down and killed by an express train in New Jersey, Carnegie ordered his financial secretary to continue paying the pension to Woodruff's only child, Mrs. I. I. Gerson.[36] For Carnegie, who liked tidy endings, there were now no loose ends left, and his venture in sleeping cars could finally be closed.

If Carnegie's entry into the sleeping-car business had been somewhat fortuitous, his involvement in telegraphy during this same period was a natural development of an interest that dated back to his first years in business. For Carnegie the telegrapher would always be a romantic and heroic figure, and the click of the telegrapher's key could always recall the wonderfully magical days when as a boy of fifteen he had first learned to translate those cricket sounds directly into words. It is not surprising that Carnegie very early in his career as an independent businessman should turn to telegraphy as a field in which he thought he could operate successfully and happily.

Telegraphy was rapidly becoming a big business in the 1860's. The early crude days of O'Reilly, Ezra Cornell, and Amos Kendall, when men with very little capital could haphazardly string wire across the country, were over. With the formation of the Western Union Telegraph Company in April 1856, through a merger of the Erie and Michigan Company and the New York and Mississippi Valley Printing Telegraph Company, a potential giant entered the field. Ezra Cornell, who gave the company its name and his claim on the Morse patents, was its godfather, but the organizing geniuses of the company were Jeptha Wade and Thomas T. Eckert of Michigan, who brought into the company the lines throughout the Old Northwest, and Hiram Sibley of Rochester, New York, who had been instrumental in raising the capital for the formation of the New York and Mississippi Valley Telegraph Company.[37] Western Union had an initial capitalization of $500,000.

The Western Union hoped from the beginning to create a monopoly. It planned to extend its lines westward along the transcontinental railroad to the Pacific, to bring order out of the chaos of the many small and hastily constructed lines throughout the eastern third of the country, and to absorb rival companies by offering the tempting bait of Western Union stock.

From the moment of its organization Western Union proved spectacularly successful in moving toward its objective. "As fast as we could make a line pay 7 per cent," said Sibley, "we put it in." [38] Within a year the company was able to declare four dividends, totaling 41.5 per cent. Soon thereafter, the prosperous Atlantic and Ohio Company, with lines between Philadelphia and Pittsburgh, was brought into the ever-expanding network of Western Union. Then there followed the New York, Albany and Buffalo Company and the Pittsburgh, Cincinnati and Louisville, the main support of the dying O'Reilly system. By the time the Civil War began, Western Union controlled a vast system—from the Atlantic to the Mississippi and from the Great Lakes to the Ohio River. Its capital had been increased to over $2,000,000, and, because it held no lines south of the Mason Dixon, the coming of the war meant no loss of its property to the Confederacy.

During the war years, when the telegraph became an essential weapon, the Western Union profited beyond the most optimistic hopes of Sibley and Wade. In March of 1863, a stock dividend of 100 per cent was declared, and an additional 33 per cent dividend was declared just nine months later. By May 1864, the capital had been increased to over $10,000,000, and still the unprecedented dividends could be paid.[39]

The very success of Western Union, however, tended to create further competition that had to be eliminated. Many small companies sprang up with but one purpose—to become successful enough to attract the attention of Western Union and force it to make an offer of its stock for their holdings. Carnegie, with some of his former railroad associates, first organized the Keystone Telegraph Company under a charter from the state of Pennsylvania in April 1867. Whether he had Western Union stock as his objective is difficult to say. The evidence extant would indicate that at the time he had his eye not on Western Union, which was generally disliked and distrusted by the old-time telegraphers of Pennsylvania, but upon a rival concern, the Pacific and Atlantic Telegraph Company. This concern, under the able direction of James L. Shaw of Pittsburgh, was the only competitor at that moment which promised to give Western Union a real contest for control of the wires in the expanding territory of the West and South.

The Keystone Company had an initial capitalization of $50,000. Its most valuable asset, however, was a concession from the Pennsylvania Railroad granting the right to erect two wires on the Pennsylvania's poles across the state of Pennsylvania, from the Delaware River to the Ohio state line, for an annual rental of $4 per mile of wire.[40] With this important concession in his pocket, Carnegie began negotiations with the Pacific and Atlantic Company before the first wire had been strung. So eager was Shaw to obtain this valuable east-west connection with the Pennsylvania Railroad that within five months Carnegie was able to bring about a merger of his Keystone Company with the Pacific and Atlantic Company. The 1000 shares of the Keystone Company, with a par value of $50,000, were exchanged for 6000 shares of Pacific and Atlantic—valued at $150,000.[41] Carnegie had trebled the value of Keystone in less than a half year, without having had to string a foot of line.

Carnegie, as the representative of the original investors in Keystone, now controlled nearly one-third of the stock of the Pacific and Atlantic Company, and he began preparing to fight Western Union. He immediately worked out plans for the extension of the P. and A. lines to Chicago, St. Louis, and Cleveland before the following winter. Writing to George H. Thurston, president of the company, in November 1867, Carnegie implied that this extension was to be only the first step and that he and Thurston were in agreement that eventually the Pacific and Atlantic should justify both its name and its charter by pushing its line to California. "The end you aim at is a great one & it will require much time & attention to accomplish it; I know if once arrived at, you will have one of the most prosperous enterprises of the day." [42]

Carnegie's interest in this rapid extension of the Pacific and Atlantic lines was motivated by more than the fact that he was now a major stockholder in the company. He and David Brooks, his former supervisor in the O'Reilly telegraph office, had received a contract from Thurston to string the wires for the Pacific and Atlantic Company. By the terms of this agreement, he and Brooks were to receive $3.00 in company stock for every $1.00 they spent in laying wire.[43] With this as an incentive, the lines between Philadelphia and Pittsburgh along the Pennsylvania tracks were quickly strung.

Carnegie was also instrumental in getting his old friend David

McCargo, whom he regarded as the ablest telegrapher in the country, to join the company as general superintendent. With what he regarded as a strong company, ably manned, behind him, and with a lucrative contract for the actual construction of its lines in his pocket, Carnegie was now ready to do battle with Western Union.

Even though he himself had taken full advantage of the exclusive contract between the Keystone Company and the Pennsylvania Railroad in his negotiations for the merger of Keystone with the Pacific and Atlantic Company, Carnegie now raised the cry of monopoly against Western Union because it had acquired the same exclusive rights to place its lines along the tracks of several railroad lines in the Middle West. Although the railroad industry, with a few notable exceptions, had been unbelievably slow in realizing the significance of the telegraph, by the late 1860's all of the major lines in the country had at last accepted telegraphy. It was essential to efficient operations. Again, with few exceptions, the most notable being the Baltimore & Ohio, each railroad line, instead of building its own telegraph system, had entered into an agreement with one of the several available telegraph companies. By the terms of the agreement, the railroad company granted to the telegraph company the exclusive right to erect its poles and string its wires along the right-of-way of the railroad. The railroad agreed to transport the poles, wire, and other equipment where needed free of charge, and further agreed to inspect the lines, reset poles and repair wires as necessary, and pay the telegraph operators' salaries. In return, the railroad had free use of the telegraph system, and its business had priority over all other messages on the wire.[44] It was, of course, of primary importance for a telegraph company to acquire a railroad contract if it was to be successful in extending its lines. For this reason the Pacific and Atlantic had been willing to pay such a high premium to the Keystone Company even before that company had erected a single telegraph pole.

Unfortunately, however, for Carnegie's ambitious plans for the expansion of the Pacific and Atlantic, Western Union had already gobbled up most of the valuable railroad contracts in the West, including the Central Pacific from San Francisco to Salt Lake City. Another rival concern, the Atlantic and Pacific, had the even more important franchise with the Union Pacific from Omaha to Utah, as well as shared rights with Western Union on the Central Pacific. Hence Carnegie's anguished cry of monopoly and his determination to break these exclusive franchises between the railroads and rival companies.

His close association with railroad executives, particularly with Tom Scott, now took on an even greater significance than before. Writing to one railroad president in Cleveland, Carnegie put the case succinctly: "The R.R. Co. simply says to Western Union, 'We cannot fight your battles. We stand neutral as between the rival Teleg. Cos. and as the law prohibits us giving exclusive rights to any party, we must give the P. & A. equal rights on our poles' & so on. If you and your friends can get this right, you can make a nice margin." [45]

In January 1869 Carnegie also put pressure upon Tom Scott to permit the Pacific and Atlantic to place "two or more wires upon the poles of the Terre Haute and Vandalia Railroad Co. We'll be glad," he concluded, "to arrange for this privilege upon similar terms and conditions to those governing the Western Union Company. But in addition, we will also pay rental of the use of said poles of $4 per mile per year, this being what we pay the Pennsylvania Railroad." [46]

Carnegie's efforts to break in upon the exclusive rights held by Western Union were moderately successful. Scott granted the Pacific and Atlantic the right to string wires and maintain service along the St. Louis, Terre Haute and Vandalia line, and Carnegie, for his services in providing the wires, pocketed 2913 additional shares of Pacific and Atlantic stock, which amounted to $5.00 worth of stock for every $1.00 Carnegie had invested in building the line.[47] At the annual meeting of the Pacific and Atlantic Telegraph Company in the spring of 1869, the directors announced that its stock capital was $807,025, and listed as property assets 2146 miles of pole line, 4183 miles of wire line, and 264 miles of leased wires. The company now had lines extending from New York to St. Louis and south to New Orleans. The business had prospered, and over the preceding three-year period the original stockholders had received dividends totaling 37.5 per cent.[48] Hopes ran high that the Western Union stranglehold on the telegraph business could be broken.

But within the next three years these hopes had faded. In every direction the Pacific and Atlantic sought to move on the continental telegraphic chess board, there stood Western Union, ready to check. Western Union, with forty times the capital, and lines that competed directly with every wire of the Pacific and Atlantic, could and did slash prices to weaken its competitor. From September 1870 on, each month saw a drop in Pacific and Atlantic earnings, from $10,000 down to $3665 by July 1871.[49] David McCargo blamed the leadership of Thurston, the president, and Edward Allen, the secretary, for this slump, and warned Carnegie that there could be no improvement in the business until "these shysters" were forced out.[50]

By December 1872, the directors of Pacific and Atlantic had to report to the stockholders that no further dividends could be anticipated within the foreseeable future. At that point Carnegie joined McCargo in an open struggle to take control of the company away from Thurston and Allen and give it to General Thomas J. Wood, who would serve as a convenient front for their management. Thurston, who was old and tired of the battle, resigned early in 1873, but as a last act of authority he, along with Allen, stopped Carnegie's move to have Wood elected president. Instead, the presidency went to W. G. Johnston, whose task it would be to preside over the liquidation of the company.[51]

Allen and a few other members of the board of directors had tried desperately in these last few months of the company's life to prevent it from falling, as so many other companies had, into the insatiable maw of Western Union. They had fought the monopolistic designs of Western Union for too long a time to yield gracefully now, even if it should mean great personal profit to themselves. Consequently, they began negotiations with the Automatic Telegraph Company of New York, which held valuable patent rights for a system of automatic operations, as well as a profitable wire line from New York to Washington. Allen hoped that by introducing automation on the Pacific and Atlantic system the company could once again successfully meet the competition of Western Union.

The contract was actually negotiated and duly executed, but it came too late to save the Pacific and Atlantic.[52] For Carnegie, realistically assessing the situation, was now more than ready to yield to the inevitable, providing the proper terms could be arranged. Since December 1872, when he had first broken with Thurston and Allen, Carnegie had been engaged in quiet, exploratory discussions with the Western Union management. Western Union agreed to exchange one share of its stock, then selling at $85.06, for six shares of Pacific and Atlantic, which had dropped to $12 a share on the open market. With these very favorable terms of exchange, the fortunate holders of Pacific and Atlantic stock stood to make $13 for every six shares of stock they could exchange for Western Union. Johnston, the new president of the Pacific and Atlantic, felt none of the sentimental loyalty to the company that Thurston and Allen had felt, and he was quickly won over to the scheme. He, Carnegie, and McCargo quietly sent out word to a few trusted stockbrokers throughout the country to buy up for them all the Pacific and Atlantic stock they could get their hands on.[53]

Such a bonanza could no more have been kept quiet than the discovery of gold at Captain Sutter's sawmill. Brokers immediately became suspicious when there was a sudden bull market for the stock of a company that was generally reputed to be facing bankruptcy and had declared no dividends for the past twelve months. Suddenly the price for Pacific and Atlantic stock began a dramatic advance, from $12.00 to $12.50 to $13.00. McCargo wired Carnegie asking whether he should continue buying at these advanced prices. Carnegie replied, "Think not—some time necessary to effect exchange." McCargo at once wired their agents in New Orleans, Memphis, and Cincinnati to stop all further purchases,[54] while Carnegie at the same time put additional pressure upon Western Union to consummate the exchange. "I have on hand," he wrote William Orton, president of Western Union, "between 9 & 10,000 P & A shares for transfer—All of it from first hands & friends. Mostly from Penn R. R. men & I am getting into trouble with them, daily—nay almost hourly telegrams asking how soon I shall remit Western Union & c. Will you please give me an order to transfer today & let me get it settled. This transfer, I find takes a good deal of time." [55]

Carnegie's remark that "this transfer takes a good deal of time" was something of an understatement. Anyone who owned a share of Pacific and Atlantic and who could make the slightest claim on Carnegie's friendship sought his good offices in making an exchange for Western Union stock. Johnston wrote that certain New York brokers were apparently having more success than Carnegie was in effecting an exchange. "Now Mr. McCargo and I think it would be decidedly better if you desire to protect our friends who write you—to answer—'Call on Mr. Johnston and show him my letter.' I can then take care of all you desire. To others who have no claim on friendship should be informed that you cannot do anything for them." [56] Johnston's boast that he could take care of all that Carnegie desired was premature, for unless Carnegie could be more effective in pushing the exchange of shares with Western Union, the whole scheme threatened to topple and bury Johnston and McCargo under an avalanche of worthless Pacific and Atlantic shares. Ten days later Johnston wrote in a more desperate note, "We are satisfied beyond doubt that we can handle as much and probably far more of the stock than any other parties if we can just have a speedy exchange effected. Now if you will attend to that exchange—and post us as to the limit at which to purchase—and authorize us to draw at sight for all purchases—we will divide ⅓ profits to yourself and ⅔ to Mr. McCargo and myself—If this arrangement is satisfactory telegraph me." [57]

It was a tempting offer, but Carnegie could do little to take advantage of it. The truth was, had Carnegie been candid enough to admit it, that Western Union was having very sober second thoughts about its initial arrangement to exchange any or all Pacific and Atlantic shares for Western Union stock at a rate of six for one. William Orton, a more conservative president than his immediate predecessor, Jeptha Wade, had been struggling for the past several years to meet dividends in a capital stock of $41,-000,000. In his opinion Western Union was greatly overcapitalized as it was. Only the smooth, persuasive talk of Carnegie, plus the tempting bait of the Pennsylvania Railroad franchise, had lured him, against his better judgment, into an arrangement in which it had been necessary to further increase the capitalization of Western Union in order to absorb the Pacific and Atlantic stock. Having already swallowed up in the past decade its two largest rivals, American Telegraph and the United States Telegraph Company, Western Union, like a gorged boa constrictor, needed now, more than anything else, a period of dormancy in order to digest what it had consumed. Moreover, the cry of monopoly, first raised against Western Union by its competitors, was now to be heard with ever more alarming frequency on Capitol Hill, and there were pending in Congress several bills which sought to make telegraphic communications, like the postal service, a governmental monopoly. So it is very doubtful if Carnegie, press as he might for a continuing, speedy exchange of stock, could have moved Western Union to complete the arrangement at this time.[58]

In actual fact, Carnegie was not pressing too hard for a continuation of this exchange.[59] He was enough of a realist to understand the situation, and having taken care of his own stock and those of his most important friends, including the 450 shares owned by J. Edgar Thomson, he was prudent enough—and selfish enough—not to want to weaken valuable property already acquired for the sake of additional quick profits on a further exchange. Having already exchanged 5898 of his own shares of Pacific and Atlantic for 983 shares of Western Union, Carnegie's own interest now, as a major stockholder, was to be as zealous in promoting the welfare of Western Union as Orton himself.[60]

The difficulty was that Western Union, having partially swallowed Pacific and Atlantic, must now ingest it completely in one way or another, since regurgitation was impossible. The business panic of September 1873 did not make the process of ingestion any easier. With Western Union stock dropping sharply on the market, an exchange of six for one no longer offered any profit to the unfortunate holders of Pacific and Atlantic stock who had not as yet effected an exchange. There was, therefore, no great outcry from these shareholders when, in January 1874, after months of laborious negotiations, Johnston and Carnegie at last arranged a contract with Orton by which Western Union leased the franchises, wires, and all other equipment owned by Pacific and Atlantic for an annual payment of 4 per cent on $2,000,000 worth of capital, the first payments to be used for the liquidation of the outstanding debts of the Pacific and Atlantic Company. As J. D. Reid, chronicler of the history of telegraphy in the United States, wrote, it "was a desirable arrangement for both parties." [61]

A less desirable result in the long run for Western Union—in part due to its complicated maneuvers at this time with Carnegie and Pacific and Atlantic—was that it missed its opportunity to buy out at a very reasonable figure the more important Atlantic and Pacific Company, which had valuable transcontinental franchises with the Rock Island, Union Pacific, and Central Pacific railroads. Had Orton not been so preoccupied with settling his unhappy involvement with the Pacific and Atlantic as well as being concerned with Western Union's already overcapitalized corporate structure, he surely would not have let this valuable opportunity slip by. Jay Gould, who had control of the Atlantic and Pacific, would later make Western Union pay dearly for this oversight, for eventually it would cost Western Union $20,000,000 to buy what it could have had in 1873 for half that amount.[62] Quite inadvertently, Carnegie had proved an useful agent for Jay Gould. It would not be the last time that the paths of these two men would cross or that Carnegie would render service to the "Mephistopheles of the stock market."

It cannot be said that Carnegie's role in the development of the telegraph industry was a very creditable one. He had, to be sure, been instrumental in the construction of several hundreds of miles of wire. He had also added considerably to his personal fortune, but this was through his success in speculation more than in construction—in burying, not building, a company of his own. In view of his later strictures against stock speculation, it is not surprising that in his autobiography he had little to say about his interest in telegraphy beyond those early years when he had been a bright young messenger boy on the streets of Pittsburgh.

In the late summer of 1867 Tom Carnegie married Lucy Coleman, the daughter of William Coleman, Carnegie's neighbor and former partner in the oil fields. Carnegie, because of the increasing complexities of his financial affairs, took this opportunity to move to New York. He and his mother gave their house in Homewood to Tom and his bride, and in the fall of 1867 they took up their permanent residence in the St. Nicholas Hotel, on Broadway between Broome and Spring streets in lower Manhattan.

The six-story St. Nicholas, with its white marble front, was the show place of New York and the nation. Even visiting Parisians and Londoners were impressed by its splendor. A British M.P. who visited it in 1854, the year after it was opened, wrote that its furnishings were "worthy of Windsor Castle." Margaret Carnegie, who could remember only too vividly their first arrival in New York just nineteen years before, could now stroll leisurely over "carpets of deep velvet pile," sit on "chairs of satin damask" and sleep under "the embroidery of the mosquito nettings that might be exhibited to royalty." [63] As she gazed at her own reflection in the great gilt-framed mirror in her bedroom, she must have found it impossible to find any connection between the plump, expensively dressed little figure that looked back at her and the over-burdened, shabby steerage passenger of two decades before. Nor did she really try. Now she had what she had sought —and what a spoon it was!

Her son could have told her precisely how rich the spoon was, for Carnegie had always found a certain beautiful simplicity in numbers. No matter how large they might be, figures, unlike words, could always be depended upon to state the exact situation. It did not matter whether one was listing the profits in pence from gooseberry-selling in Dunfermline or the profits in hundreds of dollars from dividends on stock in New York. All one needed to do was to put down those numbers in a column and the magic of arithmetic would give the simple answer. And so, one evening at the end of 1868, after a year in New York, Carnegie, writing as he frequently did, with a blunt stub of a pencil on an odd piece of paper that he might have found in a wastebasket, put down the following list of figures: [64]

Keystone	1170 shares @70	81,900	15,000
Union	2873 " @40	114,920	20,000
Central	890 " @60	53,400	6,000
Southern	106 " @40	4,240	300
U Pacific	373 "	30,000	3,000
Furnaces		10,000	—
Rail mill		10,000	6,000
Lochiel		4,000	400
Bitner		5,000	2,000
Columbia		12,000	2,000
Third Bk		3,500	300
Union Line		4,200	360

Empire Line	5,000	450
Fort Pitt	10,000	—
Locomotive	5,000	—
North Amer Ins	2,000	—
Min. & others	500	—
Surplus	3,000	300
	358,660	$56,110
others	1,340	
	360,000	
Cincinnati, Pioneer & Superior	40,000	
	$400,000	

There it all was in neat columns: investments in sixteen companies along with a few odds and ends, assets of $400,000, and an annual income of $56,110. And it had all begun with $817.50 of borrowed money, invested thirteen years before in Adams Express and the T. T. Woodruff Company.

How gratifying it all should have been! How many hours of planning, of scheming, of cajoling, and of playing lucky hunches it represented! Yet, in a curious way, it was not that satisfying, for it had all been too easy. Carnegie had for some time realized, with a sophistication beyond his years, that most of the successful men he had encountered were men with but one ambition—money, and with but one talent—the ability to get it. Scott, Thomson, Pullman, Orton, Gould—each a great man in his own world, but how small their worlds were, and how easy it was for a Gulliver to stride among these islands of Lilliput and Blefuscu. He had met only one successful businessman, John Garrett, president of the Baltimore & Ohio, who could quote from memory a single line of Burns or Shakespeare. He could not help comparing these business associates with the heroes of his childhood, Uncle Tom Morrison, Uncle Lauder, and his father, men who would discourse at length upon topics drawn from literature, history, politics, and economics.

Carnegie, to be sure, had been as ambitious and greedy for success as Pullman or Gould. He had eagerly accepted Scott and Thomson as his mentors, and their values had become his values, their goals his vision of success. But unlike these men, who had never had any other dream, and unlike Margaret Carnegie, to whom the past was something best forgotten—a dreadful memory of stitching shoes by candlelight, of silent looms, of two upstairs rooms on a mud alley in Slabtown—for Carnegie the past had held a purpose, an ideal that had not been fulfilled by these columns of figures. In the midst of success, Carnegie would know moments of ennui and restlessness that few of his associates could understand. Early in 1865, he had urged Scott to use his influence with Simon Cameron to get him a consular post in Scotland. Scott uncomprehendingly but obligingly had written to the Pennsylvania political boss: "My young friend Carnegie retires from Railway life 1st April next—having struck it rich in large quantities is now financially independent and intends to spend a few years in Europe—being one of Scotland's boys he has a strong desire to go there in some official capacity and has set his heart upon the Consulship of Glasgow . . . read Carnegie's letter and can anything be done for him?" [65]

Apparently Cameron did nothing, and Carnegie had to be content with a five-month tour of Europe at his own expense. He returned to America and to the world of business with an obvious zest for the struggle. Still the old nagging questions remained. Now, in the St. Nicholas Hotel at the end of the year 1868, having totaled up the fruits of that struggle, Carnegie was again struck by the discrepancy between the Dunfermline past and his American present. The end of the year for a Scottish Calvinist is a time for sober reflection, for pondering upon man's sinful frailty and God's awesome majesty. Carnegie had never accepted the Calvinist view of either man or God, but the ethos of Scotland had been bred into him. With all the introspection of an Edwards or a Knox, he took a hard, unpitying look at himself. Then with pen and ink, and in a neater hand, he wrote down another kind of balance sheet to accompany his statement of business holdings:

Dec. '68
St. Nicholas Hotel
N York

Thirty three and an income of 50,000$ per annum.
By this time two years I can so arrange all my business as to

secure at least 50,000 per annum. Beyond this never earn—
make no effort to increase fortune, but spend the surplus each
year for benovelent [sic] purposes. Cast aside business forever
except for others.

Settle in Oxford & get a thorough education making the acquaintance of literary men—this will take three years active
work—pay especial attention to speaking in public.

Settle then in London & purchase a controlling interest in
some newspaper or live review & give the general management of it attention, taking a part in public matters especially
those connected with education & improvement of the poorer
classes.

Man must have an idol—The amassing of wealth is one of
the worst species of idolitary [sic]. No idol more debasing than
the worship of money. Whatever I engage in I must push inordinately therefor should I be careful to choose that life which
will be the most elevating in its character. To continue much
longer overwhelmed by business cares and with most of my
thoughts wholly upon the way to make more money in the
shortest time, must degrade me beyond hope of permanent recovery.

I will resign business at Thirty five, but during the ensuing
two years, I wish to spend the afternoons in securing instruction, and in reading systematically.[66]

This remarkable document of self-analysis and adjuration is
surely unique in American entrepreneurial history, for neither
Rockefeller, nor Ford, nor Morgan could have written this note,
nor would they have understood the man who did. It is not surprising that of all the many books and articles that Carnegie was
to write, this little note, which was intended only for himself, has
been since Carnegie's death more widely quoted than any other
piece of his writing.

By 1870, when Carnegie had reached the age of thirty-five, he
was busily engaged in promoting his interests in telegraphy, the
Pullman Palace Car Company, the sale of bonds, and the building of bridges. His associates saw no evidence of his wanting to retire from "business cares" and to them his thoughts, like theirs,
seemed "wholly upon the way to make more money in the shortest time." The note still lay in his desk among his personal papers, undisturbed, yet still disturbing to his self-esteem. Although

it did not deter him in his quest for profits, it must have diminished somewhat his pleasure in achieving them.

Of all his many activities in these early postwar years, the one that apparently gave him the most satisfaction in retrospect was that of bridge building. Here at least he could feel that he was instrumental in building the kind of permanent monument appropriate to the new industrial order in America: vast iron frameworks that achieved beauty in their practical structure and the symbolic significance of union in their functional use. These great bridges over the Ohio, the Mississippi, and the Missouri, joining East to West and North to South, had for Carnegie's career a personal symbolism that was also significant. Built of iron and steel to serve the railroad industry, they also served to bring together Carnegie's many railroad interests and his increasing involvement in the making of iron. It would be in iron making that Carnegie was to find the basket he should watch. Through it he was to acquire wealth that would make an even greater mockery of his 1868 New Year admonition, and yet, paradoxically, provide him with the means to sustain "a hope of permanent recovery." It was to bridges and to iron for bridges that Carnegie's attention was increasingly to turn.

CHAPTER IX

A Basket of Iron
1865-1872

In the spring of 1865, after having resigned his position with the Pennsylvania Railroad Company, Carnegie left for his Grand Tour of the European continent. He would have been hard put to list his occupation in the ship's registry of passengers except by the generic term, capitalist. His interests were so diverse as to make any more specific statement impossible. If he had had to choose any one of his many interests to emphasize, however, it would undoubtedly have been bridge building, for this he always felt was peculiarly his own creation. With both sleeping cars and telegraphy, he had pushed his way into the concerns of other men, but the Keystone Bridge Works he regarded as his own, "always a source of satisfaction to me." [1]

The Keystone Bridge Company had been formed in April 1865, only a month before Carnegie was to leave for his European tour, but it was only a new name with a larger capitalization for the bridge firm of Piper and Shiffler which Carnegie had been instrumental in establishing in Pittsburgh during the first year of the Civil War. The genius of the organization from its inception had been J. L. Piper, whom Carnegie had first met in the Pennsylvania Railroad's machine shops when he went to Altoona in

1856. Piper, a big hulking man, generally regarded as the best mechanic on the Pennsylvania line, had been immediately attracted to the small, slender Scots boy, as diminutive as Piper was Gargantuan, for both shared the same fierce passion for fast horses. It had been Piper who had found and trained the stallion, Dash, for young Andy, and had thereby won the youth's affection and respect.

Piper also interested Andy because he had a vision, and however slow and stumbling he might be in articulating it, he was able to transmit that vision to Carnegie. As chief mechanic for the Pennsylvania shops in Altoona, Piper was responsible for keeping the tracks as well as the trains in operating order. One of his most troublesome recurrent problems, certainly his biggest headache, was the destruction of railroad bridges by fire or flood. The Pennsylvania line had many small wooden structures spanning the mountain creeks and deep ravines of the Alleghenies, and whatever the time of day or the weather conditions, Piper was on call to go to the scene where a bridge had broken down, to supervise its reconstruction. Although he never complained about the demands made upon his time and physical comfort, Piper did object to the futility of the whole process. He knew that the bridges he was building as solidly as he could were just as vulnerable and temporary as their predecessors. He had heard of experiments in constructing bridges of iron, and he dreamed of building such structures, which would be impervious to fire or water. Happily, he had found a fellow visionary in J. H. Linville, the chief bridge engineer for the Pennsylvania. The two men had spent long hours discussing designs for such bridges and had even taken out patents on some of their ideas for giving iron bridges the flexibility of wood.

Soon after Carnegie's arrival in Altoona, Piper and Linville had been given the authority by the Pennsylvania to construct a small iron bridge as a replacement for one of the bridges along the line. When Piper took Carnegie to the machine shops in Altoona to show him the blueprints for the bridge, along with the beams and trusses assembled there ready for construction, Carnegie was at once enthusiastic.[2] The simple blueprints were the harbinger of the future. When Carnegie took over the supervision of the Western Division from Scott in 1859, he realized more fully

228

than ever before the value of Piper's and Linville's ideas. The success of their first iron bridge had also convinced Aaron Shiffler, the general bridge supervisor of the Pennsylvania, that it was only a question of time until all the wooden railroad bridges must be replaced with bridges constructed of iron. Consequently, in 1862 Piper, Linville, and Shiffler were all amenable to Carnegie's suggestion that they come to Pittsburgh to form a new bridge company dedicated exclusively to the building of iron railroad bridges.

The company was a success from its very start. Within a year, Carnegie was able to note down in his neat year-end balance sheet a profit of $7500 from his initial investment in the Piper and Shiffler Company. This was but the beginning. By 1865, when Carnegie left the employment of the Pennsylvania and reorganized Piper and Shiffler into the Keystone Bridge Company, the company was receiving as many orders as it could handle with its limited capital and shop space. Carnegie could tolerate no such limitations. He saw the bridge company as he saw his sleeping-car company, playing a key role in the building of the great transcontinental railway that awaited only the end of the Civil War to be properly launched. Now that the great conflict was at last approaching its inevitable conclusion, Carnegie was in a frenzy of impatience; he wanted to be as prepared in bridge building as he was in telegraphy and sleeping cars to take advantage of any opportunity to supply the demands of a vast continental railroad system. The small iron bridges the firm of Piper and Shiffler had built across the creeks of western Pennsylvania were but toys compared with the monumental structures that would be needed to span the Ohio, the Mississippi, and the wide and treacherous Missouri. Hence the rush in 1865 to reorganize and to increase the capitalization of the bridge company. Once again, Tom Scott stepped in as a silent angel to support Carnegie's dreams and ambitions. He subscribed to half of Carnegie's $80,000 of stock investment in the newly organized Keystone Bridge Company— although the stock and presumably the voting rights remained in Carnegie's name—on the promise that he should be paid one-half the profits earned by these shares.[3]

The reorganization of the bridge company under the management of Piper and Shiffler was completed by the first of May

1865, and Carnegie, along with his friends Henry Phipps, Jr., and John Vandevort, was then able to leave for Europe. It was to be a tour in the grand style of the nineteenth century. They sailed on the steamer *Scotia* the second week in May, and although Phipps was miserably sick during the entire crossing, Carnegie, as always, was exhilarated by the sea voyage, busy making the acquaintance of the important people on board and entering enthusiastically into shipboard games. He wrote home that he had met a Mr. Hawkesworth of the steel trade in Sheffield, and also, "Mr. Morrison, prest. of the Manhattan Bank, a cannie Scotchman . . . His wife would suit Mother exactly, as she is thoroughly Scotch." [4]

The trio went directly from Liverpool to Dunfermline. Carnegie's second visit to his native town was far more pleasant than his first had been. On their last night in Dunfermline, Uncle Lauder invited a party of gentlemen over, "most of whom were shopmates and companions of my Father. Many knew grandfathers Morrison and Carnegie well. . . . It was 'ondrous strange to be surrounded with old men who were our father's boon companions. In America we are an entirely new family, and outside of Aunts Aiken and Hogan we have no relatives nor associations. Here we have a local history extending to the third generation, and many a one speaks kindly of our ancestors. You may well believe this seems a very great change." For all of his planning for the future, Carnegie could still find deep satisfaction in claiming a heritage from the past.[5]

From Dunfermline the trio returned to Liverpool, where they joined John Franks, a distant relative of Phipps, who was to accompany them on their tour of the Continent. Franks kept a travel journal for his sister in Liverpool, which gives a graphic account of Carnegie on this tour—his enthusiasm, his vigorous pursuit of culture, his cocksureness, and his charm. He was that kind of aggressive innocent abroad, guidebook in hand, who would always typify the American tourist in Europe. "He is full of liveliness, fun and frolic," Franks wrote of Carnegie in his journal. "His French is to carry us through when Vandy's German is no longer required. I had to acknowledge my obligation to him no later than yesterday when, wishing my portmanteau forwarded by rail and the German porter being so stupid as not to understand my good English, Andy kindly stepped forward to the rescue with

'Voulez vous forward the baggage to Mayence?' It is, I expect, needless to tell you that in time I found my portmanteau at its destination." [6] In other entries Franks wrote: "Visited the theatre one evening to witness the performance of the 'Biche au Bois' by Parisien Actors. This was Andy's desire who, having seen it in Paris, was in raptures with it." [7] "We are all occupied in our usual Sunday avocation of establishing lines of communication to our respective homes. Harry is writing to his sister, Vandy to his brother, and Andy is engaged in communicating his constant experiences to the Editor of the Pittsburgh Commercial." [8] "As to Andy's health, this is so overflowing that it is extremely difficult to keep him within reasonable bounds, to restrain him within the limits of moderately orderly behavior, he is so continually mischievous and so exuberantly joyous." [9] Vandy, Franks wrote, received the least amount of criticism from the others. "He is our prime minister, or our Chancellor of the Exchequer I should say. . . . Vandy praises everything as the finest thing he has ever seen, whilst Harry exclaims, 'Ai, my, ain't this nice. Ain't this grand.' Andy joining the praises with 'By golly boys, there's a great treat in store for us here.' " [10]

In his letters to his mother and brother at home Carnegie gave his own characterizations of his traveling companions: "Vandy is by far the most useful man in the lot, more useful than all of us together. He is rarely or never at fault. . . . He earns *his* grub. . . . To Harry is given the Post Office department. He mails all letters, gets them out . . . goes back after coats forgotten or guide books left at the hotel, and is par excellence the accommodating member of the quartette. Franks is a burly Englishman who has been spoiled by his sister Emma, who keeps house in Liverpool. She attends to his wants as Mother does to ours, and consequently when he is turned out into the world at large, he is as helpless as a child—can't buy anything, couldn't find his way to the station under two hours, and then would have left his overcoat or bag behind him. He depends entirely upon Harry for everything but his French, which I correct." [11]

Carnegie's travels, however extensive they were, did more to strengthen his already well-established prejudices than to broaden his outlook. He was content to stay in Paris and London while the rest of the party went on to Switzerland, for "I have seen enough mountain scenery in Scotland to satisfy me for a time." [12] And no monument on the Continent in his eyes could compare with the Scott monument in Edinburgh.

"Indeed, that is *the* monument of the world, in my humble opinion, and I think I am getting to be no mean judge of such things. The Arc de Triomphe in Paris is grander, probably cost five times as much to build it, but still give me the Edinburgh structure." [13]

Indeed, there was very little about France in these last years of the Second Empire that did please him. "In France, all seems dead. The soil is miserably farmed, and one is at a loss to account for the leading position which the Gauls have attained. I am one of those who hold that they cannot maintain it long—that they must give way to the German element which, you know is Anglo-Saxon and therefore has the right 'blend.' " [14] He was impressed with the grandeur of Baron Haussmann's Parisian boulevards, but "still I would not like to live here. Give me grim, overcrowded London, where men work as if they had other aims than pleasure, and live under a Government where individual liberty is never denied." [15]

London he found to be as vigorous as Paris was decadent. Here was the world's true capital of wealth and power, and, as Carnegie wrote, there was "nothing like being at headquarters . . . all other places are villages compared to London." He even mentioned the possibility of moving his own center of operations there. "I wish I knew the ropes and points in business affairs in London, as well as I do in the Iron City. I would certainly try to persuade the family to come there and try it for a while at least. . . . How would you like to try a residence near Hyde Park, eh? Or if Tom *will* insist on getting married (a very proper thing to do), he might run the machines in America and I do the foreign business. Seriously, however, I am quite taken with London and would like to spend a year or two there." [16]

This trip began Carnegie's long love affair with the Germans, and in the emerging German federation Carnegie foresaw a potential threat to France's military domination of the Continent. Louis Napoleon might be at the pinnacle of power just then, "but I have faith in the Germans, and expect to live to see a united Germany under a government somewhat like England (it would be rather too much to wish for a perfect thing, a Republic), taking the lead in Continental affairs. It is all wrong that a people like the French should be allowed to control matters to so great an extent." [17]

Carnegie was a nearly indefatigable tourist. He drove his companions on from gallery to opera to monument to mountain with the same relentless energy he had used in driving his railroad crews in Pittsburgh: "We make up a splendid whole and go laughing and rollicking through, meeting with many laughable adventures and exciting much merriment. We rise and breakfast by eight o'clock, begin work if we are doing a city. At one we go into a café and get something to eat . . . at two we are off again and get back to the hotel for tea. If there is an opera or amusement worth while we generally attend, although we are oftener too tired, for there is no work so exhausting as seeing picture galleries, churches etc." [18]

Museums, cities, and countries were ticked off with conscientious regularity. "Did Heidelberg today. . . ." "Climbed on our knees the sacred Santa, the identical marble steps, 28 in number, which Christ descended." . . . "Go to Naples tomorrow—visit Pompeii . . . will have seen all we expected to see except Spain. Foreign travel I have found to be more than all that is said of it and to an enquiring mind, no mode of obtaining knowledge is to be compared with it." [19]

Much of that knowledge had to do with business affairs, for, however preoccupied Carnegie might seem to be with madonnas, grand opera, and ruined monuments, his mind was always open to new manufacturing processes and techniques that were relevant to his own interests. Early in the tour, Carnegie's traveling companions went to Switzerland while he stayed behind in Paris. Although the explanation he gave them was his physical fatigue after the exhausting walking tour of England and Wales, the real reason was revealed in his letters home. He was at that moment negotiating what he considered to be a very important business deal. Earlier that summer, while in London, he had first heard of the Dodd patented process of fusing a steel facing on iron rails to give them greater durability and strength. Carnegie's interest in the manufacturing of rails was at this time of minor significance compared with his other business ventures, but he had no difficulty in seeing the potential advantage of holding the American patent rights for any process that would improve the cast iron rails upon which the railroad systems of the world at that time depended. For cast iron, being brittle and inflexible, was severely affected by extremes in temperature, and with the ever-increasing weight demands of American railway traffic, the problem of weak, easily cracked rails was becoming more acute each year. Carnegie was convinced that the railroads would pay a premium for any rail that promised to give more durable service than cast iron could provide. An all steel rail would, of course, be the answer, but in these pre-Bessemer days such a rail was prohibitively expensive. If the Dodd process of steel coating could give iron rails the strength of steel at a fraction of the cost, then the man who held the American monopoly on its use would have a very rich plum indeed. After his first inspection of the process, Carnegie was somewhat skeptical. "Yesterday [Cousin] Dod and I were busy looking at two new inventions destined, in the opinion of the inventors, to revolutionize former practices," he reported home to Tom. "One makes paper pipes stronger than those made from cast iron at ⅕ the price, another succeeds in running a face of steel upon an iron rail and welding it so thoroughly as to defy separation. . . . I have sufficient faith only to be interested. You need not fear, therefore, that I shall invest largely for the American right, but I intend to watch practical results." [20]

Nothing more was heard from Carnegie about the paper pipes, but his cautious interest in the Dodd process of steel facing soon gave way to the same excited enthusiasm he had shown for Piper's bridges, and he was quickly involved in negotiations for the American patent rights. With his customary exuberance and self-confidence, he was able to convince the English patent holders that no other man in the United States would be as useful as he in selling the American railroads the idea that they must have the Dodd processed rails. A few weeks later he reported home, "This gives you information you will be glad to have. Have had to exercise every whit of my business ability to convince these gentlemen that it was far better to give our party their patents without any cash down than to get 5,000 pounds gold from others, but I have succeeded, and feel repaid for the three weeks I have lost for Switzerland." [21]

After closing negotiations in London, Carnegie caught up with his companions in Mayence. His friends had had "a glorious time of it in Switzerland, but I have to show for my month, an important business negotiation successfully closed, from which I may reasonably expect to be able to 'do the States some service,' as it will be a great gain for America if we can do what I think we can. I have made a number of valuable and pleasant acquaintances in London during the time. . . . I have further to show a knowledge of the French language, which enables me to travel without serious difficulty wherever it is spoken." [22]

As his circle of European business acquaintances widened, his self-importance also expanded. "I am going next week among the Iron Works of Prussia on business connected with my London arrangements and hope to be much interested in their operations," he wrote to Tom in November. "At Ruhwort on the Rhine, the headquarters of the 'Dodd' German manufacturing is situated, and we will be there, I think on Wednesday night. From thence I go to Magdeburg, about two hundred miles further east, and remain Thursday or Friday to see a new idea for hardening cast iron, which is making a great noise in Britain, and the agents for which came to me to say that they will be glad to place their patents in my charge for America. I know you will share the satisfaction I have at my success in London. I can scarcely account for the manner in which I have been treated by everyone there with whom I have come in contact. The Dodds parties even told Dod [George Lauder] who was in London a short time since that they did not care whom I interested in America, or what I did, they were satisfied to leave everything in my hands." [23]

Carnegie undoubtedly hoped by these reports to give his brother the impression that his time in Europe was not devoted entirely to the selfish pursuit of pleasure. It was a point upon which Carnegie was somewhat sensitive, for this nine-month Grand Tour of Europe had been made possible only by Tom Carnegie's willingness to assume the full burden of Carnegie's business interests at home. It was a tremendous responsibility to hand over to a twenty-two-year-old youth, particularly at this moment when the nation's economy was making the difficult readjustment from war to peace. Businessmen everywhere were cautious about expansion, credit was tight, and returning veterans swelled the unemployment lists in the cities throughout the North. It was a time of general business stagnation and a groping for new fields of development now that the demands of war had at last been satisfied.

Yet Carnegie, writing from Europe, seemed to have little conception of the problems his young brother faced. He kept exhorting Tom to expand, to push for new customers for the bridge works and the iron mills, and to drive hard in developing what Carnegie saw as the potentially great new market that lay in the prostrate South. Every one of his letters home carried these persistent notes of prompting and urging: "We must pull up and develop the Union Mills sure. . . . How is the Brick concern doing? . . . Am glad to see you are pushing around after trade, but my dear boy, the South is our future market. The Freedom Iron Co. made most of its large profits from Southern trade. . . . I beg to urge upon you the importance of sending a first class man to Nashville, Memphis, Vicksburg, etc. at once. . . . Will you please carry out these views regardless of expense or anything else? . . . The Carnegie family, my boy, are destined always to be poor, but I am poorer than I expected if $8,000 in debt. We must work like sailors to get sail taken in. . . . What about Pit Hole? My interests there requires your attention, I think." [24]

And so the notes continued, week after week, filled with advice, often contradictory, to expand and at the same time to take in sail—and always, the implied criticism that Tom could be doing better than he was. Carnegie had, of course, paid his brother the highest of compliments by entrusting all of his numerous business affairs to him, but at times the beleaguered youth, treading water as hard as he could to keep from sinking, must have felt it a very dubious honor indeed. It was particularly hard to take all of this advice when it was accompanied with Carnegie's rhapsodizing over the sunrise at Snowdon or the majestic beauty of Raphael's madonnas. Finally, the point of exasperation must have been reached, even by one so quiet and even-tempered as Tom, for, somewhat contritely, Carnegie replied to one of Tom's letters:

> You wonder if we ever think of one who has notes to meet, etc. Indeed, we often do, and the more I feel myself drinking in

enjoyment, the deeper is my appreciation of your devoted self-denial and the oftener I resolve that you shall have every opportunity to enjoy what I am now doing. I'm sure you have had a trying time of it and often you must have felt disposed to throw up the game and write me advising my return, but I trust the skies are brighter now . . . and I am happy to believe matters are hereafter to be easier upon you. It is a heavy load for a youngster to carry, but if you succeed, it will be a lasting benefit to you. Talk to Mother freely; I always found her ideas pretty near the right thing. She's a safe counsellor, safer than I, probably, who have made money too easily and gained distance by carrying full sail, to be much of an adviser when storms are about, or sail should be taken in.[25]

Carnegie's disarming letter so mollified Tom that when Carnegie suggested that perhaps he should cut short his tour and come home with Phipps, Tom insisted that he stay on and complete the tour as planned. Carnegie replied, "We will go and do what we intended, always holding ourselves ready to quicken our pace, provided the tenor of your letter seems to require it. I just feel this way about it—twenty Italy's wouldn't keep me if my brother was having too much anxiety about matters. I feel that very few persons of your years have ever had such a load to travel under. I don't know anyone, I'm sure, whom I would consider able for such a task." [26]

Carnegie's confidence in his brother was thoroughly justified, for in spite of his youth, Tom Carnegie was better qualified than anyone else could possibly be to safeguard Carnegie's interests for such an extended period of time. Certainly no one else, with the possible exception of his mother, knew as much about Carnegie's various enterprises and investments. Besides giving Tom the formal education which he himself had missed, Carnegie had seen to it that Tom was trained in the same practical schools as he: telegraphy, the Pennsylvania Railroad, and now Carnegie's own business office. Tom had also been an investor, if only a minor one, in most of Carnegie's enterprises: the Storey farm oil fields, the Central Transportation Company, the Pacific and Atlantic Telegraph Company, and the Keystone Bridge Works. Even in physical appearance, Tom looked like a younger model of Andrew Carnegie—the same pale blond hair, square face, and small delicate frame. It always came as a surprise to others that two men so similar in appearance and background could be so different in personality. Andrew himself was surprised that Tom had turned out to be so different from him, and, indeed, it is doubtful if Carnegie ever understood his younger brother or fully appreciated those qualities in Tom's character that attracted the loyalty and respect of other men. Tom was everything that Andrew was not: cautious, where Andrew was impulsive; skeptical of new ideas, which Andrew would enthusiastically embrace; conservative in financial matters, where Andrew was, in his opinion, reckless; tongue-tied and ill-at-ease in social gatherings, where Andrew was at his loquacious best; wanting his own private family life completely separate from his business world, while Andrew could never separate the two and would play out his full life upon a well-lighted stage. Every man who had a nodding aquaintance with Andrew felt that he knew him well, for his moods and feelings could be read as easily as a book. No man, including Andrew, would ever feel that he really knew Tom, for the younger Carnegie always kept his own counsel, and seldom did a word or gesture betray his real feelings.

Yet, curiously, Andrew felt men trusted his brother in a way that they did not trust him. Their business partners almost always sided with Tom, partly, of course, because his policy of using profits for dividends instead of expansion was more to their immediate interest than were Andrew's grandiose plans for the future, but also, Andrew sensed, because they trusted Tom more. Andrew drove men hard with both the carrot and the stick, but Tom could get their wholehearted co-operation through quiet conversation. Had there been no Andrew Carnegie, Tom Carnegie would undoubtedly have been a highly respected and prosperous Pittsburgh businessman, but certainly there would have been no Carnegie steel empire, no multimillion-dollar fortune, and the Carnegie name would have had meaning only in the local business history of western Pennsylvania. "Tom was born tired," Andrew would occasionally say in exasperation, when his brother showed reluctance in supporting one of his ventures. But what would have become of Andrew Carnegie in these early formative years of business building if there had not been a Tom Carnegie to get credit from local banks, to soothe wounded feelings of partners and employees, and to hold some kind of rein upon Andrew's imagination was a question that the elder brother probably never asked, even of himself.[27]

Carnegie returned home in the early spring of 1866. He had written his mother earlier that "I begin to get just a little homesick, to tell the truth, feel like getting back and pitching into all kinds of business enterprises and driving things generally," which is just what he proceeded to do.[28] As the plans for the long-awaited transcontinental railroad were already well developed, he had no time to lose if he was to promote his sleeping-car, telegraph, and bridge-building ventures, all of which were dependent upon this great national railroad enterprise.

Yet almost immediately upon his return, he had to give a great part of his attention to the manufacturing of iron, which heretofore had been of secondary importance to him. Carnegie, to be sure, had very early in his career made some investments in iron. One could not be an active participant in the business affairs of Pittsburgh without having some concern for the city's basic industry. In 1861, he and Tom Miller, his old friend, neighbor, and early traveling companion, after making their investments in coal, had formed the Freedom Iron Company, a small company concerned with the manufacture of iron for railroad rails. But Carnegie's main interest at this time was in finished products—in Piper and Shiffler and such other diverse companies as the Pittsburgh Locomotive and Car Works and the Central Transportation Company, in which he had large investments.

It was Tom Miller who, having joined Carnegie in many other business ventures, would now bring a somewhat reluctant Carnegie into the actual manufacture of iron. Miller's own involvement in the iron business was the fortuitous result of his interest in railroading as a career. During the years that Carnegie was employed by the Pennsylvania, Miller was with the Fort Wayne, Pittsburgh and Chicago Railroad. Shortly before the outbreak of the Civil War, while he was acting as the purchasing agent for the railroad, he had become acquainted with two German brothers, Anthony and Andrew Kloman, operators of a small forge in Allegheny, who produced a particularly fine railroad axle. Miller had made many purchases from the Klomans, and by his easygoing gentle manner had gained their friendship and confidence.

The Kloman brothers, born in Treves, Prussia, where they first learned the iron trade, had come to western Pennsylvania in the early 1850's. By 1858 they had saved enough to open their own small forge shop at Gerty's Run in Millvale, across the Allegheny River from Pittsburgh. With one small steam engine and a single wooden trip-hammer they began their production of railroad axles, forged out of scrap iron. As their reputation for excellent craftsmanship grew so did their business, and at the time Miller made his first purchases from them the Kloman axle was generally recognized in Pittsburgh as being the finest on the market. Both brothers had a true talent for mechanical invention, and their axle owed its special strength to their having devised a method of twisting the component iron fibers of the axle while it was being forged. Mechanical genius and great physical strength were the only two characteristics that the brothers shared, however. For while Anthony, the elder, was easygoing, good-natured, and overly fond of spending his time drinking beer in one of the many taverns in Allegheny, Andrew was tight-fisted, hard-working, and entirely preoccupied with the business of running their little shop. Knowing almost no English upon their arrival in Allegheny, each brother responded to this alien environment in his own way. Anthony trusted everyone, believed everything he was told, and saw in each new acquaintance a possible friend and new drinking companion; Andrew could trust no one, was constantly fearful that because of his ignorance of the language he would be cheated in every business transaction, and saw in every associate a potential threat to his own position. Prosperity did not improve either man's character. It made Anthony more indolent and Andrew more tensely suspicious.[29]

It is perhaps a measure of Miller's personal charm that Andrew Kloman in 1859 would confide in the railroad executive his hopes and plans for the future. Or it may have been simply that Kloman was so eager to obtain capital for expansion that he had to turn to the only man he knew who had funds available for investment. In any event, Miller advanced the money that enabled Kloman to buy a second trip-hammer, and for this investment Kloman promised Miller one-third of the yearly profits. This informal arrangement was the beginning of Miller's involvement in the firm of Kloman and Company, an association which would eventually bring Carnegie into the manufacture of iron.

Miller asked that his name not appear in the contract as a partner, perhaps because, as purchasing agent for the Fort Wayne railroad, he made purchases from the Kloman firm. Instead, he insisted that a fourth party be brought into the business, a man who could hold Miller's interest in his name. Miller at first suggested Carnegie, but Kloman, his suspicions at once aroused, demurred. Carnegie was already much too imposing a business figure in Pittsburgh, and Kloman knew too much of his aggressive business tactics to want him as a partner even if Carnegie would have consented to associate himself with such a small firm.

It was then that Miller thought of a boyhood acquaintance from the Slabtown days, Henry Phipps, Jr. Phipps was several years younger than Miller and Carnegie. It had been Henry's older brother, John, who had been their friend, but after John's tragic death at the age of eighteen, the two older boys had kept a friendly, brotherly interest in young Harry, who had become Tom Carnegie's close companion. Miller had seen little of Harry Phipps in the last few years, but knew that he was employed at the firm of Dilworth and Bidwell and had a reputation for industry, seriousness, and considerable competence as an accountant. The Klomans and Miller would not only be getting in Phipps a new partner who could hold Miller's interest in his name, but the company would also be getting a first-rate bookkeeper, which, Miller told Kloman, the firm badly needed. Not even Kloman could be suspicious of the quiet, timid, self-effacing young bookkeeper and, eager to get the $1600 for the new trip-hammer, he agreed to the arrangement.

Young Phipps was more than eager to accept this invitation that Miller, acting as his patron, had arranged. The only difficulty was that Phipps could not raise the necessary $800 to take half of Miller's investment in the company. Miller then agreed to put up the entire amount, with the understanding that Phipps would repay him out of the dividends earned, and that Phipps would keep their joint one-third interest in the company in his name and protect Miller's interest as his own. Phipps still put in a full day's work at Dilworth's, but, for Miller's generous arrange-

241

ment, Phipps was more than willing to walk the three miles out to Kloman's shop every evening, post the Kloman books, and then walk back again late at night along the canal tow path to his father's cobbler shop home on Rebecca Street.[30]

With the coming of the war in the spring of 1861, Kloman and Company soon had more orders from government contracts than the small forge in Millvale, even with two trip-hammers, could possibly handle. Again Kloman turned to Miller for financial assistance. Kloman proposed leasing land directly across the river in Pittsburgh proper and building a new mill which could accommodate this wartime boom in orders. Miller was definitely interested, but insisted that there be a reorganization of the company under a new partnership agreement. The articles of agreement were drawn up and signed on 16 November 1861, to go into effect on the first of January 1862. The new Kloman and Company of Pittsburgh was capitalized at $80,000, with the rather casual provision that the capital stock should "be paid in from time to time as the wants of the business may demand." Again, there were only three named partners in the articles of agreement, the two Kloman brothers and Henry Phipps, Jr., who was, of course, to hold in his name both his own and Miller's interest in the company. "The said Henry Phipps, Jr. shall keep the books of the firm, or exercise a supervision over them during such evenings as he can devote thereto . . . ," which, as before, proved to be every workday evening.[31]

It seemed a happy situation for all involved. The Klomans had the capital they needed and the devoted services of an excellent accountant, Miller had a profitable investment which made no demands upon his time, and young Phipps had his first great opportunity to be something more than a bookkeeper for Mr. Bidwell. Unhappily, no legal articles of agreement could achieve personal agreement within the company, for Andrew Kloman was concerned with more than financial prosperity. He resented the increasing intrusion of Miller and Phipps—whom he still considered as outsiders—into the affairs of the company, and he became even more distrustful when he learned that Miller, without consulting him, had sold half of his and Phipps's interest in the company to two friends, William and Alex Crowley. Kloman and his brother had built the company out of their joint inventive talents and his own hard labor—and he could feel the control of that company slipping away.

Yet it was against his own brother that Kloman turned first, thereby ironically allowing the outsider to gain a majority interest in the company. Anthony's indolence and drinking habits had long been a source of friction between the two brothers. By 1862, when Andrew Kloman was working night and day to fill the ever-increasing war orders for axles and gun carriages, Anthony's indifference to the demands of the business had become intolerable. Andrew was convinced that such conduct could not help but set a poor example for the workmen in the mill, and he was determined that Anthony should leave the company. Miller, who was at the time in Scotland with Carnegie and his mother, was advised by a letter from Phipps that there was trouble in the Kloman mill and that Miller's return to Pittsburgh would be a "source of relief to them all." [32]

In the late fall of 1862 Miller returned home. He was immediately approached by Andrew Kloman, "who stated that the business was growing too great for him, that his brother was getting careless in business, and that he [Andrew] could not sleep at nights owing to his many cares, and desired to know if I would take an active interest in the concern and buy his brother out." [33] Miller accordingly began negotiations with Anthony, who was as eager to be free from his brother's nagging as his brother was to have him out of the company. Anthony's investment in the company and the current value of his one-third share in plant equipment were together estimated to be around $17,000. Anthony Kloman thereupon agreed to sell out to Miller for $20,000. The transaction was settled on 16 April 1863, and for the first time Miller's name appeared publicly on the articles of agreement as a partner in the firm.

The departure of Anthony from the firm did not bring peace to Andrew Kloman's troubled spirit. Belatedly, he realized that Miller and Phipps now held a two-thirds interest in the company, and this was a very different thing from his having in his control the one-third interest of his complaisant and indifferent brother. Kloman objected so loudly and strenuously to the very turn of affairs he himself had arranged that Miller, in the hope of establishing harmony in the management, sold to Kloman one-half of his brother's former share, so that Kloman would have an interest in the company equal to the combined holdings of Miller and Phipps. This gesture of conciliation did not appease Kloman for long, however. He turned an aggressively hostile eye on Phipps and demanded that Phipps sell his interest back to him so that he could once again have the major interest in his company.

Phipps refused. He saw his hopes for the future slipping away, and in desperation, he turned to Miller to save him. "If I am put out," Phipps is reported to have said to Miller, "I shall spend the rest of my life keeping books for Dilworth." [34] Miller, always fiercely loyal to his friends, assured his protégé that Kloman could not touch him. Miller and Phipps would stand together and defy Kloman. It was then that Kloman, frustrated in his attack on Phipps, swung around against Miller. Here he found the weak sector in the Miller-Phipps line that he needed, for Phipps, only too relieved to have Kloman's attack no longer directed against him, did not resist Kloman's attack upon Miller. Indeed, Miller was later convinced that Phipps was the one who directed it. Certainly the stage was set for an Iago, and Kloman was an eager Othello, ready to believe any rumor of Miller's aggressive designs against him. One rumor Kloman heard was the Dempsey story. According to this account, Miller one day, in a burst of expansive optimism, foolishly told a drayman by the name of Dempsey that his present interest in Kloman and Company was but the camel's head inside the tent. He had his head in Kloman's firm and soon he expected to occupy the whole tent. Dempsey is supposed to have immediately reported this conversation to Kloman. Although it is questionable that Miller could have been so unsubtle and indiscreet in his conversation with a chance acquaintance, it took only a suggestion of this kind to inflame Kloman's suspicious nature. [35]

In any event, soon after Miller had purchased Anthony's interest, Andrew Kloman, without any legal authority to do so, inserted a notice in a local Pittsburgh newspaper that "Thomas N. Miller is not a member of our firm nor has he any real authority to transact business on our account." War had been declared, and when Miller, in anger, turned to his ally in the partnership for support, he found to his consternation that Phipps was now on the other side. For poor little Harry Phipps, who would all his life live in fear of those stronger and more bellicose than he, had only one defense for survival in this jungle of rugged individualism, and that was to attach himself to the strong and hang on. At the moment, Andrew Kloman appeared the stronger of the two protagonists, and to him Phipps, with parasitical tenacity, attached himself.

Miller knew that his position in the company was legally secure and that Kloman and Phipps could not dislodge him by meaningless notices in the newspaper or by wild tantrums. But Miller also was enough of a realist to know that the business could hardly survive such disharmony within its ownership. He turned to his friend Andrew Carnegie and asked him to step into the troubled situation as arbiter. Phipps and Kloman accepted this arrangement, and in that manner Carnegie made his first appearance in the Kloman firm.

Carnegie would always maintain that he accepted this assignment with reluctance and only out of friendship to two of the parties involved in the dispute, Miller and Phipps. Hostile critics, however, have insisted that Carnegie's motive from the very first was selfish, that by appearing as a disinterested outside party he hoped to insert himself into the center of the firm.[36] Such an interpretation is the kind of false distortion obtained when an event is viewed in the light of later developments. The facts do not substantiate the charges that Carnegie was engaging at this time in a Machiavellian strategy of divide and conquer. He was so preoccupied with his other interests, including another iron manufacturing firm, that he very probably regarded Miller's request to intervene in the affairs of the relatively unimportant Kloman company as being little more than an intrusion upon his time. His own account of the part he played in the controversy was later verified by both Miller and Phipps as being an accurate statement of the situation:

> For some weeks, scarcely a day passed that I did not see one or more of the parties. Hearing both sides, I was fully satisfied I could not establish harmony upon the basis of a common partnership. I finally got all three together in my office and proposed that Miller should have his one third interest and be a silent (not special) member, Phipps and Klowman [sic]

transacting the business. This was agreed to; but unfortunately ill feeling was created about a trifle, the result aimed at was lost, and the conference separated under angrier feelings than ever. Time only served to increase the violence of the quarrel. . . . But I considered it so essential to Miller's standing that the notice [the newspaper notice denying Miller's partnership] be recalled, as enemies were not wanting who began circulating slanderous reports about his clandestine arrangement with Klowman while acting as agent of the Fort Wayne Road, that I insisted upon Miller agreeing to anything that would reinstate him in the eyes of the public as a legitimate member of the Klowman concern.[37]

It must have taken much insistence upon Carnegie's part to get Miller to agree to the settlement, for the terms of the new partnership agreement were anything but favorable to Miller's interest. By the terms of this agreement, dated 1 September 1863, a new partnership was established, known as Kloman & Phipps, capitalized at $60,000. Of this capital interest Kloman was to hold $30,000, Phipps $20,000, and Miller $10,000. Miller's interest in the company had thus been reduced from four-ninths to one-sixth. Even more alarming to Miller, there was an added clause in the agreement which provided that "if at any time . . . Kloman and Phipps shall desire to terminate the same as to the said special partner, then upon the said Kloman and Phipps giving to the said Thomas N. Miller sixty days' notice in writing . . . the interest of him, the said Thomas N. Miller, shall at the end of said sixty days, and upon the payment to him of the capital invested by him and share of profits coming to him . . . retire from said firm, and his interest therein shall at that time wholly cease, and the same shall in such case accrue to the said Henry Phipps, Jr., as having a pre-emptive right thereto, upon his paying in the capital for the purchase thereof." [38]

Clauses in partnership agreements providing for the purchase at book value of the interest of one partner at the desire of the other partners were, to be sure, a fairly common business practice at that time. What was unusual, however, was to have such a clause directed specifically and exclusively against one party named in the article of agreement. Quite naturally, Miller balked at signing this agreement, but he finally did, though with reluctance and under protest. To get Miller's signature required all of Carnegie's persuasive powers (including a telegram to Miller stating that, should Miller refuse to sign, "the position in which I would be placed would be that of an agent whose acts were disavowed by his principal, and this would be the first time during my life in which I had been so placed") [39] and Phipps's solemn pledge that the clause had been inserted only to appease Kloman and that never would he, Phipps, agree to its being used.

Carnegie's insistence upon Miller's signing a contract so prejudicial to his interests as this one naturally gave rise then and later to speculation about Carnegie's motives. Carnegie by then, however, must have been thoroughly weary of the whole affair, and he was eager to reach a settlement on almost any terms. He did not have the strong suspicions that Miller had against Phipps and was quite willing to accept Phipps's pledge as honorable and binding. Finally, it must be added that Carnegie had now a personal family interest in getting the Kloman partnership settled, for at this time his young brother was brought into the affair. To Harry Phipps there had been only one difficulty in the way in which the controversy was to be settled: he did not have the necessary $20,000 to invest in the new partnership, and fearful as always of going into debt and mortgaging his future in an enterprise that might fail, he had asked Tom Carnegie to take one-half of his interest in the company. Young Carnegie, eager to emerge on his own, out from under his brother's protective tutelage, readily agreed. So now there was a Carnegie in the firm, and Andrew had an added reason to push for settlement.

Miller's suspicions of Phipps were fully justified. Within three months after the new partnership went into effect, he received a terse note, properly signed by Kloman and Phipps, requesting his withdrawal from the firm and the sale of his interest to Henry Phipps, Jr. With Tom Carnegie's backing, Phipps now had the capital to finance this betrayal.

Miller had no choice but to comply. He could understand Kloman's behavior, considering the German's morbidly suspicious and possessive nature, but Phipps's perfidy he could neither understand nor forgive. Miller exemplified the business ethics of his day. He could be somewhat devious himself, concealing his direct interest in the Kloman firm at a time when, as purchasing agent

247

for the Fort Wayne railroad, he might be embarrassed by public knowledge of such a connection. But this was a common practice: J. Edgar Thomson, Tom Scott, and nearly every other railroad executive had hidden interests in manufacturing concerns with whom they did business. Carnegie, in fact, was one of the few railroad officials at that time who never made any attempt to conceal the multiplicity of his interests in other concerns and was quite willing to let men like Scott use his name to cover their own investments.

Nor was Miller unduly sensitive to the fierce competitive spirit in business. From the day he made his first investment in a second trip-hammer for Kloman, he had been ambitious to enlarge his interest in the company and to have a voice in its management. He was ready at all times to fight to protect his interests, and he could understand such zeal in others to promote their own ambitions. But even in this melee of entrepreneurial warfare there was a vestigial code of honor, and Phipps, in breaking a solemn promise to his friend and former patron, had violated it. Miller could never grant pardon to or again be reconciled with such an offender.

Carnegie's response to Phipps's betrayal was characteristically aggressive. He and Miller would take the offensive by forming a rival concern that would bring Kloman & Phipps Company to terms. Carnegie was, to be sure, motivated to this precipitate action by more than a desire to exact satisfaction for his outraged friend. The increasing demands of the Keystone Bridge Company for structural beams and plates had convinced Carnegie of the wisdom of controlling his own source of supply. It was his first momentous move directed toward the creation of a vertical organization in business, and it is important to note that at this stage the manufacture of iron was still secondary to his interest in bridge building.

Carnegie's proposal received immediate and enthusiastic approval from Miller, who was motivated entirely by a desire for revenge. Miller already had in mind an excellent location for their mill—an open field only half a mile up the Allegheny River from the Kloman plant. The land was leased from the Denny estate, and the first outlay of capital that Carnegie and Miller had to make for their proposed venture was $400 to a truck gardener named Cummings, who was using the field as a cabbage patch.[40]

The Cyclops Iron Company was formally organized as a joint partnership on 14 October 1864. Miller held the controlling interest in the firm, with Carnegie and his Keystone Bridge partners, Piper and Linville (Shiffler having left the firm), taking the remaining shares. Miller and Carnegie were prepared to invest heavily to obtain the most efficient equipment for the rolling of structural parts for bridges. Here they would have a distinct advantage in the immediate postwar period, for the rival Kloman plant was geared for war production and would have to make the painful readjustment to a peacetime market.

The businessmen of Pittsburgh watched with great interest the rapid construction of the Cyclops mill in the winter of 1864–65. The whole business community knew of the Miller-Phipps conflict, and the fact that there was a Carnegie in each of the two companies added spice to the promised rivalry. But the exciting contest between former friends and between brothers never materialized. Miller, of course, wanted a fight to the finish with no quarter given, but Carnegie from the first had quite another objective in mind. For him the appropriately named Cyclops would have its one eye fixed on Kloman & Phipps—not as a potential rival, but as a subsidiary. Carnegie was ready and eager to open negotiations with the badly frightened ironmakers down the river before the first ingot bloomed that spring in the Cyclops mill.

He did not have long to wait. In March 1865 the partners of Kloman & Phipps indicated their interest in joining forces with the Cyclops Iron Company. The resulting merger was largely the work of the two Carnegie brothers, for they were the only ones on speaking terms with all of the parties involved. Tom Carnegie, of course, had no interest in perpetuating a feud that predated his entry into the business. He wanted only to protect and strengthen his interest in iron manufacturing, and this proposed merger was certainly far more attractive to him than a prolonged rivalry with his own brother's firm. Andrew Carnegie too had very good reasons for promoting this merger. Always eager to "gain distance by carrying full sail," he was particularly eager to combine forces with Kloman & Phipps, not so much for the added capital and plant equipment that this merger would provide as for the personnel involved. Capital he could raise and equipment he could buy, but the Cyclops Iron Company needed the mechanical genius of Kloman and the business talents of Phipps and Tom Carnegie, and these assets were not purchasable on the open market. Carnegie would always put a premium on men and organization, and therein, he felt, lay the source of much of his strength and success.

Phipps certainly offered no objections to the proposed merger. He had no stomach for mortal combat with Miller, now his implacable enemy, and was willing to accept any terms that would protect his own interest in the company. The objectors to the proposal as arranged by the Carnegie brothers were, of course, Kloman and Miller. Apparently Kloman was simply outvoted by Phipps and Tom Carnegie, although Andrew Carnegie's offer to put Kloman in complete charge of the mechanical supervision of the two plants at a substantial salary, over and above his quarter-share in the capital of the combined companies, probably did much to mollify Kloman's initial opposition.

Miller, however, was quite another matter. He had entered into the Cyclops venture with Andrew Carnegie for the avowed purpose of driving Kloman & Phipps into bankruptcy. Now, before the first beam had been rolled in their new plant, Carnegie was proposing a merger with the enemies. Again Carnegie had to strain his persuasive talents to their utmost to win Miller's consent. "You return as a conqueror," Carnegie told him, and indeed he did, for part of the agreement, at Miller's insistence, was the provision that his share in the new company would be slightly larger than that of any other single holding—larger than Kloman's, larger than Andrew Carnegie's, and, above all, larger than the combined shares of Phipps and Tom Carnegie. Miller laid down one other condition to his joining forces with his former associates. "I'll do anything you desire," Miller told Carnegie, "save personal association with my old protégé." [41] This, too, was accepted, even though it created the anomalous situation of having the largest holder in the partnership refuse to attend any director's meetings or take any active part in the management of the business.

Carnegie found it appropriate that this merger should be completed at the very moment that national Union was being reestablished. The name he gave the new partnership combining the rival mills was the Union Iron Mills, and thereby he commemorated both his own and the nation's triumph. With the re-organization of the bridge company also completed at this time, Carnegie's triumphal mood as he left for Europe in May 1865 is not surprising. That he asked Harry Phipps to accompany him is a clear indication of his eagerness to forget the past. "Let bygones be bygones" would be his motto for the day, he told Miller, and he strongly advised Miller to adopt the same.[42] This Miller would never do, and he must have found it difficult to understand how Carnegie could so lightly dismiss the recent unhappy experience.

Andrew Carnegie returned to Pittsburgh in the spring of 1866 eager to push his various interests and plans for the future. He was annoyed to find that the Union Iron Mills, which he still regarded as mainly a subsidiary supply mill for the Keystone Bridge Company, was not doing as well as he had expected. Tom pointed out the generally bad economic situation throughout the nation in this first year of peace, but Carnegie would never accept what he regarded as the easy excuse of hard times. He insisted there was always business to be had if one pushed for it hard enough. He blamed the difficulties of the Union Iron Mills in part on the failure of the Keystone Bridge Company to get the orders it should have. He intended to direct his major efforts in that area. In the meantime, all the Union Mills partners were to devote their best efforts to the success of the company. This was no time to nurse old grudges and protect hurt feelings. Carnegie demanded that Miller contribute more than money to the success of the business. He wanted Miller to attend directors' meetings and to serve actively as a responsible partner in the firm. But Miller was intransigent. He would come to directors' meetings only if Phipps were not on the board, and he would come to the mills only if he would not have to see "his former protégé," Phipps. With some exasperation, Carnegie acceded to Miller's terms. Phipps was persuaded to resign from the board of directors, although, of course, he remained a partner in the firm. Miller then took his place on the board, and for fifteen months there was harmony among the partners in the Union Mills.[43]

Tom Carnegie, however, believed that Harry Phipps had been unfairly treated. Tom always felt a sense of obligation to

Phipps for having brought him into the firm, and he now became Phipps's champion on the board. Andrew Carnegie became increasingly sympathetic to Phipps's case as the months passed, for the simple truth was that Phipps was a better businessman than Miller. Even Miller admitted that "no one could keep a check longer in the air without funds to meet it [than Phipps], and I had not that faculty." [44] When a vacancy occurred on the board in the spring of 1867, Carnegie asked Phipps to fill it. Unfortunately, neither of the Carnegie brothers thought it necessary to inform Miller of their decision. Perhaps they felt that Miller would acquiesce to a *fait accompli*. If so, they underestimated the intensity of Miller's feelings. Miller, in ignorance of what had been done, came to the next regular board meeting, and it was only after he had hung up his topcoat and hat and had turned toward the directors' table that he saw Phipps sitting there. As one of the board members would later remember the incident, Miller, white with anger, demanded to know where "that man" came from.

"Oh, Tom," Carnegie replied, "stop your foolishness and take your seat."

Miller's only answer was to grab his coat and hat and slam the door behind him as he stomped from the room. [45]

For once Carnegie's persuasive powers were of no avail. After cajolery had failed, he wrote Miller a letter peremptorily demanding Miller's service if he expected to continue as a partner in the firm.

> I received yours of the third with regret partly upon your own account, for so large an interest as yours should receive your attention—principally upon my account, for so far from your presence being an embarrassment it would be esteemed of great value.
>
> Our Union Iron Mills are very far from being in a satisfactory condition—financially it requires close and anxious exertion to keep matters moving. There are only two parties whom I know of able to carry this department, yourself and Mr. Phipps. You couldn't give it the necessary attention. He is doing it without compensation except that deserved in common with others through proprietorship, even with his aid we are very closely pressed. It is simply out of the question to think that without one or the other of you that Tom could manage

matters. I do not expect to be able after a short time, even to visit the mill, or to be within reach. Some one must be put in training to manage that concern or you will find it will do no good. We want a business head there with more experience than either Tom or Kloman. I believe Phipps to be the only one in interest available for operating as a safeguard against such blundering as you had an example of in the purchase of the old book a/c's of Pipe Works for our good paper. . . . I want all parties in interest to understand that I have worked to bring matters right about as long as I intend to do so. When you know how we are placed I think instead of embarrassing us by resigning you should put your shoulder to the wheel with us. We never needed the efforts of all more urgently than now. You have of course aided us in money matters for which we are duly thankful, but your presence at the mill every morning for twenty minutes would double this obligation.[46]

Miller, however, would not retract his resignation from the board. Carnegie had had his choice of Miller's or Phipps's services—he could not have both. Apparently, Carnegie had preferred those of Phipps. Miller therefore was determined to sever all connections with the Union Mills. He asked Carnegie to buy out his large interest in the partnership.

Only when Carnegie finally realized that Miller was not going to yield, no matter what pressures might be put upon him, did Carnegie begin dickering with Miller over price. He started negotiations by deprecating the value of the partnership shares and his own interest in the Union Mills: "I want to get out of them, and will do so before long. Even if I can't sell my stock it can go . . . $27.40 will be gladly received." He also blamed Miller for getting him involved in the business: "I knew you had been previously wronged & I felt you should forget it. I did what I could at the time to redress that wrong & went into the most hazardous enterprise I ever expect to have any connection with again—the building of a rival mill. You were carried back to the business you were unjustly thrust from, were the largest owner in it—this should have satisfied you—but I could not expect you to forget the past." [47]

It was the old Scottish game of haggling, and Miller knew the rules as well as Carnegie. He held out for more than the $27.40 a share that Carnegie had proposed, and he finally received, including the cash payment as an option to purchase his shares, an average of $32.75 a share for his 2203 shares in the company. Thus Miller sold out his major interest in the Union Iron Mills for $71,362, an interest that he would live to see be worth two thousand times as much as he had received for it.[48] But Miller never had any regrets for his action, nor felt that he could have done anything else and still have kept his honor. He was to write Carnegie many years later:

> You say in your precious note, "It was a pity, a foolish quarrel between you and your pards"—truly it was—in a *commercial* sense—in me a folly, but, do you know, I never regret that day! I could not stand the stink of such treachery as his conduct had been in 1863—indeed after 40 years, while I have forgiven him, I cannot meet him comfortably. As to yourself, what you did then was wise, you had no quarrel with Henry Phipps, you advised me well to "Let bygones be bygones"—and I loved you then Andy, as I have *ever* loved you, but Phipps had stabbed me at a critical time in my life—but why weary you with dirty linen of the past— [49]

And in a letter to a Pittsburgh paper Miller took satisfaction in thinking that he had had his revenge on Phipps after all. "The whirligig of time brings its revenge to see $800 loaned a friend turned to the burden of $50,000,000. Surely that is sweet revenge. . . . To my many friends who daily sympathize with me that I am not a multi-millionaire, I simply say that like Goldsmith's 'Vicar,' I am 'passing rich on'—just what St. Paul prayed for."

In this same newspaper statement, Miller repeated publicly what he had written many times to Carnegie privately, that for Carnegie himself Miller had only love and respect. "I asked Andy to buy me out, as he was wedded to one I could not associate with; and Andy did buy me out, but at my own price, and I was glad to get out at that time. Apart from sentimentalism, Andy was right in standing for the other director. . . . Andy took no advantage of me. He never did; all was strictly straightforward negotiations." At the same time, however, Miller made a most perceptive observation about Carnegie, applicable not only to the Miller-Phipps incident, but also to Carnegie's entire business career. "The only fault I found, and in the business world it is rarely deemed a fault, was that to Andy, Napoleon that he was in business, blunder was worse than a crime. He could forgive the one; he could never excuse the other, and we parted as business associates on this line." [50]

When the partnership broke up, Union Mills was renamed Carnegie, Kloman & Company, although it was still called Union Mills. Of Miller's 2203 shares in the Union Mills, Carnegie himself took 1656 shares, which, in addition to a small number of shares he purchased at the same time from the holdings of Phipps, Linville, and Tom Carnegie, gave him 3000 shares in the company, the controlling interest, which he would hold and add to during the next thirty-three years.[51] Carnegie had found his basket, but at the time he apparently did not realize its full importance, He had too many eggs in too many other nests to give to the Union Mills more than a part of his attention and interest.

Even within the field of iron manufacturing itself, the Union Mills were not Carnegie's sole interest. In fact, he seemed at this time more concerned for the success of his investment in the Dodd process of steel-faced rails than he was in the activities within the two rolling mills along the Allegheny. He had written confidently to Tom in the fall of 1865 about his success in getting the exclusive American rights to the Dodd invention, and of his "satisfaction of knowing that not only the Messrs. Dodd but their London friends are quite confident that they have secured a reliable and competent person with whom they are perfectly satisfied to trust their interest." In the months after his return to America, if he had occasion to remember these boastful, self-assured words, he should have blushed for his own simple naïveté in assuming that he could so easily arrange for the American patent rights to a British invention. It was Carnegie's first experience in the complicated world of patents, and he was quickly to learn that there was never to be a simple and easy patent arrangement.

Soon after his negotiations with Carnegie had been completed, Thomas Dodd had hurried over to the United States to set up the American Steeled Rail Company for the processing of his steel-faced iron rails, and he had put Thomas Blair in charge of the company. Carnegie had assumed at the time that there was no question about the validity of the Dodd patent or of his own claim to the American rights, and as a consequence he invested heavily in the Dodd plant even before he returned to the United States. Upon his arrival in Pittsburgh, however, Carnegie discovered that the Dodd patent was anything but secure. His efforts to arrange matters with the Dodd brothers by correspondence proving futile, Carnegie hired James Livesey, an engineer living in London, to act as his agent in further negotiations with the Dodd family. Livesey, however, found the Dodd brothers as difficult to deal with by personal contact as Carnegie had by correspondence. "I made an appointment by letter to meet Mr. Thos. Dodd," Livesey wrote Carnegie in June 1866, "but as in most things connected with them I was unsuccessful." Livesey said that he could not seem to make Mr. Dodd understand even the most elementary fact—that Carnegie needed to have the name and date of his patent. Livesey did discover, however, that apparently the Dodd brothers had been as generous to others who had applied for their American patent rights as they had been to Carnegie. They had granted similar rights to a Mr. Henry Bakewell of St. Louis, Missouri, as well as having their own agent, David Burr, in Washington to negotiate with the United States Patent Office.[52]

Two months later, Livesey reported that he was "at last beginning to get some light on the patent question." It seemed that the Dodds had a patent agent in London by the name of Spence, who had taken out both the English and American patent rights, and it was Spence who had hired Burr as his agent in Washington.[53] Carnegie wrote to Burr that he understood that Burr had "in hand the obtaining of the patents for his process of hardening Railway bars. These patents I have arranged to purchase & would be pleased to hear from you whether Mr. Dodds has given you any instructions as to what disposition you are to make of them when obtained. Also what shape the matter is in at present, whether patent has been granted, &c."[54]

Burr's reply was not encouraging. Carnegie wrote Livesey that he had arranged a meeting in Washington, but that "Burr says he has no authority to recognize us—nor has Mr. Bakewell either—however, I hope to convince them we labor for the best interest of Mr. Dodds." Carnegie was not discouraged by these rebuffs because, as he wrote Livesey, "We have Mr. Blair with us." As long as Carnegie controlled the actual mill that processed the rails, he felt that about the patents "we need not be particular." [55]

The patent arrangements were never to be completed. In December 1866, Livesey reported that the Dodd brothers had lost control of their own mill in Sheffield and "are now in the hands of their creditors." [56] Carnegie continued negotiations for control of the Dodd patent rights for three more years without success. What finally caused Carnegie to abandon the Dodd process, however, was not his failure to secure the patent rights, for he and Blair continued to produce "Doddized" rails at the American Steeled Rail Company without legal authority. Rather it was simply the fact that the Dodd process did not work. No one could say that Carnegie had not tried to make a success of the Dodd process. He used every public-relations technique he could think of to persuade the conservative and skeptical railroad lines to adopt the Dodd rails: advertising pamphlets, statements from British railroad men, and sample lots of rails sent out to various railroad executives.[57] He got a few small orders, but in every instance these orders were soon followed by angry demands from the railroad companies that the Dodd processed rails be replaced by regular iron rails. Carnegie wrote to Bakewell a year after production had begun at the American Steeled Rail Company: "The fact is that we have been terribly put back by the bad failure of the Rails Mr. Dodd sent to us as a trial lot. They failed during the cold weather & the steeling pulled away—they were removed although the ordinary Iron Rails alongside, which we had laid to demonstrate what we claimed for the Dodds, showed but little wear." [58]

J. Edgar Thomson, who had accepted a small order of processed rails for the Pennsylvania only after the most earnest entreaties from Carnegie, advised Carnegie to abandon the project after these rails failed to stand up under test on the Pennsylvania lines. "Private—a word to the wise. The experiments made in relation to the strength of the Doddized Rails has so much impaired my confidence in this process that I didn't feel at liberty to increase our order for these rails. . . . Unless you can overcome this difficulty—which I fear is impracticable—the process is not a success. . . . You may as well abandon the patent." [59]

257

But Carnegie kept doggedly on, even using the Pennsylvania's single order as an advertisement of their success. "Mr. Thomson's report estimates the process to extend the life of the Rail three fold," he wrote without a blush to the president of the Chicago and Northwestern.[60] It was only after the cancellation orders began to pile up, and the word of the dismal failure of the Dodd processed rails had been circulated by railroad officials throughout the United States, that Carnegie finally had to admit defeat.

In the meantime, with the same enthusiasm he had once shown toward the Dodd process, he was now backing another British invention, the Webb process, which Livesey had come upon in England while negotiating with the Dodd brothers. Livesey had written that here at last was the answer to a cheap durable rail. Like the Dodd rail, it consisted of putting a steel facing on an iron rail, but unlike the Dodd method, the Webb process was for "the re-rolling of *old* iron rails with steel heads. . . . Now I shall feel dreadfully vexed if you allow some other party to get hold of this as an opponent when you had the chance of the thing yourselves. I am doing all I can to get Webb to wait until I get a reply from you. . . . In this system there is no expense whatever to start it. It is not like the Dodd requiring furnaces and special machinery to work it. You want nothing. You could commence to re-roll old rails and put steel heads on them at once." [61]

Carnegie snapped eagerly at the bait. "We will agree to pay the 4¢ royalty per ton," he wrote Livesey, "and stipulate that whenever the patent fails after 1868 to return to Mr. Webb or owners 200 pounds per annum I shall revert [the patent] to them." [62] Unfortunately, it was a re-run of the Dodd plot with a slightly different cast of characters: the same confusion over patents, the same frustrating negotiations with various agents all claiming to represent the Webb interest, and, finally, the same failure in the product itself.

This second failure evidently served as a check upon Carnegie's enthusiasm, for in 1869, when Tom Scott wanted him to invest in a new chrome steel process, his reply showed a certain weary skepticism. "My advice (which don't cost anything if of no value) would be to have nothing to do with this or any other great change in the manufacture of Steel or Iron. I know at least six inventors who have the secret, all are so anxiously awaiting.

. . . That there is to be a great change in the manufr. of iron & steel some of these years is probable, but exactly what form it is to take no one knows. I would advise you to steer clear of the whole thing. One will win, but many lose & you & I not being practical men would very likely be among the more numerous class. At least we would wager at very long odds. There are many enterprises where we can go in even." [63]

This skepticism of innovation was only temporary, however, and Carnegie's often quoted dictum, "Pioneering don't pay," was, like his aphorism of putting all his eggs in one basket, an expression of his later years. It was certainly not representative of his thinking in these early years of business activity. The records show that time after time Carnegie was only too eager to blaze a trail across terrain where angels, not to mention pioneers, might fear to tread. Yet much nonsense has been written by those who have accepted Carnegie's later dicta at face value and would present a single-minded, ever-consistent Carnegie, who resisted the new and untried and had to be pushed by more imaginative and venturesome partners into the successful innovation that would bring him fame and fortune.

Such accounts always show Carnegie steadfastly refusing the pleas of his partners to expand their iron manufacturing interests into the manufacture of Bessemer steel. They would have the reader believe that it was not until the spring of 1872, when Carnegie took a trip to England and visited the great Bessemer works at Derby, that he became convinced of his partners' counsel. There, in the blinding glare from the Bessemer ladle, Carnegie, like Saul on the road to Damascus, is supposed to have been converted to the true faith, and immediately to have sailed home to join his brethren in their great enterprise.[64]

Highly dramatic—and quite inaccurate. Carnegie, several years before his celebrated trip to England in 1872, had built his own Bessemer steel plant. The Freedom Iron Company, which he and Miller had been instrumental in forming in 1861 for the manufacture of iron rails, was the agency for Carnegie's first tentative venture into the making of Bessemer steel. In 1866, the company was reorganized under the new name of the Freedom Iron and Steel Company, and the slow process of converting the mill into a Bessemer steel plant was begun.[65] By September 1867, Carnegie wrote to John Wright, treasurer of the company, that he should inform James Livesey that "we will be ready Jan'y 1st to make Bessemer & during the next year will develop this Rail matter thoroughly at our own works (Freedom) as we know how essential it is to get everything exactly right at first." [66] It was Carnegie's intention to put the Webb process in the Freedom plant, where the rerolled rails could be headed with Bessemer steel produced there in the plant.[67] Carnegie himself wrote Livesey later that fall: "The Freedom Iron Company is pushing ahead with Bessemer & is going to be, I think, the only really successful Bessemer Manfr. in the United States for the reason that it makes its own pig & all of its charcoal. . . . They are experiencing difficulties at Penna. Steel Works, Harrisburg from not getting uniform pig metal & must undergo a year or two experimenting. We will be in position to give the Webb a fair test before long—but we want to do it at our own works (Freedom) and be sure it has full justice." [68]

By the spring of 1868, the Freedom Iron and Steel Company was producing Bessemer steel in limited quantities, but in sufficient amounts to satisfy the demand for the Webb processed rails which Carnegie was so energetically pushing, and enough in addition so that the mill could roll a small number of rails made entirely of Bessemer steel. Carnegie even offered disgruntled "Doddized" rail purchasers Bessemer steel rails on their next order "if that should be preferred." Although most buyers of Dodd and Webb rails would have preferred anything to these unsatisfactory processed rails, the price that Carnegie quoted for his steel rails must have discouraged them from accepting his offer.

Thus Carnegie's experimentation with Bessemer steel long pre-dated his visit to the Bessemer works. Although he had a heavy investment in iron manufacturing and in these years was an outspoken advocate for iron over steel, nevertheless he was canny enough to keep a foot in the other camp and venturesome enough to experiment with any process that seemed to him to give promise of solving the problem of a durable rail of uniform quality within a price range acceptable to the railroad companies.

Carnegie's hesitation in going into full-scale production of Bessemer steel in the late 1860's cannot be attributed to an overly cautious attitude toward the new and the experimental. Nor does it seem probable that even his great outlay of capital and effort to make a success of the Union Iron Mills would have served to inhibit him. Carnegie was skeptical about the Bessemer process for the same very good reason most American iron manufacturers were. The supply of iron ore then available in America that could be successfully used in the Bessemer process was so limited in quantity as to make Bessemer steel too expensive to be used in rail manufacturing. Hence the futile attempts to find a compromise between iron and steel, in which the precious Bessemer steel would be used only as a heading on iron rails.

Henry Bessemer's great discovery in 1856 of making steel out of pig iron by blowing cold air through the molten pig is one of the most dramatic stories in the history of modern industry, and it has been told so often that it needs no detailed elaboration here.[69] Bessemer's process created a heat so intense as to burn out the carbon and silicon that is found in all iron ore, and had thus opened up the dazzling possibility of making steel as easy to obtain as pig iron itself and transforming that hitherto precious metal, used only for such small high-priced items as knives, razor blades, and surgical instruments, into the basic metal of the modern industrial world. Bessemer proclaimed a new age for mankind —the Age of Steel, which would mark as significant a change from the preceding Age of Iron as that epoch had from the earlier Bronze Age. Unfortunately, however, Bessemer had announced his victory too soon. Later tests showed that, although his process successfully burned out carbon and silicon, whose removal was essential to the making of steel, it left another hostile element, phosphorus, totally untouched. Phosphorus within the ore in any appreciable quantity made Bessemer's steel a friable mass that disintegrated into fragments under the slightest pressure. Quite by accident, in his early successful tests in his London laboratory Bessemer had used an iron ore from certain Welsh mines where the phosphorus content of the ore was less than 0.4 per cent. With that ore his experiments had been highly successful. But when British steel manufacturers tried to use his method on the ordinary run of iron ore from the mines throughout Britain, the result was a total failure. Bessemer was branded as a charlatan, and the dream of obtaining steel in unlimited quantity and of uniform quality seemed as illusory as ever.

When Bessemer finally understood the cause of the difficulty and purchased only the selected, phosphorus-free ores of Wales and Sweden, he could produce steel of the highest grade. But since most of the known sources of iron ore in Britain and the United States had a high phosphorus content, it did not appear that Bessemer's discovery could have any significant practical application. "British pig iron abounded with this fatal enemy," the unhappy inventor wrote, "and I could not dislodge it." [70]

At this dark moment, however, Bessemer found other British mines whose ore was relatively free of the contaminating phosphorus, and even more extensive ore sources with a very low phosphorus content were developed in Spain. With these new sources, Bessemer's success in England was assured. At the very period when American railroad building was reaching its peak of activity, British manufacturers were prepared to offer the American lines rails made of the finest quality of Bessemer steel.

Small wonder that the American iron manufacturers felt threatened and that Carnegie should futilely chase one substitute process after another. At the same time, he felt obliged to trumpet loudly the advantages of iron over steel, as he did in this letter to H. J. Lombaert, vice president of the Pennsylvania Railroad:

> You have been so consistent in your advocacy of wrought iron for axles that we have pleasure in submitting to you an extract which I happened to see yesterday in the London Engineer. I wish you would submit it to Mr. Thomson, the great pillar in this country of "steel for everything."
> "193 axles broke during 1865 upon German Railways
> Of all the axles above mentioned 17 cast steel axles, journey 18,927 German miles a peice [sic] . . .
> 46 of fine hammered wrought iron, 25,461 miles
> 38 of rolled wrought iron, 22,959. . . ."
> The axles of hammered wrot iron appear therefore to have been the most & those of cast steel the least durable. . . . We are content to await the result of steel axles upon the Pennsylvania Rr confident that they will not come nearer to our "Kloman" than they have done to Wrot Iron axles in Germany.[71]

This letter was only one small part of a bold front to conceal a growing concern that the day of wrought iron was nearly over.

The Pennsylvania was using steel—steel made in Britain, and unless American manufacturers could find an adequate substitute, or produce steel themselves, no amount of carefully garnered statistics, or blatant advertising, or patriotic appeals to "Buy American" could save them.

Carnegie's search for a substitute had failed. Even more discouraging was the prospect of making Bessemer steel in America in sufficient quantity and at a low enough cost that would permit the American manufacturer to compete with his British rivals. The ores from the traditional sources in eastern Pennsylvania were so high in phosphorus content that they were unsuitable for the Bessemer converter.

To complicate the problem even further, there was the bitter litigation over patent rights in the United States, between the Bessemer agents who sought an American patent on their process and the lawyers for the American inventor, William Kelly of Eddyville, Kentucky. Kelly's lawyers could offer indisputable evidence that Kelly had discovered the secret of decarbonizing iron ore nine years before Bessemer did. And Kelly had patented it. But Kelly, like Bessemer, had run into the problem of phosphorus in the ore, and he had abandoned the whole project. Several years later, Bessemer, in total ignorance of the American's prior discovery, had begun his experiments in London. Nevertheless, Kelly still held his patent on approximately the same process as Bessemer's, and the Patent Office in Washington had therefore denied Bessemer's agents a patent right in the United States.

Blocked by both nature and law from using the Bessemer process, American iron manufacturers at the close of the Civil War could see no alternative but to hold fast to the traditional method of making wrought iron products, in the hope that Bessemer steel would prove to be but another will-o'-the-wisp. To protect their rails from the threatening competition of British steel, they got from an obliging Republican Congress a high tariff on imported iron and steel products, and behind this dike they sought uncertain refuge from the threatening flood.

Then suddenly, in 1866, the obstacles that had blocked the development of the Bessemer process in the United States were unexpectedly removed. The syndicate of American businessmen who had purchased Kelly's patent rights reached a settlement with Bessemer's agents. The two rival camps pooled their patent rights, and the United States Patent Office at last gave official sanction to the Bessemer process. Protected by patents, engineers acting for Henry Bessemer could now build in America the great steel converters that bore his name.

Of even greater importance for the practical use of the Bessemer process in the United States was the opening of iron ore fields in the upper peninsula of Michigan. These fields were not only the richest yet found on the North American continent; the ore there was almost entirely free of phosphorus. Here was a vast treasure house of ore, beyond the wildest hopes of Henry Bessemer. The United States now had the potential for becoming the greatest steel producer in the world.

The iron fields of Michigan had first been detected by a government surveyor, William Burt, who had gone into the untracked wilderness of upper Michigan in 1841 to map the region and divide it into townships and sections for future settlement. It was Burt who had first reported the presence of iron ore lying close to the earth's surface, and on his map, along the southern shore of Lake Superior, he had written the single word "iron." Four years later, a small company of prospectors, led by a Connecticut farmer, Philo M. Everett, had come into the region looking for gold and copper. An Indian guide named Majigijig had led them into the forest, and a few miles beyond Teal Lake had pointed ahead to a place he called Iron Mountain.

Iron Mountain it was indeed—a hill of pure iron ore. Everett, in a letter dated 10 November 1845, described his discovery. "We incurred many dangers and hardships. We made several locations, one of which we called Iron at the time. It is a mountain of solid iron ore, 150 feet high. The ore looks as bright as a bar of iron just broken." [72]

The ore was there in unbelievable quantities. The problem was how to utilize it. The first attempts to build furnaces and rolling mills in this remote wilderness all ended in failure. The distances to the markets were too great and the transportation facilities too primitive to make of this northern peninsula a new Pittsburgh, as Everett and the other early iron prospectors had hoped. The East had the mills, and it needed the ore. If a means could be found to transport the ore in its raw state to Pittsburgh and Bethlehem and the Eastern seaboard, then the prospects for utilizing these rich discoveries would be dazzling.

In 1855, the Federal government built a canal around the impassable rapids at Sault Ste. Marie, and a group of Eastern capitalists financed a small railroad line from the mine fields to the small town of Marquette on Lake Superior. Now from Marquette through Lake Superior, down Lake Huron and across Lake Erie, and then by canal and river there lay an all-water route to bring the rich ore down to the railroad terminals of Ohio, Pennsylvania, and New York. The hungry mills of the East could feast on the purest and most easily extracted iron ore that had yet been found on the earth's surface. When the first Bessemer plants were opened in America in the mid 1860's, the ore was already available to feed them, although no one at the time realized this. It was not until the first tests were made on the Lake Superior ores in 1868 that it was discovered how truly valuable they really were. Only then did Eastern capital provide the necessary funds to improve the railroad from the iron fields, and enlarge the port facilities at Marquette, so that a large flow of ore to the Great Lakes could be handled. All of this took time, but by 1870–71 America was at last ready for the Age of Steel.

During this time, Carnegie had been in the vanguard of those preparing for the future. The Freedom Iron Company had begun its conversion into a Bessemer plant in 1866, as soon as the patent negotiations had been completed. At this time Carnegie was still skeptical about the future of the Bessemer steel process in the United States because of the limited phosphorus-free ore resources. It was not until it was demonstrated that the Lake Superior ore was admirably suited for the Bessemer converter and there were adequate facilities available for the inexpensive transportation of the ore to the Pittsburgh area that Carnegie was ready to act. By 1872, when he went to England on a bond-selling mission, the problem of ore supply had been solved, and Carnegie already had in mind ambitious plans for the expansion of his Bessemer interests.

Carnegie's tour of the Bessemer plants in England did not provide him with a sudden revelation of truth. But this tour did convince him that his plans for the expansion of the small Freedom Iron and Steel Company were much too limited. After viewing the great converters in Sheffield and Birmingham and hearing the plant managers discuss their plans for future development, Carnegie realized that only by building on a scale comparable to that of the British mills could he hope to compete in the Age of Steel. What he needed was not a converted plant of limited facilities but an entirely new mill with the most up-to-date equipment available. As he watched the silver-white stream of steel pour out of the great pear-shaped vessel, his plans for the future expanded with the heat that engulfed him. It was a prospectus for new worlds to conquer that he was to carry back to his doubting partners in the Union Mills.

CHAPTER X

Bridges and Bonds
1868-1872

Up until 1872, when Carnegie became committed to the idea of building an entirely new steel mill, he had continued to regard his ventures in iron manufacturing as subsidiary to his main interests in bridge building, telegraphy, and sleeping cars. In spite of the great amount of effort, time, and money he had put into the creation of the Union Iron Mills, he saw them mainly as a source of supply for the Keystone Bridge Company. "The Keystone Works have always been my pet," Carnegie wrote, "as being the parent of all the other works." [1] He of course took an active interest in those products, particularly iron rails, which the Union Mills produced, but his main concern was to ensure for his bridge company the best available material at the lowest possible cost. Keystone should not only be in a highly favorable competitive position with other major bridge building concerns, but it must ready itself for assignments beyond the scope of any existing bridge company at that time. The two greatest American rivers, the Mississippi and Missouri, remained to be bridged, and Carnegie was determined that Keystone would do it.

This ambition was aided immensely by the inventive and adaptive talents of Andrew Kloman, as Carnegie himself readily admitted. According to Carnegie, it was Kloman who was the first to introduce the cold saw that cut cold iron into exact lengths, who invented upsetting machines to make bridge lengths, and who built the first "universal" mill in the United States.[2]

This last innovation, the universal mill, was not only illustrative of Kloman's talents at adaptation but of Carnegie's good fortune, which would repeatedly toss into his lap the golden apples of success. In the summer of 1867 the Union Iron Mills had its first serious labor difficulty, when the puddlers throughout the Pittsburgh area, organized in a small crafts union called the Sons of Vulcan, refused to accept a managerial order for a reduction of wages and went out on strike. The several iron companies affected raised a fund to bring in European workers to replace the striking puddlers, and Kloman, representing the Union Iron Mills, asked for German workers. Among those he received was a bright young metal worker named Johann Zimmer. Zimmer told Kloman about a rolling machine he had worked on in Prussia, on which it was possible to roll plates of various widths with finished rolled edges. This remarkable mill not only had the usual horizontal rolls of the plate-mills used in America, it also had two movable vertical rolls for rolling the edges of the plate, and these rolls could be widened or narrowed at the will of the operator. Kloman at once saw the possibilities in such a mill, and, from the specifications that Zimmer gave him from memory, he designed and put into operation the first American universal mill, capable of rolling plates seven to twenty-four inches wide. Zimmer's small universal mill would be improved and enlarged in the years that followed and would enable the Union Mills to roll plate of almost any desired thickness and length, with finished edges.[3] With such talent backing him up, Carnegie could enter into contract negotiations for bridge construction, confident that he could meet specifications.

Carnegie always had a partiality for the Keystone Bridge Company, even though it was never to be the most profitable of his many enterprises, and he insisted that Keystone was his favorite because of the pleasure he took in directing the construction of those great edifices, the best in American architectural design, engineering skill, and iron manufacturing—mighty monuments that would endure for generations as testimonials to the practical application of technical genius. The great bridges over the Ohio, Mississippi, and Missouri not only fulfilled the urgent practical need of carrying traffic across the continent, but they were aesthetically and philosophically satisfying as well. There was a beauty of design, given its reality in great iron beams, cables, and stone pylons. There was the symbolism of Union, so meaningful to a nation that had been but recently torn apart by civil war. All of this Carnegie found deeply moving and gratifying. "We were as proud of our bridges as Carlyle was of the bridge his father built across the Annan. 'An honest brig,' as the great son rightly said." [4]

To this list of the attractions that bridge building held for him, Carnegie might well have added others, for satisfying as these structures were, they were never for Carnegie an end in themselves. They were the means of passage into many other interests, far more financially profitable than the bridges themselves. Bridges would determine the routes of the as yet unconstructed railroads across the great plains of America. He who controlled the bridges could, like a medieval feudal lord in possession of a toll crossing, exact his tribute from trade far out of proportion to the cost of the bridge itself. For Carnegie this tribute would take many forms: profits on the iron for the beams, plates, and posts which the Union Mills furnished the Keystone Bridge works; the bridge contracts themselves; shares in the railroad companies that would use the bridges; and finally, and perhaps most importantly, commissions on selling the bonds of these railroad companies in the financial centers of Europe and America. A vast, intricate web of finance, manufacturing, and transportation hung on these bridge strands, and across the network Carnegie would move with amazing alacrity, always ready to rush in any direction where something of value had been caught in the fibers of the web.

The most spectacular of the bridges that Keystone constructed, and the one that was to test the technical skills of Piper and Linville to their utmost, was the great St. Louis bridge across the Mississippi, designed by James B. Eads. Carnegie was particularly eager to get this contract, not only for the handsome dividends it promised the constructors, but for the promotional value the bridge would have in obtaining other important contracts. Had he known in advance what difficulties lay ahead for any contractor who attempted to build from the visionary blueprints and specifications of Captain Eads, his enthusiasm might have been less pronounced.

As early as 1839 there had been discussions both in Missouri and in Washington, D.C., of a bridge that should cross the Mississippi River at St. Louis. In the two decades prior to the Civil War, such a bridge had been an integral part of the plans that St. Louis had for being the eastern terminal of a trans-Mississippi railroad to the West Coast, but sectional differences in Congress, delaying all transcontinental railroad development during these years, had also meant a postponement of plans for the St. Louis bridge. In 1864, however, in the midst of the war, a company composed largely of St. Louis businessmen was finally organized for the purpose of constructing a rail, highway, and footbridge across the Mississippi. A charter for the St. Louis and Illinois Bridge Company was approved by the Missouri legislature on 5 February 1864. Two years later a bill authorizing the construction of a bridge across the Mississippi at St. Louis, as an extension of the National Post Road, was introduced into Congress by Senator B. Gratz Brown of Missouri. The bill was passed by Congress and signed by President Johnson early in the spring of 1866.[5]

With the approval of both the state and the Congress to support them, the directors of the St. Louis and Illinois Bridge Company were now able to push ahead with their plans. It was hoped that the bridge could be completed by summer 1871, and to ensure that this monumental structure would be of the most advanced design, the company employed the services of Captain James B. Eads as engineer-in-chief for the planning and construction of the bridge. Captain Eads, a former army engineer, had won his fame during the Civil War by constructing armor-plated gunboats for use on the Mississippi and other inland waterways. Although a novice in bridge building, Eads was reputed to know more about the Mississippi River, its treacherous currents, channels, and shoals, than any man alive.

Carnegie had had his eye on the contract for the bridge's superstructure for his Keystone Bridge Company since he first heard of the organization of the St. Louis and Illinois Bridge Company in 1864. He urged the other directors of Keystone to expand the plant facilities of the company by building a new

270

blacksmith shop, purchasing additional machinery, and acquiring land across the Allegheny River for a new foundry, so that the company would be ready for the really "big bridges at St. Louis and Omaha." [6]

Once again his close association with Scott and Thomson was to bring its reward, for the Pennsylvania Railroad had a direct interest in and would be one of the principal beneficiaries of a bridge across the Mississippi at St. Louis. Carnegie persuaded Scott to use his influence with the St. Louis Bridge Company to have J. H. Linville, the bridge engineer for the Pennsylvania Railroad, appointed chief consultant to Eads for the design of the bridge. That Linville was also a director of the Keystone Bridge Company was, of course, for Carnegie a quite happy and anything but accidental coincidence. With this kind of inside position, it is not surprising that the Keystone Bridge Company secured the contract for the superstructure, although L. B. Boomer, head of the American Bridge Company of Chicago, offered spirited, if futile, competition. Carnegie's company had furnished the chief consulting engineer, and more important, Carnegie, as he pointed out to Eads in a confidential note, could provide the financial backing of both Thomson and Scott as well as his own highly useful services as a bond salesman in negotiating for needed capital abroad.[7]

Against such weighty inducements from Carnegie, Boomer could offer nothing but potential trouble if the contract for the superstructure should not be awarded him. Boomer made good his threats by forming a rival syndicate, the Illinois and St. Louis Bridge Company, which acquired a charter from a compliant Illinois state legislature recognizing it as the proper agency to finance and construct a bridge across the Mississippi starting from the Illinois side of the river. In the end, Boomer's efforts to drive the St. Louis syndicate from the field failed. The two rival agencies were consolidated under the authority of Eads and the original board of directors of the St. Louis company, and with proper compensation for his Illinois charter, Boomer retired from the field. But these protracted negotiations delayed the start of construction for another year, and it was not until summer 1868 that work on the foundation piers could be started.[8]

Having secured the contract for the superstructure of the

bridge for Keystone, Carnegie next wanted to have a hand in the financing of the bridge. This could be more rewarding to him than the actual bridge contract, and, as always, he turned to Scott and Thomson for support. Dr. William Taussig had been appointed chairman of the executive and finance committee of the St. Louis Bridge Company, and it was to him that Carnegie, backed by Thomson and Scott, applied for the commission to negotiate the sale of $4,000,000 of first mortgage bonds in New York and London. Taussig and his colleagues, William McPherson and Amos Cotting, agreed to Carnegie's proposition: a commission of $50,000 of stock in the St. Louis Bridge Company if the entire bond issue was subscribed to on a basis of 85 per cent of face value.[9] Armed with letters from Thomson and Scott in support of the bridge plans and the bond issue, Carnegie set off for London to negotiate with Junius S. Morgan for the sale of the bonds.[10]

No other type of selling mission was quite as enjoyable as bond negotiations, particularly with foreign capitalists. There was a heady atmosphere of wealth and power in the offices of J. S. Morgan and Baring Brothers in London and of Sulzbach Brothers of Frankfurt, and in this atmosphere Carnegie could luxuriate as nowhere else. More fascinating than any game of chess were the delicate and cautious gambits with which these financiers would open the negotiations: so courtly, so unhurried, so apparently casual, and yet always so clever. They won Carnegie's admiration even while he was plotting his countermoves. How easy it all was once the terms had been agreed to: a few simple figures on a slip of paper, a warm handshake, perhaps a glass of sherry and a few words of small talk. And that was all it took to move into the market the necessary gold to heat the foundries in Pittsburgh and put iron beams across a muddy river 5000 miles away. Here was capitalism in its most powerful form, and Carnegie would never tire of watching its quiet, smooth operation. And what a pleasant and simple way to earn $50,000 in stock, which would make him and his silent partners in Philadelphia part owners of the very company from whom they held the construction contract. Within a week after his arrival in London, Carnegie was able to inform the finance committee in St. Louis that Junius Morgan had agreed to take at least $1,000,000 of the bonds at 85 per cent of the face value.[11]

There were other benefits that might accrue to the bond salesman besides his commission, if he was clever enough to detect
them and brash enough to ask for them. Carnegie was both. Quite
casually, a few weeks after the negotiations with Junius Morgan
were completed, Carnegie wrote to McPherson and Taussig suggesting that "if entirely satisfactory to you, we should like to be
allowed to retain say $200,000 of the proceeds of the Bonds sold
by us, until a final settlement is had between us, or for a specified
time if you prefer. We to pay such rate of interest as you receive
for surplus of funds from other parties, or say 7%. Your security
is ample consisting as it does, of 500,000$ Stock Bonus, & also
cash Bonus due upon completion of Contract by Keystone Bridge
Co. We have occasion to use funds, just now, for the completion of
Keokuk Bridge & the arrangement indicated would be an accommodation to our party, but, please understand, we hope you will
not comply if in your opinion the interests of your Company
would in any way be affected injuriously thereby." [12]

It was an interesting little proposal that Carnegie had made in
this offhand manner. Anticipating a favorable reply, he wrote
somewhat smugly to Phipps the next day, "Money is dearer with
you than elsewhere. I expect to have 200,000$ surplus belonging
to Keokuk [13] next week, which I could invest in 2, 3, 4, and 6
months paper & if you can get 8 or 9%, I may send it to you for
that purpose." [14]

Taussig and company did not prove quite so simple-minded as
Carnegie would have them, however. In the end, Carnegie had to
put up considerably more in the way of collateral than his own
stock bonus in the St. Louis Bridge Company, including securities and shares in the Pennsylvania Railroad and Central Transportation Company. Nevertheless he got the use of the $200,000
with a rather neat little profit accruing from the difference in interest rates.[15]

In the long months that stretched ahead, from the laying of
the cornerstone on the western abutment of the bridge until the
bridge was finally completed in late spring 1874, three years after
the originally scheduled date for completion, Carnegie felt he had
more than earned any extra dividends garnered from such little
side arrangements as the use of surplus funds. Never had he encountered such a difficult client as Captain Eads, who, it seemed

to Carnegie, demanded nothing less than the impossible in his specifications for quality, strength, and durability. He asked for tests on material that had never before been demanded of a bridge contractor or iron manufacturer, and special machines had to be developed for this testing. Carnegie fussed and fumed over these demands and laid all the blame on Eads for the long delays which were doubling the originally estimated cost of the bridge.

When Taussig, in December 1870, wrote to Carnegie complaining about the Keystone Bridge Company's failure to keep up with the agreed time schedule and accusing Keystone of being concerned only with its own profits, Carnegie answered with some heat:

> Capt. Eads had expected that the steel would be rolled so as to require no planing. Now, every bar must be planed. All holes are to be drilled—a thing unheard of! . . . Capt. Eads must only require the custom of the trade. Everything beyond that must be allowed for in time and money. Piper thinks the Bridge as now designed will require fifty per cent more time than as designed when our contract was made. This Bridge is one of a hundred to the Keystone Company—to Eads it is the grand work of a distinguished life. With all the pride of a mother for her first-born, he would bedeck the darling without much regard to his own or other's cost. Nothing that would have pleased and does please other engineers is good enough for this work. All right, says Keystone, provided he allows the extra cost and extra time. . . . Meanwhile Keystone is only experiencing the fact that your man of real decided genius is the most difficult to deal with practically. But he will come out all right. The personal magnetism of the man accounts for much of the disappointment. It is impossible for most men not to be won over to his views for the time at least. Piper and Katte come to us after their sober second thought prevails and give way to expressions of fear of pecuniary results, while the same men in St. Louis seem incapable of telling the Captain how far he travels out of the safe practical path. . . . You must keep Eads up to requiring only what is reasonable and *in accordance* with *custom*.[16]

Carnegie had a grudging admiration for this "man of genius" who did not want a bridge "in accordance with custom" but rather a

274

custom-made bridge, which was quite another thing. In the end, Carnegie would regard the St. Louis bridge as one of his proudest achievements, but the parturition was prolonged and painful. One major source of difficulty between Eads and Carnegie was that Eads insisted upon steel for certain parts of the bridge: the major bolts on the piers and the staves that would make up the tubes to support the superstructure. Carnegie had made sure that his own company, Carnegie, Kloman & Company (the Union Mills), got the subcontract for all of the iron work on the bridge, and Eads's subsequent refusal to accept iron throughout the construction was particularly galling to Carnegie. It placed him in the embarrassing position of being involved in a highly publicized bridge enterprise which would proclaim to the world the superiority of steel over iron. In letter after letter, Carnegie hammered away at this question of the use of steel: the difficulty of finding a steel manufacturer who would agree to Eads's specifications, the unreliability of delivery, the exorbitant costs.[17] "You may all think that self-interest comes in here as we manfr. Iron," he wrote to Taussig, "but if so you are simply wrong. I have a much deeper interest at stake in rendering the St. Louis Bridge a success. . . ."[18]

The captain was adamant, however. The steel parts that met his exacting specifications were finally obtained, and the general agreement among professional engineers throughout the country that Eads had been right in his insistence upon steel may well have been a major factor in convincing Carnegie at this time that the Age of Steel was close at hand and could not be denied.

There were times during the long building period when Carnegie despaired of ever seeing the bridge successfully completed. In November 1871, six months after the original date set for completion had passed, and with the construction of the superstructure hardly begun, Carnegie wrote to J. Edgar Thomson: "I had an offer of 10,000$ for 1,000 shares of St. Louis Bridge Stock Saturday & have accepted it—because I am not in position to invest more in that enterprise. I do not believe Capt. Eads will get through without trouble—at all events I wished to get rid of so much liability. If you wish to join in the sale, I shall be glad to have you do so, although it looks like a great sacrifice at present. . . . The Bridge will cost at least 60% uncalled on Stock to finish it—say 2,400,000$ more. . . . In short, I am disgusted with the affair, throughout, & may have sold at panic prices. . . ." [19]

The distrust was mutual. Eads and Taussig were convinced that Carnegie, who faced them in many different roles—as a major stockholder in their own company, and as chief spokesman both for the contracting structural firm of Keystone and for the subcontracting iron producer of Carnegie, Kloman & Company—was a ubiquitous Little Jack Horner, intent upon pulling out the plums from all the pies. "It is not to be wondered at, perhaps," wrote Calvin Woodward in his history of the St. Louis bridge, "that the St. Louis Company was urged to break with the Keystone Company; on the other hand, one may perhaps find, in the intimate relation which the Keystone Company sustained to important railroad interests, a sufficient reason for the forbearance which was exercised." [20] This delicately worded reference by Woodward to "important railroad interests" was, of course, Carnegie's real source of strength in dealing with the St. Louis board in whatever guise he might appear before them. Behind Carnegie there were always Thomson and Scott, as Eads and Taussig knew only too well, and in spite of the sharp letters of criticism, of accusations made, and of excuses offered by both sides, there was never any question of the contract's being broken. Carnegie could hold fast to the agreement made by the St. Louis Bridge Company that "upon the completion and opening of the Bridge over the Mississippi River now in the course of construction, there will be due by said Company to Andrew Carnegie and associates . . . the sum of two hundred and fifty thousand." [21] As Carnegie had learned early in his business career, it was one's associates that counted.

In spite of all the difficulties encountered, the bridge slowly began to assume shape across the broad expanse of river: three magnificent arches of steel and iron, one 520 feet long and the other two each 502 feet long, containing the longest beams ever rolled in America. By December 1873 Carnegie could write to Junius Morgan, "I desire to report, that, extraordinary accidents excepted, the arches will all be closed ere this reaches you. . . . The entire work—Bridge, tunnel & approaches, are magnificent —only they cost double the money that should have been expended in such an enterprise. However, there can be no doubt as to the enormous revenues which will soon accrue—These must swell year by year without a corresponding increase of expenditure." [22] Carnegie, who only two years before had been eager to sell his stock in the bridge company at $10 a share, was now singing a different tune. In a letter written from London to Gardner McCandless, his business secretary, he counseled, "I would not be in a hurry to sell St. Louis B. Stock. It looks better than I expected here—don't sell without first telghing. me and entertain no offer below 33⅓." [23]

There remained one final dramatic encounter between Carnegie and the St. Louis Bridge Company before their association was terminated by the completion of the bridge. On 15 April 1874, the upper roadway was finished and it was agreed by all parties concerned that it should be opened to foot and carriage traffic three days later. But on the evening of 17 April, Carnegie informed the directors of the St. Louis Bridge Company that upon legal advice the Keystone Bridge Company would not deliver up the bridge or any portion of it "until all fees and bonuses due Keystone" had been paid. When the uninformed public showed up early the next morning, eager to be among the first to walk across the Mississippi into Illinois, they found the Keystone Bridge workers, led by the stalwart Colonel Piper, standing guard at the approaches to the bridge. Carnegie later recounted with amusement how he had had to resort to trickery to keep Piper in St. Louis. Piper, now that the bridge was finished, was eager to return to Pittsburgh, but on the pretext that he wanted Piper to help select a pair of horses for his sister-in-law, Carnegie managed to keep his general in the field. "We held the bridge. 'Pipe' made a splendid Horatius." The disgruntled crowds were turned away, and the exasperated officials of St. Louis could only stand helplessly by while the Keystone workers, under court authority, proceeded to tear up the east and west ends of the roadway that had been so recently completed.[24]

New acrimonious discussions and negotiations followed. One month later, the Keystone Bridge Company received the payment demanded, the roadway approaches were relaid, and on 23 May 1874 the first foot traffic crossed the bridge. On 2 July, General William Sherman drove the last spike connecting the bridge with the railway line on the shore. Then fourteen heavy locomotives with tenders full of coal and water moved slowly on the track across the bridge. "The excitement was intense as with almost breathless interest they [the crowds] watched the immense load move from the West Abutment upon the eastern span. To the unskilled it seemed incredible that the slender arches could support such a burden. Men swarmed over the engines, and to the crowd below a thousand lives seemed hanging by delicate threads." [25] Eads had planned well and the Keystone Bridge Company had built well. The bridge stood the test, and two days later, on the Fourth of July, St. Louis celebrated the completion of the bridge "in magnificent style." Senator B. Gratz Brown, nine years after he had introduced his bill in Congress for a bridge across the Mississippi at St. Louis, was, appropriately, the main orator of the day.

The building of the St. Louis bridge clearly reveals the intricate pattern of business activity with which Carnegie would surround most of his Keystone contracts. First, he would establish a sound alliance with those railroad companies who would be the chief clients of the completed bridge. Then, if possible, he would invest directly in the business syndicate holding the charter for the bridge. The contract for the bridge's superstructure would then be awarded to his Keystone Bridge Company, which would, in turn, subcontract the iron structural parts to Carnegie, Kloman & Company. For frosting, there would be the commission to Carnegie, bond salesman extraordinary, to negotiate the financing of the bridge in New York and Europe. The resulting business structure was as complicated and as carefully engineered as the bridge itself. Stress and support had to be determined with the same exactness and the same insistence upon perfection that Eads had shown in his engineering specifications. Had Carnegie been as willing as Eads to submit his blueprints to public scrutiny, the student of commerce might have found the St. Louis bridge enterprise as instructive as did the mechanical engineer.

Carnegie's most elaborate design in business structure, however, was the one he erected for the building of the Keokuk-Hamilton bridge across the Mississippi between Iowa and Illinois, some two hundred miles north of St. Louis. Here his interlocking business interests would make the celebrated Crédit Mobilier in

278

comparison appear as simple and straightforward as a cash purchase across the counter of a country general store.

Although the Keokuk bridge was a much simpler engineering feat than the St. Louis bridge, the demands it made upon Carnegie's talents were far greater, for in this instance Carnegie was involved not only in bridge construction but in the financing and building of a railroad across southern Iowa which would furnish the necessary traffic for the bridge. Almost as soon as he secured the contract for the bridge from the Keokuk and Hamilton Bridge Company on 10 December 1868, Carnegie started working on the more important project of railroad construction across the prairie to the Missouri River. The Iowa Contracting Company was formed—in which, as usual, Scott and Thomson were heavy subscribers—for "the building of a railroad from Keokuk through southern Iowa via Memphis, Missouri to Nebraska City, there connecting with the line almost built to Lincoln, thence to Fort Kearney on the Union Pacific Railroad line." [26] Scott's and Thomson's interest indicated that this new line would be subsidiary to the Pennsylvania Railroad empire and would strengthen the Pennsylvania's connections with the Union Pacific.

Carnegie had so many wheels within wheels in this operation —his direct investments in the Keokuk Hamilton Bridge Company itself (eventually he was to accept the presidency of the company),[27] that company's contract with the Keystone Bridge Company, Keystone's subcontract with Carnegie, Kloman & Company, the Iowa Contracting Company and its contracts with Carnegie and Kloman, as well as Carnegie's various commissions to sell bonds and stocks for both the Keokuk Bridge Company and the railroad contracting company—that even Carnegie's closest associates lost track of him in the maze. Tom Carnegie wrote in all innocence to Gardner McCandless, saying that he had received a substantial order for rails from an outfit unknown to him calling itself the Iowa Contracting Company. Did McCandless think that this was a sound enough concern to extend credit for the rails? McCandless replied: "We consider the Company good. . . . We would add that such men as Messrs. J. Edgar Thomson, Thos. A. Scott &c &c are interested in the building of the road, and the Treasurer of the Company is a reliable New York gentleman, a

Mr. Andrew Carnegie with whose name you are perhaps not unfamiliar." [28]

A similar pattern was followed farther to the north, in connection with the bridge across the Mississippi between Rock Island, Illinois, and Davenport, Iowa. Here, however, Carnegie was apparently not involved in the bridge building itself, but he was instrumental in the formation of the Davenport and St. Paul Construction Company which would build a railroad line north from Davenport through Rochester, Minnesota, to St. Paul, the capital of Minnesota. This construction company syndicate, which Carnegie served as treasurer, not only included the old familiar names of Thomson and Scott, but also Oakes Ames and John Duff, representing the Union Pacific interests, Benjamin Smith, president of the Columbus, Chicago and Indiana Central Railroad, and William Dennison, governor of Ohio.[29]

This was Carnegie's most ambitious venture yet in railroad building, but from the first the enterprise did not go well. There were serious disputes between William Holmes, an old friend of the Carnegie family from Allegheny who served as consulting engineer for the construction company, and Hiram Price of Davenport, president of the railroad company, over the route the railroad line should take through Iowa.[30] Presumably, the construction company had been formed as a separate corporation to serve the Davenport and St. Paul Railroad Company, but the list of investors in the two companies was nearly identical, and from the first it was the tail that wagged the dog. When Holmes offered convincing evidence that Price, whose interest was solely in the railroad company, was attempting to assert his independence from the dictates of the construction company, Scott, Carnegie, and the others stepped in. Price was forced to resign, Governor Dennison of Ohio became the titular head of the as yet unconstructed railroad, and George French, secretary for the construction company, became the vice president and actual authority in the railroad company. From then on, the railroad would serve only the interests of the construction company.[31]

Although Carnegie was deeply involved in the affairs of both the construction and the railroad companies, his major interest was in serving as the bond salesman for the railroad company. On 1 August 1871 he was authorized by Benjamin Smith, president of the construction company, to negotiate $6,000,000 of first mortgage bonds of the Davenport and St. Paul Railroad Company. Six thousand bonds at $1000 each were to be issued, and J. Edgar Thomson and Governor Dennison, very respectable fronts indeed, agreed to serve as trustees. The New York banking house of Drexel, Morgan was the American agency for the disbursement of funds.[32]

With this impressive support, Carnegie set out with a light heart for Frankfurt-am-Main to take on the redoubtable German banking house of Sulzbach Brothers. The negotiations were unduly protracted, for the brothers Sulzbach were understandably cautious about assuming the responsibility for the financing of such a large bond issue as Carnegie proposed. First, they demanded letters from leading officials not connected with the railroad company stating that the prospectus describing the venture and its potential value and future earnings was substantially true. George French, back in Davenport, Iowa, hurriedly provided signed statements from United States Circuit Court Judge John Dillon, Governor Carpenter of Iowa, and the mayor of Davenport, endorsing the prospectus.[33] This seemed to satisfy the Sulzbachs, but they then demanded that the construction company's assurance of equipping the line be guaranteed not only by the officers of the construction company but by a third party, inasmuch as "the construction company is itself the contracting party for the bond issue."[34] The fact that the list of directors and subscribers to the construction company was nearly identical to the list of names given as directors and stockholders in the railroad company made this request for a third party guarantor not unreasonable. Drexel, Morgan promised to furnish such a guarantor.

Then followed a lengthy period of negotiations in which the various documents requested by Sulzbach Brothers were studied by them and their lawyers with a Germanic meticulousness maddening to those back in the United States eagerly waiting for funds. To George French, especially, who continually had to put off the company's creditors in Davenport, these weeks of negotiation seemed endless. The Frankfurt bankers' caution even exhausted the patience of A. J. Drexel, who might have been expected to sympathize with such scrupulous attention to detail. "What do they mean by 'nature's act,'?" Drexel, in exasperation, wrote Carnegie in July, after three months of negotiating. "They don't know what they are about." [35] Twice Carnegie left Frankfurt to visit Scotland, thinking the matter finally settled, only to be called back for further consultation. "I enclose the two documents, which being properly executed, should close Davenport," Carnegie wrote to his secretary, Gardner McCandless. "It was very awkward having three of the former documents dated 'New York' instead of *Davenport*—please see that these are exactly right, also take occasion of meeting in Davenport to get copies of the other documents which Messrs. Sulzbach ask copies of, passed at *Davenport*." [36] J. P. Morgan was himself brought into the negotiations. "Your note received," Morgan wrote Carnegie, "and I immediately telegraphed Sulzbach in the exact words you sent me. I hope they will now be satisfied. . . . I hope you will see that their telegram to New York is simple. It should read, 'You can draw for Davenport.' There is no necessity of mixing up any points which may mislead them in New York and induce them to delay drawing. Don't let's have any more slip ups if they can be avoided. . . . Don't leave Frankfort again till all O.K." [37]

The only one who apparently did not lose his patience and temper during these negotiations was Carnegie himself. Having established contact with the leading German banking house, Carnegie, with an eye to future business, was determined to keep the relationship as harmonious as possible under these difficult circumstances. As always, he found the German temperament curiously attractive, and all the while that Drexel and Morgan were fuming over the delays, and French was desperately imploring Carnegie for funds, Carnegie served the Sulzbachs with the self-effacing eagerness of a courtier and met their most punctilious demands. No request for additional documentation seemed too absurd for him to comply with, no demands upon his time too much of an imposition, and finally, by the end of July, he could inform Drexel that the Sulzbachs had taken three million of the bonds and had accepted an option on the remaining three million, which he was confident they would take. Well satisfied with his three months' work, Carnegie left for his long-delayed vacation in Switzerland.[38]

Not all of Carnegie's bond negotiations turned out quite as satisfactorily as those with the Sulzbach brothers. There was that heady moment a year before the Sulzbach affair when Carnegie felt certain that he had caught the biggest financial fish of all, the Baring banking house, with his tempting bait of railroad securities, only to have it wriggle off the hook at the last moment. This negotiation involved a very complicated arrangement between the Allegheny Valley Railway and the Pennsylvania Railroad. Again J. Edgar Thomson was the central figure in the proceedings. Colonel William Phillips, president of the Allegheny Valley Railway, came to Carnegie one day to say that he needed money badly. He had $5,000,000 in bonds, bearing 7 per cent interest, guaranteed by the Pennsylvania Railroad, which he was eager to sell. Unfortunately, the bonds were redeemable not in gold but in American currency, which made them unmarketable on the foreign exchange, and Phillips had been unsuccessful in selling them to American banking houses at ninety cents on the dollar, which is what he demanded. Carnegie, who knew almost as much about the holdings of the Pennsylvania Railroad as Thomson himself, remembered that the Pennsylvania held a large amount of Philadelphia and Erie 6 per cent gold bonds in its treasury, and saw the brilliant prospect of an exchange that could result in a double commission for him on a $5,000,000 bond negotiation. He proposed to Thomson that the Pennsylvania Railroad exchange its P. and E. bonds with Phillips for his Allegheny Valley bonds, and thereby save 1 per cent interest on its bonds. Thomson agreed to the proposal. Phillips got the P. and E. gold bonds with the understanding that Carnegie should have the commission to sell them for the Allegheny Valley Railway on the foreign market.

Carnegie at once left for London and en route he decided to aim high. From Queenstown, he cabled Baring Brothers that he had for sale a security which "even your great house might unhesitatingly consider." Upon his arrival in London, he found a note at his hotel from Barings' requesting him to call. The next morning, Carnegie was ushered into the inner sanctum of British finance, and there he was at his most persuasive best. "Before I had left their banking house, I had closed an agreement by which they were to bring out this loan, and that until they sold the bonds at par, less their two and a half per cent commission, they would advance four millions of dollars at five per cent interest. The sale left me a clear profit of more than half a million dollars." [39]

Awed by his own success in selling the bonds at par, less the customary commission, when the highest price he had ever hoped for anywhere else had been 90 per cent of face value, Carnegie was eager to get signatures down on the contract. Russell Sturgis, Barings' representative, at that critical moment, however, was informed that Mr. Baring would be in town the next day, and Sturgis thought it only appropriate to have the great man himself sign the papers. If Mr. Carnegie would call at two o'clock the following day, the transaction would be completed, and Carnegie would have the honor of concluding the matter with Mr. Baring himself.

Carnegie, who for the preceding half-hour had been composing in his mind the exultant cable he would send Thomson and Phillips, left the banking house feeling vaguely uneasy. He decided not to send the cable until he had the signed contract in his pocket. He walked the four miles back from the banking house to his suite in the Langham Hotel. There he found a telegram message from Barings'. News had just been received that Chancellor Bismarck had impounded several hundred millions of sterling in Magdeburg, in order to protect the German mark. "The financial world was panic-stricken, and the Barings begged to say that under the circumstances they could not propose to Mr. Baring to go on with the matter. There was as much chance that I should be struck by lightning on my way home as that an arrangement agreed to by the Barings should be broken. And yet it was. It was too great a blow to produce anything like irritation or indignation. I . . . merely congratulated myself that I had not telegraphed Mr. Thomson." [40]

Carnegie had rarely been forced to consider the possibility that any political action in the United States might adversely affect his economic activities, and he must have been shocked to discover that in Europe the state could still autocratically alter the existing business situation. It would not be the last time, however, that a German ruler would upset his carefully laid plans.

With the $5,000,000 of bonds still unsold, Carnegie had no alternative but to turn to that banker who had never failed him, Junius Morgan. The arrangements were far less satisfactory to Carnegie than the Baring contract would have been, for Morgan was an old and experienced negotiator in American railroad securities. He took the bonds at 87 per cent of par.[41] Carnegie did have the satisfaction of seeing the bond sale greatly oversubscribed when Morgan offered the bonds on the open market. "For the 5,000,000—13,500,000$ was offered *in one day,*" Carnegie took pleasure in informing Phillips.[42] He also took a wry satisfaction in letting Baring Brothers know what they had missed: "Upon receipt of your telegram stating that you were not prepared to entertain any proposal I had no recourse but to accept an arrangement elsewhere. As you will no doubt have seen the Loan proved a decided success. Two & a half millions Sterling were offered at once, nevertheless, I find myself keenly regretting my failure to bring your house, & our great Pennsylvania Railroad Co. into business relations with each other. . . . Perhaps Mr. Thomson may entrust me with some of his loans in the future & I may succeed in my wish to do the business through your house." [43] In short, Carnegie would continue to keep a baited line in the water, for, good fisherman that he was, he had an axiom, "When one party to a bargain becomes excited, the other should keep cool and patient." [44] "I would keep steadily in view having a strong connection with the Barings," was his advice to Thomson.[45]

Actually, Carnegie had done rather well financially in this transaction even though he had not established a connection with Barings'. Not only did he earn his customary 2.5 per cent commission plus expenses on the sale of $5,000,000 of the Philadelphia and Erie bonds for the Allegheny Valley Railway, but the heavy oversubscription enabled him to persuade Thomson to sell an additional two million P. and E. bonds that the Pennsylvania Railroad held.[46] A short time later he also arranged, through Junius Morgan, the sale of the Allegheny Valley bonds which Thomson had obtained on exchange from Phillips for the P. and E. bonds.[47] For Thomson, however, Carnegie always gave a special discount commission charge of 1.25 per cent. "I am not extravagant in my views," Carnegie wrote Thomson in asking for his commission on the sale of the bonds, "having learned through many years experience in your service, that the Officers of the Great Corporation are paid only about one half of the value of their services in cash, and the other half in the honor which is conferred upon them by being connected with so great an institution. I would therefore propose that you settle with me upon the usual basis; give me one half of the ordinary two and a half per cent commission." [48] Thomson would have been justified in replying to this letter by pointing out that Carnegie got more than "honor by being connected with so great an institution." Nearly all of Carnegie's bond sales were in one way or another dependent upon the co-operation of Thomson and the Pennsylvania Railroad.

The most spectacular venture in railroad financing for Carnegie, Thomson, and Scott came early in 1871, when Carnegie was informed by George Pullman that the Union Pacific Railway needed $600,000 in cash immediately. Carnegie knew that the Union Pacific was in difficult financial straits, and he also knew that, in addition to the Pennsylvania Railroad, there were at least two other railroad syndicates, the New York Central and the so-called Boston group—which included such men as James Joy and John Forbes, who had financed the Michigan Central and the Hannibal and Burlington lines—who would be only too pleased to take advantage of the Union Pacific's difficulties to extend their interests to the West Coast.

Carnegie did not hesitate to seize this opportunity. He hurried to Philadelphia and laid his plan before Thomson. If Thomson would turn over to him enough securities of the Pennsylvania Railroad for him to secure a loan of $600,000 for the Union Pacific, he and Thomson would then be in a position to dictate their own terms to the directors of the Western railroad.

Thomson was dazzled by the prospects of this proposal. The Pennsylvania was in the midst of a great expansion program at this time and had extended its lines throughout the Middle West, so that it now controlled a network of roads from Chicago and St. Louis to the East Coast. Moreover, Scott had recently become a member of the board of directors of the Kansas Pacific, thus giving the Pennsylvania a dominant position on this line, which ran from Kansas City to Denver. The possibility of now exerting an even greater influence over the Union Pacific, which could in effect make the Pennsylvania the first truly transcontinental road in America, aroused the excitement of even the usually phlegmatic Thomson.

The transaction was quickly completed. Thomson gave Carnegie securities sufficient to secure the necessary loan for the Union Pacific. In return for this needed capital, the Union Pacific agreed to the election of Scott, Carnegie, and Pullman to the board of directors, and, as an added assurance of the Pennsylvania's dominant position within the Union Pacific, Scott was to be elected president of the board.

It was a major *coup d'état* for the Pennsylvania Railroad, and, in February 1871, when Scott's election to the presidency of the Union Pacific was officially announced, the railroad industry throughout the nation was shaken. *The Railroad Gazette* pronounced that the consequences of this move would be that the Pennsylvania Railroad would "control all the transcontinental traffic for many years to come." [49] The Boston financiers, the aging Cornelius Vanderbilt, and the wily Jay Gould suddenly realized that they had been outwitted by Thomson, Scott, and Carnegie.

The triumph of the Pennsylvania was short-lived, however. The Union Pacific, as security for the loan made to it by the Pennsylvania Railroad, had given to Thomson 30,000 shares of its own stock with a face value of $3,000,000, which Thomson had turned over to Carnegie for safekeeping. As part of the arrangement for the loan, Thomson, Scott, Carnegie, and Pullman, the four partners in the transaction, had been given an option by the Union Pacific to buy any or all of these shares at the current market price.

As might have been expected, the announcement that the Pennsylvania had moved in to shore up the shaky financial structure of the Union Pacific and that Scott, generally regarded as one of the most astute railroad managers in the country, had been elected president, had had an immediately favorable effect upon the value of the Union Pacific stock. The quoted price for the shares that were locked up in Carnegie's safe advanced enormously over the option purchase price which was still open to any of the four partners. The temptation to make a large and quick profit proved irresistible. As Carnegie would later remember the event, it was Scott who succumbed to this temptation:

> At this time I undertook to negotiate bonds in London for a bridge to cross the Missouri at Omaha, and while I was absent upon this business Mr. Scott decided to sell our Union Pacific shares. I had left instructions with my secretary that Mr. Scott,

as one of the partners in the venture, should have access to the vault . . . but the idea that these should be sold, or that our party should lose the splendid position we had acquired in connection with the Union Pacific, never entered my brain.

I returned to find that, instead of being a trusted colleague of the Union Pacific directors, I was regarded as having used them for speculative purposes. No quartet of men ever had a finer opportunity for identifying themselves with a great work than we had; and never was an opportunity more recklessly thrown away. Mr. Pullman was ignorant of the matter and as indignant as myself, and I believe that he at once invested his profits in the shares of the Union Pacific. I felt that much as I wished to do this and to repudiate what had been done, it would be unbecoming and perhaps ungrateful in me to separate myself so distinctly from my first of friends, Mr. Scott.

At the first opportunity we were ignominiously but deservedly expelled from the Union Pacific board. It was a bitter dose for a young man to swallow. And the transaction marked my first serious difference with a man who up to that time had the greatest influence with me, the kind and affectionate employer of my boyhood, Thomas A. Scott. Mr. Thomson regretted the matter, but, as he said, having paid no attention to it and having left the whole control of it in the hands of Mr. Scott and myself, he presumed that I had thought best to sell out.[50]

Carnegie wrote this account many years later, long after all the other principals in the transaction had died. His memory of the event was seriously at fault. The existing records do not support his claim of wounded innocence and his attempt to shift the entire blame upon Scott. For, on 6 March 1871, Carnegie wrote from London to John Duff, "Please place 11,000 shares of Union Pacific which you hold as Trustee for me with Messrs. J. Morgan Sons Bankers." [51] One month later, he received confirmation from his secretary, Gardner McCandless, that 11,250 shares of Union Pacific shares had been sold, and that "I will today invest proceeds 343,799.94 as you ordered in Govt. 6% currency." To this letter was appended a receipt, dated 15 April 1871, and signed by Scott, stating that he had "received of Messrs. Morton, Bliss and Company their check for $240,000 on account of sale of Union Pacific stock sold under Mr. Carnegie's instructions." [52]

The following month, Carnegie wrote to Pullman, enclosing a

check for $16,375.96 and 100 shares of Union Pacific stock. "You will see we have sold on our joint account, 29,600 shares of stock, retaining of the 30 thousand, 100 apiece—400 shares. There is still a balance in the hands of Messrs. Morton, Bliss and Company of $60 thousand drawing interest from April 15th and 5 thousand shares of stock." [53]

It would appear that, with the possible exception of Thomson, the sale of the Union Pacific shares hardly came as a surprise to any of the four partners, least of all to Carnegie. What probably did come as a shock to Scott, Carnegie, and Pullman was the retaliatory action by the other directors of the Union Pacific in dismissing the three from the board. This punishment bore the most heavily on Scott, who had the most at stake both in position and in power. He irrevocably lost his opportunity to extend the control of the Pennsylvania Railroad into the Far West, and, even worse, he was replaced as president of the Union Pacific by H. F. Clark, Cornelius Vanderbilt's son-in-law. The New York Central quickly filled the vacuum left by the abrupt departure of those who had represented the Pennsylvania Railroad.[54] Scott was deeply hurt by his public humiliation, and Carnegie was at least correct in saying that the unfortunate sale of the Union Pacific shares was the cause of "the first serious difference" between him and his former patron.

Aside from the personal embarrassment of the public disclosure of this transaction, Carnegie and Pullman had little cause for complaint. With the ousting of Scott the Union Pacific stock immediately dropped in value, and Pullman was able to buy back a large part of his share of the stock at a considerably lower price than that for which he had sold it. Carnegie had a better use for the profit he had made on the transaction. He informed his brother that he had available from his sale of Union Pacific securities some ready cash "and can lend you $80 thousand if you can use it." [55]

Carnegie, to be sure, must have had some sincere regrets over having lost the most powerful position of authority that he had yet achieved within the railroad world, for during the brief time he had held it his directorship in the Union Pacific had been a source of immense personal satisfaction to him. He had written exultantly to a business associate when the Pennsylvania–Union

Pacific transaction had first been announced, "You see we have Union Pacific. I go on the Executive Committee in March." [56] It was the pride of a field marshal who, by a brilliant maneuver, had surrounded and captured an entire army intact. During the few short months of triumph, Carnegie had regarded the Union Pacific as a personal possession. He had delighted in making casual references to it ("On Saturday, the Executive Committee of our Union Pacific meets at my office") [57] to impress associates in his many other business enterprises.

Now all this had been lost, and he had in effect been court-martialed, found guilty, and drummed out of the service of the Union Pacific by his fellow directors. It was a sobering and most unusual experience, for one of Carnegie's great talents in business was his sensitive, almost intuitive perceptiveness of the boundaries beyond which one could not step with impunity. To most of his associates, including his own brother, Carnegie seemed audacious to the point of foolhardiness. To others, such as Scott, who more than once was to transgress the permissible limits, he seemed incredibly lucky. But to Carnegie himself, it was simply a question of good, if uncommon, sense. There was a time to move boldly, a point to stop, and, on occasion, a time to retreat. He did not brood over the Union Pacific and its lost opportunities, as Scott did, but he was not to forget its lesson.

There was no time for brooding. His ejection from the Union Pacific came at a moment when the insistent demands of his many other activities could not be ignored or postponed. Carnegie continued to "push inordinately," but never blindly, in all directions. As his reputation was enhanced by the bridges and bonds for St. Louis, Omaha, Hannibal, Steubenville, and Keokuk, so did the permissible boundaries expand, allowing him to make ever greater demands upon his prospective clients. Writing to A. G. Eastman, regarding a proposed bridge at Hartford, Connecticut, Carnegie made his position quite clear:

> The control of the Railroads to Hartford must be absolutely ours through a majority of the shares—otherwise, we might be left with several millions of an investment in a Bridge, without obtaining an outlet for our traffic. It would, no doubt, be the

aim of rival interests to place us in just this fix. . . . We must own a majority of the Stock of the connecting Lines, that is certain, & I shall hope to hear soon from you upon this subject. The Stock in question has no value without the Bridge. If the Lines are made links in the Great Trunk Line between New England & the West, one half of the Stock will inevitably become far more valuable than the whole. At all events we cannot risk building a Bridge & being left without an outlet.[58]

No opportunity for a possible bridge contract was too slight for him to pass by. "Of course you are in communication with the New York, New Haven and Hartford Railway Company," he wrote to one of his subordinates at Keystone, "in regard to the Bridge at Coscob [sic] that has been recently burned." [59] Nor was any job thought to be too large, difficult, or remote for Keystone to handle. Carnegie was a member of the committee in charge of the exhibition buildings for the Centennial Exposition in Philadelphia in 1876, and, almost single-handedly, he persuaded the committee to change its original plans for the construction of the main exhibition hall from a wooden structure to an iron and steel structure and to give the construction contract to Keystone and the iron order to the Union Mills. It was an impressive advertisement for iron and led to Keystone's securing a few years later the contract to build the skeleton for the first steel-frame office building in America.[60] Carnegie was the successful low bidder for the superstructure for the Brooklyn Bridge in 1878,[61] and Keystone received contracts to build bridges in Mexico and South America, and a lighthouse at Tampico, Mexico.[62]

Carnegie's opportunism, which would frequently give him the initial advantage over his competitors, is but one factor, however, in explaining his remarkable success as an entrepreneur in these years. Carnegie knew that successful salesmanship must be reinforced by something more substantial than quick wit and audacity if there were to be repeated opportunities for advancement. As the chief salesman for all of his many enterprises, he insisted that he should be provided with a product of superior quality, for however sensitive he might be to production costs, he regarded quality of even greater importance. Writing to Linville concerning the projected bridge over the Susquehanna, Carnegie stressed this point:

> I agree with you that it is vital to the interest of our Keystone Bridge Co. that we should get this contract to keep our men together. It is out of the question to expect profit out of it: However this may be, we must maintain our policy: put nothing but the best triple rolled iron in our structures, and let concerns like the Edgemoor, which buy the cheapest and meanest stuff in the merchant market, run their course.
> We cannot afford to have an accident to one of our bridges . . . if we stand firm on quality, we must win.[63]

When Keystone did not meet these standards that he had set, he was not slow in berating Linville for this failure: "If the Keystone Br. Co. has come to the pass of having to excuse work which does not give satisfaction to its customers, I wish to know it. For one I shall protest against it. No matter at what cost we must not go further in the direction which almost compelled the Erie RR Co. to omit sending us plans to bid upon—Go and fix this so it gives satisfaction. . . ."[64]

He was equally selective in the type of bond that he would accept on commission for sale to the financial houses of Europe. He refused all assignments that struck him as being too speculative in nature. "It would not do for me to try London on any mining scheme," he wrote Edward Jay Allen, who had wanted him to float a loan for the development of a mine in Utah. "I must stick to my role of first class steady-going Security man—very adverse to anything speculative, or 'too good.' Among the class I have been dealing with you frighten if anything much beyond six per cent is talked of."[65]

At a time when business too often seemed to borrow both its ethics and its techniques from the fast-talking, quick-moving hawker of bottled snake-oil, Carnegie's standards for quality were certain to attract attention. For Carnegie himself there was not only the assurance that such standards were good business; there was also the kind of personal satisfaction in the completed project which the Drews, Goulds, and Fisks were never to know.

292

Seldom did Carnegie's various enterprises come into conflict with each other, but in those rare instances in which they did, Carnegie did not hesitate to force upon them a disciplined order that would secure the greatest benefit to his investments in their totality. On one occasion, in 1871, when Carnegie was in Pittsburgh visiting the Keystone works, he noticed that a large upsetting machine for the manufacture of iron links had been ordered by Keystone for its plant. This could only mean that Keystone intended to produce its own iron parts rather than to obtain them from Carnegie's Union Iron Mills as it had in the past. Furious at this indication of independence, Carnegie wrote to Linville that such intramural competition could not continue:

> The Union Iron Mills to meet your wants, constructed machinery and risked the experiment. . . . Under every rule recognized among fair men—unless you and the Mills had been competitors in trade—an attempt to interfere with what thus became a branch of business to which they had made themselves fairly entitled, would have been considered injudicious—scarcely creditable.
>
> But you are not competitors; on the contrary you are necessary to each other—the true policy is to work together. Each has its special business and happily both have been too successful to render it necessary for one to interfere with the other. . . . Let me ask you to consider whether the profits to be made by entering into competition with a friendly interest, are sufficient to counter-balance the weightier considerations connected therewith. . . . As a Director in your Company, I might also protest as in my judgment it is as unwise, as unfair, as it is unnecessary and uncalled for, that we should attack our neighbor in this manner. . . .[66]

When, after this protest, Keystone still gave no indication of abandoning its plans for self-sufficiency, Carnegie resorted to a more direct attack.

> I met Tom, Phipps & Schroyer at Cresson Sunday & as we unanimously decided that we were prepared to undergo any pecuniary sacrifice to protect our property from the proposed interference, I have nothing to do but resign. . . . We have ap-

plied for an injunction against you & if defeated there we propose to have a settlement of a/c's with Keystone Co. & let her seek elsewhere what we have hitherto supplied her. Our Mills can run half time if necessary, that we can stand . . . but one thing we can't & won't do, no set of men shall attempt to render any part of our property useless & succeed, if we can help it. The Keystone Bridge Co. never took so dear a step as this will prove, I think.[67]

Against these threats of boycott by the Union Mills and, even more alarming, of Carnegie's resignation and demand for a full settlement of his large interest in the company, Keystone had no alternative but to yield. The appropriately named upsetting machine was dismantled and sent back to the company from which it had been ordered. Keystone from then on stayed in line and dutifully bought its iron parts from the Union Mills. There was to be no internal competition within Carnegie's community of interests.

This brief encounter between Keystone and the Union Mills, occurring when it did, is also significant in pointing up the shift that was beginning to take place in Carnegie's established order of priorities. Heretofore, it had been Keystone that had occupied the preferred position in Carnegie's hierarchy of business interests. The Union Mills, into which he had been drawn by quite fortuitous circumstances and which he had regarded as being more Tom's concern than his own, had now apparently become Carnegie's central interest. No longer were the mills simply a source of supply for Keystone, rather Keystone had become a market for the Union Mills, and in a head-on collision between his bridge and iron interests, it was now Keystone that had to yield to the dictates of the iron manufacturer.

Few, if any, of Carnegie's closest associates in 1872 would have suspected that at the very moment when his business activities appeared to be expanding in every direction Carnegie was actually entering a transitional phase that would lead to a contraction and a consolidation of his investments, talents, and interests into one area of concentration—a kind of reverse metamorphosis, in which the butterfly would abandon its imaginal state of flitting for chrysalid security.

Apparently Carnegie himself at first was only dimly aware of this transition. It was not an abrupt change, and for several years he was to keep an active interest in telegraph lines and sleeping cars and those railroads in which he had already invested. But the days of restless searching were over. When he returned from England in 1872, determined to build a new Bessemer steel plant to replace the Freedom Iron and Steel Company, he was making a commitment that would prove to be total and irrevocable. In time, he would look back on these years of commercial exploration, if he remembered them at all, as the quixotic adventures of a stranger. By then, he would have coined his axiom of putting all his "eggs in one basket and then watching that basket." He would pontificate solemnly to rising young entrepreneurs: "I have no faith in the policy of scattering one's resources, and in my experience I have rarely if ever met a man who achieved preeminence in money-making—certainly never one in manufacturing— who was interested in many concerns. The men who have succeeded are men who have chosen one line and stuck to it. . . . My advice to young men would be not only to concentrate their whole time and attention on the one business in life in which they engage, but to put every dollar of their capital into it. . . . As for myself my decision was taken early. I would concentrate upon the manufacture of iron and steel and be master in that." [68] And with the reformed inebriate's intolerance of the saloon, he would in later years rail against speculation as the gravest of all business sins.

This radical transition in Carnegie's business attitudes and practices was effected by a variety of circumstances, some of which Carnegie did not clearly perceive and could not have himself articulated. Exciting and financially rewarding as these past years had been, and superb as his talent was as a juggler in keeping so many different enterprises whirling about him at once, still Carnegie must have realized that much of his success had depended upon sheer luck and that to continue this whirligig game indefinitely was to court disaster. There had been enough slip-ups and minor failures to serve as warnings that Carnegie was putting his luck to too severe a test as it was. Most of the railroad ventures in the Middle West had turned out to be dismal failures. There were protracted delays in the actual construction of both the Davenport and St. Paul and the Missouri-Iowa-Nebraska lines, quarrels and litigation with rival lines such as the Des Moines Valley Railroad over right-of-way and bridge approaches, inept management and default on the subsidies promised by various communities along the projected routes. Debts and expenses mounted, and long before the final chapters of these ventures were written in the courts, Carnegie was trying to extricate himself as painlessly and inexpensively as possible from these financial embarrassments. In 1878 he demanded that Henry Hill, the current superintendent of the Iowa Contracting Company in charge of constructing the Missouri-Iowa-Nebraska line, initiate bankruptcy proceedings, as the company had debts outstanding of $233,500, including a debt to Carnegie himself of $40,000.[69]

The Davenport and St. Paul Construction Company and its railroad affiliate had an even more protracted and painful demise. The Sulzbach Brothers, for all the care they had taken in collecting notarized affidavits, had not been able to secure that kind of warranty which would guarantee successful and honest management. All of the bright promises that had been solemnly sworn to by such reputable citizens as J. Edgar Thomson, the governor of Iowa, and the mayor of Davenport eventually proved to be as bankrupt as the companies themselves. Refusing to accept without protest their unhappy fate of having exchanged gold for pyrite, the Sulzbachs took their case to court and sought to collect full indemnity for their loans from the officers and trustees of the Davenport and St. Paul venture, including Carnegie. They were joined in their suit by several American investors in the Davenport and St. Paul Construction Company. Starting in 1874, the cases dragged on through the state courts in Iowa and the Federal court in Philadelphia for many years. Carnegie felt that, after six years of fruitless litigation, the Sulzbachs should become discouraged, and then they would give up. "The truth probably is," Carnegie's secretary wrote to one of the co-defendants, "that the Germans have spent all the money they propose to in these useless suits and they will soon die the death they deserve." [70] But the Sulzbachs seemed to be as immortal and inexorable in their pursuit of justice as Zeus himself. It was not until 1884 that a judgment by the Federal Court of Appeals finally dismissed the claims against Carnegie and the other stockholders in the company, who were held to be not liable for the debts of the corporation. J. Edgar Thomson, as a trustee for the ill-fated construction company and railroad, was not to escape as easily, however. Although Thomson had died in 1875, while the suits were still making their slow way through the courts, his estate was held liable for the contractual agreements. "I am sorry that in congratulating you, I have to add what I know will pain you to hear," George Dallas, Carnegie's lawyer, wrote immediately after the Court of Appeals decision. "Mr. Thomson's Estate has been held liable and the Court has referred it to a Master to fix the amount of liability. It will probably be about one million dollars." [71] The court had held that Thomson, as one of two trustees, was in quite a different relationship to the corporation than a stockholder, whose liability was limited to his investment. Fortunately for Carnegie, Thomson had not lived long enough to witness this concluding act to their long and involved business association. Mr. Scott's Andy had led his former employers down many a path with glib promises of pots of gold at the end of the trail. Being mere mortals, Scott and Thomson had been more often mocked than rewarded. As is always true in the Gaelic folk tales, it is the leprechaun who escapes with his gold intact.

When Scott and Thomson on occasion tried to reverse the plot, however, and draw Carnegie more deeply into speculative ventures of their own choosing, Carnegie showed all the canny suspicion of his Highland ancestors toward a Lowlander's smooth blandishments. It was Carnegie's refusal to endorse one of Scott's speculative schemes that was to cause the final break between the two men.

So unexpected and complete was this severance of ties between two men, whose alliance had long been regarded in the business world as something as fixed and dependable as that bond which united the Rothschild family, that it is not surprising there was much conjecture as to the cause for the rupture. A favorite explanation among the romantically inclined was that the break resulted from Carnegie's introducing Scott, the handsome widower, to Anne Dike Riddle, the Pittsburgh girl in whom Carnegie himself apparently was very much interested. In a matter of weeks Scott had won the girl's affection, and Carnegie's "best girl" had become the second Mrs. Scott. But those who thought that rivalry in love had separated the two men knew little about Carnegie's nature. This incident had had no effect on the relationship between the two men. Carnegie at the time had told his friend Tom Miller, "If anybody else in the world can win her, I don't want her!" [72] Indeed, Carnegie, instead of being upset, seemed to give his warm blessing to the marriage. At this point in his life he wanted no close alliance with any one woman, and he probably was grateful to Scott for having extricated him from what might have become too demanding an affair.

Several of Carnegie's less successful investments which he had induced Scott to enter with him had served to cool their friendship, and both had been somewhat embittered by the unfortunate consequences resulting from their speculative sale of Union Pacific stock. But they had entered these ventures together, had stood by and supported each other at the time, and their firm alliance apparently had not been shaken. It was not until the panic year of 1873, when, in the greatest financial crisis of his life, Scott turned to Carnegie for help and Carnegie refused, that their alliance was completely and permanently dissolved.

Scott, to be sure, had only himself to blame for his financial difficulties. As expansive and optimistic as Carnegie, Scott lacked the discretion of his former protégé. Unlike Carnegie, he was never cautious enough to make sure in advance that in any investment his liability was limited to that amount which, if things went wrong, he could afford to lose. Like most of his business contemporaries, Scott's method of measuring the depth of the water was to dive in head first. Carnegie preferred to use a sounding line.

Scott's most spectacular plunge, which was to lead to his difficulties the following year, had taken place in 1872, when he and several other Eastern railroad financiers took over the affairs of the all but defunct Texas and Pacific Railroad. This company had been organized soon after the Civil War and had been given a generous land grant for the construction of a rail line from the Louisiana-Texas border west to San Diego. Not a mile of track had been laid, however, when Scott assumed the presidency and the financial control of the company. With his usual enthusiasm, Scott envisaged a new southwestern railroad empire that would not only cover the vast state of Texas from Texarkana to El Paso and westward to the Pacific, but would also make connections by means of subsidiary lines to St. Louis and there, via his Pennsylvania Railroad line, have access to the East Coast. It was to be Scott's challenge to, and, he hoped, revenge against, the board of directors of the Union Pacific for having summarily dismissed him from the presidency of that company the year before. He was willing to gamble everything he had on the success of the venture, and he expected Carnegie, his companion in exile from the Union Pacific, to give him strong support with both his money and his managerial talents.

At the same time that Scott was offering and expecting Carnegie to seize the opportunity to enter railroad building on a scale that would make Carnegie's ventures in Iowa and Minnesota seem inconsequential by comparison, Carnegie received another invitation for an even more spectacular railroad venture from a quite unexpected source. There had been at least one railroad financier in America who had been favorably impressed with Scott's and Carnegie's conduct in the Union Pacific stock-selling affair. Carnegie had demonstrated a shrewdness at the expense of ethical considerations that Jay Gould thoroughly appreciated, and so, to Carnegie's surprise, Gould made a direct approach to him one morning in the Windsor Hotel with the proposition that he, Gould, would buy the Pennsylvania Railroad and give Carnegie one-half of all the profits if Carnegie would manage the railroad for him.[73]

At that very moment Carnegie was considering the prospects of entering into the manufacture of Bessemer steel on a large scale. And now he was presented with two opportunities for resuming a career in railroads in a much more important capacity than he had ever held before. Either offer promised to restore the prestige he had lost with his dismissal from the Union Pacific board: he could join Scott in building up a potential transcontinental rival, or, under Gould's sponsorship, he could take the Pennsylvania away from Scott and Thomson and emerge as the most powerful railroad entrepreneur in the country. He would then be in a position to assert his power over the Union Pacific, for Gould had already made investments in Union Pacific stock and undoubtedly had begun to lay plans for his eventual acquisition of that line.[74]

Interesting as these propositions were, Carnegie was wary of both. Vindication was not so sweet as to be purchased at the price of prudence, and Carnegie had serious doubts about both Gould as a partner and Scott as an empire builder. Nevertheless, these offers, coming at this particular time, did serve a useful purpose, for they forced Carnegie to consider the direction he wished to take in his pursuit of wealth and power. If he accepted either Gould's or Scott's offer, it would mean in effect a continuation and intensification of his present life, with all of the prospects for quick profits, the thrills of speculative gambling, and the hazards, as well. Against these proposals, Carnegie had the alternative of abandoning his extensive business investments in order to concentrate upon one field of manufacturing. There were great hazards in this course too, for if the handle on this one basket should give way all of the eggs would be broken. But at least the basket would be in his own hands, and his fortune would not be in hostage to others.

Carnegie, always keenly aware of changes in the wind, must also have sensed that the future belonged not to the freebooter but to the specialist. American business, which in the 1860's had been inchoate and amorphous, was now assuming a form and structure. Men like Gould, and to a certain degree, Carnegie himself, who had profited enormously in the chaos that had resulted from flinging down railway tracks whenever a land grant had been obtained, or digging an oil well wherever a dowsing stick dipped downward, would in the future have to yield to the planners and the experts. As American business became bigger, order would most certainly be imposed, and the businessman had the choice of being with the imposers or with the imposed-upon.

An even more important consideration to Carnegie than the question of business success—although the two could not be entirely separated—was the question of his own self-esteem and respect. One could draw a moral from the contrasting careers of two men with whom Carnegie was well acquainted, George Pullman and Jay Gould. Both men, to be sure, were products of this age of business. Both had been equally ruthless in their determination to succeed, and neither could point to many instances in his conduct of business affairs that would have met the standards of Christian ethics. Yet there was a basic difference, both in their

300

goals and their achievements, which could be given an ethical evaluation.

For Gould, the meaning of life could be expressed in a simple formula: wealth equals success. There were no qualifying plus or minus values on either side of the equation. How one achieved wealth in no way affected the positive value of success, and since, in this era of unregulated and amoralistic business practice, it was often as easy to achieve wealth by destroying as by building, distinctions between looting and laboring were meaningless. One built an unnecessary railroad only to profit from its losses, or issued shares not to provide capital for industry but to sell the water that was in them to those stupid enough to drink. Fortunately, the hunting ground was amply stocked with sheep, and it mattered little whether they were gored to death by the bulls or clawed to death by the bears. This was the credo that Gould was asking Carnegie to accept as his own.

For Pullman, however, the formula would have to be stated in a somewhat more complex form: wealth plus pride of achievement equal success. Pullman had clawed his way to the top at the expense of many associates and competitors, but at the same time he had given to the public something it had wanted, and he had insisted upon certain standards that the public, in demanding his product, had given its approval. For this reason, Pullman's success had a qualitative difference from Gould's. Pullman's name would become a common noun in the languages of the Western World. The most that Gould might hope for would be to have his name forgotten long before his accumulated wealth could be spent by him and his heirs.

To Carnegie, who had taken as his personal motto "Thine own reproach alone do fear," the distinction between the two equations was important. Even though he had ignored his own injunctions, expressed in the memorandum he had written to himself five years before, Carnegie nevertheless had not suppressed the introspective self-concern that had forced him to write that remarkable document. And so he rejected Gould's offer with thanks. He gave as his reason that "although Mr. Scott and I had parted company in business matters, I would never raise my hand against him" (i.e., by being a party to Gould's plan to take control of the Pennsylvania away from Scott and Thomson).[75] This sense of loyalty to Scott and the past was certainly a basic consideration in Carnegie's decision, but the question of the future must also have been a major determining factor. "In fact the whole speculative field was laid out before me in its most seductive guise," Carnegie would later write in recalling this incident. "All these allurements I declined." [76]

Carnegie's sense of loyalty to Scott was not so strong, however, as to compel him to accept Scott's offer to participate fully in his plans for the Texas and Pacific Railroad. With reluctance, and only because Scott had reserved it for him in advance, Carnegie did buy $250,000 worth of shares in the company, but all other demands from Scott for him to give more of his talents and money to the enterprise Carnegie adamantly refused.

When the business panic of 1873 hit, Scott and his associates found themselves in a desperate situation. For the preceding year, their Texas and Pacific construction company had been subsisting largely on temporary short-term loans at high rates of interest which Scott and his fellow investors had lavishly endorsed. Now their creditors, forced by the panic to meet the demands of their own debts, insisted upon payment. Scott's only solution to the difficulty he found himself in was to negotiate new loans and to call upon his friends with capital assets to endorse his notes. The friend he thought of first was, of course, Carnegie. Carnegie had both the assets and the credit rating that would make his endorsement of Scott's notes invaluable in the negotiation of new loans. A meeting in Philadelphia of the several men most involved in the Texas and Pacific enterprise was arranged for late September, and Scott urged Carnegie to attend. Carnegie did so, and Scott wasted no time in putting the matter squarely before his longtime associate. Junius Morgan and Company had agreed to the renewal of a large loan that had fallen due, provided that Carnegie would join the other parties to the loan and endorse the notes. Carnegie's answer was flat and unequivocal:

> I declined. I was then asked whether I would bring them all to ruin by refusing to stand by my friends. It was one of the most trying moments of my whole life. Yet I was not tempted for a moment to entertain the idea of involving myself. . . . I told Mr. Scott that I had done my best to prevent him from be-

ginning to construct a great railway before he had secured the necessary capital. I had insisted that thousands of miles of railway lines could not be constructed by means of temporary loans. Besides, I had paid two hundred and fifty thousand dollars cash for an interest in it . . . but nothing in the world would ever induce me to be guilty of endorsing the paper of that construction company or of any other concern than our own firm.[77]

His own pleas having failed, Scott urged Thomson to use his influence with Carnegie. Thomson, who was also deeply involved in the Texas and Pacific affair, wrote Carnegie a strong note demanding his co-operation. "You should tax your friends, if you have not the means yourself, to meet the calls for the Texas concern." Thomson admitted that Scott was largely to blame for the difficulty: "The scheme in itself was good enough, but it has been most wofully [sic] mismanaged financially, Scott having acted upon his faith in his guiding star, instead of sound discretion. But," Thomson continued, "Scott should be carried until his return, and you of all others should lend your helping hand when you run no risk—If you cannot go further. P.S. I shall be glad to get out of this Texas matter with a loss of three times your subscription." [78]

But Carnegie was as impervious to Thomson's appeal as he had been to Scott's. A few days later he discovered how right he had been to deny their appeals. Knowing that Carnegie had made an investment in the Texas and Pacific, and that he and Scott had always been deeply involved in each other's financial affairs, businessmen in Pittsburgh naturally assumed that he had been caught up as short in the current debacle as Scott himself. Since Carnegie had borrowed heavily from the Exchange Bank of Pittsburgh for the construction of his new steel plant at Braddock, the directors of the bank were quite naturally disturbed. They sent a wire to Carnegie in New York, asking him to come to Pittsburgh immediately to discuss his loans outstanding with their bank.

Carnegie took the first train to Pittsburgh. There in the directors' board room, quietly and self-righteously, he answered all of their questions without a moment's hesitation. The answers he gave were not what the bankers had expected to hear. His total commitment to Scott and the Texas and Pacific Railroad was $250,000 of stock in the construction company, which he had paid for in cash. He stood in danger of losing that, to be sure, but it was his alone to lose, and he thought in the long run even that money would be secure, for Texas was a vast and potentially profitable area for railroad development in the future. He expounded on his faith that American business would weather the temporary stress of panic, and he must have enjoyed the bankers' squirming impatience as he delivered this short homily of patriotic optimism, for he knew how eager they were to ask the next question. Surely, they thought, if he had not borrowed money in order to invest directly in the Texas and Pacific, he must have endorsed some of Scott's notes and thereby endangered his own assets and property—for the bankers had heard of Scott's desperate efforts to obtain endorsers. Again, Carnegie could reply with a little sermon—this one against note endorsement, which he regarded as a dangerous evil, comparable to gambling on the stock exchange. Any stories in circulation to the effect that he had backed Mr. Scott's notes were false. He had refused Scott's pleas, even though he had found it very painful to deny the claims of friendship that Scott could make upon him. In short, Carnegie had avoided the pitfalls into which his closest associates had fallen. The bankers' loans were safe, and with his own capital and assets secure, Carnegie was prepared to take full advantage of the economic depression to expand his manufacturing interests. In the words of his biographer, Burton Hendrick, Carnegie "rose from the cross-examination a new man—new, at least, in the estimation of his own community. The steelmaker whom the bankers had regarded as the weakest and most likely to collapse with hard times suddenly appeared as practically the only one who could successfully ride the storm." [79]

Carnegie had followed a financially sound course, to be sure, in refusing to endorse Scott's notes. It is doubtful that, even if he had backed the loans the Texas and Pacific sought, his backing would have made any significant difference in Scott's futile efforts to save the company from bankruptcy. Carnegie would certainly have endangered his other investments and those of his partners at the Union Mills, and in the long run all he would have contributed would have been companionship for Scott's misery. Yet one can believe Carnegie when he later said that "it gave more pain than all the financial trials to which I had been subjected up to that time." [80] Carnegie had paid a high price for financial solvency. It had cost him the friendship of the one man who, since they first met in O'Reilly's Telegraph Office twenty years before, had been closer to him and more responsible for his success in the business world than any other person. Scott's failure, and the bitterness he felt toward his former friend, continued to haunt Carnegie long after Scott's death. In time, Carnegie would find justification for his personal decision not to endorse Scott's notes by impersonalizing and elevating it to the position of a cardinal principle of business virtue. In a commencement address, "The Road to Business Success," delivered at the Curry Commercial College of Pittsburgh in June 1885, he warned the students "against three of the gravest dangers which will beset you in your upward path." These deadly dangers were drinking liquor, speculating on the stock exchange, and "the perilous habit of indorsing—all the more dangerous, inasmuch as it assails one generally in the barb of friendship. It appeals to your generous instincts, and you say, 'How can I refuse to lend my name to assist a friend?' It is because there is so much that is true and commendable in that view that the practice is so dangerous." Nevertheless, Carnegie continued, a man has a greater and more honorable responsibility toward his own capital and his own debts. "When a man in debt indorses for another, it is not his own credit or his own capital he risks, it is that of his creditors. He violates a trust. Mark you then, never indorse until you have the cash means not required for your debts, and never indorse beyond those means. . . . I beseech you avoid liquor, speculation and indorsement. Do not fail in either, for liquor and speculation are the Scylla and Charybdis of the young man's business sea, and indorsement his rock ahead." [81] Probably no one in the audience understood why Carnegie spoke with such an emotional fervor against note endorsement. But Carnegie did.

The question Carnegie never answered, in all his later self-justification for his failure to help Scott, was why he did not, as Thomson suggested, ask his friends to help, if he felt that he himself was not in a position to do so. This action would not have directly affected either his capital or his debts. The problem may have been that by Carnegie's "friends" Thomson probably meant Junius Morgan and his son, and Carnegie would not have wanted to lose their good will and confidence by persuading them to back what he knew was a highly questionable project. He was counting too much on the financial help of the Morgans to implement his own plans for expansion.

In any event, the pain, if not a sense of guilt, persisted, and even when Carnegie was an old man, writing his autobiography, he could not ignore this episode as he did the many other unpleasant incidents of the past. He felt compelled to recount the whole story and once again justify his decision. His concluding sentence to the story showed that the pain was still there: "I fear Mr. Scott's premature death can measurably be attributed to the humiliation which he had to bear." [82] This passage is notable for being one of those rare instances in his autobiography in which Carnegie expressed regret for things past.

The year 1872–73 marks the great transitional period of Carnegie's life. It was then that he made the decision to concentrate his business interests and specialize in the manufacture of steel. Old associates had to be cast aside. Former practices—stock manipulation and selling short on the exchange—were now scorned as sinful speculation. The stock and bond salesman extraordinary had found a new line, and although he kept his office on Broad Street, neighboring Wall Street was now to be shunned as a gambling den. It is a mark of Carnegie's character that he could shut the door on the past with so resolute a slam and with hardly a backward glance.

CHAPTER XI

Steel Is King

1873-1881

In January 1901, Carnegie was asked to write an article on "Steel Manufacture in the United States in the Nineteenth Century," for a special "Review of the Century" edition of the New York *Evening Post*. He concluded his piece with a ringingly enthusiastic, if somewhat confused, trope: "Farewell, then, Age of Iron; all hail, King Steel, and success to the republic, the future seat and centre of his empire, where he is to sit enthroned and work his wonders upon the earth." [1] This was a curiously belated *vive* from one who had been largely instrumental in enthroning steel as monarch some thirty years earlier and who had benefited so immensely from its reign.

Steel was already heir apparent to the ancient throne of iron when Carnegie returned from Europe in 1872, determined to enlarge his Bessemer steel production by building an entirely new plant somewhere on the outskirts of Pittsburgh. Among his business partners in the manufacture of iron, the only one who showed any marked enthusiasm for Carnegie's ambitious plans was William Coleman, his former associate in the Storey farm oil wells, and now Tom Carnegie's father-in-law. Coleman, always restless and eager for new ventures, had the year before made an

extensive tour of the then existing Bessemer steel plants throughout the East—at Johnstown, Troy, Cleveland, Harrisburg, and
Scranton. Like Carnegie, he had become convinced that the Age
of Iron was past and that the future belonged to steel. He had
even taken an option to purchase 100 acres of farm land, a dozen
miles south of the Pittsburgh city limits, up the Monongahela
River, as a possible site for a steel plant. This tract of land was
called Braddock's Field. Here, over a century earlier, General
Braddock's army, on its way to attack Fort Duquesne, had been
routed by the French and Indians. Coleman, who was an amateur
military historian, had often tramped these woods and fields looking for relics of that engagement—rusted bayonets and swords, ar-
rowheads and horn powder cases—and he knew the land well. Although the smoke from Pittsburgh's chimneys could be seen from
the river banks, Braddock's Field had changed little from colonial
days, and the poorly tilled farmland and virgin timber seemed a
remote retreat from the urban industrialism just a few miles
down the Monongahela. Nevertheless, Coleman perceived the
real value of Braddock's Field as an industrial site. The land
could be obtained at a fraction of the cost of a tract of the same
size in Pittsburgh or up the busy Allegheny River and, most happily, it was close to both the Pennsylvania and the Baltimore and
Ohio railroad tracks and fronted on the Monongahela, a natural
highway down to Pittsburgh and the Ohio and up to the coal
fields around Connellsville. Coleman had no difficulty in convincing Carnegie that he had found the right location for a new Bessemer steel plant.[2]

With Coleman's support, Carnegie was more than ready to organize a company and begin construction of the steel mill. His
partners at the Union Mills, however, were considerably less than
enthusiastic about Carnegie's proposals to shift the major emphasis of their manufacturing from iron to steel. Tom Carnegie,
Phipps, and Kloman were iron men, and they regarded the intrusion of steel into their domain with as much friendliness as cattle-
men in the West greeted the sheep ranchers. They raised all of
the old doubts about steel—the tremendous cost for equipment,
the difficulty of obtaining ore, the long, slow process of educating
their customers to accept a much more expensive product. With
customary impatience, Carnegie brushed all of these objections

aside. If his Union Mills partners wished to join him, there would be a place for them in the new organization. In the meantime, he would find new partners and new financial backing for the Bessemer plant, which he could already envision on the banks of the Monongahela.

Carnegie quickly found impressive backing in Pittsburgh. In addition to Coleman, there were David A. Stewart, a nephew of Thomas Scott and president of the Columbia Oil Company; John Scott, banker and administrative officer in the Pittsburgh, Virginia and Charleston Railroad; and, perhaps most important for his prestige within the Pittsburgh business community, David McCandless, whose friendship with the Carnegie family dated back to their first arrival in Allegheny, when McCandless, together with Will Carnegie and Aunt Annie Aiken, had founded the local Swedenborgian church. Although not a man of great wealth, McCandless was one of the most highly respected businessmen in Pittsburgh, and Carnegie knew that his support would be most valuable in opening bank doors and other sources of credit to the new company. Carnegie valued McCandless's prestige so highly that he named the new organization Carnegie, McCandless & Company.

The new company was formally organized on 5 November 1872, with a capitalization of $700,000. Of this sum Carnegie contributed $250,000, part of which was his accumulated commissions from recent bond sales. With over one-third of the total capital, Carnegie held two and a half times as great an investment as the next largest investor in the company, William Coleman, whose shares were valued at $100,000. Stewart, McCandless, John Scott, and William P. Shinn, vice president of the Allegheny Valley Railroad, each invested $50,000 in the company. Urged on by Coleman and Carnegie, the Union Mills partners, Tom Carnegie, Phipps, and Kloman, using recently acquired profits from the sale of some land near their blast furnaces, also invested $50,000 each in the new manufacturing enterprise, although they still regarded it with skepticism.[3]

Thomson and Thomas Scott also became investors in the company by taking a small part of Carnegie's share, largely at his insistence, because he still had an almost superstitious fear of entering upon any venture without the support of his oldest and most faithful business associates. But their participation as investors in the company was of brief duration. Their difficulties with the Texas and Pacific Railroad in 1873, and the resulting open breach between Scott and Carnegie, caused both Scott and Thomson to sell their small interests to Carnegie. Carnegie, who had expected much greater financial support from his old associates than they had been willing to give, was more than a little piqued by their complete withdrawal. With some acerbity, he wrote to Shinn, who had been elected secretary-treasurer of the company, "Mr. Scott was alarmed at danger of becoming a partner & I relieved him of that. I only hope he will never be involved in anything worse." [4]

Carnegie would not break all ties with Thomson, however. The new plant at Braddock needed a name, and Carnegie had a happy inspiration. He wrote to Thomson:

What to call the Works was a question until "Edgar Thomson" was suggested & carried by acclamation. "Just the very thing" was the unanimous expression. The fear had been that upon your return you would object to our use of your name, but earnestly trust you will not do so. . . . If we felt that calling our Works after you were an honor conferred upon you we could readily offer reason why you deserve it, but as we all sincerely feel that this honor will be entirely upon our side in being permitted to do so, we have nothing to say except to assure you that there is not one of our party who is not delighted that an opportunity has arisen through which expression can be given, however feebly, to the regard they honestly entertain for your exalted character & career.[5]

Thomson's reply was cautious and constrained. "As regards the Steel Works, you can use the name you suggest, if the names you sent me are individually liable for its success and as I have no doubt will look after its management. I have no funds at present to invest, having been drained by the Texas & California—and Sanborne's Mexican project. But can give you Keokuk & Hamilton Bridge bonds if you can make use of them." [6]

Carnegie, however, hoped to obtain something more important than a few bridge bonds for the name of his new steel plant.

His primary object was to win Thomson's good will, and through him the good will of the Pennsylvania Railroad. Carnegie fully appreciated that he was even more dependent than before on railroads, now that he was primarily a manufacturer rather than a financier. The railroads were the customers for his one major product, steel rails, and they also must carry the raw materials to his plant and the finished products to their market. As both producer and seller he was at the mercy of the railroads, and anything to attract their friendly recognition, even the revival of that old game of rabbit-naming, was worth a try. He was also aware that there had been a coolness within the Philadelphia office of the Pennsylvania railroad toward his new Bessemer steel plant, even before his open break with Scott, because it was located along the tracks of both the Pennsylvania and the B. & O. railroads. He needed to use every stratagem possible in order to get a friendly hearing among his old Pennsylvania associates. They had the power either to make or to break him.

Another smaller railroad that he had to placate was the Allegheny Valley Railroad, for its vice president, William Shinn, had now become one of Carnegie's partners and the secretary-treasurer of Carnegie, McCandless & Company. Carnegie wrote a long letter to Colonel William Phillips, president of the Allegheny Valley Railroad, explaining why it had been necessary for him to locate the Edgar Thomson Steel Works up the Monongahela, rather than along the Allegheny River as Phillips had hoped and expected him to do. He promised to give even more business to the Allegheny Valley road in carrying ore to Carnegie's blast furnaces, if the line would only double its tracks from the furnaces to the lower Union mills at 29th Street.[7] Carnegie tried to touch all the bases, anticipating future markets and transportation contracts, keeping the necessary contacts alive by flattery and optimistic promises for the future.

He was equally zealous in his careful scrutiny of every detail in the planning of the new plant on the banks of the Monongahela. Here again, he knew that only the most careful and rational planning would enable the Edgar Thomson Steel Works, or E.T. as it was always called, to compete with the already well-established steel plants in western Pennsylvania and along the Atlantic seaboard. If these older companies had the advantage of an established reputation and market, E.T., by starting late, would have the advantage of profiting from their pioneering mistakes, and, by the introduction of the latest and most efficient machinery, would be able to pare costs and compete with the steel Establishment in both quality and price. Knowing that quality can build a reputation and old customers can be lured away by even a 25¢ price differential, Carnegie was not frightened by gloomy predictions of Pittsburgh businessmen, including some of his partners in the Union Mills, that his brazen challenge to the steel giants, Cambria, Lackawanna, and Troy, could end only in his own defeat.

In order to succeed, though, he must have the best plant that money and talent could build, and then he must obtain the most dedicated management that high salaries and stock bonuses could procure. In his quest for both equipment and talent, Carnegie's luck did not fail him.

To supervise the building of the Edgar Thomson Steel Works there was only one real choice—Alexander L. Holley, the greatest authority on Bessemer steel mills in America, if not in the world. Holley was a kind of Renaissance figure, strangely out of both time and place in late-nineteenth-century America. A large, handsome man, whose mere physical attractiveness would have been enough to command attention wherever he went, Holley had been thrice blessed—with a poetic imagination, mechanical aptitude, and inventiveness. He could have had a brilliant career in any field that interested him, and he seemed to have an interest in everything. Poet, novelist, journalist, scientist, railroad engineer, mechanic, orator—he had dazzled his contemporaries in all of these roles. In the midst of the Civil War, at the age of thirty, Holley had been sent by the Federal government to England to study methods for the improvement of armament matériel. There he had become acquainted with Henry Bessemer, and after witnessing one performance of the magical converter in Bessemer's laboratory, Holley had been bewitched. Bessemer had found his first, most ardent, and certainly most talented disciple.

At the moment he saw the small trickle of bright steel poured out of Bessemer's model ladle, Holley, the man of many talents and interests, knew he had found his specialty. He quickly signed a contract with Bessemer for the exclusive use of his process in the United States. There had followed the long bitter years of patent fights with the owners of the Kelly patent, the discouraging search for phosphorus-free ores, and the slow process of educating both the ironmakers and their customers to the inevitability of steel as a successor to iron.

During these years of discouragement, Bessemer himself had often been driven to that point of nervous exhaustion where he was ready to give up the struggle and admit his defeat. But his American missionary never flagged in his confident assurance that the Bessemer process must succeed. Finally, a settlement was reached with the Kelly men, the proper ores were found in southern Europe and northern Michigan, and most important for Holley, a few venturesome iron companies had been willing to try out the Bessemer process and convert their iron mills into steel plants. Holley built his first Bessemer converter at the old Albany Iron Works in Troy, New York. Contracts followed—with the Pennsylvania Steel Company in Philadelphia, the Bethlehem Iron Company in Bethlehem, Pennsylvania, Jones & Laughlin in Pittsburgh, the Joliet Steel Works in Illinois, and finally and most importantly, the Cambria Iron Works in Johnstown, Pennsylvania. With each new contract, Holley improved upon Bessemer's basic design and his own previously installed converters. Holley made so many adaptations basic to the successful operation of the Bessemer method that his name is linked forever with the great English inventor as the creator of the Bessemer process: elimination of the deep English casting pit and the elevation of the converters to obtain working space on the ground floor underneath the converters, a removable bottom for the converter, a substitution of cupolas for the reverberatory furnaces, and the introduction of the transfer ladle.[8] By the time Holley had finished with the construction of the Cambria steel plant in Johnstown, he had made of Bessemer's laboratory model a giant instrument of production capable of turning out steel in quantities that were limited only by the sources of available ore and the production capacities of the blast furnaces.

Holley was obviously the one man to whom Carnegie should turn for the construction of the Edgar Thomson Steel Works, and so, in the summer of 1872, when Holley wrote to William Coleman, offering his services as consulting engineer, his offer was quickly accepted.[9] Holley's terms were moderate, to say the least.

He agreed to furnish all the necessary working drawings for the steel works and to stay on at Braddock as supervising engineer until the plant was in actual production—for a fee of $5000 plus a yearly salary of $2500.[10] Within six weeks, Holley was able to report that the details of the plans for the buildings and machinery "are well-developed and can be put in hand as soon as required."[11]

Holley could furnish the drawings and the supervisory engineering talent, but he could not with his own hands construct the giant converters and the long sheds that would house them. He needed skilled supervisors and foremen, men who knew these cumbersome but delicately intricate machines and could translate his drawings and specifications into an operating plant. There were skilled workmen at the Union Mills, but these were iron men, trained in the operation of blast furnaces and puddling, who regarded Holley's curious, pear-shaped, steel converter with suspicion and fear. Carnegie needed new men who knew and appreciated steel, and once again luck was with him. He did not need to embark upon what could have been a difficult search throughout the country for talent. Holley, quite by chance, was able to bring this talent along with him in the person of one man, Captain William Jones, recently of the Cambria Iron Works in Johnstown. It might be argued that in the long run this fortuitous acquisition was Holley's greatest contribution to the Edgar Thomson works, for it is no exaggeration to say that the initial and continuing success of the steel mill at Braddock can be attributed to the talents of William Jones.

Jones, the son of the Reverend John G. Jones, a dissenting minister, was born in Luzerne County, Pennsylvania, in 1839, not long after his father immigrated from Wales. Because his father was poor and ill, young Jones was forced to be self-supporting from the age of ten, when he was apprenticed to the foundry department of the Crane Iron Company of Catasauqua, Pennsylvania. He could hardly remember a time when he had not been seared by the heat of blast furnaces, deafened by the noise of metal rolling over metal and nearly blinded by the white, incandescent heat of molten iron. He loved every minute of it. "This is my home," he would say to visitors in whatever iron mill he might be working at the time. "A good preparation for the next world."

In 1857, in the midst of economic depression, Jones went to Tyrone, Pennsylvania, and worked with a lumberman, a fellow Welshman named Evans. The clean, cool lumberyards and forests, the sweet smell of pine and spruce, had no attraction for him. He missed the smoke and stench of the iron foundry, and by 1859 he was back in the environment he thrived in, working as a machinist for the Cambria Iron Company in Johnstown. In July 1862, he enlisted as private in the 113rd Pennsylvania regiment, served with the Army of the Potomac, fought at Fredericksburg and Chancellorsville, and was mustered out two months after the Civil War had ended with the rank of captain, a title he was proud to keep for the rest of his life.

He returned at once to the Cambria Iron Company, and soon became chief assistant to George Fritz, the general superintendent of the Johnstown mills. It was Captain Jones who worked with Holley when Holley came to Cambria to introduce the Bessemer steel process there. Holley at once recognized Jones's talents. He would not forget him.

The Johnstown mill at this time was sharply divided into two factions, one headed by Fritz, the other by Daniel J. Morrell, the general manager. A major point of difference between the two men was over the question of wages. Morrell wanted to reduce wages to cut costs. Fritz insisted upon keeping the wage scale high and increasing production. Although Morrell was nominally Fritz's superior in the company, Fritz refused to yield on the wage question, and so impregnable was his position within the company and so solidly was he supported by all of his men in the mill that it was Morrell who had to give way on the wage question.

In the spring of 1873, Fritz died. Captain Jones expected to be chosen as Fritz's successor, but he was too closely identified with Fritz's wage policies, and Morrell was only too happy to pass him over and to name one of his subordinates, Daniel Jones, as the new mill superintendent. Captain Jones neither argued with Morrell nor chafed under the slight. He sent in his resignation and left the next day for New York, where he went to Holley's office. Holley was then busy with the plans for the Edgar Thomson plant, and he welcomed his former associate at Cambria most cordially. He took Jones with him to Braddock as his chief assistant. When the plant was finished Holley told Carnegie that Jones was

315

invaluable, and on Holley's recommendation, Carnegie appointed Jones general superintendent. The E.T. Steel Works had obtained its captain, and Carnegie had obtained his most valuable employee.[12]

Jones served the mill not only as its captain, but also as the chief recruitment officer. With the death of Fritz and the departure of Jones there had been no effective leadership left at Cambria to oppose Dan Morrell's policies, and the general manager had wasted no time in putting into effect a general wage reduction throughout the mill. The foremen and workers, their wages cut, and with no one left to speak on their behalf within the management of the company, were more than susceptible to the siren calls coming from the employment office of the Edgar Thomson plant down the Monongahela. Jones knew the workmen at Cambria as well as he knew the members of his own family, and he could pick and choose the most able men in each department to join him at Braddock. In all, over two hundred men followed Jones from Cambria to the Edgar Thomson Steel Works, including many experienced department superintendents—Captain Thomas H. Lapsley, head of the rail mill; John Rinard, superintendent of the converting works; Tom James, superintendent of machinery; Thomas Addenbrook, head furnace builder; F. L. Bridges, superintendent of transportation; and C. C. Teeter, the chief clerk.[13] It was a raid of major proportions, and relations between Cambria and its new rival down the river were unusually strained during the first years of E.T.'s existence.

Several years later, when Carnegie was sedulously courting Morrell and E. Y. Townsend, the president of Cambria, in order to win from them a more friendly consideration and some measure of co-operation within the Bessemer Steel Association, he invited the two to look over the E.T. plant. As Morrell was conducted down the long sheds, past the converters and rollers manned and supervised by many men whom he could have greeted by their first names, Carnegie looked up at him in beaming pride and asked, "Well, what do you think now of our set-up at E.T.?"

Morrell's answer was a short and pointed admission of past error: "I can see that I promoted the wrong Jones." [14]

If Carnegie had been spectacularly fortunate at the beginning in acquiring the services of both Holley and Jones as well as in Coleman's choice of location for the E.T. Steel Works, he must have felt that his luck had deserted him by the time actual construction got under way. For in September 1873 the great banking house of Jay Cooke and Company of Philadelphia suddenly failed, and business firms across the country collapsed after it. The towering, shaky house of cards that was the postwar boom economy tottered and fell. What had begun as a bankers' panic became an extended nightmare of depression, the most serious economic depression in the history of American business up to that time. Banks that had eagerly extended loans to almost any businessman who could sign his name to a note now feverishly attempted to call in those loans and, having failed to get payment, were forced to close their doors. Railroads, bloated with watered stock and overextended across empty prairies and deserts in the optimistic belief that, if a track were laid anywhere, people and produce would quickly come to it, were forced to go into bankruptcy. Iron mills and steel works which had expanded in the warm air of prosperity resulting from railroad construction now found themselves with no market and were forced to stop production and dismiss their workers. It was a most inauspicious moment to begin the construction of a new steel mill in the congested and depressed Pittsburgh area.

Yet, with ruin all around him, Carnegie never for a moment wavered in pushing the project he had begun. Phipps rubbed his hands in misery and croaked his jeremiad of impending doom because there was no credit available anywhere, even for established concerns like Jones & Laughlin, or Cambria, and certainly not for a business that was only a muddy, excavated hole in an abandoned farm field. Tom Carnegie sat dourly in his old office in the 29th Street iron mill, and although he did not say anything, his brother could detect "I told you so" in every dark line in his face. To his Union Mills partners, Carnegie had become a second General Braddock who had bumblingly led his men to unnecessary catastrophe along the Monongahela.

But Carnegie never permitted himself the luxury of stunned despair. There were many things that he could be thankful for— above all, that he had not let friendship draw him into the real slough of despondency that surrounded the Texas and Pacific, even though it had meant cutting the rope that had bound him to Tom Scott and letting his friend sink. He could also be grateful that the E.T. was not being built out of the marginal sale of stock to hundreds of investors. The partners in the association had the funds available to pay cash for their subscription, and this in itself was a most impressive point to dwell upon in this winter of 1873 when he would meet with his present and hoped-for creditors. Finally, if more money was needed to realize Holley's plans for the most advanced steel mill in the world, and credit was not available in the United States, then Carnegie could turn again, this time for himself, to those familiar banking houses in London where he had so often gone for others.

In December 1873, in the midst of the first bitter winter of the long depression, Carnegie wrote to J. S. Morgan and Company in London, "We are steadily outgrowing the foolish panic here. It is mostly a fright—& the spring will see things prosperous again —but we must drive slower." [15] This letter was an unusual communication to come from America at this time. In part, of course, Carnegie's optimism was a kind of whistling in the dark to bolster up not only his own courage but also that of others to whom he was about to turn for financial aid. But, to a great measure, this note was a sincere expression of Carnegie's unwavering, optimistic faith in America's economic growth and development. Depressions were temporary and even necessary cyclical phenomena, in which the economy, as a man in a fever, burned out of its system that which was dross. Upon its recovery the economy would be stronger and more fit than ever.

A depression could also be a moment of opportunity for those who had the courage and the resources to take advantage of it. With steel mills across the country standing idle, Carnegie found manufacturers more than eager to supply the necessary equipment for his new plant, and at greatly reduced prices. Railroads lowered their freight rates for the transportation of supplies. Idle construction workers were readily available at cheap wages for building the plant. By conservative estimate, the Edgar Thomson Steel Works, built in the years from 1873 to 1875, cost Carnegie, McCandless & Company only three-fourths as much as the same plant would have cost two or three years earlier or later. As it was, Carnegie got the most modern and most efficient Bessemer steel plant in America, including the $11,000 in patent fees paid to Bessemer and Holley, for $976,103. When the costs for real estate and tenement housing for the workers were added, the total figure came to less than $1,250,000.[16] Many years later, a close associate of Carnegie, Henry W. Oliver, speaking at a public dinner in Pittsburgh, would pay tribute to Carnegie's courage and to the faith he had in Pittsburgh by having "risked his fortune" to build a new steel plant in the Pittsburgh area "on a grand scale at a time when others were timid and fearful." Oliver praised Carnegie for having "pushed Pittsburgh into an unrivaled position as a producer of steel, set a new manufacturing standard and vastly increased his operations while other steel producing centers had languished and dwindled almost to the point of extinction." [17] It was a judgment in which Carnegie concurred. He stated much the same idea more succinctly in his testimony before a Congressional committee on the tariff: "The man who has money during a panic is the wise and valuable citizen." [18] A truism which can hardly be gainsaid.

Of course there were some anxious moments for Carnegie at the onset of the depression, as he later admitted. For a few weeks, work on the plant had to be suspended while he gathered his financial resources. He was forced to sell some of his shares in the Pullman Palace Car Company and in Western Union. He might have added, as a corollary to his testimony, that the man who has sound and valuable stock to sell during a panic is also a most fortunate citizen. When still more ready capital for initial operating expenses was needed, and the Union Mills were unable to collect from their customers and "even our own banks [in Pittsburgh] had to beg us not to draw upon our balances," then Carnegie was forced to turn to English banking houses for additional funds.[19] Taking Alexander Holley with him, Carnegie left for London in the early summer of 1874. The two were an effective selling team. Carnegie had an easy entry into the house of Morgan, and his customary enthusiasm, backed up by Holley's technical knowledge, proved to be an irresistible argument in winning the support of Junius Morgan and his junior partners.

At Carnegie's request, Holley had prepared a short statement on the cost of the E.T. Steel Works, its equipment, and its production potential, which provided Carnegie with the most impressive prospectus that he had ever brought to London. The capital of $1,000,000 had been fully subscribed and, in Holley's opinion, should be sufficient to complete the proposed works. They would consist of two five-ton Bessemer converters, a rolling mill, and a pair of five-ton Siemens open hearth furnaces. There would be a gas-producing department, a boiler department, machine and smithy shops, an electric railway over the boilers and producers, and a complete waterworks. The buildings were all fireproof. At the time that Holley and Carnegie left for London the works were two-thirds completed, and Holley hoped that the plant could be put into operation by the first of January 1875.[20]

As for the production potential of the works, Holley estimated that E.T. could produce 30,000 tons of steel rails a year. The cost for producing a ton of steel rails, according to Holley's best estimate, would be $69. The average market price for steel rails over the past several years had been $110 a ton, the lowest price so far having been the current price, $97.50. Assuming that the current low price on the market, due to the depression, would remain the new average price for steel rails, the E.T. Works should make a profit of $855,000 a year—or, in other words, in one year the works should nearly pay for themselves and their site.[21] Carnegie's exuberant comment, "Where is there such a business!" [22] clearly was reflected in the thinking of Messrs. Morgan and Company, although they were too discreet to express themselves so openly. The bond issue of $400,000 was quickly arranged.

Within a short time after production began at E.T., the company realized that Holley's estimate of the market price of steel rails was much too optimistic. But, happily, his estimate for the cost of producing a ton of rails was equally pessimistic. The net result was that within a very few years profits exceeded even Holley's high expectations.

As Holley's statement indicated, the new Bessemer plant would include two Siemens open hearth furnaces. The Siemens furnace, which worked on a quite different principle than Holley's beloved Bessemer converter, had been invented as early as 1861, by a German mechanic, Charles William Siemens. It had not been accepted by the steelmakers in England because the cost of production was too high, and the process was almost totally unknown in America in the 1870's. Carnegie, however, had heard of it, and in January 1873 he had entered into negotiations with the firm of Richmond, Potts and Loring, the American agents for Siemens, to have open hearth furnaces installed at the E.T. Works.[23] Holley undoubtedly had no great enthusiasm for a rival process to Bessemer's, but at Carnegie's insistence E.T. got two open hearth furnaces. The furnaces produced an excellent steel, but, again, as the English manufacturers had discovered, cost of production was so high that they were impractical to use for anything but special orders of high grade steel. It was not until the late 1880's, when basic changes in the process of steelmaking permitted the use of low grade ores with high phosphorous content, that the open hearth furnace would assume a new importance and become a real rival to the Bessemer converter. Nevertheless, Carnegie's insistence upon trying out the open hearth process in the mid-1870's, thus making Edgar Thomson the only steel works in the Pittsburgh area and one of the few in the United States so equipped, proved to be wise. The Siemens furnaces not only enabled the company to produce a higher grade of steel for special orders, but they also proved to be a valuable laboratory for experimentation that would eventually prove the practicality of the open hearth system for the mass production of steel.

Carnegie's introduction of the Siemens process at this early date gives further evidence that he did not follow his own dictum, "Pioneering don't pay." Few American manufacturers were so eager to break with tradition and to embrace the new as Carnegie. One of Holley's assignments on his trip to England with Carnegie in 1874, in addition to the bond-selling quest, was to "take note of new ideas and improvements in the manufacture of iron and steel as you may find there." [24] Carnegie himself never made a trip to England or the Continent in these years without trying to pick the brains of the managers and researchers of the European steel industry. For Carnegie, "pioneering" paid very well indeed.

In spite of the ease with which Carnegie negotiated the bond sale in England to provide funds for the initial operating expenses at Edgar Thomson, he could not have been happy about putting his plant in mortgage. It was, however, much more preferable than the alternative—increasing the capitalization of Carnegie, McCandless & Company by selling stock in the open market. He was determined that his company should remain a tight association of a relatively few investors who would be active participants in the operation of the company. What he wanted, in effect, was a simple partnership, but with the advantage of the corporation in having limited liability for the partners. "Association" was a vague and broad enough word to cover what he had in mind, and it would be this that he would call his organization, rather than a corporation.

The depression served to reinforce two precepts of business policy that Carnegie had already become committed to before he entered the steel business.

His first precept was to avoid overcapitalization as one would shun the plague. He had seen too many businesses, particularly railroads, collapse in the first shock wave of depression because they could not meet the dividends on stock that was grossly inflated over the real value of the company's holdings and potential earning power. Carnegie was now convinced that it was just as dishonest and dangerous for a private corporation to finance itself by printing stock shares as it was for a government to finance itself by printing money. Currency must be backed by gold, and stock by plant, equipment, and product. He would never put his company in mortgage to the New York Stock Exchange.

His second precept, to which the 1873 depression had given particular emphasis, was to hold back as large a percentage of the profits as possible as a financial reserve, rather than to distribute the profits to the investors in the form of dividends. Let the high prices of prosperity finance plant expansion in time of depression when costs would be low. It would be hard to make "valuable citizens" out of his reluctant partners, who wanted to feast on fat dividends in the prosperous years without worrying about further expansion during future panics that might never come. Carnegie, however, was as sure that there would be panics and depressions as he was sure that they would be of short duration. In fact, depressions were a necessary and not entirely unwelcome factor in his scheme of things. The question of dividends versus investment would always remain the sharpest point of difference in business policy between Carnegie and his partners, particularly his brother, who was the chief spokesman for high dividends at all meetings of the board. Only by holding a majority of the stock could Andrew be assured that his policies would prevail. On a simple head count of the partners, he would have been a minority of one in 1873. Carnegie was determined in the very near future to control over 50 per cent of the capital in the company. Then there could be no question of the acceptability of his policies.

One reason Carnegie was forced to turn to London for funds, quite apart from the depression and the tightness of credit at home, was that the Edgar Thomson Works was not the only facility that he and his partners had been engaged in expanding. For a long time the Union Iron Mills depended upon various small blast furnaces in the immediate area to provide them with pig iron. Carnegie had resented this dependency on others, and the frequent highly competitive bidding for the product of these furnaces had been a major factor in keeping costs of production high. As early as 1870, two years before Carnegie had begun planning for a new steel mill, the Union Mills partners had decided to build their own blast furnace. On 1 December 1870, the Carnegie brothers, Kloman, and Phipps had formed the new company of Carnegie, Kloman & Company, and in the early spring of 1871 construction had begun on a blast furnace at 51st Street in Pittsburgh. The furnace was completed in the early summer of 1872, and, following the custom of naming furnaces after women, it was christened Lucy, to honor Tom's wife, Lucy Coleman Carnegie, the daughter of William Coleman. Instead of following the then accepted American design of building several relatively small furnaces, Kloman had decided to follow the British practice of building one large furnace, much higher and much wider at the point of its greatest diameter (called the bosh), hoping thereby to increase production with less fuel, ore, and lime. The Lucy was a giant, towering over Pittsburgh, 75 feet high, with a 20-foot diameter of bosh.[25]

At the same time that the Lucy furnace was being constructed at 51st Street, a syndicate of several smaller iron manufacturers in the Pittsburgh area, also interested in supplying their own mills, had constructed a blast furnace a few blocks away. This furnace, the Isabella, was of the same dimensions as the Lucy, and very soon after the two furnaces went into production, in the early summer of 1872, a heated (certainly the appropriate word in this case) rivalry developed between their crews. At that time a good average production for a furnace was considered to be 50 tons of pig iron a day, or 350 tons a week. Both furnaces quickly passed that mark, and by the end of the year, the Lucy was averaging 500 tons a week, or about 72 tons a day, and the Isabella was close behind with just over 70 tons a day. The next year both furnaces were breaking all records for both America and England. In 1873 the Lucy was producing an average of 593 tons a week, only to be passed by the Isabella with 612 tons. In October 1874, Lucy jumped ahead with 642 tons, and late in the month there was great celebrating at 51st Street when the Lucy broke the record by producing over 100 tons in a single day. Then the Isabella on Christmas Eve passed that mark with 112 tons for the day.

The rivalry by this time had caught the attention of iron men throughout the country. Trade journals carried the weekly totals as other papers carried baseball scores, and wagers were made on what the daily production for each furnace would be. There now seemed to be no limit to the production capacity of these giants. By 1881, the Isabella was producing 215 tons in a single day, and had far outdistanced the Lucy. But two years later, the Lucy, under the gifted supervision of Julian Kennedy, passed the 300-ton mark, and daily production continued to climb.[26] Just over ten years after the Lucy and Isabella furnaces were first tapped, American blast furnaces had increased their daily production to what had once been a good weekly production for a single furnace. This revolution in the production of pig iron was as necessary for the success of the Edgar Thomson Works as were the improvements that Holley and Jones were making on the Bessemer process itself.

On 6 August 1875, the Edgar Thomson Steel Works received its first order—2000 steel rails, appropriately enough from the Pennsylvania Railroad.[27] Two weeks later, on 22 August, the first blow was made. Blasts of cold air shot through the tuyères in the lower end of the great, delicately balanced converter, trembling with the movement of the chemical agitation that was going on inside as the atoms of the various elements within the molten pig iron, manganese, silicon, and carbon, united with the oxygen and roared out of the top of the converter. The heat increased tremendously, and the roaring flame rushing from the mouth of the converter changed its color from violet to orange and finally to a pure white flame. Carnegie had often seen the process in Besse-mer's laboratory and in his own small Freedom Iron plant, but he had never seen this magnificent spectacle on so large a scale. He must have stood entranced as the final white heat was reached and then the great converter was tapped and the silver white liquid poured out of the converter into the waiting molds that would form the ingots of steel—ingots that would then be reheated and rolled into blooms to be cut into billets and re-rolled into rails, beams, or plates. Especially rails, rails made entirely of steel to re-place the crude, iron rails and the unsatisfactory steel-faced iron rails on the railroad tracks of the nation. For Carnegie it was a proud moment, spectacularly ushered in with the greatest fire-works display that modern industry can produce.

Carnegie now had his steel plant. He had the workers to man it, the blast furnace to supply it with the crude pig iron, the or-ganization to supervise it. It would be his task to sell the rails and, more importantly, to supervise the supervision. Never could he forget that. The organization could only be as good as he made it, and his standards were very high, as all the men connected with E.T., from the sweepers on up to the general manager, soon discovered.

In William P. Shinn, Carnegie felt he had found the right general manager. A very different personality from Carnegie, sol-emn, unemotional, and apparently having no other interest than business and the making of money, Shinn seemed to be just the kind of hard taskmaster that the new plant needed. He had the kind of logical, orderly mind that Carnegie appreciated. He knew how to present a statement of costs and prices in a simplified form that could be read at a glance. Above all, Carnegie liked Shinn's ambitious nature, for if that ambition for personal success could be bound to the fortunes of E.T., then it would serve Carnegie's own interest well. But Shinn was not yet as completely committed to the steel mill at Braddock as Carnegie wanted him to be. For a time he kept his position with the Allegheny Valley Railroad and continued to give part of his time and energy to various other en-terprises in which he had an interest. Shinn's lack of complete de-votion to E.T., together with his secrecy regarding just what his other interests were, bothered Carnegie, for Carnegie wanted Shinn to be completely his own. When Carnegie received Shinn's confidential statement of costs for production and profits at the end of the second month of operation, he was quite certain that he had been right in his appointment of Shinn as general manager. Shinn's note read:

October costs—cost per ton of rails:

Labor	$8.26
Metal	40.86
Lime, fuel, etc.	6.31
Total	55.47
Bess. & Siemens royalties	1.17
	56.64

Sold at an average of $66.32 per T, so our profit of $9.86 per T is pretty good for second month. We made $18,000 in second month of operation.[28]

After reading this impressive little note, Carnegie was more determined than ever to have Shinn's undivided attention given to the welfare of the E.T. Works. To obtain this, Carnegie would be generous in bestowing his favors, both in flattery and in financial form, upon Shinn. "I like the tone of your personal letter much," he wrote to Shinn a few months after production had begun at Braddock. "Have always known you would find it necessary if E.T. proved what was expected to give it all your time & thought. It is a grand concern, and sure to make us all a fortune. With you at the helm, and my pulling an oar outside, we are bound to put it at the head of rail-making concerns. My preference would be for you to double your interest & manage it to the exclusion of everything else—we to carry the second 50,000 until you could pay it & allow you to draw on profits any sum required for expenses—but this shall be as you prefer—we shall not quarrell [sic] about your compensation. The only objection I think of to increasing your salary directly would be that $5,000 is considered the figure for partners. Tom, Harry, Piper, Linville, Shiffler and Kloman all get this, and it would cost me a pretty penny should they raise the standard, quoting you as precedent, but this may be arranged. You shall be satisfied one way or another if you take command. . . . You may depend upon one thing—Harry, Tom &

I want your entire time & am only too anxious to be able to feel
you are enlisted thoroughly in the work. It is a great one and
means $40,000 a year profit on $100,000—on an average. . . ."[29]

A few months later Carnegie was again writing Shinn, in
much the same vein:

> I have your letter. I am naturally anxious to get all of you for
> E.T. I do not know your equal as an Ex. officer & I always feel
> with you at the helm E.T. is safe but it makes all the differ-
> ence whether your entire mind is bent on the concern. The fu-
> ture will show you that it is a large thing to handle, & you
> should not have anything to do but run that establishment.
> Take Ingalls case for instance. My idea of efficient or at least
> close & rigorous management would be that he was met face to
> face in his own office within 48 hours after receipt of his letter.
> Depend upon it he would have felt bound to close with you
> then & there. Now it is *loose* and *in danger*—correspondence
> cannot effect what personal attention does. Had you been E.T.
> all over & nothing else, heart and soul devoted to its success,
> you would have probably felt this. . . . Remember I can see no
> fault with your management as it is, on the contrary I assure
> you—there are few nights in which before going to sleep I
> don't congratulate myself its our good fortune in having you
> there—Tom & Harry ditto—but we don't think we can have
> "too much of a good thing" & want somehow or other to get
> you root and branch—compensation can be arranged—I don't
> care about money so much as about success.[30]

Under this kind of pressure, Shinn yielded. He resigned his
position with the Allegheny Valley Railroad and, ostensibly at
least, had no other business interest except that of E.T. But before giving himself "root and branch" to Carnegie's interest, he
exacted his compensation. He not only had his interest in the
company doubled from 50,000 to 100,000, making him equal to
Coleman and second only to Carnegie in his share of the company's capital, but after repeated requests he also got his salary
raised from $5000 to $8000 a year.[31] This was a major accomplishment, for Carnegie was far more reluctant to grant a salary increase than he was to double the size of Shinn's interest in the
company.

Salaries, Carnegie would frequently say, were the badges of servitude, and his proudest boast was that after the age of thirty, when he retired from the Pennsylvania Railroad, he never received another salary check in his life.[32] This was not quite an accurate statement, for he did draw a salary of $1000 a year the first few years after the formation of the Union Iron Mills,[33] but in principle it is true that Carnegie had not been dependent upon a salary for his main source of income since he had gone back to Pittsburgh as superintendent of the Pennsylvania's Western Division in 1859. But Carnegie's aversion to salaries for his partners in the steel company was not motivated by a desire to release them from servitude. Quite the contrary, it was based upon a conviction that the way to bind a man to a business was not to pay him a high salary, but rather to give him a share in the company itself. High salaries were constantly negotiable, and they greatly increased the cost of production. Moreover, a good man could always be enticed away by a rival company if his only tie to his employer was a monthly salary check. But if an employer gave a manager a small share in a company where the policy was not to distribute profits but rather to re-invest them in the company, then that employer not only kept down costs—he also owned that man body and soul. The company's success was the manager's success, and the able manager could not leave without losing his interest in the future growth of the company. Carnegie was a pioneer in the policy of compensating valuable employees at the supervisory level by means of company shares. It appeared so sound to him in both principle and practice that he was always amazed that his competitors did not follow his example. He was to make only one other important exception to this policy—that of Captain William Jones, where the circumstances made no other alternative possible. It is a measure of the regard with which Carnegie considered Shinn and of his desire to placate him that Carnegie, very begrudgingly, raised his salary to the then unprecedented level of $8000 a year.

In the first few years of operation at E.T. Carnegie was convinced that his concessions to Shinn's demands were justified. E.T. had gone into full production with a gratifyingly small number of hitches, delays, and false starts. Of course, this was to a great extent a result of the skilled draftsmanship, careful planning, and expert construction of the plant itself. E.T. was Holley's masterpiece in Bessemer design, and it had been constantly improved upon in small details by the practical experience of Bill Jones.[34] It was Jones, for example, who insisted on using four-inch square steel bolts instead of three-inch round iron bolts in the open-topped housing for the rail mill.

It was Shinn, however, who had co-ordinated the various parts and created an effective unit of production. Shinn was neither a very familiar nor a very popular figure among the workmen in the plant, and very early there developed at first slight and then more serious differences of opinion between him and Jones. But Shinn was too well aware of Jones's value to his own reputation as a successful manager to let these differences come to a head or to bring them to Carnegie's attention. As long as each month showed a gratifying increase in production and a slow decrease in cost, Carnegie was happy to assume that his choice in top personnel had been most astute. By early summer of 1876, Carnegie could write to his London financial backer, Junius S. Morgan:

> In steel rails, we have made a wonderful success—every sanguine prediction I have made is more than verified & we are making today a ton of steel rails for less that 50$ per ton—cost of fuel, smelting, pig included—(we get the dross from our best coal delivered at our works for one cent per bushel). Product last month 4173 gross tons of rail—will probably be 4500 this month.

Carnegie was so exuberant that he then made an admission which would have been a little embarrassing had his letter to Morgan fallen into the hands of certain newspaper editors or politicians in America. "Even if the tariff were off entirely, you couldn't send steel rails west of us." [35]

The activity on the banks of the Monongahela was bound to attract the attention of the American Bessemer steel industry. Even before the first ingot had been heated and rolled in E.T., word had been widely circulated of Holley's great work at Braddock. The established steelmakers—the Fathers-in-Israel, as Carnegie called them—recognized E.T.'s existence by having Daniel J. Morrell, who, to his pain, was more acutely aware of the existence of E.T. than any of his fellow steelmakers, invite Shinn to a meeting of the Bessemer steelmakers to be held in Philadelphia on 15 June 1875 "for the purpose of considering questions connected with the trade, and it is hoped your establishment will be represented." [36]

It was at this meeting of the leading steelmakers of the country that the Bessemer Steel Association was formed. As first organized, it was to be little more than a loose trade association for the exchange of information and the promotion of lobbying activities to support favorable tariff legislation. It had the potential, however, for developing into an effective pooling arrangement to control prices through the regulation of production and the assignments of market areas, a potential that Carnegie was fully cognizant of and one that he prepared for very cleverly, by buying a few shares in each of his competitor's companies, thus receiving their annual stockholder's report. His own company, being a closed association with no shares on the open market, was not subject to the same kind of scrutiny—one more argument Carnegie had for his kind of business organization.

The potential co-operation became an actuality the following year, when the market was fluctuating. The Bessemer Steel Association met in Philadelphia to form a pooling agreement on prices and to assign quotas to its constituent members. Carnegie did not entrust attendance at this meeting to his general manager. He appeared there himself, smiling and warmly greeting his reserved and solemn colleagues in the Association, who barely nodded their recognition of his existence. The Fathers were all there—Samuel Felton of Pennsylvania Steel, E. Y. Townsend and Daniel Morrell of Cambria, Joseph Wharton of Bethlehem, Walter Scranton of Scranton Iron and Steel, and Benjamin Jones of Jones & Laughlin. They were prepared to divide up the Bessemer steel rail pie, but hardly in equal portions.

Carnegie later regaled his delighted partners with his account of the proceedings. Everything had been carefully arranged among the Fathers well before the Association assembled. The meeting was called simply to ratify the decisions already made. After the usual formalities, the secretary of the Association came to the real heart of the matter at hand, rising to read the list of companies and their respective shares of the rail market for the forthcoming year. Most of the Fathers were well aware of what the distribution was to be, so for them there could be no surprises. They sat back comfortably in their chairs, quietly waiting to give formal approval to their earlier arrangement. But for Carnegie, sitting on the edge of his chair eagerly awaiting the name of Edgar Thomson, there was no boredom in hearing the list slowly read out by the secretary: Cambria, 19 per cent; Pennsylvania Steel, 15 per cent; and so on down to the last on the list, Edgar Thomson, 9 per cent.

The secretary finished his reading, and the report was duly moved and seconded, while the Fathers, solemnly and a bit sleepily, nodded their heads in quiet approval. But their somnolence was rudely shattered. Before the formal vote could be taken on the motion, Carnegie was on his feet. The others looked at this brash young man, this diminutive newcomer who had pushed his way into their company, with no attempt to disguise their distaste. It was easy to look down in haughty majesty upon this youth, looking even younger than his years, who stood barely five foot three inches, even when he pulled himself up to his most commanding stance. It was not so easy to keep from laughing when Carnegie pounded the table under the startled secretary's nose and roared that the Edgar Thomson Company would have as large a share of the market as Cambria itself. Then, as Carnegie told his partners back in Pittsburgh, he made a speech.

I informed each of the other representatives, all Presidents of their companies, that I was a stockholder in their concerns and as such had access to their financial reports. I singled out each President and said, "I find that you receive a salary of $20,000 a year and expenses of $80,000," etc.—instancing each one, telling him just what his salary was, and how much he spent in expenses, etc. Then I told him that the President of Edgar Thomson received a salary of $5,000 a year and no expense allowance. Moreover, I said Mr. Holley, the engineer who built the Edgar Thomson works had informed me that it was the most complete and perfect in the world and would turn out steel rails at cost far lower than its competition. "So, gentlemen," I concluded, "you may be interested to know that I can roll steel rails at $9 a ton." [Pure bravado on Carnegie's part, the lowest cost he could achieve at that time being just $50 a ton, but apparently an effective bluff.] "If Edgar Thomson Co. isn't given as high a percentage of this pool as the highest, I shall withdraw from it and undersell you all in the market—and make good money doing it." The committee at once got off its high horse, stopped snickering at me and met my demands.[37]

The story undoubtedly lost nothing in the telling, but that Carnegie was successful in pushing himself to the top position within the Bessemer pool during the first year of its organization is a matter of record. The Bessemer Association had acquired its most aggressive, most volatile—and most undependable— member. For Carnegie's attitude toward pooling agreements would always be mercurial. Some of his colleagues in the Association would use a much more pungent adjective to describe Carnegie's policies and tactics. Carnegie would push very hard for the formation of a pool on rails, beams, or plates—and then, without warning, when the market weakened or he felt he had gained some technological advantage over his competitors, he would break the agreement, take orders for whatever price he could get, and run the mill full. It is small wonder that certain associates, such as Alexander Forbes-Leith of the Joliet Steel Company, were so distrustful of Carnegie's co-operation that they sought to form pools that would exclude his organization from participating.[38] These gestures of defiance were futile. No pool could be organized unless Carnegie would accept an invitation to join it; no pool could last a week after he withdrew.

In these first years, when it was necessary for Carnegie to establish his markets and build a strong reputation within the trade, he was zealous in promoting pooling arrangements. He had had some experience in conducting these frequently delicate and always difficult negotiations when, in the late 1860's and early 1870's, he had set up several pooling agreements involving the Union Iron Mills for regulating prices for iron beams and channels.[39] Most of these pools were of brief duration, and exploratory negotiations would often end in total failure, as Carnegie's letter to Samuel Reeves of the Phoenix Iron Company in December 1870 indicates:

The last effort at reconcilliation [sic] having finally failed; I beg to express my regret at the sad spectacle soon to be afforded

to the public in general at the sole cost and expense of four unfortunate manufacturers who prefer to waste their energies and
profits in an unwise attempt to injure each other. When the day
of sober sense and due repentance arrives, you will always find
us ready to cease the discreditable warfare.[40]

The difficulty lay, of course, in trying to reconcile the desire
for fixed prices with the equally strong desire to have the freedom
of action "to take the market where they could find it," as Carnegie expressed it. These staunch proponents of laissez faire,
through their own efforts in arranging pools and by government
help in the form of high protective tariffs, were trying to eliminate the only regulatory device that they insisted was needed in a
healthy capitalistic society—free competition. Fortunately for the
consuming public, however, businessmen were as resentful of
their own self-imposed regulations as they would have been toward government controls. In 1872, Carnegie wrote his brother,
telling him of a new pool arrangement for iron beams. This letter
shows how inconsistent and basically inimical these pooling arrangements were. He concludes it with this advice to Tom: "Depend upon it, recent rate of pig metal must fall therefor I wish to
be on record in favor of selling for Oct. Nov. Dec. & so on at anything like present prices—Now is the time to get back what we,
constructively, lose upon past sales. The way to do is to be sold
ahead when depression comes." [41] When Carnegie discovered that
his competitors were doing the same thing—selling wherever they
could at any favorable price offered—his anguished cry against
betrayal was quick. "I must confess the explanation in regard to
sale of Beams to Messr. Cook & Bradley is not at all satisfactory as
given to me," he indignantly wrote the Cooper and Hewitt Company. "Our agents report themselves caught entirely out of the
mkt. . . . For one found not proved, we naturally imagine twenty
—indeed confidence gone, all is lost. We shall probably have to
break the agreement & assume trickery if we don't get a share of
N. York trade." [42]

Only in eliminating foreign competitors by means of the tariff
were these aggressive capitalists successful in fighting free competition. Among themselves, they were intensely suspicious of each
other's good faith in abiding by the terms of any agreement, and
with good reason. As John D. Rockefeller was demonstrating in

so brilliant a fashion in the oil business, if you were really serious about ending harmful competition, you didn't do it by signing a "gentleman's agreement" with your competitors—you eliminated them. It was as simple as that.

But no one in the steel business in 1875 was strong enough to follow Rockefeller's example. And so the efforts continued. Whenever prices were rising and demand was brisk, the Fathers would gather, like undaunted diplomats at an international conference for disarmament, to profess brotherly love and sign a new treaty denouncing warfare. But let the market become the least bit shaky and demand begin to fall off, and they would dispatch their salesmen out into the enemy's territory as eagerly as generals would send troops into battle. And from Carnegie, at least, there would be a sigh of relief that the unnatural constrictions of industrial peace were at an end. He would write his partners at the Union Mills:

> I telegraphed you last night the Beam arrangement was at an end as from last evening—December statements will be settled of course, after that all is gone and we go free— . . . Let us fill our Beam Mill *full* if we can even at 5$ per ton profit, run it double time & see just what we can do. . . . In conclusion having abandoned the idea of small tonnage & exorbitant profits there is but one sound idea to embrace & *that heartily*— immense tonnage, small profits—let us take the beam orders of the country.[43]

One might well wonder why Carnegie, having had this kind of experience with pools in the iron trade, should work so assiduously in the creation of similar pools when he moved into the Bessemer steel field. Of course, such pooling arrangements did provide for a temporary division of the market that was extremely useful to a new company attempting to establish itself within the trade, particularly when that new company could demand and get the largest allotment within the pool. It was therefore well worth Carnegie's time and effort to work for this temporary advantage, even though he was realistic enough to know it could not last more than a few months and aggressive enough not to want it to last for a much longer period. Like a sovereign nation entering into regional pacts within the larger structure of an international organization, in these early years Carnegie, McCandless & Company used the Bessemer Steel Association as a kind of umbrella under which it sought bilateral arrangements with its powerful neighbor, the Cambria Iron and Steel Company. Carnegie made repeated gestures of friendship and co-operation to E. Y. Townsend of Cambria for their mutual benefit and security. In June 1876, he offered to share with Townsend an order for 5000 tons of steel rail from the Grand Trunk line in Montreal.

If we must fight—fight it is but it doesn't seem sane to me to do it in this case.[44]

In the following year he again wrote to Townsend:

The Pennsylvania and Westmoreland Coal Cos. are exactly in point,—a short war and they came together probably ten years ago— . . . In like manner, if our two works obtain a lead & go forward prosperously, we shall both grow in various directions & make always a large proportion of the steel made in this country—I have been charged with demoralizing the Rail Mkt. but should war between our concerns result in prices now almost undreamt of, I decline to share the responsibility.[45]

These efforts to achieve what amounted to a virtual partnership with Cambria were frequently successful. "The division of orders, between Cambria and ourselves, will be made by dividing each order as far as practicable," Carnegie wrote Shinn two weeks later, "and I will guard the matter of division, otherwise, very carefully." [46] These arrangements with Cambria, with only occasional breaks, lasted throughout the rest of the decade. Orders were shared and profits divided.[47] There were also co-operative ventures between the two companies in that most troublesome problem for all Bessemer steel companies—an adequate and inexpensive source of phosphorus-free iron ore. The E.T. Works and Cambria had an arrangement whereby Daniel Morrell did the purchasing and arranged for the transportation of the Michigan ore across the Great Lakes for both companies. Since the greater volume cut costs, both companies achieved a considerable saving at the mines and on the lake barges. Carnegie hoped to push this

arrangement further. "Now about foreign ores," he wrote Townsend, "I should like to have the same understanding with you—
We ought both to buy some even if we save nothing—The Lake
people have been extorting from us & now is the time to show
our partial independence of them." [48]

There were many advantages that might accrue to the participant of a pool, and even more if one was able to make separate
agreements inside the pool with one's chief competitor. One advantage that Carnegie especially appreciated in these pooling arrangements when E.T. was getting its start was the opportunity to
share cost figures, particularly on labor, with his leading competitors. Later, of course, when the Carnegie works had far
outdistanced the field, cost figures in the various departments
were the company's most jealously guarded secret. But at this
stage of development it was of vital importance for the company
to know how its cost figures compared with more experienced
firms in the field. Carnegie was far more interested in having
accurate figures on his competitors' expenditures than he was in
knowing their incomes. He sent repeated letters to Cambria, the
Pennsylvania Steel Company, Bethlehem, and others for their cost
figures,[49] and if that failed to bring the desired information, he
did not hesitate to make personal calls at his competitors' plants
to gather what information he could. After one such trip, he
wrote John Fritz of Bethlehem Steel,

> Nothing during our trip surprised me more than the low cost
> at which you could handle ores per ton of metal—My memo-
> randum about your lime seems uncertain. Did I understand
> you to say that your lime was 48 to 50% of your mixture? . . .
> If you can give me your cost of labor per ton I should like to
> have it. I might say that everything I saw tended to convince
> me that, on the Darwinian principle of the survival of the fit-
> test, you have no reason to fear the future. With many thanks
> for courtesies extended . . .[50]

The information Carnegie garnered was quickly relayed back to
Braddock.

> The most surprising fact discovered during our trip was the low
> price for ores at Bethlehem per ton of Bessemer pig. I enclose

their mixture based upon the rate at which they are now contracting for next year. Mr. Fritz says he will reach $9.00 per ton for ore per ton of pig iron. Their fuel is say 1½ Tons at 2.45 per ton—total $3.67 per ton of iron. Their labor I have not yet ascertained, but shall have it soon. . . . Scranton Pig iron cost them not less than $22.50 cash— . . . Their labor is $3.50 per ton. . . .[51]

Costs would always be Carnegie's obsession in business, and his constant concern to reduce them in every department was to a large measure the secret of his success. "Carnegie never wanted to know the profits," one of his partners once said. "He always wanted to know the cost." [52] Where other companies measured success in terms of dividends on stock, E.T. measured it in cost reduction, as Carnegie's partners, hungry for dividends and driven mercilessly to lower costs, could well testify. Carnegie's competitors would only belatedly discover that the reason his company in times of depression could have cash on hand for remodeling and expansion was that in good times Carnegie had considered costs, while they had pushed profits. In a business that had to cope with a wildly fluctuating market price, cost of production was the only variable that the steel manufacturer could control. With prices for steel rails ranging from $43 a ton in 1877, up to $85 in 1880, and then down again to the ruinously low level of $27 a ton in 1885, only a company that used the fat profits of the boom years to modernize its equipment and rationalize its operations to cut costs could continue to show a profit in the lean years and be in a position to buy out its less prudent competitors. Carnegie made sure he was in that position.

As David Brody has observed in his book, *Steel Workers in America,*

The future rested with Carnegie Company. . . . That impulse for economy shaped American steel manufacture. It inspired the inventiveness that mechanized the productive operations. It formed the calculating and objective mentality of the industry. It selected and hardened the managerial ranks. Its technological and psychological consequences, finally, defined the treatment of steelworkers. Long hours, low wages, bleak conditions, antiunionism, flowed alike from the economizing drive that made

337

the American steel industry the wonder of the manufacturing world.[53]

It was difficult for Carnegie's competitors to swallow this un-palatable truth of economy that Carnegie was taking in large doses. Because of their corporate structure, the other steel compa-nies did not find it easy to deny dividends to their stockholders in the prosperous years; while Carnegie, holding an absolute major-ity of the stock, could—and did—refuse dividends to his small number of partners. The grasshopper philosophy of enjoying the sunshine was natural to most businessmen, but Carnegie took the way of the ant, and his partners had to accept his philosophy or get out of the colony. The attitudes of two of his earliest partners toward this harsh policy of self-denial are illustrative of the two extremes of acceptance and rejection of Carnegie's business poli-cies by his associates, and their fate pointed a moral for all others to profit from if they would.

It would be difficult to find two men more different in tem-perament and mentality than Andrew Kloman and Henry Phipps. Kloman from the beginning had had Carnegie's respect and was the first within the company to win Carnegie's highest tribute, that of being called "a genius." With his inventive tal-ents, his mechanical ingenuity, and, above all, his imagination, Kloman could apparently take any machine, tinker with it, adapt it to a new situation, and put it into a successful operation that exceeded even the hopes and expectations of its inventor. From the blast furnace to the universal mill, he knew every process in the manufacture of iron, and he had a kind of magic hand that shaped and developed the new machines. Although most of his improvements were of such a nature that they could not be pat-ented, neither could they be duplicated. Irascible and suspicious of all his associates, Kloman was a difficult man to work with, but Carnegie was more than willing to put up with his temperamen-tal outbursts in return for the great contributions he made to the successful operation of the company. Time after time Carnegie would send him out to visit other plants, for Kloman could tell at a glance whether or not a competitor's new machine or opera-tional process was effective.

But Kloman had ambitions and dreams that did not fit into

Carnegie's birthplace, Dunfermline. *Carnegie Library, Pittsburgh.*

Thomas Morrison Carnegie, age 10.
Carnegie Library, Pittsburgh.

The Lucy Furnace. *Carnegie Library, Pittsburgh.*

Beehive coke ovens at the H. C. Frick Coke Company
near Connellsville, Pennsylvania.
Courtesy Helen Clay Frick Foundation.

Below: A rare photograph of Andrew Carnegie with members of the Frick family:
Mr. and Mrs. Frick (back row); Frick's sister-in-law, Martha Childs;
and the two Frick children, Helen and Childs.

Henry Clay Frick, circa 1897.

The Homestead Steel Works, 1892. The tents of the state militia can be seen on the crest of the hill. *Carnegie Library, Pittsburgh.*

The Edison Laboratory, showing the Material Stock, c. 1908. Courtesy Helm Glen Enjoh Foundation

Carnegie's scheme of things. He never accepted Carnegie's basic policy of plant expansion at the expense of immediate cash return. The bitter memories of an impoverished childhood in Prussia and the long hard years of toiling day and night in the heat of his little forge at Gerty's Run should have their compensation in gold, he felt, now that his single trip-hammer forge had grown into this giant enterprise of iron mills, blast furnaces, and steel works. He did not understand Carnegie's financial gibberish. Why should they re-invest in plant growth and build an equity for the future? All it seemed to mean was that on paper he was, or sometime in the future would be, a very rich man. But Kloman wanted the feel of coin in his pants pockets now, and, unlike the other partners who were easily cowed into submission, he decided to do something about it. He was persuaded by a group of speculators, led by a smooth-talking stock salesman, Joseph Kirkpatrick, to join them in a venture for the mining and smelting of iron ore in the upper Michigan area. Using his interests in the Union Iron Mills, the Lucy Furnace, and the Edgar Thomson Steel Works as security, Kloman borrowed heavily and invested in the Cascade Iron Company and its subsidiary, the Escanaba Furnace Company. Innocent of financial matters, he accepted a partnership in these companies without noting that they were not incorporated and that there was no limited liability protection. When, in the midst of the depression in 1874–75, both companies failed, Kloman soon found himself liable for the debts of both Cascade and Escanaba to the full extent of his personal assets.

This blow struck the Carnegie enterprises just at the time when the production at E.T. was getting under way. To Carnegie, Kloman had committed the unpardonable sin. He had, by his own foolish investments, endangered the holdings of his partners; he had made the very mistake that Carnegie had so carefully avoided in the Texas and Pacific affair. "Kloman will have to give up his interest," Carnegie told Shinn.[54] The Carnegie partners quickly rallied their resources, bought out Kloman's interests in their three companies to prevent outside creditors from getting a foothold within their domain, and retained Kloman within the company as a salaried employee. When, after a couple of years, Kloman had settled his debts, paying fifty cents on the dollar, and had received a discharge from his creditors, Carnegie relented somewhat and offered to take Kloman back in as a partner with an interest of $100,000 in the various companies, on the promise, in writing, that should he ever again engage in outside business investments his interest would revert to the other partners. Intractable to the end, Kloman refused Carnegie's offer, demanding instead that he be reinstated with the same interest that he had formerly held in the companies. When Carnegie refused, Kloman was enraged. He left the company, leased a rival steel mill, the Superior, in Allegheny, and used this as a bargaining tool to force his way into the newly organized Pittsburgh Bessemer Steel Company, which was constructing a new steel works at Homestead, Pennsylvania. Kloman died while the Homestead mill was still under construction. He left his son nothing but a small interest in the Pittsburgh Bessemer Steel Company and an unfulfilled desire for revenge against Carnegie and company.[55]

As founder of what was to become the Carnegie empire, Kloman deserved a better fate. His own ambitions, running contrary to the welfare of the company, destroyed him. He was the first partner to leave because he sought quick wealth outside of the purview of the organization. But he was not the last. Private speculation was the forbidden fruit denied to all who would dine at the Carnegie table.

Henry Phipps, unlike Kloman, seemed to have no other life, no other will, than that of the company. Kloman had tried to vault the wall; Phipps huddled against it for security. The most unprepossessing of men, unattractive, totally lacking in charm, and singularly uninteresting as a companion, Phipps seemed to have almost no characteristic that would have appealed to Carnegie. Among his associates in the company, the only emotional response he seemed to evoke, other than dislike, was pity.[56] "Poor little Harry," so obviously unfit for this Darwinian world of struggle for existence, seemed a sport in the evolutionary design of things. By temperament and natural ability he should have remained, his associates felt, where Miller had found him—a mere clerk, sitting on a high stool and keeping the books for Dilworth and Bidwell. Only the capriciousness of fate that could mock the natural order of things had lifted Phipps out of taking careful count of pen nibs and paper clips in a bookkeeper's office into a concern that would do business in the millions. Yet here, cu-

riously enough, in this world of Big Business, Phipps, with his nig-
gardly habits, had his role to play. What might look like crumbs
to others was a feast to him, and he was able to prove the importance of crumbs to a company that put an emphasis upon costs and
not upon profits.

Two spectacularly successful instances of Phipps's gathering of
crumbs dropped from competitors' tables were more than enough
to prove his worth to the company and to endear him to Carnegie. In the first instance, Phipps, who for a time took the Lucy
Furnaces as his special area of supervision, was bothered by the
piles of what was called flue cinder dumped outside of the furnaces on the river banks. Steel men considered this flue cinder a
waste product of the furnaces, but the very word waste troubled
Phipps. He knew that in making mill-iron the blast furnace used
a mixture of 75 to 80 per cent of Lake Superior ore and 20 to 25
per cent of puddle-furnace cinder. Would it be possible to substitute the flue cinder, which was going to waste, for the puddle cinder, which they either had to produce or had to buy from the puddle furnace? He took a sample of the waste flue cinder to a chemist for analysis and discovered that the flue cinder was not just
as good as the puddle cinder—it was far better, because it was
much lower in phosphorus content. In making mill-iron, one
could use a mixture of 60 per cent flue cinder and only 40 per
cent iron ore and still get a better mill-iron product than the old
formula of 80 per cent ore and 20 per cent puddle cinder. Very
quietly, Phipps sent out agents to buy up flue cinder from other
furnaces, whose owners were more than glad to sell what was
simply an indisposable waste for 50¢ a ton. The Carnegie firm
found itself in the enviable position of selling its own puddle cinder to its competitors for $1.50 a ton and getting in exchange
three tons of far more valuable flue cinder. No wonder Phipps
saw the immense value of having a trained chemist on the staff,
and persuaded the company to employ the first full-time research
chemical engineer in the iron and steel business.[57]

Phipps then turned his investigations to the rolling mills, and
here his eye was attracted by the ever-growing pile of thin steel
shavings, called scale, that were thrown off as the hot metal passed
through the rollers—much in the same way that sawdust is when
lumber goes under the trimming saw. Scale was also regarded as

waste, and it was swept out each day by young boys employed as sweepers. But it was high grade steel. It could be reheated and rolled. It was a shocking waste. Again, Phipps sent out his emissaries to the competing rail mills. For several years, until, very belatedly, the competition caught on to what was happening, Phipps was able to buy scale for little more than it cost to carry it away, and thousands of tons of the finest steel from Bethlehem, Cambria, and Scranton went into rails bearing the name Carnegie.[58]

Coupling this amazing talent—one of the partners called it "cheese paring"—with the strictest honesty in handling the company's finances and a subservient loyalty to Carnegie's policies, it is easy to understand Phipps's invulnerable position within the company, and it is just as easy to see why he alone, of all the early partners, was with Carnegie to the end. Like Abbé Sieyès, after the storm of the French Revolution had subsided, Phipps might well have congratulated himself: "*J'ai vécu.*"

In Carnegie's opinion, Phipps could well have served as a model for all the other partners, managers, and workers in the Carnegie companies to emulate. No other man better exemplified Carnegie's dictum: Watch the costs and the profits would take care of themselves. Letter after letter—to Shinn, to Tom Carnegie, and to Captain Jones—harped on this single theme. Carnegie asked and received from Shinn each month a simple statement of costs per ton of rails for metal, spiegel, molds, refractories, repairs, fuel, and labor. And with this sheet in front of him he studied every detail, no matter how small it might appear.[59]

I cannot understand *Lime,* 13 tons of lime used to each ton of metal. It can't be lime, that is certain, half rock—I suspect.[60]

I have known from the first that our hope for profit lay for sometime to come in the fact that our cost was less than others, that is, it will be, when you start double turn and we can soon do if I get New Haven & Lake & B&O orders for rails— Cincinnati Southern is ours. We can go $61.50 there on double turn & make $5 profit.[61]

I am surprised at two items in cost. Coke ½ ton per ton rails— 8 bushels should smelt the pig and certainly 4 bushels the Spiegel. How do you account for the remainder? Refractories?[62]

At times, Carnegie's efforts to achieve economies seemed penny-wise but pound-foolish. During the first year of E.T.'s operation, he had heard that another steel manufacturer had dispensed with some of Holley's improvements on the Bessemer process. He suggested to Shinn that they do the same. Then they would not have to pay the yearly patent royalties to Holley. Shinn balked at this suggestion. He told Carnegie bluntly that on this issue "You are entirely mistaken. We could not abandon the use of Holley's patents for a cost of $100,000, as it would involve a re-construction of our converting works and then it is doubtful if we could manage economically to carry on the process." [63] On this issue Shinn stood his ground, and he won.

On another proposal for economy, which shocked his partners even more than his suggestion to give up the Holley patents, Carnegie could not be dissuaded. One day, while going over the account sheets, he noted the premium paid each year for fire insurance, understandably large, for there was no business outside that of oil in which there was a greater risk of fire than in an iron mill. To the consternation of Tom Carnegie he proposed that they cancel all fire insurance.

> We are paying double the Insurance on Buildings that we could collect in case of fire. Forty thousand dollars would replace our wooden buildings with iron. . . . I hope someday we shall have the entire building fire proof. If any parts of it require renewal from time to time let us put in Iron. Insurance is a deceptive thing.[64]

Carnegie had earlier written to Jones that he wanted his "written assurance that there is not a stick of timber in our mill at Braddock below the doorstep. I shall feel relieved when you are ready to send me this." [65] Once the various Carnegie buildings had been converted from wooden to iron structures, all fire insurance was canceled, and Carnegie never again carried such insurance either for his business property or his personal dwellings.

Labor costs were particularly irksome to Carnegie. He constantly imagined that other companies were more successful than he in reducing the cost of labor per ton of finished steel rails. No other cost figures was he more eager to get hold of from his competitors than those for labor. He wrote Shinn:

> I learn that the Crane Iron Company is now paying but sixty cents a day for labor and that the result is better than when they gave two dollars.

For whom the result was better he did not say.[66]

Captain Jones was a particularly easy victim for Carnegie's constant goading on costs and production, for he carried much of the fierce competitive sportsmanship that he demonstrated in playing baseball, which he dearly loved, into the mill. Carnegie knew this and played upon it very effectively, making wagers of a new suit of clothes or a $50 gold piece that Jones could not beat Cambria in tonnage for the coming month, or, if that was too easy, could not reduce his own costs from what they were the previous quarter. With a snort of defiance, Jones would take up the challenge, usually win it, and then write back in triumph that Carnegie owed him two new suits. "Now in conclusion, you let me handle this nag in this race. I think I will keep her on the track, and may keep her nose in front. I think at the end of this year, I will have her ahead, and when we stop to rub down, you will find her in excellent condition." [67]

Jones was tremendously proud of his plant and the quality of his work. At Carnegie's constant prodding, he made a conscientious effort to reduce labor costs. At the end of 1877, he reported a labor saving of 6¢ over November, and in figuring a schedule of wages for 1878 he anticipated a saving of 53¢ per ton. "Have cut pretty close all around," he admitted.[68] It was hard for Jones to take Carnegie's constant complaints that other plants were doing better in labor costs than his. He hotly denied that the Pennsylvania Steel Works' labor costs per ton were $1.00 less than E.T.'s. "In conclusion I do think that no works in the world can point to so successful a record as we can claim—and show, and today I am in receipt of letters making inquiries, 'how we do this,' and 'how we do that?' the oldest in age asking the youngest for information." [69] But there was a point in wage reduction beyond which Jones refused to go. He had been too well trained by George Fritz at Cambria to accept the prevailing sentiment among managers to approach as near as possible Ricardo's iron law of wages. When Carnegie asked for a sharp reduction in wages in the spring of 1878, Jones argued successfully against it.

I must earnestly say let us leave good enough alone. Don't think of any further reductions. Our men are working hard and faithfully, believing that hard pan has been reached. Let them once get the notion in their heads that wages are to be further reduced and we will lose heavily. . . . Now mark what I tell you. Our labor is the cheapest in the country. Our men have "Esprit de Corps." . . . Low wages does not always imply cheap labor. Good wages and good workmen I know to be cheap labor.[70]

Jones was the only supervisor in the company who could and would serve as labor's spokesman to Carnegie.

Jones nevertheless drove his men hard, on twelve-hour shifts, even in the heat of July and August when temperatures in the mill would be over 100°F. Every day was a workday, Sunday included. When some of the local ministers protested the breaking of the Sabbath at the E.T., Jones told Carnegie how he took care of them.

I have notified our bigoted and sanctimonious cusses that in the event of their attempting to interfere with these works, I will retaliate by promptly discharging any workman who belongs to their Churches and thereby get rid of the poorest and most worthless portion of our employees. If they don't want to work when I want them, I shall take good care that they don't work when they want to. We bet a dollar they will be glad to drop the agitation.[71]

The only holiday that the E.T. scrupulously observed was the Fourth of July. Carnegie, who had been the one boy in his neighborhood allowed to skate on the river on Sundays, as an adult had imbued his entire business with secularism.

If cost figures were Carnegie's primary concern in the efficient operation of his iron and steel works, this did not mean that the meeting of production quotas was not stressed. Indeed, Carnegie saw these two factors of cost and production as the inseparable twins of business success. The managers of the various departments were more conscious of the problem of costs in seeking Carnegie's approbation, but the workmen were far more conscious of the drive for ever higher production. It was not enough for the

Lucy furnaces to compete with the Isabella; a second Lucy furnace was built in 1877, and it was pitted against Lucy furnace number one. But within a few years the two Lucy furnaces could not meet the growing demand of E.T. for more and more pig iron, and two new blast furnaces were constructed at Braddock itself and put under the supervision of that furnace wizard, Julian Kennedy. Although of smaller capacity than the two Lucy furnaces, their production was phenomenal—442 tons for Furnace A in its first week of production. Now there were four furnaces within the Carnegie domain to race against each other. A giant steel broom, raised high on the smoke stack, was the trophy that went to the furnace with the largest weekly production, and the men drove themselves as if they were rowing for an Oxford blue. It was excellent psychology from a managerial point of view, for a true competitive spirit was generated without a penny's cost to the company in additional wages. The English industrialist, Sir Lowthian Bell, who visited the United States in 1890, was shocked at the "reckless rapid rate" of driving "the furnaces so that the interior of each furnace was wrecked and had to be rebuilt every three years. 'What do we care about the lining?' replied a furnace superintendent. 'We think that a lining is good for so much iron and the sooner it makes it the better.' " [72] Sir Lowthian evidently did not ask about the men who tended the furnaces, but apparently they too were "good for so much iron," and the sooner they made it the better for the company, if not for themselves.

In every department the race was on. In the first quarter of 1877, E.T. produced 14,940 gross tons of rails and billets, and in just over a year of production the works had passed in production every steel rail establishment in the country.[73] Each quarter was to better the record set by the previous one, and still Carnegie asked for more. The stories concerning his insatiable demands were legend: "We broke all records for making steel last week," one manager telegraphed Carnegie proudly. "Congratulations!" was the reply. "What about next week?" "No. 8 Furnace broke all records today," wired a blast furnace supervisor. Carnegie asked, "What were the others doing?" [74]

Generally, Carnegie was only too happy to give his weekly and quarterly production figures the widest publicity he could, in the

346

Pittsburgh press and especially in such trade journals as *Iron Age*. But occasionally the production figures were so good that their publication was actually dangerous to the company. When the editor of *Iron Age* published the production figures for the Lucy furnaces for three days in April 1877, showing an average of nearly 118 tons a day, "surpassing anything yet known in the world," Carnegie sent him a memo, boasting that the total production for the Lucy furnaces for the week was 1612 tons, "but it is so large we want to keep it quiet." [75]

With high production and low costs, profits were assured, Carnegie felt. He found it necessary to remind Shinn constantly of this basic tenet, which so few of his partners—and almost none of his competitors, happily for him—appreciated. "Please call our people together & advise me just how low you are willing to go. You know my views—fill the works at a small margin of profit— get our rails upon the leading lines next year. The year after, take my word for it, you will make profit enough." [76] And again: "Don't be too greedy—'small profits & large sales' in golden letters above your desk is respectfully recommended." [77]

Because high production was of far greater importance than high prices in Carnegie's scheme of things, it is not surprising that he found pooling arrangements particularly irksome—once E.T. began to leave its competitors far behind in production. On the other hand, the Bessemer Association could be most useful to Carnegie's purposes in restricting production of local concerns and allotting quotas for all members in a new territory into which Carnegie wished to expand. In the late 1870's, in the trans-Mississippi West, new plants were built, and when they threatened to take over the local market, Carnegie was most eager to establish a pool. On this occasion, restriction of production went further than it had ever gone before. In 1878, largely at Carnegie's prompting, the established steelmakers in the East and in the Chicago area paid a bonus of $75,000 to the Vulcan Iron Company of St. Louis for not making steel rails—anticipating by some fifty years government subsidies to farmers for not raising crops. [78] This was an expensive ploy, however, for those companies that had to pay their share of the bonuses but did not have as much ready cash on hand as Carnegie did. When Carnegie wanted to make the same arrangement with the Troy

Iron Company, the other members of the Association refused.[79] Soon, however, such arrangements became quite unnecessary. Carnegie's company was prepared to go anywhere and beat any local producer on his own home ground. From then on, Carnegie's support for the Bessemer Steel Association was largely restricted to encouraging its Congressional lobbying activities for high tariff and its sponsorship of technological and scientific advancements in the making of steel.

However successful the blast furnaces and the steel works might be in achieving high production at a low cost, the rails, billets, beams, and plates still had to be sold in the open market, and in these early years Carnegie served his company as its sales manager. He was admirably qualified by both temperament and experience. Over 90 per cent of E.T.'s steel output in the period from 1875 to 1885 went into rails, and no other man in the steel business had had more experience in railroading or had made more useful contacts in the railroad world over the preceding twenty years. His years as divisional superintendent, bridge builder, and bond salesman worked for him now, as he went out seeking rail orders. There was not a railroad president or purchasing agent in the entire country with whom he was not personally acquainted and few with whom he had not had business in some capacity or other. Frequently, through personal friendship with the railroad officials concerned, he was able to discover in advance of making his own bid for a rail order what the bids of competing firms had been, and he would lower his own price accordingly. Shinn frequently found him a little too eager in this, and once he had the temerity to suggest to Carnegie:

> The feeling is that we are incurring unnecessarily the opposition of the older Companies & getting down so low on our first bids as to have no room for further reduction when other large contracts are in the market. . . . The Cambria people are becoming very bitter against us for making, as they claim, unnecessary concessions in prices, so early in the season.[80]

To this reprimand from his subordinate, Carnegie made a sharp retort,

Of course Cambria is bitter—she has herself to blame. Her co-operation in the maintenance of prices in the West was all that was necessary. . . . I think you should ask why a negotiation I had on foot was interfered with by their agents . . . & our price cut under one dollar per ton. Let us get bitter too at such a thing. . . . Let us manage our own business—take orders whenever a fair profit is secure.[81]

Writing in much the same vein to justify his price policy in making contracts with the railroads, Carnegie told Shinn,

Two courses are open to a new concern like ours—1st Stand timidly back, afraid to "break the market" following others and coming out without orders to keep our works going—that's where we are going to land if we keep on.
2nd To make up our minds to offer certain large consumers lots at figures which will command orders—For my part I would run the works full next year even if we made but $2 per ton.[82]

It was difficult for Shinn to understand how anyone could think they were "standing timidly back, afraid to break the market" as long as Carnegie served as their chief salesman. How Carnegie loved his self-appointed role in the company! There was almost no occasion that might not present an opportunity for promoting his business affairs, from a private dinner in Gramercy Park to intermission time at the Metropolitan Opera. He could not even discuss paintings with an artist friend without instructing him in proper selling techniques:

I told him [an art dealer] to let me know any offer as you [an artist] and I agreed the policy was to make sales cheap—to get your pictures in the hands of purchasers & then the prices could be raised. . . . These are fearful times & you must not expect sales to any extent but we will try to do something—Meanwhile keep hard at work—be economical & I will try to see you through.[83]

Carnegie anticipated Madison Avenue advertising techniques by many years. He loved publicity in an age when most businessmen shunned the limelight, for he realized that a man and his business could be so identified in the public mind that whatever the man did became an advertisement for his product. An interview on board ship in New York harbor with a group of newspapermen who had come down to write up a story of distinguished passengers returning from Europe would permit Carnegie to expound on business conditions in Europe—and at the same time say something about steel production in the United States. These shipboard press conferences became a regular feature of Carnegie's frequent trips to and from Europe. Always he was selling rails—Carnegie steel rails, "the best in the world." Carnegie never needed to hire an advertising agency to build up his public image.

Some of his methods might appear a bit too crude and direct to a later generation of public relations advisers for the large steel companies, who refined the process into "institutional advertising." But to Carnegie's contemporaries in the steel business, who had never considered the necessity for advertising a product like rails, his use of testimonials from satisfied customers seemed bizarre, and unfair, especially because they were most successful. W. R. McKeen of the Vandalia Railroad wrote Carnegie a brief note of appreciation for his fine rails, saying that "Your rails worked like Brown Rails [John Brown of England, whose steel rails were at that time considered to be the best in the world] and the others did not and were inferior." [84] Carnegie had copies of this note made and sent to railroad presidents and purchasing agents all over the country along with his own personal letter asking for orders. The Fathers-in-Israel scorned Carnegie's techniques of hawking rails as if they were patent medicine, but their disdain for his methods cost them orders, and Carnegie could not have cared less what they might think of him. He went right ahead with his advertising campaign, gathering testimonials from satisfied railroad executives who apparently enjoyed being quoted to each other.[85]

Carnegie insisted, however, that he be provided with a quality product to sell, for he knew that one adverse comment on his rails circulated by word of mouth among the railroad offices could offset a dozen testimonials in writing that he might distribute throughout the country. His anger whenever he got a complaint on an order of rails exceeded his celebrated outbursts in the Keystone office against faulty construction of bridges. When the New Haven Railroad officials reported a shipment of faulty rails, Carnegie wrote them a very apologetic letter. "I am surprised to hear of the defects in the New Haven Rails and can only account for this first and only complaint upon the hypothesis that having to divide the forces into day and night gangs to run double turn compelled us to employ ½ green men and the imperfect rails may have been shipped at night." [86] He at once dispatched an inspector to report on the rails in question and then blasted Shinn for the occurrence.

> Mr. Roysten's report on the New Haven Rails is very sad indeed. No one can hold his head up when he looks at them. Now this will not do and should not be repeated. It is ruin to send out a bad rail especially to Eastern lines where inspection is always severe. . . . Mr. Bishop wants 3,000 tons more and a good lot of rails might have given us the order. I cannot approach him at present. . . . I would rather today pay out of my own pocket 5000 dollars than have had this disgraceful failure occur.[87]

Carnegie made sure that such failures were rare.

The success that Carnegie had as chief salesman for E.T. depended upon more than flashy and hard-selling advertising of a quality product. Above all, he had an almost uncanny ability to prognosticate future trends in supply and demand. He was so justifiably confident of his ability to judge the market that he would issue flat statements to his partners on price levels six months in the future, with no qualifying "perhaps" or "I think it possible" attached. His prognosis was usually correct, and his competitors would discover that he had made the right contract at current prices for future delivery when prices would be down, or had held up on accepting orders in anticipation of a rising market—as if he were endowed with a kind of Gaelic second sight. But there was more shrewdness than supernaturalism in his insights, for Carnegie, conveniently located on Broad Street in New York, never missed an opportunity to sound out leading financiers, bankers, and stockbrokers on business conditions and trends. Nor did he ignore international affairs. No one in American manufacturing was more thoroughly conversant with European industry than he. He kept close touch with current trends in European finance and business, not only by means of the British trade journals but through personal acquaintances in London, Paris, and Berlin. Unlike his parochially minded colleagues, Carnegie appreciated the fact that business was international in scope and that a colonial clash between France and Britain in Africa could affect the price of steel in Pittsburgh. He had never forgotten that commission with Barings which had been lost because of Bismarck. He regularly drew upon all of these sources, gathered his information, and put it into a predictable pattern—which seemed as if it could have come only from crystal ball gazing.

One of the many Carnegie myths widely circulated over the years was that, although he may have been a promoter and salesman extraordinary, he knew nothing about how his product was made. Stories were told of his conducting such distinguished friends as Matthew Arnold or Herbert Spencer through his steel works and asking the foreman questions even more simple and naïve than those asked by his visitors. Carnegie's partners and supervisors must have laughed at the absurdity of such stories. The daily communiqués that they received, dealing with every detail of the manufacturing process from the amount of limestone to be used in the blast furnace charge to the relative merits of hammered versus rolled blooms for rails, left no doubt in their minds that Carnegie knew his product probably better than most of the workmen, for his knowledge of the process was not of a special but rather of a general nature.[88] In an industry as adaptable to technological change as steel, no one concerned with innovations that would reduce costs and increase production could neglect keeping informed on the latest developments in the manufacturing process. Carnegie had to argue with the traditionally conservative nature of operations men who found it easier to keep to the old familiar patterns. He could not afford ignorance, and if on his periodic visits he appeared rather simpleminded to the workers, it may have been a role that he found amusing, or, more likely, a means of finding out what the workmen knew. He did not fool the department superintendents with his wide-eyed innocence, for they well knew the intensive grilling session that awaited them at the end of the tour.

It is easy to understand how such stories of Carnegie's ignorance of steel gained currency; New York and Europe, where he spent most of his time, seemed far removed from the steel works at Braddock. But from every trip to England and the Continent, Carnegie brought back new ideas and new techniques, and he would tell his partners, "All this I have from personal observation." [89] Thomas Whitwell of the Thornaby Iron Works in Stockton, England, met with Carnegie, and gave him vital information on recent experiments on the optimum size and shape of bells for the blast furnaces, which, when tried out in Pittsburgh in 1877, put the Lucy furnace well ahead of the rival Isabella. "How can we express our sense of obligation to you?" Carnegie wrote Whitwell. "You have placed our business of Pig manufacture upon a new basis, and we look forward to the blowing in of our second stack, in August, with much pleasure, even in such times as these." [90] There are many ways of keeping shop, and Carnegie had made his office worldwide.

When Carnegie received the first six months' report on profits from E.T. in April 1876, his exultant shout back to Shinn, "Where is there such a business!" served as the prefatory statement to his proposal to Shinn to limit even further the diners at the feast. "I want to buy Mr. Coleman out & hope to do so," he frankly admitted, and continued:

> Kloman will have to give up his interest, these divided between Tom, Harry, you and I would make the concern a closed corporation—Mr. [John] Scott's loan is no doubt in some banker's hands and may also be dealt with after a little, then we are right and have only to watch the Bond conversions which will not be great as our foreign friends will want to stick to the sure thing I think.[91]

Kloman's difficulties with his creditors had effectively removed him from the table. Then it was Coleman's turn. Coleman had not wanted to sell out of what promised to be his most profitable venture since the Storey farm oil wells, but he, like Tom Scott, was overextended when the 1873 depression hit, and by 1876, he desperately needed cash to save some of his other investments. Carnegie offered to buy his $100,000 interest at face value over a period of five years at 6 per cent interest. Coleman at first refused, but Carnegie was not discouraged. "He wanted a much better bargain, but I would do no better. Finally he said to write Tom what I offered & he would talk over it. I suppose it will be arranged." [92] And so it was. On 1 May 1876 the agreement between Coleman and Carnegie was signed, whereby Coleman sold out his interest on Carnegie's terms.[93]

The company's business expanded, and so did Carnegie's appetite for a larger slice of pie. He wrote to Shinn:

> There are possible Combinations in the future. It isn't likely McCandless, Scott & Stewart will remain with us—I scarcely think they can. I know Harry & Tom have agreed with me that you out of the entire lot would be wanted as a future partner & I think we will one day make it a partnership Lucy F Co., U Mills, ET &c. &c. & go it on that basis the largest Concern in the country.[94]

In the winter of 1878 McCandless died, and his interest was bought by the company at face value. The number of partners in the firm continued to shrink like the Ten Little Indians. The death of McCandless gave Carnegie an opportunity to take the first steps in consolidating the various allied companies along the lines he had suggested to Shinn. A long continuing disagreement between the Lucy Furnace Company and E.T. over the prices charged E.T. by the blast furnace for its pig iron was a strong motive for consolidation. Although a temporary settlement had been arranged between Shinn, as manager of the E.T. Works, and Tom Carnegie, representing the Lucy Furnaces, whereby on a sliding scale basis the price of pig iron charged to E.T. would be in part determined by the current market price for steel rails, the situation remained unsatisfactory. Carnegie did not like this kind of conflict within his domain, and consolidation seemed the only ultimate solution.

A move toward consolidation of Carnegie's interests had been taken in 1872–73 when the older and less efficient Lower Mills of the Union Iron Mills had been sold to a new firm, Wilson, Walker & Company. Although Carnegie held a sizable interest in this firm, too, he had nevertheless reduced the number of plants directly under his control, making the consolidation he had in mind more manageable. With the departure of Kloman from the partnership in the old Union Iron Mills, the old company changed its name from Carnegie, Kloman & Company to Carnegie Bros., with a capitalization of $507,629, of which Carnegie held just under 50 per cent.[95]

When Coleman sold out to Carnegie in 1876, the firm of Carnegie, McCandless & Company was dissolved and a new company organized as the Edgar Thomson Steel Company, with a capitalization of $1,000,000. Two years later, the capital stock of the company was increased to $1,250,000, Carnegie taking the entire $250,000 stock increase for himself. It was an easy way to obtain what he had long sought, an absolute majority of interest in E.T. With profits for that year alone at over $300,000, or nearly one-fourth of the capitalization of the company, no one could accuse the E.T. Steel Works of watering its stock.[96] Carnegie was now in a position to dictate the terms of reorganization.

In October 1878 Carnegie left for a long-dreamed-of trip around the world. "Good bye my friend," he wrote on the eve of his departure, "I feel so perfectly satisfied to leave E.T. in your hands. This absolute confidence is worth everything & I daily congratulate myself that I have met you & got such a man bound in the closest manner to our party. Your fortune is secured that I do know." [97] This was unusual praise to come from Carnegie, but it seemed entirely justified by the accounts that Shinn submitted monthly for Carnegie's study. From the first year of operation, E.T. never made less than 20 per cent on capital invested, as Carnegie could proudly boast to the president of the National City Bank when offering notes of the company for a loan.[98]

Perhaps Carnegie's praise was too strong; it aroused in Shinn old ambitions and new desires. In any event, while Carnegie was marveling over the ancient civilizations of the Orient and finding new confirmation for his cultural relativism and religious skepticism, his philosophizing was disturbed by new demands from Shinn for a more exalted position in the company. The death of McCandless, while Carnegie was in India, left the chairmanship of the company vacant, and Shinn at once applied to Carnegie for the position. Carnegie's answer gave him little encouragement.

Your personal was a genuine surprise. It never occurred to me
that you would prefer to be called chairman rather than genl.
manager, on the contrary the latter was your own choice. You
made the organization to suit your views. I think you once explained to me Genl. Mgr. suited you best, as indication direct
management of the works, Engineering &c. . . . Let the matter
rest until my return, & we will meet as friends, desirous of
pleasing each other & I am sure our happy family will remain
one. Tom cares as little for names as I do, I think, and that is
simply nothing—its the prosperity of the works we seek *That's
our pride*. . . . It is not six mos. since you asked me to allow
$8000 salary which would satisfy you. If I understand you have
taken $2000 more—now an asst. mgr. & Sec. & Tr. under salary
are proposed. Let me get a little time for breathing please—
You travel fast in this direction.[99]

Five thousand miles away from the mills, Carnegie began to
have some doubts about his unreserved confidence in Shinn's
judgment. Writing to John Scott from Rome, he expressed his
general dissatisfaction with the way things were going during his
absence.

I think Mr. Shinn might have spared me his long letter of complaint. It has of course cut my holiday short & made me uneasy.
Surely he couldn't expect me to act on such a matter until my
return. What use then in annoying me. I would not have done
it to him had he been away. You have increased his salary to
10,000$. I consented to 8,000$ reluctantly explaining to him I
had doubled his interest from my own stock expressly to compensate him. . . . His action after what I have done for him
seems to me ungracious. Then he has gone into a damned gambling operation contracting for 45,000 tons low priced rails without first covering with Pig Iron. I can't trust such speculative
people as you & he appear to me to be. Gas Mills, Old Blast
Furnaces & c. Why can't you try to reform & make yourselves
respectable manufacturers in which hope your friend Andrew
will offer up today in St. Peter's a solemn prayer.[100]

Upon Carnegie's return home in midsummer of 1879, he was
given even more disturbing evidence of Shinn's ambitions, which
included not only a desire for a more exalted title but also private

business deals to augment what Carnegie considered his already inflated salary. The most disturbing of these stories, later proved valid, concerned Shinn's having discovered from the company's engineer that a certain limestone in the Pittsburgh area was so low in phosphorus content that it was ideal for the Bessemer converter. Instead of sharing this knowledge with the company, Shinn had quietly formed a separate firm, the Peerless Lime Company, which bought up a major portion of the limestone beds, and then Shinn had sold the lime to E.T. at a considerable profit to himself. There was also evidence that Shinn planned to do the same thing with iron ore. Carnegie later reported that the other partners, having suspicions of these matters, upon Carnegie's return refused to consider Shinn for the chairmanship—a judgment in which Carnegie heartily concurred.[101]

Shinn then threatened to resign as general manager if he could not be chairman. Carnegie answered that if Shinn wished to make an issue of the chairmanship, then the board would have to accept his resignation. If Shinn could not be content in his proper role as general manager, "then go, but in that case I cannot concur with your idea that you should remain interested with us at all—surely you don't want your colleagues to do all the work & you sit down only to share ingloriously in their triumphs. No, no, if you go, go. Sell out & try another party. We want no drones in the E.T. if we can help it." [102] It must in all fairness be pointed out that Carnegie did not seek this break with his general manager and major partner of the E.T. Steel Company, even though his break with Shinn was to give him the opportunity for consolidation that he wanted.

Shinn had already accepted part of Carnegie's advice in advance. At this time, he was negotiating with the Vulcan Iron Company to become its general manager at a salary of $10,000 a year plus an interest in the company of $120,000 to be paid out of future dividends. As an added bonus for engaging him, Shinn assured Vulcan that he would bring with him Captain Bill Jones, the genius of the E.T. Steel Works. There was a certain ironic humor in the fact that Vulcan, which had been paid a bonus to stop rail production for a year, and that largely at Carnegie's urging, should now plan to go back into production by hiring his general manager and his plant superintendent. Carnegie failed to see the humor in the situation, however. When he learned that Shinn had not been up the St. Lawrence River valley on a vacation as he had said but instead had been in St. Louis, negotiating with the board of directors of Vulcan, he was more angry with Shinn than he had ever been toward an associate before.[103] Carnegie was particularly incensed over Shinn's attempts to lure Jones away from E.T. This was the unforgivable crime. Many years later, when Carnegie wrote that there had been only one rotten apple in the thirty years of his business organization, he was referring to Shinn.

Shinn's ejection from the company brought the issue of the settlement of his interest to a head. A committee to abritrate the value of Shinn's holdings had already been selected by Shinn and Carnegie together in an apparently amicable fashion,[104] but then acrimonious testimony presented by both sides led to a breakdown in negotiations, and Shinn withdrew his offer to arbitrate. Carnegie wanted to pay Shinn only $100,000 for the book value of stock in Shinn's own name, while Shinn insisted that he had a claim upon some of the interest of both Kloman and McCandless that had been assumed by the company. Shinn took the case to court to obtain his rights and secured a court order to produce the company books as testimony of his value to the company. As Carnegie had no desire to have information on the company's costs, production, and profit become part of the public record, an agreement was reached out of court. Shinn received a settlement of $200,000 for his interest in the company, but lost his contention that he had a right to continue to keep a part of that interest invested in the company after he had left its employ and had accepted a position with a competing firm.[105]

It had been a bitter and costly fight for both sides. Shinn had lost his position in a most profitable business. Carnegie had lost a general manager of unusual competence, and it would be several years before he would find a better man to replace him. The only apparent victor in the struggle was Bill Jones. The fact that Shinn had threatened to take Jones away from E.T. made Carnegie realize as never before how dependent he was upon the services of the Welsh steelmaker. In characteristic fashion, Jones laid his case openly before Carnegie.

I am now in the full vigor of manhood, and giving to this company all the brains I possess, backed up with all the energy I
have. On my present salary, I can never expect to accumulate a
competency for myself or family. . . . I want you to clearly understand that I wish to be connected with no other concern but
the E. T. Your Brother, T. C., suits me exactly, and is far more
sagacious business man than the late Gen. Man. It is a pleasure
to me to be associated with him . . . and I only give utterance
to my earnest convictions when I say of him that he is the clear-
est brained business man I ever had connections with.[106]

Carnegie wasted no time in quibbling over terms. "I like
yours of 5th much,—always be frank with us. . . . Tom & I appreciate you I believe more than you do yourself. All you have to
do is say what you want & *don't put it low either.* . . . Tell me
confidentially what would not only satisfy you—but *gratify* you as
well." [107]

Carnegie would have preferred to have made Jones a partner,
but the Captain wanted instead a "hell of a big salary." Replying
to Carnegie's request to name his own figure, Jones answered that
the general manager at Bethlehem got $20,000 a year. "I am ego-
tist enough to say that I can walk right around him on all points
connected with a work of this kind." Then Jones added hastily,
"After re-reading this letter, I find that it would leave the impression in your mind that I think $15,000 would be right. I will say
this, I will be satisfied with less." [108] He got more. Carnegie, making the one big exception to his policy on salaries for top managerial posts, decreed that hereafter Jones's salary would be
$25,000—the same as that of the President of the United
States.[109] Jones accepted with a whoop of joy. "We will lather the
very devil out of [Cambria] in 1881. Give us the material is all we
ask. You let little Tom attend to this and then look out for 1881.
Maybe you would like to bet on 1881. If so, name your bet." [110]
Carnegie lost his "bet" and won the race. For the first four
months of 1881, Cambria produced 34,443 tons of rails, E.T.,
42,071 tons.[111]

Carnegie got more than a big tonnage of rails in 1881. With
Shinn gone and the partnership even more limited, the consolidation that Carnegie had been seeking was at last effected. On

1 April 1881, Carnegie Bros. & Company, Ltd., was formally organized. The shareholders included the two Carnegie brothers, Henry Phipps, David Stewart, John Scott, Gardner McCandless, and Carnegie's old traveling companion, John W. Vandevort. The new company represented a consolidation of the Edgar Thomson Steel Works, the Union Iron Mills, the Lucy Furnaces, coal mines and coke ovens at Unity, and a four-fifths interest in the Lorimer Coke Works. It was capitalized at $5,000,000. Tom Carnegie was chairman of the board.[112] Andrew Carnegie had no official title in the firm, but he had 55 per cent of the capital. As he had explained to Shinn, names meant "simply nothing" to him. In that same year, the $5,000,000 partnership made a profit of $2,000,000.[113] With steel as king, where else could one find "such a business"?

CHAPTER XII

Unnatural Selection
1878-1887

When Andrew Carnegie and John Vandevort left San Francisco on 24 October 1878 aboard the S. S. *Belgic,* they were fulfilling a promise they had made to each other twelve years before. While standing at the bottom of the crater of Mount Vesuvius, they had agreed "that someday, instead of turning back as we had then to do, we would make a tour around the Ball." [1] Now, more than a decade later, they were on their way, sailing westward to the Far East and still west through the Indian Ocean, into the Mediterranean to arrive back at the Bay of Naples, where the promise had been made.

Carnegie's numerous trips to Europe since his last Grand Tour with Phipps and Vandevort in 1865 had always been motivated in part by the demands of business: the selling of bonds, the pursuit of patents, and the investigation of British and German manufacturing techniques. But he could not justify this trip on business grounds to his hard-working and envious partners back in Pittsburgh. "I'm off for a holiday," he frankly admitted in his travel diary, "and the rise and fall of iron and steel 'affecteth me not.' " [2]

If this round-the-world tour was not to serve an immediate

361

business advantage, it was to provide Carnegie with further documentation in support of Herbert Spencer's evolutionary doctrines. Just when Carnegie first encountered the writings of Herbert Spencer and the heady excitement of the theory of evolution is a matter of conjecture. To Carnegie it would later seem as if he must have innately known what he regarded as the basic truth of science and philosophy, yet it is doubtful if he had even heard of either Spencer or Darwin before he went to live in New York in 1867.[3] There, quite fortuitously, he had been introduced into the intellectual life of New York by Courtlandt Palmer, the son of a wealthy New York merchant, who shared with Carnegie an interest in technical education as opposed to classical education.

One center for the intellectuals of New York, and perhaps the most celebrated, was the Murray Hill home of Vincenzo Botta, professor of Italian literature at New York University. Professor Botta was a distinguished scholar in his own right, but it was his wife, Anne Lynch Botta, who dominated the circle, as she had for thirty years. In the 1840's, as Miss Lynch, she had had her Saturday "evenings at home" and had attracted such diverse celebrities as Edgar Allan Poe, William Cullen Bryant, George Ripley, Delia Bacon, N. P. Willis, Fitz-Greene Halleck, Bayard Taylor, Daniel Webster, and Ralph Waldo Emerson. Madame Botta was something of an anachronism even in her youth. Her salon gatherings were more congenial in spirit to eighteenth-century France than to nineteenth-century Jacksonian America. In the post Civil War period she was a still more remarkable cultural phenomenon. Nearly sixty years old when Carnegie first met her, Anne Lynch Botta, a "lithe, gentle little woman," to quote Carnegie, with her white hair and her black gowns of fine lace and silk, might have been regarded by the new generation of New York society as a delicate period piece, worth preserving and cherishing for the memories of the past which her presence evoked. But Madame Botta, proud as she might be of the past triumphs of her salon— which included Poe's first recital of his poem "The Raven"—had no intention of being placed carefully away on the shelf like a fragile piece of Meissen porcelain. She had moved with the times, and she was always eager to meet anyone new who might have something to contribute to her "evenings at home." Many were introduced to her select group, but only the most interesting or those who were demonstrably successful in the arts and letters were invited to return. And if the group of regulars who met in Madame Botta's drawing room in the 1870's were not as gifted or as illustrious as those who had met with Miss Lynch in the 1840's, if Henry Ward Beecher and Charles Dudley Warren had replaced Poe and Washington Irving, it was a sad commentary on the times rather than on Madame Botta's personal attraction.[4]

For Carnegie, newly arrived from Pittsburgh and Homewood, Madame Botta's Murray Hill salon was glittering enough to excite him tremendously, but not enough to overawe him into silence. No gathering, however notable, would ever be able to do that. On his first visit he quickly caught the attention of his hostess, and at the close of the evening he was invited to return. Years later, Madame Botta would tell Carnegie that "she had invited me because some words I had spoken the first night struck her as a genuine note, though somewhat unusual." [5]

It is not surprising that Carnegie could not remember what he had said that had attracted Madame Botta's interest, for there were undoubtedly many words spoken by Carnegie that night and on the evenings that followed at the Botta home. What probably prompted Anne Botta to include Carnegie among her regulars more than anything he had to say that evening was the very novelty of the man himself—a man from Pittsburgh, a manufacturer of iron and a salesman of bonds, a representative extraordinary of the *nouveaux riches,* who had climbed from the poverty of Slabtown into a suite at the Windsor, just north of Murray Hill—in short, everything that Madame Botta's pre Civil War circle would have scorned. But now Beecher and Warner were delighted to make his acquaintance, and even John Bigelow and Richard Watson Gilder were impressed. It must have amused Madame Botta to capture and exhibit so rare a specimen of *Homo croesus americanus* as this, and the joke became doubly amusing when this busy little millionaire, taken out of his native habitat of iron mills, proved not to be a tongue-tied boor but, on the contrary, an eager and effective disputant with Bigelow on Christian theology, with Gilder on the relative literary merits of Burns and Tennyson, or with Andrew D. White on the values of a classical education.

Carnegie's triumph at Madame Botta's opened other doors to

him in New York, Boston, and even in England, for the circle that had as its center the Murray Hill salon was wide in diameter and overlapped many other cultural circles on both sides of the Atlantic. Because of Madame Botta, Carnegie was to meet men both in New York and in London who were far more attractive to him and would become closer in terms of personal friendship than anyone he was to be associated with in the business world of Broad and Wall Streets or in Braddock, Pennsylvania: the Gilder brothers, Andrew White, and from Britain, Charles Kingsley, James Anthony Froude, Justin McCarthy, and Matthew Arnold.

Unlike most of his millionaire peers of the Gilded Age, Carnegie was curiously lacking in the usual social ambitions of that day. He never made the expected obeisance to Mrs. Astor, and he could hardly have cared less that he was not even considered for admission into that charmed, if not charming, company of Ward McAllister's Four Hundred. From 1884 on, he dutifully paid his annual dues to the Union League Club, but he regarded this strictly as a business expense; club life per se held no attraction for him. But there was one organization, the Nineteenth Century Club, to which he was proud to belong. Founded by Courtlandt Palmer in the 1860's as a discussion group, the Nineteenth Century Club consisted largely of New York intellectuals interested in discussing questions of religion and philosophy as well as the major social and economic issues of the day. Regarding themselves as free and enlightened thinkers in an age of scientific advancement, most of Palmer's group were strongly attracted to the Positivist ideas of Auguste Comte and his English disciples, George Henry Lewes and Frederic Harrison, who were seeking a new "religion of humanity." There were also representatives of traditional religious viewpoints in the group, Protestant ministers, Jewish rabbis, Catholic priests. The discussions as a consequence were lively, stimulated in no small degree by the booming, oratorical voice of Colonel Robert Ingersoll, who, as an ardent—one might say even devout—agnostic, accused many of his religious humanist friends of merely substituting one form of hagiolatry for another.[6]

It was through the sponsorship of Palmer and other friends whom he had met at Madame Botta's salon that Carnegie became a member of the Nineteenth Century Club. It was probably there that he first became familiar with the names of Darwin and Spencer. His interest was quickly aroused, for since that day, many years before, when he and Tom Miller had announced their disbelief in the Reverend Mr. McMillan's Calvinist God, Carnegie had been searching for a faith that might serve in place of the Presbyterianism of his Scottish forebears or the gentle Swedenborgian mysticism of his father. It had not been an anguished search, for, like his mother, Carnegie apparently needed no strong spiritual sustenance. But Carnegie did like to argue questions of theology and philosophy with his more religiously orthodox friends, and it was somewhat disconcerting to him, after having attacked their Protestant faith, to have no ready response to the inevitable question that would follow such a discussion: "Well then, what *do* you believe in?" Carnegie was not even religiously oriented enough to be a dedicated atheist, and he found agnosticism, simply another way of saying "I don't know," to be a pallid and ineffective answer to theological orthodoxy.

Having been introduced to the new evolutionary doctrines that were being so freely discussed with this circle of new friends, Carnegie waded boldly into the writings of Herbert Spencer, and, with his feet barely wet, he imagined himself to be swimming in the strong current of a new faith. His discovery of evolution came as a thrilling revelation. Carnegie would remember "that light came as in a flood and all was clear. Not only had I got rid of theology and the supernatural, but I had found the truth of evolution. 'All is well since all grows better' became my motto, my true source of comfort. Man was not created with an instinct for his own degradation, but from the lower he had risen to the higher forms. Nor is there any conceivable end to his march to perfection. His face is turned to the light, he stands in the sun and looks upward." [7]

Armed like a Christian missionary in the righteousness of his new faith, Carnegie departed for the Orient in 1878, determined to see the world as an operating laboratory for Herbert Spencer's *First Principles*. "Seek and ye shall find," an injunction given in quite a different context, now became an appropriate motto for Carnegie's tour. Everywhere he went, he was delighted to find evidence of the truth of Herbert Spencer's faith in progress through evolution toward perfection. He could agree with the master himself when Spencer wrote, "It appears that in the treatment of every topic, however seemingly remote from philosophy, I found occasion for falling back on some ultimate principle in the natural order." [8]

Even in the midst of the great expanse of the Pacific Ocean, Carnegie saw the inexorable force of the evolutionary process at work.

A good chart shows islands dotting the South Pacific Ocean, all of coral formation; these millions of toilers are hard at work, and it is only a question of time when our posterity will run by rail from the Sandwich to the Philippine Islands, always provided that the work of these little builders is not interfered with by the forces which destroy. Thus the grand, never-ending work of creation goes on, cycle upon cycle, revealing new wonders at every turn and knowing no rest or pause. [9]

Progress through evolution, both biological and technological, bringing nature and man, "the machine and the garden," toward perfect harmony—this was to be the essence of Carnegie's faith in the ultimate perfectibility of the universe, and he would hold to that faith for the next thirty-five years.

With that customary talent for table mismatching for which ship stewards are always noted, the steward on board the *Belgic* assigned Carnegie and Vandevort to a dining table with "a reverend missionary and wife, with two young lady missionaries in embryo, who are on their way to begin their labors among the Chinese." The table talk must have been as lively as any session of the Nineteenth Century Club, for Carnegie made no effort to conceal his disbelief in his dinner companions' faith or his disapproval of their efforts to impose that faith upon another culture. "Poor girls! what a life they have before them!" he wrote in his diary. [10] The second Sunday at sea, bored, and mildly curious as to what sort of sermon the missionary might deliver to the other passengers, Carnegie decided to attend the services. "I trust he will be moved to speak to us, away in mid-ocean, of the great works of the Unknown, the mighty deep, the universe, the stars, at which we nightly wonder, and not drag us down to the level of dogmas we can know nothing of, and about which we care less." The worthy missionary disappointed Carnegie. "The sermon is over. Pshaw! He spent the morning attempting to prove to us that the wine Christ made at the marriage feast was not fermented, as if it mattered, or as if this could ever be known! and I was in the mood to preach such a magnificent sermon myself, too, if I had had his place. No; I shall never forgive him—never!" [11]

Nor the minister's fellow missionaries, for that matter. Nearly twenty years later Carnegie received a note from one of the young lady missionaries, Ella Newton, who had shared his dining table on the *Belgic*. "Although you were so kind to us, I remember you did not have very much faith in our mission to China, but you did have faith in your mother, and in her religion, and I have hoped that anchor might hold you from drifting away from God. Well, Miss Rankin and I are still in China, though we seldom meet." Miss Newton concluded her letter by asking Carnegie for $4000 for a new dormitory for her mission in Foochow, China. In denying her request, Carnegie answered:

> And so you have remained all these long years in China, and you are doing what you think right. Happy woman! How it must surprise you to know that I am led to the contrary conclusion. I think that money spent upon foreign missions for China is not only money misspent, but that we do a grievous wrong to the Chinese by trying to force our religion upon them against their wishes. I could not contribute toward this work conscientiously and I know that you would not have me do it otherwise.
>
> I believe that all religions are adapted to those for whom they are provided. The ten great religions are very much alike in their fundamental ideas, and I do not wonder at the attacks made upon foreign missions by the Chinamen. If the Chinamen were to come here protected by warships of their government and try to prove the falsity of our religions, against our earnest protests, I fear they would not meet with better treatment. Besides, I think that to force our religious views on others is not Christ-like. He never used force, but was always gentle and persuading. I commend his example to all your missionary friends in China, who are there simply because our warships or guns protect them.[12]

Already a scientific humanist at the time of his departure, Carnegie was to return from his trip around the world a convinced cultural relativist. The best features of Christianity he found to be inherent in all of the great world religions:

It is an old and true saying that almost any system of religion would make one good enough if it were properly obeyed; certainly that of Confucius would do so. . . . If any of my readers wish a rare treat, I advise him to add at least the first volume of the Rev. Dr. Legge's Life of Confucius to his library immediately, and let him not entertain the idea that the sage was a heathen or an unbeliever; far, very far from that, for one of his most memorable passages explains that all worship belongs to Shangti (the Supreme Ruler); no matter what forms or symbols are used, the great God being the only true object of worship. . . . Meanwhile, remember well what Matthew Arnold says:

"Children of men! the unseen Power, whose eye
    For ever doth accompany mankind,
Hath look'd on no religion scornfully
    That men did ever find." [13]

Yet Carnegie would qualify Arnold's poetic religious universalism by insisting that the Supreme Ruler would certainly scorn many of the religious practices that were performed by men everywhere in the name of the Deity whom they would honor. Here again, Carnegie found himself to be as much a universalist in what he rejected as in what he accepted. Although he was especially appalled by the excesses of religious superstition that he found among the Hindus in India—the "terrible car of Juggernaut," the blood sacrifices to Kali, the erotic sandstone carvings "too gross to speak of," and the bathing in the foul, polluted water of the sacred well at Benares—he found them to be, if more exotic, certainly no more monstrously degrading to man and God than the creed of the Christians. "The whole scheme of Christian Salvation is diabolical as revealed by the creeds. An angry God, imagine such a creator of the universe. Angry at what he knew was coming and was himself responsible for. Then he sets himself about to beget a son, in order that the child should beg him to forgive the Sinner. This however he cannot or will not do. He must punish somebody—so the son offers himself up & our creator punishes the innocent youth, never heard of before—for the

368

guilty and became reconciled to us. 'Very good my demon you may be reconciled to me. But I am not reconciled to you.' I decline to accept Salvation from such a fiend. This is the natural reply that rises in my heart. . . . It is libellous. The Unknown does not deserve such abuse." [14]

For the bloodthirsty Kali and the wrathful Jehovah, Carnegie would substitute the Supreme Force of the universe, who, although remaining the Great Unknown, had at last revealed his grand design for mankind through the writings of his latter-day and true prophet, Herbert Spencer. The only sin was ignorance, and man's mind was his endowment of divinity; his salvation lay in education and his evolutionary progress toward perfection was inevitable. Now that man, thanks to Spencer, understood these inexorable laws of nature, progress toward perfection would move at an ever faster rate. "All is well since all grows better," even among the Hindus, the most burdened with ignorance of all the peoples whom Carnegie met on his global tour.

Carnegie's evaluation of the three major Oriental cultures he saw was largely determined by the evidence each offered of moving forward in the mainstream of progress. In this the Japanese were certainly the most impressive. Only twenty-five years after Commodore Perry's entry into Tokyo Bay at Yokohama, Japan had already accomplished what it had taken Europe four centuries of painful transition to effect: the feudalism of the Shogunate had been replaced by Western parliamentarianism of the most advanced order; England's industrial evolution, of a century's duration, had been for Japan a true revolution, accomplished within two decades. As easily as they could process tin from the East Indies or mould glass into the bright, cheap baubles for the notion counters of the Occidental world, Japan's newly imported machines were now also converting the peasantry of an ancient agrarian economy into urbanized, factory-housed workers, hardly distinguishable from their Western counterparts, the former crofters of Yorkshire and Scotland, now the machine tenders of Birmingham and Sheffield.

All of this should have been, and was, impressive evidence to Carnegie that the world moves on and "all grows better." Japan was leaving the ancient past far behind. Her Shinto temples were already becoming tourist attractions, relics of a superstitious religion that had as little meaning to modern Japan as the ruined Catholic cathedrals in the border country had to industrialized southern Scotland. Nevertheless, Japan left Carnegie feeling vaguely dissatisfied. Perhaps the transition had been made too quickly and easily; perhaps Japan was too imitative of the West. In her frantic eagerness for modernity her parroting of Western ways had become a parody of the evils as well as of the blessings of industrial civilization. The sleek new warships at Yokohama, which Carnegie detested, were as true a reflection of Western advancement as the efficient new factories in the outskirts of Tokyo, which Carnegie admired. All was bright and shining and markedly progressive, but Carnegie felt there was an unreal quality; Japan was all too like the models children punch out of cardboard and set up on the dining-room table for the foreign visitor to take her seriously and to accept her at full value. "The odor of the toyshop pervades everything," was Carnegie's final opinion of Japan.[15]

India stood in stark contrast in almost every respect to the busy little nation of the northern Orient. At the very moment when Japan was hastily casting aside her feudal traditions and emerging as a modern, sovereign state, ready and eager to challenge the great Western countries for a position of power in the Orient, India, still bound by the ancient laws of caste and the dark compulsions of degrading superstition, had been transformed into an imperial domain of Britain, and if not "the brightest crown jewel" in Victoria's ill-fitting diadem, certainly the largest and most impressive.

Poor, unhappy India, divided into fiercely jealous and contending ethnic factions, held in the straitjacket of caste, she was unable to move either out or up without risking bloody class war and disintegration. So she had permitted the newest sahib from the West to impose the order of the barrack room on her divisions and had thus achieved a measure of unity within colonialism.

Appalled as Carnegie was by much of what he saw in this vast subcontinent, his usual optimism asserted itself, and he saw signs of hope even in India. The very hypocrisy of the Hindu priests encouraged Carnegie to believe that the savage gods of India were as doomed to mortality as the raucous Olympian deities of ancient Greece. "The germ is there," he wrote in his diary.[16] He saw far greater promise in the Moslems for future leadership of India than in the Hindus.[17] The English, whose domination of India he protested as loudly as any Indian nationalist, nevertheless served a temporarily useful role in the evolution of these nobly miserable people. The introduction of Western journalism and railroad transportation into India would doom the caste system. "India is thus in a state of transition, her caste and religion both passing away. The work before this generation and probably the next is to pull down and destroy. It will remain for those who come after to begin the more difficult labor of building up." [18]

It was China that held the most fascination for Carnegie, however. If India's problem lay in the slowness of her evolutionary development and Japan's in the speed of hers, China's difficulty had been that she had evolved to a high degree of civilization too early in the history of the human race. At a time when India was being invaded by the first of the nomadic Caucasian tribes from the West, and Europe had barely emerged from the Neolithic Age into a culture based upon the use of metals, China had already achieved a high degree of civilization in the arts and the sciences, a civilization in which aestheticism and urbanity were qualities valued more highly than efficiency and utilitarianism. In a world of barbarism, China had somehow first imagined and then effected a true civilization of poetry and astronomy, of sophistication and mannered restraint. This achievement marked man's most spectacular leap forward since the invention of agriculture and placed China so far ahead of any other culture as to make comparisons impossible. The advance had been too great and too early, leading first to an unquestioning complacency and then to stagnation. For a thousand years, China had been preoccupied only with the further burnishing of the already highly polished surface of her culture, claiming dominion over all other peoples, exacting tribute from her near neighbors when she could, and contemptuously ignoring those more distant barbarians of whom she had only the vaguest knowledge and even less interest. When these primitives, with their ugly but effective weapons, crude manners, and compelling hunger, broke into the Celestial Kingdom, China conquered them by absorbing them, softening them, civilizing them. By then they had lost all separate identity and were a part of that vastness that was China.

371

In the eighteenth century, at first only tentatively, and later, in the nineteenth century, with the serious purpose of permanent domination, new barbarians had come out of the West, and their instruments of warfare were more powerful than the wise old men of China could have ever imagined. These were barbarians who refused to be overawed by China's culture, who grabbed her treasures but would not acknowledge the superiority of a culture that had produced them, who came with their icons and holy scriptures and insisted upon an absolute single truth which Chinese culture denied. These frightening new men of the West resisted the softening, absorbing culture of China and instead attempted to impose their faith, their laws, their society upon China.

Japan had foiled the plans of these new barbarians by joining them; India had simply capitulated to them; but China would not admit defeat either by imitating their ways or by surrendering outright. The barbarians might seize her coastal cities, capture her trade, send their missionaries into her villages to force their faith upon her peasants. Their warships might patrol her coasts, and their businessmen, operating under their own laws and protected by their own troops, might ruthlessly exploit her resources, markets, and labor, but China continued her resistance in the only way she knew, by keeping intact and undefiled that inner essence of her culture which had sustained her through the many millennia of human history: the wisdom of moderation and the dignity of old age, those ancient truths which Confucius had exalted through aphorism; the beauty to be found in a single tree branch against the sky; the delicate nuances of meaning that were possible only in her language; the knowledge that the shadow was often more important than the substance. These were the things that belonged to China that could not be sold, or seized, or converted by the West.

Being a Westerner, Carnegie did not understand much of China's culture, but his perception of and sensitivity to the essential meaning of China were nevertheless remarkable. Like any good Western businessman, he decried China's lack of industry; her indifference to railroads; and the primitive, unchanging methods of her agriculture. To his credit, he also realized that one needed another kind of yardstick to measure China's stature than that used in Birmingham or Pittsburgh. "Amid much which causes one to mourn for the backwardness of this country," he wrote in his diary, "here is the bright jewel in her crown. China is, as far as I know, the only nation which has advanced beyond the so-called heroic age when the soldier claims precedence. . . . No general, no conqueror, be his victories what they may, can ever in China attain the highest rank that is held only by successful scholars who have shown the possession of literary talent. . . . These are the mandarins, and there is no other aristocracy in China." [19]

It would be this aristocracy of intellectuals, Carnegie was convinced, which would eventually revolutionize China, not in the manner of Japan by servile imitation of the West, but by an adaptation that would be meaningful to China's own culture. With prophetic insight, Carnegie wrote:

> Here in Asia the survival of the fittest is being fought out. . . . In this struggle we have no hesitation in backing the Heathen Chinese against the field. Permanent occupation by any Western race is of course out of the question. An Englishman would inevitably cease to be an Englishman in a few, a very few, generations, and it is therefore only a question of time when the Chinese will drive every other race to the wall. No race can possibly stand against them anywhere in the East." [20]

A remarkable statement to come from one whose professed faith in Social Darwinism should have led him to the only conclusion acceptable to most of his fellow evolutionists—the supremacy and inevitable worldwide domination of the white race, and, more particularly, the Anglo-Saxons.

On Thursday, 20 March 1879, Carnegie and Vandevort arrived in the Bay of Naples. "Early morning!" Carnegie wrote in his diary. "Yes my dear friends, *it is round.* Here stands Mount Vesuvius in full view this morning, making for itself pure white clouds of steam, which float in the otherwise clear, cloudless sky of Italy. No entering the crater now as we did before, for the volcano is no longer at rest. Vandy and I shake hands and recall our pledge made in the crater years ago, and say, 'Well, that is now fulfilled, and may life only have for us in its unknown future another such five months of unalloyed happiness . . . as those we have been so privileged to enjoy.' " [21]

For Carnegie, this tour had been as much a testimonial to Spencer as the fulfillment of a pledge made with Vandevort. Like any returning Pilgrim who has had his faith certified by a papal blessing in St. Peter's or the muezzin's call to prayer in Mecca, Carnegie returned from his global trip confirmed in his belief in evolution by everything he had seen, from the lonely coral atolls in the Pacific to the crowded bazaars in Cairo. Everywhere he saw signs of progress, of men either being pushed slowly but inexorably by nature or being propelled more rapidly by their own insatiable desires and dreams into a change which, in Carnegie's opinion, was for the better. Nevertheless, even if Carnegie returned from this trip a more dedicated evolutionist than ever, he had "suffered a sea-change, into something rich and strange"—at least as a Social Darwinist. He was no longer so ready to assert dogmatically how evolutionary progress should be effected, and his perceptive knowledge of the world would make it impossible for him ever again to accept those parochial prejudices and false claims of superiority that most of his fellow countrymen subscribed to in their attitude toward the peoples of the exotic East.

Go, therefore, my friend . . . go and see for yourselves how greatly we are bound by prejudices, how checkered and uncertain are many of our own advances, how very nearly all is balanced. No nation has all that is best, neither is any bereft of some advantages, and no nation, or tribe, or people is so unhappy that it would be willing to exchange its condition for that of any other. See, also, that in every society there are many individuals distinguished for traits of character which place them upon a par with the best and highest we know at home, and that such are everywhere regarded with esteem, and held up as models for lower and lesser natures to emulate. The traveller will not see in all his wanderings so much abject, repulsive misery among human beings in the most heathen lands, as that which startles him in his civilized Christian home, for nowhere are the extremes of wealth and poverty so painfully presented. . . . Another advantage to be derived from a journey round the world is, I think, that the sense of the brotherhood of man, the unity of the race, is very greatly strengthened thereby, for one sees that the virtues are the same in all lands, and produce their good fruits, and render their possessors blessed in Benares and Kioto as in London or New York; that the vices, too, are akin, and also that the motives which govern men do not differ, and so the heart swells and the sympathies extend, and we embrace all men in our thoughts, leaving not one outside the range of our solicitude and wishing everyone well. The Japanese, Chinese, Cingalese, Indians, Egyptians, all have been made our friends through individuals of each race of whom we have heard much that was good and noble, pure lives, high aims, good deeds, and how can we, therefore, any longer dwell apart, believing our own land or our own people in any respect the chosen of God! . . . Wherever we have been, one story met us. Everywhere there is progress, not only material but intellectual as well, and rapid progress, too. . . . We saw no race which had retrograded, if we except Egypt, which is now in a transitional state, and will ultimately prove no exception to the rule. The whole world moves, and moves in the right direction—upward and onward—to things that are better than those that have been and those to come to be better than those of today. The law of evolution—the higher from the lower—is not discredited by a voyage round the world and the knowledge of what is transpiring from New York round to New York again gives us joy this morning as we sum it all up.[22]

For someone who, at the outset of his trip, was hesitant about seeing the Taj Mahal in Agra lest "even Walter Scott's monument at Edinburgh—my favorite piece of stone and lime—must be surpassed by this marvel of perfection," [23] Carnegie, in this summation, gives striking evidence of the degree to which his own vision and understanding had been broadened and extended by his global tour. Indeed, it is no exaggeration to say that what Mont St. Michel and Chartres would be to Henry Adams, so Tokyo, Shanghai, and Benares were to Carnegie in providing for his education. No other experience of his adult life was to be quite so important as this trip, not only in confirming and strengthening the social views he had already acquired, but also in qualifying and modifying those views in such a way as to give to Carnegie's social philosophy a peculiar quality of cosmopolitanism that is not usually associated with Social Darwinism.

The identification of the self-interest of the post Civil War industrialists with the social philosophy of Herbert Spencer has long seemed to most American social and intellectual historians a fact so obvious as to need little or no examination or questioning. It has been granted, of course, that the earlier, cruder buccaneers on the American industrial scene—such men as Cornelius Vanderbilt and Daniel Drew—had felt no need to disguise their simple, unabashed acquisitiveness with any scientific or philosophical rationalization. For old Commodore Vanderbilt, acquisition was a simple matter of lawless and ruthless exercise of force. "Law! What do I care about law? Haint't I got the power?" [24] was as close as he had ever come to a philosophic justification of the means he had used to acquire wealth. No need for him to prattle about American Beauty roses being created by a process of ruthless pruning or about God's having given him his wealth. As for Daniel Drew, that great benefactor of future Methodist seminary students was blissfully ignorant of all evolutionary theories. Indeed, had he ever heard of them, he would have been as shocked and outraged as William Jennings Bryan and the good citizens of Dayton, Tennessee.

If these proto-tycoons of American industrialism apparently had no more need for a knowledge of Spencerian theory than did beasts of prey in the jungle, nevertheless it has been generally accepted that they, like their predatory counterparts, acted out in their daily lives the stern dicta of Darwinian evolution. The weaker were devoured, the fittest survived, and American industry and consequently American society benefited from this competitive struggle for existence. Richard Hofstadter, in his classic study of *Social Darwinism in American Thought*, has expressed the considered judgment of most American historians by identifying the social outlook of post Civil War American businessmen with the Spencerian philosophy. "Successful business entrepreneurs," Hofstadter wrote, "apparently accepted almost by instinct the Darwinian terminology which seemed to portray the conditions of their existence. Businessmen are not commonly articulate social philosophers, but a rough reconstruction of their social outlook shows how congenial to their thinking were the plausible analogies of social selection, and how welcome was the expansive evolutionary optimism of the Spencerian system." [25] Herbert

Spencer's popularity in the United States throughout the Gilded Age has seemed to provide for historians all the evidence necessary to substantiate the business world's acceptance of Social Darwinism. This unqualified acceptance of a single philosophic point of view by the businessmen in the post Civil War period has become so standard a conclusion as to be axiomatic among historians.[26]

Few, however, have been inclined to ask the most pertinent question: Who was reading Herbert Spencer in these years and directly applying his theoretical propositions to the practical American business scene? It was enough for the historian to show that not only had Spencer offered a convenient justification for American business practices by placing them outside of the old traditional moral judgments—"beyond good and evil," as it were —but also that American entrepreneurs could use Spencer's theories to reinforce the popular acceptance of laissez-faire so as to make this economic doctrine into a law of nature as inexorable as Newton's law of gravity. In short, historical logic, if not historical evidence, has strongly supported this easy identification of American business interests with Herbert Spencer's social philosophy.

Did the American businessman himself understand and make use of Spencerian evolution to justify his mode of operation? Textbook authors and other general historians of the period have found it so convenient to accept Hofstadter's thesis as an easy explanation for the businessman's social behavior that most of them have failed to note that Hofstadter qualified his statement by restricting it to the *successful* business entrepreneur. This is an important and relevant qualification, for it is highly questionable whether those who failed in this "struggle for survival" in the business world would want to attribute their own failure to being personally too weak and unfit for the contest. In all the voluminous testimony given either to Congressional committees or to muckraking journalists by the victims of the competitive business system of that day, one cannot find any suggestion that there was an inexorably just evolutionary law that had doomed them to failure.[27] Rather, these unsuccessful business entrepreneurs would attribute their failure, as men have always done, to the unethical behavior of their competitors or to the inexplicable vagaries of chance. By limiting the acceptance of Social Darwinism to those businessmen who only revealed their latent "instinct" for Darwinian terminology *after* achieving success, Hofstadter was making a generalization that would be applicable at most to only one-third of the business community.[28]

What of the survivors in entrepreneurial struggle for existence? How congenial did they find the Darwinian theory as an explanation for their success? Richard Hofstadter's study of Social Darwinism first appeared in 1946, and it was not until some fifteen years later that a few historians began to question his thesis that successful businessmen were professed and practising Social Darwinists. Most notable among the recent historians who have raised questions about the impact of Social Darwinism upon the thought of the business community has been Irvin G. Wyllie.[29] Wyllie concluded his critical evaluation, "Social Darwinism and the Businessman," with this challenge to the historical profession:

> [The critical historians] will also discriminate between positive social Darwinists and mere biological or religious evolutionists. They will ask whether competitive social Darwinism did fit the businessman like a glove, whether it served all of his interests and satisfied his every aspiration. Was he a Spencerian when he cooperated with other businessmen in pools and trusts that throttled competition? What did he contribute to the survival of the fittest when he practiced philanthropy? From a public relations point of view, who profited most from the claim that he was a social Darwinist, the businessman or his critics? As historians undertake to explain what the businessman actually thought about social Darwinism, they will recognize that their greatest single need is a need for more direct reliable evidence on all points at issue. This means evidence out of the Gilded Age, and evidence supplied by businessmen themselves, not by outside observers. It also means testimony that . . . ties ideas to their actual and not assumed sources. My prediction is that such evidence will force us to revise downward our estimate of the impact of social Darwinism on American business thought. The businessman drew his ideas and social values from many sources, not just one. He would not have been ideologically naked without the Spencerian formulation.[30]

The great problem, of course, in determining the sources for those ideas to which the business community subscribed—indeed, the problem of determining the ideas themselves—lies in obtaining the kind of evidence Wyllie asks for. As Hofstadter has said, "Businessmen are not commonly articulate social philosophers," and the records they have left in business letters, minutes of board meetings, memoranda, and contractual agreements are not, by their very nature, useful sources for determining the ideological positions of their authors. Very few entrepreneurs had either the time or the inclination during their active business careers to articulate their philosophical position—assuming, of course, that they had such a position.

A few of the great entrepreneurs, after having achieved their fortune, were moved to write, or to have ghostwritten, the story of their success, but one looks in vain through the pages of these success manuals for an expression of the Social Darwinist credo. They themselves attributed their success to a faithful observance of those traditional American expressions of thrift, sobriety, and hard work that are derived from the axioms of Benjamin Franklin, rather than from the scientific theorizing of Darwin or Spencer. Thomas Mellon probably spoke for most of his associates when he said, "I regard the reading of Franklin's *Autobiography* as the turning point of my life. . . . Here was Franklin, poorer than myself, who by industry, thrift and frugality had become learned and wise, and elevated to wealth and fame. The maxims of 'Poor Richard' exactly suited my sentiments." [31]

As John G. Cawelti has written in his *Apostles of the Self-made Man,* "There was considerable continuity between the traditional ideal of self-improvement and the new philosophy of success. In many respects—its insistence that the key to success lay in individual character, its emphasis on the productive and self-disciplinary virtues of work, economy, and temperance, and its basically religious orientation—the philosophy of success was . . . a refurbishing of the Protestant ethic." [32]

These basic American virtues, drawn from the stern doctrines of Calvinistic puritanism and the harsh realities of a frontier culture, were deeply embedded within the American ethos long before Darwin took his celebrated voyage on H.M.S. *Beagle* or Spencer pondered the significance of the slug crawling through the rotting compost heap in his vegetable garden. Lincoln's oft-repeated theme of "bettering one's condition"—never more forcibly or effectively stated than in his speech to a New England audience in March 1860, when he concluded with the classic line, "Then you can better your condition, and so it may go on and on in one ceaseless round so long as man exists on the face of the earth"—struck a responsive note among Americans everywhere. This was what America was all about. This was the promise it had always held out to the newly arrived immigrant, to the restless farmer moving ever westward, and to the country boy riding the canal barge into New York City or hopping a freight car that would take him to Chicago.

Lincoln's words of "one ceaseless round" gave no explicit promise of societal progress through evolutionary advancement. Quite the contrary. The hope for betterment that Lincoln expressed was entirely individual and personal, and this is what America wanted to hear. If asked, most Americans would have agreed that "the ceaseless round" did move upward like a spiral and society was the ultimate benefactor of the single individual's ambition for self-advancement. Had not Adam Smith, the high apostle of laissez faire, stated a fundamental truth when he wrote that "self-love" was the real basis for the wealth of a nation?

The important goal, however, was individual betterment through one's own efforts and strength of character. And if Americans in this post Civil War age believed implicitly in the "myth of the self-made man," if they made heroes out of those who had achieved wealth in the Horatio Alger tradition, they were, at the same time, not at all averse to accepting, as an important qualification of the "rags to riches" theme, another typically American folk adage: "from shirtsleeves to shirtsleeves in three generations." In short, they wanted to believe that this great race for worldly success was always open, that it must start anew for each generation under approximately the same conditions. They feared the consequences of dynastic wealth that would restrict the list of entrants more than they welcomed the possibility of society evolving toward perfection if societal advancement depended upon a closed society. The log cabin and the tenement flat must not be eliminated as birthplaces of ambition, for it was an essential part of the American dream to believe that the most fit sons in the race for material success were sired by fathers who had failed in that race. The Social Darwinists might be useful for rationalizing

380

competition, but in America, at least, they would have little success in promoting the idea that the winners in the great race of life were determined by the ruthless operation of the principle of natural selection. There was as little sympathy in America for a Darwinian class division as there was for a Marxian. Far from being "ideologically naked without the Spencerian formulation," most Americans, entrepreneurs and working men alike, felt that the old, familiar dress of egalitarian individualism, which they had taken from the wardrobe press of Franklin, Jackson, and Lincoln, was all that was necessary in the way of an ideological costume to protect themselves from the elements.[33]

But if most successful American businessmen, when called upon to discuss the topic of achieving success in a ruggedly competitive world, drew upon Benjamin Franklin and Abraham Lincoln, rather than Herbert Spencer and William Graham Sumner, as sources for their inspiration and quotations, Andrew Carnegie was the notable exception. Indeed, he has been the prime exhibit of those historians who have stressed the importance of Social Darwinism in molding the thought of the late nineteenth century American business community. Even Irvin Wyllie has felt obliged to accept without question Carnegie's Social Darwinistic faith and to concede that "it would be impossible to deny his [Carnegie's] Darwinist orientation."[34]

This acceptance of Carnegie as a Social Darwinist *par excellence* is hardly surprising, for Carnegie from 1870 on loudly trumpeted to the world—in public speeches, books, and articles, and in private conversations and personal letters—his intellectual and spiritual indebtedness to Herbert Spencer. As Carnegie would say repeatedly, "Before Spencer, all for me had been darkness, after him, all had become light—and right."

Nor had it been enough for Carnegie to worship the master from afar. He wanted to pay homage in person, and in return for his oath of fealty he wanted Spencer's friendship. Some of Carnegie's friends made use of their great wealth to bring back from Europe paintings of Rubens and Rembrandt, first editions of Milton and Blake, Louis XIV chairs, and titled husbands for their daughters. Carnegie's collecting proclivities never took these forms. It seemed to him only too easy to make this kind of ostentatious show of wealth. Any fool with a checkbook could capture culture as a trophy and either hang it on his wall or seat it in his parlor. Such easy acquisitions satisfied neither Carnegie's vanity nor his intellectual curiosity. To win the friendship of great men and, if possible, to bring them to America for display were triumphs requiring more than cash. And there was no prize that Carnegie sought more eagerly than Herbert Spencer. So began the long, patient courting of his hero, a courtship that was not without its difficulties. Carnegie quickly discovered that Spencer hardly had the same philosophic detachment and objectivity in small matters touching upon his personal convenience and comfort that he had in viewing the cosmos. Hypochondriac that he was, Spencer guarded himself zealously against any painful contacts with that teaming, competing world that lay outside the quiet sanctity of his study and bedroom. He might extol the snarling rule of the jungle for the world at large, but for himself he sought the Brahms lullaby peacefulness of a well-tended nursery.

After much effort, Carnegie did get to meet Spencer briefly sometime in the early 1880's. He is not specific in his autobiography as to either the time or place, but one can assume that, with the brashness which never deserted him, even in the presence of the master himself, he undoubtedly pressed upon Spencer an invitation to visit America at his earliest convenience.[35] Had Spencer's convenience been the only consideration, the trip would never have been made, for the Sage of Brighton had little stomach for the rigors of a trans-Atlantic voyage and the exhausting demands of a grand American tour.

Eventually, however, Spencer yielded, not to Carnegie's hearty and eager invitation, as Carnegie later liked to believe, but to the demands of his American publishers and to his own vanity. By 1882, having survived (to his surprise) a sea voyage to Alexandria, Egypt, Spencer felt he could no longer deny his American reading public, many times greater and more enthusiastic than that in England,[36] the privilege of seeing the master in person. And so the elaborate plans were made to carry Spencer as comfortably and happily as possible across the Atlantic to meet and greet his enthusiastic American supporters. His closest friend, Edward Lott, would accompany him and act as his constant shield and buffer against the bruising impact of a too eager and overly cu-

rious public. Friends in America had given their solemn assurances that his sensitivity would be respected and that all tours,
public appearances, and speeches would be arranged only to suit
his personal convenience. Although Spencer could have used
the money, he adamantly refused all offers to promote a lecture
series. "The giving a lecture or reading a paper," he wrote to one
American friend, "would be nothing more than making myself a
show; and I absolutely decline to make myself a show. What I do
while with you I mean to make entirely subordinate to relaxation
and amusement; and I shall resist positively anything which in
any considerable way entails on me responsibilities or considerable excitements. I suppose you have long ago discovered that I
have a faculty of saying No, and that when I say No I mean
No." [37]

Under these strictures and conditions, the plans for Spencer's
tour painfully materialized. He and Lott would sail from Liverpool on 12 August 1882 aboard the Cunard's finest passenger
ship, the S. S. *Servia*. Carnegie, in England at the time, heard of
these plans and hurriedly made his own arrangements to return
to the United States on the same ship. Armed with a letter of introduction from John Morley, editor of the distinguished English
liberal periodical, *The Fortnightly Review*, Carnegie lost no time
in re-establishing his acquaintanceship with Spencer. A few discreet words and other, more tangible evidence of Carnegie's importance undoubtedly impressed the chief steward enough that
Carnegie was assigned to the same table in the dining room as
Spencer and Lott. As Carnegie would later recall the voyage,
"[Being] an older traveller, I took Mr. Lott and him in
charge." [38] For nine, uninterrupted days, Carnegie could revel in
this close association with the master.

Carnegie could never play the role of sycophant, however,
even to Spencer. Both he and Spencer would later recall in their
autobiographies an incident that revealed Carnegie's irrepressibly
bold forthrightness, characteristic of his dealing with all men.

One day [as Carnegie recalled the incident] the conversation
fell upon the impression made upon us by great men at first
meeting. Did they, or did they not, prove to be as we imagined
them? Each gave his experience. Mine was nothing could be

more different than the being imagined and that being beheld in the flesh.

"Oh!" said Mr. Spencer, "in my case, for instance was this so?"

"Yes," I replied, "You more than any. I had imagined my teacher, the great calm philosopher brooding Buddha-like, over all things, unmoved; never did I dream of seeing him excited over the question of Cheshire or Cheddar cheese." The day before he [Spencer] had peevishly pushed away the former when presented by the steward exclaiming "Cheddar, Cheddar, not Cheshire; I said *Cheddar*." There was a roar in which none joined more heartily than the sage himself.[39]

Spencer, in concluding his account of the same incident, wrote,

Nor is it only in respect of intellectual manifestations that too much is looked for from authors. There are also looked for, especially from authors of philosophical books, traits of character greatly transcending ordinary ones. . . . The identification of philosophy with stoicism still prevails very generally, and continually crops up in unexpected ways and places.[40]

Certainly no one who knew Spencer even slightly would ever identify him with stoicism.

This "Cheddar cheese" attitude of Spencer was to manifest itself in many different and more unpleasant forms throughout the grand tour, and not even his most ardent and uncritical American friends would find Spencer an easy guest. They judged his visit a disaster for all concerned. Carnegie had used all of his persuasive powers during the nine-day voyage in order to wring from Spencer a promise to include Pittsburgh on his itinerary. He had described the great Edgar Thomson Bessemer steel plant in all of its majestic power and had insisted that it was the sure harbinger of that industrial order which Spencer had declared as the next and final stage of man's social evolution. Spencer could hardly deny the force of Carnegie's argument and remain true to his own philosophy, and so he had given his promise that he would visit Pittsburgh.

As soon as the *Servia* docked in New York, Carnegie hurried to Pittsburgh to make arrangements for the great man's visit.

Spencer, exhausted by the trip and complaining bitterly of the ag-
onies he had endured, went into seclusion in a hotel in the Catskills for five days before heading north up the Hudson to Lake
Champlain and Montreal. There was little in this tour that interested or pleased Spencer. He kept aloof from those disciples who
were eager to meet him. Although Edward L. Youmans, editor of
the *Popular Science Monthly* and Spencer's most active publicist
in America, tried to get him to grant interviews to the press and
appear at receptions in his honor, Spencer, begging fatigue, declined all such offers. When he discovered upon his arrival in
Montreal that the meeting of the British Association for the Advancement of Science, to which he had been invited as an honored guest, had ended, he expressed no disappointment, but on
the contrary felt "this was fortunate; for probably, had it been
going on, further mischiefs would have been added to those
which I had suffered." [41]

After Canada, which he sharply criticized for having obtained
capital from British investors for its railroads by making promises
which "have proved far more wide of the truth than such statements usually prove—so wide of it that the undertakings have
been extremely disastrous to investors," [42] Spencer journeyed
down the St. Lawrence and across Lake Ontario to Niagara. If his
anxious guides expected that at least this mighty spectacular of
nature would arouse from Spencer some enthusiasm, they were
once again to be disappointed. Spencer's comment in his diary
after viewing the Falls was that Niagara was "much what I expected . . . the Falls neither came short of my expectations nor
much exceeded them." [43] With that curt dismissal of America's
most publicized natural wonder, Spencer and company departed
for Cleveland and then, in reluctant fulfillment of his promise, on
to Pittsburgh.

Carnegie, in the meantime, had been making extensive preparations for the great man's visit. When at last the impatiently
awaited guest arrived, Carnegie and his partners were at the station to welcome Spencer to what Carnegie regarded as the Sage's
true philosophic home. For here in the Pittsburgh area was surely
the model for the world of the Spencerian future, when man
would have achieved his final stage of evolutionary development
—the industrial society everywhere triumphant, a peaceful, co-op-

erative society undefiled by any military order or compulsory state regulation. Here along the Allegheny, steel was rolled for plowshares and rails and construction beams, not for swords or cannons or armor. Here men lived and worked in a co-operative society as well-defined and as self-regulating as a beehive. Spencer had written that the industrial society as he envisioned it no-where existed in its purest and most fully developed form, but Carnegie wanted to show him that America, with its minuscule army and its great industrial potential, had come closer to the ideal than any other nation on earth, and nowhere in America was the ideal more fully realized than in Pittsburgh.

Unhappily, the Sage of Brighton did not recognize utopia when it was shown to him. Indeed, his major complaint seemed to be that in this smoky, polluted air a man would be fortunate if he could recognize his own hand held close to his face. Carnegie, brother Tom, and Henry Phipps hurried Spencer and his party off to Braddock to show them the wonders of the world's most modern and efficient Bessemer steel mill. But the heat and noise of the mills reduced Spencer to a state of near collapse. When the tour was over, he could only gasp out to Carnegie, "Six months' residence here would justify suicide." [44]

To add subtle insult to painful injury, Spencer from the moment of his arrival in Pittsburgh seemed to be more attracted to Tom Carnegie than to Andrew. Tom's reticence and natural shyness apparently came as a relief from Andrew's volubility and over-eager desire to please. Although Spencer throughout his American tour had insisted upon staying in hotels rather than in private homes, so that he would not be at the mercy of zealous hosts, in Pittsburgh he was to make an exception to this rule. "The repulsiveness of Pittsburgh," he later wrote, "led me to break through my resolution always to stop at an hotel." [45] He quickly accepted Tom's suggestion that he might be more comfortable with him in his house in Homewood. Carnegie, who had engaged the best hotel suite in Pittsburgh for his noted guest and had planned a small reception to show off his prize to the civic leaders of Pittsburgh, was forced to accept the sudden change in plans. Apparently, the evening spent with Tom Carnegie was one of the most pleasant of Spencer's entire American tour. Tom had read more thoroughly in Spencer's philosophic works than Andrew had, and the questions he posed to Spencer that evening both intrigued and stimulated the philosopher. Indeed, Spencer was so impressed with Tom that he asked him if he would care to accompany Spencer and his party to Washington and New York. Tom, although flattered, pleaded business responsibilities in Pittsburgh. The next morning, Andrew reclaimed his prize and hurriedly drove Spencer off to his summer home, high up in the Alleghenies at Cresson, Pennsylvania.[46]

The cool, clear air of Cresson (where, incidentally, Spencer stayed at an inn rather than in Carnegie's summer home) helped somewhat in Spencer's physical and mental rehabilitation after his disastrous foray into the heart of the new industrial order that was Pittsburgh. After two days at Cresson he felt strong enough to continue his American tour, which included visits to Washington, Baltimore, Philadelphia, New York, and New England, and was to reach its climax at a great farewell dinner at Delmonico's in New York on 9 November 1882, two days prior to his departure for home.

The closer the time came for the great testimonial dinner, however, the more frightened Spencer became over the prospects of having his praises sung in public by this glittering collection of intellectual and business leaders and, even worse, of then standing up before this assembly to deliver a public lecture.

By the afternoon of the dinner, Spencer was nearly in a state of shock. As he wrote later in recalling those painful hours, "An occasion on which, more perhaps than on any other in my life, I ought to have been in good condition, bodily and mental, came when I was in a condition worse than I had been for six-and-twenty years. 'Wretched night; no sleep at all; kept in room all day,' says my diary; and I entertained 'great fear I should collapse.' "[47]

Carnegie picked Spencer up at his hotel and drove him to the dinner. Carnegie saw that "the great man was in a funk. He could think of nothing but the address he was to deliver. I believe he had rarely before spoken in public. His great fear was that he should be unable to say anything that would be of advantage to the American people, who had been the first to appreciate his works."[48] Spencer stayed in an anteroom of the banquet hall until the last possible moment, "so that I might avoid all excitements of introductions and congratulations; and as Mr. Evarts, who presided, handed me on to the dais, I begged him to limit his conversation with me as much as possible, and to expect very meagre responses." [49]

In spite of this inauspicious beginning, the dinner was generally regarded as a great success by those who attended. The glowing tributes were made by such diverse persons as Carl Schurz, William Graham Sumner, John Fiske, and Henry Ward Beecher. And Spencer managed to read through his speech to the very end "without difficulty, though not with much effect." [50]

The dinner, however, has long been a disappointment to those historians who have sought to use it to mark "the peak of Spencer's American popularity." [51] Certainly this great testimonial to Spencer by American intellectuals and business leaders of the 1880's would appear to be the kind of official seal of endorsement to the Social Darwinist philosophy that most American historians have accepted as the prevailing thought of the day. Here was Spencer, the great teacher of evolution, and here were all his eager disciples ready to carry his tenets back to indoctrinate their colleagues in their respective professions and business callings of theology, law, history, politics, manufacturing, and transportation. But, unfortunately, none of the actual participants played his part quite according to the Social Darwinist script: Schurz stressed Spencer's moral and ethical probity, Carnegie stressed Spencer's detestation of the military, Fiske announced that Spencer had contributed as much to religion as he had to science, while Henry Ward Beecher, carried away with his own rolling oratory, told the startled Spencer that they would meet once again beyond the grave in that great banquet hall in Heaven.[52] These tributes, however flattering they may have been to Spencer personally, are not the stuff of which Social Darwinism is made.

At least equally disappointing to later historians of the Social Darwinist movement was Spencer's own speech, which did not furnish his followers with a clarion call to competitive battle. Indeed, it must have come as something of a surprise to his audience, once they had accustomed themselves to his faltering and barely audible delivery, to hear what he was actually saying. For Spencer was reacting to all he had seen in America—to the crowded sidewalks of New York, to the feverish activity in the steel mills of Pittsburgh, and to the commercial strife of Cleveland and Boston—not in approbation but in shocked exhaustion. His message to the illustrious gathering in Delmonico's that evening was to relax, to slow down the fierce competitive struggle and to learn how to find and enjoy leisure time. Carnegie, who had early learned this lesson, was perhaps the only man in that audience who heartily approved of what Spencer was saying. One might argue that, of all Spencer's tenets, this quite unexpected one on the art of relaxation was the only one that Carnegie throughout his life would scrupulously observe.

Two days later Spencer sailed home to England, his tour of the provinces, that Spencerian utopia, thankfully over. As he stood on the deck just prior to the ship's departure, he suddenly, in a spontaneous gesture of warm friendship quite uncharacteristic of him, grasped the hands of Carnegie and Edward Youmans, who had come down to the ship to see him off. Holding their hands, Spencer turned to the crowd of reporters, who even in this last moment were still hoping to obtain an interview, and said, "Here are my two best American friends." [53] Carnegie would never forget this proud moment—nor would the historians. Carnegie, by his own frequently proclaimed admission and by Spencer's personal endorsement, would be accepted both by his contemporaries and by future historians as Herbert Spencer's "best American friend," America's most notable example of the Social Darwinist businessman.

Certainly, there is much in the Carnegie record that apparently substantiates this judgment. Not only in his published articles and books but also in his personal letters to business contemporaries, Carnegie makes frequent and easy allusions to the Social Darwinist credo. Phrases like "survival of the fittest," "race improvement," and "struggle for existence" came easily from his pen and presumably from his lips. He did see business as a great competitive struggle and he was always painfully aware of the weak who did not survive.

Carnegie attributed to Spencer even greater influence on his own philosophic position than he did to Burns or Shakespeare. Carnegie's devotion to Spencer's writings was demonstrated one summer day on a picnic on the Scottish moors. "After lunch, as we lay upon the heather," Sir George Adam Smith, the principal of Aberdeen University, remembered, "someone started the question, which was the favorite book of all of us, which ultimately became: If each of us were condemned to live on a desert island and allowed to take with him only one author, what author would he choose? (It was understood that the Bible was not to be discussed.) Someone said 'Shakespeare.' 'Well,' exclaimed Morley, 'I don't agree with you. You would be disappointed, for two-thirds of Shakespeare is mere padding.' Carnegie said, 'But the rest is worth a lifetime's study by itself.' Dr. White said, 'I would choose Dante.' Either Carnegie or Morley replied, 'Fancy Dante for a desert island! How gloomy!' 'And you, Mr. Carnegie,' said someone, 'What would you take?' 'Herbert Spencer,' said Mr. Carnegie at once. 'Worse and worse,' cried Morley, lifting his hands." [54]

This choice made by Carnegie was no idle summer afternoon fancy intended only to impress his intellectual associates with his unorthodox literary taste. Carnegie sincerely believed that Spencer was the greatest mind of his age or of any other, and that in the ponderous volumes Spencer wrote lay the final essence of all truth and knowledge. Shakespeare had had a profound understanding of human nature, Burns was the great troubadour of human freedom, but Herbert Spencer surpassed both by revealing to man his own destiny. And it was a destiny that Carnegie was only too impatient to see fulfilled: a new industrial world, without war and physical violence, in which, through the genius of invention and the miracle of mass production, the fruits of industry would become so abundant that they could be made available to all. It would be a new Garden of Eden without the snake of discontent, and with no fruit forbidden man to eat, least of all the fruit of knowledge. In short, Spencer had provided a teleological science to replace the static mechanistic science of Newton and Malthus. He had given purpose to man's existence that was infinitely more believable and satisfying to Carnegie than that divine purpose that had been provided by the Christian theologians. Above all, Spencer had provided a happy conclusion to man's striving that was neither dependent upon the violent destruction of the existing order as envisioned by Marx nor clothed in the gossamer of fancy as spun out by such utopian dreamers as Bellamy and Howells. Carnegie's happy little

390

slogan, "All is well, since all grows better" was for him the satisfying distillation of thirty volumes of Spencer's philosophical speculation.

For Carnegie, Spencer provided a satisfactory "scientific" substitute for the orthodox theology that Carnegie had long ago rejected. That was reason enough for Carnegie to hail Spencer as the greatest philosopher of all time. Clearly Carnegie belongs in that group of so-called "Social Darwinists" which Irvin Wyllie categorizes as "the mere biological or religious evolutionists." But the larger question remains: is it correct to assign Carnegie to the "positive Social Darwinists" who would justify existing business practices and social ethics of the late nineteenth century as a manifestation of Spencer's natural order of things?

In answering this question, it should be noted that, in the first place, Carnegie, like most American businessmen in the post Civil War period, did not accept the doctrine of laissez faire in its classical, Smithian purity. Like his fellow steel manufacturers, he supported financially and politically the American Iron and Steel Association in its efforts to lobby for a high protective tariff on all iron and steel products. And of even greater importance to Carnegie than tariff in the way of government protection were the patent laws, which he vigorously defended and utilized. Nor did he hesitate to enter pooling agreements for the restriction of free competition in order to support prices and productions when it was to his advantage to do so. All of these activities were not only antithetical to laissez-faire economics but also to Spencerian social ethics, for they had as their purpose the material reduction of free competition by artificial means. Spencer's injunctions against such activities were as much ignored by Carnegie as they were by all other American businessmen.

Carnegie, however, went far beyond most of his contemporaries in the business world by advocating a debasement of the purity of the Spencerian social philosophy in favor of providing for the general welfare through legislative action. In a remarkable interview which he gave to an Aberdeen reporter in 1891, Carnegie told the startled Scottish journalist that the only way to achieve the eight-hour day in industry was through state action. "It is well that the hours of labour shall be shortened. . . . I sympathize with the desire to have shorter hours." When asked if the eight-hour day would be achieved through union negotiation with management, Carnegie replied, "No, I do not think that trade union action would be strong enough with us to affect it. Organized capital can beat organized labour. . . . Laws to that effect must be passed by all the States. That is one advantage you would have in this country—such a law would be operative all over the land." The reporter then asked how Carnegie, as a disciple of Herbert Spencer, could possibly regard the general regulation of the hours of labor as "a fit subject for legislation." Carnegie's reply was blunt and unequivocal. "I cannot agree that the State should not interfere. The Factory Acts already interfere with child and female labour, and everything that has been done so far in that way has been beneficial. I differ from my great master Herbert Spencer in regard to the duties of the State. No hard and fast laws can be drawn in this matter. Whatever experience shows that the State can do best I am in favour of the State doing. . . . I believe we shall have more and more occasion for the State to legislate on behalf of the workers, because it is always the worst employers that have to be coerced into what fair employers would gladly do of their own accord if they had not to compete with the hard men." Unrestricted competition, in short, was not the best regulator of an industrial society.[55]

Nor did Carnegie hold firm to the Social Darwinist creed when it came into conflict with his views on philanthropy. Although he agreed with Spencer that almsgiving was worse than futile—it was socially pernicious—nevertheless, Carnegie was among the first of the American multimillionaires to develop the altruistic impulse of philanthropy into a social gospel of wealth and to preach, with Calvinistic fervor, the social responsibility of men of wealth. Here, too, he was severely qualifying the doctrine of the acquisitiveness of the fit by advocating support for the weak. He simply dismissed Spencer's strictures against philanthropy, and more significantly, he pointedly ignored the purest of all American Social Darwinists, William Graham Sumner. There is no evidence that he ever communicated with him or even read a line written by the Yale professor who was to carry the doctrines of Social Darwinism to their ultimate conclusions.

Carnegie's loudly professed belief in biological evolution, at least as drawn from Spencer's essentially Lamarckian doctrine of the inheritance of acquired characteristics, can also be questioned, for Carnegie neither consistently held to nor fully accepted this doctrine in its full implications. Like most Americans, he totally rejected the idea of eugenic superiority. On the contrary, he believed that it would be from the families of the poverty-stricken, who, according to Spencer, were the unfit, that would come those natural leaders who would dominate the society. He felt only pity toward the sons of men of great wealth, for he expected only physical and moral degeneracy to be their natural lot.

Poor boys reared thus directly by their parents [he wrote in an article entitled "The Advantages of Poverty" in 1891], possess such advantages over those watched and taught by hired strangers, and exposed to the temptations of wealth and position, that it is not surprising they become the leaders in every branch of human action. . . . Such boys always have marched, and always will march, straight to the front and lead the world; they are the epoch-makers. Let one select the three or four foremost names, the supremely great in every field of human triumph, and note how small is the contribution of hereditary rank and wealth to the short list of immortals who have lifted and advanced the race. It will, I think, be seen that the possession of these is almost fatal to greatness and goodness, and that the greatest and best of our race have necessarily been nurtured in the bracing school of poverty—the only school capable of producing the supremely great, the genius.[56]

Genius was a favorite word with Carnegie. He was overly generous in bestowing it as an accolade on others whose work pleased him. Almost all of his business partners were "his young geniuses," as well as those writers, artists, critics, and even politicans who for one reason or another had attracted his attention and won his approval. Carnegie had complete confidence in his own ability to recognize genius when he saw it, but he could offer no explanation of how genius was created. The inspiration of genius remained as mysterious and inexplicable to him as it had to the Greeks, the only difference being that he lacked the Hellenic faith in the gods and the muses to provide an answer. Never did he suggest, however, that the evolutionists had found the answer to the question of individual superiority. Genius was engendered not by any Darwinian process of natural selection of fit mating with fit to create the more fit, but, on the contrary, it sprang, sport-like, from the most unlikely parentage and the most uncongenial environment: an illiterate, unwed peasant girl of North Italy giving birth to a Leonardo, or a shiftless Kentucky ne'er-do-well siring a Lincoln. Genius was the mysterious product of unnatural selection, "a wild flower," Carnegie wrote, "found in the woods all by itself, needing no help from society." [57] "The spark," Carnegie insisted, "must be there," and neither breeding, nor education, nor wealth, nor social environment could create it, or even do much to feed it into full flame. Carnegie found no answer in the writings of Spencer or Darwin to explain the triumphs of the individual man. What the Spencerian philosophy did promise, Carnegie believed, was the gradual evolution of the entire human race toward perfection, but man's evolutionary ascent would be propelled upward by those individual sparks of spontaneous inspiration that owed their creative source to no established laws of nature or of man.

Finally, it is clear from his own writings that Carnegie did not even understand Spencer's teleology. In perhaps his most widely quoted statement, Spencer had attempted to give in a single sentence an outline of the whole evolutionary process toward a purposeful end that was immanent in the laws of nature: "Evolution," he wrote in *First Principles,* "is an integration of matter and concomitant dissipation of motion, during which the matter passes from an indefinite incoherent homogeneity to a definite coherent heterogeneity." William James delighted generations of Harvard students with his mocking parody of Spencer's definition of evolution: "Evolution is a change from a nohowish untalkaboutable all-alikeness to a somehowish and in general talkaboutable not-all-alikeness by continuous sticktogetherations and something elseifications." [58] Carnegie, quite unwittingly, exceeded James in his mockery of Spencer's doctrine of evolution by innocently reversing the whole Spencerian order of evolutionary development. In a defense of the concentration of capital, Carnegie, thinking that he was quoting Spencer, wrote: "The concentration of capital is a necessity for meeting the demands of our day, and as such should not be looked at askance, but be encouraged. There is nothing detrimental to human society in it, but much that is, or is bound soon to become, beneficial. It is an evolution from the heterogeneous to the homogeneous, and is clearly another step in the upward path of development." [59] By reversing the order, Carnegie proved himself to be far more accurate than Spencer in predicting the development of capitalistic institutions, but at the same time he revealed his ignorance of the most basic premise of Spencer's doctrine. Carnegie could well have used that time on a desert island reading Spencer if he was truly interested in knowing what the master had actually said. Apparently Carnegie had found little time in his busy life for a serious study or very profound understanding of the man whom he was proud to hail as his teacher.

Not only did Carnegie reverse the Spencerian order of development, at least in human institutions, he was not essentially in sympathy with the philosophic attitude that lay behind Spencer's teleological doctrine of rigidly defined order that led toward a single conclusion. For the true Spencerians, there was a determinism in the laws of nature as pre-ordained and inflexible as the determinism the Calvinists found in the laws of God or the Marxists found in the ordered development of society. Carnegie, at a very young age, had totally rejected Calvinistic determinism as being fiendishly depraved, and he later dismissed Marxist determinism as being atavistically absurd. It is hardly surprising that he would not find any other form of determinism congenial to his concept of human freedom. Determinism was for him, as it was for most Americans, an alien and suspect doctrine, having its origins in a static feudal past in which the individual was bound by the tradition of social class, religion, and geography to live out a prescribed role. Even Calvinism, which of all the doctrines of determinism was to have the greatest influence on American thought, was not long accepted in its pure Geneva form by the New England Puritans. Within one generation it had been qualified by the Half-Way Covenant and the acceptance of good works. Determinism, be it religiously or scientifically inspired, was contrary to American egalitarian optimism when it promised salvation or survival only to a predetermined few, and Carnegie, in rejecting Calvinism and Marxism, was also, whether he realized it or not, rejecting a premise implicit in Social Darwinism. He was suspicious of all firm promises, and he denied that even the American

395

Declaration of Independence and the Constitution, America's Magnae Cartae, guaranteed anything but the opportunity for the individual to achieve success through his own efforts. "The Republic," he wrote in *Triumphant Democracy,* "may not give wealth, or happiness; she has not promised these, it is the freedom to pursue these, not their realization, which the Declaration of Independence claims; but, if she does not make the emigrant happy or prosperous, this she can do and does do for everyone, she makes him a citizen, a *man.*" [60] In short, democracy was vitally important to Carnegie precisely because, in emphasizing egalitarianism, it denied a fixed and predetermined order.

Why then, if so much that was implicit in the Spencerian evolutionary doctrine was antithetical to Carnegie's own fundamental beliefs, did Carnegie so loudly proclaim himself a disciple of Spencer that he convinced his contemporaries as well as future generations of historians that he was a genuine Social Darwinist? In part, of course, Carnegie's acceptance of Spencer can be explained in terms of his ignorance of what Spencer had actually said. Tremendously impressed by those intellectuals whom he had met in Madame Botta's drawing room and at the Nineteenth Century Club, and eager to become a part of their circle, he had, with his usual lack of restraint, trumpeted his commitment to Spencerianism. And Spencer provided an easy and impressively scientific rebuttal to the orthodox theology which Carnegie had never accepted. Carnegie wanted to believe in something, and he seized hold of the doctrine which at the moment was most acceptable among the intelligentsia with whom he wished to identify himself.

Then, too, Spencerian philosophy, in its broadest outlines, appealed to Carnegie's belief in progress. Spencer seemed to offer scientific proof that man was improving his world through technological advancement, and that the new industrial society would make obsolete the old militaristic order of things which Carnegie despised. Accepting that broad framework, Carnegie tended to ignore the rest of the Spencerian doctrine and filled in his own details. It is significant to note that when he came to know Spencer personally, and attempted to discuss specifics with him, the self-proclaimed disciple found himself in disagreement with the master in almost every instance: tariffs, patent laws, social legislation,

396

philanthropic gifts to communities, inheritance taxes, public education, and even the proper philosophic attitude to make sickness, pain, and public criticism endurable.[61] Eventually Carnegie was to abandon even the pretense of accepting Spencerianism, and after 1900 he would fully embrace the new doctrine of Progressivism with an exuberance that indicated how superficial his understanding of and commitment to Social Darwinism had been.

Carnegie, above all else, was a romantic. Like all nineteenth-century romantics, he glorified the improbable event, and he denied the predictable pattern, be it Christian, Marxist, or Spencerian. By what law of history or biological science could one accommodate the career of a Saint Joan, a Lincoln, or for that matter, a Carnegie? Who were the fittest at any one moment in human history, and what did the Spencerians mean by "survival"? In answering a letter in which Spencer had complained that he had been either ignored or unfairly criticized by his fellow countrymen, Carnegie gave the romantic's rebuttal to the Spencerian's test of success:

> When have the Prophets not been stoned, from Christ down to Wagner? Crazy, enthusiastic, or madmen all of them. Take the philosophers, from Socrates, or before Socrates' time, Plato to Spencer, the martyrs to Science, from Bruno, Galileo, Copernicus.
>
> Why, my dear friend, what do you mean by complaining of neglect, abuse, scorn? These are the precious rewards of the teachers of mankind. . . .
>
> I could wish that you had been imprisoned, tortured on the rack. This would have been no greater reward than is your due. The Philosopher who is sensitive to contemporaneous criticism is a new type, and I do not wish you to pass into history as its founder.[62]

To his own generation, Carnegie may have seemed to be the living embodiment of the Horatio Alger dream, and no one could deny that he fully enjoyed his success. In that industrial world of the late nineteenth century into which he had "pushed so inordinately," he had proved his fitness, and he had survived and had flourished. But there were times when he romantically hankered for the hemlock cup, and he placed high in his own pantheon of heroes not Alger's Dauntless Dick, but Ayrshire's Bobby Burns.

CHAPTER XIII

Courtship and Marriage
1880-1887

In 1867 Carnegie and his mother moved from Pittsburgh to New York, and, in the decade that followed, their lives settled into a comfortable and, at least to Margaret Carnegie, entirely satisfying routine. At first they lived in the best suite available in the old but still elegant St. Nicholas Hotel, but a few years later they moved to an even more luxurious suite in the new, ultra-fashionable Windsor Hotel on Fifth Avenue at 46th Street. Carnegie opened a New York office at 19 Broad Street, which served as headquarters for supervising his many business projects.

During these first years in New York, however, Carnegie did not spend a great deal of time there. He made frequent trips to Europe on bond-selling missions, hurried overnight railroad journeys to Pittsburgh, and even longer junkets to Illinois, Iowa, St. Louis, and Omaha in the interest of his various railroad enterprises. For some time the hotel life at the St. Nicholas and later at the Windsor was quite satisfactory to him as a substitute for a home. Nevertheless, he looked forward eagerly to the long summer months when, in order to escape the unendurable heat of New York and Pittsburgh, he and his mother retired to their summer home at Cresson, Pennsylvania.

Here, high up in the Allegheny mountains, some fifty miles to the east of Pittsburgh, the Carnegies had purchased a summer home, situated on the highest hill in town. They named it Braemar Cottage. It was a roomy Victorian Gothic house, with large rooms and high ceilings, deeply recessed floor-length windows with fancy stained glass panes, and a wide, open verandah which embraced two-thirds of the house. For the Carnegies it was a cool, dark retreat from the oppressive heat of the Ohio River valley and the Eastern coastal plain. The air was pure and unpolluted by the steel mills far down in the valleys below. There were mountain trails to follow on horseback, wild flowers in abundance to gather, and an excellent Mountain Inn where they could dine and where the many visitors, whom Carnegie delighted in inviting up to his mountain retreat, could be housed.

From early June until late October the Carnegies stayed at Cresson. To Carnegie these months were in some respects the happiest in the year, for at Cresson he could enjoy the nearest thing he had to a real home. Hotel life in New York had begun to pall for him. But not for Margaret Carnegie. Her spoon had long since been made, and she never ceased to delight in dipping it deep into the rich creamy luxury of life that was now presented to her on a silver tray. She had no desire to manage a home again, no matter how many servants she could have to do her bidding. She reveled in walking on the thick carpet in the lobbies and corridors of the Windsor. She liked having her meals brought to her suite, with no responsibility for giving orders to a cook or employing a staff who would serve her. When Carnegie was out of the city, it was much easier to accept his absence from the busy, crowded life of a hotel than it would have been from the quiet life of a mansion where only servants would be left for company. With each passing year, Margaret became more possessive of her older son and more demanding of his attention. Tom, whom Andrew always felt his mother secretly favored, had successfully broken free from Margaret's domination. With a family that now included nine children, Tom had little time or inclination to devote much attention to his mother, and consequently Margaret depended even more upon Andrew than she had in the past. When Carnegie from time to time remarked that the daily routine of hotel life tired him or that it would be nice to have his own dining room in which to entertain guests, she would determinedly shake her head and push these suggestions aside with a brusque, "We canna do better than this." [1]

Margaret apparently had no fear that Andrew would ever revolt and declare his personal independence from her matriarchal control. His sense of indebtedness to her was too great. Nor did Andrew for many years have any desire to alter this state of mutual dependency. An aging mother as dependent as Margaret was gave him an excellent excuse for not becoming entrapped in a permanently entangling alliance.

Margaret knew that her son had many young girl friends and was involved in what she chose to regard as innocent flirtations. She encouraged Andrew to invite several young girls at a time to their summer retreat in Cresson, where they could be properly accommodated at the Mountain Inn and diligently chaperoned by her on summer afternoon picnics. Margaret firmly believed that there is safety in numbers, and as long as Andrew flirted with all the girls, giving no undue attention to any one, she felt secure.

So the years passed. It seemed as if nothing other than death could change the fixed pattern of their lives, a pattern Margaret accepted with satisfied complacency as her due. In the early 1870's Margaret Carnegie accompanied her son on most of his trips to Europe. After their trip to Dunfermline in 1875, when Carnegie gave to the city its first public swimming baths, Margaret reluctantly had to admit that the frequent trans-Atlantic voyages were tiring and that she would have to curtail her activities somewhat. But this slight modification did not change the essential pattern of their life, nor did it lessen the ties that bound the two together.

It was not until 1880, when Margaret was nearly seventy and Andrew Carnegie was forty-five, that for the first time there appeared a genuine threat to Margaret Carnegie's place in her son's life. In that year, Carnegie became acquainted with Louise Whitfield, and with a maternal instinct that could not be deceived, Margaret sensed that this rapidly developing friendship between her son and Miss Whitfield was of a different character than the many others which had preceded it.

It began casually enough with a few horseback rides in Central Park. Louise was the daughter of a fairly well-to-do merchant,

John W. Whitfield. The family lived in a substantial brownstone house on West 48th Street, only two or three blocks away from the Windsor Hotel. Carnegie had first met John Whitfield in 1870, through a mutual friend, a Scottish-born thread merchant, Alexander King. King had brought Carnegie along with him to call on the Whitfields on New Year's Day 1870, and from that time on Carnegie had included the family on his list of New Year's Day calls. On these visits, Carnegie was aware of but scarcely gave notice to the quiet and shy but not unattractive daughter who occasionally helped her mother in serving him lemonade and sandwiches.[2]

John Whitfield died in April 1878, at the age of forty-six. Louise, who had been educated at Miss Henrietta B. Haines's School for girls in Gramercy Park, was twenty-one at the time of her father's death, and with a semi-invalid mother and a young sister and brother still in school, the main burden of caring for the family now fell upon her. There were no great financial problems to contend with, but the management of the household was demanding. Louise proved to be more than capable for the task, but in performing it she sacrificed her own freedom. For the time being, she gave up any girlhood dream of romance.

Louise's father had kept horses in a nearby stable and had taught his daughter how to ride. After her father's death, Alex King occasionally asked her to ride with him in Central Park. Louise would later remember that "Mr. Carnegie was also fond of riding and took several of his young lady friends out with him. Mr. King told him how much I liked to ride and suggested that he take me; so, after getting my mother's permission, he often invited me. This is how our friendship began." [3]

Carnegie also recalled these early days of their friendship in his autobiography. "For several years I had known Miss Louise Whitfield. Her mother permitted her to ride with me in Central Park. We were both very fond of riding. Other young ladies were on my list. I had fine horses and often rode in the Park and around New York with one or the other of the circle. In the end the others faded into ordinary beings. Miss Whitfield remained alone as the perfect one beyond any I had met." [4]

Certainly Louise Whitfield was different from the other young ladies on Carnegie's list, the pretty young things who were vivacious and coquettish, who giggled appreciatively at his little sallies of humor, and who were tremendously impressed with his wealth and position in life. These girls, who had been invited in large numbers to Cresson in the past, and who had accompanied Carnegie on his Central Park rides and to operas and musicals in New York, presented no real threat to Andrew Carnegie's bachelorhood or to Margaret Carnegie's role as *materfamilias*.

Louise Whitfield was not of this type. She was not pretty in the conventional way. Tall and graceful (she was at least three inches taller than Andrew), with dark hair and eyes, a strong chin, and a quiet dignity, Louise could more appropriately be described as handsome. Nor was she adept in the pleasant little wiles and graces of the New York debutante. If anything, she was overly serious and tended to take every passing remark too literally. But Carnegie liked her assurance in handling a horse, and he was flattered by the sober consideration which she gave to his conversation. The scribbled notes from his office or hotel inviting her to go riding came ever more frequently, and even casual friends began to note that he had apparently found "his favorite equestrienne." [5]

By the early spring of 1881, their friendship had developed to a point that Carnegie asked Louise to join his mother and him and a very select group of friends on a trip to Britain in late May. He had decided to make a long coaching trip from Brighton on the south coast of England to Inverness far up in the Scottish Highlands. Undoubtedly Carnegie had planned this coaching trip many years before, when, as a young boy living in abject poverty in Slabtown, he had seen his mother weeping in an unaccustomed moment of despair. In an effort to console her, he had grasped her hands and told her not to cry. "Some day," he had promised, "I'll be rich, and we'll ride in a fine coach driven by four horses." At which Margaret had snorted, "That will do no good over here, if no one in Dunfermline can see us." At that moment, young Andrew resolved that someday he and his mother would sweep into Dunfermline in their own coach and four, and the whole town would know about it.[6]

Now that childhood promise could be realized. In July, Carnegie was to present a free public library to Dunfermline. His mother had been asked to lay the cornerstone, and he was determined that they should arrive by coach in triumphal entry, having traveled the length of England.

Louise Whitfield was highly flattered to have been asked to be a part of so royal a procession as this promised to be, but she had considerable doubts about the propriety of accompanying the Carnegies, and she knew that her mother would be even more reluctant to agree to such a proposal. In order to allay Louise's doubts and to obtain parental permission, Carnegie persuaded his mother to call on Mrs. Whitfield to urge the invitation he had extended to Louise and to give assurances of proper chaperonage.

The very earnestness with which Andrew pleaded with his mother for her support of his invitation to Louise confirmed Margaret's suspicions that this friendship was not the usual passing fancy. There were to be other young girls on the tour—Alice French of Davenport, Iowa, and Jeannie Johns of Pittsburgh, as well as Mrs. Aggie King—but quite clearly, if Louise were to go along, Andrew would have eyes only for her.

Nevertheless, at her son's bidding, Margaret reluctantly put on her best black silk dress, black plumed hat, and grimmest look and made a call on the Whitfields. She formally and briefly extended an invitation on behalf of her son and herself for Miss Whitfield to accompany them on their tour. Both Louise and her mother could sense the lack of warmth. Mrs. Whitfield protested mildly that it somehow did not seem quite proper that an unattached young lady should accept this invitation, and she asked if Mrs. Carnegie did indeed think it correct for Louise to accompany them. This was the question Margaret Carnegie had been waiting for. Drawing herself up in awful dignity, she fixed her bright, piercing eyes on Mrs. Whitfield and snapped out the blunt answer. "If she were a daughter of mine she wouldna go." [7] That settled the matter. Louise wrote in her diary that night, "I am so unhappy about the trip. I want to go so much and yet I see it is impossible." [8]

On the evening before they were to depart, Carnegie invited Louise to dinner at the Windsor Hotel with the assembled coaching party. Carnegie undoubtedly meant the invitation to be a kind gesture of consolation and farewell, but for Louise it was agony. She sat at the table and listened to the excited conversation, in which no one participated more eagerly and more pointedly than Margaret Carnegie. Louise's diary entry for that day read: "Was very sorry I went but did not know how to get out of it." The next morning she wrote, "I suppose the party got off this morning. I must learn to be satisfied with what I have and not long for more." [9] But Louise could never forgive Margaret Carnegie, sitting proud and happy and self-assured at the head of the table, confident that she had met the threat and had turned it aside. Even as a very old lady, Louise would remember how Margaret had humiliated her, and in an interview with Carnegie's biographer she would confide that Mrs. Carnegie had been the most unpleasant person she had ever known.[10]

Carnegie himself was apparently oblivious to the hurt and embarrassment inflicted upon Louise at the farewell dinner. He was, of course, disappointed that she was not to accompany them, but the excitement of the trip drove from his mind all other considerations.

As with his trip around the world, Carnegie kept a travel diary of the coaching trip with an eye for future publication. The Gay Charioteers, as they called themselves, sailed from New York on 1 June 1881, aboard the Cunard liner *Bothnia*. There were eleven in the party. Carnegie called the roll: "Lady Dowager Mother, Head of the Clan (no Salic Law in our family); Miss Jeannie Johns (Prima Donna); Miss Alice French (Stewardess); Mr. and Mrs. McCargo (Dainty Davie); Mr. and Mrs. King (Paisley Troubadours, Aleck good for fun and Aggie good for everything); Benjamin F. Vandevort (Benjie); Henry Phipps, Jr. (H.P., Our Pard); G. F. McCandless (General Manager); ten in all, making together with the scribe the All-coaching Eleven." [11]

After disembarking at Liverpool and spending five days in London, the coaching party went on to Brighton, where they were to find their coach with "four noble bays," Perry, the coachman, and Joe, the footman, waiting for them. On a bright, sunny morning on 17 June, the coach wheeled out from the drive of the Grand Hotel at Brighton and headed north, with Inverness, Scotland, 831 miles away, as its destination. "All seated! Mother next the coachman, and I at her side. The horn sounds, the crowd cheers, and we are off." [12]

For the Gay Charioteers, the coaching trip north along country roads and through the old market towns of England surpassed even their most exuberant expectations. Carnegie wrote in his diary: "It was soon discovered that no mode of travel could be compared with coaching. By all other modes the views are obstructed by hedges and walls; upon the top of the coach the eye wanders far and wide. . . . Everything of rural England is seen, and how exquisitely beautiful it all is, this quiet, peaceful, orderly land!" [13] The coaching trip brought back to Carnegie memories of riding the canal boat many years before—the same sense of detached observing, the paradox of aloof intimacy that Carnegie thoroughly enjoyed. The neat cultivated gardens, ordinarily hidden by hedgerows and fences, in the towns and on the country estates, and the wild flowers growing in profusion in the open fields were all theirs to behold and enjoy.

The weather held amazingly well as they slowly rolled northward through Guilford, Reading, and Oxford, on to Banbury Cross and Stratford-on-Avon, spending the nights at country inns and dining at noon, picnic style, in the meadows of central England. But even in this idyllic setting, so far removed from the Thomson mills in Braddock, Carnegie did not entirely forget the interests of his business. While spending a day at Windsor, Carnegie made a special point of inviting a young amateur chemist, Sidney Gilchrist-Thomas, and his sister, Lillian, to join the party for sightseeing and dinner. Three years before, Thomas had developed the Thomas basic process which made it possible to remove phosphorus from iron ore, thus opening up vast new sources of iron ore for the making of Bessemer steel. Only a month prior to his departure for England Carnegie had succeeded in selling the American franchise on Thomas's patent rights to the Bessemer Steel Association for the sum of $250,000. Carnegie's commission was $50,000.[14] It is not surprising that Carnegie entertained Thomas while in England. His commission alone had paid for the coaching trip several times over, and the ultimate benefits he would derive from the use of the Thomas process would amount to several million dollars. He praised Thomas for having "done more for England's greatness than all her kings and queens and aristocracy put together." [15]

Carnegie tried to persuade Thomas and his sister to join the coaching party and continue on to Scotland with them. Much to Lillian Thomas's disappointment, however, Thomas refused. Miss

Thomas had found the whole group of Americans fascinating, particularly Carnegie and his mother: "His [Carnegie's] devotion to his mother, a trenchant old lady who called a spade a spade with racy Scottish wit, was delightful to see." [16]

After leaving Coventry on 24 June, the coaching party was forced temporarily to abandon the idyllic beauty of rural Britain for the "Black Country" of the industrial Midlands. Once again, Carnegie revealed how superficial his personal attachment to the new Spencerian manufacturing order was, for the bleak, raw, industrial landscape of urban England offended his aesthetic sensibilities as much as it would the sensibilities of any Lake Country poet who might decry the "Rapine, avarice, expense" which had turned England into "a fen of stagnant waters." Carnegie wrote in his travel diary,

> We see the Black Country now, rows of little dingy houses beyond, with tall smokey chimneys vomiting smoke, mills and factories at every turn, coal pits and rolling mills and blast furnaces, the very bottomless pit itself; and such dirty, careworn children, hard-driven men, and squalid women. To think of the green lanes, the larks, the Arcadia we have just left. How can people be got to live such terrible lives as they seem condemned to here? Why do they not all run away to the green fields just beyond? . . . But do not let us forget that it is just Pittsburgh over again; nay, not even quite so bad, for that city bears the palm for dirt against the world.[17]

From Birmingham, the coaching party drove northwestward to Wolverhampton.

> The eleven miles between Birmingham and Wolverhampton are nothing but one vast iron-working, coal-mining establishment. There is scarcely a blade of grass of any kind to be seen, and not one real clean pure blade did we observe during the journey. . . . O mills and furnaces and coal-pits and all the rest of you, you may be necessary, but you are no bonnie! Pittsburghers though many of us were, inured to smoke and dirt, we felt the change very deeply from the hedgerows, the green pastures, the wild flowers and pretty clean cottages, and voted the district "horrid." Wolverhampton's steeples soon came into

406

sight, and we who had been there and could conjure up dear, honest, kindly faces waiting to welcome us with warm hearts, were quite restored to our usual spirits, notwithstanding dirt and squalor. The sun of a warm welcome from friends gives many clouds a silver lining, and it did make the black country brighter. The coach and horses, and Joe and Perry, not to mention our generalissimo Graham, belong to Wolverhampton, as you know, and our arrival had been looked for by many.[18]

The "generalissimo Graham" was Thomas Graham, a Scottish-born merchant who lived in Wolverhampton. It had been Graham who had secured the coach, with driver and footman, for Carnegie and had met the party in Brighton. Graham had a special reason for donating his services, for he was at this moment in negotiations with Carnegie to enter into partnership with him for the establishment of Radical newspapers in the Midlands.

The establishment of these papers was but part of an ambitious plan Carnegie had in mind for a chain of Radical newspapers throughout England to preach the doctrines of republicanism and the disestablishment of the Anglican Church. Carnegie had never forgotten the old Dunfermline dream of a charter for Britain. Nor had he forgotten his promise to himself in 1868 to "purchase a controlling interest in some newspaper or live review and give the general management of it attention, taking a part in public matters." But just as his income had grown far beyond the limits he had set for himself in 1868, of $50,000 per annum, so had his journalistic ambitions expanded from a single newspaper into a vast chain of papers which would trumpet the cause of political and social democracy. Graham was to play a key role in this ambitious design, and consequently, somewhat to the impatience of the other members of the coaching party, the Brighton-to-Inverness non-express coach was delayed six days in Wolverhampton while Carnegie and Graham plotted out their journalistic campaign.

It was not until the first day of July that the coach began to roll again, through the remainder of the Black Country, "but near Lichfield we reached once more the rural beauties of England. How thankful to get away once more from the dirt and smoke and bustle of manufactories." [19]

The Lake Country charmed them, and there for the only time on their trip they abandoned the coach and traveled by boat up Lake Windermere from Bowness to Ambleside. They paid the proper reverential respects to Wordsworth's grave, but Wordsworth lacked true greatness, in Carnegie's opinion. He was a proper poet for this gentle country of placid lakes and low rolling hills. "Great mountains always carry one upward, but these hills are not great, nor is there anything great in the region. All is very sweet and pleasing and has its own peculiar charm, like the school of Lake Poets." [20] By this time, Carnegie and his mother were eager to cross the border into Scotland, where the mountains were great and where there had lived a poet equal in power to the land that had produced him.

The border was crossed on Saturday, 16 July. "The bridge across the boundary-line was . . . reached. When midway over a halt was called, and vent given to our enthusiasm. With three cheers for the lands of the heather, shouts of 'Scotland forever,' and the waving of hats and handkerchiefs, we dashed across the border. And oh Scotland, my own, my native land, your exiled son returns with love for you as ardent as ever warmed the heart of man for his country. It's a God's mercy I was born a Scotchman, for I do not see how I could ever have been contented to be anything else. The little plucky dour devil, set in her own ways and getting them too, level-headed and shrewd, with an eye to the main chance always and yet so lovingly weak, so fond, so led away by song or story, so easily touched to fine issues, so leal, so true! Ah! you suit me, Scotia, and proud am I that I am your son." [21]

After exploring the Burns country around Dumfries, they headed east along the Nith River to Edinburgh, where they spent five days at the Royal Hotel on Princes Street. But however impressive "the Queen of the Unconquered North" might be to the other coach passengers, it was for Carnegie and his mother but a resting place, a prelude to their triumphal entry into Dunfermline. For this would be the high moment of the trip, the old ambition realized, the moment of pride at hand. On the morning of 27 July, "we left Edinburgh and reached Queensferry in time for the noon boat. . . . Upon reaching the north shore we were warmly greeted by Uncle and Aunt Lauder, and Maggie and Annie." They drove on to a country inn near Rosythe Castle, "but we were met at the door by the good landlady, who, with uplifted hands, exclaimed: 'I'm a' alane! There's naebody in the house! They're a' awa' to Dunfermline! There'll be great goings on there the day.'" So they prepared what they could for themselves in the inn's kitchen and hurried on to the top of the Ferry Hills. "How beautiful is Dunfermline seen from the Ferry Hills, its grand old abbey towering over all, seeming to hallow the city and to lend a charm and dignity to the lowliest tenement. . . . What Benares is to the Hindoo, Mecca to the Mohammedan, Jerusalem to the Christian, all that Dunfermline is to me." [22]

At four o'clock in the afternoon, the coach and four rolled up St. Leonard's Street, past banners reading "Welcome Carnegie, generous son" and the national flags of Scotland, England, and the United States, to meet the great procession of workers' guilds and unions, eight thousand strong, assembled at Bothwell Place to greet the Carnegie party. Then the parade commenced, the guilds carrying their banners, the Lord Provost and town councilmen riding in open carriages, and the coach and four bringing up the rear, and they proceeded up Netherton and Moodie Streets to the top of the hill, where the whole entourage stopped in front of the little stone cottage where Carnegie had been born. From another such cottage, just down the street, the poverty-stricken family had fled thirty-three years ago. And now Margaret Carnegie, like Lady Bountiful, was riding back into Dunfermline in a magnificent coach, with the frenzied shouts and applause of the whole city ringing in her ears, to bestow a new handsome library, paid for by her son, on the city of her birth. For the only time during the entire trip Margaret Carnegie asked to ride inside the carriage instead of on top beside her son, so that she could weep unabashedly in her pride for the triumph of this day.

The two nights and a day that were spent in Dunfermline were filled with ceremony: Margaret's laying of the memorial stone for the library and being presented with the silver trowel to commemorate Carnegie's first gift of a library outside of the United States, the formal dinners, the toasts, the speeches of praise approaching adulation. How thoroughly and openly the Carnegies enjoyed every moment of it all! No other reception to be given him could ever match this high moment of his life.[23]

After Dunfermline, the rest of the trip, no matter how thrilling the scenery of the central Highlands might be, was for Carnegie and his mother something of an anticlimax. On 3 August they reached the Caledonian hotel in Inverness and the end of their tour. "Farewell the neighing steeds, the spirit-stirring horn, whose sweet throat awaked the echoes o'er mountain and glen. Farewell, the Republican banner, and all the pride, pomp and circumstance of glorious coaching, farewell! The Charioteers' occupation's gone. . . . It was all up after this. Perry and Joe, the coach and the horses were speeding away by rail to their homes; we were no longer *the* coaching party, but only ordinary tourists buying our tickets like other people. . . ." [24]

Half of the company they left behind in Britain. The others bade their farewells in New York, when the *Algeria* docked on 24 August. "Two or three of the most miserable hours I ever spent were those at the St. Nicholas Hotel, where mother, Ben and I lunched alone before starting for Cresson. Even Ben had to take an earlier train to Pittsburgh, and I said to mother: 'All our family gone! I feel so lonely, so deserted; not one remains.' But mother was up to the emergency. 'Oh, you don't count me then! You still have one that sticks to you.' Oh, yes, indeed sure of that, old lady." [25]

Louise Whitfield, spending this summer in the Catskills with her mother, could have told Carnegie something more about "miserable hours" spent alone. The one letter she had received from Carnegie on the trip, mailed from Reading on 21 June, describing in detail the joys of the trip—"not one mishap, nor an ache, nor a pain so far," and concluding with "Oh my Friend! Would you were with us," did little to assuage the pain she felt.[26]

A year later, she could read a full account of the whole trip in Carnegie's privately published account, *Our Coaching Trip,* which he distributed with lavish hand to his friends and business contacts. Louise, perhaps more than any other reader, must have noted with special interest the central role that Margaret Carnegie played in the story. She could picture Mrs. Carnegie sitting regally in the front of the coach close beside her son, and she could well believe the final quotation in the book: Carnegie still had one "that sticks to you." And there were those casual remarks made by Provost Mathieson at the great dinner for the Carnegies in Dunfermline that must have had a particular message for

Louise. In extolling Carnegie's many virtues, Provost Mathieson had observed that "the only flaw in Mr. Carnegie's character is that he wanted a wife. (Laughter and cheers.) I attribute that very much to the fact of his having a mother. (Laughter.) His mother has taken good care over him, and has showed that she does not want to hand him over to the tender mercies of some half-cousin, or any of the half-dozen young ladies who are with him today. (Laughter.)" [27] Whatever Louise Whitfield's reaction to this account, it seems certain that it was not "Laughter and cheers."

In the following autumn, when the Carnegies returned to New York from Cresson, his friendship with Louise was renewed in precisely the same way that it had begun eighteen months before: rides in the park, an occasional opera or concert, and then long weeks of silence upon Carnegie's part, and mixed emotions of relief and tears upon Louise's part.

Louise in the months that followed was not sure of her own feelings. Nor was Carnegie sure of his. Louise had by now come to realize that Carnegie would probably never marry anyone until he was released by his mother, either by her own volition, which seemed impossible to imagine, or by her death—and she was a most vigorous old lady, who could ride ten hours a day on top of a swaying coach and still dance a Highland fling at the end of the day. As Carnegie had written, "To be a wee lassie at seventy-one is a triumph indeed; but as the Queen Dowager says, that is nothing. She intends to be as daft for many years to come, for my grandfather was far older when he alarmed the auld wives of the village on Halloween night, sticking his false face through the windows." [28]

There was also considerable uncertainty in Louise Whitfield's own mind about accepting Carnegie as a husband, even if he had felt himself free to marry. For he was not the suitor she, as a young romantic girl, had imagined. He was nearly twice her age and only a few months younger than her mother. Louise had always pictured herself as the bride of a struggling young man whom she could encourage and help to achieve success in the business world, as her mother had helped her father when he was beginning his business career in New York. Carnegie, a multimillionaire, who was already being hailed on both sides of the Atlantic as America's steel king, hardly needed the kind of helpmeet she wanted to be. It was questionable whether he needed a wife at all, for he had apparently gotten along admirably for twenty-five years of his adult life without one.

As for Carnegie, he seemed no more willing to settle down in one place in these early years of the 1880's than he had been previously. It is true that he would occasionally drop hints to Louise that he was weary of hotel life and longed for a home of his own, but in the next moment he would be eagerly planning his next trip to Britain or the Continent. Margaret Carnegie should not be held solely responsible for Carnegie's failure to marry. Like anyone who remains unmarried into middle age, Carnegie had become so accustomed to being free to go when he desired to do so, to being concerned primarily with his own convenience and preferences, that it was almost impossible for him to imagine a situation in which he would have to consider the wishes and needs of someone else, even his mother. For Margaret Carnegie may have held one end of the tether tightly in her own hands, but the rope was long and it allowed Andrew considerable freedom of movement.

Carnegie was also at this moment deeply involved in business and political affairs which he considered most pressing—the expansion and reorganization of his steel companies in Pittsburgh and the establishment of a syndicate of newspapers in Britain.[29] But in spite of the psychological obstacles and these demands on his time and energy, he and Louise Whitfield became secretly engaged in September 1883. It proved to be a troubled betrothal. Neither was quite sure of the other's real feelings, and Carnegie, in particular, was reluctant to make any precise commitment for a marriage date. Louise's diary for these months of their short engagement reveals the varying moods of happiness and despair, of certainty and indecision, that she felt.

"Had a delightful ride with Mr. Carnegie." And then, the next day: "Am so unhappy, so miserable." On New Year's Eve, in the deeply introspective mood that the last night of the old year tends to induce, she wrote, "And now we come to the last night of the old year again. What a changed girl it finds me! Life seems so hard. I feel so old and strange. Nothing is certain, nothing is sure. I am striving so hard to do what is right but I cannot see the light." [30]

412

In the spring of 1884, Carnegie went off to Europe again for another coaching trip. He and Louise had a long talk before his departure, and, by mutual consent, the engagement was broken. Carnegie had been unable to commit himself to marriage in the foreseeable future, and Louise saw no alternative other than to end their engagement. She recorded in her diary on 23 April: "In the afternoon, took the last sad step. Felt it was best. Mother and I have decided to go to Grant House for the summer." [31]

Even with their engagement broken, however, Carnegie could not forget Louise. He sent her a brief note in mid-June from the Dartmoor, describing his coaching tour and telling her that he would be returning home aboard the *Servia* on 5 July. He would go directly home to Cresson, "so keeping my promise to Mother. . . ." He hoped that she would write him there.[32]

In July, while in New York on his way to Cresson, Carnegie took the time, as he later wrote Louise, to walk "past your house to see it all closed . . . not a soul in town I knew, or cared to know that night, except I did want to find you, and you were gone, too. Just as well, better no doubt, I said, and walked back to the hotel." [33]

Also revealing was the paragraph Carnegie added to his coaching trip manuscript as he prepared it for commercial publication by Scribner's that summer. This paragraph had not appeared in the earlier, privately published account and seemed to have been written especially for Louise.

> As we bowled along the conversation turned upon horseback riding, and someone quoted the famous maxim, "the outside of a horse for the inside of a man." "But what about a woman?" asked F. "Oh," answered Puss, "the outside of a horse for the inside of a woman and the outside as well, for in no other position can a woman ever possibly look so captivating as on a horse. Girls who ride in the park have double chances." A voice from the front—[Carnegie's?] "You are quite right." . . . A woman looks her loveliest on horseback.[34]

In any event, when Carnegie returned to New York, the rides with Louise in the park were resumed. But for several weeks the renewal of their friendship did not bring more understanding, nor did it seem any more likely to lead to a definite commitment. At one point Carnegie wrote that he would not see her again, for apparently his presence "has brought you only dead sea fruit." Louise's response, that this was not true, that indeed she did not care "who knows that the serene happiness of the past two months has been caused by your presence," changed his mind.[35] He called for her the next afternoon, and after a long ride together in which they discussed their relationship and feelings toward each other, they once again became engaged. The letter Louise wrote to him two days later reveals how certain she now was that their love for each other was true:

> We have had rain and snow since you left. You and I enjoyed the last bright, warm day together. Shall you ever forget that view of the dark cloud rolling aside, and allowing the sun to burst forth in all its splendor, and forming a golden pathway across the river? It seemed to me as typical of our lives—all the clouds gone at last.
>
> I have had a busy day, but oh, what a light and happy heart. Surely it seems to me that this must be the "peace which passeth all understanding." [36]

Nevertheless, the clouds were not gone entirely. The months after their second engagement were often as troubled and the outlook as uncertain as during the time that had preceded the breaking of their first engagement. Carnegie, even during the winter months, was away from New York more often than he was there, for he was in the process of reorganizing the entire corporate structure of his steel mills and blast furnaces. His letters to Louise were often as impersonal as if he were writing to a casual acquaintance. He would, on the other hand, frequently complain that in her letters she did not demonstrate that depth of feeling toward him that he expected. Certainly, Louise's patience and real love for Carnegie must have been tested to their utmost.

In the early spring of 1885 Carnegie told her that the Phipps family were going to Europe and wanted him to go with them. He implied that, due to his mother's ill health and his unwillingness to be away from Louise for that extended a period, he did not think he would go. Then, late in June, he quite suddenly announced that he would go after all. "Now what news I have for

414

you! I sail Saturday next, 9:35 for Liverpool. Gone till August 22nd. . . . Mr. Phipps and Mr. Lauder go along and Mother really asked me to go . . . and really my newspaper business demands my presence for a week or two in London. Then two weeks in Scotland is all I have." [37]

Louise Whitfield in answer indicated that the news was hardly as surprising as Carnegie thought it would be. "I felt from the first that you would go with Mr. and Mrs. Phipps. How delightful it all is!" [38] Carnegie's letters from England that summer did little to console her: "Rather lonely some mornings, at breakfast in my room alone, but I like it in some ways. So quiet (Bachelordom has its advantages). Miss Mother much in such big rooms. Wish a certain young beautiful lady were only here to brighten them up with her smiles and silvery laugh, but she is having fine hours with many admirers, no doubt. . . ." [39]

Louise was actually having a miserable summer, at Gilbertsville, Pennsylvania, in a resort hotel which she described as a "regular sanatarium." When later, after his return, Carnegie complained once again about the indifferent tone in her letters and how she seemed to have found happiness that summer without him, he finally exhausted her patience, and Louise replied with some heat, "My dear Andrew what a goose you are! . . . Shall I tell you the truth of the summer? . . . The summer stretched away such a long dreary space before me and it seemed to me such a sacrilege to even talk about 'having good times,' but I said to myself, 'He evidently enjoys himself just as much with others as he does with me. . . . I will pretend that I enjoy it too.' If I had had the opportunity, I should have done my utmost. As it was, the few men that were there were not at all congenial, so I retired within myself and occupied myself with my painting. All this time everything was so dreary and quiet. . . . Mother kept urging me to brighten up and I did try, oh, so hard, but it was no use. I was utterly miserable. . . . I lived in the hope you would come. When you went abroad, I wrote to you trying to be as cheerful as possible, for the lonelier I felt, the more I tried not to show it. A young lady at Gilbertsville also had friends on the 'Etruria,' and we both looked for letters. Hers came, mine did not, and my heart turned to stone." [40]

This frank expression of feeling helped clear the air between them. After this letter Carnegie did not again complain of Louise's indifference and lack of feeling. The question of whether they should marry had been resolved, but there still remained the question of when. Louise surely realized by now that Carnegie would not marry as long as his mother lived, but in the summer of 1886, just prior to Louise's first visit to Cresson, he made sure that she did understand.

> I count the days. The mountain will come alive when you are on it. I have not written to you because it seems you and I have duties which must keep us apart. . . . Therefore I have stood back, as it were, and resolved that it was best to let you alone and free, but now when I hear the 29th I thrill with gladness and await your coming, even if I do not see that we can go beyond our present relations at present. I did not want to write because you were to be here soon, and we could talk over all this and decide upon our course. Mother *seems* really better; it is miraculous. I trust yours is also better. Everything does hang upon our mothers with both of us. Our duty is the same—to stick to them to the last. I feel this every day. . . . Come and let us confer with each other. I do hope you will like Cresson.[41]

Carnegie made a valiant effort to place the responsibility for the delay in the marraige upon both their mothers, but it was a quite futile gesture. Louise and Carnegie knew that Louise's mother would welcome their marriage at any time.

Thus Carnegie, at the age of fifty, when most men of his age were celebrating their silver wedding anniversaries, found himself belatedly and cruelly caught in an emotional trap of youth from which there could be no easy release. Louise's visit to Cresson increased his desire for her. He wrote to her shortly after she returned home, "What nonsense for us to dwell apart very much longer! I sometimes feel I can't endure separation." [42] At the same time, he would not consider marriage in defiance of his mother's wishes. And so, ironically, Carnegie, who had always aggressively gone after and obtained everything he had ever wanted, was now being deprived, by his own conscience, of that which he wanted most.

There must have been, of course, basic psychological reasons for his inability to defy his mother. All of the psychological expla-

416

nations so dear to the amateur Freudian could be brought forth in way of explanation: a weak, ineffectual father who had been unable to provide for his sons; a domineering, ambitious mother who *had* provided; an unduly prolonged childhood innocence of sexual knowledge; a sense of competition with a younger brother for his mother's affection; a personal vanity so strong as to indicate latent narcissism. There is evidence in Carnegie's background and personality for all of these diagnostic evaluations. But the historian lacks the competence to probe so deeply into Carnegie's psyche as to offer an explanation for Carnegie's attitudes toward his mother and marriage. That Louise Whitfield accepted the situation with patience, if not understanding, does reveal a great deal of the depth of her love and the strength of her character.

The spring and early summer of 1886 had been particularly difficult for Carnegie. He had had an unusual number of business problems to worry him in addition to his personal difficulties. He had been involved for many months in the reorganization of his company, which now included the recently acquired Pittsburgh Bessemer Steel Company at Homestead. The sale of rails was low, and his company had to decide whether or not to enter bids to the government for armor and guns for the new naval construction program being pushed by the Cleveland administration. Carnegie had given a flat "no" on the question of guns, but he still had not resolved to his own satisfaction as to whether the building of armor plates would violate his pacifist principles.

Also, during the preceding year he had been busily engaged in his own ambitious writing projects. Besides writing several magazine articles, he had finished the manuscript of what he would always regard as his magnum opus, his remarkable book, *Triumphant Democracy*. He wrote exultantly to Louise, "My book *all right*. I worked till Wednesday and am satisfied. Have not been till now. It's going to be a stunner. 'Triumphant Democracy' is now fairly in the graces of the author, but there's 'Triumphant Louise,' far, *far* in his graces, beyond anything." [43]

All of these activities, business, political, and literary, in addition to his worries over personal matters—the health of his mother and his brother Tom, and his own romantic problems—had exacted a toll upon his physical stamina that he did not fully realize. Summers in Cresson had always before been wonderfully restorative to his physical and mental health, but the summer of 1886 did not have this effect. By the time Louise ended her visit to Cresson the summer was nearly over, but Carnegie felt more exhausted than he had felt when the summer retreat began. Although he regretted the reason, Carnegie welcomed the doctor's suggestion that, due to Margaret's precarious physical condition, the Carnegies should delay their return to New York for as long as possible. Carnegie made a few quick trips to his offices in New York in September, but each time he hurried back to the peace and quiet of Cresson as quickly as he could.

Both Margaret and Andrew were concerned about Tom, who lay seriously ill in Pittsburgh. Carnegie went into the city several times on business matters, and he called at Homewood to see Tom whenever he did. What he saw and what the doctors told him did not encourage him. Tom was not responding to treatment; he seemed to have lost any real desire to live. Carnegie, who had never really understood his younger brother, had found him in the last few years even more withdrawn and inaccessible. The truth was that Tom had been drinking heavily over a period of five or six years, far in excess of anything that his family, and especially Andrew, knew about. Tom had never been an active supporter of Andrew's grandiose dreams of business expansion. Left to his own devices, he would have conducted a small, sound, conservative business operation in Pittsburgh. He had always resented the constant pressure from Andrew to acquire more and more. He had been mistrustful of Andrew's reckless gambles, and in the early years he had tried, with occasional success, to hold his older brother in check. But the gambles he could not stop had paid off, and the business had expanded beyond Andrew's wildest dreams and Tom's worst fears. Tom felt more and more isolated and unnecessary. Although he still had loyal support—from the other partners, the plant superintendents, and even the workers —which Carnegie never had, Tom had lost all real influence in directing the company's policies and operation. Perhaps it was for this reason he had sought escape in drinking. Now, stricken with fever, he had neither the physical strength nor the will to recover. Andrew on his visits could do nothing to arouse Tom's spirits or encourage his recovery.[44]

In Cresson, Margaret Carnegie also lay dying, of pneumonia.

Her spirit was still indomitable, but her heart was weak and she was physically tired. She could not command her own body in the way that she could order the nurses and her son around.

Early in October, Carnegie made another hurried trip to New York, and upon arriving back in Cresson, he wrote a brief note to Louise, saying he had a bad cold. "Am keeping in the house and hope to be all right in the morning. . . . Yours miserably, A.C." [45] But he was not all right the next morning. For two weeks he lay in bed, and finally the doctors diagnosed his case as typhoid. Then he received word that Tom was dead, and he had a serious relapse. [46] For four more weeks Carnegie lay in a semiconscious state in his darkened room in Cresson. James Bridge, his secretary, who was with him at Cresson, kept Louise informed daily by telegram. On the morning of 10 November, Louise received from Bridge a telegram reading, "Mrs. Carnegie died this morning. Andrew doing well." [47] Carnegie was not informed of his mother's death until a week after it occurred. Her coffin was lowered out of her bedroom window so that it would not have to pass her son's door. [48]

Late in November, Louise finally received a scrawled note from Carnegie. "It is six weeks since the last word was written and that was to you as I was passing into the darkness. Today as I see the great light once more my first word is to you. . . . Louise, I am now wholly yours—all gone but you. . . . I live in you now. *Write me*. I only read yours of six weeks ago today. Till death, Louise, yours alone." [49]

There followed long weeks of recuperation for Carnegie, weeks that to him and Louise seemed even longer than they were, now that there remained no obstacle to their marriage. As soon as he was able to travel, Carnegie went south, to the estate that his brother Tom had bought a few years before in Dungeness, Florida, a small island just off the coast at the Florida-Georgia border. There, in the warm sunshine which Carnegie found almost too hot, he slowly recovered his strength. By mail, he and Louise made plans for their marriage. But the presence of Margaret Carnegie was still felt. Carnegie begged Louise to continue to keep their engagement secret. He wanted no public announcement of their marriage until after it had occurred. [50] With scrupulous care, Louise respected his wishes.

In early April, Carnegie returned to New York. The wedding

had originally been planned for 12 April in the Whitfield home, but at the last moment Carnegie had to ask Louise to postpone it. He had to go to Pittsburgh, for a court case required his presence.[51] Louise was at least reassured that he had fully recovered in every respect.

From Pittsburgh, Carnegie sent a brief note to the Reverend Charles Eaton, Louise's pastor in New York: "My dear Mr. Eaton. I am so fortunate as to be about to marry Miss Whitfield, who would scarcely think the ceremony properly performed were she to have anyone but you. Could you oblige by marrying us at her residence Friday evening next, 8:00 p.m. 22nd inst.?" [52]

On 22 April 1887, Carnegie was at last free to attend his own wedding. It was an informal affair. Only thirty people were present, all relatives and close friends. Within an hour after the ceremony, Mr. and Mrs. Andrew Carnegie were driven by carriage to the North German Lloyd pier. There they boarded the steamship *Fulda* that was to take them to England, where they were to spend two weeks at Bonchurch on the Isle of Wight.

The New York newspapers that carried the brief announcement of the Whitfield-Carnegie wedding revealed that "Mr. Carnegie's present to his bride was the handsome house at 5 West 51st St. and securities from which an income of twenty thousand dollars may be derived." [53] Andrew Carnegie, at the age of fifty-one, at last had a home and wife.

CHAPTER XIV

The Two Worlds
of Andrew Carnegie
1881-1896

Following his marriage in 1887, Andrew Carnegie's trans-Atlantic travels, although no more frequent than during the preceding twenty years, assumed a new regularity in pattern. Ever since he had suffered a sunstroke in Virginia during the first year of the Civil War, Carnegie had felt it imperative to escape to a cool climate each summer. This had been his reason for purchasing Braemar Cottage, high up in the Alleghenies at Cresson. But after that last sad autumn of 1886, Carnegie had never wanted to see Cresson again. He seemed determined to shut the door tightly on the dead past, and the cottage had been quickly sold. All pictures and mementos of his mother were packed away, and for many years he would not mention the name of Margaret Carnegie to anyone, not even to Louise.

When Carnegie brought his bride to Britain he had the idea of seeking out a summer home in Scotland to replace the lost Cresson. For this first summer he leased Kilgraston House in the Valley Tay, near Perth. Here the newlyweds established their first home, after having spent the month of June in London observing the festivities in celebration of the Golden Jubilee of Victoria's reign. Happily for both of them, Louise fell in love with Scotland. Her enraptured account of this first Scottish home, written to her mother, was all that Carnegie could have asked for as an expression of enthusiasm for his native land:

> I wish I could describe this lovely place. Just now roses are in full bloom around one of my windows with white jessamine around the next one filling the room with the most delicious perfume. The beautiful lawn in front where we play tennis and the Scotch game of bowls, lovely shady walks on one side and in the distance a new mown field with hay cocks. Oh! why aren't you all here to enjoy it too? [1]

Within a month after the arrival at Kilgraston, Carnegie was able to boast to an Edinburgh audience that he saw in his wife "the great danger that exists in all converts—she is beginning to out-Herod her husband in her love and devotion to Scotland. . . . Believe me, my wife is as thoroughly Scotch already as I myself. . . ." [2]

The following year the Carnegies were back in Scotland as tenants of Cluny Castle, the ancestral home of the Macpherson chieftains, situated on an open hill overlooking the Valley Spey, near Kingussie in the central Highlands. Near by was one of the high mountains of Scotland, Ben Alder, and some of the most rugged and heavily wooded lands of North Britain. It was a landscape designed for the romances of Stevenson or Scott, and history, with a rare sense for the appropriate, had obliged. For here in a cave on the side of Ben Alder, the then ruling chieftain of Cluny, Ewen Macpherson, had hidden Bonnie Prince Charlie after his disastrous defeat at Culloden, until the Young Pretender could escape to France. To the Carnegies, Stevenson's recently published *Kidnapped* had the special flavor of personal involvement, and Carnegie, the arch-republican foe of monarchy, delighted in playing the role of Laird (pro tem) of Cluny and protector of the Stuart legend. The faithful Louise reported back to her mother the wonders of their Highland estate.

We are all in love with Cluny already. Such walks, such drives, such romantic little nooks! Imagine the most beautiful mountain brooks on each side of the Park with rustic bridges, beautiful waterfalls, plenty of shade trees and shrubs all surrounded by high rocky mountains. . . . It looks in places just like the scenery in Die Walküre, and we are constantly pointing out where Brunhild is lying on the rocky summit surrounded by fire. . . .[3]

For the next ten summers, with the single exception of the year 1892, the Carnegies leased Cluny Castle, and their trans-Atlantic migrations became as regular in pattern as that of migratory birds: from late October to the first of May in New York, and the remaining six months of the year in Britain. Because it was still too cold to be comfortable in the unheated halls of Cluny in early May, the Carnegies usually spent the first six weeks of their annual British sojourn in a country home near London. For several years they rented the Coworth Park estate in Sunningdale, Berkshire, and later they rented the home of Lord Cantelupe, Buckhurst, in Hampshire.[4]

Carnegie had neatly divided his life into two parts—the British half-year and the American half-year, and he was not hesitant about playing an active role in the social, political, and intellectual life of either country. There was no question for him, however, about any divided loyalty, which this migratory life might easily have induced. His fundamental allegiance belonged to the United States of America—of that there was no doubt either in his own mind or among his contemporaries. He never missed an opportunity to draw comparisons, politically, socially, or economically, between what it pleased him to refer to as his motherland and his wifeland, to the obvious advantage of the latter. But because he regarded the American political and social system as being as nearly perfect as any human institution could be, he gave far more attention to the British half of his life than to the American. He believed Britain needed to be awakened to the need for reform, while America needed no such alarm clock. Consequently, most of Carnegie's strident calls for action were directed at his motherland. Except in the most unusual circum-

423

stances, the United States could get along very nicely without his advice and warnings. But there was so much to reform in Britain that Carnegie was often at a loss in deciding which crusade was in the most urgent need of his backing: Home Rule for Ireland, the dissolution of the British Empire, the abolition of the monarchy and the House of Lords, the disestablishment of the Church of England, land reform, or a new public educational system.

Carnegie was not averse to taking on all of these causes simultaneously, for he saw them all as but various manifestations of the need to reform the basic evil existing in the established order, that of an archaic military feudalism to which the British upper classes clung with perverse obstinacy. Carnegie's direct involvement in British politics antedated by a number of years his marriage and the establishment of regular residency in Scotland. Ever since his teens he had carried on the running trans-Atlantic debate with his cousin Dod, regarding the relative merits of American republicanism and the British monarchical system, and their arguments had given Carnegie a keen interest in British political reform. But it was not until 1880 that he had the financial resources and the time necessary to engage actively in British politics.

Carnegie entered into the British political scene at what appeared to be an opportune time for genuine Liberal, if not Radical, reform. In 1880 the Disraeli government was defeated, and the Grand Old Man of British Liberalism, William Gladstone, was asked by his reluctant sovereign to form a Liberal ministry, the second under Gladstone's leadership. Cousin Dod had written Carnegie in joyous exultation over the defeat of Disraeli, "that man whom none equals in wickedness but Stafford. He [Stafford] tried to destroy the liberties of England and lost his head. Beaconsfield the same and he has lost his place. In his fall, he has sacrificed the honor of his party and what I regret most the popularity of our good kind Queen. She and the royal family has [sic] played into his hands—the more the pity for themselves." [5]

Carnegie, who shared none of his cousin's loyalty to the "good kind Queen," could only hope that Victoria had so tied the monarchy as a tail to Disraeli's high-flying imperialist kite that the sudden downdraft which had sent Disraeli plummeting to the ground would also bring down the monarchy. In any event, Carnegie was now ready to move boldly to the front of the British political stage.

He entered under impressive sponsorship. His zeal for collecting distinguished British philosophers and literary figures and bringing them in triumph to the United States had drawn him into the center of Britain's tight little island of intellectuals. And how immensely Carnegie enjoyed his associations, however forced, with these notables! He had never found any intellectual stimulation from his business associates in Pittsburgh and New York. It is doubtful if Henry Phipps ever in his life read an entire book purely for pleasure or intellectual interest,[6] and almost all of Carnegie's other American business friends were equally dull when removed from their railroads and steel mills. Although Carnegie would probably never have admitted it, he was clearly in agreement with his friend Matthew Arnold, who had written that life in America "compared with life in England, is so uninteresting, so without savour and depth." [7]

Carnegie had found intellectual excitement in the salon of Madame Botta and in the meetings of the Nineteenth Century Club in New York, but he sought to add to these moments by importing from Britain that on which happily there was no tariff— the intelligentsia of London. Herbert Spencer was only one of these importations which Carnegie arranged and exploited to the fullest. Matthew Arnold's visit was perhaps Carnegie's greatest triumph. He had been introduced to Arnold at a dinner party in London, given by Mrs. Henry Yates Thompson, the wife of the proprietor of the *Pall Mall Gazette,* in June 1883. Carnegie had at once been fascinated by Arnold, "the most charming man I ever knew," and immediately began his campaign to bring Arnold on a lecture tour to the United States. Somewhat to his own surprise, Arnold suddenly found himself in October accompanying Carnegie home to America for a whirlwind lecture tour and social lionizing for which the gentle and reserved classical poet was ill-prepared.

The Arnold lectures were not a success. The great impresario of the lecture circuit, Major J. B. Pond, who arranged the tour, later recalled that "Matthew Arnold came to this country and gave one hundred lectures. Nobody ever heard any of them, not even those sitting in the front row." [8] This was something of an exaggeration, for Margaret Carnegie was present at the first lecture to hear what her son's latest find had to say, and when later asked by Arnold what she thought of his lecture, she was her usual candid self. "Too meenisteerial, Mr. Arnold, too meenisteerial." [9]

However much Arnold and his audiences may have suffered through his lectures, Carnegie regarded the entire tour as a grand triumph. Like a mother hen showing off her only chick, Carnegie clucked and hovered over the bewildered poet throughout his visit, arranging elocution lessons for him in Boston, leading him through the frightening smells and sounds of the Chicago stockyards, and proudly displaying him to the bemused steelworkers at Braddock. Curiously enough, Arnold was fascinated by all of it, amused by Carnegie's enthusiasms, delighted by his intellectual naïveté, and almost hypnotized by his solicitous care. The two became close friends, and their friendship endured until Arnold's death four years later.

On occasion, Carnegie could be too solicitous of an eminent guest's welfare. Edwin Arnold, whose poetry Carnegie admired more than he did that of Matthew Arnold, came over for a lecture tour in 1891. Again Pond, serving as impresario, was to be disappointed in Carnegie's importation. Upon Arnold's arrival in New York, Carnegie thought he looked unwell and insisted upon calling a doctor. The doctor told Arnold that he was a sick man and must cancel all of his engagements. Pond had to return $1800 in advance ticket sales, and for days Arnold lay in his hotel room under the constant ministrations of Carnegie and his personal physician. In despair, Arnold confided to Pond, "Oh, Major, if I don't get out of this country soon, I will never be able to go at all." As soon as he could totter to his feet, Arnold left for Japan where, free from Carnegie's care, he carried on his scheduled engagements.[10]

With the two Arnolds and Herbert Spencer as his close friends, Carnegie could move with ease and confidence into a quite different world in Britain from that in which he earned his fortune at home. It was a world of poets, novelists, philosophers, editors, politicians, and even the nobility, whose collective existence he sought to terminate but whose individual members he thoroughly enjoyed. At the age of forty-five, he felt all the joy and excitement of a teen-ager in finding the first truly close friends of his adult life.

The closest of these friends proved to be John Morley, who at the time Carnegie met him was editor of both the *Fortnightly Review* and the *Pall Mall Gazette,* two of Britain's most distinguished Liberal periodicals. A strong supporter of the more Radical elements in Gladstone's government, Morley abandoned his editorial career in 1883 to enter Parliament. Three years later he became part of the Gladstone cabinet as Secretary of State for Ireland. An avowed agnostic and positivist, who accepted the Social Darwinian promise of progress through evolution, Morley shared most of Carnegie's views on philosophy and society. It was this doctrinal compatibility that brought and held the two men together, for in personality and temperament it would have been difficult to find two men more different than Carnegie and Morley—the one impetuous, enthusiastic, democratic in his personal relationships; the other cautious, reserved, and a democrat only in theory, not in practice. Yet each seemed to find in the other those qualities of character and spirit that he was aware he himself lacked. Over the years each became more and more dependent upon the friendship of the other. This was especially true of Carnegie, who was never happier than when Morley was visiting him at his Scottish estate. Carnegie gave to Morley the supreme accolade of being "the old shoe" type of house guest—"as comfortable to have around the house as an old shoe." A curious tribute in the eyes of Carnegie's servants, who found Morley the most difficult, demanding, and snobbish of all Carnegie's many visitors.[11] With Morley, Carnegie felt no need for pretense; there were no thoughts or inner feelings that could not be bared and shared.

The highly sensitive and introspective Morley on occasion found Carnegie's friendly candor a little too forthright. When he informed Carnegie that he was contemplating the writing of Oliver Cromwell's biography, Carnegie without hesitation wrote back that he thought Morley should stick to his role of statesman on the current political scene. There had been too many biographies of that grim old Calvinist Puritan already. With some heat, Morley replied, "Why do you frown on every literary project of mine. . . . Would I discourage you from making steel plates just

427

because someone else manufactures them." [12] After such a sharp thrust Carnegie might momentarily retreat, but not for long; he was irrepressible. Somewhat to his own surprise, Morley would be eager to welcome him back. In time, Morley, who could never give of himself to anyone as completely as Carnegie gave of himself to almost everyone, came to regard Carnegie as "almost my oldest friend, and assuredly the most devoted." [13] The letters written during the six months that Carnegie spent in America passed ever more frequently between them, and Morley greatly regretted Carnegie's departure from Britain each autumn. "I do not feel as if I had had talk enough with you this year. The stars have fought in their courses against us—worse luck to them for it," [14] which was about as an emotional expression of regret as Morley ever permitted himself to display about anything or anyone.

It was Morley, the rising young Radical Liberal in Gladstone's second ministry, who brought Carnegie into close contact with the leaders of British politics—Joseph Chamberlain; Henry Fowler; Henry Labouchère; Lord Bryce; the Earl of Rosebery, grandson of Lord Dalmeny, who had so frequently been taken to task by Carnegie's grandfather Morrison; and, of course, the great Gladstone himself.

Carnegie exulted in being a part of this distinguished company. How he enjoyed the gracious little notes written from the Athenaeum Club or the Home Department Office by Chamberlain or Fowler inviting him to dinner or to an evening at the club "to meet several interesting people whom you will enjoy." [15] And on high, rare occasions, there would be a summons to Hawarden, to stroll in the gardens with the Prime Minister, which to Carnegie was comparable only to having dinner at the White House and a far greater honor than being received by the Queen at Buckingham Palace.

It was quite clear to Carnegie, of course, that he was being courted for a more ulterior purpose than his congenially Liberal political views or his personal charm and wit. None of his exciting new political friends was at all hesitant in asking for financial assistance in meeting the pressing demands of a Parliamentary campaign, Gladstone least of all.

> Very recently your bountiful disposition gave me an opening which I felt it my duty not to pass over, for representing to you

the difficulties as to money in which the Liberal party is now placed. . . . Knowing your desire to apply funds to great and beneficial public purposes, I hoped you would consider this a fit case for the exercise of your liberality which I know it is your practice to put in action on a truly "liberal" scale. . . . It is of the utmost public importance to raise at once a considerable fund, which will give efficacy to the operations of the party.[16]

And Carnegie usually responded. "I send my contribution to you direct. It is so largely a personal admiration for your own self that prompts me to contribute at this time (I mean when a general election is not on) that I wish you to have the disposal of the enclosed." [17] Carnegie responded generously not only to Gladstone, but to Radicals Samuel Storey, John Burns, William Digby, I. G. Manen, and John Morley. Especially to Morley.[18]

Gratifying as Carnegie found these demands upon his time and purse, he wanted to play a more direct role in British politics than simply serving as angel to the party. Like so many persons with a limited formal education but a genuine interest in intellectual concerns, Carnegie had an exaggerated notion of the power of the pen to influence human behavior and to direct the course of history. From the time when, as a young boy in the Webster Literary Society in Pittsburgh, he had enthusiastically argued the affirmative for that old, debate-worn topic, "Resolved: That the pen is mightier than the sword," Carnegie had been convinced that although faith might not move mountains, books and newspapers certainly could. In that almost forgotten memorandum written to himself in December 1868, he had dreamed of purchasing "a controlling interest in some newspaper or live review and . . . taking a part in public matters, especially those connected with education and improvement of the poorer classes." That dream had persisted, even if the rest of the message had been ignored. Now he had the wealth and time to turn that dream into a reality. His talks with Thomas Graham of Wolverhampton while on the coaching trip in 1881 convinced Carnegie that a journalistic venture such as Graham was promoting would not only be ideologically gratifying but would prove to be a moneymaking proposition as well. Graham, an old hand at selling, had never before had so eager a customer as Carnegie.

Carnegie's new and rapidly developing friendship with John

Morley had definitely turned his thinking once again in a literary direction. And the wide acclaim he had received for his two privately published travel accounts, *Round the World* and *Our Coaching Trip,* had inflamed anew his old ambitions for a literary career. Carnegie had used both of his travel journals for didactic and propagandizing purposes: *Round the World* to preach the doctrine of evolutionary progress, and *Our Coaching Trip* to attack the grotesqueries of the British political and social system.

For Carnegie, in spite of his eager commitment to late-nineteenth-century scientism, had remained the child of early-nineteenth-century Chartism. His political heroes were still Cobbett and Cobden, Grandfather Morrison, Uncle Tom Morrison, and his father, Will. In America, under its political institutions as determined by its great democratic charter, there was no limit to what the individual could achieve—as his own remarkable success story showed. This was the basic lesson in political economy and individual liberty that Britain had yet to learn. Carnegie was determined to subsidize a new Chartist movement in his native land, not only through financial support of the Liberal party, but also by the establishment of a syndicate of Radical newspapers throughout Britain.

It has been suggested by some critics that Carnegie, in attacking the special privilege of monarchy and aristocracy, was simply setting up "an excellent straw man to pommel" in order to direct attention from basic economic and social reform which he genuinely feared.[19] Such a suggestion is in contradiction to Carnegie's most fundamental political beliefs. For Carnegie, the king, the bishop, and the lord of the manor were no straw men. He could not have been more serious than he was in this campaign against the British Establishment. He regarded himself as the Scottish Chartist come home again to pick up the battle standard that his father had been forced to lay down, and, with a wealth his father could not have imagined, to give substance to his army.

Nor would either he or his Radical friends in Britain have agreed with a later, twentieth-century judgment that "the medieval privileges which still survived in England . . . in the 1880's were hardly worth mentioning."[20] Hereditary privilege remained nearly as strongly entrenched in 1880 as it had been in 1830 when the Chartists were beating the drums for revolution. It is true that the Reform Act of 1867 had extended the suffrage to nearly all adult males except agricultural workers, but the old order had been hardly touched, let alone toppled, by this concession. In the fifteen years that had passed since this extension of the franchise, there had been no land reform, no Irish Home Rule, no weakening of the position of the hereditary House of Lords as the upper chamber, no extension of higher educational opportunities to the general population. Above all—and it was this which Carnegie found particularly irksome—there was no change in attitude among the common people from their age-old compliant acceptance of their "status in life." It was this submissiveness of the people to the old order that Carnegie wished to shake, and the best way to do this, he felt, was through a popular and cheap ha'penny press that the poorest mill hand or domestic servant could afford to buy.

Carnegie's decision to enter the newspaper business in order to reawaken the old Chartist movement had been strongly supported and encouraged by Samuel Storey, a member of Parliament from Newcastle, the most Radical center for republicanism in Britain. Storey, a six-foot-two giant, was an appropriate representative for his Radical district. A maverick who refused to belong to any established party, Storey thundered out his denunciations of the royal family and the House of Lords from his privileged position within the House of Commons and from his less protected position as publisher of the Radical Sunderland *Echo* and Tyneside *Echo*. Carnegie had been quickly captivated by his vitality, his intelligence, and by his cocksure confidence that the advent of a Republic of Britain was imminent. All the old order needed to fall flat on its face was a hard shove from the people who stood behind it. And what better way was there to stimulate the people into giving that shove than through the popular press? If a chain of newspapers could be set up throughout Britain, run by Storey and Graham, who had the journalistic competency, and paid for by Carnegie, who had the ready cash, the death of hereditary privilege in Britain would be inevitable. So Storey reasoned, and Carnegie was quick to agree.

As an important step in establishing his journalistic empire, Carnegie acquired two-thirds interest in the London *Echo* from its owner-editor, John Passmore Edwards, in 1884. Edwards, the son of a Cornish carpenter, was one of the most interesting figures in late-nineteenth-century English journalism. He had begun his newspaper career in Manchester as a reporter for the *Sentinel*. In 1846 he had come to London, where he worked at several editorial jobs. Then, in 1850, he founded a Liberal monthly magazine, *The Popular Good*. In 1876 he purchased the London *Echo*, a small, insignificant daily, from Albert Grant, and immediately transformed it into a crusading, Liberal journal which sold for a halfpenny on the London streets. Edwards, like his American counterparts Pulitzer and Hearst, whose journalistic methods and style he anticipated by a decade, was not averse to making use of sensationalism to sell his papers and promulgate his Liberal reform ideas.[21] "For two or three years," Edwards wrote in his autobiography, "I staggered under the obligations. . . . But with diligence, fledged with hope, the paper grew prosperous and became a substantial London daily organ."[22] Edwards, who had had no intention of retiring from journalism so soon after having made a success of the *Echo*, found Carnegie's cash offer and the promise of carrying the *Echo*'s Liberal reform message throughout Britain irresistible. He agreed to sell the controlling interest of the paper to the Carnegie-Storey syndicate, but he insisted upon keeping one-third interest.

The acquisition of the London *Echo* completed a chain of newspapers controlled by Carnegie and Storey that extended from Portsmouth on the southern coast of England to Sunderland and Newcastle on the northeast coast. By the end of 1884, Carnegie owned or held a controlling interest in seven daily newspapers and ten weeklies, with a heavy concentration in the Black Country of central England and in the manufacturing centers to the north.[23] A few of these papers, such as the Midland *Echo* (Birmingham) and the *Midland Counties Guardian* (Wolverhampton), were newly founded, but the majority were well-established papers, including one, the *Hampshire Telegraph*, which dated back to 1799. In most cases, the acquisition of the paper by the Carnegie-Storey syndicate meant a rather abrupt change in editorial policy, but the change was most radical in the Wolverhampton *Evening Express and Star*, which had been the voice of Tory reaction in the Black Country until Thomas Graham took it over in 1882. The incredulity and anger expressed in letters to the editor by the old subscribers were a delight to Carnegie and Graham.

The syndicate made no major change in either the format or the editorial policy of the London *Echo*. Although the Edwards brand of Liberalism was somewhat milder than the radicalism Storey and Graham advocated in the Black Country, the London *Echo* staunchly supported Irish Home Rule and free compulsory education, and its success with the London public convinced Carnegie it should remain unchanged.

But in the north country, where Storey and Carnegie hoped to arouse the coal miners, mill hands, and the sullen unemployed to desperate action, the newly acquired papers were remarkably alike in editorial tone. Their calls for the abolition of the monarchy and the House of Lords and the disestablishment of the Church of England were consistent and strident. Frequently the same editorial would appear in two or three of the syndicate's papers at the same time, but whether or not the editorial pages for the various papers were written by the same hand, they all carried the same message. They were selective in their backing of candidates for Parliament, but it was usually the Liberal candidate who most nearly met their democratic standards. As might have been expected, John Morley had a very good press in the syndicate in his campaign for Parliament from a Newcastle constituency. Carnegie's journals attacked resurgent imperialism of the Conservative government in sending troops to the Sudan; they supported labor strikes of the coal miners in the Black Country; they upheld the sacred Liberal principle of free trade; they even espoused such extreme reform as the abolition of capital punishment—as well as the granting of women's suffrage, which was generally regarded by the Conservative press as being just as iniquitous as free love. The syndicate's biggest campaign, however, was reserved for the Reform Bill of 1884. This final extension of manhood suffrage became for Radicals the essential first step in the disestablishment of the old order. When, in July 1884, it appeared that the House of Lords might be successful in blocking the Reform bill after it had passed the House of Commons, the Wolverhampton *Evening Express and Star* spoke for the entire syndicate when it demanded that "the existence of the House of Lords be painlessly terminated." The Radicals, the paper pointed out, "long before and quite apart from the present Franchise crisis, have urged reform of the House of Peers. . . . The Lords, in the Radical view, come before the country for judgement much in the position of a well-known and hardened offender brought before the magistrates with a record of fifty previous convictions against him." [24] When the Reform bill became law in the fall of 1884, the syndicate press regarded the enactment as a personal triumph. The Tyneside *Echo* jubilantly proclaimed that the Radicals "are becoming more important all the time. They will soon be the rulers, and no longer thwarted and hampered by Whigs, they will put many aristocratic anomalies in order." [25]

Unfortunately, if the Radicals were increasing in numbers, they were not buying more newspapers. The syndicate, with the exception of the London *Echo,* was in serious financial difficulties. At first, with his natural optimism, Carnegie was not discouraged over the debts the various papers were running up, and he wrote encouraging notes to his partner, Storey: "Yours rec'd. Don't be discouraged—I never mounted a horse first time that had go in him which didn't kick. All our enterprises have gone wrong at first. All came right when reconstructed. You are the sole manager of business matters. *Go ahead.*" [26] He also put up a brave front before John Morley: "Let me tell you the Midland Echo is no longer an experiment. Its swelling daily has taken firm root. Portsmouth papers also. Ditto at Wolverhampton but the latter, slowly. It will soon kill the other paper however (Conservative)." [27]

But the Conservative press proved stronger than Carnegie had thought. Soon he was writing anxious notes to Storey suggesting a solution that had worked in the iron and steel business:

"I shall be in Wolverhampton a few days after you receive this, and we can then consider the situation together. I hope you are ready with your scheme to consolidate all the papers: Reid's Tyne-side, and Sunderland. I do not feel inclined to go on investing more capital at present but of course will pay my share of any assessment made. We would be a strong power were all of our papers merged into one, and could then strike as a thunderbolt, whereas we are now merely showering the enemy with small darts none of which are strong enough to pierce their armor. Even the London 'Echo' should be merged." [28]

434

Edwards, however, protested the merger of his old paper, in which he still held a sizable interest, with the struggling papers in the north, and, after further consideration, Carnegie and Storey agreed that it would be best to keep the separate identity of each paper. "I agree about small bright papers," Carnegie wrote Storey. "The London Echo is highly creditable, one *must* read *it*. Wolverhampton & Birmingham flat penny beer—" Graham had now become Carnegie's whipping boy, the easy explanation for the failure of the papers to catch on with the reading public. "Put a man at Wolverhampton in *full* charge as you suggest. No divided authority. This is essential. Graham had a good business & profitable one—I agree he lacks the 'go.' Your man should be told he is to have a fair trial. But we know one test only— success. We will change till we get an augur that will bore. I have already written Graham before yours rec'd. that on his statement of loss that was an end of our *business* cooperation, as for friendship, that was always as before. . . . Don't give up Birmingham. We don't know how to give up." [29]

In the spring of 1884, while in the midst of these financial difficulties with his newspapers, Carnegie arrived in Britain for his second coaching trip through the island. This tour was to be quite different from the earlier one, for it was planned for English celebrities rather than for old friends and relatives. The party consisted of the English novelist, William Black, whose book, *Adventures in a Phaeton,* had been a source book for Carnegie's first coaching trip; the painter and illustrator for *Harper's Magazine,* Edwin A. Abbey, the only American other than Carnegie in the party; Edwin Arnold; Matthew Arnold, his wife, and his daughter; the son and daughter of William Gladstone; and Carnegie's journalistic partner and favorite M.P., Samuel Storey. It was a more leisurely coaching trip than the first had been; it was confined to England, and the party took six weeks to travel from London through the southern counties to Ilfracombe on the Bristol channel in Devonshire.[30] With this influential group, Carnegie and Storey lost no time in promulgating the Radical republican doctrines their papers were disseminating. That this anti-monarchical propaganda became a bit tiresome to most of Carnegie's traveling companions is evident in the travel notes on the trip which William Black wrote for an American magazine a few months later. Dubbing Carnegie "the Star-Spangled Scotchman" (apparently it was Black who coined this celebrated phrase, in which Carnegie took great pride), Black pictured Carnegie as spending most of his time either singing "John Brown's Body" or proclaiming the glories of the United States. He described in detail one picnic as being typical of so many others on the trip. Happily, he wrote, "John Brown's . . . ghost was left undisturbed for a while. On the other hand, we had such a discourse on the freedom and purity and incorruptibility of the United States of America that more than ever we longed to fly away and be at rest in that happy land. Why should we be lingering here in slavery? . . . As we listened, the land of promise became more and more fair, more and more dismal and desperate became the results of a monarchical system of government. We couldn't see any of them, it is true; for the Wiltshire hawthorn bushes are thick, and around us were only pleasant meadows and rippling streams, but they were there somewhere; and we wondered that the birds, in such a condition of affairs, could sing so carelessly." [31]

While Carnegie and company were ambling through the countryside of southern England, the political crisis over the Reform Bill of 1884 was reaching its climax. In midsummer the House of Commons passed the bill only to have it rejected by the House of Lords. The Carnegie-Storey syndicate became more vociferous than ever in demanding the end of the House of Lords, that "bastion of special privilege which stands in the way of the will of the people." In late autumn, driven by rising pressure from the public, the Gladstone ministry, and even the Queen herself, the upper house capitulated, and universal manhood suffrage, the first plank in the old Chartist program, became a reality.

Carnegie, back in New York at the time, regarded this achievement as a victory not only for the Gladstone ministry but for his newspapers, which he was sure were responsible for arousing public opinion. Hopes were bright in that autumn, and the Chartist republican millennium seemed close at hand. For a brief time, Carnegie, whose citizenship had always been somewhat cloudy, even toyed with the idea of entering Parliament himself. He wrote to a friend that the American Minister to Britain, James Russell Lowell, "had heard I intended to enter public life in England & sometimes I feel it is my mission to do so—but only to give my native land some of the political justice enjoyed by my adopted one." [32] But Carnegie was willing to postpone his personal political ambitions. For the time being, he had felt he could play a more powerful role as a publisher than as an M.P. He told a Philadelphia reporter, "I do not think I would care much to enter Parliament even if I were a British citizen. The press is the true source of power in Britain as in America. The time of Parliament is consumed discussing trifling affairs, which should be relegated to local assemblies. Members of Parliament sit merely to carry out the plans dictated by the press, the true exponent of the wishes of the people." [33] To his potential British constituents, however, Carnegie was not so resolute in denying any desire for office. When a Liberal party leader in Edinburgh sent out a polite and discreet feeler on whether Carnegie might be willing to stand for Parliament from an Edinburgh district, Carnegie did not shut the door to the opportunity:

> That I should be thought of, by the advanced wing of the Great Army of Liberalism as, perhaps, a man worthy to represent the capital of my native Land in Parliament—and the capital is Edinburgh—is indeed flattering. I am compelled to say that as at present situated, I am not yet prepared to enter public life and devote myself wholly to the advocacy and support of those radical reforms which I have so much at heart. If, however, it ever happens, in some future day, that, after a full and frank exposition of my political convictions before the advanced Liberals, they select me as their standard-bearer, and elect me, I should much rather rise in the House of Commons, to speak in Edinburgh's name for some great reform than to play at "King of Great Britain." [34]

In the meantime, Carnegie had been indefatigable in making "a full and frank exposition of his political convictions," not only before the advanced Liberals but before the whole British nation. Through the Radical expressions of his newspaper editors and by his own remarks before political rallies in Scotland and England, he left no doubt about his opinions on the monarchy and the aristocracy. When the reactionary *St. James's Gazette* accused Carnegie of being engaged in a conspiracy against the British Empire,

Carnegie replied with an attack upon the monarchy so vitriolic that even his Liberal friends were alarmed. Carnegie found it necessary to write to one of the Liberal party leaders the following defense of his position:

> You regret that in the published interview I attacked the Crown. What I then said was in reply to the charge of the St. James's Gazette that I was engaged in a conspiracy against English institutions. This charge I resented. I am no conspirator; but I am, as you are well aware, and as I would have all the world know, a man who regards the doctrine of the political equality of man as man, as the very soul of politics; the precious root from which spring manly self-respect and all its attendant virtues. . . . Cobden, Bright, and all their colleagues gave you Free Trade, but the men who bring the day to England, when her flag no longer decrees a single privilege to one citizen which is denied to another, but proclaims equal privileges to all: these men will have accomplished a task as much nobler than theirs as the things of the spirit are nobler than the things of the body.
>
> Holding these opinions, I should not have been honest had I not admitted that I would destroy, if I had the power, every vestige of privilege in England; . . . but at the same time, I would not shed a drop of blood, nor violate a law, nor use violence in any form, to bring about what I so much desire. It is not necessary to do so. It will all come in good time, and come the more quickly and the more surely from the gradual spread of education, and by peaceable discussion, than by any other means.
>
> The first duty of a Republican is to bow to the decision of the Ballot box.
>
> The weapon of Republicanism is not the sword, but the pen.
>
> I am glad to note that you are abreast of John Morley. He is a safe leader and a growing power. I should be very much surprised if he would reply in the affirmative, were he asked whether he believed that the hereditary in any form, to use the language of Mr. John Bright, as applied to the Hereditary Chamber, "could be a permanent institution in a free country." Even if he did reply in the affirmative, I would there part company with him, and say to him, as I now say to you: "The dawn has come, and the full day approaches when there shall be no officer in any free state who does not derive his authority

438

direct from the vote of the people, and submits himself, and his
acts, from time to time for their august approval. When that
day comes in England, believe me that the spirit of the nation
will be sensibly raised. Your young men will be freer from
snobbery—your middle aged men will be more self-reliant—
your old men free from the pitiful hunt after rank and title,
and all classes will be prouder, and will have good reason to be
prouder, of the glorious little isle which we are so privileged to
call our mother land.[35]

These were brave and hopeful words, and Carnegie sought to implement them by public agitation for land reform, Irish Home
Rule, and the abolition of the House of Lords as the first steps toward a republican form of government for Britain. He entered
into public controversy over land reform by advocating that Britain adopt the land laws of Denmark, which had a heavily graduated tax on all land holdings above 250 acres. "Denmark," he
wrote to Professor J. Stuart Blackie of Edinburgh University, who
was interested in Carnegie's proposal, "has increased her land
owners from, I think, seventy to some fifty-three thousand by cu-
mulative taxation. . . . I believe that we have in this simple law
the remedy for the Land trouble in England." [36]

Gladstone had been Carnegie's political hero for fifteen years
because of his brilliant achievements during his first ministry, and
particularly because of his acceptance of the arbitration of the Alabama claims. But during these years of Gladstone's second ministry, Carnegie was beating the drums for truly revolutionary innovations and associating closely with the most extreme elements in
British politics, including such Radicals as Charles Dilke, Labouchère, and John Burns.[37] Carnegie's newspapers were frequently a source of embarrassment to Gladstone, for they associated his ministry with Storey's and Carnegie's Radicalism.
Gladstone could never be and had no desire to be the kind of
Radical innovator that Carnegie wanted. Nevertheless, for Carnegie he was the best that Britain had to offer in the way of enlightened leadership. Carnegie was quite willing to ride along on
Gladstone's back and serve as his gadfly, even if Gladstone did not
appreciate those services.

But Britain's reforming zeal seemed to have spent itself with
the passage of the Reform Act of 1884 and the redistribution of

Parliamentary seats in January 1885. Even the mild expression of Radicalism, Home Rule for Ireland, was doomed to failure. After having briefly lost control of Parliament to the Conservatives late in 1885, Gladstone, in order to form his third ministry in 1886, had come to terms with the stern, unyielding Charles Parnell, leader of the Irish Home Rulers in Parliament. Parnell, however, demanded too much. He wanted all of Ireland, including Protestant Ulster, and Gladstone, desperate for Parnell's block of eighty-five votes in Parliament, acquiesced. This, as G. M. Trevelyan has said, "was more than an error in tactics. It flew in the face of racial and political possibilities." [38] Carnegie not only supported the Gladstone-Parnell alliance; he went much further than Gladstone. He suggested a federal union for Britain similar to that of the United States. "Your position upon the Irish question," he wrote Gladstone at the beginning of the third ministry, "seems to me certain to win and crown your career with the most important legislation you have ever carried." He went on to assert that Parnell was now receiving financial and moral support, not just from Irish-Americans but "from real native Americans. . . . I suggest therefore that you take an early opportunity to refer to the rights of States in the American Union as being the proper position for Ireland. Such a measure will strengthen the bonds of union between Ireland and Great Britain; for America has proved through the federal system that the present self-government of the parts produces the strongest government of the whole." [39] Carnegie quite clearly had in mind eventual statehood for Scotland and Wales as well as Ireland. Gladstone was so impressed with Carnegie's suggestion that he made marginal comment on the letter, "A movement of the kind he indicates wd. draw much notice. Let Mr. Morley see this." [40]

But in spite of Carnegie's assurances of American moral support, in spite of Gladstone's magnificent oratory in presenting the bill in Parliament—a speech that has sometimes been called the greatest ever delivered in the House of Commons—and in spite of Parnell's solid block of votes, the bill was defeated and with it Gladstone's power. Too many English Liberals put ancient prejudices above party loyalty. In the ensuing election, the Parnellites lost their position of strength as the balance of power between the two major parties. That position now belonged to the dissident

Liberal Unionists, who cast their lot with the triumphant Conservatives, and Lord Salisbury took over the government. Gladstone went into retirement at Hawarden.

At the same time Gladstone's third ministry collapsed in defeat to a resurgent Conservatism, so did Carnegie's Radical newspaper empire. For the past several months all of the papers in the syndicate, with the exception of the London *Echo,* had consistently lost money. New management and more money from Carnegie had failed to get them off the ground. Now with the defeat of the Liberals, Carnegie abruptly decided to get out of the enterprise completely, to stop pouring good money after bad, and to sustain what losses were necessary in order to extricate himself from this unhappy venture. Fortunately, Passmore Edwards was eager to get full possession of his London *Echo* once again, and he offered to pay Carnegie and Storey £100,000, double what they had paid him for their two-thirds share of the paper.[41] The gain made on the sale of the *Echo* to Edwards helped to offset Carnegie's losses on his investments in the other papers. Neither Storey nor Graham wanted to give up their interests in the papers in Newcastle, Birmingham, and Wolverhampton, so Carnegie agreed to accept their notes for several thousand pounds and to hold shares in the various newspaper companies which they owned as security. A settlement was not reached with Graham until 1902, when Carnegie surrendered the remaining 268 shares of the Midland News Association stock which he still held as collateral and accepted a promissory note for the £5000 which Graham still owed him.[42] There is no further record in Carnegie's accounts that would indicate that Graham ever settled his remaining debt to Carnegie. It was quite probably still outstanding at the time of Graham's death in 1909.

For the few thousand pounds which he may have lost in this newspaper venture, Carnegie felt that he had learned a lesson that was worth several times the loss he had sustained. Never again after 1886 would he be tempted to subsidize any journal or publication pleading a special cause, although many requests for such subsidization would continue to come to his desk.[43] Carnegie's answer to the brilliant but erratic editor of the *Review of Reviews,* W. T. Stead, who had wanted Carnegie to endow "a first class newspaper" to combat the jingoism of the day, indicates

441

how completely he had learned his lesson. "Cannot agree with you about supported newspapers to support an idea. They never amount to anything." [44] When Stead continued over the years to pester him for support of such a journal, Carnegie finally became even more explicit: "Frankly, I have little faith in the advocacy of publications especially founded for that end. They are devoted to the one subject entirely and only those will read them who are already converted. The same money paid in advertising our views in the ordinary periodicals would, in my opinion, have a much greater effect." [45]

Although the failure in 1886 of all the bright hopes Carnegie shared with the triumphant Liberals in 1881 marked the end of his newspaper syndicate, his basic optimism was not daunted. The war for Radical reform, he was certain, had not been lost—only a minor engagement. New tactics were required, both in politics and in propaganda. Carnegie would now preach to the British public through general publications, in those journals directed at the intellectuals and the political leaders of both parties, and in those newspapers among whose readers one could find every shade of political thought in the country.

Carnegie was not at all averse to propounding his political and social ideas under his own byline rather than second-hand through the medium of hired editorial writers. With the publication of his first article in the *Fortnightly Review* in 1882, an essay entitled "As Others See Us," Carnegie's literary ambitions were vigorously stimulated. From that time on, his articles were frequent features in the more liberal journals of Britain.

He also found a convenient means of getting his views published in *The Times* of London and in the provincial papers of Britain by writing letters to the editor and by holding elaborate press interviews whenever he was given the opportunity to do so. By these tactics he was able to present his Radical ideas in Conservative journals that would not touch his signed feature articles. All of these ways of carrying on the crusade were far more satisfying to his ego than his role of being the silent owner of seventeen newspapers had ever been.

His greatest literary accomplishment in these years of Radical agitation, however, was the publication of *Triumphant Democracy*. This appeared at the very moment he was extricating himself from the unhappy venture into journalism, and it did much to assuage his feelings of failure as a crusading newspaper publisher.

Carnegie had reason to be proud, for *Triumphant Democracy* created a sensation on both sides of the Atlantic. In the United States it went through four printings and a second completely revised edition, and eventually it sold over 30,000 copies. In Great Britain it went through several printings, including a cheap paperback edition which alone sold 40,000 copies. It was translated into French and German and had a sizable sale on the Continent. Above all, it became the subject of controversial reviews and editorials, both pro and con, on both sides of the Atlantic, which delighted the publishers and the author. Carnegie knew that he had touched the quick of the British Tory soul when both the *St. James's Gazette* and the *Saturday Review* lambasted it in their editorial columns as if it were a new and more dangerous Marxist Manifesto for revolution.

From the outside cover, designed by Carnegie himself, which showed two golden pyramids, one standing firmly on its base and labeled "Republic" and the other teetering precariously on its apex and labeled "Monarchy," to the final sentence, some 509 pages later, the book is an exultant paean of praise to his adopted land. The opening sentence states the basic thesis of the entire book: "The old nations of the earth creep on at a snail's pace; the Republic thunders past with the rush of the express." [46] Carnegie's method of proving his thesis was the simple one of presenting statistical information from the 1880 census and from *Scribner's Statistical Atlas,* which revealed the spectacular growth of American population and material wealth as expressed in its agricultural production, manufacturing, mining, trade, and commerce, and in its transportation and communication facilities. But Carnegie was not content to "let the figures speak for themselves." "As the pile of reference books, census reports and statistical works lay around upon tables and shelves," Carnegie wrote in the preface, "the question suggested itself, 'shall these dry bones live?' I hope, therefore, indulgent readers that you will not be warranted in accusing me of giving too much solid information. I have tried to coat the wholesome medicine of facts in the sweetest and purest sugar of fancy at my command. Pray you, open your

443

mouths and swallow it in small doses, and like the sugar even if you detest the pill." [47]

Curiously enough, the "dry bones" do live, for the book is filled with anecdotes, editorial comment, and, above all, Carnegie's own ebullient personality. The reader, to be sure—to continue with one part of Carnegie's own mixed metaphor—frequently finds the sugar coating a bit too sweet and sticky and would welcome just a suggestion of the medicinally bitter acid of criticism. Carnegie was immediately attacked, even by some American critics, for being effusive in his praise of everything American. George William Curtis said that Carnegie's book reminded him of the Californian's boasting about the weather in his state. "It's all sunshine, sunshine, sunshine," wrote Mr. Curtis. "Where are the shadows?" To which Carnegie had a ready reply, "The book was written at high noon when the sun casts no shadows." [48] And when a somewhat skeptical Scottish reporter in Aberdeen asked him during an interview, "But you mean to say in America you have no long standing abuses to correct as we in Britain have?" Carnegie, with quiet assurance, replied, "No, that is true, and it is a blessing. The system is perfect. . . . We have only the proper administration of perfect institutions to look after." [49] Against such a faith, the shafts of criticism were useless.

It has been easy ever since the book's first appearance for critics to point out how naïve Carnegie was in confusing the material progress of a nation with true cultural greatness. For quite clearly Carnegie did just that. Here is a book that anticipates by forty years and quite unconsciously out-parodies Sinclair Lewis's *Babbitt* in its expression of the American "booster" spirit. Matthew Arnold wrote from America to a friend: "You should read Carnegie's book, *Triumphant Democracy*. The facts he has collected as to the material progress of this country are remarkable. . . . He and most Americans are simply unaware that nothing in the book touches the capital defect of life over here; namely, that, compared with life in England, it is so uninteresting, so without savour and without depth. Do they think to prove that it has savour and depth by pointing to the number of public libraries, schools and places of worship?" [50] Of course, the answer that Carnegie would give to Arnold's rhetorical question would be a ringing "yes."

Arnold's advice to his friend that he should read Carnegie's *Triumphant Democracy* is valid for the historian today, for in spite of its obvious defects—or, perhaps, because of its obvious defects—it remains one of the most important documents of America's Gilded Age. It is the kind of testimonial of faith that the great majority of Americans of all classes, occupations, and regions would have made, had they had the time, money, and literary talent to do so. Carnegie's book, which is a Fourth of July oration with statistical tables, expresses the genuine American beliefs of the late nineteenth century in the signal value of material progress, in the supreme importance of the political forms of democracy, in individualism, and in numbers. *Triumphant Democracy* explains much about the American society which the European observer found bewildering and inexplicable: the lack of any real distinction between the two major political parties because of an absence of any real ideological conflict, the failure of Marxism to take root in this industrial nation because the working class tended to identify itself with the middle class, the essential isolationism in foreign policy because America felt itself apart from and peculiarly blessed above all other nations in the Western World. In short, all of the basic themes which Ralph Gabriel was later to find as the essential "doctrine of the American democratic faith," a belief in natural law, in the free and responsible individual, and in the mission of America to set an example of democracy for the rest of the world, found full expression in Carnegie's *Triumphant Democracy*.[51] One can learn more about the actual tenets of faith of the American businessman in the Gilded Age, and of the American workingman as well, by reading this book than by reading all eighteen volumes of Herbert Spencer's collected works.

This implicit faith in democracy, so fervently expressed by Carnegie throughout the book, does much to explain why the European doctrinaire found few rewards in the United States. The Spencerian evolutionist and the Marxist socialist both failed to understand America, for both tended to see political bourgeois liberalism as product rather than producer. Spencer and Sumner believed that American political democracy was the result of the free enterprise system. Marx saw all forms of government as but manifestations of the prevailing economic order. But Carnegie's entire book is devoted to the basic thesis, held to by most of his countrymen, that America was rich, progressive, and capitalistic *because of the political order* that had been established in 1787. He totally rejected the naturalistic social theories of Spencer and Sumner which held that all political and legal institutions were but superstructures, dependent upon the industrial economic base of a society.[52]

Triumphant Democracy is but another expression of the simple Chartist faith in form. At the same time, it is as basic to American thought as Lincoln's "Fourscore and seven years ago" philosophy or Jefferson's "When in the course of human events" Declaration.

The question has been frequently raised of why Carnegie, as preoccupied as he was at this time in his various business enterprises, should have taken the time and effort required to write *Triumphant Democracy*. Carnegie thought he had anticipated and answered this question by his dedicatory preface: "To the Beloved Republic under whose equal laws I am made the peer of any man, although denied political equality by my native land, I dedicate this book with an intense gratitude· and admiration which the native-born citizen can neither feel nor understand," or as he put it more succinctly, it was "a labor of love," an expression of gratitude for all that America had given him.[53]

And so it was. But there were reasons for writing this book at this particular time more complex than the one Carnegie stated in his preface. Historians have suspected that in part Carnegie was attempting to justify himself and the major role he had played in creating the kind of America that had emerged in the post Civil War decades. Robert McCloskey has written: "It seems reasonable to believe that he wrote *Triumphant Democracy* because he had an imperious need to explain and justify himself and his environment, because he had to convince both the world and himself that what he was doing was good and that the context within which he operated was just. The book appears to be a defense of democracy; actually, it is a defense of nineteenth-century capitalism—and Carnegie." [54]

There is much truth in this statement. For, whether or not he would ever have admitted it, even to himself, Carnegie was motivated by "an imperious need" to justify himself. This book was

446

part of that continuing search for a reconciliation between his Radical Dunfermline past and the plutocratic present which was to engage Carnegie throughout most of his life. In this the book was only partially successful. The reconciliation was not achieved with the publication of *Triumphant Democracy,* and the uneasy Carnegie had to seek elsewhere for a more satisfactory justification of his life.

Quite obviously, the book was also part of Carnegie's continuing campaign to bring the Charter of republicanism to Britain. Having failed in his newspaper campaign to exhort the British public into action in the name of justice, he was with this book appealing to British nationalism, by showing how democratic America was surpassing monarchical Great Britain in almost every area of economic endeavor. He was attempting to arouse the competitive spirit of the British people by the hard sell of the sideshow huckster. In effect, what he was saying was, "Do you want to be rich, powerful, and happy? If so, take Uncle Sam's easy-to-swallow political institutions. There's a sure-cure for all your ailments in every election." It was as simple as that, and Carnegie had the advantage over most patent medicine salesmen in that he believed fervently in his own remedy.

Carnegie, as the author of *Triumphant Democracy,* had now achieved a measure of fame in British Radical political circles that extended far beyond the narrow confines of the Liberal party leadership in London. He was courted by the Radical Association in various cities throughout his native Scotland, and nothing delighted him more than to be asked to mount the platform and thunder out against special privilege, as he did before the Glasgow Junior Liberal Association in September 1887. How he revelled in the shouts and foot-stamping that greeted his remark, "We have our executive in the President. We make our king every four years. . . ." The demonstration continued until he had repeated that remark three times.[55] At that moment, Carnegie sincerely believed the monarchy was dead in Britain.

There was a very special pleasure for him in the tribute paid to him by the Dunfermline Radical Association in the same year. The spokesman for that group, which included the sons and grandsons of his father's Chartist associates, said that Carnegie had already done more to bring about democracy in Great Brit-

447

ain than any thousand other men in Britain. In reply, Carnegie brought out all of the old familiar charges against every aspect of the Establishment—the monarchy, the church, the House of Lords, and the landed gentry. But lest his audience might think he was more of a Radical than he was, he concluded his speech by reminding them that by democracy he did not mean "equality of condition, physical or mental, or equality as to property." He meant only political equality. He did not want his audience of working men to confuse republicanism with socialism.[56] There was a decided limitation to his radicalism even in Britain.

Such public gatherings were an intoxicant to Carnegie, and he himself felt at a loss to judge whether he was more effective in working for the cause as an orator or as a writer. Certainly there was enough of the showman's vanity in Carnegie to make him a highly dramatic figure on the public platform. Frequently rising to his tiptoes and pumping his short arms vigorously, to his critics in the audience he looked like a bantam rooster ready to crow. But to his Radical supporters he was the tough little man ready to take on all comers in the ring. Even the highly critical Scottish weekly, *The Bailie,* had to admit that "nowhere is Mr. Carnegie stronger than in his oratorical instincts. His speech is occasionally marred by an American accent, but his feeling is always Scotch and his Americanisms soon relapse into his mother tongue. . . ."[57]

So energetically did Carnegie plead the cause of republicanism during the six months each year that he spent in Britain that both the outraged Conservative and the somewhat embarrassed Liberal party leaders were relieved when, with the first cold, damp days of October, Carnegie would head back to his utopian Republic across the Atlantic.

The more cynical of the Conservatives, however, took great delight in pointing out that, in his annual migration, Carnegie, the flaming Radical of Britain, was miraculously transformed into the conservative Republican of America; the decrier of special privilege became the outspoken advocate of protective tariff; the supporter of John Burns, the workingman's candidate, became the confidant and close political associate of James Blaine—so much so, indeed, that he would not even mention Grover Cleveland by name, for Cleveland was "no gentleman."[58]

It was only too easy for such Conservative British journals as *St. James's Gazette* and *Blackwood's Magazine* to point out these remarkable discrepancies in Carnegie's political views. They accused him of hypocrisy and asked why, if he was so concerned with the rights of the common man, he did not stay at home and cultivate his own American democratic garden, which was badly in need of weeding.

There was enough truth in these charges to make Carnegie a little uncomfortable. Particularly difficult for him to explain were the differing points of view he held on the tariff, depending upon which side of the Atlantic he was viewing it from. Nothing alarmed him more than the growing movement among British Conservatives to abandon Britain's policy of free trade in favor of a program of imperial preference, particularly since that program might effect American-Canadian trade relations. Joseph Chamberlain, his former friend and Liberal associate, who had broken with Gladstone and the Liberal party over questions of Empire and Home Rule for Ireland, was the chief promoter of this "abomination." Carnegie railed and fumed against the imperial preference policy in angry letters to *The Times*, threatening all kinds of dire consequences for Canada should this rich market for rails and beams be no longer free to American steel plants.[59]

For the United States, he championed the cause of protective tariff with equal vigor. For many years Carnegie Brothers had made their large annual payment to the American Iron and Steel Association for the services of the Association's indefatigable lobbyist, James M. Swank, to keep the steel schedules high in all proposed tariff legislation. It was money well spent, for Swank did a good job, ably assisted by most of Pennsylvania's congressmen and senators in the nation's capital. In a letter to Swank in 1895, following a brief scare when it appeared that Matthew Quay's seat in the United States Senate might be in jeopardy, Carnegie expressed his gratitude for the long years of faithful service that Swank and Quay had given: "Your cable gave me much pleasure and relief. Senator Quay's defeat would have been more than a State—a national calamity. It is necessary to know, as you and I do, what services he renders to Pennsylvania, to keep him in the Senate as long as he can be induced to serve. I am also glad to know that you are well enough to be still *active* in the good cause.

You are another man to whom Pennsylvania owes an unpayable debt." [60]

Carnegie did not usually take nearly as direct and active a role in American elections at the local, state, and national level as he did in British elections, nor in specific measures pending before the Pennsylvania legislature or before Congress. Whatever promoting or repelling needed to be done was ably handled by his subordinates and by paid lobbyists such as Swank. As long as the Republican party remained in control at Harrisburg and Washington, God was in His Heaven and all was well. But on matters of tariff, Carnegie would with painstaking care go through each scheduled item in the proposed legislation that affected iron and steel products and send his specific recommendations to key congressmen and senators. "Schedule No. 108—Pig Iron," he would advise Senator Arthur Gorman, one of his staunchly Protectionist Democratic friends, "the lowest duty that will keep Southern and Eastern furnaces from disaster is 2/10¢ lb. . . . No. 112 Boiler Plates etc. Present duty 5/10 to 3½¢. Might be reduced to 5/10 to 8/10. 5/10 is required as a minimum upon the lowest qualities of plate." [61]

Such efforts, of course, over the years had paid off handsomely, and few men in America had benefited so directly and bountifully as Carnegie. During the 1870's, when there had been a duty of $28 a ton on steel rails, the Edgar Thomson steel mill had been built, had grown, and had flourished, protected and nourished by such beneficent welfare legislation as has seldom been given by any government to any single group of private citizens. Carnegie was certainly not going to deny the advantages of protective tariff for the sake of trans-Atlantic consistency.

He did, however, seek to reconcile his support of Manchester Liberalism in Britain with his protective Republicanism in America. He had the opportunity to make public a full statement justifying his two positions in 1890, when he was asked by the editors of the *North American Review* to conclude a series of articles which this distinguished journal had run over the past several months on the tariff question. The debate had opened with articles by Carnegie's two great political heroes of the day, William Gladstone, writing on behalf of free trade, and James G. Blaine, supporting protection. There had been other articles by

Congressmen Roger Mills of Texas and William C. B. Brecken-
ridge of Kentucky, arguing for "a tariff for revenue only," and by
Senator Justin Morrill and Congressman William McKinley for
protection. The editors of the *Review,* in choosing Carnegie to
sum up the discussion, had clearly tipped the scales toward protection, and difficult as it may have been for Carnegie to take up
the debate in opposition to his hero, Gladstone, he was not at all
hesitant in doing so.

Carnegie met the argument of contradiction head on, by immediately admitting that in Great Britain and in the United
States he had and, indeed, should have, diametrically opposite
views on the tariff. Inasmuch as Britain had been first in the industrial race and had for a long time produced more than enough
goods to satisfy her internal market in every field of manufacturing at a lower cost than any other nation could produce such
goods, a tariff for Britain had meant only a tariff in agricultural
products. Consequently, free trade, which Britain had adopted in
1846 with the repeal of the Corn Laws, was simply the freeing of
trade for the importation of absolutely essential food products
and the ending of what Gladstone had called "the immorality" of
the British landlord's monopoly of grain. "All that Mr. Gladstone
says in regard to the 'folly' and the 'immorality' of this attempt to
maintain a monopoly and starve the people is true and well deserved. But how different the meaning of protection when used
by the American. . . . Given a world within itself, with every
requisite for manufacturing the various commodities required by
its people, was it wise to give the necessary concessions and bounties to induce skill and capital to establish manufactures within this
world? and, if it were found that the easiest and surest mode of
building up manufactures was by taxing the manufactures of
other nations, so that the product of experimental factories in the
undeveloped land should be shielded from the competition of
fully-developed factories abroad, should this protection have been
given or not, and should it be maintained as far as may be found
necessary? How interesting it would be to have Mr. Gladstone's
answer to this problem—the only one which our country has to
consider." [62] Carnegie took delight in quoting the Radical leader
in Parliament, "that thorough man of the world, Mr. Henry Labouchère, who has recently explained that the question of free

trade or protection is one of condition; not a science applicable everywhere. It is good for some countries, bad for others. 'As I am an Englishman,' says he, 'I am in favor of free trade; but if I were an American I should be in favor of protection.' " [63] Carnegie's implication here, in using this quotation was clear. If what Labouchère said was true, why should Carnegie, a resident of both countries, be criticized for being a free trader in Britain, where he was simply a consumer of food, and a protectionist in America, where he was a producer of steel?

For the remainder of his lengthy essay, Carnegie considered and, by means of statistics, logic, and arguments *ad horrendum,* demolished, at least to his own satisfaction, every argument against protection that had been advanced by the free traders and the "tariff-for-revenue-only" Democrats: First, Protection is "immoral" (it was only immoral in Britain, where it was applied to absolutely essential trade in foodstuffs); second, "that the infantile stage in American industry had passed" (American industry was not yet mature, and still needed considerable protection); third "that if we do not buy abroad, foreign nations cannot purchase from us" (numerous people would always buy in the cheapest market, and besides, we had a large domestic market, making foreign trade unnecessary for a national well-being); fourth, "that our nation's prosperity and wealth are to be best gauged by the extent of its dealings with other countries" (again, nonsense, the value of our foreign trade has gone down in direct ratio to the increase in our national wealth over the past ten years); fifth, "that protection creates monopolies" (no monopolies exist in the United States); and, sixth, "that protection is artificial and unnatural" ("What is there of man's triumphs in any branch of his activity that is not artificial," from cultivating the soil preparatory to planting, to fashioning cloth out of raw wool or steel out of red ore dug from the ground).[64] With a triumphant flourish, Carnegie concluded:

> There is no place for partisanship in this question. It is simply a matter of figures. They tell their own story, and it would seem that only a very obtuse legislator could fail to read correctly the lesson they convey. In all cases of doubt he should err on the safe side. Much better continue protection, even if it be

a shade higher than actually necessary, than run the risk of crippling any branch; because, as we have seen, it is not easy to establish new industries in a country, and it would be much less easy to resuscitate one which, having made a fair start, had gone down in the struggle.[65]

On that note, the *North American Review* ended its great debate on the American tariff question.

Whether or not the statistical figures that Carnegie presented "told their own story," certainly he had told his. But it was not the whole story. His rather glib assumption that the tariff was "a tax upon the manufactures of other nations" missed the whole point of the tariff reformer's argument—that the protective tariff was in actuality a tax upon the domestic consumer, not on the foreign manufacturer. The farmer who sent his wheat to market over rails manufactured at Braddock, the businessman who constructed his warehouse and office building out of structural beams rolled at Homestead, the Southern planter who bound his bales of cotton with steel ties made at Duquesne, were all paying "the necessary concessions and bounties," amounting to nearly $28 a ton, in order to induce Carnegie to establish his "manufactures within this world." To paraphrase Carnegie, "How interesting it would have been to have had Mr. Carnegie's answer to this problem."

Nor was Carnegie's justification for protection on the ground that the cost of labor in the United States was double that of Great Britain a convincing argument to the free traders. For they could reply that the high cost of labor in the United States was in great part a result of the high cost of living which the protective tariff had effected. Although reliable statistics on international wage comparisons were not available to the tariff reformers in the nineteenth century, it was apparent to even the most casual observer that the differential in *real* wages between Great Britain and the United States was nothing like the 100 per cent that Carnegie claimed by quoting the nominal wage scales.[66]

Finally, Grover Cleveland, Congressman William Wilson, Henry Watterson, David Wells, and the other worshipers of the "Star-Eyed Goddess of Tariff Reform" were not at all convinced by Carnegie's blandly pious assurances that protection would slowly disappear as the need for it diminished by the growth of American industry. Such indefinite promises for future freedom of trade inspired about as much conviction as Marx's prediction of the withering away of the state following the dictatorship of the proletariat. Men never give up power or privilege willingly, and the tariff reformers felt that Carnegie was being far more candid when he urged that "in all cases of doubt, it is better to err on the safe side. Much better continue protection . . . than run the risk of crippling any branch." The halls of Congress echoed with the lobbyists' cries of "crippling," whenever there was the faintest suggestion of tariff reduction, and it was hard to imagine Carnegie or Quay or Swank ever crying, "Enough. We are big boys now and can walk alone."

Yet in the years that followed his classic defense of the protective tariff Carnegie did appear to moderate his position. Perhaps, as some of his critics suggested, he simply grew more sophisticated, more ingenious in his arguments. At least he was flexible enough to adapt to the changing times. When President Cleveland opened his administration's war on the tariff in his State of the Union message of December 1887, he took his cue from those reformers who were urging a tariff for revenue only, and he justified tariff reduction on the ground that it was bringing in too much revenue to the Federal government. Carnegie found this an absurd argument. In an angry article in the *North American Review,* he demanded to know "how can there be a surplus when we have a thousand million of dollars of debt outstanding? When we have paid off that debt, and not until then, can there be any true surplus whatever. The reduction of taxation, internal or external, will then be in order, but not till then." Carnegie insisted that a reduction in the tariff would actually increase the surplus as it would increase foreign importations. "Let those gentlemen masquerading about disguised as surplus reducers, tell us what they mean when they advocate a policy certain to increase revenues. Give us your *real names,* gentlemen! And you Mr. Surplus Reduction President, suppose you begin!" [67]

But after four years of Benjamin Harrison's administration, with its generous pension policy to Civil War veterans and its heavy monthly purchases of silver bullion, there was no surplus left, and when Cleveland returned to the White House in 1893 for his second term, both he and Carnegie found it expedient to change their lines of argument. Cleveland now urged tariff reduction, not because it produced an unnecessary surplus in the treasury, but rather because it was an unfair form of taxation which burdened those least able to pay. He favored an income tax to replace revenue lost by reducing the tariff schedules. Carnegie, on the other hand, eagerly took up the old cry of the tariff reformers of the 1880's and insisted that the maintenance of a protective tariff in the 1890's should be for reasons of revenue only.

In a remarkable essay published in *The Forum* in March 1895, entitled "What Would I Do with the Tariff If I Were Czar," Carnegie argued that

> my aim would be to keep free of duty the necessaries of life used by the many, and to tax highly the luxuries of the few. The masses who wear and consume home products I should not tax, but the luxurious man and woman of fashion who will wear at whatever cost the fine woollens and exquisitely fine silks and the delicately fine linens of Europe should pay the duties. . . . The increased duties proposed upon foreign articles *de luxe* would not be levied with a view of protection, but purely for revenue. That incidentally this policy might slightly benefit the manufacturers at home would not be considered an objection, but this advantage, if any, could be but slight. . . . Home manufacturers almost completely control the market for goods of ordinary quality which are used by the masses. . . . If 50 per cent additional duty were tried, the revenues would soon be increased to almost the whole of the extra tax. This is neither protection nor free trade, and has nothing to do with either. It is simply a question of revenue." [68]

Well and good—a clever argument for protection that Carnegie knew would appeal to the Populist sentiment of the day. But what about those products, such as steel rails and structural beams, which were not used directly by the individual consumer, be he rich or poor? Carnegie slid past this point rather quickly:

> In regard to coal and iron ore, so-called raw materials, the new tariff should make no further reductions, because a reduction of nearly one-half of the duty at one time, just made, is se-

rious, and time is needed before any industry can adjust itself to so great a change. Besides the tax of forty cents per ton upon ore and thirty cents per ton upon coal is comparatively trifling. This applies to iron and steel generally, which have suffered two reductions recently.[69]

And that was all that Czar Carnegie had to say about the tariff on those products in which he had more than a passing interest.

Nevertheless, this essay represents a moderation in Carnegie's position on protection. It is not the strident call for a high tariff of his earlier articles. In the troubled days of Cleveland's second administration, as the winds of change blew cold and bitter from out of the West, there were other perils to fear, perils more dangerous to the established order than tariff reform. There was more than a hint of these perils in the Wilson Tariff Act, and they had nothing to do with reduction of schedules for beams or boiler plates. For the so-called Wilson Tariff Reform Act of 1894, which, by the time it got out of the Senate, was more tariff than reform, had carried a provision for a straight, ungraduated tax of 2 per cent on all annual incomes above $4000. Carnegie, in his essay in the *Forum,* clearly revealed why he was now insistent upon regarding the tariff as a revenue, not a protective measure, when he wrote:

> There would be no income tax. I know of no statesman or authority who does not denounce an income tax as the most objectionable of all taxes. . . . While it is in theory a just tax, in practice it is the source of such demoralization as renders it perhaps the most pernicious form of taxation which has ever been conceived since human society has settled into peaceful government. Any measure is justifiable in time of war, but the only excuse for an income tax is imperative necessity. There is at present no such necessity. The Government revenues must soon produce a surplus over expenditures, if from no other cause than the increase of population and wealth, and they can be made to do so now, as previously pointed out, by taxing higher only the extravagances of the few.[70]

In a letter to President Cleveland, he was even more urgent in pressing his proposal for higher duties on luxury items in order to avoid the necessity of an income tax:

My suggestion, therefore, is that a short bill be passed increasing for two years the duties upon these articles de luxe, used only by the extravagant few, at least 50 per cent. . . . I should go even beyond this. . . . The Income Tax could readily be abandoned and yet the increased duties proposed would come as exclusively as the Income Tax will from the few having more than four-thousand dollars income per annum and require no increase of officials or entail additional cost; besides these duties would yield double any estimate made of the Income tax revenue. It is a new policy Mr. President, and I cannot but think one worthy of you, and one which requires just such a man to propose and establish.[71]

Neither Congress nor the President gave much heed to Carnegie's "new policy," however. Yielding to the same old pressures from the lobbyists of special interests, Congress had raised, not lowered, tariff duties on most articles, not just on articles *de luxe*. But as a sop to the reformers, Congress had kept the mild income tax feature in the bill. The bill was enacted over the President's veto, not because Cleveland objected to the income tax provision, but because the bill did not represent true tariff reform. To Carnegie, the two parties were fighting the same old battle at the wrong time. In a letter to the editor of the New York *Tribune*, written while the Wilson bill was still before Congress, he had urged "that it would be infinitely better to have a moderately satisfactory tariff bill passed by the Democratic party than even a more satisfactory bill as the work of the Republican party. . . . What seems most desirable in the interests of manufacturers of the United States, is, that a tariff bill should be passed by the Democratic party, and thereby, that the suspicion that even one 'Robber Baron' exists in the broad domain of the Republic, cannot remain in the mind of the most ignorant citizen. For one, I should gladly accept greatly reduced duties—judiciously formed —to accomplish this result." [72]

Happily for Carnegie, the Supreme Court was more cognizant of the danger to men of property that was embodied in the Wilson Act than were the other two branches of government. In two cases brought before it within a year after the passage of the income tax provision, this august tribunal, in audacious defiance of both precedent and popular will, declared the income tax unconstitutional. A few years before, Carnegie had described the Supreme Court as being "beyond and before, and higher than House, or Senate or President. . . . Does any court in the world command greater respect than this Supreme Court? Are abler, purer lawyers, men clearer in their great office, to be found elsewhere? Certainly not. Even my Lord Salisbury regrets that there is not such a tribunal in Britain." [73] Carnegie's faith had been amply justified.

But the Supreme Court, however obliging, could not silence the angry voices of protest that were raised against the established order in these years of bitter economic depression. Frustrated by both Court and Congress in their attempts to obtain relief, Western farmers and Eastern laborers alike were becoming more desperate in their quest for social justice. The genteel reforms of the Mugwump liberals, the civil service acts, and the lower tariffs, had proved to be illusionary and totally irrelevant as a means of combating the forces of monopoly and reaction that were aligned against the people. If Carnegie truly hoped that "a moderate" tariff bill, passed by the Democratic party, would dispel "the suspicion that even one 'Robber Baron' exists in the broad domain of the Republic," he would in the next few years be rudely shaken out of his foolish illusion. These were the years of the hobo and the tramp, of Coxey's army and the soup lines in the cities, of the debt-ridden farmers wanting "to raise less corn and more Hell," and of the dejected, gray-faced unemployed who no longer had the energy even to raise Hell.

It was a time ripe for the dreamer and the demagogue. And so they came, these utopian hopefuls, each with his own panacea for the nation's woes: the scholarly Henry George, with his single land tax; the poetic Edward Bellamy, with his proposal to nationalize industry; and then the more angry apocalyptic visionaries— Ignatius Donnelly, with his terrifying vision of the immolation of man to form *Caesar's Column;* Johann Most, who would cleanse with dynamite; and Daniel De Leon, forming and then breaking one radical organization after another.

These were lonely apostles on the fringe of action. They did not speak to or for most Americans, who still believed so much in the existing capitalistic system that all they wanted was to participate more fully in it. Something was wrong, of that they were sure, for they had not known of any recent triumphs in Carnegie's "triumphant democracy." They were ready to question whether, indeed, there was a democracy, when the courts could halt their strikes by injunctions, jail their labor leaders, declare laws taxing men of wealth unconstitutional, and smile indulgently on monopolistic trusts. Congress seemed eager only to protect those who were already secure, and the President looked to Wall Street, not Main Street, for support and guidance.

It was in this time of trouble and despair that the People's party was formed, seeking to gather together all of the dissident elements in the country, to provide simple solutions to the great problems of the day, and to give the government back "to the plain people." The Populist leaders, meeting in Omaha on 4 July 1892, drew up a platform that they hoped would cut across sectional and partisan lines and appeal to farmers and workers alike. Here was the cry of the "Have-Nots" against the "Haves": "We meet," Ignatius Donnelly announced in the preamble to the platform, "in the midst of a nation brought to the verge of moral, political and material ruin. . . . The fruits of the toil of millions are boldly stolen to build up colossal fortunes for a few, unprecedented in the history of mankind; and the possessors of these, in turn, despise the Republic and endanger liberty. From the same prolific womb of governmental injustice we breed the two great classes—tramps and millionaires." [74]

Although the adopted platform laid as great a stress upon measures to better industrial workers' conditions as it did upon action to ameliorate the situation of the farmers, from its very beginning the Populist party failed to bring about an effective alliance between the Southern and Western farmers and the Eastern laborers. In the ensuing election, James B. Weaver of Iowa, the Populist candidate for the presidency, polled over a million popular votes and received twenty-two electoral votes in six states, the most impressive record for any third-party candidate between 1860 and 1912. But an analysis of Weaver's vote reveals that he received all of his electoral votes and 60 per cent of his popular votes from the states of the Great Plains and the Far West. From the New England, the Middle Atlantic, and the industrial states of the Old Northwest, Weaver received less than 4 per cent of his total vote.[75] Whatever hope for future success the Populist party might have had lay in its becoming truly a "party of the plain people," but from the first it was to be largely a party of the people of the plains. Its real concern was for the debt-ridden farmer, seeking an inflated currency, and not for the wage-earning laborer, seeking higher purchasing power for his dollar. It looked for and found its votes among the red-necks of Georgia and the dirt-farmers of the Dakota plains, and eventually all of its bold, comprehensive demands for all the Have-Nots would shrink to the single demand for the free, unlimited coinage of silver. Inevitably, it would find its appropriate leader in William Jennings Bryan of Nebraska, not in John Peter Altgeld of Chicago. The Populist story is but one more chapter in the long history of American native Radicalism, which, from Bacon's rebellion of 1676 to the Farm Holiday movement of 1932, was rural, and not urban-centered.

Since the days of the Greenback craze in the early 1870's, Carnegie had been an outspoken opponent of cheap currency. He had vigorously fought against the Bland-Allison Act of 1878, which had required the Federal treasury to purchase from two to four million dollars' worth of silver bullion a month and coin it into dollars. He had written angry letters to Senator J. Donald Cameron and Representative William A. Wallace (both from Pennsylvania), protesting their having supported the measure against the best interest of their state.[76] In spite of his warnings that "should the curse of a depreciated currency be brought upon us, those who inflict it will lose the confidence of intelligent men," both Cameron and Wallace apparently felt that there were more votes to be had among the unintelligent, and for once they failed to do the steel master's bidding.

These currency tempests of the 1870's, born out of the depression of those years, happily dissipated in the sunshine of prosperity in the 1880's. The treasury continued dutifully to purchase the minimum amount of silver bullion each month, but with business expanding and a strong demand for money and credit the dollar suffered no appreciable devaluation as a result of this mild dose of currency inflation.

In these years, which he would later look back upon nostalgically as the "Golden Age of American business," Carnegie felt there was little need for him to give much time or attention to American politics. For a man of his active, restless temperament, the American political system was dull—perfect, but dull. It was much more gratifying to play the active reformer in Britain, where he felt so much needed reforming, than it was "to look after the proper administration of perfect institutions." [77] He had, of course, been deeply committed to James G. Blaine's campaign for the presidency and had been thoroughly confident that Blaine would win. He had even dreamed that he might be sent as America's Minister to the Court of St. James's to replace James Russell Lowell, whom he regarded as "a Tory snob." [78] Blaine's defeat by that "coarse and low character, [whose name] I don't like even to write," came as a great shock to Carnegie.[79] But, except for his provokingly insistent demand for tariff reform, this coarse, low character, Cleveland, turned out to be a surprisingly good fellow after all—in fact, one of the best conservatives ever to occupy the White House. Contentedly, Carnegie could turn his attention back to really exciting political issues such as Home Rule for Ireland and salaries for the members of Parliament, and rail against the victorious Conservatives who controlled Parliament from 1886 to 1892.

After 1892, however, when the Liberals came back into power again, and the aged Gladstone emerged from Hawarden to form his fourth and last ministry, for the first time in many years Carnegie failed to take an active role in British politics. There would be one more try for Irish Home Rule, and John Morley would dutifully keep him informed on that futile campaign, but Carnegie remained strangely inconspicuous on the British political scene. After the bloodshed at Homestead in the summer of 1892, he had few friends left among the Radicals, and the Tories took delight in taunting him on his "Triumphant Democracy." Moreover, the political pace in America was quickening. There were issues at home, particularly a new demand for an inflated currency, that needed his close attention. So Carnegie left Britain to its own devices for the time being, and the British were quite happy with that arrangement.

The revival of the silver craze in 1890 had come like a bolt out of the blue to Carnegie. It was a bitterly ironic fact that the door to inflation should have been opened by his own party in order to woo the newly admitted silver states of the West and to win their votes in Congress for Congressman McKinley's high protective tariff. With the passage of the Sherman Silver Purchase Act in 1890, which, going far beyond the Bland-Allison Act, required the Treasury to purchase a total of 4,500,000 ounces of silver monthly—the total output of American silver mines— Carnegie with a snort sprang into action. All other issues paled in importance compared to the question of the honesty of the American dollar. If the Eastern Republican leaders thought they had made a good bargain in exchanging silver votes for tariff votes, they were to be rudely informed to the contrary by Carnegie. Dashing off a long article entitled "ABC of Money," which the *North American Review* eagerly accepted, Carnegie warned his party that "I, a Republican and a believer in the wisdom of protection, tell you that I would rather give up the McKinley Bill and pass the Mills Bill, if for the exchange I could have the present Silver Bill repealed and silver treated like other metals. In the next presidential campaign, if I have to vote for a man in favour of silver and protection, or a man in favour of the gold standard and free trade, I shall vote and work for the latter, because my judgment tells me that even the tariff is not half so important for the good of the country as the maintenance of the highest standard for the money of the people." [80]

Carnegie's article, which was curiously elementary considering the audience to which it was originally directed, proved in the long run to be one of the most effective and certainly the most widely read article he ever wrote. Cleverly, he began his essay with a note of humble defensiveness:

> Perhaps someone in the vast audience which I have imagined I am about to hold spellbound cries out: 'Who are you—a gold-bug, a millionaire, an iron-baron, a beneficiary of the McKinley Bill?' Before beginning my address, let me therefore reply to that imaginary gentleman. . . . So far as the McKinley Bill is concerned, I am perhaps the one man in the United States who has the best right to complain under it, for it has cut and slashed the duties upon iron and steel, reducing them 20, 25, and 30 per cent; and if it will recommend me to my supposed interrupter, I beg to inform him that I do not greatly disapprove of these reductions . . . and that I am not in favour of protection beyond the point necessary to allow Americans to retain their own market in a fair contest with the foreigner.

It does not matter who the man is, nor what he does—be he worker in the mine, factory, or field, farmer, labourer, merchant, or millionnaire,—he is deeply interested in understanding this question of money, and in having the right policy adopted in regard to it. Therefore I ask all to hear what I have to say, because what is good for one worker must be good for all, and what injures one must injure all, poor or rich.[81]

What followed was a basic, elementary economics lesson in the history of money, beginning with the simple barter system, through commodity "money," to the establishment of metals, gold and silver, as legal tender and the development of the more sophisticated instruments of exchange, checks, bank drafts, and bills of exchange. As the title indicated, Carnegie was spelling out for illiterates in economics the monetary alphabet, preparatory to the establishment of his thesis, which was equally elementary. Bi-metallism was a delusion, no matter how rigidly it might be written into law or how widely accepted it might be by International Monetary Conferences. No nation could keep gold and silver in balance in order to maintain a bi-metallic standard. The value of one metal would always fluctuate with the value of the other, and the metal that was over-evaluated by the official monetary ratio in terms of its world market price would always drive the under-evaluated, more valuable metal out of circulation. Since it is always silver that fluctuates, and tends to be over-evaluated, Carnegie argued, we cannot maintain a bi-metallic standard for long. If we continue the present totally unrealistic fixed ratio of 16 to 1, when the market value is closer to being 32 to 1, we will certainly drive gold out as a currency, and shall join such backward countries as India and the Argentine in being on a silver standard. The consequences of continuing our present policy of buying 4,500,000 ounces of silver a month and issuing Treasury notes on this silver, redeemable in either metal, will be dire indeed:

When the farmers' alliance shouts for free coinage, this is exactly what it supports—a scheme to take from the people twenty-two cents upon each dollar and put it into the pockets of the owners of silver. . . . We are told that they [our farmers] are in favour of silver. If this be true, there can be only one reason for it—they do not understand their own interests. . . . If the

463

American farmer agrees to take silver in lieu of gold, he will enable the Liverpool merchant to buy upon the lower silver basis, at present seventy-eight cents for the dollar; while for all articles coming from abroad that the farmer buys he will have to pay upon the gold basis. . . . He will thus have to sell cheap and buy dear. . . . How then can the working people or the farmers be benefited? It is the owners of the silver, who will give the government seventy-eight cents' worth of bullion and get for it a dollar, who will make the profit. Surely, this is clear.[82]

Basic to Carnegie's thesis and argument was his faith in gold as being "steady, pure, unchangeable." From a professed agnostic and evolutionist, such blind, unquestioning faith in the immutability of anything in this world was both remarkable and touching. In his long article, Carnegie brought forth every argument and appealed to every occupational group (except the silver mine owners) and social class in the country. For the cause, he would even wring the British lion's tail, in hopes of the Irish vote, by pointing out that of all the countries in Europe that were burdened with silver bullion in their treasuries there was one, "our principal rival, Great Britain," who has *not one dollar* in silver. "Wise old bird . . . sits upon her perch, whistling away out of all danger from this silver trouble. . . . What she is praying for is that the United States will continue to go deeper and deeper into silver until retreat is impossible, and she will keep her old policy, which has made her supreme in finance. . . . What a grand thing for Britain if our country could be brought down to a silver basis —forced to relinquish the one standard which can alone give a nation front rank in the financial world! Silver for the republic, Gold for the monarchy: this is what Great Britain is hoping may come to pass, and what every American should resolve never shall." [83] Carnegie concluded with choked emotion,

Do not think, however, that I despair of the republic—never; even if dragged into the difficulties inseparable from silver and matters become as bad with us as they are today in the Argentine Republic. . . . The good senses of the people will restore the gold basis after a time and the republic will march on to the front rank among nations. . . . The stamp of the republic must be made true, the money of the American people kept the highest and surest in value of all money in the world, above all doubt or suspicion, its standard in the future, as in the past, not fluctuating Silver, but unchanging Gold.[84]

Carnegie needed all the faith that he could muster in the Republic and the good sense of the people in the years that lay ahead. When his article first appeared it received little notice, there was "no vast audience" which he had imagined to heed his warnings, and his party continued to play its dangerous game of purchasing silver and spending the Treasury's gold reserves. John Sherman, who had given his name if not his enthusiastic support to the purchase act, sent a polite little note in acknowledgement after receiving a copy of Carnegie's article. He too professed horror at the idea of the unlimited coinage of silver, but added, "I cannot agree with you as to the danger of buying silver bullion at gold prices. It can safely be made the basis of treasury notes equal in amount to the cost of bullion and thus furnish a convenient mode of increasing the paper currency at about the rates of the increase of population. At all events, it was the best compromise to prevent the free coinage of silver, which would otherwise have passed Congress, and, perhaps have become a law." [85]

Although Carnegie dutifully made his contribution to the campaign for President Harrison's re-election, there was no great weeping in the Carnegie household, as there had been in 1884, when Grover Cleveland won the presidency this time. Immediately upon taking office, Cleveland demanded and within a year got a repeal of the hated Sherman Silver Purchase Act. The gold outflow was checked by selling government bonds through the House of Morgan for gold, and the sanctity of the gold dollar was at least temporarily preserved. Cleveland became Carnegie's new political hero, someone to cherish and preserve and to admit into that company of "real inner circle dwellers" along with Andrew White and Richard Watson Gilder.[86] When he heard of Cleveland's illness in 1894, Carnegie was as disturbed as if the President were a member of his own family. He sent anxious notes to Cleveland's secretary, asking for daily reports on the President's condition and offering him "Scotch whisky from a vat which is reserved for Queen Victoria & *myself*. . . . I think the President & the Queen should drink the same article. . . . Her majesty has trouble in her knee and this Scotch whisky is her only tipple—no wine allowed—probably the President is likewise restricted. It will be a bad day for the Country if the President's health gives way." [87]

Although President Cleveland was more seriously ill than Carnegie knew, he proved as resolutely unbending before the ravages of cancer as he did before the angry dissensions within his own party. As long as he remained in the White House, he would do all within his constitutional powers to hold the line for gold. But not even Cleveland could prevent the currency crisis in American politics from reaching its stormy climax in the summer of 1896. There was a strong movement among the Gold Democrats to urge Cleveland to seek a third term—a movement which Carnegie would have supported—but Cleveland was tired, and he was quite sure he could not get the nomination for a third term even if he should try for it. Events in Chicago were to prove him to be absolutely right. In that tumultuous city, on those hot July days of 1896, all of the frustration and bitterness of the past twenty years and all of the hopes for a new age in a new century were poured out. It was as if a tight cork, which had bottled up all meaningful political activity since the end of Reconstruction, had been suddenly pushed out by the growing fermentation within, and the resulting explosion shook the nation. Historians have argued ever since about whether the Democrats had seized control of the Populists, or the Populists of the Democrats—but for the Clevelands, the Whitneys, the Belmonts, and the Ryans, it made little difference. Madness had seized the party, and suddenly there was a thirty-six-year-old unknown standing before the convention, shouting, "You shall not press down upon the brow of labor this crown of thorns. You shall not crucify mankind upon a cross of gold." In that moment, the convention, the nomination, and the party belonged to William Jennings Bryan.

Carnegie was, of course, far away in Scotland when these momentous events occurred on the shores of Lake Michigan, but to him and to the stalwart conservatives of both parties who for the past four years had depended on Grover Cleveland to hold the fortress against revolution it seemed that the nation also belonged to Bryan. Carnegie later wrote that he was convinced, if the elec-

466

tion had been held in July, "that light-headed, blathering demagogue would have been President of the United States." [88]

After the initial fright, however, Carnegie, as always, was optimistic about the results of the campaign and election. Happily,
the Republican party put aside the vacillating weakness of Harrison and the temporizing expediency of Sherman, and Carnegie
did not have to make the unhappy choice between tariff protection and the gold standard. He got both in a single package, labeled William McKinley, that had been carefully wrapped, tied,
and delivered by that stalwart of stalwarts, Mark Hanna.

Carnegie wrote exultantly in the *North American Review,*

> The great party which sprang to the defence of the Union is
> again in the line of battle, ready to fight for the preservation of
> all that makes that Union worth fighting for—the reign of law,
> order, honesty; and, as in the war for the Union, so in this war
> for the rights, liberties, and safeguards of the Constitution,
> under the Union, and for honest money, that party finds at its
> side, fully abreast and equally loyal, the mass of sterling men of
> the Democratic party who hold party subordinate to country.
> . . . Such a spectacle has not been seen since the shot fired at
> Fort Sumter.[89]

That fall Carnegie and his business partners made far larger
contributions to the Republican party than they ever made before. But to Mark Hanna, Carnegie's most important contribution was not the thousands of dollars which he poured into the
overflowing campaign chest, but rather the essay he had written
five years earlier for the *North American Review*. In this massive
campaign of public education on the currency issue, Carnegie's
"ABC of Money" was precisely the kind of primer which the
Gold men needed to offset the effectiveness of W. H. Harvey's
Coin's Financial School and the speeches of Bryan. Hanna wrote
to Carnegie late in the campaign:

> It required but a moment for us to see that the leaflet was ad-
> mirably calculated to make the money issue of this campaign
> clear to the simplest mind. We therefore printed and have cir-
> culated more than 5,000,000 copies of the leaflet, and the de-

mand for it was as great as for that of any document we have issued. This of itself is evidence of its worth, but the scores of letters we have received commending the paper, attest its value, and the powerful influence for good we feel it has exerted. The beneficial results that will inure to our cause from the circulation of this document cannot, I feel, at this time be determined, but we all appreciate its value . . . and at this late day, I want, in the name of and on behalf of the National Republican Committee, to thank you for your work, and assure you that we appreciate the service you have rendered the party and the country.[90]

Carnegie was delighted and his optimism soared. In a letter to the editor of The (London) Times, he predicted, "Mr. McKinley is probably to be elected by the largest popular plurality ever given to any candidate for the Presidency. . . . Mr. Bryan, attended by a few nobodies, is usually left to do all the speaking himself." [91] In private correspondence to Henry Yates Thompson of the Pall Mall Gazette, he was even more sanguine: "The Majority of the popular vote will be enormous for McKinley, the largest ever obtained by any candidate; perhaps, he will have the largest majority in the Electoral College. The Bryan campaign promises to collapse. Once more virtue triumphs in the Republic." [92]

The triumph of virtue was not quite as overwhelming as Carnegie had hoped for. Actually, Bryan carried only one state less than McKinley. But those states Bryan carried were the sparsely settled states of the mountains and plains and the traditionally Democratic states of the rural South. Just as in 1860, the nation had divided along sharp sectional lines. For the Republican party and for the Gold conservatives of both parties such a division was certainly preferable to that of a class division that threatened to pit the "Have-Nots" against the "Haves." The Populists, by concentrating on the single issue of currency inflation, had alienated the Eastern laborer and had assured the victory of McKinley.

In a post-election article for the North American Review, which served as his happy valedictory statement on the currency crisis that had preoccupied him for the past four years, Carnegie, in victory, could afford to be magnanimous even toward Bryan. "There is such evidence here of indomitable pluck that we cannot help admiring, much as we find ourselves admiring Milton's Satan, strive as we may against such deadly sin." And with more perspicacity than many of his jubilant fellow Republicans, Carnegie accepted the fact that a new and vital personality had emerged on the American political scene, a young man who in all probability would be around for a long time to come. "It need not be assumed that with the passing of Mr. Bryan's . . . platform there comes also the passing of Mr. Bryan himself; on the contrary it is far from improbable that he may yet play a great part. . . . His is an interesting individuality, whom one cannot help wishing to follow and study." With a final note of condescension which Bryan must have found particularly irritating, Carnegie praised both Mr. and Mrs. Bryan for "their gentle, sweet sympathy." They were simply "too young to understand the real problems of the day." [93]

Soon after the final results of the election had come in, Carnegie in exultation had written to a Scottish friend, "Triumphant Democracy is once more Triumphant. All is well." [94] One cannot help wondering, however, what Carnegie's reaction would have been had the election results been different. Would the election of Bryan have been enough of a political shock to have caused Carnegie to question the principles of democracy? Carnegie's abiding faith in the essential wisdom of the people had never really been tested, for, since 1860, with only minor exceptions, the democratic process—legislative, executive, and especially judicial—had always worked to Carnegie's personal benefit, just as it had been in harmony with his philosophic ideals. Even the election of a Democratic President, the steadfast Grover Cleveland, had in the long run proved, as Carnegie freely admitted, the infinite wisdom of the American people. It was not hard for Carnegie, during these thirty years following the Civil War, to preach the gospel of democratic republicanism in Britain when it served him so well at home that he need never question its efficacy and justice. And so he had found it easy to move between his two worlds, that of a Radical republican in Britain and of a conservative Republican in America. If his contemporaries both at home and abroad found him difficult to understand, it is only because Carnegie himself did not understand the true potential of the democratic process, and, consequently, did not fear shaking the feudal Establishment in Britain while safe within his middle class order at home. Only rarely in these last decades of the nineteenth century had the curtains surrounding his well-ordered security been parted even slightly to permit him a glimpse of what real revolution might be like. He had heard its growl in 1892, coming from the throats of angry strikers, lining the banks of the Monongahela. He had had a frightening, fleeting look at its face in 1896, when "demagoguery," personified by Bryan, had tried unsuccessfully "the fomenting of strife between the 'Haves' and 'Have-Nots,'" compared with which, as Carnegie frankly admitted, "even the question of the money standard was as nothing." [95] Democracy, however, as defined and understood by Carnegie, had apparently triumphed once again, and all was well. Carnegie, nurtured in the simple faith of Dunfermline Chartism, had throughout his life never really feared the people, and the election of 1896 seemed to him to be but a confirmation of that faith.

CHAPTER XV

Enter Mr. Frick

1881-1892

The business reorganization that Carnegie effected in 1886, just prior to his illness and his brother Tom's death, was an acknowledgment of the tremendous expansion of the Carnegie steel business since the last reorganization of the company in 1881. In that year, Carnegie Bros. & Company, Ltd. had been organized with a capitalization of $5,000,000. The Edgar Thomson Steel Company, with a capital evaluation of $2,385,000, had lost its separate corporate identity and was brought in as part of a single firm, which then included the Union Iron Mills, the Lucy Furnaces, the Scotia Ore Mines in Center County, and several coal fields and coke ovens Carnegie had acquired at Unity in the Connellsville coal area, as well as four-fifths of the Larimer Coke works in the same district. Tom Carnegie became chairman of the newly consolidated company. Andrew Carnegie, whose only official position was member of the board of managers, held $2,721,550 of the capitalization, or 54.4 per cent, in his name. At Carnegie's insistence, all of the others in the partnership, which included Tom Carnegie, Henry Phipps, David Stewart, John Scott, Gardner McCandless, and Andrew's traveling companion, John Vandevort, had had to give up a small fraction of their holdings in order to provide a

471

$30,000 interest in the company for Carnegie's cousin, George "Dod" Lauder,[1] for it was apparently at this time that Carnegie persuaded Lauder to come to the United States.

This first consolidation of all of Carnegie's interests in iron and steel was of very short duration, however, for two months after the act of association setting up the organization of Carnegie Bros. & Company, Ltd., had been duly recorded in Pittsburgh, the company sold the Lucy Furnaces to Wilson, Walker & Company, which had earlier purchased the Lower Union Mills.[2] Thus the first venture into developing a truly vertical steel organization had been quickly dissolved. At this point neither Carnegie nor his associates saw the advantages of having within one company the entire process, from the mining of raw iron ore and coal through the manufacturing of pig iron to the converting of pig iron into steel. Carnegie, however, kept a personal interest in verticality, for rarely did he ever give up control of anything he had once possessed, particularly if it was related to the making of steel. He continued to hold a 42 per cent interest in the Lucy Furnaces, which, with the shares he had kept in the Lower Union Mills, gave him by a considerable measure the largest interest in Wilson, Walker & Company.[3]

In the five years that had elapsed between the organization of Carnegie Bros. & Company, Ltd., in 1881 and the organization of Carnegie, Phipps & Company in 1886, the Carnegie steel interests had experienced a great expansion both in production, profits, and facilities. In that five-year period, in spite of a severe slump in the rail market in 1883, and again in 1885, the E.T. works had made a profit of $7,641,207.17, or an annual average of $1,250,000,[4] two and one-half times greater than the best year the company had known in the decade of the 1870's. During these years the market price of rails went steadily downward, but with Carnegie's constant goading of his departmental supervisors, costs went down even faster, so that in 1886, at the time of reorganization, the Carnegie steel interests realized a profit of $2,925,350, the highest in the company's history.[5]

An annual net profit representing 60 per cent of the capitalization of a company is a remarkable return upon investment under any circumstances, but in this era of watered stock and gross overcapitalization the financial records of Carnegie, Phipps

& Company, Ltd., would have dazzled the financial world, had they been made public.

With such profits Tom Carnegie and the other partners in the association were more than a little disgruntled that Carnegie permitted them small enjoyment of these profits in the form of dividends. Most of the profits each year went back into plant improvement and expansion. Carnegie was convinced that one way to keep costs down was to make sure that the equipment was the most modern and efficient that technology and inventive genius could provide. No matter how new or expensive the machinery for a particular process was, if that process became obsolete then his orders were to scrap the machinery and install new machinery for the more efficient process. In this policy he had the complete support of Captain Bill Jones, whose own inventive mind and restless, unsatisfied nature were responsible for many of the advances in the steelmaking process in these years. J. H. Bridge has precisely stated the Carnegie-Jones policy of innovation: "The famous scrap-heap for outgrown, not outworn, machinery was instituted by Jones, who never hesitated to throw away a tool that had cost half a million if a better one became available. And as his own inventions saved the company a fortune every year, he was given a free hand." [6] Carnegie and Jones, of course, could promote such a policy with equanimity, for Carnegie's interest in the company was so large that even the smallest annual dividends provided him an exceedingly lucrative cash income, while Jones repeatedly refused a partnership share in the business and, instead, demanded and got "a hell of a big salary." But to Tom Carnegie, Phipps, and the other hard-working associates, the tangible returns that they could deposit in their personal banking accounts seemed pitifully small in comparison with the annual profits that had been credited to them on paper. The debate over cash dividends versus capital investment was vigorously argued each year, but it was a debate which Carnegie, with his 54 per cent interest in the company, always won.

A problem inherent to industrialism, one that had manifested itself repeatedly from the time of the first mechanical developments within the textile industry in Britain in the eighteenth century, constantly plagued the steel industry during these years of rapid expansion. This was the problem of keeping the various stages of processing, from raw material to finished product, in proper balance with each other. In this, steel could be compared to the cotton industry, whereas iron manufacturing, like the woolen industry in Britain, was much more firmly entrenched in traditional methods and less subject to innovation and hence less subject to imbalance. A company that so eagerly pushed innovation and the rationalization of method as Carnegie Brothers did was constantly involved in the never-ending struggle to keep all stages of processing in reasonable balance with each other. The fact that throughout the 1880's the company was more horizontal than vertical in structure of course made the problem even more acute. With horizontal structure, much of the imbalance occurred in areas outside the company's control—the acquisition of raw material and the finishing processes of goods manufactured out of steel.

For a short period of time in the late 1870's, after the Edgar Thomson works were in full production, the Bessemer converters were producing far more steel ingots than the rail mill could roll. Although the greatest profits in these years were obtainable from rails, the rail mill could roll only so many rails a day, and as a result steel ingots began to pile up. It was then discovered that this Bessemer steel could be used for a great variety of products: buggy springs; railroad car axles; stovepipes; and even plowshares, for which, up to that time, it had always been thought only specially produced crucible steel was suitable. The Edgar Thomson works was delighted to sell the excess steel ingots as merchant steel to local manufacturers, who would then finish the steel into a great variety of special products. The result was that E.T. stimulated small manufacturing throughout the Pittsburgh area and created a large market for merchant steel.

In 1879, improvements were made in the rail mill so that a far greater number of rails could be rolled each day than had been possible. The E.T. works no longer had an excess of steel ingots to sell as merchant steel, and it abruptly cut off the supply to those finishing manufacturers whose expansion for the past two years it had been encouraging. Several of these manufacturers, desperate to find a source of supply for merchant steel, formed a syndicate for building their own steel plant to provide the needed material for making buggy springs and stovepipes. The syndicate,

474

consisting of representatives of five manufacturing companies, was incorporated in October 1879 as the Pittsburg Bessemer Steel Company, with a capitalization of $250,000, and began its search for suitable location for a new steel mill. It found the right place on the banks of the Monongahela, about a mile down and across the river from Braddock, in a small, newly established community, called Homestead. The company at the same time found an important ally who had the technical knowledge to supervise the building of a new plant and put it into operation. This was Andrew Kloman, still bitter over what he regarded as the gross injustice done to him by the Carnegie brothers, and still holding fast to his dark, sweet dreams of revenge. Kloman was only too eager to co-operate with the syndicate, but he was determined to build not just a small steel mill to provide Pittsburgh manufacturers with merchant steel, but a steel works capable of producing steel rails that would rival the product of the hated E.T. works up the river. Kloman had already bought a small tract of land, adjoining the property of the Pittsburg Bessemer Steel Company in Homestead, where he was erecting a 684-foot long building which would contain a rail mill, two Universal mills, a 16-inch bar train, and a muck train. In combination with Pittsburg Bessemer, which would build the converting works and blooming mill on the adjoining land, Kloman estimated that he could produce 50,000 tons of steel rails and 30,000 tons of structure material annually. "The result," as J. H. Bridge has written, "was unsurpassed not only in the completeness and efficiency of the works, but in the rapidity of their construction. While the Edgar Thomson plant was over three years in building . . . the Homestead works were put in operation fifteen months after the land was bought." [7] It was as if Kloman, driven on furiously by his own internal demons, knew that he did not have a moment to lose if he was to enjoy that revenge for which he thirsted. Even so, Kloman died before the mill was completed, but ultimately Homestead would provide a kind of perverted revenge upon Carnegie which even in his wildest fancies Kloman could not have imagined.

The Carnegie associates, next-door neighbors on the Monongahela, had at first regarded Kloman's latest venture with amusement and condescension. Having outstripped their old rivals in western Pennsylvania—Cambria and Jones & Laughlin—they could hardly have been expected to take seriously this new fly-by-night enterprise of local manufacturers who had allied themselves with that lost and wandering Kloman. If Pittsburg Bessemer wanted to make merchant steel for the use of its own members in their individual factories, well and good. Carnegie Brothers had no longer any need for that market. But if it had ambitions to compete with E.T. in the making of rails in E.T.'s own home district, clearly Kloman had infected the whole syndicate with his paranoiac madness.

Unfortunately for the Carnegies' sense of security, an entirely new mill, providing it has been wisely planned by men with competency in the field, always has a technical advantage over an older mill, even one managed by so enlightened and progressive a policy as was the E.T. Just as the Edgar Thomson mill had had a distinct advantage over Troy and Cambria in 1875 simply because it was new, so now Homestead could claim for itself the same advantage over E.T. The first rail was rolled at Homestead on 9 August 1881, and within three weeks Homestead was turning out 200 tons of rails a day and had already accepted orders for 15,000 tons at what presumably were highly profitable prices. The E.T. works, to be sure, had advance orders for 80,000 tons of rail at this same time. The fact that an entirely new and untried concern, however, could crowd into Carnegie's own domain and within two months of operation obtain a market for its product that was nearly 20 per cent of E.T.'s market meant that the Carnegie associates could no longer be complacent about their position. The irony that it had been the mere fluke of the temporary imbalance of the rolling process with ingot production which had given cause for the creation of this rival must have made the situation even more galling to Andrew Carnegie and company.[8]

Homestead's smokestacks, a mile down the river, served as a constant reminder to the men in Braddock of the importance of keeping in balance the various processes within their huge sheds, from the first heating of the raw ore in the great blast furnaces to the last flange-shaping roll in the rail mill. But no matter how smoothly these various processes might be co-ordinated, with no one part of the whole operation lagging behind any of the others, the hard fact remained that the production of steel at E.T. was still affected by the availability of raw material, over which, except for a few small mines of limited production, the company had no control. The three basic raw materials essential to steelmaking were, of course, the iron ore itself, limestone—which apparently was available in abundance and never presented any serious problem—and coke, processed coal, which had replaced charcoal as the basic fuel for smelting in the English blast furnaces as early as the mid-eighteenth century but did not assume its primary importance in American blast furnaces until the 1870's. It was Andrew Carnegie's quest for this third basic material, coke, that led him in 1881 to take the most important step he had yet made in giving his company the vertical structure essential to keeping the whole operation of steelmaking in balance. The quest for coke also led him to a new partner, the most influential of all his associates in achieving the ultimate financial success of Carnegie Steel.

Ironmaking owed its initial start in Pittsburgh to the availability of iron ore in Pennsylvania. But Pittsburgh remained the nation's major center for steelmaking long after the Bessemer process had forced manufacturers to turn to other, far more distant sources for their iron ore, because of the easy availability of coke in the Pittsburgh area. It was nature's gift of coal, not iron ore, to western Pennsylvania that built modern Pittsburgh, for manufacturers early learned it was much less expensive to transport iron ore great distances than the much more bulky coke.

Coke (the word is derived from a contraction of coal-cake) is simply soft, bituminous coal that has been baked to remove the sulphur and phosphorus that exist in greater or lesser quantities in all soft coals. The ovens in which coke was produced in the late nineteenth century were so-called beehive ovens, built of brick, with a circular vent in the roof through which the soft coal was fed, and an oven door in front which was sealed during the cooling process. When the coal was baked to a certain heat, most of the sulphur and phosphorus was burned out of it in the form of flaming gases. The coal then fused into a cake, which was cooked slowly at an even temperature for from two to four days. At the end of this time, little remained of the original coal substance within the oven except pure carbon. While still in the oven, this carbon cake was drenched with water, and it was then quickly pulled out. The sudden cooling of the coal-cake, or coke,

477

splintered it, and it was then ready to be mixed with the iron ore and lime in the blast furnace. When the mixture was heated, the lime and the unwanted elements in the ore combined to form slag, leaving the gleaming metallic liquid of molten iron. At the time the first Lucy Furnace went into operation it took one and a half tons of coke to smelt one ton of pig iron, but as furnace practices advanced, and the process of making coke was improved by washing the coal before baking it, the amount of coke necessary to smelt a ton of pig iron was reduced to 1700 pounds.[9]

As early as 1770, it was known that there was coal lying just under the surface soil on the western slopes of the Alleghenies along the Yonghiogheny River. George Washington, who visited the farm of William Crawford in this region in October of that year, wrote: "We went to see a coal mine . . . on the banks of the Yonghiogheny River. The coal seemed to be of the very best kind, burning freely, and abundance of it." [10] Near by Crawford's farm, a small village was laid out in the 1790's and was named Connellsville, after Zachariah Connell, an early pioneer settler in the area. Washington had been right when he judged the coal he saw there "to be of the very best kind," and Connellsville would give its name to the finest grade of coke which America has produced.

The first attempt to sell coke made from the coal in this region in 1842 proved to be a failure, however, and for several years thereafter no one was interested in developing the coal fields there. The coal was easily accessible, and the farmers in the area dug it out of their fields for their own domestic purposes, but the iron manufacturers in Pittsburgh and on down the Ohio River valley to Cincinnati were still committed to the use of charcoal and had only contempt for what they called "cinders."

It was the introduction of the Bessemer process in the late 1860's that changed the traditional blast furnace practices and gave to the Connellsville area its wealth and fame. And it was a slightly built, delicate-looking young man named Henry Clay Frick who appropriated most of this wealth and fame for himself. In so doing, he attracted the attention of Carnegie, who needed what Frick had in such abundance to sell, Connellsville coke.

Henry Clay Frick had been born on the farm of his maternal grandfather near the small village of West Overton in the center of this rich coal region. His grandfather, Abraham Overholt, was perhaps the wealthiest man in the Westmoreland County, owner of a prosperous farm which his father, Henry Overholt, a Mennonite from eastern Pennsylvania, had acquired in 1800. But Abraham Overholt's great fortune had not been derived from the rich, rolling fields of grasses and corn with which he fed his livestock, nor from the coal that cropped out in those fields. It came from the excellent rye whiskey that he produced from his own distillery on the farm. "Old Overholt" was a deservedly famous name throughout all of trans-Appalachian America, and it brought wealth and distinction to the strict Mennonite farmer who produced it. In 1847 Abraham's youngest daughter, Elizabeth, married a handsome but impecunious youth named John Frick. The Overholts were not pleased with their daughter's marriage, but in order that she and her husband might have a roof over their heads, Overholt gave them the old spring house at the rear of the Overholt farmyard for their first home. It was here that their first son was born on 19 December 1849. He was named after his grandfather's political hero, Henry Clay.

Clay, as he was called by his family, was a sickly child, and his parents and grandparents frequently despaired of his ever reaching maturity. There was about him, however, even as a small boy, a kind of inner strength and inflexibility of purpose that must have surprised and puzzled his easygoing, good-natured father. Clay always knew what he wanted, and what he wanted from the time he was a child could be stated in one word—money. His boyhood hero was not his father, who could barely provide for his family, but his grandfather, who lived in the big house on the hill. Clay's proudest moment as a boy was to sit beside his grandfather in the Overholts' fine carriage and be allowed to drive the team of horses. If Grandfather Overholt, as he had been told, owned a fortune of half a million dollars, then Clay resolved to have a million, "and I propose to be worth that before I die." [11]

After several years of schooling at the West Overton Independent School and at Westmoreland College in near-by Mount Pleasant, young Frick continued his formal education at Otterbein College in Westerville, Ohio, until he was seventeen. Mathematics was the only academic subject which interested Frick and in which he excelled, for only in it did he see any relevance to his purpose of acquiring "a good business training." He eagerly left school to acquire practical training as a clerk in a store run by his uncle Martin in Mount Pleasant.[12]

Frick's demonstrated ability as a salesman and his ambition soon secured him a position in the large department store of Macrum and Carlisle in Pittsburgh. His industry, his eagerness to please, and his success in "waiting upon lady customers" soon boosted him to the top of the list in sales among the store clerks, and his salary was increased to $12 a week. A severe case of typhoid fever brought an end to his potential career in merchandising, forcing him to return home. Upon his recovery he was offered the position of chief bookkeeper in his grandfather's distillery at the salary of $1000 a year.

Young Frick was back in the country of his birth. Many years later, he must have found special meaning in Russell Conwell's celebrated sermon, "Acres of Diamonds," so admired by generations of Americans who had been raised on Horatio Alger stories, for Frick, unlike Conwell's Persian farmer, had found his "acres of diamonds" in his own farm country. It might have been iron ore in northern Minnesota, or copper in Montana, or silver in Nevada, or even real diamonds in South Africa, but it turned out to be the black, soft coal that the furnace men in Cincinnati thirty years before had contemptuously dismissed as "cinder" and that his own father had cursed when his plow had dug too deeply, scraping along a seam of it. Here was the stuff out of which Frick would fashion a fortune that would multiply his grandfather's fortune a hundred times over.

Frick got his opportunity to plow these backyard acres of diamonds quite fortuitously, through what appeared to be an unwise investment of his older cousin, Abraham Overholt Tinstman, who, in 1859, along with Joseph Rist, had bought 600 acres of coal lands. In 1868, Tinstman and Rist had joined their coal holdings with those of Colonel A. S. M. Morgan for the purpose of manufacturing coke. At that time there were less than twenty-five coking plants in the country, but, even so, there was not enough demand for the produce of these few plants to make them profitable. After a few months Morgan abandoned the enterprise, but Tinstman was so deeply in debt that he could not pull out. He talked over his problems with his young bookkeeper cousin during their frequent evening games of chess. It did not take many sessions to convince Frick that this was the opportunity he had been waiting for. He asked to come into the operation, and Tinstman, eager for support from wherever he could find it, even from a virtually penniless twenty-one-year-old, quickly consented. Frick's solution to his cousin's difficulties was not to liquidate his coal holdings, but to expand them. Together with Rist and another Overholt cousin, who was engaged to marry Frick's sister Maria, Tinstman and Frick formed a new company and boldly purchased 123 more acres of coal land near Broad Ford, on borrowed money, for the sum of $52,995.[13] The company was incorporated under the name of Henry C. Frick Coke Company, for the older partners did not wish to lend their names to what promised to be a dubious and short-lived venture. Frick had no such doubts and no hesitancy in stamping his name on what he had become convinced was the enterprise that would give him his million.

From that moment on, although he prudently kept his $1000-a-year job at the Overholt distillery for some time, Frick thought of nothing but coke—more coal lands, more beehive ovens, more coke. How he financed these constantly expanding operations, no one, probably not even Frick himself, could ever adequately explain. He borrowed on his own future legacy from his grandparents and on the legacy that would go to his mother and sister. He borrowed from his uncles. Even his father, who had little to give, was persuaded to mortgage his small farm to provide ready cash for this strange son of his. When familial resources were exhausted, Frick turned to local wealthy farmers. Finally he was made bold enough by his obsessive dreams to appear before the conservative Pittsburgh banker, Judge Thomas Mellon, to ask for and, surprisingly enough, to get a loan of $10,000, which he used to build fifty more coke ovens. There was something about his quiet but obsessive insistence upon the unlimited future of Connellsville coke that inspired, if not confidence, at least a kind of awe in even the most cautious bankers. This loan was the beginning of a long and most profitable association between the Mellon family and Henry Clay Frick. Judge Mellon's son, Andrew, became perhaps the only intimate friend that Frick was ever to have.

The Frick Coke Company had been organized in 1871 with

holdings of 300 acres of coal lands and 50 ovens. Within a year, Frick, on borrowed money, had built 150 more ovens and had acquired 100 more acres of the best coal lands. By 1873 Frick was able to sell all the coke his ovens could produce. After paying his most pressing debts, he was already considering further expansion, but at this moment the panic hit, and within the year there was no market left for his coke at any price. This seemed to mark the end of all his plans, but his neighbors and creditors who so predicted did not know Frick. Like the Carnegie associates some fifty miles down the Monongahela, who had been caught by the depression just as they were beginning construction of the Edgar Thomson works, Frick took full advantage of the depression, and he used this period of business stagnation not for retreat but for advance. Again with borrowed capital, largely from the Mellons, he bought out his frightened partners. With coke now selling for 90¢ a ton, if one could find any purchasers, it was not difficult for Frick to buy out several of his discouraged competitors in the region. His faith in the future of his product was amply rewarded. By 1877, with steel plants throughout western Pennsylvania back in production and the insatiable maws of the Lucy and Isabella furnaces demanding more and more fuel each week, the price of coke rose to $2, $3, then $4 a ton. On the night of 19 December 1879, on his thirtieth birthday, he dropped into the small store in Mount Pleasant where he had begun his career as clerk, bought a five-cent Havana cigar, his one personal extravagance, and lighted it with satisfaction. On that day, his carefully kept books showed he had achieved his first million. Frick's personal fortune was twice as great as his grandfather's had been at the time of his death nine years before.[14]

In spite of this early achievement of his boyhood ambition, Frick was not ready to retire. Indeed, his childhood dream would now seem as confining as if he had tried to wear the same suit of clothes he had worn at the age of ten. There was no particular magic or real satisfaction in his million. The only satisfaction lay in pushing harder than before. More coal, more ovens, more freight cars and barges to move the coke to the mills—this had become the only meaningful rhythm of his life. By 1880, Frick had nearly 1000 ovens and close to 3000 acres of coal land. In that year, he took a vacation from business for a trip to Europe with Andrew

Mellon, and, having checked off that experience, he was ready for another the following year. On 15 December 1881, he married Adelaide Childs of Pittsburgh, and the two left for an extended honeymoon trip through the major cities along the East Coast.

Two vacations in as many years must have caused some surprise among his neighbors in Mount Pleasant. This did not seem like the Clay Frick that they had known. Perhaps his first million had gone to his head. But Frick, as he did in everything, found a substantial business purpose in each trip. On his trip to Europe the preceding year, he had asked Andrew Mellon if he would be agreeable to their having an older business acquaintance accompany them. Mellon acquiesced, but with some surprise at his friend's choice of a traveling companion, for the man whom Frick had suggested was a business rival in the coke business, and even within that stolid business community he was known to be extraordinarily dull. Before they had reached Venice, however, Mellon had an explanation for the invitation. By that time, Frick had persuaded his rival that a life of leisure and travel was what he needed. Frick had bought his coal fields and ovens, and the erstwhile rival was now busily preparing to continue his trip alone around the world.[15]

Now, in 1881, as Frick set off for Washington and New York with his young bride, he had in his valise a note of congratulations and a cordial invitation from his largest customer of coke, Andrew Carnegie, to have dinner in New York with him and his mother at the Windsor Hotel. Frick sensed that this invitation promised more than simply an opportunity to drink a toast to his blushing bride. And he was quite correct.

At a formal midday dinner at the Windsor Hotel, where Carnegie had gathered a few friends and business associates, the two men met for the first time. It would have made an interesting study in contrasts if there had been a detached observer at the table. Carnegie was in his best form, laughing and joking, giving the Fricks a full, running account of his coaching trip through Britain the previous summer. He flattered the new Mrs. Frick outrageously, and he gave rapt attention to every word, rare as each was, that Frick uttered. Clearly, something was up. The whole company sensed it. It could hardly be said that Frick participated in these hilarious proceedings, although they were clearly designed for him. He occasionally ventured an icy smile or a mono-syllabic response to a direct question, but he was warily waiting for the denouement to this Carnegie-staged drama. It came with the explosive abruptness which Carnegie delighted in. After the company had drunk toasts to the happiness of the newlyweds, Carnegie arose from the table, and with his glass held high, pro-posed a toast to Henry Clay Frick, and to the success of the Frick-Carnegie partnership.

The sudden silence at the table was broken by the brusque query of Margaret Carnegie: "Ah Andra, that's a verra good thing for Mr. Freek, but what do we get out of it?" [16]

One can be assured that long before he had proposed this momentous toast, Carnegie had obtained for himself an entirely satisfactory answer to the very question that his mother now raised. He knew precisely what he was going to "get out of it." Coke was indispensable to his operations. The most easily accessible coke, as well as the best that could be obtained anywhere in the world, was Connellsville coke. Henry Clay Frick, by a perspicacity and audacity which Carnegie could not help but admire, had managed in ten short years to acquire an 80 per cent control of the coal fields and coke ovens of the Connellsville region. Frick was looking for more capital and an assured market in order that he might expand his operations even further. What was more natu-ral that this happy combination of producer and customer to the mutual advantage of both? Carnegie, first among the major steel producers of the country, was taking a decisive step which would ultimately give him, as a manufacturer, control of his own sources of raw material.

It is doubtful that at this particular moment Carnegie looked much beyond the immediate gain of combining Frick's coke and his own steel. He could hardly have anticipated that the result of this combination would give the Carnegie steel interests its most determined and effective manager. And, had he been truly gifted with the Celtic powers of prophecy that his associates attributed to him he might have found that his mother's provocative ques-tion had such a fateful answer as to cause him to request that his toast be stricken from the record.

Frick's attitude toward the proposed merger was also deter-mined by the prospect of immediate gains. The idea of admitting the Carnegie associates into partnership with his coke business did not, of course, come as a complete surprise to Frick. It was only Carnegie's flat, unequivocal dinner announcement that for the moment caught Frick off guard. There had been discreet feelers from the Carnegies in the fall of 1881, feelers which Frick had in no way discouraged. Nor had Frick made any secret of the fact that he was considering reorganization of his company, now that he had bought out his old partners, and was looking for outside capital in order to increase the capitalization of his proposed new organization. Frick was fully aware of the prestige that would accrue to his new coke company if it had the open backing of the Carnegie steel interests. And the distinct possibility exists that Frick, more than Carnegie, realized that once an entry had been opened to the Carnegies into his company, the flow of traffic could be in two directions: if the Carnegies could move into the coke business, then there should be no obstacle to prevent Frick from moving into the steel business. Perhaps it was Frick who was gifted with a second sight, for he predicted the consequences of this proposed partnership more fully than Carnegie did.

In any event, Frick accepted Carnegie's toast, and within a month the Henry C. Frick Coke Company was reorganized, with a capitalization of $2,000,000, representing 40,000 shares of stock, each with a par value of $50. Prior to his alliance with the Carnegies, Frick had interested two Pittsburgh brothers, E. M. and Walton Ferguson, in investing heavily in the proposed company. When the 40,000 shares were distributed, the Ferguson brothers got 23,654 shares; Frick got 11,846; and the Carnegie associates got 4500.[17] The Carnegie associates thus held a minority interest of only 11.25 per cent of the total stock. But this situation did not last for long.

During the next year and a half, Carnegie pressured the Ferguson brothers into selling to him a large share of their stock, so that by the summer of 1883, at the time when Frick was seeking a further expansion of his coking facilities, Carnegie had become the largest single shareholder in the company.[18] Carnegie somewhat reluctantly agreed to a further increase of the capital of the company to $3,000,000. When, however, in November of the same year, Frick offered Carnegie more stock—enough to give him a 50 per cent interest in the company—on the provision that Carnegie assume all the outstanding debts which Frick had contracted in his previous expansion, Carnegie jumped at the chance.[19]

By December of 1883, only two years after his little dinner party for Frick and his bride, Carnegie and his partners in Carnegie Brothers owned over 50 per cent of the Frick Coke Company. A continuing supply of coke was now assured. Frick, of course, remained in charge of all operations of the company he had brought into existence, even though he was now only a minority stockholder. Carnegie regarded Frick's managerial ability as being at least as important as the physical assets which the company controlled.[20]

As long as Frick continued to supply the Carnegie blast furnaces in Pittsburgh and Braddock with their weekly needs of coke, Carnegie had no complaints and asked no questions about the management. And this was the way Frick wanted it. What Carnegie liked even better was that as fast as his blast furnaces' capacities for producing pig iron increased, so also did Frick's facilities for producing coke. No wonder Carnegie regarded Frick as having "a positive genius for management." [21] It appeared to be a very happy arrangement for all concerned.

Frick, on the other hand, was delighted with the excess capital he had acquired, which, for the first time since he had entered into partnership with his cousin thirteen years before, enabled him to be entirely free of debt. And if Carnegie supported the expansion of his coking facilities, Frick was even more pleased to have an enlargement of the Carnegie steel facilities. That was a major consideration in his decision to offer Carnegie Brothers a majority interest in the Henry C. Frick Coke Company at the time he did. For Carnegie had just made his most important acquisition of facilities since the building of the Edgar Thomson works a decade before. In October 1883, Carnegie Brothers took over their near-by rival at Homestead.

Carnegie's success in obtaining the virtually new and impressive facilities of the Pittsburg Bessemer Steel Company at Homestead almost at cost was the result of two factors: constant labor problems at Homestead and the depressed condition of the rail market. Once again, Carnegie was taking full advantage of an economic recession to enhance his own position.

Almost from the first, Homestead had been plagued by labor

difficulties. The skilled workers were mostly union men, members of the Amalgamated Association of Iron and Steel workers, one of the most powerful labor unions in the country. Although the union was organized on an industry-wide, national basis, and included workers engaged in both iron and steel manufacturing, it was a craft union in spirit: it sought members only from the skilled workers in every department of the trade. The unskilled were denied membership and were left to fend for themselves in individual hiring arrangements with management. The most that the great mass of workers could hope for was to share indirectly in any wage-and-hour benefits the Association succeeded in obtaining from management on a contractual basis for the skilled workers.

William Clark, whom the Pittsburg Bessemer board of managers had put in charge as general superintendent of the Homestead works, was a notorious union-hater, and from the first he was determined to break the Association's strength among the skilled workers at Homestead. Seeking trouble, he quickly found it. Within four months after the plant went into the production of rails, Clark issued an order requiring all employees to sign a "yellow-dog" contract, renouncing their right to belong to a labor union. Not one member of the Association would sign such a contract, and, consequently, on 1 January 1882 Clark issued orders for a lockout until the skilled workers should agree to sign. A week later he followed up this order with an announcement that even those who did sign would now have to accept a reduction in wages. The result was a strike by the entire labor force that lasted for ten weeks. On 11 March 1882, the strike appeared to be settled with a victory for the workers, but on the following day a dispute arose between Clark and the Association on the terms of the verbal agreement between labor and management. Immediately, a second strike was called. On 20 March, the board of managers, who had taken over the negotiations from Clark, capitulated. It was an even more complete victory for the Association than the previous settlement, and it was made all the sweeter by Clark's resigning in disgust over the terms that the board of managers had accepted.

But it was a short-lived truce. In August 1883, because of the severe slump in the rail market, Homestead was forced to close down for two weeks. When it resumed operations in September, a minor dispute concerned with the firing of a union man boiled up, and the six local lodges of the Association in the plant threatened to call another strike. By this time, the stockholders had had enough. Doubly discouraged by the depressed rail market and the apparently unending labor strife, a group representing the syndicate approached the Carnegies and offered to sell out.

Carnegie, who for the past several months had been expecting such an overture from his luckless rivals, was most gracious in offering the terms of surrender. He offered to buy at face value all shares of the company, and he gave an option of payment in cash or in stock in Carnegie Brothers. With one notable exception, the relieved stockholders took the cash and felt that they had been fortunate indeed to get out of a bad situation with their original investments still intact. Only W. H. Singer accepted Carnegie's offer of stock. He thus became a partner in Carnegie Brothers, and the $50,000 he had invested in Homestead eventually would be worth $8,000,000.[22]

Carnegie could congratulate himself upon having acquired at little more than original cost the most modern rail mill and Bessemer steel plant in the country. He had eliminated an embarrassing and potentially dangerous rival in the Pittsburgh area, and he had acquired facilities that could easily be adapted to the rolling of structural beams. Carnegie had the foresight to know that a market of increasing importance for steel manufacturers, now that the rail market was glutted, would develop in structural steel material, and he was anxious to prepare facilities to supply this market. By June 1885, less than two years after acquiring Homestead, the first steel beams were being rolled out from its former rail mill.[23] Unfortunately for Carnegie, he also acquired, along with its rolling mills and Bessemer converters, the same old labor difficulties that had forced the Pittsburg Bessemer Steel Company to sell out to him at a bargain price. The full price for Homestead had not been paid on that October morning in 1883 when a smiling Carnegie had handed out checks to Homestead's disgruntled former owners.

It was the acquisition of Homestead and its adaptation to the production of structural beams that forced Carnegie and his associates to reconsider the organizational structure that had been in existence since 1881. Homestead appeared to be too large to fit into the existing Carnegie Bros. & Company, Ltd., without greatly increasing the capitalization of that company, which Carnegie did not wish to do. Moreover, Carnegie had decided to take back the Lucy Furnaces from Wilson, Walker & Company and have them directly under his name. As a result, a second Carnegie company, named Carnegie, Phipps & Company, was organized on 1 January 1886. John Wilson sold his interest to Carnegie, and John Walker, in return for his agreeing to the merger, was made chairman of the new company, which included the Lucy Furnaces and the Homestead mills. Both companies, Carnegie Brothers and Carnegie, Phipps, now represented two complete and separate units, from blast furnace to finished, rolled rails and structural beams. Carnegie personally held a majority interest in each. He was, for the time being, content with this dual organizational structure and saw no necessity for further consolidation. First, two separate companies tended to allay the public's apprehensions over the possibility of a trust, and second, this dual organization avoided heavy capitalization which might result in even stronger demands from his associates for increased dividends. Carnegie was still not prepared to put all of his eggs in one organizational basket.

The one company in which Carnegie now had a majority interest that was not included in the dyarchy created by Carnegie in 1886 was the Hartman Steel Company. This was a finishing mill for the manufacturing of merchant steel, wire, and nails, located in Beaver Falls, some thirty miles northwest of Pittsburgh on the west bank of the Beaver River. It had been built by a group of Pittsburgh businessmen in 1882, and was called the Beaver Wire Company. Within a few months after operations began, the owners approached Phipps and offered to sell out to the Carnegie interests. Phipps urged Carnegie to buy, and in January 1883 he did so. H. W. Hartman was made chairman of the company, which was renamed for him. The plant was never a success, however, and from the first it was the only one of Carnegie's steel plants that consistently lost money. This was in part due to poor planning in the original construction of the plant, and in part due to inefficient management and to the fact that the plant lay some distance outside the circle of Carnegie's main iron and steel activities in the Pittsburgh-Monongahela area and was therefore not so closely supervised by the Carnegies and Phipps as were the blast furnaces and steel mills at Braddock and Homestead. All through the 1880's, Carnegie had to make repeated loans to the managers of the Hartman company to keep it out of serious financial difficulties.[24] The lack of success of the Hartman Steel Company considerably cooled Carnegie's interest in pushing further in the direction of finished small steel products.

The death of Tom Carnegie in the fall of 1886 had a far-reaching effect upon the entire Carnegie organization, not the least part of which was the opening both in shareholding and in management which Henry Clay Frick was to fill. There was little question in the minds of most of Andrew Carnegie's associates that brother Tom, although he was frequently ignored, had served as a conservative restraining force on Andrew's natural impulsiveness and eagerness to push ahead regardless of the consequences. After Tom's death, curiously enough, Carnegie himself became more conservative and cautious in extending himself, and it was frequently his junior partners who had to prod him into taking action that would prove to be of immense benefit to his own and his company's fortune. It was only after 1886 that Carnegie coined his much quoted phrase, "Pioneering don't pay," a slogan that belied all of his previous strategy and activities for success. Perhaps Carnegie needed Tom, for, from the time they were small children, Andrew had always considered Tom a rival, a foil. Tom's caution had been for Andrew a goad to drive him on. Now, with Tom gone, Carnegie's natural Scottish conservatism asserted itself, and he was far more inclined to listen to Cousin Dod's constant advice for caution than he had ever been to accept the same counsel from his brother.

At the time of his death Tom held a 17.5 per cent interest in Carnegie Brothers and a 16 per cent interest in the newly formed Carnegie, Phipps & Company.[25] His interest in the two companies was equal to Henry Phipps's and second only to Andrew Carnegie's. In early October 1886, while Tom lay dying at his home in Homewood, and Andrew was gravely ill with typhoid fever at Cresson, Henry Phipps had gone to John Walker in great consternation. "Tom Carnegie is sick with pneumonia," Phipps wailed, "and is going to die. Andrew Carnegie is sick with typhoid fever and is going to die too. That's going to leave Carnegie Brothers in a nice mess. You know our finances are not in any too good condition. We shall be called upon to settle with their estates and it will ruin us."

Walker took a more sanguine view. "Don't worry," he told Phipps. "Tom Carnegie probably will die for he has been a hard drinker. But Andrew has lived an abstemious and regular life and will probably recover." [26]

Walker proved to be a sound prophet. Andrew Carnegie's death, which would have required a full and immediate settlement of his 54.5 per cent interest in Carnegie Brothers and his 52.5 per cent interest in Carnegie, Phipps, would have bankrupted both companies. Tom's interest, upon his death, was not so large as to make a ruinous demand for settlement. Andrew absorbed most of Tom's interest himself and came to an amicable arrangement with Lucy Coleman Carnegie, Tom's widow, whereby he could buy this interest over an extended period of time.

Nevertheless, Phipps had been badly frightened, and he was determined to make arrangements whereby the company would never again be faced with bankruptcy because of sickness or accident threatening the life of Andrew Carnegie. As a result, early in 1887, Phipps, with legal counsel, drew up the first of the famous "Iron Clad" agreements, which all partners in the association were required to sign. The idea for this dated back to the early partnership arrangement of Kloman, Phipps, and Miller, an arrangement which Kloman and Phipps had found useful in ousting Miller from the business.

But the motivation for the Iron Clad of 1887, Phipps always later insisted, was solely to provide for a way in which the company could, over an extended period of time, purchase for itself at book value from the heirs of a deceased partner his share of the company's interest. The Agreement provided that if the interest in the company did not exceed 4 per cent, the company had four months' time in which to purchase the interest. The time allowed increased with the size of the share, so that, in case of Carnegie's death, the company had fifteen years in which to purchase his interest.[27] Clearly, Phipps and the other associates were concerned with the major problem of settling Carnegie's estate and the tremendous strain that this would place upon the company if ample time were not allowed to purchase his majority interest. For this reason, even the most junior partners were eager to sign the Iron Clad Agreement.

It is specious, however, to argue that Phipps's only concern was for the welfare of the company. Both he and Carnegie clearly intended to use the Agreement as a means of forcing the sale at book value of the interest of any other partner whose continued presence in the association might prove to be detrimental to their and the company's best interests. The opening statement of the Agreement was quite explicit on this point:

> Each of us moving, do hereby covenant, promise and agree to the party of the first part that . . . when three-fourths in number of the parties holding interests in said first part, and three-fourths in value of said interests shall request us to sell, assign and transfer to said first party all of each of our interests in the limited partnership of Carnegie Bros. and Co., Ltd. The interest shall be assigned free of all liens and encumbrances or contracts of any kind, and this transfer shall at once terminate all our interests in and connection with said Carnegie Bros. and Co. Ltd. . . . This agreement is hereby declared to be irrevocable. Death shall not revoke or alter any of the terms of this contract. . . . This agreement is hereby declared to be a lien and encumbrance upon each of our shares in said Carnegie Bros. and Co. Ltd.[28]

The memory of the William Shinn affair was still fresh in both Carnegie's and Phipps's minds, and both senior partners were determined that never again would they be brought to court by a recalcitrant partner who might demand more for his interest than the book value. After the Iron Clad Agreement went into effect, Carnegie was more reluctant than ever to overcapitalize the company, which would increase the book value of each partner's interest.

The one party to which the Iron Clad did not apply, of course, except in the case of death, was Andrew Carnegie. Since it required "three-fourths in value of said interests," as well as "three-fourths in number of the parties holding interests" in the company, the Agreement in effect excluded any partner whose interest was over one-fourth of the total capital of the company from being forced out of the association. There was only one such partner. Andrew Carnegie would never have consented to any Agreement which put his own interest at the mercy of three-fourths of his associates. Surprisingly enough, Phipps did not at first see the threat to his own security within the company that was implicit in the Agreement. He was so eager to provide for the exigency that would arise in case of Carnegie's death that he was the most outspoken advocate of the Iron Clad among all of the partners.

While Carnegie was still recuperating from his serious illness in Florida, and prior to his marriage and departure for Britain, he took the first step in bringing Frick officially into the Carnegie steel interests. On 31 January 1887, Carnegie agreed to sell to Frick $100,000 of par value, or 2 per cent, of the total capital of Carnegie Brothers for the book value of $184,000. Frick was not required to put up any cash for this share, but the share would be held in trust for him by Phipps until such time as the full amount had been paid for out of the declared dividends of the company.[29] It was an easy, inexpensive way to become a Carnegie associate. All that Frick had to agree to in return for this assignment of interest was to sign the Iron Clad Agreement. Frick had invited Carnegie into his tent, now Carnegie was returning the compliment. For better or for worse, the two men's destinies were now joined together.

Carnegie thought it was for the better. Ever since his disappointment in Shinn, he had been looking for a general manager with all those attributes he considered essential for managerial success: drive, ambition, and imagination, balanced by a sense of what was practical in any given situation. Tom Carnegie, who had succeeded Shinn as general manager, was a good businessman, excellent in dealing with those under him and in getting their full co-operation. But he was a poor competitor. Phipps's succession to the chairmanship of Carnegie Brothers upon the death of Tom was purely a stopgap measure. Everyone knew that, including Phipps himself, whose only ambition was to sit at the feet of the mighty, not on the throne itself. Now, Carnegie felt, he had at last found the right director for his steel interests. Many years later, in recalling his considered opinion of Frick at this time, he was to write that Frick was "a man with a positive genius for management." [30] Hence the offer of an interest in the company that cost Frick not a cent of his own money. Soon Carnegie would be urging Frick to take more. He was clearly interested in getting Frick deeply involved in the Carnegie steel interests.

Although the Carnegie associates had held a majority of the stock in the Frick Coke Company since 1883, Frick had remained general manager and chairman of the board, and he still regarded it with parental pride as his creation. As it had for the preceding fifteen years, the company still occupied almost all of Frick's thought and attention during his waking hours and quite probably it also intruded into his dreams. Carnegie thus had ample opportunity to observe Frick in action as general manager of a concern that Carnegie largely owned. What he saw had encouraged Carnegie to pull Frick in his direction.

Carnegie must have had some misgivings, however, about Frick as a potential manager of the steel companies soon after he had given Frick his first financial stake in Carnegie Brothers. For in the late spring of 1887, while Carnegie was still on his honeymoon on the Isle of Wight, a strike was called in the coke industry by the local lodges. The target was a wage settlement that had been fixed by a board of arbitration and accepted by the national unions, the Knights of Labor and the Miners' and Mine Laborers' Amalgamated Association. The national officers of the Knights of Labor branded the strike as illegal, but this did not bring the coke men throughout the Connellsville region back to work. Rather it increased the tension, which led to several isolated acts of violence upon the part of the wildcat strikers who felt they had been betrayed by their own unions' acceptance of the wage reduction scale proposed by management. Frick, who had ruthlessly suppressed previous strikes in his coke company, took the leadership in getting agreement from all the owners of coal fields and coke ovens in the region to hold firm, refuse to yield an inch, and, if necessary, import strikebreakers to get the fields back in production. But with the market for both rails and structural beams strong and the blast furnaces and steel mills at Braddock and Homestead running full with thousands of tons of back orders to fill, Phipps and John Walker, as chairmen of the two Carnegie companies, had a quite different view. They cabled their account of the problem to Carnegie, who at once instructed Frick to accede to the strikers' demands.

Frick, although furious, had no choice but to yield to the majority interest of his company. It was particularly galling for him to be the first to break the managerial agreement which he himself had promoted. The rest of the coke owners condemned Frick's defection as being more reprehensible than the workers' refusal to accept their own union settlement. Frick, the tough man of Connellsville, burned with shame over being branded a traitor and labor appeaser by his fellow manufacturers, and his reaction was violent and extreme. It must have come as a shock to Carnegie and the others in the association, who thought they knew Frick, and had regarded him as a man with ice water in his veins who never acted imprudently or hastily, to realize that, when crossed, he could be a man of violent passion and extravagant action. Phipps and Walker were startled to receive this brusque communiqué from Frick the day that the strike against the Henry C. Frick Coke Company was settled:

Gentlemen:

As you hold a majority of the stock and are entitled to control in the Frick Coke Company, and in viewing what has passed between us on the subject, I feel compelled to vacate my position as its President. I therefore enclose, herewith my resignation.

But I accompany it with this serious protest against the course you propose to take regarding the pending strike. I am satisfied that it must occasion heavy loss to the Coke Company. Besides the loss occasioned by granting the men's present unreasonable demands, it will only lead to still more unreasonable demands in the near future. The loss to the Coke Company may be far more than made up, so far as you are concerned, by gains in your steel interests, but I object to so manifest a prostitution of the Coke Company's interests in order to promote your steel interests.

Whilst a majority of the stock entitles you to control, I deny that it confers the right to manage so as to benefit your interest in other concerns at the loss and injury of the Coke Company in which I am interested.[31]

Eventually, however, Frick's anger subsided. Carnegie from Scotland courted him with flattering letters, while Phipps and Walker, as well as those associates who were his men on the board of managers of the H. C. Frick Coke Company, begged him to reconsider. What proved more effective as an emollient were the monthly account sheets, which showed that even with the 12.5 per cent higher wage scale at Frick's coke plants over any of its competitors, the profits were still enormous. Six months after his resignation, Frick accepted his re-election to the presidency of the company by the board of managers.

This incident, however, proved useful in giving both Carnegie and Frick a fuller picture than either had had before of the other's character and the nature of their relationship. Frick, by nature suspicious of the motives of all men, was now more than ever convinced that Carnegie had to be watched at all times. He knew now that in a showdown Carnegie would always sacrifice the best interests of the coke company to protect his larger steel interests. Frick would be defenseless against the greater voting power of the Carnegie associates within the management of his beloved coke company if another crisis, such as that over the strike issue, should arise. The best that Frick could hope for would be the avoidance of such head-on confrontations regarding company policy by having a voice in the management of the steel companies; in other words, by entering the enemy's camp and influencing policy from within its inner council. Hence Frick, after he had had sufficient time to let the cold reason of logic dominate his hot passion of anger, became outwardly more cordial toward Carnegie than he had ever been in the past. He was not only amenable but eager to accept Carnegie's suggestion that he take a more active interest in Carnegie Brothers.

As for Carnegie, he came out of this direct confrontation with even more respect for Frick than he had had before. He could understand Frick's sense of frustration and anger in having the rug jerked out from under him in the labor dispute, and he rather admired Frick's reaction—of accepting the cold necessity of having to carry out an order that he detested and then of resigning in protest. Here was a tough horse; if he could ever be coaxed into harness and trained to pull in the right direction he would plow a deep furrow indeed.

Carnegie understood the primacy of Frick's loyalty just as fully as Frick understood his. Frick would place the interests of his coke company over that of Carnegie's steel companies, Carnegie believed, as long as that remained Frick's only major interest. The best tactic, then, in redirecting Frick's loyalty would be to give him a larger share in the Carnegie association and, if possible, persuade him to accept a responsible position within the management of the company. And so, for quite different reasons, Frick and Carnegie arrived at the same conclusion: Frick must be given a position of managerial authority within the Carnegie steel domain.

This was accomplished in January 1889, when Frick replaced Phipps as chairman of Carnegie Bros. & Company. His interest was also increased, from 2 per cent to 11 per cent, again without Frick's having to pay a cent in cash. Carnegie wrote to his new chairman in happy confidence over the future: "Take supreme care of that head of yours. It is wanted. Again, expressing my thankfulness that I have found THE MAN, I am always yours, A.C." [32]

Frick proved his worth within a year after taking over the chairmanship of Carnegie Brothers by acquiring for the Carnegie interests the Duquesne Steel Works, in Duquesne, Pennsylvania, some five miles up the Monongahela River from Homestead. This area had been open country as recently as five years before. Then a group of businessmen and manufacturers organized the Duquesne Steel Company, capitalized at $350,000, and bought up farmland as a site for their steel mill. Construction got under way in the summer of 1886, but work had to be suspended due to serious disagreements among the partners. It was not until the company was reorganized as the Allegheny Bessemer Steel Company, with an increased capital of $700,000, that construction was resumed in March 1888. The principal promoters of the reorganized company were E. F. Clark, of the Solar Iron Works, and two brothers, William G. and D. E. Park, both of the Black Diamond Steel Works.[33] These men, experienced in steel processing, introduced radical innovations in steel mill operations. Of particular interest to steel men everywhere was the introduction of the process of running ingots directly from the soaking pits into the rollers, and making billets and rails without further heating. This eliminated one entire and expensive process in the production of rails. Carnegie immediately saw the cost threat of this innovation, and before the first rail had been rolled at Duquesne he had drafted a circular to railroads throughout the country warning them that the process being used by Allegheny Bessemer would result in defective rails, because for lack of a second heating the steel in the rails would not have "homogeneity" of structure. No one in the Carnegie mills knew what this meant, but it sounded impressive, and railroad purchasing agents were reluctant to take a chance on rails which lacked "homogeneity." Later, when one of Carnegie's partners was asked if he considered this tactic a legitimate form of competition, his reply was that "under ordinary circumstances we would not have thought it legitimate; but the competition set up by the Duquesne people was also not legitimate, because of their use of this direct rolling process. . . . They were a thorn in our flesh, and they reduced the price of rails." [34]

What followed was the story of the Homestead purchase repeated in almost every detail. Carnegie's false charges had seriously hurt Allegheny Bessemer's ability to obtain initial orders, and there was continuing disharmony between the partners and the plant managers. Then, too, there were serious labor disturbances and short periods of work stoppage during the first months of operation. More capital was needed, but the partners were reluctant to subscribe it, and Frick saw his opportunity. Late in the fall of 1889, he offered the major stockholder, William Park, $600,000 for the entire plant. As the shareholders had put nearly twice that much capital into the company, the offer was summarily rejected. But Frick could afford to wait and negotiate further. Nine months later, he offered $1,000,000 in bonds, and the offer was quickly accepted. Carnegie Brothers received for their bonds—which would not mature for five years—two seven-ton Bessemer converters, six cupolas, seven soaking pits, four trains of rolls, and all the boilers, engines, and other equipment necessary for the successful operation of a blooming and rail mill. Before the bonds matured, Duquesne had paid for itself six times over without Carnegie Brothers having paid a dollar of its own capital for its purchase.[35] Frick had more than earned his unpaid capital interest in Carnegie Brothers, and the last potential rail rival in the Monongahela River valley had been eliminated. The Duquesne purchase became a legend among steel manufacturers everywhere as the greatest bargain in the history of steel manufacturing. Carnegie's exultant shout when he heard that Duquesne was theirs gave credit where credit was due: "F is a marvel. Let's get all F's." [36]

From the time that Carnegie Brothers took over the Duquesne plant, strangely enough, nothing more was heard against the direct rolling process or that rails so produced lacked "homogeneity." Not only was this process kept at Duquesne, but it was also quickly introduced into the mills at Edgar Thomson and Homestead, and it soon became standard practice throughout the trade. It proved to be one more important step in reducing costs.

Costs remained Carnegie's greatest concern, of far greater importance, he felt, than either production or prices. One of his plant superintendents would remember that Carnegie "would say: 'Show me your cost sheets. It is more interesting to know how cheaply and how well you have done this thing than how much money you have made, because the one is a temporary result, due possibly to special conditions of trade, but the other means a permanency that will go on with the works as long as they last.' " [37]

In this policy of taking care to keep costs down and the profits would then take care of themselves, Carnegie and Frick were in complete agreement. Carnegie felt that none of his other partners (except Phipps, of course, who was the greatest cost-parer of the lot) ever really understood this principle. They measured success in terms of profits and wanted their dividends now. But profits used within the plant to bring about greater efficiency and greater production at less cost meant far greater profits in the future. It seemed so elementary to Carnegie that he was always amazed that other companies did not follow his example.

One way of achieving cost reduction was through technological improvement and innovation in method. Carnegie had been genuinely frightened by the Duquesne direct rolling process because of the potential competition in cost factor it represented. Of course this was the reason he fought it in the underhanded way he did when it was introduced by a rival company—and then quickly adopted it when that company became his property. Immediate expense meant little to Carnegie, if spending big money now could mean the saving of small sums over a very long period of time. Once, without a moment's hesitation, he told Charles Schwab, plant manager at Homestead, to dismantle a mill that had been in operation only two months when Schwab expressed dissatisfaction with it and felt that it should have been built differently.[38]

One of the technological advances in the making of steel that Carnegie promoted vigorously in the 1880's was the Thomas basic process. Sidney Gilchrist-Thomas, the young Englishman whom Carnegie had so assiduously courted on the 1881 coaching trip, was an amateur chemist. In his off hours from serving as clerk in a London police court he had played around with the puzzle that had baffled chemists and metallurgists for a generation—how to remove phosphorus from iron so that it would be suitable for the Bessemer converter. Since the early 1860's, when Henry Bessemer learned to his chagrin that not all iron ore could be changed into steel by his converter method, but only that ore which contained less than .02 per cent phosphorus, men had been seeking an answer to what seemed an insolvable problem. British steel manufacturers were particularly interested in finding a way to remove phosphorus from the ore, for nearly all the iron ore to be found in Britain contained a high percentage of phosphorus. This had meant that Britain, with an ample supply of ore for producing cast iron or wrought iron, now in this age of Bessemer steel had had to import most of its ore from Spain or Sweden. The problem was not so acute in the United States, inasmuch as most of the Lake Superior ore was low in phosphorus content. Nevertheless, anyone who could discover a method of removing phosphorus from the molten iron before it was converted into steel would be rendering a service of inestimable value to steelmakers everywhere, for vast new resources of raw material would be made available throughout the world.

Young Thomas had become fascinated with the problem, and for years he experimented in the small laboratory he had set up in his lodgings. Here he had a miniature converter, "a toy pot," Carnegie later called it, "that deserves to rank with Watt's tea-kettle." And then one evening, he came upon an answer—or, at least, half an answer. Building upon previous work of Lowthian Bell, Thomas discovered that at a very high temperature, 2500°F., which was 500°F. above the usual heat used in the converter, the phosphorus in the iron acquired a strong affinity for

500

lime. If lime was placed in the converter along with the iron, the phosphorus at this temperature left the iron and attached itself to the lime, which then floated to the top and could be removed as slag. The iron that was left, regardless of its previous phosphorus content, had been converted to steel.

The only problem remaining was that of temperature. Unfortunately, neither the fire-brick lining nor the metal converter itself could stand up under the very high temperatures demanded by the process to force the phosphorus out of the iron. Some kind of lining in addition to ordinary fire brick had to be provided if the process was to have any practical use. Again months of experimenting followed, until Thomas finally devised a protective inner wall, a "basic lining," as he called it, for the converter.

At the spring meeting of the Iron and Steel Institute held in London in 1878, this quiet young clerk, totally unknown to the great majority of distinguished steel manufacturers, chemical engineers, and metallurgists, got up and made a simple announcement. "I have successfully eliminated phosphorus in the equivalent of the Bessemer converter and at a future meeting I hope to have an opportunity of telling you how it has been accomplished." This announcement should have exploded with the force of a bomb, but to the delegates present he was simply another crank inventor who somehow had managed to sneak into their assembly. His promise of a revolution in the steel industry did not even seem worthy of the simple question, "How?"

In the following autumn, when the Institute met in Paris, Thomas managed to get a leave from his job in the police court and showed up with a technical paper in hand to explain his process. He was not allowed to deliver it. But Alexander Holley, the great engineer of the Bessemer converter, was there, and Thomas, rebuffed by the Institute, approached him and asked him to read his paper describing the process he had invented. Holley, who had the imagination so often lacking in his colleagues, consented, and was at once excited by Thomas's idea. He sent the paper to an American mining and metallurgical engineer, George W. Maynard, who was at that time in England, serving as a consultant for the Standard Iron and Steel Works at Gorton. In an accompanying note, Holley wrote: "This looks like a good thing and if you think it is you had better secure it for the United States."

Maynard, after reading the paper, agreed, and persuaded the

Standard Works at Gorton to give the Thomas process a test with pig iron containing a heavy concentration of phosphorus—2.75 per cent. The results of the test were all that Thomas had claimed for his process, and Maynard at once applied for and obtained a commission to be Thomas's agent in the United States.[39] The first large-scale commercial application of the Thomas "basic process" was made by E. Winston Richards, plant manager of the largest steel mill in the world, at Eston, England.

Carnegie first heard of the Thomas discovery while in Europe in the summer of 1879. He was at once interested, and after consulting with Richards in Eston, he got in touch with Thomas, who agreed to sell the rights to Carnegie for $300,000. When he returned home in the late autumn of 1879, Carnegie got in touch with Maynard and informed him that Thomas had agreed to sell the American rights for $300,000. Maynard felt that Thomas had sold out too cheaply, and he strongly resented the fact that Carnegie and Thomas had made their arrangements directly without consulting him. Since Thomas desperately needed ready cash, however, Maynard agreed to the transaction.[40]

Carnegie undoubtedly would have liked to have kept the Thomas franchise as the exclusive possession of Carnegie Brothers, for it would have given E.T. an immense advantage over all of its American competitors. But Thomas's demand for cash payment, in full, was more than Carnegie cared to manage alone. Then, too, as soon as the Thomas discovery became public knowledge, an American inventor by the name of Jacob Reese came forward, claiming that he already had an American patent for exactly the same process. It was Bessemer versus Kelly all over again, and Carnegie needed the combined strength of all the major steel manufacturers in the Bessemer Steel Association to help in securing a patent settlement.

The result was that Carnegie worked very hard for the next two years to sell the Thomas franchise to the Bessemer Association, thus making it available to all of the major steel producers in the country, and he also had to persuade the Association to buy up Reese's patent. Many of his competitors who had not seen the process in operation in England were not as convinced as Carnegie that the basic process as developed by either Thomas or Reese was the solution to the old problem of phosphorus-bearing

502

pig iron. In February 1880 Carnegie wrote in triumph to Thomas saying that the Bessemer Association had agreed to pay $50,000 for a year's option on purchasing the franchise. Carnegie said that Captain Jones would come over to England immediately to see the process in operation at Eston. "There is no time to be lost as our Lake ores have risen to extreme prices and we have Phosphorus ores near at hand which can be mined very cheaply. Indeed the Thomas [process] seems a necessity for us." [41]

Carnegie was a little premature in considering the matter settled. A few months later, he was writing in disgust to E. Y. Townsend of Cambria Iron, his one associate in the Bessemer Association who seemed as interested in the Thomas process as he was:

> For my part I live in daily apprehension of our finding this process in other hands. We *deserve* to lose it. It is pitiable to see men like Messrs. Felton & Kennedy [officers in the Bessemer Association] playing with such a question & no doubt pluming themselves on driving a "good bargain" & perhaps saving each of us a couple of thousand dollars. I have felt many times that I would buy those patents & own them & let the Bessr. Ass'n go to the devil. If it were not that you have fully supported me in the matter & done good work in getting action upon it I should certainly close with Thomas at once.[42]

It was not until May 1881, and then only after six of the eleven member companies of the Bessemer Association had agreed jointly to the purchase of the patent rights, that the Bessemer Association finally purchased the Thomas basic process for $275,000.[43] The Association also purchased the Reese patent for $15,000.[44] Carnegie came out very well in this transaction. It is true, he had to forgo the privilege of exclusive American ownership of the patent, but in recognition of his "generosity in introducing the Thomas basic process to the United States and in making it available to the entire Bessemer Steel Association," his company was not assessed any portion of the purchase fee.[45] In addition, Carnegie received a commission of $50,000 from Thomas for his services in selling the patent rights to the Association. In other words, Carnegie was paid a rather handsome sum for the privilege of using the Thomas process free of charge, whereas his competitors had to pay nearly $30,000 for the same rights.[46]

There were problems, however, in using the Thomas basic process in the Bessemer converters for which it had been designed. American manufacturers, eager to make use of local ores, regardless of quality, charged their converters with pig iron which was not only excessively high in phosphorus content but also high in other impurities. The resulting product was not the high grade of steel the promoters of the Thomas process had promised. Some manufacturers had excellent results with the basic lining, but a large number felt that they had been deceived, and went back to the old methods and used ores with very low phosphorus content. The British manufacturers, however, did not have as wide a choice in ores as the Americans. The Thomas process was their only hope for staying in the world steel market with competitive prices, and in 1885 it was proved in Britain that, whereas the Thomas process was not an unqualified success in the Bessemer converter under all circumstances, it worked perfectly in the Siemens open hearth furnaces regardless of the quality of pig iron used. So the British manufacturers with their own ores could produce a steel purer and more ductile than the best grade of Bessemer steel.

Once again, Carnegie was in on the ground floor of a new development in steel manufacturing. Visiting in Britain in the summer of 1885, he received information on the increased use of the open hearth furnace before any of his American competitors did. Carnegie, as early as 1875, had had an open hearth furnace installed at Edgar Thomson, but it had been used only for special orders, and its total annual production of steel had been very small. Now his British associates were predicting that, with the adoption of the Thomas process, the open hearth method would eventually replace the Bessemer converter that had dominated the field for the past two decades and had changed the material structure of civilization from iron to steel.

Carnegie believed them to the extent that he ordered an open hearth furnace for his newly acquired plant at Homestead. In March 1888 the first run of open hearth steel using the Thomas basic process was made. Carnegie was so pleased with the results that he urged a rapid expansion of open hearth facilities. In October 1888 he wrote to William Abbott, who had succeeded John Walker as chairman of Carnegie, Phipps & Company:

> It strikes me our most important step just now is to hasten the completion of the four open hearth furnaces agreed upon, by working day and night. We are certain to be followed sooner or later in Basic, and every day we gain is just so much clear, now since we have proved its success.

And, as always, costs were a major concern with Carnegie:

> I suspect that we are losing a dollar and a half to two dollars per ton in labor, owing to faulty construction of our open hearth. The true plan is to build the new furnaces upon the most approved system, even if this involves additional expenditures and we should look forward to changing the present furnaces so that they also can be run to the one or two great pits, like the Scotland Steel Company. Even if we save half a dollar per ton by the changes, it would justify a large additional expenditure now.[47]

By December of the same year, Carnegie had become so convinced that open hearth represented the trend of the future that he was prepared to install the process in the Edgar Thomson plant, the very temple of American Bessemer steel. He wrote Abbott: "The Captain [Jones] has satisfied me that it would be best to erect two open-hearth furnaces, Basic, at Edgar Thomson." And again, two weeks later, "I notice that the Board of C.B. & Co. has required Capt. Jones to submit estimates and plans for Basic Hearth Furnaces. . . . I think it not objectionable to get estimates of cost, but really hope that the work will not be delayed waiting for detailed plans which no one in the Board can intelligently understand. Every day's delay in building Basic furnaces is just so much clear profit lost, as we are bound to be followed very soon after we get started." [48] Even though Carnegie had hundreds of thousands of dollars invested in Bessemer converters, he was ready to scrap them in favor of a better and more economical process. Construction costs never bothered Carnegie. It was operational cost that mattered, and that simple truth was a major reason for his success. Frick better than anyone else among his partners understood this and was prepared to carry out Carnegie's policy. It is quite natural that Carnegie felt he had at last found THE MAN.

The agreement between Frick and Carnegie on cost of production gave promise of a harmonious relationship between chairman and major stockholder. Both were eager for technological improvements that would lower costs, even if these improvements meant a large initial outlay of capital expenditure. Frick, in carrying out this program, supported Carnegie's long-established principle of returning to the partners only a small fraction of the profits in the form of dividends so that there might be capital funds available for plant expansion and improvement. Unlike Tom Carnegie, Abbott, Walker, Phipps, and others who had been in positions of managerial authority, Frick did not wear the blinders of immediate personal gain. He shared with Carnegie the same visions of empire and of future greatness. The strong bond of understanding in basic policy and entrepreneurial philosophy had from the beginning tied together these two men so different in personality and temperament, and that bond was in large part responsible for making the Carnegie-Frick alliance last as long as it did.

In their concern over cost, however, each man had a different and specific *bête noire* which he wished to attack in order to lower substantially the cost of production. For Carnegie, the villain was the railroad. No other item on the cost sheets upset him as much as transportation costs. From the moment the first rail rolled out of the mill at E.T., Carnegie carried on a relentless war against the railroads to reduce cost of transportation. On this subject he was almost paranoiac. He was convinced that other steel companies were getting a better deal than was he on freight rates. With his railroad background and early close ties to Thomson and Scott, one would have thought that he might have been sympathetic to the railroad's position, but, on the contrary, these early associations had made him extraordinarily sensitive to railroad tactics. As assistant to Scott and later as superintendent of the Western Division of the Pennsylvania Railroad, Carnegie knew all about secret rebates and the great discrepancy between published rates and the actual rates paid by certain favored customers of the railroad. He resented the monopolistic position that the Pennsylvania Railroad held in Pittsburgh, and a consuming ambition which constantly tormented and goaded him was to break the Pennsylvania's monopoly by a competitive road, preferably one that he himself controlled. It had been the close proximity of Braddock to both the Baltimore & Ohio and the Pennsylvania lines that had persuaded him in 1872 to accept Coleman's choice of a site for the Edgar Thomson plant. Unfortunately, however, the B. & O. did not have the facilities in either track or rolling stock to make it a true competitor of the Pennsylvania in handling the freight demands of the E.T. Consequently, Carnegie found himself as much a subject of the Pennsylvania's monopoly at Braddock as he had been at 29th Street in Pittsburgh.

Carnegie assiduously sought and learned, by one means or another, the rates that his competitors were being charged for the shipment both of raw material to the plants and of finished products to the market, and these he used effectively in his annual bargaining with the officials of the Pennsylvania Railroad. In 1881, he wrote to Alexander Cassatt, then vice president of the Pennsylvania Railroad Company:

> Before you take final position upon the issue before us, may I take this occasion to point out, in a friendly way, just what it is you will have to defend—to wit—
>
> | | | |
> |---|---|---|
> | The justice of levying upon us for 38 miles distance | 86 ¾¢ | |
> | While you charge others for 65 miles (Isabella) | 70 | ¢ |
> | & Cambria for 65 miles | 84 | ¢ |
> | The justice of levying upon us for 49 miles distance | | |
> | *to Pittsburgh* | 1.16 ¾¢ | |
> | While you charge others for 65 miles, as above | | |
> | *to Pgh* | 70 | ¢ |
>
> That the traffic is *West bound* in our case as against Cambria, will not be urged by any Competent Railroad officer as a reason for charging more.
>
> And now let me say, in all seriousness, that it is beyond the power of anyone to sustain such discrimination. It is no crime to manufacture in the Pittsburgh district, and I shall be much disappointed, if you, or Mr. Roberts, when fully informed of the question, will be a party to the attempt.[49]

507

Backed by such specific, detailed information, Carnegie usually carried the argument and succeeded in getting rates that the company could live with for the coming year. The acquisition of a major share of the Frick Coke Company was a particularly strong weapon during the years 1881–83 in obtaining favorable rates on coke shipment from both the B. & O. and the Pennsylvania.[50] But early in 1884 another crisis arose between Carnegie and the Pennsylvania over freight rates. A new general freight agent for the railroad, John S. Wilson, refused to give Carnegie the yearly guaranteed rates to which he was accustomed. After several unsuccessful efforts to arrive at an agreement, Carnegie wrote to him:

> We have waited and waited upon you. Three of our most important men have made trips to see you at your request. Our Scotia mine stands idle awaiting your decision. We have not shipped one ton of ore this year and we cannot ship any until your decision is made. Hundreds of poor men await your decision whether they are to be permanently displaced or not. . . . We do not wish to reflect upon you, fully appreciating the fact that you have recently come to the management of the vast and intricate system and that you have necessarily much to learn. We have, therefore been patient and waited upon you until it is no longer possible to do so without serious detriment to our business. We have not appealed to your superior officers as we do not wish to give offense. As a last resort, we have been forced to decline to pay your freight bills till we know what rates we are to pay, as the only means of obtaining a decision from you.[51]

Carnegie's patience was a trifle shorter than this letter indicates, however, for he had already written Frank Thomson, vice president of the company, an indignant letter on the coke rates that Wilson had apparently established for the year, but not to Carnegie's satisfaction:

> Mr. Wilson telghs. me our coke rates are to be advanced 20%. If this advance is made to other Steel Rail manfrs. on your line we have nothing whatever to say. We have always told Mr. Roberts & Mr. Cassatt we would gladly pay any rates

508

they fixed for other Steel Rail Manfrs. Our present rates are the result of an appeal to Mr. Roberts & a decision made by him. . . . We agree to any general advance. We do not agree to be singled out & discriminated against. Please accept this notice.

We appeal to you first as we did to Mr. Cassatt—failing equal treatment here we appeal again to Mr. Roberts, failing here, we appeal to the Directors, failing here, we send a circular to every shareholder & failing here, we make our appeal to the great public whose opinion no corporation these days can successfully withstand—

Your charge of a dollar per ton for fifty-five miles *Westbound* transportation to Pittsburgh, as against ninety cents for coke seventy-five miles East will not stand publicity. Every manfr. in Pittsburg & in the West will rise in indignation. It is infamous & I give you due notice you can't impose upon us.[52]

The Pennsylvania in its favored position not only could but did impose the advance on freight rates for coke. Wilson proved to be a tougher agent than his predecessor, and Roberts, Cassatt, and Thomson held firm in supporting their new manager. For a time, Carnegie toyed with the idea of a mass protest of enraged citizens of Pittsburgh workers and manufacturers, marching in unison to end the stranglehold that this railroad octopus held on trade in western Pennsylvania. Visions of justifiably enraged citizenry assembled in the spirit of the great Chartist rallies of his childhood flashed through his mind. But further reflection and the counsel of his more conservative colleagues caused him to abandon such an exciting and melodramatic response to the Pennsylvania's obduracy. In the first place, he was not at all sure he could get the citizens of Pittsburgh to a fever pitch of anger over a 20 per cent advance in freight rates for Carnegie Brothers. And, in the second place, as Phipps and Tom Carnegie pointed out, once a mob was aroused there was no assurance that it would direct its hostility only toward the freight offices of the Pennsylvania. There could be awkward questions raised about the recent reduction in the hourly wage scales that had more than offset the advance in freight rates. The Carnegies had too much invested in the prevailing order of things to be mounting soapboxes and lighting torches, much as these actions might appeal to Carnegie's sense of the dramatic.

It was just at this moment, when Carnegie was searching desperately for weapons to use against the Pennsylvania, that an opportunity was offered to him to participate in a venture which promised to be a much more effective and permanent solution to the freight problem than mobs marching in Pittsburgh streets. The New York Central was at this moment involved in one of its periodic disputes with a competing line. This time it happened to be the Pennsylvania Railroad Company, with whom it had heretofore been at peace, inasmuch as neither had directly threatened the other's territory. But in 1883, a new railway company was organized, the New York, West Shore and Buffalo Railway, which proposed a line up the west bank of the Hudson and then west to Buffalo—in direct competition with the New York Central's main line. It has been generally believed that the Pennsylvania Railroad was secretly backing this company, although the Pennsylvania was always to deny it and no specific records have ever been found that would confirm this suspicion.[53]

William Vanderbilt and the other officials of the New York Central were convinced, however, that the proposed West Shore Line was but a shadow company for the Pennsylvania. If the Pennsylvania Railroad was now invading the New York Central's most sacred inner domain, Vanderbilt was determined to retaliate in kind. He had long had his eye on the rich market of southwestern Pennsylvania and knew how desperately the great industries of that region longed for effective competition to the main Pennsylvania line. There had existed since 1854 a charter from the state of Pennsylvania to a corporation to build a railroad in a westerly direction from Harrisburg to the coal fields of southwestern Pennsylvania. Further extension of the charter to the South Pennsylvania Railroad Company had granted it the right to build on west to the Monongahela River—in effect, to Andrew Carnegie's back door at Braddock and Homestead. Although the railroad existed only on paper, the paper was important, and it was this that Vanderbilt, working through the Reading Railroad, took over in 1883.[54]

Carnegie, quite naturally, heard of this interesting development in its formative stage, and was eager to promote it. He and Henry Oliver of the Oliver Iron Works, along with a few other

Pittsburgh manufacturers, quickly subscribed $5,000,000 to the enterprise, an amount which represented a third of the capital stock.[55] At long last, Carnegie saw an end to the Pennsylvania monopoly. In the summer of 1884 the difficult work of grading, building bridges, and digging tunnels that would take the South Pennsylvania across the broad Susquehanna and through the Allegheny Mountains to the banks of the Monongahela began, and Carnegie could hardly wait for the road to be completed. In November he wrote to W. C. Whitney, chairman of the board, urging that the construction be speeded up. Carnegie felt that there was no need to waste time on double trackage; a single track would do. "It is, believe me, folly to prepare for more business than a single track is amply competent to carry for some years to come. . . . By pursuing the policy suggested communication can be opened for about the $15,000,000 we have." [56] A single line would be all that was needed to run alongside the Pennsylvania's main line to force that company to listen to reason.

By midwinter of 1884–85, Carnegie confidently expected to see the South Pennsylvania open for traffic by July of the following year. The orders were in for the rails, and these orders, one can be sure, were given top priority at the E.T. plant in Braddock. Already, without a single rail or tie laid, the prospect of real competition in western Pennsylvania was having a most salutary effect upon the attitude of the Pennsylvania Railroad in fixing freight rates for the coming year. Carnegie had little difficulty in December 1884 in obtaining the rates he wanted. In January he was able to write to President George Roberts:

There remains under your administration only one survival of the previous policy which made every manufacturer in Pittsburgh a bitter enemy of the Penna. R.R. Co. While you have removed every other flagrant case of injustice, I have often wondered why you permitted this to mar your reputation. I allude of course to the charge made on Ore from Cleveland to Pittsburgh and Johnstown. . . . I wish you could find time to give this matter your personal attention not allowing your subordinates to deter you from going to the bottom of it. I know the transporter is suffering equally with the manufacturer and I dislike very much to say to you that we must have lower rates. I

511

can only say, we believe the best policy for both is to meet low rates and run our mills and our tracks full, thus producing lower cost.[57]

In tone this was quite a different letter from that of a year before when Carnegie had screamed "infamy" and had threatened mass public protest. One did not have to threaten verbally when a more powerful threat was at that moment being constructed with pickaxes and steam shovels in the Allegheny wilderness. One could even be somewhat deprecatory in suggesting lower rates. It was a lovely, comfortable feeling, and it is hoped that Carnegie enjoyed it to the fullest, for it was not to last long.

All of the industrial and financial powers in America were watching the approaching battle between the two titans of the railroad world, the New York Central and the Pennsylvania, with quite varied reactions. For the great coking and steel industries of western Pennsylvania, it was with unfeigned joy; for the steel industries of Chicago, who had long enjoyed the advantage which competitive freight rates had given them over Carnegie and Cambria, it was with deep regret; and for certain financial interests on Wall Street, it was with outright consternation.

One of this last group was J. P. Morgan, the son of Carnegie's old London banking patron, Junius S. Morgan. And Morgan, more than anyone else, was in a position to do something to end what he could only regard as insane competition. As a member of the New York Central's board of directors, he had a direct and personal interest in the welfare of that company. But unlike Vanderbilt, who sought revenge against the Pennsylvania and the immediate gains that might accrue from this open invasion of the enemy's territory, Morgan had a long range view of rail transportation. He was an international banker first, and his railroad directorship was quite secondary to this large interest. He had a responsibility to those clients of his, both domestic and foreign, to whom he had sold the bonds of both the New York Central and the Pennsylvania. He could not allow them to be placed in jeopardy by ruinous competition. He decided to use his directorship in the New York Central to intervene directly and to bring about an agreement between these great rivals, if it was at all possible to do so.

In the spring of 1885, Morgan hurried off to Europe to meet William Vanderbilt, who was vacationing there, and to accompany him home. In that period of time, he was able to persuade the reluctant Vanderbilt to accept his larger, ecumenical view of the business world, in which there was no place for destructive competition, but rather a need for what Morgan chose to call that "community of interest" which fostered co-operative agreements and mutual respect for "spheres of influence" to the profitable advantage of all concerned. With Vanderbilt's begrudging consent, the stage was set for that momentous summer meeting which Morgan had worked so hard to arrange, bringing together the principals in the dispute.

On a hot July morning in 1885, George Roberts, president of the Pennsylvania Railroad, and his able vice president, Frank Thomson, accepted J. P. Morgan's kind invitation to join him on his yacht, *Corsair,* ostensibly to escape the sweltering heat of Philadelphia. But Morgan hoped to bring about more than climatic relief by this little outing, for aboard the *Corsair,* in addition to Roberts, Thomson, and Morgan, was the affable and conciliatory Chauncey Depew, recently appointed president of the New York Central. Depew was under instruction from Vanderbilt to get an agreement with the Pennsylvania on the terms outlined by Morgan. Depew did most of the talking while Morgan sat silently by, wagging his big cigar in assent; for, after all, Morgan had coached Depew carefully. Depew was already on his way to becoming America's most famous afterdinner speaker, and on this hot afternoon, while sitting under the gaily striped awning aft of the *Corsair*'s single stack, Depew had ample opportunity to put his oratorical skills to test. He was at his most affable and persuasive best. And the terms he outlined were simple—an easy exchange of *quid pro quo*—the New York Central's as yet unconstructed South Pennsylvania line *quid* for the mysterious owner's West Shore line *quo.* The New York Central would turn over the South Pennsylvania charter, rights-of-way, and construction so far completed to the Pennsylvania Railroad for its disposal in any way it saw fit. In exchange, the New York Central would be permitted to buy the West Shore line out of bankruptcy and take a long-term lease on its operation. Both companies, in short, would recognize the other's territorial integrity and sovereign rights.

Thomson was easily convinced, but Roberts proved to be much more suspicious of Morgan's and Depew's motives. The exchange looked too good, and Depew was a little too glib. All this talk must mean that Vanderbilt had some trick or other up his sleeve. It was not until shortly before the *Corsair* pulled up to the dock in Jersey City, when Morgan himself took over the negotiations and with irrefutable logic pointed out the folly of this competition, that Roberts relented in his stubborn opposition. As he stepped upon the gangplank, he quite abruptly shook Morgan's hand and said, "I will agree to your plan and do my part." [58]

For Carnegie, this meeting aboard the *Corsair* between the presidents of America's two most powerful railroads was something like the meeting between the Emperor Napoleon and Czar Alexander I, aboard a raft on the river Nieman near Tilsit, with Carnegie playing the luckless role of the Prussian king, Frederick William III. The only difference between Carnegie and his Hohenzollern counterpart is that Carnegie was not subjected to the anguish of pacing the river bank while the mighty rulers deliberated. He knew nothing about Morgan's little cruise up the Hudson until he was informed by a brief communiqué from the South Pennsylvania directors a week later that all construction work on the line would be suspended indefinitely. The secret was soon out—the New York Central had sold out the line to the Pennsylvania, and in so doing they had sold out their friends in Pittsburgh. For once, Carnegie did not own the controlling interest in a company in which he had heavily invested. His protests were unavailing. He could do nothing except curse the peacemaker. How appropriately named was Morgan's yacht, *Corsair,* for, like the old pirate ships, it had suddenly appeared over the horizon and in a matter of hours had snatched away the prize that Carnegie had worked for years to obtain. From that time on, Carnegie's long-standing amicable relations with the House of Morgan were terminated, and thereafter he regarded J. P. Morgan with the greatest suspicion.

The Pennsylvania was now free to do with its projected rival anything it chose. It chose to do nothing. No superstructure was ever built across the magnificent bridge piers in the Susquehanna, no rail laid upon the carefully prepared grades or through the tunnels that had been blasted out of solid rock. A roadbed that had been cut through part of the most rugged terrain in the eastern United States—at a cost of more than two thousand lives—was allowed to revert back to its wilderness state. Grass and weeds crept over the embankments, the headless bridge piers stood like ancient ruins in the rivers, and the tunnels were left to the bats and lichen. Fifty years later, however, engineers working for the Commonwealth of Pennsylvania in building the nation's first great superhighway would find the grading and the tunnels still intact, and would build the Pennsylvania Turnpike on the very same roadbed that had been constructed for the South Pennsylvania Railroad.[59] Eventually Vanderbilt's and Carnegie's road did provide a rival transportation line to the Pennsylvania after all. The great semitrailers and buses that roar down the four lane concrete road and through the tunnels of western Pennsylvania today carry the freight and passengers that once belonged exclusively to the Pennsylvania Railroad.

Such a far-distant triumph over the Pennsylvania's monopoly could provide no solace or relief for Carnegie. Once again he had to resort to the annual freight rate negotiations, the angry hagglings, the protests, the conniving maneuvers for rebates with the constant, gnawing suspicion that other steel companies were getting better rates or bigger rebates than he. The same old letters to the detested Wilson had to be written: "Our people here show me some rather startling freight bills. For instance: limestone which you have been sending us in your empty westbound cars at 60½¢ per gross ton, freight is now billed at $1.37 per gross ton." [60]

In another letter, again protesting a raise in rates, Carnegie wrote Wilson, "As the State has not interfered with you it seems you have if not wantonly—at least prematurely, created a great disturbance in the business affairs of your best customer, which a little patience upon your part might have shown you to be unnecessary." [61] The more Carnegie thought over that initial phrase, "as the State has not interfered with you," which he had written in anger, the more pregnant with possibilities it seemed when studied with sober rationality. He had tried all the other expedients, appeals to the president and stockholders of the Pennsylvania, threats of mass meetings, even the effort to construct a rival line. Why not state action? There had been effective laws

515

passed in the Midwestern states. There was now Federal legislation in the form of the newly enacted Interstate Commerce
Commission—though it, unfortunately, did not affect a great percentage of Carnegie's freight traffic with the Pennsylvania Railroad, most of which was intrastate. What Pennsylvania needed
was its own Granger Law. And so, quite easily and quickly, Carnegie tossed aside any laissez-faire or Social Darwinian scruples he
might have professed and became an outspoken proponent of legislation that would permit the state government to intervene directly in the conduct of a private business enterprise.

Carnegie's effort to get state regulation of the Pennsylvania
Railroad reached its climax in the spring of 1889, when the issue
was brought before the state assembly at Harrisburg. Carnegie
was invited to state his views. His address, which was later published under the title "Pennsylvania's Industrial and Railroad
Policy," was a masterful summary of the problems facing Pennsylvania, and, particularly, western Pennsylvania industrialists. In a
wholly realistic manner, he presented the natural advantages that
Pennsylvania as a state held in the development of its industrial
potential, and he quite properly assessed its major advantage to
be fuel—the anthracite coal deposits in the eastern part of the
state and the soft, bituminous coal, best in the world for coke,
and the natural gas of western Pennsylvania. The state's greatest
disadvantage lay in its distance from the best iron ore sources of
the continent and the necessity for the long, overland transportation of this basic raw material. All of this was, of course, but a
preface to the main purposes of his remarks, which were to attack
the monopolistic position of the Pennsylvania Railroad and to ask
for remedial legislation from the state.

"As a result of careful investigation," he announced to the
startled legislators, "I have reached the conclusion that a reduction of one third in the present freight rates would still leave the
railway companies a fair profit." [62] He then gave precise figures
of profits earned by the principal railways of the country per ton
of freight carried one mile during the years 1885 through 1887:
New York Central 5.9 mills; New York, Lake Erie, 6.27 mills;
and, as could be expected, the highest profits went to the Pennsylvania, 7.52 mills.[63] "This gigantic corporation," Carnegie
charged, "exacted last year upon its mainline and branches be-

516

tween Pittsburgh and Philadelphia $13,171,604 profit, no less than 93½ per cent of all its traffic being local, that is *Pennsylvania* traffic . . . not a single combination of properties owned by the Pennsylvania Railroad Company beyond the limits of the state, either East or West, paid its expenses and charges. All entailed a loss, to be made up by profits charged upon Pennsylvania traffic of the main line. Here we have a Pennsylvania corporation levying upon the state, whose creature it is, a tax of fully $3,000,000 per annum beyond a fair return upon its stock." [64]

The *Corsair* peace settlement between the New York Central and the Pennsylvania still rankled. Carnegie made the charge, which he could not substantiate, that it was the Pennsylvania, not the New York Central, which was paying off the investors in the now defunct South Pennsylvania line. "The money paid to the South Pennsylvania people is not Vanderbilt's money; it was or is to be taken from the Pennsylvania Railroad Company in some form or other; so that the Pennsylvania Railroad Company has used the millions extracted unjustly from the state of Pennsylvania to prevent the southern counties from obtaining railroad facilities. . . . The Pennsylvania Railroad Company has killed the South Pennsylvania Railroad, your courts and your Constitution to the contrary notwithstanding. Such is the melancholy story of the effort to develop still further the resources of our state." [65]

Carnegie then gave illustrations of what this monopolistic situation meant in terms of freight costs at Pittsburgh compared with costs at terminals such as Chicago, where there were competing facilities: two and a half times the cost for bringing coke from Connellsville to Pittsburgh for those trains marked for Carnegie Brothers as for those marked for Chicago: 50 per cent more for bringing ore to Pittsburgh from the Great Lakes than to the Hocking Valley of Ohio, which was fifty miles farther. "Is not this monstrous?" Carnegie shouted.[66]

He concluded by demanding from the legislature "the passage of a State Commerce law similar in scope to the Interstate Commerce law, and the appointment of suitable commissioners to supervise the transportation charges of our railways. . . . If there be not time this session for a complete act, give us before you adjourn a simple act . . . making it unlawful . . . for a Pennsylvania railroad to charge more for similar service in the state

517

upon materials for Pennsylvania manufacturers than they charge manufacturers beyond the state. This would remedy nine-tenths of our wrongs." [67] Again Carnegie threatened that the people of Pittsburgh might be forced to take to the streets to demand justice if relief were not given. "The people of Pittsburgh lined the streets on a memorable occasion before the rebellion broke out, and prevented guns being taken from the arsenal to be shipped South. . . . Are they to be forced into a similar protest against the Pennsylvania Railroad Company carrying supplies past Pittsburgh furnaces to furnaces in other states upon terms they refuse us?" [68]

It was a powerful speech—the speech of a Radical Populist demanding governmental regulation, not a Social Darwinist preaching laissez faire. The legislators may have been moved, even frightened, by Carnegie's precise statistics and impassioned oratory, but the good old days, when it was said that the Pennsylvania legislature could not adjourn until Tom Scott dismissed it, were not entirely past. The Pennsylvania Railroad, embracing the whole state, was a far more powerful lobby than Carnegie, who spoke only for the Pittsburgh district. President Roberts could still snap his fingers and the legislature would obediently adjourn with no action taken. Carnegie had yet to find an effective ploy to use against the power of the Pennsylvania.

Freight costs remained Carnegie's special concern in the years after Frick took over the active management of Carnegie Brothers. But it was a concern that Frick did not share. On the contrary, he was frequently embarrassed both by the nature of Carnegie's suggested remedies and the language in which these proposals were couched. State laws to regulate private business and to set an upper limit in profits, mob action in the streets to prevent the through transit of trains—these to Frick were the crazy ideas and intemperate language of a socialist demagogue, not a respectable leader of industry. There was also the foolish expenditure of capital funds in a futile attempt to build a rival line to compete against the power of the great Pennsylvania. Frick felt that Carnegie would have been far better off to have kept that $5,000,000 to pay his freight bills. The Pennsylvania gave good service, better than any other line in the country. When it promised delivery, it delivered the correct amounts, and delivered them on time.

Nor could Frick ever forget, as apparently Carnegie frequently did, that not only was Carnegie Brothers a customer of the railroads but that the railroads were also the most important customers of Carnegie Brothers. How could you expect to sell rails to clients if you kicked them in the teeth or threatened to refuse to pay their legitimate bills? Frick was determined that under his management the long-standing feud between Carnegie and the Pennsylvania would be muted as much as it was in his power to accomplish. Soon after Carnegie's inflammatory speech to the Pennsylvania legislature, Frick wrote: "It is very much pleasanter to agree than differ with you and in most things I would and will defer to your judgment because there is no one whose attitude I hold in as high esteem, but I always hold to the opinion that your attack on P.R.R. was wrong and I should deprecate its renewal." [69]

Frick was perhaps more aware than Carnegie was of the generous contribution that the Frick Coke Company received annually from the Pennsylvania in the form of secret rebates. He tried his best to convince Carnegie that "our interests lie in the future with the P.R.R." [70] But Carnegie remained unconvinced. He continued to scream about the high cost of freight rates and to dream about an escape from the net of the Pennsylvania's monopoly. Sometime, some way, he would break out.

If Carnegie remained obsessed with the problem of freight rates, Frick's special villain was labor costs. It is not that Carnegie ignored the largest and most important item in the cost of production. Long before Frick joined the Carnegie associates, Carnegie was constantly prodding and needling his managers and individual department heads to get labor costs down by hiring fewer men, reducing hourly wages, and, whenever possible, introducing mechanical improvements that could replace human labor. In 1883 he asked all department heads to give him an evaluation of labor costs in their departments in a simplified form:

1st column —Pres. number of men employed
2nd column —No. which Capt. Jones thinks sufficient
3rd   "   —Compensation per ton
4th   "   —Compensation thought sufficient
5th   "   —Saving in no. of men
6th   "   —Saving in no. of dollars

519

Capt. Jones should be invited to make any remarks bearing
on the subject.[71]

Just as with freight costs, Carnegie was always convinced that
other mills were doing better on labor costs than he was. He was
continually begging rival plants to give him their monthly or
yearly wage scale figures, and if this information was not voluntarily given, he would send out directives to his salesmen to get him
the information even if they had to bribe rival plant foremen to
get it. He wrote to A. L. Griffin, the company's agent in Chicago,
asking him to get the current wage scale at Joliet in any way he
could. "I know we are paying our men too much and if you can
get me desired information, not opinions but *exact figures,* you
will do a great service to our firm." [72]

Armed with this information, he would then go to Jones to
argue labor costs with him. "Please read the enclosed information
carefully. The writer states the truth when he says 50 men per
furnace are all that are allowed in the West Coast District for 150
tons of iron. If we ever get up to the fair average of 180 tons per
day 60 men should be more than enough. . . . We cannot have
North Chicago or anybody else beat us on the Furnace practice." [73]

Carnegie needed all the ammunition he could get in his arguments with Jones over labor costs, for this was the only major area
in which the two men had sharp differences of opinion. Jones believed in working his men hard during the hours that they were
on the job, but he also believed in paying them well for that
work. Just as he demanded "a hell of a big salary" for himself, so
he also demanded good wages and fair treatment for his men.
And as long as he remained as general superintendent of the
Edgar Thomson works, his policy prevailed, in spite of Carnegie's
protests and figures to prove that E.T. was paying more in wages
than its competitors.

It was also Jones who, soon after taking over the management
of the E.T. plant, persuaded Carnegie to abandon the traditional
two-turn, twelve-hour shift in favor of the three-turn, eight-hour
shift. Jones was convinced that more productive work could be
obtained from men working only eight hours a day than could be
obtained from tired and careless men working half again as long.
What would be gained in attracting skilled men to Carnegie's em-

ployment as well as in reducing the amount of absenteeism and the number of expensive accidents would more than offset the cost of increasing the labor force by one-third. Speaking before the British Iron and Steel Institute in London in May 1881, Jones explained that the amazing production record of the Edgar Thomson works was in part a result of this revolutionary labor policy:

> In increasing the output of these works, I soon discovered it was entirely out of the question to expect human flesh and blood to labor incessantly for twelve hours, and therefore it was decided to put on three turns, reducing the hours of labor to eight. This proved to be of immense advantage to both the company and the workmen, the latter now earning more in eight hours than they formerly did in twelve hours, while the men can work harder constantly for eight hours, having sixteen hours for rest.[74]

Persuaded that if Edgar Thomson adopted the eight-hour day, other steel mills would have to follow suit, Carnegie had consented to this radical innovation in labor policy in his steel mills. In time this, along with what he regarded as the high wages paid by Jones to his men, came to be proud evidence of the enlightened labor relations in the Carnegie works.

But that old devil cost remained, and so Carnegie was torn between two desires: to reduce labor costs to a level competitive with rival steel manufacturers and, at the same time, to appear before the world as America's most enlightened and progressive employer of a mass labor force. Because there was no easy way to reconcile these two contradictory policies, critics have often raised the cry of hypocrisy against Carnegie, charging him with preaching one doctrine while practising quite another.

It was precisely on this charge of hypocrisy that Carnegie differed from his new partner and company president, Henry Clay Frick. No one could ever accuse Frick of hypocrisy in regard to labor policy. No talk from him on the inalienable rights of labor to organize in order to protect jobs, no softness on the eight-hour day, no backing down in a strike situation. Even in the notoriously antilabor coal fields of Connellsville, Frick was known as a tough man who brooked no nonsense from labor organizers.

521

Frick and Carnegie were united in their desire to reduce costs wherever possible, but just as Frick looked askance at some of Carnegie's methods to beat down freight rates, so Carnegie was reluctant to support Frick's simple, uncomplicated attitude toward labor, to regard men as a commodity like anything else used in manufacturing—something to be bartered for as cheaply as possible, to be used to its utmost capacity, and to be replaced by as inexpensive a substitute as was available.

If Carnegie could have subscribed wholeheartedly to Frick's position he would have saved himself a great deal of anguish and would have avoided the epithet of hypocrite that was to be hurled at him by both contemporary critics and later historians. To call Carnegie a hypocrite in his labor policy as stated in theory and as put into practice is too easy. For such a charge leaves unanswered the question of why Carnegie found it necessary to propound the doctrines that he did in the age in which he lived. No one expected the late-nineteenth-century industrialist to provide labor with a Bill of Rights. Frick, not Carnegie, was the norm, and to deviate from that norm was to ask for trouble. Then what compelled Carnegie to write his two remarkable essays for *Forum* magazine in 1886? Why had he gone out of his way to spell out a policy which could not fail later to embarrass him and make him vulnerable to the charge of hypocrisy?

To answer these questions requires a far more profound insight into Carnegie's personality and career than the simple charge of hypocrisy can provide. In part, the answer lies in Carnegie's vanity, in his desire to be loved and admired by all Americans. A special drawer in his big roll-top desk was labeled "Gratitude and sweet words," and it was one of the tasks of his personal secretary to clip out any flattering notice of Carnegie that appeared in the public press and to file it in this drawer for Carnegie's later perusal and enjoyment. And in part, the answer may be found in the ability of Captain Jones to convince him that an enlightened labor policy was good business practice, and that his two basic desires, to make money and to be a kind and good employer, were not antithetical, but rather complementary. A well-rested, well-paid, highly trained employee could produce twice as much with far less waste of raw materials than an under-paid, over-worked, ignorant peasant brought over from the steppes of

eastern Europe. Jones's favorite workers were what he called
" 'Buckwheats'—young American boys judiciously mixed" in
their ethnic background.[75] As long as Jones remained the dominant figure in the Carnegie steel mills, his influence prevailed in
labor policy.

But, above all, the answer lies in Carnegie's lifelong quest to
reconcile the Radical egalitarianism of his Dunfermline childhood with the capitalistic success that he enjoyed in manhood.
For his own peace of mind he had to believe that he had not betrayed the faith of his fathers when he became a multimillionaire
and an employer of tens of thousands of men. He once wrote that
of all the lines in Robert Burns's poems he loved, the one that
meant the most to him was "Thine own reproach alone do fear."
Indeed, Carnegie was so confident of his own abilities that it was
the only reproach he *could* fear. But fear it he did, and somehow
he had to justify his kind of life to himself. This was the motivation that had impelled him to write the *Forum* essays on labor
that he was never allowed to forget.

The first essay, which appeared in April 1886, painted a picture of sweetness and light between capital and labor in the
United States. He stressed the remarkable advances that labor had
made in the preceding 300 years, moving from serfdom to a position of "equal terms with the purchaser of his labor. He sells or
witholds it as may seem best to him. He negotiates and thus rises
to the dignity of an independent contractor." Carnegie had to
admit that friction still existed between capital and labor—an occasional "collision where there should be combination. . . . A
strike or a lockout is, in itself, a ridiculous affair. . . . In this it
resembles war between two nations." Carnegie looked forward to
the time when such "collisions" would be as rare as international
war appeared to be in the late nineteenth century. He discussed
various suggestions that had been proposed to eliminate such
strife, including co-operatives, compulsory arbitration, and trade
unions. It was the last which he regarded as the best hope for
peaceful co-operation between management and labor. "Some establishments in America," he wrote in his defense of unions,
"have refused to recognize the right of men to form themselves
into these unions; although I am not aware that any concern in
England would dare to take this position. This policy, however,

may be regarded as only a temporary phase of the situation. The right of the working men to combine and to form trades-unions is no less sacred than the right of the manufacturer to enter into associations and conferences with his fellows, and it must be sooner or later conceded. . . . My experience has been that trades-unions upon the whole are beneficial both to labor and capital." He concluded this article with a special plea for the adoption of a sliding-scale plan in wage compensations. "What we must seek is a plan by which the men will receive high wages when their employers are receiving high prices for the product, and hence are making large profits; and *per contra,* when the employers are receiving low prices for products, and therefore small if any profits, the men will receive low wages." [76] This was Carnegie's version of profit sharing, and it was to be adopted in all of his plants.

Carnegie had bad fortune in timing: his Pollyanna-like article appeared at the very moment when all hell was breaking loose on the American labor front, culminating in the Haymarket Square affair and the national hysteria that followed that explosion. Carnegie felt obliged to rush back into print with another article for *Forum.* He attempted to minimize the significance of the disorders, pointing out that there had been only 250,000 men involved in the strikes out of over 20,000,000 workers employed in the United States. He blamed the press for magnifying the crisis and creating a national panic. Most significantly, he placed the major responsibility for the strikes upon management, not labor. "We expect from the presumably better-informed party representing capital much more than from labor; and it is not asking too much of men intrusted [sic] with the management of great properties that they should devote some part of their attention to searching out the causes of disaffection among their employees, and where they exist, that they should meet the men more than half way in the endeavor to allay them." On the other hand, he warned labor that the nation could not tolerate violence and lawlessness. "The 'deadline' has been definitely fixed between the forces of disorder and anarchy and those of order. . . . Rioters assembling in numbers and marching to the pillage will be remorselessly shot down; not by the order of the government above the people . . . but by the masses of peaceable and orderly citizens of all classes in their own community." He hastened to add that violence was no longer necessary, for "Public sentiment now supports the rights of labor not only in wages but in hours. . . . And the time approaches, I hope, when it will be impossible in this country to work men twelve hours a day continuously."

Carried away with his own enthusiasm for occupying Solomon's throne in industrial America, he then wrote the fateful paragraph which would come back to mock him in the years ahead:

> While public sentiment has rightly and unmistakably condemned violence even in the form for which there is the most excuse, I would have the public give due consideration to the terrible temptation to which the workingman on a strike is sometimes subjected. To expect that one dependent upon his daily wage for the necessaries of life will stand peaceably and see a new man employed in his stead is to expect much. . . . In all but a very few departments of labor it is unnecessary and I think improper to subject men to such an ordeal. In the case of railways and a few other employments it is, of course, essential for the public wants that no interruption occur, and in such case substitutes must be employed; but the employer of labor will find it much more to his interest, wherever possible, to allow his works to remain idle and await the result of a dispute than to employ a class of men that can be induced to take the place of other men who have stopped work. Neither the best men as men, nor the best men as workers, are thus to be obtained. There is an unwritten law among the best workmen: "Thou shalt not take thy neighbor's job."

He concluded by paying special tribute to such men as T. V. Powderly, head of the Knights of Labor, and "Messrs. Wihle [sic] and Martin of the Amalgamated Iron and Steel Association. . . . The disturbance is over and peace again reigns; but let no one be unduly alarmed at frequent disputes between capital and labor. Kept within legal limits, they are encouraging symptoms, for they betoken the desire of the working-man to better his condition; and upon this desire hang all the advancements of the masses." [77]

This remarkable essay, coming from America's leading steel industrialist at the very moment that the country was still gripped by hysteria over the recent labor disorders, created a national furor. Organized labor, quite naturally, regarded it as a kind of Magna Carta, handed down by a new and far more benevolent and genial King John. What matter if Carnegie was so ignorant of union affairs even within his own industry as to misspell consistently throughout both of his essays the name of the able national president of the Amalgamated Iron and Steel Association, Weihe. Had not Carnegie, with that beautiful statement, "Thou shalt not take thy neighbor's job," given to unionism the very slogan it needed as the rallying cry against the hired Pinkerton mercenaries and the poor, frightened, and exploited scab labor, with which management was trying to beat back the forces of organized labor? "Little Andy" had overnight become the worker's hero, and that desk drawer of his was filling up nicely with congratulatory letters and editorials from trade union publications. The Brotherhood of Locomotive Engineers was sufficiently moved to name a division after him and to make him an honorary member. Carnegie, in happy acceptance of these honors, responded: "As you know, I am a strong believer in the advantages of Trade Unions, and organizations of work men generally, believing that they are the best educative instruments within reach. . . . I feel honored by your adopting my name. It is another strong bond, keeping me to performance of the duties of life worthily, so that I may never do anything of which your Society may be ashamed." [78]

The managerial class and the conservative press reacted quite differently. His own partners were highly embarrassed by his remarks. Frick, who must have read these essays in grim, tight-lipped silence, later credited to their unfortunate appearance part of his own difficulties with labor in the coal fields the following spring and Carnegie's quick surrender to labor's demands in that incident. Frick's temporary resignation from the presidency of the coke company in May 1887 was in no small part due to the effect that Carnegie's articles had had on both workingmen and Carnegie alike. Most of Carnegie's other partners kept a disapproving silence. Only Cousin Dod Lauder dared to reprimand Carnegie, and he only by a parable. He told Carnegie the story of a man, killed by a streetcar, who had no papers upon him and was placed on public view in an undertaker's parlor for identification. After a while a wealthy woman drove up, identified the corpse as her husband, and then ordered the most expensive funeral the establishment had to offer. As she was leaving, the eager undertaker's assistant, in showing her to the door, inadvertently bumped against the slab upon which the corpse was displayed. The jolt knocked the dead man's mouth open, revealing a handsome gold tooth. The lady, taking another look at the corpse, at once canceled the order, saying that she must have made a mistake because her missing husband had no such gold tooth. As she went out the door, the disappointed undertaker turned angrily on the corpse and cried, "What kind of an idiot are you anyway? If you'd only known enough to keep your damned mouth shut—!" [79] Carnegie got the point and laughed uproariously, but neither then nor later could he ever keep his mouth shut.

Labor lost no time in giving Carnegie an opportunity to test his theories in practice, and in these first trials Carnegie, with some difficulty, passed labor's examination standards. In the first test, which was directed against the Frick Coke Company, Carnegie could naturally pass with a very high mark from labor, for it was to his distinct advantage as a steel manufacturer to yield quickly to the coke workers' demands. But in so doing, he temporarily lost Frick's services to the company and permanently acquired Frick's distrust.

In the second test of his principles Carnegie did not do well at all, for this involved a question of retreating from a position he had taken both in practice and in theory in regard to the eight-hour day. The adoption of a three-turn operation at Edgar Thomson had not brought about an universal acceptance of this practice throughout the steel industry as Carnegie had hoped. By 1887, ten years after its adoption by Jones at E.T., the eight-hour day could be found in no other major steel plant in the country. Carnegie became convinced he could no longer afford a three-shift labor force, and ordered the reluctant Jones to announce that beginning on 1 January 1888, Edgar Thomson would adopt the standard two-turn, twelve-hour shift. The E.T. workers immediately went on strike. After lengthy conversations with Jones to make sure he had his support, Carnegie announced that the plants would stay closed until the men would accept his terms. When a group of labor representatives from the local strike com-

527

mittee of the Association showed up at his home in New York in April, after the strike had been on for four months, Carnegie knew he was winning. He wined and dined them, showed them the sights, and sent them home with a promise that he would come to Pittsburgh soon with a profit-sharing plan he was sure the workers would like.

Three weeks later Carnegie appeared before the assembled workers of E.T. The atmosphere was tense, and Lauder and Phipps feared an explosion. After a few placatory remarks, Carnegie asked for individual statements of grievances from the men. There was an awkward silence, then one worker stood up, and tremulously began, "Mr. Carnegie, take my job, for instance—" He got no further. Carnegie, with ready wit, interjected, "Mr. Carnegie takes no man's job." The men roared with laughter, stamped their feet, and shouted their approval of "Thou shalt not take thy neighbor's job." The ice had been broken in a most satisfactory way. Carnegie outlined his proposal of a sliding scale of wages as he had stated it in his *Forum* article, and then gave the men an option, to vote for a continuance of the eight-hour day with reduced wages and no sliding scale, or a return to the twelve-hour day with a profit-sharing sliding wage scale. Carried by the momentum of the meeting, the men hardly realized that what was being offered them was an option of "heads-I-win, tails-you-lose." By secret ballot, a thousand workers voted for the twelve-hour day and the sliding scale. The plant was able to start work the next day, and the union then quickly capitulated. Carnegie had got what he wanted, and ever afterwards he could and did maintain that the twelve-hour day existed in his plants by the democratic process of the men themselves electing that system in order to receive higher pay. It was a nice sophistry which in time deceived even Carnegie himself.[80]

The third test came at labor-restless Homestead, in the summer of 1889. Carnegie was in Britain, as usual, but he had left the United States knowing that there was apt to be trouble over an attempt to institute the same sliding-scale policy at Homestead as had existed at E.T. since the settlement of the strike there the previous year. When Carnegie took over Homestead in 1883, the skilled workers were organized into six lodges of the Amalgamated Iron and Steel Association, numbering about 800 skilled workers out of a total labor force of 3800. They represented the most powerful labor organization anywhere within the Carnegie companies, and they were paid on a flat tonnage basis. With the recent mechanical innovations at Homestead, production had greatly increased, and with this tonnage increase, the men had, of course, greatly benefited. Any attempt to adopt a sliding scale at Homestead, no matter how generous, would in effect mean a reduction in wages for the skilled tonnage men. The Association was prepared to resist the scale. The current contract was due to expire on 30 June, and on 18 May the management announced that the contract would not be renewed on a tonnage basis, but rather on a sliding-scale basis, and that "men desirous of employment will be required to sign an agreement" with management to work under the sliding-scale plan. It was the phrase "required to sign an agreement" that appeared ominous to the Amalgamated Association, for it implied individual contracts between workers and management and the exclusion of the union from its bargaining position. It was largely for this reason that the lodges were determined to fight, and they urged the men not to sign the new contract. The affirmative response of the men to the union's request was nearly unanimous, and on 1 July Homestead shut down.[81]

Carnegie from his post abroad urged Abbott to stand firm. "Homestead is settled. No use fighting there. If it never runs it will not start except with rates it can run upon steadily and compete with others." [82]

Abbott, however, became panicky in this first major strike situation under his presidency of Carnegie, Phipps. Disregarding Carnegie's orders, he advertised for strikebreakers in early July. Fortunately, when a small group of immigrant and Negro laborers showed up at the plant under the escort of the sheriff and 125 deputies, the huge crowd of strikers—nearly 2000 men—frightened the sheriff, the deputies, and the would-be strikebreakers away. Had the sheriff elected to make a stand, blood might have flowed at Homestead in the summer of 1889.

In the meantime, the workers at E.T. threatened to walk out in a sympathy strike. Carnegie had left instructions that if this should happen, Captain Jones should talk with the workers and say to them, "Now boys, keep clear of this fight. *Don't agree to act until I return*. Keep free and I'll try and get the firm to let us run another year under the scale." [83] Whether or not Jones would be effective in playing this kind of conciliatory role Abbott did not wait to see. Threatened by violence at Homestead and a mass walkout throughout all of the Carnegie plants, Abbott capitulated. A meeting was held with the strike leaders and "a compromise" was reached. The union accepted the sliding scale and was formally recognized as the sole bargaining agent for Homestead. A new contract was signed; it was to last for three years and to expire on 1 July 1892. All of Homestead celebrated that night, and there were frequent cheers for both the union and "the little boss," the man who would not take his neighbor's job. The men had reason to cheer. For, in spite of the sliding scale, the union was more strongly entrenched than ever before. Because it was now accepted as the only bargaining agent with management, not a man could be hired or fired at Homestead without the union's approval.[84]

Carnegie had passed the third test that labor had given him with flying colors, but at considerable discomfiture to management and at considerable cost to his own pocketbook. He was no longer quite so pleased with the plaudits of labor as he had been. He wrote to Abbott after the settlement:

> I understand how trying the position was. Reductions seem big in tonnage with men of three mills, a move in right direction the effect of which will be permanent. So much is clear gain. The great objection to the compromise is of course that it was made under intimidation—our men in other works now know that we will "confer" with law breakers. At this distance one can be very brave no doubt, [but] I don't like this feature at all. Seems to me a curt refusal to have anything to do with these men would have brought matters right in less time than to you seems possible. Whenever we are compelled to make a stand we shall have to shut down and *wait* as at E.T. until part of the men vote to work, then it is easy. I am glad however we have three years of peace under sliding scale. Your statement published in New York Tribune about this was to the point— admirable—Scale can be made fair where it is not and then we are at peace.
>
> So glad Schwab proved so able. If we have a real manager of

men there Homestead will come out right now. Everything is in the man. . . . Mrs. Carnegie sends her congratulations on end of troubled days. "I know Mr. Abbott did the best thing." Good bye. Yours ever, A.C.[85]

Carnegie's flattering reference to Charles Schwab indicates how fast and how far this ambitious young man had risen since he had first joined the Carnegie ranks only eight years before as a lowly stake driver in the E.T. mill at a dollar a day. Schwab, the son of a German livery stable operator, had been born in Williamsburg, Pennsylvania, in 1862. When Charles was only a few months old, his family moved to the small, entirely Catholic settlement of Loretto, Pennsylvania, high up in the Alleghenies near Cresson. There he had helped his father in the livery stable and on occasion had ridden with his father on the daily trip to Cresson, carrying mail and bringing back supplies. This was Loretto's only contact with the outside world. As a small boy, Schwab frequently saw the great Andrew Carnegie at his summer home in Cresson, and on one proud occasion he got to hold Carnegie's horse for him.

Schwab briefly attended St. Francis Academy in Loretto, but he was impatient to start making money, an ambition which his father, with a large family to support, encouraged. After several years of working in his father's livery stable, young Charlie, seventeen years old, went to Braddock and got a job as a clerk in a grocery store. Captain Jones patronized this store, and Schwab lost no time in striking up an acquaintance with the almost legendary steelmaker, the hero of all young men in Braddock. Never one to be shy about advancing himself, Schwab, a month after meeting Jones, asked him for a job at Edgar Thomson. Jones sized up the husky young lad with the cheerful grin, and replied that he reckoned Schwab knew enough to drive stakes. Jones told him to be at the plant at seven the next morning.

Thus began Schwab's meteoric rise in the Carnegie steel world. Six months after beginning work as a stake driver he was made superintendent in charge of the construction of new blast furnaces at Edgar Thomson. His work was a tremendous success, Carnegie asked to meet him, and from then on things went very well indeed for the eager young man from Loretto. From the first

531

moment, Carnegie liked Schwab immensely. Here was a young man who knew how to laugh, and Carnegie saw so few smiling faces among his harried and worried plant officials that Schwab's appearance was a welcome change. Charlie could make a joke out of anything and leave the old man doubled up and hooting with laughter. Jones quickly discovered that if he wanted a report approved by Carnegie, Charlie was the boy to take it to him. Schwab had become Carnegie's court favorite—chief jester and skilled acrobat, with a little juggling thrown in for good measure. What a relief his charm and good humor were from the grim seriousness of Frick or the rabbit timidity of Phipps! So, at the age of twenty-five, Schwab became superintendent of Homestead. He came out of the Homestead strike of 1889 smelling very fragrant indeed. Abbott got the blame for conceding too much, and Schwab got the credit for preventing violence. Carnegie had great plans for Schwab's future.

These plans were to materialize much more quickly and dramatically than Carnegie had expected or wanted. On the night of 26 September 1889, one of the newly constructed blast furnaces at Edgar Thomson suddenly exploded. Captain Jones, who was standing close by, jumped backward and fell onto the lower level car tracks, striking his head on the side of an ore car in falling. He died two days later without regaining consciousness. The greatest steelmaker in America was dead, killed by an accident on the job, as so many of his men before him had been.

No one could ever take the Captain's place. Edgar Thomson was Jones's masterpiece. He had built it, run it, improved upon it, year after year. He had more patents to his credit than any other single individual in the history of steelmaking. The Jones Mixer, a huge iron chest capable of holding 250 tons of liquid pig metal from many different blast furnaces, had revolutionized the making of steel by dispensing with the re-melting of pig iron in the converter's cupola. This one invention alone had saved Carnegie Brothers hundreds of thousands of dollars in the cost of producing steel. In Jones's desk there were patent rights for a dozen other major inventions for the making, rolling, and cutting of steel, dating from 1877 to 1889.[86] There were also hundreds of small improvements in the design, construction, and operation of the machinery which Jones had considered too trivial to patent but which had made significant contributions to the efficient operation of the Carnegie steel plants.

Jones had generously made available his patented inventions to all of Carnegie's plants, exacting only a small royalty fee on their use. The full value of these inventions, which now belonged to his estate, could not be accurately appraised, but Lauder and Phipps, checking over Jones's papers the day after his death, realized how important it was for the company to take possession of these patents. Two days after Jones's funeral, Lauder hurried over to Jones's home and got from his widow a bill of sale for all of Jones's patents, for which Carnegie Brothers paid Mrs. Jones the sum of $35,000. The amount that the company ultimately realized from these patent rights can never be calculated, but one can safely assume that Jones's patents proved to be at least as spectacular a bargain as the Duquesne plant was when Carnegie bought it the following year.[87] Jones's inventive genius, his skillful handling of workmen, his restless drive and energy in promoting the company's success, his beneficial influence upon Carnegie, could not, unfortunately, be so easily purchased as his patent rights.

But E.T. needed a new chief superintendent, and Schwab was promoted to Jones's position. Schwab was only twenty-seven when he stepped into Jones's office, and he had many excellent qualifications for the job. There was a great deal more to Schwab than the charm of manner which had first attracted Carnegie's notice and favor. He knew far more, through diligent study of chemistry and metallurgy, than Jones had ever known about the science of making steel. He had something of Jones's personal magnetism in dealing with workmen and subordinate officials. He worked himself and others equally hard, and he set high standards for performance. The company was fortunate to have him in line as a successor to Jones. But he lacked Jones's intuitive feel about the making of steel which could not be compensated for by a technical knowledge of chemistry. His ambition was much more self-centered and less company-centered than Jones's had been, while at the same time he lacked Jones's independence. Carnegie liked Schwab because he carried out all orders given him, with no questions asked. And if there were no specific orders, Schwab could improvise brilliantly and then make Carnegie and the others believe that they had been Carnegie's orders all along. It would never occur to him to resign with periodic regularity, as Jones had, or, in yielding to a direct order, to mutter, as Jones did, in sarcastic parody of Carnegie's telegraphic orders from abroad, "Puppy dog number three, you have been beaten by puppy dog number two on fuel. Puppy dog number two, you are higher on labor than puppy dog number one." [88] There was no spirit of the maverick in Schwab. He was exceedingly well-trained in every way, and life for Carnegie would be much easier with him than it had ever been with Jones. But an age had ended with the death of Captain Jones. The days of Andrew Kloman and Captain Bill Jones were over. Steel would no longer be made by intuitive feel, nor steel companies directed by seat-of-the-pants drivers. It was now the age of the chemist and the corporate director. The future would belong to Frick and Schwab, and even Andrew Carnegie had become something of an anachronism.

The death of Jones, whom Frick had never liked because of his maverick spirit and his "softness on labor," in addition to Abbott's troubles at Homestead, convinced Frick that now was the right time for the company reorganization that he had long had in mind. He proposed to Carnegie that there be a single company to replace the dual organization of Carnegie Brothers and Carnegie, Phipps. He also argued strenuously for a much larger capitalization that would more realistically represent the true value of the Carnegie steel holdings. This increase in capitalization would also permit many of the able young men in the operational departments of the company to be rewarded with a partnership and a small interest in the company. This aspect of reorganization appealed strongly to Carnegie, who had always favored partnership interests rather than big salaries as the proper way to give compensation to his "young geniuses."

There remained one strong financial argument for keeping the fiction of two separate companies, even though the ownership of each was identical with the other. It had proved exceedingly useful to maintain two legally separate companies in order to provide working capital by discounting notes given by the one company to the other, and thus having the "two-name paper" required by banks and other credit facilities. Either company could also borrow from the surplus funds of the other when a short-term loan was needed, without having to resort to outside borrowing.[89] Frick, however, had an answer to that argument. In a letter to Carnegie of 10 February 1890, he pointed out that at present "there is outstanding $1,185,000.00 of paper made by Carnegie, Phipps & Co., to the order of Carnegie Bros. & Co., $860,000.00 of paper made by Carnegie Bros. & Co., to the order of Frick Coke Co., the proceeds of which was paid to Carnegie Bros. & Co., $590,000.00 of paper made by Carnegie Bros. & Co., to the order of Frick Coke Co., for the accommodations of the Frick Coke Co." In short, the Frick Coke Company was already being used and could continue to be used as the second company for financial arrangements without the necessity of keeping Carnegie, Phipps & Company alive for that purpose. "So you see," Frick continued, "a few months of such earnings as we are now having will enable us to get along without the necessity of taking paper from C.P. & Co. If anything of the kind is needed, the Frick Coke Co. can be used. Had a talk with Abbott who favors making one company." [90]

Frick had reason to be boastful of "the earnings we are now having." In the year that he had been in charge of Carnegie Brothers, profits had nearly doubled, from $1,941,555 to $3,540,000.[91] Carnegie's last argument against consolidation had now been disposed of. After months of study of the legal and financial issues involved, the consolidation was accomplished. Under the terms of the charter, which was to go into effect on 1 July 1892, Carnegie, Phipps & Company and Carnegie Brothers & Company were to sell their physical assets to, and be dissolved by, the Carnegie Steel Company, Limited. The combined capitalization of the two companies at the time of the merger was $10,000,000. Carnegie Steel was to be capitalized at $25,000,000, of which Andrew Carnegie would hold $13,833,333, or 55.33 per cent; Frick and Phipps would each hold $2,750,000, or 11 per cent, and the other nineteen partners would each hold 1 per cent. The remaining capital, 3.66 per cent, would be held in trust by Francis Lovejoy, secretary of the company, to be divided among deserving young men in the organization whom Carnegie might later wish to admit into the partnership.[92] Schwab, who in 1892 still did not have a partnership interest in the company, had his eye on that reserve. He was soon to get his reward.

The consolidation of all of Carnegie's steel operations had at last been effected, thanks to Henry Clay Frick's persistence. The new company included the four major steel plants—Edgar Thomson, Homestead, Duquesne, and Hartman—and the Upper and Lower Iron Mills, the Lucy Furnaces, the Keystone Bridge works, the Scotia mines, and the Larimer and Yonghiogheny coke works. Only the Henry C. Frick Coke Company kept its separate corporate existence. Of the original nine partners who had formed Carnegie, McCandless & Company for the manufacture of Bessemer steel in 1873, only Carnegie and Phipps remained as partners in the new Carnegie Steel Company. The twenty-two partners of Carnegie Steel elected Henry Clay Frick as chairman of this new association in recognition of his services in creating it. Andrew Carnegie's name for the first time did not appear as a member of the board of managers, but with a clear majority of the interest in his pocket, Carnegie remained as secure as ever in his position as the final authority in the company.

In September 1889, six months after Frick had taken over as president of Carnegie Brothers, Carnegie had written him a note of thanks: "Let me express the relief I feel in knowing that the important departments of our extended business are in the hands of a competent manager. Phipps and I exchanged congratulations upon this point. Now I only want to know how your hands can be strengthened." [93]

Two and a half years later, in looking over the profit sheets for that period, Carnegie had no reason to regret his earlier congratulatory message. With profits averaging $4,500,000 annually, he could now exclaim more fervently than before, "Was there ever such a business!" And Frick's hands had been considerably strengthened. He now headed a $25,000,000 company, the largest steel organization in the world. As for Carnegie, he was quite willing for others to move to the front and center, providing, of course, that the script for the show remained in his hands, and that he could scrutinize and criticize every gesture made, every line spoken, on this impressively large new stage.

CHAPTER XVI

Homestead 1892

On 1 July 1892 the Carnegie Steel Company came into being. It was the largest steel company in the world, capable of producing steel equal in amount to over half of the total production of steel in all of Great Britain.

Carnegie and Frick were inordinately proud of their creation, but, unhappily, they had selected a singularly inauspicious birth date for their new giant. For on that hot July morning all was not well within this vast corporate body that lay sprawled out from 33rd Street in Pittsburgh down along the steaming valley of the Monongahela to Duquesne, Pennsylvania, some fifteen miles to the south. The strong, right arm of the company, the recently acquired plant at Homestead, which had been converted into America's largest open hearth steel mill, lay paralyzed by strike and lockout, a paralysis that threatened to spread from the newest mill at Duquesne to the oldest at 29th Street in Pittsburgh.

It had been persistent labor difficulties at Homestead in the early 1880's that had enabled Carnegie to purchase at cost this impressive and dangerous new rival, only a mile down the river from Braddock. The Homestead plant, which had been built only three years before Carnegie acquired it on what had once been a prosperous farm called, ironically, the Amity Homestead, had the most modern and efficiently designed rail and beam rolling mills in the country. Carnegie was as pleased to acquire its remarkably well-designed facilities as he was to eliminate it as a rival to Edgar Thomson.

Unhappily for Carnegie, along with the purchase of Homestead's Bessemer converters and rolling mills came six highly organized and well-disciplined labor lodges of the powerful Amalgamated Association of Iron and Steel Workers. Carnegie, who was in the process of eliminating the Association from his plant at Braddock at the very moment he was buying Homestead, did not regard the acquisition of his labor organization as an asset. He was well acquainted with the Association and its effectiveness in organizing the most highly skilled workers within the iron and steel industry, for there had long been lodges of the Association within the company's Union Iron Mills at Pittsburgh as well as at Edgar Thomson.

If Carnegie did not like the Association for its constant potential threat to management, he had watched its development and had admired its effectiveness as an organization. The Amalgamated Association had been formed in 1876 by the merger of the three existing craft unions within the trade: the United Sons of Vulcan, a union of iron puddlers; the Associated Brotherhood of Rail Heaters; and the Iron and Steel Roll Hands Union. At the time of its formation, the Association had only 3000 members, but within fifteen years it had increased its membership eightfold and had become one of the most powerful craft unions within the country. Like the railroad brotherhoods, it remained fiercely elitist in its philosophy, refusing to consider the nonskilled and semiskilled workers for membership and resolutely opposing the efforts of the Knights of Labor to organize all iron and steel workers into one large industrial union. During the relatively prosperous years of the 1880's within the trade, the Association had had remarkably strong national leadership and had entrenched itself into the most important steel mills in the country, including those in the Pittsburgh, Youngstown, and Chicago-Joliet areas.[1]

Following the successful strike at Homestead in 1889, when William Abbott, the president of Carnegie, Phipps & Company, had agreed to the union's terms on tonnage scale rates and a terminal date for the three-year contract in exchange for the introduction of the sliding scale of wages at Homestead, the Association had emerged more powerful than ever before. Although it admitted only some 800 of the 3800 workers at Homestead, it could count on the loyalty and support of all the employees in any future labor disputes. To the disgruntled Frick, who, as chairman of the other company, Carnegie Brothers, had had no voice in the management of Homestead, it appeared that Abbott had in effect turned the management of the company over to the labor union. Technological improvements at Edgar Thomson in 1885 had displaced 57 of the 69 men on the heating furnaces, and 51 of the 63 men on the rail-mill train, so depleting the membership of the lodges there that Carnegie Brothers succeeded in closing down the union at the plant.[2] Frick now had no desire to see the remaining skilled workers at Edgar Thomson reintroduce the union in emulation of the victorious rollers and heaters at Homestead. Abbott, he felt, had been so frightened by the strike that he had, by the terms of the contract, given to the union full authority to hire and fire as well as to determine the working conditions within the plant. When Frick took over full authority of all plants within the Carnegie empire in 1892, he was determined that there would be no repetition of Abbott's soft-headed mismanagement when the contract with the Association at Homestead came up for renegotiation in the spring of that year.

Although the Association, having won out over management in the showdown with Abbott in the summer of 1889, looked forward with confidence to a similar success when the contract expired on 30 June 1892, it had little reason for that confidence. During those three years much had happened that would place the Association in a far more vulnerable position than it had been in 1889. First, and of primary importance, the lodges were dealing with quite a different man as managerial director than they had faced across the bargaining table three years before. Actually, the Association welcomed this challenge of management. Knowing Frick to be the toughest antilabor man in the industry, the Association felt that, if it could successfully bargain with him, it could meet any other challenge throughout the iron and steel industry. Indeed, all other steel companies were looking toward Homestead in that spring of 1892, as they had in 1889, knowing that they would be affected by the outcome of the confrontation of labor and management there. An official of Jones & Laughlin had spoken for the whole industry when he said, "This company will make no terms with its men until there is a settlement at Homestead." [3]

Frick had more than his iron will and grim determination to back his position, however. The 1889 strike and resulting confrontation had occurred at a moment when prices on steel rails and beams were high, and the company was behind in meeting its orders. But the situation in 1892 was quite the opposite. With overexpansion of facilities and technological improvements, production had increased even faster than demand. The obvious result was that prices continued to fall for both iron and steel. Carnegie announced in April 1892 in the trade journal *Engineering and Mining Journal* that "The making of pig iron has developed faster than the demand for it, resulting in large stocks in hand and low prices. . . . There must be a check on production . . . or prices will go lower yet." [4] The company, with the market in this condition, had no great fear of a prolonged cessation of work and, indeed, saw this as a most opportune time for a decisive confrontation with the union.

The Association, moreover, had been even further weakened during the preceding three years by technological advancements within the industry. Because the Association admitted only the highly skilled workers, it was particularly vulnerable to the introduction of new machinery, which reduced the number of skilled workers needed in any particular process of steelmaking.

The reduction of skilled workers was brought about not only by the new machines, but also by the simplification of the training process for a particular skill, making it easier for management to instruct new men in a shorter time to replace the skilled workers. Schwab boasted that he could take an untrained man with some basic intelligence about machinery—an American farm boy, for instance—and make a skilled melter of him within six weeks. [5] The potential for the use of strikebreakers was a growing, not a diminishing threat to the unions, in spite of Carnegie's noble words against the practice.

Finally, the rapid increase in the urban population during these years, caused by the expansion of immigration from central and southern Europe and the depressed farm conditions in America that brought an ever-increasing number of farm boys into the cities, meant that there was no shortage of labor available to industry in 1892. Hungry men were no more scrupulous in their observation of Carnegie's eleventh commandment, "Thou shalt not take thy neighbor's job," than was management. So, although national membership in the Amalgamated Association of Iron and Steel Workers had grown impressively in the preceding decade, and its success at Homestead in 1889 had enabled the union to obtain favorable contracts throughout the industry, the Association was actually in a far more precarious position in the summer of 1892 than it had ever been before. And it was then that it faced its greatest test.

There were long and serious talks between Frick and his major shareholder before Carnegie prepared to depart for Britain in late April 1892. Both the defenders of Frick and those of Carnegie have tried, ever since the calamity of Homestead, to place the responsibility for the decision to break the union on the other man. Although there were private conferences held in Carnegie's home in New York, for which no minutes nor written reports were kept, it is apparent from what evidence we have at hand that both men agreed that this was the proper time to end the Association's power at Homestead. They disagreed only on tactics to be used. Carnegie preferred to meet the issue head-on. On 4 April 1892 he prepared a notice which he asked Frick to post at the Homestead plant. It read in part:

> These Works having been consolidated with the Edgar Thomson and Duquesne and other mills, there has been forced upon this firm whether its Works are to be run "Union" or "Non-Union." As the vast majority of our employees are Non-Union, the Firm has decided that the minority must give place to the majority. These works therefore will be necessarily Non-Union after the expiration of the present agreement.
>
> This does not imply that the men will make lower wages. On the contrary, most of the men at Edgar Thomson and Duquesne Works, both Non-Union, have made and are making higher wages than those at Homestead which has hitherto been Union. . . . A scale will be arranged which will compare favorably with that at the other works named; that is to say, the Firm intends that the men of Homestead shall make as much as the men at either Duquesne or Edgar Thomson. Owing to the

great changes and improvements made in the Converting Works, Beam Mills, Open Hearth Furnaces, etc. . . . the products of the works will be greatly increased, so that at the rates per ton paid at Braddock and Duquesne, the monthly earnings of the men may be greater than hitherto. While the number of men required will, of course, be reduced, the extensions at Duquesne and Edgar Thomson as well as at Homestead will, it is hoped, enable the firm to give profitable employment to such of its desirable employees as may temporarily be displaced. . . .

This action is not taken in any spirit of hostility to labor organizations, but every man will see that the firm cannot run Union and Non-Union. It must be one or the other.

To this notice Carnegie added a personal note to Frick: "Should this be determined upon Mr. Potter [John A. Potter, superintendent of the Homestead Works] *should roll a large lot of plate ahead,* which can be finished, should the works be stopped for a time." [6] This note referred to the contract for armor plate which the Carnegie Steel Company had obtained from the Department of the Navy, and it was the only urgent order that the plant had to complete at this time.

Carnegie's tactics were clear: an open disavowal of the union at all plants within the Carnegie companies; a continuation of the sliding scale of wages, as established at Homestead in 1889; and the reduction of existing tonnage rates for those few skilled employees who were paid by tonnage production rather than by hourly rates. If the workmen refused to accept this policy decision, then Carnegie's private instructions to Frick were to close the plant and to wait the men out.

Carnegie's decision that the works within his company could no longer continue part union, part non-union, and that since "the vast majority of our employees are non-union, the minority must give place to the majority," seemed to be in flat contradiction to his warm acceptance of unionization in his *Forum* articles. It is hard to reconcile this proposed notice with his flat, unequivocal statement, written only six years before: "The right of working men to combine and to form trade-unions is no less sacred than the right of the manufacturer to enter into associations and conferences with his fellows, and it must sooner or later be conceded. . . . My experience has been that trades-unions upon the whole are beneficial both to labor and capital." [7] Carnegie's biographer Burton Hendrick attempts an explanation of this remarkable switch in sentiment by claiming that Carnegie was opposed not to unions in general but only to the Amalgamated Association because of its elitist policies. In a rather effusive defense of Carnegie's basic democratic principles, Hendrick wrote: "The Amalgamated was an anachronism, an old-fashioned puddlers' union, that had survived into the age of machinery. A genuine organization, representing modern ideas, all-embracing in its membership, would not have aroused Carnegie's hostility, but a feudal group, whose policy was one of exclusiveness and chauvinism, . . . could not be permitted to tyrannize indefinitely over their fellow workers and their employers. . . . Had it been modernized in keeping with the progress of the art, it could have maintained its position with the complete approval of Carnegie and his associates, but, in the progressive era now dawning, the Amalgamated, unchanged from the seventies, could hardly be endured." [8]

Of course, we cannot be sure as to exactly what Mr. Hendrick meant by his use of the word "modernized," but it is difficult to follow the logic of his argument that Carnegie sought to cure the exclusiveness of the Amalgamated Association by the rather drastic remedy of excluding unionism from all of his works. Nor does the attack that Carnegie made upon the Knights of Labor for being too all-inclusive help Mr. Hendrick's argument. In an interview given only six months before he wrote his notice to the employees at Homestead, Carnegie told a Scottish reporter, when asked if the United States did not have a trade union called the Knights of Labor, "Say rather, we *had*. It was one of those ephemeral organizations that go up like a rocket and come down like a stick. It was founded on false principles; viz., that they should combine common unskilled labour with skilled. . . . One mistake that many writers make about labour is in holding that it is one class. There are more grades and ranks in labour than in educated society." [9]

No, the efforts of Carnegie's more sympathetic biographers to portray him as an egalitarian democrat, valiantly battling against the elitism of the craft unions on behalf of modern industrial unionism, are not successful. They are rendered futile by Carnegie's own words. The only way Carnegie's actions in 1892 can possibly be related to his pro-labor sentiments of 1886 lies not in underplaying Homestead but rather in giving a more critical examination to his *Forum* articles. A careful reading of those essays reveals that, in spite of his praise for William Weihe and the Amalgamated Association, the kind of unionism that Carnegie really approved of was company unionism, not national trade unions, either craft or industrial in type. In his summary of the main points of his first essay, Carnegie made this quite clear, when he wrote that one of the next steps that should be taken "in the advance toward permanent, peaceful relations between capital and labor" is "a *proper* organization of the *men of every works* . . . by which the natural leaders, the best men, will eventually come to the front and confer freely with the employers." [10] By this statement, he defined the "proper" organization of labor as that formed by the men within each plant, not by a national organization. With company unionism, Carnegie had no quarrel. Unfortunately, organized labor did. If labor would not buy the company union, then Carnegie felt the only alternative was nonunionization, with the employer dealing with each employee on an individual basis.

Frick, in preparing for the battle with the Amalgamated Association, was in an enviable position compared with Carnegie. He had written no embarrassing *Forum* articles on the rights of labor to which his detractors could point and cry "Hypocrite!" In attacking the union at Homestead, he was remaining true to his reputation and to his principles. Yet, curiously enough, Frick rejected Carnegie's notice and advised against posting it for the employees to read. Although he agreed entirely with Carnegie's position that unionism would eventually have to be eliminated from all branches of the Carnegie Steel Company, he was not prepared to take on the union everywhere it existed at the same moment, especially in the Union Iron Mills, where relations with the union were good. He was also more realistic than Carnegie in anticipating that there could be serious trouble at Homestead over the refusal to grant a new contract to the local lodges of the Association, and from the first he sought to place the onus for any trouble that might ensue upon labor, not management. Although not sensitive to general public opinion, Frick was very much aware that the confrontation would take place in the summer of a presidential election year. He did not wish to make Homestead into a campaign issue for the Democrats, who were already making alarming noises about protective tariff, monopoly, and a growing plutocracy.

Consequently, Frick favored more devious tactics than Carnegie's flat announcement that unionism was to end within the Carnegie empire. He proposed instead that the company offer to the lodges terms for the renewal of the contract so severe as to make acceptance by the union impossible, and then hold to these terms no matter what action labor might take.

Carnegie was at Coworth Park, in Sunningdale, England, and had conferred with Phipps and Lauder, who had come over to England with the latest instructions from Frick. Upon further reflection about his own position and reputation, he changed his mind as to tactics. He wrote to his chairman:

> You remember I wrote you a type-written slip, which I suggested you might have to use. . . . But I hope you will make this change in it: I did not get it quite right, because I think it said that the firm had to make the decision of "Union" or "Non-Union." This I am sure, is wrong. We need not make that point, and we should not.
>
> We simply say that consolidation having taken place, we must introduce the same system in our works; we do not care whether a man belongs to as many Unions or organizations as he chooses, but he must conform to the system in our other works. . . .
>
> One thing we are all sure of: No contest will be entered in that will fail. It will be harder this time at Homestead than it would have been last time when we had the matter in our own hands, as you have always felt. On the other hand, your reputation will shorten it, so that I really do not believe it will be much of a struggle. We all approve of anything you do, not stopping short of approval of a contest. We are with you to the end.[11]

Having sent Frick this *carte blanche,* Carnegie left England for Scotland. Unlike every previous year since their marriage, the Carnegies in 1892 did not go to Cluny Castle. The Laird of Cluny wished to make some necessary repairs on his family residence, and he planned to occupy the castle himself during the summer to supervise the work. Carnegie had thus been forced to look elsewhere for a home. Through the agency of J. Watson Lyall in London, he had signed a lease with Sir Robert Menzies for the rental of Rannoch Lodge in the central Highlands of Perthshire. The somber, dark, gray stone lodge, located at the west end of Loch Rannoch, was in one of the most remote and isolated parts of Scotland. When the heavy gray mists hung low over the loch and the dark green forests along its shore, as they frequently do in July, the occasional visitor to this lonely land could easily be convinced that it was here that Macbeth must have met the three weird sisters, beckoning him on to fame and infamy. Although the North British Railroad line did make a stop at Rannoch Station, some ten miles away from the lodge, there was no coach road with public transportation to the lodge, and visitors had to be met at the station and brought to the lodge by private carriage.[12] This summer Carnegie did not expect the usual crowd of visitors and the gay festivities that he had always had at Cluny. He had left his address only with Frick, his secretary, and a few close friends in New York, and he did not issue his usual generous invitations to friends in Britain to visit him "at any time."

Indeed, so secretive had Carnegie been about his summer plans, and so remote was his retreat, that when Homestead broke into open warfare reporters on both sides of the Atlantic, trying to find him for comment, would accuse Carnegie of deliberately hiding out in anticipation of the trouble that was coming. There is some measure of truth in this, but the design in this arrangement was more at his partners' insistence than it was Carnegie's. The last thing in the world that Frick and Phipps wanted, aside from having Carnegie directly on the scene, was to have him easily available to the press. Knowing Carnegie's impetuosity and his great proclivity to talk more than he should, Frick and Phipps were obsessed with the desire to keep Carnegie out of sight—and out of sound.

Carnegie himself did not anticipate any great trouble. He wrote to Frick in June, "Of course you will win, and win easier than you suppose, owing to the present condition of the market." [13] Frick, however, prepared for the worst. In late spring, the workmen at Homestead were startled to see a stout stockade of planks, pierced with holes suitable for rifle barrels and topped with barbed wire, erected around the entire plant and running down to the river bank on each side of the piers where barges came for deliveries. The intent of this fence was only too clear. It was built, as Frick admitted later to the House of Representatives' Judiciary Committeee, "for the purpose of putting the property in a position that it could be defended against an assault." [14]

Frick had also entered into negotiations with the Pinkerton Detective Agency, asking that he be furnished with 300 guards for his property sometime during the first week in July. Further details would be forthcoming at a later date, he said. Frick had made use of this agency on two earlier occasions during labor trouble in the coal fields: in 1884, to protect Hungarians and Slavs whom he had brought in as strikebreakers, and, more recently, in 1891, to protect Italian strikebreakers, brought in against the Hungarians and Slavs, who were themselves on strike.[15] Frick's only complaint against the system was that, no matter how ignorant and illiterate the recent immigrants brought in to break a strike might be, they learned only too quickly to ask for more. Then it became necessary to search for a new ethnic group who would not be able to communicate with those who were on strike. Happily, Europe was richly stocked with diverse ethnic groups. If one wore out the Hungarians, there were the Italians, and if it became necessary to replace them, then there were the Poles and the Ukrainians.[16] As for the Pinkertons, Frick had no complaint against them at all.

The Pinkerton National Detective Agency, which provided useful guard service to many employers of mass labor, had been founded by a young Scottish immigrant, Allan Pinkerton, in 1850, quite by accident, after he had successfully captured a counterfeiting band for the United States government. Pinkerton, whose very name was to become the symbol of labor oppression in the late nineteenth century, had, curiously enough, a Radical background very similar to that of Carnegie. As a young man in Scotland he had been a Radical Chartist, and he had been forced to flee his native land to escape arrest. His detective agency received nationwide prominence in 1861, when Abraham Lincoln made use of its services for protection on his way to Washington for his first inaugural. Pinkerton continued his investigations for the Federal government during the Civil War, but soon thereafter he was incapacitated by a paralytic stroke, and he turned much of the direction of the agency over to his two sons, William and Robert. In the frantic postwar years of business expansion and violent labor trouble, the agency increasingly moved into the more lucrative field of business protection.[17]

The Pinkerton Agency was, in its own way, filling a need that had arisen as America changed from a nation of rural isolated communities into one of highly industrialized urban centers. During the colonial period our institution of local law enforcement had been brought over intact from Britain, where it had remained unchanged since the thirteenth century, when Robin Hood was successfully outwitting the Sheriff of Nottingham. The county sheriff system seemed even more impervious to change in the United States. If trouble arose, the sheriff, along with his deputies, was expected to enforce order and protect property within the community. If necessary, he could deputize private citizens and form a *posse comitatus,* in the old Norman tradition. By the end of the Civil War, however—if not long before—the system had become totally inadequate. The sheriff of Cook County in the 1870's was not being challenged by a "Tom, Tom, the Piper's Son, who stole a pig and away he run," but by hundreds of desperate men, battling their railroad employers and destroying millions of dollars' worth of property. Because the local governments were unable to enforce the laws, business began to look for its own private protection. It turned to the Pinkertons, who would provide any number of guards at $5 a head to furnish the protection business was desperately seeking. Like the Italian merchant-princes of the cities of the Renaissance, the manufacturing and transportation entrepreneurs of America in the late nineteenth century were hiring their own private armies, and Pinkerton captains, resplendent in blue livery with brass buttons, had become the *condottieri* of America's new industrial age.

To make themselves appear even more indispensable to their employers, the Pinkerton agents were not above acting as *agents provocateurs* to foment strife where it did not exist and to turn legitimate demands for the remedy of grievances into acts of violence against the established order. No labor union meeting could ever be certain that it did not harbor in its midst a Pinkerton spy, ready to report its real plans to management and equally ready to report false plans for rapine and destruction to the press. Naturally, labor everywhere hated and feared the name Pinkerton as the Devil Incarnate. At the same moment that Frick was laying his secret plans to bring 300 Pinkerton guards to Homestead, the Populists, meeting in Omaha, were including in their platform a plank denouncing the existence "of a large standing army of mercenaries, known as the Pinkerton system, as a menace to our liberties," and demanding its abolition.[18]

Frick, early in the year, in anticipation of the termination of the union contract, had asked the representatives of the local lodges to submit their contract proposals. The members of the Association submitted the contract in early March. Labor's proposals were simply to renew the 1889 contract. They asked for the same tonnage rate for those union men who were paid on a tonnage rather than an hourly basis. For those who were paid on a sliding scale, based upon the market price of steel billets, they asked that the minimum rate, below which hourly wages would not be reduced, be kept at $25 a ton, as it had been in the 1889 contract. That is, if the price of steel billets went above $25, hourly wages would rise accordingly, but if the price fell below $25, wages would not be cut. In 1889, when the contract had been negotiated with Abbott, the market price for billets was $27 a ton, and $25 seemed a fair minimum. But in 1892, with a depressed market condition, billets had fallen to $24 and promised to go even lower. The union, however, proposed $25, believing that this was a point upon which there could be reasonable and adjustable negotiations with management. Finally, the lodges asked that the new contract again be for a three-year period, to terminate on 30 June 1895.

In spite of the general depressed market within the trade, the Amalgamated Association at first felt fairly confident that its demands, except for some adjustment on the minimum price for the sliding scale, would be met by management. The men were prepared to strike if a reasonable settlement could not be reached by 30 June, and they were assured of the backing of the some 3000 employees in the plant who were nonunion. The Association's confidence in success was based upon several factors: the pressure upon the company to produce the armor plate to fulfill the government contract, their belief that they had an assurance from Carnegie that he would not use strikebreakers in the event that a strike should be necessary, and management's reluctance to have serious labor trouble in an election year.

The confidence that the skilled workers at Homestead felt because of the Navy contract was revealed by a government inspector, A. C. Buell, in a letter to an official in the Navy Department in January 1892. He reported a conversation he had had with a man named J. W. Allen, who posed as a reporter from the United Press seeking information on the armor contracts. But Buell had recognized him. Allen was an organizer of the Amalgamated Association.

> He [the labor organizer] began by saying that he desired to prepare an article for the Sunday papers throughout the country on the manufacture of armor and that he had been referred to me by Mr. Coolidge and others as a man familiar with that subject. He proved to be very shrewd and smart, and, but for my having previously seen him in his real capacity, I might easily have given him the whole armor situation as far as I know it.
>
> He told me that it was generally believed by the mill men here that there was a "bonanza" in armor contracts and, as the number of men in this district competent to work the armor-mill was comparatively small, they were disposed to get their share of it, together with many other interesting points. In fact, I brought my old newspaper training to bear on him and did the "interviewing" myself.
>
> Among other interesting things, I learned that the Committees of the Amalgamated have discounted the "boom" in ship, bridge, railroad and structural steel and have decided to force the hands of mill-owners all along the line. . . . He made one remark that seemed particularly forcible. It was this: "The mill-owners," he said "are constantly improving their plant. With automatic tables and hydraulic jacks and furnace-jacks and all that sort of thing they are making one man do the work that four and five men used to do, and yet they say that because they have invested so much capital in labor saving plant, the few men who are still necessary to run the plant should accept

lower 'scales' on account of the increased output capacity." "This matter," he continued, "has been under advisement for some time, and the Associations have decided that they will not accept the principle that is involved; that is, the doctrine that because one man, with these improved plants, can do the work that four or five used to do, he must at the same time accept a lower scale than used to be allowed in the days of handwork. . . . At Homestead, at Edgar Thomson, at Par's new mill, at Otis' 124 inch mill in Cleveland, and at South Chicago, you will see seven men doing the work that formerly required 24 men in a crew and yet they say that the seven ought to be content with a lower scale than used to be paid to the 24."

There was much more of the same sort, but the upshot of the whole was an impression that a great strike is impending in the steel industries. I considered the information I got from Mr. Allen valuable. In fact, it afforded me the first real insight in the workings of the Amalgamated Associations that I have ever enjoyed. Perhaps I ought to add that during the above described conversation, Mr. Allen was in possession of all his faculties, he having declined two or three "invitations" which I tendered him for the purpose of more completely thawing him out.[19]

Whether or not this interesting conversation was ever conveyed to Frick, he was fully aware of the need to roll as much armor plate as possible during the spring of 1892. The plates rolled at Homestead were stockpiled in an unfinished state, inasmuch as they could be given their final treatment at either Edgar Thomson or Duquesne.

Having taken these necessary steps to prepare for the contingency of work stoppage at Homestead, Frick then summarily rejected the lodges' proposals for a new contract and in return submitted his own. His proposals, of course, were totally unacceptable to the Association. The major points were these: first, the minimum price on steel billets below which the sliding scale would not go would be $22, not $25; second, the termination date for the new contract would be 31 December 1894; and third, the tonnage rate would be cut 15 per cent to allow management to get a share of the advantage of the increased production resulting from the new machinery. It was quite apparent to the

Association that "it was simply a proposition made by the firm that they knew we would not accept." [20] Even the Pittsburgh press could see through Frick's obvious ploy. As one local paper editorialized, "It was not so much a question of disagreement as to wages, but a design upon labor organizations." [21] Frick quite clearly was maneuvering the union into either a strike or an abject surrender of all its recent gains. Either way, he stood to win.

Sensing the trap, the Association sought to avoid a showdown by keeping negotiations open. William T. Roberts of the workers' committee told the company that labor was willing to make reductions in the minimum for the sliding scale as well as for the tonnage rates if management could show that it was necessary. "We want to settle it without trouble. We don't want a strike." [22]

But Frick was obdurate. On 30 May he sent his ultimatum to the men in the form of a letter to Superintendent Potter:

> Referring to my visit to the works this morning, I now hand you herewith Homestead Steel Works wage scales for the open hearth plants, and No. 32 and 119 inch mills, which you will please present immediately to the joint committee, with the request that its decision be given thereon not later than June 24th.
>
> These scales have had most careful consideration with a desire to act toward our employees in the most liberal manner. . . . You can say to the committee that these scales are in all respects the most liberal that can be offered. We do not care whether a man belongs to a union or not, nor do we wish to interfere. He may belong to as many unions or organizations as he chooses, but we think our employees at Homestead Steel Works would fare much better working under the system in vogue at Edgar Thomson and Duquesne.[23]

Potter, at Frick's instruction, informed the workmen's committee that, unless the lodges accepted his terms by 24 June, the company would negotiate with the men individually and not through the Association. Roberts's response was, "Do you think this is fair, Mr. Potter?" To which the superintendent replied, "I cannot help it. It is Mr. Frick's ultimatum." [24]

Frick was strongly supported in these maneuvers by Carnegie, who wrote to him in June: "As I understand matters at Homestead, it is not only the wages paid, but the number of men required by Amalgamated rules which make our labor rate so much higher than those in the East. Of course you will be asked to confer, and I know you will decline all conferences, as you have taken your stand and have nothing more to say. It is fortunate that only part of the Works are concerned. Provided you have plenty of plates rolled, I suppose you can keep on with armor." And, again, later that month, he wrote: "Cables do not seem favorable to a settlement at Homestead. If those be correct, this is your chance to reorganize the whole affair, and someone over Potter should exact good reasons for *employing every man*. Far too many men required by Amalgamated rules." [25]

This was the crux of the matter as far as Carnegie was concerned, and it was the major reason he had for wishing to break the union. As one of Carnegie's partners later remarked, "The Amalgamated placed a tax on improvements, therefore the Amalgamated had to go." [26] But although the local lodges had been given a considerable voice in hiring and firing practices at Homestead by the contract of 1889, it was basically an unfair charge that Carnegie had made in claiming that "Amalgamated rules" forced a company to keep "far too many men." Compared with later union policy, the Amalgamated Association was remarkably tolerant and understanding of technological replacement. President Weihe later testified to the House Judiciary Committee, "The object and motive of the Association has been for years to get the cost of labor as nearly uniform as possible, where the work is similar. . . . The Association never objects to improvements. If there are improvements that do away with certain jobs, they make no objection. They believe in the American idea that the genius of the country should not be retarded." [27] That Weihe was speaking the truth about union policy can be substantiated by the fact that when Carnegie Brothers was able to dispense with four-fifths of certain types of skilled operators at Edgar Thomson, and had thereby destroyed the two local lodges that existed there, the national Association had made no protest whatsoever.

Carnegie, in his correspondence with Frick, also misstated the situation by overemphasizing the high wages at Homestead. For years there had circulated throughout the trade wild stories of workers in the Carnegie plant who made $25 a day and were driven to work in their own carriages by servants. These stories, which were in no way discouraged by the company, were of course pure fabrication.[28] When Frick, on the witness stand, was forced to give Congress the wage scales at Homestead just prior to the strike, he told them that four men at Homestead received from $10 to $12.65 a day; twelve from $8 to $10; thirty from $6 to $8; eighty-two from $4 to $6; 443 from $2 to $4; and 335 men received under $2 a day. These, of course, were only the skilled men, who came under union contract, but even these figures were inflated, for they were based only upon the May wage and tonnage scales, when production had been abnormally high as the company feverishly attempted to stockpile armor plates. The actual averages over the preceding year were considerably lower: the top four men at Homestead received $7.60 as a daily average; and the next twenty-three highest received from $5.40 to $7.04. Of the 3800 employees at Homestead, only 113 had an average of from $4 to $7.60; 1177 had an average of from $1.68 to $2.50; and 1625 had an average of $1.40 a day or less. It was difficult for the workers to understand why wages now should be cut 15 per cent on tonnage and 8 per cent on scale by reducing the minimum below which the sliding scale would not fall. The workers had begun to suspect that Carnegie, with all of his talk of their sharing in the profits of the company, had in effect sold them a false bill of goods when he had persuaded them to accept the sliding-scale principle. Why should prices determine wages? Were not the English steelworkers better off under a system whereby wages determined price? [29]

The workers' committee took its proposals to the annual meeting of the Association in early June and received support from the national organization. President Weihe, however, urged further negotiation with the company, and the local committee eagerly complied. As the deadline of 24 June approached, the committee once again asked for further negotiations. Frick informed them that they had had his first and only offer, but he reluctantly agreed to a conference on 23 June, one day before his ultimatum would expire.

At that meeting, Frick, along with Otis Childs, his brother-in-law and partner in the company; Francis Lovejoy, secretary of the company; and John Potter, met with the representatives of labor from all the departments at Homestead working on a tonnage basis. Again, each side repeated its proposals, but only on the question of the minimum for determining scales did there seem to be any indication from either management or labor that it would yield. The workers said that they would consider a new minimum of $24, inasmuch as steel billets were currently selling at $22.50. Frick said he would not yield even on this point, but after he had left the room, Potter told the committee that he thought he could get the company to agree on a $23 minimum instead of the $22 offered. On the other two points, tonnage rates and the terminal date for the next contract, neither side would yield.[30]

Because management and labor had apparently come close to an agreement on the minimum to determine the sliding scale, with only a one-dollar difference separating the two sides, most contemporary writers commenting on the tragic strike that ensued felt that it had been totally unnecessary. It was generally accepted by the public that, had management and labor shown any willingness to bargain, surely a compromise could have been reached. Such commentators, in making this judgment, however, tended to minimize the other two points that divided labor and management. Men ignorant of the labor situation seemed to regard the terminal date, in particular, as being of little consequence.[31]

To the workers in the plant, however, the terminal date for the contract was of crucial importance. To have to negotiate the next contract in mid-winter, as the company insisted upon, would mean that the union would be severely handicapped in calling a strike should negotiations break down. Men who are out of work in July can subsist much more easily and cheaply, with no fuel bills to pay, fewer clothes to wear, and their own garden produce to eat, than can men who are out of work in January. Frick knew this very well, and for this reason he had insisted upon 31 December terminal date. The conference broke up on this point and did not even discuss the tonnage rates.[32]

The confrontation Frick had sought was at hand. The men returned from the conference still hoping that management would ask for another conference, still expecting Carnegie at this point to intervene, as he had against Frick in the coal fields strike of

1887. But this time there was to be no word from Scotland. The deadline of 24 June passed, and the lodges still refused to accept Frick's offer of a new contract. On 25 June a notice was posted throughout Homestead that thereafter the managers of the company would deal only with individual workmen, not with the Association. The workers' answer to this notice was to hang Frick and Potter in effigy. On 28 June the company began closing down the four departments that had tonnage men under contract with the company. By 30 June all four departments of heating and rolling were closed. The following morning the 3500 other employees of Homestead, skilled and unskilled alike, walked out. The great plant at Homestead was dark and empty, closed by both lockout and strike. The stage was set for war.

With punctilious correctness, Frick had waited until the deadline for accepting his offer had passed, and then, on 25 June, he wrote to Robert Pinkerton to ask for the 300 guards to arrive at Homestead on the early morning of 6 July. "These guards should be assembled at Ashtabula, Ohio," he told Pinkerton, "not later than the morning of July 5th, when they may be taken by train to McKees Rocks, or some other point upon the Ohio River below Pittsburgh, where they can be transferred to boats and landed within the inclosures of our premises at Homestead. We think absolute secrecy essential in the movement of these men so that no demonstration can be made while they are en route. . . . As soon as your men are upon the premises, we will notify the Sheriff and ask that they be deputized either at once or immediately upon an outbreak of such a character as to render such a step desirable." [33]

In the meantime, the men at Homestead were busy taking countermeasures. The entire work force of Homestead was divided into three divisions for an around-the-clock watch of the plant, the river, and all roads leading into the borough. Knowing Frick's previous tactics, the advisory committee fully expected the company to attempt to bring Pinkerton guards and strikebreakers into the plant. The advisory committee, consisting of representatives from each of the lodges, assumed full command, and Hugh O'Donnell, a skilled roller, was elected chairman. There was full co-operation from the municipal government, for the mayor of the town, John McLuckie, was one of the skilled workers at the plant and an ardent supporter of the strike. And, for that matter, the entire population of Homestead supported the strikers. An elaborate alarm system was set up to warn all the inhabitants of the arrival of any of Frick's "visitors," and there were watchers posted on bridges in Pittsburgh and patrol boats sent out to cruise the Mononghela to give the word of any unusual movement up the river.

For four days the tension at Homestead built. On 5 July, at the official request of the Carnegie company managers, the sheriff of Allegheny County, accompanied by a few deputies, appeared at Homestead to provide protection for the property. The advisory committee politely conducted the law officers around the high wall of the plant and informed them that not a living creature could make a move toward the plant without being observed and stopped. No property in the nation, including the government mint, was as well protected as Homestead. The committee in all seriousness asked Sheriff McCleary to deputize their guards as official law officers. Bewildered by this unexpected request, the sheriff hurried back to Pittsburgh, and his deputies were politely but firmly escorted out of the plant by the advisory committee.[34] Frick, having failed to get protection from the law officers of the county, was assured by his legal counsel that he was now acting properly in bringing his own private guards. He informed the sheriff that, on the early morning of 6 July, he was planning to send by river barge 300 Pinkerton guards into the Homestead plant. He asked the sheriff to send a deputy sheriff with the guards with authority to deputize them should the need arise. The sheriff sent Colonel Joseph H. Gray, a deputy sheriff, to Bellevue to join Potter and the 300 guards on the barges, but he explicitly denied Gray the authority to deputize the Pinkerton men.

The details of that bloody 6 July on the Monongahela have been told so often that they need no elaboration here. The Homestead strike was not the most violent uprising in American labor history. Considering the ferocity of the battle, which raged for nearly twelve hours, the casualties were surprisingly low, and only the two river barges that had brought the guards down to Homestead were destroyed. The plant itself was untouched, and it was in operation again within ten days. But Homestead has become a part of the American union man's legend, a symbol of the injustice and perfidy of "the bosses," in much the same way that Haymarket Square has served as a symbol of the anarchy and terrorism of labor organizations for conservative business interests.

One reason that Homestead has been given a prominent position in American labor history is certainly the high drama—one might say melodrama—of the situation: there were the darkened barges moving quietly up the Monongahela in the heavy, sultry fog of a hot summer night; the alert guard from Homestead, who spotted the barges as they passed under the Smithfield Street bridge in Pittsburgh and speedily sent an alarm to the strikers; the sirens and factory whistles that roused the entire town out of its uneasy sleep at four o'clock in the morning; the thousands of men and boys who grabbed up rifles, hoes, and the staves off picket fences and rushed to the river bank to confront the barges as they came into dock.

There is also the classical unity of time, place, and theme in the ensuing battle that is worthy of Greek drama: the narrow stage of this violent action, along the crowded river bank and aboard the dirty, cramped barges drifting just off the shore; the furious fighting that raged all through the hot day, with only occasional lulls as the men on shore brought in new weapons of attack; and the single intensity of purpose of the entire population of Homestead, battling for jobs, homes, and the only kind of life these people knew and desperately wanted to keep.

Along with the tragedy, there were in this drama touches of the opera bouffe. These valiant but inexperienced fighters, clambering over piles of steel beams and crawling in the mud of the river bank, were constantly thwarted by their own ineptitude and by the whimsical vagaries of chance: the novice serving as artilleryman, who charged the town's only cannon (taken from the courthouse square) with dynamite, and blew it up; the ingenious crew who pumped a stream of oil into the river, in an effort to set the barges on fire, only to be frustrated by a sudden surface breeze that blew the burning oil away from the barges; the foolhardy young fighter who ran down the dock and successfully hurled a lighted stick of dynamite on to the roof of one of the barges, only to see it roll off into a bucket of water on the deck and splutter out; the sweating gang of men who loaded a flatcar with burning boxes and rags and pushed it down the track that led to the dock, only to see the car running off the track before it got to the dock and burning harmlessly on the shore. It was as if the gods themselves were laughing at these clumsy Trojan heroes, fighting to hold their Ilium.

Finally, in the last scene to be enacted on that tragic day, there was sheer horror mixed with a pathos which has haunted the memory of Homestead: The Pinkerton guards, who had lain all day cramped in the infernal heat of the barges, had at last, around four o'clock in the afternoon, been able to raise a white flag and get the strikers to cease firing. Hugh O'Donnell then came aboard. He promised the Pinkertons safe conduct into town if they would depart immediately. The frightened Pinkertons agreed. They dropped their guns, jumped off the barges, and waded ashore. But O'Donnell and his committee, who had maintained a disciplined order in Homestead for five days, could no longer speak for the people of the town. The fury of the day had touched the whole community and had transformed it into a howling mob. The Pinkerton men now had to run a gauntlet of screaming, cursing lunatics. The women of Homestead were worse than the men. They beat the hated "Pinks" with stockings filled with iron scraps, gouged at their eyes with pointed umbrellas, threw sand and dirt in their faces, and kicked them when they fell. Only one Pinkerton man had been killed and eleven injured during the long day on the barges, but on the walk into town, three more were killed, and every one of the 300 suffered at least some minor injuries before they reached the sanctity of the village jail. Their bright new uniforms had been torn to shreds. Naked and bloody, these miserable wretches staggered down the streets of a place once known as Amity Homestead, totally defeated.

But they had been the defeated and abused before they had entered the barges. These were men who could not find employment elsewhere, and so, for a dollar a day and the chance to wear a bright blue uniform with shiny brass buttons, they had entered the employment of the Pinkerton National Detective Agency. Hated symbols to working men everywhere of everything despicable in the existing order, they had become the tools of the oppressors because they had been the most oppressed. They were the tragic waste products of America's industrial order. Now on this day of madness these "Have-Nots" had become the victims of the

"Have-Littles." Homestead had written a new preamble to the platform of the Populists that exceeded even the fertile imagination of Ignatius Donnelly. It is not surprising that this drama on the banks of the Monongahela has lived on as the "blackest scene in American labor history." [35]

Unquestionably, Homestead has also been given an added significance because it took place within the Carnegie empire. There had been and would be many other bloody and tragic encounters between management and labor—against Frick in the coal fields of Westmoreland County, against George Pullman and his "model town" in Illinois. The Fricks and the Pullmans of American industry were the known enemies of organized labor. Neither quarter nor compassion had been expected in any struggle with them. But Carnegie had sung a different tune—about the dignity of labor, the sanctity of a man's job, of profit-sharing and the Gospel of Wealth, and of democracy triumphant. "Where was Andy, the good little boss, on this dark day? Why, he was over in Scotland, and far away." Had he known in advance of Frick's plans for Pinkerton guards and strikebreakers and state troopers? Most of Carnegie's older employees at Homestead could not believe it. If only Andy had been here, they told the others, things would have been different. But the younger workers at Homestead, and labor throughout the country, drew quite a different lesson from the situation. "You can't trust any of them," was the moral they drew from Homestead, "and it is better to confront a Frick with a hard heart than a Carnegie with a false tongue."

What, indeed, was Carnegie thinking in his remote Highland fastness when he got the news of the battle of Homestead? His first reaction was panic. He cabled Frick that he was coming back home to take charge of the situation. This struck terror in the hearts of the senior partners, Lauder and Phipps, for they felt sure that if Carnegie came this would mean the repudiation of Frick, Frick's resignation, and the triumph of the union, none of which they wanted. Phipps and Lauder, who were in England at the time, hurriedly sent letters telling Carnegie to stay where he was and to keep quiet about the situation.[36] Given the awful choice of losing face or losing Frick, Carnegie swallowed his pride and complied with his partners' request. There was no retreat now. But he was angry at Frick, first, for having ignored his repeated instructions that in case the men refused to accept the company offer, he was simply to close the plant and wait them out; and second, after deciding on a different course, for having bungled the job. Carnegie wrote Lauder in anger, "Matters at home *bad*—such a fiasco trying to send guards by Boat and then leaving space between River & fences for the men to get opposite landing and fire. Still we must keep quiet & do all we can to support Frick & those at Seat of War. I have been besieged by interviewing Cables from N York but have not said a word. Silence is best. We shall win, of course, but may have to shut down for months." [37]

For four days after the Pinkerton guards were routed and order had been restored by the workers' committee and the local municipal government, the strikers were in full control of Homestead. Their victory, however, was to be of short duration. On 10 July, Governor Robert Pattison, at last convinced that local law officials could not maintain order and restore the property at Homestead to its owners, ordered out the state militia. The following morning, 8000 troops arrived on the scene, and the gates of Homestead were once again opened to management, on its own terms. Within a week, certain departments were back in operation with newly employed help. Frick posted a notice at the plant informing the strikers that "Individual applications for employment at the Homestead Steel Works will be received by the General Superintendent either in person or by letter until 6 p.m. Thursday, July 21, 1892. It is our desire to retain in our service all of our old employes whose past records are satisfactory and who did not take part in the attempts which have been made to interfere with our right to manage our business. Such of our old employes as do not apply by the time above named will be considered as having no desire to re-enter our employment, and the positions which they held will be given to other men. . . ." [38]

The discipline of the Association still held, however, for both members and nonmembers, and would continue to hold for many months. Homestead reopened with 700 imported strikebreakers, who were given little welcome in the community. But in spite of the loyalty of the 3800 employees to the union cause, the war was over. It was only a question of time, of waiting for winter to force hungry and cold men to try "to re-enter our employment," providing, of course, their jobs were still open.

In the meantime, there was to be an epilogue—one more scene of insane violence acted out before the drama of Homestead could be complete. On Saturday afternoon, 23 July, Frick was sitting in his office, talking with the vice president of the company, J. G. A. Leishman, when a pale, nervous young man, a recent immigrant from Lithuania by the name of Alexander Berkman, burst in and shot Frick twice with a small pistol at close range. The first bullet pierced the lobe of Frick's left ear, then entered his neck near the base of the skull and penetrated to the middle of his back. The second lodged in the right side of his neck. Before Berkman could fire a third time, Leishman struck his arm and the shot went into the ceiling. As Berkman and Leishman grappled together, Frick grabbed his assailant around the waist and all three men fell to the floor. Berkman managed to extricate from his pocket a crude dagger fashioned from a file and stabbed Frick three times in the hip and legs. Then the office clerks rushed in and tried to subdue Berkman. A deputy sheriff arrived in the midst of this scuffle, and he raised his gun to shoot the would-be assassin. Frick, leaning against his desk, cried, "Don't shoot. Leave him to the law but raise his head and let me see his face." Frick then pointed to Berkman's jaw, which was moving as if he were chewing. The deputy forced the man's mouth open and found a capsule containing enough fulminate of mercury to blow the room to bits. This was too much for Leishman, who fainted dead away.

The indomitable Frick sat quietly in a chair and, without an anaesthetic, allowed the hastily summoned surgeon to probe his neck and back, telling the doctor when he had reached the bullets. When the slugs were extricated and his profusely bleeding wounds staunched and dressed, Frick insisted upon returning to his desk. He wrote out a telegram to his mother, "Was shot twice but not dangerously," and a similar cablegram to Carnegie to which he carefully added the sentence, "There is no necessity for you to come home. I am still in shape to fight the battle out." While his office force and the doctor stood by in silent wonder, for no one dared to interrupt him, Frick then completed the paper work on an essential loan he was negotiating, signed several letters, and prepared a statement for the press: "This incident will not change the attitude of the Carnegie Steel Company toward the Amalgamated Association. I do not think I shall die, but whether I do or not, the Company will pursue the same policy and it will win." Having then completed all of his tasks for the afternoon, Frick informed the doctor he was ready to be taken home by ambulance.[39]

The story of the attempted assassination of Frick made front-page news around the world. Berkman, a young Nihilist activist, had no connection whatsoever with the labor union. But his attack upon Frick was inevitably associated in the public's mind with the strike at Homestead, and some of the popular sympathy that had gone to the strikers was lost. The effect on public opinion would have perhaps been even greater if the Frick story had not been immediately followed by newspaper accounts of the overzealous commanding officer of the troops at Homestead, who hung a young private by his thumbs for over a half an hour until the boy lost consciousness. Private Iams's offense had been to shout, "Hooray for the anarchist," when he heard the news of the attack on Frick.[40]

The union made one final attempt to enter into negotiations with the company. Hugh O'Donnell, under arrest on the charge of murdering Pinkerton guards, fled to New York and there hastened to the Republican headquarters, where he suspected there might be considerable concern over recent events at Homestead. He was quite right. Whitelaw Reid, editor and publisher of the New York *Tribune,* who had been recently nominated for the vice presidency at the Republican National Convention, was greatly alarmed over the impact that Homestead would have, not only on the labor vote, but also in giving substance to the Democrats' charge that Big Business had become autocratic and bloated with wealth because of the protective tariff. Reid was more than receptive to O'Donnell's plea that an effort be made to communicate to Carnegie the concessions that labor was willing to make in order to reopen negotiations. Reid suggested that O'Donnell write a letter to him (Reid) as if O'Donnell were still in Homestead. Reid would then transmit this letter by cable to Carnegie along with his own message supporting the workers' proposals. So O'Donnell, in Reid's office, wrote this letter:

Honorable Whitelaw Reid,
Dear Sir:

I address you in behalf of the 12,000 inhabitants of Homestead, Pennsylvania. In their name, I ask that you interest yourself in the unfortunate controversy still pending between them and the Carnegie Steel Company by whom the majority of the adult population of the town is employed. In presenting this matter to you I have no desire to dwell upon the merits or demerits of the conflict. I am looking toward the future, not the past. . . . I simply therefore lay before you the situation as it exists today. . . . It is in the interest of no one that this state of affairs should continue; that it should not, there is but one, and only one, course to pursue. . . .

But before submitting my proposition permit me to say a word in reference to the course of procedure which appears to be in the minds of the Carnegie Company. I mean their express determination to put non-union men at work in the place of our people by the aid of the State authorities. . . . This will only intensify the internecine strife at Homestead—most of the union men own their own homes, and they will not give them up without a fight. [A virtual paraphrase of Carnegie's *Forum* article.]

. . . But further trouble can be prevented. How shall it be done? Simply let the Carnegie Company recognize the Amalgamated Association by re-opening the conference doors, and I have no hesitation in saying that there is no disposition on the part of the employees to stand upon a question of scale or wages, or hours, or anything else. The spirit that dominates them is conciliatory in the extreme, for they deplore the recent sad occurrence as much as any other class of people in the whole country. . . . That it is true is sufficiently clear to my mind to cause me to ask you to do what you can in every honorable way to bring about an amicable settlement.[41]

Having written his letter to Reid and indicating that the Association would reconsider its position on every issue, including the terminal date for the contract, O'Donnell hurried back to Pittsburgh to surrender himself to the sheriff. Reid had at this moment very tender feelings about putting personal welfare above party welfare, for he had just agreed, for obvious political reasons, to allow the Typographers Union to establish a local in the *Tribune* office for the first time. He was eager to send O'Donnell's message to Carnegie, but Frick refused to give Reid Carnegie's address. Finally, in desperation, Reid sent the message to Carnegie in care of the American Consul General in London, John C. New, along with his own message urging Carnegie "to weigh it most carefully before deciding, for so small a reason as the objection to continued recognition of their organization, which you have heretofore recognized, to prolong this distressing and bloody strife which may spread so widely." Reid told Carnegie that O'Donnell "assures me that if your people will merely consent to reopen a conference with their representatives, thus recognizing their organization, they will waive every other thing in the dispute, and submit to whatever you think it right to require, whether as to scale or wages or hours or anything else. . . ." [42]

Because the messages were delayed, Carnegie did not hear from Reid until 28 July. Carnegie's first reaction was to accept O'Donnell's proposal. Smarting under the personal attack upon him in the British press, Carnegie was eager to get the whole matter settled and forgotten as quickly as possible. Consequently, he cabled Frick in the company's code, "We have a telegram from Tribune Reid through high official London Amalgamated Association reference Homestead. The proposition is worthy of consideration. Replied 'Nothing can be done. Send H. C. Frick document.' You must decide without delay. Amalgamated Association evidently distressed." [43] For the moment, Carnegie had apparently forgotten that what Reid had referred to as "for so small a reason—the continued recognition of their organization" had been the main reason for the contest. Upon further reflection, "his intellect and sense of justice, however, at once supervened," as Carnegie's biographer, Burton Hendrick, so generously put it. [44] After all, Carnegie, on the day after the Homestead battle, had wired Frick, "Cable received. All anxiety gone since you stand firm. Never employ one of these rioters. Let grass grow over works. Must not fail now. You will win easily next trial." [45] Could Carnegie now do any less than stand firm himself? As a consequence, Frick received a second cablegram the following morning: "After due consideration we have concluded Tribune too old. Probably the proposition is not worthy of consideration. Useful showing distress of Amalgamated Association. Use your own discretion about terms and starting. George Lauder, Henry Phipps, Jr., Andrew Carnegie solid. H. C. Frick forever!" [46]

Reid, who had been hopeful for the outcome since receiving a cablegram from Consul General New that Carnegie had accepted the proposal but wanted Frick to be consulted, hurriedly sent his representative for the Republican National Committee, John E. Milholland, to Pittsburgh on 30 July to talk with Frick. Milholland found him at home in bed, where he had lain for the past week, recuperating from his wounds. He did not find Frick in a conciliatory mood. In the account he sent to Reid, Milholland reported Frick's response:

> Mr. Frick declared emphatically that he would never consent to settle the difficulties if President Harrison himself should personally request him to do so. Notwithstanding the fact that he was a Republican and a warm friend and admirer of the President, the whole Cabinet, the whole leadership of the party might demand it but he would not yield. He was going to fight the strike out on the lines that he had laid down. I remarked, "If it takes all summer?" "Yes," he said, "if it takes all summer and all winter, and all next summer and all next winter. Yes, even my life itself. I will fight this thing to the bitter end. I will never recognize the Union, never, never! . . . It makes no difference to me what Mr. Carnegie has said to [Consul] General New or to anybody else. I won't settle this strike even if he should order me peremptorily to do so. If he interferes every manager that he has will resign and of course I will get out of the concern. But I do not think he will interfere." [47]

Hugh O'Donnell, out of jail on $13,000 bond, was in despair. He blamed Frick's intransigence upon the fact that he had been murderously assaulted by a fanatical anarchist. In a letter to Edward Bemis, he wrote, "Thus it would seem that the bullet from Berkman's pistol, failing in its foul intent, went straight through the heart of the Homestead strike." O'Donnell was one of the most pathetic victims of the Homestead strike. Although he was ultimately cleared of all charges of murder, he was blacklisted from ever again obtaining work in any steel mill in the country. He was also an object of suspicion to his fellow workmen for having, on his own, gone to Reid and for having promised too much in the name of the union. "I am now shunned by both labor and capital, a modern Ishmael, doomed to wander in the desert of ingratitude," he wrote in 1894 to Edward Bemis, a political scientist who was writing an article on the Homestead strike.[48]

It is highly doubtful, however, if the personal assault on Frick had had the slightest effect on his attitude toward the union. He would have proved just as intransigent had Berkman stayed in Vilna, for as Frick himself wrote immediately after the attack, "This incident will not change the attitude of the Carnegie Steel Company toward the Amalgamated Association." As far as Frick was concerned that attitude had been determined three years before, when William Abbott had been so pusillanimous as to accept the Association's terms without a struggle.

The Republicans, to be sure, lost the election, and Harrison and Reid forever after blamed Homestead for their defeat. They pointed to the effective use of the strike by the Democratic press, particularly Joseph Pulitzer's *St. Louis Post-Dispatch* and Carter Harrison's *Chicago Times*. President Harrison said that he was defeated by "the discontent and passion of the workingmen growing out of wages or other labor disturbances." [49] Chauncey Depew, the toastmaster-general of the G.O.P., put it more bluntly, "As a matter of fact the Homestead strike was one of the most important factors in the presidential contest. . . . It happened at a crisis and injured us irremediably." [50] Whitelaw Reid, who had had the most at stake because of his active role in trying to bring about negotiations between Frick and the workers, never forgave Carnegie for his betrayal. Nor did Carnegie's ingratiating little note the following spring mollify him. Carnegie had written:

> I feel it is too long to wait to express my sincere and heartfelt thanks for the noble effort you made to settle that Homestead blunder. I assure you my partners Messrs. Phipps and Lauder, whom I had summoned to Scotland to confer with me, agree with me in feeling ourselves under a debt of gratitude to you. We supposed the matter would be promptly settled, as a conse-

quence of your action. I never suspected that the seven hundred men reported at work were *new* men. I rested believing them to be our former employees. Between ourselves, no manufacturer is wise who attempts to employ new men. My partners thought the three thousand old men would keep their promise to work and therefore opened the works *for them*. The guards were intended only to protect them. . . . But I only started to express myself your debtor and assure you that all three of the principal owners are very grateful to you.[51]

After reading this letter, which was so patently distorted by falsehood as not to be worthy of a reply, Reid would be inclined to agree with the Republican congressman from Ohio, Charles Grosvenor, who called Carnegie "the arch-sneak of this age."[52] A year and a half after the election, Reid was still smarting over his defeat. He wrote to Senator W. E. Chandler, former national secretary of the Republican party, "It was Homestead more than any other agency—I am not sure but it was Homestead more than all other agencies combined that defeated us in 1892. As you probably know, there is an interesting story, which the labor people are likely some day or another to bring out, of their efforts to adjust that difficulty through me, of their offering to accept Mr. Frick's terms, of Carnegie's assent to the arrangements, and Mr. Frick's refusal. For the present, however, all this must be considered confidential. But it is in the line of your letter, and serves to show how much the Republican Party is indebted to this concern." Reid was convinced that Carnegie's recent letter, expressing a desire to compromise on the tariff, which the *Tribune* had reluctantly published, showed Carnegie's eagerness to put personal gain above principle and party loyalty. "He has been coddling Cleveland obviously with an eye to those contracts [the armor plate contracts]. He undoubtedly meant to please the Democrats, and particularly the Administration Democrats, as much as possible by his letter, no matter what it cost the Republicans;—and he took pains to compel the publication of his letter by having his partner, Frick, advise the Pittsburgh papers of its existence and call for copies."[53] The *Tribune* for many years afterwards never missed an opportunity to give Carnegie a poor press.[54]

Carnegie and Frick thus served the Republican party as useful scapegoats upon whom to load the burden of its defeat. Most historians have since accepted the strike as a major contributory factor. Unquestionably, Homestead did cost the Republicans some votes, but it is highly doubtful that this tragic event was in any way decisive in determining the outcome. Cleveland, who actually had received a larger popular vote than Harrison in 1888 but had lost the election in the Electoral College, was not to be denied a second term in 1892. The congressional elections of 1890, which had gone heavily Democratic, showed the growing dissatisfaction of the people with the policies of the Grand Old Party. The unprecedented victory of a Democratic presidential candidate in Illinois and Wisconsin was the result of growing farm unrest as well as a switch in the city vote in Chicago and Milwaukee. All of this had been indicated in the congressional elections two years before. It is significant to note that Pennsylvania, which should have been most affected by Homestead, remained in the Republican column; Cleveland actually received fewer votes in Philadelphia in 1892 than he had in 1888. There was one city, however, in which Homestead did have a decisive effect, and that was in Homestead itself. Homestead had always voted two-to-one Republican, but in 1892 the beleaguered town voted Democratic by the same wide margin. It was the only way left for the strikers to register a last protest against their former bosses.[55]

The scapegoats themselves, however, bore their burden of guilt with a greater equanimity than might have been expected from such staunch Republicans. Frick wrote Carnegie immediately after the election, "I am very sorry for President Harrison but I cannot see that our interests are going to be affected one way or the other by the change in administration." On the same day, Carnegie was writing to Frick, "Cleveland! Landslide! Well we have nothing to fear and perhaps it is best. People will now think the Protected Manfrs. will be attended to and quit agitating. Cleveland is pretty good fellow. Off for Venice tomorrow."[56]

A major reason for Frick's and Carnegie's sanguine outlook at this time was that the Homestead strike was at last coming to an end. On 18 November, Frick sent a single word cablegram to Carnegie, "Victory!" and three days later, a longer message reading, "Strike officially declared off yesterday. Our victory is now complete and most gratifying. Do not think we will ever have any se-

569

rious labor trouble again, and should now soon have Homestead and all the works formerly managed by Carnegie, Phipps & Company, in as good shape as Edgar Thomson and Duquesne. Let the Amalgamated still exist and hold full sway at other people's mills. That is no concern of ours." Carnegie, from Italy, responded, "Life is worth living again—Cables received—first happy morning since July—surprising how pretty Italia—congratulate all around—improve works—go head—clear track—tariff not in it —shake." [57] From Rome, Carnegie wrote at somewhat greater length,

> I am well and able to take an interest in the wonders we see. . . . Shall see you all early after the New Year. Think I'm about ten years older than when with you last. Europe has rung with Homestead, Homestead, until we are sick of the name, but it is all over now—So once again Happy New Year to all. I wish someone would write me about your good self. I cannot believe you can be well. Ever your Pard, A.C.[58]

But Carnegie was mistaken. Homestead was not "all over now," nor would it ever be over for those who had been involved, willingly or not, in this conflict. The Republican candidates felt that they had been forced to pay too high a price for the Carnegie-Frick victory, and the bitterness the party leadership felt in November 1892 would last for a long time. The targets of this bitterness had also paid a high price for their victory over the Amalgamated Association. On the day of the riot, Mrs. Frick, distraught with worry, had given birth prematurely to a son, Henry Clay, Jr. She barely survived the birth, and the infant died four weeks later, while his father lay stricken with the wounds inflicted by Berkman.

As for Carnegie, he would later write, "Nothing I have ever had to meet in all my life, before or since, wounded me so deeply. No pangs remain of any wound received in my business career save that of Homestead. It was so unnecessary." [59] Carnegie had reason to feel pangs of pain, for the wounds inflicted upon him by press, pulpit, and political platform were deep and came from all directions—right, left, and center. Carnegie did not have a drawer on the other side of the desk labeled "Harsh words and bitter thoughts" to counterbalance his drawer for "Gratitude and sweet words," but had he had such a compartment, it would have been overflowing in the weeks and months after Homestead.

In Britain the cry raised against him was both bitter and taunting. Every major newspaper carried full front-page accounts of the events at Homestead, and most of them editorialized at length on Carnegie's deficiencies as an employer and a man. The Old Thunderer, *The Times,* with pointed reference to Carnegie's active role in the Irish Home Rule campaign, said that it hoped America would remember Pittsburgh the next time it tried to tell Great Britain how to run Ireland. "Every country, however fortunate, will always have its hands full if it attends to its own affairs." Although certainly not pro-labor in its editorial policy, *The Times* condemned Frick's tactics. "The employment of a private police force is a thing that should neither be permitted nor required in a civilized community. Such a force, at the disposal of any capitalist . . . is a standing provocation to the labouring class." [60] The Edinburgh *Dispatch* called Carnegie's position "certainly a most unenviable one. . . . We on this side of the Atlantic, where the bitterest labour quarrels have never attained such a degree of intensity as exists at Pittsburgh, may well feel thankful that neither our capitalists nor our labourers have any inclination to imitate the methods which prevail in the land of 'Triumphant Democracy.' " [61] Even the *Journal* in Carnegie's beloved Dunfermline raised its voice against the town's most noted son and taunted that "even in the boasted 'land of freedom' the sons of toil are still a considerable distance from an 'industrial millennium.' " Although the *Journal* opposed the workers' taking over the plant, it said they had "a perfect right to refuse to submit to a reduction" of wages. It blamed all of America's industrial woes on "this wicked impost," the McKinley Tariff Act.[62] The Sheffield *Daily Telegraph* sneered, " 'The Tyrannies of Democracy' would be a good title for a companion volume to its 'Triumphs' as recorded by or for that millionaire 'man of the people, the great protected of tariffs and Pinkertons, Mr. Andrew Carnegie.' " [63] The press of Great Britain was finding sweet revenge at last on the former owner of that radical syndicate of penny papers who had jabbed so viciously into England's most sacred institutions.

571

Even more irritating in their condescending scorn for Carnegie were such arch-Tory journals as *St. James's Gazette* and *Blackwood's Edinburgh Magazine*. The *Gazette* carried a full account of the events at Homestead and then editorialized:

> Pleasant news this morning for Mr. Andrew Carnegie, iron master, millionaire, philanthropist, and free lecturer to the inhabitants of Great Britain! Mr. Carnegie's iron works at Pittsburgh, U.S.A., have been the scene of a labour riot, which is simply the nature of civil war. . . . Let us just think what would be said of this kind of thing if it happened in England! . . . At Pittsburgh the Government of the County, as a Government, has been powerless. The maintenance of "order" has been left to a hired band of private mercenaries. . . . A strike is one thing, and we know what a strike is; but armed private mercenaries are another, and they are a thing which in this effete old country we emphatically would not tolerate. . . . That is the lesson of liberty which England can still teach her forward children. Freedom can only exist where all rights are safely secured. Mr. Andrew Carnegie has preached to us upon "Triumphant Democracy," he has lectured us upon the rights and duties of wealth. . . . It is indeed a wholesome piece of satire.[64]

Carnegie received no kinder treatment from the American press: the New York *World*, the *Chicago Times*, even the Pittsburgh papers. The cruelest editorial of all appeared in the *St. Louis Post-Dispatch*. It was reprinted widely throughout the country.

> Count no man happy until he is dead. Three months ago Andrew Carnegie was a man to be envied. Today he is an object of mingled pity and contempt. In the estimation of nine-tenths of the thinking people on both sides of the ocean he had not only given the lie to all his antecedents, but confessed himself a moral coward. One would naturally suppose that if he had a grain of consistency, not to say decency, in his composition, he would favor rather than oppose the organization of trades-unions among his own working people at Homestead. One would naturally suppose that if he had a grain of manhood, not to say courage, in his composition, he would at least have been willing to face the consequences of his inconsistency.

But what does Carnegie do? Runs off to Scotland out of harm's way to await the issue of the battle he was too pusillanimous to share. A single word from him might have saved the bloodshed—but the word was never spoken. Nor has he, from that bloody day until this, said anything except that he had "implicit confidence in the managers of the mills." The correspondent who finally obtained this valuable information, expresses the opinion that "Mr. Carnegie has no intention of returning to America at present." He might have added that America can well spare Mr. Carnegie. Ten thousand "Carnegie Public Libraries" would not compensate the country for the direct and indirect evils resulting from the Homestead lockout. Say what you will of Frick, he is a brave man. Say what you will of Carnegie, he is a coward. And gods and men hate cowards.[65]

To Carnegie's former Radical labor friends in Britain, he had become a leper, a man whose money was tainted and whose support had now become the kiss of death. The Glasgow Trades Council, before whose cheering members Carnegie had so recently extolled the glories of republicanism, now formally declared him to be "a new Judas Iscariot"—but thanked him for calling world attention to the plight of labor. The Labour Representation League urged all workers in Great Britain to refuse any future gifts from Carnegie, and the London Trade Council passed a similar resolution. George Bateman, Carnegie's former ally in the Liberal party, urged that Carnegie be kicked out of the National Liberal Club, and Kier Hardie, the Radical M.P. from Scotland, who had, not long before, received a £100 contribution from Carnegie for his campaign fund for the 1892 Parliamentary elections, sent the money to the workers at Homestead to be added to their strike fund.[66] Back in America, Carnegie was even blackballed from honorary membership in so conservative an organization as the Cleveland, Ohio, Chamber of Commerce,[67] while thousands of laboring men in all fields of industry in Pittsburgh protested to the Pittsburgh Art Association and the Pittsburgh municipal government against accepting Carnegie's gift of a public library and art museum.[68]

For someone as proud as Carnegie all of this was very hard to bear. But he could find solace in other letters that were written to him in these dark days. Gladstone himself wrote in September to express his sympathies and to say that he, at least, remembered Carnegie's great gifts of philanthropy: "I do not forget that you have been suffering yourself from anxieties, and have been exposed to imputations in connection with your gallant efforts to direct rich men into a course of action more enlightened than that which they usually follow. I wish I could relieve you of these imputations of journalists, too often rash, conceited or censorious, sometimes ill-natured. . . . No one who knows you will be prompted by the unfortunate occurrences across the water (of which manifestly we cannot know the exact merits) to qualify in the slightest degree either his confidence in your generous views or his admiration of the good and great work you have already done." [69] To which a grateful Carnegie replied: [70]

It was just like your noble self to write us such a kind sympathetic note. This is the trial of my life (death's hand excepted). Such a foolish step, contrary to my ideas, repugnant to every feeling of my nature. Our firm offered all it could offer, even generous terms. Our other men gratefully accepted them. They went as far as I could have wished but the false step was made in trying to run the Homestead Works with new men. It is a test to which workingmen should not be subjected. It is expecting too much to expect poor men to stand by and see their work taken by others. *Their daily bread.* In all my experience I have had only one grossly unfair action on the part of 178 secretly sworn *Irishmen* to combat—just such men as render Homestead Works (which we bought with its men) a nest of dissatisfaction. I said, "Gentlemen, we cannot do what you demand, but we will wait. You have stopped the Works, *let us see you start them*—not till a majority work shall a wheel turn."

It was all quietly settled, this our partners should have done, & I had written sketching the plan, alas, too late—my letter did not reach. Feeling had been aroused—Sheriff's aid called in, his Deputies halted—then other Guards sent for with *Sheriff's approval,* these attached & then the military.

All this time I heard nothing until days had elapsed & as the way *easiest to peace* going on was then best—returning being impossible, for the State of Penna. could not retire troops until they had established & vindicated *Law.* The pain I suffer increases daily. The Works are not worth one drop of human blood. I wish they had sunk.

574

I write this to you freely, to no one else have I written so—I must be silent and suffer but after a time I hope to be able to do something to restore good feeling between my young & rather too rash partner & the men over at Homestead. . . . I retired from active management three years ago to devote my time to other aims. I have a book about ready for the press dealing with the "Burning Questions," Wealth, Labor, Short Hours, Trade Unions, &c. &c. It is intended for my "Fellow Workmen" and I think will do good both to Capital & Labor —enough about self. . . . I have one comfort, self-approval & a second—the support of a Wife who is as strong & as wise as she is gentle & devoted—so I shall sail on & let the tempest howl. . . . With grateful thanks for your extreme consideration, believe me, Devotedly yours,

Andrew Carnegie

There were other kind letters. Lord Rosebery wrote, saying that he knew "nothing of the rights and wrongs of the Homestead case, but I cannot believe that you would ever be illiberal or unjust." [71] And, of course, there were letters from Morley: "We've had a good deal of tribulation during the last twelvemonth both you and I. . . . As I told you, the world is often harsh to its benefactors. But this philosophic truth does not make me the less angry at the odious line taken about you by English newspapers and Scotch. However, it is past, and by now pretty well out of your memory, I'll be bound." [72]

Not out of Carnegie's memory, certainly—Homestead could never be out of his memory. But gradually, with time, the facts were becoming blurred. He came to believe that he was on a coaching trip and not at Rannoch when the trouble broke out; that he was not informed of the riot until three or four days after it had happened, rather than within twelve hours; that he actually thought the men being hired when the gates to the plant opened again were his old employees returning to work; that O'Donnell's and Reid's proposals came too late for him to do anything that might have achieved an amicable settlement. A blurred memory is often far better than complete forgetfulness in helping a man to justify himself to himself, in holding tightly to that "one comfort—self-approval" of which Carnegie had written to Gladstone. In time, Carnegie even became convinced that the workers had sent him a telegram that read, "Kind master, tell us what you

575

wish us to do and we will do it for you." Unfortunately, nowhere in his personal papers could he find such a telegram. He wanted it when he wrote his account of Homestead in his autobiography, and for weeks he had a top executive in the company, Alexander Peacock, at work trying to trace down the telegram or getting former employees to say that they had signed such a telegram. But Peacock had no success.[73] Carnegie, without any corroboration, told of the telegram in his autobiography anyway.[74] Undoubtedly, he had confused the wish for such a telegram with the fact of O'Donnell's letter to Reid. The interesting part of the story, however, is that Carnegie should have actually believed that his workmen would address him as "Kind Master." That in itself reveals a great deal about Carnegie's attitude toward his workers. An European who visited Homestead some years after the strike made the perceptive comment: "The managers represented 'Triumphant Democracy,' but nearly all that I saw while with the men might be described under the title of 'Feudalism Restored.' " [75] Carnegie would resent such a judgment as being antithetical to everything he stood for and believed in about America, but that he could describe himself as being "Kind Master" to his workmen without understanding the full import of what he was saying is perhaps more damning than anything that was said about him by others.

In January 1893 Carnegie returned to New York and at once hurried off to Pittsburgh. He insisted upon visiting Homestead, and there, before the collected workers, new and old, he read a prepared speech:

> I have not come to Pittsburgh to rake up, but to bury the past. It should be banished as a horrid dream, but the lessons it teaches should be laid to heart for future application. For twenty-six years our concerns have met with only one labor stoppage. I trust and believe that this record will be equalled in the next twenty-five years. When employer and employed become antagonistic, their antagonism can only be described as a contest between twin brothers. No genuine victory is possible for either side, only the defeat of both. . . . I made my first dollar in Pittsburgh and expect to make my last dollar here also. I do not know any form of philanthropy so beneficial as this; there is no charity in it. I have hoarded nothing, and shall not die rich

apart from my interest in the business. Unless the Pittsburgh Works are prosperous, I shall have nothing. I have put all my eggs in one basket right here, and I have the satisfaction of knowing that the first charge upon every dollar of my capital is the payment of the highest earnings paid for labor in any part of the world for similar services. Upon that record I could stand.

He concluded by praising Frick:

I am not mistaken in the man, as the future will show. Of his ability, fairness and pluck no one has the slightest question. His four years' management stamps him as one of the foremost managers of the world—I would not exchange him for any manager I know. . . . His are the qualities that wear; he never disappoints; what he promises he more than fulfills.

I hope after this statement that the public will understand that the officials of the Carnegie Steel Company, Limited, with Mr. Frick at their head, are not dependent upon me, or upon anyone in any way for their positions, and that I have neither power nor disposition to interfere with them in the management of the business. And further, that I have the most implicit faith in them.[76]

It took courage for Carnegie to come to Homestead to make his first and only formal public statement regarding the recent difficulties. Considering the circumstances, the reception he received was good. He had said all the right things with the proper note of conviction, and at least Frick and the other company managers were satisfied. For them, Homestead could now be considered a closed book. Both they and the workers knew that Carnegie had been wrong when he said that no victory was possible for either side, but it was to be expected that he should say that.

Carnegie also knew that his strong endorsement of Frick and his management of the affair was what he should say, and he said it forcibly and well. But he had implied something quite different to Gladstone and Morley, and in time the rancor Carnegie felt over Frick's management of the Homestead confrontation would fester and erupt. It would contribute to the open break between them.

Perhaps Carnegie had been right, after all, in saying "no genuine victory is possible for either side." Certainly it had proved no genuine triumph for him. His own role, his actions, and his lack of action had been so ambiguous and contradictory that they cast doubt on the sincerity of anything he later said or did. The impartial judge, if there had been one, might at least have recognized Carnegie's genuine sincerity on two points. First, he was sincere in not wanting to use force by bringing in strikebreakers. He had given explicit instructions to Frick upon that point, and he was genuinely horrified when he heard that deaths had resulted because his instructions had been disobeyed. Second, he was sincere in his desire to break the union at Homestead. He had proposed an open confrontation with the Association on this issue, and he fully backed Frick in achieving that goal. That these two positions came into open conflict with each other was largely due to Frick, not to him. Had Carnegie been at Homestead, as he had been at Braddock in the winter of 1887–88, it is quite possible that rioting and bloodshed would have been avoided. Carnegie might have simply closed the plant and waited the men out. But the union would have been broken, in any event. So for Carnegie, Homestead brought both pain and gain. He wrote Morley soon after his visit to Homestead: "I went to Homestead & shook hands with the old men, tears in their eyes & mine. Oh, that Homestead blunder—but it's fading as all events do & we are at work selling steel one pound for a half penny." [77] With that letter, Carnegie accurately summed up the credit and debit sides of the ledger on Homestead as it affected him.

The American trade union movement in general, however, could find very little in the Homestead ledger that marked a gain for them. It is true that there was a wider sympathy for labor throughout the country as a result of the strike and its suppression than had ever existed before. The majority opinions of the House and Senate committees' reports were generally favorable to labor, and sharply critical of the use of Pinkerton guards by management.[78] In the wave of public indignation over Pinkertonism that followed Homestead, state after state passed laws against the hiring of outside guards. By 1899, twenty-six states had passed such laws—including Pennsylvania, which had outlawed Pinkerton guards in 1893 without one dissenting vote in the Assembly.[79]

578

The question of hiring guards was only one aspect of the problem of labor relations, however. Unionism throughout the steel industry was effectively destroyed by the victory of the Carnegie Company over the Amalgamated Association. In 1897 and 1899, the Association lost its last major strongholds in Jones & Laughlin and Illinois Steel without putting up a fight. It did make a last desperate show of strength against United States Steel, when that huge combine was formed in 1901, but it was totally defeated. The last lodge in a steel plant gave up its charter in 1903, and for the next thirty-four years there were no unions within the steel mills of the nation.[80]

It was the individual workers at Homestead who paid most dearly for the strike, however. Some of the leaders continued to pay throughout their lives. They lost everything they had possessed in Homestead—their jobs, their homes, their personal possessions. And through the efficiency of the blacklist throughout the trade, they were denied employment in the steel industry for the rest of their lives. O'Donnell was only one victim. John McLuckie, the former mayor of Homestead, was discovered by one of Carnegie's friends working as an unskilled laborer in a Mexican mine near the Gulf of California. He had lost everything but his pride. He refused financial help from Carnegie when it was offered him.[81]

Those old employees who were able to get their jobs back after the strike found conditions changed under the new "non-union order" that prevailed. Within a year, tonnage rates for rollers, shearmen, tablemen, and heaters were cut more than half, from an average on all these skilled jobs of 9.6¢ down to 4.4¢ a ton.[82] The minimum for the sliding scale was abolished in 1892, and the entire sliding-scale principle was abandoned in 1894. In the next few years, the price of steel billets, which had once been used to determine the wage scale, rose 40 per cent, but wages at Homestead and Edgar Thomson increased only 10 per cent. The twelve-hour shift, seven-day week prevailed now throughout the industry.[83] And Carnegie went on giving libraries and wondering why so few adults made use of his magnificent gifts.

Worst of all was the general atmosphere of Homestead. Every visitor commented upon it. Charles Spahr, in *America's Working People,* commented on the bad impression that he received of

Homestead in 1900. "This came from the spirit in which workmen did their work. They were cheerless almost to the point of sullenness. . . . The sullen attitude, indeed, was absolutely intangible, and when my escort said that he had not observed it, there was really nothing that I could point to as evidence." After living in Homestead a few weeks, Spahr could be more specific. "The atmosphere was at times heavy with disappointment and hopelessness. Some of the men were afraid to talk, even the Catholic priest—to whose class I am accustomed to go for fair statements of the relations of men to their employers—was unwilling to make any statement." One worker told Spahr that what he wanted above anything else was an education. "But after my day's work, I haven't been able to do much studying. . . . After working twelve hours, how can a man go to a library." [84]

Ten years later, John Fitch and Margaret Byington, who spent months in Homestead in the preparation of their reports for *The Pittsburgh Survey* under the auspices of the Russell Sage Foundation, received much the same impression. Fitch said that "the overwhelming majority of them are resentful and bitter toward their employers. . . . These men with spirit dead, face a future in which they expect nothing and ask for nothing. They look dull-eyed on a world from which the brightness is gone." [85]

Hamlin Garland discovered there were worse roads to travel than those "main travelled roads" of rural poverty and social isolation. For in 1894, Garland visited Homestead. He was frightened by what he saw:

> The town, infamously historic already, sprawled over the irregular hillside, circled by the cold gray river. On the flats close to the water's edge there were masses of great sheds, out of which grim smoke-stacks rose with a desolate effect, like the black stumps of great trees. Above them dense clouds of sticky smoke rolled heavily away.
>
> Higher up the tenement-houses stood in dingy rows, alternating with vacant lots. . . . The streets of the town were horrible; the buildings were poor; the sidewalks were sunken, swaying, and full of holes. . . . Everywhere the yellow mud of the street lay kneaded into a sticky mass, through which groups of pale,

lean men slouched in faded garments, grimy with soot and grease of the mills.

The town was as squalid and unlovely as could well be imagined, and the people were mainly of the discouraged and sullen type to be found everywhere where labor passes into the brutalizing stage of severity. . . . Such towns are sown thickly over the hill-lands of Pennsylvania. . . . They are American only in the sense in which they represent the American idea of business. . . . [Inside the sheds] we moved towards the mouths of the pits. "It takes grit to stand there in July and August," said my guide. "Don't it, Joe?" The man nodded. . . . "I'd as soon go to hell at once," I replied. He laughed.[86]

Yet men had fought here, for this ugly town, for these jobs, for this way of life. They had felt that they had acquired a proprietary interest in the mill, for if it possessed their minds and bodies most of their working hours, then surely they also possessed it. But this was something that almost no one else seemed to have understood. Certainly Frick had not understood it. One might as well have said to him that the mill also belonged to the iron ore or to the limestone as to have said that it belonged to the men who labored there. The conservative press that screamed for law and order did not understand it. Nor did the liberal press and the Democratic congressional committees, who condemned the Pinkertons, but who also rebuked the workers for "taking private property into their own hands." Even the national officers of the Amalgamated Association had not really grasped the idea. William Weihe, when asked by the Senate committee if he thought labor objected to troops protecting property, had replied, "Not that I am aware of. . . . Working men that have given the matter study know law and order must be maintained. All that they desire is that proper authorities should have charge of it." [87]

Ironically enough, it had been Carnegie himself, six years before the strike, who had best expressed the feelings of those men who stood on the banks of the Monongahela on that hot July morning. Carnegie had written, "I would have the public give due consideration to the terrible temptation to which the working man on a strike is sometimes subjected. To expect that one dependent on his daily wage for the necessaries of life will stand

581

by peaceably and see a new man employed in his stead, is to expect much. This poor man may have a wife and children dependent upon his labor. No wise employer will lightly lose his old employees."

And that is what the fighting at Homestead had been all about.

CHAPTER XVII

Mr. Carnegie's
Empire of Business
1892-1900

In the immediate aftermath of Homestead, in the winter of 1892–93, Carnegie assessed the position of the newly organized Carnegie Steel Company within the industrial world. In so doing, he had reason to view the future with both confidence and uncertainty. It had been only twenty years ago that Carnegie had gone with his neighbor, William Coleman, out into the country to inspect a few acres of land that Coleman owned at Braddock's Field. After considering its strategic location, Carnegie had agreed with Coleman that this was the proper site for the new Bessemer steel plant that he proposed to build. Construction of the Edgar Thomson Steel Works had begun on the eve of the 1873 panic, in a moment of high prosperity, but it had been finished in the midst of economic depression, and had not only survived but had profited from that depression.

Now, twenty years later, Carnegie held a majority interest in a company capitalized at $25,000,000, with annual earnings of $4,-000,000. It was the largest and most profitable steel business in the world. It owned four major steel plants, two iron mills, several blast furnaces, and its own internal rail system. Its owners held a majority interest in and managed the largest and finest coke company in the country. The tragic Homestead strike, costly as it had been to the company both in loss of production and in prestige, had been a victory of management over the trade unions, and there was to be no further serious trouble from labor throughout the Carnegie companies. Quite clearly, Carnegie had reason for confidence.

But not for complacency. Carnegie could never be complacent or satisfied. Although he could not know in the winter of 1892 that the country once again, as in 1872, stood on the brink of a major depression, he was canny enough to realize that difficult times lay ahead for business in general, and for the steel industry in particular. There was the continuing turmoil over the currency with the demand of the Populists for silver inflation, which the Sherman Act had in no way satisfied. To be sure, the President-elect, Grover Cleveland, promised to be much more vigorous in his support of "honest, sound money" than his predecessor had been, but still business was uneasy and credit was increasingly hard to come by. The production facilities of the country, both agricultural and industrial, had expanded too rapidly in the relatively prosperous decade of the 1880's. This was particularly true of the steel industry. "It seems to me," Carnegie was to say repeatedly in the next few years, "that while a large amount of steel will be used, yet the demand will just fall short of the capacity to produce, therefore a struggle must ensue among producers for orders wherever percentages cannot be arranged. The sooner you scoop the market the better." [1]

If this advice sounded all too familiar to his partners, it was because Carnegie saw no reason to change his basic business practices that had proved so spectacularly successful over the past quarter of a century: "Run our works full; we *must* run them at any price. . . . Cost if it can be had, but any price for cash or undoubted buyer. Keep this in mind—all other considerations secondary." [2]

The fact that Carnegie's basic principles remained the same did not mean he was inflexible in meeting changing conditions. To "scoop the market" would mean something quite different in the 1890's than it had in the 1870's and 1880's. First of all, the demands of the market were changing. For twenty years, rails had dominated the steel market, but now, as the country faced its second great depression in less than a generation, the age of railroad building was coming to an end. There would always be a market for rails, for replacements and new feeder lines, but the great railroad systems had now been built, and steel manufacturers must look elsewhere for the real bread-and-butter of the trade. Carnegie was one of the first to see that, with the fantastic growth of the urban centers, steel beams for multi-storied structures, made possible by the invention of the elevator, would serve in the future as rails had in the past. The full potential for steel products had hardly been imagined. He had therefore pushed the development of open hearth steel production at Homestead and the rolling of structural beams from open hearth steel.

Not only was there a change in the kind of product demanded, there was also a change in the source of markets. Reluctant as Carnegie was to admit it, America no longer represented an ever-expanding domestic market whose needs could never be satiated. Increasingly, it appeared, foreign trade would become important, and Carnegie Steel must be prepared to compete for a world market. Carnegie's realization of this change explains his growing indifference to high protective tariffs, much to the concern of the tariff lobbyists such as Swank, who had always regarded him as a stalwart in matters of tariff.

Up until the 1890's, Carnegie had been somewhat contemptuous of foreign trade considerations. As late as 1889, in an address before the Pennsylvania legislature, he had dismissed foreign trade: "The relative importance of these two branches of commerce [foreign and domestic] is seldom considered. We hear so much of foreign commerce and so little of internal commerce; and yet the latter represents over 95 per cent of the commerce of the United States and the more noisy branch counts for less than 5 per cent." [3]

In the midst of the depression of the 1890's, however, Carnegie was willing to listen to this insignificant "noisy branch." For the first time, the company had a sales manager employed full-time to seek out the European market, and in 1897 sales agents were also appointed for China and Australia.[4] Carnegie was not

585

happy about this development. "Just received cable, 'sold Japan 14,000 tons steel rails.' This is the third order," he wrote to Henry Yates Thompson. "Bad days for us when we have to take foreign trade. . . ." [5] At the same time he felt pride in the company's foreign business. "I hope you will go ahead and send not less than five thousand tons into the British market no matter what we lose," he wrote to the president of the company, J. G. A. Leishman, in 1896, and he concurred with the "general opinion of the Board . . . to sell a limited amount of product to foreign markets even though prices are low just so as to keep up connections there." [6] He even entered into negotiations with the Royal Bank of Scotland regarding a loan to establish "a London Branch for our foreign business," but this was never pushed beyond the planning stage.[7] He was ready to pursue the Russian market for both rails and armor plate, even though he was skeptical of the reliability of Russian private capital in paying its bills and preferred to deal directly with the Czarist government.[8] By the end of 1897, he could boast to his British friends that "the exports of the Republic will exceed the exports of Great Britain for the first time." [9]

"Scooping the market," both domestic and foreign, required something more than an aggressive sales force, however. In reassessing the company's position in the depression of the early 1890's, Carnegie became convinced that there needed to be an emphasis upon two factors in business operations—one old and one new. The first was the old story of concentrating upon the cost of production. This had been Carnegie's favorite theme since he had joined Kloman and Phipps in the operation of the iron forge on 29th Street in Pittsburgh. Profits were incidental to and only a by-product, however desirable, of cost. One could never hope to run full and scoop the market unless one was continually concerned with keeping costs below those of one's competitors in order to maintain the lowest price. With the vivid metaphor of which he was a master, Carnegie constantly reminded his partners: "It has never failed that the lowest price given has proved to be a high price at time of delivery on a falling market. When you want to capture a falling stone, it won't do to follow it. You must cut under it, and so it is with a falling market." [10]

The second factor in business operations which Carnegie now

wanted to stress was the achievement of verticality, so that there would be within the company all three stages of manufacturing: the production of raw materials, the conversion of those materials into basic product, and finally the fashioning of basic product into finished articles. Carnegie's interest in verticality as a major goal came only in the 1890's. In the beginning, Carnegie's company had been concerned principally with the second stage of manufacturing, the conversion of raw materials into steel. By 1892, the company had dominated this stage for ten years, and Carnegie believed it was time for management to turn its attention to the first and third stages, and by so doing achieve a verticality of organization and operation unknown within the trade.[11] By giving it vertical structure, Carnegie, by the end of the decade, changed his company from a highly successful business into an industrial empire.

It was to stage one, the acquisition of raw materials, that Carnegie first turned his attention. He had taken a major step in the early 1880's by acquiring Frick's coal fields and coke ovens, but at that time he had not pushed verticality any further. Now it was time to go further, and he did not have to prod his partners, for they fully appreciated the necessity of controlling the sources of the basic raw materials needed for the production of steel. Actually, Carnegie's junior partners would have to prod him into risking capital for the acquisition of iron ore.

Of the three basic materials needed to produce steel—coke, limestone, and iron ore—the company had an invaluable and seemingly unlimited source of coke through its connections with Frick and his company. It also had easy access to limestone, having three-quarters of the ownership of the Pittsburg Limestone Company. Iron ore, however, had always been a problem to Carnegie's company, as it was to every other steel company in the world. The Bessemer process had required an ore low in phosphorus content, which had greatly limited the sources available to steel manufacturers. The Thomas process had come as an answer to the steel man's prayer, for now not only could ores relatively high in phosphorus content be used in the Bessemer converter, but the open hearth method of producing steel had become practical from the point of production costs.

Thomas's invention had radically changed the quest for iron

587

ore among American steel producers—from high grade, low phosphorus ore to any ore that could be cheaply obtained. The most important single area for Bessemer ores in the United States had been the rich deposits of the Marquette Range, just south of Lake Superior in the upper peninsula of Michigan. Seemingly inexhaustible when first opened up in the late 1840's by Philo Everett, this supply was noticeably depleted by the heavy demands of America's rapidly expanding steel industry. By the early 1880's it was apparent to the more farsighted of the large scale producers that new sources of ore would have to be found in the relatively near future if the current rate of steel production was to be maintained. There were frantic searches for ore in other areas of the upper peninsula of Michigan, the northernmost part of Minnesota, the mountains of West Virginia, and the highlands of northern Alabama. In 1872, iron was found in the Menominee Range near Green Bay along the Michigan-Wisconsin border. From 1875 to 1880, a group of mining engineers and adventurers, including George Stone of Duluth, Samuel Munson of Utica, Charlemagne Tower, a Pennsylvania millionaire who financed the operation, and Tower's son-in-law, R. H. Lee, explored and opened up the valuable deposits around Lake Vermillion in northern Minnesota near the Canadian border. This was the first significant discovery of iron on the north side of Lake Superior.[12] At about the same time, a third iron range, the Gogebic, was discovered in the upper peninsula of Michigan, and it was opened for mining operations in 1884.

These were important and valuable discoveries to supplement the rapidly diminishing Marquette source, but all of these ranges lay in the remote forest wilderness of the north. Transportation facilities had to be built over difficult terrain to take the ore down to Lake Superior. The transportation costs were not as formidable as those of labor, however. There was no local population from which to draw a labor force, skilled or unskilled. Miners had to be brought in from great distances, housing and food had to be provided, and a premium in wages had to be paid to compensate men for working in this isolated wilderness, far from any towns and women.

The iron deposits in these Lake Superior ranges, furthermore, were located in fairly deep and sharply inclined veins. In order for the miners to get at the ore, it was necessary to develop a new and rather hazardous method of shaft mining, known as sublevel stoping, in which the men, working at cross-cut, horizontal sublevels, loosened the ore and allowed it to drop through holes into chute-raises at the haulage level below. If the walls were too soft, a great deal of waste material would be loosened along with the ore and would drop into the chutes. If the ore veins were too hard, as was frequently the case, the cost of driving the sublevels and drilling the ore was greatly increased.[13] These factors added considerably to costs and made the problem of labor procurement even more difficult.

Indeed, it had been the labor difficulties that had defeated Carnegie in his one early attempt to develop his own source of iron ore. At Kloman's insistence, Carnegie and his partners had provided capital for the development of the Kloman Mine on the Marquette Range in Michigan in 1872. Kloman had promised an annual production of 50,000 tons, but in the two years 1873–74 the mine had produced only 36,000 tons at a cost of $2.76 a ton, simply to get it out of the mine. Then there were heavy transportation costs by rail and water to be added before the ore finally reached the Lucy Furnaces in Pittsburgh. By 1875 the mine had been closed because it had become too expensive to operate, and in 1880 Carnegie was relieved to be able to sell the company's controlling interest to an outsider, P. B. Shumway.[14] It is not surprising that, after this fruitless venture, Carnegie was wary of entering into any further mining ventures, and for some time preferred to buy his ore on the open market, searching for the best price available, either domestic or foreign.

His early unsuccessful mining venture explains why, in spite of his stress on verticality at this later date, he was not enthusiastic about taking advantage of the greatest opportunity of his entire business career in the fall of 1892. This was the chance to acquire an important interest in a newly opened range of iron ore lying to the west of Duluth and south of the Vermillion Range, variously known as the Missabe, Missaba, or Mesabi Range, which was to prove the most valuable iron deposit ever to be discovered on the entire North American continent.

The Mesabi Range, approximately 120 miles in length, lies across north central Minnesota and serves as the watershed for that part of the continent. It separates those streams which flow north to the St. Lawrence or Hudson's Bay from those—including the Mississippi—which flow south to the Gulf of Mexico. For this reason the Indians of the region named it Mesabi, meaning "Grandmother of Them All."

Trappers who knew nothing about the theory of geological formations suspected that there might be iron in this range because they had occasionally seen pockets of red ore. As early as 1870, an explorer by the name of Peter Mitchell had tramped over the whole range from Beaver Bay westward, guided by Indians from the Vermillion district. He collected some samples of a fine, powdery ore which he sent to some mining friends in the Marquette region. Perhaps because of these samples, a mining expert from Hamilton College in New York, Professor A. H. Chester, visited the region in 1875. After examining the topography, he came to the perfectly rational and apparently scientifically sound conclusion that no iron in any meaningful amounts could possibly be found in the Mesabi area.[15]

The reason for this scientific skepticism is not hard to understand. Although traces of iron can be found almost everywhere on the planet's surface, commercial mining possibilities were then believed to be limited to particular and easily definable geological formations. What the learned scientists and experienced miners could not know was that the Mesabi Range was in reality one of nature's most freakish and spectacular phenomena. Along this range there had once been deep valleys and hollows that over eons of time, by a process that cannot be explained, had been filled with particles of iron as smoothly and evenly as a measuring cup is filled with flour by a housewife in baking. Then the glaciers had pushed down from the north, covering these pockets of ore with drifts of gravel and sand to depths of from a few inches to seventy or more feet, and topsoil was laid over that. Great forests of pine had completed the camouflage, and only occasionally, when one of these coniferous giants was toppled by storm, did its exposed roots reveal the hidden caches of wealth that lay under the surface. Trappers and foresters saw these bits of evidence and wondered about them, but few had seemed willing to believe the evidence of their eyes against the overwhelming authority of science and experience. The few attempts that had been made to explore this area for commercial exploitation had proved futile, and the "Grandmother of Them All" continued to guard her secret well.

Now, however, her days of secrecy that had lasted for millennia were numbered. So frantic was the search for ore in the 1880's that there were men willing to look in improbable places and other men willing to back their absurd ideas with funds. In 1887, a mineral explorer, James B. Greggie, working out of the Vermillion Range, found what he considered conclusive evidence of iron in the Mesabi area. Hurrying back to Duluth, he discovered that ten local businessmen in the city had an option to buy 800 acres of land in the area he had explored. "I bought the option from that syndicate," he later wrote, "and commenced exploration . . . finding evidences of iron in every pit and in some clean, soft ore as fine as flour. You will notice that this was before the discovery of soft ore at Mountain Iron by the uprooting of a tree. No one suspected soft ore could be found in the State, and I was looking for a vertical vein of hard ore such as were being operated on the Vermillion at Tower."

Greggie was able to interest George Stone, the man largely responsible for opening the Vermillion Range, and with Stone's encouragement and some financial assistance from Captain Joseph Sellwood, Greggie organized a mining company for the development of the Mesabi Range. The first serious drillings in the Mesabi, however, failed to open significant deposits of ore. Further operations were abandoned and the company dissolved. The scientists and businessmen of Duluth who scoffed at the suggestion of ore along the Mesabi had apparently been right all along.[16]

Nevertheless, the rumors persisted and the dreams would not die. Within three years after Greggie's abortive attempt to unlock her secret, there came out of the woods of northern Minnesota a band of lusty young men who were determined once and for all to conquer "the Grandmother," and open her secret charms to the world. If she had to submit to man, it was highly appropriate that her first ravishers should be the Merritt boys, four brothers and three nephews, who were nearly as much the natural children of the northern forest lands as were the Indians who had named the Mesabi.

The Merritt brothers had come with their parents from Chau-

591

tauqua, New York, to Duluth in the 1850's. Their father, Lewis Merritt, was a dreamer of fantastic dreams, who sought gold in the pine woods of Minnesota. All he ever found was "fool's gold," —that, and a small package of powdered red iron ore, which he had collected far to the west of Duluth in an area sacred to the Indians of the forests. This, he told his sons, was iron ore, and if found in sufficient quantity could be as valuable as gold. So he gave to his sons, and especially to Leonidas, their dream of wealth, which in time, for Leonidas at least, became an obsession. The boys grew up to be powerful figures, both in physical size and in woodland skills. They tramped the forests of northern Minnesota and soon knew the whole region from Duluth to Grand Rapids as well as any Indian. Because of their ability in surveying and in selecting choice timber for lumber companies, they were able to build collectively a modest capital for which Leonidas—Lon, as he was called by his brothers—had definite plans. Knowing nothing about the sciences of geology and minerology, Lon, the natural leader of the group, was convinced that the Mesabi was rich in iron ore, no matter what the scoffers in Duluth might say.[17]

With his brothers and nephews, he set off in 1885 to open up his first mine. Taking along the traditional tools of the miner's trade—drills, pick axes and explosives, the Merritts were prepared for the traditional methods of mining. But that was not the way to win the Mesabi. As Lon Merritt later recalled the story before the Stanley Committee of the House of Representatives, at one particular spot he asked one of the miners with them to start drilling a test hole. The miner, an experienced German, refused, saying that there could not possibly be iron ore there, and he would not waste his energy so foolishly. "If we had really got mad," Merritt testified, "and kicked the ground right where we stood, we would have thrown out 64 per cent ore." [18]

Merritt had happened to strike one of those pits in which the topsoil covering was only a few inches thick. Picking up the loose soil in his hands, he saw the red ore underneath. "If this is iron ore," he shouted to his brothers, "all we have to do is swing a shovel." With that, the secret of Mesabi was revealed.[19] Here indeed was a new mining method—mining with a shovel. No dark, narrow subterranean tunnels with men inching forth like moles, blasting and chipping their way through rock, but rather steam shovels, clawing up ore, like a child filling a sand bucket on the beach, and creating vast amphitheatres a mile across and 400 feet deep. This revolution in the iron industry had begun with Lon Merritt's grubbing up a handful of the precious ore.

Filling what containers they had with the ore, the "seven men of iron" trudged through the wilderness back to Duluth. Tests showed that what they had brought in was indeed almost pure Bessemer ore, with only minimal traces of phosphorus, but of a quality so fine and powdery that experienced furnace men felt that it would be useless. Nature had indeed mined the ore and hidden it neatly in caches, but she had refined it also, grinding it to the softness of sifted cake flour. When tested in a furnace, the ore either caked or else was blown out of the chimney along with the gas. The men of Duluth now found a new way to jest about Mesabi. "If you tried to load an ore car with this stuff," they said, "half of it would blow away like dust before you ever got to the docks." [20]

The Merritts had not been deterred by laughter before, and they would not be now. By 1890, they had gained possession of the tract of land where they had made their first important discovery and which they named Mountain Iron. They were fifty miles away from the nearest railroad line, and there was nothing but a trail into their mine. Nevertheless, they managed to get scoop shovels and other equipment into Mountain Iron to begin large scale excavations. What they needed now was capital to finance a railroad spur line that would connect with the Duluth and Winnipeg line, giving them access to docks on Lake Superior. Lon Merritt's first thought was of the steel master of America, Carnegie. If he could interest Carnegie in his project, his dreams of wealth would be realized. So in the spring of 1891 he went to Pittsburgh, where he saw not Carnegie but Frick.

Frick's supporters have always delighted in dwelling upon Carnegie's later reluctance to get involved with the Mesabi ores and how it was only the foresightedness of his astute chairman, Henry Clay Frick, that gave to the Company its greatest wealth. They do not mention that the first refusal came not from Carnegie but from Frick.

Lon Merritt on his first visit to Pittsburgh got a very cool reception indeed. "Frick did not use me like a gentleman," Merritt later testified, "and cut me off short and bulldozed me." [21] To the hardheaded and coolly practical Frick, this burly giant standing before him and shouting about scoop-shovel mining must have seemed a raving wild man just escaped from his forest wilderness. Carnegie Steel was definitely not interested.

Merritt returned to Duluth, and by stock manipulation and fancy credit transactions that would not stand the scrutiny of even an amateur auditor he somehow managed to finance his railroad line. By 1892, the first shipments of ore were arriving in Duluth from Mountain Iron. It is true that adaptations had to be made in existing blast furnaces before the soft hematite could be used. Furnace men, however, because of the low cost in labor to extract Mesabi ore compared with conventional ores, were willing to pay for such adaptations. Eight men working a large steam shovel could load more ore in one hour than several hundred highly skilled miners could blast and chip out of an underground mine in a day. The difference in price to get the ore out of the ground was the difference between $3.00 and 5¢ per ton.[22]

If Frick and Carnegie were not interested in the Mesabi in 1892, there was another Pittsburgher, Henry Oliver, who was. Little "Harry" Oliver, Carnegie's boyhood chum on Rebecca Street in Slabtown, whom Carnegie had persuaded the telegraph company to employ as a messenger back in 1850, had had quite a career since he and Andrew had scurried through the streets of Pittsburgh delivering messages. Pittsburgh's prototype of Mark Twain's Colonel Mulberry Sellers, Oliver in the intervening forty years had made and lost half a dozen fortunes in iron, steel cars, railroads, and anything else that looked promising. Now in 1892, he was down on his luck again, heavily over-invested in blast furnaces and with hardly a dollar of free capital in his bank account, but with no depletion in his enthusiasm and with his usual optimism that something good would turn up. In the summer of 1892 he was in Minneapolis as a delegate from Pennsylvania to the Republican National Convention. It was there that he heard the magic word "Mesabi" for the first time, and all interest he might have had in the process of renominating Benjamin Harrison disappeared. Without a moment's delay, Oliver set off for the northern frontier.

By this time, the great Mesabi "iron rush" was on. In the five months since the first ore trains had come down from Mountain Iron on the Merritts' little spur line, grandiosely named the Duluth, Missabe and Northern Railroad, fifty-one other iron mining companies had been organized to develop the Mesabi Range. John McCaskill had opened the Biwabik mine to the east, and new explorations were feverishly being conducted around Embarrass Lake further to the east and at Hibbing and Nashwauk to the west by such adventurous mining engineers as Edmund Longyear, A. J. Trimble, and Frank Hibbing.[23]

Duluth had the excitement and fever of San Francisco in 1850. Men with shovels in their hands and wild hopes in their hearts were arriving from all over the northern range country. The land office was swamped, for it was still possible in 1892 to file homestead claims for this hitherto undeveloped wilderness.[24] It was just the kind of milieu in which Harry Oliver was at his best. He wasted no time in finding the Merritt brothers, who were now the respected lords of Duluth. With his easy charm, fast talk, and Pittsburgh connections, he had little difficulty in impressing the unsophisticated Lon that here was precisely the connection with Pittsburgh's steel and finance that Merritt had sought in vain when he had called upon Frick. The Merritts, as always, desperately needed cash, and without a moment's hesitation, Oliver wrote out a check for $5000 on his nonexistent cash balance in a Pittsburgh bank. He implied with a wink and a smile that there was plenty more where that came from, and the Merritts were only too happy in return to admit him into their partnership.

The first thing Oliver had to do was to make sure the check would not bounce by arranging a loan from the bank upon which he had written his check. This arrangement was made with no great difficulty. Oliver had been involved in far more complicated credit transactions in the past. The second task he set for himself proved more troublesome. He hurried back to Pittsburgh determined to do what Merritt had tried and failed to accomplish—to bring the Carnegie Steel Company into the operation as a partner. He encountered none of the problems that Merritt had in his interview with Frick. By this time, Mesabi ore with its cheap cost of production was the talk of the trade. Frick was definitely interested, but unfortunately Carnegie was not.

Just as Frick had regarded the burly giant of the north woods with cold suspicion two years before, when Lon Merritt had come bursting into his office, now it was Carnegie who distrusted his old friend, Harry Oliver. For Oliver, with his wild enthusiasms, his proclivity toward reckless speculation; and his many, varied interests, was everything that Carnegie had once been but now despised. When Carnegie got word from Frick of Oliver's overtures, he wrote back from Rannoch Lodge: "Oliver's ore bargain is just like him—nothing in it. If there is any department of business which offers no inducement, it is ore. It never has been very profitable, and the Massaba [sic] is not the last great deposit that Lake Superior is to reveal." [25]

In Frick's opinion, however, Oliver's offer was too good to miss. Oliver offered one-half interest in his mining company, which he had hastily organized with the Merritts, for a loan of $500,000, secured by a mortgage on the ore properties which Oliver and the Merritts would develop. Frick took pains to point out to Carnegie that they were getting half interest in a company simply by making a loan, not an investment. Supported by the other partners and business managers, Frick, in his capacity as chairman of the company, completed the negotiations with Oliver soon after the Homestead Strike was settled.

Carnegie remained unhappy about the business alliance with the mercurial and overly expansive Oliver. All through 1893 and 1894, in letters and comments on the minutes of the board meetings, he continued to grumble. "The Oliver bargain I do not regard as very valuable. You will find that this ore venture, like all our other ventures in ore, will result in more trouble and less profit than almost any branch of our business. If any of our brilliant and talented young partners have more time or attention than is required for their present duties, they will find sources of much greater profit right at home. I hope you will make a note of this prophecy." [26] His talented young partners did indeed make a note, and in later years it was often a source of consolation to remember that "the old man" could, on occasion, be quite wrong in his predictions.

Almost as if he were trying to draw his partner's attention away from Oliver's enticing siren calls from the north, Carnegie was at this same time taking an active interest in ore properties in West Virginia. With some excitement, he wrote to President Leishman in 1895:

Coming in here from Pittsburgh, Mr. Curry and I conversed about ore supply. . . . It flashed upon me that here was something of great importance. . . . Mr. Curry talked here with Gayley one morning and the latter told him that he received a letter from Mr. Catlett, a young mining engineer, whom he had seen a great deal of when in West Virginia. . . . Mr. Curry showed me that letter, and it seemed to be just what was needed. Mr. Catlett spoke of several of the finest properties now being within reach. I suggested that they should telegraph Catlett to come here. He did come and we had a most interesting meeting. The supply of ore around the White Sulphur Springs is unlimited. He named four properties, the option of which he felt sure could be got for a year at low prices. . . . The freight rate upon these Virginia ores to Duquesne or Edgar Thomson would be less than we are paying from the Lakes, from 75 to 80 cents. They can be concentrated to yield a 55 per cent ore. Messrs. Curry and Gayley are to lay the matter before you; I need not expatiate upon the possibilities. As usual I am very sanguine.[27]

A few weeks later he was encouraging Henry Curry, the treasurer of the company, to get options upon all available properties, but to do it secretly. "I do not think we should try to take up all the territory, but we should certainly have the option upon any proved mines that we know of. I wonder," he mused to Curry, with an almost Oliverian optimism, "if we are to look back upon this enterprise as one of the most remarkable in your long and illustrious career." [28]

Carnegie's optimism was unfulfilled. Within a year the West Virginia ventures had come to nothing. Carnegie put the reason for this in succinct fashion to H. E. Davis, who had been promoting the options to gain traffic for his railroads: "In reply to your note of the 16th inst., I am sorry to tell you that we did not find anything suitable in West Virginia. The Mesaba ore field with mines each containing from thirty to fifty millions of tons of proved ore, which has only to be shovelled into cars, renders competition from other fields almost impossible. . . . It is quite a disappointment to us, but we have dropped the matter." [29]

It must have been disappointing to Carnegie to have failed in his diversionary tactic against Oliver and the Mesabi Range. It was never easy for Carnegie to admit he had been wrong, but he could not compete against ore sold at 5 ¢ a ton, and he never allowed personal pride to stand in the way of profits. He later testified before the House Committee in 1912: "Fortunately, I woke up in time. . . . The truth of the matter is until I went to Lake Superior and saw and studied the question, I was averse to buying ores at all. I felt we had enough to do at home developing the finished product. . . . Harry Oliver, my fellow messenger in the telegraph office, was one of the brightest men Pittsburgh ever could boast of, and he saw far ahead, and went up to that region and loaded himself with ore leases. . . . He came to us and said he would like us to buy five-sixths of all his mining leases. That was a big order and I went to Lake Superior myself, because at that time I had thought we would not engage in the risk of mining; but I went up myself and looked over the whole question of ore there, and I saw those immense steam shovels shovelling up this ore at 15 or 20 cents a ton—and changed. 'We will go and own our own ore.' " [30]

That was not quite the way it happened, nor was it as simple and graceful a surrender upon Carnegie's part to the reasoned arguments of the ledger sheet as his testimony would indicate. And the hurt pride remained long after the profits had been gathered. In Carnegie's autobiography there is not one word about Mesabi or Harry Oliver's contribution to Carnegie Steel.

Considering the tangled web of the Merritts' finances and Oliver's past history of feast and famine, however, it is not altogether surprising that Carnegie should have been hesitant about associating his company's good name with such entrepreneurial instability as these men represented. And almost as soon as Frick had made the decision to join forces with Oliver and the Merritts by loaning them $500,000, Carnegie's worst fears seemed to have been proved true. The depression of 1893 hit the iron range country with a stunning blow. The Merritts had not only extended their credit, but had manufactured it when necessary, to build their railroad lines and open up new mines. And now their bills came due. Mesabi was far bigger than their most grandiose dreams, and certainly its demands for capital far exceeded any financial resources they could call upon in Duluth, or had been able to get from Carnegie Steel. Nor did they, even with Oliver's help, have the entrepreneurial skills necessary to manage an enterprise of this magnitude. It was at this moment, in the midst of depression, with the Merritts' creditors demanding payment, and steel mills no longer demanding their product, that John D. Rockefeller stepped in. It is not necessary in this account to deal with the complicated story of the Rockefeller-Merritt alliance that ultimately resulted in a civil suit which dragged through the courts for years. A cursory glance at the record would indicate that Frederick T. Gates, the former Baptist minister who became Rockefeller's most important associate in developing the iron ore interests, was right when he said that Rockefeller had saved the Merritts' skins.[31] At the Merritts' request and upon Gates's recommendation, Rockefeller in 1894 took over the major share in the newly formed Lake Superior Consolidated Iron Mines Company, which included the six mines the Merritt brothers had opened and held independent of Oliver, plus their railroad and ore docks.[32] Oliver and Carnegie Steel kept the mining company that was in Oliver's name.

The entry of Rockefeller into the iron ore business of Mesabi at once raised speculation that he would do for iron and steel as he had done for oil—create a new trust in another one of America's basic industries. Financial journals and the popular press alike were filled with stories of Rockefeller's acquisition of the richest iron ore deposits in the world, and with this control, the potentiality of his becoming the leader in the steel industry. To the nation it now seemed inevitable that there should be a confrontation between the two most noted figures in American business. Rockefeller and Carnegie, the two richest men in the world, were about to contend for control of the industrial world in open battle, like Alexander and Darius. Rockefeller did nothing to dispel the rumors that he planned to build a magnificent new steel mill near Cleveland, for such rumors could not help but strengthen his position in any negotiations with Carnegie. But Rockefeller never had any intention of entering into the manufacture of steel. Even his interest in the ore was far more involved in its transportation across the Great Lakes than in mining. This being so, the possibility for a co-operative alliance rather than a bloody battle between the Carnegie and Rockefeller forces became apparent to Oliver. As he opened the delicate negotiations, with Gates and Rockefeller on one side and Frick and Carnegie on the other, he was fully aware that, if successful, he would achieve the most spectacular agreement in the history of the iron trade.[33]

Carnegie continued to express doubts about Oliver's reliability, and he even cast some aspersions upon Rockefeller's business ability. He wrote to his partners in 1894, soon after Rockefeller's acquisition of the Merritts' interest became known: "Remember Reckafellows [sic] & Porter will own the R.R. and that's like owning the pipe lines—Producers will not have much of a show. We are big enough, however, to take care of ourselves and if *forced* could make another outlet somehow. . . . I don't think Standard people will succeed in making ore a monopoly like oil, they have failed in every new venture and Rockefeller's reputation now is one of the poorest investors in the world. His railroads are almost worthless. Note Troy, Cotton Seed, etc., etc." [34]

Nevertheless, when serious negotiations between Gates and Oliver got under way, Carnegie gave them more than his tacit assent. In a letter to Rockefeller (whom he persisted in addressing as Rockafellow), written in October 1896, he indicated his strong interest in an alliance:

> Our people have been conferring with your Mr. Gates upon an alliance which would give us all the ores we can use from your properties. The differences between the two seems to have been so great as to cause a failure of the negotiations. They came to see me today and explained these differences, which do not seem to me too irreconcilable, if both parties realized as I do, the mutual advantage of such an alliance, and were prepared to meet each other halfway.
>
> When Mr. Gates submits the matter to you, as I suppose he will, and you concur in this, I believe you and I could fix it in a few minutes, and I shall be very glad to go and see you if you think it worth while to take the matter up. It is a big operation, and needs to be looked at in a broader light than either Mr. Gates or Mr. Leishman, perhaps, are justified in taking.[35]

Carnegie and Rockefeller must have had a successful meeting, for shortly thereafter Carnegie was writing to Cousin Dod, "I think we shall ally ourselves with Rockafellow [sic]—Oliver showed me yesterday a sketch of alliance which is good. Will get Mesaba ore mostly Bess^r Limit at not over $4\frac{1}{2}$ ¢ a unit—from Mo Iron. Hope it will be closed this week." [36]

The terms of alliance were indeed good, and Rockefeller had gone more than half way to ensure an accommodation with Carnegie. The agreement provided that the Oliver Mining Company and the Carnegie Steel Company were to lease all of the Rockefeller ore property in the Consolidated Mining Company and were to pay a royalty of 25¢ for each ton of ore extracted. Carnegie and Oliver were to guarantee to take at least 600,000 tons of ore a year out of the mines and were to ship this ore, along with an additional 600,000 tons from the Oliver property, over the Rockefeller railroads and Lake steamships to the port near Cleveland. Rockefeller promised not to engage in the manufacture of steel, and in return Carnegie and Oliver agreed not to lease or purchase any additional Mesabi mines without Rockefeller's permission. The contract was to run for fifty years.[37]

Small wonder that Carnegie was pleased with these negotiations and could write Curry, "You should be thinking of how to provide two million tons of Mesaba ore next year. . . . If Rockefeller has no other desirable mines to lease upon the same terms, Oliver should be looking after others; but of course, we want to deal with the Rockefellers' if they have the article." [38]

The journal for the trade, *Iron Age,* hailed this contract as Carnegie's greatest triumph: "[It] completes the last link in a chain which gives the Carnegie Steel Company a position unequalled by any steel producer in the world. . . . With the Duquesne furnace in full operation, the Carnegie Steel Company will be unapproached in the world, not only as the largest works, but also as the concern who can market at the lowest prices." [39]

On the last day of 1896, Carnegie viewed the past year with great satisfaction. Bryan had been defeated, the gold dollar was now safe, and all was very definitely well within his own company. "Gentlemen," he addressed the officers of Carnegie Steel, "Let me wish you all the best of New Year's, and congratulate you upon the prospects of THE CARNEGIE STEEL COMPANY, and also THE FRICK COKE COMPANY. You have read the paragraph in to-day's 'Iron Age,' . . . which does not exaggerate, I think, what the company is to do, but which is slightly premature. . . . All hail 1897!

No New Year in the history of the Company so heavy with results ensuring our preeminence." [40]

The very success of the Carnegie-Oliver-Rockefeller negotiations had an effect upon the ore properties of the northern ranges which neither Carnegie nor Oliver had anticipated but which was to extend their control over the ore market. Rockefeller had accepted a royalty of only 25¢ a ton on the ore from all the properties leased to Carnegie and Oliver, which was 40¢ below the standard royalty fee of 65¢, and in addition, Rockefeller had granted very favorable transportation rates of 80¢ a ton by rail to Duluth and 65¢ a ton on the Great Lakes. This contract was given wide publicity, and it caused a panic among the other owners of ore property on the Mesabi, Vermillion, and Gogebic ranges. Shareholders were eager to sell out before the Carnegie-Rockefeller combination should reduce prices to a ruinous level. Within a few months after the contract went into effect, the price of Norrie ore, from the largest and best mines on the Gogebic Range, dropped from $4 a ton to $2.65, delivered on the docks at Cleveland. [41]

Carnegie had indicated in his letter of 22 December to Curry that, in anticipation of a need for 2,000,000 tons of ore in 1897, he hoped that Oliver would attempt to secure other leases for the Oliver Company. Oliver needed little encouragement in that direction. Having sold, at Carnegie's insistence, an additional one-third of his mining company to the Carnegie Steel Company, Oliver now held only one-sixth of the company that bore his name, and consequently he was eager to have that one-sixth interest represent as large an amount of ore tonnage as possible.

Restricted by the terms of the contract with Rockefeller from buying or leasing additional mines in the Mesabi Range, Oliver at first turned his attention elsewhere—to the Vermillion and Gogebic ranges. In the depressed condition of the market, he had a brilliant opportunity. By July 1897, he was able to report to Frick that he could acquire, either by leasing or purchase, three important mining areas: the Norrie and Tilden mines on the Gogebic Range, and the Pioneer, owned by a syndicate which included Senator John C. Spooner of Wisconsin, on the Vermillion Range. "The Carnegie and Oliver furnaces," he told Frick, "will require about four million Ts of ore per annum. Our minimum under my proposition would stand as follows: Mesaba—1.2 mills, Norrie—700 thousand Ts; Tilden—400 thous Ts; Pioneer—500 thous. Ts. The only cash obligation will be the purchase of the Norrie stock. The Mesaba leases we can throw up on 6 months notice, and the Tilden and Pioneer leases on 3 months notice. The amount we invest in Norrie is a very small item."

Fearing possible opposition from Carnegie, Oliver presented Frick those arguments which he knew would have the greatest chance of impressing Carnegie:

Excuse me for bringing to the attention of yourself and your associates the fact that the Carnegie Company never heretofore hesitated to invest millions of dollars to save 25¢ to 50¢ per ton in the manufacture of pig iron. You destroy old plants and erect new ones to save a quarter of a dollar per ton. . . . I propose at a risk of using our credit to the extent of $500,000, or possibly one million dollars, to effect a saving, in which our competitors will not share, of four to six million dollars per annum. On the Gogebic Range, the mines I have selected comprise over 80% of developed ore or "ore in sight." They comprise in this year's pool about 60% of the allotment. . . . An important point, in making the venture in the Gogebic region and securing a large body of ore, is the effect it will have upon the guarantee made us, by the Rockefeller party, that our ore shall be as low as any other Mesaba ore at Lake Superior ports. The possession of a large body of ore in the Gogebic Range will strengthen our position, in holding the Rockefeller people down to low freight rates from the Mesaba Range.

I am not ignoring the strong position we hold on the Mesaba Range. . . . More Mesaba ores can be used in our mixtures, but it is not a wise policy to quickly exhaust the rich quarry we have on the Mesaba Range, taking off rapidly the surface ore. Although we are mining it at present for less than five cents per ton for labor, we must look to the future, when we will have to go deeper, pump water and lift the ore. We should rather prolong the period of cheap steam shovel mining, take in the other Range properties I suggest for mixture; and by working one Range against the other, keep down the costs of freights. I desire to impress upon you the fact that if it had not been for our Rockefeller-Mesaba deal of last year, with the consequent demoralization in the trade caused by the publication thereof, it

603

would not have been possible for us to now secure the other
Range properties I propose to acquire, either by lease or for
any reasonable price. We simply knocked the price of ore from
$4.00 down to say $2.50 per ton. Now let us take advantage of
our action before a season of good times give the ore producers
strength and opportunity to get together by combination.

Then, realizing how Carnegie regarded his enthusiasm for plung-
ing, Oliver added a personal note:

I trust that when you read this letter and my reports you will
not attribute the strong position I take to my usually optimistic
nature. . . . You do not hear of the many properties I have condemned and turned down as being not worthy of your consideration. I have selected, for the decision of the associates only the
very best. . . . Please recall that . . . I only brought before you
for approval the magnificent properties on the Mesaba Range
that we are now operating. Pardon me for mentioning the
above. I only do it to impress upon you the fact that I have analyzed this question most thoroughly. . . . I know I am right
and trust you and your associates will give me the opportunity
to prove it.[42]

These were powerful arguments, which easily convinced most
of the board, but, unfortunately, not Carnegie. Carnegie wanted
to lease ore fields but did not want to buy mines, particularly on
the Gogebic and Vermillion ranges. "We should think twice before embarking in mining underground ore," he had counseled
his associates.[43]

Undaunted, Oliver had gone ahead making his arrangements
for the acquisition of the ore of all three mines. The Keweenaw
Association, headed by T. M. Davis, owned both the Norrie mines
and the Tilden mines. The Tilden mines had been leased to
Rockefeller, and Oliver had been able to secure an agreement
with both Davis and Rockefeller to sublease the Tilden, paying
to each a 25¢ royalty per ton, providing a minimum of 400,000
tons were mined each year, and Carnegie readily assented to
this.[44] With the owners of the Pioneer mine on the Vermillion
Range, Oliver was able to secure an option to lease with a royalty
of 35¢ a ton and the possibility of later purchasing the mine out-

right. Carnegie noted on the back of this proposal from Oliver, "This is the most attractive of all—Think we should cable to get option. Yes Tilden., Yes Pioneer. AC." [45]

On the Norrie, however, Oliver reached an impasse with both the owners and Carnegie. Carnegie wanted to lease, the owners wanted to sell. Oliver had spent many trying weeks writing to minority stockholders all over the country to get options to buy their stock, and by the end of July, he felt he had secured enough options to give the Carnegie-Oliver interests control over the concern. Schwab strongly favored the proposition, and he wrote to Frick: "Cost of stock would be 2.68 mill; quick assets of Co. such as ore on hand, bills receivable, etc. would be 1½ mill. over liabilities, leaving net cost of mine at 1.380 mill. There is beyond any doubt 2.8 mill tons of ore in sight so that if there were no other ore it would mean that we would have to charge against our cost of mining 50¢ per ton. . . ." (To which Carnegie made a marginal notation, "and interest 80,000 per yr—25¢"). "I think," Schwab continued, "there is no doubt whatever but that there is much over 5 mill Ts of ore to be had. . . . With this quantity of ore, it would mean charging off of only 25¢ per ton against our cost of mining." ("And *interest,* 80,000 per year. A.C.") At the bottom of this letter appeared Carnegie's notation: "Means an investment of say 3,000,000. Could not and should not try to freeze out other stockholders—litigation, censure etc. Can make three times any probable profit out of 3,000,000 in manfg." [46]

Two weeks later, Schwab received a cable from Carnegie flatly rejecting the Norrie proposition. "Norrie rejected owing minority stockholders. Tilden Pioneer favored." He followed this up the next day with a memo to the board of managers, which, among other matters discussed, amplified somewhat his strong feelings on the subject: "Norrie Mine declined. Policy of firm not to invest Capital in mining, but to lease mines upon favorable terms." Carnegie also feared that, since there would remain some minority stockholders whose shares they could not buy, there might later be trouble with them. "It is not wise for the Carnegie Steel Company Limited ever to buy trouble trying to deal with them." [47]

In spite of this rejection, Schwab would not give up. He wrote Carnegie immediately after receiving the cable that Oliver had obtained 19,400 shares at $20 a share. "This makes a total of 75 thousand we have options on. . . . I believe that Norrie is the property we should have, and I now believe that the objection on account of the minority of stockholders is not a good one." [48]

Frick, surprisingly enough, in view of later claims made by his supporters for his foresightedness, was with Carnegie in his lack of enthusiasm for purchasing the Norrie mines. In a letter to Phipps at this time, he said, "I feel just as I did when in consultation with Mr. Carnegie, yourself, and Mr. Lauder that we should not buy ore property. . . ." To the board of managers, he was even more explicit in his uneasiness about Oliver's business judgment. He said Oliver had acted foolishly in giving a $5000 advance to Rockefeller for the option on the Tilden mine, which would have to be forfeited if the option were not taken. "I do not believe that Mr. Rockefeller, personally, would have asked such a payment, and think it is a reflection on us to have an Agent make such a payment. . . . Mr. Oliver is a valuable man, properly controlled, but if he is allowed to run loose, he would soon wreck the credit of any concern that he attempts to do business for." [49]

The Norrie mines option would expire on 30 September. With less than three weeks to go, Frick suddenly had an inspiration, which he hastened to pass on to Carnegie. Since Oliver had now collected options on 87,300 of the 100,000 shares and thought that he would have the remainder by 20 September, why not offer these options of stock to Rockefeller? The oil magnate could then own Norrie as he owned the Mesabi mines, and Carnegie and Oliver could lease from Rockefeller on the same terms that they had arranged before. "This would be far better than purchase of even a minority interest at $20 a share. . . . Fortunately, Mr. Rockefeller's Mr. Gates has left for California, to be absent six weeks, so that there can be no impropriety in Oliver going direct to Mr. Rockefeller. . . . If you see any objections to taking this up with Mr. Rockefeller, please cable." [50]

Carnegie, of course, was delighted with this suggestion. Back came his answer in code, "Thoroughly approve of action. Whirlpool [John D. Rockefeller] buy we lease. Our buying intundit [not entitled to consideration]. . . . Wesenlos [Oliver] needs careful watching." [51]

Unhappily for Frick and Carnegie, Rockefeller was not in the market for more ore properties and he declined Frick's offer to

606

serve once again as their genial landlord. With only five days left on the option, Oliver decided to make one last appeal to Carnegie to change his mind. On 25 September, he sent this historic cable:

> I am distressed at indications here that Norrie options expiring on Monday are to be refused. It would be a terrible mistake. The good times make it that I could not possibly secure these options again at fifty per cent advance. The Norrie mines control the whole situation. They have sold over one million tons this year with the additional property we will get from the fee owners we secure fifteen to twenty million tons of the ore that the Carnegie company are purchasing this year five hundred and fifty thousand tons. I will guarantee counting the surplus they have in the treasury to return in profits every dollar we invest in two years. Do not allow my hard summer's work to go for naught.[52]

Although Carnegie had always distrusted Oliver's proposals on the personal ground of having known him too well in the past, it was, paradoxically, this final plea of Oliver's, couched in personal terms of past friendship, that caused Carnegie to relent. He replied to Oliver, "Board decides. Think myself true policy only lease best mines," To the board, he sent the following cable, "Always approve unanimous action of board after full expression views. Sure leasing true policy but if board decides this exception all right." [53]

The board met in emergency session on the same day that Carnegie's cable was received, on 27 September, and unanimously approved the purchase of the Norrie stock. Even Frick announced that he had changed his mind since last Saturday. He then sent a cable to Carnegie, "Board unanimously decide will purchase all stock Norrie Mines. This removes the Carnegie Steel Company, Limited from the Bessemer Ore Market. Business broadening; outlook good." [54]

And indeed it was. The Carnegie Steel Company was now self-sufficient and would never again have to buy a ton of Bessemer ore on the open market. Oliver's victory was complete, but never did a man have to work as hard to present a fortune to others as he had.

Iron Age noted this latest acquisition with some concern for the independent producers of steel in the trade:

> Announcement is made that the Oliver mining Company have acquired by purchase control of the stock of the Metropolitan Iron Company, owning the Norrie and adjoining mines and have also leased from John D. Rockefeller the Tilden mines. Both are located on the Gogebic range. . . . The Carnegie-Oliver interests are, therefore, largely independent of any wide fluctuations in the cost of raw materials. . . . The iron trade in this country will study the situation with special references to its effects upon the interests of each concern and each district. . . . [There is] `a belief prevalent that a few persons, using the tactics of John D. Rockefeller, will try to do in the iron business what was done in oil. . . . It would be better for the country to have a large number of independent producers, each supporting a community, than one or two great concerns. . . . It is to be hoped that the project of controlling the iron trade of the Central West will be found too great to be accomplished, even with the colossal funds at the command of those who are undertaking it.[55]

Iron Age had reason to be concerned about the fate of the numerous independent producers. After September 1897, it would be increasingly difficult for anyone to compete with Carnegie Steel. As Carnegie had written several years before, in the mistaken notion that he was quoting Herbert Spencer, it was "an evolution from the heterogeneous to the homogeneous, and is clearly another step in the upward path of development"— certainly, at least, for Carnegie Steel Limited.

Having reluctantly taken his first taste of mine ownership, Carnegie, as was always the case, became voracious in his appetite, and wanted much more. He encouraged re-opening negotiations with Senator Spooner and his associates, from whom the Carnegie company had a lease on the ore from the Pioneer mine in the Vermillion region. Carnegie now wanted to own it.[56] That Spooner was receptive to this suggestion is indicated by the letter he wrote one of his partners: "It looks to me that with the reservation left in the Carnegie agreement to throw up the lease at any time, . . . we will be entirely in their power. . . . It strikes me that it would be a great deal safer for us to make a contract with the Carnegie's, or the Oliver Mining Co., to transfer to them the present lease at 57. as Oliver wanted it. . . . I only suggest this. Probably there is no danger that they would throw up the lease, but I learned a long time ago not to put much faith in Princes." [57]

Oliver kept the pressure on Spooner, and a few months later Spooner was writing to the same partner: "I have no apology to make . . . for talking to Oliver, or to anyone else, about purchasing our stock. . . . I would rather sell out our stock at ten or twelve dollars than have the lease extended on a five hundred thousand ton maximum . . . giving them the right to throw it up at anytime they saw fit. With our party, that would leave us with a bear's grip on our throat all the time." [58]

Soon thereafter the final arrangements were made. The Oliver Mining Company purchased Spooner's shares in the Pioneer, giving the Carnegie-Oliver interests a majority interest in the mine.[59] Spooner wrote to a friend, "I am sorry we had to sell the Pioneer stock, but I have been very glad every moment since it was sold that we sold it. With the consolidations that are taking place, I think we would have been smashed if as individuals we had attempted, without large capital, to develop it and run it. I do not know that we could have done it successfully with large capital." [60] *Iron Age* again had to report a major acquisition by the Carnegie-Oliver interests. It called the purchase of the Pioneer mine by Oliver "his most brilliant accomplishment yet," for with this purchase, Carnegie and Oliver "now control the Gogebic, Mesaba and Vermillion ranges." [61]

The indefatigable Oliver was not finished yet, however. By the end of 1899, he and Carnegie Steel controlled through lease or ownership 34 working mines, including 10 mines on the Marquette range, 7 on the Gogebic, 5 on the Menominee, 4 on the Vermillion, and 8 on the Mesabi. In addition, they had acquired 16 areas for exploratory purposes, located on every range except the Mesabi.[62] Their monopoly of the Lake Superior and Minnesota iron ranges, the most valuable known iron deposits in the world, was virtually complete.

In accumulating this impressive list, however, Oliver had not been overly scrupulous about the contract agreement with Rocke-

609

feller. The Stephens mine at Biwabik had been leased from another company, and the Security and the Rouchleau mines had been purchased outright in direct violation of the contract.[63] When, in September 1899, Gates rather belatedly heard of this from outside sources, he quite properly entered a vigorous protest to Oliver. He quoted from a letter, signed by both Leishman and Oliver, dated 4 December 1896, in which, on behalf of their companies, both men promised "that it will not be our purpose, certainly within the first ten years of the existence of the Mountain Iron lease, to lease, or purchase any fee in further Missabe properties." He also quoted a letter from Oliver of 12 May 1898 in which Oliver said that other properties, including the Rouchleau mine, "have been pressed upon us. . . . *There has been nothing equivocal in our answers* to these people, and you must allow me to say that it is thoroughly well known on the Range that it is *no use approaching us, on account of our relations with you.*" Gates concluded his letter by saying, "Further comment is unnecessary. These facts speak for themselves. I do not pretend in these letters to exhaust our files in these quotations. I am simply giving you a few salient points. Of course, I need not tell you that this matter cannot be dropped or overlooked." [64]

The Carnegie Steel Company had no choice but to acknowledge that it and the Oliver Mining Company had broken the contract with Rockefeller. There followed months of negotiations, in which James Gayley and Daniel Clemson, as board members, represented Carnegie Steel. In February 1900, a tentative agreement was reached, that, all things considered, was remarkably generous to the Carnegie-Oliver interests. By the terms of these negotiations, the Rouchleau mine was turned over to Rockefeller, as was the Stephens mine. But in return, Carnegie and Oliver got a lease on the Stephens mine and also a lease on the much more valuable Ohio mine located near by, as well as on the Shaw mine. In reporting this settlement to the board of Carnegie Steel, Gayley and Clemson wrote, "After a careful examination of the original papers, with memoranda thereon by Mr. Carnegie, Mr. Leishman and Mr. Curry, we are entirely of the opinion that we have no grounds whatever to justify our purchases of these properties. The demand of Mr. Gates that we turn over to them without condition the 75,000,000 tons of ore we had secured was fully justified within the letter and spirit of the agreement entered into. It is difficult to play a game of bluff when the other party holds the card, and you know it; nevertheless, we have been able to retain 60,000,000 tons out of the 75,000,000 tons that we acquired during the past year." [65] For the next five months, both sides worked out in minute detail twenty-eight separate contracts, covering every possible facet of the mining agreements between Rockefeller's Consolidated Company and the Oliver Mining–Carnegie Steel companies. [66]

As for Oliver, he was quite unabashed by having broken the previous contract. He wrote a hearty letter of congratulations to Gayley on his new agreement:

> The advantageous features are twenty to one in our favor, and are over and over much better than I expected we would be able to obtain. I congratulate you and Mr. Clemson most heartily on your success. I am delighted that our plan of campaign has worked to such a favorable result. From your experience and working with our friends, I think you will acknowledge that there would have been no concessions . . . if we had not made the radical and pronounced change in our policy, and purchased and leased the properties now in question. . . . I note that you could do nothing in the Rouchleau matter and can easily see that that was a sore point with our friends, and that they think they are punishing us in holding it out. You will recall that I always stated that I intended to trade the Rouchleau for the Ohio, Etna, etc. You have done this in a grand way, far better than I originally anticipated. [67]

As Carnegie always said, "Oliver needs watching." But then, so did Carnegie and company.

With the acquisition of the Norrie mines on the Gogebic Range and the Pioneer on the Vermillion, it could be safely said that Carnegie Steel Company, Limited had successfully completed stage one. It now had almost unlimited control over the basic raw materials needed in the production of steel, and did not need to go into the open market for either iron ore or coke. During the 1899 season alone, the Carnegie Steel Company shipped 3,500,000 tons of iron ore on lake freighters to the docks at Conneaut on Lake Erie at an average rate of $65\frac{1}{2}¢$ a ton. [68]

Unfortunately, however, the long trip of transporting ore from the Michigan and Minnesota mines was not over for Carnegie Steel when the ore boats came into dock, as it was for Illinois Steel or the Lorain Steel Works. The Carnegie Company had then to reload the ore into railroad cars and take it 150 miles across the rugged terrain of western Pennsylvania to Pittsburgh.

Having obtained bargain rates on transportation from Rockefeller, on both his Duluth, Missabe Railroad line and his "whaleback" ore freighters on the Great Lakes, Carnegie more than ever resented having to pay the freight rates of the Pennsylvania Railroad. He continued to be obsessed with the idea that the Pennsylvania was taking full advantage of its monopolistic situation to extort rates twice as high from him as it did from his competitors, who were more fortunately located at points where there was competition among several roads for their freight.

Even before he had entered into an alliance with Rockefeller on the Mesabi Range, and while he was still buying Marquette ore on the open market, Carnegie was looking around for a way out of the Pennsylvania snare in which he felt himself trapped. In 1894, he had his very able general freight agent, George E. McCague, obtain for him the freight rates being paid by his competitors on raw materials. By methods which he never revealed, but which must have involved the bribing of railroad personnel, McCague got the figures on the freight rates for the raw materials necessary to produce one ton of steel at the Lorain and Youngstown steel works. These figures Carnegie found most interesting when compared with freight costs to Bessemer, Pennsylvania, the terminal point for rail shipments to the Carnegie works at Braddock, Homestead, and Duquesne. Lorain, being located on the Lake Erie shore, had no freight rates for ore, so comparisons were as follows: [69]

Iron Ore:

Bessemer	1.6 tons of ore at $1.15 a T	$1.84
Lorain	no charge	0
Youngstown	1.6 tons of ore at 67½¢ a T	1.08

Coke:

Bessemer	.85 tons at 55¢ a T	.468
Lorain	.85 tons at $1.65 a T	1.402
Youngstown	.85 tons at 1.25 a T	1.062

Limestone:

Bessemer	.4 ton at 80¢ a T	.32¢
Lorain	.4 ton at 30¢ a T	.12¢
Youngstown	.4 ton at 30¢ a T	.12¢

Total Cost of Freight Rates on Raw Material
To Make One Ton of Steel:

Bessemer	$2.628
Lorain	1.52
Youngstown	2.262

Carnegie, after perusing these figures, could not accept the conclusion drawn by his freight agent that "our rates are not unreasonable as compared with the rates of our competitors," or that "the P.R.R. . . . have pursued a liberal policy toward us during recent years." [70] Nor could Carnegie agree with Frick's note added to McCague's letter: "The Pennsylvania Railroad has really been assisting us in the most satisfactory manner. Believe we have their confidence, and they will do everything possible to assist this concern in holding its own against all comers." [71]

Carnegie could never understand Frick's tolerant attitude toward the Pennsylvania Railroad when the figures McCague obtained, not only in this instance but on several other occasions, clearly showed that Pittsburgh, and most notably the Carnegie Steel Company, continued to pay a high premium of freight rates to the Pennsylvania. Frick, however, wanted no trouble with the railroad that continued to be their best customer for rails, that always took care of the company's shipments, no matter how large, efficiently and expeditiously, and, above all (although Frick would never have admitted this), that was extremely generous in its rebate payments to the Frick Coke Company. He was always cautioning Carnegie not to disrupt their amicable relations with the Pennsylvania. "It has been our policy," wrote Frick to Carnegie in December 1894, "to tie to them [the Pennsylvania Railroad]." [72]

But Carnegie took the good service for granted, and as for the rebates, he was sure that other companies were getting larger rebates simply because they could bid for them with one railroad against another. After the acquisition of the Mesabi mines, Carnegie was determined to get his own railroad line to the Lake ports.

This time he was not going to be foiled by a deal arranged by Morgan between competing lines. Against the advice of Frick, who felt he had made a very fair arrangement for transportation for the coming year, 1896, Carnegie started negotiations for a railroad to the Lake Erie port of Conneaut, Ohio.

Frick had made one major contribution to offsetting the high freight rates, for which Carnegie was most appreciative. Soon after taking over the management of the company, he had planned and successfully completed the building of the Union Railway, a company-owned railroad that served all of the company's various plants, steel mills, and furnaces in the Monongahela Valley and Pittsburgh areas, and that connected with the Pennsylvania Railroad. Prior to the building of the Union Railway, both the Pennsylvania and the B. & O. railroads had had control of all tracks and sidings within the plant areas. The savings in switching charges alone that Carnegie Steel had previously had to pay to the railroads was enough to pay the interest on the cost of building the Union Railway. Although it covered a distance of less than a hundred miles, the Union Railway carried as much freight as many of the major railway systems of the country—16,000,000 tons in 1899.[73]

If this railway could be connected with a line to the Great Lakes, Carnegie reasoned, then at least a part of the ore required could, after being unloaded at the docks, be brought directly to the furnaces in Pittsburgh without paying tribute to the Pennsylvania monopoly. There existed at that time a small, nearly bankrupt line called the Pittsburgh, Shenango & Lake Erie Company. The lengthy name represented more aspiration than reality, for actually it ran only from Conneaut, Ohio, on Lake Erie to Butler, Pennsylvania, some thirty miles north of Pittsburgh. To call it a railroad was in itself something of an exaggeration. Its road bed was in a deplorable state—"little more than a right of way and two streaks of rust" was the description one writer has given of it.[74] Nevertheless, it did have the all-important charter from the state of Pennsylvania, giving a right of way through the Alleghenies to a port on the Great Lakes. This charter alone made the railroad highly attractive to Carnegie. He entered into negotiations with its president, Colonel S. B. Dick, late in 1895, to reorganize the nearly defunct company and to extend its line from Butler to Bessemer, where a junction could be made with the Union Railway.

Colonel Dick soon proved himself to be as full of promise and as empty of performance as the line he headed. For several months, he kept assuring Carnegie that with the guaranteed tonnage which the Carnegie Steel Company could furnish the railroad there would be no difficulty in forming a syndicate of wealthy Boston financiers to finance the railroad improvements and the extension of the line. But there were continuing delays, excuses, and not very subtle suggestions from Dick that other, unnamed interests were eager to buy Pittsburgh, Shenango & Lake Erie stock.[75] It was not until the middle of April that the required $3,000,000 to extend the line to Bessemer was subscribed, and then only by Carnegie's contributing $2,000,000 and Frick $300,000, as well as Phipps, Lauder, and Singer adding another $150,000. It was thus from the first controlled by and exclusively for the Carnegie Steel Company.[76]

So determined was Carnegie to get this railroad project under way and to control it that he did something he had not done in many years. He borrowed on his own personal note $1,000,000 from the United States Trust Company of New York, secured by $1,500,000 worth of his Frick Coke Company stock.

There was a rather interesting little by-play in Carnegie's obtaining this loan which Lucy Carnegie, Carnegie's sister-in-law, might have appreciated had she known about it. A favorite story in her family concerned the time that she complained to Carnegie, who was visiting her in Florida, that she never could get her son and his namesake, Andrew, to write to her while he was away at college. Carnegie replied that he would bet her ten dollars that he could get an answer from his nephew by return mail. She immediately accepted the wager, so Carnegie sat down and wrote a nice, newsy letter to young Andrew. At the conclusion he added the postscript that he was enclosing a check for ten dollars as a little gift. Then Carnegie deliberately failed to enclose the check. Within two days, there was a letter from his nephew, thanking Carnegie for his gift but telling him that the check had not been enclosed. Lucy had to pay the wager, which Carnegie then promptly sent to her son.[77]

Whether or not Carnegie deliberately used the same tactics in obtaining a favorable response from John Stewart, president of the United States Trust Company, is a matter of conjecture, but the end result proved to be just as successful. Money was not easy to come by in the spring of 1896, as the silverites threatened to take over the country and to inflate the currency. Carnegie nevertheless needed $1,000,000 quickly to meet his promised subscription of $2,000,000 to the railroad syndicates. So he wrote his request to Stewart, and concluded by saying, "You would also have something unique—my note. It is many years since I have had a personal obligation, and I have none now, nor do I intend to have any but this, which would be about one million for 12 mos. $80,000 each mo. 1 year." [78]

Then, curiously enough, Carnegie failed to enclose the letter in the envelope. Stewart, upon receiving an empty envelope, at once wrote back to Carnegie, asking what Carnegie had intended to send.[79] Carnegie replied the next day by sending the original letter and adding the postscript that after he had written the letter he had decided not to send it as he did not really need to borrow the money after all, "but the envelope was already addressed and in the rush, had got mailed anyway." But if Stewart wanted to lend him money, he would accept $1,000,000 with the Frick stock as collateral.[80] Stewart apparently came through, for the following week Carnegie wrote to his business secretary, Robert Franks, that he had been successful in borrowing $1,000,000 from John Stewart, "which I have turned over to the Carnegie Steel Company. I pay 5% interest and the Carnegie Steel Co. credits me only with the same, namely 5%." [81]

With the money thus raised, the negotiations were quickly completed and construction of the railroad got under way. Carnegie was now ready to talk tough to the Pennsylvania Railroad. The most in the way of tonnage that could be expected to be carried on the new line was 1,500,000 tons a year, about one-half of the total amount of ore used each year. So Carnegie would still have to depend upon the Pennsylvania to carry the balance, but he now felt in a position to bargain. As he wrote Frick, "Now please understand, I do not blame Mr. Roberts, Mr. Thomson, Mr. McCrea or Mr. Caldwell for combining and getting the best rates they can from us. . . . I am sure that you feel with me that if we were in Mr. Robert's place, it is very probable we should do

616

exactly as he does. I quite appreciate this. I would not reduce rates until I thought it was necessary." [82]

Carnegie felt the time had come when the Pennsylvania managers would see that a reduction was necessary. On 5 May, he wrote to Frank Thomson, the vice president of the Pennsylvania Railroad, enclosing a copy of the contract with Colonel Dick regarding the extension of the Pittsburgh, Shenango & Lake Erie line:

> The Pennsylvania Road cannot afford to stand by and see its principal customers assailed by competitors who get lower rates, and you know this as well as I do, that sooner or later you must protect your manufacturers.
>
> I have no doubt of being able to get equal rates as soon as our line is finished to a connection with Baltimore & Ohio, New York & Erie, Nickel-Plate and the Lake Shore. Two of these have already told how anxiously they await our coming. Therefore the advantages you give to us are slight.
>
> You will observe that coke is included in the contract. An extension to the coke region was part of the scheme, but it did not seem to me necessary to go forward with this. It will, however, be promptly done, unless the matter is closed between us by Saturday. It is already, and I have only to say the word when I go to Pittsburgh on Monday. . . .
>
> I think the great Pennsylvania Railroad has come to a sad condition, when it is only not willing, but not anxious to stand behind its own customers, and give equal rates per ton per mile to those which its competitors receive. The idea that Chicago can send ten-thousand tons of plates to Newport News for three dollars a gross ton, and the P.R.R. Co. tried to get four dollars net ton; and that billets reach New Jersey as cheaply from Chicago as from Pittsburgh! [Carnegie here refers to a recent bid on a contract by a foreign government for ship plates which his company had expected to win but had lost to Illinois Steel. Carnegie blamed the loss of the contract on the high freight rates charged by the Pennsylvania Railroad to Newport News, Virginia.] If the thousands of idle men in Pittsburgh to-day knew that this was one reason for its [sic] idleness, I would not give much for the receipts of the Pennsylvania road in and around Pittsburgh after a month or two. Even if you do not arrange with us, something must be done soon, or an explosion will take place.

I send the enclosed contract to you personally and not as an official of the Pennsylvania Railroad, and I depend upon you returning it by messenger, and not taking a copy. Any notes you may desire for your personal use, of course, are all right.[83]

Whether or not Thomson kept notes on the contract, there is no doubt that he and President Roberts understood what Carnegie was driving at. Carnegie did not have long to wait for an invitation from Roberts to come to Philadelphia to see him and Thomson about freight rates. Armed with additional secret information on rates paid by his competitors which McCague had obtained for him, Carnegie on 11 May set off for Philadelphia and the main offices of the Pennsylvania Railroad with a light heart. In later years, in an article in *Century Magazine,* "My Experience with Railway Rates and Rebates," he took delight in recalling that meeting. Never had he received a more cordial and friendly reception from the executive officers of the Pennsylvania. Both Roberts and Thomson were shaken when he produced exact rates paid by his competitors on freight tonnage hauled on competing lines. "Tell us what you want," Thomson asked. Carnegie's answer, according to him, was a simple request for justice. "Gentlemen, all we have ever asked was that rates charged us shall be at all times as low as those which competitors on other lines are paying on the same articles for similar distances. We ask for nothing else. Other lines are carrying freight for our competitors cheaper than you are carrying it for us, and you take part of this freight at the cut rates. We cannot stand that." Roberts and Thomson promised Carnegie the same rates if he would stop building his own line to the Lakes. This, Carnegie said, he could not do, but he did agree not to build an extension to the coke fields. "This," he recalled, "they gladly accepted. The result of the meeting was that I got all I asked for. . . . Everything was satisfactorily arranged, and we were all 'boys together again.' "[84]

The agreement was indeed all that Carnegie could possibly have hoped for: instead of paying $1.15 a ton for ore, the new rate was fixed at 63 ¢; coke was reduced from 55 ¢ to 35 ¢ a ton at Bessemer and 45 ¢ a ton at the Lucy Furnaces; and limestone from 80 ¢ to 55 ¢ a ton. In return, Carnegie agreed not to build any more railroads or to allow any rival roads to enter the various works.[85]

Carnegie estimated that by the terms of this settlement the company would save $1,500,000 annually in freight costs for raw materials. It was his proudest moment in the long history of his struggle with the Pennsylvania Railroad. Regardless of the reduced costs, the Pittsburgh, Shenango & Lake Erie had already more than paid for itself in terms of Carnegie's own personal satisfaction.

Replacing the inept Colonel Dick with Judge James H. Reed, who had successfully managed the Union Railway, Carnegie demanded quick action on the construction for his new railroad. The old road bed from Butler to Conneaut was regraded and new ties and new rails, sturdy enough to bear the heavy burden that was expected to be placed on them, replaced the "two streaks of rust" through the mountains of western Pennsylvania. As always, Carnegie pushed Reed and his employees inordinately. He wanted the railroad completed within fifteen months and to do that he was willing to lash Reed with tongue and pen. The patient, hard-working Judge was not surprised by these tactics for, as he said, "I know the 'Carnegie' policy is no credit for what has been done but constant spurring up for the future. . . ." [86]

Within fifteen months ore and other materials could move from Conneaut to the furnaces at Duquesne and Homestead on Carnegie's own railroad. In line with the removal of Colonel Dick, Carnegie wanted to erase all other traces of the old railroad's luckless past. The Pittsburgh, Shenango & Lake Erie line was merged with the new extension from Butler to Bessemer and renamed the Pittsburgh, Bessemer & Lake Erie Railroad. It was more familiarly known as "Carnegie's model railroad"—but not in a diminutive sense. Frank McClure wrote in the *National Magazine* that it was probably the finest, most modern and efficient freight line in the world. Its rolling stock was the wonder of the railroad world, for it had two of the biggest locomotives ever built up to that time. The total weight of each locomotive, McClure reported, was 391,400 lbs., and each was capable of pulling twenty-five of the large steel ore cars fully loaded, the heaviest freight train ever drawn by a single engine.[87]

With the completion of the railroad in the fall of 1897, there remained the question of docking facilities to complete Carnegie's railroad system. In the spring of 1898, Carnegie Steel purchased the entire area around Conneaut harbor. The existing docks and car-loading equipment were modernized and, where necessary, replaced with new facilities, at a cost of $250,000.[88]

Carnegie made sure that the Pennsylvania Railroad was kept fully informed on the progress of the Carnegie Steel Company's venture in railroad building. In November 1896, with construction well underway, Carnegie wrote with cocksure pride, "When the improvements are finished, we shall transport ore south, coal north in 1200-ton trains at one mill per ton per mile, or thereabouts. One mill per ton more will pay the interest on every dollar invested, say total .30 cents per ton. We shall reach Chicago and New York at not exceeding $1.30 per ton from our works during water navigation from Conneaut. Pittsburgh is to be once more the best point for manufacturing and marketing steel, better even than Lorain. This railroad has saved our property." [89]

As Carnegie had anticipated, the Pennsylvania Railroad, which had backed down in 1896, proved even more tractable in 1898, when the new road from Bessemer to Butler was opened and merged with the old Pittsburgh, Shenango & Lake Erie. Thomson, the newly chosen president, agreed to a further reduction in freight rates on ore from 63 to 53¢ per gross ton, the same as the charge on the new Pittsburgh, Bessemer & Lake Erie, and 46¢ per ton on lime. "And the PRR agrees that upon finished products of the Carnegie Steel equal rates per ton per mile will be given to those given from time to time by other railway companies in other districts to steel manufacturers upon similar traffic." In return the Carnegie Steel Company agreed "not to embark upon or aid in building new roads to Pittsburgh, nor to contract with other railways for a portion of its traffic, and that it will consult the first Vice-President of the P.R.R. in regard to all its traffic, and do all that it properly can do to give the PRR as much of its traffic as it can without creating a rupture with other lines. . . . This understanding is meant to bring the PRR and the CSCo. into close alliance, and is never to be referred to, except to the parties hereto. It is in nowise intended to be a legal document, on the contrary, it is not. It is however an honorable understanding between the parties. It is subject to five years notice by either party, and we pledge ourselves upon our honor to carry out this understanding in accordance with the spirit which created it, namely, a mutual desire to enter into close alliance." [90]

In the warm glow of this newly created alliance, Carnegie wrote Thomson quite a different letter from the one he had written him two years before:

> You took up none too soon the question of our rates upon finished material. Let me say how delighted I was to hear of the broad and able manner in which you met and solved that vital question. When Mr. Schwab advised me of your decision I had no hesitation in approving future extensions which I hope will give the dear old Pennsylvania Rail Road a great deal more traffic than ever. . . . It was Lorain that made our railroad to the lakes a necessity. Pittsburgh had to become practically a Lake Port or be bottled up. Now we must prepare to meet this far more serious competition than ever existed before. The Lorain concern will grow and of course as you know its business goes to the Lake Shore lines. . . . We shall need the lowest possible rates to and from the lakes to compete with Lorain. Most of these of course we can take care of upon our own line if we have to, but rates to Cleveland Toledo &c you will have to take care of for us. Newport News we should also reach at low rates. [That loss of contract on ship plates still rankled.] . . . Meanwhile permit me again to express my appreciation of your action and, if I may say so, of your wisdom in giving us today rates which I think are fair to both and which we are only too glad to pay as long as our competitors do not force your rivals to give even lower rates. With sincere congratulations upon the obvious success of your administration. Always yours." [91]

As for Frick's coal fields, they did quite all right with the Pennsylvania Railroad too. The Pennsylvania's published rates proved, under Thomson's new liberality, quite fictitious and for public consumption only. Frick quietly arranged with Thomson and McCrea the most generous rebates that he had ever obtained in return for Carnegie Steel's not extending its railway lines to Connellsville. Some years later, the former secretary of the H. C. Frick Coke Company, M. M. Bosworth, after reading some of Carnegie's pious statements in the public press, that he and his partners had never benefited from the rebate system, wrote Carnegie an angry letter in which he pointed out how false Carnegie's professions of innocence were:

> Through your great wealth and your philanthropy, libraries, etc., you have become a public character of prominence and international interest. Some of your public utterances and writings are read with interest. To some of your old employees they are both interesting and highly amusing. Recently you publicly referred to persons who buy and sell stocks in Wall Street as stock gamblers. . . . Why don't you tell the public that through the great volume of your business, you were able to take railroads by the throat and to compel them to secretly violate state and Federal laws . . . ? Why are you apparently afraid to acknowledge that you were the "chiefest rebater" of the Pennsylvania RR Co. as charged in last June's Pearson's Magazine by James Creelman."

Bosworth then proceeded to list the rebates obtained from various railroads for the coke company for the one month of December 1899, which he, Bosworth, as secretary of the company, had arranged. The rebates for that month totaled $1,105,243.57. Bosworth's real complaint was, of course, that, although he had been "your partner in *crime,*" he had not shared in the plunder, and he concluded by saying, "Thieves obtain their plunder through violations of law but they are honest enough to divide the 'swag' with their pals. It takes Carnegie-Frick millionaire hogs to receive vast financial benefits through secret violations of state and federal laws . . . and leave old pals in the lurch." [92]

To Bosworth's angry charges, Carnegie, of course, made no response. Bosworth's letter, however, with its specific figures showing the amount of rebates received on coke from each railroad which the company patronized, can hardly be denied, and it does much to explain Frick's friendly and tolerant attitude toward the Pennsylvania Railroad. Nor is it surprising that for a time at least Carnegie was quite satisfied with the alliance with Thomson. Carnegie had not given the public a full understanding of how varied and rich his "Experiences with Railway Rates and Rebates" were, in his celebrated article in Century Magazine.

After building the railroad from Bessemer to Conneaut and

acquiring the harbor and docks of that Lake Erie port, there remained only one additional step to complete the Carnegie transportation system to the rich ore fields of Lake Superior and northern Minnesota. By the terms of the lease with Rockefeller, the Carnegie Steel Company had agreed to ship a minimum of 1,200,000 tons of ore on the Rockefeller ore boats across Lake Superior and down Lake Erie each year. At the time the leases were made in 1896, this had seemed to be an impressively large figure, and, indeed, one reason for Carnegie's hesitancy in taking up Oliver's proposal had been the magnitude of this guarantee. But within a year Carnegie Steel was taking more than 3,000,000 tons of ore out of the northern ranges, and the most that the Rockefeller lake freighters could handle was 1,500,000 tons. In order to transport the remaining half, it was necessary for Carnegie Steel to bargain with various steamship companies who were not as generous in their terms as Rockefeller had been. As a result, Carnegie, for once, was more than receptive to a proposal from Oliver, when that busy little man suggested that the Carnegie-Oliver interests should acquire their own steamship company. Early in 1899, Oliver arranged to purchase the Lake Superior Iron Company's fleet of six ore vessels, each of which could carry 3000 tons of ore. The Pittsburgh Steamship Company, capitalized at $4,000,000, was organized, controlled, and directed by the managers of the Oliver Mining Company and the Carnegie Steel Company, but its corporate identity was kept separate from that of its owners.[93]

Thus, by 1899, Carnegie could take pride in the fact that his steel company was now in control of stages one and two of manufacturing, as he had outlined those stages. From the moment the soft, red ore was shoveled out of the ground in northern Minnesota by one of Oliver's giant steam shovels until the bright new steel rails rolled out of the mill at Edgar Thomson and were cut and stacked on the company's flatcars, the Carnegie Steel Company controlled every step in the manufacture and transportation of its own products, except for the short rail trip on Rockefeller's Duluth, Missabe line. On the day the first Carnegie ore boat left Duluth for its long run to Conneaut harbor, there to meet up with the Pittsburgh Bessemer line, Carnegie wrote proudly to Frick, "Today Pittsburgh becomes a lake port."[94] The transportation battle appeared to be over, and Carnegie was confident that he had won.

The other major item in addition to the acquisition and transportation of raw materials in the cost of producing steel was labor, and after Homestead there was little difficulty in arranging wage scales that were satisfactory to management. Both the depression and the elimination of the Amalgamated Association from all of Carnegie's steel plants were major factors in keeping labor costs low. Carnegie, even during the depression, liked to boast that his company paid the highest wages in the trade. In a letter to the editor of *Outlook* magazine in 1896, in commenting upon a series of articles the magazine was running on labor and capital, Carnegie objected vigorously to the references to him in those articles:

> In his last article, [the author] speaks of myself, and thinks, perhaps, it would be better to distribute in higher wages among the workmen the money with which I build libraries, etc., etc.
>
> You see, Mr. Editor, I differ from him in toto, but perhaps he will be surprised to know that we do pay the highest wages in the world. Every man employed at Homestead last year made two dollars and ninety cents per day average. This embraced common labor as well as skilled. Perhaps an "Employer" can find something like that elsewhere, but I have never known of it.[95]

Unfortunately for Carnegie's argument, these wages could not be found at Homestead either. The average wage at Homestead prior to the strike and the depression had been less than $1.40 a day. In December 1893, the *Pittsburgh Post* announced that new wage scales at Homestead represented cuts as high as 60% for skilled workers. "These are the lowest scales of any in this section, union or non-union," the paper reported. "The men at Homestead are disgruntled." [96] It is true that the steel industry generally cut wages in 1893–94 due to the depression, but the over-all average reduction in annual earnings for the blast furnaces and rolling mills of the country was 14%, not the 60% reported at Homestead.[97]

Carnegie Steel Company's distinction in wage payment lay not in average daily wages, as Carnegie boasted and as the general public believed, but rather in keeping the mills running and the men employed even during the worst days of the depression. The *Pittsburgh Times,* which usually gave Carnegie a more favorable press than its local competitor, the *Pittsburgh Post,* reported in December 1893, at the same time that the *Post* was emphasizing the wage scale reductions, that all of the Carnegie mills would start running full time the first week in January. It also praised Carnegie for having given $1000 during the previous two months "for the relief of the poor in Pittsburgh." [98] Carnegie's generous act of charity was commendable, as was his decision to keep as many men as possible employed and the mills running during the lowest period of the depression. Nevertheless, working twelve hours a day for wages that were the lowest in the district quite naturally led the men to believe that they were being exploited. After all, Carnegie was not running his mills, even in 1893, for reasons of charity. As he had done in previous periods of depressed market, Carnegie was "running full" to capture the market with whatever prices he could get. W. M. Garland, the newly elected president of the Amalgamated Association, spoke for many of the men of Homestead, Edgar Thomson, and Duquesne when he criticized Carnegie for cutting wages drastically even though he kept his mills open. "Mr. Carnegie seems to think that what the workmen want is work and not money. He coincides with President Cleveland's statement that it is better for men to work steadier for less wages than intermittently for higher pay. . . . But intelligent workmen do not see it nor will they. . . . It's the money not the work we are striving for." [99]

Carnegie and Frick continued to strive to get the work done for as little money as possible. They kept the pressure on their managers and plant superintendents to reduce labor costs even further, by replacing men with machinery wherever practical, and by stepping up production and hours of labor. There was no detail too insignificant to escape their notice, and the ambitious foremen and superintendents in every department and mill knew that the surest way to catch Carnegie's attention was to show a marked decrease in cost of production over the previous report. Charles Schwab, who had succeeded the hapless Potter as superintendent of Homestead after the strike, was particularly assiduous in this respect, for, as he wrote Frick, "The task, therefore, which

I have set for myself for the year 1895, is to save one-half million dollars in the cost of manufacture [at Homestead] over the cost of the year 1894. In other words, expect to make a clear saving by practice, labor, running expenses, etc. of one-half million dollars for this year." [100] Schwab slashed expenditures on items that no previous superintendent had ever before even considered. He figured that the drinking water for the men in the mill at Homestead cost from $8000 to $10,000 a year, and he proposed pumping water from "the well we have at hand" rather than bringing cold water in from the outside in water tanks.[101] When he submitted the labor scale for Homestead for the coming year, Schwab could proudly boast, "I beg to say that the reductions we have made are the very lowest I can possibly make, considering the wages paid by ourselves at other works and other people in the neighborhood. . . . It is my opinion that no trouble will result from the adoption of this scale. There may be a very slight chance of some trouble in some departments by reason of the heavy cuts contemplated by this scale. . . . For instance, I plan to re-arrange the open hearth so as to do away with melters entirely. . . . While it is also true that a few of our men may quit work on the first of January, I think not a sufficient number, if any, to give us any difficulty whatever. I therefore recommend the adoption of this Scale." [102] Carnegie regarded Schwab as "a wonder," and he was quite clearly in Carnegie's eyes the heir apparent to Leishman for the presidency of the company.

All of the other plants were forced to follow Schwab's lead for 1895 by reducing wages an additional 15 per cent, in spite of the fact that business generally was showing signs of improvement.[103] By the late spring of 1895, however, the market had improved so greatly that, even though the wage contracts would not be up for consideration for another six months, the board of managers felt that they would have to grant a wage increase over Schwab's scales if only to meet the competition for labor from other steel companies. When Frick reluctantly broached this matter to Carnegie, he got the following cabled answer from Scotland, "Object of scale [is to] throw all labor questions to January first. Nothing but crisis will justify departure. Present excitement probably flash in pan but if all agreed crisis arisen which must be met suggest best form of notice would be   In addition to scale rates from June first until further notice a bonus of blank per cent will be paid. This would leave scale untouched as basis. Board should consider well before throwing away three quarters million yearly. Bonus should be restricted if possible to common and Furnace labor earnings." [104]

Carnegie's suggestion was adopted, and a notice of a 10 per cent bonus effective 1 June was announced by Frick, who said that "the business outlook justifies this bonus." [105] The great advantage of the bonus, as Carnegie had made clear, was that, unlike raises in the wage scale, it could be given—and also taken away—at the pleasure of management quite independently of any negotiations with the workers.

The same wage scale and bonus was kept throughout 1896, and in December of that year it was announced that both the scale and the bonus would be kept in 1897. In February 1897, however, the Pennsylvania Steel Company announced that it was reducing its wages by 10 per cent. Carnegie at once wrote Frick, "I think this forces us to take off the bonus to teach our competitors that they cannot take any advantage over us by the reduction of wages." [106] How simple it all was now: no union with which one had to bargain. It was not even necessary to adjust the prevailing scale. The bonus was one of Carnegie's cleverest practices in the field of labor management.

Although no action was taken in February, there was continued pressure throughout the spring, particularly from Schwab, who had now replaced Leishman as president of the company, to remove the bonus. At the meeting of the board in the first week of July, Schwab proposed that the bonus be removed as of 1 August. Lauder, and, interestingly enough, Frick were hesitant. Frick felt that "we should not interfere with a fight between the Amalgamated Association and our competitors, and we should not assist our competitors by making a cut. We should remove the Bonus at a proper time when wage matters are settled." [107] With such dissent, the proposal was allowed to rest for the time being.

At the following two meetings of the board Schwab again brought up the question of the bonus. As reported by the secretary in the minutes of the meeting, Schwab stated that it was his belief that business would not improve immediately, but that if it did, "we will be expected to advance wages. This we cannot do unless we take the Bonus off now. The order books are practically filled for the next six months with sales made at very low prices. The result will be that our profits will soon be at a point where we must take the Bonus off, to have anything left for ourselves." With profits that year at $7,000,000, the highest in the history of the company, 14.5 per cent over the previous year, and representing a return of 28 per cent on the capital invested in the company, this did not seem to be a very legitimate fear on Schwab's part. Francis Lovejoy, the secretary of the company, quickly pointed out that "we haven't quite reached that point yet." Lovejoy then offered some very cogent arguments for postponing any decision for at least a month. "I think our announcing that Bonus in 1895 materially helped business in general, and its discontinuance just at this time, when everyone is prophesying better times, will have the contrary effect." He also pointed out that their competitors, including Jones & Laughlin, who had cut wages, had "very little stake in asking reductions. They have few orders on their books and can stand a lock-out as easily as they can stand a shut-down for lack of orders." Finally, taking cognizance of who would be reading these minutes with meticulous care, Lovejoy offered as his clinching argument, "Another thing, business reasons being equal, we must consider the effect on Mr. Carnegie's position before the public. He will be severely criticized for a reduction just at this time." Lovejoy's last argument proved effective in swinging a majority of the board to his side. The managers agreed to postpone further consideration until 17 August. The disgruntled Schwab, eager to make as impressive a record as possible during his first year in the presidency, had to yield. "Then we will postpone action until August 17th, but I wish to be placed on record as saying this is the most serious mistake we have ever made concerning labor, and you will all be of that opinion within the next six or eight months." [108]

Evidently, Carnegie had been properly impressed with Lovejoy's arguments, for when the board met on 17 August to reconsider the bonus question, there was a telegram from him, "Advise leave bonus alone." [109] With this advice at hand, Schwab, of course, capitulated. "We were to have discussed the Wages' Bonus matter today," Schwab reported to the board. "But I do not think it necessary. I think we should have taken it off July 1st or August 1st, but I am not in favor of taking it off now. We will have some adjustments to make January 1st, and the whole thing can be fixed at one time." [110]

Highly conspicuous by its very absence in this managerial debate on wages was the question of the collective attitude of the laborers. The fact that a wage cut by its competitors was not so crucial as one would be for Carnegie Steel, the impact a wage reduction by Carnegie Steel would have on general business conditions, and the possibility of an adverse public reaction to Carnegie personally were all seriously debated and given great weight. But the possibility of labor's organizing to take collective action against losing the bonus was, after Homestead, too remote to need debate. As Schwab said in reporting to Frick, "I really think there would be no risk whatever with reference to our men; still there might be and no doubt we would be seriously criticized by this administration [McKinley's] if we were to take off this Bonus at the same time the Tariff Law is passed." [111]

Not even the question of working the mills on Sunday needed to be discussed with the workers. For the past several years, after 1893, the mills had not only been on a two-turn day, but also on a seven-day week. Frick first brought up the question of Sunday work to the board in January 1899. He feared adverse publicity. "Will not the Churches and the newspapers take it up and reflect upon us for doing Sunday work?" Lovejoy and Lauder joined him in opposing Sunday work, but Alexander Peacock, the general sales agent, was a strong proponent of continuing the present practices. He reported that there was no pressure from the local ministers, "as Carnegie Steel has always been generous to churches throughout the area." After further discussion the board agreed to continue Sunday work until the improvements in the mills were completed and then to discontinue it.[112] Eight years later, when John Fitch made his Pittsburgh study for the Russell Sage Foundation, he found that the blast furnace men and about 20 per cent of the labor force in the rolling mills were still working a seven-day week.[113] It had, of course, not occurred even to Lovejoy or Lauder to consult with the workingmen as to what a seven-day week, month in and month out, meant to them not only in physical well-being, but also in mental health, family relations, and community life.

629

In 1898 and 1899, however, as business continued to improve and the company's profits increased ever more rapidly, the workers, particularly the newer and younger men who had not been personally involved in Homestead, began to grow restless. The Amalgamated Association had been so thoroughly crushed in 1892 throughout the Carnegie domain that none of the officers of the company ever expected to see unionism try to raise its head again in any of the company's steel mills. Chairman Frick had hailed that victory in 1892 with the statement, "Do not think we will ever have any serious labor trouble again," and the years that followed had so far proved him right.

To make sure of this situation, the company since 1894 had established its own Bureau of Information, which employed labor spies, euphemistically called operatives, to report on any signs that indicated potential trouble within the mills. The operatives were requested to give names of men "loafing on the job," wasting material, or making critical remarks about company policy. The greatest danger, of course, lay in any attempt among the men to form an organization, and the Bureau was constantly on the alert for any movement in that direction.[114] "We are advised and on pretty good authority that there is a move on foot to organize the Structural and Shop men in all the Bridge Works in this district," J. R. Mack, director of the Bureau of Information, wrote to one of the operatives in 1896. "Please keep your eyes and ears open and the minute you get onto anything of this kind, advise us at once. Be especially particular to give the names of anyone connected with this movement." [115]

Because in the early years after the break-up of the Amalgamated at the Carnegie mills there was not a great deal to report, the operatives were hired on a temporary basis at such times as just after the announcement of a new wage scale when trouble might reasonably be expected. The men selected for these "reporting jobs" had been carefully screened in advance by the company from among the workers themselves without their knowledge. Considering how amateur the operation was at first, it was remarkable that the company was never itself betrayed by someone acting as a double agent. The records do not show how much the operatives were paid for playing their Judas goat role, but they do indicate that for several years each operative received a turkey at Christmas time from his grateful employers. This practice was continued until it was discovered that the workers at Homestead had caught on to the system and were identifying the spies among their fellow workers by noting who received a package, with its obvious contents, by express the week before Christmas. This rather festive little holiday tradition in Homestead and Braddock then had to be abandoned by the Bureau.[116]

In the spring of 1899, the operatives, like the mills, had their busiest season yet. Schwab reported to Carnegie in May, "Labor seems to be giving us some little trouble in all directions. This week at Homestead there was an effort on the part of some men to reorganize a union. We promptly took action and discharged a half dozen of them yesterday and will do the same to-day. I feel this will nip the move in the bud." [117] But it did not. In June, seven more men were discharged from the Open Hearth department at Homestead, and the faithful Schwab reported to Carnegie, "We are watching the labor situation very carefully in every department. Homestead Steel Works has given us some little trouble, as you know from previous reports, but I think we have the matter now well in hand. There is a scarcity of labor at our works and our scale of wages, especially for common labor and at our blast furnaces is lower than at other furnaces in this district and in the valley. It is just possible if pig iron continues to advance that higher wages may have to be paid. Our superintendents, however, think an advance unnecessary at this time, with which I agree." [118]

The movement toward organization continued to grow, and by the second week of June the situation at Homestead was serious enough for Schwab to bring it to the board for full discussion. The minutes of that meeting reveal how completely in agreement all the managers were over keeping any organization of labor out of the Carnegie works:

Schwab: The Labor problem is one I want the Board to be familiar with and clear upon. The Amalgamated Association is making a very strong effort to get into our Homestead Steel Works. They are able to make a better effort in this direction just now because of the large percentage advances in tonnage rates they have been able to obtain from other Iron and Steel Companies, and because of the misleading ways in which these

631

advances in rates are spoken of in the newspapers. There is no question of wages or earnings involved, but the Amalgamated officials are working on the organized labor basis. They have had organizers at Homestead for several months, and John Jarrett tells me he is informed that 900 of our men at Homestead Steel Works have obligated themselves to join any movement toward organization. I do not believe anything like this number are implicated. We have agents in the Mills, and as fast as we learn the names of any men taking active part we discharge them. We should not permit the Amalgamated Association to get into Homestead again—we should keep them out at any cost, even if it should result in a strike. . . . I would like to know what the Board thinks of the situation.

Peacock: I would certainly do everything possible to keep them out.

Singer: I would not let them get a foot-hold under any circumstances—not under any condition—stop it at once. I would mean not only Homestead but the rest of the Works. We have gone through that condition of affairs, and it cost us a good deal of money to get our works back again; but it was money well spent. . . .

Gayley: I certainly would resist their getting any foot-hold.

Corey: Every man we discharged, excepting one, on being asked if he was satisfied with the wages, replied that he was, but that he preferred to work in a union mill.

Schwab: It is a singular fact that all those concerned in this movement are young men; none of the older men who had belonged to the Amalgamated Association, appear to be interested.

Clemson: I would go to the limit against their getting in, and would stop the Works if necessary.

Morrison: If we postpone decided action, we will have that much trouble later on. I do not look for much trouble at this time—have had none at all at Edgar Thomson.

Lovejoy: I would rather see the Works blown up with dynamite than turned over to the control of those scoundrels.

Phipps: There would be nothing so detrimental to our organization and business as to allow the Amalgamated Association to get a foot-hold in our Works. We can make the fight very much better now than if we let them get a start.

Curry: We should maintain our position at all the Works, and take all chances necessary.

Lauder: I quite approve of everything that has been done but do not like to make resolutions that we will do so and so without first consulting with the absent Partners.

Schwab: But we are confronted with this:—If the men go to Mr. Corey, and demand the re-instatement of the men who have been discharged for attending Amalgamated meetings, and say, "If those men are not taken back, we will go out." Mr. Corey must be in a position to make immediate answer, and not appear to hesitate in the least.

Lauder: I would let them go, but that does not necessarily mean a strike.

Singer: As long as we are paying as good wages as other Plants, it is not such a hard problem. If we were paying less, it would be a different matter.

Lauder: I would certainly wait until we can hear from absent Partners. You may do something you will be sorry for afterward.

Schwab: I really do not think there is much prospect of trouble, but it may come, and we must be prepared to meet it. I do not think as many men are involved as rumors say. We get very full reports and they do not show that the movement is widespread. It may be summed up that everyone present, except Mr. Lauder, is in favor of the utmost resistance to the Amalgamated Association getting any start in any of our Works, and especially Homestead.

Lauder: I think it would be best to get opinions from the absent Partners, on a matter of so much importance.

Schwab: No formal action is necessary at present; we simply wanted the matter discussed at the Board meeting . . . with the minutes . . . our absent Partners will be kept informed.[119]

This discussion, as reported by Lovejoy in the board minutes, reveals as much about the board members themselves as it does about the labor situation: Schwab, eager to dominate and lead, somewhat impulsive and always ready for action; Lauder, cautious and hesitant about doing anything without first getting Carnegie's approval, remembering only too well the anger that his cousin had shown toward Frick for having taken too drastic an action in the trouble of 1892; the rest of the board ready to follow Schwab's leadership unless given orders to the contrary, and, above all, the intensity of feeling they all expressed, Lovejoy included, against the Amalgamated Association.

Within two weeks, Schwab had the answer necessary to convince Lauder from "our absent Partners," Carnegie, Phipps, and Frick, who were together in Scotland. "We heartily endorse views of Board of Managers with regard to Amalgamated Association. Stop Works if necessary to hold present position." [120] Carnegie followed this up with a coded cable to Schwab, "Seems to me best plan you strike first blow, post notice understand effort organize union. Desire notify men we never will recognize Amalgamated because it broke agreement. Men can decide stop or run just as they please. Every member firm determined never recognize Amalgamated." [121]

Schwab, with Carnegie's full backing, was only too happy to strike the first blow. The notice was duly posted, and forty men known to be members of a revived Association lodge were summarily dismissed. A committee of workers headed by T. Gehm, the reputed president of the Homestead lodge, called on William Corey, then superintendent at Homestead, and demanded that the discharged men be re-instated, threatening a strike if this were not done. Corey's answer was to fire these men. The Amalgamated Association then placed pickets at each gate to meet the men as they came off the day turn to get them to promise to go on strike. "They succeeded in keeping out fifty-one men that night, and the next morning, by intimidation, they kept out seventy-six men," Corey later reported to the board. "Friday night and Saturday, the mills were running full, although Open Hearth No. 2 and the 10 " Mill were somewhat crippled. Sunday night, they made their strongest effort to keep men out, but only eighty-eight stayed away. At one of the gates, there was considerable disturbance and intimidation; men were seized, their dinner buckets kicked out of their hands, but nothing serious followed—there was no riot. Monday morning everything in the Mill was in good shape and running. At 3:00 o'clock Monday afternoon, a meeting was held, after which Gehm made a personal canvass, telling all the men to go to work. The strike was given up."

Schwab complimented Corey on the good work. "I think Mr.

Corey should have the congratulations of the Board for the way in which he has handled this matter. Any other course of action would have caused us a great deal of trouble."

Corey was generous in giving some of the credit to others: "Thank you; but I think our thanks are also due Mm. Lindsay and Milton for the manner in which they have kept us posted. They covered every meeting, and gave us most thorough reports from inside on all that was going on." [122]

The following day, Schwab was able to write Carnegie that "we have completely knocked out any attempt to organize Homestead workmen. . . . I now feel satisfied no further attempt will be made for sometime at least." [123] It was one of Schwab's more prophetic statements. Never again would there be an attempt to organize any of his works as long as Carnegie remained in control of the company. Homestead had at last been tamed. But if there was now docility, there was no amity.

The year 1899 marked the point of a new dramatic high in the success of the Carnegie Steel Company, for the full benefits from the recent acquisitions in ore resources and transportation facilities began to be realized. Profits in that year amounted to $21,000,000—almost equal to the total capitalization of the company. No one could ever accuse Carnegie of watering his stock. But the dividends paid to the partners remained low in spite of this unparalleled prosperity. Most of the profits were poured back into the company for new open hearth furnaces, for improvements on existing facilities, and for adapting machinery and men to new techniques.

Carnegie's insistence upon using profits for the further expansion of facilities and the reduction of costs did not find favor among most of his partners. This was particularly true of his senior partners, Phipps and Lauder, who held a sizable interest in the company and had the seniority that emboldened them to speak out against Carnegie's policy. The question of dividends had been a sore point between Phipps and Carnegie during most of the time they had been partners, beginning with their association in the Carnegie, Kloman Company in the 1860's. As the profits grew, so did Phipps's feeling about dividends, until he finally exploded in a letter to Carnegie in 1895:

It surely must be in manufacturing—say C.S.Co.—that man never is—but always to be blest! If a man wants spread—reasons are plentiful—opposition unpopular. Would much prefer increasing our cash capital and have it ready to pay retiring Partners. If I withdraw I get no benefit of tieing up my money —and thus losing interest—courting trouble.

I know it must annoy & bore you my giving opposite views —have not hesitated much when it seemed duty. . . .

Quite sympathize with Jack's [John Vandevort's] wish for money—he is tired—discouraged with expansion. Hope tells a flattering tale, never otherwise with us. We get in sight of div^d. then like Phillip Nolan ('man without a country') he sees his native land—then a new ship, a new voyage—and never lands, each time a new & deeper disappointment, so with our divd^s.[124]

Cousin Dod joined in this protest. "I have a long communication from Harry on the question of dividends v. improvements," Lauder wrote to Carnegie a few days later. "His position seems to me unassailable. But apart from all urges, I cannot see why you do not make dividends. . . . Lovejoy has just been shewing me a statement that shews we are in a better condition financially than we have been since 1888—on the first of May we were about 1,000,000 ahead with all fixed capital left out—add May earnings & stocks & bonds which are really available assets & there is between 6 & 7 millions. If I am not right about this I would like to know it. If I am, why do you not make dividends?" [125]

Carnegie refused to alter the dividend policy that he had established long ago. In standing firm he had the support of Frick, who had followed much the same policy in building up the vast coal field holdings and the number of coke ovens in the Henry C. Frick Coke Company.[126] Schwab also enthusiastically supported Carnegie's policy, not just to court the favor of his employer, but because, like Carnegie and Frick, he too was interested in the building of a business for its own sake. The majority of the partners in the Carnegie Steel Company—Phipps, Lauder, Singer, Vandevort, and most of the junior partners—could never understand what motivated Carnegie, Frick, and Schwab. Phipps and Lauder were always ready to believe at any given moment that, to use Phipps's metaphor, the journey was over, the desired harbor had finally been reached, and it was now time to cast anchor and start enjoying the rich cargo they had brought with them. Why continue this seemingly interminable cruise, seeking ever more booty and risking the loss of what they already had acquired on the wild, tempestuous seas?

For Carnegie, the metaphor Phipps used was totally wrong. Carnegie regarded his activities of the past thirty years not as a cargo-gathering cruise, but as the creative building of a great enterprise. Nor could Carnegie accept that other metaphoric figure of speech which equated him and his fellow industrialists with the "robber barons" of medieval Europe, who exacted their outrageous tolls from the honest traveler at mountain passes and river crossings.

This highly colorful term, first popularized by the Populist press in the 1880's and 1890's, was revived by Matthew Josephson in the 1930's and quickly became as widely accepted among journalists and historians in the New Deal period as the term "Industrial Revolution" had long been accepted. Later revisionist historians of the 1940's would reject the term as being historically false. For them, Rockefeller, Carnegie, Morgan, Harriman, and Hill were not "robber barons," but "industrial statesmen," who through their business activities of consolidation and improvement had built for America the greatest industrial strength the world had ever known and had enabled her in the years from 1941 to 1945 to preserve Western culture from the barbarism of Nazi totalitarianism.

Carnegie had objected to the term on less grandiose grounds. He argued it was basically false in its premise that he was engaged in robbery. On the contrary, it was because of his superb industrial organization that the general public could obtain steel at an unbelievably low price. In an interview given to the New York *Herald* in 1893, he pleaded not guilty to the charge: " 'The robber baron' has ceased to rob and is now being robbed. The eighth wonder of the world [Carnegie was not hesitant about mixing metaphors] is this—two pounds of iron-stone purchased on the shores of Lake Superior and transported to Pittsburg; two pounds of coal mined in Connellsville and manufactured into one and one-fourth pounds of coke and brought to Pittsburg; one-half pound of limestone mined east of the Alleghenies and brought to Pittsburg; a little manganese ore, mined in Virginia and brought to Pittsburg, and these four and one half pounds of material manufactured into one pound of solid steel and sold for one cent. That's all that need be said about the steel business." [127]

The arguments used by both Carnegie and the later revisionist historians against the use of the term "robber baron" are at best only partial truths and fail to get at the real error in the metaphor. If Carnegie was not robbing the consumer in selling steel at one cent a pound, he was certainly not being robbed. His annual profits would indicate that his cost for producing steel, even with all the preliminary transactions in obtaining the raw materials, as he outlined them, was considerably below one cent a pound. As he acquired the ownership of sources of raw materials and transportation facilities, the difference between cost of production and market price became ever greater, of course, with the result that Carnegie's annual profits in a period of five years increased by over 500 per cent.[128]

As for the "industrial statesmanship" thesis of the revisionist historians, it comes perilously close to being based on the logical fallacy of *post hoc, ergo propter hoc.* Certainly Carnegie was not thinking of his nation's needs fifty years hence as his steam shovels clawed the very best surface ore out of the Mesabi Range at an ever-increasing rate. Indeed, so rapidly did the amount of tonnage taken out of the range increase that even Oliver became alarmed at the rate at which the Carnegie Steel mills were using up the best Bessemer ores of Mesabi. He counseled, "It is not a wise policy to quickly exhaust the rich quarry we have on the Mesaba Range, taking off rapidly the surface ore." He urged Frick and Carnegie to "look to the future" and "prolong the period of cheap steam shovel mining" by taking in other ores for mixture.[129]

It was not Oliver's prudent advice, nor some altruistic regard for future generations, that kept Carnegie Steel from exhausting the best iron resources of the northern ranges long before the democracies of the West had to meet the threat of a Nazi totalitarianism. Only the abundant richness of nature itself, which vastly exceeded even the ravenous appetites of the Lucy furnaces, kept America's steel mills supplied with ore through World War II. America's "industrial statesmen" were singularly blind to any concept of conservation throughout the nineteenth century. They laid waste to great forests, feverishly mined out the mineral resources of the nation, polluted the streams and air—without considering what they might be doing to America by their exploitation of her natural resources. They were, it is true, creating the industrial might of the nation as they built their railroads, erected their steel mills, and laid their pipelines. They were, however, building for themselves, and not for, but rather frequently in defiance of, the future.

There is also an implied assumption in the "industrial statesman" thesis that only by the means the Rockefellers, Carnegies, Goulds, and Harrimans employed could America have achieved its industrial supremacy. Such a supposition cannot be sustained when subjected to a comparative historical study of modern economic development. No other nation that has engaged in industrialization, since Great Britain first led the way, has done so with as little planning and with such a great waste of natural resources, manpower, and capital as did the United States in the post Civil War period. Only the uniquely favorable conditions of vast physical resources, unrestricted immigration, and the political security provided by her geographical location gave the United States the freedom to industrialize in the manner in which she did. Every European visitor to America in the late nineteenth century was appalled by the waste and lack of order in America's industrialism. The great English steelmaker, Sir Lowthian Bell, who visited the United States in 1890, could hardly believe what he saw at Pittsburgh and Johnstown—the "recklessly rapid rate of driving" blast furnaces that brought "the interiors to a wreck about every three years." [130]

Workers were driven and burned out with the same reckless disregard. Hamlin Garland found not one man over forty in the steel mill at Homestead. Sir James Kitson, the president of the British Iron and Steel Institute, also visited the United States in 1890. While inspecting one of Carnegie's works, he met a former employee of his, who told Kitson, "I am quite a different man here from what I was in the old country; I don't know why it is so. . . . I can do more work; I feel that I have it in me; but I also feel and know that it won't last. I shall be done in ten years." Kitson's conclusion, after visiting many mills, was, "No, it won't last. The extreme physical effort put forth results in greater production, but it saps the vital energies and cuts short the career. This

639

continual work at high pressure does not pay in the end. 'It won't last; and the remark applies with equal force to the employers as well as to the workers." [131]

Even if the criticisms offered by Carnegie and revisionist historians to the term "robber baron" are inaccurate, nevertheless the phrase can still be judged an inappropriate metaphor to describe the business activities of America's great entrepreneurs of the late nineteenth century. Meant quite obviously to be a term of reproach to the methods and goals of these industrialists by those who coined it in the 1880's and those who popularized it in the 1930's, the term is more belittling than it is condemnatory in its judgment. Whatever else Carnegie and Rockefeller may have been—ruthless, selfish, and wasteful of men and resources—they were not petty "barons-of-the-crags," seeking only to rob the innocent passer-by who came down their road. Carnegie himself provided a much more appropriate phrase in the title he gave to a volume of his collected essays—*The Empire of Business*. He, Frick, and Schwab were empire builders, not extortionists, and it is that drive for imperium that distinguishes them from their partners in Carnegie Steel. If they are to be metaphorically transplanted into the historic past, given their temperament and ambition, men like Carnegie and Rockefeller deserve to be assigned the more illustrious—or more infamous—roles of Charlemagne, Tamerlane, or Suleiman the Magnificent. Of course they were wasteful of men and resources, as much so as any conqueror building an empire by military force. They were as self-centered as Alexander or Caesar. Their historical perspective, as it related to industrial development, was always from a personal point of view, not from a societal or even a national one. "What's good for Carnegie Steel is good for the country," could well have been said by either Carnegie or Schwab. Their own empire comprised as much of the economic world as their entrepreneurial statesmanship could encompass.

It would be wrong to suggest that this ambition for building an empire of business was totally negative or destructive of the best interests of the nation. There was a pride in this creative activity that ensured certain standards of behavior and a certain quality of product which a Gould or a Drew would never understand. Carnegie was quite sincere when he said that he had never

640

knowingly turned out a rail or structural beam that he was not proud to see his name stamped upon: "We are not in for dollars," Carnegie wrote to Schwab in January 1900. "Fortunately, you and I and all our partners have plenty, or are getting plenty. We have pleasure in business, performing useful parts—this is our great reward." [132]

Carnegie, to be sure, was overly sanctimonious when he wrote this. He was always "in for dollars," and the accumulation of wealth was a major motivation for his business activity, as all his partners knew full well. But it was an over-simplification to answer the question of "What makes Andy or John D. run" with a dollar sign, as many of the Populists, muckrakers, and the later New Dealers did. In so doing, these critics of "the economic royalists" failed to understand how intense and sustained this drive for economic success was among these titans of the business world. If the accumulation of dollars had been the sole motivation for Carnegie, Frick, or Rockefeller, this purpose would have been amply satisfied long before their business activities were actually concluded. As Carnegie said, "You and I have plenty." Carnegie found "pleasure in business," quite apart from monetary gain. Wealth, beyond a certain point, cannot be an end in itself. It serves only as a yardstick.

The desire for power, however, is not so easily satiated as is the desire for wealth. It is not subject to the same law of diminishing returns as is the acquisition and consumption of material goods. It was imperial power that Carnegie, Frick, and Rockefeller sought—empires of steel, coke, and oil in which each would reign supreme. Although based within and legally created by a political state, these economic empires, in time, became international—or perhaps more accurately, supranational, carving out their own boundaries and operating in accordance with their own code of laws.

These empire builders all professed a belief in laissez-faire economics, but they were by no means purists of the Manchester school of economic liberalism. They did not deny the role of government in economic affairs, nor did they agree with Jefferson and the Physiocrats that that government is best which governs least. Political government performed important functions within their economic empires. Government would, of course, be concerned with the preservation of law and order, the protection of private property—even the Manchester liberals would accept these activities of the political state. American empire builders expected political states also to take a positive role in sustaining and supporting business activities. Of primary concern, of course, was the protective tariff, anathema to the traditional English liberal economists, but vigorously lobbied for by American industrialists. Tariff rates were written by the trade associations and dutifully passed by Congress, with only minor variations, and no industry had a more effective or powerful Washington representative than the Iron and Steel Association had in its secretary, James M. Swank. "I have placed in Quay's hands [Senator Matthew Quay of Pennsylvania] a complete typewritten analysis of the rates in the metal schedule of the House and the Senate tariff bills, with reasons in detail why in some cases we do not want the Senate rates," Swank wrote Carnegie in May 1897 as Congress was deliberating upon a new tariff bill to replace the Wilson-Gorman Tariff Act. "Our whole case is in his hands and he will be backed up by Penrose in every demand we may make. I will go to Washington tomorrow and Wharton will go down on Monday. We will be all right in the final round-up." [133] Indeed they were all right in the resulting Dingley Tariff Act, as they had been in all previous tariff legislation.

Government provided another form of legal protection for the individual industrialist through its patent laws. This area of governmental protection has not been given the attention it deserves, for—in theory at least—a patent granted not just domestic protection to industry in general but an absolute monopoly to the individual patent holder. A patent was not subject to legislative debate or political compromise, and it was upheld by the national judicial system. Carnegie gave far more attention to acquiring and protecting patent rights than he ever gave to promoting tariff legislation. A letter to Leishman in 1895, regarding Captain Jones's Bessemer mixer patent, which the company had acquired at the time of Jones's death, indicates the importance of patents to Carnegie:

> Yours received in regard to our Mixer Patent. I feel very strongly about the action of our friends the Illinois and the

Pennsylvania Steel Companies. No one pretends that a mixer was ever used successfully except ours. These companies saw the results and had already realized that a mixer was necessary for the direct process. They deliberately appropriated our invention without arranging with us for a liscence [sic].

We can prove that the invention was worth to the Illinois Steel Co. at least $150,000 per year probably $200,000, and it will be worth the same to the Pennsylvania and the Sparrow Point works. Stated truthfully, it was nothing but a pure theft of our property by men who were in close relations with us, and with whom we were co-operating. In my whole experience as a business man I have never known anything so flagrantly dishonest. . . .

As if to add to the injustice done us, they now endeavor to rake up some old trumpery claims that the mixer was known before Captain Jones invented it. Everyone knows that the most important inventions have been thus assailed, but fortunately, our Courts are more and more strenuously vindicating the claims of those who put the invention into practical use. . . .

Our patent is recognized everywhere throughout Europe, and we can obtain from parties using it, testimony proving its value. . . . I think that if you will see Mr. Potter of Chicago and Mr. Morris of Philadelphia, and lay the matter before them, they will repudiate the action of their officers and pay us the small sum we are now willing to take amicably; but failing this, I do hope you will employ the best Counsel and prepare to test the question in the highest Court of Appeal. I have no fear of the verdict. We can put the officers of these two Companies upon the stand, and compel them to admit that they never thought of using a mixer until they saw ours in successful operation, and therefore, that they stole our property; a nice position in which to place the Illinois and the Pennsylvania Steel Companies.

It is not a question of money with me, but of honorable dealing between concerns which should be friends and not pirates preying upon each other's property.[134]

Carnegie's letter reveals the gap between the theory and the reality of governmental protection offered by the patent laws. It was too easy in the field of mechanical invention for a process or device to be copied and duplicated by others. These disputes over patent claims were frequently settled out of court, but whenever this was done the protective power of the patent was weakened.

Nevertheless, over the thirty years that Carnegie was engaged in the iron and steel business, the many patents that he acquired through purchase from his inventive partners and employees such as Kloman and Jones, or leased on a royalty basis from Bessemer and Thomas, had netted him millions of dollars and were a major factor in his acquiring dominance in the field. There were good reasons for him to prosecute vigorously any infringement of patent rights, no matter how costly and lengthy such suits might prove to be. "Anything to win from the robbers of our Mixer Patent," he wrote Lauder two years after he had begun his suit against Illinois Steel.[135] After winning his case before the United States District Court of Western Pennsylvania, Carnegie had his victory snatched from him by the Circuit Court of Appeals in August 1899, and the case was still pending before the Supreme Court in 1901 when the Carnegie Company was sold and the suit was dissolved.[136]

Carnegie and his fellow industrialists saw government not only as a protector and patron of their business activities but also as a potential customer, particularly after 1882, when both Republican and Democratic administrations became interested in a big Navy program. In these circumstances, it became increasingly important to have friends in Washington. Carnegie, of course, made it a point to be on as familiar a basis as possible with each succeeding President, even the Democrat Cleveland. It was often more important to have close friends in key subordinate positions, such as Blaine as Secretary of State and George Shiras on the Supreme Court. Even lieutenants could be important. Carnegie had little luck at first in getting appointments in the new McKinley administration, even though he felt that McKinley and Mark Hanna owed him a great deal. There seemed to be a chance that Carnegie Steel Company's own lawyer, Philander C. Knox, might get the nod from President-elect McKinley for the office of Attorney General. Frick had written to Carnegie urging him to push the nomination. "Am satisfied you could secure the selection of Mr. Knox for this position, as I know the President-Elect would do almost anything you asked." [137] Although Carnegie did not often personally petition for patronage favors, preferring to work through subordinates, he found this too good an opportunity to miss. He wrote McKinley the following day, "If there was one thing which I had resolved upon, it was that you should never be troubled by me about appointments. I pity you too much . . . I cannot refuse, however, to comply with Mr. Frick's request to say a word about Mr. Knox, who ranks with me as the best lawyer I have ever had for our interests, a veritable 'little giant,' and one of your *real* friends from the start. . . . Should you like to adopt Mr. Knox as one of your 'happy family'—which I hope it is to be—I for one will rejoice." [138]

Carnegie had no occasion to rejoice at this time. The President-elect might, as Frick thought, be prepared to do almost anything Carnegie asked, but he was not prepared to grant his request in this instance. McKinley chose Joseph McKenna for the spot. Four years later, McKinley chose Knox as his Attorney General, in which position Knox was better known to the public as "sleepy Phil" than as "the little giant." [139] Unfortunately, his appointment in 1901 did Carnegie little good, as it came after he had retired from business. United States Steel, however, was to appreciate his somnolence very much.

The national government had made its first tentative moves toward the creation of that vast industrial-military complex of the mid twentieth century under the otherwise quite innocuous presidency of Chester A. Arthur. At that time a reluctant Congress approved an administrative budget of four new warships, the first modern steel vessels in the American navy. Warships made of steel and armed with heavy guns meant business for the iron and steel industry of a magnitude that could not easily be ignored. Carnegie's initial attitude toward seeking out the government as a potential customer for these kinds of goods was highly ambivalent. He had so long trumpeted his pacifist beliefs before the world, and had specifically praised the United States for its obsolete navy, that it would be difficult now for him to enter into competitive bidding to provide steel plates and gun forgings for these new warships. On the other hand, it would be equally hard to see these lucrative contracts going to his competitors. After much internal anguish, he decided against militarism. He wrote to Louise in 1887 that he had decided against building armor plate for the government, to which she responded that she was very proud of him.[140]

He kept to his resolve for some time as the naval building program expanded under the Cleveland administration. He wrote to Cleveland's Secretary of the Navy, W.C. Whitney, in 1886 that his company would make no bids for armor plates. He also enclosed two pages from his *Triumphant Democracy,* on which he had underlined the sentence, "It is one of the chief glories of the Republic that she spends her money for better ends and has nothing worthy to rank as a ship of war." To which he had added, as a postscript on the back, "Compliments to my friend the Sec'y of the Navy who I am sorry to see trying to rob his Country of one of its chief glories." [141]

His noble resolve did not last long. By the end of the year, he was writing quite a different note to Whitney: "You need not be afraid that you will have to go abroad for armour plate. I am now fully satisfied that the mill we are building will roll the heaviest sizes you require, with the greatest ease. I also find that our people have already contracted for the armour plates for one of the ships you have let and are negotiating for the plates for the others." [142]

Quite clearly, Carnegie had given in to the pressure of his partners and his own desire for the profits and prestige involved in these contracts. He regarded it not as a surrender, but only a minor compromise of his pacifist principles. He would only make armor plate—a defensive item of armaments, not guns. On this point he was, at first, very insistent.

By 1889, with a new Republican administration committed to an even more ambitious naval program, Carnegie was very actively engaged in the armor plate business. He wrote to W. L. Abbott, "Sec'y Tracy [Benjamin F. Tracy, President Harrison's Secretary of the Navy] told me that Bethlehem seemed disinclined to put their plates against compound armour tests. . . . Hopes we will 'read up' on it and be prepared to offer Armor. Wants to ask bids soon as tests are made—Ritchie, our Akron, O. friend, has the big nickel mine and is selling to Krupps & c. . . . There may be millions for us in armor. To one man should be assigned 'Armor' and he should read up and keep up on the subject." [143]

In the fall of 1890, Carnegie, Phipps & Company signed a contract with the United States government to provide six thousand tons of armor plate made of nickel steel. Millard Hunsiker was selected as the company's "armor" man. He was active in arranging for the use of the patented ferro-nickel process of compound nickel-steel plates with the Abel Ray Company of London, which held the patent. Carnegie, Phipps finally obtained the American rights to use the patent at a royalty of 2¢ a pound.[144]

Throughout the years that Carnegie dealt with the government in providing armor plates, he was aided immensely by having key men in the Department of the Navy provide him with advance information on contract specifications for proposed warship construction. The naval attaché in London, W. H. Emory, sent Carnegie the following information in June 1890, prior to Carnegie's making his first bid for armor plate:

> I am truly glad to enclose . . . what you wish. Enclosed you will find the thickness of the armor and number of tons to each thickness. Besides, I also give a detailed list of everything composing the hull of the ship except the fittings—as I think they would come under the list of what could be made at your works. . . . In sending this list I have to request that it will only be used by you personally and that the source of your information or anything which would point to me will be carefully avoided. . . . I owe a deep debt of gratitude to Mr. Blaine [Secretary of State] and I know that he will be gratified to have me place myself at your service. . . . In considering the particulars I send, I have good reason for saying that you will be *able to base your calculations and action upon the figures given.* You can rely absolutely that there will not be any decided departure from the weights given. . . . Only kindly do not let anyone this side or at home see this list of weights. I do not know what the size of the two other cruisers appropriated for is to be. When it is ascertained you can easily form an estimate by the comparative tonnage. If I can be of further service please commend me.[145]

There was also Lieutenant C. A. Stone, whom Secretary of the Navy Tracy had assigned to the Carnegie plant as consultant on naval specifications. Stone shortly thereafter retired from the navy and entered Carnegie's employment, but kept his close navy contacts. He proved invaluable in obtaining for Carnegie a contract for armor plate for the Russian navy, for, like Emory, he was able to give advance information on specifications that the Russian admiralty would call for. Captain Mertwago of the Russian navy gave Stone drawings of the armor required, which Stone promptly passed on to Hunsiker. "The specifications will give all the details but the above which you have in advance of Bethlehem, give the requirements near enough. . . . I saw Lt. Singer, who is also a class-mate of mine, and now in charge of the Office of Naval Intelligence here in the Department. . . . He told me what I knew before, that the Naval Attachés are forbidden, by order of the Department, from giving to anyone any information whatever. They send all the information they obtain to the office of Naval Intelligence. I have explained to Singer that it would be of advantage to our government that certain information obtained be given to us, and he has taken quite kindly to the idea, and will talk to the Secretary about it. He appreciates that it would be to the advantage of the U.S. that we keep running on the armor manufacture for others, if the U.S. cannot keep us employed. We improve by continued manufacture, while a stoppage would prevent such continued improvement." [146] The arguments for Carnegie's getting inside information were ingenious indeed.

The Secretary of State, James G. Blaine, was also most co-operative in using his influence in getting foreign contracts. Carnegie wrote to Blaine asking him to "speak to your friend, the Russian minister upon the subject." Blaine responded, "The Russian minister arrived here about four weeks ago. I lost no time in seeing him and in seeing him a second time. He has written very earnestly to the Russian Naval department." [147]

In time, Carnegie Steel came to an agreement with its only rival in the field of armor plate manufacturing, Bethlehem Iron, so that there was no longer competitive bidding. The government had to take from each company a certain percentage of production at a single price agreed to by the two companies, an arrangement which ran counter to Carnegie's usual reluctance to enter into pooling agreements. It was a very cozy deal, with Carnegie Steel getting 60 per cent of the orders and Bethlehem Iron the remaining 40 per cent at a fixed price of $450 a ton. The only real competition left between the two companies was for foreign government contracts. Carnegie tried to reduce competition in this area also. He wrote to Robert Linderman, president of Bethlehem, regarding a Russian contract which Bethlehem had won:

> I said from the first to our people, that I did not favor taking the whole of the Russian order. I foresaw the objections that might arise to either one of the two Companies putting itself in the attitude of exacting more from its own country than from the foreigner, and I still believe that it would be good policy for your Company to divide that order rather than occupy the position it does before the masses of the people. There is not much money in the order, but there is a great deal in the armor-making plants working in perfect union. But this is a matter for your Company to decide for itself. As to the future, we are together, and that is all right, as far as armor is concerned.[148]

Within three years, such an arrangement was reached, and the two companies divided all foreign armor contracts.[149]

It was fortunate for Carnegie that he had the assistance he did by means of secret, inside information and pooling arrangements, for no other field of manufacturing that he ever engaged in was to cause him as much difficulty as did armor plate. The immense profits and the further extension of his business enterprise sustained Carnegie's enthusiasm for armor in spite of all the problems involved. Although no secret was more carefully guarded within the company than the actual cost of producing a ton of armor plate (even references to cost in Carnegie's letters have been carefully clipped out),[150] one letter from Schwab to Carnegie that is still intact reveals in regard to one special order of Russian armor that "while . . . difficult to make, we shall manufacture it at a cost of about $175 a ton." [151] If this special order, "difficult to make," cost the company only $175 a ton to produce, the regular armor plates ordered by the United States navy probably did not cost the company more than $150 a ton, once the mill was tooled and the men were trained for this kind of product. With the government's paying $450 a ton for armor, it is not surprising that Carnegie would write exultantly to Abbott, "Best specialty going sure. Millions in it." And to Frick, "Sure we never had such a chance for returns." [152]

There were times, however, when Carnegie must have felt

that he more than earned his 300 per cent profit. In the late fall of 1893, the nation was startled by the announcement that formal charges were being brought by the Secretary of Navy, Hilary A. Herbert, against the Carnegie Steel Company for certain "irregularities" in the Homestead armor plant. Four employees at Homestead had turned "informer" and had provided the Department of the Navy with information that "blowholes" appearing in the plates had been concealed by "plugging." A second and more serious charge was that the plates selected by naval inspectors for ballistics testing had been carefully marked by company employees and, during the night before the test, after the inspectors had gone home, had been re-treated to make them of superior quality, thereby earning premium payments for the company.

The press of the nation had a field day in exploiting this sensational news. One cartoon showed a trembling Carnegie wearing the kilt and cowering behind a steel plate, while an U.S. naval officer pointed a cannon, labeled "Investigation," at him. The caption beneath read, "Hold on! Don't shoot. I made this plate." [153]

In the resulting investigations, the "blowhole" charge, even though it had received the most publicity, was easily dismissed as being unimportant. Steel plates and rails always contain small bubbles ranging in size from that of a pin head to that of a marble. These bubbles, or "blowholes," do not affect the quality or strength of the steel. It is common practice to plug the larger blowholes at the time of finishing the steel in order to provide a smoother surface. There was no intent upon the part of the company at deception here, for the plugging was done with full knowledge and approval of the naval inspectors.[154]

The charge of giving special treatment to the plates selected by the naval inspectors for testing could not be so easily dismissed, however. On this charge, the company was found guilty of fraudulent practice by a special naval board, even though, ironically, the plate that had been given special treatment did not measure up as well as those chosen at random that had not been treated.[155] Carnegie, in a confidential letter to President Cleveland, angrily protested against having "been accused, tried, found guilty & sentenced without ever having been heard. . . . The so-called Board who should have been our Judges were not allowed to judge. They were *instructed practically* what to find. The Secretary called them together only once I think. *Instructed them* as to the *Law,* gave them a long lecture as to the enormity of the offence &c. Instead of acting in the capacity of an Impartial Judge, he has been as if Attorney for these informers. Of course this is chargeable to overzeal. . . . Inspectors now will not pass what should be passed & the money of the Govt is to be wasted. Irregularities there are & must be in production of such masses of steel. We need an officer of Highest rank stationed at the Works immediately with *discretionary power* of the ordnance Bureau to pass promptly upon emergencies as they arise. . . . This is a serious business for us not as to more money though that is important these times—I feel like Hotspur after he had won the battle. . . . Spent millions, subordinated every other Branch of our business to the Govt's needs, succeeds—& then upon the testimony of spies we are charged with irregularities & our men with fraud—I cannot stand this—even at the risk of offending the Secretary, good honest man, but overzealous in this affair." [156]

The following week, Carnegie sent to Cleveland a copy of a telegram he had received from Frick saying that at the latest tests ordered by Secretary Herbert the Carnegie armor plates "passed a very successful acceptance test." To which Carnegie added a note to the President: "I told you that fifteen thousand dollars of the Government's money was to be wasted this week. Enclosed shows you I was right. . . . This is 'inspection' run mad, caused by the hasty, overzeal of an inexperienced Secretary who charges 'fraud' upon people (Mr. Schwab & others) quite as incapable of attempting to defraud the Government as the Hon. Sec'y himself. A chance to explain & defend ourselves before an impartial board will however soon dispel the slanders of informers, & this we ask at your hands if our legal position does not protect us." [157]

Carnegie got his opportunity for a hearing both before a House of Representatives subcommittee on naval affairs and before the Bureau of Ordnance the following spring. The Bureau found that the allegations of the four employees were correct and recommended penalties of 15 per cent of the cost of the armor delivered to the government as well as the return of all premiums paid. President Cleveland, however, tempered justice with mercy, and ruled that only 10 per cent of the price should be levied as a penalty over the period from 3 November 1892 to 16 September

1893. The value of the armor plates delivered in that particular period was $1,404,894.41, thus making the fine $140,489.44. Carnegie Steel had to suffer the further indignity of paying to their four former employees $35,121.23, being the 25 per cent of the penalty to which the men, as informers, were entitled under law.[158] At least four workmen at Homestead that year were the highest paid laborers in the United States, even though their "bonus" was also their severance pay.

Nevertheless, in spite of all the notoriety and penalties imposed, it should be noted that all of the armor plates tested easily passed the rigid ballistics tests of the navy and that Carnegie Steel continued to get its contracts for armor plate from the government.[159]

The next difficulty with the government came over the question of cost. The indefatigable and troublesome Mr. Herbert first raised the question in the summer of 1896, and Captain William Sampson, chief of the Bureau of Ordnance, with dogged persistence, kept at Carnegie Steel and Bethlehem Iron to show their costs of production. This the two companies refused to do. Sampson then made his own estimate of what costs were. He refused to tell Schwab what his estimate was, but Schwab reported back to Leishman that he had information that "their report will show cost of Armor at about $350 per ton, which won't be unfavorable to us." [160] As indeed it would not. Captain Sampson was a long way from the truth, but he and Herbert kept digging.

On 5 January 1897, Secretary Herbert, with only two more months to serve, sent to Congress a report on the cost of armor in which he estimated the cost to be $250 per ton. He pointed out that Bethlehem had furnished a bid to the Russian government for armor at $249. He concluded that both Carnegie Steel and Bethlehem Iron should furnish armor to their own government at no more that $400 a ton. If they could not do so, he wanted the Secretary of the Navy to have the authority to erect or buy or lease its own armor works. Carnegie Steel's response was that if the government would give the company an average of 2000 tons of armor per year, Carnegie Steel would gladly provide it at $400 a ton.[161]

In response to Secretary Herbert's threat that the government would run its own armor plate works if necessary, Carnegie decided to take the offensive. When the new Republican administration came into office, and there was still no let-up in the pressure exerted from the Bureau of Ordnance to reduce the price of armor, Carnegie, in a letter to the Secretary of the Navy, offered to sell his armor plant to the government for $3,000,000. Schwab reported that he didn't think the government "w'll take our plant at cost, because the Secretary of the Navy thinks a new plant can be built for 1½ million." [162] Carnegie responded by urging Schwab to offer the plant to the government for $2,000,000, "letting them know that this is one million less than it cost, in return we will furnish the steel for the armor at prices to be fixed by mutual agreement or by arbitration. . . . My idea is that we should force our Works upon the Government at a price that will appear to the country much below what would be required if the Government were to build. . . . Another advantage of this plan seems to me that Bethlehem could not possibly follow us, or, if it did, that its price would be necessarily much higher than we are willing to take. Indeed, I should offer the plant at one half what it cost us and if it were taken, we should have the supply of steel and natural gas, by arbitration, which, I am sure, would net us handsomely." [163]

Carnegie's partners did not warm to this idea, however. Nor did the government, upon further investigation, show any inclination to build its own plant or to buy Carnegie's. As the nation prepared for war in 1898, the navy was happy to buy its armor for new construction from Carnegie Steel and Bethlehem at $400 a ton, and the profits continued to roll in.[164] Indeed, so essential had the armor business proved to be for the company during the depression of the 1890's, when other kinds of orders fell off drastically, that Carnegie was prepared to sacrifice the last of his scruples against military production. As early as 1894, he was urging his partners to enter the business of gun forgings.[165] In a remarkable show of independence, however, his partners opposed him on this. They did so not on any ideological grounds, but as Phipps said, in answer to Carnegie's renewed urgings in 1898, "the tonnage is too small and the profits no greater than on armor." Lauder also opposed guns. "Projectiles," he felt, "might pay us better than forgings. Guns fire many times their own weight in projectiles." [166]

Against such united opposition Carnegie was forced to yield. Nevertheless his enthusiasm for producing finished manufactured goods had in no way been dampened by the difficulties he had experienced in the manufacture of armor plate. There had been "millions" in it, and Carnegie was sure there were more millions to be had in the manufacture of other goods. Of more interest to Carnegie than the money involved was the vertical structure to be achieved for his company. It was high time, he felt, to dominate stage three in manufacturing. "The next step—and it is coming," he wrote in 1898 to the board of managers, "is to go into the manufacture of finished articles. At all events, the concern that does this first, will remain first." [167]

To Carnegie, the direction that the steel business must take in the immediate future was so obvious that he could not understand how anyone could fail to perceive it. In an interview given to *Iron Age* in 1895, he put it succinctly, "The railroad system is practically developed. . . . We can never expect again to build railways at the rate of 13,000 miles a year. . . . The rail mills must now adapt themselves to other purposes. . . ." [168] Carnegie had been one of the first in the trade to convert rail mills into mills for the rolling of structural beams. His friend Edward Atkinson had written a letter to J. S. Jeans, Secretary of the British Iron and Steel Trade Association, when the Boston textile manufacturer was visiting Carnegie at Cluny Castle during the summer of 1895. Carnegie read it with great approval—he was so impressed that he made a copy of it. Atkinson had written, "The use of structural steel is increasing with enormous rapidity. Steel beams for long spans and heavy loads are now on the market at less than the cost of hard Southern pine beams, such as would be required for similar stresses." [169] Carnegie Steel was successful in getting the contract for the structural beams, braces, and plates for the celebrated Brooklyn Bridge. To get this contract, it was necessary to adapt their open hearth furnaces to the making of acid steel, since that was what the builders wanted. No expense or trouble was too great, however, for this contract was valuable not only for the amount of steel involved but, even more important, for the publicity connected with it.[170] The company also got the major portion of the contracts for the elevated railways in New York City, with much the same public fanfare.

The production of structural material was an obvious and generally easy adaptation from rail manufacturing. But Carnegie had far more ambitious plans for the future of his company than beams and plates. In a long letter to Schwab in 1898, he outlined what he meant by "Stage Three":

> Our policy should be to make finished articles, Bridges among them. We should make the best Bridge Shop in the United States as soon as you get time to build it.
> We want to sell finished [railroad] Cars as soon as you can do it. We shall want to make Wire, and I think nails, as soon as we can. I suggested also Boilers, and hope that some of the members of the Board will find some other special articles.
> The concern that sells articles finished, will be able to run all weathers and make some money while others are half-idle and losing money.[171]

The members of the Board, however, far from finding "some other special articles" for the company to manufacture, were singularly disinterested in if not outright hostile to Carnegie's vision of the future. Frick and Schwab seemed far more concerned with spending capital and profits on improvements for the existing works than in launching upon new manufacturing ventures. Peacock, the General Sales Manager, was fearful of alienating present customers of billets by entering into competition with them. Phipps, always sniveling about dividends, seemed afraid to spend money for anything. In commenting upon some of Schwab's projected plans for expansion, Phipps showed the kind of timidity that Schwab and Frick regarded as disastrous: "My breath was taken away. Better some opportunities be missed, than this fast jumping at things. . . . By all means, do let us go a little slower, my heart is often in my mouth, when I read of their rushing way in *big* things." [172]

The steel car issue was a case in point. Carnegie early in 1898 began pushing the board to enter into the manufacturing of pressed steel railroad cars in direct competition with one of their larger customers of steel billets, the Schoen Pressed Steel Car Company. "The Car matter is already upon us—Steel cars really a step forward." But Frick, speaking for the board, replied that "the car matter is quiet now—too many other interests to concern us and take our money." [173]

As Carnegie continued to push the matter, Schwab countered with another proposal. He reported that he had talked with Charles Schoen and found that his capital stock was excellent, but that he needed some immediate cash. For a loan of $300,000 to $400,000, Schoen would give Carnegie Steel a five-year contract for all steel used by his car works and could guarantee production of 40 to 50 cars a day. This would amount to 80,000 to 90,000 tons of steel a year that Schoen would purchase from Carnegie Steel.[174] Further investigation revealed, however, that Schoen was not in as strong a financial condition as Schwab had thought. There was already a first mortgage in his works, and Carnegie flatly refused to agree to a loan. After months of discussion of various proposals from Schoen and Charlie Schwab, who was Schoen's chief supporter on the Carnegie Steel Board, Carnegie, in opposition, at last convinced the board that Carnegie Steel should enter into no agreements with Schoen or any other producer of railroad cars but should instead erect its own car works. He made one of his rare appearances at a board meeting in November 1898 and apparently carried the day.[175]

There were, however, protracted negotiations over the proper site for their car works, and when the board met again at the end of January to discuss the matter further, there was quite unexpected opposition to the entire plan from Peacock. When Frick began the discussion by saying, "I believe we are a unit and in favor of going ahead with the Car Works," Peacock answered bluntly, "No, we are not a unit." He pointed out the amount of steel tonnage they were presently selling to the three largest car works in the country. "We have seldom, if ever, gone into any business unless we were in shape to control it, but that would not be the case with Steel Cars. We cannot control the Car business; we would have to buy many parts, springs, buffers, wheels, brakes, etc. . . . What we wanted particularly was a market for our material, and I believe we can sell many times the tonnage through the Pressed Steel Car Company than we can if we antagonize them and undertake to sell Cars ourselves." There was also a letter from Phipps, which was not unexpected, opposing the venture. Frick, obviously nonplussed by this development, coldly concluded the discussion by saying, "As I understand it, we are going ahead as fast as possible with plans for the Works. I think we need take no further motion at present." [176] Carnegie, upon reading the minutes of the board meeting, must have been as surprised as Frick, for Peacock was usually the most compliant and malleable of all the partners. Indeed, it had been he who had made the motion in favor of the erection of the car works at the meeting at which Carnegie had been present. Carnegie wrote to Cousin Dod, "It is all right for Peacock to submit his views. . . . We have decided to build Steel Cars, that settles it unless contrary action be taken." [177]

The issue was not settled after all. Peacock's arguments made too much sense to his fellow managers. Carnegie was obliged to write to a board that was now nearly unanimous against him: "Now to give up this business is pretty bad. I should be sorry indeed, and would want a pretty big reward." [178] The result was that Carnegie got his "pretty big reward" instead of his car works. So eager were Schoen and the officers of the Pressed Steel Car Company to keep Carnegie out of their field that they agreed to buy all their steel plates, angles, bar beams, channels, and axles from Carnegie Steel at a fixed price for a ten-year period. In addition, Schoen, who had once had the naïve hope that he would get a $400,000 loan from Carnegie, now had to pay him $1,000,000 in $100,000 yearly payments simply not to manufacture cars.[179]

It was a hard bargain, but still Carnegie was not satisfied. He wrote to Lauder, "Much prefer that we build our Car works, no reason why we should not. . . . Please say to Frick I favor our building our car shops even if they stand idle." And to the board, "I promised to write my views. . . . I am not managing the business. If the Board decides otherwise, I shall have nothing to say and no reflections to cast on anyone. I think that prestige means dollars and even on the dollar platform I think giving up our own idea will cost us dollars. . . . The contract as proposed giving us right to terminate on a year's notice being only a *postponement* is the utmost I would agree to. We are still free. . . . If we postpone for a year, Pipe should be pushed in place of cars." [180] Clearly, Carnegie was simply biding his time until he could persuade his lieutenants to follow him into battle.

It was much the same situation in the other fields of manufacturing finished articles. For five years Carnegie continued to push tubes, wire, hoops, and pipes, only to meet resistance from his partners.[181] They were impressed with the monopolistic trusts that were being formed in all these fields during these years and the promises of large purchases of steel from these trusts. Carnegie, on the contrary, was highly suspicious of them. "In these days of Trusts and other Swindles, I think Carnegie Steel Company should keep a pure record," he wrote to the board in 1899. "I do not favor the contract as made [a contract to sell steel billets only to the Tin Plate Company and to no other company making tin plate]. I do not believe it is legal; I do not believe it is right, besides. I believe that independent concerns will soon beat the Trust and we shall lose more business ultimately by antagonizing these than by now trying to aid the Trust to maintain an unfair monopoly. We should stand as that large Manufacturer in Philadelphia stands, open to do business with all, and I beg this to be recorded on the minutes." [182]

Nor was Carnegie afraid of the trusts, as his more timid associates were: "In the case of the Tin Plate Company as in the case of the American Wire Company, if our President steps forward at the right time and in the right way, informs these people that we do not propose to be injured . . . but that we require this arrangement:—then specify what is advantageous for us, very advantageous, more advantageous than existed before the combination, and he will get it. If they decline to give us what we want, then there must be no bluff. We must accept the situation and prove that if it is fight they want, here we are 'always ready.' Here is a historic situation for the Managers to study—Richelieu's advice: 'First, all means to conciliate; failing that, all means to crush.' " [183]

To his more cautious partners, however, Carnegie appeared to be a very trigger-happy Richelieu. His idea of conciliation was his opponent's surrender. He seemed always eager for the moments to crush, and he never gave up trying for new conquests. In June 1900 he was writing to the board of managers: "I should not allow present drop to postpone our going into Tubes. This is a dead sure thing for us, a clear track all the way. The tube people do not give us trade any more as they used to. We have only to build the works to make a satisfactory division of the tube business with one party in it, the Trust. . . . Don't be scared into postponing, the cost of works will now be less and by the time you are ready to make tubes, chances are the market will be good." [184]

But the board of managers held back, content to sell its billets to the trusts and reluctant to march out with pennants flying against these formidable combinations. Carnegie was not the first empire builder to learn that his real enemies were not the hosts on the opposing hill, but the timidity and inertia within his own ranks.

To be sure, the attitude of independence that first Peacock and then the other partners manifested in the steel car case did show they had a certain courage in resisting the wishes of the partner with the majority interest, even if it was only the courage of not taking action. This was not atypical, however, for there seemed to be an unwritten law within the company that, although Carnegie had an absolute veto on any positive action by the board, particularly if it involved the spending of either surplus or capital, he, on the other hand, could not by the sheer weight of his interest in the company force the board to take positive action against its better judgment. The result was that the burden of proof was on anyone, Carnegie included, who wished to embark upon a new venture. Although this could have led to total inaction and stagnation, in general it would appear that this was a salutary policy. It meant that all major proposals, even those which Carnegie sponsored, had to meet the open and searching scrutiny of all the partners. Unquestionably, the company was saved from entering into the kind of highly dubious ventures that wrecked so many American business concerns in a period of expansion. Fortunately, the company working under this tacit agreement did not miss any great opportunities, although it came perilously close to doing so in the case of the Mesabi leases and the purchase of the Norrie mines. In any event, it was the kind of policy that Carnegie wanted and was willing to live with even when it hampered or blocked his own more daring proposals.

The executive management of the company was as simple in structure as was the corporate organization itself. What started off as a simple partnership arrangement under Kloman, Phipps, and Miller remained that, even though the company had expanded to be the biggest steel company in the world and in terms of capitalization one of the largest business concerns in all American industry. The board of managers consisted of five—later expanded to nine—men, who were also actively engaged in supervisory positions within the operations of the company. The three senior partners, Carnegie, Phipps, and Lauder, were not originally members of the board of managers, although during the last few years of the company's existence Lauder did serve on the board at Carnegie's specific request. After the organization of the Carnegie Steel Company in 1892, Frick at first served as chairman of the company, and was the sole executive head of the consolidated company. In 1894, he resigned his position as sole executive head of the company and became chairman of the board of managers. At this time a new executive position was created, that of president of Carnegie Steel Company. The president was to be in direct charge of the actual operations of the company. Carnegie was not too happy with this arrangement. As he often said, "A company cannot have two heads any more than a ship can have two captains." For several years, however, under the presidency of first Leishman and then Schwab, this executive arrangement worked quite satisfactorily. Frick, in almost every respect, was a superb executive. He dominated Leishman, an essentially weak and ineffective man, and kept the company moving forward during Leishman's presidency. Against the much stronger and extremely ambitious Schwab, Frick served as a whetstone held against a blade. Sparks were struck, and the blade was sharpened.

No man who held a supervisory job in Carnegie Steel Company could regard his position as either easy or secure. And the higher the position, the less easy and secure it was. Of all the executive heads of the steel companies in which Carnegie held the major interest, only Schwab survived to the end. Schwab had the unique distinction not only of surviving but of growing stronger and more certain of Carnegie's favor with each passing year. The rest, beginning with Shinn in 1881, all either died, resigned, or were forced out: Tom Carnegie; David Stewart, who died soon after taking over the presidency of Carnegie Brothers; Phipps, whose brief presidency was regarded by all, including Phipps himself, as only an interregnum; William Abbott, who never enjoyed the fierce competitiveness of business and was happy to resign in 1892 when the two companies were consolidated; Leishman, who was lashed unmercifully by Carnegie until he was forced out; and finally even Frick, who resigned the chairmanship of the company in 1894 of his own free will and was later to be ousted as chairman of the board.

The way in which Leishman was treated as president of the company is illustrative of how Carnegie could drive an ordinary man to the point of distraction. Leishman had begun his career in the iron and steel business with a Pittsburgh manufacturing concern, Schoenberger and Company. He then had headed his own company, Leishman and Snyder, which manufactured finished steel articles. It was there, as a customer of Carnegie, Phipps, that he had come to the attention of Frick and Carnegie. On 1 January 1887, he joined Carnegie Steel as vice chairman; and, upon the resignation of Frick as chairman in 1894, Leishman was promoted to the presidency, at Frick's suggestion. Almost at once he came under attack from Carnegie.[185]

Probably Carnegie realized from the start that the board had made a mistake in electing the genial, easy-going, but generally ineffective Leishman as president. Frick had pushed this appointment, perhaps in part in recognition of the fact that Leishman had saved his life at the time of the Berkman attack, but more probably because he had worked closely with Leishman for several years and knew that he could dominate and direct him. None of this background had particularly endeared Leishman to Carnegie, and it took only the suspicion that Leishman was engaged in speculative activities to set Carnegie against him. For to Carnegie in these later years, there was no offense more deplorable than that of speculation. Like the retired high-wire artist who refuses to climb a stepladder, Carnegie, the old master of high finance and stock manipulation in railroads, telegraphs, and sleeping cars, now feared the stock exchange and was determined to keep his partners innocent of its allurements. Speculation in commodities basic to their business was especially to be eschewed by all of Carnegie's "boys," if they knew what was good for them. But Leishman had come to the Carnegie brotherhood late, and it was difficult for him to refrain from those practices which were generally considered quite normal in the world of business. Carnegie—with good reason—suspected his president of speculating in pig iron and ores and was quick to let Leishman know of his displeasure:

> When a President has left business methods and brought a great concern into disrepute many tongues wag which otherwise would remain silent. . . . It appears you speculated for ore in Minnesota Ore Stock, which you bought when already in debt, simply because you thought it would rise in value and pay you more than the interest upon the loan. The stock has been of less value than your debt upon it. Like your purchase of pig the speculation has been a mistake—the gamble didn't win.
>
> Now there may be other complications in your private affairs. *You conceal,* keep silent, when no man can obtain firm standing with partners who keeps any business investments from them. Our President should have reputation, hence influence and financial strength, if not from capital, yet from *character.* The Carnegie Steel Co. is daily compromised by its President owing private debts. I am told of an instance where you borrowed from a subordinate. This is madness, and proves to me and to others that you do not realize what the Presidency means, just as little as you admit you do in regard to your gamble in pig. . . . Every dinner you attend, every lunch at the Club at which you may linger, every act affects the Company; every word you speak; but every financial step in your private affairs has serious consequences. It was for this reason I put you out of debt, as I thought, but *you concealed from me again your true position.* . . . The President must have no private affairs which his Board does not know. He must sell out all investments carried on margins, or by loans; he must make no contracts of importance, except as the Board after full discussion as a Board, directs him to make.
>
> We all appreciate your ability in some directions, but you have much to do before you regain the confidence of your partners as a safe man to be the Executive head of the Company. I cannot read a trade paper without being stabbed to the heart—even the Philadelphia Press, which I picked up yesterday morning, wounded me sorely. It places your speculation at 250,000 tons.[186]

After this Leishman could do nothing right in Carnegie's eyes. Every major act or decision upon Leishman's part brought a critical comment from Carnegie: "The Annual Statement shows a charge for adjustment of pig iron of $988,000. I had figured that it could not amount to more than, say, $400,000. . . . The best plan for you is to take Mr. Lovejoy's statement, analyse it item by item, and then make a report to the Board, showing just how each loss occurred, also giving such explanation as you may have to make." [187] Again, the following day, Carnegie wrote, "Have you noticed that your Stock of Materials On Hand amounted January 1st to $6,639,000. January last year to $4,687,000. Now there is no use in your thinking of going abroad and leaving the business in this condition. Your task is to get the Stock On Hand down one and three-quarter million dollars. Nothing you can do abroad in armor, or anything else will make up for failure to attend to this vital point. . . . Frankly, I must say, that if you do not look out, you will bring even our firm into serious trouble. . . . I scarcely know what next to expect. These things cause me great anxiety." [188]

Leishman was to give the senior partner more surprises. The following week, Carnegie was again writing in great consternation:

> I was surprised to find upon the statement that the Carnegie Steel Co. had purchased two bankrupt furnaces in the Valley called the Douglas. . . . I leave you to imagine how unsatisfactory it is to have such surprises sprung upon one. In all your communications to me not one word have you ever said about this important purchase of Furnaces involving, as I think it does, an unwarranted stretch of authority upon the part of yourself and the other members of the Board, and certainly a violation of every sound principle governing business affairs.
>
> I am sorry to have to write this, but I cannot live and have the Carnegie Steel Company degraded to the level of speculators and Jim Cracks, men who pass as manufacturers, but who look to the market and not to manufacturing. . . . If the Board of Managers wish to do me a great favor, let them get the Douglas Furnaces off our books at any cost.[189]

What Carnegie was also saying, of course, was that the board of managers, if it wished to do him a great favor, would get rid of Leishman at the earliest opportunity. For Leishman, there was more relief than despair in this prospect. As he wrote after one of

Carnegie's angry outbursts, "While my position is an exalted one it is not an enviable one as I certainly require not only all my strength but also a clear head to look after the many important matters that turn up every day in a large concern like ours—and the way you have treated me for the past two weeks has worried me more than a year's hard work—and if it was going to continue I simply could not stand the strain as you would soon have a broken down man on your hands and it would be better for me to quit business at once and not wait until I become a physical wreck." [190]

Leishman was saved from further anguish on 12 February 1897, by being relieved as president of the company. To the public he gave poor health as the reason, which by this time was undoubtedly true.[191] He happily retired to the relative peace of the American embassies abroad, where he served as Minister to Switzerland and later as Ambassador to Italy and then Germany. After Carnegie, the Kaiser held no terrors for him.

The presidency of Carnegie Steel then went to Charles Schwab, which is what Carnegie had wanted all along. At last, the company had an executive who not only had the talents and drive to manage the company to Carnegie's satisfaction, but also had the temperament and sense of humor to withstand every insult the Old Man could offer.

Leishman's anguish, which all officers in the company had to endure in some degree, raises the question of why any man, unless he had a hide as tough as Schwab's, would endure such torment. The answer, of course, is simple. The prospect for rewards was so great that every employee throughout the Carnegie domain dreamed of the opportunity to subject himself to Carnegie's criticism in return for an interest in the company. Even the bedeviled Leishman received over $800,000 when he retired and was required to sell his interest at book value. A man will take a great deal of punishment at this price, and there was never a shortage of employees eager to become one of Carnegie's "associates."

Carnegie was generous in admitting employees into this charmed circle. He was to use an interest in the company as effectively as his plant superintendents used the bonus to drive ambitious young men on to ever greater achievements. Every January the question of partners' interests came before the board, and

Carnegie's wishes were scrupulously respected in this area. As the wealth and potential value of the company grew, the shares of interest for new partners became smaller and smaller, but ever more valuable. Men were willing to work beyond their physical capacities to give to the company their bodies, minds, their souls if that were necessary, to get that one-ninth of 1 per cent of interest, knowing that in time, if they survived, that fractional interest could be worth a million.

Carnegie knew precisely the value of the partnership system. "Mr. Morgan buys his partners," he was fond of saying, "I grow my own." Burton Hendrick has compared "life in the Carnegie kingdom . . . to a perpetual race, in which each contestant put forth his finest effort, understanding that, at the goal, there was a splendid prize." [192] Carnegie's associates would have disputed this analogy on one point. There were rewards all along the track and the promise of a splendid prize at the goal, it is true, but the goal seemed never to be reached. It was always, "more, more, faster, faster." The race went on and the casualties were heavy. But still they ran, with Carnegie alternately cheering and cursing them on. "Every year should be marked by the promotion of one or more of our young men," Carnegie wrote to Frick in 1896. "I am perfectly willing to give from my interest for this purpose, when the undivided stock is disposed of. There is Miller at Duquesne, and Brown, both of whom might get a sixth of one per cent. It is a very good plan to have all your heads of departments interested, and I should like to vote for the admission of Mr. Corey; and if there is a Sixth left, perhaps Mr. Kerr of the Edgar Thomson Blast Furnaces deserves it. We cannot have too many of the right sort interested in profits. What says the good book. Something like this: There be those that gather and yet scattereth abroad. I should like to see all these interested, and next year I shall be glad to give for others." [193]

One cannot help but be impressed with the fact that Carnegie not only knew the names of his employees in supervisory positions throughout his vast domain, but also knew precisely which ones were producing and should receive the rewards. This is what made his partnership system highly effective. The Millers and the Browns, toiling away at the mills at Duquesne or Homestead or Braddock, worked with the knowledge that at any moment they might feel the golden touch on their shoulder. So they worked harder and lived in hope. Just as Napoleon drove his soldiers on with the slogan that every foot soldier carried a marshal's baton in his knapsack, so Carnegie had taught his men to believe that every worker carried a partnership in his lunch pail. And as Carnegie scattered the prizes, he richly gathered in the fruits.

With the partnership came more responsibility on the "new Pard." The insults were frequent, and if the partner failed to meet Carnegie's expectations, he was removed from his position and eliminated from the partnership by being forced to sell his interest back to the company at book value. If Carnegie was quick to criticize, he could be unexpectedly generous in his praise. He like to refer to his associates as his "young geniuses," and for a job well done there could be a doubling of a partner's interest at the next January meeting. "Prospects never were so bright," he wrote to Schwab at the end of the year 1898. "Please present to all parties my cordial congratulations upon the prosperity of our concern, a concern which may now be said to have made a good start, the result of exceptionally able management by the most wonderful organization of young geniuses the world has to show—or ever had to show. I mean this, every word of it." [194]

Carnegie, a hard taskmaster, was paradoxically overly generous in his general estimate of the talents of his associates. The great majority of them were far from being geniuses, even within their narrow field of competency. They were, generally speaking, very ordinary men. If they had any trait not possessed by the common run of employees, it was not brilliance of mind, but a consuming ambition to get wealth. "Take from me all the ore mines, railroads, manufacturing plants, but leave me my organization, and in a few years I promise to duplicate the Carnegie company," Carnegie would frequently say in these later years of success.[195] This simply was not true. With the two notable exceptions of Frick and Schwab, Carnegie could have easily replaced all of the men in his organization with others equally as talented as they, and the company would have been little affected one way or another.

For someone supposedly as tough in personnel matters as Carnegie, it is indeed surprising that he should have tolerated, even encouraged, the amount of nepotism that existed within his organization. Among his partners were his second cousin Tom Morrison, and his beloved Cousin Dod, George Lauder, who, according to most of his associates, contributed almost nothing to the organization except to serve as a spy for Carnegie at the managerial level.[196] J. E. Schwab, another partner, was Charles Schwab's brother, and A. C. Dinkey was Schwab's brother-in-law. Lawrence Phipps, second vice-president and treasurer of the company, was Henry Phipps's nephew, and Otis Childs, still another associate, was the brother of Frick's wife.

Sentiment also played a role in the personnel policies of the company. There was a widely held belief in Dunfermline that any young man of that town who decided to emigrate could get a good job in Carnegie's steel mills. The remarkable success of Alexander Peacock, a Dunfermline salesman of ladies' fineries, did much to perpetuate this legend. Peacock came to the United States in the late 1880's and first found employment with a linen company in New York. The pay was low and the future not bright. Peacock knew nothing about steel, but he had a letter of introduction from Uncle George Lauder, so he called on Carnegie and was given an important position in the sales department.[197] Within three years he was a partner and general sales manager of the company. By 1897, he was first vice president, next in line to Schwab, yet there is nothing in the business records to indicate any superior talents that would merit the encomium of genius. Like so many other partners and members of the board of managers, men like James Gayley, Daniel Clemson, and A. M. Moreland, Peacock worked up to the best of his capabilities within his own specialty, knew how to drive his subordinates to get the most out of them, stayed in the good graces of Carnegie to the extent that that was possible, and did nothing to rock the boat.

Something of an exception in this group was Francis Lovejoy, the secretary of the company. Of all the men on the board, except for Frick, he was the most independent, could always be counted upon to speak his mind freely regardless of the consequences, and his advice, frequently because it was different, appears in the minutes to be the most imaginative and sagacious of any given. He tended to be more sympathetic toward labor than his colleagues, although he too was violently opposed to labor organizations.

The minutes of the board meetings that he kept were models of reporting in their completeness and accuracy. He also held uncompromisingly to his high principles, a characteristic which was later to cost him dearly.

Of the whole association of partners, the only two men who might be regarded in a broad stretch of the term as geniuses were Schwab and Frick. Schwab was, of course, Carnegie's all-time favorite. Their relationship was not unlike that which had at one time existed between the young Carnegie and Thomas Scott. Schwab in many ways was the son that Carnegie never had. Although he could do many wrongs in Carnegie's eyes, he could never commit an offense that was unforgivable. Whereas Abbott and Leishman were castigated unmercifully and eventually driven out of the firm for their speculative tendencies, Schwab could gamble recklessly at the card tables of Monte Carlo and not lose his favored position within the company, although he would have to suffer much verbal abuse from his master. The story frequently told in Pittsburgh is of Schwab's being scolded vigorously by Carnegie for some peccadillo. Schwab in self-defense replied that at least he never did anything, unlike some people he knew, that would have to be done behind closed doors. To which Carnegie is supposed to have replied, "You damned fool. What do you suppose doors are for except to be closed?" Although probably apocryphal, this story does illustrate the easy and candid relationship that existed between the two men.

Schwab's greatest contributions to the company were in terms of personality and imaginative vision. He could take over the tragic wreck that was Homestead in 1892, get the men back to work, and ease the tenseness of the situation as no one else could. Although often more harsh in his labor policies than Frick, he got the co-operation and support of his men in a way that can only be compared with that of Captain Jones. He did it by the force of personality. "Genial Charlie," always smiling, always slapping a man on the back, always ready with a joke or friendly quip, was the man who got things done to Carnegie's satisfaction. More than that, he had a vision for the growth and success of the company that was surpassed only by Frick and Carnegie. No man in the whole organization was as imaginative as he in seeing what improvements could be made to reduce costs and increase production. Like his two superiors, he was a true empire builder, and it is this that set him apart from his colleagues on the board.

Frick, of course, was the greatest executive whom Carnegie was to employ during his forty years in business. No two men could have been more unlike in temperament and interests than Schwab and Frick. His associates could never remember Frick's telling a joke or indeed conversing on any subject not related to the business at hand. His concentration on business affairs appeared to be almost monomaniacal in its intensity, and quite frightening to ordinary men. But there was no shrewder, more perceptive businessman in all America. As "coke king," he deserves to rank in the same company as Rockefeller, Carnegie, Hill, and Ford.

Frick's greatest mistake was to have joined Carnegie Steel as a partner and chairman of the company. It brought him immense wealth, to be sure, far more than he could ever have attained in his chosen field of coke, but this wealth was acquired at the expense of his own self-esteem. In the long run, he could not tolerate his own empire's becoming but a satellite of the larger concern, even though he was director of both. His associates regarded him as cold and unemotional, a man whose every action was carefully and rationally premeditated. But in his personal life, what little he had time for, he was a most affectionate father. He doted upon his only surviving daughter, Helen, and she in turn was zealously to guard the memory of her father as having been a paragon of all virtues. He on occasion could even show more sympathy toward his subordinates than Carnegie. He had a sense of justice tempered with mercy that occasionally surprised his colleagues. For instance, he wrote to Carnegie:

Do not think it quite fair that you should be so severe on McCague, as the Judge [Reed] told me you were in your letter to Mr. Lauder, and which Mr. Lauder showed to McCague. This, on the part of Mr. Lauder, does not seem to me to be prudent. No one knows better than you the immense freight business of the Carnegie Steel Company, but I doubt whether you are fully aware of the little deals the Freight Agent has to make of one kind or another to secure best rates, which he really takes great risks in doing. McCague is an exceedingly sensitive man, and it unfits him for business. In some respects, he probably is not as able as he should be, but I'm sure he at all times does his best for the concern. Being on the ground, and keeping on to matters pretty closely, I'm in a position to speak on these matters, and am satisfied, if you could view the whole situation as I do, you would thoroughly agree with me.[198]

That Frick could be overcome by towering, blinding rages Carnegie was to discover on several occasions. Under Frick's usually cold, unemotional exterior, there was a very passionate man, but only on rare occasions did he reveal himself publicly.

John Walker, a close associate of both Frick and Carnegie, told Hendrick that the Carnegie works had both a Napoleon and a von Moltke. "And don't ever forget that Carnegie was the Napoleon—that is the commander and intuitive genius, who planned campaigns and executed them with a rapidity and boldness that swept all enemies from his path; while Frick had the calm qualities of a von Moltke—long-headed, deliberate, a great tactician,—a man who acted from carefully reasoned premises, while Carnegie struck out boldly, burning all his bridges behind him, not necessarily knowing himself the stages of reasoning by which he reached his results. In fact, he didn't reason much—he acted on impulse; but his impulses were usually far more accurate than others' logical processes. But both were very big men—too big to enjoy each other's presence in the same organization." [199]

This is a very perceptive comparison that Walker drew. It errs in only one respect. Von Moltke had been content, like a good Prussian general, to subordinate his own ambitions to that of Bismarck. The Iron Chancellor had built the German Reich; von Moltke had carried out orders without question. Frick had come to Carnegie after his own successful venture in Reich-building. He could never accept gracefully or for long the subordinate position of being the expediter of another's will. Therein lay the seed for division within this empire of business.

Finally, there was Carnegie himself, who never held an official position within the company that bore his name. But he held 58 per cent of the capital shares, and Carnegie Steel belonged to him. Seldom in Pittsburgh, only rarely present at any board meeting, he nevertheless kept himself completely informed on every detail of the business. To the delight of later historians, he demanded and got the fullest minutes of board meetings that probably ever existed in business history. "Some suggestions I made to Mr. Frick are, I think important," he wrote to Secretary Lovejoy, "that the votes of each member, pro and con, in the board shall be recorded; that no new undertakings be gone into except by a two-thirds majority of the total number of the Board, nor new methods adopted; and their [sic] are several other points which may be important." [200] In another letter to Lovejoy he wrote, "The minutes should, in addition to this, record every reason or explanation which a member desires to give. If this were properly done then any of us looking over the minutes would be able to judge of the judgment displayed by the voter, which of course would affect his standing with his colleagues. It would bring responsibility home to him direct. The minutes cannot err in being too full, the fuller the better. They can err in being too much curtailed." [201]

Accordingly all board discussions were fully and faithfully reported by Lovejoy. This policy must have both inhibited and encouraged discussion, for it became as important to get into the minutes with sagacious remarks as it had been to get the position of *valet de chambre* at the court of Versailles. A single proper comment could catch the attention of the king. On rare occasions, to be sure, the minutes could become too full. Carnegie wrote Leishman somewhat petulantly, "Mr. Hunsiker's interesting but very detailed reports, occupy far too much space. . . . It is not possible that Mr. Hunsiker can have something interesting to say every week." What Carnegie wanted was facts. "A serious omission is that Mr. Curry does not report for the important department of Furnaces and Ores. . . . Mr. Peacock's reports are interesting, but he fails to give any proof of what we should have, viz.: Amount of orders received during the week; Amount produced; Gain and Loss. His report should wind up with such a statement in 'Rails,' 'Billets,' 'Beams,' and 'Channels,' 'Miscellaneous,' so that we could see at a glance whether we were gaining or losing upon our orders." [202]

After Lovejoy had sent out the report to Scotland or New York, Cannes or Cairo, the board would wait for the inevitable "Thoughts on the Minutes." In a week or a month, back would come the response, often as detailed as the minutes themselves:

671

First, MIXER: If you will stand for ten cents per ton royalty, the Supreme Court will give it to you. . . . My vote is to go ahead and bring suit against Illinois Steel Co. . . .

NATURAL GAS: I am very clear that we should go ahead preparing to use coal. . . . We are wasting a great deal of money using gas. . . .

RAIL MILL: Why should we wait till Fall to take up plans for necessary finishing additions. You should not lose a day. . . . Pray, put this in train at once.

KEYSTONE BRIDGE: This does indeed, make a sad showing. . . . We cannot stand this. . . . I should not wait until I ran across the proper man, I should try one within ten days, and if he does not suit, get another.

EDGAR THOMSON FURNACES: Cost of pig both at Edgar Thomson & Lucy's is higher than I had expected. . . . Please give me items justifying this. Sorry that Kerr is not keeping up to the record. Note that five of our Furnaces are beyond 400,000 tons product, and one beyond 600,000 tons. . . . A private word to Kerr might give him the necessary impetus. We lag at times.[203]

And so on, item after item. Carnegie could be maddeningly forgetful at times when one of his decisions had been proved wrong, but never did he fail to catch a point of trouble anywhere within his entire steel domain. Never could it be said he failed to see either the trees or the forest.

In short, Carnegie and Carnegie Steel were one and the same. He built it, sustained it, expanded it into America's most successfully unified business enterprise. He frequently was wrong on specific issues, but never wrong in direction for the goal he sought. William Abbott perhaps best summed up Carnegie's role when he told Hendrick, "Most of Andrew Carnegie's partners were most ordinary men. . . . Yet Carnegie could take this commonplace material and make out of it a truly great organization." [204] That, of course, is the peculiar talent of builders of empires.

CHAPTER XVIII

Mr. McKinley's
Business of Empire
1898-1900

In the decade of the 1890's, while Carnegie was engaged in building his empire of business, he also became deeply involved with those political empires that were being built or dreamed of by the jingoists of the Western World. Typically, Carnegie was anything but consistent in his attitude toward the nationalistic imperialism that had become a dominant force in London, Paris, Tokyo, Berlin, Rome, and even Washington.

It would hardly be surprising to find that Carnegie found some attraction in political empire building, for there was an obvious relationship beween the goals of his business activity and the ambitions of the imperialistic statesmen of the day. Both were concerned with consolidation and expansion; both were expressions of a particular kind of creative drive that seemed endemic throughout the trans-Atlantic world in this last decade of the nineteenth century. The same compulsive urge for acquisition and conquest that drove men like Schwab and Frick and Hill to build more blast furnaces, open up new coal fields, and push railroads

673

across the northwest wilderness of America, led other men to attempt to plant the British Union Jack or the French Tricolor in the Sudan, the Sahara, or on the Transvaal veldt of South Africa. All of this political aggressiveness Carnegie should have understood and even applauded.

On the other hand, for one who had worked within the Liberal party in Britain for Irish Home Rule and had loudly trumpeted the glories of American democracy and the wisdom of its anti-militaristic policies, the very word imperialism should have been anathema. And so it was for Carnegie when he considered the British governor in India or the French soldier in Indochina or the American missionary in China. Closer home, this expansive drive was for Carnegie no longer imperialism, with its connotative image of Roman emperors wearing the purple; rather, it was the extension of American democracy in the spirit of those great patriots Jefferson, Polk, and Lincoln. Like most Americans, Carnegie had never thought of the white man's drive to the Pacific, riding roughshod over the original inhabitants of this vast territory, as possibly being imperialism. The American people were simply fulfilling their destiny, made manifest by nature itself, by the rough but noble frontiersman and by the singing lyrics of Whitman.

Nor would that destiny be complete until the American Republic incorporated within itself all land north of the Rio Grande. To Carnegie, as to millions of his fellow citizens, the Dominion of Canada was a sorry anachronism of the monarchical past. The fact that Queen Victoria still held scepter over a larger area on the North American continent than that occupied by the American Republic infuriated and baffled him. Surely the Canadians were being held against their will or were duped by British officialdom and propaganda into continuing to hold to an ancient and wrong sense of loyalty. If the former was the case, then Britain must be made belatedly to accept the fact that the Western Hemisphere was a new world having no place within it for European colonies and monarchical loyalty.

If Canada still remained outside the American Union due to some perverse sense of loyalty upon the part of the Canadian people themselves, then the people must be educated as to where their true interests lay. Carnegie's unequivocal feelings on the subject were expressed to Secretary of State Blaine: "America is going to control anything and everything on this continent. That's settled. The more this is argued against the stronger the determination of the American people will be. No joint arrangements, no entangling alliances with monarchical, war-like Europe. America will take this Continent in hand alone. . . ." [1]

Holding such views, Carnegie was an early and enthusiastic subscriber to the Continental Union movement, founded in the 1880's by Goldwin Smith, a distinguished British professor of literature and history and an amateur politician, then living in Toronto. Carnegie wrote to Gladstone on this subject in the spring of 1891: [2]

> We may be on the eve of grave events upon this side. Nothing can long keep the English-speaking race under different governments upon this continent. Sir John Macdonald's victory is really a defeat, the centre provinces having voted against him and he is in power today by the votes of the remote and unimportant districts.
>
> I have just returned from Washington where I saw the President and Mr. Blaine. There is no use in any Canadian delegation going to Washington in the hope of effecting reciprocity. If Canada wants the advantage of the American market, it must become American.[x]
>
> Always, Very truly yours.
>
> [x]*Republican*

In September 1891, Carnegie published in the *Nineteenth Century* magazine a lengthy essay entitled "Imperial Federation," in which he attacked two organizations in Britain, the Imperial Federation League, headed by Lord Rosebery, and the United Empire Trade League, whose idea of an imperial preference tariff was to be vigorously supported by Joseph Chamberlain. Carnegie's major criticism of the Imperial Federation League was not against its basic idea of stronger political and cultural ties among the peoples of British ancestry, but that it proposed "to combine only the minority of the English-speaking race in a solid phalanx, leaving out the majority."

He directed his more pointed shafts of criticism against the United Empire Trade League, for in this proposal to end Britain's traditional free trade policy Carnegie saw a distinct threat to American trade and industry. He pointed out that Britain's trade with the United States was greater than with all of her colonies combined, and Germany took more British products than did Canada. He threatened retaliatory discrimination on the part of the United States, which might include an outright prohibition of all trade with Britain, should the United Empire Trade League's ideas be adopted by Parliament. "Close the ports of this island for a year, and her people would suffer for food," was Carnegie's ominous warning. "Britain's house is a whole Crystal Palace—she of all nations should be the last to begin stone-throwing." [3]

Having thus brushed aside the British federationists, he then proposed a "race alliance" of his own which went considerably beyond the dreams of Rosebery, Chamberlain, and the other new imperialists of Britain and which, of course, gave the central role not to the "motherland" but to the "majority portion of the English-speaking race," namely, the Republic of the United States. "Impossible Imperial Federation and Empire Trade League should give place to Race Alliance, and so embrace all in one common bond, the only test being

> If Shakespeare's tongue be spoken there,
> And songs of Burns are in the air." [4]

We had taken the first steps in such an alliance, Carnegie maintained, by the arbitration of differences, as in the case of the *Alabama* claims. The resulting situation was that "Henceforth war between members of our race may be said to be already banished, for English-speaking men will never again be called upon to destroy one another. . . . Is it too much to hope that . . . another step forward will be taken, and that, having jointly banished war between themselves, a general council should be created by the English-speaking nations to which may first be referred only questions of dispute between them? This would only be making a permanent body to settle differences, instead of selecting arbiters as required—not at all a serious advance, and yet it should be the germ from which great fruits would grow." From this beginning would come an alliance of the English-speaking nations that would be a real "Kriegsverein with power so overwhelming that its exercise would never be necessary." The result would be that ancient dream of mankind, world peace, achieved by a true *pax Anglicae*.[5]

Because it hinted strongly at the union of Canada and the United States when it stated that "the unions of England and Scotland should be held up to [them]," Carnegie's article was hailed by Goldwin Smith and the other Continental Unionists. With funds provided by Carnegie, the article was distributed widely throughout Canada and the United States. To a supporter in Hamilton, Ontario, who had written him after receiving a copy of his pamphlet, Carnegie replied, "I am glad to see the subject of the union of the race upon this continent is attracting attention. We have only to consider the benefits flowing from the union of Scotland and England to realize what a similar union of Canada and the United States would bring to both. It seems to me little less than criminal to remain apart." [6]

There were also encouraging words from more important sources. Herbert Spencer wrote Carnegie upon receiving his pamphlet that the ideas in it were sound, and "I should be glad if your essay could be more widely distributed." [7] Carnegie, however, had more ambitious plans for the "race" than a simple Continental Union between Canada and the United States. He wrote an article for the *North American Review*, which he planned to use as the final chapter in a new edition of his *Triumphant Democracy*. "My last chapter T/D 'A Look Ahead' restores the Union between the Old and New Lands—makes Britian [sic] permanently prosperous, access to this enormous market *free of all* duty," he announced proudly to Morley. "Have read it to Goldwin Smith & some other Continental Unionists, & they are startled, naturally. Join the new idea, Federal alliance. Canada, United Kingdom & the United States—am fascinated with this subject—Ireland is ready. Scotland gets national Parliament, Wales ditto. All states in the Reunion." [8]

If Goldwin Smith and the Continental Unionists within the United States and Canada were startled by Carnegie's proposals, his British Liberal friends were struck speechless. Morley did not even reply but maintained a discreet, and one may assume, shocked silence, as did Gladstone, Rosebery, and the other party leaders. The Tory press, however, had a field day, claiming that Carnegie's earlier political activities on behalf of republicanism in Britain had had all along as their ulterior motive the aggrandizement of the American empire. Such a conclusion seemed warranted, for what Carnegie proposed was a simple extension of the American union which would bring England, Scotland, Ireland, and Wales in as new states, each with its own state legislature, and each sending representatives and senators to the national Congress in Washington.

There were, Carnegie admitted, certain difficulties standing in the way of an immediate realization of his proposal, such "impediments to reunion," as he phrased it, as Britain's colonial possessions, the Indian empire, Britain's role in European affairs, the monarchical form of government, and the Established Church. To Carnegie these were not insurmountable difficulties because they all could easily be removed by Britain with simple legislative enactment if Parliament were only willing to do so. The colonies could be turned loose, and India could become a great independent power. Nor would Britain, as part of the American union, "need to worry about Europe. Everything she now seeks would be hers—namely, protection of her soil and command of the seas." As for her monarchical form of government, Carnegie admitted that this was a real problem, "but not eternal . . . From what wise friends who know the Prince [of Wales] tell me, I am persuaded he is the last man in the world to stand in the way of healing a separation which he so constantly deplores; and unless the estimate formed by all the patriotism, virtues, and character of Her Majesty herself be strangely awry, she would give up much beyond her crown to be the peacemaker who brought reunion to her race. . . . She is the only one who could by a sublime act reunite the separated branches of her race. Never in the history of the world has it been in the power of any human being to perform so great an act. . . . There would be but two names set apart forever in the annals of the English-speaking race . . . Victoria and Washington—patron saints of our race. . . . For such a mission and such a destiny even Queen Victoria on bended knee might pray."

How simple it all seemed to Carnegie to achieve this "reunion of race":

It would be so easy a task that its very simplicity amazes and renders us incredulous, but most of the important successes and valuable discoveries have been remarkable for this very feature. . . . This may all seem Utopian but we have had many prophetic voices . . . more than fulfilled, which were at the time of their inspired utterance much wilder than anything herein suggested. It may be all a dream, and I but a dreamer of dreams. So be it. . . . And if it be a dream, it is a dream nobler than most realities. . . . I believe it will be [realized], for all progress is upon its side. . . . The tendency of the age is towards consolidation. . . . Readers will kindly note that this is A Look Ahead—how far ahead I shall not attempt to guess— nevertheless, it is ahead, and sometime, somehow, it is to come to pass.[9]

Anthropologists and biologists might well dispute Carnegie's rather casual use of the term "race" as applied to a linguistic grouping of peoples, but Carnegie was clearly in tune with his times when he referred to an English-speaking race and advocated a race alliance. Race, as identified with language, had become a powerful buttress to national unification and territorial expansion. In these last decades of a century that had seen the rapid rise of ambitious new nation states—Germany, Italy, the United States, Japan—it had been the word as much as the sword that had brought about a sense of national identification.

These new national states might be culturally and linguistically monolithic as Japan, or highly pluralistic as the United States, but it made little difference to the dominant nationalist group. The Blaines, Carnegies, Lodges, and Mahans of the United States, when presenting their country to the outside world, assumed a racial homogeneity with as much confidence as any shogun or admiral of Japan. An uninformed reader of a distant land would never guess from Carnegie's articles urging an Anglo-Saxon race alliance that there existed within the continental limits of the United States any other peoples or culture than that of white Anglo-Saxon Protestantism.

Carnegie differed from most of his contemporary race-alliance advocates only in rejecting the racial supremicist arguments of Comte de Gobineau or Houston Stewart Chamberlain. Although he assumed the superiority of the Anglo-Saxon peoples just as he

assumed their commonality of interest, he did not favor the imposition of this culture upon other peoples living outside the Atlantic community of the British Isles and the North American continent. The lessons in cultural relativism which he had learned in
his trip around the world in 1878–79 had not been forgotten and
remained as an important and somewhat unusual qualification to
his ideas about race alliance.

Carnegie sincerely believed that an Anglo-Saxon race alliance
was the surest way to help bring about world peace, not world
conquest. With Britain, the United States, Canada, Australia, and
New Zealand united under one republican form of government,
there would be no need for military conquest. As the re-united
states of the Anglo-Saxon race, they would establish a global order
of the kind that the Latins had once imposed upon the Mediterranean world. When it was suggested to him that there were a
hundred points of conflict between Britain and the United States
that militated against such an alliance, Carnegie's answer was the
worn, old aphorism that "Blood is thicker than water."

But not even Carnegie, it turned out, could live with his own
aphorisms. When the first real test of his Anglo-Saxon "blood alliance" came with the Venezuelan boundary crisis of 1895, just four
years after his widely publicized "Look Ahead," Carnegie, by his
own words and actions, proved just how right the doubters had
been. Water, particularly if it happened to consist of the Atlantic
Ocean, separating the New World from the Old, was considerably
thicker than blood—thick enough, indeed, to serve as a fortress
wall to shut out completely one's blood brothers.

The largely uninhabitable and inhospitable jungle land that
lay south of the Orinoco River and north of the Guiana highlands
of South America might seem a curiously insignificant area of the
globe to be the focal point for a confrontation between the two
great English-speaking nations that could well lead to war. Nations, however, have never been very particular about geographic
sites when national pride is at stake, as witnessed by the Anglo-
French confrontation in the Sudan in this same decade, or the
Franco-German crisis over the vast swampland of equatorial Africa. The disputed territory lying between Venezuela and British
Guiana had, moreover, in spite of the nature of the terrain, more
tangible value to the two main parties to the dispute than simply

the question of national honor. Gold, discovered in the area in the 1880's, held keen interest for several British mining companies with the equipment and capital necessary to go into the jungle to exploit these discoveries. Venezuela's chief concern was to protect the lower basin of the Orinoco River, and in particular to possess Point Barima, which commanded the broad delta region at the mouth of the river.

What brought the United States into this far-distant dispute was primarily the magic name "Monroe." President Cleveland, to be sure, was one of the least jingoistic of American Presidents, a man who consistently discouraged imperialistic ventures into the Sandwich Islands and the far reaches of the Pacific Ocean beyond those islands. At the same time, he was no Anglophile, and like most Americans, he regarded the Monroe Doctrine as being in reality an integral part of the Constitution, which he had sworn to uphold and defend. During his first term of office, when the Venezuelan boundary dispute had first flared up into crisis proportions, he had urged arbitration upon the British government and had offered his services as honest broker. Britain, with good reasons, could not see any American President playing the role of a Bismarck in a situation that involved an European colonial possession in the Western Hemisphere. London politely but firmly refused the American invitation to arbitration.

So the matter rested until late in Cleveland's second term, when the issue was once again raised by a former minister to Venezuela, William L. Scruggs, who had served under Benjamin Harrison. This ex-diplomat was still involved in Latin American affairs, but now as the employee of the Venezuelan dictator to lobby in Washington and New York on behalf of Venezuela's territorial claims. Scruggs gave full service for whatever lobbying fees he may have received. His most effective effort in Venezuela's behalf was a pamphlet written in 1894 entitled "British Aggression in Venezuela, or the Monroe Doctrine on Trial." This clever piece of propaganda went through four editions and was widely read and discussed by newspaper editors throughout the country.

Congressmen, always hypersensitive to any testing of Monroe's sacred tenets, were easy targets for Scruggs's propaganda shots. Early in 1895, both Houses of Congress in a joint resolution urged immediate arbitration. This was all very well as far as it went, but for the young Anglophobe senator from Massachusetts, Henry Cabot Lodge, it did not go far enough. The "or else" threat was implied in the resolution, but Lodge was determined to make it explicit. In the June 1895 issue of the *North American Review,* he pronounced his own ultimatum: "If Great Britain is to be permitted . . . to take the territory of Venezuela, there is nothing to prevent her taking the whole of Venezuela or any other South American state. . . . The supremacy of the Monroe Doctrine should be established and at once—peaceably if we can, forcibly if we must." [10] It was, of course, precisely this attitude of pre-judging the case in Venezuela's favor, so strongly expressed by Lodge, that made Britain reluctant to agree to arbitration.

Carnegie, watching the intensification of the crisis with mounting concern, was torn between his desire for world peace and his insistence upon American hemispheric power. At this troubled moment, when Lodge was thundering out his belligerent "or else," Secretary of State Olney was proclaiming for the United States continental sovereignty, and even the usually phlegmatic Cleveland was bristling in a message to Congress that the United States "must resist by every means in its power" any British expansion upon territory that "we have determined of right belongs to Venezuela." [11] A more cautious and prudent man than Carnegie might well have elected to stand clear of this imbroglio. Certainly these were difficult times for a pacifistic jingoist. But Carnegie apparently was as eager as Lodge to propound his views. Ever since his appointment by Secretary of State Blaine as a delegate to the first Pan-American Congress in 1889 (the only governmental office he was ever to hold), he had regarded himself as being something akin to a minister without portfolio for Latin American affairs. He now felt it incumbent upon himself to speak to an eagerly expectant world. Making use of the same medium of communication as Lodge, Carnegie, in the *North American Review* for February 1896, analyzed the situation for the enlightenment of the British and American governments.

Starting out moderately enough, he expressed regret that the President had couched his message in terms of a hardly veiled threat of force. "Insisting with an adversary upon the duty of accepting peaceful arbitration is one thing, insisting upon peaceful arbitration, *or ——*, quite another." He was even more sharply critical of Secretary Olney's manifesto:

Lord Salisbury had received great provocation in Secretary Olney's dispatch. It is an able paper upon the whole, but how a man capable of writing such a paper should permit himself to depart so far from fact as to say that the United States is sovereign upon the American continent and its fiat law, passes comprehension. This is not the case, as every schoolboy knows, and the effect of such a claim upon the sister Republics of the South must be most injurious. Had Mr. Blaine, when presiding over the Pan American Conference, even intimated that the United States claimed anything beyond equality with these republics, the Conference would have dispersed at once. . . . Fortunately for us the pride of the Spanish race in South America is not to be trifled with. It was not for nothing that President Harrison, on receiving these delegates when their labors were ended, said to them: "We have had in your honor a military review, not to show you that we have an army, but to show you we have none." . . . It may take several wise Secretaries of State succeeding Secretary Olney fully to erase the suspicions which he has so recklessly created. One can understand how Great Britain, who still owns so much of the American continent, must have felt when the alleged sovereignty of the United States over its possessions was thus flaunted in its face. The truth is that neither Lord Salisbury nor Secretary Olney has conducted this correspondence in a manner creditable to his reputation as a diplomat; for their communications have needlessly irritated the nations to which they were addressed.[12]

This was Carnegie the pacificist speaking. No jingoism here. But as he warmed to his subject, the jingoist began to take over —in the name of peaceful arbitration, of course. He pointed hopefully to signs of British public opinion swinging to the side of arbitration, and he quoted Gladstone, Sir Edward Clarke, the former Solicitor General, and even the Prince of Wales in support of amicable negotiations. But there remained the recalcitrance of the Salisbury government to accept the American offer of arbitration, and the more Carnegie pondered this, the angrier he became. The result was that his article was concluded with a stern warning that differed very little in tone or diction from the bellicosity of Olney or Lodge:

There comes in the life of every manly man a time when he has to assert his own manhood. . . . The republic has become of age and entered into the possession of his heritage. It has so much room that its desire does not go in the direction of acquiring non-coterminous territory to which alternative his parent land is reduced. It is as the elder brother of the sixteen [sic] republics upon this continent that it intends to act. . . . It is time that the people of Great Britain understood that if war be still possible between the two countries, it is not the fault of the republic but of their own country, not of President Cleveland and Secretary of State Olney, but of Prime Minister Salisbury and the leader of the House of Commons, Mr. Balfour, who do not accept the offered treaty which would banish war forever between the two nations of our race. . . . [T]he American is sensitive in regard to affairs of this continent. . . . He sees clearly that, the principle of arbitration destroyed, the introduction of the European mode of settlement, war, follows. Hence, he feels it to be his stern duty to preserve the Union. He sees that it would be better to rally this continent to its defence, and secure perpetual peace thereafter, by fighting against the first attempt, should any be made, to render this continent now dedicated to Arbitration, the prey to war as other continents are.

John Bright, Quaker as he was, nevertheless pronounced the war for the preservation of our Union a duty. Were he alive today, he would tell his countrymen that if they persisted in rejecting the American policy of arbitration upon questions affecting the American Continent and lighted the torch of war upon it, all the crimes recorded in human history would pale before this.[13]

So, as it turned out, Carnegie could scream for "peace, by God, even if we have to fight for it" as loudly as any man. Not even Lodge had been quite so extravagant as to call Britain's stubbornness a crime to surpass all crimes in recorded history.

In his private letters to friends in Britain, Carnegie was equally strident in his warning that a refusal upon Britain's part to arbitrate clearly meant war with the United States. "Any President," he wrote the Duke of Devonshire, "can rouse the people and carry all classes with him. . . . Those of us who have done our best to allay the present excitement are not deluded upon this point." [14] And to Morley, he was even more blunt: "I have been wondering why no word was flashed across the Atlantic from you in support of the Granville-Gladstone Agreement to arbitrate with Venezuela in 1885, which Salisbury has reversed. . . . If Mr. Gladstone were only your age, we should have the Liberal Party back to power on the issue, Arbitration. . . . Here is a moral question worth all your other questions put together, petty Home Rule included. If you ever mean to be Leader of the Liberal Party, here is your chance. You will never probably have so grand an issue. . . . There is but one voice now from the whole of the United States, East, West, North and South—Arbitration, and to this it must come. . . . Unless the Venezuela question be settled, it is even possible that we may have Cleveland for a third term. . . . Cleveland has only to insist upon arbitration to carry everything before him, as the country is unanimous upon that point, and determined. Do read my article." [15]

Carnegie's article probably did more harm than good in promoting a peaceful settlement. For like Olney's pontificating, Carnegie's moralizing inflamed the jingoistic mood of British nationalists. William Black, Carnegie's one-time coaching companion, wrote in some heat:

I see you are still calling out for arbitration. Is there no sense of humour left on your side of the water? Of course everyone understands why the United States should clamour for arbitration on every possible point: it is because they alone among the nations of the world know how to manipulate it to their own advantage. When the award is given in their favour, as in the Alabama case, they accept and walk off with a Surplus buttoned up in their breeches' pocket ("shameful" was the epithet I heard Herbert Spencer apply to that transaction.) Then when the award is against them as in the Behring Sea instance, all they have to do is to declare by a vote of Congress that they won't pay. And this is the standard of national honour to which Triumphant Democracy has attained.[16]

Fortunately, however, as so often had happened in the long history of Anglo-American relations, Britain had more pressing concerns in other parts of the world. Alarmed by Germany's naval building program and the Kaiser's ambitions to find his place under a tropical African sun, even the touchy Salisbury finally yielded pride to persuasion. In mid-August of 1896, Morley wrote joyfully to Carnegie, "You would see, my good friend, from Balfour's answer to Harcourt, that all is right about Venezuela. The whole claim is to be submitted to arbitration. Now we must see what can be done to provide the larger issue of a permanent tribunal." [17] Carnegie replied with considerable satisfaction, "I have not ceased to rejoice at intervals over Balfour's answer to Harcourt. Sir Richard Webster is with us [at Cluny Castle], and we have had a good deal of talk over ARBITRATION. If I were you, or in public life, I should make that my question. It will be a clear distinct step forward in the history of man when the English-speaking race abolishes war among its members, and this is substantially what a Treaty of Arbitration will do." [18]

Carnegie, in fact, never before had felt so close to his native land and to its venerable institutions as he did in the months immediately following the settlement through arbitration of the Venezuelan boundary dispute. In an article with the provocative title, "Does America Hate England?" published in *Contemporary Review* in the autumn of 1897, Carnegie insisted there was frequent irritation, but "not true hatred." To be sure, there was still the old sore, called Canada, and those new smarting irritants called imperial preferential tariffs, but deeper than these surface abrasions were "the genuine respect, admiration and affection for the old home. The pride of race is always there at the bottom." [19]

On 22 June 1897, Britain celebrated the Diamond Jubilee of Victoria's reign. Carnegie was one of the hundreds of thousands who witnessed the gaudily triumphant and exultant procession that wound through the streets of London to Buckingham Palace to pay tribute to the little old woman who for sixty years had held the imperial scepter over the greatest empire the world had ever known. Even Carnegie, that professional arch-foe of monarchy, the son and grandson of Radical Republican Chartists, was affected by the spectacle, and was moved to write in the *North American Review:*

> The principal figure of the Jubilee, Queen Victoria herself, and the position she has gained and will hold to the end of her days, is worthy of study. It is not possible for any American, however well informed of British affairs, to quite understand the feelings with which this human being is now regarded. If he

can imagine Old Glory and *Old Ironsides,* Washington and Lincoln, Bunker Hill and "My Country, 'Tis of Thee," rolled into one force, and personified in a woman, he may form some conception of the feelings of the average Briton for "the Queen," for she in her own person symbolizes today the might and majesty of the land, and its long, varied, and glorious history from the beginning. "The Queen" means everything that touches and thrills the patriotic chord. That both as a woman and a sovereign, she has deserved the unique tribute paid her goes without saying; the wildest radical, or even republican, will concur in this. Sixty years of unremitting work—she still signs every state paper herself, including lieutenants' commissions in the militia—prudence, patience and rare judgment have made of this good, able, energetic, managing, and very wise woman a saint, whom her subjects are as little capable and as little disposed to estimate critically as the American schoolboy can imagine or is disposed to imagine, Washington as possessed of human frailties. Washington, Tell, Wallace, Bruce, Lincoln, Queen Victoria or Margaret are the stuff of which heroes or saints are made, and well it is for the race that the capacity for hero worship and for saint worship remains with both Briton and American wholly unimpaired.

When a nation ceases to create ideals its glorious days are past. Fortunately for the world, both the republic and the monarchy have the future before them.[20]

A remarkable tribute from a man who as a boy had had the ambition to kill a king. But then, in June 1897, Carnegie was for once at peace with both of his two worlds. Bryan had been defeated, and conservative Republicanism, as embodied in William McKinley, was safely entrenched in the White House at home. Britain had yielded to the force of American public opinion, and had accepted arbitration of the Venezuelan dispute. The sacred tenets of Monroe's Doctrine had been upheld without recourse to war.

To be sure, in Britain, his other world, Irish Home Rule was dead, Gladstone was dying, the Liberals were divided and defeated, and the triumphant Conservatives under the detestable Lord Salisbury now controlled Parliament and the Empire. Carnegie, in writing his tribute to Victoria, must have realized that he and the Radicals had failed in their efforts to remake Britain in America's republican image; but in spite of Disraeli and Salisbury and even Victoria herself, it was not the same empire to whose throne she had ascended in 1837. Canada was now virtually independent, Australia and New Zealand would soon follow, and "it is clear to all that the colonies are, and must hereafter be, recognized as the equals of the parent." [21] Who, then, on this glorious June day would deny the aged "widow of Windsor" her one last hurrah?

Carnegie had a personal reason for feeling as satisfied and content as he did, for in the spring of this same year, at the age of sixty-one, he had become a father. After ten years of marriage, on 30 March 1897, Louise, at the age of forty, had given birth to a daughter, who was named Margaret after Carnegie's mother. Carnegie exulted in his new status.

He had been delighted to hear that the tenants of Cluny on receiving the news had celebrated the event in true Gaelic manner by lighting nine bonfires on the hills surrounding the castle.[22] But however loyal the tenants of Cluny might be to the Carnegies, unfortunately the Carnegies were also tenants, and Cluny did not belong to them. Although Carnegie had tried several times to buy Cluny Castle, the chief of the Macpherson clan would not sell. Now with the birth of Margaret, Louise was determined that they should have their own home in Scotland. Carnegie tells in his autobiography of Louise's calling him to her bedside in their New York home soon after Margaret's birth and telling him, "Her name is Margaret after your mother. Now one request I have to make.

"What is it, Lou?"

"We must get a summer home since this little one has been given us. We cannot rent one and be obliged to go in and out at a certain date. It should be our home. . . . I make only one condition. It must be in the Highlands of Scotland." [23]

To this Carnegie had readily agreed, and so now in this summer of the Queen's Jubilee, the Carnegies were spending their last summer at Cluny, while Carnegie began his search for their own castle in Scotland. He told his friends and the many realtors who were only too eager to serve that on any estate he might purchase he wanted three things: a view of the sea, a trout stream and a waterfall. It was Hew Morrison, the librarian of the Carnegie Public Library in Edinburgh, who found for Carnegie an ancient manorial estate, that of the Roman Catholic Bishops of Caithness, which had in the sixteenth century belonged to John Gray. It was called Skibo. It lay in Sutherland County, in the far northeast corner of Scotland on the Firth of Dornoch. Two rivers, the Shinn and the Evelix, lying twenty miles apart, formed the boundaries of this estate. Although Skibo is in the same latitude as Juneau, Alaska, it is protected by the long narrow firth and the surrounding hills of Sutherland from the cruel east winds off the North Sea. The air is soft and mild throughout most of the year, rhododendrons have been known to bloom in January, and, in a country where there is little competition for such honors, Skibo has more hours of sunshine a year than any other part of Scotland.

The ancient castle of Skibo lay in ruins when Carnegie first drove up the long winding road from the little village of Bonar Bridge. There was no waterfall on the estate, but the sea was there, gleaming silver in the distance, the sun was shining, and the thousands of acres of empty moor were a hazy green with only a slight lavender suggestion of the deep purple heather that would later bloom. Carnegie fell in love with the place at first sight. Here at last was his Scottish Highland home. The estate was purchased from the current owner, George Dempster, for £85,000, and Carnegie immediately began making plans for the building of a new baronial castle—and a waterfall.[24]

As, first, a new father and now as Laird of Skibo, Carnegie might well view the world in the summer of 1897 with equanimity. Never had his favorite motto, "All is well, since all grows better," seemed more apropos than at this moment.

But the bright peaceful sunshine of this Jubilee summer would not last long. If anyone had told Carnegie then that within less than two years he would be weeping over the lost ideals of his beloved Republic, would have broken with the McKinley administration, and would be seriously considering open support for that wild demagogue, William Jennings Bryan, Carnegie would have dismissed him as being mad. Carnegie had truly believed in November 1896 that with the election of McKinley, Triumphant Democracy had achieved its greatest triumph. Order had been preserved; democracy, as Carnegie defined it, had been saved. What Carnegie failed to understand was that order must exact its own price. The two worlds, which he had to his own satisfaction kept so distinct and separate, were now beginning to merge. The conservative forces, so vigorously supported by Carnegie, that had put McKinley instead of Bryan in the White House, were not all that different from the conservative forces, so vigorously opposed by Carnegie, that had given the Parliamentary majority to Lord Salisbury. Carnegie had not sold the American brand of republicanism to Britain. On the contrary, it would now be the British brand of imperialism that would be sold to America. Carnegie had once predicted that his "two worlds of motherland and wifeland" would inevitably move closer and closer together until eventually they would be one world again.[25] Now under McKinley and Salisbury, the two great English-speaking nations were moving in concert, but hardly in the direction that Carnegie had hoped. Rudyard Kipling, not Bobby Burns, was to be the poet laureate of this new Anglo-Saxon world.

When America first set out on its great imperialistic venture in the spring of 1898, however, Carnegie did not immediately raise his voice in opposition. Unlike Henry Clay Frick, who was writing anxious letters to senators and congressmen, urging them to support McKinley's attempts to avoid war with Spain,[26] Carnegie, who was in Cannes at the time, seemed remarkably unconcerned about the prospects of war. When war did come late in April, Frick and other conservative businessmen, who feared the effects of war on business conditions, blamed McKinley for yielding to the popular clamor for war. "A stronger man," Frick wrote Carnegie, "would have held the Jingoes in check, and avoided war, at least until there was a good cause for one." [27] Carnegie, however, already felt there was a good cause for this one. He believed implicitly in McKinley's assurances that it was a war only to give Cuba its independence and to drive one more European nation completely out of the Western Hemisphere. Like his good friend, John Hay, Carnegie regarded this as "a splendid little war," one that would cost America little in either men or material resources. He also saw the war as bringing America and Britain closer together. The continental powers, he wrote McKinley immediately after the declaration of war, were all hostile to the

United States, but there was a "genuine attachment of Britian [sic] to the American people and its Government. . . . Mr. President I have ventured to say that in supreme crises the racial element will be found most potent, and it is that that will control action. Without exception, the British are our friends." Never adverse to a little name-dropping, he added, "I had a talk with the Prince of Wales here referring to the changed feelings between the two nations & their evident drawing together as members of the great 'English speaking race'—he said very decidedly *Yes I like that. I like that.* It is no secret that from the Queen down they are with us—Germany, Russia & France, they regard with suspicion and antipathy—evident that a combination against Britian is only too probable in the opinion of England. With Britian standing by us you have nothing to fear from European action." [28]

Caught up in the martial spirit of the moment, Carnegie laid aside his pacifist sentiments for the duration and soon was sending not just diplomatic advice to the President but also military advice to General Nelson Miles, commander of the American forces in Cuba. In July, he cabled Miles, "Believe you wise bold enough withdraw Santiago. Proceed full force Porto Rico. Object Santiago expedition attained. Town worthless. Capture Porto Rico would tell heavily Spain and Europe." [29] Miles, in his autobiography, would later acknowledge that he had regarded this advice highly and had laid it before the President. The President soon afterward authorized the Puerto Rican campaign.[30]

To old friends in the international peace movement, who had expected Carnegie to oppose the war, his new position was difficult to understand. But Carnegie had an answer for them. Writing to Dr. Adolf Gurlt of Bonn, he explained why he could not speak out against this war: "No power on earth can stop the American people doing what has now become their duty—Cuba must be freed from Spanish oppression. When Spain realizes this there will be peace, but not till then. Knowing this as I do I remain silent. When the proper time comes, when I can urge liberal treatment of Spain and the surrender of the Philippines, believe me, you shall again find me, as you say you did before, pleading the right in the North American Review and elsewhere. The true friend of Spain is he who tells her that there is no possibility for her again exercising dominion over Cuba." [31] Moreover, Frick's fears were groundless. As Carnegie wrote Cousin Dod, "Business is great. War bound to end—probably before this reaches you negotiations will be begun. Spain is done." [32]

How good such splendid little wars, fought out of a sense of duty and for the right, were for everyone concerned. Even for Spain, who was learning her lesson very fast. And so the United States took Cuba, took Puerto Rico, and then rather surprisingly, half way around the world, took the Philippine Islands. Spain in July asked for terms. Then belatedly, Carnegie realized what those terms might be, what, in short, might be the real cost of this war. Quite suddenly, it was no longer such a little war, and it was not splendid at all. For the unleashed dogs of war were now baying after larger imperial game, and Carnegie's promise to Dr. Gurlt that he would again speak had now taken on a greater urgency than he could have imagined when he wrote those complacently reassuring lines.

McKinley, the somewhat reluctant and bewildered war President, had had to get out an atlas to find out just where the Philippine Islands were when he was informed by the Navy Department that Commodore Dewey had seized these far outposts of the once glorious Spanish Empire. At first, it appeared that McKinley, by nature no more of a jingoist than Cleveland had been, would resist the pressure of the war hawks and the Big America imperialists and would return to Spain or set free this exotic tropical domain that had been so easily and so surprisingly won. But just as he had yielded in April to the strident clamor for war, so now he gave in to the equally raucous cry for conquest. It was, after all, hard to stand up against the scholarly Admiral Mahan, the bumptious Colonel Roosevelt, the political Senator Beveridge, and apparently even God Himself. In a speech to the General Missionary Committee of the Methodist Episcopal Church, McKinley told how he arrived at his momentous decision to keep the Philippines as an American colony:

> I walked the floor of the White House night after night until midnight, and I am not ashamed to tell you, gentlemen, that I went down on my knees and prayed Almighty God for light and guidance more than one night. And one night it came to me

692

this way—I don't know how it was, but it came . . . that there was nothing left for us to do but to take them all, and to educate the Filipinos, and uplift them and civilize and Christianize them and by God's grace do the very best we could by them, as our fellow-men for whom Christ also died. And then I went to bed, and went to sleep, and slept soundly, and the next morning I sent for the chief engineer of the War Department (our map-maker) and I told him to put the Philippines on the map of the United States, and there they are, and there they will stay while I am President.[33]

On one point, however, McKinley was adamant and showed that his backbone was not entirely made of the chocolate éclair substance which Theodore Roosevelt claimed it was. Against all pressure of historic covetousness and immediate avarice to keep Cuba as our own now that we had defeated Spain, McKinley stoutly resisted. The war had been fought for *Cuba libra,* and free she should be, if only nominally, in order to redeem that pledge. For this Carnegie was grateful. He wrote a letter to the anti-imperialistic New York *World,* praising McKinley for having kept the faith, in this respect at least. "The war was not undertaken for territorial aggrandizement. . . . The President is the real leader, the first to speak again the magic words 'Free and Independent,' temporarily lost in the struggle. . . . All honor to him for this." [34] To his old friend, John Hay, McKinley's newly appointed Secretary of State, Carnegie wrote that the President's "grand position as to Cuba makes me a happy man. I see daylight out of our danger cloud and have nothing but praise for the President since he took his rightful place, *that of Leadership.*" [35] These were to be about the last kind words Carnegie was to have for the McKinley administration for some time. The "danger cloud" soon blotted out all the daylight as far as Carnegie was concerned.

That Carnegie had had some premonition that war with Spain might lead to imperialist ventures is evident by the fact that at the same time he was supporting any means necessary to free Cuba from Spanish rule, he was also making generous contributions to the newly formed New England Anti-Imperialist League, which the Boston manufacturer, Edward Atkinson, had founded in the early spring of 1898.[36] Now with the opening of negotia-

tions with Spain in Paris, when it had become all too apparent
how real those premonitory fears were, Carnegie threw himself
into the battle to preserve what he regarded as the basic principles of American republicanism with a vigor he had never shown
for any political issue before, even including the fight against silver in 1896. In August, with the opening of the Paris conference,
Carnegie rushed into print in his favorite journal, the *North
American Review,* with an article entitled "Distant Possessions—
The Parting of the Ways." It was a bitter, unequivocal attack
upon American imperialism. "Are we to exchange Triumphant
Democracy for Triumphant Despotism?" he cried. "Is it possible
that the Republic is to be placed in the position of the suppressor
of the Philippine struggle for independence? Surely, that is impossible." He accepted annexation of the Hawaiian Islands because "it is ours by a vote of its people, which robs its acquisition
of many dangers. Let us hope that our far outlying possessions
may end with Hawaii." He pointed out there were two kinds of
possessions, one colonies, the other dependencies. "In the former,
we establish and reproduce our own race. The world benefits
from this. But with dependencies it is otherwise." Britain in
India he regarded as the classic example of the tragic folly of a
great nation's acquiring an hostile dependency. In contrast to
Britain, he pointed out that "today two great powers in the world
are compact, developing themselves in peace throughout cotermi-
nous territories. . . . These powers are Russia and the United
States. . . . As long as we remain free from distant possessions we
are impregnable against serious attack. . . . I am no 'Little'
American, afraid of growth, either in population or territory, provided always that the new territory be American and that it will
produce Americans, and not foreign races bound in time to be
false to the Republic in order to be true to themselves." [37]

This article, which he sent out broadcast, gave to Carnegie a
prominent position in the anti-imperialist movement. As always,
Carnegie was confident that reason and justice would carry the
day, that once the American people were informed on the basic
issues, they would force the administration to abandon its foolhardy venture. But Morley, to whom he sent a copy of his article,
did not place as much confidence in *vox populi.* "I like your arti-

cle. . . . it is extraordinarily well-written and sound." Morley said he showed it to W. T. Stead, who also liked it but said that Carnegie would never carry his people with him. Morley agreed. "Satan is in splendid form just now on two continents." [38]

Carnegie's initial opposition to the acquisition of the Philippines was prompted more out of concern for what it would do to the character of the American Republic than out of sympathy for the Filipino people's aspirations for independence. This lead him into making some highly unorthodox proposals, much to the dismay of some of his anti-imperialist friends. For example, late in August, he wrote a letter from Skibo to the editor of *The* (London) *Times,* suggesting that we give the Philippine Islands to Britain in exchange for all of the British possessions in the West Indies plus Bermuda.[39] There was no response from Whitehall to this suggestion.

Undaunted, he dashed off to Washington when he heard that by terms of the proposed treaty the United States was going to give Spain $20,000,000 for the Philippine Islands, and offered the President the same amount to purchase them from the United States in order to give them their independence—surely the only time in our history that a private citizen offered to buy an empire from a sovereign nation. When later asked if this report were true, Carnegie replied, "Quite true. I would gladly pay twenty millions today to restore our Republic to its first principles." [40]

Having failed in his efforts to swap empires with Britain or to buy up his own, Carnegie was forced to resort to less flamboyant but more practical methods of thwarting imperialism. There began a long and sustained attack on the administration by means of the public forum: letters to the editors, particularly in the highly friendly, anti-administration papers, the New York *World* and the New York *Evening Post;* articles in monthly periodicals; and speeches whenever and wherever the opportunity arose. There was also the almost constant flow of letters to senators, cabinet officers, and to the President himself.[41] As the moment approached for the treaty to be signed and to be sent to the Senate for ratification, Carnegie grew more and more vituperative against the President and everyone closely associated with him, including Carnegie's dear friend, John Hay. Carnegie was particularly infuriated by McKinley's tour of the Midwest, when the President tried to drum up support for the treaty by speaking out of both sides of his mouth at the same time. At about this time, Carnegie wrote to Hay:

> My friend, I have never had such an unpleasant task to perform in my life. I wish I could feel that it was unnecessary. If the President's message to Congress is direct and outspoken and he takes one side or the other, we can all respect him, although we may differ from him, but if his message is to be like his speeches in the west, and reveals Mr. "face both ways," he must expect to get such a castigation as a President of the United States never got before.
>
> When a jelly-fish wishes to conceal its whereabouts it does so by ebullitions of blubber—this is what people say the President did on his western tour. The Springfield Republican has a column showing his sentiments one morning after another—I had it put up to send you, but really I refrained. I am so sorry for the President—I do not think he is well, and yet I see that if one American soldier's blood is spilt shooting down insurgents, either in Cuba or the Phillipines, he is like another Mac, he shall sleep no more. . . .
>
> Why does he not speak out one way or the other, for Imperialism I believe we can kill it, if for adherence to the policy of the fathers, believe me the leaders and thinkers of his party will follow greatly relieved. . . . It is a great strain which the President is putting upon the loyalty of his friends and supporters. Many are bearing it—it has proved too great for me.[42]

Secretary Hay did not exactly appreciate the almost daily communiqués from Carnegie berating the administration. He wrote to Whitelaw Reid, the New York *Tribune* editor, who was a member of the Peace Commission: "Carnegie really seems to be off his head. He writes me frantic letters, signing them 'Your Bitterest Opponent.' He threatens the President not only with the vengeance of the voters, but with practical punishment at the hands of the mob. He says that henceforth the entire labor vote of America will be cast against us and that he will see that it is done. He says that the administration will fall into irretrievable ruin the moment it shoots down one insurgent Filippino [sic]. He does not seem to reflect that the government is in somewhat robust condition after shooting down several American citizens in his interest at Homestead." [43]

A cruel thrust—the reference to Homestead. But Reid appreciated it, for he would always believe that he had been deprived of election to the vice presidency because of Homestead. And he too was the recipient of letters in a similar vein from Carnegie. "It is a matter of congratulations," Carnegie wrote him, "that you seem to have about finished your work of civilizing the Fillipinos [sic]. It is thought that about 8000 of them have been completely civilized and sent to Heaven. I hope you like it." [44]

Hay was not the only person to draw a parallel between Homestead and the Philippines. In a muckraking book on labor conditions in the United States published at this time, Charles Spahr dwelt at length on Homestead. He was impressed with the library, the baths, and gymnasium that Carnegie had built for the workers at Homestead. McKinley and Carnegie were really very much alike, Spahr asserted, in being zealously attentive to their subjects' welfare, one for the Filipinos, the other for his workers. "But the fatal defect which Mr. Carnegie observes in the President's policy in the Philippines permeates his own policy at Homestead. The government at Homestead aims to be the government for the people, but its fundamental principle is that there shall be no government by the people." [45]

Carnegie, however, could not be deterred by his opponents who tore open old wounds or who considered him a traitor to the party, if not to his country. In a speech at the Lotos Club, he proudly asserted, "The country is fortunate that boasts a class of men which rises on occasion superior to party. . . . To be popular is easy; to be right when right is unpopular, is noble. . . . I repudiate with scorn the immoral doctrine, 'Our country, right or wrong.' " [46]

Carnegie sought to make his position both right and popular. If he had lost some old friends like Hay, Hanna, and McKinley by opposing the government's foreign policy, he had found strong support from other old allies, Grover Cleveland, E. L. Godkin, and, of course, on the other side of the ocean, John Morley. Carnegie continued to pour out letters and articles. If the New York *Tribune* and his favorite newspaper, the New York *Sun*, refused to print his Letters to the Editor, he found an eager market for them still in the *World,* the *Evening Post,* and *The New York Times.* In a two-part article entitled "Americanism versus Imperialism," which appeared in the January and March 1899 issues of the always faithful *North American Review,* he attempted to destroy every possible argument being used by his opponents to justify imperialism: the economic costs, rather than gains, of possessing distant colonies; the dangers of tying ourselves to British imperial foreign policy, thus making ourselves more, not less, vulnerable militarily; and the historical precedents of Washington, Jefferson, and especially Lincoln. He saved his sharpest attack for the "White Man's burden" argument, that it was our mission under Divine sanction to civilize the Filipinos. There will be no civilizing influence from us, he maintained, because "the only Americans that will come in contact with the Filipinos will be soldiers, not mothers or children. And the soldiers require missionaries themselves more than the natives. . . . Our 'duty' to bear the 'White Man's Burden' is to-day's refrain, but Lincoln tells us: 'When the white man governs himself, that is self-government; but when he governs himself and also governs another man, that is more than self-government, that is despotism.' " Carnegie ended the article with an emotionally charged peroration: "Oh, the pity of it! the pity of it! that Filipino mothers with American mothers equally mourn their lost sons—one fallen, defender of his country; the other, the invader. Yet the invader was ordered by those who see it their 'duty' to invade the land of the Filipinos for their civilization. Duty, stern Goddess, what strange things men sometimes mistakenly do in thy name!" [47]

There were encouraging reports from allies throughout the country which Carnegie seized upon and magnified to convince others as well as himself that the battle was being won: labor, the farmers, businessmen were all reported as organizing in opposition to the administration.[48] With great bravado, Carnegie wrote in the New York *World* early in January 1899, as the Senate began its consideration of the treaty: "The Republican party, with President McKinley as its standard bearer, could not carry a State to-day against a candidate pledged to rescue the farmer and wage-earner from the impending danger, and who insured them a return to the true policy of 'America for the Americans.' " [49]

Carnegie's anti-imperialism brought him even stranger bedfellows than party politics had. Late in December of 1898, there was a report in *The New York Times* that Carnegie had had a long private interview with Colonel William Jennings Bryan when Bryan had visited the city during the preceding week. According to the *Times* story, Carnegie had written Bryan, "I want you to come to see me. I would go to you, but am sick and unable to leave the house. I believe you to be the only man in the country to-day who can save us from the twin evils of imperialism and militarism." But the *Times* reporter, when calling at the Carnegie home, was informed by a secretary, that Carnegie was not in and had left word that "Mr. Carnegie has nothing to say upon the subject." [50]

If Carnegie had nothing to say, the press throughout the country had a great deal to say. That America's wealthiest citizen, a loyal angel for thirty years of the Republican party, and a man who had called Bryan the most dangerous demagogue in the history of the Republic, should now regard the Nebraskan Populist as the only man who could save the country was indeed sensational news. The fact that the usually voluble Carnegie had nothing to say on the subject added both mystery and veracity to the reports.

The truth is that as early as November Carnegie had been discreetly sending out feelers to friendly Democrats in the Senate as to the availability of Bryan for taking the national political leadership of the anti-imperialist forces. Whether Carnegie at this juncture wanted from Bryan only his influence in blocking the treaty in the Senate or whether Carnegie was indeed looking to 1900 is difficult to say. Wilkinson Call, Democratic Senator from Florida and a strong opponent of the administration's foreign policy, was one of those whom Carnegie contacted. Call, a conservative, clearly interpreted Carnegie's overture as pointing to the presidential election, for he replied: "Mr. Bryan's personality is a great factor, but not sufficient of itself. . . . Much has to be done and a large expenditure and it will require all the time between this and the election to make it. I think Mr. Bryan will have to be brought more in accord with the business men on other questions to have their support. The Southern states will have to be kept in line and New York carried for him and Indiana. I doubt if this can be done without your aid—and if done the country will owe it to you. The spirit of militarism and conquest is about and to keep it within bounds will require all possible effort. I hope these considerations will induce you to give your time and ability and means to making an organization of vital forces to which you refer." [51]

Bryan, who had, of course, soon heard of Carnegie's interest in him, actually made the first move for a meeting. Arriving in New York on 17 December, he sent a telegram asking Carnegie to visit him at the Bartholdi Hotel.[52] Carnegie asked Bryan to call on him instead, which Bryan did. There is no record of what topics were actually discussed in their private conversation. There is no doubt, however, that the two men found themselves in complete agreement on foreign policy. How deeply they may have explored domestic issues together is quite another question. Carnegie apparently believed that Bryan was ready to abandon his 1896 silver Populism in the interest of the larger issue of imperialism and for reasons of his own political ambitions. At the end of this conference, the covers had been pulled back on the bed, even though this strangely matched pair were not quite yet ready to announce that they were climbing in together.

Carnegie, to be sure, was more than ready, and it was Bryan who suddenly drew back. Home again in the capital of Midwestern Populism at the moment the story broke in the national press, Bryan suddenly panicked over the consequences of this possible liaison. He hastily sent a telegram from Lincoln, Nebraska, to Carnegie on Christmas Eve:

> Am informed that you have prepared a public statement discussing our interview and suggesting possibility of your supporting me in 1900. I hope report untrue. I have not discussed interview publicly and prefer that you do not. I am not a candidate for any office at this time. Whether I ever shall be depends upon circumstances. I not only ask no pledge of support conditional or unconditional but believe a pledge or prophecy likely to injure the cause of constitutional government against imperialism, a cause which is more dear to me than political preferment. I am making this fight in my own way and hope to see the question disposed of before 1900 so that the fight for silver and against trusts and bank notes may be continued. You and I agree in opposing militarism and imperialism but when those

700

questions are settled we may find ourselves upon opposite sides as heretofore. Let us fight together when we can and against each other when we must, exercising charity at all times.[53]

One could not be more explicit than that. Bryan was not going to fall into any plutocratic trap, and sell his pieces of free silver for any soul. The press, however, would not leave Bryan alone, and he was forced to admit to the public that he had indeed conferred with Carnegie while in New York, as he hastened to explain to his would-be supporter:

> I wired you this morning in regard to report that you had prepared an article suggesting your possible support of me in 1900. . . . I fear that a promise or even suggestion of support from so prominent a republican might embarrass me in the work I now have on hand. . . . I am pleased to find our Democrat Populists, Democrats and Silver Republicans practically unanimous in their opposition to imperialism. Many of our Republicans are outspoken against it and others are thinking and investigating. Am sure we are right and that our fight will win. . . . You will not agree with my reference [in a St. Louis press interview] to the gold standard, the trusts and bank paper, but I have lost none of my interest in these things and our people are as determined as ever. The fact that you and I differ on these subjects will not prevent our working together against militarism and imperialism. My work must be done among Democrats, Populists and Silver Republicans, yours can be done among Republicans. We shall differ in methods but agree in purpose, namely, the rescue of our country from the perils of a colonial policy. . . . Then we can return to the old questions.[54]

A few days later, when Carnegie seemed still to be suffering under the delusion that Bryan was going through the old 1896 oratory *pro forma*, Bryan was brutally direct: "I believe that the gold standard is a conspiracy against the human race. I am against it. I am against the trusts. I am against bank currency. Just now I am talking against imperialism not because I have changed on the other questions but because the attack of the imperialists must be met *now or never*. The lines of the next campaign cannot be seen at this time but you need not delude yourself with the idea that

701

silver is dead." [55] This was to be no marriage of love, and, as it turned out, not even one of convenience.

Bryan had warned that they might differ in methods for achieving those goals upon which they were agreed, and so it proved. When the formal debate on the treaty opened in the Senate on 4 January 1899, Carnegie's immediate objective, along with a majority of the anti-imperialist leaders, was to block the treaty in the Senate. Then a counterproposal would be introduced as a resolution to grant the Philippines their independence and to prevent a treaty of peace from being ratified until the administration should accept this resolution. Carnegie and his anti-imperialist cohorts in the Senate fully expected Bryan to accept these tactics and to use his not inconsiderable influence as titular head of both the Democratic and Populist parties to swing the necessary support that would make this plan effective. Senator Call wired Bryan: "Come here and aid your friends including Mr. Carnegie in amending Treaty. It will help you and your friends." [56]

But Bryan had quite different plans in mind. Quite unexpectedly, he announced that were he in the Senate he would vote for ratification. Carnegie simply could not believe this and urged Bryan to join him in Washington to work against the treaty or at least wire his friends in the Senate to defeat the treaty.[57] Bryan's reply revealed how far apart the two men were:

> Your telegram was rec'd & answered. . . . I fully realize the responsibility which rests upon anyone who can influence a vote at such an important crisis as this and note what you say. I commenced worrying over this matter as soon as the Battle of Manila was fought. . . . I considered very carefully the best way to meet our opponents and after mature deliberation decided upon the plan set forth in last Monday's Journal. . . . Your letter commending my views contained no criticism of my plan. My faith in the plan has increased as I have considered it. Sentiment is turning our way, why risk the annihilation of our forces by rejecting the treaty? To reject it could throw the subject back into the hands of the administration and those who prevented the ratification would be held responsible for anything that might happen. We can support a resolution and call public sentiment to its support. If the republicans delay it or

defeat it we can renew it before the people. If you have watched my speeches you will see that I lose no opportunity to present an argument against imperialism. . . . I expect to speak in Washington on February 22 & my subject will be "America's Mission." I am going to keep up the fight until victory is won —as I am sure it will be won—not by a *minority* of the Senate but by a *majority* of the people. If we get the treaty out of the way we can prevent an increase in the standing army. If the treaty is rejected, it will be hard to defeat the army increase. Am sorry to differ from you & some of the others as to the method of procedure but each person must be governed by his own judgment and my judgment leads me to adhere to the position taken in my first interview and elaborated in my *Journal* article. I can not wish you success in your effort to reject the treaty because while it *may* win the fight it *may* destroy our cause. My plan can not fail *if the people are with us* and we ought not to succeed unless we do have the people with us.[58]

Carnegie, of course, was not convinced by Bryan's arguments, and for one who had always stoutly maintained his faith in the voice of the people, he must have found it particularly irritating to have Bryan lecture him on the democratic process.

Angered by Bryan's stand in support of ratification, Carnegie dashed off a blistering letter to the New York *World* accusing his erstwhile ally of playing directly into McKinley's hands:

President McKinley, our "War Lord," is beginning to see that he can agree to pay twenty millions for an opportunity to shoot down people only guilty of the crime of desiring to govern themselves, but that he cannot get even his own party as whole to ratify his un-American purchase, while the Democratic is almost solidly against this intended violation of American principles. If the President gets his bargain ratified he has Mr. Bryan alone to thank for his success.

Mr. Bryan can defeat President McKinley by a word upon this question in the Senate to-day. He will not say the word simply because he knows if the treaty is ratified President McKinley is tied to his ruin. The appeal is then to the people, where verdict is certain. The votes are against imperialism. . . . No war for us, thank you, to suppress the aspirations of any people, however backward, for independence. . . . We are republicans who believe the government derives its just powers from the consent of the governed.[59]

Bryan made one last attempt to try to convince Carnegie of the wisdom of his tactics. In a letter written a few days prior to the vote on the treaty, which was scheduled for 6 February, Bryan argued, "Senator Davis is quoted as saying that no vote will be allowed on the treaty unless he is sure it will be ratified. What advantage is there in putting off ratification until new Senate is convened. New Senate has increased republican majority & will ratify. Why not ratify now and make a fight for a resolution declaring our Policy? Such a resolution gives a basis for a fight which can be continued until we win. The results are too important and the dangers of imperialism too great to risk a fight against the treaty when a vote can be prevented or the treaty withdrawn. Get the treaty out of the way and let us begin a fight for the Independence of the Filipinos." [60]

Even without Bryan's support of the treaty, however, Carnegie was assured by his friends in the Senate that the treaty could be blocked. They had not taken into account, however, the determined efforts of Henry Cabot Lodge, Mark Hanna, Nelson Aldrich, and other jingoist supporters of the administration. Senator Richard Pettigrew of South Dakota, a silver Republican opponent of ratification, was so outraged by Aldrich's and Lodge's efforts that he complained to Senator Cushman Davis, chairman of the Senate Foreign Relations Committee, of "the open purchase of votes to ratify this treaty right on the floor of the Senate," which included the buying of one Democrat whose vote had remained in doubt until the final session.[61] Certainly, promises in the name of McKinley for patronage in post offices and federal judgeships were handed out by Hanna, Lodge, and Aldrich with great abandon. Lodge wrote to Theodore Roosevelt that "it was the closest, hardest fight I have ever known. . . . We were down in the engine room and do not get flowers, but we made the ship move." [62]

Events in the Philippines also aided the pro-administration forces. On 23 January, Emilio Aguinaldo, the Filipino patriot, who had co-operated with the Americans against the Spanish forces, proclaimed the free, independent Philippine Republic, and on 4 February actual fighting began between the American occupation forces and Aguinaldo's nationalist army. The anti-imperialists hoped that this news, arriving in Washington on the eve of the Senate vote, would shock the waverers into voting against a policy that had led to imperial combat. But if anything, it seemed to have had the opposite effect. "Old Glory" had been fired upon, and a nation flushed with an easy victory over an ancient imperial European power was not going to yield to force exerted "by half-naked Asiatic savages."

On the morning of 6 February, when the vote was to be taken, Carnegie must have realized his side was in trouble when he received an urgent cable from Senator W. E. Mason of Illinois, one of the most staunchly anti-administration Republicans in the Senate. Mason requested, "Wire your present views, sign same 'C'. I am assured plan suggested by you and by our friends has been agreed up at White House and that treaty will simply give legal title which will be used to temporarily defend us but will not be used for purposes of annexation. Rush answer please." [63]

Carnegie's views were still the same, block the treaty at all costs. But Carnegie's views made very little difference now. By a vote of fifty-seven to twenty-seven, one vote more than the two-thirds necessary for ratification, the treaty was approved. The party line-up was 41 Republicans, 10 Democrats, 4 Populists, and 2 Independents, Aye; 22 Democrats, 2 Republicans, 2 Populists and 1 Independent, Nay. Mason's vote could have blocked the treaty. It made little difference that Mason, full of contrition, wrote Carnegie two days later: "I have, with several other men in the same circumstances, been successfully 'buncoed.' I wish I had time to write you, and the courage to take your time to read just what happened. I can only say now that I did not receive your letter or telegram until after the vote was taken. The trade was made for four votes and on an absolute agreement to pass the McEnery resolution. My legislature at the last moment instructed me, but of this there is no need of writing further. I feel that I ought not to have allowed the ordinary confidence game to have been played in the manner it was. However, the fight is just begun, and although I have noted carefully what you say in your telegram as to relying upon the White House, nevertheless I believe that the President intends to keep the agreement to get rid of the Philippines as early as possible, giving them the same treatment that he gives Cuba. The next few days will tell whether I am right or not." [64]

Senator Mason was to be "buncoed" a second time. The administration, having got its precious treaty, had no intentions of giving away any of the spoils of victory. A resolution by Senator Augustus Bacon of Georgia, by which the United States would hereby "disclaim any disposition to exercise sovereignty, jurisdiction or control over said islands," [65] was defeated by a tie vote in the Senate, with Vice President Hobart then casting the decisive negative vote. The Senate did pass the McEnery resolution, which merely expressed the hope that "in due time" the Philippines might be granted their independence. Since even this weak and vague resolution died in committee in the House, the Administration was committed to nothing. With the treaty, it had a free hand to annex the Islands and subdue its rebellious subjects in the best of imperial traditions, which it then proceeded to do. The Bryan plan had failed. The treaty had been ratified with no formal and binding statement as to American colonial policy.

In a vote as close as that on the treaty had been, with only one vote determining the decision, any number of factors could be credited for giving the administration the victory. Carnegie, of course, always blamed Bryan for the ratification of the treaty, and made bitter reference to this in his autobiography: "One word from Mr. Bryan would have saved the country from the disaster. I could not be cordial to him for years afterwards. He had seemed to me a man who was willing to sacrifice his country and his personal convictions for party advantage." [66]

Most historians writing of this period have accepted Carnegie's interpretation, and have placed the blame for the passage of the treaty squarely on Bryan's shoulders and have assumed that his motivation was to have the issues of imperialism and militarism to take to the country in 1900.[67] The number of votes that Bryan is reputed to have influenced has varied from Carnegie's estimate of seven to that of George F. Hoar, who counted eighteen.[68] Surely it cannot be denied that Bryan's position must have influenced at least one Senator to vote for the treaty. Having said that, the historian moves to much less secure ground in assigning the reason for Bryan's stand to political expediency—getting an

706

issue for the next presidential campaign. There is no evidence either to support this conclusion or to refute Bryan's own often expressed desire that the imperialist issue would be settled before 1900 so that he could get back to the domestic issues that he thought were the basic points of difference between the two parties: silver versus gold, control of the trusts, and bank currency. Bryan, like some of Carnegie's own allies in the Senate, including W. E. Mason, was sincere in believing that with the treaty there would be a definite commitment on Philippine independence which the administration would have to respect. Bryan, to be sure, underestimated the resources of the administration, and the determination of the jingoes who had captured that administration, but in this Bryan was no more in error than Carnegie.[69]

Moreover, Bryan was right when he wrote Carnegie that the failure to ratify the treaty on 6 February would make very little difference. The 55th Congress would adjourn no later than 4 March, and the new Senate, with a larger Republican majority, would have easily produced a two-thirds majority for the same treaty, should it be resubmitted, as the administration had every intention of doing. Carnegie was far more correct in laying the blame on McKinley, as he did in a bitter letter to the editor of the New York *World* shortly after the Senate vote, than he was in trying to make Bryan the scapegoat. When McKinley in a public statement said that the Philippines, like Cuba and Puerto Rico, were "entrusted to us by the war," Carnegie's retort was:

> The Philippine burden is not chargeable to the war. This is the President's own Pandora box, his New Year's gift to his country, for which he alone is responsible. Neither Congress nor the people had any voice in the matter. But one need not wonder why he should now attempt to evade the responsibility since he tells us that "every red drop, whether from the veins of an American soldier or a misguided Filipino, is anguish to my heart." His conscience smites him. No wonder. The guilty Macbeth also cried out, "Thou canst not say I did it."
>
> Whether the acquisition of the Philippines was wise or foolish, they are upon our hands not by the war but by the President's own act, and he had better stand up like a man and assume the responsibility, asking his countrymen to forgive his mistake if he now sees he has made one.[70]

After the debacle over the treaty fight, the anti-imperialists set their sights on the 1900 presidential election. A few of Carnegie's friends, such as Edward Atkinson, still pinned their hopes on Bryan. Atkinson wrote to Carnegie that he had just had a long conversation with Louis Ehrich of Colorado Springs. "He is a personal friend of Bryan in whose sincerity he has entire confidence. He thinks it possible and even probable that Bryan is big enough to come out and declare that while he still thinks his crusade on behalf of unlimited silver is right, the country and the world have decided against him; he therefore puts it aside as a back number and proposes to enter the field on the present great issues. If he does that he may be the next President, and that move will compel the Republicans to put McKinley aside and put up Tom Reed or some other strong man. I think we have won." [71]

Carnegie, however, no longer was naïve enough to believe in a new Bryan. For him, that sorry little flirtation was quite finished. But Carnegie was naïve enough still to believe that the great majority of American people were opposed to McKinley's foreign policy, or would be once they had given sober second thoughts to the road down which McKinley was leading them. "We are mad over here just now," he wrote to his old friend, Andrew White, then Ambassador to Germany. "Passions, always inflamed by war, must have their fling; but of the ultimate result I am certain. Our party is doomed next election. The masses of the people are not with the leaders. The wage-earners and farmers are opposed to the desertion of American ideals. President McKinley's drifting policy is bringing the Republican party to ruin. . . . For all that I do not for a moment despair of the Republic." [72]

For anyone less congenitally sanguine than Carnegie, however, there were reasons enough to despair, not only of the American Republic, but of his "English speaking race." Britain in these last months of the old century went to war against the Boer republics in South Africa while the United States continued its slow, grinding conquest of the Philippines. The ancient and cynical Herbert Spencer wrote to Carnegie, "No one can more fully agree than I do with your denunciations of the doings of our race in the world. And not only our race but of all races. And yet we are asked by the Comtists to worship humanity!" [73]

As the presidential campaign of 1900 approached, it was ap-

708

parent that the Democrats had nominated the same old Bryan of 1896, while the Republicans, by acclamation, nominated the same old McKinley, made even more imperialistic by the vice presidential choice. Carnegie wrote to Andrew White, "I had hoped you would be Vice-President instead of Roosevelt. He is a dangerous man." [74]

Because the Democratic platform was an unequivocal denunciation of America's forcible conquest of the Philppines and the Republican platform was as vague on imperialism as the genius of the platform writers could make it, there were many who felt that Carnegie would be obliged to support the Democratic ticket, free silver and all. Late in August, the Anti-Imperialist League somewhat prematurely announced in *The New York Times* that Carnegie would soon return from Scotland to assist in the campaign against McKinley by taking "the stump for Bryan, speaking under the auspices of the Anti-Imperialist League." [75]

Carnegie quickly put such rumors to rest by contributing an article to a symposium the *North American Review* planned to run in the October issue, on "Bryan or McKinley." Writing to Morley, he explained his support of McKinley's re-election. "I have just finished my article for North Am Review, 'The Presidential Election—Our Duty.' I decide it is to continue the Republican in power even though its failure, or, as I believe, *only its postponement* to do its duty to the Filipinos as to the Cubans. Remember, never have I doubted this would be done—never. I am delighted with McKinley's attitude re China, he will not be bitten again with foreign possessions." [76]

Carnegie's article appeared in distinguished company, along with articles by former Vice President Adlai Stevenson, Senator Ben Tillman, and Erving Winslow, Secretary of the Anti-Imperialist League, all of whom were supporting Bryan; and Postmaster General Charles Smith, Senator Thomas Platt, and Senator George Hoar (who, like Carnegie, had to put his anti-imperialistic views to one side) in support of McKinley. For Carnegie, it took a considerable amount of gulping to get the bitter pill down, but swallow it he did. He admitted that there were times, such as 1896, when "an issue transcends party loyalty," and he attacked the slogan "My Party or My Country, Right or Wrong." Apparently 1900 was not such a year. He was also forced to admit that the Democratic platform in "its Americanism, as opposed to Imperialism, rings true. It stands, as the writer feels, for the true policy, the only policy consistent with the fundamental ideas which gave birth to the Republic. . . . It is also American in every syllable against militarism. . . . It is right upon Porto Rico. . . . It is right in regard to Cuba; but here our party, the writer rejoices to say, is in full accord. It is right, also, in regard to expansion. . . . It is right in condemning the Hay-Pauncefote Treaty as Un-American. It is right in regard to the Boers. . . . This being said, all has been said that can be urged in favor of the Democratic ticket." Apparently for Carnegie that was far from being enough to win his support for the Democrats. Bryan was still hopelessly wrong on silver, the Supreme Court, and the income tax. "McKinley," Carnegie concluded, "stands for war and violence abroad, but Mr. Bryan stands for these scourges at home." [77]

With the support of anti-imperialists, like Carnegie, being given to McKinley, and that of Southern jingoists like Senator John T. Morgan of Alabama being given to Bryan, the election of 1900, like most presidential elections, was hardly a national referendum on an important issue. In electing McKinley by the largest popular and electoral majority since that given to Grant in 1872, had the people voted for imperialist expansion or against silver and the income tax? Politicians could and did interpret the results in any way they wished, but however much the people might grumble about the continuation of war taxes and the mounting casualty lists in Luzon, they had not only accepted but took pride in their new empire. Even Bryan, in the last days of the campaign, had found it expedient to play down the imperialist issue and to play up the old familiar themes of 1896. By 1900, however, silver was a dead issue, and imperialism had never really been a live one. Bryan failed to carry even his home state of Nebraska. All that was left to him was the loyalty of the Solid South and the silver dreams of four western mining states. For better or for worse, the United States was now an imperial power, whose ensign waved across the vast expanse of the Pacific nearly to the coast of China.

The anti-imperialists could not believe that the issue had been decided. There remained one last hope: the Supreme Court. Edward Atkinson wrote Carnegie soon after the election,

710

I believe there will be a vigorous opposition headed by Hoar, Hale, Spooner and others, against the continuation of conquest, and that under existing conditions McKinley will lead our forces out as fast as he led them in, especially since two Judges of the United States District Court and one Massachusetts Judge has held that the Constitution goes with the flag. If the Supreme Court should sustain that view, as I doubt not they will, how quickly our course would be reversed and what a mess we shall find we have been put into, wasting money and life in the conduct of arson, robbery and murder.[78]

Former President Benjamin Harrison also wrote Carnegie, "My whole heart has been aflame with indignation against the monstrous proposition that Congress has absolute power in the territories, and that none of the guarantees of personal liberty and civil rights in the Constitution apply there." Harrison had an interesting suggestion for a way out of the Philippines, so that the United States might not continue to have blood on its hands. ". . . a rather curious interview that I had while in Belgium [has] bred a suggestion. In a brief conversation with him, King Leopold told me of his very profitable business ventures in the Congo Free State, and then said, 'By the way, I see your country is having a good deal of trouble with the Philippines. Now I would like to lease those islands. We are quite accustomed to dealing with such people.' . . . The suggestion that occurred to me in Washington was that we might make a sort of Congo Free State of the Philippines, under the control of some one of the small powers of Europe." [79]

That Carnegie would be willing to accept Harrison's Pilate-like solution to the Philippine question is highly doubtful, but he did agree with Harrison that the Supreme Court in the forthcoming so-called Insular Cases would have to accept the fact that with possession of new territories the United States was obligated to extend to the inhabitants of those territories all the rights of American citizenship, including trial by jury, representative government, and the right to import their goods into the United States duty free. Carnegie had great faith in the Supreme Court. Indeed, one of the blackest marks against Bryan, in his opinion, had been his attack upon the Supreme Court. "There is nothing

711

more American than the Supreme Court," he had written in his article justifying his support of McKinley.[80] His close friend on the Court, Justice George Shiras, however, in a response to a letter from him, had given Carnegie a hint of what was to come. "It is not easy to see how," Shiras wrote just as the Court had begun to hear arguments on the Insular Cases, "if we are now to hold that Porto Rico and the Philippines are within the meaning of the term 'the United States,' in such a sense that their exports into the ports of the United States cannot be subjected to duty, unless a similar and uniform duty is imposed on all other imports from the States into such ports, we could hereafter refuse to regard the inhabitants of those islands as citizens of the United States—a most undesirable conclusion to reach! However, the subject in every point of view, will be thrashed out by able counsel; and it can only be hoped that the result will be for the best." [81]

Thrashed out it was, and the Court in a remarkable series of decisions proved its Americanism, but not exactly in the way Carnegie had anticipated. For as Mr. Dooley said in commenting on the decisions to his good friend Hennessy, "Whether th' Constitution follows th' flag or not, th' Supreme Court follows th' iliction returns." Coming up with a totally new principle in American Constitutional law, the Court decided that Puerto Rico, Hawaii, and the Philippines were "unincorporated" territories, a kind of territory that the United States had never before possessed, and that as such they did not have the same rights as guaranteed in the American Constitution to citizens of the several states and of "incorporated" territories such as New Mexico or Alaska. It was a happy solution for the jingoists. America could have its imperial cake and eat it too. As Mr. Dooley shrewdly observed, "Ye can't make me think th' Constitution is goin' thrapezin' around ivrywhere a young liftenant in th' ar-rmy takes it into his head to stick a flag pole. It's too old. . . . It wudden't last a minyit in thim tropical climes." [82]

The great debate on imperialism was over. It was, indeed, as Carnegie had said, "a parting of the ways," and the United States was to enter the twentieth century quite a different nation from that which she had been in the nineteenth, a colonial power now, building a great navy and seeking to turn the Pacific into "an American lake."

Carnegie had good cause for despair and pessimism, but such were not in his nature. In yet another letter to the New York *World* which appeared on the last day of the old century, Carnegie wrote, "No matter what trials the coming century may have for humanity, it must close with a civilization higher than that of to-day. All goes well, upward and onward. I believe that as the twentieth century closes, the earth will be purged of its foulest stain, the killing of men by men in battle under the name of war and that the profession of arms, hitherto the most and until recently the only profession thought worthy of a gentleman, will be held the most dishonorable of all and unworthy of any being in human form. To kill a man in that day will be considered as disgusting as we in this day consider it disgusting to eat one." [83]

It was at this time that Morley wrote to him, "I thought of you t'other day when I came across a line of Wordsworth,—'a man of cheerful yesterdays and confident tomorrows.' Quite right, too. That's the temperament that wins. Only it does not win everything, recollect. There is a crumb or two for people of the other sort, who like to see things as they are, such people as

> Your friend
> J.M." [84]

CHAPTER XIX

Exit Mr. Frick

1899-1900

The last two years of the old century were perhaps the most difficult years of Andrew Carnegie's political and business life. This
should not have been the case, for prospects had never appeared
brighter than they did in 1897. Bryan had been defeated, McKinley was in the White House, business was booming, and the Carnegie Steel Company was making more steel and more dollars
than had ever been made in the history of the industry. But
within a year both Carnegie's Grand Old Party and Carnegie's
company were to be torn by internal dissension, and in both instances he was a major factor in that dissension. There were moments, indeed, when it seemed to Carnegie's associates that he,
like a goaded and blind Samson, was determined to tear down the
pillars of his party and his company and see them both crash into
rubble if he could not have his way. Carnegie, of course, did not
see himself in such a role. He was the true conservative, attempting, against the perfidy, avariciousness, and plain stupidity of men
in positions of power, to preserve the old ideals, the old order. In
politics and in business, however, he would be forced to yield to
the new order of a new century.

In his assessment of his chief opponents in these two great in-

714

tramural fights, Carnegie had a much sounder perspective on President McKinley than he did on his major adversary within his company, Henry Clay Frick. McKinley he saw as being basically conservative like himself, a good man, who if only left alone would have eschewed both militarism and imperialistic ventures. In a letter to John Hay, after the treaty with Spain had been ratified, Carnegie exonerated McKinley from any willful wrongdoing:

> Thus in each of the three crises which have arisen [war with Spain, acquisition of Philippines, free trade with Puerto Rico], we find the President differs from Philip, who began drunk and only ended sober. The President begins right & the party will do well to note that fact & hereafter follow his first advice. Our party in Congress has been wrong in opposing the President's first decision & the President has been wrong in being so easily frightened by threatened opposition. . . . Whether by Congress or People, the President's first decision was opposed instead of being loyally supported by the Party & that is what is important for us to remember. We need more backbone in the President, that is all.[1]

In short, Carnegie saw McKinley more as a weak-kneed victim of the new forces at work in the world than as a leader of those forces.

With Frick it was quite a different matter. Carnegie, of course, had to recognize that there were new forces also at work within the business world, forces not dissimilar to those set loose by aggressive nationalism within the field of international politics. Carnegie's own company, in its moves toward true verticality of structure, toward concentration and expansion, was a major contributor to those forces. Yet in his business, too, Carnegie wanted to preserve the old even while benefiting from the new, and he saw Frick not as a compliant tool (certainly no one, least of all Carnegie, would ever accuse Frick of lack of backbone), but as a positive, malignant force attempting to wreck the old order that Carnegie cherished.

That ultimately these two strong men would confront each other in open combat might have been foretold by any close observer of human personality at the very beginning of their association. Unlike Carnegie's other associates on the board of managers, Frick had not risen through the ranks but had joined the company as the proud and successful head of a major industrial concern which bore his name. The union of the Frick Coke Company and Carnegie Steel had been more an alliance of two sovereign powers than it had been an annexation. Because Carnegie and his company came to own a majority of the interest in the Frick Coke Company, and because Frick became a partner and employee of Carnegie Steel, it was difficult for Carnegie not to regard Frick as simply another of "his boys," an able manager, working for the glory and profits of Carnegie Steel, and holding a small interest in it through the generosity of Carnegie himself. Frick, of course, saw their relationship quite differently, and for him the Henry C. Frick Coke Company, his own creation, would always have the paramount place in his plans and aspirations. Should there be any conflict of interest between these two allied sovereignties, neither man would be inclined to yield gracefully.

That Carnegie appreciated the talents of his able chairman could not be doubted, even by Frick himself, who was the recipient of many warm and complimentary notes from Carnegie over the course of their business association. The two men had very little in common outside this association, however. Frick took almost no interest in politics, other than the direct effect of governmental policy on business; seldom read a book not related to the science of coke and steelmaking; was something of a social recluse; and was not actively interested in philanthropy. Frick's only interest outside of his business and his family was one which Carnegie did not share—the collection of great art, particularly of the late Medieval and Renaissance periods. What responsive chord of appreciation was struck in this business ascetic's soul by the rich, sensuous canvases of Titian, Tintoretto, and Velásquez is difficult to say, for Frick, unlike Carnegie, always kept his feelings and most of his thoughts to himself. It was only when Carnegie's daughter, Margaret, was born, a few years after the birth of Frick's youngest daughter, Helen, that the two men at last had something in common outside of business, something in which they could delight and were willing to share with each other.

There had been strain and tension in the two men's relationship from the very moment that Frick had joined the Carnegie company. To Frick Carnegie's impetuous pronouncements on labor policy were both hypocritical and foolhardy. He had opposed Carnegie's constant war with the railroads, particularly the Pennsylvania Railroad. And Frick did not find it easy to accept the constant nagging memoranda from Carnegie for more production, lower costs, and greater sales—especially since they were sent from the Highlands of Scotland or the beaches at Cannes or Florida. Homestead had also been a severe strain for both men. Although Carnegie had stood by Frick in his public pronouncements, he had privately blamed Frick for the bloodshed and the resulting calumny that had shattered the image of benevolent paternalism that Carnegie had so assiduously tried to build up. Frick, on the other hand, deeply resented Carnegie's holier-than-thou attitude, held at the same time he was enjoying the major share of the pecuniary benefits of Frick's tough labor policy. Frick could hardly have appreciated the ad lib remarks Carnegie made at the dedication of the new Carnegie Public Library at Homestead in 1898. Carried away by the emotion of the moment, Carnegie looked down from the platform at the assembled workmen and said he could not believe there would have been the tragedy at Homestead had he been present to talk with his men.

With such differences in temperament, interests, and methods of doing business, the surprising fact is that the two men were able to work together as long as they did. It was because Carnegie respected Frick's ability as a manager, and Frick, in turn, accepted the realities of Carnegie's majority interest and did his best to accommodate himself to Carnegie's absentee management, that their association could survive Homestead and the other disagreements. If the business had not been prosperous, undoubtedly the confrontation would have come much earlier, but the balm of profits soothed like an unguent a multitude of minor irritations.

By 1898 Carnegie Steel clearly dominated the steel industry of America, and consequently of the world. Profits in that year came to $10,000,000, an increase of $3,000,000 over the preceding year, and representing nearly 50 per cent return on the total capitalization of the company. And Schwab and Frick were estimating that, with the immediate postwar boom, profits for the coming year would be nearly double that of 1898 and would come close to being equal to the entire $25,000,000 capitalization of the company. Still the dividends paid out to the partners remained small, in spite of the protests of Phipps. Carnegie, of course, was pushing his partners to invest more and more of the profits into new ventures in the manufacturing of finished products: steel freight cars, gun forging, wire, nails, and tubes, as well as armor plate and structural steel beams in which the company was already engaged. Carnegie's partners had so far resisted these pressures, but quite clearly the rapid build-up of surplus profits would force either an unprecedented expansion of facilities or a total reorganization of the company. Phipps, Frick, and most of the junior partners favored reorganization, while Carnegie stood alone in pushing for new plants, at the same time keeping the organization, with its capitalization still set at $25,000,000, intact.

That the company had within six short years vastly outgrown its organization as established in 1892, both in value of assets and in profits, could hardly be denied, even by Carnegie. Yet he feared any reorganization which would truly represent its present size and power within the industrial world, because such reorganization might change the simple partnership association which owned and governed the company. The last thing in the world that he wanted was to open the company to public ownership and have its stock bartered and speculated on in the open market. But the very success of his enterprise made it inevitable that his organization, as he had built it, was doomed.

Of all the many scientific discoveries and achievements made later under grants provided by his philanthropy, the one that seemed to please Carnegie the most was the discovery in Colorado and Wyoming of the fossil remains of a gigantic herbivorous dinosaur, one of the largest vertebrates to inhabit this planet. Carnegie delighted in this graphic proof of evolutionary development, and had copies of the original skeletal structure, named *Diplodocus carnegiei* in his honor, reproduced for numerous museums throughout the world. Here was a classic instance in biological evolution of an organism so successful in its physical development that it outgrew the brain and nervous system necessary to control and direct it. Ironically, this instance of nature's having reached a dead end through evolution, which so greatly interested Carnegie, might well have served as a symbol for his own business organiza-

718

tion. Carnegie Steel, with its vast resources—in iron mines, fleets of barges, railroads, blast furnaces, Bessemer converters, open-hearth furnaces, rolling mills, and finishing mills—could no longer function successfully as a simple partnership organization with such limited capitalization. The body had become too vast for so small a head, but Carnegie could be as blindly stubborn as nature itself, and with 58.5 per cent of the interest of the company no one could gainsay him.

The only solution was for Carnegie to sell out. Although decidedly ambivalent about this, Carnegie by 1899 was at least willing to listen to any reasonable proposal. It was now thirty years since he had written that memorandum to himself in the St. Nicholas Hotel, promising himself an early retirement—thirty years in which he had "pushed inordinately" and made every conceivable "effort to increase fortune." The $50,000 per annum, which he had set as an upper limit beyond which he felt he would be "degraded beyond hope of permanent recovery," now represented less than half of his potential weekly income, should the real value of his interest in the company be converted into liquid assets. And the years that might be left to him to dispose of this ever mounting surplus "for benevolent purposes" were limited. Surely it was time at last to play Laertes, and heed his own Polonian advice.

For an eighteen-month period, from May 1897 to October 1898, the Carnegies lived abroad, spending the winter at Cannes and the summers in Scotland, without once returning home. It was during this period, in his ecstatic letters to his partners about the climate of the Riviera and the glories of Skibo, that Carnegie clearly indicated he would not be averse to selling out and making his vacation from business cares a permanent one. Frick and Phipps needed nothing more than hints such as these to initiate action to effect that desired end.

There were two possibilities open to the board of managers in closing out Carnegie's majority interest: first, to buy out Carnegie's interest in both Carnegie Steel and the Frick Coke Company, and then to combine the two companies into one, keeping the same associational partnership but greatly increasing the capitalization of the company; or, second, to sell Carnegie Steel outright to outside parties, who would undoubtedly make the company into a corporation with stocks open to the public on the New York Stock Exchange. Of the two proposals, Carnegie and, of course, his alter ego, Lauder, preferred the first alternative. Frick, Phipps, and the junior partners preferred the second, inasmuch as it promised a greater return for their interest in the two companies, even though they would lose their managerial-ownership control.

Although Carnegie had stated his preference, he was not adamant in his position, and in December 1898 he told Frick to go ahead and see what he could come up with as concrete proposals for either option. The most obvious possibility for an outside buyer was the syndicate headed by J. P. Morgan that had recently created the Federal Steel Company out of Illinois Steel and several smaller companies. Another possibility was to offer Carnegie Steel to the Rockefeller interests, who owned many of the iron mines leased to Oliver-Carnegie and the ore barges on the Great Lakes. Frick and Carnegie had agreed that the price to outsiders for Carnegie Steel should be $250,000,000 and for the Frick Coke Company $70,000,000, although Carnegie in a letter to the board of managers—a letter he would later regret having written— stated that he thought Carnegie Steel was by itself worth at least $300,000,000.[2] The Federal Steel syndicate, however, having bitten off more than it had as yet been able to digest comfortably, could not even consider such a large deal as this, while Rockefeller, in spite of rumors prevalent in the trade journals, had no desire to extend himself further into the steel business. Carnegie was not disappointed at Frick's failure to find an outside buyer. ". . . , Standard Oil, and Federal said truly too big a dog to be wagged by so small a tail," he reported to Lauder. "Now H. C. F. and I talked over the matter. He will proceed, get plan new charter, bonds, &c. as proposed."[3]

There had been a meeting at Carnegie's residence on 5 January 1899, with Frick, Henry Phipps, Lauder, Schwab, Peacock, Lawrence Phipps, and Lovejoy being present. At that time it was agreed that, providing there was no outside buyer available, the company would consider reorganization and consolidation with Henry C. Frick Coke Company. This new company would be known as Carnegie Company, Limited, capitalized at $60,000,000, "to be subscribed by the present shareholders of the

Carnegie Steel Company, Limited in proportion to their present holdings in the Carnegie Steel Company, Limited. This capital shall be paid in cash at the rate of six million dollars per month." In addition, the new company would purchase

all the property and business of H. C. Frick Coke Company; Yonghiogheny Northern Railway Company; Yonghiogheny Water Company; Mt. Pleasant Water Company; Trotter Water Company; and the Union Supply Company, Limited . . . for the sum of thirty-five million dollars. . . . The Carnegie Company, Limited shall purchase all the properties, assets and business of the Carnegie Steel Company, Limited . . . for the sum of $125,000,000, sixty million dollars of which shall be paid in cash in ten monthly instalments of six million dollars each. A general mortgage shall be created by the Carnegie Company, Ltd. to secure an issue of one hundred million, fifty year, five per cent gold bonds. These bonds to be free of all taxation . . . the interest on the Bonds to be paid semi-annually at the office of the Trustee in New York. . . . The mortgage shall cover all the properties of the Carnegie Company, Limited . . . and all the properties of the H. C. Frick Coke Company. . . . The mortgage shall contain a provision for a sinking fund of ten cents per ton on all coal mined and sold as coal and fifteen cents per ton on all coke made and sold from lands owned by the H.C. Frick Coke Company or the Carnegie Company Ltd. . . . In addition to the above and beginning ten years after the date of the mortgage, the Carnegie Company, Ltd. shall pay into the sinking fund the sum of $500,000.00 annually until all of the bonds are paid.

"I may add," Frick said in reporting this plan to the board on 16 January, "that the question of buying and selling value of capital stock in the new company, that is, what will be paid to retiring Parties, or what will be paid by new shareholders admitted, is having careful consideration, will be fixed on a fair basis, and will be set forth in an agreement similar to our present 'Iron Clad Agreement,' to be signed when the new Company takes possession." [4] Carnegie himself would receive, both in cash and in mortgage bonds, $75,000,000 and would then retire completely from the business.[5]

Carnegie was genuinely interested in this proposal and wrote to Lauder for his opinion. Lauder, as usual, suspected that others were benefiting more than he and Carnegie were, and he objected to paying $35,000,000 for the Frick Coke Company: "There seems to me no earthly reason for the Coke works to be jumped up 5 mill. If we keep fooling around much longer it will go to 50 or 75 M without any trouble. Apart from money value, however, I cannot see wherein the advantage comes in, from consolidating steel & coke, the businesses are separate & must be practically run as separate whether they are owned by one set of persons or not & why we should be asked to agree to pay such an inflated price for this property is more than I can quite get into my head." [6]

Lauder's suspicion, as was always the case, gave Carnegie cause to hesitate. "Rest assured," he answered, "your views have great weight. I haven't gone contrary to those upon a mining question (your dept.) and I am just toward you in this Dept. . . . There will be nothing done in a hurry. Plenty of time—plenty." [7]

The other partners, however, were not as willing to be leisurely in resolving the question. At a special meeting of the board, held on 19 January, all of the board members present—except Lauder—voted to purchase the Frick Coke Company for $35,000,000. Lovejoy spoke the most strongly in support of the proposition as being a fair price. He pointed out, quite correctly, that the Frick Coke Company had 40,000 acres of unmined coal, and that the market value of each acre was $1,000, making a total value of $40,000,000 for the land alone, without taking into account the coke ovens, water works, railroads, stores, etc.[8] Clearly Frick was not exorbitant in setting the price for his company at $35,000,000. Lauder was effectively silenced, but not satisfied. "Have just had the juniors together," he reported to Carnegie. "They all seem to be in favor of taking the Coke Co. at 35 M., or rather leaving it to you & Frick to fix the price. I have nothing more to say on the merits of the question." [9]

At this point, in spite of Lauder's opposition and Carnegie's hesitation, the matter seemed to have been settled. Frick wrote to Carnegie that he liked the plan because it would "keep it all within ourselves, which looks to me to be the prudent thing to do." Prudence had its price, however, and Frick could not resist adding, "Of course it would be far better for stockholders of the

A Pittsburgh steel mill. *Courtesy Helen Clay Frick Foundation.*

A western Pennsylvania patch (the local term applied to company-owned coal towns) at the turn of the century. The caption for the company photograph reads: "This is a sample of a mining village (back-yard view) at Shaw Mine, showing how miners' houses can be kept and how they should be kept at all the mines of the Pittsburgh Coal Company."

Courtesy Helen Clay Frick Foundation.

Andrew Carnegie (left) and his mother with the coaching party, Brighton to Inverness, June 17–August 3, 1881.

Carnegie Library, Pittsburgh.

Skibo Castle, *Carnegie Library, Pittsburgh.*

Mr. and Mrs. Andrew Carnegie, circa 1917.
Carnegie Library, Pittsburgh.

Andrew Carnegie on the terrace at Skibo.
Carnegie Library, Pittsburgh.

and Grover Cleveland at Princeton.
Carnegie Library, Pittsburgh.

first of the endowed Carnegie libraries.
Dedicated March 30, 1889.
Carnegie Library, Pittsburgh.

Carnegie, the builder of libraries.
Cartoon by Peter Newell.
Carnegie Library, Pittsburgh.

Frick Coke Company to see a sale made at figures that have heretofore been mentioned for both properties, . . . yet I believe, with the organization we have, more money, greater satisfaction and contentment would be secured in the long run, by retaining the property under some such arrangement." [10]

Still, the difference in the value of interest based upon $320,000,000 as opposed to $125,000,000 kept dancing through Frick's, Phipps's, and the junior partners' heads. And through Carnegie's, too, for that matter. As was his practice, he was at that point going over the account sheets of profits and of value of individual interests as of the end of the calendar year 1898. The combined profits of the two companies were $10,250,000, and the value of Carnegie's interests in the two companies at book value was $48,000,000. [11] In a memo to Lauder, he estimated profits for the coming year of 1899 to be at $20,000,000. "Just as likely to be above as below, I think. In 1899, we add—Big Plate, Steel Car Shops, new axle plant, Car wheel foundry. . . . Also two new Blast Furnaces at Carrie. . . . I am certain that in two years hence we shall be on a basis of 25,000,000$ net yearly even at low prices —We have to supply the world—note last weeks British advances —Less ore this year than last from Foreign points great scarcity. Prices wild. Coke up to 15^{00} at works best grades hard to get at that near 3.75$ per ton—and scarce. Impossible to increase supply of either coke or ore. Since we reach Atlantic ports at 1$ per ton we have all the trade of the world. I favor holding on for two or three years. No question but we can sell. . . . Why then not wait." [12]

Clearly, it was going to be difficult to get the Old Man out of harness after all. Frick and Phipps, however, did not wish to wait. As Frick had written Carnegie earlier, "It is surprising the amount of money awaiting investment in this City [New York]. On all sides you find people who are looking for investments." [13] And Frick and Phipps were looking on all sides for investors.

Early in April, their search was apparently successful. While Carnegie was busying himself with a new plan for reorganization that would keep the ownership largely within the present association but would increase the capitalization of the new company to $300,000,000, double that of the earlier proposal, [14] Frick and Phipps came up with a mysterious syndicate which was appar-

ently ready, willing, and eager to purchase Carnegie Steel for
$250,000,000 and the Frick Coke Company for $70,000,000. Frick
told Carnegie that for the moment he had to keep the names of
the men in the syndicate secret, but he assured Carnegie of their
honorable intentions. Here it was at last—the apparently definite
offer to purchase Carnegie's empire at precisely the figure he himself had set. It was now a case of agreeing or shutting up about
wanting to retire. Pressured by Phipps and Schwab, and even
Lauder, who was eager to get out, Carnegie agreed to the proposal. He was to receive $157,000,000 for his share of the two
companies: $100,000,000 in first mortgage, 5 per cent gold bonds,
and the remainder, $57,000,000, in cash.

Somewhat suspicious of the anonymous source of this offer,
and of the fact that the syndicate, according to Frick and Phipps,
wanted a ninety-day option to raise the capital, Carnegie demanded that, for this option, the syndicate deposit in trust
$2,000,000 in cash, of which $1,170,000 would be in his name,
representing his 58.5 per cent of the companies. Should the
option to purchase not be taken up during the ninety-day period,
the deposit would then be forfeited. After all, Carnegie reasoned,
for any group of financiers who proposed to raise $57,000,000 in
cash within the ninety-day period, an immediate deposit of
$2,000,000 should prove no difficulty.[15]

When Frick and Phipps hurried back to their principals, however, they discovered that this deposit did present a serious obstacle. The most that the syndicate would or could put up was
$1,000,000. As Carnegie was scheduled to sail for Britain on 26
April, there was no time to be lost in haggling. Frick and Phipps,
eager to have the deal consummated by getting Carnegie's signature on the paper granting an option to purchase, took the
$1,000,000 from the syndicate and put up $170,000 of their own
money, thus themselves covering that portion of the two million
which Carnegie insisted be deposited in his name. Carnegie then
signed the paper giving both Frick and Phipps the power of attorney to negotiate the sale in his name. With Carnegie safely off to
Europe, the two senior partners then presented the problem of
the option to the board on 26 April—the same day Carnegie left
for Europe. Still without revealing the names of the promoters of
the syndicate, Frick explained to the board how the $1,170,000

that Carnegie had demanded as an option deposit had been raised. He then said that both he and Phipps not only had put up $170,000 of their own money, but would of course waive their percentage of the deposit representing their shares in the two companies. The junior members were then told that they had the choice of waiving their deposit shares or of having the whole arrangement fall through. Not surprisingly, all of the partners came in line, waived their deposits, and the option to purchase was duly signed by all concerned and delivered to Frick and Phipps to negotiate with the syndicate.[16]

What Frick and Phipps did not reveal to the board at this time, according to later testimony by all the other members of the board, was that they had not been motivated out of sheer altruism to contribute $170,000 in order to secure the option from Carnegie. By the terms of the agreement drawn up with the syndicate, $10,000,000 of the total stock issue were to be used as bonuses for consummating the sale and paying for legal fees. Of this, $5,000,000 were to go to the promoters of the syndicate and $5,000,000 were to go to Frick and Phipps for having arranged the option. In effect, the two senior partners had themselves, by the terms of the option, become members of the syndicate and, should the sale be effected, were to be handsomely rewarded.[17]

Carnegie, taking the proposal in good faith, prepared a long letter in his own handwriting, which his business secretary, Robert Franks, was to release to the press as soon as the sale was effected. It was Carnegie's farewell address to the business world: [18]

> I wish to take our officers & employees & indeed all the people of Pittsburgh into my confidence. I recently gave my partners an option to buy my interests in Carnegie Steel & Frick Coke Co[s] & this they have done & determined to change the partnership into a Corporation & have sold so much of their interests as was required to pay what was still owing to the firm upon these. The remainder they hold & it is not expected that any change will occur in their position, each will continue to perform his accustomed duties & I doubt not help to carry the Carnegie Steel Co onward to further triumph.
>
> My young partners, thirty odd in number, have naturally been concerned as to the future of the firm in case of anything occurring to me. They have always said if we could only ensure

725

a continuance of existing conditions nothing would induce them to think of any kind of change for a moment—as this was of course impossible, human life being so uncertain, I felt it my duty to help them while still with them to place affairs in a more permanent form & relieve them from debt. Personally I know it will be a long time until I can cease to feel that a serious change in my life has occurred. It will seem so strange & cause a pang to visit the Works and see all our men in whom I have taken such pride no longer "ours." Yet I flatter myself that the bond of sympathy still vibrates between us & binds us together.

To the people of Pittsburgh I say that in no sense is this complete retirement from business to be construed as a retirement from Pittsburgh—very far from that—as the future will show. No change of condition could make me less devoted to her. I have even indulged the hope that perhaps being now entirely free from connection with one company only I may come to be regarded as belonging in a sense to every Pittsburgh concern.

General interest can now be my care unbiased by personal interest. I should be most unhappy if I thought my ability to serve Pittsburgh here was to be lessened by my laying down the cares of business life.

I retire while I see Pittsburgh the metropolis of the Central West, the best point in all the World to manufacture Steel & also many kindred articles. I leave the Carnegie Steel & Frick Coke Co^8. more prosperous than they have ever been & with such prospects before them as never entered my dreams until the past two years, since Pittsburgh has obtained fair rates of transportation.

In the next few years I am confident I could have added to my fortune a second fortune but one in his sixty second year should have other ambitions than to add dollars to dollars when already blessed with enough. I leave all pecuniary considerations without one shadow of regret, but the progress of the firm—the new methods & inventions—the grander machinery —the greater effluency in manufacture which has enabled Pittsburgh to make the world's markets tributary to her—the wonderful development of the Steel Age—these I shall miss— greatly miss—but more than all I shall miss the relationship of a senior partner with his juniors who have grown up with me and to whom I am affectionately attached. This change is what is to cause the heart aches but even here I am consoled by the knowledge that though we may no longer be partners in business we can never cease to be friends, staunch & true to each other through all our lives, but the pang of separation in business comes nevertheless as I write.

I have often said that this matchless organization was worth more than our works. If I had to choose upon entering manufacturing anew between "the Works" and my partners, these being without a dollar of Capital, I should let all the works go & hang on to the boys and to our unrivalled workingmen. Such men as these have enabled Pittsburgh to lead the world in manufacturing. No other nation has such men.

Andrew Carnegie

This sentimental letter was never to be published, but another letter, which was intended for publication before the sale, nearly queered the deal. In response to a request from A. I. Findley, editor of *Iron Age,* for his views on the formation of new consolidated companies, such as Federal Steel, Carnegie wrote on 19 April in his usual forceful style:

> Putting together weak concerns does not make a strong one. . . . The present craze for consolidation in the iron and steel business is due to the fact that manufacturers have for a long time been doing business at little or no profit, and they are glad of the opportunity to sell out. . . .
>
> Individual management will show its superiority in the future as in the past—What has been is still to be. And when depression comes, as it surely will, some of the consolidations will not even pay their bonded interest. When a concern becomes the football of Wall Street, it is owned by nobody or anybody, nobody knows who—a waif that will become a wreck at the first storm. Some corporations there are, in which a few persons are prominent as owners and in which individual management is marked, that are exceptions to the rule; but where stock is held by a great number, what is anybody's business is nobody's business. "The eye of the owner maketh a fat horse, not the eye of the salaried official." [19]

No one could deny that this statement was an honest expression of Carnegie's views in regard to management. His own company was proof of that. Nevertheless, with its gloomy prediction of depression and of resulting inability to pay bonded interest, it was hardly the kind of document to serve as a companion piece for the glowing prospectus that Frick, Phipps, and the syndicate were preparing to release. When Frick saw a copy of the letter Carnegie had sent to Findley, he told Carnegie that it simply could not appear in this form, for it might wreck the whole deal and cause a panic among those consolidated companies already formed. At Frick's insistence, Carnegie hurriedly wrote a follow-up letter to Findley: "There was mailed you an unfinished article which I should have revised. I should ask you to return it for this purpose, but I am sailing for Europe. Please strike out several penciled passages in which I was altogether too hard upon new combinations. What I said may be all true, but it is not my part to say it. Please stop with the remark that 'individual management will show its superiority in the future as in the past,' and leave out all other penciled matter, especially the remark that 'some will not pay interest on bonds.' " [20] But even this expurgated version seemed too dangerous to Frick and Phipps, and after further pleading on their part, Carnegie sent word to Findley to kill the letter in its entirety.

For one as enamored of his own literary compositions as Carnegie, this act of verbicide shows how co-operative he was trying to be in making the arrangements for the sale. But the incident should also have revealed to Carnegie the real purposes of the syndicate—to use Carnegie Steel and the Frick Coke Company as powerful weapons for building a gigantic steel trust in the United States. If Carnegie had any such suspicions he did not express them, and it was not until he was safely in Britain, three thousand miles from the scene of operations, that Frick disclosed to him just who the mysterious syndicate was. On 10 May he received from Frick and Phipps a long cable giving details of the proposed organization—as drawn up by William H. Moore of Chicago with the backing of John W. ("Bet a Million") Gates. Carnegie, who had thought that the syndicate might be headed by the Mellon family, who were close friends of Frick, or even by Rockefeller, who might have reconsidered his earlier refusal, was outraged. To anyone who had made a creed out of opposition to "Wall Street jobbing" and stock market speculation as Carnegie had, the names of Moore and Gates were anathema. No two men in American financial history had earned a more notorious reputation than these two.

William Moore, with his brother, James Hobart Moore, had first burst upon the American financial scene three years before, in the organization of the Diamond Match Company. The financial maneuverings in that instance of trust building had been so wild that they forced the Chicago Stock Exchange to close for three months, and the Moore brothers, along with several others caught in the mesh, were driven into bankruptcy. Undaunted, the two brothers had then moved into the baking industry and had formed the National Biscuit Company. From there, for men of their talents, it had been but a short step into steel, where they formed the American Tin Plate trust, the American Steel Hoop trust, and the National Steel company, all companies which Carnegie had publicly excoriated and privately had been reluctant to do business with. Gates, as his sobriquet would indicate, had had an equally spectacular career in Wall Street gambling. Now these "Chicago adventurers," as Carnegie had contemptuously referred to them, had their hands on his company. Carnegie knew exactly what they would do with it if they were successful in raising the funds to purchase it. As Herbert Knox Smith would later summarize in his report to Congress, the Moore brothers' activities might well be damned with the single line, "The Moore Concerns were the most heavily over-capitalized and suffered from a distinctly speculative backing." [21] With the addition of Carnegie Steel and the Frick Coke Company to the several steel concerns and trusts they had already acquired, the Moores and Gates would be in a position to create a super-trust of incredibly inflated capitalization and to dominate if not wreck the American steel industry. The irony of the whole situation did not escape Carnegie. Nor did it amuse him.

On 20 May Carnegie received another cable from Frick and Phipps:

> Moore's plan cabled was not made public but requiring our aid consented to Pennsylvania charter. Present plan capital Two hundred and fifty millions of one kind of stock to be sold at par subject to bonds. Proceeds of fifteen millions stock to go

into treasury and fifteen millions to bear expenses. One third of the balance to Moore, one third to us and one third to be held for deserving young men, thus carrying out your long cherished idea. Expect to offer public soon. After allowing fair premium on bonds you will see we are offering the stock at less than paid you. Bonds are a serious objection, perhaps fatal. The sum needed is immense, hence uncertainty. Frick. Phipps.[22]

One can imagine Carnegie's reaction upon reading this latest communiqué from his busy partners—particularly the phrase, "thus carrying out your long cherished idea." What a gratuitously insulting touch that was! As if $5,000,000 in stock put aside for deserving young partners could gloss over and hide the $5,000,000 bonus that Frick and Phipps were getting for arranging the deal.

If the full details of the Moore syndicate's plans had not been made known, apparently not even to the other partners, enough now was public knowledge for Carnegie to be mortified. From 5 May on, the American press was filled with sensational headlines: "Andrew Carnegie's Retirement," "The Great Steel Amalgamation," and "Carnegie Stock To Be Placed on Market." [23] The English press was not far behind in heralding the news. The irrepressible W. T. Stead jumped into print with a pamphlet entitled "Mr. Carnegie's Conundrum: £40,000,000. What Shall I Do With It?" which inspired an enterprising advertiser of soap to run a contest offering prizes for the best letters answering Carnegie's conundrum.[24] It was one of the rare times in his life when the publicity-minded Carnegie had more public attention than he wanted.

As Carnegie would later tell the Stanley Congressional Committee investigating United States Steel, "I never knew [at the time the option papers were drawn up] that Judge Moore was a party to it. I would not have given them an option upon any account." [25] Nevertheless, the option had been given, and Carnegie's only hope now lay in the last line of Frick's and Phipps's cable, "The sum needed is immense, hence uncertainty." Unless the $100,000,000 in bonds could be sold and the $57,000,000 in cash could be raised by 4 August, the deal was off. But this possibility carried its own embarrassment, for it would mean that the Moores, Gates, Frick, and Phipps, working both sides of Wall

Street, were unable to find purchasers for Carnegie bonds or enough confidence in the future of the company to raise the necessary cash.

By early June it was apparent that the money would not be forthcoming in time to meet the option deadline of 4 August. Both Moore and Frick always felt that it was the sudden death of Roswell Flower, head of one of the largest brokerage houses on Wall Street, that frightened financiers away from so large an undertaking. It is doubtful, however, that Flower's death had as adverse an effect as the notoriety of the Moores in frightening away the really big and sound capital on Wall Street. J. P. Morgan later revealed that he had been approached and would not touch an undertaking with this kind of backing.[26]

In any event, Frick and Phipps hurried off to Scotland in mid-June to see if they could get an extension for the option.[27] Carnegie, knowing why they were coming, gave them a warm welcome, but when they asked for an extension he was adamant. "HP and HCF came & told me Moore wished an extension," Carnegie reported that same day to Cousin Dod. "I said not one hour. They were delighted, both wished the matter ended altho they left me to decide not knowing their views. I said business was to be so fine & next year would show 40 to 50 m. Steel was going to be scarce for sometime & not likely to remain as low as it had been &c. They concurred. I said no trouble selling out at 320m. That I thought partners would be glad to take it for themselves and on that basis. It would enlarge mortgage & make Bonds 4% if necessary. Frick said just his idea. Harry ditto. Partners would buy, a plan could be devised, &c. Meanwhile nothing to be said to our people except that option ceases Aug. 4th & they needn't be thinking over anything but attention to business &c." [28]

It is doubtful if Frick and Phipps were quite as "delighted" with the abortive ending to their plans to sell out as Carnegie indicated. Nevertheless, their cablegram to the board was properly noncommittal: "Pleasant interview at Skibo. Will not extend or modify present option." On the back of the board minutes in which the text of this cablegram appears is the following notation in Carnegie's handwriting: "Frick and Phipps. Secret bargain with Moores to get large sum for obtaining option. Never revealed to their partners." [29]

If the Skibo interview went off pleasantly enough, the whole Moore affair had left additional wounds for the three principals, Carnegie, Frick, and Phipps, that would not heal. Frick and Phipps were outraged when they were informed by Carnegie's secretary that Mr. Carnegie intended to keep their $170,000 option deposit along with the Moores' $1,000,000, even though at the time of the option he had written a note to the board saying, "Of course any part paid by my partners I shall refund." [30]

Carnegie, for his part, could never forgive Frick and Phipps for having made arrangements with the Moores in the first place and for having secured for themselves alone a $5,000,000 bonus should the deal be consummated. He felt no obligation under these circumstances to return their part of the deposit. By coincidence, the elaborate additions to the old Skibo Castle, completed at this time, cost just over $1,000,000. In later years, after his break with Frick was complete, Carnegie delighted in telling visitors, awed by the crenellated grandeur of Skibo, "The whole thing is just a nice little present from Mr. Frick." [31]

Frick returned home in August, determined to draw up plans for reorganization along the lines suggested by Carnegie—plans that would greatly increase the capitalization of the company and would provide for buying Carnegie out. In September such a proposal for capitalization at $250,000,000, but without any mortgage bonds, was approved by the board and submitted to Carnegie.[32] Carnegie, however, would not consider any proposal that provided for buying his interest with stock rather than with first mortgage bonds. Let others play with stocks if they wished, but here was one tough old sheep that was not going to be sheared by either the bulls or the bears. Before any further proposals could be made, however, a crisis arose within the management of the company that for a time halted any further consideration of the buying out of Carnegie's interest.

The issue that brought this crisis to a head concerned the price for coke that Carnegie Steel was willing to pay the Frick Coke Company. Considering all the other conflicts that had arisen between Carnegie and Frick—Homestead, railroad policy, and the Moore affair—this would seem to be a rather trivial issue to cause the final break, but it touched upon the very heart of their relationship. That this dispute proved to be as acrimonious and

732

as final as it did is strong evidence of the fallacy in the "robber baron" thesis. If the desire for monetary gain had been the motivating force that drove men like Carnegie and Frick, as the "robber baron" proponents argue, then this dispute would never have arisen, for neither man had much to gain whichever way the issue was settled, and everything to lose if the issue should end in an open break. For every ton of coke sold by the Henry C. Frick Coke Company, Carnegie and his steel company took the major share of the profits. For every ton of steel sold by Carnegie Steel, Frick's interest in that company became more valuable. Both companies were so interrelated that the success of the one could not help but profit the other. Here was a classic example of a community of interest that, according to the "robber baron" argument, should have led to a totally harmonious relationship. But this argument fails to take into account other forces that motivate men besides the profit motive. One of the strongest of these forces is self-pride—the pride a man has in his own name, be it borne by a son he has sired or by an organization he has created. Carnegie Steel and the Frick Coke Company might be economically complementary and have essentially the same group of men as owners and managers, but each remained a separate creation; each flew its own proud ensign bearing its creator's name. It is strange that Carnegie could never understand the thrill of pride that some of his jingoistic compatriots felt in knowing that the American flag was flying over the Philippine Islands, for it was precisely the same thrill of pride he felt in knowing that the rails connecting East with West, and the structural beams in the Brooklyn Bridge, all bore the imprint of that magical name, Carnegie. Both Carnegie and Frick were quite prepared to do battle to protect their respective ensigns, no matter what the cost might be.

In any such engagement, of course, Carnegie had the distinct advantage, for he and his company controlled the major share of the Frick company. Frick, on the other hand, was the chairman of both boards, and by his astute management of both companies was in a position to protect the interest of the Frick Coke Company. That Frick was highly sensitive about his precious coke company was certainly well known to Carnegie. Twice before Frick had exploded in awesome rage when Carnegie had interfered in the affairs of that company in a manner that Frick considered deleterious to its best interests. In 1887 Frick had resigned as president of his own company when the Carnegie interests had forced a settlement with labor that Frick found unacceptable. Carnegie had had to beg him to take back the presidency with the assurance that thereafter he could settle labor disputes within his company in his own way. Again, in the winter of 1894–95, Carnegie had interfered in the internal affairs of the coke company without consulting Frick, by trying to arrange a merger with Frick's largest competitor, W. J. Rainey and Company. Frick had as little regard for Rainey as a businessman and competitor as Carnegie had for William Moore, and when Carnegie entered into discussions with Rainey about changing the name of the Henry C. Frick Coke Company to the Frick-Rainey Company, with Rainey having an interest as large as Frick, Frick again exploded. This time he resigned as president of both companies, and asked Carnegie to buy out his interest in Carnegie Steel. Carnegie did not retract on the Rainey deal. It fell through, not because of Frick's opposition, but because Rainey demanded too high a price for consolidation. Once again, however, after a flurry of angry letters between the two men, cooler tempers finally prevailed. Frick was persuaded by Phipps, Schwab, and others on the board to reconsider his withdrawal from both companies, and Carnegie was persuaded to have him appointed chairman of the board.[33] It was an uneasy truce. Carnegie did not like having two heads to the company—Frick as chairman of the board and Leishman, and later, Schwab, as president. Frick, on his part, was undoubtedly convinced there could be no real peace or security within either company for him and his friends until Carnegie agreed to bow out completely.

This third and final crisis came late in the fall of 1899, some three months after the Moore fiasco, and was due basically to a misunderstanding between Carnegie and Frick over an agreed price on coke. Several months earlier, Carnegie had appeared in Henry Phipps's office with a satisfied smile that indicated he had successfully completed another business arrangement. He told Phipps that he had just arranged for a three-year contract with Frick for all the coke that Carnegie Steel should want for $1.35 a ton. As this was some 15¢ below the then prevailing market price,

Carnegie had reason for satisfaction. Phipps, with his usual habit of anticipating the gloomiest contingency, replied, "And suppose coke falls below $1.35 on the open market, do we still have to pay the set price?" Carnegie had not thought of that possibility, but of course it was a real one, for coke, even more than iron ore or pig iron, was subject to wild fluctuations on the market. Carnegie thanked Phipps for his suggestion and assured him that he would get Schwab to speak with Frick and have a provision inserted into the contract to take care of such a contingency. Schwab did not have much luck with Frick, who was already regretting his verbal agreement with Carnegie. Frick told Schwab that he had been in error in making such an agreement with Carnegie, that neither he nor Carnegie had the authority to make contracts, and that Schwab, as president of Carnegie Steel, should negotiate directly with Thomas Lynch, the president of the Frick Coke Company. Schwab reported this to Carnegie just prior to the Carnegies' departure for Europe, but Carnegie was so taken up with arrangements over the option to buy his interest that he apparently paid little attention. Schwab was reluctant to go ahead with negotiations with Lynch until he had Carnegie's approval, and with no further word from Carnegie, the matter was allowed to rest.[34] In the meantime, however, the price of coke went through one of its wild fluctuations, not downward as Phipps had feared, but fantastically upward. By late fall it was selling on the open market for as much as $3.25 a ton at the ovens.

Carnegie had completely forgotten about the conversation with Phipps and his desire to renegotiate the contract with Frick. He had also forgotten about Schwab's account of why he had failed to get a written contract, if he had ever paid any attention to it. As was often the case, Carnegie remembered only those arrangements that were favorable for him. In January, he had written with some satisfaction to Lauder that there was now a fixed rate on coke. As far as he was concerned, that was that.[35]

That was not that, as far as the Frick Coke Company was concerned. Beginning in the first quarter of 1899, the coke company began billing Carnegie Steel at $1.45 a ton; for the second quarter, $1.60 a ton; and after 30 June through the balance of the year, $1.75 a ton, f.o.b. at the ovens. Although this was considerably below what the company was getting from its other steel

735

customers—$2.50 a ton from American Steel Hoop Company, $3.25 from the Duluth Furnace Company, and $2.60 from Federal Steel—it represented a sizable increase over what Carnegie considered to be the fixed price agreed upon.[36] When these increased charges started coming in, Schwab, to avoid a storm over the issue while the reorganization and sale of the two companies were being considered, instructed A. M. Moreland to pay the bills as charged, but to mark all charges above $1.35 a ton as "payment on advance accounts only," thus indicating that Carnegie Steel did not recognize the advance in prices.[37]

Matters were allowed to continue in this way until Carnegie returned home in October, when the issue could no longer be avoided. Carnegie at once demanded that the Frick Coke Company recognize the agreement that he had reached with Frick late in the previous year. The issue then came to the board of managers of the Frick Coke Company. The minutes of that meeting of 25 October 1899, presided over by Chairman Frick, set the stage for the final break between Carnegie and Frick:[38]

> *Mr. Lynch*: There is another matter that I would like to submit to the Board for an expression or instructions. While the Carnegie Steel Company has been paying us each month for the coke we shipped them at the price which it was billed, they have paid the money "on account"—for the reason, it is stated, they "have been advised by Mr. Carnegie that he made a permanent contract with Mr. Frick at a fixed price per ton, commencing January 1st last." We have no record of any such contract, and I have repeatedly so informed the proper officers of the Carnegie Steel Company. [Lynch then gave the prices during each quarter of the current year that the Frick Company had been charging Carnegie Steel.] The claim of the Carnegie Steel Company is that the price should be only $1.35 under the contract alleged to have been made by Mr. Carnegie and Mr. Frick.
>
> *Mr. Lauder*: I think that is a question between Mr. Frick and Mr. Carnegie.
>
> *Mr. Frick*: Mr Carnegie and I had considerable talk about what the price of coke should be for, as he called it, "a permanency." For the sake of harmony, I was personally willing to agree to almost anything. I am willing to talk over the matter with Mr. Carnegie at any time. Mr. Lynch, what action do you wish the Board to take in this matter?

736

Mr. Lynch: I think the Board should take some action. My suggestion is that this Resolution, or a similar one, should be adopted. *Resolution*: That the President be authorized and instructed to notify the Carnegie Steel Company that the existence of any Contract is denied, and

That no claim to settle in accordance with the terms of the alleged contract for past or present or future deliveries of coke to the said Carnegie Steel Company will be recognized or entertained by this Company.

Mr. Walker [John Walker, a major shareholder in Frick Coke Company who held no interest in Carnegie Steel] : I think some action should be taken.

Mr. Lynch: I move the Resolution just read be adopted.

Mr. Lauder: Of course, I would naturally dissent from any action of that kind. I think it is entirely a question between Mr. Frick and Mr. Carnegie, and that they should settle it.

Mr. Frick: I have no authority to make contracts for the H.C. Frick Coke Company.

Mr. Lauder: You and Mr. Carnegie represent a vast majority of stock in the two companies, and if you cannot fix the matter, it is a strange thing.

Mr. Frick: I have had a great deal of talk about the matter with Mr. Carnegie personally. I think this Resolution is perfectly proper. I have no authority to make contracts. We have By-Laws and they provide who should make contracts.

Mr. Lauder: Let me look at the Resolution. It seems too much like a declaration of war. Don't you think we had better leave the matter for Mr. Frick and Mr. Carnegie to settle?

Mr. Lynch: I think the Board should take action on the matter.

Mr. Frick: All in favor of the motion say Aye.
(Responded to by MM. Lynch, Walker and Bosworth.)

Mr. Lauder: I wish my dissent recorded. I think it should be settled by Mr. Frick and Mr. Carnegie.

Mr. Frick: I am Chairman of the Board of both the Coke Company and Carnegie Steel Company, and I have no authority to make contracts. We have officers for that purpose. Mr. Lynch is President of the Coke Company and Mr. Schwab is President of the Steel Company. Mr. Lynch and Mr. Walker have no interest in the Steel Company, and they would naturally object to me making any contracts for the sale of coke.

Mr. Lynch: I say frankly I would not be satisfied to have Mr. Carnegie and Mr. Frick fix the price to be paid for coke by the Carnegie Steel Company. I think the stockholders in the Coke Company, who have no interest in the Steel Company, are also entitled to a voice in the matter.

. . .

Mr. Walker: As long as I am a member of this Board, I feel that I should at least be consulted on these matters; and even as a stockholder, as I have a large proportion of what I am worth in the Coke Company, and as I have no interest in the Steel Company,—from that standpoint, while I think that the Carnegie Steel should not pay the highest price, yet I feel that we should get a fair average price. That is my individual opinion, but I would rather take a little less, but not much less, than have any feeling in the matter.

Mr. Lauder: You need not have any feeling at all. It is a question that can be fixed without any trouble. But I think if it had not been for the Carnegie Steel Company, the Coke Company would not be as big a company as it is to-day.

Mr. Frick: I don't know about that.

Mr. Lauder: Well, that is a matter of opinion. That is my opinion and you can give yours. That is all right. Through good times and bad, the Coke Company has been supported by the Carnegie Steel Company. The question is surrounded by a great many circumstances that should be taken into consideration. If you and Mr. Carnegie will take it up, I am sure I would be delighted to submit it to arbitration.

Mr. Walker: It strikes me that that would protect my interests as nearly as well as they could be protected.

On motion, the meeting adjourned.

Bosworth, Secretary

Lauder was right. This was a declaration of war, as Frick well knew. Perhaps Frick welcomed it. All of the frustrations of the past several months, of trying to reorganize the company on terms Carnegie would accept, of trying to find outside purchasers, and of searching fruitlessly for financial backing, had entirely used up his never large reserves of patience, tact, and discretion. Now, no more compromise. If there was to be a confrontation, let it come.

Carnegie, just back from Europe, hurried to Pittsburgh for a meeting of the board of managers on 6 November 1899. Curiously enough, there was no discussion of coke prices and of the action of the Frick Coke Company at its last meeting. The only important decision taken was to agree to purchase some land that Frick had acquired above Peters Creek, some six miles down the Monongahela river from Homestead. Frick now offered this to Carnegie Steel for $3500 an acre, either for future expansion or to prevent another steel company from building on that site. The board was eager to purchase it, and without dissent, or a word from Carnegie, the sale was agreed to by all present.[39]

If Carnegie kept strangely silent at the board meeting, he did a great deal of talking privately afterwards with the junior partners about his plans to force the Frick Coke Company to agree to his terms. He said he would buy up other coke lands if necessary and start a separate coking operation. Carnegie also made some sneering remarks about the impropriety of Frick's buying land and making a profit off it by selling it to his own partners. All of these remarks of course got back to Frick in rather short order.

In his direct communications with Frick, however, Carnegie apparently was still willing to arrive at an amicable solution of both problems—the price of coke and the reorganization of the company. Shortly after his visit to Pittsburgh, he wrote to Frick:

> There's one question I wish you would fix up—coke prices.
> . . . Do get at this and fix it and always remember that none of your partners can or will regard you as only the representative of a seller company to them, they will not argue or object freely but they *think* all the same. None of them want to stir up things with F. & Co.—very foolish when it's only business with nothing personal in it. Isn't it? Yet so it is. Do get at a permanent arrangement and greatly oblige. You want to make your pard a Charistmas gift anyhow. I'll not look for a $40,000 thing. Give me a settlement permanent on coke and I'll bless you.
> We've never had friction before—it annoys me more than dollars—even than Philippines.[40]

When this brought no response from Frick, Carnegie reverted to his argument that the verbal contract between them was binding, and no further arrangements were necessary.[41]

739

It's all settled anyhow. Schwab writes me they are willing to pay $1.35 permanently. I think it's high. It is your own terms and ends it.

My friend, you are so touchy upon F.C. Co. (fortunately the only point you are), and we all have our "crazy bones." . . . But now all's over and you have a mighty good bargain and a big profit. I had no part fixing price. It's all the same to me provided there is no more dissatisfaction. I believe all back things are also settled—so now all's well.

A. C.

Positive thinking, of which Carnegie was surely the country's leading proponent, might be able to move mountains, but it could not move Frick. For all was certainly not well with Chairman Frick. He could not agree with Carnegie's glib statement that after all "it's only business with nothing personal in it." Carnegie's private remarks while in Pittsburgh Frick regarded as not only personal, but personally insulting.

Nor were the efforts at this time to come to some sort of agreement on reorganization any more fruitful. Carnegie proposed that the two companies be merged and that Frick receive for his interest in the Frick Coke Company a corresponding interest in the new consolidated company. Frick was willing to listen to this proposal, providing the book value of the new company be made not less than $150,000,000. To this Carnegie would not agree, so once again a dead end had been reached.[42]

Believing that there was nothing more to be gained by playing these negotiating games with Carnegie, Frick, grim-faced and determined, went before the Board of Managers of Carnegie Steel at their regular meeting on 20 November and read the following statement:

I learn that Mr. Carnegie, while here, stated that I showed cowardice in not bringing up the question of the price of coke as between the Steel and Coke Companies. It was not my business to bring that question up. He is in possession of the minutes of the Board of Directors of the Frick Coke Company, giving their views of the attempt, on his part, to force them to take practically cost for their coke. I will admit that, for the sake of

740

harmony, I did personally agree to accept a low price for coke; but on my return from that interview in New York, President Schwab came to me and said that Mr. Lauder said the arrangement should provide that in case we sold coke below the price that Mr. Carnegie and I had discussed, the Steel Company was to have the benefit of such lower price. I then said to Mr Schwab to let the matter rest until Mr. Carnegie came out (he told us he intended to come), and we would take up the question of the coke contract. He changed his plans, and did not come out. I saw him in New York before he sailed, and told him that Mr. Lauder had raised that question, and suggested that he write Mr. Schwab, and let Messrs. Schwab and Lynch take up the question of a coke contract. Mr. Schwab, I believe, never heard from him on the subject, and Mr. Lynch, . . . very properly, has been billing the coke, as there was no arrangement closed, at a price that is certainly quite fair and reasonable as between the two companies, and at least 20 cents per ton below the average price received from their other customers. . . . Why should he [Carnegie] whose interest is larger in Steel than it is in Coke, insist in fixing the price which the Steel Company should pay for their coke? The Frick Coke Company has always been used as a convenience. . . . The value of our coke properties, for over a year, has been, at every opportunity, depreciated by Mr. Carnegie and Mr. Lauder, and I submit that it is not unreasonable that I have considerable feeling on this subject. He also threatened, I am told, while here, that if the low price did not prevail, or something was not done, that he would buy 20,000 acres of Washington Run coal and build coke ovens. That is to say, he threatened, if the minority stockholders would not give their share of the coke to the Steel Company, at about cost, he would attempt to ruin them.

He also stated, I am told, while here, that he had purchased that land from me above Peters Creek; that he had agreed to pay market price, although he had his doubts as to whether I had any right, while Chairman of the Board of Managers of the Carnegie Steel Company to make such a purchase. He knows how I became interested in that land, because I told him, in your presence, the other day. Why was he not manly enough to say to my face what he said behind my back? He knew he had no right to say what he did. Now, before the Steel Company becomes the owner of that land, he must apologize for that statement. I first became interested in that land, as I told you, through trading a lot in Shady Side that I had owned for years. The land is six miles away from any land owned by the Carnegie Steel Company. The Steel Company does not need it now, and will not need it for a long time in the future, if at all; but of course, if they owned it, it might keep another large works from being built, or enable the Steel Company to go into competition with some other large industry.

Harmony is so essential for the success of any organization that I have stood a great many insults from Mr. Carnegie in the past, but I will submit to no further insults in the future.

There are many other matters I might refer to, but I have no desire to quarrel with him or raise trouble in the organization; but in justice to myself, I could not at this time, say less than I have done.[43]

The silence from New York was nearly deafening in its ominous heaviness. Carnegie made no direct reply to Frick, and of course made no apology for any remarks he had made while in Pittsburgh. He waited a week to see if the board would approve of the minutes as they stood without repudiating the remarks of the chairman. On 27 November, the board approved of the minutes without a demur. Carnegie realized that he himself would have to act quickly and decisively if Frick were to be put in his place, and that place would surely be out of office. Lauder had written Carnegie in great consternation soon after the board meeting, asking, "Would any possible sacrifice that could be entailed be too much in order to cut loose from such a disturbing element? I am well aware the steps to be very grave but an enemy outside your lines is always less dangerous than inside no matter what the apparent sacrifice may be in putting him there. . . . To my mind the chairman seems to have deliberately burned his boats, & the issue is now Carnegie or Frick pure & simple. Should you make any arrangement that leaves him in power everyone will practically look on the settlement as your virtual abdication from the control of the affairs of the firm, . . . and opinions have been expressed that this will be the outcome of the crisis." [44]

Carnegie needed no urging on this score from Lauder. He promptly answered his cousin: "You voice my views exactly. Frick goes out of Chairmanship of Board next election or before. That's settled days ago. Have no fear of opposition whatever—none. . . .

742

You may tell CMS he will be the man & the only man & that next election Chairmanship will be abolished. Now CMS must see that his men stand firm for that policy, must express opinion. . . . CMS can manage all this nicely. Everyone likes him at heart, not like Frick. I have nothing but pity for Frick not one iota of temper. His recent exhibition is childish. . . . My birthday—never better or happier especially since I decided to tell Mr. Frick in kindest manner that I mean divorce under 'Incompatibility of Temper.' I shall tell him never had anything but happy family until he came into it & I am not going to have anything else. It is divorce between us as far as management of our business is concerned. No feeling—only I believe our best business interests demand an end of quarreling." [45]

Schwab, upon whom Carnegie was depending to carry out his orders, was placed in a most difficult position by this crisis. He had worked closely and harmoniously with Frick for eleven years and had the highest respect for Frick's managerial talents. On the other hand, as he hastened to write Carnegie, "Aside from personal regard and feelings for you, you have heaped honors and riches upon me and I would indeed be an ingrate to do otherwise. My interests and best efforts will always be for you and the old firm. . . . Believe me, Dear Mr. Carnegie, I am always with you, and yours to command." [46]

Schwab's great fear, as was true of the other junior partners, was that he would commit himself to one side, and then have the ground cut out from under him by another Frick-Carnegie reconciliation. He put this rather bluntly to Carnegie. "Naturally the members of the Board would hesitate about taking any initial steps in this matter and if I were you, would not ask them to do so until you have definitely instructed them as to your wishes. The boys are, I am sure, most loyal to you, but knowing Mr. Frick's power in the past, will hesitate to do anything against him, fearing the matter might ultimately be fixed up, and if it was would injure or end their career. The only way for you to do is to take *decisive action yourself first*." [47]

A hurried trip to New York convinced Schwab that Carnegie was prepared to do just that. Nevertheless, "genial Charlie" attempted to maintain congeniality to the last moment. Upon getting back to Pittsburgh, he wrote Frick: [48]

743

I write you confidentially. I just returned from New York this morning. Mr. Carnegie is en route to Pittsburgh today— and will be in the offices in the morning. Nothing could be done with him looking towards a reconciliation. He seems most determined. I did my best. So did Mr. Phipps. I feel certain he will give positive instructions to the Board and Stockholders as to his wishes in this matter. . . .

I believe all the Junior members of the board and all the Junior Partners will do as he directs. Any concerted action would be ultimately useless and result in their downfall. Am satisfied that no action on my part would have any effect in the end. We must declare ourselves. . . . Personally my position is most embarrassing as you well know. My long association with you and your kindly and generous treatment of me makes it very hard to act as I shall be obliged to do. But I cannot possibly see any good to you or anyone else by doing otherwise. It would probably ruin me and not help you . . . I beg of you for myself and for the Junior Partners, to avoid putting me in this awkward position, if possible and consistent. . . . Please consider confidential for the present, and believe me

As ever
C.M.S.

What Schwab was clearly hoping for came to pass. When Carnegie called on Frick the next morning and asked if he would resign voluntarily as chairman of the board of Carnegie Steel, Frick said he would oblige. The board and Schwab were spared the embarrassment of having to ask Frick for his resignation. At a special meeting of the board, called on 5 December, Frick sent the following brief communication: [49]

Gentlemen:

I beg to present my resignation as a member of your Board.

Yours very truly,
H. C. Frick

On a motion by Clemson, seconded by Peacock, Frick's resignation was accepted, "the vote being unanimous, and all present concurring." [50]

Most of the junior partners and Phipps would have been more than happy to have had the quarrel end there. Frick had been punished. He no longer had an official capacity in the company. But there were still unresolved issues: the question of the price of coke from the Frick Coke Company, the fact that Frick was still chairman of the board of that company, and, finally, that he still held a valuable 6 per cent interest in Carnegie Steel, the third largest interest in the company, and this interest would certainly affect any plans Carnegie might have for reorganization. Carnegie was by no means finished with Frick.

The first and most pressing issue was that which had precipitated the quarrel, the price of coke. For a time Carnegie had thought to resolve that by buying up valuable coal lands in Fayette County, reputed to be nearly as good as the Washington County coal owned by the Frick Company. He had entered into serious negotiations with J. V. Thompson, the owner of the coal lands, through an agent, Emmett Queen.[51] But even if these lands could have been purchased at a reasonable price, as Carnegie hoped, it would be at least two years before the necessary ovens, washing mills, and rail transportation could be provided to make the fields usable, and in the meantime Carnegie Steel needed coke, and needed it from the Frick Coke Company. By the time Carnegie came to Pittsburgh in December, he had devised a plan to get the coke at the price he wanted to pay.

The solution was really quite simple for anyone who knew the history of the British reform movement, and Carnegie, child of Radical Dunfermline, knew that history well. He had often heard his father and uncle tell how the Great Reform Act of 1832 had been pushed through a recalcitrant House of Lords by the King's threatening to create enough new Peers to ensure its passage if the House as then constituted would not approve it. The analogy seemed quite appropriate. If Frick and his board of managers continued to refuse to recognize what Carnegie regarded as an existing and binding contract, Carnegie would create enough new board members to vote in the price of $1.35 on coke for Carnegie Steel. Carnegie revealed his plan to Lauder in two memos, late in December: "Mr. Lovejoy should get at Bye Laws of Frick Coke Co.—don't be put off—see if a majority of interests and number be required to elect Board. Of course such a Bye is illegal in corporations but if it be there suggest to Mr. Schwab to transfer 100 shares to each manager and make them eligible—want this done and *certificate of stock got* for them before Jany 9th sure." Shortly thereafter: "Say to H.P. that since I have seen those memos and also know that contract was in operation three months. Mr. Frick will not be elected to Frick Coke Co board Jany 9th unless that contract is restored. No Sir—no repudiation of contracts for me. He had better exchange his CS Co Stock for Frick Co Stock as I suggested and get control of Frick Co. This he is entitled to and I shall be glad to give it to him. CS Co to get third of Frick Coke land and property and make coke best suited for Furnaces. Mr. Frick can then manage Frick coke to suit himself. He can't repudiate contracts for any company which myself and friends control —we are not that kind of cats." [52]

Carnegie also toyed with the idea of buying up the entire Frick Coke Company for $35,000,000, which had been the evaluation Frick had put on the company earlier in discussing consolidation. "If your judgment goes with Schwab's," Carnegie wrote Lauder, "better make the offer & let us own it all—no minority stockholders & no fuss—just gobble it." [53] But the cautious Lauder responded, "I don't think you ought to be in any hurry about making changes in the Coke Co—better let it alone & see what Frick does. . . . I believe History will repeat itself & that after this boom, coke will go to $1.00 or maybe 90 cts. as it did before." To which Carnegie agreed, "Probably you are right. . . . We only need a majority interest & I don't think it's a very good bargain to take more at over 30M." [54]

In the meantime, Schwab had been setting the stage for Carnegie to take over control of the management of the Frick Coke Company. He assured Frick that, with the combined holdings of Andrew Carnegie and of the Carnegie Steel Company comprising a majority of the interest in the coke company, enough new managers would be elected at the annual meeting to enable Carnegie to dominate it. Frick, always a realist in business matters, saw that this was inevitable. On 27 December, Schwab wrote Carnegie, "Frick left yesterday for 10 days in the South. Before leaving arranged Coke Board matter with him: to be 7 members of the board, he to name 2 and we to name 5. He named himself and Lynch. I suggest we name: Lauder, Clemson, Moreland, Gayley and Morrison. Lynch is to be elected President and the office of chairman is to be abolished." [55] At a special board meeting of the Carnegie Steel Company on 2 January 1900, shares of stock in the Henry C. Frick Coke Company, held by Carnegie Steel Company, were transferred to individual partners in Carnegie Steel. Schwab, Peacock, L. C. Phipps, Clemson, Morrison, Gayley, Moreland, and Lovejoy each suddenly became a proud owner of five shares of Frick Company stock and thus eligible to vote in the annual meeting.[56]

Carnegie arrived in Pittsburgh on 7 January and the following morning called a secret meeting of the board of managers of Carnegie Steel, a meeting of which Frick was not notified. The purpose of this exclusive gathering was to discuss and take action to resolve the present confused state of the famous Iron Clad Agreement, under which, since 1887, all partners in Carnegie Steel Company had held their interest in their company. This, of course, was the Agreement that had been drawn up at the instigation of Henry Phipps at the time of Tom Carnegie's death, when Andrew Carnegie was himself seriously ill. It had provided a means by which the company could assume the interest of any of the partners at the time of the partner's death and pay the estate the book value of that interest over an extended period of time, depending upon the size of that interest. The Agreement had gone even further, by also providing that, at any time three-quarters of the interest in the company and three-quarters of the number of associates in the company requested it, an individual associate would be obliged to assign, transfer, and sell his interest back to the company at book value. This meant that each of the partners, with one notable exception, continued to hold his interest in the company at the sufferance of three-fourths of the other individual associates and of three-fourths of the total interest of the company. The only partner who could not be forced to sell his interest at book value was Carnegie himself. By holding over half of the interest in the company, he could quite obviously prevent three-quarters of the interest from demanding that he sell, even if three-quarters or more of the individual partners should so desire it.[57]

When the company had been reorganized in 1892, the Iron Clad Agreement had become a part of that organization, and over the years some fifteen partners, either through death or voluntarily, as in the case of Abbott and John Walker, or by demand, as in the case of Leishman, had had their interest transferred back to the company, and either they or their estates had been paid the book value for that interest. Up until 1895 this had caused no great difficulty, inasmuch as the book value very nearly approximated the actual value of the partner's interest. After 1895, however, it had become quite a different matter. The acquisition either through purchase or lease of the incredibly rich iron ore fields in the northern range country of Mesabi and Lake Superior and the rapid growth of annual earnings of the company were not fully reflected in either the capitalization of the company or in the book value of the individual associate's interest in the company. With each passing year, book value had less and less reality in terms of actual value of the interest held.

Actually, by 1897 it was apparent that even the book value of the shares had increased so much that the company would be in serious difficulty in trying to meet the payments required by the Iron Clad Agreement if one of the senior partners, such as Phipps, who held an 11 per cent interest, or Frick, who held a 6 per cent interest, should die. If Carnegie himself should die the company might well be forced into bankruptcy in order to meet the scheduled monthly payments on his 58.5 per cent interest. Both Frick and Carnegie had seen that it was essential to re-design and re-execute the Iron Clad Agreement. As early as January 1896, Carnegie had written to Lovejoy, "Now will you take up the subject of each member signing what we call 'The Iron Clad Agreement.' It is highly important that every shareholder shall sign that, just as he has signed these By-Laws, because we do not know what day someone may 'fall from grace,' or do something which will require the interests of the firm to sever connection with him." [58]

Everyone within the company could see the danger of trying to pay to Carnegie's estate, in the event of his death, the book value of his interest, even over the extended period of fifteen years provided in the Iron Clad Agreement. Either the period of time to buy his interest would have to be greatly extended or the Iron Clad principle would have to be abandoned in favor of permitting Carnegie's heirs to inherit his interest directly. Carnegie

748

vigorously opposed the abandonment of the Iron Clad principle, just as he opposed the idea of Carnegie Steel's becoming a corporation with its stock sold on the open market. As long as he remained within the company, he wanted to keep the ownership limited to those actively engaged in the management of the company. "No outsiders for us," was his stock answer to any suggestion of change.

It was the problem of paying for Carnegie's interest if he should die that forced the question of the Iron Clad Agreement in 1897. In June, Carnegie proposed that in the event of his death the company should have the option of purchasing his interest from his estate over a fifty-year period in registered, first mortgage gold bonds bearing interest of 5 per cent. Frick and the other partners at first objected that, with a blanket mortgage on the entire property of the company for fifty years, 5 per cent seemed to be an excessively high interest rate.[59] After several weeks of discussion among the board members and further letters from Carnegie, the board accepted Carnegie's proposal, and the way seemed clear for a new Iron Clad Agreement.[60] Thereupon a new Iron Clad Agreement, containing these provisions, was drawn up by the secretary with the approval of the board, dated 1 September 1897.[61] Then they hit a snag. Henry Phipps, who had been the instigator of the original Iron Clad Agreement, now refused to sign. He, who had been party to its use against many of his former partners, now in the last years of his business career saw the full potential of the Agreement for perhaps the first time. There were long dark memories that could frighten a man as nervous as Henry Phipps had always been—memories of Thomas Miller, forced out by him and Kloman; of Kloman himself, forced out by him and Carnegie; of Shinn and Abbott and, most recently, Leishman. If these men, why not Frick, why not he himself, why not, indeed, anybody and everybody except, of course, the one man who could not be touched except by death itself, Andrew Carnegie? All of these long years of toil, of living more in hope than in realization, all of that vast wealth accumulating and so little of it being distributed—now at last when the end of the game was surely in sight, just before the score would be tallied and the rich prizes would have to be given out, would he too suddenly be yanked out of the game and be given a mere fraction of his true reward? "My dear Andrew," he wrote on the 25 September, "I am very sorry that I have to tell you that for reasons with which you are familiar, and others equally obvious and good, I have fully decided not to sign the 'Ironclad' or other similar paper. I therefore returned the proposed agreement with my regrets." [62]

Carnegie was nonplussed. He could not really believe that Phipps meant what he said. "Mr. Phipps sails on 16th," Carnegie wrote Frick in early October. "You may find him all awry in regard to Iron Clad Agreement, but if you will have Lovejoy get all the signatures promptly, the Squire [Phipps] will be all right. He seems unduly alarmed about matters. Thinks we give young men interests unnecessarily large, favors getting in capital; in other words he would make the firm like the corporation Mr. Hasbey describes, the secret of our success has been that we have done just the opposite and I have written him that next to taking care of our own families, I think our young partners have the greatest claim upon us old fellows, for whom they are working, making fortunes. . . . You can no doubt smooth him down; calm his fears and get his signature to the Iron Clad, which I think it is important to close." [63]

Frick, ironically enough, was a strong supporter of the Iron Clad. Upon getting notice of Phipps's refusal to sign he reported to the board that "Mr. Phipps certainly believed [at one time] the Agreement to be both legal and wise, or he would not have taken an active part in its execution. On the question of policy, it is certainly better for this Association to control the ownership of its capital by such an Agreement . . . and as the present form is satisfactory to every member of the Association who has examined it, with the exception of Mr. Phipps, I am of the opinion we should proceed to print and execute the Agreement. Mr. Phipps is a fair man . . . and I fully believe will withdraw his objections after he has talked the matter over with Mr. Carnegie and with the members of the Board." [64]

Mr. Phipps, however, did not withdraw his objections and would not sign the agreement. But Frick did not see this as an impediment to the continued enforcement of the Iron Clad. As he told the board, in words he would later regret, "The old

750

Agreement we believe to be legally operative until this revision has been signed, as the only changes made, other than the extension of the stipulated times of payment, are for the better understanding and carrying out of the details." [65] As late as 3 January 1899, the company had made use of the Agreement to buy out John Pontefract's 0.5 per cent interest in the Company, as Pontefract found it necessary to resign from active business due to ill health. Carnegie suggested to the board that his interest be bought out at book value and that he then be given an additional sum as an honorarium. "I think this would be better. We might have other Estates to deal with, and a precedent might be troublesome." The board had been unanimous in carrying out Carnegie's suggestion. [66]

Now, however, a year later, as some, but not all, of the board members met secretly at Carnegie's call, Carnegie was worried about the legal status of the Iron Clad. Did the Agreement of 1897, signed by all the members except Phipps, have any real legal standing? More troublesome than that was the possibility that the board, by passing the 1897 revision, had made inoperative the earlier Iron Clads of 1887 and 1892. By now Carnegie was determined that, should the plans for the annual meeting of the Frick Coke Company set for the following day go awry, he would use the Iron Clad against Frick as his ultimate weapon to bend Frick to his will or to crush him. Better to get rid of that troublesome 1897 Agreement which muddied the legal waters. Therefore, Carnegie read the following resolution to the assembled board: "Whereas, as appears by the Minutes of October 19, 1897, a proposed Supplemental Agreement, dated September 1, 1897, to the original Agreement, appearing in the Minutes of January 18, 1887, was signed by Andrew Carnegie, conditioned upon all members signing the same, but was objected to by Henry Phipps, who refused to sign the same; and, consequently, that it has not been signed by several other members, and is, therefore, of none effect;
Now, therefore, be it
RESOLVED: That the Resolution of October 19, 1897, approving said Supplemental Agreement, passed in the hope that Mr. Phipps would upon reflection withdraw his opposition and all

751

members sign, is hereby rescinded, and the Board decides that no further steps be taken with the proposed Supplement, thus leaving the original Agreements in full force." [67]

It was a sheer inspiration on Carnegie's part to refer to the 1897 Agreement as "a proposed Supplemental Agreement," thus making it appear to be a mere, incidental addendum to the original Agreement of 1887, and leaving that original Iron Clad still legally in effect and binding upon all members.

The remaining minutes of this 8 January meeting read as follows:

"On motion, L. C. Phipps and Peacock, this Resolution was adopted, vote unanimous.

"Without a motion, the Secretary was directed to obtain to the Supplemental 'Iron Clad Agreement,' dated July 1, 1892, the signatures of the present members of this Association who have not signed the same, it having not been presented for signature to the members admitted while the aforesaid Supplemental Agreement of September 1, 1897 was being drawn up, considered, revised, and after its adoption." [68]

Thus armed for combat, Carnegie faced the annual meeting of the Frick Coke Company the following morning with equanimity. Schwab had set the stage well. There were many new faces present, and the steam roller operated without a hitch. The number of board members was increased from five to seven. Frick, Lynch, and Lauder were re-elected. Walker and Bosworth, both Frick men, were dropped, and Gayley, Moreland, Clemson and Morrison, all members of the board of Carnegie Steel, were elected as new members. Carnegie thus had five members bound to him, Frick only himself and Lynch. Lynch was duly re-elected president, but the office of chairman of the board was abolished.

The newly elected board then took up as its first item of business a resolution to rescind the resolution of 25 October, which had denied the existence of a contract to deliver coke to the Carnegie Steel Company at $1.35. By the not surprising vote of five to two, this resolution was passed. Then there was a motion instructing the president to enter into formal contract with Carnegie Steel to provide all of the coke that company should care to order from Henry C. Frick Coke Company at $1.35 a ton, delivered f.o.b. cars at the oven. Again, the vote was five to two. This was enough for Frick, who got up, stalked to the door, and there declared, "You will find that there are two sides to this matter." With that he left the meeting to consult with his lawyer regarding the possibility of a court injunction to prevent the Frick Coke Company from making any deliveries of coke to Carnegie Steel under these terms.[69]

Carnegie called on Frick the next morning at his office, ostensibly to persuade him not to seek a court injunction but to accept the settlement as an accomplished and irreversible fact. It was the last face-to-face meeting the two men would ever have. Frick sat in stony-faced silence while Carnegie, holding all the cards, tried with sweet reasonableness to obtain Frick's co-operation. Finally, having heard Carnegie out, Frick said, "And if I don't accept this contract and am successful in enjoining the Frick Coke Company from making any deliveries to Carnegie Steel, what then?"

Well, then, Carnegie replied, the company would have to make use of the Iron Clad Agreement and take over Frick's interest in Carnegie Steel at book value. The threat of the ultimate weapon had at last been used. Frick, in towering rage, jumped from his chair, shouting, "For years I have been convinced that there is not an honest bone in your body. Now I know that you are a god damned thief. We will have a judge and jury of Allegheny County decide what you are to pay me." With fists clenched, Frick advanced from around his desk toward the shaken Carnegie, who never before in his life had been spoken to in this manner. With more speed than dignity, Carnegie made his exit, and Frick slammed the door behind the retreating Carnegie with a bang that startled the terrified clerks and stenographers throughout the outer offices.[70]

Without slackening his pace, Carnegie went directly from Frick's office to the board room of Carnegie Steel. He sent word by a secretary for all of the managers present to assemble immediately for an extraordinary session of the board. He gave to the board members assembled a brief account of his meeting with Frick. He then demanded that the board at once institute proceedings to have Frick's 6 per cent interest in the company transferred to the company under the Iron Clad Agreement. The frightened managers, who had come running at Carnegie's angry call, hastily passed a resolution invoking the Iron Clad and asking

Henry Clay Frick "to sell, assign and to transfer to Carnegie Steel Company, Limited all of his interest in Carnegie Steel Company, Limited by 31 January 1900." The resolution was then signed during the next two days by thirty-two of the thirty-six associates in the company.[71]

Of the four who did not sign, Frick was, of course, not asked. H. M. Curry, who was at home desperately ill, refused to sign when the resolution was taken to his bedside. He told Moreland that he intended to "go to my grave with the marks of an honest man, just as I lived." [72] For Phipps, the whole quarrel had become his worst nightmare realized. It was the fear of having precisely this sort of thing happen that had kept him from signing the 1897 Agreement. He could do nothing else but stand by Frick, but he knew that if they lost in their battle with Carnegie, he would go down tied to Frick. Phipps, who never in his life had wanted to play the role of the hero, much less the maverick, now to his despair found himself a leader in the rebellion. It was cruelly insane, but there was no escape. He did not sign.

The only other holdout was the secretary of the company, Francis Lovejoy, whose defection came as a surprise to Carnegie and Schwab. Lovejoy, who had stood by Carnegie in all the steps leading up to this moment—the ousting of Frick as chairman, the taking over of the Frick Coke Company, even the rescinding of the 1897 Agreement in order to make sure the 1887 Agreement would still be legally effective—could not countenance this final step of taking Frick's interest from him at only a fraction of its real worth. It was a particularly embarrassing situation, inasmuch as, under the terms of the Agreement, the secretary was the officer in the company who was to serve as trustee to hold any former partner's interest that was transferred to the company. Lovejoy had no alternative but to resign as secretary and also as a member of the board. Moreland replaced him as secretary, and Singer was added to the board.[73] Lovejoy wrote to Carnegie,

> I fully appreciate and sincerely thank you for the kindness shown by your favor of yesterday, and thank you also for pointing out my wisest course, under existing circumstances.
>
> I have placed my written resignation in the hands of the President, and have also said to him that my services are at his

disposal, for such time as he may deem advisable, in the closing up of last year's business, or in any other matters entirely apart from the transactions of the Board in this one controversy. I have no desire to discuss the question, nor, I am sure, have you; so I will only add that I can now have no regret whatever for my decision. . . ."[74]

Frick, at the conclusion of his explosive meeting with Carnegie, as soon as he had cooled down a bit, hurried over to John Walker's office. "John," he said, "I lost my temper this morning."

"Well," Walker remarked, "I knew you had one to lose."

Frick then told Walker the whole story. The usually imperturbable Walker was outraged at Carnegie's threat to take Frick's interest away from him at book value. Although Walker had never admired Frick as a person in a way that he admired Carnegie, having always considered the coke master to be far too narrow in his interests and totally lacking in a sense of humor, his sympathies in this instance were entirely with Frick. It was decided then and there that, should Carnegie proceed to carry out his threats, both in forcing the Frick Coke Company to sell its coke to Carnegie Steel and in taking Frick's interest way from him, Walker and Frick would present the Carnegie associates with two separate suits. One suit would be to enjoin the Frick Coke Company from selling coke to Carnegie Steel, and the other would be to force a fair evaluation of Frick's interest in Carnegie Steel or to bring about a liquidation of the company's assets and a dissolution of the company.[75]

Carnegie, of course, fully intended to carry out both threats. The resolution of the board of Carnegie Steel requesting Frick to transfer his interest to the company was delivered to Frick on 12 January 1900, and in a board meeting of 24 January, a resolution formally ratifying the verbal contract between Frick and Carnegie setting the price of coke at $1.35 a ton was unanimously passed. A contract with the Frick Coke Company was then approved, making the price retroactive to 1 January 1899.[76] Frick and Walker had their answer to the question of Carnegie's plan for attack.

They lost no time in their counterattack. Meeting with Frick's attorney, D. T. Watson, whom, incidentally, Phipps had employed in 1886 to draw up the first "Iron Clad Agreement," Frick and Walker decided, at Watson's suggestion, to engage the services of John A. Johnson of Philadelphia, perhaps the most distinguished trial lawyer in America at that time. Frick said he would write Johnson that day. "No," said Walker, "telephone at once; you can't afford to take any chances." So Frick put in a call, and within two minutes Johnson was retained to represent both Frick and Phipps, for Phipps had also joined in the suit. The next morning, Carnegie, who had the same idea, hurried down to Philadelphia to try to get Johnson to represent the Carnegie Steel Company. For once in his life, Carnegie had moved a little too slowly.[77]

Frick and Phipps, within the week after the board meeting that had invoked the Iron Clad Agreement, sent formal notices of protest against the action, Frick on the grounds that the proceedings were "illegal and fraudulent" against him, and Phipps, as a major stockholder, in objection to "the right of our Company to use its capital in the purchase" of Frick's interest.[78]

These letters were followed by a joint communication from the two men on 29 January, stating that the fair values of properties of Carnegie Steel Company were not shown on its books. "We insist that the books shall be so kept that they will be an aggregation of all accounts, fairly show the present real value, as a whole and going concern. . . . We believe that said value considerably exceeds the sum of two hundred and fifty million dollars. If you dissent from this, we are willing to refer this question of value to three satisfactory and disinterested business men to be agreed upon by you and ourselves." [79]

The board of Carnegie Steel ignored this communication, and Frick not having voluntarily transferred his interest as of 31 January, the Board formally passed a resolution on 1 February transferring Frick's holdings of 6 per cent over to the company, to be held in trust by A. M. Moreland. Schwab, who had power of attorney by terms of the Iron Clad Agreement, signed the transfer for Frick.[80]

Schwab had fully expected Frick would seek an injunction preventing the transfer, but he did not.[81] Instead, Frick, working closely with Phipps and his lawyers, D. T. Watson and John A. Johnson, spent the month of February preparing Frick's brief for an equity suit in the Court of Common Pleas of Allegheny

County. The irony of the situation could hardly be missed and should have amused William Abbott and John Leishman. Here were Phipps, the instigator of the Iron Clad, and Frick, the chief employer of that Agreement, now attempting through court proceedings to prove that the Agreement had never had validity, and for this purpose they had employed the services of the same lawyer who had drawn up the Agreement in the first place and who had assured Phipps then that it was "so legally perfect that it could never be broken in court." But if some of the former partners and the public in general found the situation amusing, the principals on both sides did not.

The official legal counsels for Carnegie Steel, J. H. Reed and P. C. Knox, refused to touch the case, inasmuch as it involved a suit among partners within their company. Deprived of Johnson's services, Carnegie turned to George T. Bispham, Richard Dale, Clarence Burleigh, and the one lawyer within the company who would work on the case, Gibson D. Packer. Carnegie faced the prospects of a trial with a great deal of confidence. He felt sure that the action he had obtained through the board of rescinding the 1897 Agreement had made the Iron Clad Agreement of 1887, with the Supplementary Agreement of 1892, entirely legal and binding. Unexpected complications arose, however. It was discovered to everyone's surprise that the 1892 Agreement had never been signed by any of the partners, including Carnegie himself. Although it was a simple matter to get all of the partners except Frick, Phipps, Lovejoy, and Curry to sign the Agreement now, still, the omission of those four names brought into question the validity of the Agreement. As for the original Iron Clad Agreement, it certainly bore both Phipps's and Frick's signatures, but it applied to Carnegie Bros. & Company, Ltd., and Carnegie, Phipps & Company, both of which had gone out of legal existence with the reorganization of 1892. Nevertheless, Packer, in a long letter to Carnegie early in February, assured him that the Iron Clad Agreement would be held valid by the court. He interpreted the Agreement as a contract between each individual member of the association with the association collectively, and reorganization and consolidation of the two companies in 1892 had not abrogated those contracts. On the contrary, the board, by passing the 1892 Agreement, had reaffirmed those contracts, even

757

though individual members might not have signed the Agreement. Furthermore, "there is no better evidence of the intention of the parties to an Agreement than their own construction as evidence by their acts under the Contract. The managing officials of this Company have uniformly for years enforced this Contract according to its true intent against deceased and retiring members. The Contract does not mean one thing for the Company and another for the partner, and when the officials of the Company have by acting under it, and in various other ways, given it one construction as against outgoing members, they cannot face about, and say it means an altogether different thing as to them individually." [82] Here, of course, Packer had touched on Frick's and Phipps's most vulnerable point, the fact that both men had actively participated in the use of the Iron Clad against some fifteen partners over the preceding thirteen years.

In addition to the legal action brought by Frick and Phipps, there was also the suit of Walker and the other minority stockholders in the Frick Coke Company who submitted their individual letters of formal protest to Carnegie Steel and to Thomas Lynch, the sympathetic president of the Frick Coke Company, on 1 February 1900.[83] Carnegie had no intention of rescinding the highly favorable contract he had forced through the Frick Coke Company, but on the other hand he had no particular desire to become embroiled in a secondary suit with his old friend, John Walker, and with Lynch and the other minority stockholders in the Frick Coke Company who were not directly involved in his life and death struggle with Frick. Carnegie, therefore, tried to come to an agreement through Lynch with these minority interests by which Carnegie Steel would "release the Frick Company from delivering that amount of coke under such contract which such dissatisfied interests represent and we will obtain this portion of our supply from others. This will enable you to sell the percentage of coke to best advantage which would represent the amount such small dissatisfied interests would contribute to our supply and hand over to them the proceeds during the operation of our contract. By this means all supposed threatened injury to said small minority interests would be entirely removed." [84] Quite naturally, Lynch and the others turned down this ingenious scheme, since the dividends on their interest were based on the total profits of the coke company. They were not interested in having only the small percentage of the product based on their percentage of ownership exempt from the contract. They wanted the total production exempt from the $1.35 price. After this fruitless effort at buying off the minority interests, Carnegie ignored the Walker suit and turned all of his attention to Frick.

Like Carnegie, Frick was confident that he would win his suit in equity, which he formally filed in the Court of Common Pleas in the second week of February 1900. In Frick's suit, the profits of Carnegie Steel during the preceding several years were for the first time revealed to the public. The profits in 1899 were $21,000,000, and in 1900, $40,000,000 were expected in profits—all this for a company capitalized at only $25,000,000. On the basis of book value, Frick pointed out, his 6 per cent interest was worth only $4,900,000, but in actual value it was worth at least $15,000,000. He quoted Carnegie to the effect that the company's true value was at least $250,000,000 and he could probably sell it on the London market for $500,000,000. Frick also claimed that it was an act of larceny on Carnegie's part to force the Iron Clad Agreement on him, inasmuch as Carnegie would personally gain over $5,000,000 on the deal, since he would get over half of Frick's interest, and the difference between book value and actual value was $10,000,000. The now-famous Iron Clad Agreement of 1887, under which this transfer had been effected, Frick maintained had been inoperative and null and void since 1892. Frick in his request for "equitable relief" asked for a permanent injunction against Carnegie Steel Company Limited, enjoining the defendants from transferring his interest and from denying him the right to participate in the operations of the company. In case the defendants should refuse to comply, Frick asked the court to dissolve the company and bring about a liquidation of its affairs.[85]

In the first week of March, Carnegie personally, and Carnegie Steel Company, Limited, as co-defendants, filed a response to Frick's case in Equity. In this response, the book value of the company as of 31 December 1899 was shown to be $75,610,104.06, which was arrived at by totaling the capitalization of the company with the undivided profits of $49,350,000 and the contingent fund of $1,260,104.06. As for Frick's interest, Carnegie in response pointed out that Frick had paid only $300,000 for an interest worth nearly $5,000,000, and of that $300,000, less than half had come from his own pocket, the remainder having come from credit in dividends. The response also pointed up the number of partners (sixteen) whose interest in the company had been settled under the Iron Clad at book value, at a total amount of $6,270,288.99. Nor could Carnegie resist the personal argument in stressing "Mr. Frick's unmanageable temper" and his threat of physical attack upon Carnegie.[86]

All of this made lively reading, and the American press did not underplay the story. This was the most sensational law suit in the history of American industry. Both sides were confident of victory, and Frick and Carnegie, at least, were eager to press the suit to its bitter conclusion. Johnson had assured Frick that the Iron Clad could easily be punctured, while at the same time Carnegie wrote in high spirits to Cousin Dod, "We are not worrying much anent suit—Our four lawyers, one after the other, after study report not the slightest doubt about Iron Clad, and nothing in Frick's bill we need fear. The Minority Coke suit probably instigated by Frick file bill, but that's easy. Our reply goes in next week—absence of Hunsiker in London, Taylor and your present suit being pressed until middle April or thereabout. Judge sails May 12th for Europe. It will go over until Dec. probably. Give time for all to quiet down. The administration anxious not to have it until election over & we all are. Think Hanna will ask other side not to object to delay. . . . Lovejoy as expected goes with Frick. . . . All our managers so happy. . . . All very well indeed—very." [87]

If neither Carnegie nor Frick had any misgivings, their respective partners did. W. H. Singer reported to Carnegie that Phipps and Walker had called on him. "They stated Watson had substantially agreed with . . . Johnson that the Carnegie Steel Co. L. was not organized properly and was simply an individual partnership and could be dissolved and thrown into liquidation, &c. . . . As our charter expires April 1901 when a new organization would take place, I was in hopes the matter of publicity which is deplorable would be avoided. As their first intention was to attack the validity of the ironclad (and it may be yet) but this other attack I fear will expose the business much more. As it will be such a rich thing for the lawyers and a great gratification to our competitors and the public I dread the attack." [88] Schwab, writing the same day, presented another disturbing argument:

> Knox told me this morning that he had decided to leave for California tonight as he was satisfied that Frick could not be brought to any reasonable position. . . . The only thing Frick will say is that he thinks the property is worth 250 m. and would rather buy than sell at that figure. . . . Knox very strongly advised settlement with F on any reasonable basis. Says that if at any time we want to dispose of our reorganized stock proceeding in court to show a low valuation will injure us. Knox evidently gets this from Frick. My own impression is that Frick is much more anxious for a settlement than we are. But I can't help think that reorganization at an early date is the proper step.[89]

So the pressure on Frick and Carnegie began to build, not only from their partners and allies within the company but from friends and political associates outside as well. Colorful as the personal argument between such giants as Frick and Carnegie was, the press almost forgot the two men in their excitement over the facts revealed by the sworn statements of both sides. Even the respectably conservative *New York Times* gave great play to the profits that this tariff-protected industry had made, while the Democratic press, with the New York *World* in the vanguard, for the moment forgot the Philippines and dwelt fondly and at length upon "Mr. Carnegie's and Mr. Frick's Revelations." "Surely there is something wrong," the *World* editorialized sarcastically, "when capital must go dragging for a pitiful return of less than 200 per cent. Plainly, Mr. Frick has revealed deserving industry's great need for protection." [90] *Iron Age,* in shocked disgust, commented: "The part of the Frick-Carnegie conflict that has caused the most talk is the revealed profits of the Company. It has aroused all of the old anger against trusts. There is much free trade talk in the newspapers." In a classic understatement, it concluded, "The quarrel is bound to have an effect on the whole industry." [91]

George Westinghouse, in Washington, was alarmed. He wrote to Carnegie, "I have just seen in tonight's Chronicle that a suit is to be filed by Mr. Frick against you or the Carnegie Company to determine the value of his interest. I believe such a step will be almost a calamity by reason of the fact that the private affairs of your company will undoubtedly be made public. Can I be of any assistance to you in an attempt to adjust the matter? . . . Will you allow me to say, at the risk of being considered officious, that this matter is looked upon by mutual friends as not only very harmful to your own interests but to Pittsburgh generally. . . . I may add that Mr. Frick has recently spoke [sic] to me in such terms that I feel there must be a way to adjust matters between you and him." [92]

If industry was alarmed, the high command of the Republican party was almost desperate in its desire that this suit be brought to an end before any more facts were revealed about the operations and success of Big Business. Carnegie in his letter to Lauder had indicated that Mark Hanna wanted the trial postponed until after the election. But Hanna wanted much more than that. He wanted the whole argument settled out of court without further delay. The bitter memories of 1892 and the impact of Homestead on that presidential election were still sharp in the minds of Hanna, McKinley, Reid, and others. How ironical it would be if McKinley should lose this election to Bryan, not because of Carnegie's deliberate and purposeful attacks upon McKinley's foreign policy, but because of Carnegie's quite unintentional aid to Bryan's Populist attack upon Big Business.

By the middle of March, both Carnegie and Frick came to the same conclusion—that they were embroiled in a controversy which neither could really win. It had become simply a question of how much either was willing to lose in order to satisfy his pride. If Carnegie should win, it would be only because, by the judgment of the court, his company was worth as little as he was maintaining it was. What would become of his plans to sell out for $250,000,000 or $300,000,000 after he himself had won an argument by proving his company was worth only a fraction of that amount? On the other hand, if Frick should win, thereby forcing the dissolution of the company and the liquidation of its assets, the vultures that would swarm in to pick its carcass would quickly reduce his 6 per cent interest to such a pitiful scrap that Carnegie's present evaluation of that interest would appear generous in contrast.

Both men were foolishly proud and profoundly angry, but not to the point of madness. Therefore, the compromise solution was found. It had been there all along, of course, but at last Frick and Carnegie were ready to accept it. There would be a consolidation of the two companies with a greatly increased capitalization. Frick and all of the other partners would keep their present interests, readjusted to reflect the increased capitalization. Both the Frick and the Walker suits would be dropped, but under no circumstances would Henry Clay Frick ever again have an official position, other than as shareholder, in the company.

The two sides met on neutral ground, in that playground of American middle class society, Atlantic City, New Jersey, on 22 March 1900. One small satisfaction remained to Carnegie. He would refuse to go or allow his loyal partners to go to any meeting at which Frick was present. So Frick's interest at the meeting was represented by Francis Lovejoy and Henry Phipps. And Phipps was only too happy to play the role, no longer of maverick, but once again of mediator. The details were quickly settled: a new company was created, the Carnegie Company, under which both Carnegie Steel and the Frick Coke Company remained as separate subdivisions. The new company was capitalized at $320,000,000, organized under the laws of New Jersey, with $160,000,000 in common stock and $160,000,000 in 5 per cent, first mortgage bonds. Carnegie's interest was fixed at $174,526,000, of which $86,379,000 were in stock, $88,147,000 in bonds. Frick received for his interest $15,484,000 in stock and $15,800,000 in bonds—a rather substantial increase over the $4,900,000 offered him under the Iron Clad Agreements.[93]

And so was concluded a bitter chapter in Carnegie's life. Frick had been forced out of the company as an active participant, but he made his exit with pockets bulging. There remained for Carnegie only the pleasant task of rewarding with an increased interest in the company those "boys—the young geniuses" who had remained loyal to the end. All of them got an increase in interest, and, of course, the biggest increase went to Charlie Schwab, a whopping 2 per cent, taken out of Carnegie's own interest.[94]

The bitterness remained in spite of the "spirit of Atlantic City." For most of the participants, part of that bitterness in all honesty would have to be directed against themselves. John Walker was quite right in saying that Carnegie had not been motivated in taking the action he did out of avarice, as Frick charged, but out of principle. For the first time, Carnegie's authority had been openly challenged, and his response had been ruthless in its totality. For Frick and Phipps, on the other hand, it must be said that it was not "the principle but the money of the thing" that motivated them. Neither had had the slightest compunction about utilizing the Iron Clad Agreement until suddenly it seemed to threaten them. As for Schwab and the lesser partners, their behavior could be interpreted as being opportunistic. Although they surely felt a strong sense of loyalty to Carnegie, they must also have realized that his action against Frick was unjust. At the same time, they knew that Carnegie had the power, and all, with one exception, stayed in his camp. The one exception, of course, was Francis Lovejoy, the only man in Carnegie Steel to emerge from this imbroglio with his honor intact. He kept his honor, but very little else. His small interest in the company was not taken away from him, but, like Frick, he was forever barred from active participation in the company. Cut off from Carnegie Steel, which had been his life, he soon dissipated his fortune. Eight years later, his wife, unknown to him, wrote a pathetic letter to Carnegie asking for a loan in order to save their home.[95] Some time after that, Peacock, who was doing research for Carnegie to aid him in the preparation of his autobiography, wrote, "All agree needless to talk with Lovejoy. He seems to have gone all to pieces, physically and mentally." [96] Virtue, in the world of Big Business, had its own peculiar rewards.

As for Frick and Carnegie, they never saw each other again. Several years later Frick moved to New York, where he built his marble palace just off Fifth Avenue, some twenty blocks from Carnegie's new home. A story was told that Carnegie, who could never with any pleasure nurse hatred and bitterness, sent a note down to Frick, suggesting that since they were both growing old, perhaps they might forget the past and meet once again. The messenger who delivered the note, according to the story, brought back a curt response. "Tell Mr. Carnegie," Frick answered, "I'll meet him in Hell." [97]

CHAPTER XX

The Contract Closed

1901

Upon receiving the news from Carnegie that a settlement had been reached in his quarrel with Frick, John Morley sent his congratulations. "I cannot tell you how much I rejoice at the end of your break with Mr. Frick. I know your horror of the waste of life in lawsuits and the like, and felt sure that somehow your active mind would find a way out." [1]

After those long weeks of bitter dispute, when it must have seemed to Carnegie's frightened associates that their two former partners would destroy the very empire that they had together built, the sense of relief in having found "a way out" was indeed profound for all concerned. The settlement was a true compromise, for the men on both sides could regard it as a personal triumph, and not a defeat. Frick had not only kept his interest, but had had it augmented in value beyond all expectations. Carnegie had "gobbled up" the coke company (no problem now about coke prices), and Frick was forever banished from the managerial operations of the two companies. True, Carnegie, who had always opposed large capitalization, now found himself the majority shareholder of the largest capitalized company in the history of American manufacturing—three times the capitalization of

Standard Oil of New Jersey. But Carnegie had had his way in keeping the entire capital within the small band of associates, now only slightly increased by the addition of the minority stockholders in the Frick Coke Company. Not a share of stock had fallen into the hands of "outsiders," to be bartered and gambled on the Wall Street Exchange. In the immediate afterglow of Atlantic City, it must have seemed to all of them, from Carnegie with his $174,526,000 interest down to Emil Swenson with his $38,000 share, that the future was very bright indeed. "Isn't it wonderful we are to have such a good year," a happy Carnegie wrote to Cousin Dod.[2]

The industrial world, however, had not stood still in quiet abeyance while the Carnegie associates were absorbed in their own civil war. Carnegie and Schwab awoke shortly after Atlantic City to the realities of a new industrial order which presented as great a challenge as they had ever known before. And they had to meet this challenge without the managerial talents of Henry Clay Frick to aid them. Frick, exiled from the two companies he had done so much to build, could not resist one last communiqué to his senior partner. Some six months after the settlement he sent a cablegram to Carnegie in Scotland: [3]

> You being in control, stockholders and public look to you to see that the great Carnegie Company is managed successfully and honestly. Five year contracts for coal fifty per cent above the lowest price paid, and six per cent above prices now currently paid by smaller concern. Ruinous. Scrap unloaded on you at fancy prices, while others were selling, now being sacrificed abroad. Look into these and other matters yourself. Do not let them hide things from you. You cannot trust many by whom you are surrounded to give you facts. You need commercial rather than professional ability to cope with the concerns managed by brainy and honest men trained to the business. You are being outgeneralled all along the line, and your management of the Company has already become the subject of jest.
>
> Frick

Frick expected and got no response to this gratuitous piece of advice. Carnegie could well dismiss much of it as the embittered remarks of an ousted chairman, but there was enough truth in what Frick said, of which Carnegie was undoubtedly aware, to add to his concern for the future of the Carnegie Company. The giant *Diplodocus carnegiei* had suddenly developed an immense head of capital. If this huge capitalized beast was to be properly nourished, it would require all of the aggressive drive, imaginative innovations, and cost cutting of which the managerial leadership was capable. Profits of $20,000,000 a year, so impressive for a company capitalized at $25,000,000, were hardly adequate for the survival of a company with a capitalization twelve times that amount.

The most immediate threat to the Carnegie Company's domination of the steel industry lay in the aggressive determination of the newly organized manufacturing trusts of finished steel products to achieve verticality of organization. The American Steel and Wire Company, the American Tin Plate Company, the American Sheet Steel and the American Steel Hoop Company and the National Steel Company, all organized by the Gates-Moore syndicate, were either already engaged in producing their own steel billets or were making definite plans to do so. The National Tube Company, recently organized by J. P. Morgan, had become in a relatively short time a major producer of steel billets. There was also the Federal Steel Company, another Morgan creation, fabricated out of that old rival of Carnegie's, Illinois Steel, and several lesser companies. When it was formed in the summer of 1898, Carnegie had sneered contemptuously, "I think Federal the greatest concern the world ever saw for manufacturing stock certificates—we are not in it—but they will fail sadly in Steel." [4] But in two short years, while the Carnegie Company, incidentally, was manufacturing a great many stock certificates, Federal Steel had jumped into second place in the nation in the production of steel—1,225,000 tons in 1900. This was still less than half of the Carnegie Company's 2,970,000 ton production, but Federal Steel could no longer be dismissed as a stock jobbing outfit. [5]

There were two ways to meet the threat of these aggressive new trusts who no longer were giving Carnegie Company large orders for billets. One was to eliminate the competition by entering into pooling agreements with them. The other was to beat them at their own game by pushing verticality in the direction of the manufacture of finished products. Carnegie, always wary of

767

pooling arrangements, strongly favored the second of the two alternatives. This did not mean that he was unalterably opposed to pools under any circumstance. In 1899 the rail market was depressed, and the major producers made pooling agreements on rails and structural beams, giving Carnegie Steel 30 per cent of the market. He certainly favored that. Any arrangements on plates, however, he felt should be regarded as temporary and should be entered into reluctantly. He wrote to Schwab in the early summer of 1900, "I concur in the policy you are pursuing, trying to keep prices up as high as practicable owing to the large number of high priced orders in the books yet unfilled. But it is probable you will be met by the problem before long whether to do as we did before or to continue cooperating with others trying to keep up prices. I am inclined to think that in regard to rails you may be able to do this, although Cleveland [the Lorain Steel Co.] and perhaps others will interfere. . . . Structural steel, probably one half of all the steel made, at tolerable prices would be better than a large amount at lower prices, and it would be a pity to disturb an agreement that has worked so satisfactorily. In plates, and all other things except these, I see nothing for it but the old policy, take orders." [6] When, however, the producers of finished products stopped buying their billets from Carnegie Company, then Carnegie was ready for direct confrontation in their own arena. "I notice that the American Steel Hoop Company are taking only 3,000 tons per month from you. That should be stopped, or we should go into making their product directly." [7]

His partners varied in their attitudes toward these alternatives. Lauder and Phipps almost invariably opposed any new ventures that would take precious capital and would expand the operations of a company whose lines were already drawn out too far and too tightly. They much preferred the security of the pool, where each company had its allotted share, competition was eliminated, and risks were reduced to a minimum.

Frick, during the years in which he had served as chairman of the board, had vacillated between the two possibilities. Not as opposed to pooling arrangements as Carnegie, he had nevertheless supported Carnegie in the manufacturing of steel cars and had been aggressive in pushing armor plates. On the other hand, he had opposed pipe manufacturing when Carnegie was pushing it hard. "We should not go in unless we do it right," he told the board in April 1899. "Anyway we should not go into it this year, we have so much on hand, and are so busy." He quoted with apparent approval a letter from Phipps, who was unalterably opposed: "Let us develop what we now have . . . and no groping in the dark, such as a new venture would involve. Why then hasten; why look beyond our own business." [8]

Schwab, who was by temperament the aggressive plunger, was almost always sympathetic to Carnegie's proposals for new manufacturing ventures. It was one major reason that his star shone so brilliantly in the Carnegie Steel constellation. More than any other partner, he listened eagerly to Carnegie when the Old Man wrote, almost weekly, urging that "the concern that sells articles finished, will be able to run all weathers and make some money while others are half idle and losing money. . . . Our policy should be to make finished articles. . . ." [9]

Now that Frick had been eliminated as a somewhat conservative and restraining force, it would be expected that Carnegie and Schwab would aggressively push the manufacturing of finished articles. "I have had to take general charge of the business for next year," Carnegie wrote Morley at the time of Frick's forced resignation from the board. "Some means to be made to meet these huge Combinations which are really at our mercy. But my being at helm makes victory easier. So thought my partners, but it is only a short postponement of withdrawal. Ashamed to tell you profits these days. Prodigious." [10]

With Carnegie "at the helm," as he put it, and Schwab as the executive officer, the Carnegie Company had steam up for a new voyage of plunder. But not without some mutinous mutterings among the officers. The minutes of the Board meeting of 16 July 1900 reveal how sharply divided the board was on the question of expansion into manufacturing. The issue under discussion was whether or not the company should build a wire and nail mill at Duquesne.[11]

Lauder: This is a very dangerous time in our history, in my opinion, and I want to say distinctively [sic] and positively that I cannot vote for any more appropriations for improvements at the present time. With the present cuts in prices and the very doubtful state that the business is in I think we should defer action for a time. . . . I say 'nay' to any further expenditures.

Schwab: I do not agree with Mr. Lauder; if we had adopted the policy of holding back because we were to meet a panic, we should never have developed our business to its present state. We would have no Structural Steel Departments, no Open Hearth furnaces; we have got to move in some direction to take care of our billets, or shut down our plants. We have no outlet for our billets. The wire people have given us notice of the cancellation of their contract, also the American Steel Hoop Company. . . . I do not think there is anything left for us to do but to put our billets into the same products that others have been doing. I would like to call Mr. Lauder's attention to the fact that he opposed a great many improvements that have been advocated and I would like to know where we would be today if we had not gone ahead with our Open Hearth Furnaces and other things.

Lauder: If you make it a personal question, I have at times been on the opposite side but not exactly against the improvements themselves. I have asked for further and more serious consideration of the propositions. . . . I am not opposed to the present improvements, as improvements; I am only questioning the time; I would like to see the matter postponed for a time. . . . We have been through several panics and I, for one know the effect of them. I fear, as I have said before, that with the market we have now we may see considerable trouble financially.

Schwab: Of course this matter is an honest difference of opinion, but I do not think it is right for me to hold back in advocating improvements just because I have had no experience in panics. We must dispose of our billets.

Lauder: I do not know now but that if times improve we can dispose of our billets just as we did in the past. . . . How much business has the American Steel & Wire Co. at the present time?

Schwab: I do not think they are running to one-half of their capacity; not more than that. . . . Still that does not alter the fact that we are not disposing of our billets. . . . We certainly should have faith in our ability to not only meet our interests on Bonds, but have money besides for improvements and for progress.

770

Blackburn: I favor improvements now.

Moreland: I too favor the building of the wire and nail plant now.

Morrison: We must prepare to go into the wire business. But I do not favor the manufacturing of hoops.

Clemson: We have to go into the business. There is one thing, however, that I would not do: I would not sell Bars at 1¢ per pound for a year; I would rather have the mills idle than to do so. . . .

Gayley: I do not favor going into rods; I prefer the tube business. Why can't we do this at Duquesne?

Schwab: We can't use Duquesne for tubes—it requires a separate plant. The whole question is that we have from 35,000 to 40,000 tons of steel that has been going into such products as rods, wire, nails, hoops, etc. and our mills are constructed for supplying the same. Now we cannot sell the tonnage. Should we finish it? We are talking of a Bessemer plant and of billet mills.

Gayley: I understand the question. I presume that we will have to finish the product, but I would not favor going into rods. I would make the finished articles.

Singer: It is probably necessary, but I am not sure that it should be done immediately.

Lauder: I would like to see this matter postponed until the middle of September, till I can have an opportunity to confer with Mr. Carnegie and inform him of the actual condition of affairs existing here and I will report by cable the result of the conference.

Singer: I favor the delay.

Schwab: If we want to drop back into an old fashioned way of doing business I want to be counted out of it. We already have Mr. Carnegie's approval, by letter and by cable.

Clemson: I am opposed to delay.

Lauder: I still want to wait until I can talk with Mr. Carnegie.

Schwab: I do not see how we can defer any longer; it simply means the shutting down of Duquesne. The American Steel and Wire and the American Steel Hoop Company say that they are not going to buy billets from us. . . . To say that we are going into the business will not bring out a contract; that time has passed. I am very willing, indeed, to have my self placed on record as stating that it is decidedly wrong to defer.

Lauder: I move that we postpone the authorization of improvements contemplated until the middle of September.

Mr. Gayley seconded.

The vote: Lauder and Singer, aye: Schwab, Moreland, Gayley, Clemson, Morrison, nay. The motion lost.

Lauder: I am opposed to going ahead notwithstanding we have had the approval of Mr. Carnegie. When he returns in October or November and finds business in a bad way he won't care anything about his cablegrams but will tell us we should have known better than to have plunged ahead and contracted for large expenditures in doubtful times, or bad times. I wish these remarks put on the record.

Schwab: I would state that the question I wish to have decided by the Board now is whether or not we will appropriate $1,400,000 for the Rod, Wire and Nail plants to be built at Duquesne Steel Works in accordance with the plans we have made.

Motion made by Morrison and seconded by Gayley.

The vote: Aye: Schwab, Singer, Morrison, Moreland, Gayley, Clemson. Nay: Lauder.

There was, of course, considerable truth in Lauder's observation: Carnegie frequently had pushed some idea, only to have it go wrong, and he would then blame the board for having been so rash and precipitate as to have acted without proper consideration. This time, however, Carnegie was firmly and irrevocably committed to entering into the manufacture of finished articles. Neither the cautious "go slowly" advice of Lauder, which often had a sobering effect on his enthusiasm, nor the possibility of a postwar slump could deter him this time. All through the summer he sent impatient letters and cablegrams, urging action:

> You are face to face with the great question, the parting of the ways; the country cannot take the product of the steel works. Are we to decide that we will take the business at the best price possible and run the works full, independent of all other concerns, managing our business in our own way, or are we to take percentages of the business with these and try to maintain prices.[12]

My recent letters predict present state of affairs; urge prompt action, essential; crisis has arrived, only one policy open; start at once hoop, rod, wire, nail mills, no half way about last two. Extend coal and coke roads, announce these; also tubes. Prevent others building; not until you furnish most staple articles can you get business among them sufficient if costs are high. Never been time when more prompt action essential, indeed absolutely necessary to maintain property. It will be made poor affair if failure now when challenged; have no fear as to result, victory certain. Spend freely for finishing mills, railroads, boat lines. Continue to advise regularly by cable.[13]

Still later, Carnegie wrote:

Confirming my wire upon the situation let me say that all is coming just as expected. There is nothing surprising; a struggle is inevitable, and it is a question of the survival of the fittest. For many years we have seen that the manufacturer must sell finished articles. One who attempts to stop halfway will be crowded out. We have a great advantage over others, running non-union, but I do not believe that we shall be allowed to run non-union peaceably unless we give our men steady work; unless we run when others stop as we did for some years previous to the boom. The result of our decision to take orders and run was a great triumph and has given us the position we occupy. . . . Briefly, if I were czar, I would make no dividends upon common stock, save all surplus and spend it for a hoop and cotton tie mill, for wire and nail mills, for tube mills, for lines of boats upon the lakes. . . . You have only to rise to the occasion, but no half way measures. If you are not going to cross the stream, do not enter at all and be content to dwindle into second place. Put your trust in the policy of attending to your own business in your own way and running your mills full regardless of prices and very little trust in the efficacy of artificial arrangements with your competitors, which have the serious result of strengthening them if they strengthen you. Such is my advice.[14]

It was almost as if the Old Man were starting afresh in the early days at Braddock. And of course, his use of the subjunctive in the phrase "if I were czar" was an amusing conceit. He was czar. It was no longer a question of whether they should build the mills for finished products, but where. Here, too, Carnegie had very definite ideas, the more he considered the proposition. "If can't get site on river for tube works, should locate elsewhere. . . . Of course, we will push our own line to the coke field. The Pennsylvania Road broke its engagement with us in changing the rates and the time is upon us when we shall have to avail ourselves of every chance to save a cent per ton. . . . Conneaut Harbor might be a good place for the tube works." [15]

The more Carnegie thought of it, the more ideal Conneaut appeared to be. The land was cheap and available. It was located at the terminal point of their own railroad, and it had excellent docking facilities on Lake Erie. There were problems to be sure, as Lawrence Phipps pointed out to the board: "The objectionable feature is that workmen will have to be brought there. There is no other settlement than Conneaut, where workmen could live, and get to their work. We could not draw many men for a plant from the present town of Conneaut, and the country is not thickly settled." In Lawrence Phipps's opinion, however, the advantages outweighed the disadvantages. "On the whole, I am very favorably impressed with the whole matter. I believe the property is everything that could be desired for a manufacturing plant, and I do not think we would have any difficulty in getting proper railroad facilities at a moderate cost." [16]

It was that last feature, inexpensive railroad facilities, that made Conneaut particularly attractive to Carnegie, for Carnegie was once again engaged in combat with the Pennsylvania Railroad. For three years he had been at peace with his ancient ally and foe, since establishing a highly favorable modus operandi with Frank Thomson in 1896. The secret rebates, particularly on coke shipments, had been dutifully paid, and for perhaps the only time during his long years of dealing with the Pennsylvania Railroad, Carnegie felt that he was getting at least as good a deal on freight rates as any of his competitors.[17] Then in 1899, Thomson died, and Alexander J. Cassatt took over the presidency of the Pennsylvania.

The honeymoon with Carnegie was over, for Cassatt was quite a different man from his predecessors, George Roberts and Frank Thomson. No opportunity here for appeal to boyhood sentiment, and absolutely no sympathy for the nefarious system of rebates which was bleeding the major trunk lines of the country white. Long a foe of the practice of giving rebates, Cassatt, while vice president of the Pennsylvania, had given testimony on rebates in hearings conducted by the Commonwealth of Pennsylvania. He had been candid as no railroad official had ever been before on how railroads had been coerced into giving secret rebates to large shippers. The evidence he gave, in specific figures, substantiated the claims of small oil refining companies that the Pennsylvania had reluctantly become the tool of the Standard Oil Company. Soon after those hearings Cassatt left the railroad, and it was only after several years that he returned. But during those years he had not lost interest in striking at the rebate system. Now, as president of the company, he was in a position to take action. Realizing that it was hopeless to expect effective action from the Interstate Commerce Commission, which by 1899, through unfriendly court decisions, had been reduced to little more than a debating society, Cassatt saw that the only solution lay in joint action by the railroads. Such co-operation could only be achieved by developing a "community of interests"—a euphemism for the old pooling arrangements—that was strengthened by the creation of interlocking directorships. Cassatt got together with Vanderbilt of the New York Central, and they developed these directorships with the Baltimore & Ohio, the Chesapeake & Ohio, and the New York Central. With this kind of united front to back it up, the word went out late in the fall of 1899 that no more secret rebates would be given to any shipper on these lines. This unexpected edict, which caused a deep cut into the profits of the Frick Coke Company, undoubtedly was a major reason for the sudden rise in coke prices, which in turn helped to precipitate the Frick-Carnegie dispute.[18]

In the midst of all his other troubles, Carnegie was outraged by what he regarded as duplicity on the part of the Pennsylvania Railroad in breaking the Thompson agreement. As usual, Carnegie regarded any increase in freight rates as a personal affront to himself and a direct attack on the city of Pittsburgh. Frick, he had always felt, had been far too lenient with the Pennsylvania, and he did not have too much confidence in Schwab's ability to deal with "these people." "Schwab wrote very hopefully about PRR giving rates we asked," Carnegie wrote to Lauder, "but he does not know r r. officials. He is being 'played with' after the

old fashion. He will learn by and by that 'fight' is the cue with
r r. people." [19]

Carnegie was determined to teach Schwab. He himself took
over the railroad question as his special assignment while Schwab
was busy planning the new manufacturing plants at Duquesne
and at Conneaut. The beauty of Conneaut, of course, lay in its
lakeside location. A major manufacturing plant developed there
could bring in iron ore from the Minnesota and Michigan areas
almost entirely by water, the cheapest form of transportation. An
added advantage would be that the boxcars that now carried ore
from Conneaut to Pittsburgh on Carnegie's own railroad line, but
had to make the return trip empty, could be loaded with coke to
transport to the new plant at Conneaut at virtually no cost to the
company. The finished manufactured articles, fabricated at Conneaut, could move both east and west on competing rail lines at
favorable rates, and hopefully even by water, providing the old
Erie Canal was improved, to New York and the markets of the
world. Carnegie looked with great favor on the 4500 acres of lake
shore that lay on the Ohio-Pennsylvania border near the small
village of Conneaut.[20]

Nevertheless, there still remained the problem of railroad
service in the Pittsburgh area, where the major facilities of Carnegie Steel would always be located. Carnegie was quite prepared to
take the fight to Cassatt, as he had done with all his predecessors, to
get what he considered fair freight rates in and out of Pittsburgh.
As in the past, he turned to George McCague, with his remarkable talent for ferreting out the rates given to other major shippers. This time, however, McCague's report was not very helpful
—for the simple reason that there were no secret rebates being
given to other shippers. The railroads for the first time were actually charging their published rates.[21]

Carnegie's next line of attack was on the legal ground that
Cassatt was violating the Constitution of the Commonwealth of
Pennsylvania by owning stock in the competing line of the Baltimore & Ohio. He also talked wildly, as he had in the past, of
arousing public opinion against the railroads:

> Of course no railroad official will be permitted to sit down
> and with a stroke of his pen injure, and in many cases destroy

776

the value of all the manufacturing property of a district. No country permits this, and you may be sure ours will not. We can arouse public sentiment to the fighting pitch in three days if we have to. The Board of Trade in Britain controls the rates, and in every country in Europe railroad rates are regulated. So they will be with us unless these two reckless men are brought to their senses. I intend to have the Chamber of Commerce of Pittsburgh call a meeting of our citizens in Pittsburgh, and invite all the manufacturers and business men of Western Pa. and Eastern Ohio to attend a mass convention in Pittsburgh, which I will address. My plan is appoint a Committee to have charge of the matter, employ the highest legal training and attack the Penna Railroad for violation of the Constitution, and expose the whole matter to the people.

Imagine the people of Pittsburgh permitting two people two men, Messrs. Cassatt and Vanderbilt, to sit in an office and decree that Pittsburgh as a manufacturing centre is stricken. . . . He [Cassatt] will carry the Pittsburgh traffic at the same rate per ton per mile as the Penna Road receives upon its western traffic. I have no doubt of this. Pittsburgh has suffered long enough. . . . The deliverance of Pittsburgh is my next great work, and this time it will be thoroughly done once for all, if I live.[22]

These old threats were a bit threadbare now. Too much had been revealed publicly about Carnegie Steel's profits during the Frick suit to expect the people to mount the barricades for "fair" freight rates for Carnegie. It was necessary to use more sophisticated and rational arguments to have any effect on Cassatt, and in a long memo of 7 December 1900, Carnegie tried to do just that. He pointed out that it was much more economical for the railroads to ship steel than it was to ship grain—"perhaps as much as 10%"—inasmuch as steel rails and billets could not be damaged in transit, could be shipped in any kind of car, including open gondola, and did not require expeditious handling as did grain.[23] He also appealed to Cassatt's sense of reason by pointing out that he was destroying his best customers, who were located in the Pittsburgh region. "It is not possible that a broad able man like yourself can long sit and see new manufactories building in rival districts while no new concern would think of locating on your line. . . . My dear sir, I think I know you well enough to rely upon your awakening very soon and announcing to all those Rail-roads that there is nothing they could do for their manufactors [sic] that the Pennsylvania will not do for hers. I shall take my chances upon that. You have returned to harness after years of recreation and rushed into a policy which, being unsound, as I believe, you will soon abandon. I am looking forward with great interest to the new rates which you are to make early next week. No half way business will do any good." [24]

For a brief moment Carnegie believed that he had succeeded in persuading Cassatt to restore the old favorable rates. "Cassatt is going to reduce rates heavily but owing to prosperous conditions reductions just now may not be as great as intended," he wrote Lauder, "but with dull times we shall get more concessions." [25] He was even more optimistic when he wrote Schwab a few days later, after having consulted with Cassatt. "I had a very satisfactory interview with Mr. Cassatt today upon his invitation. Mr. Cassatt told me, as at our first interview, that we have only to show that Pittsburgh manufacturers were not getting the same rates on steel as other manufacturers were in other districts, to have him protect them. He stated that the extreme low rates shown to prevail would soon be advanced, he thought, but if not, he would meet them whenever necessary. . . . Mr. Cassatt talks just right, what he declares he would do is exactly what I would do in his place, namely protect his home concerns by giving them any rates that their competitors had." [26]

Carnegie's optimism was short-lived. Apparently he had mis-understood or had been misinformed by McCague on what the new rates would be. He had thought the rates to New York would be 4.8 mills per ton per mile. "I now find," he wrote Cassatt three days later, "that you propose to charge 6 mils per ton to New York, not 4.8 mils . . . and 6⁸⁄₁₀ cents [sic] per ton per mile to Phila and Baltimore. This is disappointing indeed. . . . I need all my philosophy every time I remember that we ship our products over your lines to Chicago, and you assess us 6 mils per ton per mile, but whenever we get out of your grasp, railroads are delighted to take the same freight at just half what you extort. How you can see this to be politic, not to speak of its fairness, I cannot conceive . . . 6⁸⁄₁₀ mils per ton per mile on steel today for long distances is a rate that nobody but the Pittsburgh combination would seek to exact." [27]

Carnegie's papers reveal, however, that all during this period of negotiation with Cassatt he was not putting as much faith in the reasonableness and good will of the Pennsylvania Railroad as he indicated to his partners or tried to make Cassatt believe. Long before he wrote this last letter, expressing his complete disillusionment with the Pennsylvania and giving up any hope that Cassatt would "play fair" with Pittsburgh, Carnegie was already deeply involved in several schemes that would free Pittsburgh and the Carnegie Company from the encumbering embrace of Mr. Cassatt's railroad line. These were intricate and involved schemes indeed, and they reached both east and west. Carnegie already had his own line north to Conneaut and the Great Lakes, but he was eager to reach New York, Philadelphia, and Baltimore by a more direct route than the Lakes and the Erie Canal. So through Judge Reed, his able director of the P.B. & L.E. Railroad, he made contact with a small but strategically located line, the Western Maryland Railroad Company, which could be tied up with the P.B. & L.E. and which could take the products of Carnegie's mills directly into Baltimore.[28] Another possibility was the Buffalo, Rochester & Pittsburgh Railway Company. It connected with Carnegie's line at Butler, Pennsylvania, and also connected with the Reading Railroad, which had direct access into New York and Philadelphia.[29] Both of these lines, although they would need considerable work on roadbeds to carry the heavy freight Carnegie projected, were available for purchase at no great cost. Like a frustrated Peter the Great, searching desperately for his "window on the sea," Carnegie was looking at all possibilities.

The most exciting possibility lay to the west. Many years before, Carnegie had had dealings with that freebooter in railroad building and railroad wrecking, Jay Gould. Carnegie had not at that time entered into an alliance with Gould, but now Gould's son, George, who was no less ambitious than his father, if more circumspect, had a grandiose dream. He wanted to put together the first truly transcontinental railroad line, extending from Baltimore on the East Coast through Maryland and West Virginia to

779

Pittsburgh and from there to St. Louis and the gateway of the West. It was Gould who got control of the Western Maryland, and at that point the Carnegie Company signed a contract with him, promising one-fourth of its tonnage to Gould as soon as the terminus in Pittsburgh should be completed.[30] Undoubtedly even larger contracts were in the offing, once the way to the West was cleared.

These were busy and exciting times. Carnegie had not felt so involved in the affairs of his company since the time Frick had taken over the management of the company in 1889. It was as if Carnegie were beginning his business career, not bringing it to a close. Schwab and the other junior partners were caught up in the same excitement of these new ventures into railroading and manufacturing. Only Lauder and Henry Phipps, among the partners, were dismayed by Carnegie's new creative burst of energy. All that Lauder and Phipps wanted was to get out with their fortunes in their pockets and not invested in new railroad lines and Conneaut manufacturing plants.

There was another man who was watching these developments with a highly critical eye. This was J. P. Morgan, the king of American high finance, who, like Carnegie, was entering into his most creative period in his mid-sixties. Morgan, like Rockefeller, was an orderly, systematic man. He felt that the American economy should ideally be like a company organizational chart, with each part in its proper place, and the lines of authority clearly designated. He did not really believe in the free enterprise system, and, like the most ardent socialist, he hated the waste, duplication, and clutter of unrestricted competition. Basically, the only difference between men like Rockefeller and Morgan on the one side and the socialists on the other was over the not insignificant issue of who was to control this co-ordinated economic system, the state or an oligopoly. While the vast majority of Americans of all classes were contemptuous of Marxist socialism and loudly professed their belief in the "American system" of free enterprise and unrestricted competition, a few men like Morgan, with an efficiency and power that the socialists could never achieve in America, went about in their quiet way, building combines and trusts and interlocking directorates that would forever eliminate that wasteful competitive system.

By 1901, Morgan could look upon his colleagues' work with considerable satisfaction: railroad combines and agreements, steel trusts and oil trusts, and interlocking directorships within the world of finance that controlled the credit and currency of the nation. In these last few years, Morgan himself had been particularly interested in steel. He had looked with favor on the results, if not on all of the actual promoters, of the trusts in steel products—the various "American companies" in hoops and wire and nails, built by the Moore brothers. And, of course, he took particular pride in his own creations: Federal Steel and the National Tube Company.

Now all of this beautiful construction, both in steel and in railroads, was being threatened by the range-riding, fence-cutting tactics of this man Carnegie, who had long been notorious in the trade for entering into and dropping out of pooling agreements whenever it suited his convenience. It was men like Carnegie, the fierce, undercutting competitors, who played havoc with the orderly world of Rockefeller and Morgan. These competitors pushed their way in, like unwanted children in the nursery, smashing down the neat pyramids of blocks that had been so precisely and delicately balanced. Rockefeller had taken care of such unruly characters in the oil industry with dispatch and finality. Morgan had also, with ease, taken care of Carnegie back in 1885, when the steelmaker had attempted to ally himself with the New York Central to build a line from Pittsburgh to Philadelphia in direct competition with the Pennsylvania Railroad.

But the Carnegie of 1900 was not the Carnegie of 1885. He now had behind him the vast ore resources of the northern iron ranges, and he had controlling interest of the largest capitalized manufacturing company in America. His annual production of steel was 85 per cent of the combined production of all of the Moore and Morgan trusts, and he had twice the number of coke ovens and double the coke production of all these same companies combined.[31] Now he was threatening once again to ally himself with the notorious Gould syndicate in the railroad field and build totally unnecessary and destructively competitive lines to the East and West, simply to protect his own interests. The most insulting challenge of all was his threat to build a magnificent new tube plant on the shores of Lake Erie, a plant which would not only compete with but could also destroy Morgan's favorite child, the National Tube Company. Morgan, who heard most of the important stories in the industrial world, did not miss the one about Carnegie asking Schwab, "How much cheaper, Charlie, can you make tubes than the National Company?" And when Schwab had answered that he could save at least $10 a ton, Carnegie had ordered, "Go on and build the plant." Not only would this be a far more efficient plant in cost of production, but it promised to turn out a radically different type of tube, a seamless tube which the Shelly Steel Tube Company had recently developed and which the Carnegie interests were prepared to take over.[32] In short, Carnegie could not now be dismissed so peremptorily by Morgan as he had been in that famous meeting on board the *Corsair* fifteen years before—the meeting to which it had not even been necessary to invite Carnegie.

What would Carnegie's price be to stay out of the manufacture of tubes? Morgan decided to find out. Late in October, he sent word to Schwab that he would like to see him, but the canny Schwab declined the invitation. A week later Schwab reported to the board: "I did not comply for several reasons. I thought it was about railroad matters, but I did meet Mr. Steele, who is his chief assistant, and was informed it was in reference to tubes; that the Morgan people had financed and put through this new tube combination, and were much alarmed about our going into tubes. I think when Mr. Carnegie comes out here next week and we have definitely decided as to site, we should make a definite announcement of our intentions." [33]

If Morgan intended at this time to restrict his negotiations with the Carnegie Company to the question of tube manufacturing, his associates in his many different enterprises would soon disabuse him of that intention. The most concerned people were the railroad directors, who knew Carnegie was not bluffing in his threats to break the Pennsylvania's and B. & O.'s monopolistic community of interests in western Pennsylvania. Carnegie's old friend, Wayne McVeagh, now chief legal counsel to the Pennsylvania Railroad, made heroic efforts to serve as peacemaker between Carnegie and Cassatt. "Now I cannot reconcile myself to the idea that two such men should differ about a plain proposition," McVeagh wrote Carnegie. "You wish all you can properly get for your Co., Cassatt wishes all he can properly get for his Co., then there must be a common meeting point of these two interests, and you two men can find it if you desire to find it." [34] Scurrying between Philadelphia and New York on numerous peace missions, McVeagh failed to find that common point. He begged Carnegie not to demand the reopening of the railroad differential rate question between long and short hauls which Judge Thomas Cooley and his arbitration board had supposedly settled once and for all back in the 1880's, and he tried to get Carnegie to see Cassatt's point of view on rebates.

> You fail to give proper weight to the fact that the rebates you were getting were not only unlawful but if he had continued them after he knew all about them, he would have been committing a criminal offense while you in taking them ran no risk whatever of that kind. Of course you may reply that your steel rail pool is equally unlawful & yet it is maintained; but in maintaining it you are not committing a criminal offense; and that is a serious difference. If maintaining that pool put you in danger of the criminal bar, I don't believe you would take that risk. . . . Don't suppose I don't appreciate your side of the case. I am perfectly sure you believe Pittsburgh as well as yourself badly treated. All I can say is that it is preposterous to assert that two such men as you and Mr. Cassatt both desiring to reach a basis productive of a fair proposition of advantage to both parties cannot do so. *I know you can.*[35]

McVeagh's appeals had no effect. It is doubtful whether Carnegie really wanted another settlement with his old antagonist, the Pennsylvania Railroad. He was caught up in the excitement of railroad building and would not retreat. After all, he had vowed he would free Pittsburgh once and for all from the Pennsylvania monopoly, and what a perfect conclusion to his business career it would be for him, who had begun as a telegrapher for the Pennsylvania, to end it by being the organizer of a whole new railroad system.

The calls on Morgan became more frequent, from the railroad men and from steel men, and their cries were as one: "Carnegie must be stopped." Morgan, who never gave press interviews and seldom said much even in private conferences, sat in his inner sanctum at 23 Wall Street, listening to these anguished cries, and then he uttered one of his rare and succinct oracular statements, "Carnegie is going to demoralize railroads just as he demoralized steel." [36] His associates knew precisely what Morgan meant by "demoralize." Carnegie was to Morgan what the Anabaptist had been to Calvin, the fanatical enthusiast who in an excess of fervor would destroy God's and Calvin's orderly plans for the universe. Clearly, Morgan now intended to stop Carnegie, but he could not banish him, as Calvin had so effectively dispatched the Anabaptists from his theocratic state. There was only one solution—buy Carnegie out.

How Morgan arrived at this answer has always been clouded by mystery and legend. To what degree was Morgan influenced by Carnegie's frightened rivals, and to what degree was he led, by his impressive nose, by Carnegie's own associates, particularly Schwab? Probably both groups were influential. Certainly Schwab was ready and eager to play his part in the delicate negotiations. On 12 December 1900, a famous dinner was given at the University Club in Manhattan by J. Edward Simmons and Charles Stewart Smith, two New York financiers who had recently visited Pittsburgh. They had been entertained there by Schwab, and were now returning the favor by giving a dinner in his honor. Who did the real planning and staging of this affair is hard to say. If Schwab had not himself done the arranging, clearly he understood the purpose. For he was to speak that night, and Morgan was to be seated at his right hand.

It was a magnificent speech. Schwab was never in better form, and in less than a half hour he laid out the blueprint for the development of a new organization within the steel industry. It was precisely the kind of plan that Morgan would heartily approve— a colossal organization of specialized plants, a super-trust of true verticality, made up of many parts. Each part would make, under the most rational and efficient methods possible, its particular contribution to the over-all objectives of the organization, which were simply to produce the world's best steel and steel products —not at inflated monopolistic prices, but at prices so low as to bankrupt any existing company or combination of companies producing steel at that time. No wasteful competition, no unnecessary duplication among individual plants, no faulty planning in plant location, no inadequate transportation facilities. Morgan sat there, imperturbable as always, but obviously fascinated by Schwab's vision, for the cigar he held in hand remained unlighted throughout the speech. Schwab had been speaking to only one man in that assembled group of eighty influential leaders of American industry and finance, and he knew he had been a success when Morgan took him aside after the dinner, asked him several questions, and indicated that he would welcome a longer session in the immediate future.

That session occurred in early January, in Morgan's home at 219 Madison Avenue. Present besides Morgan and Schwab were Morgan's partner, the suave, sophisticated New Englander, Robert Bacon, and the rough, but equally sophisticated—in quite a different manner—Wall Street manipulator, "Bet a Million" Gates. The session lasted all night, and what the four men talked about involved more millions than even Gates could easily imagine. There, in that mahogany-paneled library, its walls covered with priceless paintings and worthless framed mementos of trips abroad, the United States Steel Corporation was conceived.

Dawn comes late in January, but the sky was a gray light when Schwab stepped out onto 36th Street, to ponder, as he rode in a cab back to his hotel, the one question asked by Morgan for which he had no easy answer: "Would Carnegie sell?" Schwab simply did not know.

How much did Carnegie know of this planning? Of course he knew of the dinner, had been delighted that "Charlie" was to be so honored, and had even made a brief appearance at the dinner before hurrying off to another engagement.[37] He knew nothing, however, of the secret meeting in Morgan's home. Schwab had gone to this meeting in considerable trepidation, because he had not consulted Carnegie first. While Carnegie slumbered soundly in his bed that night, for all he knew Schwab was back in Pittsburgh, working on plans for Conneaut, not just fifteen blocks away, sketching diagrams for Morgan.

The great banking and brokerage houses that line Wall Street are built like massive fortresses of stone and concrete, but they might as well be built of glass for the amount of privacy they provide. This most notorious street in all America is seismographically sensitive to any rumor. A whispered secret is quickly registered and then transmitted up and down that narrow street with a speed that outruns the fastest messenger boys.

It was not many hours after a tired but exhilarated Schwab checked into his hotel in the early morning that Wall Street was quivering with excitement. Of course the rumors soon reached Carnegie's ears. Horace White, his journalistic ally in the anti-imperialism fight, wrote on 14 January that he had just read in the New York *Tribune* "about J. P. Morgan & yourself—it reads like a 'cock & bull story.' I wish you would send me word this morning at my office whether you are to be diverted, in any way, from your present business plans, either by purchase or otherwise. I hope you are not. You can put this in words which will not convey any information to others, and I shall not quote you in any case without your authorization." [38]

Carnegie was certainly not ready to reveal how much credence he was giving to these stories or what his true reactions were, not even to his most trusted intimate, Cousin Dod. He wrote to Lauder a few days later, "There is no substance in the reports anent great combination—some talkee, talkee. I don't think any of us would be willing to trust our 160 M Bonds in any management but our own. These could easily be made ducks and drakes of. In our hands they can be made A-1 and the stock behind them—a couple of years will do this as I see it. . . . Judge Reed here talking with P.R. people. Gould with Wabash system coming to Pittsburgh giving us a new line to Detroit, Chicago & N. West—St. Louis and Kansas City and beyond. It is great. I suggested it to him and he came up to see me with his chief men and it is now closed. We get traffic contract at as low rates as prevail *in any* district of U.S. It seems almost too good to be true and I am not without fear that allied PR interests here and Morgan may frighten him from going to work. We shall see. If he does come to Pittsburgh, the Eastern Line is next step—but that's another story." [39]

Carnegie did not sound like a man eager for retirement. Nor did Schwab's letter to him, written that same day, indicate that any drastic changes were being considered: "I really believe that for the next 10 years the Carnegie Company will show greater earnings than all the others together. A poor plant makes a relatively better showing in prosperous years. Then we will advance rapidly. Others will not. I shall not feel satisfied until we are producing 500,000 tons per month and finishing same. And we'll do it within five years. Look at our ore and coke as compared with the others. If you continue to give me the support you have in the past we'll make a greater industry than we ever dreamed of. Am anxious to get at Conneaut. Are finishing plans rapidly & will be ready for a stand in the spring. Hope to see you next week." [40] A strange letter to come from a president who was planning to sell his company.

Schwab could not delay obtaining the answer to Morgan's question much longer, however. The pressure was increasing on Morgan, who in turn was putting the screws on Schwab. Schwab did come to New York to see Carnegie the next week, but on quite a different mission than to talk about Conneaut. And, first, he went to see Louise Carnegie privately. He told her the whole story—of his secret parleys with Morgan, of Morgan's interest in buying the Carnegie Company, and of his own concern about how best to broach the subject to Carnegie. Louise Carnegie was the sympathetic listener Schwab wanted. She was more than eager to extricate her husband from pressing business affairs, and to have him turn to the great business of philanthropy which he had talked so much about and which was her chief interest in money matters.

Louise Carnegie was at this moment weighed down with a thousand details of her own. The Carnegies were building a new home, forty blocks north of the home on 51st Street that Carnegie had given her as a wedding present. How fine it would be if they could move out of the old house and out of the old world of business at the same time! She assured Schwab that she was his strong ally in pushing the proposal with her husband. She suggested that Schwab go the next morning with her husband to the St. Andrews Golf Club in Westchester County, for Andrew was always in his best mood immediately after a golf game, particularly if he had won. Carnegie had taken the game up only two years before, at the age of sixty-three, and was already a fanatic on the subject. "Dr. Golf," he called it, and he insisted that it was the best physical therapy in the world. [41] Schwab proceeded to make the arrangements.

Carnegie won rather handily over Schwab the next morning, much to his delight and surprise. The two men then retired to

Carnegie's own small stone cottage at the edge of the links. There, over lunch, Schwab, rather shamefacedly, told Carnegie the sequence of events from the University Club dinner on 12 December to the present moment when Morgan, check in hand, was standing in the wings, waiting for his cue to enter.

Carnegie did not interrupt Schwab, nor did he have much to say when the recital was over. He said he would have to think it over. He asked Schwab to call on him the next morning, and in the meantime, he asked his junior partner to consider, as he himself would, what would be a fair price to ask in case they decided to sell.

It was not an easy night for Carnegie, for he was pulled strongly in both directions. There were the new railroads, the plant at Conneaut, and the unquestionable promise that within ten years at most—probably within five years—as much of the world of steel as he wanted would be his. He stood where few men have, on the edge of total triumph in his field of endeavor, and he was being asked to step aside voluntarily before that triumph was complete.

On the other hand, he was sixty-five. There might not be left to him five years in which to complete his work, and then no time to take up that other work which truly interested him, the business not of getting, but of giving. There were the desires of Louise, not strongly stated but strongly felt, to consider. There was also his pride in knowing that he had hurt and frightened the mighty Morgan, who now sought peace terms by asking Carnegie to name his price. This situation would do much to offset the shame of the Frick-Moore affair. The more he thought of the whole proposition, the more he realized he could do nothing else but accept Morgan's offer, providing Morgan would accept his price at his terms.

When Schwab called the next morning, Carnegie scribbled, with his usual blunt lead pencil, a few figures on a scrap of ordinary paper. He handed the paper to Schwab and told him to take it to Morgan and see if he would accept it.

The figures on the paper were big, but not elaborate in detail:

Capitalization of Carnegie Company:
$160,000,000 bonds to be exchanged
   at par for bonds in new company $160,000,000

$160,000,000 stock to be exchanged
at rate of $1000 share of stock
in Carnegie Company exchanged
for $1,500 share of stock in new
company $240,000,000

Profit of past year and estimated
profit for coming year $80,000,000

Total price for Carnegie Company and
all its holdings $480,000,000

Carnegie had only one other stipulation. For his own personal holdings in the company and those of George Lauder and of his sister-in-law, Lucy Carnegie, only first mortgage, 5 per cent gold bonds would be accepted. Carnegie had no intention of becoming the major shareholder in the new corporation. Moreover, he wished to have his payment in easily negotiable bonds, inasmuch as he intended to transfer most of this wealth to institutions and organizations, as yet undetermined, unnamed, and, for the most part, as yet not in existence.

Schwab took the paper down to Wall Street. Morgan took one look at the simple statement, which even a child could have read and understood, and said simply, "I accept this price." [42] That was that—the biggest sale in American industrial history consummated with all the formality of an errand boy's taking a shopping list to the corner grocery store.

A few days later, Morgan decided he would at least like to see Carnegie and shake his hand on the deal. He phoned Carnegie and asked if he would come down to his office at 23 Wall Street. Carnegie, with memories of the *Corsair* incident, when he had had to stand on the sidelines while the great Morgan decided his fate, replied that, as he figured it, it was about as close from 23 Wall Street to 5 West 51st Street as it was from 5 West 51st Street to 23 Wall Street. Morgan got the point. He promptly drove up to Carnegie's home. The two men met alone for precisely fifteen minutes. Then Morgan, standing in the door, shook Carnegie's hand and said, "Mr. Carnegie, I want to congratulate you on being the richest man in the world!" [43] This probably was not true, but certainly no other man in the world had a fortune as large in liquid assets that could be immediately converted into cash.

On 4 February, the board of managers of Carnegie Company, having been told of the informal agreement by a letter Carnegie had sent them two days before, answered, "Whatever pecuniary benefits we may derive from a new organization such as outlined, our first and most natural feeling is the keen regret to all of us in the severance of our business relations with you, to whom we owe so much. Your sound judgment and profound business sagacity have been the foundation stones on which has been built the fabric of our success. . . . With such feeling, knowing you to be sincere in your desire to spend the remainder of your days in those acts of generosity which have endeared you to the world, we reluctantly acquiesce in your decision to retire, and are willing that you should receive bonds of the new Company in payment for your stock in the Carnegie Company, we taking stock of the new company in exchange for our stock in the Carnegie Company." [44]

At the same time Carnegie wrote to his two closest friends. To Lauder he wrote in an exultant mood, "Morgan has taken option of our Stock. Yours, Lucy's & mine payable in 5% Bonds at par —our stock at *1500* per share. . . . I didn't expect our stock to be par for years—that we can get 50% more is 'no bad.' . . . Well, I thought they wanted C Co. pretty bad & stood there. We sold option to Moore at 1000$ per stock Par & it didn't go—We sell now to Morgan at $1500 for stock & it will go barring accident. He is confident and Steel Stocks are booming today." [45] With equal satisfaction he wrote to Morley: "Have been busy, very, ere this reaches you I may have accomplished my purpose to retire which was frustrated. Morgan, the chief banker, has taken it up & I believe will succeed. He has never failed yet. The price is 16 million stg. [£] higher than before & in 5% Bonds instead of cash which makes 15% better. I'll have *at least* 50 millions stg. all in 5% gold bonds & safe as any—and then. Ah then, well, I'll tackle it. You'll see—I could as well had 100 millions stg. in a few years, but no sir. I'm not going to grow old piling up, but in distributing." [46]

To which Morley replied, "Well, you are the industrial Napoleon—and no mistake. I am rejoiced that you are trying to draw out of active trade, but I should rejoice far more confidently, and heartily if you had ½ of 1 million, instead of 40 or

50. Still you make the best of the burden, and nobody who knows you will doubt that you will do your best to diffuse happiness & to spread light." [47] A somewhat mixed and deflating compliment, typical of Morley, but one that Carnegie would more fully appreciate as he began what would prove to be the difficult task of diffusing happiness and spreading light.

There was one senior partner whose joy and relief at the news was unmixed with either regret or a sense of new burdens to be taken up. For the first time in his life, Henry Phipps felt himself truly free. He was sick in bed with a serious bout of bronchitis when he was brought news of the sale, which Carnegie had asked Dr. Jaspar Garmany, physician to both men, to convey to him. As Garmany later remembered the incident, it was early evening when he called on Phipps. After tending to Phipps's physical condition, Garmany said that Mr. Carnegie wanted him to tell Mr. Phipps that he had just closed the deal with Morgan. It was all arranged on their terms. Phipps, who had so often despaired of ever hearing words such as these, remained silent for several moments staring up at the ceiling. Then he turned to Garmany, and with a voice choked with emotion, he cried, "Ain't Andy wonderful!" [48] The voyage had ended after all. The booty was safely delivered, magnified beyond his most avaricious dreams. No more daring adventures, no more raids, no more nightmares of having to walk the plank. Once Phipps had said to John Walker, who made fun of his penny-pinching ways, "John, I wish the time would come when I could get away from the feeling that a penny is a penny." [49] Phipps being Phipps, he would never know such a moment, but at least now all of his pennies, four and one-third billion of them, were safe. The former bookkeeper of Dilsworth and Bidwell slept soundly that night.

There still remained many details to be worked out with many different companies and men before the deal was finally consummated and the new United States Steel Corporation was a reality. During this time Carnegie alternated between being fearful that Morgan would not be able to create so vast a super-corporation and being fearful that he would. At one point, Carnegie, who still had not signed a formal contract, called Schwab in and said he wanted out of the whole deal. They would go ahead with their own plans and forget Morgan. Both Carnegie and Schwab knew, of course, that it was much too late for that kind of retreat. Morgan decided to take no chances, however, and quickly sent his chief counsel, Francis Lynde Stetson, to Carnegie's home to get a formal signed agreement to sell. By the terms of this letter, dated 26 February 1901, Carnegie agreed to sell to the newly formed United States Steel Corporation, consisting of the Carnegie Company, the National Steel Company, the American Steel & Wire Company, and the American Tin Plate Company, his interest in the Carnegie Company. For his interest of 5 per cent bonds, with a par value of $86,145,000, and capital stock, par value of $92,-996,000, he would accept in payment bonds for $225,639,000 par value of the United States Steel Corporation, "to be secured by a mortgage upon all of its property now held or hereafter required." [50]

With the signing of this formal contract, the deal was closed. Carnegie wrote to Lauder,

> I wired you Sunday eve, "Closed." . . . Morgan has succeeded as I felt he would. Now we are all right. Of course he has to issue notice & get ⅔rds of each stock in & then it is a go. The other will come of course—all the stock will come in. This is evident from the market. You are right—we did well in getting Securities—Mtge on everything—now & all they take hereafter. We are all right. . . .
>
> I feel better get Louise away from this new house—architects &c too troublesome especially on Furniture & Decorations. Have tried Kaiseren Theresa Mch 16 for Genoa intending going to Antibes &c & then to Aix & getting six weeks holiday for her free from House & Housekeeping.[51]

On 2 March 1901, the circular describing the organization and capitalization of the United States Steel Corporation, the world's first billion-dollar corporation, capitalized at $1,100,000,000, was sent out and formally filed. Carnegie wrote to Lauder that their and Lucy's bonds would be delivered within two weeks to the Hudson Trust Company, Hoboken, New Jersey, in trust to Robert A. Franks, Carnegie's business secretary.[52] There a special vault of impressive size was built to house the physical bulk of nearly $300,000,000 worth of bonds. Carnegie never wanted to see or touch one of these bonds that represented the fruition of his business career. It was as if he feared that if he looked upon them they might vanish, like the gossamer gold of the leprechaun. Let them lie, safe in a vault in New Jersey, safe from New York tax assessors, until he was ready to dispose of them.

"All seems right about Steel matter—no hitch—" he wrote Lauder, "so be it." [53]

The contract was closed.

PART III

THE
DEED
1899-1919

"The man who dies thus rich, dies disgraced."
Andrew Carnegie, "Wealth," *North American Review*, June 1889

*

"Gratitude and sweet words"
Label on one drawer of Carnegie's desk.

*

"Open no letter except such as your Secretary
lays before you as from your family."
Carnegie's advice to Mrs. Russell Sage on how to be a philanthropist,
26 February 1910.

*

"Pity the poor millionaire, for the way of the philanthropist is hard."
Letter to the Editor of *The Independent*, 26 July 1913.

*

"My chief happiness as I write these lines lies in the thot that even
after I pass away the welth that came to me to
administer as a sacred trust for the good of my fellow men
is to continue to benefit humanity for generations untold."

Carnegie's letter to the Trustees of Carnegie Corporation of New York,
10 November 1911.

CHAPTER XXI

The Gospel of Wealth
1889-1901

On 16 March 1901, Andrew Carnegie, with his family, sailed from New York for the Mediterranean aboard the *Kaiseren Theresa.* This early spring departure was a familiar enough routine for all of them—for Andrew, Louise, Louise's sister, Stella, and even for four-year-old Margaret, affectionately called "Baba" by her adoring parents. But this time it was different. Carnegie had a sense that he was sailing away from a familiar world that he would never really know again. There was the same finality about this voyage as there had been when, as a small, tow-headed boy, fifty-three years before, he had reluctantly boarded the *Wiscasset* to cross the Atlantic in the opposite direction. There were now the same mixed feelings of tears for what had to be given up and excitement for what lay ahead. Some time later, he would jot down a few brief phrases on a scratch pad, perhaps for a speech never delivered, or for a farewell statement to the press never written, that revealed some of this pain of departure: "Trial bitter— father bereft of his sons—abandoned & alone—no more whirl of affairs, the new developments in—occupation gone. Advise no man quit business—plenty retire upon nothing to return to— misery. Reading Scotch Am selections—the gods send thread for a web begun." [1]

It was a new century, and he was sailing into a new world. The familiar landmarks which had bounded his old world, and had given him the same sense of security that the bells in the Abbey of Dunfermline had given him as a child, were gone. One of his last public appearances before leaving New York had been to deliver a memorial address at the St. Andrew's Society on the occasion of Queen Victoria's death. He, the son of Dunfermline Radicals, the eager crusader for a republican Britain—imagine him weeping in public eulogy for a Hanoverian monarch! But Victoria had been the nineteenth century. It was appropriate that the monarch and the century should depart together and that even a republican should weep for the one because she had been the enduring symbol of the other. Within six months, President McKinley, America's political symbol of the nineteenth century, would also be dead, and with that "wild man Roosevelt" in the White House, the United States too would explode into the twentieth century.

Most immediate to Carnegie's sense of a shattered world was the death of the Carnegie Company, Limited—limited not just in precise, corporate, legal sense, but limited in ownership and management. The small band of Carnegie associates, who had directed this great empire under the watchful paternalism of the Old Man himself, had been replaced by a vast super-corporation, owned by thousands of stock investors and managed by salaried specialists, by bureaucrats sitting in committees, and by an intricate web of interlaced financial interests that no one would ever understand or untangle. Small wonder that the press of both England and America, either in condemnation or in praise, should view the formation of the United States Steel Corporation as the harbinger of a totally new world for a new century. "It is a revolution so radical in its sweep, so wide in area affected," wrote John Brisben Walker, the publisher of *Cosmopolitan* magazine, "that in comparison the most important movements of history become insignificant. . . . Governmental divisions will cease to exist except as means to carry out mandates decided upon in the executive offices of the world's commercial metropolis." [2] If more soberminded readers regarded this effusive hyperbole as the usual popular journalistic license, Carnegie, for one, did not. For him the transformation had been so radical and so complete that no commentary upon it could be too exaggerated to be believable. The organization that he had built and maintained and defended against all opponents both within and without was now quite as extinct as the *Diplodocus carnegiei.* The new breed of industrialists, like small boys visiting Carnegie's favorite fossil exhibit in the Pittsburgh Institute, would in the years ahead only marvel that it had been able to move at all.

The final epilogue of bitterness for Carnegie in this revolutionary change was the behavior of his associates, those "young geniuses" who he had once said were worth more to him than all the plants and railroads and mines put together. Pittsburgh would never forget that spring of 1901, when far more than pennies seemed to rain down from the heavens on the Carnegie partners. Even those with only two-ninths of 1 per cent interest in the Carnegie Company now found themselves millionaries. Long denied any large share of the rich annual profits, which Carnegie had made them put back into the company, they now enjoyed their sudden wealth, if not wisely, exceedingly well. The papers of Pittsburgh were filled with stories of lavish parties and wild spending which Carnegie heard with grim-faced, Calvinistic disapproval. He wrote in despair to Oswald Villard, who had run an editorial in the New York *Evening Post* about the extravagances of these *nouveaux riches* of Pittsburgh: "These young men were models as long as they knew they had to be—besides they had my example & they were poor. Altho making large sums, these went to their credit paying for their interests. Now they see stock gamblers prominent in the Company & behind it. They become demoralized. . . . It is too sad for me to see such ruination morally. You will see I cannot speak of it publicly. My influence is best exerted privately upon the others. I am not in the proper position to play critic of my former associates publicly." [3]

The cruelest blow of all was Schwab's fall from grace. At Morgan's insistence and to Carnegie's delight, Schwab had been elected the first president of the United States Steel Corporation. As president, Schwab had to associate once again with Frick, who had been made a member of the board of directors for his services in getting possession of the Rockefeller iron mining interests for United States Steel. Schwab had apologized profusely to Carnegie for having agreed to work with Frick, but Carnegie was not upset by the arrangement.[4] With Charlie at the head of United States Steel, Carnegie felt confident that his bonds would be safe, and Schwab could work with the devil himself if that were necessary to protect those precious bonds.

To work with the devil might be all right, but to play with the devil was quite a different matter. It was genial, fun-loving Charlie's propensity to do the latter that was to destroy Carnegie's faith in his favorite protégé. In December 1901, Schwab, who had spent a most arduous year first in negotiating the sale of the Carnegie Company to the Morgan syndicate and then in organizing and inaugurating operations for United States Steel, felt he deserved a vacation. He and his wife, emulating the Carnegies, had sailed for the Riviera. Once there, however, he did not follow Carnegie's sober habits. Joining a wealthy, rather fast-moving group that included Baron Henri Rothschild, Schwab, with the "big, fast automobile" he had purchased in Paris, cut a dashing figure along the Côte d'Azur and the Grand Corniche. It became the custom of this group, on their way back to Cannes in the late afternoon, to stop at the Casino of Monte Carlo for a quick session with the roulette wheels. Schwab would later rather lamely explain to Morgan's junior partner, George W. Perkins, that he had been going there for fifteen years: "I always visit the Casino on acct of its orchestra." On a particular evening in 1901, however, he had had sensational luck, according to New York newspapers, who had picked up the account that "he had broken the bank at Monte Carlo." When Carnegie read this headline in the New York *Sun,* he was outraged. Even Schwab had succumbed. Carnegie immediately sent a cablegram, signed with his code name "Wakeful," to Schwab: "Public sentiment shocked. *Times* demands statement gambling charges false. Probably have resign. Serves you right." [5] Carnegie followed this up with a letter to Morgan, along with a clipping of *The New York Times* editorial berating Schwab:

> I feel in regard to the enclosed as if a son had disgraced the family.
> What the Times says is true. He is unfit to be the head of the United States Steel Co.—brilliant as his talents are. Of course he would never have so fallen when with us. His resignation would have been called for instanter had he done so.

I recommended him unreservedly to you. Never did he show any tendency to gambling when under me, or I should not have recommended him you may be sure. He shows a sad lack of *solid* qualities, of good sense, & his influence upon the many thousands of young men who naturally look to him will prove pernicious to the extreme.

I have had nothing wound me so deeply for many a long day, if ever.[6]

Poor Charlie Schwab, who had not broken any bank, and had not even sat at the gambling tables, but had remained standing (this seemed to him a significant fact) throughout their brief visit to the tables, was both amazed and heartbroken by this attention. He wrote Carnegie:

Your letters also copies of New York papers just received. I am heartbroken and leave for home at the earliest available boat. My vacation has been utterly spoiled. The newspaper reports are absurd. Absolutely untrue. Of course in going to Monte Carlo, I invited this attack and will pay the penalty. . . . Mr. Morgan must accept my resignation but he has refused to do so as yet. . . . My trip through Europe has been filled with pleasant occurrences but they possess no attraction for me now. Have been feted and invited by all the distinguished people in Vienna & Berlin. Have had unsolicited interviews with the Kaiser and treated in the nicest possible manner by many of the greatest men in Europe and feel badly indeed that the Monte Carlo episode should have spoiled all. I should like to hear from you when I land. . . . I feel from your letter and cables and reports from my office that you do not care to see me any more and shall come only if you desire it.[7]

Two days later he wrote again from Paris:

When I reached Paris this evening, I found your second letter. It hurt me very much. That you would be willing to listen to and believe the stories someone has seen fit to tell you was indeed a surprise to me and would not in all probability have been told if the hearer had not in some manner signified his willingness to listen and to believe. . . . I am no gambler. . . . But be what I may, there is no condition of affairs that would make me even listen to a tale of such a character concerning

801

you. I'd defend you or any of my friends until I knew the truth.
I admit I have made a serious mistake and one I shall probably
never be able to rectify and I will pay the penalty. I have cabled Mr. Morgan again today saying that he must accept my
resignation. My chief pang is not for my loss of position . . .
but the loss of your confidence and friendship. Do not send for
me for I should not come.[8]

Morgan, whose musical taste evidently was more in harmony
with Schwab's than Carnegie's was, refused to accept Schwab's resignation. A grateful Schwab wrote to Perkins, "I'll do anything
Mr. Morgan wants. He's my idea of a great man. Carnegie has
condemned me without a hearing. Mr. Morgan, a new friend, is
broader gauged by far. I'm his to command." [9]

But as it turned out, Schwab's days with United Steel were
numbered. Late that same year, due to overwork and worry, he
became seriously ill, and took a long vacation. Returning from
this extended leave in the summer of 1903, he found that much of
his authority had been usurped by others, and Morgan, distrustful of some of Schwab's side investments, including a large interest in Bethlehem Steel, did not support Schwab's attempt to get
his power back.

Carnegie, noting all these events with shocked disapproval,
was ready to write an end to Schwab's career. "Schwab really
bad," he wrote Lauder. "Mr. Hunsicker saw him in Paris just
now & no better I'm afraid he is never to get back to work
again." [10] A few months later he wrote, "I am sad indeed about
Schwab. I didn't think he would lose his head so completely." [11]

Nevertheless, the greatest period of Schwab's career lay in the
future, when he was to take the small Bethlehem Steel Company,
then primarily an ordnance concern, combine it with the U. S.
Shipbuilding Company, and make it into one of the great steel
plants of the world, a strong competitor to United States Steel itself. Carnegie's attitude to Schwab became much more friendly
and less censorious after Schwab had left United States Steel.
There were occasional visits between the two, shared jokes, and of
course, the annual Carnegie Veterans dinner, presided over by
Schwab, when all of Carnegie's boys who had stayed by him during the Frick quarrel would meet with the Old Man and drink a

toast to his health. But things could never again be quite the same between Schwab and Carnegie. Carnegie had been too quick to cut deeply into Schwab's pride. One by one, Carnegie's ties with his old partners were being severed, which was probably just as well for both sides.

Even so, it took Carnegie two or three years to adjust to the fact that he really had nothing to say about the conduct of United States Steel, no authority to dismiss officers or to promote favorites. He had deliberately chosen bonds, not stocks, and now as a creditor he had no right to attend stockholders' meetings or vote upon policy. But he did worry about those bonds and was always fearful that this strange new breed of managers, being responsible as he felt "to everyone and no one," would somehow trick him in their financial maneuverings. There were frequent letters from Francis Stetson, general counsel for United States Steel, and Judge E.H. Gary, chairman of the board, in response to Carnegie's anxious inquiries about the security of his bonds. "Your rights do not in any wise depend upon the good faith or good intentions of the managers of the Steel Company," Stetson reassured him, "but have the legal security of the deposit of the stocks with the United States Trust Company, as Trustee, as stated in the original Indenture of April 1, 1901. . . . Answering your question specifically, I would state that there is not either latent or patent, $160,000,000 bonds, or any bonds whatever, ahead of your bonds on the property which . . . has [been] received from The Carnegie Company." [12] A short time later, after Carnegie wrote in alarm about a rumor he had heard that United States Steel was going to buy the Union Steel Company and place a mortgage on it which would have first lien, Judge Gary, with less patience, answered: "You are laboring under a misapprehension. I believe you will find our Corporation disposed to keep within the law and within the equity applicable to the whole subject." [13]

Such peremptory responses did not discourage Carnegie from sending gratuitous advice: "More and more I think the managers will see the wisdom of accumulating an enormous reserve fund by holding fast to a large portion of the earnings in prosperous years, so that regular, though moderate, dividends can be maintained." [14] Advice familiar enough to his old partners now employed by United States Steel, for they had been controlled by it for many years. It had worked when one man owned a majority of the stock and could simply deny large dividends to his partners, but it was quite meaningless to a corporation owned by thousands, who wanted dividends, not reserve funds.

Eventually Carnegie gave up. It would even sometimes seem that he took a positive delight in having U. S. Steel stock decline on the market, for it showed up the poor management of the present directors and pointed up Carnegie's wise foresight in taking bonds instead of stock. "I see U. S. stocks way down. Guess our Bonds are better than both [common and preferred stock] together—I thought they would prove so," he would write with satisfaction to Lauder.[15]

Carnegie, moreover, had many other business interests to which he had to give at least cursory attention—enough, indeed, to provide a full-time business career for almost any man: railroad stocks and bonds, individual loans, real estate investments in New York, Chicago, and Pittsburgh, even such ancient relics out of the past as the Keokuk and Hamilton Bridge Company. Of his various investments made after his retirement, certainly the most interesting to him, although not the largest by any means, was his partnership with Charles Van Hise, the noted geologist and distinguished president of the University of Wisconsin. Van Hise, who had been trained under Roland Duer Irving, a pioneer in genetic petrography in the 1870's, had spent much of his professional life as a geologist in the study of iron bearing regions around Lake Superior. Even though president of a major university, Van Hise had not given up his interest in geological explorations, and in 1903 he entered into formal partnership with Carnegie for iron ore prospecting in Canada. Under the terms of the agreement, Carnegie put up $100,000 to survey and purchase potential iron ore lands, and the two men were to divide any profits that might accrue, fifty-fifty. Later, Van Hise was given a greater latitude to explore for cobalt, silver, and other valuable minerals in Canada, but Carnegie drew the line at mining operations in Brazil. In all, over a period of fifteen years, Carnegie was to provide Van Hise with $186,000, and although the discoveries were not as impressive as both men had hoped, Carnegie received a return of about 16 per cent on his investment. But the greater value of these explorations was the sense of adventure which came to

804

Van Hise through his work in the field during the summer months and to Carnegie through the study of his partner's carefully written reports.[16]

Interesting and profitable as all of these activities were to Carnegie, they certainly worked at cross-purposes to what he fully intended to be his main business in retirement—giving, not getting. It was time now for the deeding away, not the contracting for more. He was no novice in his new preoccupation, for with his first gift of $25,000 for a public swimming bath to Dunfermline in 1873, Carnegie had begun his career as a philanthropist. Certainly no man had made as many public expressions of the obligation for men of wealth to give of their riches as he. To shirk that duty now would be inconceivable, but Carnegie was under no illusions about the problems that would confront him. Morley had written him a month after the sale to Morgan had been consummated, "I say to you what Johnson said to Burke, when B. showed him his fine house, 'I don't envy, I do admire.' You'll have some difficulty, tho' in adapting the principles of accumulation to the business of distribution." To which Carnegie replied, "Thousands of clippings from eleven thousand daily papers reach me. I read them to get my bearings in the new Line of Trade. Some are really strengthening. . . . These nerve me for the long campaign upon which I have entered. No parade to Petrovice I well know, but one requiring me to clinch my teeth & stand to it. I don't see it needs the same principles as acquisition—but it needs some of these. Tenacity and steady sailing to the haven we clear for—supreme confidence in one's own ideas, or conclusions rather, after thought—and above all, placing *use* above popularity." [17] These were qualities of character with which Carnegie had proved himself to be well endowed, but he also showed a quality of capriciousness which often made his philanthropic gestures—or lack of them—an enigma to those soliciting him for aid.

Yet Carnegie would always believe that his philanthropic practices, like his business practices, were based upon rational, systematic principles. These principles in some respects made his task of giving more difficult, but, he felt, far more socially significant and beneficial than the simple random distribution of largess. Although Carnegie reveled in the public attention that came

to him through his gifts and accepted without too much protest
the reputation of being America's first great philanthropist, he
never made such a claim for himself. Indeed, he frequently would
point out for praise his heroes who had pioneered in the field of
philanthropy—Enoch Pratt, Peter Cooper, and George Peabody.
He did, however, like to think of himself as a pioneer in "scientific philanthropy," as one of the first to analyze the problem of
the administration and distribution of great wealth and to state
specifically "the best fields for philanthropy." He had made this
analysis and statement in a remarkable two-part essay, entitled
"Wealth," which appeared in the June and December 1889 issues
of the *North American Review*. It was no accident that this essay,
along with several other of his previously published magazine articles on trusts, labor, and imperialism, was reprinted in book
form in 1900, just prior to his retirement from business. For in effect, by this essay, Carnegie was giving notice to the world of the
way in which he, as a "scientific philanthropist," intended to distribute his fortune.

His essay on "Wealth" created a considerable stir when it first
appeared, and deservedly so. The editor of the *North American
Review,* Allen Thorndike Rice, called it the "finest article I have
ever published in the Review." It was quickly picked up in Britain, where it appeared in *Pall Mall Gazette,* under the title "Gospel of Wealth," given to it by the editor of the *Gazette,* W. T.
Stead. It was further sanctified by the appearance in *Nineteenth
Century* magazine of a highly complimentary review by William
Ewart Gladstone, whose only criticism was that Carnegie had
been too harsh on inherited wealth. It caught the attention of the
reading public of two nations because of its candor, its specific
proposals for the distribution of wealth, and, of course, because of
its author, a well-known American millionaire who was openly
critical of his own class.

The thesis of the "Gospel" was simply and boldly stated: "The
problem of our age is the proper administration of wealth," and
to Carnegie there appeared only three alternatives by which a
man of great wealth could dispose of his fortune: he could leave it
to his family, he could bequeath it in his will for public purposes,
or he could administer it during his lifetime for public benefit.[18]
Of the three, the least desirable both for society and for the indi-

vidual was the first, and on this point Carnegie gave his oft repeated homily on the evils of inherited wealth. "Beyond providing for the wife and daughters moderate sources of income, and very moderate allowances indeed, if any, for the sons, men may well hesitate. . . . The thoughtful man must shortly say, 'I would as soon leave to my son a curse as the almighty dollar,' and admit to himself that it is not the welfare of the children, but family pride, which inspires these legacies." [19]

The second alternative, while socially more responsible, is frequently thwarted by disappointed heirs contesting the will. Even when a philanthropic bequest is successfully carried out, "it may be said that this is only a means for the disposal of wealth, provided a man is content to wait until he is dead before he becomes of much good in the world." Carnegie approved of heavy inheritance taxes, or "death duties," to ensure society's reaping some benefits from the accumulation of wealth if either of the first two alternatives were chosen by the man of wealth.[20]

"There remains, then, only one mode of using great fortunes; but in this we have the true antidote for the temporary unequal distribution of wealth, the reconciliation of the rich and the poor —a reign of harmony. . . . It is founded upon the present most intense Individualism and . . . under its sway we shall have an ideal State, in which the surplus wealth of the few will become, in the best sense, the property of the many, because administered for the common good, and this wealth, passing through the hands of the few, can be made a much more potent force for the elevation of our race than if distributed in small sums to the people themselves." [21] In short, the rich man should spend his fortune during his lifetime in ways that will most effectively benefit and advance society. "This, then, is held to be the duty of the man of wealth: To set an example of modest, unostentatious living, shunning display or extravagance; to provide moderately for the legitimate wants of those dependent upon him; and, after doing so, to consider all surplus revenues which come to him simply as trust funds which he is called upon to administer . . . —the man of wealth thus becoming the mere trustee and agent for his poorer brethren, bringing to their service his superior wisdom, experience, and ability to administer, doing for them better than they would or could do for themselves." [22]

In the second part of his essay, Carnegie, at the request of the editor, presented "some of the best methods of performing this duty of administering surplus wealth for the good of the people." The first requisite, of course, regardless of the field of philanthropy, "for a really good use of wealth by the millionaire who has accepted the gospel which proclaims him only a trustee of the surplus that comes to him, is to take care that the purposes for which he spends it shall not have a degrading pampering tendency upon its recipients, but that his trust shall be so administered as to stimulate the best and most aspiring poor of the community to further efforts for their own improvement. It is not the irreclaimably destitute, shiftless, and worthless which it is truly beneficial or truly benevolent for the individual to attempt to reach and improve. For these there exists the refuge provided by the city or the State, where they can be sheltered, fed, clothed . . . and, most important of all—where they can be isolated from the well-doing and industrious poor, who are liable to be demoralized by contact with these unfortunates. . . . The individual administrator of surplus wealth has as his charge the industrious and the ambitious; not those who need everything done for them, but those who, being most anxious and able to help themselves, deserve and will be benefited by help from others and by the extension of their opportunities by the aid of the philanthropic rich." [23]

The specific fields of philanthropy in which the wise trustee of surplus wealth would invest, according to Carnegie, were seven, listed in descending order of importance: (1) universities, the founding of universities, of course, being possible only "by men enormously rich"; (2) free libraries, for Carnegie himself, he said, this "occupies first place"; (3) the founding or extension of hospitals "and other institutions connected with the alleviation of human suffering"; (4) parks; (5) halls suitable for meetings, concerts, etc.; (6) swimming baths; and (7) churches, but only the buildings, not the maintenance of the church activities, which should be done by the entire congregation. "It is not expected," Carnegie added, "that there should be general concurrence as to the best possible use of surplus wealth. . . . There is room and need for all kinds of wise benefactions for the common weal." [24]

It is fortunate that Carnegie did not expect "general concurrence" on his list of proper fields for philanthropy, for he certainly did not get it. Ministers and mission boards, in particular, were outraged to find churches seventh on the list—just after swimming baths. Artists, writers, and musicians also wanted their share of patronage, as did orphanages, private schools, and other charitable institutions. The *Nineteenth Century* magazine, in addition to publishing Gladstone's lengthy and laudatory review of Carnegie's essay, carried the following month a symposium on "Irresponsible Wealth," with statements by three leading religious figures in Britain: Cardinal Manning, the Archbishop of Westminster; Hermann Adler, Chief Rabbi of the United Hebrew Congregations of Britain; and the Reverend Hugh Price Hughes, a noted Methodist minister.[25] All things considered, Carnegie came off rather well at the hands of this religiously mixed trinity. Both Cardinal Manning and Rabbi Adler praised Carnegie for his personal generosity and his large social vision of a better society, although each pointed out that Carnegie had really said nothing that was not basic to the Judeo-Christian tradition.

From the Reverend Mr. Hughes, however, Carnegie got rougher treatment. "I am quite unable to let off Mr. Carnegie in the pleasant and approving way in which Mr. Gladstone dismisses him," Hughes asserted. "When I contemplate him as the representative of a particular class of millionaires, I am forced to say, with all personal respect, and without holding him in the least responsible for his unfortunate circumstances, that he is an anti-Christian phenomenon, a social monstrosity, and a grave political peril." [26] Mr. Hughes's basic criticism of Carnegie's essay was that he did not deal with the fundamental question of society—the distribution of wealth, rather than the administration of wealth. In a true Christian society modeled after the teachings of Jesus there would be no millionaires at all. Millionaires were in themselves a symptom of a people's fall from grace. "They have no beneficent raison d'être. They are the unnatural product of artificial social regulations. They flourish portentously in the unhealthy forcing house of Protection, but everything else fades and dies behind them. We prefer fresh air. Millionaires at one end of the scale involve paupers at the other end, and even so excellent a man as Mr. Carnegie is too dear at that price." [27] Hughes took particular delight in quoting at length from *Study of Sociology,* written by the man Carnegie called his mentor, Herbert Spencer. Spencer drew an interesting parallel between the perils and hardships of life for the feudal nobleman in the Middle Ages and of the millionaire entrepreneur of the present time. The rather surprising conclusion reached by the founder of Social Darwinism was that power and wealth are not blessings but evils to those who achieve the dominant position in any society. Hughes, however, did support Carnegie's proposals for the distribution of wealth, presumably on the ground that every millionaire who gave away his wealth meant one less "social monstrosity" was at large to pollute that society which was sick enough to produce him. Hughes concluded with the warning that if Carnegie's gospel of giving was not quickly accepted by all men of great wealth, if, instead, the gulf between the Haves and the Have Nots continued to grow, then a terrible social upheaval was bound to come. "In London we are living on the verge of a volcano. . . . Never, since the downfall of the Roman Empire and the dissolution of the ancient world, has Europe witnessed so perilous a situation as exists in London today. Never has there been so vast a multitude of half-starved men, within sight of boundless wealth, and outside the control of the Christian Church." [28]

A more sophisticated, if less apocalyptic, critical view of Carnegie's gospel was offered by William Jewett Tucker, the liberal American theologian, professor of religion at Andover Seminary, and later to be the distinguished president of Dartmouth College. Writing a review of "The Gospel of Wealth" in 1891 for the *Andover Review,* a periodical he had helped to found a few years before, Tucker touched, as no other critic of the time did, to the very quick of Carnegie's gospel—and found it fallacious. First, Tucker pointed out, it was based upon a false assumption of inevitability. He quoted Carnegie as saying, "We start with a condition of affairs [referring to the prevailing competitive system] under which the best interests of the race are promoted, but which inevitably gives wealth to the few." In effect, Tucker pointed out, Carnegie has truly given us a new gospel statement: "The inevitable factor in society is not so certainly the poor as the rich. The rich ye have with you always. But this necessarian view of extreme riches is not so obvious to all as to Mr. Carnegie.

For while he is asking and answering with so much courage and assurance, this question about the disposal of the vast surplus of private wealth, society is taking hold in very serious fashion of the other end of the problem, and asking why there should be such a vast surplus of private wealth. Mr. Carnegie's scheme of redistribution is a most interesting one . . . and, within the limits in which it is likely to be carried out, not without direct practical benefit, but it is in no sense a solution of the great social question which is stirring the mind and heart of this generation. And my present concern is that it should not be accepted as such by ethical and religious teachers. For I can conceive of no greater mistake, more disastrous in the end to religion if not to society, than that of trying to make charity do the work of justice. . . . [T]he assumption . . . that wealth is the inevitable possession of the few, and is best administered by them for the many, begs the whole question of economic justice now before society, and relegates it to the field of charity, leaving the question of the original distribution of wealth unsettled, or settled only to the satisfaction of the few. . . . The ethical question of today centres, I am sure, in the distribution rather than in the redistribution of wealth." [29]

Tucker found fault also in Carnegie's plan for the redistribution of wealth, generous and praiseworthy as it seemed to be, for even if Carnegie could persuade most of his fellow millionaires to follow his example, which Tucker doubted, "Society, in its institutions of relief and of culture, in its improvements and refinements, would become the object of the bounty of the few, and rightly so, as Mr. Carnegie argues, because the rich benefactor can do better for the community than it would or could do for itself. Just as formerly it was contended that political power should be in the hands of the few, because it would be better administered, so now it is contended—I quote Mr. Carnegie's words, slightly transferring them, but not changing their meaning—that 'the millionaire is intrusted for the time being with a great part of the increased wealth of the community, because he can administer it for the community far better than it could or would have done for itself.' This, of course, if accepted and carried out in any complete way, becomes patronage . . . and, in the long run, society cannot afford to be patronized. It is better for any community to advance more slowly than to gain altogether by gifts rather than, in large part, by earnings. Within proper limits, the public is advantaged by the gifts of the rich, but if the method becomes the accepted method, to be expected and relied upon, the decline of public self-respect has begun. There is a public public spirit to be cherished as well as a private public spirit." [30]

To the Reverend Mr. Hughes Carnegie wrote a reply in the *Nineteenth Century*, in which he had great sport in turning the tables on the Methodist divine. As Hughes had quoted Herbert Spencer to Carnegie, Carnegie retaliated by quoting John Wesley to Hughes—a sermon in which the founder of Methodism had urged his followers to "gain all you can; save all you can and then give all you can to do good to all men." [31] All in all, Carnegie felt he had successfully refuted the critical and gloomy minister.

William Tucker's criticism was not as easily refuted, however, and if Carnegie ever read this review, he should have been deeply disturbed by the questions that Tucker raised. Carnegie must have expected that there would be the angry denunciations of great wealth by men like Hughes, as well as the more probing socio-economic questions of distribution that Tucker raised, but the main thrust of Tucker's criticism that should have struck home for Carnegie was philosophical, not political or social. For in seeing that the questions of inevitability and of patronage were implicit in Carnegie's gospel, Tucker was striking at Carnegie's real inner defense line that protected his self-esteem and provided a justification for his life.

In his essay, "The Advantages of Poverty," which he had offered as a rebuttal to Hughes, Carnegie made one brief statement that was far more revealing of his own motivation for philanthropy than he probably ever intended or realized. In discussing the question of why the very rich should avoid extravagant living, Carnegie made the statement that "they can, perhaps, also find refuge from self-questioning in the thought of the much greater portion of their means which is being spent upon others." [32] It is the phrase, "perhaps, also find refuge from self-questioning," that is the tip-off. This is the kind of refuge Carnegie must have been seeking for twenty years, ever since as a young man in 1868 he had written, "To continue much longer overwhelmed by business cares and with most of my thoughts wholly upon the way to make more money in the shortest time, must degrade me beyond hope of permanent recovery." Nevertheless he had continued, at an ever faster rate, to make more and more money. Had he in the process degraded himself beyond the hope of recovery? And, even more alarming to this child of Dunfermline Chartism, had he helped to change America in such a manner as to degrade democracy as well? He had written *Triumphant Democracy* to prove that this was not so. But the old doubts persisted. What was really happening to an America in which one man could accumulate a fortune that ran into nine figures? Carnegie had to justify his life to himself. Unlike some of his contemporaries—Fisk, Gould, Drew—he could not accept for himself the innocent animal amorality of the freebooter, nor on the other hand could he, having rejected the tenets of orthodox religion, now retreat with John D. Rockefeller into pious Baptism and say, "The Good Lord gave me my wealth."

Carnegie must have felt that he had at last found justification for plutocracy by his Gospel of Wealth: A man may accumulate great wealth in a democracy, but he has a responsibility to return that wealth in a way that will not destroy society's own responsibility to preserve individual initiative. To give through the usual charitable outlets is wrong, for such charity is primarily concerned with the hopeless "submerged tenth." It keeps the weak weak and upsets the equality of opportunity. To give library buildings with the provision that the community must then furnish the books is right, for this makes available opportunities for all, it encourages the "swimming tenth" and at the same time respects the responsibility of the community. And who is better prepared for such a responsible task of being steward for a nation's accumulated wealth than the man who, starting with nothing, has through his own initiative gathered in this wealth? Carnegie must have felt with the writing of "Wealth" that he had at last made peace with his conscience, had at last found that "refuge from self-questioning." [33]

But here was this Andover theologian, who with cold logic pointed out the deep cracks in the very foundations of Carnegie's refuge. If democracy meant anything, it meant freedom of choice. How could Carnegie, who denied the doctrine of inevitability for the individual, think that his gospel, which had as its cornerstone the inevitability of the concentration of wealth, was reconcilable

813

with democracy? What if the people, out of their collective, divine reason in which Carnegie loudly professed his faith, should pass an income tax so highly progressive in form as to preclude the accumulation of wealth? Would Carnegie, in the name of individualism and the inevitability of accumulation, deny the democratic process? Or would he be forced to admit that nothing in a truly free society is inevitable and predetermined?

There was the even more awkward point of patronage raised by Professor Tucker. It was particularly cruel of him to equate Carnegie's rich benefactor, who "can do better for the community than it would or could do for itself," with the old feudal concept, so antithetical to everything Carnegie professed to believe in, that "political power should be in the hands of the few because it would be better administered." Tucker, in short, was saying to Carnegie, you cannot have it both ways: you cannot reconcile true political democracy with actual economic feudalism. You can believe in inevitability if you are a Calvinist, or a Marxist, or a Social Darwinist, but you cannot believe in inevitability if you are a democrat.

Since obviously Carnegie could never be accused of being either a Marxist or a Calvinist, the logical conclusion would be that it was his belief in Social Darwinism that thwarted his belief in democracy. It seems particularly ironical that Carnegie should most closely approach the Social Darwinist position, not in his political or economic philosophy, but in the development of his philosophy of philanthropy, a field that one does not usually associate with Social Darwinism. Even here, of course, Carnegie's Social Darwinism was far from pure, and William Graham Sumner would hardly have welcomed him into the fold. Carnegie might in his essay on "Wealth" use all the proper clichés—"survival of the fittest," "the pauper is a social leper," "the rotten apple in the barrel must be removed," etc.—but no true Sumnerian could accept his basic premise that "individualism will continue, but the millionaire will be but a trustee for the poor." One can almost hear the cantankerous Sumner snort, "Pure rot," as he read that line. Nor could Carnegie have expected his great mentor, Spencer, to accept his arguments for a graduated inheritance tax, to take care of those men of great wealth who would not distribute their fortunes during their lifetime. As was so often the

814

case with Carnegie when he attempted to build a philosophy to suit his convenience, he ended up with a structure that was all doors and no roof—easy enough to get in and out of, but not much in the way of shelter.

If it is to be assumed that Carnegie read Tucker's critique, then it can only be said that it left him unmoved. Perhaps he did not see the full implications of Tucker's arguments. He never claimed to be a systematic philosopher, however, and if there were logical fallacies in his arguments that would outrage both the Social Darwinist and the social democrat, Carnegie would see no reason to change his gospel for the sake of consistency. He had found a justification for his life that was entirely satisfying to him. There was no more self-questioning, and he would hold to his gospel for all the years to come.

He, of course, had begun to practice long before he had had a gospel to preach. That is why he was convinced that he was a "scientific philanthropist." His principles of philanthropy, he felt, were pragmatically based upon experience. His earliest philanthropic bequests, however, were based on no discernible system. Sentiment and his own idiosyncratic interests dictated his choice more than any rational philosophy. By the time his essay on "Wealth" appeared in 1889, he had given a swimming bath and library to Dunfermline, a library to Braddock, Pennsylvania, and a pipe organ to the small Swedenborgian Church in Allegheny which his father and aunts had attended in the 1850's. His only gift to higher education was a grant of $6000 extended over a five-year period to the Western University of Pennsylvania (later to be the University of Pittsburgh).[34] This is not a tremendously impressive list, and sentiment was clearly a major factor. But the list is interesting in its diversity. It is evident that these early gifts determined his ideas about "the best fields of philanthropy."

After the appearance of his famous essay, Carnegie began in earnest to follow his own dictates. As he had indicated in "Wealth," libraries were to be his specialty in this early phase of his philanthropic career. In the United States, he gave libraries to Allegheny, and, at the request of Senator James F. Wilson, who had been most helpful to Carnegie in the building of railroads in Iowa, to Fairfield, Iowa; in Scotland, he gave libraries to Edinburgh, Aberdeen, Ayr, Wick, Sterling, Jedburgh, Peterhead, and

Inverness, all within five years after the announcement of his gospel.[35] After Dunfermline and Braddock, in which he furnished not only the library building but provided an endowment for the acquisition of books and the maintenance of the library, Carnegie would give only the building and insist upon the town's taxing itself for the books and maintenance. As he wrote to Senator Wilson's son, who wanted Carnegie to provide an endowment for the library in Fairfield, "I do not agree with you about endowing the institution. It has always been my aim to help such communities only as are willing to co-operate. . . . I think that an institution has not taken root, and is scarcely worth maintaining unless the community appreciates it sufficiently to tax itself for maintenance." [36] He was to make only three exceptions to this rule after having established it: at Duquesne, Homestead, and the borough of Carnegie, a suburb of Pittsburgh. Fifty years later, a report on the Carnegie library system by Ralph Munn, which appeared in the *Library Journal,* showed the wisdom of that rule. The only four libraries in the United States to receive an endowment from Carnegie, Munn reported, "still have exactly the same endowment which he gave them in the 1890's and the cities have firmly refused to give them any local financial support." [37]

It was much easier at first for Carnegie to give libraries in Scotland than in the United States, for there were no taxation restrictions on British municipalities. They could tax themselves for the support of libraries, while many cities in the United States could not.[38] Pittsburgh, for example, could not accept Carnegie's offer to provide a library building in 1881 because the city council ruled that the laws of Pennsylvania did not provide for municipal property tax assessments to be used to maintain a free library. Shortly thereafter, however, the Pennsylvania legislature specifically provided for tax assessments for libraries, and Pittsburgh quickly requested a renewal of the offer. The renewal came multiplied several times over, for Carnegie now had in mind a great civic center, the Carnegie Institute, which would include not only an imposing library but a great museum, a music hall, and an art institute, located at the edge of Schenley Park on Forbes Street.

This was Carnegie's first great philanthropic endeavor, and in these early days he could still allow himself the luxury of being consulted on and of considering almost every detail, from the architectural design of the buildings to the question of nudity in the copies of classical statuary. "I strongly recommend nude to be draped since question has been raised," he wired W. M. Frew, the president of the Carnegie Library Commission. "Remember my words in speech. We should begin gently to lead people upward. I do hope nothing in gallery or hall will ever give offense to the simplest man or woman. Draping is used everywhere in Britain except in London. If we are to work genuine good we must bend and keep in touch with masses. Am very clear indeed on this question." [39] For weeks he fussed with Frew about the names that would be carved in stone on the entablature. When he saw the proposed list in the *Pittsburgh Dispatch,* he exploded to Frew: "I cannot approve the list of names. . . . Some of the names have no business to be on the list. Imagine Dickens in and Burns out. Among painters Perugini out and Rubens in, the latter only a painter of fat, vulgar women, while a study of the pictures of Raphael will show anyone that he was really only a copyist of Perugini, whose pupil he was. Imagine Science and Franklin not there. The list for Music seems satisfactory. Palestrina rightly comes first. Have been entranced by his works, which we have heard in Rome. As I am to be in Pittsburgh very soon, I hope you will postpone action in regard to the names." [40]

In spite of Carnegie's knowing what he liked, the great Institute was completed, more or less to everyone's satisfaction and to Carnegie's immense pride. The building, of light gray sandstone, covered four acres, and Carnegie wrote to the president and the board of trustees of the Institute: "Not only our own country, but the civilized world will take note of the fact that our Dear Old Smoky Pittsburgh, no longer content to be celebrated only as one of the chief manufacturing centres, has entered upon the path to higher things, and is before long, as we thoroughly believe, also to be noted for her preeminence in the Arts and Sciences. . . . As for myself, I am amazed at what has been accomplished. I had prepared myself for years of weary waiting for the Harvest—and even for disappointment. I had not ventured to estimate at its value the mass of latent desire for the things of the spirit which lay inert in the hearts of our fellow citizens of the industrial hive, which needed only the awakening touch. . . ." [41]

817

Library giving, except for so large an undertaking as the Carnegie Institute of Pittsburgh, quickly became a business, as efficient and standardized in procedure as the filling of orders for steel billets at Homestead or Duquesne. A town council would apply for a Carnegie Library, and Carnegie's secretary, James Bertram, would acknowledge the request and inform the municipal government of the specifications to be met before the grant could be made. The town would first have to provide a site, if possible centrally located in the town, then the governing board of the community would have to pledge an annual appropriation for books and maintenance which would amount to 10 per cent of the Carnegie gift. The size of Carnegie's gift was based upon the population of the town, usually $2 per capita, which worked very well indeed for cities from 25,000 to 100,000 in population. In the latter instance, for example, Carnegie would give $200,000 for the building, and the city would pledge $20,000 a year for maintenance.[42] But in many of the very small villages that also received gifts of libraries, the annual amount pledged in order to receive the gift might be as low as $200 a year. In fact, the only major criticism made by the Munn report of 1951 was that it would have been much better if small neighboring towns had "pooled their resources for a single library," much as communities would later do in consolidating public school systems. "Too small to provide even the minimum essentials of good service, these libraries are largely responsible for the attitude of benevolent apathy with which so many people regard public libraries. We would surely have a more aggressively favorable public opinion if Andrew Carnegie had known what we know today, and had restricted his grants to governmental units which are large enough to finance the operation of well stocked and adequately staffed libraries."[43] From the professional librarian's point of view this is certainly a justifiable criticism, but who can say how many youths or lonely old people living in towns like Idaho Springs, Colorado, or Flora, Indiana, or Sanborn, Iowa, in those pre-radio-television days, found their only intellectual excitement or companionship in the Carnegie Free Public Library? In any event, Carnegie, remembering tales of his grandfather's "college" in the tiny hamlet of Pattiemuir, liked to think this was true. As he wrote to one applicant for a library building, "I believe that it outranks any other one thing that a community can do to benefit its people. It is the never failing spring in the desert." [44]

At first Carnegie made no attempt to provide building plans along with his grant of money for the building, leaving the architectural design to be determined by each locality. But there were so many bad buildings erected in these early years of library giving, and so many complaints from librarians who had to contend with functional problems, that Carnegie, and later the Carnegie Corporation of New York, sent out standard plans along with the monetary grant.[45] What may have been gained in functional efficiency, however, was lost in architectural variety. Soon, in small towns all over America, there came to be an architectural style, popularly known as Carnegie Classical, that was as easily identifiable as that other standardized small town architectual style known as Wesley Romanesque. A stranger in the community seldom had difficulty in spotting the Carnegie Library and the Methodist Church, which in many towns confronted each other across the square.

The public generally believed that Carnegie insisted that his name be engraved above the front entrance of the libraries he gave. This was not true. But certainly he never objected to its being done, and, upon request, he would provide the library with a photograph of himself, which would hang in the place of honor just inside the main door. As he made clear to applicants, the one thing he did desire was "that there should be placed over the entrance to the Libraries I build a representation of the rays of a rising sun, and above 'LET THERE BE LIGHT,' and I hope you can have this on the building." [46] Not all communities complied with this request, however. Perhaps the Methodists across the way found it a bit presumptuous for a secular institution thus to arrogate to itself Jehovah's own first command.

Carnegie frequently attended the dedication ceremonies of a major new library, particularly if it was in Britain, for there it usually meant that he would be granted the Freedom of the City, a medieval rite which he thoroughly enjoyed. He began collecting "Freedoms" in the early 1890's. The parchment scroll signifying this honor was encased in a small casket, and each town in Britain seemed to be trying to outdo its neighbor in the elaborateness of design of the casket. Carnegie, who had never before been infected with the collector mania—neither stamps, nor paintings, nor rare old books ever having had an appeal for him—entered into this hobby with all the zest of the most fanatic philatelist. It was a proud day when he broke the previous record, held by Gladstone, of fourteen Freedoms. He really hit top form when he received six Freedoms in six days.[47] They came so fast, in fact, that even *The Times,* usually so absolutely reliable, became confused, and on one occasion reported that Carnegie was to receive the Freedom of Bromley-by-Bow the following week. The citizens of that small London suburb were alarmed when they read their papers on that day, for it was the first they had known about it— no casket, no parchment, nothing was prepared. *The Times* hastily carried the next day one of its few retractions. It appeared that it was Bromley, Kent, that was prepared to honor Carnegie that week.[48]

"How dog-sick you must be of all these meetings, addresses and Hallelujah business," Morley wrote Carnegie, who was then on one of his whirlwind collecting tours. "I shouldn't wonder at your longing for Skibo, and what Mr. Smith calls 'the quiet stream of self-forgetfulness'—blessed waters for all of us." [49] But this was the kind of "quiet stream" that Carnegie never cared to fish in, and Morley's sympathy was quite wasted on him. Carnegie, for all his loudly proclaimed radical republicanism, dearly loved the pomp and circumstance of the medieval ritual—riding in an open carriage through the old twisting streets, lined with crowds and flags; being met at the Town Hall by the Lord Mayor, resplendent in his robes and silver medallion of office, who made the formal presentation of the Freedom of the City to Carnegie. Finally came the opportunity to address the assembled crowd, and to spread his Gospel of Wealth.

The reception at the ancient Abbey town of Jedburgh on 4 October 1894 was typical of the many, many such ceremonies in which Carnegie would joyously participate. The Carnegies and ever-faithful Sister Stella arrived the evening before and were met by Provost Laidlaw at the railway station. They drove to the appropriately named Spread Eagle Hotel, which was gaily decorated with the Union Jack and the Stars and Stripes. A luncheon given the next day at the Royal Hotel by the Provost was followed by the ceremony of presentation in the Sheriff's Court Room. The casket, made from the wood of an ancient oak that grew on the grounds of Ferniherst Castle, was graciously accepted by Carnegie. Then he spoke on the Stewardship of Wealth. Excerpts carried in the local newspaper would indicate that, as always, Carnegie's speech was a smashing success.

> In graduated taxation lies the key to the solution of this whole problem of grossly excessive wealth in the hands of the few. . . . I refer only to millions—moderate amounts left to dependents should not be taxed at all, for the good of the State is subserved by these moderate accumulations of property. [Hear, hear] . . . When I first said this it was from a pulpit one Sunday evening in one of the leading churches of New York city, when, much to my surprise but I think a great deal more to the surprise of my hearers themselves, the crowded audience burst into applause. Rather a strange experience in a church on a Sunday evening, but you must remember they had a strange minister preaching, and he was preaching a strange sermon. [Loud laughter.]
>
> Herein you have a power sufficient to cure the evils flowing from enormous fortunes. It is vitally important not to interfere with the motive power which leads to the creation of wealth— the desire to possess property. It would be as unwise to disturb the millionaire bees while they are making honey as to "kill the goose that lays the golden egg." Society should not do that; it should not only foster the bird but should always be careful not to disturb it, and especially leave eggs enough in the nest to encourage future deposits.
>
> The drones we can do what we like with, but we should let the slaving millionaires toil on and accumulate. . . . Let the community first get the honey safely in the hive, and the rest is easy. . . . Note also that this system of graduated inheritance taxation is strictly constitutional. The power to tax is a sovereign power, and the chief end to be kept in view in its exercise is the good of the State. All private rights of property are subordinate to this. [Applause] . . . The result of knowledge [gleaned from libraries] is to make men not violent revolutionists, but cautious evolutionists; not destroyers, but careful improvers. [Much applause.]

Carnegie then declared the library officially opened and invited the public to make free use of it.[50]

How sweet it all was! "Never so busy, never so happy," Carnegie would frequently write to Cousin Dod or Friend Morley, neither of whom could understand why he was either.

Carnegie would always insist that these shows were all for a purpose—to dramatize and publicize the Gospel of Wealth, in the hope that other millionaires might be converted. As he wrote to one friend in explanation of his "Hallelujah business," "Well do I remember my apprehensions when you advocated keeping all you did quiet. *No show.* No advocacy. Only go on & do the work in a quiet way, when I knew that advertizing was essential for success, i. e. to spreading abroad what could be done. . . . Of course its disagreeable work & puts me forward as a vain trumpeter but one who isn't willing to play this part *for the good* to be done, isn't much of a man." [51]

Carnegie enjoyed his trumpeting too obviously to convince anyone that he found it disagreeable work. The ceremonies and speeches continued, and ultimately he was to collect the Freedom of fifty-seven cities, the all-time record for Great Britain. For a time after World War II, it appeared that Winston Churchill might surpass it, but he never quite equaled this total. Carnegie remains, with his fifty-seven Freedoms, the freest citizen that Britain has ever known, which was what he had tried to tell the British for many years.

These flamboyant public displays of course enhanced Carnegie's already notorious reputation for being a publicity seeker. It was generally believed both in Britain and in America that he never gave a cent that was not returned to him tenfold in public adulation. Poultney Bigelow, the son of Carnegie's old acquaintance, John Bigelow, who worked with him for the establishment of the New York Public Library system, in his autobiography made one of the harshest indictments of Carnegie:

> Never before in the history of plutocratic America had any one man purchased by mere money so much social advertising and flattery. No wonder that he felt himself infallible, when Lords temporal and spiritual courted him and hung upon his words. They wanted his money, and flattery alone could wring it from him. Ask him for aid in a small deserving case or to assist a struggling scientific explorer—that would be wasted time. He had no ears for any charity unless labelled with his name.

. . . He would have given millions to Greece had she labelled the Parthenon Carnegopolis.[52]

Such criticism, while understandable, was quite unfair, and although Carnegie generally ignored such comments, on occasion he felt it necessary to speak out. When he offered to match the $600,000 endowment of the Franklin Institute in Boston, he was greatly disturbed to receive an inquiry from Charles Eliot, president of Harvard, one of the trustees, asking if this meant that Carnegie expected the name to be changed to the Franklin-Carnegie Institute. Carnegie felt obliged to deny this at some length:

> The idea of tampering with Franklin's name never entered my mind any more than when I duplicated Peter Cooper's gift of six hundred thousand. . . . When Pritchett told me of the Boston fund I volunteered to duplicate it, glad to do something for Boston for which it isn't easy to do much blessed as she is with a very rich and gift getting University and Public Libraries.
>
> I find it difficult to avoid having gifts for new things called after the donors. Carnegie Hall New York was called by me *The Music Hall* a la Boston. Foreign artists refused to appear in "A Music Hall"—London idea. The Board changed it in my absence in Europe without consulting me. . . . "The way of the Philanthropist is hard" but I don't do anything for popularity and just please my sel'—do what I think is useful. I never reply to attacks. Altho I confess I was surprised that you should have for a moment imagined there was a man living who could dream of coupling his name with Franklin *or with any founder*.[53]

There were many instances of Carnegie's philanthropy which, at his express order, received no publicity whatsoever. He had many people on his private pension lists, ranging from obscure boyhood friends in Dunfermline to such celebrities as Rudyard Kipling and Booker T. Washington.[54] The most interesting instance of his anonymous philanthropy was that concerned with Lord Acton's library. In 1890, Lord Acton, who was heavily in debt, had written Gladstone saying that he must sell his magnificent library of some 80,000 volumes in order to meet his creditor's demands. As it was probably the best private library in Britain, being particularly strong in French, Italian, and Roman Catholic Church history, Acton hated to have the collection broken up and sold in piecemeal lots. He thought perhaps Gladstone might know of an individual or institutional library that would purchase the entire collection.[55] Gladstone turned to his wealthiest friend, Carnegie, hoping that he would buy it and present it to some university. On 9 June 1890, Gladstone entered in his diary the notation: "Wrote memoranda on the Acton library. Then saw Mr. A. Carnegie, who outran all my expectations." [56] Carnegie offered to buy the entire library for £10,000, on the condition that Lord Acton be allowed to keep it for the rest of his life. Carnegie wrote Gladstone four days after their conversation, "Now one point, I wish no one to know about this, not even my Wife shall know. Lord Granville should understand that such an arrangement if known must make it somewhat uncomfortable for Lord Acton. I did not expect him ever to know beyond this, that a friend of his & yours had taken over the loan & security in place of the Bankers & he should never be disturbed." [57] And so the secret was kept until Lord Acton's death in 1902. At that time the story came out. Carnegie took possession of the library and gave it to John Morley for him to do with as he wished.[58] Morley gave the library to Cambridge University, where it remains intact today. Deeply touched by Carnegie's generosity, Morley wrote, "The Cambridge gift has been excellently well taken by the public here. I saw the Duke of Devonshire, and he was immensely gratified, as well he might be. Don't think me such a fool as not to know but I owe these laurels *wholly* to you, who might just as well have bound them round your own brows." [59] On occasion, Carnegie found private philanthropy quite as rewarding as public performance.

The publicity he sought and got after 1890, however, resulted in an almost unbelievable torrent of letters from individuals requesting aid for themselves or for some project in which they were interested. The faithful James Bertram, who handled all of this correspondence, estimated that Carnegie received on the average of 400 to 500 letters a day, and after the announcement of some large benefaction, this number might increase to 700 a day.[60] The great majority of these letters Carnegie, of course, never saw. They came from all over the world, from writers who could not get their books published, from inventors with patents to revolutionize industry, from persons who claimed kinship with the Carnegie or Morrison families, or simply from desperate people having no other recourse but the blind hope that a simple scrawled message to that magical name would be the "Open Sesame" to help.

No one, however, was too important, or too proud, it would appear, to write a "begging letter" to Carnegie. These letters from friends and distinguished persons he would have to see and to answer. On one day alone, he had letters from John Morley, Herbert Spencer, and William Gladstone. Morley, who never "begged," had simply written a personal letter, but Spencer was begging for help for some sociological study a friend was engaged in, and Gladstone wanted Carnegie to give money to the Bodleian Library. Carnegie was impressed. "Just think," he wrote in reply to Gladstone, "one mail brought me three letters,

> One from you—Gladstone
> One from   Herbert Spencer
> One from   John Morley

I am quite set up as no other one can say this. A.C." [61] But not set up enough to become softheaded. Carnegie politely but firmly turned down both Spencer and Gladstone.

Mark Twain, who was a frequent correspondent and who always addressed Carnegie as Saint Andrew, wrote the most delightful begging letters of all those that Carnegie received. Sometimes Twain would be quite frivolous:

> You seem to be in prosperity. Could you lend an admirer a dollar & a half to buy a hymn book with? God will bless you. I feel it. I know it. N.B. If there should be another application this one not to count. P.S. Don't send the hymn-book, send the money. I want to make the selection myself.[62]

Sometimes it would be a serious request for Carnegie to enter some business venture with him or to rescue him from one that he was already caught in, but either way, he took Carnegie's refusals with good grace.[63]

Not so with other friends. Andrew D. White, president of Cornell University, was one of the most persistent and imaginative of all the applicants for Carnegie's money. White very often got what he asked for, but when he was refused, he did not hesitate to let Carnegie know of his unhappiness. "I did not regard my letter to you as begging. . . . Doubtless you are 'bored to extinction' with requests and suggestions and my letter may have been a sort of 'last straw.' Nearing the close of life, I have been doubtless overanxious to see certain great things done before my departure:—am sorry to have vexed you and will do so no more." [64]

Fortunately for his own peace of mind, Carnegie had a tough skin. He could say "no" and not be overly troubled by the hurt and angry reactions. Anyway, he knew that most of those rebuffed would soon be back with another project and another request.

On that early spring morning in 1901 when Carnegie sailed for Europe, leaving behind him safely locked in a vault in Hoboken the world's largest negotiable fortune, he had some understanding of the size of the task that lay before him. Just prior to his departure, he had sent to the managers of the Carnegie Company, now a subdivision of United States Steel, $5,000,000 of those bonds to be held in trust for the following purposes:

> Income from $1 million to be spent in maintaining Libraries at Braddock, Homestead & Duquesne works.
>
> Income from other $4 million to be applied:
>
> 1st, to provide for employees of Carnegie Company injured in service and for dependents of those killed
>
> 2nd, to provide small pensions to employees after long service, help in old age. Not to be regarded as a substitute for what the Company is already doing. . . . I make this first use of surplus wealth upon retiring from business, as an acknowledgement of the deep debt I owe to the workmen who have contributed so greatly to my success.[65]

He also left letters granting $5,200,000 to New York City for sixty-five branch libraries throughout the five boroughs, under the same conditions as applied to all of his library gifts,[66] and to St.

Louis, $1,000,000 for branch libraries. Thus, by three letters written in a single day, Carnegie had given away $11,200,000. All of his previous gifts up to that date had totaled $16,363,252.[67] But the interest on his bonds and other investments alone amounted to over $15,000,000 a year. Carnegie knew he would have to do much better than this if he were to make any substantial cut into his vast amount of capital. He had only begun to face up to the demands of his own gospel. He had once written to a friend, "It is the *pursuit* of wealth that enlivens life, the dead game, the fish caut become offensive in an hour." [68] Now that the game had been bagged, Carnegie was in full pursuit away from wealth. And he would soon feel that never before had he had to run quite so fast.

CHAPTER XXII

Philanthropy
Becomes Big Business
1901-1911

During the long summer months spent at Skibo in this first year of his retirement, Andrew Carnegie had ample time to consider how best to disperse his vast surplus of wealth, upon which he had hardly as yet made a dent. For someone who had written so extensively and preached so eloquently as he on the duties of the man of wealth, it is rather surprising that he faced this task better armed with platitudes than with any concrete program of action. Library giving, which he regarded as his specialty, had, indeed, become systematized by 1901, with standards established and a routine procedure to handle all requests efficiently and promptly. In the years that lay ahead, up to the time of his death, Carnegie (and, later, the Carnegie Corporation of New York and the Carnegie United Kingdom Trust) would give 2811 free public libraries, of which 1946 were located in the United States. Of the remainder, there were 660 in Britain, including Ireland, 156 in Canada, 23 in New Zealand, 13 in South Africa, 6 in the British West Indies, 4 in Australia, and 1 each in the islands of Seychelles, Mauritius, and Fiji. The total cost for all libraries was $50,364,808; those in the United States cost $44,854,731.25. Every state in the Union except Rhode Island had at least one Carnegie Library, and there were also libraries in the District of Columbia and the territories of Hawaii and Puerto Rico. Most had gone to three Midwestern states—164 to Indiana, 114 to Illinois, and 104 to Iowa—and to California, which got 122.[1] Bertram, with an auditor's accuracy, kept a monthly balance sheet of libraries completed, libraries under construction, and libraries promised, and Carnegie would periodically scrutinize these reports with the same avid attention he had once given to the minutes of the board meetings of Carnegie Steel.

There continued a steady stream of criticism from those who felt Carnegie was doing too much ("better for a community to do for itself")[2] and from those who felt he was doing too little ("a building without books is not a library").[3] But of all the criticism he was to receive for his philanthropic enterprises, the critical comments on his library program bothered him the least. He knew that no other gifts were as popular or had as direct an impact upon as large a number of people as did his public libraries. Virtually nonexistent in the United States before 1880, the free library, as a result of his philanthropy, became almost as much a part of America as the schoolhouse or church. A conservative estimate of the size of the reading public making use of Carnegie libraries in the United States a generation after he began his library program would be 35,000,000 persons a day. Carnegie liked to boast that the sun never set on Carnegie Free Public Libraries. They would remain his most enduring claim to popular fame. It pleased him especially to think that his gift forced the community itself to match that gift over every ten-year period, decade after decade. "Don't congratulate me," he wrote to a friend who had praised him for giving sixty-five branch libraries to New York City. "It's the best bargain I ever made. The money I have given is a small affair. See what I have compelled the city of New York to give!"[4]

Another area of giving which had become more or less systematized by 1901 was that of church organs—a form of philanthropy into which he rather inadvertently stumbled when he presented an organ in 1873 to the small Swedenborgian New Jerusalem

Church that his father had attended. Once this gift became publicized other requests began to come in, and soon Carnegie found himself involved in a major operation. Knowing the prejudice of Scottish Calvinists against instrumental music in church, particularly the pipe organ—"a kist fu' o' whistles"—Carnegie took a certain delight in seeing a Scottish Presbyterian Church swallow its pride and ask for an organ, in the hopes that this would induce Carnegie to make other and more holy contributions to the congregation. After a time, this game became no longer a sport but a big business. A church requesting an organ would have to fill out a questionnaire, showing its financial status, and submit it to Robert Franks, Carnegie's business secretary. If the church was not deeply in debt the request was usually granted. But the correspondence was exceptionally heavy and time-consuming for both Bertram, who had to answer the initial inquiries, and Franks, who made the financial investigations.[5] Carnegie, at least, learned one lesson from this experience—one should never make a gift to an institution unless one is prepared to enter that field on a large scale. As he wrote to Elizabeth Haldane, the noted Scottish author, who was interested in a charity school in Edinburgh, "Sorry, I cannot extend my field to cover the cause you have at heart. It would be a case of Organs over again. I gave one Organ to an church in Allegheny City, my home, and it has resulted in giving or contributing to over four thousand Church Organs, and the correspondence really takes the greater part of one Secretary's time. We have seven thousand Church Organs, arranged in order awaiting attention in this one department. As for schools and institutions of kindred nature, their name is legion. Can't enlarge even for you." [6] By 1919, Carnegie had given 4092 church organs in the United States, 2119 in England, 1005 in Scotland, and an additional 473 throughout the rest of the world, making a grand total of 7689 at a cost of $6,248,312 [7]—a chest full of whistles large enough to have impressed John Knox himself.

But other than organs and libraries, which at this time his busy secretaries were handling by themselves, Carnegie had no large projects in mind when he arrived in Scotland in the summer of 1901. There was no end to the possibilities and suggestions that were coming by the bushel basketful each day. He was even greeted in Britain with large newspaper advertisements for a contest on "How Mr. Carnegie Should Get Rid of His Wealth," sponsored by the makers of Mother Seigel's Syrup. The company promised a gold sovereign to the reader or readers whose suggestions either were accepted by Carnegie or happened to coincide with his own decision on how best to dispose of his fortune. Some 45,000 suggestions were submitted, which the company tabulated into categories. These included: [8]

Begging for self (by all odds the largest category)	12246
Recommending the free distribution of Mother Seigel's Syrup	5296
Begging for others	2268
Giving to churches	2044
Giving to the poor	1562
Giving it all to Carnegie's young daughter	509
Paying off the national debt	237

Quite obviously the readers of Mother Seigel's Syrup ads had not been very careful students of Carnegie's "Gospel of Wealth." Mother Seigel was not out any gold sovereigns, and Carnegie was to receive very little help from the general public in deciding on his philanthropic projects.

It must have been quite clear to Carnegie by now that his fortune exceeded the vision of philanthropy he had when he had written his essay on "Wealth" in 1889, both in the administration of the dispersal and in the fields of philanthropy. He could hardly expect to give more administrative duties to his overworked secretaries, who were already burdened with the library and organ projects; and the dispensation of swimming baths, parks, and civic auditoriums on a mass scale would be rather difficult to arrange. He had furthermore ruled out such obvious and eager recipients of largess as churches (except for those pestiferous pipe organs), sanitariums, and charitable alms-giving organizations like the Salvation Army, orphanages, and other homes and agencies for derelicts—"the submerged tenth" of society.

There was, to be sure, the whole area of medicine, but Carnegie was always curiously reluctant to enter into this broad field of philanthropy. Very early in his career as a philanthropist, in

1885, he had given what was then for him the quite substantial sum of $50,000 to establish the first medical research laboratory in the United States, at the Bellevue Hospital in New York, and at the same time, with considerable fanfare, he had sent at his own expense four small children to Paris, to be treated by Louis Pasteur for rabies—the first Americans to receive that treatment.[9] But in later years, when there was great pressure upon him from the medical profession to build hospitals and medical laboratories, and to provide other public health services, he steadfastly refused. "That is Mr. Rockefeller's specialty," he would say, with his cryptic little smile, to applicants from leading hospitals and medical schools throughout the country, "Go see him." [10] He did make a contribution of $120,000 to the Koch Institute of Berlin for medical research, and because of Louise Carnegie's interest in the career of Helen Keller, he made several contributions to the New York and Massachusetts Associations for the Blind.[11] But most applicants for medical aid who came begging went away still begging. "I have always held that hospitals should be city institutions like prisons," he wrote the head of one large hospital in New York. "As the latter are the refuge of diseased minds, the other of diseased bodies. Therefore I have not included hospitals among the proper objects of private charity. . . . I think you should show the city the work you are doing and why it is necessary and ask its aid." [12]

Having largely excluded the spiritual and physical areas of man's nature as proper fields for his philanthropy, Carnegie really had left to him only one major possibility—other than specific projects of political or social reform—and that was man's mind. If one defines education in the broadest sense possible, which would include libraries as a form of popular, undirected education, then one can say that the great bulk of Carnegie's fortune—over 80 per cent—was to go for educational purposes: libraries, colleges and universities, institutions to promote scientific research and the diffusion of knowledge, and individual grants and pensions to college teachers. The dispersal of this vast sum, nearly $300,000,000, would require that Carnegie abandon his essentially naïve view, expressed in his "Gospel of Wealth," of the man of great wealth himself serving as the administrator for the distribution of that wealth. By the very magnitude of his fortune, Carnegie was forced to adopt and develop the modern philanthropic foundation as the only feasible means of administrating the dispersal of funds.

Carnegie, of course, did not invent the trust or foundation. The idea of the benefactor leaving a specified sum to be administered by a designated group of trustees for purposes specified by the benefactor is an old tradition in the history of philanthropy. Benjamin Franklin, Stephen Girard, and Peter Cooper, among others, had established such trust funds in the early years of the Republic. But with Carnegie and Rockefeller the modern foundation, established to organize and conduct what Rockefeller called "this business of benevolence," was truly established. The Rockefeller and Carnegie foundations were as natural a development in the field of philanthropy as Standard Oil and United States Steel were in the field of manufacturing. As Rockefeller said in 1899, to the group of leading citizens who had gathered to commemorate the tenth anniversary of the founding of the University of Chicago, "Let us erect a foundation, a trust, and engage directors who will make it a life work to manage, with our personal co-operation, this business of benevolence properly and effectively." [13]

Carnegie had come to much the same conclusion only a few years earlier. In establishing and endowing the Carnegie Institute at Pittsburgh, he had established a board of trustees to manage the "benevolent business" of the library, art gallery, music hall, and museum. This, in effect, was Carnegie's first foundation. It also marked a departure from his earlier position that a benefactor should personally administer his own benefactions. But Carnegie felt that this was simply a proper delegation of responsibilities, much as he had delegated authority to his "young geniuses" in Carnegie Steel. He made it perfectly clear to W. M. Frew, secretary of the Institute, that he expected hard-headed, practical men of broad and general interests on the board:

Let me say . . . that the last men I should appoint to manage a business are experts. The expert mind is too narrow—the artistic, very narrow. For this reason, painters of the day ridiculed Millet as vulgar; the musicians of the day, Wagner as insane; writers of the day, Shakespeare as bombastic. The future is to laugh at many pictures which experts are extolling today;

and art amateurs are buying to be in the fashion, and at many books which are supposed to have the elements of enduring fame. I wish to trust my fund to a committee dominated by able men of affairs, who have within reach the expert element with which they can confer. Besides this, I wish a larger number of officials directly from the people in the committee, as I am satisfied that unless the institution be kept in touch with the masses, and therefore popular, it cannot be widely useful.[14]

One of the strengths of the American private university system, Carnegie felt, was that these universities were corporate bodies, owned and governed by boards of trustees who generally were drawn from the affluent business community. He looked with scorn on the impractical, unworldly, internal self-governance of the Scottish universities. "Americans do not trust their money to a lot of professors and principals [presidents] who are bound in set ways, and have a class feeling about them which makes it impossible to make reforms. Americans put their money under the control of business men at the head of the Universities. If I had my own way, I should introduce that system into Scottish universities." [15]

Carnegie had some other notions about higher education that were equally disturbing to the traditional, classically trained educator, particularly in Britain. In a speech at the graduating exercises held for the Pierce College of Business and Shorthand of Philadelphia in 1891, he propounded at great length on the folly of the classical, liberal arts education, and praised the Pierce College graduating class for the practical education they had received:

> In the storms of life are they to be strengthened and sustained and held to their post and to the performance of duty by drawing upon Hebrew or Greek barbarians as models, or upon examples of our own modern heroes? Is Shakespeare or Homer to be the reservoir from which they draw? . . . What support have Greek or Latin quotations—fearfully pronounced—comparable to what we have in our own tongue? For instance, "Don't give up the ship;" or "Fight it out on this line;" or "If any man touches the flag shoot him on the spot." . . . I rejoice, therefore, to know that your time has not been wasted upon

dead languages, but has been fully occupied in obtaining knowledge of shorthand and typewriting . . . and that you are fully equipped to sail upon the element upon which you must live your lives and earn your living. Good-bye—success to you —*bon voyage*—never say FAIL.[16]

The speech was a great success, although some of his practically trained young scholars in typing and shorthand must have been a bit puzzled by that strange foreign expression he chose to use in the final sentence.

In an article entitled "How to Win a Fortune," written for the New York *Tribune,* he had been even more blunt. "The almost total absence of the [college] graduate from high position in the business world seems to justify the conclusion that college education as it exists seems almost fatal to success in that domain. . . . It is in this field that the graduate had little chance, entering at twenty, against the boy who swept the office, or who begins as shipping clerk at fourteen. The facts prove this." Carnegie did express some interest in "the polytechnic and scientific school . . . The trained mechanic of the past, who has, as we have seen, hitherto carried off most of the honours in our industrial works, is now to meet a rival in the scientifically educated youth, who will push him hard—very hard indeed. . . . Such young educated men have one important advantage over the apprenticed mechanic—they are open-minded and without prejudice. . . . Let no one, therefore, underrate the advantage of education; only it must be education adapted to the end in view, and must give instruction bearing upon a man's career if he is to make his way to fortune." Even so, Carnegie felt, it was the trained mechanics who remained the leaders in business, "the founder and manager of famous concerns . . . They are the winning classes. . . . It is they who have risen to the top and taken command, who have abandoned salaried positions and boldly risked all in the founding of a business. College graduates will usually be found under salaries, trusted subordinates." [17]

Carnegie's fellow entrepreneur and colleague in the anti-imperialist movement, Edward Atkinson, found all of this prattle about "the self-made man" a bit too thick. "Will you kindly send me a copy of 'The Tribune' of February 1st, containing your letter on the 'Classical Education,'" he wrote Carnegie.[18] "You started young without a classical education. I did the same thing. We have both accomplished something, and we have reached radically different conclusions. I should recommend every boy of capacity to make the utmost sacrifice possible and to devote the time up to twenty-three or twenty-five if necessary, to getting the benefit of a thorough University training, including the Classics. There are no dead languages. English is pervaded throughout with Greek and Latin forms, and even the little Greek that I learned at school in preparing for College, I regard a very valuable possession in giving me a command of English. Now of all the elements of life necessary to success the command of language— the comprehension of the logic of the sentence—and the faculty of definition are most important. . . . I propose to review your article, therefore I send for it." [19]

As Carnegie might have expected, the reviews in most of the British press of his views on education were far more critical than Atkinson. *Blackwood's Edinburgh Magazine* set the pace for the defenders of traditional English education:

> Mr. Carnegie has devoted his whole life to the amassing of money; and if he die poor, it will be by hastily ridding himself of the dollars he has collected. . . . Success for him is the accumulation of dollars. The "splendid" heroes, whose names he is never tired of quoting, are all money bags. . . . Maybe Mr. Carnegie has never heard the fable of Midas. If for a moment he can overcome his loathing of the past, we would urge him to read it. . . . Push and screw; buy cheap and sell dear. . . . To get money you must strangle joy and murder peace. . . . Presently the American ideal of life will be our own. . . . In old days, a rich man enjoyed his wealth—and if he did the community "no good," at least he did not insult it with patronage.[20]

Blackwood's voice was perhaps more stridently hostile than most, but many Scots shared the magazine's concern over the future of Scottish higher education when in the late spring of 1901 Carnegie announced that his next great philanthropic venture would be in the field of higher education, and that as one part of this program he proposed to create the Carnegie Trust for the Universities of Scotland, endowed with United States Steel Corporation bonds, with a par value of $10,000,000, or £2,000,000. This was Carnegie's largest single grant to that date. To the four Scottish universities of St. Andrews, Aberdeen, Edinburgh, and Glasgow, whose combined total endowment at that time was only £72,000, the prospect of a £2,000,000 endowment with an annual revenue of £104,000 was as dazzlingly incredible as if each had been told that it was about to be visited by a fairy godmother.[21] Fairy godmothers, however, usually have strings on their gifts— midnight curfews and other troublesome restrictions. When the news leaked out, there were many cautious and even alarmed voices raised that this particular fairy godmother intended to debase and vulgarize—in the quite literal meaning of that word—Scottish higher education.

The terms of the Trust were simple and direct enough: one-half of the annual income "to be applied toward the improvement and expansion of the four Scottish universities, in the Faculties of Science and Medicine, also for improving and extending the opportunities for scientific study and research, and for increasing the facilities for acquiring a knowledge of History, Economics, English Literature and Modern Languages, and such other subjects cognate to a technical or commercial education . . . by the erection and maintenance of buildings, laboratories, classrooms, museums or libraries, the providing of efficient apparatus, books and equipment, the institution and endowment of professorships and lectureships, including postgraduate lectureships and scholarships . . . for the purpose of encouraging research." The other half of the income "or such part thereof as may be found requisite, shall be devoted to the payment of the whole or part of the ordinary class fees, exigible by the universities from students of Scottish birth or extraction." [22]

Both provisions were subjected to a storm of controversy and criticism by educators, politicians, and journalists. There were many, particularly among the upper classes, who strenuously objected to the remission of fees for Scottish students, seeing in this a "pauperization" of the university clientele, a debasing of educational standards, and a populistic encouragement of the lower classes to push out of "their proper station in life."

There were others who criticized the heavy emphasis upon science and technological training. John Morley had agreed to serve on the board of trustees, along with such distinguished figures as Lord Bryce, the Earl of Rosebery, Arthur Balfour, Henry Campbell-Bannerman, Herbert Asquith, Lord Haldane, Lord Shaw, and the chairman, the Earl of Elgin. But even Morley felt obliged to enter a mild demur on this point. "The conflict is not between sciences, engineering &c on the one hand, and old Greek on the other; but between a purely and exclusively practical training on the one hand, and on the other training in which the deep matters of human life, character, and conduct, as set forth in history, philosophy & literature, shall have at least an equal place. True, literary education has had an excessive share—very excessive—but that is no reason at all why a man like you should now like Luther's drunken man on horseback having swayed violently to one side sway violently to the other. We expect you to show that you have not been the friend of M. Arnold for nothing—to say nothing of humbler folk, like the highly respectable friend who has the honour to subscribe himself Your very faithful friend." [23]

To which Carnegie had a ready rejoinder—several, in fact:

Why institute comparisons & thus provoke antagonisms? I have been repelled by such folly. We don't get it in the United States & Harvard & Yale simply could not be commanding Powers today if they ignored, *or slighted* their scientific Depts. You knew & I knew that for us—yes, even for me, practical as I am—the flavor & philosophy of Poets & wise men is the sweetest of all foods, but for others, not so & these the vast majority who must earn a living.[24]

After the Trust was formally established, he wrote again to Morley:

Glad people approve "The Trust" sorry you were absent at final meeting. I get many letters telling me how important is the remission of fees, but I don't place that feature as of first importance. *Research* is the soul. You and Principal Story are not quite right anent the Classics. One doesn't offer a millionaire a check. Classics in all Scottish Universities are provided for to the exclusion almost of all else. Had there been the reverse their claims should have been considered. Science is the Cinderella of the family of Knowledge in Britian & the prince

838

came to her as you remember. Her Haughty Sisters, Miss Greek, Miss Italian & others were not chosen.[25]

As in all good fairy tales, this fairy godmother came stocked with only one size of glass slippers, which would fit only the favored one. No amount of persuasion, even from Morley, would have any effect upon Carnegie.

Although Carnegie, for sentimental reasons, had undoubtedly intended to do something rather spectacular for Scottish educational institutions, the particular form in which it was done was largely attributable to the efforts of Lord Shaw of Dunfermline. In a series of delightful letters written to his daughter, Isabel, in 1919, Lord Shaw gave the background to the creation of the Scottish Universities Trust. In 1895 he had been a house guest of the Carnegies at Cluny Castle, and while fishing for trout on Loch Laggan he asked the young boatman who had taken him out what he wanted to do with his life. The lad replied that he would very much like to go to a university and become a doctor, but of course could not because of the expense. Shaw, who had been a poor boy himself but whose family had scraped and borrowed to put him through the University of Edinburgh, was very sympathetic. He asked the boy if it would make any difference if there were no fees charged. The boatman replied that why, of course, then he could go. Shaw told the story at dinner that night. The responses of some of the guests were typical of their class— "unwarranted ambition" and "hopelessly unprepared." Carnegie said nothing and appeared to be pondering the matter. Shaw, an M.P., later told the story in the House of Commons and within two days had an offer from a friend to pay the fees for the lad, whose career was then made.

Shaw could not forget the incident, however, and soon thereafter he wrote an article for the *Nineteenth Century* magazine, in January 1897, entitled "The Educational Peace of Scotland," in which he argued for the abolition of all university fees in Scotland as a fulfillment of John Knox's dream of free education for all Scottish youth. There was no meaningful response to this idea until four years later, when he received a cablegram from Carnegie, asking Shaw to meet him when he arrived in Britain. They met at the Langham Hotel in London early in May.

"Shaw," said Carnegie, "I read your article in the *Nineteenth Century*. . . . I am disposed to realize your idea. . . . How much do you need?"

Shaw answered £1,000,000. Carnegie wanted to know how he knew that. Shaw explained that it would take the annual income of £50,000 to pay for the present fees charged and to permit some expansion, which would inevitably come with tuition free universities. Carnegie replied, "How are we to do this? Can you manage?"

As Shaw wrote to his daughter, "Here was railroad speed! I pulled up. 'Mr. Carnegie,' said I, 'this is good business, but it is big business, too big to entrust to me or to any one man. You must get the whole nation on your side, have a live trust, put men in it of both parties . . . and meantime send for Ross; we need skilled help like his.' "

The Ross whom Shaw referred to was John Ross of Dunfermline, Carnegie's solicitor and ultimately Carnegie's philanthropic alter ego in Scotland—a James Bertram and a Robert Franks combined. Ross came the next day, a group of eminent men were decided upon to be the trustees, and it became Shaw's task to solicit their support. Many, like Lord Balfour, Secretary for Scotland, were at first cool to the idea, but at last Shaw got all whom he, Carnegie, and Ross had selected to agree to serve as trustees. Carnegie then told Shaw he wanted to contribute additional funds to the Trust for scientific research and equipment. It was decided that the Trust should be endowed at £1,500,000— or $7,500,000. The agreement was signed, and Shaw felt that his dream was about to be realized.

Shortly thereafter, however, the project, from Shaw's point of view, was in jeopardy. "And," as Shaw told his daughter, "its danger was in Carnegie himself, who naturally wanted to be associated with men of power, and who always had a real weakness towards the aristocrat. In later life, poor man, this led him far astray." Aristocrats, who strongly opposed the opening of the Scottish universities to all free of charge, got to Carnegie. Shaw was informed by Henry Campbell-Bannerman, who supported the abolition of fees, that Carnegie intended to change the Trust deed to limit the exemption of fees only to those who applied for exemption "on grounds of poverty." Shortly thereafter, Shaw received a message from Carnegie to meet him and Ross in Dunfermline.

At this dramatic meeting, as Shaw later related the story, Carnegie opened the conversation with an aggressive attack. "Shaw, you have led me into a nice fix. I feel that I have been rather affronted. I now find that your scheme is no good." Shaw knew then that the aristocrats had captured Carnegie.

"I am sorry to hear you say that," Shaw replied, "or think that anything I have ever said or done has put an affront upon you. I meant your name to be loved for generations."

"This thing will not do," Carnegie broke in. "The help is not needed."

"Who told you that? I know the kind that told you."

Carnegie was unmoved but willing to talk. He said that he had been informed that the fees were but a small part of the total cost for the session. Shaw replied that for the really poor they were the major obstacle, that he had known crofters who actually sent food to their children so they could eat while attending the university, but that "the meeting of hard cash for fees was cruel."

Carnegie said, "There is a better use for my money and I have resolved on it—to equip the Universities."

At this point, Shaw arose and began to gather up his papers. Carnegie exclaimed, "Shaw, what does this mean? Does it mean that you are not to be a trustee?"

"It means exactly that. I took you for a democrat"—Carnegie's eyes blazed at that—"and here you have been consulting with aristocrats and giving away endowments right enough—but why not build on your democracy, get the people of Scotland on your side by giving them this free charter that I want?"

"Then in the pause," Shaw later related, "and to his everlasting credit, Ross struck in, 'Would it not be possible, gentlemen, to realize both your schemes.' Carnegie looked at me; and I said, 'I could have no objection to that. I favor both.' Then Carnegie too began gathering up papers. 'You to get your million pounds,' he said. 'That would make things solid,' I replied. The next morning Carnegie gave Ross his orders. 'Shaw to get a million and also another million to Universities for equipment.'"

"Shall I now write the epilogue?" Shaw concluded in his letter to his daughter.

On the final settlement of the Deed, several of us came out of the Secretary of Scotland's room together, and of course, the warm-hearted donor was being congratulated. He—little man —took Lord Balfour—big man—by the buttonhole, and said, "Reminds me of the Sunday School collection. Each scholar had to quote an appropriate text. Number One toddles forward, puts down his dime with 'Blessed is he that considereth the poor." Number Two, with "The Lord loveth a cheerful giver." Then comes up Number Three, puts his dime in, and solemnly quotes his text—'A fool and his money's soon parted!' " [26]

The victory was not as complete for Lord Shaw as his account to his daughter would indicate. It is true that £1,000,000 were set aside for the payment of the university fees, "or such part thereof as may be found requisite." But under the terms of the Trust deed, the funds for remission of fees were not made available to all students, but only to those students who applied. The student applying, to be sure, did not have to plead poverty or have to submit a financial statement from his parents, but the fund had established a scholarship system, based on the assumption of need, rather than the free university system that Shaw had advocated.

In spite of this compromise with the aristocrats, the Carnegie Trust for the Universities of Scotland remained throughout Carnegie's life one of the most controversial of all of his large benefactions. The trustees included some of the most distinguished and respected men in Britain, and there was only praise for the unstinting efforts of the board, and particularly of its chairman, the Earl of Elgin, in the efficacious and wise distribution of funds. Nor could Carnegie's most hostile critics accuse him of interference once the Trust was established. The deed was broadly enough stated to give the trustees ample freedom. To give emphasis to that freedom of action, Carnegie later added a codicil to the deed stating that, at any time in the future when two-thirds of the trustees agreed, the deed could be amended in any way the Trustees saw fit. "I do not believe any body of men wise enough to legislate for future generations," he wrote Lord Elgin. "I know that at any time in the future, two-thirds of my Trustees will not err." [27] At a much later date, when the dream of John Knox, as interpreted by Lord Shaw, had become a reality in all of Britain, Carnegie's foresight and faith were vindicated. The provision for flexibility permitted the trustees to divert almost all of the revenue from the endowment into equipment, research, and instructional resources.

In the early years of the Trust, however, there were some who did not share Carnegie's great confidence in the trustees. There was a continuing concern that these men, however benevolent and wise they might be, by the very magnitude of their purse were playing the role of "autocrat, capricious, incalculable, and responsible to God alone." [28] The *National Review,* always highly critical of Carnegie, charged that in creating an academic dictatorship he had established a power that "runs counter to the very idea that underlies the university system." [29] One of the most probing criticisms of the Trust came from a professor, W. M. Ramsay, at the University of Aberdeen. Writing in the *Contemporary Review,* seven years after the establishment of the Trust, he pointed out that many of the things that had been feared by the early opponents of the Trust had not come to pass. The universities had not been swamped by hordes of ill-prepared students as had been predicted, nor had the classics suffered as the traditionalists had feared—and as, perhaps, Carnegie had hoped. More students in the grammar and preparatory schools were now reading the classics at a higher level than ever before in order to take advantage of the Trust funds by being admitted to the universities. "The Trust has been the main external support of the Classics." Nor could Professor Ramsay deny the boost that had been given to scientific research and consequently research in all fields by the funds the Trust provided.

He felt, however, that the trustees did have too much power in setting the whole tone of education in Scotland. They were men who had for the most part been educated at Oxford or Cambridge and knew very little about the Scottish University system. Standards, at least in some areas, had been lowered by the policy of excluding advanced classes or "extra-classes" from the benefits of the Trust. Ramsay also objected to the "one invidious feature" of the Trust, which "discriminates according to birth" by providing scholarships only to students of Scottish birth or Scottish extraction. It did not affect Aberdeen University too greatly, inasmuch as 90 per cent of the students there were Scottish, but in the other three universities, where there were many foreign students, "it is responsible for perpetrating a certain odium" against all Scottish students whose fees were paid by the Trust.[30]

Indeed, the fee question remained a source of constant irritation for university officials, students, and the general public as long as Carnegie lived. Nevertheless, many Scottish youths attended the universities and went on to distinguished careers in scholarship and the professions who might have otherwise never been educated beyond grammar school. There is no question that the Trust awakened Scottish higher education to an intellectual activity that it had not known since the golden days of the late eighteenth century. With funds available for equipment and research, Scotland was now prepared to advance into the twentieth century. Throughout Britain, to be named a Carnegie Research Fellow was a mark of distinction for any young scholar. Twice the students of the ancient University of St. Andrews elected Carnegie their Rector for a three-year term, and it was with more than the usual commencement platitudinous politeness that the Principal of the University of Edinburgh, Sir Alexander Grant, in awarding Andrew Carnegie an honorary degree in 1906, said, "Let us remember that the Carnegie Trust for the Scottish Universities is but a single chapter, so to speak, in the long story of Mr. Carnegie's benefactions. The ideals which he seeks to realise are such as command the warm approbation of the University; for the foremost objects towards which his generosity is directed are to bring knowledge within easy access of all classes, to extend the usefulness of educational institutions and enhance their efficiency, and to promote International Peace. . . . It is therefore with feelings of sincere admiration as well as of profound gratitude that the University offers her degree to the creator of the Carnegie Trust." [31]

Carnegie, somewhat scarred by his first major encounter in this "business of benevolence," must have welcomed these words as a soothing unguent. "Gratitude and sweet words" were always welcome, for they further strengthened his conviction, already strong, that he had acted wisely and well.

Carnegie was also proud of what he felt was his only direct influence upon Scottish higher education aside from providing funds—that of bringing the principals of the four Scottish universities together for the first time.[32] From 1901 until the outbreak of World War I, these four educational leaders met for several days each summer at Skibo with Carnegie, shared their common problems and discussed educational projects together. Carnegie considered this to be the best single thing he ever did for Scottish education.

Carnegie's next major venture into philanthropy, also in Scotland, was directed toward only one small part of his native land, his beloved Dunfermline. Once, in response to a letter from an acquaintance in Pittsburgh criticizing Carnegie for not having more sympathy for the "submerged tenth" and for "not giving with his heart as well as his head," Carnegie had answered, "My friend, the heart is the steam in the boiler; the head is the engine that regulates dangerous steam and prevents disastrous explosions. So far from my heart being allowed to more control, I see that wisdom requires it to be more and more repressed." [33] Dunfermline, however, was clearly an instance of Carnegie's letting off steam. Like his private pension rolls, it was to serve as a safety valve of sentiment, for which he would never make apology.

Carnegie had already made generous gifts to his native town, having provided it with his first library and with swimming baths which were the marvel of Scotland. Dunfermline, in return, had given to its most illustrious living son his first "Freedom of the City," cherished by him above all others. Carnegie was eager to do more, much more, for the "Auld Grey Toon." It was the classic case of the returning son, having achieved fame and fortune elsewhere, becoming prodigal at home because he still felt it necessary to prove himself in a place where he had once been a nobody. Carnegie's proof was to exceed all expectations.

It began in 1900, when Colonel Thomas Hunt, the new Laird of Pittencrieff, approached John Ross with the rather surprising suggestion that he might be willing to sell Pittencrieff to Andrew Carnegie if Carnegie would meet his price. Ross was amazed at this suggestion, for like all citizens of Dunfermline he knew of the old feud between the Hunt and Morrison families. Colonel Hunt's father, James Hunt, had for half a century carried on a running court battle with old Tom Morrison, Carnegie's grandfather, and with his son, the Bailie Morrison, over the rights of the people of Dunfermline versus the rights of the Lairds of Pittencrieff. The Hunts were relative newcomers to the landed gen-

845

try class of Scotland. Grandfather Morrison had known men who remembered the time when James Hunt's grandfather had earned an honest living as a barber in Dunfermline. But having acquired some wealth through fortunate investment, the Hunts had purchased Pittencrieff. The estate lay at the edge of the city, and the Hunts were constantly trying to enlarge their holding by encroaching upon the common lands of the town. The Morrisons, who always enjoyed a public lawsuit, had on several occasions brought James Hunt to court and had successfully blocked his efforts at expansion. They had also forced him to open his estate once a year in order that the historic monuments in the Glen might be viewed by the public. After one such suit, the enraged Hunt had challenged Morrison to a duel, a challenge which was quickly accepted. "All right," boomed out Andrew's Uncle Tom for all the town to hear, "I'll fight ye. As challenged party, I have the choice of weapons. I'll take my father's shoemaker's knife and you take your grandfather's razor." [34]

Such insults were not quickly forgotten, and James Hunt had decreed that thereafter no Morrison or descendant of Morrisons should ever step foot on Pittencrieff's sacred soil. Like a fabled ogre, James Hunt stood at the entrance to the estate on the one day of the year that the Glen was open to the public to make sure that no Morrison got inside—and that included the small boy Andrew, barred by his ancestry from seeing those historic ruins of Dunfermline's glorious past: Malcolm's Tower, Margaret's shrine, and the one remaining wall of the palace of the Stuarts. Now, sixty years later, James Hunt's son was offering to sell all of it to that same Andrew, thus making old Tom Morrison's grandson the Laird of Pittencrieff. Hunt's original price was £70,000, which Ross, in writing to Carnegie about the offer, thought was double what it was worth. "I cannot conceive what has put selling into the Colonel's head. I thought he would never part with the Park & the Glen." [35] After consulting with Carnegie, Ross's reply to Hunt was that the price was too high and that Mr. Carnegie was not disposed to consider the purchase further.[36]

But, of course, Carnegie was most disposed to consider the matter further. There was nothing in the world he wanted quite as much as Pittencrieff. The negotiations continued for over two years, with Lord Shaw, who was on much better terms with the

Hunt family than was Ross, acting as Carnegie's intermediary. Finally, on Christmas Eve 1902, Carnegie purchased for himself the most wonderful Christmas present of his life, the entire Pittencrieff estate, for £45,000.[37] To Cousin Dod, he simply wrote, *"Pittencrieff is ours."* [38] No need to tell Dod what the possession of Pittencrieff meant. To Morley, Carnegie had to be more explicit:

> My new title beats all. I am Laird of Pittencrieff—that's the glen & Palace ruins at Dunfermline, the most sacred spot to me on Earth. Would rather be Pittencrieff than King Edward by a long shot. I laugh at the importance of it. It really tickles me. But Oh—those who have passed should be here to enjoy it. What it would have meant to my Grandfather, Father, Uncles. Ah, Uncle Lauder more than any. He was born in Pittencrieff Glen & played on its sunny braes as a child.
>
> You remember Mr. Gladstone astounding me by quoting from Four in Hand: "What Mecca is to the Mohammadan, Benares to the Hindu, Jerusalem to the Christian—all that & more, Dunfermline is to me"—that meant Pittencrieff & the abbey bell. By the way please read in Four in Hand about the abbey bell—the only real good paragraph I think I ever wrote. It brot tears to my eyes as I read it yesterday in the Dunfermline paper.[39]

Clearly, Carnegie was in the proper sentimental mood to make a handsome benefaction to Dunfermline, and Pittencrieff was to be the first installment. In November 1903, in formal solemn rites which, unfortunately, Carnegie, by then back in New York, could not attend, the estate was transferred in perpetuity to the Royal Burgh of Dunfermline. Carnegie kept for himself during his lifetime only a small portion of the estate, including the mound upon which stand the ruins of Malcolm's Tower. Keeping this bit of land allowed Carnegie to retain his proud new title, Laird of Pittencrieff.

Carnegie asked Lord Shaw to be his representative at the formal opening of Pittencrieff. "If it were practicable to associate with you my cousin, Robert Morrison, I think it will be a fine touch. You know his father, Bailie Morrison, is to be credited with getting part of the ruins back to the nation and open to Dunfermline. The then Mr. Hunt, by special order, prohibited any Morrison from entering them. To have his son stand in Pittencrieff at your side and to be a party to presenting the whole estate to Dunfermline would be historically fine." [40]

John Ross wrote a long letter to Carnegie the day after Pittencrieff was opened as a park. As is so often true of November in Dunfermline, the weather had been bad for several days before, and on the morning of the ceremony there were showers. "Then it became so beautiful that you could not have failed to believe in a Special Providence. Never since the Park was created has it looked better, never was there a more lovely sunset, a clearer view, a lovelier moon. . . . Lord Elgin and his two daughters headed the procession, then came a carriage with Mr. & Mrs. Shaw and Mr. & Mrs. Morrison. . . . The Lauders were under the escort of Hew Morrison in full Highland costume. I must not forget to say that costume was the order of the day. I was ablaze in a scarlet robe. The wonder is I did not take fire. . . . Ah me! when shall we see the like of that procession again?" [41]

For a time, Carnegie toyed with the idea of fixing up the old high-gabled mansion on the estate as his personal residence, and he entered into discussions with Dunfermline Provost James Macbeth about it. Ross and others soon persuaded him that it would not be the proper thing to do, that if he maintained a residence in Pittencrieff, even though he might be there only infrequently, the people of Dunfermline would never regard the estate as belonging to them. So Carnegie called the whole thing off,[42] and the mansion became a recreation hall where old men would gather in the afternoons to play checkers and mothers would stop for a bit of breath after pushing their prams through the formal gardens and spacious lawns of Pittencrieff. Ever since that ceremonial November day in 1903, the gates have been opened every day of the year, and it is truly a people's park. A concert hall and tea room were built in the center of the park, along with great horticultural conservatories that brought the flamboyant beauty of the tropics to this unlikely old grey town on the cold Firth of Forth. Majestic peacocks now sweep their tails across Pittencrieff's green lawns, while, with equal incongruity, the drab native sparrows flutter through the glass enclosed tropics of the conservatories, luxuriating in the warmth as they pick up the seeds of exotic jungle plants.

Pittencrieff was but a part, though to Carnegie a very special part, of a much larger plan he had in mind for Dunfermline. During the summer of 1903, while the old Hunt estate was being cleaned up and landscaped for its opening as a park, Carnegie was busy with Ross writing several drafts of a deed that would create the Carnegie Dunfermline Trust. After several tries by Ross and many marginal corrections by Carnegie, the final deed creating the Trust ($2,500,000 in United States Steel Corporation bonds) and naming the trustees (all from Dunfermline or County Fife) was ready for publication on 3 August 1903. As a preamble to the deed, Carnegie had written:

> I, Andrew Carnegie of New York and of Skibo in the County of Sutherland, Scotland in pursuance of a duty which I have long felt incumbent on me and which I have so far already endeavored to discharge, vizt:—to distribute in my lifetime the surplus wealth which I possess in such a manner as shall best advance the well-being and happiness of the greatest number of beneficiaries; and being desirous of testing by experiment the advantages which a community may derive by having placed at its disposal, under the administration of public spirited and intelligent men chosen from among themselves, funds dedicated to the purpose of providing the means of introducing into the daily lives of the masses, such privileges and enjoyments as are under present circumstances considered beyond their reach, but which if brought within their reach are calculated to carry into their homes and their conduct sweetness and light. . . .[43]

The phrase "sweetness and light," which Carnegie had taken from Matthew Arnold, was his favorite expression when referring to the benefactions he wished to bestow upon his native town. It is interesting to note that in the first draft of the deed Carnegie attempted to cover his sentimentality for Dunfermline with a cloak of rationality, so that he might still appear before the world as the "scientific philanthropist." He had carefully made the point that he was bestowing these riches upon Dunfermline "from no partiality to my native town" but rather as a part of a larger scientific experiment in which he intended to select a town of equal size in the United States to which he would also bring the same gifts of "sweetness and light." "I have considered other communities in the new and old home of our race—hope also to select one in the former. It will be instructive to have one in each of the two branches of our race, but first this will require time." [44]

Fortunately for Carnegie's sanity this paragraph was deleted in the final draft, for one can imagine the flood of applications from towns all over the United States, putting forth claims to be part of the experiment in "sweetness and light." Carnegie was obliged to appear naked before the world as an unabashed sentimentalist. Nevertheless, it was an interesting idea, and sociologists might well have been provided with material for fascinating comparative studies between two cultures had the experiment been carried out.

In the earlier drafts Carnegie had also been quite specific as to areas of "sweetness and light" in which he expected the trustees to be active: public gardens, parks, golf links, art galleries, public exhibitions of art, lecturers, public entertainment such as theatrical and musical events, musical societies, field trips for school children to historic and scenic spots in Scotland, the restoration of the Abbey and the palace of the Stuarts, medical clinics, even model housing for the poor. These specific proposals were also deleted from the final draft, and instead Carnegie charged the trustees with the undefined task of bringing "into the monotonous lives of the toiling masses of Dunfermline—especially the young —some charm, some happiness, some elevating conditions of life which residence elsewhere would have denied; that the child of my native town, looking back in after years, however far from home it may have roamed, will feel that simply by virtue of being such, life has been made happier and better. If this be the fruit of your labours you will have succeeded; if not, you will have failed. . . . Remember you are pioneers. . . . Try many things freely, but discard just as freely. . . . Not what other cities have is your standard; it is something beyond this which they lack, and your funds should be strictly devoted to this." At the same time, the trustees were enjoined from doing those things which the community should tax itself to do for itself. "It is not intended that Dunfermline should be relieved from keeping herself abreast of other towns, generation after generation, according to the standards of the time. . . . I can imagine it may be your duty in the future to abandon beneficent fields from time to time when municipalities enlarge their spheres of action and embrace these." [45] No easy task that he had laid out for his eager but somewhat bewildered trustees.

Carnegie had granted considerable freedom of action to the trustees of all his philanthropic trusts, but in no other did he take such a personal interest from its very inception as in the Dunfermline Trust. For weeks he fussed with Ross, who was the designated chairman, over the selection of the other trustees. Carnegie had wanted a Roman Catholic priest as a member of the commission, but this was too ecumenical for Calvinist Dunfermline. Ross, in as polite terms as possible, informed Carnegie that in his opinion "no priest would care to serve and the Roman Catholics in Dunfermline would not feel such a representation necessary." Carnegie yielded: "All right, Boss. Exit Holy Father, but I like to keep in with one who can really grant absolution. It may be handy someday." [46] On one point regarding selection, however, Carnegie was adamant. There had to be representatives of the working class on the commission along with the more wealthy business and professional men and town and county officials. So John Weir, Secretary of the Fife Miners Union, John Hynd, a miner, and James Brown, a dyer, were there, along with the wealthy Beveridges, the Earl of Elgin, and Provost Macbeth.[47]

Carnegie also had definite ideas on projects, even though the specification of those projects had been taken out of the deed. As he became increasingly liberal in his political views, in reconciliation with his Radical origins, this progressivism was reflected in his philanthropic ideas. In 1911, he wrote Ross that he wanted him to look into the possibility of "model housing for the poor." Remembering his own childhood days of squabbling with neighborhood women over the use of the town pump, he said he wanted to make sure these houses had indoor plumbing, especially a bathroom. "I consider this the most important feature. . . . I know of no way of diffusing sweetness and lite more easily and practically than by improving housing conditions among the poor." [48] Again, Ross felt obliged to set Carnegie straight on the facts of life. "Where is this experiment to stop? If the Trust began they would at once create antagonism with all the present house owners, who would say that they were being subjected to an unfair competition, and there would be no possibility of satisfying the demands of those who would wish to inhabit the model houses. . . . I quite agree that the improvement of houses for the poorer classes is one of the most urgent social needs, but it is a complex question and involves a good many others, such as the wages which the tenants earn out of which the rent must be paid. It involves also the social habits of the people and their ability to do justice to the occupation of such houses." [49] Carnegie was disappointed. "The tone of yours of March 9th is indeed discouraging." But he was not ready to yield completely: "Here is a suggestion submitted for discussion by one entirely ignorant of the situation, but therefore certain he is right as usual in this." Carnegie's suggestion was that the Trust should approach the owners saying that it would fix up houses for the tenants if the owners would not then charge any more rent.[50] The trustees gave as little attention to this modification as they had to the original proposal. Britain was not yet ready for the welfare state, even if done by private philanthropy.

On the other hand, sharp disagreement on occasion arose between Carnegie and the trustees when they proposed projects that ran counter to his views. His most acrimonious dispute with Ross came over a proposal to build an extension to the Dunfermline library, which, since it was his first library, he regarded with proprietary interest. Carnegie got the idea that the extension was to be used only as a special research library for scholars, and this he vigorously objected to as not contributing to the welfare of "the toiling masses." If scholars wanted a library for research, they could go to Edinburgh. It reached the point of difference at which Ross, in exasperation, wrote a very strong letter to Carnegie, which Carnegie may have destroyed, for it is not in his papers. Carnegie replied in that tone of long-suffering martyrdom that his business partners knew so well:

You surely regret the words you have riten me but I forgive you. . . . Has it come to this, that I cannot be permitted to forcibly express my feelings? I have had and am having as much experience as you with Libraries for the Masses which is what I consider most important. Libraries for antiquarians are within reach of Dunfermline as I point out—not for working man as you have it. My Friend, beware of the weaknesses of old age—

which as I begin to learn from experience sometimes betray us into regretful words or action against those we love and honor most. I have laid aside your letter, sad, indeed, feeling that I have not deserved at your hands such a blow—not angry, no, no—but oh so sorry.[51]

At this point, the vice chairman of the Trust, Sir William Robertson, jumped into the fray and told Carnegie bluntly that his stand reflected on the judgment and good sense of the trustees. He told Carnegie that he paid too much attention to Lord Rosebery. "Nobody in Scotland pays any attention to him." Robertson said that the extension was not just for antiquarians' use. The library had outgrown its present facilities, and he for one felt they needed an entirely new building. Under such pressure, Carnegie yielded and agreed that £5000 should be spent for an extension. He would, he said placatingly, let the trustees decide on the plans—"nothing too good for their reward here or hereafter." [52]

On another trustee project, however, he refused to give in. Since 1880 he had given sums of money for the establishment of the George Lauder Technical College. In October 1899, just two years before his Uncle Lauder's death, the school was opened for students, and both Carnegie and Dod were immensely proud of this vocational school, established to honor, in the practical way which he approved, the man who meant so much to them both.[53] Eight years later, John Ross began plans for a textile school, appropriate for Dunfermline, and at once Carnegie's hackles were up. He wrote Dod, "Ross tells me he has written you anent the Textile School—It appears 'he went ahead' & many of the other Trustees did not think this a part of the Trust—in this they were right, of course, but it was a part of the Lauder Tech School undoubtedly. Now please don't answer Ross until you & I talk it over. It can all be arranged quietly between us. . . . I couldn't stand the Lauder Tech having a rival in the Trust—not much." [54] Whether quietly or not, the matter was arranged, for a few months later Carnegie was able to inform his cousin: "Ross writes me the Weaving School has to be dropt. I wrote congratulating him upon this manifest interposition of providence." [55] In this case, appropriately enough, providence was spelled with a small "p."

Considering all the restrictions under which they worked, the trustees of the Carnegie Dunfermline Trust did a remarkable job over the years in dispensing "sweetness and light" to the fortunate citizens of Dunfermline. The endowment, originally $2,500,000 but soon raised to $4,000,000, yielded an interest amounting to $200,000 annually, making Dunfermline, a town of only 27,000, the community with the largest private endowment in the world. As with all Carnegie's trusts, there were criticisms of the Dunfermline Trust: the trustees were too dictatorial and anti-democratic; they held the board meetings in strictest privacy; they used funds to establish a College of Hygiene and a Medical Clinic, which should have been established with funds of the Carnegie Trust for the Universities of Scotland; in constructing buildings for their various projects they took property and demolished dwellings badly needed "by the toiling masses," thus raising rents; etc.[56] Nevertheless, in less than a decade, the Trust had made Pittencrieff into one of the most beautiful parks in all Britain, had built new swimming baths, a gymnasium, a College of Hygiene and a clinic which provided medical and dental care for all the children of the town, a school for the training of physical education teachers for all of Scotland, a school of music providing free music lessons to all Dunfermline children wishing to participate, a school of horticulture, and a Women's Institute for training in homemaking and vocational skills, and it had set up free tours of Scotland for school children, financed a full concert series each year, and provided lectures and theatrical productions for the entire town.[57] Carnegie had reason enough to write Chairman Ross and the members of the Dunfermline Trust in 1914, not long before his last visit to his native city: "You have fulfilled the hope I indulged—the child of Dunfermline looking back will realize that 'birth in Dunfermline has given advantages which birth elsewhere would have denied.' Be of good cheer, you labor not for flattering reward from your townsmen, but from your own conscience which tells you that because you have lived and labored, the people of Dunfermline have been advantaged—glorious work this." [58]

In the years ahead, the Carnegie Dunfermline Trust would continue to provide the people of Dunfermline with special advantages not available to any other community in Britain. It would become increasingly difficult after 1945 to stay ahead of the general welfare services provided by the state, but with able and dedicated trustees and the highly efficient and imaginative administration of J. W. Ormiston, who served as secretary of the Trust from 1925 until 1959, and treasurer from 1944, the Carnegie Dunfermline Trust has provided one of the most interesting experiments in community benefits in the history of philanthropy. It is regrettable that there have not been more studies made of this town by sociologists, social historians, and psychologists, in order to evaluate the impact such an endowment has had upon an entire community.

With the establishment of the Scottish Universities and the Dunfermline trusts, Carnegie could feel that he had taken proper care of Scotland. It was time now to turn his attention back to the United States. He did not lack for prompters to call his attention to the needs of American higher education. The publicity given to the Scottish trusts had not gone unnoticed in American educational circles, and there was hardly a college president, trustee, or alumnus in the country who did not have his eye on the Carnegie fortune. Grover Cleveland, a newly appointed trustee of Princeton University, Woodrow Wilson, president of Princeton, Charles Eliot of Harvard, Daniel Coit Gilman of Johns Hopkins, Elihu Root, loyal alumnus of Hamilton College, and the indefatigable Andrew White, president emeritus of Cornell University, all knew precisely how Carnegie could best spend his money, and they were eager to teach him. He proved to be a tough pupil. As a matter of fact, he did most of the teaching—and preaching.

The headquarters for Carnegie's American philanthropic activities was his own home, his newly built mansion at 2 East 91st Street. This quickly became one of the best known addresses in America—certainly to the postal clerks of New York, who routed hundreds of letters to that address daily. The Carnegies had moved into their new home in 1902, after several years of waiting for it to be finished—too many years, in Carnegie's opinion. He wrote almost apologetically to Dod, "I don't like building any more than you do & am sorry the house grew to a mansion while my thots (new spelling) were on selling out. But I do believe it is far healthier up here & would not return to 51st St. for anything." [59]

"Up here" on 91st Street was still open country in 1900, far beyond the congestion of mid-Manhattan, the shops, hotels, and the great mansions of the Morgans, Vanderbilts, and Goulds. When Carnegie purchased several city lots some twenty blocks north of the last buildings of any consequence on Fifth Avenue, most of his associates thought him crazy. Here, on a small rise of land which quickly became known as Carnegie Hill, just across Fifth Avenue from the reservoir at the north end of Central Park, some of Carnegie's much-abused "submerged tenth," the shifting, unwanted refuse of New York's millions, had drifted and had found a squatter's haven. Here they had built their lean-to shanties and grazed their goats, unbothered by law, unconcerned about order.[60] Unfortunately for the squatters, it was the building location desired by Carnegie, who cared nothing about fashionable society and who wanted space enough for a large garden. The shacks had been razed, the hill cleared and leveled, and in 1898 construction had begun on Carnegie's mansion. In spite of what he might say in deprecation of big houses to Lauder, Carnegie wanted a mansion, and he got it. He himself had written, in his essay on "Wealth," "It is well, nay, essential, for the progress of the race that the houses of some should be homes for all that is highest and best in literature and the arts, and for all the refinements of civilization, rather than that none should be so. . . . Without wealth there can be no Maecenas." [61] The public, too, expected its millionaires to live in style in big houses; it looked with contempt upon Hetty Green, living penuriously in a small apartment in Hoboken. As Mr. Dooley said, speaking for the general public, "I'm glad there is a Newport. It's th' exhaust pipe. . . . I wish it was bigger." [62]

Carnegie wanted a big house, imposing in its exterior, sumptuous in its interior, but not vulgarly ostentatious in either. With $1,500,000 to spend, his architects, Babb, Cook and Willard, were remarkably successful in meeting these difficult demands. Carnegie's house was no French Renaissance château such as Richard Morris Hunt had built for the Vanderbilts further down Fifth Avenue, nor a de Medici Romanesque style palace by Henry Hobson Richardson, but a rather expanded Georgian brick classical, topped by a cornice and balustrade of granite, and properly set off, as the Fifth Avenue châteaux could not be, with garden and lawn. There were four stories above ground and three basement levels—sixty-four rooms in all. The entire house was a marvel of technological planning for that day. Air was brought in from the outside, filtered, and then heated or cooled to exactly the proper temperature. In the sub-basement were three large boilers, heated by coal that was brought from the huge coal bin on a railroad track by a coal miner's car that carried three-quarters of a ton of coal in one load. On a single cold winter day, it took two tons of coal to heat the house.[63] Not surprisingly, Carnegie's personal and property taxes jumped from $150,000 to $1,000,000 a year after his move to the more salubrious clime of 91st Street.[64]

In his magnificent library-study on the first floor, seated at a roll top desk so huge that it had had to be constructed inside the room, Carnegie, his feet barely able to touch the floor, would sit, contemplating how best to dispose of his wealth. All around him, carved into the wood paneling of the walls, were the slogans that had inspired him throughout his life: high above the mantle of the fireplace, "Let There Be Light," and directly below that the words which he had first seen as a young man in the Stokes's library in Greensburg, Pennsylvania, and which he had vowed would some day be in a library of his:

> He that cannot reason is a fool,
> He that will not is a bigot,
> He that dare not is a slave.

Running around the walls of the room like a frieze carved out of *Poor Richard's Almanac* were the words: "The Kingdom of Heaven Is Within You," "The Gods Send Thread For The Web Begun," "All Is Well Since All Grows Better," "The Aids To A Noble Life Are All Within," and "Thine Own Reproach Alone Do Fear." It was difficult to be other than noble in such a room.

Here Carnegie would read over the few carefully selected begging letters that Bertram would bring in to him from his outer office, and would carefully file away in his "Gratitude and Sweet Words" drawer the laudatory news stories and magazine articles found in the press. Here, too, he would receive the very important persons who came seeking funds. Off the library, connected by sliding doors, was the large reception room, where press conferences and meetings with various trustees could be held—the arrangements all very functional, yet elegant—philanthropy with flair.

Carnegie's first idea as a worthy project for higher education in America was to establish a great national university in Washington, D.C. This was an old dream of American statesmen and educators—first suggested by George Washington when plans for a new Federal capital city were being discussed. It was pushed hard thirty years later by President John Quincy Adams, only to be ignored, as so many of his great national dreams were, by Congress and the public at large. The United States remained one of the few nations in the world without a major university in its capital city. Now, in 1900, Andrew White of Cornell, being four thousand miles away from Ithaca, New York, as our Ambassador to Berlin, could take a broader perspective of American education. He revived the idea of a national university and got Carnegie excited about it.

At this same time, Carnegie met Daniel Coit Gilman, the distinguished president of The Johns Hopkins University, who, in the twenty-five years since the founding of that university, had made it into the most progressive center of graduate study in the United States. Gilman, who planned to retire shortly, had told Carnegie that Johns Hopkins planned to build an entirely new campus. Carnegie was at once inspired, and wrote to White in some excitement:

> You suggested a National University at Washington—Washington's desire, several have; but while this does, as you say, ensure immortality to the Founder, it has hitherto seemed to me not needed, and this puts immortality under foot. Recently Prof. Gilman of Johns Hopkins talked to me—they are to change it to the country near Balto. Now if Hopkins could be united with Washington neighborhood it has occurred to me, a University for Balto-Washington and the West and South might be highly useful.
>
> If you confirmed this view and thought we could approach the Hopkins people and get their views I might or you might sound them out. What do you think of the Idea? Gov. Sandford [sic] made a useless rival as you and I saw when in San Francisco, to the State University. I could be no party to such a

thing. Don't care two cents about future "glory." I must be satisfied that I am doing good, wise, beneficial work in my day.[65]

White responded with some caution. While still eager for a national university, he was not overly enthusiastic about Johns Hopkins as the major beneficiary. A joint university of Washington and Hopkins would, of course, be "perfectly feasible," he told Carnegie, but he didn't agree that Stanford had made a mistake in building his university close to the University of California at Berkeley. Stanford "has stimulated its rival, the University of California, and the latter has received more appropriations because of it. The one specializes in the scientific side, the other in the humanities." White felt that the same result would be achieved if a new university were established in Washington to stimulate universities near by.[66]

Carnegie could not be discouraged at this point. He wrote White that Gilman would come to Skibo that summer. He wanted White to come up too, and the three of them would draw up plans for the new university. "I do not see why it [Johns Hopkins] should not yield a little upon the matter of a new site. It has not much of a fund I take it except its present property in Balto, so funds for nearly all the new must be raised. . . . I guess we shall have to call you from frittering away your time as Ambassador (altho it would be delightful to be with that character the Emperor if he gave one a chance to talk freely) and put you where real work is to be done in Washington working out that great national institution." [67]

There was no record kept of that meeting in Skibo in the summer of 1901, but apparently Gilman, White, and Carnegie were unable to come to any agreement. Undoubtedly Gilman was bound by the terms of the trust that had established The Johns Hopkins University or by the specific instructions from the board of trustees not to move the university out of Baltimore. And Carnegie must have held steadfast to his conviction that it would be an unnecessary duplication to establish another university within thirty miles of Johns Hopkins. In any event, when he returned to the United States in the fall of 1901, he had abandoned the idea of a national university. He wrote a long letter to the recently installed President of the United States, Theodore Roosevelt, explaining that there would be no national university built with Carnegie money. Instead, Carnegie said, he intended to establish an Institution in Washington, D.C., that would further knowledge for all universities in the nation. He was ready at this moment to construct the appropriate buildings on a site selected by the government and to endow the Institution with $10,000,000, thus ensuring an annual revenue of $500,000. He proposed, as ex-officio members of the board of trustees of the Institution, the President of the United States, the President of the Senate, the Speaker of the House, the secretary of the Smithsonian Institution, and the president of the National Academy of Sciences.[68] Carnegie had been much impressed with a letter he had received from Prime Minister Arthur Balfour the previous summer, at the time he was considering the details of the Trust for the Scottish Universities. The Prime Minister had written that he hoped Carnegie would make ample provision for scientific research, for universities should not only be "places where knowledge already attained is imparted, but also where the stock of the world's knowledge is augmented." [69] It was for the augmentation of the world's knowledge that Carnegie now envisioned that the Institution in Washington would play a major role. His first group of trustees, all of whom quickly agreed to serve, included such distinguished men as John S. Billings, head librarian of the New York Public Library system; William N. Frew, president of the Carnegie Institute of Pittsburgh; Daniel Coit Gilman; John Hay; Abram S. Hewitt; Seth Low, Mayor of New York; Wayne Mac-Veagh; Elihu Root; and Andrew White. President Roosevelt wrote Carnegie, accepting his position as ex-officio member of the board: "I will serve with the greatest pleasure. Let me congratulate you upon the very high character—indeed I may say the extraordinary character—of the men whom you have secured as trustees; and I congratulate the nation upon your purpose to found such an institution. It seems to me to be precisely the institution most needed to help and crown our educational system by providing for and stimulating original research." [70]

Carnegie was ecstatic. With that kind of send-off from the new President of the United States, the Institution was assured of success. It was the beginning of Carnegie's fascination for the former Rough Rider, whom he had previously distrusted. He wrote to

Dod, "I have got 'my Trustees' together & President Roosevelt writes congratulating me upon the 'extraordinary high quality of the body.' We meet in Washington Jany 29th to organize. You will see general scope in the papers but do read Carl Snyder's article in this month's N.A. Review—I had no idea our country was so poverty stricken in higher scientific workers. Don't fail to read it. It is as severe an indictment as Kipling's of Britian—stunning as that is." [71]

At the first meeting of the board, John Hay presided and Daniel Gilman was elected president of the Institution. During its first year, the Institution established departments of research in experimental evolution, marine biology, history, economics, and sociology. Gilman served until 1904, at which time a new charter of incorporation, comprehensive in scope, was granted by Congress. Robert Woodward, dean of the College of Pure Science at Columbia University and editor of *Science,* succeeded Gilman as president in this same year, and under his capable leadership the Carnegie Institution successfully pushed forward in many directions of social and scientific inquiry to "augment the world's knowledge." During the sixteen years of Woodward's presidency, departments of research were set up for the study of terrestrial magnetism, astronomy (at the Mount Wilson observatory), geophysics, botany, nutrition, meridian astrometry, and embryology. The Institution also took over the Eugenics Record Office at Cold Spring Harbor, Long Island, which Mrs. E. H. Harriman had founded and endowed and then bequeathed to the Institution. Grants were also made to individual scientists, working independently of the Institution's departments of research, and funds were provided for the publication of books. [72]

Of all Carnegie's philanthropic trusts, the Carnegie Institution of Washington received the least amount of criticism from the lay public and the academic world. At the time the Institution received its new charter from Congress, the *Independent* published an editorial comparing its awards with those of the Nobel Foundation. It concluded that the Carnegie Institution had the more difficult task, for the Nobel Foundation awarded past achievement in science, but the Carnegie Institution had to speculate on the future and decide which of the hundreds of applicants were most likely to make a significant contribution to man's knowledge. The editors of *Independent* did find it some-what paradoxical, however, in view of Carnegie's own stress upon practical, applied science, that the Institution in the two years of its existence had given "the lion's share of its grants to research in pure science," astronomers having received the most grants, psychologists the fewest.[73]

Carnegie was so delighted with the work of the Institution that he more than doubled the original endowment by giving an additional $15,000,000 to the Trust. In an interview with the press in 1911, soon after making this additional grant, he boasted of the "wonders" it had done in service to the world. He was particularly delighted with the work of the sailing ship, *Carnegie*. He told reporters that "that yacht is the first ever built with bronze substituted for iron; the latter deflects the magnetic needle and bronze does not. The result is that all former observations are incorrect. The 'Carnegie' found two grave errors in the British Admiralty charts in her voyage to Britain, and returning via the Azores, she found that the Captain was not to blame who ran a great steamer upon the rocks which destroyed it; on the contrary he was sailing in his right course according to his chart, but the Institution yacht proved that chart was from two to three degrees astray. The 'Carnegie' is going over all the seas year after year, putting the world right. That one service will give ample dividend upon the whole twenty-five million dollars in my opinion." Carnegie also boasted about the Mount Wilson Observatory in California, which he had visited the previous winter. "The Institution discovered a young genius in Professor Hale, who adopted entirely new processes, including photography. His first test, taken just before my arrival, revealed 16,000 new worlds, and he has written me since that his second plate has revealed 60,000 new worlds never seen by man, some of them ten times larger than our sun. The whole world is going to listen to the oracle on the top of Mount Wilson, and in a few years we shall know more about the universe than Galileo and Copernicus ever dreamt of. A new lens 100 inches in diameter is being prepared of three times more power than any instrument yet made. I hope I shall live long enough to hear the revelations that are to come from Professor Hale on Mount Wilson. It is a triumph indeed for this young continent of ours to be the revealer to the world of the prime mysteries of the universe and I could not resist giving the Institution the second gift." [74]

The editors of *Independent* had misjudged Carnegie's breadth of interest in science. With his wonderfully insatiable curiosity about the universe he lived in, all science fascinated him, from fossils to dinosaurs to sea-charts to distant worlds as yet undiscovered. What he did want was action, regardless of the field, and as he had once boasted of American industry, he now boasted of American science pushing ahead of its European counterparts. "The declared object of the Carnegie Institution," he wrote Woodward in 1909, "was to attain preeminence if possible in investigations, discovery, etc., for the Republic. I quite agree with you that the money given in Britain, as far as I know, is not well managed. Too many doctrinaires and too little managing ability. My impression is that rather than assist projects already started, if the Carnegie Institution does anything in foreign lands it should be in some new field, where success will be credited to the Republic. Rivalry between nations is beneficent when it is rivalry for good ends." [75]

It is a safe conjecture that Carnegie would have heartily approved of the competition of American science and technology with the Russians in racing to the moon, and how he would have gloried in America's success!

Individuals within the academic world were benefiting from the establishment of Carnegie's first great foundation for education in the United States, but the Carnegie Institution of Washington left unsatisfied institutional demands upon Carnegie's philanthropy. Great universities, as well as small, private colleges, had been hopeful that something comparable to, but on a much larger scale than, the Scottish Universities Trust would be one of Carnegie's first major educational projects in this country. There was considerable speculation about what form this institutional benefaction would take. Would he bestow his favors upon a select few, such as Cornell and Columbia, whose presidents were on close terms of friendship with Carnegie? Or would he distribute his largess over a much wider field, taking a particular type of institution, such as mining schools or teachers' colleges, under his patronage? Or perhaps he would follow the example of Stanford or Rockefeller and found his own university, now that the plans for a Washington national university had fallen through. Carnegie showed little disposition to pursue any of these possibilities. Although he expressed interest in 1900 in establishing a technical school in Pittsburgh, he flatly rejected the plan submitted by a committee of educators to establish an Institute of Technology comparable to the Massachusetts and California institutes. Instead, he insisted upon setting up a group of secondary schools to produce skilled craftsmen and laborers. The administration of these schools was given to the trustees of the Carnegie Institute of Pittsburgh. It would not be until a decade later, in 1912, that he would yield on this point, and permit the reorganization of the secondary schools into an institute of higher education and professional training in engineering, fine arts, and home economics. The Carnegie Institute of Technology, with its adjunct, the Margaret Morrison Carnegie College for the education of women, received from Carnegie an endowment of $4,000,000 and an additional grant of $3,250,000 for capital expenditures, but, curiously enough, he remained rather indifferent to the only institution of higher education to bear his name.[76]

In fact, it soon became clear that he had very little interest in large universities of any sort, particularly the famous universities of the Ivy League. He felt toward Harvard, Yale, and Columbia much as he had toward Oxford and Cambridge. They had too much already and spent too much of what they had on the wrong things, like classical literature, poetry, and philosophy. Most university presidents in the country could have sympathized with the president of the University of Virginia, Edwin Alderman, who came to New York to seek money for his university from Carnegie. He had asked a friend, William Schieffelin, who, as president of the Citizens Union, knew Carnegie well, to go with him on his begging mission. For three hours, before, during and after lunch, they used every argument, every persuasive ploy they could conceive of, to wheedle some money out of Carnegie, and finally were successful in getting Carnegie to match gifts given to the Alumni Fund up to several thousand dollars.

When it was all over, Alderman and Schieffelin shook hands on their success.

Schieffelin said, "Didn't you feel you were playing a salmon? You'd get it up near by and then he'd rush off again."

President Alderman replied, "I'll tell you how I felt. I felt like backing him up in the corner and saying, 'Give it!' And then I kept saying to myself, 'It's his money, it's his money.' " [77]

Alderman should have considered himself fortunate. Very few other university presidents had even that measure of success in "playing the salmon." Carnegie's only real interest in institutional giving was to small colleges with very limited endowments. As he told David Starr Jordan, the president of Stanford University, "The colleges I have been helping for two years, already about two hundred in number, do not average more than $200,000 to $250,000 in endowments and after deep consideration, I decided it was better to help smaller colleges than larger ones. . . . The case of Stanford University fails to arouse the desire on my part to help. . . . My impression is that no University in the United States is your equal in endowment." [78] He told his old friend Andrew White much the same thing, and to Charles Eliot he was explicit as to which of those small colleges he was most interested in helping:

> I agree with you upon the importance of Tuskegee and Hampton and similar institutions and have not been unmindful of them. I have this minute signed a check for $200,000 for the Lincoln Institution, an offshoot of Berea College, which is to carry on Hampton work and starts with $400,000. Hampton's contribution from me to date has been $95,000, and I give them a sum annually [$15,000]. Tuskegee's you know is $30,000. So that our African brethren have not been overlooked.[79]

Other than the many small gifts of libraries to colleges throughout the country, the only schools that did receive substantial grants from Carnegie were schools like Berea, Hampton Institute, and Tuskegee Institute. These schools appealed to his sense of social justice. He liked their curricula and the composition of their student bodies—white youths coming from the Kentucky mountains to Berea, and black youths from the rural South to Hampton and Tuskegee—and in all three schools the students working on campus to put themselves through college while at the same time learning an useful craft or trade. Booker T. Washington had no disciple more devoted to his philosophy of education and race relations anywhere than Andrew Carnegie.

One of Berea's most persistent advocates for Carnegie's favor was Woodrow Wilson, both as president of Princeton and later as President of the United States. "We must, of course, do our best for the South Europeans who come and for the colored people already here," Wilson wrote Carnegie in 1914, asking for a sizable contribution to Berea's efforts to raise $2,000,000 in endowment, "but I feel that it is hazardous and heartless longer to neglect this great mass of people of our own stock and traditions. . . . I feel that you have a right to lasting satisfaction in the immense service to the nation you have rendered in the line of negro education, and it seems only a natural corollary that you should do for this three million white population something commensurate with their particular need. The South and the nation would certainly appreciate such action." [80]

Wilson was to have far more success in pleading the cause of Berea than he had had in his earlier and even more strenuous efforts on behalf of his own university, Princeton. Elected president of the university in June 1902, Wilson almost at once began a campaign to capture Carnegie. It would be a most impressive feat with which to inaugurate his presidency if he could succeed where such old hands in the presidential game of fund-raising as Butler, White, Gilman, and Eliot had failed. Early in the spring of his first year in office, he wrote Carnegie a long letter about Princeton and its needs. He laid great stress upon Princeton's "Scottish connections," from President John Witherspoon on, although he was wise enough not to stress Princeton's Presbyterian heritage. "She has been largely made by Scotsmen, being myself of pure Scots blood, it heartens me to emphasize the fact." Having, he hoped, established the right ancestral connections, Wilson outlined the areas of need for Princeton in which Carnegie's money could be put to good use:

(1) A Graduate College residence system
(2) A School of Jurisprudence and Government—"My idea would be to make it a school of law, but not in any narrow or

technical sense: a school, rather, in which law and institutions would be interpreted as instruments of peace, of freedom, and of the advancement of civilization: international law as the means and guarantee of cordial understandings between the nations of the world, private law as the accommodation of otherwise hostile interests, government as the means of progress. No doubt it would be wise, too, as immediately collateral matter, to expound the part which commerce and industry have played and must increasingly play, in making for international as well as national peace and for the promotion of all the common interests of mankind." [Wilson apparently believed that if a salmon was too cautious to catch with a lure, one should use a net. Almost every Carnegie cliché of the last twenty years was woven into that mesh.]

(3) A School of Science

(4) Methods of Teaching—the introduction of the tutorial system.

He then urged Carnegie to come down to Princeton, look the school over, and talk further with him on all of these points.[81]

After much further cajoling, Wilson finally got Carnegie down to Princeton. Accompanied by Trustee Grover Cleveland, who had on his own been doing a little soliciting of Carnegie in behalf of the Princeton graduate school, Wilson gave Carnegie the grand tour of Old Nassau, pointing out the inadequate library and science facilities, going over plans for new graduate school facilities, introducing him to deans, professors, and bright young Princeton scholars. Carnegie was most amiable, most interested in everything that was shown him. Wilson should have been forewarned of trouble, however, when Carnegie seemed to give undue attention to the physical education facilities, particularly those used by the varsity football team. Such questions as how many boys play football, how many casualties do you have in a year, etc., were not, if asked by Carnegie, mere efforts at small talk. They were instead related to Carnegie's latest fancy regarding higher education, a crusade to end the playing of football on college campuses —an idea which most American college alumni would find far more heretical than his earlier attacks upon the classics. One strong bond between Carnegie and President Eliot of Harvard was their common aversion to football. "I should like very much to have the paragraph in which you sum up the faults of that bloody game," Carnegie had written Eliot. "It begins by stating that the maimed and the killed are not the worst feature, it is the trickery, fraud, etc., the plot to concentrate and disable certain players on the other side, etc., that make the game so objectionable." [82] A favorite poetic line, taking care of both Britain and the United States, which Carnegie delighted in quoting, was:

> The flannelled fools at the wicket
> The muddied Oafs at the goal.[83]

Wilson would have been well advised to have steered Carnegie far away from the playing fields of Princeton.

At the conclusion of the long day, when Carnegie was at last ready to board that quaint vehicle posing as a train to take Princeton visitors back to the main line to New York and Philadelphia, he turned to Wilson and thanked him for a most instructive day. As the story would later be told by generations of delighted Princetonians, Carnegie then said, "I know exactly what Princeton needs and I intend to give it to her." His momentarily ecstatic host, who had visions of libraries, laboratories, and law schools dancing in his head, eagerly asked, "What?"

"It's a lake. Princeton should have a rowing crew to compete with Harvard, Yale and Columbia. That will take young men's minds off football."

Carnegie was as good as his word. Construction was begun that spring by the Hudson Engineering Company to build Lake Carnegie by damming up Stony Brook, east of the campus. Howard Russell Butler, Princeton class of 1872 and an avid rowing enthusiast, served as general manager of the project. Two and a half years later, at a cost of $400,000, the lake, three and one-half miles long and four hundred to one thousand feet wide, was completed and officially opened with elaborate ceremonies, attended by Carnegie, on 5 December 1906.[84] President Wilson made a long speech of welcome to Carnegie, concluding with an account of how Carnegie had visited Princeton and had "seen exactly what Princeton needed—a lake." That Wilson could say this with a perfectly straight face was a tribute to his Calvinist upbringing and an indication of how adept college presidents must become in dealing with the eccentricities of wealthy patrons. Carnegie also made a speech at this momentous occasion in the history of Princeton. He said he had been happy to give the lake in the hope that it would be used for aquatic sports to the discouragement of football. "I have never seen a football game, but I have glanced at pictures of such games, and to me the spectacle of educated young men rolling over one another in the dirt was—well, not gentlemanly." According to the newspaper reporters present, "Mr. Carnegie's remarks were received with murmurs of dissent from the undergraduates." [85] Carnegie, however, was very much pleased with both his gift and speech. He wrote to Charles Eliot, "I did what I could at Princeton to stand by your side in regard to football, and I am happy to say that everybody, from President Cleveland down, thanked me for speaking the needed word." President Eliot, in a rather neat bit of one-upmanship over his Ivy League competitor, promptly replied, "It is odd that your note of yesterday should reach me the day after Harvard won from Yale in debating. Six years ago when I was in Bermuda you congratulated me in winning in debate when we lost in football. The same thing has been repeated this year. We also won in chess." [86] It is hardly surprising that Wilson should turn his efforts thereafter to pleading the cause of Berea.

Building lakes to discourage football might be personally gratifying to Carnegie, but it hardly satisfied the needs of higher education in the first decade of the twentieth century. Nor had his gifts to individual small colleges, while meritorious and deserved, had the kind of impact upon higher education in general throughout the United States that could have been derived from a more imaginative use of Carnegie's funds. No one came forth with any remarkably innovative suggestions, however. College presidents seemed incapable of looking beyond their own institutional needs, college professors beyond their own narrow disciplines. Carnegie himself had serious reservations about the value of formal higher education if it were not technically or vocationally oriented. He was much more interested in the advancement of knowledge through scientific research conducted by organizations like the Carnegie Institution of Washington, which had no direct connection with college teaching. Yet almost in spite of himself, by approaching the problem through a side door, as it were, Carnegie was to have a greater impact upon standards of higher education than any man had had previous to this time in the history of American education. The side door that led to this major re-evaluation of American educational standards was one that involved Carnegie in an act of charity upon a major scale, something that he had previously scrupulously avoided except in a very limited and directly personal way. One of the most basic tenets in his "Gospel of Wealth" had been to avoid "indiscriminate charity. . . . The amount which can be wisely given by the individual for individuals is necessarily limited by his lack of knowledge of the circumstances connected with each." Carnegie had made individual gifts and granted individual pensions, but these had all been for close friends or for those who, he felt, had some claim out of past association upon his pocketbook, such as his former employees in Carnegie Steel, for whom he had established a pension plan immediately after his retirement from business. Now, however, he was to become involved in a pension plan for an occupational group with whom he had neither personal nor vocational connections.

The origins of this remarkable charitable enterprise upon Carnegie's part can be traced back to 1890, when he was elected a trustee of Cornell University. In attending his first meeting he had been shocked to discover how very small the salaries of college professors were, even at a relatively well-endowed university such as Cornell. Like most men of very limited formal education, and particularly men of European background, Carnegie held college professors in awe. He might regard them as unworldly and impractical, but there was a special prestige attached to their professorial status that men in other professions did not have. To discover that college professors might teach for several decades and not achieve a salary above $400 a year, with no provisions for retirement, was for Carnegie a shocking revelation. Office clerks at Carnegie Steel earned as much or more than this. But apparently such was the prevailing scale within the profession, and no one in the administration at Cornell, or anywhere else for that matter, seemed disposed to do anything about it.[87]

Carnegie largely forgot about the matter too. There were, to be sure, frequent letters from impoverished teachers unable to work, or from their wives, but these letters were of the kind that Bertram rarely showed to Carnegie. It was Henry S. Pritchett, the president of the Massachusetts Institute of Technology, who was to open the door of higher education to Carnegie by raising the question of teachers' pensions. Pritchett was visiting Carnegie at Skibo in the summer of 1904 to discuss the work of the Carnegie Institution of Washington, and in the course of their discussions he brought up a subject that was very much on his mind. As president of an institution whose faculty was predominantly in the fields of science and technology, Pritchett had a great deal more difficulty in recruiting able men than did administrative officers of the traditional liberal arts colleges. Now that the basic industries were following Carnegie's early example of employing chemists, physicists, and professionally trained mechanical engineers, educational institutions, even those as distinguished as M.I.T., did not find it easy to compete for personnel with companies in which an engineer could earn three to five times as much as a teacher could. Another college personnel problem resulted from the fact that there were no pension plans for professors. A college, out of purely humanitarian concern, was often obliged to keep an elderly faculty member, who should retire, on its active teaching staff, thus denying a place to a young and valuable instructor. This situation further discouraged young men from going into the teaching profession. Carnegie listened intently to Pritchett's arguments.

There were further discussions the following winter, and in the spring of 1905 Carnegie was ready to announce his latest philanthropic foundation, the Carnegie Teachers Pension Fund, to be endowed with $10,000,000 from his diminishing hoard of United States Steel bonds. As always, Carnegie had the administration of this Fund firmly established before he made the announcement. The list of trustees read like a selected précis of *Who's Who in American Education:* presidents A. T. Hadley of Yale, Eliot of Harvard, William Harper of The University of Chicago, Butler of Columbia, Jacob Schurman of Cornell, Wilson of Princeton, L. Clark Seelye of Smith, Alexander Humphreys of Stevens Institute, Edwin Craighead of Tulane, H. C. King of Oberlin, C. F. Thwing of Western Reserve, Thomas McClelland of Knox, Edwin Hughes of DePauw, H. McC. Bell of Drake,

George Denny of Washington and Lee, Sir William Peterson of McGill, Samuel Plantz of Lawrence College, Jordan of Stanford, W. H. Crawford of Allegheny, Provost Charles Harrison of the University of Pennsylvania, and Chancellor S. B. McCormick of Western University of Pennsylvania. The only non-academicians were Carnegie's nephew T. M. Carnegie, Frank Vanderlip, and Robert Franks. Pritchett was chosen as chairman, a position he was to hold for twenty-five years.[88]

In his letter to the trustees establishing the Fund, Carnegie set the broad outline of the plan:

> I have reached the conclusion that the least rewarded of all the professions is that of the teacher in our higher educational institutions. New York City generously, and very wisely provided retiring pensions for teachers in her public schools. . . . Very few, indeed, of our colleges are able to do so. The consequences are grievous. Able men hesitate to adopt teaching as a profession and many old professors whose places should be occupied by younger men, cannot be retired.
>
> I have therefore, transferred to you and your successors, as Trustees, $10,000,000, 5% First Mortgage Bonds of the United States Steel Corporation, the revenue from which is to provide retiring pensions for the teachers of Universities, Colleges and Technical Schools in our country, Canada and Newfoundland, under such conditions as you may adopt from time to time.
>
> The Fund applies to the three classes of institutions named without regard to Race, Sex, Creed or Color. We have, however, to recognize that State and Colonial Governments which have established or mainly supported Universities, Colleges or Schools, may prefer that their relations shall remain exclusively with the State. I cannot, therefore, presume to include them.
>
> There is another class which states do not aid, their constitutions in some cases even forbidding it, viz., Sectarian Institutions. Many of these established long ago, were truly sectarian but to-day are free to all men of all creeds or of none—such are not to be considered sectarian now. Only such as are under control of a sect, or require Trustees (or a majority thereof), Officers, Faculty or Students, to belong to any specified sect, or which impose any theological test, are to be excluded.[89]

Had Carnegie simply set up a pension fund for all college teachers in private colleges and universities, as the original title of the Fund implied, and as the first newspaper stories stated, the trustees would have had little to do but see that there was a proper administration of the pensions. It was Carnegie's strong bias against sectarianism, plus the phrase "under such conditions as you may adopt," that enabled probably the ablest group of college administrators that could have been selected at that time to set standards for higher education. Setting such standards had never before been done on a national basis, and it was to have consequences reaching far beyond Carnegie's and even Pritchett's original intentions. The Fund was at first incorporated under the laws of New York State, but within a year it sought and received a national charter by Act of Congress under a more appropriate name: The Carnegie Foundation for the Advancement of Teaching.

The first act of the trustees was to send out a questionnaire to 627 institutions of higher education throughout the United States and Canada, asking each college the size of its endowment, what educational standards it had established for admission and for graduation, what its relation to the state or province was, and what, if any, sectarian ties or obligation it had. The trustees received replies from 421 institutions, and they then proceeded to establish standards for admission to the pension fund. They first decided that no school with an endowment of less than $200,000 would be considered. No school that received a substantial portion of its operating funds from the state or province was eligible. No school that required a majority of its trustees to belong to a particular denomination, or that had a sectarian requirement for its president, faculty, or student body, or that had a required course for the teaching of the tenets of a particular religious creed or sect, would be eligible. Finally, no school that did not require of its students what the trustees would regard as a minimum of preparation at the secondary school level prior to admission to the college would qualify. Of the 421 original applicants, the trustees accepted only 52 for admission into the pension plan.[90]

There were some surprising rejections. Northwestern and Brown universities were kept out on sectarian grounds. The University of Virginia, a private university founded by Thomas Jefferson, was eliminated from the list of applicants because it required only six and one-half units of high school training for admission to the university—well below the normal fifteen units

873

of college preparatory training required by the better colleges for admission. Of the 52 institutions selected, 22 were located in New England and New York State. Only one Southern school, Tulane University, was admitted. Vanderbilt and Randolph-Macon, both of whose educational standards were such as to qualify, were rejected on sectarian grounds.[91]

Many critics of the plan, both conservatives and radicals, who had predicted that the academic profession would reject out of hand this patronizing act of charity from Carnegie, were to be sadly disillusioned in their estimate of the rugged individualism of the teaching profession. William Jennings Bryan, receiving the news in Hong Kong that the college of which he was both an alumnus and trustee, Illinois College, had been selected and had accepted the pension system, immediately sent his letter of resignation from the board of trustees. "Our college cannot serve God and Mammon," he told the president. "It cannot be a college for the people and at the same time commend itself to the commercial highwaymen who are now subsidizing the colleges to prevent the teaching of economical truth. It grieves me to have my alma mater converted into an ally of plutocracy, but having done what I could to prevent it, I have no other resource than to withdraw from its management." The college accepted Bryan's resignation and kept the pension program—one more victory for Carnegie over Populism.[92]

In other schools, not so fortunate as to be selected, the anguished cries of faculty members and the threats of resignation shook college administrations with a violence that Carnegie and Pritchett could hardly have imagined. There were emergency sessions of boards of trustees throughout the country, and charters that had once been considered inviolate were in many places quickly changed to remove sectarian requirements. Bates College went to the state legislature of Maine and successfully pushed through a new act of incorporation which changed its former relations with the Free Baptist Church. The University of Virginia raised its standards of admission, which had an immediate impact upon the secondary schools throughout Virginia and in other parts of the South.[93] Inadvertently, Carnegie, with his pension plan, had done more in a year to advance the standards of higher education within the United States than probably any carefully conceived program to accomplish that goal could ever have done.

He had also in the process knocked down a hornet's nest. State institutions, fearful of losing key faculty members, protested at being excluded. So many faculty protests at such schools as the universities of Wisconsin, Illinois, and Minnesota, and even formal applications from the administrators of those schools, poured into the Foundation that the board felt obliged in 1908 to bring the issue to Carnegie's attention. His response was that when the pension fund had been set up three years before, he had felt that it would be presumptuous on his part to extend it to those institutions supported by state taxation. But now "your favor of today informs me of the desire of professors of State Universities to be embraced by the Pension Fund, as shown by a resolution unanimously adopted by their National Association. . . . I beg now to say that should the Governing Board of any State University apply for participation in the Fund and the Legislature and Governor of the State approve such application, it will give me great pleasure to increase the Fund to the extent necessary to admit them." Carnegie then granted an additional $5,000,000 to provide funds for pensions in state universities. In closing, Carnegie commended the trustees for their excellent work. "From the numerous letters I have received from pensioners and their wives and the warm approval of the press and public, I am satisfied that this Fund is, and must be for all time, productive of lasting joy, and not only to the recipients but to the cause of higher education. Most grateful am I to be privileged as trustee of this wealth to devote it to such use." [94]

The issue of state universities was thus rather easily and happily resolved. Not so the sectarian question, which was quite a different matter. That some very distinguished colleges and universities should be excluded from participation on that ground was not easy for the faculties and administrations of those institutions to accept. The most persistent and angry protester of all was president Abram W. Harris of Northwestern University, who, in a series of letters both to Pritchett and Carnegie, argued that Northwestern was "really non-sectarian in spirit," even though its charter required that a majority of its trustees belong to the Methodist faith. The Carnegie restriction, moreover, "keeps many good schools from associating with those colleges with which they

875

prefer to associate, and can in the long run mean more denominational control as these schools will have to turn back to churches for support, particularly for pension plans." In another letter, Harris, speaking also for Brown University, wrote, "These institutions [Northwestern and Brown] ask to be judged by what they do, rather than by charter provisions inherited from a dead generation. . . . I enclose a copy of a suggested remedy. . . ." The remedy offered by Harris was to allow the Foundation "to provide for a limited number of such institutions—ten or twelve now excluded, but clearly non-sectarian in administration, even though the charter provides that a majority of their trustees must belong to a certain denomination; that these ten or twelve shall be selected by the President of the Foundation, and that he will further provide for the admission of other institutions as their liberality is made clear by examination, or as they become liberal." [95]

Even the President of the United States got involved in the controversy. Theodore Roosevelt wrote Carnegie, "Northwestern is no more sectarian than Princeton." [96] To which Carnegie replied that the Carnegie Endowment, "headed by Pritchett . . . is a model institution and is doing great work, rooting out denominational control in colleges. . . . Like yourself, we are depending less and less upon the doctrine of grace and more upon the doctrine of works, not what a man believes but what he does, which was the great doctrine laid down." [97] Pritchett, who was a tough administrator and in complete agreement with Carnegie upon the question of sectarianism, was not willing to budge and advised Carnegie to stand firm. He pointed out that a number of colleges and universities had changed their charters "without any great friction or discussion and have dropped the strict sectarian qualifications that have excluded them from participating in the Foundation. . . . All of those that are really interested can do so." [98]

With this backing from the trustees, Carnegie's response to Harris's suggested remedy was negative and final: "To permanently fasten denominationalism on Colleges would be of serious consequence to the whole country. I saw in my travels around the world what denominationalism really ment—several sects each claiming to proclaim the truth and by inference condeming the others as imperfect. So many colleges have seen fit to broaden their views and become participants in the Pension Fund that it is best to adhere to present conditions, hoping the reform may soon be complete." [99] Harris's protest ("Your letter . . . a disappointment. Will you let me reason with you?") was of no avail.[100] If Northwestern wanted in, she could change her charter.

By 1909, it was quite apparent to anyone interested in higher education that the Carnegie Foundation had become the national unofficial accrediting agency for colleges and universities. Good teachers were accepting positions on the basis of whether or not the school was a participant in the pension fund, prospective donors used participation as a major criterion in determining the status of the institution, and it even had an indirect effect upon admissions. It is not surprising that schools like Northwestern should be concerned over exclusion. Increasingly, with Carnegie's approval, more and more revenue was being used by the Foundation to broaden its investigations of higher education in the United States, to publish critiques, and to suggest standards. In a letter to Carnegie in 1911, Pritchett gave a specific example of the influence the Foundation was exerting, not only upon colleges, but upon all educational facilities:

> I was greatly pleased to have your generous words at our luncheon last week concerning the influence of the Foundation in advancing education and in helping to solve our problems of education from a national rather than from a local point of view. This is an outcome of the Pension Fund administration, which has far exceeded all our expectations. I had yesterday the entire board of the University of West Virginia discussing with me the educational program of that state, including grammar school, secondary school and college. This sort of thing does not go into the press, but it has resulted in five years in transforming the educational situation in this state. The time, in our judgment, will never come when this sort of nationwide scrutiny will cease to be fruitful. My concern is, however, that it has always been looked upon as a sort of addition to the Foundation. We pay the expense of that ministry from the income of such funds as we accumulated in the first three years. Whenever the income of the Foundation is demanded to its full limit in order to sustain our system of pensions in the accepted institutions our trustees would feel . . . that this money would have to be devoted to the pensions. I hope, therefore, that at some-

time you will place in the hands of the Foundation a moderate sum, the income of which shall be specifically available at the discretion of the trustees for the maintenance of the educational studies and publications.[101]

Pritchett might well have referred to an even more significant instance of the impact the Foundation had upon education than the case of West Virginia by citing the famous Flexner report on medical education in the country. Abraham Flexner, a young staff member of the Foundation who had no special competence in science or medicine, was assigned the task of inspecting medical schools throughout the country. For two years he did just that, and his report, when published in 1910, shocked the public and forced the medical profession into action. Flexner named names and produced irrefutable evidence that many of the so-called medical schools of the country were little more than diploma mills, with no standards and few requirements, except that of a large fee collected upon the granting of the degree. Some of these schools had even attached themselves to highly respectable institutions that had wanted the prestige of having a medical school among their graduate facilities. But with this publicity, and the resulting public furor, many such schools promptly went out of existence, while those that survived greatly tightened their standards for admission and for graduation. The Flexner report remains today a model for educational investigation. Ironically, Carnegie, who had never showed any great interest in aiding the medical profession, had provided the funds for the study that did more to improve the quality of medical education in this country than any other single act.[102] Flexner, whose reputation had been firmly established by *Medical Education in the United States and Canada,* was asked by Rockefeller to serve as secretary of the General Education Board, which gave over $50,000,000 to medical education in the next two decades.

In 1913, Carnegie, in response to Pritchett's earlier request for a separate fund for "the maintenance of educational studies and publications," gave an additional $1,250,000 to the Foundation. In the years ahead, it was to carry on investigations of legal, engineering, and graduate education, college athletics, the training of teachers, and a monumental study of the interrelationship of secondary and college education in Pennsylvania.[103]

If the work of the Foundation in advancing education from a national point of view "far exceeded all our expectations," so too did the number of faculty throughout the country who were eligible to be on the pension list. Carnegie had spoken grandiosely that "the Fund must be for all time productive of lasting joy," but by 1915 it was apparent to the trustees that the free pension system could not be continued indefinitely. A detailed study of the whole pension problem was made by the Foundation, and in 1917 its recommendations were adopted by the board. Under this plan, an independent legal reserve life insurance company was created, chartered under the laws of New York State, and called the Teachers Insurance and Annuity Association of America. The Carnegie Corporation gave $1,000,000 to the Association for initial capital and surplus, and the stock of the Association was owned by the Carnegie Corporation until 1938, at which time it was transferred to the trustees of TIAA, making it a totally independent, nonprofit insurance company. TIAA from 1918 on entered into contractual relationships with individual institutions of higher education and established life insurance and annuity programs for faculty and college administrators on a contributory basis. In most cases the institution paid one-half the premiums and the individual faculty member the other half, with the premiums based upon a certain fixed percentage of the individual's annual salary which guaranteed an annuity upon retirement. The Carnegie Foundation for the Advancement of Teaching continued, of course, to honor all obligations for free pensions incurred up to that time, but the lists were closed after 1917. It is probable, however, that the Foundation will still be paying out Carnegie pensions until at least 1980.

The free pension plan proved itself to be infeasible within twelve years after its inauguration, but it was a noble experiment, and it is fortunate for American education that it was tried. Had a system like TIAA, which, like any insurance company, sets no educational standards for admission into the program, been adopted in 1905, we should not have had the kind of national evaluation of higher education that we sorely needed. *The Times* of London was quite correct in calling the Foundation one of Mr. Carnegie's most significant accomplishments "in the supremely difficult art of spending large sums of money in undertakings to be of permanent advantage to the public." [104]

The Carnegie Foundation for the Advancement of Teaching was to be Carnegie's last major foundation in the general field of education for several years. After 1905 he became increasingly involved in politics, both domestic and foreign, because of his deep commitment to the cause of world peace. Except for various foundations he established to further this cause (some of them so peripheral to it that only he could see the direct connection),[105] he seemed to have become bored with big philanthropy and resented the time it took from his political activities. It had proved a far more difficult task than he had ever dreamed it would be when he wrote so glibly in "Wealth" about "the man of wealth . . . becoming the . . . trustee . . . for his poorer brethren, bringing to their service his superior wisdom, experience, and ability to administer, doing for them better than they would or could do for themselves." [106] He had learned over the twenty years since he had written those lines that, however superior he might think his wisdom and ability to administer were, it was no easy task to do better for others than they could do for themselves, particularly when everyone he encountered felt he could do it as well as Carnegie, if not better. As a steelmaker, he had been regarded as an expert; the public listened when he spoke. But he quickly discovered that the public recognized no experts in philanthropy— there were only men with money and other men who were trying to get it away from them. He was to say repeatedly in these years that he had not worked one-tenth as hard in acquiring as he did in divesting himself of his great wealth.

For a few years it had been fun, and he had thrown himself into the game with the same zest with which he had entered business. There was even the heady excitement of competition about it. As trade journals had once carried monthly production figures of the steel plants of the nation, pitting Carnegie Steel against Cambria or Illinois Steel, so now the daily press frequently ran stories of who was ahead in philanthropy, Carnegie or Rockefeller, and Carnegie always came in first. In 1904, *The Times* of London reported that he had given during the previous year

$21,000,000, Rockefeller only $10,000,000. By 1910 the New York *American's* box score read: total lifetime giving: Carnegie, $179,300,000; Rockefeller, $134,271,000. Whether or not these figures were accurate made little difference to the *American's* readers. The little Scotsman was far ahead.[107]

Carnegie had also enjoyed posing as the expert among his fellow philanthropists, from whom he received considerably more respect than he did from the general public. He sent a list of "do's and don'ts" to Mrs. Russell Sage at her request, and he even had the satisfaction of giving advice to John D. himself.[108] And certainly in the world of philanthropy Carnegie had met people that interested him far more than those he had known in the world of steel. He had long ago forgotten his own advice about not having experts on his boards of trustees, and one need only compare the names of men he selected for his first board, the Carnegie Institute of Pittsburgh, with the names of the trustees selected for the Carnegie Institution of Washington to see how quickly and completely he had forgotten it.

By 1906, however, Carnegie was tired of the game, and by 1910 he was desperately sick of it. He wrote to Ross, "The final dispensation of one's wealth preparing for the final exit is I found a heavy task—all sad— . . . You have no idea the strain I have been under." [109] And in Peebles, Scotland, at a jubilee celebration of the Chambers Institute to honor the memory of the Edinburgh printer and philanthropist, William Chambers, Carnegie departed from his prepared text to say, "Millionaires who laugh are rare, very rare, indeed." [110]

There were honors, to be sure, many of them—all of those Freedoms, with the caskets imposingly arrayed in Skibo Castle; twice Rector of Scotland's most ancient university, St. Andrews; honorary degrees from Oxford and Edinburgh; president of the British Iron and Steel Association (the first president who was not a British citizen); honorary president of the St. Andrew's Society of New York—the list was long and impressive.

On the other hand, there was bitter criticism, too, which Carnegie had not expected. He surely knew that he would not be able to please everyone with his philanthropy, but he had not anticipated that he would be pilloried in the way he was, both from the right and the left, because of his gifts "for the benefit of all mankind." With the possible exception of Homestead, nothing he had done in his business activities was subjected to the same scorching criticism as that which he did in the name of the love of man. The public apparently expected a wolf to act like a wolf, and this brought very little comment, but when a wolf began to bleat like a sheep and to lie down with the lambs, everyone suspected the worst. The conservatives regarded him as a socialist, and the liberals accused him of trying to prostitute the colleges, science, and the general public with his millions. Keir Hardie, the Socialist M.P. from Scotland, whom Carnegie had once helped finance back in those far distant days of his journalistic republican radicalism of the 1880's, sneered at Carnegie's gifts to Scotland: "I see nothing in it to call for special comment. He gives no indication of being in touch with modern Humanitarian thought, and appears to think that the filibusterers of commerce who have acquired millions out of natural or state-given monopolies, and who have maimed and destroyed thousands of human lives in the process—not including those shot by their hired Pinkerton thugs—square their account with humanity by agreeing that eight per cent of the swindlers' grab shall be returned to the community from whom it has been taken by force and fraud, as a kind of hush money after the robber is dead." [111]

Most discouraging of all was the fact that no matter how fast he had run during those ten years of giving, he had not run fast enough. The interest on his bonds kept gaining on his dispersal of those bonds. He had given away $180,000,000, but he still had almost the same amount left. His friend, Secretary of State Elihu Root, said to him when he was feeling at his lowest, "You have had the best run for your money I have ever known." Carnegie could not share his friend's enthusiasm. It had been a good run, all right, but the capitalistic system at 5 per cent was faster than he. He told Root that he would have to die in disgrace after all, for he could not possibly get rid of all his wealth in the few years that were left to him. Root had a simple solution. Why didn't Carnegie set up a trust, transfer the bulk of his fortune to others for them to worry about, and die happy in a state of grace? [112]

And so it was done. Carnegie created the Carnegie Corporation of New York in November 1911, and in a series of grants he transferred to it the bulk of his remaining fortune, $125,000,000, "to promote the advancement and diffusion of knowledge among the people of the United States by aiding technical schools, institutions of higher lerning, libraries, scientific reserch, hero funds, useful publications, and by such other agencies and means as shall from time to time be found appropriate therefor." [113] As a board of trustees, he simply brought together the presidents of all of his other American philanthropic trusts—Pritchett, Woodward, Charles L. Taylor of the Carnegie Hero Fund, Samuel H. Church, who had succeeded William N. Frew as president of the Carnegie Institute of Pittsburgh, and Elihu Root, president of the Carnegie Endowment for International Peace—as well as his faithful secretaries, Robert Franks, James Bertram, and John A. Poynton. He himself, as was only fitting, assumed the presidency of the Corporation. As United States Steel had been the super-corporation in industry, so the Carnegie Corporation of New York was the super-trust in the history of philanthropy. For not until the expansion of the Ford Foundation following the death of Henry Ford in 1947 would the world know a greater accumulation of capital in a single organization devoted to philanthropic causes. There remained only one last thing for Carnegie to do in this "business of benevolence"—to provide for a continuation of the library and church organ grants in Great Britain after his death. At first he thought that a simple order to the Carnegie Corporation of New York to transfer $10,000,000 to a new Trust, to be called the Carnegie United Kingdom Trust, would be sufficient. Root, however, informed him that he was bound by the terms of his own charter. The money was no longer his to spend, and the charter stipulated that the Carnegie Corporation funds had to be used in the United States and Canada. So, in 1913, Carnegie was obliged to dig down into his own remaining resources in order to endow the United Kingdom Trust.[114]

With the creation of the Carnegie Corporation of New York in 1911, Carnegie had been forced to abandon almost all of the basic tenets of philanthropy he had expressed in the "Gospel of Wealth." For the creation of this vast philanthropic corporation under the most vague stipulations was an open admission by Carnegie that a fortune as great as his could not possibly be administered and dispersed by a single man, no matter how "superior his wisdom." In compliance with his gospel, Carnegie had given 90 per cent of his fortune away during his lifetime, but it was left to other men to worry about its management.

"Now it is all settled," he wrote Ross with relief in February 1913. "We are off for Florida." [115] "What Is Andrew Carnegie Really Worth Now?" *The New York Times* speculated after the announcement of the Carnegie Corporation. "He probably still has $160 million in his personal possession." [116] With great thanksgiving, Carnegie could deny that story. The New York *Herald* ran at this time the final box score on the contest between Carnegie and Rockefeller: "Carnegie, $332 million; Rockefeller, $175 million." [117] It was no longer a contest. The public had lost interest, and so had Andrew Carnegie.

CHAPTER XXIII

The Quest for Peace
1901-1910

"We have already Peace Societies and Arbitration Societies," Carnegie wrote in October 1900 to the quixotic editor of *Review of Reviews,* W. T. Stead, who wanted Carnegie to use some of his vast wealth to found a new international society for world peace. "I do not see that it is wise to devote our efforts to creating another organization. Of course, I may be wrong in believing that but I am certainly not wrong in believing that if it were dependent upon any millionaire's money, it would be an object of pity, and end as one of derision. I wonder that you do not see this. There is nothing that robs a righteous cause of its strength more than a millionaire's money —especially during his life. It makes a serious, holy cause simply a fad. Its life is tainted thereby." Besides, Carnegie added, "I am not a 'peace at any price' man much as I should like to be. I believe it was my duty to be on the field at Bull Run. In the present state of civilization (barbarism) wicked powers will wage war, which it is the duty of righteous powers to repel. I like the revised edition of the Scriptures: 'If a man strikes you on the cheek, turn unto him the other also, but if he strikes you on that, go for him.' " [1]

Seven years later, Carnegie was writing to Charles Eliot of

Harvard, "I am hoping our people have been successful in pre-vailing upon you to come to our New York Peace Conference 15th April for truly it is to be memorable: Earl Grey, Bryce, d'Estournelles and others, Sec'y Root, Gov. Hughes. You could use the Ottawa Speech—nothing better possible. I am drawn more to this cause than to any—Just as when young I became a rabid anti-slavery zealot, so in regard to war, far more heinous than owning and selling men is killing men by men." [2] A little later he would write to American Ambassador David J. Hill in Berlin, "Don't feel like travelling to Geneva, too fond of Skibo, but I'd pilgrim-age thru Europe if I could serve the cause of Peace." [3] And on his pilgrimages he would say repeatedly, "The crime of war is inher-ent, it awards victory not to the nation that is right, but to that which is strong. It knows nothing of righteous judgment. . . . Let us rid ourselves of thinking that there are good nations who abhor war, and bad nations who lie in wait for an opportunity to attack the weak." [4] For those who, like the *London Morning Post,* in re-calling Carnegie's earlier statements about a righteous war at Bull Run, would taunt him now with the statement, "If Mr. Carne-gie's idea that war is a crime be right, then Lincoln committed a crime," Carnegie had a ready answer. "The *Post* has confounded two different issues. International war is one thing, upholding the reign of law is another." [5]

Such was the degree of development of Andrew Carnegie's views on the subject of pacifism within seven short years. During that period he was to move from being something of a jingoist, as far as the Western Hemisphere was concerned, to being a man who could without hesitation say, "The Monroe Doctrine has in-deed done its work and should be relegated to the past. All is well." [6] He had, in short, become what he had said in 1900 he wished he could be, a "peace at any price" man.

Part of the credit for the education of Andrew Carnegie must be given to his new associates, men and women with quite a dif-ferent point of view from that of the steelmakers and armor plate men of Pittsburgh—in the United States, Oscar Straus, merchant and career diplomat, Nicholas Murray Butler of Columbia, and David Starr Jordan of Stanford, and, among the international set of pacifists, Norman Angell, Baron d'Estournelles de Constant, and the Baroness Bertha von Suttner. These were people with a mission, who found in Carnegie a receptive pupil with funds more than ample to pay the tuition.

A major part of the credit for his education, however, belongs to Carnegie himself. He may not have been a self-made man in industry, in the best tradition of that venerable American myth, but he was to a great extent a self-educated man. From the time he entered Mr. Martin's Roland Street School in Dunfermline for his few brief years of formal training, his education had never ceased. He read constantly, he remembered what he read, and he was not at all hesitant about expressing his opinions either in discussion or writing. He had sought out those who could teach him more, from Courtlandt Palmer and Madame Botta in New York to Matthew Arnold, Herbert Spencer, and John Morley in England. Now, at sixty-five, he was still seeking out his own teachers. Carnegie's greatest strengths throughout his life in pushing toward the goals he sought, whether it be wealth or wisdom, were his adaptability and his eagerness to learn, even at the expense of having his fixed ideas shaken or his established procedures rendered obsolete.

Moreover, Carnegie in 1900 was clearly looking for a mission in life. He wanted something more challenging to his intellect, more demanding of his own talents as a publicist and amateur politician, more radical in its impact upon society than were the obligations imposed upon him by the Gospel of Wealth, however arduous they might be. Just as when he had first entered business he had placed his eggs in many baskets, so in philanthropy he had at first scattered his wealth in many directions. Now he was to look again for a single basket to brood upon. He found that basket in pacifism, and it became his hope that from it would be hatched a flight of doves to bring peace to the world.

In many respects, it was a natural choice. Pacifism was a part of his radical Dunfermline heritage. His earliest letters from America back to Cousin Dod in Scotland were in praise of America's not having a standing army, his admiration for Chinese culture was to a great extent based upon that nation's ancient non-militaristic tradition, and his most active interest in international affairs in the last three decades of the nineteenth century had been to promote the cause of international arbitration. Once he had risen to a position of prominence that permitted him to correspond freely with Gladstone, he had written frequently and forcibly on behalf of an arbitration treaty between the United States and Great Britain.[7] He had strongly supported the idea of an organization of the Western Hemisphere nations, and one of the proudest moments of his life was when he was selected as an official delegate to the first International Conference of the American States to be attended by the United States, in 1889.[8] He had been tireless to the point of obsession in his efforts to force Britain to the arbitration table in the Venezuelan crisis of 1894–95, bombarding his friends in the British government with frantic letters and cablegrams that alternately promised either perpetual peace or immediate war. It had been the prominent role that he had taken in the anti-imperialist crusade of 1898 to 1900, however, that had given him worldwide publicity and brought him close to the inner circle of international pacifism.

Nevertheless, in spite of his valiant efforts to prevent the American acquisition of the Philippines, which ranged from the improbable possibility of his supporting Bryan for the presidency to the impossible suggestion of his purchasing the Philippines from the United States, he was still in 1900 not beyond suspicion to such pure pacifists as Stead, David Starr Jordan, and Edwin Mead. His letter rebuffing Stead would be evidence enough to men such as these that Carnegie's pacifism was not fashioned of that pure, unalloyed metal that could withstand the test of every crisis involving the nation's honor or self-interest. He had not opposed the war with Spain, only some of the unexpected tropical fruits of that war. His race alliance theme, so blatantly broadcast supposedly in the name of world peace, smacked too much of race aggrandizement not to alarm peace societies both in the United States and Great Britain, not to mention France and Germany. Most irritating of all was his crusade for Continental Union, which frequently took on the appearance of an open threat of aggression against America's northern neighbor, Canada. That four thousand miles of undefended border between Canada and the United States was the pacifists' prize model against militarism, their brightest hope of providing an enduring example of practical pacifism to an armament burdened world. Carnegie at times, by his blustering, jingoistic speeches and articles, seemed determined to ring all the alarm bells from Halifax to Vancouver, to arouse Canadians into a panic of self-defense. His arguments against American imperialistic adventures in the far Pacific hardly endeared Carnegie to the New York Peace Society:

> It does not stand to reason that the American with his good sense will seek additional territory if he wants it in distant parts of the world; he has Canada on the north and Mexico on the south, coterminous territory.[9]

Nevertheless Canada remained Carnegie's *bête noire;* her continuing loyalty to the British monarchy he regarded as a personal affront. As late as 1903, when he otherwise seemed to be moving into the inner circle of international pacifism, a proposal by Joseph Chamberlain for a preferential tariff for British dominions set him off again. In a series of angry letters to the British Prime Minister, Arthur Balfour, to American officials, and, most damaging of all to his pacifist reputation, to the Editors of *The Times* of London, *The New York Times,* and the New York *World,* he screamed against this act of "aggressive discrimination," and threatened that the United States would surely take retaliatory measures should this tariff be imposed. Carnegie seemed to have the fixed impression that Canada was an ice-locked Siberia five months of the year, totally dependent upon American ports from November to April. He gave solemn public assurance in *The Times* of London that if an imperial preference tariff were passed, America would close all her ports to goods bound for Canada. The Western farmers in the United States, he warned, were up in arms.[10]

It did not particularly mollify Carnegie's anger to have high administrative officials in his own government unconcerned about the possibility of a British imperial tariff. Secretary of Agriculture James Wilson, himself "a Western farmer," wrote Carnegie that he knew of no serious protest from agriculture over Britain's proposed fiscal policy. In a rather unkind dig, he asserted that "the Western people are the most cosmopolitan of Americans. . . . We do not make iron, for example, out in Iowa, yet we stand solidly for protection of American industries out there and give enormous majorities to that end. . . . As strong a protectionist as I am, if I lived in Great Britain, I would sympathize with

Mr. Chamberlain." He added that he had discussed the matter with President Roosevelt in a recent cabinet meeting, and "the President said we could not afford to stoop to retaliation." [11] Even the usually trigger-happy Anglophobe Senator from Massachusetts, Henry Cabot Lodge, was unperturbed. After all, he pointed out to Carnegie, "We have a discriminatory tariff with Cuba." [12] Carnegie, all alone with his "get-tough-with-Canada" policy, dashed off more letters to editors, saying that, in the long run, British imperial tariff programs would make very little difference. "You must know that I am a race Imperialist. . . . Canada and the United States shall be one nation." Then, perhaps in the foolish notion that he was sweetening his doctrine, he added, "Canada will someday annex the Republic, just as the northern part of Great Britain, called Scotland, actually annexed the southern part, called England, and has blessed it ever since. May this be the destiny of Canada." [13] He thereby accomplished the remarkable feat of angering everybody: Scotsmen, Englishmen, Canadians, and even American jingoists.

Alarmed as the pacifists must have been by some of Carnegie's more aberrant pronouncements, they kept coming back to him. Perhaps they sensed that he was, with proper tutelage, educable and tamable. And if his pacifism was not pure and unalloyed, his gold certainly was. The letters to Carnegie from Mead, Stead, Butler, and White continued, and with each passing month they found a more positive response in Carnegie's evident willingness to contribute both his wealth and his time to the cause of international peace.

The easiest thing for Carnegie to do for the cause of peace was to give money, and that is largely all that his pacifist friends at first expected of him. They were as naïve as Carnegie in believing that with enough money one could buy anything—knowledge, health, even world peace. Large scale philanthropy became Carnegie's first weapon for peace. From 1903 to 1914 Carnegie endowed four trusts or foundations and built three imposing buildings, "temples of peace," as he liked to call them, all in the cause of international peace, at a cost to himself of $25,250,000. This was not, to be sure, his largest contribution to a single idea, but it was the project to which he gave the greatest personal attention.[14] His first two trusts for peace must have come as some-

890

thing of a disappointment to his new pacifist friends, further evidence to them of an eccentric attitude that needed correction. To Carnegie, however, the Simplified Spelling Board, established in 1903, and the Hero Fund, first set up in the United States in 1904, were not tangential but central to the cause of world peace.

It had been Melvil Dewey, the New York State Librarian who developed the Dewey Decimal library classification system, and Brander Matthews, professor of dramatic literature at Columbia University, who had first interested Carnegie in the crusade to simplify the spelling of English words. Carnegie, who himself often wrote his personal notes in a staccato, telegraphic style, omitting what he regarded as unnecessary articles, prepositions, and conjunctions, and who had frequently expressed the hope that someday, in the more efficient future, calligraphy as we know it would be entirely replaced by Pitman's shorthand, was an easy convert. Particularly in these days, when he tended to judge all political and social activities by their contribution to—or detraction from—the cause of world peace, Carnegie was impressed with Melvil Dewey's argument that the simplification of English spelling would be a major step in making the English language "the lingua franca of the whole world." What could be a more effective agency for world peace than to have all men able to communicate with each other in the same language, especially if that language were English? Carnegie agreed to contribute $10,000 a year (shortly thereafter he increased it to $25,000 a year) to carry out the work of a National Simplified Spelling Board.[15]

The Board's task was to get fifty distinguished American writers to sign a pledge card promising to use the approved simplified spelling for twelve words—program, catalog, decalog, prolog, demogog, pedogog, tho, altho, thoro, thorofare, thru, and thruout. Hardly an earthshaking revolution even in the rather rarefied air of orthography. The writers that the Board got to sign the pledge included such distinguished men of letters as George Washington Cable, Thomas W. Higginson, Henry Holt, William Dean Howells, Edwin Markham, Ernest Thompson Seton, Josiah Strong, William Graham Sumner, and Andrew White.[16] The most important pledge card, however, was received from the President of the United States, Theodore Roosevelt. Carnegie, in delight, wrote to Roosevelt, "The reform of our language may seem a small task compared to the establishment of arbitration instead of war, and so it is, yet the former is no mean accomplishment. If we can ever get our language as fonetic as the Italian and Spanish, as Pioneer you will have rendered no small service to the race. . . . I have just receved from the editor of the Worcester (Mass.) Telegram his issue of August 27th, the first paper publisht with the improved spelings—the world moves." [17] Any editor living in Worcester, Massachusetts, who favored phonetic spelling deserved Carnegie's commendation.

As for Carnegie, he was more than ready to go the whole way with simplified spelling, not just the twelve minor changes which the Board suggested as a start. The full range of simplification included the dropping of the *u* in words like honour, labour and favour; the final *e* which did not signify a long vowel for the preceding vowel, as in have, deposite, and love; the substitution of *f* for *ph*, as in phantom, sulphur, and phonetic; and the phonetic rendering of *gh* as in cough, draught, and plough. Many of these changes were already standard American usage, but the other changes caused a wild storm in the literary and journalistic teacups throughout the country, while humorists everywhere had a field day. A columnist in *The New York Times* suggested that the members of "the Bored of Speling start with their own names: Androo Karnage, Richud Watsn Gildr and Brandr Mathooz." Mark Twain, an early if somewhat bemused convert, said that his only fear was that the reform "won't make any hedway. I am as sory as a dog. For I do lov revolutions and violense." [18]

Carnegie, in spite of criticism and sarcasm, remained faithful to his pledge to the end of his life. To Whitelaw Reid, whose paper, the New York *Tribune,* was the most critical of the proposed changes, Carnegie wrote, "Amused at your calling improved spelling movement 'a fictitious movement' . . . move up, move on before old age comes—don't be an old fogey—*if you can help it.*" [19]

Often, to be sure, it was hard to remember to simplify, and one can see, in his handwritten manuscripts, how conscientiously and laboriously Carnegie would erase "have" and rewrite it as "hav." He also let it be known that he would appreciate having all of his philanthropic trusts write all official communications in "simplified English." The British trusts flatly refused. John Ross would have as willingly appeared naked in Pittencrieff Park as have dropped his final e's and gh's. Of all of Carnegie's various ventures into reform, this proved to be his most complete failure. In spite of the encouraging notes that Matthews and Carnegie exchanged year after year—assuring each other that "the work goes bravely on!"—nothing really happened after the satirists had had their fun with it. When Matthews in 1915 sent Carnegie a list of daily newspapers that had adopted the reform, Carnegie was not impressed: "Please note not one Eastern paper. I see no change in New York and I am getting very tired indeed, of sinking Twenty-five thousand dollars a year for nothing here in the East." [20]

By this time even Carnegie's own trusts in America had abandoned the ship. Robert Woodward, in sending Carnegie the annual report of the Carnegie Institution of Washington, apologized. "You will see from this report that in deference to my eminent colleagues of the Executive Committee and the Board of Trustees I have taken what we would call a step backwards in reference to spelling. My experiment with the two preceding reports met with a degree of disfavor which was unanticipated. . . . I have concluded that the relatively small question of the spelling of the English language should not be allowed to jeopardize the larger interests of the Institution." [21] The world, it would appear, was run by "old fogeys." By 1915, Carnegie had had enough—or, as he spelled it, "enuf." He wrote to Henry Holt, editor of *Independent* and director of the Board, "A more useless body of men never came into association, judging from the effects they produced. Instead of taking twelve words and urging their adoption, they undertook radical changes from the start and these they can never make. . . . I think I hav been patient long enuf. . . . I have a much better use for Twenty-five thousand dollars a year." [22] If English was to become the lingua franca of the whole world, it would apparently be the King's English, not Carnegie's.

Carnegie had considerably more luck and happiness with his next philanthropic venture, even though most of his pacifist friends, with greater plans in mind, considered it to be almost as frivolously incidental to the main issue of peace as simplified spelling. This project was the Hero Fund, which Carnegie first created in the United States in 1904 and was later to extend to most of the nations of Western Europe. Indeed, of all of his philanthropic enterprises this seemed to delight him the most. As he wrote to Ross, "It is the fund that may be considered my pet. I used to hate that word, becaus the children at school cald me 'Martin's pet,' but now I like it." To W. T. Stead, who could not understand this curious affection, Carnegie explained why: "It's my pet because no one ever suggested it. Its reception here was not universal at first, some critics thot I proposed to stimulate heroism, but now nothing I've done is so popular. It was time the Heroes of Peace had recognition." [23]

Every other philanthropic fund that Carnegie had ever established had been proposed to him—often forced upon him—by others. The Hero Fund came out of his own head and heart, and it delighted him. Dunfermline claims that he first got his inspiration for this fund in 1886 when a youth named William Hunter of neighboring Townhill lost his life in trying to rescue two young Dunfermline boys from drowning in Townhill Loch. Carnegie, hearing of the tale from his Uncle Lauder, contributed money for a monument to Hunter's memory, and a fitting epitaph, which read, "The false heroes of barbarous man are those who can only boast of the destruction of their fellows. The true heroes of civilisation are those alone who save or greatly serve them. Young Hunter was one of those and deserves an enduring monument." [24]

If this was the inspiration it was a long time incubating, for it was not until eighteen years later that Carnegie, following a mine disaster near Pittsburgh, announced that he was creating the Carnegie Hero Fund, with an endowment of $5,000,000. Its national headquarters were to be in Pittsburgh. In the opening paragraph of the deed creating the Fund, Carnegie indicated the philosophy that lay behind it: "We live in an heroic age. Not seldom are we thrilled by deeds of heroism where men or women are injured or lose their lives in attempting to preserve or rescue their fellows; such the heroes of civilization. The heroes of barbarism maimed or killed theirs." [25] Too long, Carnegie felt, had soldiers been decorated, honored, feted, and pensioned for killing other men. Small wonder that wars continued when society depended on battles to provide it with heroes. Now, Carnegie medals in gold or silver or bronze, pensions, and great publicity would go to the Heroes of Peace.

Again the cartoonists and humorists had great sport with Carnegie's latest fancy—especially Finley Peter Dunne's Mr. Dooley:

"It's no use," said Mr. Dooley, "I give it up."

"What's that?" asked Mr. Hennessy.

"I can't get away from him," Mr. Dooley went on. "I can't escape me ol' frind Andhrew Carnaygie. I've avided him successfully f'r manny years. Th' bookless libry an' th' thoughtless univarsity niver touched me. I'm not enough iv a brunette to share annything he done f'r Booker Washin'ton. Up to now, he been onable to land on me annywhere. But he's got me at last. He's r-run me to earth. I throw up me hands. Come on, Andhrew, an' paint ye'er illusthrees name on me. Stencil me with that gloryous name."

"What ar-re ye talkin' about," asked Mr. Hennessy.

"He has created a hayro fund," said Mr. Dooley. "He has put aside five millyon dollars or it may be fifty . . . to buy medals f'r hayroes in th' daily walk in life, sogers, polismen an' investors in steel common barrd. . . . Suppose f'r instance, I should save your life. . . . Th' talk gets ar-round th' neighborhood an' wan day a comity steps into me place, headed be a little dumpling iv a man, an' wan iv them pins me hands while Andhrew Carnaygie nails on me chist a medal all in goold, with this inscription—here it is—that Father Kelly wrote out f'r me:

'To Martin Dooley, Hayro
This medal is prisinted by

ANDHREW CARNAYGIE

Dulcy et decorum est pro Carnaygie
To spoil y'r Sunday Clthes.'

"I'm a hayro fr' good an' all. I'm f'iver doomed to be a sandwich man an' parade th' streets advartisin' th' gin'rosity an' noble charakter iv Andhrew Carnaygie. . . . Iv coorse, I won't be good fr' annything else. I'll have to sell out th' liquor store. . . . They'se nawthin' a hayro with a medal can do fr a livin' that ain't beneath him. . . . Afthir awhile I'll be lurkin' in the corner iv the bridge an' pushin' me friends into th' river an' haulin' thim out f'r a medal. I'll become an habichool Carnaygie hayro, an' good fr' nawthin' else." [26]

895

Carnegie's account of the work of the Hero Fund, as given to Morley—done without dialect—was almost as good. "Our Hero pension has triumphed, its last annual report swept the Country. Those papers who at first supposed my idea to be to stimulate Heroism have seen their mistake. . . . Sixteen Heroes & Heroines injured while engaged in rescuing others were placed on our list. One man (fisherman) rescued seven men when the Life Boat crew declared it impossible. Our 'visitor' went to his home, found him & his wife only one wish to give their boy a better education than they had—good, we send him to college, of course—a small mortgage on House, pay that. The Hero wasn't injured but in extreme triumphs like that we do assist pecuniarilly [sic] when money can do them such service. In case of Injury, preventing usual work, his highest wages are given, no broken time. If killed, his widow and children are paid his wages & sometime more if children need better education, &c. We also give medals. . . . No bogus heroes. Must be real thing." [27]

Carnegie was so delighted with the Hero Fund—"I don't believe there's a nobler fund in the world" [28]—that within four years he decided to make it international. In 1908 he created the Carnegie Fund Trust for Great Britain, endowed at $1,250,000. The following year, the *Fondation Carnegie* in France was established with a $1,000,000 endowment. Carnegie felt obliged to explain to Ambassador Henry White why France was getting a quarter of a million dollars less than Great Britain: "It will be found ample. Life is much more secure in France, I think, even than in Britain with its enormous number of mines and enormous amount of shipping, fruitful of accidents." [29] The following year it was Germany's turn. The *Carnegie Stiftung für Lebensretter* was endowed with $1,500,000. Germany under Kaiser Wilhelm was apparently even more fruitful of accidents than Britain. Then in rapid succession Hero Funds were created in Norway, Switzerland, the Netherlands, Sweden, Denmark, Belgium, and Italy.[30] Mr. Dooley would have to travel far indeed to escape Andhrew Carnaygic now.

The Hero Funds abroad never had the success that they did in America, however. The British were too diffident to give peaceful heroism the kind of publicity that Carnegie felt would offset the propaganda of militarism. He wrote a scolding letter to

John Ross, who was handling the British Hero Fund out of the Dunfermline Trust office, for his failure to capitalize on a particular incident:

> A live Sec'y would know to use the unsurpassed act of Heroism [reported] in the *Scotsman* (libellous to use the word *providential* but such is our theology.) Properly recorded and copy to send to each newspaper would give you a start as nothing else would and stir the hearts of the people—giving the full item as in the *Scotsman*. So much depends upon first impressions and here the fates favored you. *The very day* you began, this heroic case happened within a few miles of headquarters of Hero Fund. Something like this—"The very day the Hero Fund was formed the following incident occurred within fifteen miles of Dunfermline and the first case it is called to deal with is this: (Story in *Scotsman*) next morning the following was received from the Founder showing how his heart is in the work: The agent of the Fund is in Edinburg investigating the widow and her children who will probably be the first wards of the Fund &c &c &c." Only utilize this incident and your start is assured—nothing could give you such a start.[31]

The French, although not shy, were too bound up in bureaucratic red tape to move with enough dispatch and efficiency for Carnegie. "Why the delay?" he wrote White. "But then they manage such things differently in France from what they do in Britain or America." [32] As for Germany, it was very difficult there for a heroic miner, no matter how large his medal, to compete for public esteem against the youngest sub-lieutenant with his first duelling scar. Nevertheless, the Hero Fund, whatever its shortcomings and problems, remained Carnegie's pet. It provided the kind of dramatic human element and newspaper attention that most of his philanthropies lacked. "Someday," Carnegie was fond of saying, "when war has been relegated along with cannibalism to that position of barbarism that it deserves, the only heroes we shall have will be the Heroes of Peace."

It was not until Carnegie created the Carnegie Endowment for International Peace in 1910 that he satisfied the demands and expectations of his pacifist friends. His first two endowed trusts

897

for peace were regarded by most of them as being expensive eccentricities—colorful, amusing, but hardly germane to the serious cause of world peace. Men like Butler and Mead continued to press for a truly significant foundation, comparable to the Carnegie Institution of Washington. In 1907, the Association for International Conciliation, headed by Baron d'Estournelles de Constant of France, established a branch in the United States. Nicholas Murray Butler took the presidency, and he was gratified by Carnegie's large contribution. The pressure on Carnegie increased. In 1908, Mead, Samuel Dutton, and Hamilton Holt wrote a long letter to Carnegie, proposing a major endowed trust to work for "the education of the public for peace, to spread arbitral justice among nations and to promote the comity and commerce of the world without the dangers of war." The head of this foundation, they argued, should be a man comparable to Henry Pritchett or Robert Woodward, and they suggested Nicholas Murray Butler, who quite obviously was more than willing to take on such a position.[33] Carnegie, not yet ready for such a grandiose scheme, replied that the matter was one needing "careful and prolonged consideration." [34] Although in later years Butler took full credit for having persuaded Carnegie to establish the Carnegie Endowment for International Peace, it was actually Secretary of State Elihu Root who carefully and slowly led Carnegie to his final decision. Quite properly, when the Endowment was at last established, it was Root, then Senator from New York, who became the first president of the Board of Trustees, not Butler.[35]

On his seventy-fifth birthday, 25 November 1910, Carnegie announced the creation of the Carnegie Endowment, with a trust fund of $10,000,000.[36] The Endowment was comparable to the later Carnegie Corporation of New York in that the widest kind of latitude of action was given to its board. It was directed to spend the annual income in any way appropriate "to hasten the abolition of war." The Endowment was to be perpetual, and with that wonderfully naïve optimism that pervaded all peace movements in the first decade of the twentieth century, the deed, at Carnegie's direction, provided that "when the establishment of universal peace is attained, the donor provides that the revenue shall be devoted to the banishment of the next most degrading evil or evils, the suppression of which would most advance the progress, elevation and happiness of man." [37]

For his first board of trustees, Carnegie had collected the leaders of American pacifism, including Root, Butler, Pritchett, Joseph Choate, Eliot of Harvard, James Brown Scott, John W. Foster, Andrew White, J. G. Schmidlapp, Oscar S. Straus, and President Taft, who was honorary president.[38] In 1913, Butler reported on the organization of the Endowment, which had created several subdivisions, including the divisions of International Law, Economics, History, and Intercourse and Education. The last was the one that dealt directly with the public, attempting both to ascertain and to influence public opinion. It also helped to set up international organizations throughout the Western World, and it investigated and gave wide publicity to "the shocking conditions" in the second Balkan War, 1913–14.[39]

Praise came to Carnegie from pacifist leaders all over the world for his Endowment. Baron d'Estournelles thanked him on behalf of "the children of all the world." [40] Paul S. Reinsch, professor of political science at the University of Wisconsin, and later Woodrow Wilson's Minister to China, wrote in the *North American Review* that Carnegie "has again astonished the world with his latest benefaction . . . It is unprecedented that a social and political purpose should have been endowed in this manner and provided with so powerful and flexible an organization." The old style of peace propaganda, Reinsch wrote, is clearly outdated. "People give little heed to abstract arguments against war." Nor did he think that worldwide peace was immediately realizable. The Carnegie Endowment's trustees "believe world peace is attainable, but only slowly and after much sacrifice. It is the aim of this institution to diminish this sacrifice and to allow this great and necessary purpose toward which civilization is tending to work itself out at less cost to humanity than if forces were left blindly to find their way." The three general fields of work— study, propaganda, and action—needed to be synthesized, and this could be the Endowment's greatest service. The studies that the divisions were engaged in "will form the basis of intelligent propaganda." Reinsch praised Carnegie for having selected not only idealistic pacifists for his board of trustees, but also men of action in both commerce and government. He urged the pushing for neutrality legislation in Congress and above all "the necessity for working out an international code of law that meets the highest conception of equity and justice." The Carnegie Endowment should co-ordinate all the various efforts, such as those of David Dudley Field and Francis Lieber. The tasks that lay before the foundation were tremendous, Reinsch concluded, but here was the agency that could accomplish them and thus give hope to the world.[41]

Carnegie was most touched by Morley's encomium.

> This last noble stroke of wisdom and beneficence is the crown-ing achievement, and is universally recognized for what it is—a real ascent in the double spheres of ideal and practical. . . .
> Today, my dear Carnegie, you have truly made us, who are your friends, proud of you, including especially one who has been your friend longest of them all, to wit, John Morley.[42]

There was, to be sure, criticism from some quarters, even for this most nobly idealistic of all his benefactions. John Bigelow wrote to J. G. Schmidlapp, one of the trustees, "Your brother pea-cemaker, Carnegie, reminds me of a verse that I learned at an early period of my life: 'There was an old woman who lived in a shoe. She had so many children, she didn't know what to do.' Car-negie seems to know no better what to do with his money than this old lady knew what to do with her children. He takes three columns of a newspaper to give you ten millions of money to spend to stop people from fighting, and gives not a single sugges-tion from beginning to end of what you are to do to accomplish this result,—not even spanking. He gives you ten millions of dol-lars to promote peace, every penny of which was the Dead Sea fruit of a war tariff which he has himself admitted was unneces-sary and therefore oppressive, and he selects forty of the most con-spicuous men of his acquaintance in the country, pretty nearly everyone of whom is a stand pat protectionist, and a red-handed partisan of war upon every commercial nation, including our own, to spend millions for peace, without the suggestion of a sin-gle step they were to take to accomplish it. Why could he not have said, 'Use what is necessary to abolish the tariff and put the rest in your pockets'—for a riddance of the tariff would be a guar-antee of peace, and your Board of Trustees would be functus officio." [43]

Sir Norman Angell, a later Nobel Peace laureate, was in the

United States at this time, and he met Carnegie to discuss with him the newly established Endowment. "I remember very well," he would later recall, "the warning which I gave him. 'You are choosing for the work of this endowment people like Elihu Root and Butler, who are very good. But they shouldn't be the only people. They are conservatively minded; their thinking is along conservative lines. You want to get the interest also of the younger generation and be bold in your methods, even revolutionary. Take every means of reaching the student mind. . . . The Peace Foundation shouldn't be merely an organization of eminency, of university presidents and great public figures.' I tried to impress on him that there were two problems confronting the peacemakers. One was to establish the facts, to get at what ought to be done. The second, quite distinct from this, was to learn how the truth as to facts and what ought to be done about them could be put across to the public. I tried to impress on him the importance of the psychology of persuasion and of clarification. The enemy we fought, I insisted, was confusion in the public mind, sometimes quite elementary confusion, like the difference between owning and governing territories. . . . Carnegie was momentarily receptive to the ideas I put before him, but one must remember that after all, he was an industrialist not a political scientist. I think he felt this. He had good will, of course, to help, but thought it best to leave the details of the problems to educationalists, men like Butler and Root." [44]

And Butler, in reviewing the work of the Endowment in the late fall of 1913, was generally well satisfied with its organization and goals, even though he was critical of his own nation and the other great powers. "What of the future?" he wrote in these last bright days of peace. "It would be simple blindness to conceal from ourselves the fact that the international situation has in it many points of possible danger. The naval rivalry between Great Britain and Germany, the long-standing antagonism and jealousy between Germany and France, the constant misunderstandings between the United States and Latin American countries, the open attempts in the United States to secure action that must necessarily produce friction with Japan, and the appalling conditions that have prevailed in the Balkan Peninsula, all speak for themselves." Still, Butler felt, there was reason for hope. There had been a considerable improvement of relations between France and Germany. War was less likely now than it had been a few years earlier, and no little credit was due to the work of the Carnegie Endowment. Our biggest task, Butler concluded, was to work with our own people. The United States "had proved itself to be internationally incompetent. . . . The American public and Congress must be educated to behave like gentlemen." [45] Butler apparently felt that what was needed for world peace was an Edwardian code of proper decorum—not exactly the kind of new scientific approach that Angell and Reinsch had had in mind. The time for the Butler-Root style of gentility was rapidly running out.

Carnegie's last major endowment in the cause of peace must have pleased men like Sir Norman Angell even less, for it found its leadership and made its appeal to an even more genteel and unworldly select group than the academicians of the Old School tie who dominated the Carnegie Endowment. The Church Peace Union was founded in February 1914, with an endowment of $2,000,000 that came not directly from Carnegie himself but by his direction from the Carnegie Corporation of New York. It was surprising that Carnegie, as his last gesture in large scale philanthropy for peace, should have turned to an institution that he had largely ignored in all of his previous philanthropies—the institution of organized religion. Louise Carnegie had become interested in the idea through the persuasion of two ministers, her own pastor, Dr. William P. Merrill, of the Brick Presbyterian Church in New York, and Frederick Lynch, a young Congregational minister in Pittsburgh. Louise was largely instrumental in interesting her husband in this project, and it was to remain her favorite philanthropic organization. In his letter establishing the organization, addressed to "Gentlemen of Many Religious Bodies, All Irrevocably Opposed to War and Devoted Advocates of Peace," Carnegie expressed, in this last year of world peace, the same optimism he had earlier expressed in the deed creating the Carnegie Endowment:

> After the arbitration of international disputes is established and war abolished, as it certainly will be some day, and that sooner than expected, probably by the Teutonic nations, Ger-

many, Britain and the United States first deciding to act in unison, other Powers joining later, the Trustees will divert the revenues of this fund to relieve the deserving poor and afflicted in their distress, especially those who have struggled long and earnestly against misfortunes and have not themselves to blame for their poverty. . . . As a general rule, it is best to help those who help themselves, but there are unfortunates from whom this cannot be expected. [Apparently, Carnegie was now willing to take a new and more sympathetic look at the submerged tenth.]

After war is abolished by the leading nations, the Trustees by a vote of two-thirds may decide that a better use for the funds than that named in the preceding paragraph has been found, and are free according to their judgment to devote the income to the best advantage for the good of their fellow men.[46]

What pleased Carnegie even more about this foundation than its being dedicated to the cause of world peace was that it was truly ecumenical in the religious affiliations of its trustees. "Would you believe that I have the cordial, delighted acceptance of Cardinal Gibbons of Washington (R.C. of course) Bishop Greer, Episcopal Head, and two dozen heads of various sects, *not one* refused," he wrote to Morley. "I am so pleased at union of the separate Sects, Jews included, two Rabbies [sic], Universalists, Baptists, etc. etc., esteeming that in itself a step forward toward the coming brotherhood of man. Have called all to meet here 5th February to organize—Episcopalians here not being unfairly pampered by the nation, cooperate freely with other sects." [47]

Bishop David Greer was chosen president of the board at the first organizational meeting of the trustees, among whom were such distinguished religious leaders as Shailer Mathews, president of the Federal Council of Churches, Edwin Mead of the First Unitarian Church of Boston, and Rabbi Stephen Wise of New York. Merrill was chosen as vice president and Frederick Lynch as general secretary.[48] At this meeting it was decided to hold an international conference the following summer in Europe in order to bring together religious leaders from America and western Europe in a new organization to carry out the purposes of the deed. Lynch assured Carnegie that it would be "an informal conference, not a full scale conference. We are taking over a splendid group from America, and it will be a fine thing for the Americans and Europeans to meet in this intimate way." [49] The meeting was to convene in Constance, Germany, on 1 August 1914. Other forces, unfortunately, were to force an early and rather abrupt adjournment.

The four foundations established to further the cause of peace may have received a large amount of money from Carnegie, but they did not get as much attention from him in the planning stage as did the "temples of peace" which he contributed to international law and organization. Of these three buildings, the Palace of Peace at The Hague—the first begun and the last finished— was the largest, the most expensive, and by far the most demanding of Carnegie's attention and concern. Carnegie had been such an enthusiastic and outspoken public advocate of the efforts of the first Hague Conference in 1899 to establish a permanent court of arbitration that it was only natural for Frederick Holls, secretary of the American delegation to the Conference, and Andrew White, then Ambassador to Germany, to seek him out with their proposal to build an appropriate court house for this international judicial body. Carnegie, who had first met Holls when they served together on the New York Tenement House Committee, was pleasant but not responsive.[50] White, who knew Carnegie better, put more pressure on him, telling him that the Russian diplomat, Frederic F. de Martens, who had originated the idea of a great peace palace at The Hague, had told him "that it would render the man who makes the gift a benefactor to every nation and to all mankind—acknowledged as such through all time." [51] Carnegie was still reluctant. For three years Holls and White kept angling. At times it looked quite impossible. Carnegie, caught up in other philanthropic ventures, seemed singularly uninterested in buildings. "Please let the idea rest for the present," he wrote Holls in the spring of 1902. "Let us get our English speaking race at peace first. This forcing ourselves upon unwilling peoples & shooting resisters down is so incongruous with the Hague Peace idea that neither Britain nor America seems in place—doing right (Hague) with one hand and (Filipinoes & Boers) wrong with the other. I am not going to think of it at present." [52]

But Holls, a determinedly aggressive lawyer, and White, a veteran in pleading philanthropic causes with Carnegie, would not let him "not think of it." By late summer, they had him at least partially hooked. Carnegie agreed he would give $250,000 for a library on international law for the use of the Permanent Court of Arbitration at The Hague.[53] This was a start, but only a start. As White told Holls, it was something like the turkey of which the gourmand said, "It is too much for one & not enough for two." It was too much for a library but not enough for "a great international temple." [54] The two men pressed Carnegie further, and Carnegie tentatively agreed that if the government of the Netherlands should ask him, he might consider building a "temple of peace" rather than just a library.[55] Holls realized he must work fast to get a request from the Dutch government. He wrote to the American Ambassador to Russia, "He [Carnegie] has not absolutely decided to do this, and, of course, the whole matter is as yet very private. . . . As soon as he makes up his mind definitely —and he is rather slow to do this, besides being given to changing it with lightening [sic] quickness—the fact will be announced and this again will add to the prestige of the Court." [56] The proper assurances were given Carnegie by Baron de Gevers, Minister of the Netherlands to the United States, that Her Majesty's Government would be most pleased to accept the gift of a court house for the Hague Tribunal, and would furnish a site for the building.[57]

On 7 October 1903, at Skibo Castle, the formal deed to create a "stichting," a foundation or trust under Dutch law, for "the purpose of erecting and maintaining at The Hague a courthouse and library for the Permanent Court of Arbitration," was signed by Andrew Carnegie and W. A. F. de Gevers.[58] Under the highly unusual terms of this agreement, Carnegie promised to pay $1,500,000 out of his personal account on a bank draft by the government of the Kingdom of the Netherlands. With great relief, Holls wrote to Baron de Bildt, the Swedish Minister to the Court of St. James's, "I wonder whether he [W. T. Stead] told you anything about Mr. Carnegie's willingness to give a million and a half of dollars for a Temple of Peace—a Court House and Library—at the Hague. I have been working at that for over a year [something of an understatement] and it now seems probable that it will be accomplished. You ought to know Carnegie personally. . . . He is a very peculiar man but you will know exactly how to get along with him and he will doubtless invite you up to Skibo and I urge you strongly to go up there for it is one of the most charming places in Scotland. I shall urge him to look you up or to write to you, purely in his interest, for he is a man who needs a great deal of advice and counsel, and you are just the right man to speak to him, so far as some of his international ideas and plans are concerned." [59] Andrew White was also delighted. He wrote to Carnegie: "The gift which fairly takes my breath away is your provision for the Temple of Peace. That will result undoubtedly in saving hundreds of thousands of lives. It is an immense thing, to have made such a provision." [60]

Frederick Holls did not live to see even the laying of the cornerstone of the edifice for which he had worked so long and so hard. He was killed in a tragic accident a few months after he had finally wrung from Carnegie his assent to build the Peace Palace. He was, however, spared the agony and confusion that accompanied its construction. First, there was the controversy over the site. For two years various proposals were made by the Dutch government and the planning commission. They would not agree. Each rejected the other's ideas. It was not until the end of May 1905 that there was an agreement to build the Hague Court House on the edge of the Zorgvliet Park near The Hague, and the parliament of the Netherlands made the necessary authorization of 700,000 florins ($290,000) to purchase the land.[61] Then there followed a long and at times acrimonious debate over every detail of the construction, from the prize-winning architectural plans down to the actual building materials to be used, in all of which Carnegie played an important and highly opinionated part. David Jayne Hill, at that time our Minister to the Netherlands, was the beleaguered intermediary, and to him Carnegie wrote frequent and highly critical letters. First Carnegie apparently completely forgot that he had originally been attracted to the whole idea by the suggestion of building only a library, for he wrote Hill: "The Library contemplated [as a part of the building] is a new idea. The Directors, as I understand matters, cannot devote one-third of the funds for this purpose. . . . I have not seen a plan of the proposed Temple and therefore cannot judge of its size. A large, showy building would I feel be incongruous. A moderate structure only is needed. The Court, the principal chamber, should be small, so that the members can sit close together, in touch with each other mentally and almost physically, proximity being always conducive to friendly conference and harmony. It dampens excited oratorical discussion." [62] Two days later, Carnegie received the report of the architectural jury, who had selected the winning architect, W. M. Cordonnier of Lille, France. Carnegie wrote in great alarm to Hill, "When I expressed fear that the Library feature would be improperly accentuated, little did I ever expect to read, as in the report of the Jury, 'The Library and Court of Arbitration.' This is to me shocking. I am positively wounded. The day that a permanent tribunal was established to settle international disputes humanity took a great step forward, and when a Temple of Peace is erected it will in my opinion be the holiest structure in the world. To speak of 'The Library and Court of Arbitration' is as if a bereaved husband were to ask plans for a sacred shrine to 'my nephew and my dear wife.' " Clearly, Carnegie was also disappointed that the jury had selected a French rather than an American architect. "I never heard of the New York Architects whose plan is praised both for simplicity and for suitability of character. I am no judge, but it does strike me as nearest a 'Temple of Peace.' . . . I have neither the right or desire to counsel the Jury. They know best. Upon the union of the Temple of Peace and a Library, or rather Library and Temple of Peace, I hope I shall not be considered intrusive in calling the attention of the proper authorities to the vital importance of confining the building to the sole purpose for which the money was given." [63]

The jury would have smiled wryly had they read that line about Carnegie's having "no desire to counsel," for counsel flowed almost daily from Skibo to The Hague. Two weeks after writing the letter above, Carnegie wanted the whole prize-winning plan scrapped. "It seems clear to me that they must make a fresh start. I fear they found that such a structure as that proposed might run into several millions, and not a dollar more will I ever give. . . .

To me the building proposed is no temple of peace, but shouts all over of the pomp, pride and vain circumstance of inglorious war." [64] Hill was inclined to agree. What both men would have liked was a sort of small scale Parthenon, not a great medieval Flemish guild hall, complete with high pitched roof, towers, and an imposing brick facade, however more appropriate to the Netherlands that might be. Samuel Harden Church, director of the Carnegie Institute of Pittsburgh, who regarded himself as being the unofficial custodian of Carnegie's taste in the fine arts, hurried over to Europe to argue architectural plans with the beleaguered director of the Peace Palace, Jonkheer Van Karnebeek. Church's pontifical judgment was that all the designs were bad and the whole project should be started afresh. He invited Van Karnebeek to come to Pittsburgh the following spring to look over the Institute and see what proper architectural style was like. Apparently, Van Karnebeek found it easier to agree than to argue on most points, for Church wrote Carnegie, "The only unpleasant thing he is yet tenacious of is *red brick*. How a Peace Palace could be beautiful in red brick I fail to see. He thinks the climate of Holland will not stand stone or marble. But you can get him out of this heresy." [65]

After this devastating encounter, Van Karnebeek hurried up to Skibo in August to talk directly with Carnegie about the whole project. It proved to be a surprisingly amicable meeting. After some modification of the towers, Carnegie finally agreed to the general design of the Palace, with a library as an essential part of the building. He gave permission to Van Karnebeek to use any surplus funds after the building was constructed for the purchase of books and maps for the library.[66] The only point upon which Carnegie was adamant was the question of the red brick. He insisted upon the same stone he had used in building Skibo Castle, taken from a near-by quarry in Dornoch. Happily for the architect, it was soon discovered that Carnegie had nearly stripped the quarry in building Skibo. Carnegie then urged the same stone that was used in the major buildings in Aberdeen, Scotland. "It remains pure even in a great city. Dirt and smoke do not affect it one particle," he wrote the Dutch director.[67] The costs of quarrying and shipping the stone from Aberdeen to Holland proved too expensive, and the red brick native to the Lowlands was kept in the specifications.

With all of these problems, it was little short of a miracle that the "stichting" board was ready to lay the cornerstone for the building in the summer of 1907, at the opening of the Second Hague International Conference. It then took six more years before the Palace was completed, during which time there continued to be squabbles over details, modifications of architectural plans, and lengthy discussions about furnishings. For ten years, the Temple of Peace was a storm of controversy, but at last, on 28 August 1913, the Grand Opening ceremonies were held. The reporter from *The Times,* with proper journalistic cynicism, observed that the "inauguration took place in the happiest of circumstances." There was glorious sunshine and, more importantly, "the present lull between the last war and the next has been a propitious opportunity for offering to the world the noble gift of Mr. Andrew Carnegie." The Great Court was crowded with four hundred people. The Queen of the Netherlands was there, and so were the Carnegies. There were speeches by the exhausted but relieved Van Karnebeek and the Dutch Minister of Foreign Affairs. It was a gala day for all concerned. The reporter added cryptically that the building itself "is certainly unlike anything else in the world." [68]

On the following day, marble busts of King Edward VII and Sir W. Randal Cremer were unveiled by Carnegie in the Great Court, and in his speech Carnegie praised the Palace as a "perfect gem." He then got onto his favorite topic of race alliance among the "Teutonic nations" of Britain, the United States, and Germany. "Why should these Teutonic nations ever quarrel? Why should they not agree to demand peace upon the seas?" He urged the German Emperor to invite the chief civilized nations to confer upon the best means of ensuring peace. "The greatest advances have appeared to burst upon us suddenly although the ground has been well prepared. So it will probably be with the change from barbarous war to civilized peace." He closed in stirring fashion with this metaphor: "One small spark often creates the flame. The German Emperor holds in his hand the torch." [69]

Later events would prove that to be an unfortunate figure of speech.

Happily for all concerned, Carnegie's other two "temples of peace" did not cause as much trouble in their planning and execution as the Hague Peace Palace did. Always having regarded Latin America as his special field of competence, Carnegie was highly flattered when he was asked by his hero, Secretary of State Elihu Root, if he would consider building a new center for the Bureau of American Republics worthy of its important task of furthering closer ties among the republics of the Western Hemisphere. No years of haggling over this, as Holls and White had had to endure. Within three weeks Root had his answer: "I am happy in stating that it will be one of the pleasures of my life to furnish to the Union of all the Republics of this hemisphere, the necessary funds ($150,000) . . . for the construction of an international home in Washington." [70]

No trouble here either with foreign architects, medieval towers, and plebeian red brick. Everyone concerned was agreed on District of Columbia Classical, built of white marble. On 11 May 1908, a little over a year after Root wrote his letter, the cornerstone of the Pan American Union Building was laid, and two years almost to the day after that, at a gala ceremony, the building was opened. Everyone present from the President of the United States on down agreed that it looked just as a "temple of peace" *should* look.[71]

The last of the three buildings was also done at the suggestion of Secretary Root. In 1907 the five small republics of Central America, who for years had been nurturing an artificial nationalistic spirit by snapping at each others' boundaries, signed an agreement in Washington to establish a Central American Court of Justice where differences among them could be arbitrated. All Root needed to do was suggest that it would be a good thing for the court to have a suitable building for its important work in international arbitration, and Carnegie promptly responded. "Delighted to receive yours of May 27th this morning. One more step in the right direction—the peace of our hemisphere. All goes well. I have written Mr. Franks, Financial Secretary, to honor the calls of the proper authorities of Costa Rica to the extent of one hundred thousand dollars. I had expected the cost to be much more, but perhaps the work is very cheaply done there." [72] The more temples you built, the cheaper they got—and the more quickly they were finished. The Central American Court of Justice, located in Cartago, Costa Rica, was only a little over a year in the building. Construction was finished and the building ready for its dedication by the first week of May 1910.

How pleasant it had become to build for peace by giving money! There were times when Carnegie felt that surely all of this wealth that he was giving must be moving the world closer to that golden age of true universal civilization. At times he had the frantic feeling that if only he would spend more and spend it faster, he could hasten that day. He wrote to Judge Joseph Choate, a member of the Hague Tribunal, telling him that he knew "a friend of yours & of Peace who would esteem it a privilege to provide say six or seven millions 5% bonds 300,000 a year 7 judges at 15,000\$—300,000\$—if 20,000\$ salary then 340,000— seven millions provide 350,000\$—provided the President asked me to see that man & get the fund as Sec'y Root asked me to provide the Pan American building but that man has to be asked he wouldn't presume to intrude and suffer. Nations might not like it but if President the Peace Maker asked it then 'My Friend' would be happy to be instrumental in establishing the World's Supreme Court." [73] Choate could hardly keep the smile out of his response. He explained that the financial problem of the court was not the salaries of the Judges, "amply provided for by the powers . . . creating the court . . . ," but the cost of litigation to the parties, a "matter it is difficult to see how to regulate." He closed by saying he would "always keep in mind the very generous offer of 'your friend' which I do most highly appreciate." [74]

Hard as it may have been for Carnegie to accept the idea, money could not accomplish everything in the complex field of human relations. Nor was the giving of money entirely satisfactory to him as the form of action to further his quest for peace. Not that the giving of money was easy—Carnegie never took his philanthropic obligations lightly—but no matter how actively he might participate in the organization and establishment of a particular foundation, he could not, in the role of founder, be the policymaker, the man of action. For one with his energy and determination, this role would never be enough to absorb his interest completely. He needed to be in on high level policy discussions; he needed the satisfaction of knowing that he was manipulating forces and moving men, not just with his checkbook but also with his ideas. He would gladly have exchanged his

911

wealth for Roosevelt's position, or even for that of a lesser official such as the Secretary of State or the Chancellor of the German Empire. His letters to friends like David Hill, Andrew White, and Morley frequently expressed his frustration at being on the outside of power looking in. "Whew! wish I were von Bülow just for a month or less. Maybe President will catch on. I'm going to write Knox [Secretary of State Philander C. Knox] freely." [75] And again: "I wish I were Prime Minister . . . I'd settle matters finally, *Peace* or War for Peace." [76]

Writing was Carnegie's great outlet, and he wrote frequently not just to Knox but to Presidents, Emperors, Chancellors, Prime Ministers, Ambassadors. He took full advantage of his close friendships in the British government, with Morley, Bryce, Rosebery, and others, to obtain information useful in giving weight to his suggestions and arguments to the White House and to cabinet officers. Roosevelt was to warn his Ambassador to the Court of St. James's: "Apparently the members of the present British Cabinet talk with extreme freedom to Carnegie." [77] And Carnegie was not at all hesitant in reciprocating by sending on to Morley confidential information he received from Root and Roosevelt, as the following correspondence from Morley to Carnegie indicates: "I have yours of July 16 with Mr. Root's enclosure. I shall send it to the P.M. this afternoon, and then on to E. G. [British Foreign Minister Edward Grey]. If you think it right (to me after reading Root's letter it seems a trifle dubious)—send me the papers, and I will communicate them to E.G." There is a penciled note from Grey to Morley at the bottom of the letter indicating how eager the British Foreign Minister was to see the promised Root papers: "This is very good news. I should like the correspondence very much. E.G." And finally a postscript by Morley: "You see what Grey says. Pray, let me have it. I will be most careful not to let it fall into wrong hands." [78]

At times, Carnegie's meddling in foreign affairs came perilously close to making commitments for the government of the United States that could have proved highly embarrassing to the President and the Secretary of State. With the first news in 1911 of popular uprisings against the Manchu Dynasty in China, Carnegie enthusiastically intervened on behalf of the republican forces. He sent to Charles Hilles, President Taft's personal secretary, the following letter and copies of an exchange of cablegrams with Wu Ting Fang, one of Shanghai's leaders in the republican movement:

> Feeling that the Secretary of State has not yet returned to Washington, I send this to you; but please hand it over to the Secretary if he be present.
>
> You can judge whether to advise the President or not. Wu Ting Fang and myself were close friends, both being students of Confucius!
>
> CABLEGRAM, Sent Nov. 8, 1911 to Wu Ting Fang, Shanghai
>
> Our hearts go out to you. Success attend you.
>
> Andrew Carnegie.
>
> CABLEGRAM, Received Nov. 10, 1911 from Wu Ting Fang:
>
> Grateful good Wishes. We are fighting for liberty and good government. Kindly ask your government to recognize us.
>
> CABLEGRAM, Sent Nov. 10, 1911, from Carnegie
>
> Our country certain among first to welcome heartily sister Republic.[79]

There must have been times when the Secretary of State regretted that he himself had not been a student of Confucius in order to learn patient forbearance from that contemplative sage.

In his quest for peace, Carnegie, though perhaps more quixotic and impetuous than many of his fellow laborers in the vineyard, shared most of their naïve hopes and assumptions regarding the attainment of peace. Like them, he placed an unwarranted faith in treaties and international agreements. The pursuit of arbitration treaties was eventually for him to become synonymous with the pursuit of peace itself. Any man who, throughout his long business career, had made and then broken as many pooling agreements and commercial pacts as Carnegie had should have had a more sophisticated skepticism about diplomatic agreements, but Carnegie regarded them with more reverential awe than he did the Holy Scriptures. Also, like most people caught up in a mission, he came to believe in the efficacy of organization for organization's own sake. The more peace societies that there were meant, per se, the more peace there would be in the world. Neither he nor his brother pacifists ever stopped to consider that the membership lists were virtually the same from one peace organization to another. It was always the same weary but ever hopeful band of angels speaking to each other as they moved from conference to congress to league. And pacifists in general, but Carnegie especially, gave undue importance to the power of the single political leader. There was a strong predilection on Carnegie's part to engage in hero worship, to have implicit faith in the cult of personality. He was always looking for THE MAN, the *deus ex machina* bearing in his hands the final, irrevocable treaty that would make peace an eternal reality.

What was lacking in Carnegie's perspective on the feasibility of attaining world peace was a proper estimate of the role of the people in the modern national state. War, at least since the time of the French Revolution and Napoleon, had become a popular, democratic activity that depended upon mass participation and, above all, mass support. It was no longer the eighteenth-century game of monarchs played with hired pawns. It was totally dependent upon the whole population of a nation, and the form of government of that nation was quite incidental to how actively a nation would play the game. Russia had been playing by the old rules when she went to war against Japan in 1905. It was the case of a giant with a professional, caste-ridden army pitted against dwarf, but the dwarf had become a total war machine, and the result had been calamitous for the giant. The lesson had not been lost on the Russian government. In the next war, there would be total mobilization and total mass support of fighting and dying for Mother Russia. War, in short, had to become as democratized under Czarist absolutism as it was in republican France, if it was to be won.

All of this the warmongers throughout the world understood far better than the peacemongers. Carnegie and Butler and Root chased after arbitration treaties and talked to each other in noble platitudes about proper decorum and respect for international law, while Roosevelt and Mahan and Clemenceau spoke to the people about national pride and unsullied flags and Jeanne d'Arc. A few men like Norman Angell and Paul Reinsch had some glimmerings of reality when they urged upon the Carnegie Endowment for International Peace a new approach to peace propaganda, and asked for new leadership which had some understanding of war as a modern democratic phenomenon. But Root was the first president of the Endowment, and Butler the second. Under their leadership, sincere and dedicated men worked hard to banish war from this planet. They were unsuccessful. But they did perform one noble function—they provided funds for the restoration of Europe after two World Wars.

The warmakers, if they were aware of the Endowment's existence at all, could have found little reason to object to its activities. They needed only to fear that day when the slogan, "Suppose they held a war, and *nobody* came," should become a reality. That day was so far distant in 1910 as to be unimaginable. The generals and admirals, the war ministers and munitions makers, and even just the ordinary well-meaning politicians throughout the world, men who worried about their country's prestige and got lumps in their throats when they sang their respective national anthems, knew full well that, if a war should be held, the people would be only too eager to come.

Carnegie was never to understand any of this. If he had, he would have realized that most of his activities during the last busy years of his life would have little result in achieving peace. His sincerity in desiring to abolish war, which he regarded as being the greatest of all man's crimes, cannot be questioned. But he and his fellow pacifists were playing according to the old rules of the eighteenth-century diplomacy, when treaties could be negotiated in privy council, unbeknownst to and uninfluenced by *vox populi,* when national honor lay exclusively within the purview of the aristocracy and the people were not a factor in determining whether there was to be war or peace. The men of peace assumed, in spite of all the evidence to the contrary, that the great mass of people throughout the world, those who had to bear the burdens of modern war, wanted peace as much as they did—that it was only kings and presidents and generals who led nations, against the popular will, into war. That assumption was the fundamental error which made their whole program largely an exercise in futility. It is almost too painful for anyone living in the last half of the twentieth century to read the speeches, the letters, the conference minutes of the pacifists who labored so zealously in the first decade of this same century. Carnegie, proudly bearing his bright banner, "All is well since all grows better," was to become the eponym of this antebellum pacifism, with all its high hopes and naïve optimism for an imminent victory over the forces of darkness.

Carnegie first attracted serious attention as being something more of a force in international pacifism than just a source of money when he delivered his rectorial address at St. Andrews University in 1905. Given on 17 October to inaugurate his second term as Rector of the University, the speech was a scathing indictment of war, all war, as "the foulest fiend ever vomited forth from the mouth of Hell." For one who belittled classical education, Carnegie showed a surprising penchant for quoting from the ancient Greeks and Romans to point up the evils of war. The oratory of Daniel Webster at its most effusive best was not more replete with classical allusions than was this address. The early Christian Fathers came in for their full share of attention and praise too. "We may well ponder over the change [in Christianity] and wonder that Christian priests accompany the armies of our day and even dare to approach the Unknown, beseeching his protection and favor for soldiers in their heinous work." But happily, in spite of the failure of Christianity to live up to the tenets of its Founder, the Prince of Peace, it is possible to point "to many bright rays, piercing the dark cloud, which encourage us. Consider for a moment what war was in days past. It knew no laws, had no restrictions. Poison and assassination of opposing rulers and generals arranged by private bargain . . . were legitimate weapons. Prisoners were massacred or enslaved. . . . Women, children and non-combatants were not spared." Carnegie then traced the "history of the reforms in war which have been achieved": the work of Grotius, the Treaty of Paris of 1856, the Treaty of Washington of 1876, the Brussels Convention of 1874. "Non-combatants are now spared, women and children are no longer massacred, quarter is given, and prisoners are well cared for. . . . There is great cause for congratulation. If man has not been busily striking at the heart of the monster War, he has at least been busily engaged drawing some of its poisonous fangs. . . . Thus even thruout the savage reign of man-slaying, we see the blessed law of evolution increasingly at work performing its

916

divine mission, making that which is better than that which has been and ever leading us on towards perfection." There had been only one backward step: "It is no longer considered necessary to declare war . . . a Power may surprise and destroy while yet in friendly conference with its adversary endeavoring to effect a peaceful settlement."

Carnegie then pointed out that more constructive in the abolition of war than the amelioration of the conditions of warfare was the movement for the peaceful arbitration of international dispute. Carnegie proceeded to give a long disquisition on the history of arbitration, beginning with Emeric Cruce, "the originator of the idea," through Henry IV of France down to the calling of the First Hague Conference by the Czar of Russia in 1899, which established a Permanent Court of Arbitration, approved by every civilized nation on earth. "At last there is no excuse for war. A tribunal is now at hand to judge wisely and deliver righteous judgment between nations. It has made an auspicious start. . . . First, it settled a difference between the United States and Mexico" . . . then the Venezuelan crisis of 1902, then the Dogger Bank incident between Great Britain and Russia, and under the Hague Convention, "the President of the United States addressed Japan and Russia seeking to bring about peace. . . . There sits the divinest conclave that ever graced the earth." There have been, Carnegie sadly admitted, three incidents since the Tribunal was organized "that have caused pain—the United States refused the offer of the Filipinos for arbitration. Britain refused the offer of the Transvaal Republic, and both Russia and Japan refused arbitration." In short, there had been three international wars in the previous five years. But Carnegie was not discouraged. In the preceding two years, he pointed out, twenty-three international treaties of arbitration had been made among various powers. "The United States has negotiated ten of these with all the principal powers." True, the Senate had not ratified any of them, but its objections were over mere technicalities, which could easily be rectified.

Carnegie then proposed a League of Peace, by which the five Great Powers, the United States, Great Britain, Germany, Russia, and France, would agree never again to go to war with each other. This agreement he felt was quite possible and was what

917

men of good will everywhere should work for, although it would be no easy task. "We should delude ourselves," he warned, "if we assumed that war is immediately to cease, for it is scarcely to be hoped that the future has not to witness more than one great holocaust of men to be offered up before the reign of peace blesses the earth. . . . But that peace is to come at last, and that sooner, much sooner than the majority of my hearers can probably credit, I for one entertain not one particle of doubt." He concluded by pointing out to the students what they could do to hasten that day. "Whenever an international dispute arises in which Great Britain is involved, demand your government, whatever party is in, to seek arbitration. If necessary break with your party. . . . And young women, you should not wait until war has begun and then go to the battlefield as nurses, but now raise your united voices in stern opposition to war." [80]

The speech was an instantaneous success among pacifist groups everywhere, for it had struck precisely the right balance between pointing up the evils of war and offering constructive and hopeful suggestions for the ending of war. Here was a powerful new voice for pacifism, and, moreover, one that could finance its own broadcasting. Within a year and a half, largely through the efforts of Baron d'Estournelles de Constant and his Society for International Conciliation, several hundred thousand copies, in thirteen languages, had been distributed throughout the world at Carnegie's expense. In France alone 100,000 copies had been distributed to school teachers, and by 1909 it was in its fifth edition with well over 3,000,000 copies in distribution.[81] Carnegie was delighted. He soon became one of the most prolific publicists for peace in the Western World. In the next few years he wrote many articles and pamphlets—"The Anglo-French-American Understanding"; "The Cry of the Wolf"; "The Next Step for Peace"; "Peace versus War"; "The Crime of War Is Inherent"; "Armaments and Their Results"; "The Path to Peace Upon the Seas"; "War as the Mother of Valor and Civilization"; "The Baseless Fear of War"; and "The Decadence of Militarism." Widely distributed to government officials, newspaper editors, and teachers, they all stressed much the same themes: the folly of war and the necessity for arbitration and for the co-operation of the great powers to prevent war. Carnegie struck out against the ancient clichés about war: that it brought out the best qualities of courage and sacrifice in man, that it was the impetus to technological advancement, that to prepare for war was the best way to preserve peace, that the military was an honorable profession, and that it was inevitable that there should be a war every generation. He wrote and spoke in a vigorous style that attracted a great deal of public notice, and he reveled in this attention.

He also enjoyed working behind the scenes, using his influence with persons in power to push his proposals. Although always an opponent of large military expenditures, he was more sophisticated in regard to disarmament than were most of his fellow pacifists. He was willing to argue with President Roosevelt about the increase in the number of battleships in the American navy, but he was not optimistic about any realistic proposal for reduction of the size of existing fleets. "I agree with you about disarmament," he wrote Roosevelt in 1906. "It will be found difficult to formulate a satisfactory plan. Probably all that can now be done is to agree not to exceed present 'Dreadnought' standard. Other powers will hold that Britain's present enormous preponderance cannot be accepted as a starting point for pro rata reductions. Total naval tonnage of the five chief European powers is 2,700,000 tons; Britain alone has 2,100,000 tons." [82] The Second Hague Conference in 1907, which devoted most of its time to a fruitless wrangle over disarmament, was a great disappointment to him. "Propositions for reduction of armaments," Bryce had written Carnegie soon after the Conference ended, "never had a chance of success, against the opposition of Germany. But it seems still doubtful whether a suitable permanent court of arbitration will emerge, a thing which we really hope for." [83] Carnegie had replied: "The Hague has disappointed chiefly because we expected too much. There never was a hope of disarmament with me—Britain naval tonnage 2,100,000 tons . . . She is in no position to ask concurrent disarmament. We shall only get one step —a great one—toward Permanent Court. It will be sent to the Powers to agree upon, make selection Judges, etc. a sharp point. The So. American Republics insisting upon equality was too much. I incline to the plan of five or six Powers agreeing to the Court, and let the smaller Powers alone. They can't go far, a joint word—what we Scotch call 'an intimation' will serve to keep them from disturbing the world's peace." [84]

Carnegie was increasingly drawn to the idea, not of disarmament, but of a coalition of great powers which would police the world. As early as 1904 he had written the International Peace Congress meeting in Boston: "Suppose for instance that Britain, France, Germany and America, with such other minor states as would certainly join them, were to take that position, prepared, if defied, to enforce peaceful settlement, the first offender, if there ever were one, being rigorously dealt with, war would at one fell swoop be banished from the earth. . . . I think this one simple plan most likely to commend itself to the intelligent masses. A Committee might be formed to consider this. If a body of prominent men of each nation agreed to unite in urging the co-operation of their respective countries in the movement, I think the idea would soon spread. . . . Having secured a permanent Court for the settlement of international disputes, the time seems ripe for the same agencies to consider the one step further needed to complete the work." [85] He even hailed the military alliance between Great Britain and France in 1905 as being a step in the right direction. He wanted the United States to join the alliance also and "even better if Germany would join it. Militarism would then have received its death-blow, and Europe would soon be as free from its huge armies as America." [86] The Baroness Bertha von Suttner, Alfred Nobel's former secretary, and the first woman to receive the Nobel Peace Prize, writing in the *Deutsche Revue* at this same time, urged an international "peace army, a voluntary, unorganized army whose sole duty would consist in at once raising a protest upon every occasion against every printed and spoken word of war-baiting. The summoning of such an army would have the advantage that the number of people of the same mind could be estimated, that each one would then confidently raise his voice, knowing that there was a mighty chorus back of him." She even suggested that there be a badge of recognition similar to that of the Salvation Army. This would be a badge with a blue field upon which would be three letters in gold, "F.I.G. (*Fraternitas Inter Gentes*)." [87]

One could well imagine the sport that the punsters would have had with that one—"We don't give a F.I.G. for disarmament," and so on. Carnegie's proposal for a "Legion of Peace" was made of somewhat stouter stuff than that. Carnegie was one of the first to use the term "A League of Nations." In an article in *Out-*

look, in 1907, he wrote, "I believe the next step to universal peace to be the formation of a League of Nations similar to that formed in China recently for a specific object." This League would have at its disposal an international police force. "This is no novel suggestion, but only an extension of the practice of nations. . . . It involves no bitter contentions, arouses no suspicions such as disarmament inevitably will, since it allows every nation undisturbed control of her own domestic policy and only asks cooperation for a term for one specific purpose—the maintenance of peace." [88]

He pushed this idea hard with Roosevelt, thinking the proposal might well appeal to the energetic, aggressive President more than disarmament. "An 'International Police' that really should be the aim at the next Hague Conference. If the German Emperor could rise to his destiny & stand with you favoring this instead of pegging away trifling over petty questions. Chasing rainbows in form of a Colonial Empire which he cannot get & which would do Germany no good if he did. I think you should write him a private letter & suggest if he take the lead in Europe alongside you in America, between you, war could be banished. . . . Perhaps you know I have agreed to take Presidency of the great Peace Society about to be formed. Our first conference New York April 17th delegates from many cities. We hope to strengthen your hands & shall not fail to give you due credit as the Model Ruler for peace." [89]

In Carnegie's inaugural presidential address at the opening of the National Arbitration and Peace Congress later that spring of 1907, he again stressed the international police force idea. "Personally I am a convert to the league of peace idea. . . . [But] before resorting to force it would be well to begin by proclaiming non-intercourse with the offending nation. No exchange of products, no loans, no military or naval supplies, no mail—these restrictions would serve as a solemn warning and probably prove effective. Force should always be the last resort." [90]

By 1907 it was clear what the main points in Carnegie's program for world peace were: (1) a league of nations, consisting of the five great powers, Great Britain, the United States, Germany, Russia, and France, with the power of economic sanctions, and that failing, a combined international police force to bring an aggressor nation into line; and (2) an effective World Court at The Hague, to which all nations would agree to submit all international disputes to which they were a party. This was the ultimate goal, but Carnegie was willing to reach that goal step by step. He saw as a first step for the international police force a treaty between the United States and Great Britain which would combine their naval fleets to police the high seas. He pushed this idea vigorously with the sympathetic Lord Bryce, and with the less sympathetic Secretary of State Philander Knox, with the British Foreign Minister, the Marquis of Landsdown, and with John Morley. Morley wrote to Carnegie in response to his suggestion: "It is true and sound in spirit. Unluckily there is no man nor Party here now, that is powerful & bold enough." To which Carnegie replied, "Can't see any 'boldness' in writing Naval powers to confer & see whether some plan cannot be desined to put an end to armaments on the sea. . . . The action of the Powers upon invitation would stamp the guilty with an indelible brand before the world. I dout if anyone would dare to decline the invitation. I hope you have let it be known you are not afraid to invite them. I'm having a revised copy printed & shall send to my august friends, Emperors, Kings, Presidents, Prime Ministers & to every member Legislatures of Europe & America." [91]

Carnegie was even more eager to push the ten unratified arbitration treaties through the Senate, eager to the point of accepting the various amendments and qualifications the Senate leadership insisted upon adding to the treaties. He urged Roosevelt to accept these changes: "I found the Sec'y of State distressed about the arbitration treaties as I once before found him about the Hay-Pauncefote Treaty. Senate Amendments in both cases. I said to him these had strengthened the latter. Britain would cheerfully accept them. He thot not, but later pronounced me 'a true prophet.' I said again on Friday All nations will accept Senate Amendments, & the good effect of the Treaties will remain unimpaired. Mr. President such is the opinion of all of us who have labored for these treaties from Ex Sec'y Foster down—No one in half a million will ever note the amendments. It will be forgotten in two years that there were amendments. . . . We shall have the substance and this is what you are after." [92] Roosevelt would have no part of such a compromise, however. "I do not agree with you about the treaties. I am not willing to go into a farce." He withdrew the treaties.[93]

Carnegie and Roosevelt also differed sharply on the question of naval expansion. In 1906 Roosevelt had written Carnegie to say that "from now on I do not wish to increase our navy beyond its present size." Carnegie had been delighted and had immediately sent this letter on to Morley.[94] A year later, Roosevelt abruptly reversed himself and indicated at a White House luncheon at which Carnegie was present that he was now prepared to ask Congress for a substantial increase in the navy. Carnegie kept quiet at the luncheon, but as soon as he got home, he wrote a long scolding letter to the President. "You stand before the world today committed to the policy of only maintaining efficiently the present number of ships in the navy, the only ruler of a great nation who has ever reacht this height. . . . Pause and reflect how the world will regard and bemoan your sudden change into the ruler reversing his policy and asking the most unexpected increase. Why? Why? Verily, the question needs your most serious attention." [95] The truth was that Roosevelt had become obsessed with "the Yellow Peril," and he did not appreciate Carnegie's preaching. He answered stiffly, "I have your letter of the 18th instant. I shall recommend an increase in the navy. I shall urge it strongly as I know how. I believe that every far sighted and patriotic man ought to stand by me. I will give sufficient reason in my message. I cannot state *all* the reasons in my message, and I certainly will not state them in a letter to you or anyone else or state them verbally save in strict confidence. . . . You say the question needs my serious attention. It has had it, and, as I say, I cannot imagine how anyone . . . can fail to back me up." [96] Curiously enough, Carnegie did not fail to back him up. He wrote rather limply to Morley, "Fine visit to Washington. President excellent form—but much to regret of not a few of his 'judicious friends' his message demands *three* battleships. . . . I wrote him upon return, but he replies can only talk verbally & give me reason. I'm going down there 9th Dec. again. . . . He's a 'white soul' & surrounds himself only with such." [97] Apparently, on his next visit to Washington, Carnegie did get the real reason from Roosevelt for his sudden decision to increase the navy, but it was a reason which Carnegie must not have taken very seriously, for

923

shortly thereafter Roosevelt wrote him in an even more curt fashion, "My dear sir, it would be the very highest unwisdom for us to act on the belief that you so lightly express that 'Japan is really a negligible quantity.' " [98]

In spite of these sharp differences of opinion and these rebuffs, Carnegie, almost alone among his pacifist friends, remained one of Roosevelt's strongest supporters and defenders. For Carnegie, too, had an obsession, one that grew stronger with each passing year, and that was that the peace of the world depended upon two men, Theodore Roosevelt and Kaiser Wilhelm II of Germany. In both cases, it was hero worship, pure and simple. Carnegie had a wonderful fantasy, in which this unlikely trio of himself and his two heroes would meet together, Carnegie would outline his program for world peace and the President and the Kaiser would enthusiastically accept it. Then and there, war would be doomed, the lion would lie down with the lamb, and all the world's spears would be beaten into plowshares. Of the two heroes, Carnegie regarded the Kaiser as being the more important and the more certain of fulfilling his great destiny. In the same presidential inaugural address at the Peace Conference in New York in 1907 in which he had pressed for his "league of peace" idea, Carnegie had taken special pains to add that the success of his idea depended upon one man. "It lies today in the power of one man to found this league of peace. Perhaps our President may yet have that part to play. He seems born for great roles in the world drama. . . . At this moment, however, it is not in his hands, but in those of the German Emperor, alone of all men, that the power to abolish war seems to rest. . . . Much has been written and said of the Emperor as a menace to the peace of Europe, but I think unjustly. So far, let me remind you, he has been nearly twenty years on the throne and is guiltless of shedding blood. No war can be charged to him. His sin hereafter may be one of omission, that having been entrusted with power to abolish war, he failed to rise to this transcendent duty." [99]

Carnegie had been carefully tutored, by some of his closest friends in the diplomatic service and in the peace movement, to respect the Kaiser. Nicholas Murray Butler, Andrew White, his successor as American Ambassador to Germany Charlemagne Tower, and David J. Hill were all staunch defenders of the Kaiser. Once convinced, however, Carnegie outdid them all in his hopes and expectations of the Kaiser's fulfilling "his transcendent duty."

Calling Britain's and, to a lesser extent, America's fear of Germany as "the cry of 'wolf' " over a false, unreal danger, Carnegie in article after article played up the peace-loving nature of the German Emperor, differing sharply with his British friends, Morley and Bryce, on this issue.[100] Such favorable expressions did not go unnoticed at Potsdam, for the Kaiser welcomed whatever good press he could get in these years. In the spring of 1907, the Emperor let the American Ambassador know that he would be delighted to receive Carnegie that summer at the annual boat races at Kiel, if the great American philanthropist could arrange this visit in his busy schedule.[101] The invitation, so soon after Carnegie's speech in New York in which he had put the whole burden of success for a League of Nations on the Kaiser, meant to Carnegie only one thing—that the German Emperor was disposed to listen to the plan. Carnegie was overjoyed. He wrote Morley:

> We go to Kiel, leaving here 18th, pass thru London 19th. . . . I told our Ambr. I'd go only if H.M. *really wished the interview after my speech putting the Peace of Nations on him.* He really is responsible. No other man has the power to draw a League of Nations competent to keep the peace for an agreed upon period just as an experiment. Even if nations didn't accept he holds the Stage as world's apostle of Peace. He couldn't be held up by anyone as not having proved his apostleship. It is this point which I hope may impress him—a real great statesman must like to have a game of "Heads I win—tails you lose." He has the cards. May the "holy spirit" light upon me & lead him heavenward. Fortunately, he's very devout—very. He sent me his address to his son upon his Consecration & it wouldn't discredit a Holy Father of the Catholic Church. Well, never was a holy Father more convinced of his Mission than I am of mine. I *know* I offer H.I.M. the plan that makes him the greatest agent known so far in human history. The Peace Maker.

Such religious fervor must have been a little difficult for the gentle skeptic Morley to appreciate. He replied, "Do let us have a look at you both on your way to reform the man of might. How interesting it will be. That you can inflame him with your own Crusader's Zeal, I am not sure. But the effort is *noble*." [102]

From Carnegie's point of view, the meeting was a great success. True, there was no commitment from His Imperial Majesty on anything, but he was most gracious, and he let Carnegie do some of the talking. At least he showed no shock at Carnegie's proposals. Upon returning to Scotland, Carnegie was convinced he had planted the seeds that were bound to bear fruit. He wrote to Sir James Donaldson, Principal of the University of St. Andrews, "Delighted you are coming to us this season. We shall have much to say to each other. It is very pleasing to know that a publication is to be begun in Germany favorable to our ideas. I had three interviews with the German Emperor and dined with him twice—a wonderful man, so bright, humorous, and *with a sweet smile*. I think he can be trusted and declares himself for peace." [103] From that moment on, Carnegie never wavered in his faith in the Kaiser, not even when such a trusted friend as Elihu Root, by then thoroughly disenchanted with Germany, wrote him in 1909: "The fact is, and no well informed person can doubt it, that Germany under present Government, is the great disturber of peace in the world. . . . She looks with real contempt and loathing upon the whole system of arbitration, and she considers all talk about it to be mere hypocrisy." [104] Nevertheless, for Carnegie, the Kaiser remained the Man of Destiny, and as late as the summer of 1913 he wrote an article for *The New York Times Sunday Magazine,* entitled, "Kaiser Wilhelm II, Peace Maker." [105]

Carnegie's faith in his other hero, Theodore Roosevelt, was not to remain as constant. Their friendship, moreover, had begun under far less auspicious circumstances. Carnegie, like Mark Hanna, had not been pleased when McKinley had chosen the rambunctious victor of San Juan Hill as his running mate in 1900, and he had been appalled when an assassin's bullet had made Theodore Roosevelt President of the United States in September 1901. "President McKinley gone," he wrote Dod. "Isn't it dreadful. I was quite depressed by the shock & not very confident of Roosevelt's wisdom but power may sober him." And to Morley: "Anxious about Roosevelt, an unknown quantity, capable of infinite mischief. . . ." [106] Carnegie, however, was always attracted to centers of power, and he always tried to establish lines of communication with the occupant of the White House, even when, on those rare occasions, that occupant was a Democrat. Roosevelt had not been in office many weeks before the letters, flattering in their sentiments, began to arrive from 2 East 91st Street, New York. These were followed by visits to the White House, luncheons, state dinners, and those private little meetings *tête-à-tête* that Carnegie dearly loved. Carnegie tried to remain objective about Roosevelt, tried to keep in mind the weaknesses of character that were only too apparent but which were easily dismissed from mind in the charm of his presence. On the back of one of Roosevelt's letters inviting Carnegie to visit him at Oyster Bay, Carnegie wrote: "President Roosevelt. If he would only act as he tells one that he feels. Plenty good advice given & apparently taken & then some wild erratic outburst on the stump. Prest. Eliot Harvard sums it all up when he said recently, 'I knew Teddy when he was a boy. I know him now when he is still a boy, and I'll never know him anything else but a boy.' But one can't help loving him. He has high & pure ideals." [107] Carnegie might not trust him, but he could not help being fascinated by him—the breadth of Roosevelt's knowledge; the catholicity of his interests, ranging from the migratory patterns of East Coast water fowl to the fiscal policies of Albert Gallatin; his ability to tell a story and to laugh heartily at another man's—all of these traits made him by far the most interesting man to occupy the White House since Lincoln. Actually, Carnegie in temperament and personality was very similar to Roosevelt. Both believed in living life to the fullest, of "pushing inordinately" in any activity he was engaged in; both were egocentric extroverts who, each being supremely confident in his own judgment and ability, was not afraid to test his ideas in vigorous debate. Moreover, Roosevelt, in this first term, which had come to him by accident, was moving cautiously, to the degree that he understood that word, to make sure that he alienated no important faction that might effectively block him from a second term attained in his own name. He particularly had no desire to antagonize as affluent an angel of the Republican party and as dynamic a public figure as Carnegie. So the frequency of the meetings increased, and Carnegie, after a time, forgot his earlier reservations. Roosevelt became his hero.

Incidents like the Panama Canal, naval expansion, and the withdrawing of the arbitration treaties were quickly forgotten. Carnegie became increasingly enthusiastic over Roosevelt's domestic program and increasingly confident that he was having an influence upon Roosevelt's foreign policy. By 1907 he was loudly beating the drums for a third term for his hero.

Roosevelt, on the other hand, however ingratiating he might be to Carnegie, never really liked him. He charmed Carnegie, but was not himself charmed. He wrote quite candidly to Whitelaw Reid in 1905, after the election was safely over:

> I have tried hard to like Carnegie, but it is pretty difficult. There is no type of man for whom I feel a more contemptuous abhorrence than for one who makes a God of mere money-making and at the same time is always yelling out that kind of utterly stupid condemnation of war which in almost every case springs from a combination of defective physical courage, of unmanly shrinking from pain and effort, and of hopelessly twisted ideals. All the suffering from Spanish war comes far short of the suffering, preventable and non-preventable, among the operators of the Carnegie steel works, and among the small investors, during the time that Carnegie was making his fortune. I can respect, even though I do not sympathize with, a fanatic like "Golden Rule Jones," who applied his Utopian dreams to money-making, that is, to business, just as much as to war; but I have no respect for the business man who makes enormous sums of money without any regard whatever for advanced principles of doctrinaire ethics, but who applies these same principles in their most advanced and least rational form to war—a form of effort for which he is personally as unfit as he is fit for business. It is as noxious folly to denounce war per se as it is to denounce business per se. Unrighteous war is a hideous evil; but I am not at all sure that it is a worse evil than business unrighteousness; and as far as I can see it is a much harder thing to find a practical way of applying a high ethical standard in business matters than it is to find a practical way of applying such a standard as regards war and peace.[108]

This was quite indiscreet of Roosevelt, for Reid was a notorious gossip, and he must have delighted in relating to his friends this bit of presidential candor about a man whom he himself disliked.

But apparently Carnegie never got word of this candid appraisal of himself by his hero. And if Roosevelt felt a "contemptuous abhorrence" for the efforts of the money-maker, his abhorrence did not extend to the fruits of those efforts. As his second term approached its end, having manfully resisted the efforts of many, including Carnegie, to draft him for a third term, Roosevelt was concerned with what he should do immediately after his term was over. With a sensitivity toward the position of his successor (which also suited his own desires), Roosevelt decided to leave the country as soon as possible after the Inauguration and hunt big game in Africa. As soon as Carnegie heard of this safari retirement, he was inspired with an idea. Roosevelt had written Carnegie at the time that the latter was making plans to visit the Kaiser at Kiel and had said that he regretted the tradition that a President should not leave the country while in office, as he too would like to meet the German Emperor.[109] No such tradition bound Roosevelt now. Why not combine his African hunt for heads of game with an European hunt for heads of state? "I have written the President that the 'big game' he should bag when relieved from office are the rulers of the world," Carnegie wrote a Scottish friend. "He should go the round." [110] As Roosevelt had already agreed to deliver the Romanes Lecture at Oxford sometime in the spring of 1910, after having had a good year's hunt in eastern Africa, he was quite amenable to the idea of a grand European tour as the climax to his African junket. The arrangements were quickly and happily made. Roosevelt's mass slaughter of African wild life would be done in the name of science under the auspices of the Smithsonian Institution, but financed by Carnegie, Morgan, and a few other selected "money-making" friends. In return, Roosevelt would visit the Kaiser and press the cause for a "League of Peace." From there he would go on to Britain and meet with the leaders of both parties and again talk up a multilateral pact that would tie the Teutonic nations together in "a great power" alliance.

The more Carnegie thought about and made plans for this trip, the more excited he became. This visit of Roosevelt to the Kaiser could bring about the triumphant resolution of all he had worked for, written about, and dreamt of for the past five years: Carnegie's two heroes, at last meeting face to face, reaching an agreement, and by that agreement forcing Britain into line. "If any man can get the Emperor in accord for peace, you are that man," he wrote to Roosevelt. "He will go far to act in unison with you, of this I am certain. You are sympathetic souls." [111]

Roosevelt, who at this point was far more interested in the lions of Africa than in being lionized in Europe, was making his own elaborate plans. With every conceivable kind of gun and the most elaborate camping and field supplies available, he was better equipped for the invasion of Africa than the Italians had been when they tried to conquer Ethiopia in 1896. He had hardly arrived in Nairobi, East Africa, in June when he discovered he had already run out of funds. He wrote back to Carnegie asking for $30,000 more, "otherwise the expedition will have to go home." Carnegie immediately wrote to Charles Walcott of the Smithsonian Institution, telling him to get all the subscribers to double their contributions. "Tell them I am, Morgan will—they all will if they know T R wishes it. . . . We must not let our greatest man suffer, remember." [112] In addition to his original contribution, of which there is no record in his papers, Carnegie was to make three more payments during the course of Roosevelt's expedition, totaling $24,000. He had written Franks after Roosevelt's first appeal for more funds, "Have written Roosevelt any drafts drawn by him on you would be honored. This is to provide against any possible failure of Walcott to remit. . . . There must be no disappointment of the Ex Prest." [113]

Carnegie, of course, expected payment in full, not in kind but in services. He was in fact in an agony of impatience for the safari to end. Never had a year seemed so long, as Roosevelt wended his way down the White Nile, shooting elephants and looking eagerly for the fabled white rhinoceros. "You are supposed to be after big game, my friend," Carnegie wrote, after sending his first additional contribution. "All very well for a holiday, but, of course, unworthy as a pursuit of one who has played and, in my hope and belief, is yet to play a great part in the world." Carnegie was concerned because Roosevelt was so impetuously foolhardy. Suppose he was felled by the charge of a bull elephant, not to mention the bite of a tsetse fly, and never got out of Africa alive? "Shall be so glad when you have started upon your return, and hope you will make it a point of meeting the big men of the world. These are the big game, altho your present holiday was well-earned." [114]

Carnegie filled the long months of waiting by making the elaborate plans for the summit meetings. Letters were frequent to Ambassador Hill in Berlin and Ambassador Reid in London, as well as to Morley. At first Carnegie thought that he and Root should meet Roosevelt in Berlin and be with him when he conferred with the Kaiser. "You remember that I told the Emperor that if you and he got together I thought it would be my duty to be present, that you young colts might get into trouble, no saying what you might do. The Emperor replied, 'I see, you want to drive us, Roosevelt will be in front and I behind.'—to which I replied, 'No your Majesty, I know better than to drive two such wild colts in tandem; you never get enough purchase on the first horse. No, your majesty, I will have you both in the shafts, holding you abreast.'—at which His Majesty laughed 'consumedly.'" [115] This, however, looked a bit too much like a marionette performance. Root said he would be unable to go, and Carnegie reluctantly bowed out, promising Roosevelt he would meet him in London for the British conference. Even though Root and Carnegie could not be at Potsdam in person, they were quite prepared to write the script and Roosevelt, amazingly docile in shaft, was willing to accept it. Carnegie wrote Roosevelt in January 1910:

> In reply to yours, here is what I should say to His Imperial Majesty, were I in your place.
>
> "You talk peace, as all other rulers do, but you have also acted Peace, for your hands are giltless of shedding human blood during your long reign . . . ; but while granting all this, I confess I do not understand how Your Majesty can delay in establishing the Peace you desire among civilized nations, when you have the power to do so and are therefore responsible for the present unnecessary, costly, and dangerous era of rival armaments, which fan embers of jelousy and suspicion among the Powers, probably ending in the war you deprecate.
>
> "Your Majesty has only to propose to the two other branches of your own race, Britain and America, to form with you a League of Peace, the independence of existing territories of the

powers to be recognized and only new disputes considered; all other international disputes to be settled by arbitration; other civilized powers to be invited afterwards to join the League to intimate to other civilized Powers that the Peace of the world, in which all are so deeply interested can no longer be broken by one or two powers—disputes must be peaceably settled.

"Your Majesty, I have felt it to be my duty to lay this matter before you in the hope that you would recognize the holy mission of bringing Peace to the world rests upon you. No service ever man has rendered to man since the world began equals this.

"From what I have lernd I believe that Britain stands redy to accept your invitation. There can be no dout about France being so, and as for America, we are always for peace. I shall take occasion to confer with the leaders of both these powers so that we of America may understand just what and who bars the path to peace and consequently what policy we shall be compelled to pursue. Much depends upon your decision. . . . Assuring you of my sincere regard and cordial friendship, I leave this subject with you. It will not down, of this I am certain."

Let me assure you, dear Mr. Roosevelt, that the Emperor can be trusted. I believe in him. He is a true man and means what he says, although probably inclined to rank physical before moral force. The history of Germany favors such views, but might is not right. It is who is strong not who is right that war decides; therefore it should not be appeald to.[116]

Root also sent his suggestions via Carnegie as to what Roosevelt should do and say. For Root "the crux of the whole business" was in Berlin. "It seems plain that he can do nothing in England unless he has first accomplished something in Germany. England is ready to quit the arms race if the other fellow will. . . ." Root therefore suggested that Roosevelt say to the German Emperor, "One of those great opportunities which have been presented to a very few men in history lies before you at this moment. If you ignore it your name will live only as one of a great multitude of men who have raised and trained armies and governed states and have been forgotten because everything that they have done has been what thousands of other men have done equally well. If you seize the opportunity you render a service to mankind of such signal and striking character as to place you forever in the little group of the supremely great who, upon a review of the whole field of human history, are to be seen rising above the great mass of the ordinary great.

"The opportunity is to do this: That you having the greatest and most effective army that ever existed in the world, having the means and the constructive capacity and great advances already made for an unsurpassed navy, shall say to the world, 'I will lead you to peace. Let us stop where we are, and let us end now and here the race of competition in enlargement of provision for war." Root felt that if "such an idea were entertained by the Emperor, then our friend would have something to talk about when he got to England. . . . I am satisfied, not only by reflection upon the nature of the subject but by experience of the pour parler which preceded the last Hague Conference regarding the inclusion of a proposition for disarmament in the program of the conference, that it is hopeless to secure any agreement upon any elaborate or complicated scheme which shall seek to set a variety of limits upon a variety of countries, and that the Gordian method of cutting the knot is the only one that affords any possibility of success. The only way to quit is to quit. The Emperor can do it, and no one else can. . . . I do not know of anybody who would be more likely to make a lodgement in the Emperor's mind with this idea than Theodore Roosevelt." [117] Carnegie promptly sent this letter off to Roosevelt to serve as an addendum to his own.

Meanwhile, there were the plans to be made for the British conference that would follow the visit to the Kaiser. It was decided that this conference should be held at Ambassador Reid's country home at Wrest Park. Morley and Reid were to make all the arrangements, with constant advice from Carnegie, of course. "Do take care of yourself," Carnegie wrote Morley, "for believe me you are going to be in position to do great work in May when Roosevelt is with us there or I am mistaken. I saw Mr. Balfour in Manchester & told him we wanted a meeting & explained. He is responsive to a degree, as I expected. He & Landsdown, Asquith & Grey & you. Maybe Haldane. No more. I told you Roosevelt had written me. It is time for statesmen (not politicians) to understand each other & act in Unison re War." [118]

As the weeks passed, Carnegie kept making more and more plans for Roosevelt. He wanted the former President to include

Christiania, Norway, on his itinerary, where he had been invited, as a Nobel Peace Prize winner, to appear before the Academy and deliver an address. Roosevelt at first protested that he did not have time, but Carnegie persisted, claiming that if Roosevelt did not agree to go, it might diminish the chances for Root, whom they were both backing, to win the Nobel prize that year. Carnegie also wanted Roosevelt to visit Scotland, accept an honorary degree from St. Andrews, and then go on to Dunfermline "to see what my fund is doing in my native town in the way of bringing sweetness and light among the working people." [119] To these requests, Roosevelt replied, "All right, I have been uncomfortable about that Nobel Prize business; on receipt of your letter, I wrote that I should go. But my time is so limited that I greatly fear this makes a visit to Scotland, dearly as I should like to go, an impossibility." Carnegie was a little hurt by this. If Roosevelt could spend a year stomping through the brush of Africa, he should be able to give more time to his far more serious business in Europe. "I cannot see why you are in such a pressing hurry to get home. Since Mrs. Roosevelt is to meet you in Europe you should give her a treat; not only should you come to Glasgow and take the degree you have been offered, but you should accompany us to Skibo for a few days. Especially should you devote more time to Berlin and get to the men who really control events, because as Root says, 'It all comes back to Germany.' " [120]

Roosevelt refused to add Scotland to his itinerary. In every other respect he was most co-operative. With perhaps just a touch of sarcasm, he wrote Carnegie: "When I see the Kaiser, I will go over the matter at length with him, telling him I wish to repeat our whole conversation to you; then I will tell it all to you when I am in London. . . . I regard the proposed [Wrest Park] conference as most important. I leave absolutely with you to make the arrangements; to be made through Morley, as you suggest." Roosevelt, however, was becoming apprehensive over the high expectations Root and Carnegie seemed to have in his bringing off a miracle. "I only fear, my dear Mr. Carnegie, that you do not realize how unimportant a man I now am, and how little weight I shall have in the matter." [121] It was true that by now Carnegie seemed to have lost all perspective on Roosevelt's projected visit. He was pinning his hopes for an almost immediate realization of his League of Nations plan on a whirlwind tour of Berlin and

London, by a private citizen, albeit a very dynamic and influential private citizen, who was without portfolio and with no power to act in any official capacity. As the time approached for Roosevelt to emerge out of Africa into the bright spotlight of the European political scene, Carnegie's excitement reached a peak worthy of anticipating a Second Coming. Carnegie felt compelled to send this pep talk to his personally appointed Messiah: "I cannot but feel that if you are disposed to cooperate and take the leader's part in conferring with German rulers, and especially if you press for a League of Peace, that you would triumph. . . . The only question is whether the idea of promoting World Peace stirs you. If it does, you will not fail, but even failure in such a cause would be noble. I am willing to throw aside everything, and I know Root and Butler share this feeling, because we see success with you as the Great Peace Maker. Even if nothing definite can be accomplisht at present in Germany, the other nations can be induced to support the League idea, which must ultimately win, Germany notwithstanding." [122]

The Wrest Park conference was assuming paramount importance in Carnegie's mind. He wanted to make sure Morley was aware of his feeling. "Suppose a serious question arose between Britain and America today and that you had charge of the matter; consider the difference it makes that you have spent some days with Roosevelt and as his guest; consider what a difference it would make to Roosevelt if he were the agent of America and had to deal with you and knew you as a cherished friend. This is the reason I wish your people and Roosevelt to know each other as friends in view of what is probably to come about." To make sure that Morley and his British colleagues did not think they were dealing with a man whose days of power were behind him, Carnegie added, "In all probability he will be President again, and it will count for much that he knows your colleagues as he knows you." [123]

In March, Carnegie received a long letter from Roosevelt, who, at the time of writing, was on the last stretch of his journey down the Nile.[124]

> Well, here I find all your letters, and I guess I shall have to surrender. I'll go to Whitelaw Reid's first, and the meeting shall be at Wrest Park on May 21st, the weekend, as you desire.

I've already agreed to go to Christiania to speak to the Nobel Prize people. I am now trying to arrange to be in Berlin for a number of days, as you suggest, and have written Hill to have me meet the right public men. . . . I shall speak there on the 13th or 14th . . . ; and if the Kaiser isn't in Berlin then, I shall, if he is willing, go to see him wherever it is convenient for him.

Now, however for some reservations. First, and least important, personal. I want to go home! I am homesick for my own land and my own people! Of course it is Mrs. Roosevelt I most want to see; but I want to see my two youngest boys; I want to see my own house, my own books and trees, the sunset over the sound from the window in the north room, the people with whom I have worked, who think my thoughts and speak my speech. . . .

Second, as to the policy itself. With *your* policy, as you outline it (of course accepting it generally and not binding myself as to details) I am in hearty sympathy; what Root champions along these lines you can guarantee I will champion also; he was *the* man of my cabinet, the man on whom I most relied, to whom I owed most, the greatest Secretary of State we have ever had, as great a cabinet officer as we have ever had, save Alexander Hamilton alone. He is sane and cool headed as he is high-minded . . . —and all I say I mean, and it is said with full remembrance that on certain points he and I would hardly agree.

But you have on your paper certain names which inspire me with a most lively distrust. Stead and Trueblood for instance belong to the type that makes a good cause ridiculous. Their proposals are rarely better than silly; and the only reason that the men themselves are not exceedingly mischievous is that they are well-nigh impotent for either good or evil.

Now, with the big statesmen of Europe, Emperors, Kings, Ministers of State, I will do whatever lies in my power to help secure the adoption of the policies *you* outline in your letters, the policies for which you and Root stand. . . . But I cannot conscientiously support, nor could I persuade any sane and honest ruler or great public servant to support, the fantastic and noxious theories of such extremists as those to whom I have alluded.

My past words, and the acts wherein I have striven to make those words good, afford proof of my sincerity in the cause of peace. I will do all I can to bring about such a league of, or understanding among, the great powers as will forbid one of them,

936

or any small power, to engage in unrighteous, foolish or needless war; to secure an agreement to check the waste of money on
growing and excessive armaments. If, as is probable, so much
can be secured at once, I will do all I can to help in the movement, rapid or slow, towards the desired end. But I will not be,
and you would not wish me to be, put in the attitude of advocating the impossible, or, above all, of seeming to be insincere.
. . . Again, I would not care to spend my time in securing a
merely nominal, not a material, victory for peace. . . . I cannot
be, or seem to be, an accredited envoy; I cannot work for a policy which I think our country might repudiate; I cannot work
for anything that does not represent some real progress; and it
is useless to expect to accomplish everything at once. But I will
do all in my power, all that is feasible, to help in the effort to
secure some substantial advance towards the goal.

In France, Italy, Austria and Germany—especially Germany
—I shall go into the matter at length with the men of power,
and I will report to you in full in England. You can show this
letter to Root.

It was an honest letter. It was not all that Carnegie might
have wished for—the attack on Stead and Benjamin F. Trueblood, a close associate in the Lake Mohonk Arbitration Conferences, was disturbing—but Roosevelt had promised to do his best
along the lines laid down by Root and Carnegie. The realistic
fashion in which he faced his task may have helped a little in ena-
bling Carnegie to see the venture in a clearer, more rational
perspective.

Roosevelt left Cairo the last of March and arrived in Naples
on 2 April 1910. At long last, the European trip had begun, at
the end of which lay the Berlin and Wrest Park conferences and
Carnegie's great hopes. Except for a minor contretemps in Rome
with the Pope over the question of Methodist missionaries in
Italy, Roosevelt's tour through Italy, Austria, Hungary, France,
Belgium, Holland, and the Scandinavian countries was a triumphal procession. On 9 May Roosevelt was scheduled to leave Sweden for Berlin and the long-awaited meeting with the Kaiser. Carnegie wrote Ambassador Hill in excited anticipation, "What a
pair T.R. and H.M. to hobnob—well they will love each other
like vera brithers and I have faith in both. . . ." [125] Carnegie was

937

scheduled to sail from New York on 4 May after Roosevelt's expected triumph in Berlin. While Carnegie was on the high seas,
however, and Roosevelt was in Christiania delivering his Nobel
Peace Laureate speech, in which he stressed the League of Peace
and the Kaiser's role in it, and arbitration, and restricting naval
construction, and all the other points in which he had been carefully rehearsed by Root and Carnegie, the whole carefully
planned and constructed project collapsed about their heads. It
was almost as if the gods of war were giving warning. On 4 May,
in far-off Cartago, Costa Rica, where the final finishing touches
had been made on Carnegie's latest temple of peace, the ground
suddenly shook violently. The Central American Court of Justice
crumbled into ruins. Forty-eight hours later, the news was flashed
from Windsor Castle that King Edward VII was suddenly dead of
heart failure. All Europe immediately went into official mourning. All state affairs were canceled.

Carnegie, receiving the news aboard the R.M.S. *Adriatic*, sent
a note to Reid, "The sad news of the passing of the King sad-
dened us all. Mr. Roosevelt's visit will naturally be greatly
changed by the event." [126] Carnegie was not able at first to accept
the full impact of the disastrous turn of events. He wrote to Hill
immediately upon landing at Plymouth, "Perhaps the Emperor
may go along with Roosevelt to London for King Edward's funeral, fine if they attended together. We . . . don't reach London
until the 20th to attend Wrest Park meeting next day. . . .
Maybe I may meet H.I.M. I hope so. . . . Sorry and surprised
France is backward. Can't understand that. Perhaps T.R. saw
them and succeeded." [127] Hopes as great as Carnegie's die slowly
and hard. It was Morley's painful task to write Carnegie, "In what
a queer plight do you find us all! All engagements broken off—
including the important one for which you had taken such pains.
There is no help for it." [128] The British monarchy was getting a
belated revenge on that Radical republican from Dunfermline.

Roosevelt, in the meantime, went gamely on with his schedule, modified though it was by this unexpected turn of events.
His public address in Stockholm had to be canceled, as well as the
large state affairs in Berlin. He did meet the Kaiser, even though,
under the circumstances, he could not be a house guest at the palace. Although it would be a gross exaggeration to say that they

loved each other "like vera brithers," they did find that they liked each other better than either had expected. They talked briefly of matters of peace and both agreed that a war between Britain and Germany would be the height of madness. "I adore England," the Kaiser shouted at Roosevelt, who replied that he himself would not go quite that far in expressing his sentiments toward Britain. There seemed little opportunity to discuss the carefully detailed points of the memos that Root and Carnegie had given him, mainly because the German press had anticipated Roosevelt's visit by denouncing his expected efforts to get Germany to disarm. Clearly the Kaiser was sensitive about the subject, and Roosevelt was not eager to push it. Both men were relieved to go out and review troops for about five hours.[129] Earlier Roosevelt had written Carnegie, "You were very wise in your suggestion that I should make the Nobel Prize speech. This has proved to be desirable from every standpoint; indeed (as things look now), I believe that what I say in that speech will represent very nearly all that is efficient and useful that I can accomplish." [130] And so it proved to be.

Taft appointed Roosevelt to be the American representative at King Edward's funeral. On 20 May, the day that Carnegie had long hoped that Roosevelt would be meeting at Wrest Park with Asquith, Morley, Balfour, and Grey to herald a new day, Roosevelt was riding in a carriage with the French president and an obscure Persian prince, in the funeral procession of an age now dead. It was the last brilliant show of European monarchy on the stage of history. They were almost all there: the new King of Great Britain, George V; the Kaiser; and the kings of Greece, Spain, Portugal, Denmark, Norway, Belgium, and Bulgaria—as well as the Crown Prince of Austria, Franz Ferdinand. The funeral knell may have been sounding for their days of glory, but Roosevelt found it all rather amusing and on the whole enjoyed the show.[131]

For Carnegie, it was little short of tragic. He wrote Reid from Torquay, "The King's death has changed all and as there is to be no meeting at least for some time there is not need for my running up to London. . . . We will keep out of London hubbub and rest quietly here." [132] Roosevelt was much more cheerful in his final note to Carnegie before leaving Britain. "My last twenty-four hours in England have really been the pleasantest of all, as I spent them with Edward Grey in the valley of the Itchen and the New Forest, listening to bird songs. . . . Well, I wish I could have seen a little more of you. . . . When you reach New York, come out in an auto and take lunch with us in Oyster Bay. . . ." [133] This was not quite the way Carnegie had planned things. A superstitious man would have seen in the unexpected events of the past few weeks dark auguries for the future. A faint-hearted man would have been prepared to admit defeat. Carnegie was neither. A man having the motto "All is well since all grows better" is not easily defeated. Don Quixote might be stopped by a single swipe of the windmill's vane, but not Carnegie.

CHAPTER XXIV

Sunshine at Skibo
1901-1914

Andrew Carnegie's later life, busily spent in the dispensing of his wealth and in pursuing peace, frenetic as it may appear in any retrospective account, did not mean that he had no time for friends and family, or for the kind of leisure that he had always enjoyed. On the contrary, the years from 1901 to 1914 were probably the happiest and most personally satisfying of his life. At the age of seventy, he never felt healthier or more vigorous. The passing years seemed to have had no effect upon either his energy or his capacity to enjoy life. John Morley could never understand this vitality. Writing to Carnegie to complain, as he frequently did, of his weariness and exhaustion, Morley observed, "Of one thing be sure—that your poor friend with this load on his back craves *Rest.* That's a feeling unknown, I do believe, to Mr. A. Carnegie?" [1]

One reason for Carnegie's amazing vitality was that he had early learned the importance of relaxation. Throughout his entire business career, once he had become an independent entrepreneur, he had resolutely refused to become tied to an office. His sensitivity to summer heat had always provided an excellent excuse to escape the country for five to six months every year, and

941

when he was in the United States he never permitted himself to be imposed upon by any strict business regimen. Even more important to his physical and mental health was his ability to make a decision and then to stop worrying about it. For him there were seldom any anguished moments of indecision, or long, troubling periods of second thoughts. An act done was done, and Carnegie never knew the peculiar torture of sleepless nights spent in pointless doubts or self-recrimination. He worked hard, played hard, and slept well—that old tried and true recipe for good health.

Carnegie also knew the value of physical comfort. Quite abstemious in his eating and drinking habits, he nevertheless insisted upon the best in food and in Scotch whisky, the only spirituous liquor he ever drank. He exercised regularly, particularly after he took up golf at the age of sixty, and played every game as if his life depended upon winning. Both he and Louise enjoyed the luxury of the thermal baths in Aix, Provence, and Hot Springs, Virginia, and usually visited one or the other of these health resorts at least once a year. But Carnegie's greatest joy was Skibo, his "Heaven on Earth," as he frequently called it, and the five months spent each year at this remote Highland castle were, for him, the very elixir of living. Here, whether fishing in the rivers Shinn and Evelix, cruising down the firth in his yacht, playing golf on his private course, or swimming in his heated, salt-water pool, Carnegie felt truly alive and knew the full pleasure of what his wealth could buy. "I am so busy working at fun!" he wrote Dod. "Fishing, yachting, golfing. Skibo never so delightful; all so quiet! A home at last." [2]

Skibo may have been always delightful, but it was seldom quiet. Its remote location did not mean isolation, for here, far more than in New York, the Carnegies carried on for four of the five months they were in residence an intensely active social life. Carnegie delighted in mixing his guests with a complete disregard for social background, politics, religion, and nationality: old Dunfermline neighbors and cousins along with prime ministers, poets, university presidents, and American businessmen. Skibo was an exciting place to be, but every guest, no matter how distinguished his rank or eccentric his personal habits, had to adapt himself to the order that prevailed there. If a guest had any notion of sleeping later than eight o'clock in the morning, that expectation was rudely dispelled on the first morning at the castle. Promptly at that hour there would come a distant wail that to the uninitiated sounds like the cry of a lost soul in one of Dante's more deeply depressed circles in Hell. As it grew louder and more intense, a nervous American guest might well imagine it to be an exceptionally querulous meeting of Macbeth's weird sisters on the near-by moor, were it not for the hour and for the fact that the sun was shining much too brightly for any proper coven of witches. The fully aroused guest, looking out his bedroom window, would see a Scottish piper in full Highland dress, approaching the castle, skirling the pipes with all of the vigor of a piper leading the troops into battle at Culloden. By now, sleep was out of the question for all inhabitants of the castle.[3]

Hastily dressing, the guest would descend the grand staircase and walk, a bit self-consciously, through the front hall into the dining room, again to the sound of music, more recognizable as such to non-Celtic ears, coming from the great pipe organ in the hall. The kippers, porridge, and scrambled eggs were eaten to the majestic tones of Haydn, Bach, and even Wagner, which echoed throughout the castle. It was an experience that a visitor to Skibo would find difficult to ignore while there or to forget after he left. There were even a few cases of highly strung, probably emotionally unstable persons who after the first morning at Skibo rather abruptly cut short their visit and took the next train from Bonar Bridge south to the more predictable sounds of the cities.

Carnegie was very proud of the matutinal course in music appreciation that he offered his guests, and he selected his pipers and his organists with great care. In writing to John Ross, whose services he was utilizing for the employment of a new organist, Carnegie emphasized this fact: "We are particular about the music. . . . No fancy pieces—these prostitute the organ. The fine old hymns—Wagner's finest *religious* pieces Loghengrin [sic] — Siegfried March &c. Played slowly, feelingly—no *bounce*—no flare. . . . You ask what terms? We can't tell—we wish him to feel he is liberally dealt with—pay the best price for the best is the rule—Your musical director ought to know a real musician from a claptrap splurger. Want him Skibo early July." [4]

Following breakfast, the guest had a variety of diversions open to him—trout and salmon fishing in the lochs, stocked with fish

943

from Skibo's own fish hatchery; swimming in the salt water pool; playing golf with Carnegie; or, if it was the season, hunting grouse, pheasant, or deer. In this last pursuit, however, he had to dispense with the company of his host, for Carnegie hated guns and would never take part in a hunt, which he regarded as not a sport but a slaughter. For the guest of more sedentary habits there was the magnificent library. Here in the large sun-filled room one could find among the over eight thousand volumes almost any classic in the fields of history, philosophy, literature, biography, political science, economics, and travel.[5] Lord Acton had personally made the selections for the library, and Hew Morrison, the head Librarian of the Carnegie Library in Edinburgh, had made the purchases. In spite of this expertise in the stocking of the library, it was the only part of Skibo that was a disappointment to Carnegie. He had been delighted with Lord Acton's selections, but he had wanted Morrison to find used—obviously used—copies of these books for the library shelves. There was a kind of reverse snobbery in Carnegie's makeup that made him eschew the more obvious manifestations of wealth. Morgan's library of rare first editions had no appeal for him whatsoever. He wanted his library to look like a working scholar's library, not a rich man's hobbyhorse. He had written Hew Morrison, "Please remember that I do not wish rare or curious books or elaborate bindings. It is to be a working library, only of the gems of literature." [6] His disappointment, consequently, was keen when he received the rather sizable bill from Morrison for binding the books in gold, brown, and green bindings. He let Morrison know his feelings in no uncertain terms:

> I asked you to get the best editions of a list of books Lord Acton would furnish you. I never said one word to you about changing the bindings of these gems, never. Now I learn that you have spent more money on bindings than the precious gems cost. This is, to my mind, not only a waste of money, which is wrong in itself, but an insult to the great Teachers from whom I draw my intellectual & emotional life—my spiritual existence. I would today give 3000£ to have their messages cased in sober, cheap bindings showing it was *these* & not the bindings you have so strangely contracted for, that I value.
>
> It may be that I shall have to strip these Treasures of their

costly covers & have their ordinary shells restored. I cannot tell until I see them at Skibo. I am really hurt by the affair & as I told you, I wish one check sent to you by my cashier (for I could never sign it) & charge the matter off once for all. It has to be paid of course for you were my agent.[7]

Carnegie apparently was never reconciled to his magnificently bound library, and few of his guests must have had much leisure to do more than casually browse along the shelves, for the volumes still stand today in very nearly their same pristine, resplendent condition as when placed there by Morrison some sixty years ago. A random check of several hundred volumes reveals by the wear and by marginal notations that Carnegie had made real use of only one volume—Tom Paine's *Age of Reason*. He preferred to use his own personal, small working library in his study just off the main library.

Although Carnegie was lavish and unpredictable in his issuance of invitations to both Americans and Britons to visit him at Skibo, in time there came to be an established pattern to the entertainment. The first week in September was known as "the Principals' Week." There might be several other guests present at the same time, but this week was primarily reserved for the visit of the Principals of the four Scottish Universities, who had met each other collectively for the first time at Skibo soon after the Scottish Universities Trust had been established. They had found the experience so rewarding that Carnegie continued it each year.[8] Another week was reserved for the board of trustees of the Dunfermline Trust. Led by John Ross, these solid Fifeshire men made their annual pilgrimage northward, and Carnegie found in their natural lack of affectation and in their impassive acceptance of the splendors of Skibo a rather delightful contrast with many of his other guests.

The Fourth of July was elaborately celebrated as Fête Day. All of the school children for miles around would gather on the lawns of Skibo to run races, drink lemonade, sing songs, and salute that curiously hybrid ensign, consisting of the Union Jack and the Star Spangled Banner sewn together, that fluttered from the mast of the highest turret at Skibo. Carnegie took particular pleasure in celebrating this day of American Independence on

945

British soil, and he capered about with all of the exuberance of his most youthful guests.

Then there was the group familiarly known to the Carnegies as the "Old Shoes," who were always welcome at Skibo and needed no special invitation. These were Carnegie's oldest British friends, most of them Liberal party leaders, who had first introduced Carnegie into British journalistic and political circles in the early 1880's: Lord Armistead, Frederic Harrison, Sir Henry Fowler, the Yates Thompsons, Herbert Gladstone, and Swire Smith. A few Americans were admitted into this select company on their visits to Europe: Richard Gilder, Andrew White, and Nicholas Murray Butler.

The "Oldest Shoe" of all was, of course, John Morley. With each passing year, Carnegie and Morley seemed to come closer together, each more and more dependent upon the other's friendship. This deep attachment between two men so radically different in background and temperament was difficult to understand, even by Carnegie and Morley themselves, but its inexplicability made it even more real and unexpectedly precious to them both. For each, the other served as the one person with whom any idea, any personal problem, any hope or despair could be shared. Their exchange of letters became more and more frequent, and their increasing affinity was reflected in the changing salutations of the letters over the years, beginning with that proper English informal formality of "My dear Morley," and "My dear Carnegie," progressing to "Dear Friend Morley" and "Dear Friend Carnegie," and finally reaching the point where the reserved Morley could write, "My dearest and oldest friend," and the much more effusive Carnegie would respond, "My Chum—Dear Chum." (Who else in all the world would think of referring to—much less dare to address—Morley as "Chum"?) Upon leaving Scotland one autumn without having had Morley up to Skibo for a late summer visit, Carnegie wrote, "Disappointed we are not to meet but there's a bond between real affinities independent of space or visibility—presence Corporeal not essential to Communion. I feel you in a sense always at hand. I don't remember the poets expressing this truth, but no doubt its noted in Shakespeare somewhere—a kind of wireless telegraphy." [9] And Morley, writing to both the Carnegies, would respond, "Nobody ever had truer friends, either in great things or in small, than it has been my good fortune to find in you two. Perpetual be it—so far as perpetuity is to be hoped for in this strange, shadowy sense." [10]

Hardly a week passed during the summer months of each year that Carnegie did not write Morley, urging him to drop whatever political or social obligations he might have and come to Skibo. No matter how many others might be there, there was always a place for Morley. "Don't fail to come soon as you can next week," was a typical Carnegie letter. "You may have trouble getting a Berth—better engage it. Sunday, Aug 9th would suit. We shall be ready for you tenth & perhaps this would save you from the rush. Monday eve the tenth might be crowded—so why not Saturday eve & arrive Sunday noon. We can send for you even that day without shocking the people too much when we can urge a Cabinet official's needs. For any ordinary man this palliation would be insufficient. I hope you are to be greatly benefited by your stay with us which must not be short—stretch it as much as possible. Bryce's may be here ere you go. Montrose Room will be ready for its rightful occupant & I'll be happy." [11] Morley demurred at being assigned the "Montrose Room," which was the most luxurious suite in Skibo. He replied, "Now 'Montrose' besides being beyond my merits has one drawback. In these days I awake too early, and want to read in bed. Montrose, if I am right, does not favour this practice. If it made no difference, I'd as lief have a room where the window shines upon the pillows of the guest. Excuse me for this petition if you please. . . . I *am* looking forward to it all with infinite satisfaction." [12]

Morley definitely belonged to the more sedentary group of Skibo visitors, the inveterate readers, who would awake even before the Highland piper in order to read and who spent the day trying to avoid all of Carnegie's planned fun and games in the trout streams, in the swimming baths, and on the golf links. Only Morley, with his privileged status, could totally escape all of this vigorous activity. Carnegie quite early gave up any attempt to make an athlete out of him and was quite content to have Morley restrict his physical activity to taking long, slow walks with him along Sunset Walk, a trail that led from Skibo to Loch Ospisdale, where in the late evenings one could get a magnificent view of the setting sun over the distant moors and firth. Here on this walk, or seated on stone benches on the castle terrace, the two men would discuss current politics, argue over literature, and laugh at ancient jokes. In spite of the similarity of their views on most topics, they delighted in baiting each other, for each knew the other would be quick to respond. For Carnegie these moments were quite the best times at Skibo.

Louise Carnegie, upon whom the major responsibility fell for providing for this vast influx of visitors each summer and for managing a staff of eighty-five servants, proved herself to be a most remarkable administrator as well as a gracious hostess. If Carnegie enjoyed immensely all of this constant activity, she herself would probably have preferred a quite different life. But if the tensions upon her were great, she rarely revealed her feelings, and then only to an intimate friend like John Ross.[13] Carnegie found it hard to imagine that anyone would not be enjoying life at Skibo as much as he. It was not until their seventh season there, in 1904, that Carnegie finally realized the kind of strain that Louise was living under each summer and that she needed a respite from the constant entertaining. He wrote Principal James Donaldson of St. Andrews, "She has no long Holiday term as you lucky Scotch Professors and I have. Skibo I call one interrupted playtime. Not quite so for the 'Boss of the show' however— woman's work is never done." [14]

High up on the moors behind Skibo, there was a small stone cottage, called Auchindinagh, and here Carnegie decided that Louise and he and Baba should go for three weeks of rest. He wrote to Morley explaining why they couldn't have him visit the latter part of July as had been planned. "The family go into retreat July 22–to Aug. 10th away up the high moors . . . Cottage on the Shinn. Madam thinks higher air for two weeks best for Baba. She also gets a rest preparatory to shooting season. It is an experiment we are to try. I think a wise one. She wished to postpone it until next year when you wrote you could come but I insisted you could & would come later, or *sooner*. Perhaps you can spend sometime here before 23d July your Edinburg meeting." [15]

The experiment proved a great success, and thereafter a three-week retreat into the moors became a regular part of the Skibo summer. For Louise it was the best part of the summer; indeed, the best part of their lives. For three weeks they lived a sim-

948

ple life as an ordinary family, just she, Andrew, Baba, and Louise's sister, Stella, with only two servants. It was the kind of home life she had imagined as a romantic young girl, dreaming of her future as a wife and mother. Here Carnegie had ample time for his writing, finishing his biography of James Watt and beginning in earnest a project he had long had in mind but had made only desultory starts on before—the writing of his personal memoirs. In 1910 the Carnegies built a somewhat larger cottage, which they named Aultnagar, a short distance away from Auchindinagh, but the more spacious quarters were for their own comfort, not for visitors.[16]

The retreat into the moors became especially precious to the Carnegies after their daughter became seriously ill at the age of eight. What appeared at first to be only a sprained ankle, suffered at Skibo in the late summer, did not heal properly. When the specialists in Edinburgh examined it, they suggested that Margaret might be afflicted with a serious bone infection. Upon the return of the family to New York, Margaret's entire leg was put in a plaster cast, and the leading orthopedists could give no assurances that a cure could be effected. Carnegie, who had so rarely been touched by the normal vicissitudes of life that he was quite unprepared emotionally for any tragic occurrence, was frantic with anxiety. "We are having the first active pang of grief," he wrote Morley. "Baba's leg in plaster cast . . . leading specialist enveloped entire leg. She has fixed stilts for it & can hobble about a little. Is very patient & cheerful, but it does go deep into our hearts, deep, deep. It may be only result of sprain, but I fear Edinburg specialist Prof. Stiles believed it to be more serious. We are so anxious. Can't tell for three or four months & naturally fear the worst. It is terrible." [17]

Later diagnosis was much more hopeful. It proved to be not the deterioration of bone but, as Carnegie wrote Morley a couple of months later, "of a gouty nature & not as the Edinburg specialist feared. This seems decided, a heavy weight is lifted from our hearts." [18] Even so, Margaret had to wear splints for nearly three years. It was not until the spring of 1908 that Carnegie could write happily to Dod, "Baba attended church yesterday minus splint. First appearance—as it was mine. She asked me to go." [19]

Margaret was always precocious; she had her father's quick wit and lively curiosity. After her illness, her life became especially restricted and protected, and she had to spend her childhood largely in the society of adults, but the weeks of lonely isolation at Auchindinagh in the company of her parents and aunt did not seem as empty of companionship as they would have seemed to most children. She delighted her father with her knowledge and the kinds of questions she would ask. "I must tell you Margaret astonished me the other night by repeating the Seven Ages of Man & again she has repeated—The quality of mercy, &c. . . . All perfect & in fine style. She is developing fast—puzzles her mother about certain things in Holy Writ now & then that gives Madam some anxiety. She does her best & I say, all right, Lou— I'll not give you away. Do the best you can—but remember she'll find out the truth before long for herself & Lou agrees, Yes, she won't rest until she is satisfied." [20]

The old radicalism of her Dunfermline forebears also manifested itself anew in Margaret. Carnegie reported to Richard Gilder that Margaret's "chief work is making up parties who never had a motor ride and taking them as her guests—all our servants in turn—picnics also provided. We encourage her in doing for others, already the young socialist crops out. . . . Why should some be rich and others poor, why do we invite rich people and give them everything when they have plenty at home— and the poor haven't. Questions easier to ask than answer. Her babble for a day would enrich even the Century columns." [21]

To say that Carnegie, at the age of seventy, with an eight-year-old daughter, was a proud and doting father would be something of an understatement. If Margaret was occasionally afflicted with boredom when they were in retreat on the moors, Carnegie did his best to enliven the situation. Remembering the hours of his childhood spent with Uncle Lauder in the grocery shop on High Street, Carnegie retold all of the old Celtic legends and fairy stories, taught her the great passages of Shakespeare, and encouraged her to question everything that came to her attention. In spite of what must have been a difficult childhood for her, Margaret, because of these retreats, would cherish the memory of a special relationship with her father which most children, with much younger fathers, would never know.

The seven months of each year that the Carnegies spent in the United States also had a pattern, not dissimilar to that of their life in Scotland. They did not engage in as active a social life in New York as they did in Skibo; there was not the steady stream of guests. But 2 East 91st Street was also open to visitors, particularly to British friends—Edward Grey, Lord Bryce, Goldwin Smith, and Rudyard Kipling. For years Carnegie had been attempting to get Morley to visit him in the United States, without success. In the spring of 1904, however, when the Liberal party once again had failed to win control of Parliament, Morley felt free of any political and literary obligations that would prevent him from planning a trip to America. It was decided that he should come with the Carnegies on their return from Scotland in late October and that he would present the main address at the annual Founder's Day of the Pittsburgh Institute. Roosevelt also invited Morley to visit him at the White House immediately following the presidential election. His visit was to be climaxed with being the guest of honor at one of Carnegie's famous literary dinners, given annually to honor a distinguished writer.

All through the summer of 1904 Carnegie and Morley planned and talked over the prospective visit with all of the excitement of two youths discussing their first high school prom. Carnegie was particularly concerned about Morley's lecture in Pittsburgh. When Morley suggested as a topic, "Comparison of the world's hopes at the [time of the] French Revolution— moral, social, political hopes—and the realized results today— vindication of the dreams of progress and human perfectibility," Carnegie was enthusiastic. "I am sure it will make your visit Historical, always provided you do find progress. I am carried away with the subject *do do it.* I send Miller address to show you I find Progress." [22] Morley, after looking over the tentative program, could not resist the temptation to tease his agnostic friend: "By the way, I'm both perplexed and scandalized at the discovery that proceedings at Pittsburgh on your Day seem to begin with Invectives of the unseen & unknowable power. I don't mind this sort of thing in places of ancient endowment. It disappoints me to find theological appeals started fresh in your new foundation. I would have *no theology.*" [23]

In bringing John Morley to America, Carnegie could justifiably feel that he had captured as great a celebrity as he had in Herbert Spencer many years before. Certainly, he had a far more co-operative and far less demanding guest than he had had in the querulous Sage of Brighton. For Morley, the visit was a personal triumph, from Pittsburgh to Washington to New York. Unfortunately, Carnegie was not able to share in his friend's successful activities except vicariously, through Morley's letters. Almost immediately upon their arrival in New York, Carnegie became ill with what the doctors diagnosed as a severe case of gout. He was ordered to bed for at least a month. It seemed cruelly unfair after all these years of planning to have to spend the entire time that Morley was to be in the country in bed, but Dr. Garmany was adamant. Morley's itinerary was carried out as planned, however. He went to Pittsburgh from New York via Niagara Falls for Founder's Day, without the Founder. "Pittsburgh was an unalloyed pleasure and gratification and interest," he reported back faithfully to his ailing host. "It gave me a completely new vision of your work in the world. Of course, I have always known it in a general way; but 1) to see Homestead, its magnitude, order, system and discipline; 2) the Museum, Institute &c. &c.; 3) to hear the position you hold in so great a community, brought all home to me in a way that was at once striking, half-unexpected, and wholly delightful. The Frews were *kindness itself.* The banquet was really an immense success. When I rose and when I sat down, I felt that I heartily liked them, and they liked me. You who take such affectionate interest in my poor concerns would have been pleased. (What Vanity!!)" [24]

From Pittsburgh, Morley went to Chicago and then to Washington, to the White House. It was a memorable encounter for Morley. In Roosevelt he found someone even more given to strenuosity than Carnegie. Upon his departure, Morley was to make an observation to a newspaper reporter that would be quoted around the country, "I have seen the two great natural wonders of America, Niagara Falls and Theodore Roosevelt."

The great dinner at the Carnegies' for Morley took place on the night of 22 November. Richard Gilder, who always planned Carnegie's literary dinner, this year had to be the presiding host as well. In fact, Gilder saw a great deal more of Morley while the latter was in New York than did the miserably unhappy Carnegie. Reporting on his various social activities with Morley to a friend, Gilder seemed to find his calendar a bit crowded with Morley: "The other day I dined with Morley at President Butler's; also lunched with him to-day at ex-Mayor Low's; also lunched *him* at the Player's Club Wednesday; also go out to meet him at White-law Reid's Sunday; also spent yesterday afternoon with him, having taken Booker Washington to be catechized by him at Carnegie's; also went upstairs to Carnegie's sick-room to be thanked (feelingly) by A.C. for presiding at *his* dinner to his guest Morley on Tuesday night; where were five college presidents and I don't know how many ambassadors, poets, novelists and such. At which select banquet I had provided each guest with a stunning quotation from the Right Honorable,—which bowled the Right Honorable over,—and served as a text for a very eloquent speech; while the poor unhappy host was lying upstairs, cussing his luck, groaning with his pernickity back, and missing, in his own house, the yearly event he most cares for, and one of the greatest private dinners ever given in New York." [25]

Morley returned to Britain the first of December, and the recuperating Carnegie wrote him, "House quiet since our swell visitor left us. I am over my gout, but careful these stormy days. . . . Am busy on Watt. . . . It has been a source of great pleasure to me while cooped up. . . . I've been reading Mill's autobiography, very interesting only he lauds Mrs. Taylor rather too much. . . . How seriously you big dogs take yourselves. Mill does, recording so minutely his moods &c. Spencer ditto. Gladstone! What a prig. Pray avoid this in yours just a little." [26] Clearly, Carnegie was nearly well and quite up to teasing Morley again. Morley rose to the bait: "Your observations about Mill and Gladstone offend me mightily. Men of that stamp have a right to their foibles. Americans are apt sometimes to lack the grace of reverence. Don't forget that, my dear Sir, in the training of Miss Baba. Her mother, by the way, has plenty of it. Somebody asked Plato whether he did not find something or another amiss with an old teacher. He said, 'I am not going to lay hands on my father Parmenides.' No more will I lay hands on Mill—the most virtuous and truth-loving man that I at least have ever known." [27]

This had been Carnegie's only serious illness since he had

nearly died of typhoid in 1886. By the middle of January he was completely recovered and could write Dod, "I am quite restored again. We go to Washington to dine with President Feby 2nd & then present arrangement is I start 15th for Dungeness. . . . Bot an auto for St. Andrews runs and have been up at golf several times." [28]

The Dungeness that Carnegie referred to was the sea island off the coast of north Florida which his sister-in-law Lucy owned. Tom Carnegie had built a mansion here shortly before his death, and around it Lucy in turn built cottages for her nine children when each of them married. His brother's widow had always had a special place in Carnegie's affections. He felt much closer to her than he ever had to Tom. A large, fat woman, Lucy had an infectious good humor. Although she and Carnegie would argue over almost any topic, shouting boisterously at each other, they would usually find themselves laughing uproariously at each other's sallies. Dungeness served Carnegie as the same kind of retreat from New York during the winter months that Auchindinagh served from Skibo in the summer. Lucy—the Commodore, as Carnegie called her—could always lift his spirits, and he particularly enjoyed playing golf with her, for here was an opponent he could usually beat. "I beat Lucy today badly at golf—really broke my record & now feel I can do something creditable," was a typical boast.[29]

Louise, however, did not regard Dungeness as being anything like the kind of restful retreat that their Scottish moor cottage was. Being the serious and reserved person she was, Louise found Lucy and her whole ménage a bit overpowering. Carnegie might enjoy this irrepressible large family of relatives with "Lucy the main pillar . . . all revolving round her ample orbit," [30] but Louise too often found herself excluded from the circle, as Lucy and Andrew talked over old Pittsburgh friends, argued over names and places she had never heard of, and laughed at their own "in-family" jokes. Carnegie accused her of being a perfect hostess but a very poor guest, and to this she readily pleaded guilty. It was always a relief to her to head back north to her own relatively quiet and well-run home after the bumptiously expansive disorder at Sister Lucy's. Had she not felt that the warm winter sunshine was good for Margaret, she would much rather have forgone this annual winter holiday altogether and let Andrew visit his relatives by himself.

Louise might return from Dungeness exhausted, but Carnegie would come back exhilarated, ready for another final round of the season in the American political arena before they should leave for Scotland. Carnegie's preoccupation with American politics was somewhat of a new venture for him in this first decade of the twentieth century. In the 1880's and 1890's he had been far more engrossed in British politics, where there was so much more to reform than in a country where, by his own evaluation, there were "perfect institutions of government."

Much of Carnegie's rather belated interest in American politics came, of course, out of his intense desire to secure world peace, but this was not the sole motivating force. Theodore Roosevelt, more than anyone else, had awakened Carnegie's interest —not only by giving an excitement to the political scene that, except for the aberration of the 1896 campaign, Americans had not known since the Civil War, but also by pointing up to his countrymen the many things that were wrong with their land. Almost without realizing it, Carnegie, like millions of other Americans, had shifted over with surprising ease from complacent conservative Republicanism into Progressive reformism.

Carnegie, to be sure, already bore the mark of the maverick for having broken with the McKinley administration over its Philippine policy. This break, however, had placed him more in opposition to some of the more Progressive elements within the party, men like Governor Roosevelt of New York and Senators Lodge and Beveridge, than it did to some of the more conservative elements who feared the impact of foreign colonial possessions upon American tariff policies. But at the same time that the Supreme Court was alleviating the fears of the high protectionists by declaring that our new colonial possessions were not an integral part of the United States as far as tariff and basic Constitutional rights were concerned, Carnegie made it quite clear that his opposition to imperialism was not based upon a fear of extending the free domestic market to far distant lands. In December 1901 he startled the business community by the blunt answer he gave to the editor of the *New York Commercial,* who had asked him, along with several other prominent men, his opinion of the necessity of maintaining the present high protective tariff. "In reply to your inquiry," Carnegie wrote, "my opinion is that the Tariff as a protective measure has lost much of its importance, and is now to be considered principally in regard to Revenue." [31] His choice of words in dismissing the importance of the tariff was considered particularly infelicitous, for the phrase "A Tariff for Revenue Only," coined by the Louisville *Courier-Journal* editor, Henry Watterson, for the Democratic platform of 1880, had been the battle cry of tariff reformers ever since.

This proved to be a mild statement, however, compared to his later pronouncements in favor of Progressive reform. He vigorously backed Roosevelt's efforts to push through the Hepburn railroad rate bill in 1906. He wrote to the liberal Republican Senator from Minnesota, Moses H. Clapp, "A few great railroad organizations control the situation, combining they divide the business between them—agree not to build in certain territory, fix rates, &c. That govt. must control them & prevent unlimited sway to public or private injury seems obvious. . . . The President is right upon this question sure." [32] Actually, Carnegie's support of the Hepburn Bill was not surprising and did not represent too radical a shift in viewpoint, as he had long been an outspoken opponent of monopolistic railroad rates, threatening the retaliation of state commissions and mob action against the Pennsylvania Railroad.

In 1907, during the so-called "Bankers Panic," Carnegie began to press Roosevelt for strict federal regulations "upon issue of Capital Stocks or Bonds. We cannot trust this to the Gamblers, for such they are. All you have stood for is amply justified by recent events." [33] A little later, as the recession deepened, he wrote: "It is certain that they [the people] will sustain subjection of corporations to Law. Our railroads must be restricted as those of all other countries. Matters of Capitalization must be supervised by the Intercommerce Commission. Also Stock Dividends & Consolidations. Nothing radical needed, but this is imperative." [34]

To many of Carnegie's former associates, however, this course of action sounded radical enough, and not at all what they would regard as imperative. To them he must have appeared in these years like the reformed inebriate, who not only forgoes liquor for himself but goes around speaking at temperance meetings and

trying to break up saloons with an axe. It was bad enough to have
Carnegie making a big publicity stunt out of giving away his own
wealth; it was considerably worse for him to be seeking to deny
others the privilege of getting wealth in the same way and of the
same magnitude as he had done. But Carnegie was now convinced
that the good old days of free enterprise and unregulated competition were gone forever. "Sir Charles, the day of the multi-millionaire is over, the people won't have it," he told a fellow Fife-
shireman, Sir Charles Macmara, who had made a fortune in
Manchester textiles.[35]

Carnegie seemed determined to give validity to his assertion.
The man who had eagerly bought up Rockefeller leases on the
Mesabi range and the coal fields in Westmoreland County, Pennsylvania, in order to claw and dig out as much of these great natural resources as possible in as short a time as possible, now was an
eager participant in Theodore Roosevelt's White House conference in the Conservation of Natural Resources, held in May 1908.
Carnegie's paper on "The Conservation of Ores and Related Minerals" presented at this meeting was later printed as a pamphlet
by the Government Printing Office and given wide distribution.
In this well-documented essay he in effect presented a scorching
indictment of the policies of the Carnegie and United States Steel
companies in the preceding fifteen years. He deplored the wasteful methods that had been used in the extraction of iron ore, "our
most useful metal," and coal by the steel and coke companies of
America. Moreover, he asserted, "the same spirit of recklessness
that leads to waste in mining and in the consumption of coal
leads to unnecessary risk of human life." Nine thousand men had
been killed or injured in the preceding year alone in the mining
of coal. We as a nation were throwing away both our precious
mineral and our even more precious human resources with reckless abandon: "The production and consumption of minerals are
increasing much more rapidly than our population." Iron Mountain in Missouri, which only forty years earlier had been considered a nearly inexhaustible source of iron ore but now was completely gone, was but one example of this rapid, ever-increasing
consumption of our mineral resources. Carnegie urged that specific steps be taken to conserve mineral ores: use water transportation more extensively and thus cut down on the production of

railroad rails; use concrete, both simple and reinforced, to reduce the need for steel in buildings and bridges; push for world disarmament, not only for humanitarian but also for conservation reasons; improve coal mining methods to be less wasteful of both the mines and the miners; develop radically new sources of power, including sun power, to replace coal.

Carnegie concluded his dissertation by emphasizing that the conservation of our mineral resources, about which he felt the most qualified to speak, was only one area in which the nation was facing national disaster if it did not adopt strict conservation policies. He stressed the need for equally specific proposals to conserve our forests and rich soil resources. "Our president, with far-sighted patriotism, has arisen to lead effort and action. He deserves, and I am sure will receive, your earnest support and that of all citizens who understand the importance of the problems involved." [36] One can imagine the reactions of Schwab, Gary, Frick, and others to their former business associate's plea to the nation to use less rails, structural beams, and coal.

Having struck out at the iron and coal industries, Carnegie next turned his critical attention to another field of economic activity from which he had previously greatly benefited—the field of finance. In the winter of 1908 he gave an address before the Economic Club which was later published in *The Outlook*. As implied by the title of the article, "The Worst Banking System in the World," Carnegie, who had once insisted that every American institution, political, economic, and social, was superior to that of any other nation, now with equal insistence was maintaining that the American banking system was inferior to that of any Western capitalistic nation. Even Canada, his usual whipping boy, he felt had a far better national banking system than the one the United States had established in 1862 and had maintained ever since. Born out of desperate need to finance the Civil War, it was totally inappropriate to and hopelessly inadequate for meeting the financial needs of modern America.

Carnegie's proposed solution was a curious mixture of early-nineteenth-century Thomas Hart Benton conservatism and contemporary-twentieth-century Progressivism. It anticipated much of Woodrow Wilson's Federal Reserve banking system. For instance, he objected to the requirement under the current National Bank system that "the currency issued must be based upon an equal amount of government bonds deposited in the Treasury . . . We should have gold as our reserve—this is what all civilized countries have." [37] He was highly critical of the Aldrich bill, then before the Senate, because it would have the effect of "pushing us deeper into the mire—more currency based upon securities, when the authorities are clear upon the point that nothing is perfect but gold as a security." [38] This was straight Bentonian philosophy. At the same time, however, quite apart from having a gold reserve to replace government bonds as security, he wanted the amount of currency in circulation to be determined by the assets of the banks issuing the notes. "Currency based upon the assets of banks rests chiefly upon trade bills. In the nature of things, the bank is called upon to issue or redeem notes just as business requires; that is, as business increases or decreases, currency required is less or more. Business brisk, more notes are needed, currency remains in circulation; business dull, less notes needed, some are promptly returned to the banks for redemption. All is elastic and automatic. . . . This [in contrast to European nations] we lack." [39] This principle of the elasticity of currency would later be incorporated into the Federal Reserve Act, although the method of achieving it was not the same as that suggested by Carnegie.

Carnegie was also ideologically equivocal in regard to the role of government in banking. On the one hand, like a true Jacksonian Democrat, he wanted government entirely out of the banking business. He wanted no central United States Bank that would be even partly government owned and controlled. On the other hand, like a Roosevelt New Nationalist, he wanted the government to have the "right of supervision and the exercise of that right." [40] He was not even opposed to Representative C. N. Fowler's proposal to have the government guarantee individual bank deposits, although he would have preferred that the banks be required to have a guarantee fund to protect individual depositors.[41] On the question of a central bank that would be privately owned, he was neither enthusiastically for nor adamantly opposed. "Details should be left to the future as to whether there should be one central bank as in European countries, or the Canadian plan of establishing a point of redemption in each district." [42]

Upon the publication of Carnegie's article on the banking system, Nicholas Murray Butler wrote him a highly laudatory letter, calling his article one of the best things Carnegie had ever written—"a masterpiece . . . and every Senator and Representative should have a copy." [43] Carnegie had already more than anticipated Butler's suggestion. He had 70,500 reprints of his article made, and he distributed them not only to every member of Congress but also to nearly every bank president and manufacturer in the country.[44] Unquestionably, Carnegie's article helped to stimulate the thought and discussion that eventually led to the establishment of the Federal Reserve System.

Carnegie's biggest bombshell against the business community came late in the fall of 1908, when, in the December issue of *The Century Magazine,* he denied the need to continue a protective tariff on most products imported into the country. Even the liberal editor of *The Century,* Robert Underwood Johnson, was startled by the unequivocal stand Carnegie took. The article, which Carnegie sent in late August, had been scheduled for the November issue of the magazine, but both Johnson and his associate, Richard Watson Gilder, feared that this was such inflammatory stuff that, if it should appear just prior to the presidential election, it might have an undesirable impact upon the outcome. They sent galley proofs off to Roosevelt and his heir designate, William Howard Taft, to see if they wished it held up. "I think there is campaign dynamite in it," Johnson wrote Roosevelt, "as in the interview with the Emperor by a gentleman who recently called upon you. Both articles would be a sensation in our November number, but either would we think operate disadvantageously to the candidacy of Mr. Taft. So both would (*we* think) better go over. Personally, I think Mr. Carnegie's argument bears strongly against the whole iniquitous tariff system, but I wish Mr. Taft to be in at the revision—with a Congress of revisionists. Mr. Carnegie makes no account of the great middle class but only of rich and poor." [45] Taft, in response, counseled delay: "Mr. Carnegie's article is very interesting . . . and will prove very useful in revising the tariff. I think perhaps that some of his positions would be misunderstood or would be perverted in the campaign. We are pledged to revision now, and I don't think he really differs from the position we take, assuming his facts to be correct. As for instance, with reference to the steel industry: He says that we can produce steel, except in certain specialties, more cheaply here than they can abroad, which would certainly justify taking off the tariff altogether." [46]

The November issue appeared the last week in October with nothing more politically controversial in its pages than an article by Frederick Trevor Hill, commemorating the fiftieth anniversary of the Lincoln-Douglas debates. Taft easily won the presidency, and Bryan went down to defeat for the third and last time. It is hard to imagine that an article in *The Century* or in any other journal in the country would have made an iota of difference in the outcome. Nevertheless, when Carnegie's article appeared a month later, it caused a storm of controversy, even though the election was over. Carnegie stoutly maintained that his views on the tariff had not changed at all from what they had always been. Only conditions had changed. He made a point of quoting from John Stuart Mill's *Principles of Political Economy:* "The only case in which, on mere principles of political economy, protecting duties can be defensible, is when they are imposed temporarily (especially in a young and rising nation) in hopes of naturalizing a foreign industry, in itself perfectly suitable to the circumstances of the country. The superiority of one country over another in a branch of production, often arises only from having begun it sooner. . . . A country which has this skill and experience yet to acquire, may in other respects be better adapted to the production than those which were earlier in the field. . . . A protecting duty, continued for a reasonable time, will sometimes be the least inconvenient mode in which the nation can tax itself for the support of such an experiment. But the protection should be confined to cases in which there is good ground of assurance that the industry which it fosters will after a time be able to dispense with it; nor should the domestic producers ever be allowed to expect that it will be continued to them, beyond the time strictly necessary for a fair trial of what they are capable of accomplishing." This, Carnegie insisted, had always been his position, and justified his being in the 1880's a Liberal free trader in Britain and a Republican protectionist in the United States.

The protective tariff on steel in the United States had not only been justified in Mill's view, but it had also ultimately given steel to the whole world at a much cheaper price. Carnegie illus-

trated his point by telling the story of a dinner that he and James
Blaine had attended in London in 1888:

> Mr. Chamberlain [then a strong advocate of free trade] was
> present, and the tariff question naturally came up. Mr. Cham-
> berlain remarked that Carnegie was a good fellow, and we all
> liked him, but still he didn't see why the United States should
> present him with $28 per ton protection upon his steel rails.
> This brought laughter and applause. When quiet was restored,
> Mr. Blaine replied: "We don't look at it quite that way. I am
> interested in railroads and before we put on that tariff we had
> to pay you $100 per ton for steel rails. Just before we sailed our
> board bought a large amount from Carnegie, and he charged us
> only $30. I guess if we had not put on that tariff, you would
> still be charging us $100."
> After the laughter subsided, Sir Charles Tennant, President
> of the Scotland Steel Company, exclaimed: "Yes, $100 per ton;
> we all held to that price, and could have got it today if Carne-
> gie and others hadn't interfered."
> Mr. Blaine said, "Mr. Chamberlain I don't think you have
> made much by this frank confession."
> "No," replied Mr. Chamberlain; "how could I, with Sr.
> Charles sitting there and giving me away." [47]

In short, the experiment in initiating and fostering an American steel industry by the classic formula of John Stuart Mill, Carnegie insisted, had been spectacularly successful. But now with
that success there was no longer any need for protection. Except
for tin plate and possibly a few other minor steel specialities, all
duties on steel products should be eliminated. What was true of
steel was also true of most American manufactures. "The infant
we have nursed approaches the day when we [sic] should be
weaned from tariff milk and fed upon the stronger food of free
competition. It needs little, if any more nursing. . . ." [48] Carnegie
named three manufactures in particular, in addition to steel, that
should be immediately "weaned": illuminating oils, thread, and
cutlery. The only justifiable reason for a tariff at all was as a
source of revenue, and tariff for this purpose should be restricted
to imported luxuries, where the burden of taxation would fall entirely upon the rich or on products such as spirituous liquors and

tobacco, which, although used by the poor, were in themselves harmful to all who used them.

Carnegie's article was published just at the moment when the House Ways and Means Committee was beginning its preliminary hearings for a new tariff bill to replace the Dingley Tariff of 1897, and it created an uproar in Washington and New York. The New York *Tribune* printed four page-length columns of comment from congressmen and senators on Carnegie's article. Some of the Democrats said they wanted reprints to use as campaign documents for the next election.[49] *The* (London) *Times* correspondent cabled his paper, "It requires no particular gift of imagination on the part of those in England who are interested in the American tariff to picture the sensation created here by Mr. Carnegie's article in *The Century*. . . . The *New York Tribune* attempts to break the force of what Mr. Carnegie says. It reminds us that his *ipse dixit* is not to be accepted as convincing by any means, and thinks it would be 'an error either for protectionists to be depressed by the thought that Mr. Carnegie has suddenly become hostile to them, or for free-traders to be elated at his supposed conversion to their cause.' " [50]

But the error was on the *Tribune*'s part. The protectionists were not simply depressed; they were outraged. Eugene Zimmerman, the wealthy Ohio railroad financier whose daughter was the Duchess of Manchester, was quoted in *The Times* as saying that Carnegie was "the most selfish man in the United States. Having made his own millions, he wants to prevent others doing likewise." Willis King, a Pittsburgh steel manufacturer, flatly denied before the House Ways and Means Committee Carnegie's statement that the United States could make steel cheaper than anyone else, but when asked for evidence to refute Carnegie's claim, he refused to offer any data.[51]

The free traders, on the other hand, were elated and did indeed hail Carnegie as a "convert to their cause." The New York *World,* long a champion for lower tariffs, proudly claimed him as its ally. "Mr. Carnegie can render no greater service to the American people than to lead the fight for true tariff reform." It ran a cartoon showing Carnegie being pursued by Speaker Joseph Cannon, Representative John Dalzell, and Senator Boise Penrose, the grand old triumvirate of stand-pat Republican protectionism, with ropes in their hands, and above the cartoon the title, "Lynch Him!" [52]

Carnegie professed bewilderment at all the uproar. He wrote to his old Republican ally, the former Mayor of New York Seth Low, "You will have to agree that time brings changes, and it is fully time that the Tariff was changed to meet present conditions. As far as protection is concerned, great reductions can be made without injuring our manufacturers in any degree." He added a postscript to assure Low that he was still a good card-carrying Republican, with his credentials all in order; "I sent $20,000 to the [Republican] Campaign Fund." [53]

The worried chairman of the Ways and Means Committee, Representative Sereno E. Payne, who had been the guardian shepherd through the House for both the McKinley and Dingley protective tariff bills, wrote Carnegie asking him to appear in Washington to testify before his committee, thus hoping to bring the apostate back into the fold. Carnegie at first demurred: "I have been seven years out of the Steel business and have no detailed figures to give you, and I cannot be induced to enter into a Tariff controversy. All that I have to say upon the Tariff has been published in the Century Magazine and I beg to enclose a copy of the article." But Representative Payne had already read Carnegie's article. He sent Carnegie a subpoena.[54] Carnegie came, and like Caesar, he conquered. He wrote Lauder upon the eve of his departure, "Off for Washington tomorrow to answer Tariff Comm. They will get short responses. We are approaching great crisis in 'Combination' Monopoly vs. Competition." [55]

Within half an hour after Carnegie took the stand, Chairman Payne was fervently wishing his witness's response would be even shorter and was sincerely regretting his subpoena. Carnegie had a delightful time. He had discovered his most exciting rostrum yet —a Congressional witness stand—and one of the most appreciative audiences he had ever addressed. The room was packed with tariff reformers who roared at his every joke, applauded his every attack upon the tariff. And his attacks made his *Century* article, by comparison, seem mild indeed. When asked about the tariff on steel, he replied that the United States Steel Corporation made a profit of something on the order of $15.50 per ton. "Does that enter into your brain?" he exclaimed, pointing directly at the perspiring Chairman. "Can you arrive at any other conclusion than that the steel industry can stand on its own legs? . . . The time for free trade has come so far as steel is concerned. The total abolition of the tariff will leave the steel companies in a better position, as far as this country is concerned, than a continuance of the present coddling system." [56] Then in a prepared statement, he read:

In obedience to your subpoena, I proceed to give my views upon Tariff Revision. The object and effect of a Protective Duty is to increase the price to the consumer of the article protected, that is to say, it levies a tax upon the consumers who are the great body of the people. The only valid reason for doing so is that the tax upon the consumer is temporary and meant to ensure for them a home supply as low in price as could be obtained from any country, and this is done only by repeal of the tax. I am one of those who believe that this alone is true statesmanship, and that no government is just to the consumer, which means the great mass of the people, which taxes them permanently for the good of the manufacturer. . . . Mr. Chairman, . . . I predict that in many departments it [the Committee] will find the time has arrived when the consumer is entitled to be relieved from the tax he has so long and so patiently borne, and that our country will be greatly advantaged just in proportion as the consumer obtains his just rights.

Two witnesses, each at the head of his respective line, have declared they no longer need to tax the community, in other words that the temporary protective tax upon consumers has performed its purpose, and thus vindicated our policy of protection. Other establishments in their line will laugh at their fears today, when they see how little the protective duty was required in their cases. If there be a concern in either line that cannot today live and prosper, without still levying a tax upon the consumer, much better that establishment pass into competent hands than that the whole community should be unnecessarily taxed. . . . We have taxed the consumers for a generation, and the time has come when they can be relieved without injury to the competent manufacturer.[57]

After this oration, the Committee was pleased to dismiss Carnegie and to assure him that he need not appear on the following day. Carnegie returned home well satisfied with his day's work. When Judge Gary, the chairman of United States Steel, wrote to protest Carnegie's quoting him as saying to President Roosevelt that his company did not need a tariff, Carnegie replied, "I am done now with the subject, having done my duty when subpoened. I told the truth—the whole truth as I know it." [58]

The "whole truth" as he now knew it lost Carnegie some old friends, but it gained him many new ones. Herbert Myrick, editor of the nationally known Springfield, Massachusetts, agricultural journal, *Farm and Home,* wrote to Carnegie the day after his appearance at the Congressional hearings, "Gee Whiz! How you did do up that poor little committee yesterday! They have bully-wragged other witnesses to such an extent that it is refreshing to see them 'hoist with their own petard.' " [59] George P. Hampton, another agricultural leader, hailed Carnegie as "a powerful new champion of reform." [60]

So radically abrupt did Carnegie's metamorphosis from Conservative chrysalis to Progressive butterfly seem that many of his new friends were totally at a loss to explain the presence of this gorgeous winged creature who fluttered among them. Carnegie's old companions, like Zimmerman, had no difficulty, to be sure, in offering an explanation. It was simply a metamorphic change from aggressive industrialist to indolent philanthropist, or to put it another way, from big manufacturer to big consumer. There is a measure of truth in this explanation, for it is impossible to believe that the Carnegie of ten years earlier would ever urge the country to use less iron for the sake of the conservation of resources. These industrialists would argue that if Carnegie, in selling out to United States Steel, had been paid in common stock rather than in first mortgage, 5 per cent gold bonds, he would now not be flying quite so high with the tariff reformers.

This is an easy but not entirely satisfactory explanation. He might not now have a direct vested interest in tariff on steel, but the value of his own wealth and the holdings of the large philanthropic foundations he had created were still directly affected by the success or failure of the steel trust. Yet here was Carnegie, by the end of Roosevelt's term of office, outdoing even his trust busting, big-stick carrying mentor, in speaking loudly about Progressive reform. One could be a Progressive and Roosevelt supporter, like George W. Perkins, Morgan's partner, without shaking the whole capitalist structure; but Carnegie was writing to the Editors of *American Industries:*

> You ask an amplification of my views in regard to the proposed Tariff Commission. The difficulty with Tariff Commissions composed of the members of Congress is that these men are necessarily uninformed upon the true conditions of the varied industries. Evidence given by interested parties cannot be depended upon as disinterested. Interested people form distorted views, colored as these are by their own interests.
>
> . . . There should be a permanent staff of able, disinterested men, charged with studying the conditions in all manufacturing countries.
>
> The industrial world is about to undergo the most momentous change known in its history, even more far-reaching than was the change from the individual domestic manufacturer, manufacturing at home, to the factory system and the huge establishments of today.
>
> We are rapidly losing competition upon which nations have hitherto depended to ensure reasonable prices for the consumer. Some of our most important industries today are only nominally competitive and in reality are monopolies so far that an understanding is made as to prices that will prevail. We cannot, in my opinion, withstand this movement. It has to be received and tested, which means that these virtual monopolies must be controlled some way or another. The only force seems to be that of a national government. A supreme industrial court will have to be created and eventually it will have to pass upon prices—disguise this as we may.
>
> To leave monopolists in control would not be tolerated by the people, therefore there must be control and that control, as far as one sees, must be in the hands of the general government.
>
> This is even a larger question than the tariff, but our trouble with revisions of the tariff will be greatly overcome by a body of experts, keeping themselves fully informed of all matters pertaining to the question. . . .
>
> There is nothing alarming in this changed condition, which requires changed regulations. Change is the necessary element in all progress and there should not be the slightest apprehension that the American people will not meet this new phase and adjust it for the best interests of the nation as a whole.[61]

With this statement Carnegie went far beyond Roosevelt's Square Deal and New Nationalism, or the New Freedom of Woodrow Wilson. Indeed, few governmental spokesmen in the much later New Deal of another Roosevelt's administration would be radical enough to propose such sweeping governmental controls of the market place as Carnegie was here advocating in 1909. No longer did Carnegie dismiss with a shrug the "bugaboo of trusts" as being but brief, transient organizations which by their very success created an opposition that would destroy them. It was absurd now to believe, as he once had, that a steel trust would, by taking advantage of its monopoly, raise prices, and immediately call into existence its own manufacturing competition that would force prices down and break up the trust. Who could possibly enter the field at this late date and effectively compete with the vertical power of United States Steel? There were no new Mesabis to lease for a pittance, no new Connellsville coal fields to gobble up. The day of regulation by competition was over, and the only regulation that could be effective now was political, not economic. If Carnegie had changed his views on the viability of the free enterprise system, as he most obviously had, his explanation for that change was simple—it was but a realistic acceptance of the change in conditions. He did not find it necessary to add that he himself was, of course, as responsible as any man in America for this radically new situation.

Carnegie had, in the beginning, courted Roosevelt, about whose unstable radicalism he had had considerable fear, in order to convert him to pacifism. But the heathen had become the missionary, and Carnegie had ended up much more of a Progressive than Roosevelt had a pacifist. Carnegie, who had hoped for four more years of reform, deeply regretted Roosevelt's decision not to seek another term in 1908. "Sorry for my country that you are not to be at the helm for some years more during which I am confident you would have secured for the Republic the reforms essential for her welfare," he wrote the President soon after Roosevelt's announcement of retirement. "You have done the preparatory work which only needs continued attention to give us a prouder position than hitherto occupied in some departments. In control of corporations & in Banking and Currency no lag behind all other Civilized Nations. Interstate problems require extension of

Federal power. We must be a Nation, one central power. Not a Confederacy of States." [62]

With Roosevelt's withdrawal from the presidential race of 1908, the great guessing game as to who his designated heir would be began, for it was inconceivable that Roosevelt would remain neutral and allow the Republican party free rein in selecting his successor. Carnegie's own favorite among the more probable candidates was the liberal reform governor of New York, Charles Evans Hughes, although if he could have appointed one man in the country to be President undoubtedly that man would have been Elihu Root.[63] When it became increasingly apparent that Roosevelt's choice would be his Secretary of War, William Howard Taft of Cincinnati, Carnegie was distinctly cool to the idea. "Looks like Taft for Presidency nomination," he wrote to Morley in April, two months before the Convention. "Hard contest to elect him." [64] Actually Carnegie did not fear the difficulty of electing Taft so much as he feared what the nation would be getting in electing him. For Taft represented to Carnegie those aspects of Roosevelt's administration that he would just as soon forget—not the social and economic reforms, but the ventures in imperialism and the infatuation with "righteous" wars. Although it would be difficult to imagine a less bellicose figure than the huge, jovial Judge Taft, nevertheless he had defended McKinley's Philippine policy and for his reward had been appointed first president of the commission to America's newly acquired Pacific colony. He had also served Roosevelt for five years as Secretary of War and, presumably, at least, supported Roosevelt's expanded budget for military appropriations. At the same time he had not been an outstanding proponent of Roosevelt's Progressive domestic program, but instead represented the more conservative wing of the President's cabinet. To Carnegie, Roosevelt's choice was as disappointing as it was surprising. It was with the attitude of choosing much the lesser of two evils that Carnegie contributed generously to Taft's campaign against Bryan in the autumn of 1908. Even so, he asked that a large portion of his party contribution be designated for Governor Hughes's use rather than for the national ticket.[65]

Carnegie's last contribution to the Roosevelt era was to write the introduction to a two-volume collection of the President's speeches, letters, and state papers, entitled *The Roosevelt Policy,* which the Current Literature Publishing Company brought out in the spring of 1908. In sending the set to Morley, Carnegie wrote that the "introduction written by me has greatly pleased the President so he writes me." [66] Little wonder, for it was an extravagant eulogy to Roosevelt Progressivism. The *Times Literary Supplement,* in its review, devoted more space to Carnegie's introduction than it did to the main contents of the book. With a touch of sarcasm the reviewer wrote:

> At first sight it seems a little odd that this book, which attacks the undue concentration of wealth, and has many severe things to say about "swollen fortunes" should be sent into the world with an introductory benediction from one of the two richest men in America. But Mr. Andrew Carnegie, as we all know, has always been "on the side of the angels" and the reformers, and this is not the first time he has come forward as a Roosevelt man. Labour leaders, who do not appreciate fine shades . . . may not see much difference between the Standard Oil and Steel Corporations; but good Republicans know better, and Mr. Carnegie is not afraid to present himself as a thick and thin supporter of controlling the trusts. To him President Roosevelt is first and foremost the leader who undertook "the serious task of regulating inter-state commerce and restricting the powers of trusts and corporations which threatened the structure of good government itself." But at the same time Mr. Roosevelt is the man who "has just stated that he would never agree to establish the right of boycott in this country, and would stand firmly for the right of the working man to be either unionist or non-unionist as he pleased, and for the rights of employers as strongly as those of labour." Everybody who knows Pittsburgh . . . is well aware that the shrewdest capitalists are quite willing to submit to severe legal restrictions if they can at the same time secure such protection as this.[67]

Such comments were typical of the British Conservative press, who would never let Carnegie forget the past. The more liberally Progressive he became, the more they liked to recall old sins, to make sure that the ghost of Homestead would haunt him forever.

The reviewer was correct in saying that Carnegie had not been "afraid to present himself as a thick and thin supporter" of

Progressive reform. He had not only championed the Square Deal's economic and political programs, but its social philosophy as well. In regard to civil rights, Carnegie, like Roosevelt, was in advance of most Americans, including the liberal president of Princeton, Woodrow Wilson, who was soon to make his entry into Progressive politics. Carnegie had always been an outspoken critic of sectarianism and religious prejudice in any form. When a philanthropic organization asked him if he would sell five acres of land he owned for a free cemetery, he replied, "You ask my price for five acres of land for a Cemetery open to all Protestants. I should be happy to present the land without price provided it were open to all who desired to rest there of every sect or of none. If you will make it free, a free resting place for every human being, Pagan, Christian or Jew, it will give me great pleasure to make the gift. We poor mortals while living our short span are far too sharply separated. Surely, we should not refuse to lie down together at last upon the bosom of mother earth." [68]

He was also a strong opponent of all efforts to limit immigration by literacy tests or by nationality preference quotas, and supported the various presidential vetoes that blocked such legislative restrictions. He wrote to President Wilson in 1915, strongly opposing a new literacy test that had just passed Congress on the ground that it was grossly unfair to millions who "have no opportunity for education in their native land." He was not pleading out of his own personal experience, he carefully pointed out, because "John Knox's law which placed a primary school in every district in Scotland and required all citizens of whatever station to educate their children, gave us education. We could read and write well. Indeed, my early letters to friends in Scotland, when fourteen, are said to be better than those of this date. . . . I would not exclude illiterates. The parents may not become intensely literary Americans, but the children will. They cannot help it; such is the Republican atmosphere." [69] Edward Steiner, himself an immigrant, who had succeeded the radical Christian Social Gospel leader, George Herron, as professor of Applied Christianity at Grinnell College, sent Carnegie a copy of his book, *On the Trail of the Immigrant,* with an accompanying note, "It had its start at the National Congress of Immigration when you were present and delivered an inspiring address. May I

971

ask you to receive the book with a feeling of gratitude for what you have been to all those who are struggling to develop and teach the American youth?" To which Carnegie replied, "I am greatly your debtor for a copy of your valuable book upon an important subject, . . . as I am deeply interested in the question of Immigration. I have done the best to keep the door wide open." [70]

Carnegie, in these years, was also interested in opening doors for another group of descendants of immigrants—those who had not come to America voluntarily, and who had found here only slavery, degradation, and the cruelest forms of man's inhumanity to man. As a young boy, just arrived in the United States, Carnegie had found slavery to be the one great, unforgivable sin of what to him was otherwise a nearly perfect democracy. He had written back to Dod in Scotland that when old enough to participate in politics he would be a Free Soil Democrat, and he first entered the Republican party at the age of twenty-one as an ardent free soil, free land, Frémont supporter. During the Civil War and Reconstruction periods, he had generally supported the Radical Republican positions on the racial equality issues of the day. But for him, as for millions of White Americans, the idealism flickered out in the 1870's, and the Republican party became a source of quite different satisfactions. The Black American, conveniently isolated in the distant South, was forgotten. There were now no dramatic escapes of fugitive slaves across the Ohio to stir the conscience of the North. *Uncle Tom's Cabin* had become largely a minstrel show, performed by White actors in blackface; no longer an anguished cry for social justice, but a charming piece of American folklore out of a dim, distant past. Grant had said "Let us have peace," and the country gratefully accepted peace after twenty years of turmoil and war. But it was White America's peace, bought with the subjugation and fear of millions of Black Americans.

Carnegie had never entirely lost interest in the Blacks. Although almost none came North to work in his steel mills or mines, he early made generous contributions to Hampton and Tuskegee Institutes, and it was through his gifts to Tuskegee that he became acquainted with Booker T. Washington. Carnegie was immediately captivated by Washington's personal charm and by

Washington's views on technical and vocational education, which were very close to his own. In 1903 Carnegie gave to the trustees of Tuskegee $600,000, and Washington became a recipient of one of Carnegie's private pensions.

To some of the more radical, new militant voices in Black America, such as that of W. E. B. DuBois, Carnegie gave but slight attention. Washington was the White liberal American's ideal of what a Black leader should be, a man who worked for slow, evolutionary progress through practical education, a leader who spoke for his race in moderate, reasonable tones, who raised no embarrassing political and social questions, yet pushed surely and persistently for the economic and educational betterment of his people. Theodore Roosevelt gave the presidential blessing by inviting Washington to lunch at the White House. Carnegie did the President one better by paying all the expenses for the Washingtons to travel to Britain and visit him at Skibo. He also served as an advance publicity man in Britain, writing to friends to help promote Washington's lecture tour. "My friend, Booker Washington, perhaps the most remarkable man living today, taking into account his birth as a slave and his position now as the acknowledged leader of his people, is coming to England," Carnegie wrote William Archer. "He could be induced to give a lecture in London and one in Edinburgh. I should think he would be a drawing card. He has recently made a triumphal tour thru the Southwestern States, being received by white and black—no hall big enough to hold his audiences." [71]

In 1907 Carnegie was paid the signal honor of being asked to deliver the opening lecture at the famed Edinburgh Philosophical Institution. After considerable deliberation, Carnegie chose as his topic, "The Negro in America," and then went to work to collect all the information he could on a subject about which he actually knew very little. He hounded Booker T. Washington and his faculty at Tuskegee, and especially H. B. Frissell, the White principal at Hampton Institute, for facts and figures about the economic and social conditions of the Blacks in the South. What he ultimately produced was a kind of Black version of *Triumphant Democracy*.[72] The same hopeful note of progress as demonstrated by statistics ran throughout the address: illiteracy among Negroes cut nearly in half in thirty years, from 83.5 per cent in 1870 to 47.4

per cent in 1900; land ownership by Negroes in South Central States: 27.2 per cent of all farms in that region by 1900; in the South Atlantic States, 30 per cent. In two states, Louisiana and Mississippi, "the negro [sic] has more farms than the white, but it must be remembered that the average size of negro farms is very much less than those of the whites." [73] The increase in the Black population was equally encouraging, a 34.3 per cent increase in twenty years. "There is no trace of decline here, but a surprisingly rapid rate of increase, one of the surest proofs of a virile race calculated to survive in the struggle for existence." [74] He pointed up the number of artists, poets, professional men, and even a few millionaires that the race had produced since Emancipation, and he noted those Blacks who had made important contributions to American society throughout its history but who had been—and still are—largely ignored by the writers of American history texts: Benjamin Banneker, the distinguished astronomer and close friend of Thomas Jefferson; J. G. Groves, the "Potato King" of Kansas; and Thomas Fortune, the New York publisher. He reserved his highest praise, of course, for Booker T. Washington, "the combined Moses and Joshua of his people. Not only has he led them to the promised land, but still lives to teach them by example and precept how properly to enjoy it. . . . History is to tell of two Washingtons, the white and the black, one the father of his country, the other the leader of his race." [75]

Like his earlier *Triumphant Democracy*, the greater part of Carnegie's address on *The Negro in America* was all "sunshine, sunshine, sunshine." Neither the distinguished Harvard graduate and Black historian W. E. B. DuBois, who two years later would organize the NAACP, nor certainly the illiterate, poverty-stricken sharecropper in Mississippi, would have recognized Carnegie's idyllic picture as his own Black America. Washington may have led Carnegie into the sunshine, but the Blacks of whatever class or background lived in the dark shadows of reality. Even Carnegie felt it necessary to conclude his address in a rather abrupt about-face, which vitiated much that he had laboriously built up:

Lest you separate, holding the view that there remains little more to be accomplisht in the negro problem, let me say that

974

all that has been done, encouraging as it undoubtedly is, yet is trifling compared with what remains to be done.

The advanced few are only the leaders of the vast multitude that are still to be stimulated to move forward. Nor are the leaders themselves, with certain exceptions, all that it is hoped they are yet to become.

When you are told of the number owning land or attending schools, or of the millions of Church members, and the amount of wealth and of land possesst by the negro, pray remember that they number ten millions, scattered over an area nearly as great as Europe.

The bright spots have been brought to your notice, but these are only small points surrounded by great areas of darkness. True, the stars are shining in the sky thru the darkness, but the sun spreading light over all has not yet arisen, altho there are not wanting convincing proofs that her morning beams begin to gild the mountain tops.[76]

Carnegie, with his abiding faith in America, could not have imagined that fifty years after his death the sun still would not have risen, or that when it was at last rising, it would come up not as he had poetically pictured it, but in Kipling fashion, "like thunder" out of the ghettoes of the North as well as the tenant farms of the South.

It is noteworthy that Carnegie should have selected this particular topic for this time and place. There were precious few instances of any White American in the first decade of the twentieth century giving any attention at all to the subject of the Negro in America. Morley, to be sure, was highly gratified by Carnegie's choice of topics for the Edinburgh Philosophical Institution. He wrote Carnegie after receiving a copy of the address, "Your negro lecture interests me greatly. As you remember, I said when I left your shores, that question struck me as the one insoluble problem for you." [77]

Carnegie's actual audience on that October night in Edinburgh was not as enthusiastic. The great majority had undoubtedly come expecting to hear a discourse on peace, or perhaps an exposition of Herbert Spencer's philosophy. They were quite unprepared for, and, in the main, totally uninterested in, the racial question in America. Lord Rosebery, who was chairman of the proceedings, was nonplussed by the speech. When he arose at the conclusion to propose the customary vote of thanks to Carnegie, he quite candidly said that he for one was unable to follow Carnegie's "maze of statistics." But in any event, he added, "I have one maxim which I believe to be a sound one, which is, 'It is wise not to offer opinions as to the internal concerns of other nations.' " [78] The *Glasgow Herald* was less noncommittal on Carnegie's address. In an editorial it accused Carnegie of having ignored "the real negro problem" that existed in "these very figures" that he had offered in such great abundance, namely, "the consequent claim of the black man to compete with the white on equal terms in everything. That problem Mr. Carnegie gaily leaves to the future, being doubtless aware that it will not become acute in *his* time." Reflecting the predictable British prejudices of a majority of Carnegie's audience, the *Herald* concluded its editorial with the dire warning that Mr. Carnegie in appealing for an end to racial antagonism should realize that "the decay of race antipathy may well mean the decay of the predominant." [79]

All in all, it was not a successful evening. Carnegie, who had worked so hard in preparing the speech and had expected so much public interest in his findings, was deeply disappointed. Washington, to be sure, wrote him immediately afterwards, praising his address to the highest and urging "that it be arranged for this speech to have a worldwide circulation. Especially ought it to be circulated widely throughout the United States." [80] Except for a small printing by an Inverness publisher, which Carnegie himself distributed to friends in Britain and America, the address did not receive a wide circulation, however. It remains the least known of all of Carnegie's writings, and, significantly, Burton J. Hendrick, who in the early 1930's brought out a multi-volume edition of every book and almost every article Carnegie ever wrote, omitted the text of *The Negro in America* from that collection. Nor is there any mention of this address in his biography of Carnegie, except as it is listed in the bibliography. Yet this text, perhaps more than anything else that Carnegie wrote or said in the Progressive era, gave to his liberalism a special distinction that could be claimed by few others at that time. However complacent and smug it may appear today, this essay pointed a finger at something

976

few White reformers in the early twentieth century cared to recognize. As for the general public, it was too busy looking at D. W. Griffith's *Birth of a Nation* even to notice.

With the departure of Theodore Roosevelt from the White House on 4 March 1909, something vital and compelling was removed from American politics. Carnegie, who had been more than a little cool to Taft's candidacy, was at that moment much too preoccupied with his hero's African tour, which would reach its momentous climax in Europe in the late spring of 1910, to give more than passing notice to the new occupant of 1600 Pennsylvania Avenue. He regarded Taft's administration as a kind of caretaker's operation, during which time the real ruler of the people would tour the capitals of Europe, establish an international league, negotiate arbitration treaties with Britain, Germany and France, and then return in triumph to the United States to reclaim the presidential power and renew his efforts for Progressive domestic reform.

This glorious dream of Carnegie's was shattered in May 1910. Roosevelt had been unable, and indeed, had no authority to exact any firm pledges for international co-operation from the Kaiser. The Wrest Park conference with British leaders had been canceled because of the death of the King. Carnegie had been deeply disappointed by this unanticipated turn of events, but he was not crushed. He immediately began all over again, in a more legal if less dramatic way, to work for international agreement through arbitration treaties which would require the signatories to submit all disputes to the World Court for adjudication. To effect this goal, he was perforce obliged to seek the favorable offices of the President, and so began his courtship of William Howard Taft, as assiduously conducted as the wooing of his predecessor had ever been. Even before Taft's inauguration, Carnegie, writing to Morley from sister Lucy's Florida island, indicated that he was making an effort to adjust to the new administration: "We return March 9th to New York. I stop over in Washington to see the new President. Can hardly expect ever to get upon quite such intimate terms as with our mutual friend, but we shall see." [81]

The adjustment proved to be much easier than Carnegie had imagined. While his attention and hopes were fixed upon Roosevelt, working his way down the Nile, there began to emanate from the White House some very sweet sounds indeed. As early as May 1909 Taft indicated that he favored the arbitration of all disputes except those that involved an "attack upon a country's honor or independence." Carnegie was most gratified. "This is a decided gain upon former formulas, all 'questions that do affect *vital interests* or honor excluded,'" he wrote Morley.[82] The "former formulas" of course had been fashioned by Roosevelt, who continued to talk about "righteousness" in connection with war. Carnegie on more than one occasion had felt it necessary to lecture Roosevelt about that. "Have just read your splendid letter to the Peace Congress," he wrote Roosevelt in 1907. "Only one point that seems to me weak. 'Righteousness' vs. Peace. Disputants are both seeking 'righteousness,' both feel themselves struggling for what is just. Who is to decide? No one. According to you, they must go to War to decide not what is 'Right' but who is Strong. Pray reflect." [83]

Then, in the spring of 1910, just as Roosevelt was arriving in Europe, Taft made the boldest and most unequivocal statement that any president since Jefferson had made for the cause of international peace. On behalf of arbitration, he said, "Personally I do not see any more reason why matters of national honor should not be referred to a Court of Arbitration than matters of property or national proprietorship. I know that is going farther than most men are willing to go, but I do not see why questions of honor may not be submitted to a tribunal composed of men of honor who understand questions of national honor, to abide by their decision as well as any other question of difference arising between nations." [84]

Carnegie was elated. He wrote Taft, "Your repeated earnest utterances in favor of International Peace entitle you to rank with Washington, whose first wish was to 'banish war, the plague of mankind, from the earth.' . . . If you only prove true to your great promise and propose to Germany and Great Britain at first (other invitations to follow) that they confer confidentially with our country, basing this suggestion upon their repeated declarations that their earnest desire is International Peace, I believe you will succeed, . . . and when peace is established, as it finally must be, you would be as clearly the father of Peace on Earth as Washington is father of his country or Lincoln its preserver . . .

My dear Mr. President, compare this world-wide cause in its scope and mission divine with any hitherto accomplished by man. I say all others sink into insignificance, yes, even those of Washington and Lincoln." [85]

Carnegie needed only to compare Taft's speech on behalf of arbitration to Roosevelt's disturbing pronouncements at the Sorbonne to make him wonder if he had not spent his money to send the wrong emissary to Europe. "I notice in your speech at the Sorbonne," he wrote rather stiffly to Roosevelt, "you speak of 'righteous wars.' I am sure that upon serious reflection you will no longer be satisfied to send disputes between nations to war for adjustment, the crime of war being inherent. . . . It has no regard for 'righteous.' Every citizen in a civilized community is under the reign of law compelled to submit his wrongs to the law for redress. He is not allowed to go to war with his adversary, for either of them mite shoot the other without the slightest reference to 'righteous judgment.' Ponder over this. You have a conscience. Ask yourself the question 'Is crime inherent in war for the reason given?' As for the question of honor, no man ever dishonored another since history began. No nation ever has, nor can, dishonor another nation—'all honor's wounds are self-inflicted.' As President Taft suggests, however, a Court of Honor should determine whether one nation proposed the 'dishonor' of another, and if so disallow it. . . . The whole matter is so simple, my dear Mr. Roosevelt—Germany, Britain and America coming together and agreeing to form a joint police force to maintain peace is all that is needed. . . . It is not treating the Emperor fairly unless you deal openly and frankly with him; the same with Britain; you will find her ready to listen and even glad to hear you as the larger half of the race is not a negligible quantity." [86]

There must have been times when Roosevelt felt that he was paying a very high rate of interest for his safari funds. As for Carnegie, his doubts about Roosevelt continued to grow, even before the unexpected turn of events that dashed all chances of Roosevelt's securing any international agreement. "Had a long letter from T. R.," Carnegie wrote Ambassador Hill in Berlin. "He doesn't come out so boldly as the President, didn't expect him to do so for there's a trace of the savage in that original compound, but he will develop and become civilized by and by." [87]

Taft, however, continued to show how really civilized he was.

Soon he could do nothing wrong in Carnegie's eyes, even though, through political ineptitude, he was rendering ineffective Roosevelt's domestic program that Carnegie had enthusiastically supported. First there was the disaster of the tariff revision. Carnegie may have carried the day at Congressman Payne's committee hearings, but Payne won the war. The resulting Payne-Aldrich Tariff was all Payne and Aldrich and precious little reform. It was bad enough that Taft, who had been pledged to a lower tariff, should have signed the bill, but it was quite inexcusable for him to say in a public statement a few days later that it was the best tariff ever enacted by the Republican party. Inexcusable, that is, to almost all reformers except Carnegie. He dismissed it all as being but a natural error due to inexperience.[88] And by the time of the unfortunate Ballinger-Pinchot fiasco in the Interior Department, when Taft stuck gamely by his Secretary of Interior, Richard A. Ballinger, and thus appeared to be sanctioning the sabotage of Roosevelt's cherished conservation program, Carnegie was so preoccupied with arbitration treaties that he ignored the whole affair.

Taft's expressed willingness to submit all international differences to arbitration, including questions of national honor, was more than enough encouragement for Carnegie to push for his favorite solution for the abolition of war—a series of mutual arbitration treaties among the great powers. He dashed into print with an article in *Century Magazine,* "Peace Versus War: The President's Solution." With lavish public praise, he sought to bind the President irrevocably to what in fact had been a personal expression rather than a public commitment.[89] For the next two years, Carnegie gave little attention to any other public issue than that of the treaties. In his efforts he had powerful support on both sides of the Atlantic: Lord James Bryce, who was now Britain's Ambassador to the United States; Morley, once again in the British Cabinet as Secretary of State for India; and, not least important, Taft, whose enthusiasm for the whole idea continued to grow.

Carnegie did not, however, have any support from his former hero, Theodore Roosevelt, who, upon his return to America in the summer of 1910, was greeted by the anguished jeremiads of former members and friends of his administration, accusing his successor of having joined hands with the enemies of Progressive reform. Roosevelt was by nature suspicious of pious international agreements, which in his opinion were unenforceable. The way to win international respect and to keep the dogs of war securely leashed, he believed, was not by statesmen in striped pants signing solemn pacts, but by admirals in Great White Fleets sailing in full panoply past the Japanese islands. That Taft should now be neglecting important domestic problems while at the same time giving the proposed treaties with Great Britain, France, and Germany his full support hardly made Roosevelt less disposed to be suspicious of the whole arbitration project.

In the meantime, Congress had passed a bill authorizing the President to establish a Peace Commission to study the possibility of establishing an international naval force, drawn from the great naval powers of the world, to preserve peace on the high seas. Carnegie saw this as a possibly significant step in the direction of the ultimate creation of an international league of peace, an indispensable part of his dream for a new world order. He promptly sent off to Taft his suggestions as to who should be named to the commission: Joseph Choate, Alton Parker, Nicholas Murray Butler, John Bassett Moore, Seth Low, Charles Eliot, Richard Bartholdt, and Lyman Abbott.[90] How excruciatingly painful modesty was! For he would, of course, have been delighted to have Taft name him to the commission. Taft, however, still laboring under the illusion that "friend Theodore" was his close mentor and patron, had quite different ideas. In one of the last private conferences the two men would have, Taft asked Roosevelt to be chairman of the Commission. Roosevelt dismissed the idea out of hand. Indeed, about the only thing the two men agreed upon during that hot July meeting together was that Carnegie should not be named to the Commission. As Taft later reported to his Secretary of State, Philander Knox, "There is a suggestion of Carnegie, but Mr. Roosevelt and I both agreed, in discussing it, that he might be a hard man to be responsible for because he talked so much." [91]

Although most certainly disappointed by Taft's failure to appoint him to the commission, Carnegie's *amour propre* suffered no deep wound, for he considered the proposed arbitration treaties a much more practical first step toward world peace than any study commission that had such a long-range goal as an international police force as its objective. And on the subject of the treaties, no one could keep him quiet or push him out of the limelight. His easy access to men like Edward Grey, Prime Minister Asquith, and the German Ambassador to the United States, Count Johann von Bernstorff, made him a commission unto himself.

Work on these men he did, by numerous letters to Grey and frequent conferences in Washington with Bryce and Bernstorff—and whenever he could, with the President and the Secretary of State. Taft was far more amenable to the whole project than was his Secretary of State. Relations between Knox and Carnegie had not been exactly cordial since the Frick affair of a decade earlier, when Knox, as one of the chief legal counsels for the company, had refused his services to Carnegie against Frick's suit. They had not greatly improved after Knox became an important government official, first as Attorney General under McKinley, then as successor to Matthew Quay, as Senator from Pennsylvania, and most recently as Taft's Secretary of State. Knox was the dominant member of the Cabinet; indeed there were many insiders in Washington who felt that he had picked the rest of the Cabinet for Taft, and that the somewhat indolent President was not averse to having Knox largely direct the whole administration. While these rumors were undoubtedly exaggerated, nevertheless it could not be denied that Knox was a very powerful force in an otherwise weak administration, and, as Secretary of State, he was not simply a department head, subordinate to the President, but a true Minister of Foreign Affairs in the traditional manner of a British Cabinet member. Carnegie sensed this situation and did his best to win Knox's favor with flattery, while he offered the Secretary what Carnegie regarded as sage advice on how to direct the nation's foreign policy. Carnegie's efforts, however, were worse than useless, for Knox was an old hand by now in Washington and had no difficulty in seeing through Carnegie's never very subtle flattery. Carnegie became, in Knox's eyes, the most notorious of all those Court hangers-on whom he referred to in private conversations with the President as "the Princes of Humbug." [92] Nor did Knox appreciate Carnegie's gratuitous and constant advice. Carnegie was precisely that kind of correspondent that Knox found most difficult to bear—too important to dismiss, too insistent to ignore, too sententious to endure. But Carnegie was far too engrossed in pursuing what he regarded as the most important objective in the history of man, world peace, to be sensitive to Knox's true feelings.

As the negotiations between Britain and the United States for an arbitration treaty entered their most delicate stage, Knox's attitude toward Carnegie's incessant talking and letter-writing changed from irritation to fear; Carnegie, by his tactics, might defeat the very proposal that he himself most desperately sought to effect. Knox therefore wrote to Carnegie: "The Government of the United States feels, as it has reason to believe the British Government does also, that any premature or exaggerated public discussion of this question might perhaps have the effect of disturbing the deliberate study which the two Governments would naturally be compelled to give so important and so difficult a question as that of the possibility of an unlimited arbitration treaty between the Governments of the two English speaking peoples—a question which, I may add, has not yet passed incipient pourparlers between the two Governments." [93] One could hardly be more pointed than that, but Knox might just as well have hoped to quench Vesuvius with a dash of cold water as to repress Carnegie with a coldly formal note of caution.

The letters continued to flow and Carnegie's hopes continued to rise. By the late spring of 1911 it appeared that not only would there be a treaty of arbitration negotiated with Great Britain, but also one with France. Carnegie wrote to Knox in great elation, "Well you have it & the Republic of France to make a glorious trinity. What a hit. Must strengthen you in the Senate & check our bogus Irish-German discontents. . . . Hope Bryce will ask his Govt. if satisfactory to wire & let you present to Senate. I imagine you, pen in hand, signing the greatest document in its influence upon the world ever signed. Your *piloting* superb. I am rejoicing that I live in these days." [94]

Carnegie was doing a considerable part of the piloting on his own. To keep the treaties from becoming a politically partisan issue, he sent off letters to William Jennings Bryan, Governor Samuel Baldwin of Connecticut, Champ Clark, the Speaker of the House of Representatives, Governor Eugene Foss of Massachusetts, and Governor Woodrow Wilson of New Jersey, asking for their support. He received strong letters of endorsement from all of them.[95] Then came the most exciting and significant support of all—and all the more gratifying because it was totally unsolicited. Carnegie received a confidential message from Charles Hilles, Taft's personal secretary, that the Papal delegation in Washington had been informed that the Pope would shortly issue an autographed brief in support of the President's efforts for world peace. Hilles wrote: "It will be the duty of each priest to read this in public. I understand that the brief praises the President for his part in this stroke of statesmanship, and commends you for the interest you have taken in the cause, and the substantial aid you have rendered it." [96] Carnegie was in a transport of joy, for he knew how important the Pope's support would be in winning over or at least silencng the Irish-American opposition to any British-American pact.

At the same time, Carnegie received word that at last the draft of the treaty of arbitration had been completed and had been submitted to Ambassador Bryce of Britain and Ambassador Jusserand of France for transmittal to their governments.[97] Everything, with a rush, seemed to be going Carnegie's way. He dashed off a telegram to Morley, "Shake friend Morley, Shake. I am the happiest mortal alive. Couldn't call snakes snake this morning if naming created things." Carnegie's expression of elation completely baffled his friend. "I think my heavy labours must be turning my brain, for I cannot for the life of me quite satisfactorily interpret the enclosed wire. It was brought to me when I was hailed to the bench of the H. of L., and I've been puzzling ever since to read the words of the oracle. Do tell me. Am I wrong in supposing that it means cordial approbation? I don't believe I am. Or has it a bearing on some good news from U.S.A.? Anyhow, you would not have sent it if you had not been in tearing good spirits, and thereat I rejoice, and will rejoice." [98]

Carnegie hastened to explain to the bewildered Morley, "Sorry my telegram not understood—thot you knew the celebrated American who being elected declared he felt so happy that he couldn't libel snakes by calling them by their real name. I had just heard that the Race—our race had agreed to banish war— the greatest step upward ever taken by any race since history began. . . . Other nations will soon follow." [99]

The only discordant note during this harmonious spring was

that struck by Theodore Roosevelt. Just as the treaty draft was being completed, Roosevelt had an article published in *Outlook,* blasting Taft's willingness to arbitrate "questions of honor." [100] "The savage" in the former President was far from being civilized. This article, of course, snapped one more strand of the cord that had once bound Taft and Roosevelt together in close friendship. Neither was quite yet ready to say that the break was complete. Taft wrote to Carnegie after Roosevelt's article had appeared, "I am sorry that Theodore thought it necessary to come out in advance of a definite knowledge of what we are planning to do, but I venture to think that what he says is so much aside from the real point that both he and the public will see it, and that it will not interfere with the consummation of what you and I both desire." [101] Roosevelt himself wrote what he hoped would be a placating note to Carnegie, "You know that one reason why I hesitated long before writing that article was just because I hated to do anything that might seem distasteful to you. I finally came to the conclusion that it would be weakness on my part not to write it. . . . If it had not been for the very unfortunate statement that we would arbitrate questions of honor, I do not think any trouble would have come about the treaty at all." [102]

This was sheer hypocrisy on Roosevelt's part. He did not in the least mind doing something that would be distasteful to Carnegie, for in his letters to his close friends, Lodge and Arthur Hamilton Lee, he was quite frank in expressing his real feelings toward Carnegie: "All the male shrieking sisterhood of Carnegies and the like are quite powerless"; and "the professional apostles of peace, like Carnegie, are both noxious and ridiculous." Yet, interestingly enough, Roosevelt's chief objection to the great dream of his former benefactor was that these treaties "would mean hypocrisy, and hypocrisy is not nice . . . the whole business is tainted by that noxious form of silliness which always accompanies the sentimental refusal to look facts in the face. The sentimentalist, by the way, is by no means always a decent creature to deal with; if Andrew Carnegie had employed his fortune and time in doing justice to the steelworkers who gave him his fortune, he would have accomplished a thousand times what he has accomplished or ever can accomplish in connection with international peace." [103]

But no opposition from Roosevelt could depress Carnegie's

high spirits in these days of apparent success. Now that victory was so close, it became increasingly difficult for Carnegie to be patient while the final details were agreed upon by Knox, Bryce, and Jusserand. At least Carnegie could await developments in the delightfully cool and sunny Scotland, while Bryce had to suffer through the heat of Washington mid-summer. "You have been expecting to hear before now of the progress of the General Arbitration Treaty," Bryce reported to Carnegie in late June. "It has been very slow; you know the causes to which that is due both in Washington & in England. I had hoped that the matter would have been settled before the Senate last month and now we must stay on in this furnace of a city for we know not how much longer." [104] Edward Grey seemed also to be having difficulty with the treaty draft on his side of the Atlantic. Carnegie had written him complaining of the delay and he responded, "I could not deal with the American draft of the Arbitration Treaty as a purely Departmental matter, and the Imperial Conference has taken up so much of our time that it has been difficult to discuss together matters of importance not relating to the Conference. But we are now ready to go ahead, and I shall make the important communications by cable, to prevent any loss of time." [105]

Bryce's great worry, however, was not of differences between the British and American drafts, which were minor and could be reconciled, even if such a process was regrettably time-consuming. Rather he feared what the fate of the treaty might be when it came before the Senate for approval. "There is really very little between us & as the President is genuinely wishful to put the thing through now, this session we hope this may be achieved. The political situation in the Senate is so odd, & unprecedented, that one fears to prophesy, but I don't see why they should refuse the Treaty; it doesn't infringe what they think is their prerogative. In all our discussions over the wording of the Treaty, Knox has been very fair and reasonable; he is genuinely wishful that the thing should be done & done well." [106]

Carnegie himself was not unmindful of the potential danger that confronted this treaty, which, like all treaties, had to be ratified by the Senate with a two-thirds majority. As early as January, he had warned Knox that the "Senate's rights must be respected." [107] But Carnegie, who always had had a respect that approached the reverential for what he regarded as "the world's greatest deliberative body," could not agree with Bryce that the Senate too often acted out of "various personal motives, some of them not elevated." [108] Carnegie felt that the Senate was quite justified in zealously guarding its prerogatives, and he for one was willing to make all reasonable compromises and revisions necessary in order to get the treaty approved.

What was to follow was a repetition of that which befell the Roosevelt arbitration treaties of a few years before—the only difference being that this time Roosevelt was in the opposition and could command the powerful voice of Senator Lodge as his spokesman in the Senate. In early August the general arbitration treaties were signed by Great Britain and France and were submitted to the United States Senate for ratification. Carnegie was extravagant in his praise for Taft in his cabled congratulatory message to the President, and Taft responded, "I thank you from the bottom of my heart not only for what you have been good enough to say in this cable but for your constant and unvarying encouragement and support from the beginning of the negotiations and even before. The treaties are now before the Senate and I am hopeful that they will be ratified there; if not in the few remaining days of this session, then early in the regular session." [109]

Events, however, were quickly to prove how illusory Taft's hopes were. Almost immediately the treaties ran into difficulties in the Senate Foreign Relations Committee. The most serious objection was that raised over the third paragraph of Article III of the treaties, which provided that a Commission established by the signatory nations would determine whether a particular issue that had been raised between two of the nations fell within the scope of the treaty. If the Commission ruled that it did, that question would have to be submitted to arbitration. Immediately Lodge, Roosevelt, and Mahan, the most outspoken critics of the treaties, raised a hue and cry. The Commission could possibly be composed of "all foreigners," questions that involved the nation's honor and territorial integrity could be summarily ordered to an International Court of Arbitration, the Monroe Doctrine would be destroyed, questions involving the immigration of Orientals into the United States would be decided not by Congress but by an international court—the number of bogies that these imagina-

987

tive patriots could conjure up were numberless, and the Senate
was an easily frightened body.[110]

Carnegie, then at Skibo, optimistically had arranged with
Elihu Root that he should send the single cabled word, "Slumber," when the Senate Foreign Relations Committee was ready to
give its approval and report the treaties out of committee for
Senate action. In late August, Root was forced to write, "I cannot
telegraph 'Slumber' much to my regret because the arbitration
treaties meet with opposition in the Senate which has not yet
been disposed of. . . . The trouble could have been averted easily if some of the Senate had been consulted before the treaty
was signed; but now the Foreign Relations committee has reported for the treaty with the clause giving power to the committee [commission] stricken out and except as amended the treaty
would not get even a majority vote unless there be change." [111]

Carnegie, plunged into sudden and unexpected despair, wrote
to Bryce, "The result has been a surprise to me. I had always been
assured the Senate committee would be consulted as the various
points touching its perogatives [sic] were formed, & its counsels
duly considered. . . . The disappointment is too great to cause
annoyance, or wrath. It falls like a heavy dull load of disaster
which we must slowly surmount. It is a serious struggle to get two
thirds majority from a body that changes so slowly. I hope some
compromise can be reached. Taft's reelection, however, seems so
certain by an overwhelming majority that he may win without
changing form of treaty, but it seems more probable to me that
some change can be arranged without sacrificing much. The proposed Commission mite be made by President subject approval of
Senate—or by Senate subject President's approval. There is so
much at stake that we should not stand on forms." [112]

Root had written Carnegie that the Senate's failure to ratify the
treaty without serious amendment was not the fault of the Senate.
"Someone has blundered" in failing to keep the Senate fully informed, was Root's considered judgment. Carnegie heartily concurred in this assessment, and he had no difficulty in identifying
the "someone" to whom Root referred. It certainly was not Taft.
In Carnegie's eyes Taft in those days could do no wrong, and
in spite of the obviously growing schism within the Republican

ranks, Carnegie could "see nothing but triumphant victory for our President who as you know well deserves his second term. I have known six Presidents," he wrote Bryce, "the last not the least intimately, and Taft, take him all in all, is really the finest of them all." [113]

Carnegie needed only to compare the activities of Taft on behalf of the treaties with those of Knox to know who was the hero and who the insensitive and uncaring blunderer in the piece. The usually lethargic Taft was expending unprecedented energy and time in supporting the treaties, giving speeches in cities throughout the East and Middle West. Even Bryce, whom Carnegie regarded as unduly pessimistic about the President's chances for re-election, had to admit that "Taft's speeches have been excellent on the subject." [114] In contrast, Knox was so adamant in refusing to consider Senate amendments as to suggest that he did not really want the treaties to succeed. "I have . . . hoped Secy Knox could find *one day* for the treaty very soon . . . a couple of paragraphs [added to the treaty] would suffice," Carnegie complained to Bryce. "Perhaps you can run across Sec'y Knox and refer casually to the matter." [115]

Carnegie himself took to the stump to plead for the treaties. He appeared at a huge rally at Carnegie Hall on 12 December along with Henry Watterson, the *Louisville Courier-Journal* editor, who, quite surprisingly, in view of his usual militant views on foreign policy, was now giving speeches throughout the country in favor of arbitration. The Carnegie Hall meeting proved to be a rather boisterous affair. Although both Carnegie and Watterson were at their oratorical best, they were frequently drowned out by raucous cries from the balconies, which Under Secretary of State Francis Loomis, in writing to Carnegie to apologize for the disturbances, said was "largely the work of ignorant Irish Americans." [116]

Carnegie himself was not particularly disturbed by the affair, for the great majority of the audience had been enthusiastic in their applause and cheers, and Watterson assured him that such was the case throughout the country: "You may be interested to know that my recent meetings in swinging around the circle were immensely successful and very far beyond what I had myself expected. The meetings at St. Louis, Kansas City, Atlanta and Richmond, Va. were especially so, monsters in their way. I make no doubt of the ultimate ratifications of the treaties. . . ." [117]

Taft, who was searching desperately for a popular issue to offset the growing boom within the party for Roosevelt's nomination, was greatly impressed with these "monster" rallies and apparent popular clamor. Peace through arbitration might well provide just the issue that Taft needed to convince the politicians, who were then selecting delegates to the national convention, that he was the people's favorite. "I propose to ask the Republican National Convention to adopt a resolution endorsing them [the treaties] and recommending them for ratification, as a part of the party platform," he wrote Carnegie in March, after Roosevelt had declared that he was a candidate for the nomination. "The people of the country have manifested a very general and unusual degree of interest in these treaties and I believe that the preponderance of public sentiment is overwhelmingly in their favor. . . . If we get them made a part of our party's creed, I believe we shall have very little difficulty in getting them through the Senate in their original form." [118]

Although Carnegie was more than pleased with this suggestion, he was not happy by the phrase "original form," which indicated that Taft, like Knox, was adamant against any compromise with the Senate. He wrote a long, earnest letter pleading with Taft to accept the treaty amendments proposed by the Senate. "I hope that you will accept the situation. The Senate's rite under the Constitution cannot be impaired as they know well." [119] Carnegie's arguments had no effect. Taft had become convinced that if he should yield to Senate pressure for amendments, he would then lose the other signatories to the treaty. "I have a letter from Bryce," Taft wrote Carnegie, "in which he suggests that no amendments as to the treaties would be acceptable. He says, 'My government do not at all like the "Root resolution"; and Jusserand tells me that he said the same to you as the view of his Government.' I think it wise for us to go for the full treaties as they are. We can get them by a majority vote, and I am hopeful that we will have a majority. Don't let us give up in advance." [120]

Taft's tactics were now clear—to win the nomination and re-election to a second term, and with that election as a mandate from the people, force the Senate to accept the treaties as they had been negotiated. With some misgivings, Carnegie yielded to the Taft-Knox line. He wrote Morley, "The Treaty agreed upon is much better than expected, not a word changed. . . . President is satisfied. Root & I spent an evening with him in Washington recently no one else present & we 'shook hands.' " [121] Nevertheless, as he told both Morley and Edward Grey, Carnegie felt that the Senate was justified in insisting that it must keep its Constitutional right of approving of all treaties that might emerge out of any future arbitration.[122]

By April it was clear that there could be no ratification of the treaties until after the election. Depending upon the results of that contest, either the President would force the Senate to accept the treaties without change, or the people would have forced a change in the Presidency. The important thing now was to get Taft re-elected, and for the duration of the political battle Carnegie was willing to put aside any differences he might have with Taft and Knox on the form of the treaties. Carnegie had no illusion about the difficulty Taft faced in seeking a second term. He must have found it particularly galling to recall that he had once fondly dreamed that Roosevelt, after a short interim, would return in glory to the White House. But the script had turned out to be quite different from his dream. Roosevelt was not the hero, but the villain, usurping power that rightfully belonged to another. Carnegie expressed his vexation to Morley, "I am mourning over the pitiable disagreement between Roosevelt & Taft. . . . Roosevelt wrong in not agreeing second term for President who has done so well—Roosevelt & Niagara. Quite true. Both uncontrollable." [123]

Carnegie was under the illusion, however, that he still had some influence upon Roosevelt and that he might succeed in getting a personal arbitration treaty between Taft and Roosevelt. He wrote a long letter to the latter a few days after Roosevelt had declared his candidacy for the Republican nomination in 1912:

My dear Friend:
  When we last talked at Oyster Bay your position was right—although you had no expectation of being called to the Presidency you could not pledge yourself not to perform any public

duty you might be called upon to undertake. Sound dictum this. So you remained until the other day when you changed and became an aspirant against the second term due the President. . . . Four years more given President Taft, your protege, would have made all the difference and then your protege would have rejoiced to play the part you did for him by exerting all his influence for his dearest friend, completing an idyll unequalled in history. All this I have pleased myself in dreaming, never for a moment believing you would discard your impregnable position.

To see you and your protege now rivals, each strongly for the nomination overwhelms me—both men to whom I have become deeply attached for their virtues. Every panegyric you paid President Taft I know he has deserved. Every word he has spoken to me of you has shown intense devotion. "Whatever he may say or do can never destroy my gratitude and affection for him. I know what I owe him; I owe the presidency to him and this I can never forget." These were his words when I told him of our interview. Two men who should have remained as twin brothers and passed as such into history—a glorious idyll. . . . Now history is to record the failure of this idyll; the two heroes at variance, stabbing each other and blasted hopes of the friends of both alone remain—"What fools these mortals be."

. . . What a service would that man render who could induce you and the president to meet face to face and just let your hearts speak. It is not too late. You are both big enough to discard mean petty trifles and renew your idyllic relations before history records you as false or worse. . . . Do remember me to your *dear perfect* wife. . . . Listen to her in this matter. Remember the terrible load your protege is carrying, a sick wife, incurable I fear, the greatest of all misfortunes.[124]

It is difficult to imagine an emissary from the Taft camp less likely to be successful in a quest of reconciliation than Carnegie would be. Every word in his letter smacked of precisely that kind of sentimental bathos that Roosevelt found repugnant and typical of that "shrieking male sisterhood" to which he had assigned Carnegie. Roosevelt's answer, while civil, was blunt and direct:

I thank you for your kind letter. You are, however, mistaken when you say I have changed. I have not changed. My reply to the Governors [Roosevelt's letter of 24 February sent to the governors of seven states, accepting their invitation to be a candidate] was precisely what I had said in private to you and everyone else, namely that if called upon to undertake a duty to the people, I would undertake it. . . .

You oblige me to speak frankly by what you say about Mr. Taft—I would not say this for publication. I have never been so bitterly disappointed in any man. I care not one whit as to his attitude toward me. But I care immensely as to his attitude toward the people. He has completely reversed the position he held when he was my lieutenant. Everything I said of Taft as a member of the Cabinet and Governor of the Philippines was deserved. I have not reversed my position. He has reversed his. . . . He has not a chance of being nominated if he relies merely on the people. His sole chance, and an excellent one, lies in having the wish of the people thwarted by the activity of the Federal officeholders under him, by the unscrupulous use of patronage and by the successful efforts of his and my former foes, his present allies—Penrose, Crane, McKinley, Aldrich, Barnes and all the other bosses to whom he seems to have surrendered himself. That Mr. Taft should feel grateful because I put him in the presidency and should so express himself to you is of very little consequence; but it is of great consequence that his deeds should falsify his words. . . .[125]

The battered emissary, after this blast, crawled back to the Taft camp. "No more of this," Carnegie, in retreat, wrote in reply to Roosevelt. "It will work out somehow. The republic is invulnerable." [126]

The republic, perhaps, but not the Republican party. Events worked out much as Roosevelt had said they might. Taft had the support of the party machinery, if not the people, and without great difficulty won the nomination on the first ballot in Chicago. But it was the sort of victory that King Pyrrhus could have appreciated. Taft had the official and worthless title of nominee of his party. Roosevelt had his bitter dreams of revenge. And Wilson, who emerged the victor after a long and gruelling contest for the Democratic nomination at Baltimore, had all the smiles that go with the faint but unmistakable scent of victory.

The election results were virtually a foregone conclusion as soon as the final gavel had sounded at the Republican convention in June, and Roosevelt and his dissident Progressives stormed out of Chicago to "battle for the Lord." Actually, they were battling for the Democrats, as Roosevelt himself candidly admitted when he decided to break with the G.O.P. and head the newly formed Progressive party. "In strict confidence," Roosevelt wrote to William Dudley Foulke, president of the National Municipal League and a former civil service commissioner in his administration, "my feeling is that the Democrats will probably win if they nominate a progressive. But of course there is no use of my getting into a fight in a halfhearted fashion and I could not expect Republicans to follow me out if they were merely to endorse the Democratic Convention. So I hoisted the flag and will win or fall under it." [127] He fell, but in true Rooseveltian style, with a gloriously resounding crash. And he had the satisfaction of crushing the hapless Taft in the ruins.

Carnegie tried to keep up a brave front throughout the campaigns for Taft's nomination and for his election. "Roosevelt grieves me deeply but a Niagara will swell and overflow its banks," he wrote Morley. "President Taft behaves as a gentleman should & is rapidly gaining. . . . *Cheer up,* cheer up. No use looking on the dark side of things. . . . All's rite with the world or will be later. She's on the upward path, by the law of things can't go backward tho it may have a jolt or two now & then." [128] Never had Carnegie whistled a braver tune in a gloomier political graveyard. That tune was particularly appreciated at Taft headquarters, for it was accompanied by the sweet ring of hard cash—$100,000, to be exact, the largest contribution that Carnegie ever made to a presidential candidate, with the possible exception of that given to McKinley in 1896.[129]

For Carnegie, Taft's humiliating defeat in November was in part mitigated by the fact that Roosevelt was also soundly beaten. But this balm could not soothe the deep pain of having lost the arbitration treaties upon which Carnegie had pinned his hopes for a better world. Bryce resigned as the British Ambassador to the United States a week after the election, and Carnegie wrote to him in sorrow, "I hoped your crowning glory was to be The Treaty, which was lost by poor management, nothing else. It will come some day." [130] Bryce agreed with Carnegie's assessment. "As you say, the Treaty was lost for want of promptitude & management. But we mustn't say that except to each other. It grieved me sorely as it grieved you. How often do great enterprises fail for the want of a little tact or a little energy at the right moment." [131]

Bryce's advice to Carnegie, that they should keep their thoughts about the failure of the treaties to themselves, was a piece of caution which Carnegie would not heed. In those gloomy days following Taft's defeat, the more Carnegie thought of the lost opportunity the angrier he became. On 15 December, he wrote the lame duck President a long scolding letter:

> Why did you fail? The answer given by Republicans and Democrats alike was you failed to remember that the Constitution gives the Senate the right not only to consider and approve or reject, but also to advise. With Japan Treaty you invited the Committee on Foreign Relations to dine with you and so prompt was their response to your wishes the new treaty was law in a few days. You told me this policy was to be adopted re arbitration. When I learnt in Scotland the treaty had been sent to the Senate duly signed I concluded you had submitted it to the Senate Committee and cabled you my joy. I lived for days in a happier world. . . . Believe me, failure to consult the Senate Committee was the *fatal* mistake; keeping leading Senators ignorant of your presuming to make a treaty which they read for the first time to their surprise in the morning papers. Whether it be Root, Crane, or O'Gorman or others, I found them unanimous upon this point. The President is necessarily overwhelmed with business and is to be pardoned, but Secretary Knox knowing the success of the Japan Treaty example might have suggested following it and obtained your cordial assent and all would have been well. All this is past and past forever. Another is no doubt to take up the task some day. . . . [132]

Taft, who had staked his political future on those treaties, could not have read this bit of gratuitous, *ex post facto* advice with good grace. He scribbled at the top of Carnegie's letter instructions to his secretary, "Refer to Sec. Knox. Isn't it pleasant to be told how it could have been done. WHT."

For some inexplicable reason, this letter did not come to Knox's attention until he was cleaning up his papers on the day before he was to leave office as Secretary of State. Upon reading the three-month-old letter, he exploded in fury. This was for him the final, insufferable bit of "I-told-you-so" pomposity that he would take from his former business associate. He wrote in white heat to the President: [133]

As an exhibition of ignorance, mendacity and impudence, this communication of Mr. Carnegie's is quite up to his well known and well deserved international reputation for these mental and moral failings. It should be appropriately tagged and filed and given no further attention. His statement that we did not consult leading Senators about the peace treaties is untrue. His statement that the Senators knew nothing of the treaties until they had been negotiated and appeared in the morning papers is untrue. His quotations of what Senators have said upon the subject are untrue. His characterization of your making a treaty without consulting the Senators as presumption upon your part is an exhibition of pitiable ignorance and a piece of colossal impudence.

The facts are that even in Great Britain, a quarter in which Carnegie renders the obsequious service he demands from his pensioners and near pensioners at home, the openness and frankness of the negotiations of the peace treaties and the publicity given at every stage of the proceedings . . . moved the London Times to state editorially on August 4, 1911, the day after they were signed, that "the tenor of the treaties has been so well known for a long time past as to make a detailed consideration of their provisions unnecessary."

When Carnegie's epitaph is honestly written, its author may well use the monkish rhyme:

"Mel in ore, verba lactis
Fel in corde, fraus in factis."

And so the four year Taft-Carnegie romance ended in bitterness and reciprocal recriminations. Carnegie, however, could not long endure bitter hopelessness, nor live without a hero. Providentially, there was a new hero already on the scene. Two days after the election, Carnegie was writing to him. "Having done my best to elect President Taft to the second term I now find myself impelled to congratulate you upon your election to the hiest office upon the earth—the elected ruler of the majority of the English speaking race. My second choice. My friends for International Peace have not forgotten your reply to my circular letter addrest to seven leading Democrats, yourself among the number; all of whom rose above partisanship to Statesmanship when a great issue presented itself. Britian, France, *Germany* stood ready to sign the treaty but alas, it miscarried. Some day I hope to be permitted to tell you why it miscarried. What the fates have in store for you is unknown. Perhaps you are destined to succeed in banishing war between the most enlitened nations where President Taft failed. . . . I am sincerely your admirer and cannot help it." [134]

President-elect Wilson's response to this congratulatory letter was most gratifying: "I note with the greatest interest what you say about the effort to get a definite foundation of treaty of the international peace for which we are all striving, and I need not tell you again what my own sympathies and feelings are in the matter. I shall always be on that side." [135] Carnegie by this time could write Morley about the election with no regrets. "The election has not surprised many—Roosevelt's power for mischief is unlimited. . . . Have written Wilson, of course, a nice letter. You knew he is on the board University Professor's Trust, & has been at Skibo with his wife. *He is for Peace* & will I think manage better than Taft who really failed in Treaty thru poor management." [136] With this judgment Morley was in hearty accord: "I confess that I was not sorry *your* election went as it did. Mr. Taft is a fine fellow, but he had no giant in the State Department, and he is himself—if a foreigner has any right to judge—not quite the man to 'wield your fierce democracy.' Still, whatever Mr. Wilson may turn out, it is a comfort that *Theodore* has had a check. I fear your pungent sentence is only too true, that 'his power for mischief is unlimited.' Well, though America has plenty of qualities that one might wish otherwise, . . . I retain a mighty confidence in her shrewd political instincts." [137]

All in all it seemed to Carnegie that as usual things had turned out quite for the best. He gave short shrift to the chairman of the Republican State Committee who came to him, hat in hand, for another $10,000 to help keep the Republican state headquarters open after the huge deficits resulting from the disastrous campaign. Carnegie had his secretary answer curtly, "Mr. Carnegie . . . asks me to say that he has not recovered from the effects of the campaign and must have a rest for a time before considering anything of the nature you suggest." [138] Carnegie's interest in the Grand Old Party was at lowest ebb ever, for the Wilson administration gave every promise of being the new wave of the future. Here was the scholar in politics, an occidental version of the Chinese mandarin concept that had enchanted Carnegie when he had visited China many years before. There was, moreover, evidence of a renewal of the *élan vital* that had made the Roosevelt era exciting. The reforming zeal of Progressivism had not been killed during the Taft administration; it had not even slept very easily. And now it was fully awake and stirring again.

Carnegie had not given much attention to domestic affairs during the past four years, so preoccupied had he been with the fight for arbitration. It is perhaps symbolic of his relations with the Taft administration that his only public appearance on a major domestic issue had been as a witness in 1912 before the so-called Stanley Committee in the House of Representatives, which was investigating the United States Steel Corporation as a trust. Once again, Carnegie was the star of a Congressional Committee show. After two days of testimony, the wife of Representative Jack Beall of Texas told Carnegie that he was "the foxiest old man I ever heard and you have more brains than all the members of the Committee put together." Henry Watterson, a fellow Kentuckian and friend of Chairman A. O. Stanley, wrote to Carnegie to congratulate him on his performance. "I long ago told Stanley he would catch a tartar when he caught you; and I guess by this time he too thinks so." [139] Carnegie was up to all of his old tricks, remembering whatever it was to his advantage to remember, conveniently forgetting or playing innocent when the questions became too personal or embarrassing for him to deal with, and doing it all with humor and charm. To the delight of the press, he once again showed how a witness could be an effective foil to the most penetrating thrusts of the Congressional investigator. But it was a quite different situation from his last Congressional appearance three years before. Stanley belonged to the new politics of Progressivism, not to the old stand-patism of Sereno Payne, and Carnegie was perforce obliged to play the Conservative role, to recall the days when he was demanding special rates from the railroads, getting the best of Rockefeller on iron ore leases, and building his empire of business.[140] It was all looking back with pleasure, rather than forward with concern, and, although appropriate to the Taft era, it was not a congenial role for Carnegie to play since his liberal conversion.

Now with the new administration, Carnegie could once again become the vigorous champion of Progressive reform. When the editor of the conservative *Pittsburgh Dispatch* wrote him soon after the election, expressing great concern over the victorious Democrat's promise to lower tariffs drastically, Carnegie wrote with great equanimity, "In reply to your inquiry . . . I beg to say that I have no apprehension of disaster arising from the change of administration. On the contrary, I think we are now in a position to reduce the tariff on manufactured articles. Protection should be temporary affair. . . . People need not lie awake nights fearing disaster to the business of the country from any legislation that is to come in the opinion of Yours very truly, Andrew Carnegie." [141]

In the months that followed, the new legislation that came in a flood from the White House to Congress and then back to the White House for Wilson's signature caused for Carnegie no sleepless nights but instead many pleasant days. The Underwood Tariff, the Clayton Anti-Trust bill, the Federal Reserve Banking proposal, which incorporated many of the ideas that Carnegie had earlier suggested as ways to correct "the worst banking system in the world"—all met with Carnegie's enthusiastic approval. Not even the income tax, which he once had regarded as being legalized theft, disturbed him now. "So we have a tax at last—1% on everyone's revenue over 5000$. So we go. Untaxt wealth and Rank to become things of the past. Common sense." [142] After eight months of the new administration Carnegie had become a staunch Wilsonian Democrat in everything but formal affiliation. "President Taft demoralized the Senate & lost his treaty thereby" but Wilson is "everything that could be wisht," Carnegie wrote Bryce. "He is with us heart and soul. Tariff is out of the way. Banking Bill soon will be & Panama Tolls also I think will be arranged. He is advanced in all these good causes & will be hard to beat, a great contrast to his predecessor. . . . Root is here & I am to attend a meeting tomorrow with him re Republican Party policy in future. Sad demoralization with Roosevelt's revolutionary ideas." [143] It did not appear that Carnegie would be one of the louder wailers at the funeral bier.

It was Wilson's foreign policy that interested Carnegie even more than domestic reform, for the quest for peace remained his greatest concern. "I have no party where Peace is concerned," [144] was Carnegie's proud boast, and on this issue he did not need to make even a ritualistic gesture of being a Republican. Even before Wilson took office, Carnegie was convinced that the President-elect would be "sound on arbitration . . . Have great confidence in him. He's Scotch." [145]

Wilson did not fail Carnegie's expectations. He, and particularly his Secretary of State, William Jennings Bryan, were eager to pick up the arbitration treaties where Taft had been forced to drop them. Moreover, Bryan, unlike Knox, was a consummate politician, and his tight control over an important segment of the Democratic party, especially the jingoist South, would prove decisive in obtaining the Senate's approval, for the majority party in the Senate was now the Democratic party. Nor did Bryan make the mistake of his predecessor in failing to consult with and exert his influence on key committee members. It was almost as if Carnegie were writing the script for the action.

The only criticism that Carnegie could offer to the whole proceedings was that Bryan seemed more interested in the quantity rather than the quality of the treaties. "Bryan's treaties," as they became labeled in the press, were not true arbitration treaties on the model of the Taft-Knox treaties, but rather treaties of conciliation, or, as Bryan preferred to call them, "cooling off" treaties. They provided that in case of a dispute between the United States and any one of the nations with whom she had ratified such a treaty, each party to the dispute would select one of its own citizens to serve on a Commission of Inquiry. Then each of these two commissioners would select one citizen from the other nation, and the four members would select a fifth member. The Commission would study the issue for no longer than a year, during which time the two parties to the dispute would agree not to go to war. It was this "cooling off" period that Bryan considered important, more so than the actual inquiry and the recommendations for settlement that would result. He believed that wars between nations were analogous to fist fights between men; they were always the result of giving way to immediate passion. Time provided for reflection would effectively deter any war. As the

Brooklyn Eagle somewhat sarcastically saw it, Bryan's plan was but an international application of that old childhood maxim, "When angry count to fifty, when very angry, count to one hundred." [146]

Although Roosevelt would have found it impossible to believe, Bryan was even more naïvely idealistic about the importance of getting peace treaties than Carnegie was. Carnegie saw the flaws in Bryan's conciliation treaties, for there were no provisions for enforcement or even for agreement to abide by arbitration. There was also something approaching a parody of Carnegie's efforts to get treaties with France, Great Britain, Germany, and Japan in Bryan's frantic zeal to get treaties with everybody. The Memphis *Commercial-Appeal* mocked Bryan with the editorial comment, "Secretary Bryan's completed arbitration treaties with Switzerland, Denmark, and Uruguay take a great load off our minds. The thought of war with them was terrible." [147] Still, the treaties were a step in the right direction, and as Carnegie would say, "Onward and upward, the world moves." He dashed off a note of hearty congratulations to Bryan upon successfully negotiating the treaty with Denmark. "I wish you speedy success, and more treaties of the same character." [148] Bryan was happy to oblige.

Bryan's "cooling off" treaties were not, in Carnegie's opinion, as significant an indication of the Wilson administration's good faith in promoting international harmony even at the expense of national pride as was the stand the administration took on the Panama toll issue. By the terms of the Hay-Pauncefote treaty, which had given to the United States exclusive rights to build and own an Isthmian Canal, the United States had agreed that all nations would be treated exactly the same in respect to toll charges through the Canal. In 1912, however, as the Canal neared completion, Congress had passed a law exempting "American coastwise shipping"—that is, American ships going from East Coast ports to West Coast ports—from paying Canal tolls. This was a clear violation of the Treaty, and Britain, quite properly, protested. Congressmen of both parties, playing for the Irish vote, seemed determined to defy British objections. It was our Canal, we had built it, and we could jolly well do what we wanted with it. Carnegie, knowing how strongly the British felt on this matter, and he himself believing that this was indeed a question of national honor—of being true to one's given word—was outraged by the stand taken in Congress and by Taft's agreeing to that position. He wrote to Robert Underwood Johnson, the editor of *Century Magazine,* "The spectacle which we present before the nations of the world is pitiable indeed. The nations were ready to receive the gift our country was providing for the world in the Panama Canal with unbounded enthusiasm and gratitude. The action of Congress and the Executive has shocked them and should sober us. . . . The result to us even if we gain all that we claim is so pitiably small, our national humiliation so great." [149]

The position Wilson was placed in by this issue, still unresolved when he took office, was highly embarrassing. He had campaigned and won on a platform which strongly supported the exemption act. Yet he personally considered it a violation of our Treaty agreement. He allowed the whole question to lie dormant, however, during the first six months of his administration while he pushed through Congress the major domestic legislation that he wanted. Then in October he sent a message to Congress asking that the discriminatory clause be repealed. Carnegie was elated, and he cabled the President, "Greater far than your tariff victory, great as that is, greater than your banking bill . . . is your noble stand for equal tolls to all lands. This touches our country's honor; the people will support you, ensuring victory." [150] To Morley, who had been chiding him on American honor, Carnegie wrote in pride, "What a bold earnest man can accomplish! Naturally I think it's the Scotch in him, the do or die." [151]

The Congress, however, was not as easily moved as Carnegie thought it should be. It took a precedent-shattering appearance of the President before both Houses of Congress to get the House of Representatives to vote for repeal, and even then the Senate held out. For the first time Carnegie had some doubts about the integrity of the upper House. "The Irish extremists here are doing everything to defeat repeal of Canal Tolls. Senator Gorman of New York, their Leader, is rampant, even our Peace Fund denounced as British & Anti-American, Root included, as traitor to his Country," was Carnegie's unhappy report to Morley.[152]

It was not until June that Wilson was able, by a vote of 50 to 34, to get the Senate to repeal the clause, and then only by making the issue one of a vote of confidence in his administration. "By your heroic stand and victory," Carnegie cabled, "you have become one of the Immortals." [153] By the summer of 1914 the last important difference between the United States and Great Britain still outstanding had been settled to Britain's satisfaction and to America's honor. Carnegie felt that at last here was a hero that had proved himself as no President since Lincoln had done.

Not even Wilson's Mexican adventure, which occurred at the same time as the glorious Canal triumph, could do more than shake, not destroy, Carnegie's confidence in the President. The Mexican Revolution, which had been raging spasmodically and ineffectively since 1910, in February 1913 had thrown to the top a new caudillo, in the unattractive person of General Victoriano Huerta. Taft refused to recognize Huerta's government, and Wilson followed the same policy when he assumed office. Carnegie, as a self-appointed expert on Latin American affairs, wrote a long letter to Wilson, giving his advice on the tense situation. Carnegie had long been an admirer of the deposed dictator, Porfirio Díaz, and he hoped that in Huerta Mexico once again had a man who could restore law and order, even if at the expense of liberty. But, above all, he advised Wilson, "If I were you I'd let Mexico manage her own destiny, limiting my charge to taking care of our citizens there." [154]

That same high sense of moral rectitude in Wilson, which Carnegie had found so very appealing in the Canal toll issue, was not so attractive when it manifested itself in the Mexican crisis. Wilson not only refused to recognize Huerta, he demanded that the "desperate brute" resign. Carnegie, like the soothsayer croaking out a warning to Caesar on the steps of the Capitol, immediately wrote Wilson, "Beware! Beware Invasion." [155] But Wilson's moralism was as strong as Caesar's ambition. Huerta would never be recognized, American honor would not be sullied. The test of that honor came in April 1914, fifteen months after Huerta seized power. A crew of American sailors, loading supplies on a boat in Tampico, were arrested by local Mexican troops and held briefly in jail. Shortly afterwards they were released with an apology, but the irate commanding admiral of the American fleet in the Caribbean demanded that the Mexican officer salute the American flag with a twenty-one gun salute. Huerta ordered his officers not to salute the American flag unless the American fleet saluted the Mexican flag. The American press screamed for war, and when Wilson received word that a German merchantman was landing a cargo of arms at Vera Cruz, he ordered the American fleet to seize and hold the city, the ancient gateway of invasion into Mexico. Carnegie's faith in Wilson had reached its severest test. In great anxiety he wrote to the President: "Such a war as seems pending will in after years be held akin to the fabled war of the two kings to decide which end of the egg should first be broken. 'How or when shall the salute be fired' is a trifle unworthy of consideration. 'What fools these mortals be.' I am very sorry for you. Just on the eve of your unequalled triumf, the gods threaten you with defeat; but I still hope for a miraculous triumf. War is defeat, no true victory is possible here." [156]

Fortunately, the gods were working overtime, and the "miraculous triumf" that Carnegie—and probably Wilson as well—hoped for came to pass. The "ABC Powers"—Argentina, Brazil, and Chile—offered to serve as mediators, and Wilson promptly accepted. Even then, Carnegie thought the President needed further advice: "If mediation fails," he counseled, "you can still blot out the past by prompt withdrawal, and inform your countrymen that your desire to save poor Mexico . . . from a reign of misrule had been found wholly impracticable." [157] It was not until July that Carnegie could feel that the danger of full war with "our sister republic" had been narrowly averted. "Rejoicing this morning that our noble President is likely to escape from his Mexican blunder," he wrote Morley after receiving the news that Huerta had resigned.[158]

The end result of the Mexican affair was not to diminish, but on the contrary, to increase Carnegie's admiration for Wilson and to strengthen his optimism for world peace. After an egregious blunder, the President had accepted arbitration, thereby strengthening the force of international law and order. Upon receiving word that the last troops were being withdrawn, Carnegie wrote Wilson "congratulating you from heart and brain upon our troops being recalled from our sister Republic. That is a providential escape. You are indeed a favorite of the Gods." [159]

The years 1913 and 1914 mark the high point of Carnegie's optimism in believing that world peace was virtually ensured. Al-

1004

though the preceding five years had provided a catalogue of disappointments and failures, beginning with the inconclusive Second Hague Conference of 1907 and concluding with the miserable failure of the Taft-Knox arbitration treaties, the advent of the Wilson administration gave promise of a new era of progress toward peace. And even if there had been great disappointments in the five years prior to Wilson, there had also been encouraging signs in the fact that the recurring crises in the Balkans and the imperialistic ambitions of the Great Powers in Africa, serious as these incidents were, had not been able to precipitate a general European war. In an article entitled "A Silver Lining to War Clouds," which he wrote for *The World To-Day* in 1912, Carnegie pointed out that the Morocco crisis of 1911, had it occurred at an earlier time, "would have plunged Great Britain, France and Germany into war. Instead, it was diplomatically and peacefully settled . . . and here let me state that, from the writer's own knowledge, the statement of the Earl of Northumberland that peace was maintained through the increasing efforts of the Emperor of Germany, is true." [160]

Now, more than ever, the Kaiser was Carnegie's "Hero of Peace," and Carnegie enthusiastically backed Nicholas Murray Butler's proposal to present the Kaiser with a memorial signed by seventy officials "of the leading Societies and Corporations of the United States" offering the German Emperor "cordial congratulations upon your twenty-five years of peaceful and prosperous reign . . . We thank your Imperial Majesty as the foremost apostle of peace in our time. . . ." [161] Carnegie, along with Joseph Schmidlapp, went to Berlin in June 1913 to present the memorial to the Kaiser in person. As he handed the document to Wilhelm, Carnegie hailed the Emperor as "our strongest ally" in the cause of peace. [162]

In his rectorial address, delivered to the students of Aberdeen University in the summer of 1912, Carnegie spoke in a markedly more complacent tone than he had dared use in his rectorial address at St. Andrews University only seven years before. He now spoke as if world peace had been virtually secured:

We hav past the stage of barbarism when there was constant danger, and hence heroism in the profession of arms—all this

1005

has gone. The safest occupation in the land today, either in
Britain or America, is that of a soldier, who rarely or never sees
a battle or fires a hostile shot, but marches from youth to age in
perfect safety, unmolested. . . . The military age is rapidly passing. We cannot imagin that many students who hav received
years of precious education will hereafter dedicate themselvs deliberately to this profession. . . .[163]

There was not the slightest indication in any of the speeches,
articles, or letters Carnegie wrote in these last years of the golden
age of *Pax Britannica* that time was rapidly running out for all
his hopeful dreams. Carnegie was not alone in his belief that the
millennium was at hand. Most of the statesmen, journalists, and
academicians of the Western World shared his delusion of security. In spite of all the evidence to the contrary—the armament
races, the military alliances, and the heightened spirit of nationalism throughout the world—a general war seemed inconceivable.
Crises and threats of war would undoubtedly continue until more
effective peace-keeping machinery could be adopted, but the designs for that machinery were already drawn, and the Great Powers with each passing year seemed more amenable to the idea of
adopting those designs. Indeed, many had already been imple-
mented by the establishment of co-operative international unions
to regulate postal service, trade, and communications. Peace societies continued to proliferate and to expand in membership, and
for the first time in the history of the Christian era, the world
seemed ready at last to join Christ in saying "Blessed are the
peacemakers, For they shall be called the children of God."

Carnegie would have had to be a far more humble man than
he was not to have exulted in his own beatification which came to
him in these years from many hands. There was the remarkable
public letter from the Holy Father himself, calling Carnegie
"peacemaker." There was the tribute from Baroness Berthe von
Suttner: "America is in advance in many things over Europe—but
in the peace-movement the advance is a stupendous one. And most
of it is due to *you*." [164] There was the heart-warming praise from
Nicholas Murray Butler on Carnegie's seventy-fifth birthday:
"Tomorrow you will be 75 years young! What a grand 75 years
they have been! Lincoln was a raw-boned young man when you

were born & Napoleon had not long been dead. Think of the change! Today Napoleon is unthinkable. Peaceful industry and enlightenment are putting an end to war. Just think how much you have helped it all on, & are helping it on. Thank God for your health & strength & broad vision." [165]

There were the honors that foreign governments bestowed upon him, largely in response to his creation of a Carnegie Hero Fund in each of their respective countries: France, Germany, Belgium, the Netherlands all gave him their highest civilian medals of honor. Edward VII wanted to grant him a title, but Carnegie settled for an autographed picture. He was proposed for the Nobel Peace Prize of 1912, and although it did not go to him, he at least had the satisfaction of seeing it awarded to his favorite candidate, Elihu Root.[166]

The greatest tribute of all, in his own estimation, came in 1911, when he was presented with the first Pan-American Gold Medal by the governing board of the Pan-American Union. Carnegie, at the elaborate presentation ceremony held in Washington, D.C., and attended by President Taft, Secretary Knox, and official representatives of all twenty-one American republics, expressed his gratification at receiving the honor. He told the distinguished audience that he had been sitting at his desk in the Highlands of Scotland "when I received a telegram which I opened and read without seeming quite to grasp the meaning of the words. I was stunned. Was I dreaming? . . . My hands went to my forehead and I bent my head to the desk. Slowly the truth developed and established itself, and I began to realize what it all meant. . . . Truly, my friends, I never before felt so completely overwhelmed and crushed as it dawned upon me that the honor which the Conference had voted to confer was without parallel; 160 millions of people, forming twenty-one sovereign nations, bestowing upon poor me an honor the like of which had never before been bestowed upon a human being." [167] To Morley, Carnegie wrote: "The medal presentation in Palace So Am Republics Washington, 160 millions of people contributing, was the crowning honor of my life. Nothing can ever equal that. Must try to live up to it." [168] He at once began preparations to extend the Carnegie Hero Fund to every nation in the Western Hemisphere.

Always sanguine about the future, Carnegie felt he had more

reason than ever before to be optimistic about world peace. The words of an old spiritual that he had often heard at Fisk University and Hampton Institute seemed beautifully appropriate to him now: "Ain't gonna study war no more." And the Carnegies' New Year greeting bore the cheerful note: [169]

> We send this New Year Greeting January 1, 1914, strong in the faith that International Peace is soon to prevail, thru several of the great powers agreeing to settle their disputes by arbitration under International Law, the pen thus proving mitier than the sword. . . . Be of good cheer, kind friend.
>
> > "It's coming yet for a' that!
> > When man to man the world o'er
> > Shall brothers be and a' that."

Carnegie may not have been aware that time was running out for world peace, but with his seventh-fifth birthday he was acutely conscious of the fact that time was running out for him. Carnegie had always had an almost morbid fear of dying. The deaths of his mother and brother, occurring at the same time, had been so painful to him that for years afterwards he avoided any mention of their names and refused to have any memento of them in his presence which would remind him of their deaths. In middle age he changed the date of his birth from 1835 to 1837, and for many years thereafter he succeeded in convincing himself that the later date was the actual year of his birth. It was not until he was past sixty-five, and then only at the insistence of his friends, that he wrote John Ross to ask him to examine the official Register in Dunfermline to ascertain his correct birth year. "I thought it was 1837, but some say 1835. Sorry if am to lose 2 years." [170] He lost the two years, and had to change his records accordingly. But he was so vigorous in energy and in health that he resented any imputation that he was an old man. When his friend, W. T. Stead, who was always chasing after one chimerical panacea after another, wrote to him to urge him to apply for "a wonderful elixir of life that comes from the Atlas Mountains in Africa," Carnegie snapped back, "No Elixir for me, thank you." [171] Most of his associates felt that Carnegie had already found such an elixir. At the age of seventy-five he appeared to be no older than fifty, a more appropriate age to be the father of a thirteen-year-old daughter. In his daily activities—attending ceremonials, running off to Washington or London, writing articles and delivering speeches —he exhausted secretaries and friends who were half his age. He kept physically fit by playing golf, walking, and swimming, and he never indulged in over-eating or drinking. With this vitality and zest for life, it was even more difficult for him to reconcile himself to the fact that he was old. But the ever more frequent deaths of close friends who were his contemporaries were a constant reminder of his own mortality. Richard Gilder, Grover Cleveland, Mark Twain, Henry Campbell-Bannerman, W. T. Stead—all died within three or four years of each other, and the narrowing of his circle of friends forced him, most reluctantly, to get his own affairs in order. In 1913, when he had made the final disposition of his fortune, had set up trusts for his wife and daughter, and had made provisions for all of his personal pensioners, he wrote John Ross that he had found all these preparations "a heavy task—all sad—deep regrets that one isn't allowed to live here in this *heaven on earth forever,* which it is to me. None other satisfactory." [172]

For Carnegie there was no consolation of orthodox religion which promised reunion in Heaven. To Elizabeth Haldane he wrote, "More and more I realize we should think less & less of 'Heaven our Home!' more & more of 'Home our Heaven.' Wish I could get an option to leave this heaven only when I wisht." [173] But it was not in Carnegie's nature to brood long upon unpleasant subjects, and most of the time he was quite successful in shutting out thoughts of old age and death completely. Too much of life was passionately absorbing for him to surrender to senile melancholia. A much more typical expression of his temperament was a note written to Morley in 1911: "Skibo never so beautiful. I mourn our departure in many respects, but I am going to begin my memoirs up on the moors, opening with my retirement from business eleven years ago. I have a new life to describe, acquisition & distribution of surplus wealth, & as I have had to organize & gather sound men above the sordid love of gain & adhere myself to my vow never to make another dollar, it is an interesting development. At least it should be—I dout if any business man so far as I have known them could perform the task I'm going to try." [174]

Carnegie needed none of Stead's magic potions from the Atlas Mountains—for Carnegie there was always "a new life to describe," a new cause to fight for, a new hope to sustain him. Butler was quite right—What a grand 75 years they had all been! No man living had more reason to call "Home our Heaven" than Carnegie.

On 23 May 1914 the Carnegies left New York for their annual migration to Great Britain. It was Carnegie's sixty-fourth crossing of the Atlantic, and as he outlined his program to Morley, this summer promised to be as busy as ever: "Due Plymouth 31st [May]—Coburg Hotel for four days, then Freedoms of Coventry & Lincoln enroute to Skibo, join Madam &c on northward at York for Skibo. Return London for Liberal Club address 16th & Burt banquet—& Aberdeen University Society these two following 17 & 18th, then am free." [175] Louise Carnegie might have had a different idea about being free, for after Andrew's "Freedom" collecting and speech-making jaunts were over, the usual busy social season at Skibo would begin. But in mid-July came the retreat to the moors, and this summer Carnegie assured Louise he would finish writing the autobiography in which he had been engaged for the past three summers.

The summer of 1914 was a particularly good one all over northern Europe, from Scandinavia to Scotland—long days of warm, bright sunshine, followed by short white nights in which the light never really left the sky, and the air had a peculiar, exhilarating quality that made of it an almost tangible substance to savor and enjoy. For fifteen years Carnegie had largely ignored British politics. He had been thoroughly engrossed in the anti-imperialist, the Progressive, and the peace crusades at home. But now he evidently felt that America was safe enough in the hands of Wilson and Bryan to permit him once again to concern himself with the domestic affairs of Great Britain. He had much to catch up on, for during the preceding five years a quiet revolution had been effected within his native land. Organized labor had become an independent political force, and it threatened to upset the traditional Whig-Tory political balance that had endured for a century and a half. To counteract the socialism of the aggressive new Labour party, the Liberal party had abandoned its nineteenth-century Manchester laissez-faire liberalism in favor of state social welfare legislation. The Constitutional crisis that had resulted from the rejection of David Lloyd George's budget by the House of Lords in 1909 had ended with the complete triumph of the Commons over the Lords, for the King, like William before him, had threatened to pack the House of Lords with new peers if the Lords would not bow to reform. And so the old Chartist dreams of seventy years before had, quite suddenly and easily, become a reality. Britain had achieved a democracy that went far beyond the Jacksonian political democracy of America, which had long been the model Carnegie had held up to Britain for emulation. The New Liberalism of Asquith and George even went beyond the New Nationalism of Roosevelt and the New Freedom of Wilson in providing old age pensions and health and unemployment insurance for the workers. Here was a "triumphant democracy" that Carnegie had not anticipated.

But certain things are constant, even in a nation going through the process of revolutionary modernization, and the British in the summer of 1914 still had the Irish question, like an ancient family curse, to plague them. No amount of progressive legislation could successfully exorcise this particular political devil. Catholic Ireland threatened war if it was not granted Home Rule over the entire island. The Protestant Irish of Ulster threatened civil war if they should be abandoned by Britain and annexed by a Free State of Ireland. By July 1914 the apparently unsolvable problem was rapidly approaching what most Britons feared would be a tragic climax. Carnegie was full of advice and counsel to Prime Minister Asquith, John Morley, and anyone else in the British government who cared to listen. To Morley, Carnegie wrote in great concern, "You made a clear strong speech the other day. The situation seems incredible—to think of a Civil War in Britian. Surely impossible. I have faith in Landsdown. He seems reasonable—but Shylock's contempt—'there be your Christians' is not going too far. Religious bigotry in our day surprises us. Nothing Religious about it. Pure bigotry—Well, well, let it pass. If *possible Compromise.*" [176]

For Carnegie, and for most Britons, everything on the international scene was obscured by this black cloud of Irish civil war. Indeed, on the very day that Austria-Hungary declared war on Serbia, 28 July 1914, Carnegie wrote a long letter to *The Times* expressing his "anxiety . . . regarding the perils in which the Mother Country is becoming involved." There was not a word about the crisis in the Balkans, or about the diplomatic threats that were being exchanged among the capitals of Europe—only Carnegie's expression of incredibility over the possibility of a "civil war between English speaking peoples." [177]

Any outbreak of violence anywhere would seem incredible when viewed from the terraces of Skibo this glorious summer. "We are off to our retreat in a few minutes where we spend two or three weeks," Carnegie wrote Morley on 16 July, "and then return to greet coming friends, among them yourself and Lady . . . The 'sunset walk' is a thing of beauty these lovely days." [178]

The Carnegies were in their retreat at Aultnagar when the news reached them that the Great War had begun. For Carnegie it was as if the very planet had cracked—suddenly, senselessly, without any warning. On the day he received word that Great Britain, France, and Russia were at war with Germany and Austria-Hungary, he had just finished his autobiography—the self-portrait of a self-satisfied man, with all the turmoil, all the "pushing inordinately," that might have been included, carefully expunged.

The last page of his memoirs was entitled "The Kaiser and World Peace," and it concluded with Carnegie's account of his meeting the German Emperor the year before and presenting him with "the American address of congratulation" upon his peaceful reign of twenty-five years.

> As I approached to hand to him the casket containing the address, he recognized me and with outstretched arms, exclaimed:
> "Carnegie, twenty-five years of peace, and we hope for many more."
> I could not help responding:
> "And in this noblest of all missions you are our chief ally." [179]

It was a happy ending to a happy book. Like *Triumphant Democracy*, his *Autobiography* had been "all sunshine, sunshine,

sunshine." And then the sun was suddenly blotted out. Carnegie had to add a final section that he never could have imagined would be necessary:

"As I read this today, what a change! The world convulsed by war as never before! Men slaying each other like wild beasts."

But even in this dark moment Carnegie could not really believe that all was lost. He continued:

I dare not relinquish all hope. In recent days I see another ruler coming forward upon the world stage, who may prove himself the immortal one. The man who vindicated his country's honor in the Panama Canal toil dispute is now President. He has the indomitable will of genius, and true hope which we are told,

"Kings it makes god, and meaner creatures kings." Nothing is impossible to genius! Watch President Wilson! He has Scotch blood in his veins.

To which John C. Van Dyke, who edited Carnegie's memoirs in 1920, added:

"[Here the manuscript ends abruptly.]" [180]

And so, in reality, did Carnegie's life. In a preface to her husband's autobiography, Louise Carnegie wrote:

For a few weeks each summer we retired to our little bungalow on the moors at Aultnagar to enjoy the simple life, and it was there that Mr. Carnegie did most of his writing. He delighted in going back to those early times, and as he wrote, he lived them all over again. He was thus engaged in July, 1914, when the war clouds began to gather, and when the fateful news of the 4th of August reached us, we immediately left our retreat in the hills and returned to Skibo to be more in touch with the situation.

These memoirs ended at that time. Henceforth he was never able to interest himself in private affairs. Many times he made the attempt to continue writing, but found it useless. Until then he had lived the life of a man in middle life—and a young one at that—golfing, fishing, swimming each day, sometimes doing all three in one day. Optimist as he always was and tried to be, even in the face of the failure of his hopes, the world disaster was too much. His heart was broken.[181]

With the news of a general war, Carnegie's first thoughts were of the Church Peace Union. At that very moment the associated councils of churches of Great Britain, Germany, and the United States were holding the Union's first Peace Conference, in Constance, Germany. The conference, which had been planned by Frederick Lynch, had been scheduled to convene on 1 August. On the following day, with Germany's having already declared war on Russia, Carnegie, still at Aultnagar, sent a cable to the British pacifist J. Allen Baker, who was the leader of the British delegation. "We shall be with you all today in spirit, and full in the faith that our cause is righteous and therefore must prevail amid many deplorable catastrophes such as the present outburst. We know that man is created with an instinct for development, and that from the first he has developed to higher and higher standards and that there is no limit to his future ascent." [182] How hollow the old "onward and upward" cry sounded now as Europe plunged downward into Hell.

On the day that Britain declared war on Germany, Morley, true to his pacifist principles, resigned from the government. He wrote to Carnegie that evening,

> You will tomorrow see in the papers . . . that I have left the Government. You may be sure that the strain of the last five days has been severe. . . . You will know that I do not leave Asquith, who has been my friend for 30 years, without a mortal pang. As we shall meet on Monday next, I won't go into details now. I cannot imagine men showing loftier temper and tone than our cabinet yesterday: not a single unkind or wounding word.
>
> But what a black panorama!! To nobody will it seem blacker than to you. Hell in full blast. This is a sorrowful night for me —probably the last of my public life. . . .[183]

The following morning, 5 August, Carnegie received a telegram from Lynch that the American delegation to the Constance Peace Conference had made it safely out of Germany to Britain but were stranded in London and desperately in need of funds to get back to the United States. Carnegie immediately sent a wire to the branch of the Royal Bank of Scotland in London: "Party of 40 delegates from our Peace Conference in Germany have reached London but are in trouble and need money to take them home. Should be greatly obliged if you will furnish their Secretary, Frederick Lynch, with the funds they need. I shall promptly reimburse you." [184] The next day Lynch wrote Carnegie a long letter describing in detail the escape of the American and British delegations from Germany. They had taken the last train out of Germany before the border was closed.

> You will be glad to know that our conference has been held clear through and while the world was rushing into war, we went right on and talked peace all the more . . . There were three meetings in Constance on Sunday [2 August], . . . They were very remarkable because everyone was burdened with sadness. Every speech was like a prayer. It was something never to be forgotten that while Englishmen, Germans and French were everywhere beginning to fight one another, here these three peoples were together in perfect brotherhood and affection. No one will ever forget that day. . . .
>
> [Sunday night the British and American delegations received word from the German government that they would be given safe conduct to the border in two train cars leaving the next morning. The conference unanimously agreed to adjourn, and to reconvene in London. Lynch then described for Carnegie their journey through the hell of war.]
>
> We had a remarkable journey. All along the way we saw pitiful scenes. We saw all the men being taken from work and corralled at every railroad station. We saw one young man go crazy at being torn from his wife and children. We saw four foreigners shot deliberately down because they would not take arms for Germany. We saw lines of women weeping and wailing. Worst of all, we saw great crowds of young men in mad orgies of drink and war fever, howling, with wild eyes for the blood of Russians and French and Englishmen. I saw a Russian family pulled out of a train by the German soldiers and the mother so frightened that her milk stopped and the poor little baby got nothing to eat for two days. We took them along in our party and on the steamer Lady Barlow, one of our group,

found a mother with a baby who offered to give the little Russian baby a drink from her breasts. The poor little thing snatched at the breast with a cry that was pathetic. Everywhere we saw soldiers yelling as they marched. We saw officers taking the horses away from farmers in the fields. We saw all the schools being closed and every boy and girl in Germany was ordered into the fields to take the places of the men seized. Most pitiful of all we saw German families fleeing from Paris, and French families fleeing from Germany. It was heart-rending. In Paris, the Gare de l'Est was packed with German families—the poor little children screaming all night, the parents bent with the little luggage they could take. . . . The French soldiers were howling "a Bas" at them all the time ("to Hell") and only kept from striking them by the officers. . . .

When we got to the mouth of the Thames we found it had been planted full of mines and a naval pilot came aboard and we proceeded to creep through them. . . . At last we reached London. . . . There are about 10,000 Americans stranded here I am told. . . .

[The next day, the Conference reassembled at the Westminster Palace Hotel.] It was the unanimous feeling of everyone present that we must devote our lives to it [peace] as never before. Many felt that the very fact that the world was now witnessing the collapse of the military system as the preserver of peace, the utter incapacity of the present international political order to secure justice for any nation, would reach in our favor. Never again can anyone say that armaments make for peace.

Today after the adjournment yesterday, the American delegation of about forty met and had a very extraordinary meeting —a sort of consecration to go home and call upon the United States to be Moses to lead Europe out of this awful wilderness she has become. At this meeting a statement was drawn up by Dr. Douglas, Hendrix, Wilson, Merrill, Macfarland and myself to be presented to the churches of the Federal Council (practically all the churches) in America. We voted to send you one at once, and I am forwarding it and think you will like it.

. . . So long as this awful calamity has had to be, it is a good thing our American delegates were on the continent and saw even the beginning of it. They have become the most radical peace men. They are all going back to America converted absolutely, if they ever faltered before, to the fact that militarism is an unmitigated curse, and was the great crime of civilization.

They know now that the old order has proved a sham and a delusion and that some new order must rise out of the old. I think too that they feel that there is no hope except in democracy. . . .

I hope you have not lost courage. You must have felt heartsick and dejected as have we all. But I believe this catastrophe will witness the beginning of the end of trust in might and brute force. That trust has failed at last.[185]

This letter by Lynch to Carnegie serves as an appropriate epitaph to Carnegie's long quest for peace. All of the hopes and illusions, the naïveté, and the futility of the quest are here. So many peace conferences, leading inevitably to this last conference where, "while the world was rushing into war, we went right on and talked peace all the more." So many millions Carnegie had spent in search of peace, now shown to be but pennies compared with the billions spent in preparation for war. So much faith in democracy, sustained by the belief that "the people" wanted peace and that it was only "the leaders" who planned for war, while "worst of all, we saw great crowds of young men . . . howling . . . for blood." Everything that Carnegie had believed in had been held up before the world, had been weighed, and found wanting, and had been smashed on the ground.

But even in this tragic moment neither Lynch nor Carnegie could give up his illusions and accept the truth. They clung to what was left to them out of the debacle, their faith in democracy, their belief that the United States could be a "Moses to lead Europe out of this awful wilderness she has become." As a churchman, Lynch should have been more careful in his choice of metaphor—he should have remembered that Moses wandered for forty years in the wilderness and died there without ever reaching the promised land. But men cannot live long without some faith, and the few illusions that were left to Carnegie were to sustain him for yet a few more months. Although the world had entered the gates of Hell, Carnegie had not quite yet abandoned all hope.

The last few weeks at Skibo were the only dark days that Carnegie had ever known there, even though nature mocked them all by continuing to give them one bright, sun-filled day after another. Morley came for his usual late summer visit, as did a steady stream of other English and American visitors. But with each passing day, the horrors of the war were brought closer to this unreal Camelot: the growing casualty lists printed daily in *The Times* and *The Scotsman;* the tears that were shed as young men on the staff at Skibo and from the many tenant farms of the estate left for the army. Carnegie wrote to Ross in mid August: "Thanks for your notes. We are in perilous times. Our horses, traps &c commandeered—our territorials, ditto. All the household servants included steadily at work, sewing & knitting for the Army. It is all too sad to contemplate but we can indulge the hope that out of this eruption there is to spring the resolve to form an organization among the nations to *prevent war* hereafter. In this I hope our race will tell. . . ." [186]

Morley lived under no such illusions. Writing to Carnegie soon after his last visit to Skibo, he could offer no words of comfort:

> The only days of peace and refreshment in this Trough of Despair, for me at least, have been my fortnight at Skibo. The company was both genial and understanding. The young people were most delightful. The weather was ideal. The host and hostess were almost kinder, more considerate, and more sympathetic than usual. We are keenly alive to it—and only regret that my wife's illness gave such trouble.
>
> There is evidently to be no speedy ray of light upon the European scene; nor will the Devil be chained safely up again in your time and mine. We are seeing evil war at its worst—worst in carnage, worst in its depravation of all moral sense, worst as a murderous gamble. For the moment, there is nothing for people like you and me, but *an iron silence*. We can keep a vigilant eye upon events—Words are vain or worse than vain.[187]

Carnegie fully intended to keep "a vigilant eye upon events," but he had no intention of heeding Morley's other bit of advice about maintaining "an iron silence." For Carnegie words were never vain, and never did he feel it more important for men of good will to speak out than at this darkest moment in world history. The most pressing business of the moment was to get back to the United States as soon as possible, and, from that haven of sanity in a world gone mad, to lay plans for the American government to take the leadership in bringing a halt to the war. After a great deal of difficulty and several changes in plans, the Carnegies finally managed to book passage on the *Mauretania,* sailing from Liverpool in mid September.[188]

The Carnegies made their annual farewell to the household staff at Skibo on the morning of 14 September, about a month and a half earlier than was their usual custom. As might be expected, the parting was more tearfully emotional in this sad autumn, but no one, least of all Carnegie, realized that it was his final farewell. Driving by auto to the train station at Bonar Bridge, the Laird of Skibo had an opportunity for a good view of his estate. The trees that he had had planted along the roads were in brightest autumnal foliage, and the hills beyond were at their deepest heather purple, the traditional color for royalty—and also for mourning.

The last night in Britain was spent at a hotel in Liverpool. Morley, as he frequently had done in the past, came up to be with the Carnegies on the eve of their departure and to see them off in the morning. The two old friends sat up far later into the night than was their practice, talking over many things. Morley was in a state of deep depression; Carnegie, as usual, was resolutely hopeful, outlining his plans for a world peace council which he intended to persuade President Wilson to call, as soon as he got home. Only when they touched on the past, old friends, old political triumphs and defeats, old jokes shared and old disputes engaged in, did Morley shake off his gloom. Even then the talk was not the same as it always had been before, yet neither was willing to have it end. In the morning, the Liverpool Station was filled with tearful people whose anxious faces showed their concern for the fate of those who must cross the Atlantic in the midst of war, and of those who must stay in England and endure that war.

In that crowded station farewells could only be hurried and brief, and so the parting was made easier for Carnegie and Morley. Nor could there be any lingering backward look for the Carnegies as the ship sailed down the Mersey and out to sea, for the fog lay heavy over the entire Irish Sea, and Britain was quickly blotted from view.

CHAPTER XXV

Shadows at Shadowbrook
1914-1919

The long trip home across the Atlantic in September 1914 was the most difficult crossing the Carnegies had ever made. Louise, never a very good sailor, was so worried about sailing on a British ship in time of war that she was ill most of the way. Carnegie described the voyage to John Ross: "Consider what it means to go upon a small steamer across the Atlantic, lites all out, shut in every evening—all dark until the sun rises—crawling along on the look-out for bergs—such our experience home." [1] Carnegie, however, used these long days aboard ship to good advantage, and before the ship had docked in New York he had a proposal for ending the war ready to send to the President. Wilson replied on 29 September, "I have your letter written from the Mauretania and also the little note which followed it after you reached this country. I am warmly obliged to you for lodging in my mind a suggestion which may later bear fruit." [2]

The suggestion which Carnegie had "lodged" in Wilson's mind found well-tilled ground, for it was one that the President had been considering since August. The plan was for Wilson to offer his good offices to serve as arbitrator of the European conflict, and for all of the warring nations to call for a cease-fire while

the President of the United States sought for a settlement suitable
to both the Central and the Entente powers. To effect this plan,
Wilson was prepared to send his close friend and personal ad-
visor, Colonel Edward M. House, to Europe to visit with the
heads of state of each of the warring powers. Carnegie was delighted with Wilson's plan, but Morley saw little hope in such a
proposal. "You say you are 'trying your hand' at a presentation of
the case for abolishing war," he wrote Carnegie in late November.
"I fear the time has not yet come. People will not listen. There is
not a place in Great Britain today where you could hold an open
meeting to criticise the war—either its origins, its circumstances,
or its consequences. The president of the Peace Society is a member of the Cabinet!! You may call me a Wet Blanket, if you like. I
am not. But any form of remonstrance against the war will—*for
the moment*—do more harm than good. Scotland is worse than
England." [3]

Carnegie, however, would not let Morley's realism suffocate
his idealistic hopes. Nor did he feel that he could call a morato-
rium on efforts at international co-operation just because Europe
was presently at war. In October he wrote an article for *Independent,* entitled "A League of Peace—Not 'Preparation for War.'"
It was as if for Carnegie time had stopped in 1913. The same old
arguments were offered: once again international war was compared to dueling, and once again the Kaiser was praised for having reduced the amount of dueling among military officers in the
German army! And the same old solutions were offered: arbitration treaties, a league of the great powers, especially Great Britain, Germany, and the United States, to preserve peace. "One
thing is certain," he concluded, "peace upon earth can never
come from 'preparation for war,' hence let us discard that fallacy
and try other means. It is submitted that a League of Peace embracing the chief nations is worthy of consideration." [4] But before
there could be a League of Peace there had to be a world at
peace. As Morley tried to tell Carnegie, nothing "fills our thought
and vision here" but "the savage and mournful trail of bloodshed
and ruin." [5]

Carnegie, in these first months of war, acted at times as if he believed that by ignoring the war he could make it go away. And so
he went right ahead, working to get a "cooling-off" treaty with

Germany along the same lines as the earlier treaties which Bryan had arranged with France and Germany. In these efforts, he had the active co-operation of Secretary of State Bryan. Between the two of them it was arranged that Carnegie would serve as a direct intermediary between the State Department and the German Emperor. "I'm enclosing you copies of the British, French, Russian and Netherlands treaties for your own information and that you may transmit them to the German Emperor," Bryan wrote Carnegie on 7 October. "I most sincerely hope your words will have weight with him." [6]

Along with the copies of the treaties Bryan had furnished him, Carnegie sent a personal letter to the Kaiser. But he was careful first to get Bryan's approval. After Bryan suggested a few minor corrections, Carnegie wrote to Wilhelm II:

May it please Your Majesty:

Of your earnest desire for World Peace I am convinced. This you probably know, since I have not failed repeatedly to proclaim it here.

I could not refuse the request of our Secretary of State, who has undoubtedly risen greatly in public esteem, . . . that I write your Majesty. . . . In my opinion, nothing would please or affect our people so much as your participation in the proposed treaty, thus giving additional proof of your devotion to International Peace. . . .

I had opportunity yesterday morning of consulting at Hamilton College your friend and admirer, Charlemagne Tower, who introduced Mrs. Carnegie and myself to your Majesty at Kiel, and found him enthusiastic upon the proposed treaty of giving statesmen a year to cool, which would generally ensure peace upon some terms. . . .

Meanwhile I find accord among statesmen of both parties here. All support our President in maintaining strict neutrality between the two unfortunate warring nations. Silence for the present; but also I find remarkable unanimity in the belief that this unparalleled war is at last to result in a stern resolve among the best of the nations that men shall no longer be permitted to slay each other, as they are now doing. War must be abolished by a union of the civilized nations, possessing the will and power to maintain peace.[7]

1022

The Kaiser, who must have decided that at this point he had very little to lose and possibly something to gain in preserving American neutrality, agreed to the treaty. But after finally getting the German government's acceptance of a conciliatory treaty, Bryan's and Carnegie's hopes were once again thwarted by the United States Senate, which delayed considering ratification until after the *Lusitania* was torpedoed in the spring of 1915. By then it was too late to hope for ratification.

Another area of Bryan-Carnegie co-operation was in resisting the growing demands for military preparedness, led by Theodore Roosevelt and the military professionals of the country. Carnegie wrote long, earnest letters to Secretary of the Navy Josephus Daniels and to the press arguing against increased naval expenditures.[8] The final political irony of Carnegie's life was that of finding himself in close harmony with Bryan, Senator "Pitchfork" Ben Tillman, and all the other old-time Populists, whom he had once feared as mad demagogues,[9] and in resolute opposition to his one-time hero, Theodore Roosevelt. The former President, who was vigorously beating the drums of war throughout the country, in turn showed openly and publicly his contempt for "the pacifist crowd . . . above all Carnegie" for having "occupied a peculiarly ignoble position . . . and who seemingly are willing to see the triumph of wrong if only all physical danger to their own worthless bodies can thereby be averted. . . ."[10]

How thankful Carnegie was now that the election of 1912 had turned out the way it had! The American people, in their infinite wisdom, had rejected both the well-meaning but ineffective Taft and the mad militarist Roosevelt, and instead had elected as President the greatest man since Lincoln. Wilson, in turn, for whatever reason may have motivated him, had had the good luck to appoint the best Secretary of State, with the possible exception of Root, in the history of the Republic. Things could indeed be much worse than they were, and on 1 January 1915 Carnegie was moved to send out one of his annual, cheery New Year greetings, this time in the form of a letter to the editor of the *Pittsburgh Dispatch:* [11]

> Thanks for your kind favor in which you suggest that I say a few words upon "America's Opportunity."

1023

First: Our beloved Republic has no enemies in the world: neither personal nor national. She covets no new territory and wishes all nations peace and prosperity, setting an example to all the world. She is the foremost of nations in longing for international peace, knowing that "peace hath her victories much more renowned than those of war."

Immigrants come to her from many nations, all certain of being classed under the laws of our own citizens. She welcomes all, and shares her privileges with them. In due time, these arrivals apply for citizenship and become Americans—one man's privilege, every citizen's right—their children educated at our schools, free of expense. She is the pioneer nation proclaiming the brotherhood of man.

She needs no increase in army or navy. The latter is today quite sufficient, better that it were not so large; and as for the army—16,000,000 militia, subject to call, and if called to repel invaders, our only difficulty would be how to provide for the surplus millions who would report. Men who advocate increased armies for us can be likened only to those who are afraid to step out of their homes without a lightning rod down their backs, because men have been known to be struck by lightning. Our Republic has nothing to fear, our march is onward and upward. She leads the procession, other nations must follow.

Andrew Carnegie

New York
December, 1914

This statement, so typically Carnegiean, proved to be his valedictory statement to the American people. The circle was complete. Any one of his letters to Cousin Dod, written when he was fifteen, sixty-five years before, could have been substituted for this letter, and no one could have told the difference. The message was the same: "We have the Charter. Onward and upward with our Beloved Republic."

Carnegie's closest friends and associates, when the first news of the outbreak of the war had come, had been fearful that Carnegie might not survive the blow. So identified was he with the international peace movement that his secretaries in particular had come to regard world peace as Carnegie's own personal possession, and now they feared that his reaction to the failure to maintain it would be the same as if, twenty years before, he had been told that Carnegie Steel was bankrupt. "The war news is terrible and shocking," Robert Franks had written to Carnegie's personal secretary, John Poynton, on the day that the German armies marched toward France. "I do feel so sorry for Mr. C. after having peace so close to his grasp." [12] And Morley had written, "It is impossible that a man like you who has Peace for the deepest cause in his whole soul, and who has made such manful effort to spread the light of Peace over the civilized world should not watch this war with daily horror." [13]

Yet after the initial shock was over and the Carnegies were aboard ship headed back to America, Carnegie, with vigor, energy, and even optimism, had begun to lay plans for the American government to initiate a peace conference and then to assume leadership in achieving an effective international organization of peace. Indeed, so absorbed did he become in co-operating with Bryan to attain these goals, that it was almost as if there were no general war, as if he indeed had peace closer "to his grasp" than ever before. He made nearly as many trips to Washington as he had done in the days of Taft. There he found a much warmer welcome in that quaintly ornate museum that served as an office building for the State Department than he had ever known when Philander C. Knox served as chief officer. When in January 1915 Ross wrote him urging that he come to Scotland for the summer in spite of the war, Carnegie had answered with the impatience of a man too involved to be distracted by trifles like summer vacations: "I am here in constant touch with our President and Secretary of State. . . . Several points between my native and adopted lands require very gentle handling indeed to prevent serious consequences. Anxious as our President and Secretary of State are to do justice to the Old Home, I have a part to play here. I know, or at least I feel that from this point of view I may be of use here." [14] Carnegie felt needed by his country, and this feeling was very important in sustaining him at this dark moment. "These are troublesome times, never was so prest with matters," Carnegie wrote to his cousin Dod,[15] and there was comfort for him in this pressure of affairs, as there is for one obliged to attend to the funeral details for someone whom one has loved deeply.

In early February 1915 Carnegie was once again supoenaed to
appear before an investigating committee. This time it was a special Industrial Relations Commission, appointed by President
Wilson to study the whole field of labor-management relations in
the United States. Among the many topics of interest to the Commission was that of the philanthropic foundations created by men
of immense wealth. Quite obviously, Carnegie and Rockefeller
would be the leading witnesses in such an investigation, and they
were asked to appear before the Commission on the same day,
Rockefeller in the morning and Carnegie in the afternoon.

Carnegie arrived in the hearing room to find a large crowd
present, a great number of whom, according to the New York
Herald reporter covering the interrogation, were "socialists, sin-
gle-taxers and members of the I.W.W." Carnegie could sense the
hostility in the air, and, challenged by this cold reception, he
turned on all his charm. When the chairman of the Commission,
Frank P. Walsh, asked him to state his business, Carnegie turned
to the audience, and addressing them instead of Walsh, replied,
"My business is to do as much good in the world as I can; I have
retired from all other business."

Carnegie then took the offensive by asking permission to read
a prepared statement, a statement in which he anticipated all the
embarrassing questions that he might be asked, and gave in advance his replies to Homestead, labor unions, wages, collective
bargaining, co-operative stores for the workers, and profit-sharing.
All the old chestnuts were dragged out, and re-told with a born
actor's consummate skill and charm, everything from the "Kind-
master-tell-us-what-to-do" cablegram, supposedly sent to him during the Homestead strike, to the "Mr. Carnegie takes no man's
job" story that never failed to bring laughter. According to the
Herald reporter, long before Carnegie had finished his statement,
all the hostility that had initially confronted him had dissipated,
and Carnegie had "a rapt audience" who resented the futile efforts of Chairman Walsh to bring this story hour to an end and to
get down to the business at hand. Carnegie was particularly
courtly and gracious to the many young militant suffragettes and
female socialists in the audience. "One of the greatest triumphs of
this age is the elevation of women," Carnegie joyously shouted,
and was greeted with a storm of applause. "He stood beaming like

a veritable Santa Claus before the Commission," the reporter noted.

Chairman Walsh finally managed to break in and interrupt this fascinating soliloquy.

"Now, I just want to ask you a question or two, Mr. Carnegie, and then we will excuse you."

"Oh, I am not in any hurry. I am enjoying this immensely," Carnegie said.

Walsh gamely persisted. Had Carnegie ever considered "the possibility his foundations might exert undue influence over the beneficiaries"?

"I cannot imagine any injury coming from that."

"President Eliot has said—whom of course you know—"

"Well, I ought to know him. He is drawing one of my pensions." Great laughter and applause.

"He says that the giving of large sums of money does influence the directors, but that the influence has always been for the good."

"Yes, I think it has."

When asked if he thought that the state or Federal government should exercise any supervisory control, Carnegie replied, "Why, I would be delighted to welcome them."

"Do you believe full publicity should be given to the activities of these foundations?"

"Well, I have heard that story—it is one of Burdette's, the publisher of the Burlington [Iowa] Hawkeye—who said, 'The Reverend Mr. Taylor is to preach Sunday night upon "Why Was Lazarus a Beggar?" We have never thought there was any doubt upon the question. It was settled long ago. He did not advertise.' "

There was a roar of laughter at this sally. Then Carnegie continued, "Now, I believe in advertising. I would like more men, more people to get interested in my foundation."

Walsh interrupted. "Now we are going to excuse you permanently, Mr. Carnegie, and thank you very much for what you have told us."

To which Carnegie graciously replied, "The thanks are reciprocated. I have not spent a more agreeable afternoon, I cannot tell you when."

The reporter concluded his story, "It had become almost a love feast now. He had met them and they were his." [16]

It was Carnegie's last public appearance, and he left the stage, as any actor would like to do, with the laughter and applause of his audience ringing in his ears. It had been a brilliant performance, but exhausting, and Carnegie returned home tired and suffering from a slight cold which he felt he had caught from being in the crowded, over-heated conference room.

At home, the weariness persisted for days, and he could not seem to shake off the cold, which developed into bronchitis and then into pneumonia. By the middle of March he was seriously ill, and although the doctors assured Mrs. Carnegie that his heart was strong and that there was no immediate threat to his life, still his recuperation would be slow and prolonged. With the coming of the first warm days of spring, however, Carnegie was well enough to be wheeled out into his garden. Some six weeks after he had been first stricken with pneumonia, his physical recovery was complete, but it was apparent to everyone, and most painfully to Louise, that he was sorely stricken in spirit. He would sit for hours, staring off into space, saying nothing and showing no interest in anything or anyone.

The doctors blamed his state of depression on his recent severe illness. A man of eighty, no matter how vigorous he might be, could not be expected to have the recuperative powers of a man of fifty. But Louise knew that Carnegie's illness was more deeply rooted in the soul than it was in the body. Two months before the onset of his illness, he had given indication that the full brunt of the horror of the war had at last struck home. Since August he had been sustained by a forced activity which numbed his initial grief and kept him alive and in motion. But now the funeral of his hopes was over—there would be no quick ending of the war, and the slaughter would continue grimly and endlessly for as long as he could see into the future. With the burial of his optimistic dreams now done, the full understanding of the loss could at last be realized.

The letters from old friends in Britain were in part responsible for shaking him out of anesthetized trance into painfully cruel reality—letters like the one from the English Positivist, Frederic

1028

Harrison, who, like Carnegie, had once believed that man moved ever onward and upward:

> There is, I fear, no prospect of your visiting Britain whilst the horrors continue; and I am some years your senior—when this letter reaches you, I shall have completed my 85 years on earth—so there is little chance of my being here should you come across the Atlantic when this war is ended. It must end one day from sheer exhaustion if nothing else. So, whilst I have strength to write I send you a few words to express my grateful sense of our friendship in happier days and my profound sense of admiration for the long and universal efforts you have made in the Old & the New Worlds to avert the cataclysm that is a menace to human civilization.[17]

Most painful of all were the letters from Morley, who, unlike Bryce and other close friends, could not accept the premise that Britain had no alternative but to go to war once Germany had invaded Belgium in order to attack France:

> I wrote to you two or three weeks ago—saying little, in truth, saying nothing. Now, when the blasting and desolating curse of War is enveloping the world, what is there to say. The war fever is raging here in heavy strength. It is not yet realised that we at any rate might well have kept out of it; that its results can bring us no solid gain; and that the cost in carnage, waste, and demoralisation of the public mind, will be monstrous.[18]

And a few weeks later:

> It seems a long time since we exchanged letters. The reason, I suppose, is the painfully simple one, that the world gives us nothing on which either of us can say to the other a single, new, fresh, cheering instructive word—not one word. . . . There is no opening, nor possibility for active public operations at the moment. Our people are opening their eyes, as there dawns upon them the huge magnitude of the policy to which they have committed themselves . . . and the impossibility of setting out in clear words what it is exactly that we hope to attain, as the end and object of it all. . . . When the present

ministers—no longer liberal in any sense whatever—continue their journey towards *conscription,* that will probably stir people a little to the criminal folly of first starting that journey.[19]

Letters such as these could not help but have their effect. But when Carnegie, by January 1915, began to express his own growing sense of despair, these same friends were frightened to hear him repeating their sentiments, and they tried desperately to lift his spirits. It was as if each of them felt that if Carnegie should give up hope, then everything would indeed be lost. When Carnegie wrote Ross that he would never come to Skibo as long as the war continued because it would be "too cruel and too sad," Ross at once protested:

> On the contrary, I feel sure that the very fact that you abstain from coming here will increase the sadness. . . . Your presence will tend to encourage and comfort them [the tenants] far more than any letters you could write. . . . Your position as a public man raises a much larger question than a domestic one. You are so much committed to the "Peace Crusade," and you have been so often the exponent of the belief that amidst all the contradictions in this world, the world grows better, that if you now make a public announcement that your sadness has altered your life, it would be accepted as a confession that your faith has been shattered. This will never do. No matter whether the Heavens fall your hope must not be broken. Out of this immeasurable evil you must continue to believe that good will come. . . . In short, you must remain the same happy, optimistic person as ever you were, and there is room enough in your constitution to entertain, at one and the same time, both the optimism and the despondency, but the former must be the more powerful.[20]

Even Morley became alarmed at the mood of Carnegie's letters in the last months of 1914, and he found himself in the unaccustomed role of trying to lift Carnegie's spirits: "It cuts me to the heart that you of all men—the bravest and most confident of men—should write that 'happiness is all over for the nonce.' Today is black—yes, black at the best. But you have a right—and a duty—to find several hours of happiness *per diem* in thinking

1030

that you have fought your best and hardest for your fellow creatures." [21]

But his friends asked too much of Carnegie. The Heavens had fallen, and his hope was now finally broken. As the bright days of spring 1915 came to New York, he sat in his garden, a tiny, motionless figure, wrapped in a cocoon of blankets, unwarmed by the sun, unmoved by the vernal renascence of nature that surrounded him. When the time approached that in every past year had meant the beginning of preparations for their annual migration to Scotland, his depression seemed to deepen. The only thing in the world that he seemed to want now was to go back once again to Skibo, and Louise would have to say, "No, not this year, but surely next."

In June, in accordance with the plans they had made before Carnegie became ill, the Carnegies went to Pointe d'Acadie, Bar Harbor, Maine, where they had leased a summer home built by George Vanderbilt. Louise now felt that if she could get Andrew near the sea again, and if he were strong enough physically to take an occasional short cruise on their yacht, he would surely recover. There was no question that the change was good for Carnegie. He became physically stronger, and Louise kept up a brave front, writing cheerful notes to her friends, "I am delighted to tell you that Mr. Carnegie is very much stronger and spends most of his time on the yacht, the strong sea air proving the very elixir of life for him." [22] But it would break her heart to see him start to write a letter to Morley, and then after a few words, shake his head, push the paper aside, and lapse back into a silent inner retreat that could not be penetrated.

As the summer wore on, he slowly began to come back to life. There was the happy moment in August when Louise could write to Robert Franks, "I have still further good news of Mr. Carnegie. He wrote Lord Morley a most delightful letter last week which we were able to send!! But of course he will not be allowed to write another for a long time. The weather is very trying, so much fog & rain, but we all keep cheerful." [23]

The Carnegies spent most of the winter of 1915–16 in Florida, cruising aimlessly on their yacht. These were trying months for Louise, who never enjoyed travel and was always happiest when she was in her own home in New York or Scotland. But the sunshine and mild sea air seemed to be the best medicine possible for Andrew, and she did not complain. In January, they received news that Lucy Coleman Carnegie had died. Louise wrote Robert Franks, "The whole family revolved around her, and life can never be quite the same to any of us. Mr. Carnegie bore the news better than I expected. I tried to break it very gently, and his quiet acceptance of it was very pathetic. He does not say much, but he is not brooding over it." [24] Death no longer held the terror for Carnegie that it once had.

In April the Carnegies returned to New York. Margaret graduated from Miss Spence's School in May, and then the family went to a new home, the Brick House, in Noroton, Connecticut, on Long Island Sound. Maine had been too damp and foggy the previous summer, and Louise was desperately searching for a suitable substitute for Skibo. Noroton was not the answer. It was hot and humid, and Carnegie, who could never tolerate summer heat, was uncomfortable and miserably lonely for Skibo. Louise knew that Carnegie would probably never be able to undertake another trans-Atlantic journey, even if the war should end during the coming year, and she was determined to find a summer home that would be their own. She asked her friends to help in the search. In the fall of 1916 the Carnegies bought a large stone mansion near Lenox, Massachusetts, called Shadowbrook, which had been built by Anson Phelps Dodge in the 1890's. It was situated on a high hill overlooking Lake Mahkeenac far below. Surrounding the lake were the lovely, wooded Berkshire Hills, which in fall glowed with the color of flame. Louise, visiting Shadowbrook in October, knew that no place in all America could come closer to matching Skibo for natural beauty, and the estate was promptly purchased.[25] Carnegie was pleased, and with a new home to look forward to, some of his interest in living seemed to return to him. Falteringly, hesitantly, he began his correspondence with Morley again, although Louise often worried that Morley's letters were not good for him. They were too sad and sentimental:

> My best of friends. Here's the last day of the year—the worst of years! . . . The political skies do not clear, in whatever aspect you care to look to them. The carnage is hideous. . . . The Britain that you and I have known all these long years is

pretty rapidly disappearing. Well, we must face our fates as we best can. . . . I often think of that parting night in the Liverpool hotel.[26]

Morley wrote often of coming to America to visit them, either in Florida in the winter or to see their new home in the Berkshires. Louise had mixed feelings about that proposed visit, but Carnegie lived in the hopes of having one more good talk with his friend.

As relations between the United States and Germany reached the breaking point in the late winter and early spring of 1917, Carnegie's interest in world affairs revived. He once again read the newspapers and would dictate an occasional letter of advice to the President. Strongly influenced by Louise and by John Poynton, who were devoted Anglophiles, Carnegie by February 1917 had finally become convinced that the only way now to achieve world peace was for the United States to enter the war and defeat Germany. On 14 February 1917 he wrote to Wilson urging war. His letter had all the vigor of expression and the conviction he had used in addressing McKinley and Taft:

> Sometime ago I wrote you "Germany is beyond reason." She has ever since become more and more so until today she shows herself completely insane. . . . Were I in your place there would soon be an end to this. There is only one straight way of settlement. You should proclaim war against her, however reluctantly, and then settlement would soon come. Britain and France cooperating with us, would insure peace promptly beyond question, and at the next meeting at the Hague, we would abolish war forever. . . . Let me predict you will have the greatest of all careers before you; hope it will be soon clearly defined. Be of good cheer.[27]

Carnegie had good company in his move from pacifism to militarism. J. Allen Baker, the great English pacifist, was now begging the United States to enter the war as Britain's ally. Lord Bryce wrote Carnegie frequently to say that Britain could not endure another year of war without America's help. Even the Carnegie Endowment for International Peace passed a resolution in support of Wilson's strong stand against Germany. Only Morley stood firm, in proud isolation, holding to his principle that all war was criminal folly.[28]

Following the declaration of war by Congress on 6 April 1917, Carnegie sent a telegram to Wilson, "You have triumphed at last. God bless you. You will give the world peace and rank the greatest hero of all." [29] Wilson had taken America into the Great Crusade, the war to end all wars, and Carnegie from the sidelines cheered him on. He sent a telegram to Franks, "Would like to subscribe for about two hundred thousand dollars of Liberty Bonds. All should rally to the country's call. Madam concurs. Please wire if this can be arranged." [30]

The Carnegies made other contributions to the war effort that were far more of a personal sacrifice than their monetary contributions. Harry Whitfield, Louise's brother, received a commission as a lieutenant in the army, and was prepared to be sent to the front. Hardest of all for Carnegie to give up to the war was his valet, Robert Morrison, who had attended him faithfully for many years. Morrison enlisted in the Marines, and no one else in the Carnegie household could be a satisfactory substitute.

Shadowbrook proved to be all that Louise had hoped it might be. It was not Skibo, but it would certainly serve until the war should end. "Andrew is a new man since coming here," Louise wrote to Franks during their first summer in the Berkshires. "We take a motor drive every day and we are so delighted with this beautiful country. Andrew sleeps well & has a good appetite. . . . We love our home already & we are fast getting settled. . . . Andrew misses his yacht but we have bought him an electric launch which is to be here next week and he is keenly looking forward to fishing on the lake." [31]

It was almost like the old times at Skibo—fishing, reading, walking slowly on the terrace and watching the sunset on the lake —even making plans for the important tasks that lay ahead. "Glad to say I am much stronger than I have been for months, and able for serious work which is sure to come very soon," Carnegie wrote Lord Bryce in October 1917. "We are on the eve of Germany's defeat that is certain. President Wilson's detailed statements settled this. By the end of the year you will be out of anxiety. Germany will deserve her fate. We hope to see you & Madam in London soon & of course you visit us at Skibo as usual." [32]

But there was a loneliness now that Carnegie had never known at Skibo, and the long summer days, waiting for the war to end, waiting for the triumph of peace, waiting for Skibo, seemed interminable. George Lauder came up to visit him, but after the first flurry of greetings they had very little to say to each other. The world of business seemed so far distant in the past and so unimportant that Carnegie had no interest in talking about that, and Lauder had never paid much attention to American politics. So after a few efforts at conversation, they spent the remainder of Lauder's visit fishing, or trying a few desultory games of checkers, or simply sitting and looking at the distant hills, each lost in his own world. Carnegie felt more lonely than ever.[33]

What meant more to Carnegie than any of the few visitors he had in these months was receiving an advance copy of Morley's memoirs. Reading his dearest friend's autobiography brought back a flood of memories which, fortunately, were more real to Carnegie than the present could possibly be. It was as if the long-hoped-for Morley visit had actually occurred.

> Your wonderful book of recollections has given me rare and unalloyed pleasure. You have dealt with matters of state as no others could in my opinion, especially those of India and Ireland. . . . I have read every word and it is as if I were again talking these things all over with you face to face on the terrace at Skibo. Your references to me are all too flattering, but I am not altogether displeased, though you know my modest nature.
>
> I feel confident that with America's help, the great war cannot last much longer, and Madam and I are thinking and talking of the time when we will return to Skibo and have you with us once more.[34]

To which Morley responded:

> I never had a letter that gave me more peculiar pleasure than yours of January 21. First of all, it was delightful to think of you in full health and strength to write it, and besides to do the long spell of reading through a couple of heavy, and not light-handed volumes.
>
> As for my book, the critics here have been wonderfully indulgent; but your warm liking for it, and interest in it, moves me more than all the critics put together. I seem to hear your very

voice, as if we were pacing the Skibo terrace arm in arm, together. . . . We have done a good space of our long journey
with substantial understanding of one another, and unbroken
sincere sympathies. As I think of it, . . . I have something of
the feel in me that I used to have as I heard the organ of a
morning at Skibo.[35]

The basic difference in temperament between the two men
was still apparent. Carnegie spoke of Skibo as the future—"when
we will return to Skibo"; Morley spoke of Skibo as the past—
". . . I have something of the feel that I used to have. . . ." Old
and tired as he was, Carnegie was still reaching out toward the future.

In spite of his easy assumption that America's entry would
bring a speedy end to the conflict, the war continued to drag on,
through the long winter, and with the coming of spring 1918
Skibo remained as far away and inaccessible as it had been for the
last three years. The Carnegies returned to Shadowbrook for another summer of waiting. Wilson's phrase, used to describe his
policy during the Mexican crisis, of "watchful waiting" had taken
on a new and terribly personal significance for Carnegie. Only the
thought of Skibo and the hope for the new world order that Wilson promised gave to Carnegie the strength and the will to live.

The Carnegies had planned to return to New York during the
last week of October, but the autumn of 1918 was so unusually
warm and beautiful in the Berkshires that they stayed on at Shadowbrook during the first week of November. "We made the decision yesterday," Louise wrote Franks, "and as we are all packed
& ready to go this week, the few extra days are like our former sea
voyages, a real rest between our two big houses." [36]

By the time they came back to New York, it was apparent to
the whole world that at last the war was finally coming to an end.
The Kaiser had abdicated, Austria-Hungary had capitulated, and
an excited Carnegie was full of plans and advice for the President.
On the tenth of November, less than twenty-four hours before the
Armistice, he wrote to Wilson, "Now that the world war seems
practially at an end I cannot refrain from sending you my heart-
felt congratulations upon the great share you have had in bringing about its successful conclusion. The Palace of Peace at the

Hague would, I think, be the fitting place for dispassionate discussion regarding the destiny of the conquered nations, and I hope your influence may be exerted in that direction." [37]

Carnegie had offered much advice to many Presidents, but he had never offered sounder counsel than this. It is possible that at The Hague a quite different treaty might have been written. Certainly the site for the Peace Conference that was chosen—the Palace at Versailles, with its historical connotations that evoked memories both of the French arrogance of Louis XIV and of the French humiliation of surrender in 1871—was the last place in the world in which there could be any "dispassionate discussion regarding the destiny of the conquered nations."

Wilson, however, in responding to Carnegie was quite noncommittal: "I know your heart must rejoice at the dawn of peace after these terrible years of struggle, for I know how long and earnestly you have worked for and desired such conditions as I pray God it may now be possible for us to establish. The meeting place of the Peace Conference has not yet been selected, but even if it is not held at The Hague, I am sure you will be present in spirit." [38] As indeed Carnegie was! He exhausted himself in reading every word he could find in the newspapers about Wilson's proposed League of Nations, which closely followed—even to the name— the proposal Carnegie had made several years before in what now seemed like a different century and was certainly a different world.

Carnegie's eighty-third birthday came two weeks after the Armistice, and it was the happiest birthday that he had known in years. The war was over, and all of Carnegie's hopes for international peace and order were now formulated and secured in the portfolio which the President of the United States would carry with him to Paris the next month to present to the nations of the world as the non-negotiable basis for any peace treaty. In addition, Louise and Andrew had a very personal reason for regarding this particular birthday celebration as being something extraordinarily momentous and pleasurable. Margaret, who had grown into a beautiful and gracious young lady, had during the summer fallen in love with a young ensign, Roswell Miller. His sister, Dorothy, had been a close friend of Margaret's at Miss Spence's School, and she had introduced Margaret to her brother. Carnegie had known Roswell's father, the former president of the Chicago, Milwaukee & St. Paul Railroad, for many years.

Compared with her parents' extended engagement, Margaret's romance was a whirlwind affair. Upon returning to New York in November, she and Roswell told her parents that they wished to marry, and it was agreed that the engagement would be announced at Andrew's birthday celebration. The wedding was set for the following spring. And so all through this first winter of peace, the Carnegie family were busy with preparations—for Margaret's wedding in April and for the Carnegies' departure for Scotland in May.

Morley had written to Carnegie a few days after the war had ended: "I sometimes dream that you may cross the Atlantic this summer. Shall I? 'I hae ma doots.' Do you reproach me? You were always far the bolder and more valiant of the two." [39] Carnegie had no "doots" at all about his and Louise's crossing the Atlantic that summer. This was what he had been waiting for, for nearly five years. Against what must have been Louise's better judgment, the plans for sailing were made and the instructions sent to John Ross and to the factor at Skibo for assembling a household staff and making the necessary preparations for the opening of Skibo.

On 22 April 1919, the thirty-second wedding anniversary of the Carnegies, their daughter Margaret was married to Roswell Miller at the Carnegie home. Frail and feeble as he was, Andrew insisted upon escorting Margaret down the stairway to the altar that had been erected in the dining room. Louise wrote in her diary that evening:

> Glorious bright spring day. Our darling's wedding day and our own 32nd anniversary. Ceremony at noon . . . Margaret made a lovely bride . . . Andrew so well and alert. He and I gave Baba away and later we walked down the aisle together. After greeting the bride and groom he went upstairs and rested . . . Andrew up in the evening. Backgammon.[40]

By the first of May, it was apparent to Louise that they must give up their plans to return to Skibo that summer. Andrew, weak as he was, could never survive the long trans-Atlantic trip.

"I talked Shadowbrook to him yesterday," Louise wrote to her daughter, "and told him all about giving up Skibo this year . . . he made no fuss, he fully understands that it was impossible to go across this year and is looking forward to the fishing from the *Shiela* this summer. So the disappointment I dreaded for Daddy has passed almost without a ripple." Louise was apparently still trying to keep up the pretense of next year with her husband. When she told Carnegie that they couldn't go this spring after all, because of the difficulties of transportation and the shortage of food in Britain, she added, "But surely next year, we can go." Carnegie looked up at her with that sharp, penetrating glance that his business associates had once known so well, and replied, "There won't be a next year for me." Neither of them ever mentioned the return to Skibo again.[41]

In late May the Carnegies went back to Shadowbrook. The children drove up to visit them for a few days. On the day they left to return to Connecticut, Louise noted in her diary, "Margaret and Roswell left by their motor at 9:30 and I am left alone with Andrew, so frail and feeble and so very weak." The long days of summer dragged slowly by. There was no fishing for Andrew this summer, only quiet, patient waiting. "Andrew is so weak and weary," Louise wrote on 5 August. "I played the little organ for him on the verandah after tea." [42] The only comfort for Louise in this sad summer was that Morrison, Carnegie's devoted valet, had been released from military service and was there at Shadowbrook to take care of Andrew.

On 9 August Carnegie was stricken once again with pneumonia. Both Louise and he knew that the end was near, but Carnegie was so very tired that he welcomed it. In the early morning hours of 11 August the nurse aroused Louise and told her she should come to Andrew's bedside. "I was called at 6 A.M. and remained with my darling husband, giving him oxygen until he gradually fell asleep at 7:14," Louise wrote in her diary. "I am left alone . . . Margaret and Roswell such comforts, relieving me of details. Telegrams pouring in. I think he knew me but he did not speak." [43]

Of all of the hundreds of letters and telegrams that came to Shadowbrook from around the world, the one that touched Louise Carnegie the most was from John Morley.

I cannot realise that my most steadfast of all friends has gone, nor do I realise that this letter will find you lonely in your home. Though he was far from me in place and sight, in thought he was close and constant. How little when we last said goodbye at the Liverpool Station, could we suppose that we were to meet no more, and that the humane hopes we had lived in, and lived by, were on the very eve of ruin. Our ideas and aims were just the same, but the fire and glow of his spirit was his own, and my debt to him from the year when Arnold made us acquainted, was more than I can find words for. His interest in me and my doings was for all this long span of time active, eager, indulgent, long-sighted, high pitched. My days of survival cannot be very far prolonged, but they will be much the more dull now that the beacon across the Atlantic has gone out.[44]

There were many besides Morley who would find the world a much duller place without Carnegie. He had, it is true, been a long time in passing from the scene—nearly nineteen years since he had left the world of business, seven years since he had given up the direct supervision of his philanthropic interests, four years since he had been an active force in politics. Yet, until the moment of his death, he had remained to millions of his countrymen their prize showpiece of what they liked to think was the real essence of the American experience—the Americanized immigrant, the rugged individual, the self-made man, the Horatio Alger hero, the beneficent philanthropist, the missionary of secular causes, the democrat who could not only walk with but argue with kings. The public library was his temple and the "Letters to the Editor" column his confessional. With his death the editorial writers throughout the country solemnly proclaimed the end of an era in American history. Carnegie knew it had ended long before 1919, and he also knew that by his very success he had done more than any socialist, any labor leader, any academic theorist to kill the very system under which he had flourished. He knew in 1901 what it had meant to have his simple "associational" partnership be replaced by America's first billion-dollar corporation. He knew what it meant to have his personal philanthropy, once handled by a single secretary, replaced by a $125,000,000 corporation. A decade before his death he had written that the day of the free enterprise, competitive system of American capitalism had ended, and that these new "virtual monopolies" must be controlled by the national government. Carnegie may have been an idealist in believing that the world moved ever "onward and upward," but he was also a realist in knowing and accepting the fact that change was inevitable.

At his own request, Carnegie was buried in the Sleepy Hollow Cemetery in North Tarrytown, New York. His grave was marked by a Celtic cross, cut from stone quarried near Skibo. The cross bore the simple message:

Andrew Carnegie
Born in Dunfermline, Scotland, 25 November 1835
Died in Lenox, Massachusetts, 11 August 1919.

Five years later, Samuel Gompers, head of the American Federation of Labor, was buried in an adjoining lot. The villagers report that they lie at peace with each other, for there are no new tales of ghosts walking uneasily to add to the Legend of Sleepy Hollow.

Epilogue:
The Deed Continues
1919- —

The probating of Andrew Carnegie's will two weeks after his death was a major news story throughout the world, for there had been much speculation as to whether or not he had succeeded in giving away his immense fortune. The opinion expressed in the New York *Sun,* that Carnegie's fortune must have exceeded $600 million, of which it was believed he had given away $350 million, leaving for his family a balance of $250 million, was typical of the general attitude of doubt that Carnegie had died in the state of grace that he had sought.[1]

But when the will was opened, the shelves were nearly bare. The *Literary Digest* helpfully listed for its readers an itemized account of Carnegie's principal benefactions, which came to the precise total of $350,695,653.[2] Of what remained of his fortune to dispense by his will—a sum of $30 million, which was less than one-tenth of his fortune, two-thirds of even that went to the Carnegie Corporation of New York. Of the remaining $10 million, $4 million were set aside to provide yearly pensions of from five to ten thousand dollars to Dunfermline relatives and to old friends: Annie and Maggie Lauder and John Morley each received an annuity of $10,000. Carnegie also remembered the old Radical associates he had once worked with in British politics: Thomas Burt, John Wilson, and even John Burns, who had scornfully rejected Carnegie's contribution to his Parliamentary election campaign following Homestead. Carnegie also provided a $10,000 annual pension for David Lloyd George and former President Taft. Long an advocate of state pensions for the widows of former Presidents, Carnegie apparently hoped to shame the government into action, for he provided pensions for Mrs. Theodore Roosevelt and Mrs. Thomas Preston, Grover Cleveland's widow. There were lesser amounts left to personal servants and to the tenant farmers of Skibo. "We are blessed with fine people on the Skibo estate," Carnegie had written by hand in his will. "A sum equal to two years rent shall be remitted to each crofter as rent accrues who is in good standing among his neighbors." [3]

Except for the real estate that Carnegie had owned, there was no other monetary bequest at all. Instead he wrote, "Having years ago made provision for my wife beyond her desires and ample enough to enable her to provide for our beloved daughter, Margaret, and being unable to judge at present what provision for our daughter will best promote her happiness, I leave to her mother the duty of providing for her as her mother deems best. A mother's love will be the best guide." [4]

The remaining one million dollars were divided among Hampton Institute, Pittsburgh University, Stevens Institute, Cooper Union, the Relief Fund of the Authors Club of New York, and St. Andrew's Society. The will was Carnegie throughout, an expression of his loves, his interests and concerns, couched in his own forceful style. As *The New York Times* stated in editorial tribute: "In this [will] the dead man seems alive and speaking to us." [5]

And so it was finished for Carnegie. Not a single bond was left in that once imposingly filled vault in Hoboken, New Jersey. He had not died in disgrace. The press in general was impressed. The New York *Sun* called Carnegie "the personification of 'Triumphant Democracy.'" An enterprising reporter from the New York *Globe*, however, went out on the streets and asked fourteen working men what they thought of Andrew Carnegie. The answers ranged from "He was a good man," and "I believe he was a just employer," to "All businessmen is crooked, you know," and "I never seen a book yet that would keep a man from starving to death." One old blacksmith, a Scotsman, appropriately enough, best summed up the average workingman's view: "Maybe you've heard the saying, that every honest man has hair growing in the palms of his hands." No "gratitude and sweet words" here, but no particular anger or bitterness either—just a cynical Diogenesian acceptance that no man is honest, and millionaires, of necessity, being the most successful, are the least honest of all. Carnegie was simply a product of his society.[6]

Carnegie might have wished for a better epitaph, but he should not have been too surprised at this expression of the voice of the people. There were, to be sure, magnificent words of tribute from leaders in business, government, education, and humanitarian organizations throughout the world. Carnegie would have enjoyed these, but he certainly would not have been surprised at them either.

One tribute to his memory which he would have desired above any other he was to be denied, however. Three months after his death, the United States Senate, of which he once wrote, "I regard as the wisest body of legislators in the world," [7] in its own peculiar wisdom voted down "Mr. Wilson's Treaty," which had incorporated Wilson's—and Carnegie's—best hope for world peace, the League of Nations. Wilson, as President and as a man, was destroyed by this act. Carnegie, mercifully, was spared the knowledge of his latest defeat. Had he lived to witness it, however, he would probably have not given up hope even then. He certainly would have applauded one of Woodrow Wilson's last comments on the failure of their mutual dream. "Perhaps," Wilson told his daughter, "it was best after all that the United States did not join the League of Nations." When she, in surprise, asked why, he replied, "Because our entrance into the League at the time I returned from Europe might have been only a personal victory. Now, when the American people join the League it will be because they are convinced that it is the right thing to do, and then will be the *only right* time for them to do it." Carnegie could not have said it better for himself.[8]

Carnegie's natural optimism could have survived this defeat of the League, for a single lost engagement might temporarily delay but could not permanently arrest man's steady "onward and upward" progress. Carnegie's view of history had always been linear and vertically inclined—*ad astra per aspera.* America's history, he believed, was the Q.E.D. of his historical theorem, and this view had sustained him even in the last, dark days of his life.

But history can trace a quite different pattern from that of the oblique line. It can also be seen as moving in a plane orbit back upon itself. In the quarter-century after Carnegie's death, it was this inane cruelty of circular repetition that would make a mockery of Carnegie's simplistic faith in progress.

For Louise Carnegie, who was sixty-two years old when Andrew died, and who faced the prospect of long years of widowhood, there was at first comfort in preserving the traditional pattern of their lives. The first summer after Andrew's death, she returned to their beloved Skibo, and the old familiar transatlantic migrations were renewed once again: winter and spring in New York, summer and autumn at Skibo. No longer the crowds of people, to be sure, and even fewer of the "Old Shoes" to come up on the little train to be met at Bonar Bridge. John Morley died in 1923, and after that there was really no one left from the old days. The retreat to Aultnagar was no longer necessary. Skibo was now filled with Margaret's four children and their many friends, and there was great joy for Louise in this.

She held fast to Andrew's interests, dutifully read the reports of the various Carnegie foundations, closely followed international events, and continued to work for the League of Nations. She was deeply touched by the many ceremonies in both Britain and the United States that celebrated the centenary of Andrew Carnegie's birth in November 1935. In one of her rare public speeches, she spoke with all of the optimism of her husband: "I believe the day will yet come when his hope shall be realized and the world shall become a family of nations. For many years the subject of internationalism has interested me more deeply than any other, and if the years have taught me anything it is that no man nor nation can do any effective work in the world alone. It is only by working together for a common cause that civilization can be carried forward." [9]

1045

That day was as far off in 1935, however, as it had been in 1913, when Carnegie had delivered his tribute of peace to the Kaiser. In August 1939, Louise was at Skibo when the news was received that Britain and France were again at war with Germany. There was no comfort in this repetition—the same departure that she had made with Andrew twenty-five years almost to the day. There was the quick packing, the sad farewells, and then Louise Carnegie left Skibo for the last time, clutching a gas mask under her arm.

She was older in 1939 than Andrew had been when they had left Skibo in 1914, and these years of war would be even more difficult for her, for part of her family remained in Scotland, and the peril was much greater. She was old and tired, and she was more of a realist than Andrew had ever been. Weeks after she had left Skibo, one of the few servants who remained in the castle found a small bouquet of flowers, with a note in her handwriting, "Farewell to Skibo. September 1, 1939." [10]

Back home in New York, she gave Christmas parties for servicemen,[11] sent checks to the Red Cross, bought war bonds, and waited for this war to end. The first spring of peace in 1946, she thought again of Skibo, but she knew she could not return. The farewells had been said, seven years before. On 24 June 1946, Louise Carnegie died at her home in New York. The circle was complete.

But Carnegie would not have accepted this as an ending to his and Louise's life. There was always the possibility of another try, always the hope of a better tomorrow. His memorials were not mausoleums built to celebrate death, but great foundations for the celebration of hope. In 1911 he had endowed the Carnegie Corporation of New York with $125 million, "for the advancement and diffusion of knowledge." He had wisely given the trustees the freedom to carry out this charge as they saw fit, with no mortmain of the past to restrict their effectiveness.

Ever since that day, when as a young boy, he had received his first dividend check from his ten shares of Adams Express, and had shouted, "Eureka! Here's the goose that lays the golden eggs," Carnegie had put his faith in the capitalistic system. The Carnegie Corporation of New York has been the justification of that faith. In the fifty years since Carnegie's death, the Corporation has made grants that almost total Carnegie's entire fortune. Yet the latest quarterly report of the Corporation shows that its present assets total $324 million—again almost equal to Carnegie's total wealth—and all of this from an endowment of $145 million.[12] Here was the proof of a kind of immortality that Carnegie could understand. The good deed would continue—onward and upward, forever and ever. As Carnegie would say, "So be it."

Notes

CHAPTER I

1. Robert Southey, *Journal of a Tour in Scotland in 1819*, London, 1929, 136; Macqueen, *A Letter to his Grace, the Duke of Hamilton and Brandon*, Glasgow, 1820.
2. Philip Guedalla, *Wellington*, New York, 1931, 423.
3. Southey, op. cit. 37.
4. See D. G. D. Isaac, *A Study of Popular Disturbances in Britain, 1714–1754*, unpublished doctoral dissertation, University of Edinburgh, 1953.
5. Henry W. Meikle, *Scotland and the French Revolution*, Glasgow, 1912, 79f.
6. William Law Mathieson, *The Awakening of Scotland*, Glasgow, 1910, 140–41.
7. See Agnes Mure Mackenzie, *The Kingdom of Scotland*, Edinburgh, 1957; W. T. Barr, *For a Web Begun*, Edinburgh, 1947, 18f; J. M. Webster, *Dunfermline Abbey*, Dunfermline, 1948.
8. In the 1831 census Dunfermline's population was 10,625; by 1841 the population had increased to 13,323. Peter Chalmers, *Historical and Statistical Account of Dunfermline*, Edinburgh, 1844, 327.
9. Ibid. 375.
10. Ebenezer Henderson, *The Annals of Dunfermline*, Glasgow, 1879, 171.
11. Alexander J. Warden, *The Linen Trade, Ancient and Modern*, London, 1867, 554; Daniel Thomson, *The Weavers' Craft*, Paisley, 1903, 148, 219.
12. The story of James Blake is repeated in nearly all accounts of the weaving industry in Scotland. See Barr, op. cit. 40f; Thomson, op. cit. 194; Henderson, op. cit. 400. Barr and Thomson give the date as 1719; Henderson, who is usually more reliable, gives 1718.
13. W. H. K. Turner, "The Textile Industries of Dunfermline and Kirkcaldy, 1700–1900," *The Scottish Geographical Magazine*, Vol. 73, December 1957, 131; Henderson, op. cit. 640.
14. Chalmers, op. cit. 381.
15. Thomson, op. cit. 352.
16. Barr, op. cit. 95–97. See also Albert V. Dicey and Robert S. Rait, *Thoughts on the Union Between England and Scotland*, London, 1920.

1049

17. John Naismith, *Thoughts on Various Objects of Industry Pursued in Scotland*, Edinburgh, 1790, 113f.
18. *Parliamentary Papers, 1835. Reports from Committees, Session* 19 February—10 September 1835, Vol. 13, xiii, Bodleian Library, Oxford University.
19. Barr, op. cit. 50–51; Thomson, op. cit. 352.
20. Turner, op. cit. 136.

CHAPTER II

1. *The Dunfermline Almanack and Register for 1835*, No. 7, Dunfermline, 1836.
2. *The* [Edinburgh] *Scotsman*, Vol. XIX, Wednesday, 25 November 1835.
3. *Dunfermline Almanack*, op. cit; Alexander Stewart, *Reminiscences of Dunfermline Sixty Years Ago*, Edinburgh, 1886, 25.
4. Henderson, *Annals of Dunfermline*, 638.
5. Burton J. Hendrick, *The Life of Andrew Carnegie*, (hereafter cited as Hendrick, *Life*), I, New York, Doubleday, Doran, 1932, 11.
6. Marjorie Plant, *The Domestic Life of Scotland in the Eighteenth Century*, Edinburgh, 1952, 253–54, 44.
7. Letter from Mrs. M. C. Douglas of Stonehaven to the writer, 19 March 1958; note from the Earl of Southesk to Andrew Carnegie, undated, but probably in December 1899, Andrew Carnegie Papers, Library of Congress (hereafter cited as ACLC), Vol. 70.
8. J. B. Mackie, *Andrew Carnegie: His Dunfermline Ties and Benefactions*, Dunfermline, 1916, 5–6. This is the best account of the family background. Also, Henry Carnegie to a Mr. George, 19 December 1907, ACLC, Vol. 146.
9. Mackie, op. cit. 7.
10. Joseph Frazier Wall, "Andrew Carnegie: Child of Chartism," *History 4*, 154.
11. Andrew Carnegie, *Autobiography of Andrew Carnegie* (hereafter cited as *Autobiography*), Boston, 1920, 2. Quoted by permission of Houghton Mifflin Co.
12. Ibid. 3; Daniel Thomson to Henry Carnegie, 9 July 1906, ACLC, Vol. 131.
13. John Pattison, "Genealogy of the Morrison Family," handwritten manuscript, dated Pittsburgh, 1935, in the Carnegie papers, Carnegie Museum, Dunfermline (hereafter cited as AC, Dunfermline).
14. See Carnegie's testimony before the Stanley Committee, House of Representatives, as reported in the New York *Herald*, 13 January 1912.
15. Hendrick, *Life*, I, 8–9.
16. Pattison, op. cit. 6.
17. William B. Dickson, ed., *History of the Carnegie Veterans Association*, Montclair, N. J., 1938, 5.
18. Henry Cockburn, *Journal of Henry Cockburn, 1831–1854*, Edinburgh, 1874, Vol. 1, 14 November 1831 and 26 April 1832.
19. Henderson, op. cit. 632.
20. Cockburn, op. cit. 22 May 1832.
21. Ibid. 6 August 1832.
22. Ibid. 11 August 1832.
23. See Simon Maccoby, *English Radicalism, 1832–1852*, London, 1935, 41ff.
24. *The Dunfermline Universal Sufferage Associations Principals and Rules*, Dunfermline, 1832.
25. Clipping from the *Glasgow Free Press*, 5 October 1832, copy in ACLC, Vol. 1.

26. Thomas Morrison, *Rights of Land,* unpublished holographic MS, AC, Dunfermline, 25.

27. Ibid. 44–45.

28. Ibid. 49–53.

29. William Cobbett, *Rural Rides,* edited by G. D. H. and Margaret Cole, London, 1930, Vol. 3, 781.

30. Wall, op. cit. 159.

31. A copy of this issue may be seen in the Carnegie Public Library, Dunfermline.

32. *The Precursor,* Dunfermline, 1 February 1833.

33. Morrison, op. cit. 37.

34. Thomas Morrison to Lord Dalmeny, 3 December 1834, ACLC, Vol. 1.

35. Thomas Morrison to Lord Dalmeny, 24 April 1835, ACLC, Vol. 1.

36. Mackie, op. cit. 11.

37. Extract of notice of marriage from an entry in the register kept at the General Registry Office, Edinburgh, copy in ACLC, Vol. 1.

38. *Autobiography,* 23.

CHAPTER III

1. Chalmers, *Historical and Statistical Account of Dunfermline,* Edinburgh, 1844, 378.

2. John K. Winkler, *Incredible Carnegie,* New York, 1931, 3.

3. Andrew Carnegie, "From Bobbin-Boy to Millionaire," *The Golden Penny,* London, Vol. 8, 28 January 1899, 87.

4. See letter from Daniel Thomson to Henry Carnegie, dated 9 July 1906, ACLC, Vol. 131.

5. From a scrapbook of newspaper clippings on Andrew Carnegie, Vol. 1, Carnegie Public Library, Pittsburgh.

6. Andrew Carnegie, *Our Coaching Trip,* New York, 1882, 185 (hereafter cited as *Our Coaching Trip*).

7. An Old West Fifer Abroad, *When We Were Boys,* Dunfermline, 1911, 27.

8. *Dunfermline Journal,* 26 February 1841.

9. Alexander Stewart, *Reminiscences of Dunfermline Sixty Years Ago,* Edinburgh, 1886, 87–90.

10. Ibid. 152–55; *Autobiography,* 20.

11. Stewart, op. cit. 148; Mackie, *Dunfermline Ties and Benefactions,* 40.

12. See a collection of these broadsides, undated, Carnegie Public Library, Dunfermline.

13. *Autobiography,* 15–16.

14. Ibid. 16, 20.

15. Andrew Carnegie, handwritten MS dated 28 December 1889, ACLC, Vol. 10.

16. Bernard Alderson, *Andrew Carnegie: From Telegraph Boy to Millionaire,* London, 1902, 16.

17. Hendrick, *Life,* 1, 14.

18. Stewart, op. cit. 40; Winkler, op. cit. 33.

19. *Autobiography,* 23–24.

20. Ibid. 13.

21. Mackie, op. cit. 36–39; *Autobiography*, 14; MS by Thomas Clark, schoolmate of AC, dated 12 October 1901, Carnegie Public Library, Dunfermline.

22. Hendrick, *Life*, I, 20–21, 27.

23. L. C. Wright, *Scottish Chartism and Its Economic Background*, unpublished Ph.D. thesis, University of Edinburgh, 1951, 59–60.

24. Daniel Thomson, *The Weavers' Craft*, 362–63.

25. Ibid. 364.

26. F. C. Mather, *Public Order in the Age of the Chartists*, Manchester, 1959, 208–9.

27. *Niffler Society Records Book, 1776–1885, Nethertown*, Carnegie Public Library, Dunfermline.

28. Tom Morrison to his children, 1837, ACLC, Vol. 1.

29. Stewart, op. cit. 115.

30. *The Edinburgh Monthly Democrat and Total Abstinence Advocate*, No. 1, July 7, 1838.

31. William Thom, *Rhymes and Recollections of a Hand-Loom Weaver*, London, 2nd Edition, 1845, 21ff.

32. Thomas Johnston, *The History of the Working Classes in Scotland*, Glasgow, 1912, 314–17.

33. F. C. Mather, "The Government and the Chartists," in *Chartist Studies*, 385–90; F. C. Mather, *Public Order in the Age of the Chartists*, 15–16.

34. Stewart, op. cit. 115.

35. Wright, op. cit. 221. See also *The* [Edinburgh] *Scotsman*, 27 August and 3 September 1842.

36. *Autobiography*, 8–9; Mackie, op. cit. 15–16.

37. See copy of the broadside in the Thomas Morrison Collection of MSS, Carnegie Public Library, Dunfermline.

38. Notes of James Shearer, who lived on Moodie Street near the Carnegies, ACLC, Vol. 244.

39. *Dunfermline Journal*, 26 February 1841.

40. *Autobiography*, 9.

41. Mackie, op. cit. 16–17.

42. Hendrick, *Life*, I, 25.

43. *Autobiography*, 10.

44. *Autobiography*, 12–13; Hendrick, *Life*, I, 39.

45. *Autobiography*, 13.

46. Hendrick, *Life*, I, 247–48.

CHAPTER IV

1. Quoted in John W. Dodds, *The Age of Paradox: A Biography of England, 1841–1851*, London, 1953, 212.

2. Frederich Engels, *The Condition of the Working Class in England in 1844*, London, 1952 reprint (Social Science Series), 298.

3. Johnston, *History of the Working Classes*, 308; Stewart, *Reminiscences of Dunfermline*, 114; Thomson, *The Weavers' Craft*, 336.

4. Henderson, *Annals of Dunfermline*, 655; Stewart, op. cit. 114.

5. Table of Prices, Weavers Collection, Carnegie Public Library, Dunfermline.

6. *Parliamentary Papers*, 1834, Vol. X, quoted in Lucy Brown, "The Chartists and the Anti-Corn Law League," *Chartist Studies*, 350n.

7. Mackie, *Dunfermline Ties and Benefactions*, 53–54.

8. Hendrick, *Life*, I, 38.

9. *Autobiography*, 12.

10. Annie and Andrew Aitkin to William and Margaret Carnegie, 10 October 1840, ACLC, Vol. I.

11. Annie Aitkin to Margaret and William Carnegie, 11 April 1842, ACLC, Vol. 1.

12. Annie Aitkin to Margaret Carnegie, 30 May 1844, ACLC, Vol. 1.

13. *Autobiography*, 25.

14. See Frank Thistlethwaite, *The Anglo-American Connection in the Early Nineteenth Century*, Chap. 2.

15. John Saville, *Ernest Jones: Chartist*, London, 1952, 30; E. L. Woodward, *The Age of Reform*, Oxford, 1938, 138–39; Dodds, op. cit. 328–30.

16. Ibid. 331.

17. See *Dunfermline Journal*, 31 March 1848.

18. *Autobiography*, 25, 28.

19. D. Younger to AC, 9 October 1913, ACLC, Vol. 218.

20. Reminiscences of Charlotte Carnegie Drysdale, quoted in Hendrick, *Life*, I, 42–43.

21. Ibid. 42.

22. *Autobiography*, 26.

23. Ibid. 28.

24. W. A. Carrothers, *Emigration from the British Isles*, London, 1929, 305.

25. *Autobiography*, 28.

26. Ibid.

27. Seymour Dunbar, *A History of Travel in America*, Vol. III, Indianapolis, 1915, 850–52.

28. Horace Greeley, *Recollections of a Busy Life*, quoted in Dunbar, op. cit. 871.

29. Thomas S. Woodcock, *New York to Niagara*, 1836, quoted in *A Mirror for Americans*, I, edited by Warren S. Tryon, Chicago, 1952, 113.

30. *Autobiography*, 30.

31. *The Ohio Guide*, the Ohio Writers' Program of the Work Projects Administration, New York, 1940, 169–70.

32. *Autobiography*, 30.

CHAPTER V

1. This selection is taken from *Immigration as a Factor in American History*, edited by Oscar Handlin, Englewood Cliffs, N.J., 1959, 48.

2. *Autobiography*, 30.

3. Andrew Carnegie, "How I Served My Apprenticeship as a Business Man," *The Youth's Companion*, 23 April 1896, 217.

4. *Autobiography*, 13.

5. Winkler, *Incredible Carnegie*, 33.

6. Andrew Carnegie, "The Road to Business Success: A Talk to Young Men," reprinted in *The Empire of Business*, Garden City, N.Y., 1933, 13 (hereafter cited as *The Empire of Business*).

7. *Autobiography*, 33.

8. Ibid.

9. Ibid. 34.

10. Ibid. 35.

11. Carnegie, "How I Served My Apprenticeship As a Business Man," loc. cit. 217.

12. *Autobiography*, 35.

13. Ibid.

14. Ibid. 35–36.

15. Ibid. 36.

16. Authorities differ as to the location of the O'Reilly Telegraph Office. Some assert that it was on the corner of Fourth Avenue and Wood Street, others that it was in the old Odeon building, on the south side of Fourth, near Wood. I have accepted the statement of David Homer Bates, in "The Turning-Point of Mr. Carnegie's Career," *Century Magazine*, Vol. 76, July 1908, 335. This article presents the best account of Carnegie's early career in telegraphy.

17. AC to the president of the U.S. Military and Old Time Telegraph Association, Pittsburgh, 10 August 1896, ACLC, Vol. 38.

18. *Autobiography*, 39.

19. James D. Reid, *The Telegraph in America*, New York, 1879, 176; T. B. A. David to AC, 20 May 1903, ACLC, Vol. 96.

20. *Autobiography*, 43.

21. David to AC, 20 May 1903, ACLC, Vol. 96.

22. *Autobiography*, 43–44; AC to William B. Wilson, 12 December 1909, ACLC, Vol. 172.

23. *Autobiography*, 54–57.

24. Interview of AC in the *Philadelphia Press*, reprinted in the Newton (Iowa) *Daily News*, 30 November 1903.

25. *Autobiography*, 57.

26. AC to Dod (George Lauder, Jr.), 22 June 1851, ACLC, Vol. 1.

27. *Dunfermline Journal*, 29 September 1848.

28. Mary M. Goodall, granddaughter of Tom Morrison, Jr., to AC, 5 November 1907, ACLC, Vol. 145; official papers on the suit in the Tom Morrison, Jr., MSS, Carnegie Public Library, Dunfermline.

29. AC to Uncle George Lauder, 30 May 1852, ACLC, Vol. 1.

30. AC to Dod, 1 June 1853, letter in possession of E. E. Moore, Pittsburgh.

31. AC to Dod, 18 August 1853, ACLC, Vol. 1. Italics mine.

32. AC to Dod, 12 November 1855, letter in possession of E. E. Moore, Pittsburgh. Dod's letters to AC, unfortunately, are not extant, and the contents must be inferred from AC's letters to Dod.

33. AC to Uncle George Lauder, 30 May 1852, ACLC, Vol. 1.

34. AC to Dod, 22 June 1851, ACLC, Vol. 1.

35. AC to Uncle George Lauder, 30 May 1852, ACLC, Vol. 1.

36. AC to Dod, 22 June 1851, ACLC, Vol. 1.

37. *Autobiography*, 26.

38. AC to Uncle George Lauder, 30 May 1852, ACLC, Vol. 1.

39. David to AC, 20 May 1903, ACLC, Vol. 96.

40. *Autobiography*, 60.

41. Ibid.; Winkler, op. cit. 54–55.

42. AC to Uncle George Lauder, 14 March 1853, ACLC, Vol. 1.

43. AC to Dod, 22 June 1851, ACLC, Vol. 1.

44. AC to Uncle George Lauder, 30 May 1852, ACLC, Vol. 1.

45. *Autobiography*, 62–63.

46. Ibid. 59.

47. AC to Uncle George Lauder, 30 May 1852, ACLC, Vol. 1.

48. Carl Engel to Robert M. Lester, 24 April 1935, letter in files of Carnegie Corporation of New York.

49. Thomas N. Miller to AC, 10 April 1903, ACLC, Vol. 95.

50. Collection presented by the Carnegie Free Library of Allegheny to the Carnegie Birthplace Memorial Building, Moodie Street, Dunfermline.

51. Hendrick, *Life*, I, 65–66.

52. Speech at Grangemouth, Scotland, September 1887, quoted in Hendrick, *Life*, I, 67.

53. Ibid. 69.

54. Ibid. 70.

55. *Autobiography*, 45–46.

56. AC to Dod, March 1855, letter in possession of E. E. Moore, Pittsburgh.

57. AC to Dod, 8 February 1854, letter in possession of E. E. Moore, Pittsburgh.

CHAPTER VI

1. H. W. Schotter, *The Growth and Development of the Pennsylvania Railroad Company*, Philadelphia, 1927, 35.

2. *Autobiography*, 63.

3. Samuel H. Church, "Scott, Thomas Alexander" *Dictionary of American Biography* (hereafter cited as *D.A.B.*), Vol. 16, New York, 1946, 500.

4. Schotter, op. cit. 120.

5. Ibid. 34.

6. *Autobiography*, 63.

7. T. B. A. David to AC, 20 May 1903, ACLC, Vol. 96. See also J. P. Glass's letter to AC, 15 March 1858, ACLC, Vol. 1.

8. AC to Uncle George Lauder, 14 March 1853, ACLC, Vol. 1.

9. *Autobiography*, 65–66.

10. David to AC, 20 May 1903, ACLC, Vol. 1.

11. *Autobiography*, 66.

12. For a brief description of Altoona's early history see *Pennsylvania: A Guide to the Keystone State*, the Writers' Program, Work Projects Administration, New York, 1940, 525.

13. Ibid. 391. Quotation is from Charles Dickens, *American Notes*.

14. *Autobiography*, 67.

15. Ibid. 67–68.

16. Ibid. 73–74.

17. Ibid. 81–82.

18. Ibid. 71–72.

19. Ibid. 72.

20. Ibid. 73.

21. See Winkler, *Incredible Carnegie*, 59.

22. AC to John Bigelow, 6 January 1907, ACLC, Vol. 139; *Autobiography*, 51.

23. See the notarized copy of the official record of the Clerk of Court, Allegheny County, Pa., in ACLC, Vol. 1.

24. See M. F. and J. C. Campbell, *Anti-Carnegie Scraps and Comments*, Pittsburgh, 1899.

25. *Autobiography*, 63.

26. For example, see Winkler, op. cit. 66.

27. *Autobiography*, 52; see also Mrs. Francis C. Cooper's letter to Burton J. Hendrick, 5 July 1927, ACLC, Vol. 239.

28. *Autobiography*, 75-76.

29. AC to Dod, 8 February 1854, letter in possession of E. E. Moore, Pittsburgh.

30. AC to Dod, 15 July 1854, letter in possession of E. E. Moore, Pittsburgh.

31. *Autobiography*, 68-69.

32. AC to Dod, 8 February 1854, letter in possession of E. E. Moore, Pittsburgh.

33. Transfers of stock, dated 11 April and 17 April 1856, ACLC, Vol. 1.

34. See Hendrick, *Life*, I, 92, and Winkler, op. cit. 64.

35. Note of AC to Thomas A. Scott, 17 May 1856, ACLC, Vol. 1.

36. Ibid.

37. Note dated 1 November 1857, ACLC, Vol. 1.

38. See note giving a mortgage on the house owned by Margaret Carnegie to Richard Boyce for a sum of $500, payable within a year, dated 27 March 1858, ACLC, Vol. 1; see also letter to AC from I. Bennett (in whose home Margaret Carnegie was helping out as a nurse to his sick children), 11 March 1858, ACLC, Vol. 1.

39. *Autobiography*, 80.

40. Ibid; Andrew Carnegie, "How I Served My Apprenticeship as a Business Man," loc. cit. 217.

41. *Autobiography*, 84.

42. Ibid. 85.

43. Ibid. 86.

44. "Carnegie on the Verge of Seventy," *Current Literature*, Vol. 42, May 1907, 502.

45. Thomas N. Miller to AC, 10 April 1903, ACLC, Vol. 95.

46. *Autobiography*, 90.

47. Miller to AC, 10 April 1903, ACLC, Vol. 95.

48. Hendrick, *Life*, I, 95-96.

49. Andrew Carnegie, *Triumphant Democracy*, London, 1886, 297-99 (hereafter cited as *Triumphant Democracy*).

50. T. T. Woodruff to AC, 12 June 1886, as it later appeared in the *Philadelphia Sunday News*, November 1886 (no day given), ACLC, Vol. 9.

51. See Carl W. Mitman, "Woodruff, Theodore Tuttle," *D.A.B.*, Vol. 20, 497. See also obituaries of Woodruff in the *Philadelphia Record* and the *Public Ledger* (Philadelphia), 3, 4, and 5 May 1892.

52. Schotter, op. cit. 87.

53. AC to T. T. Woodruff, 15 June 1886, ACLC, Vol. 9.

54. *Autobiography*, 87-88.

55. Ibid. 91.

56. Ibid. 91–92; Hendrick, *Life*, I, 92.
57. Copy of General Order No. 10, 21 November 1859, in ACLC, Vol. 1.

CHAPTER VII

1. *Autobiography*, 93–94.
2. Hendrick, *Life*, I, 98.
3. See Solon J. Buck, "Wilkins, William," *D.A.B.*, Vol. 20, 221.
4. *Autobiography*, 96.
5. For a full account of the Club's activities, see letter from R. Taggart to Thomas N. Miller, 4 April 1909, ACLC, Vol. 165; see also *Autobiography*, 61.
6. *Autobiography*, 93.
7. Miller to AC, 10 April 1903, ACLC, Vol. 95.
8. George M. Alexander to Miller, 12 May 1903, ACLC, Vol. 96.
9. Ibid.
10. Hendrick, *Life*, I, 91.
11. *Autobiography*, 94.
12. Winkler, *Incredible Carnegie*, 69.
13. *Autobiography*, 26.
14. Ibid. 97.
15. Ibid. 82–83.
16. Andrew Carnegie, "Stanton, the Patriot," address delivered at Kenyon College, Ohio, 1906, reprinted in *Miscellaneous Writings of Andrew Carnegie*, I, New York, 1933, 217.
17. *Pittsburgh Gazette*, 13 April 1861.
18. Carnegie, "Stanton, the Patriot," loc. cit. 223.
19. Joseph A. Borkowski, "Camp Wilkins, Military Post, 1861," *The Western Pennsylvania Historical Magazine*, September 1962, 229–30.
20. Samuel R. Kamm, *The Civil War Career of Thomas A. Scott*, Ph.D. dissertation, University of Pennsylvania, Philadelphia, 1940, 34.
21. Ibid. 35; Schotter, *Pennsylvania Railroad*, 53–55; Allan Nevins, *The War for the Union: The Improvised War 1861–1862*, New York, 1959, 77.
22. Nevins, op. cit. 83.
23. Ibid. 84–85; David Homer Bates, "Lincoln in the Telegraph Office," *Century Magazine*, May 1907, 124–25; Carnegie, "From Bobbin Boy to Millionaire," loc. cit. 88; Margaret Leech, *Reveille in Washington*, New York, 1941, 63–67; W. R. Plum, *The Military Telegraph During the Civil War in the United States*, Chicago, 1882, I, 66–67.
24. Nevins, op. cit. 85–86.
25. D. H. Bates to AC, 8 May 1906, ACLC, Vol. 129; Kamm, op. cit. 41.
26. Kamm, op. cit. 42.
27. Nevins, op. cit. 159.
28. Ibid. 216.
29. Ibid. 214–21; *The West Point Atlas of American Wars*, edited by Col. Vincent J. Esposito, New York, 1959, I, Maps and text, 18–24.
30. Bates, op. cit. 125–28; *Autobiography*, 100–101.
31. For a copy of this dispatch, see letter to AC from John P. Cowan, Editor, *Pittsburgh Chronicle-Telegraph*, 29 April 1911, ACLC, Vol. 192.

32. AC to W. H. Holmes, 26 July 1861, ACLC, Vol. 1.

33. *Autobiography*, 109.

34. Ibid. 101.

35. Ibid. 102–3.

36. Nevins, op. cit. 226.

37. AC to John B. Dailey and William Mills, 7 June 1861, ACLC, Vol. 1.

38. See Nevins, op. cit. Chaps. 14 and 15 for an excellent account of McClellan's preparation in the summer and autumn of 1861.

39. AC to W. R. Plum, 25 November 1879, Letterbook, 1879–80, Andrew Carnegie Papers, United States Steel Corporation, 525 William Penn Place, Pittsburgh (hereafter cited as ACUSC). Hendrick is mistaken in saying that Carnegie stayed with the Telegraph Corps until November 1861 (Hendrick, *Life*, I, 109). Letters from Carnegie, written from Pittsburgh in October, indicate that he had been back on his job with the Pennsylvania Railroad for the preceding six weeks.

40. See letters of AC to Enoch Lewis, 4, 5, 9, and 10 October 1861, ACLC, Vol. 1.

41. AC to Lewis, 5 October 1861, ACLC, Vol. 1.

42. Paul H. Giddens, *Early Days of Oil*, Princeton, 1948, 1–3.

43. Allan Nevins, *John D. Rockefeller*, New York, 1940, I, 151.

44. Giddens, *Early Days of Oil*, 4–6, and Paul H. Giddens, *The American Petroleum Industry—Its Beginnings in Pennsylvania*, Princeton, 1959, 8.

45. Giddens, *American Petroleum Industry*, 11.

46. *Autobiography*, 137.

47. Hendrick, *Life*, I, 120; Giddens, *Early Days of Oil*, 26.

48. Giddens, *Early Days of Oil*, 12.

49. Giddens, *American Petroleum Industry*, 12; *Autobiography*, 138–39; Andrew Carnegie, "The Natural Oil and Gas Wells of Western Pennsylvania," reprinted in *The Empire of Business*, 224–25.

50. Giddens, *Early Days of Oil*, 26.

51. *Autobiography*, 139.

52. AC to Dod, 26 May 1862, ACLC, Vol. 3.

53. Miller to AC, 5 April 1903, ACLC, Vol. 95.

54. *Autobiography*, 110–12.

55. Ibid. 110–11.

56. See AC's letter to Dod after his return to Pittsburgh, 21 June 1863, ACLC, Vol. 3.

57. See *Dunfermline Journal*, various issues: 30 May, 27 June, 1 August, 26 September 1862.

58. See Royden Harrison, "British Labour and the Confederacy," *International Review of Social History*, Vol. 2, 1957, 78–105, for a thorough account of the attitudes of British labor journals toward the American Civil War.

59. See Henry Phipps to AC, 26 November 1909, ACLC, Vol. 171. In his autobiography Carnegie claims for himself a much more significant role than a single letter to the editor in protest. He asserts that on the day Lincoln's Cabinet was to discuss the issue and decide what action to take, he was able to convince Scott, who in turn convinced Secretary of War Cameron to join Seward in urging the release of the two prisoners. But the *Trent* incident occurred in November 1861, and by that time Carnegie was back in Pittsburgh. It is doubtful that he had the direct influence upon the Cabinet discussion he claims to have had. *Autobiography*, 102.

60. Robert Botsford, *Scotland and the American Civil War*, unpublished doctoral dissertation, University of Edinburgh, 1955, 434ff.

61. *The* [Edinburgh] *Scotsman*, 29 January 1862.

62. Thomas Morrison, *Rights of Land*, 55–56.

63. Troup, quoted by Botsford, op. cit. 363.

64. For an excellent account of Harriet Beecher Stowe's visit to Scotland, see George S. Shepperson, "Harriet Beecher Stowe and Scotland, 1852–53," *Scottish Historical Review*, Vol. 32, April 1953, 40–46.

65. *Triumphant Democracy*, 454.

66. *Autobiography*, 113.

67. AC to Dod, 21 June 1863, ACLC, Vol. 3.

68. Miller to AC, 2 April 1903, ACLC, Vol. 95.

69. *Autobiography*, 139–40; see also letter from William Dixon, manager of the Brick House farm, Duck Creek, Ohio, to AC, 26 February 1865, Early Investments File, ACUSC.

70. See letters and Articles of Agreement for various investments Carnegie made during 1863–64, Early Investments File, ACUSC.

71. See Articles of Agreement for Piper and Shiffler Co., 1 February 1862, Early Investments File, ACUSC; *Autobiography*, 115–16.

72. Memorandum in AC's handwriting, income in 1863, ACLC, Vol. 3.

73. T. B. A. David to AC, 20 May 1903, ACLC, Vol. 96.

74. *Autobiography*, 106–7.

75. See receipt for the sum of $850 in full payment for furnishing Carnegie a substitute, dated 19 June 1864, and Certificate of Non-Liability, dated 19 July 1864, issued to Carnegie, Miscellaneous Papers File, ACUSC.

76. AC to the Officers and Employees of the Pittsburgh Division of the Pennsylvania Railroad Company, 28 March 1865, ACLC, Vol. 3.

77. AC to Dod, 21 June 1863, ACLC, Vol. 3.

CHAPTER VIII

1. See Thomas C. Cochran, "Did the Civil War Retard Industrialization?" and Stephen Salsbury's reply, "The Effect of the Civil War on American Industrial Development," both reprinted in *The Economic Impact of the American Civil War*, edited by Ralph Andreano, Cambridge, Mass., 1962, 148–68.

2. Stephen Vincent Benét, *John Brown's Body*, Holt, Rinehart and Winston, Inc., New York, 1928, 333–34. Copyright 1927, 1928, by Stephen Vincent Benét; Copyright renewed, 1955, 1956 by Rosemary Carr Benét, Reprinted by permission of Brandt & Brandt.

3. *Autobiography*, 36.

4. AC to Margaret and Tom Carnegie, London, 26 July 1865, and business memorandum to Tom Carnegie, undated (autumn 1865), Travel Letters, in the possession of Margaret Carnegie Miller (hereafter cited as Travel Letters, 1865–66). See also memorandum, dated March 1865, Early Investment File, ACUSC.

5. *Autobiography*, 139.

6. See AC's letter to John Scott, 30 April 1883, Longstreet–Pennsylvania Railroad File, ACUSC.

7. Joseph Husband, *The Story of the Pullman Car*, Chicago, 1917, 75–82.

8. Ibid. 76.

9. AC to Jonah Woodruff, 9 January 1868, Letterbook, 1866–69, ACUSC.

10. *Autobiography*, 158.

11. Husband, op. cit. 27.

12. Husband, op. cit. 30–32.

13. Mitchell Wilson, *American Science and Invention*, New York, 1954, 224.

14. Ibid. 225.

15. *Autobiography*, 160.

16. AC to George M. Pulman [sic], 29 May 1867, Letterbook, 1866–69, ACUSC.

17. AC to Pulman [sic], 16 June 1867, Letterbook, 1866–69, ACUSC.

18. Contract in AC's handwriting, undated, Letterbook, 1866–69, ACUSC.

19. See various drafts of contracts, including the final one accepted by all parties, drawn up by William M. Harbaugh, dated 30 November 1867, Central Transportation Company File, ASUSC; see also Agreement between Pullman and Carnegie, February 1868, Letterbook, 1866–69, ACUSC.

20. AC to Pullman (by this time Carnegie had learned to spell his partner's name), 4 March 1868, Letterbook, 1866–69, ACUSC.

21. See AC's letter to C. S. Bushnell, 18 February 1868, offering him 400 shares of stock in the Pullman Pacific Car Company for $18,000, and his letter to Pullman, 10 February 1868, in which he sent a draft for $12,000 as payment of the first installment ($10 a share) for 1200 shares in the company. Letterbook, 1866–69, ACUSC.

22. AC to Charles W. Angell, 21 May 1868, Letterbook, 1866–69, ACUSC.

23. AC to Pullman, 22 February 1869, Letterbook, 1866–69, ACUSC.

24. AC to Pullman, 8 March 1869, Central Transportation Company File, ACUSC.

25. AC to Angell, 7 June 1869, Central Transportation Company File, ACUSC.

26. See AC's letter to C. A. Carpenter, 3 November 1871, Central Transportation Company File, ACUSC.

27. Account dated 31 August 1869, Central Transportation Company File, ACUSC.

28. Draft of the contract in AC's handwriting, Central Transportation Company File, ACUSC.

29. AC to J. Edgar Thomson, 29 March 1872, Letterbook, 1872–73, ACUSC.

30. Pullman to AC, 19 March 1872, Central Transportation Company File, ACUSC.

31. See AC's letter to F. Rohan, 9 April 1877, Letterbook, 1877, ACUSC.

32. William Addison to AC, 9 January 1873, Central Transportation Company File, ACUSC.

33. See letters from J. F. Cottringer to AC, 3 October 1876, 1 January 1877, Central Transportation Company File, ACUSC.

34. AC to Jungerich and Smith, Brokers, 25 September 1875, Letterbook, 1875–76, ACUSC; Cottringer to AC, 18 January 1884, Central Transportation Company File, ACUSC.

35. *D.A.B.*, "Woodruff, Theodore Tuttle," Vol. 20, 497.

36. AC to Robert A. Franks, 11 December 1891, Letterbook, 1888–92, ACUSC; R. A. Franks to Mrs. I. I. Gerson, 30 June 1892, Letterbook, 1888–92, ACUSC.

37. The best single source for the early history of the telegraph is still James D. Reid, *The Telegraph in America*, New York, 1886. See also Alvin F. Harlow, *Old Wires and New Waves*, New York, 1936.

38. Quoted in Harlow, op. cit. 255.

39. Ibid. 256–57.

40. Reid, op. cit. 448–49.

41. Agreement between Pacific and Atlantic Telegraph Co. and AC, dated 13 September 1867, Telegraph File, ACUSC.

42. AC to George H. Thurston, 9 November 1867, Letterbook, 1866–69, ACUSC.

43. See AC's letter to David Brooks, 11 November 1867, Letterbook, 1866–69, ACUSC.

44. Harlow, op. cit. 213–14.

45. AC to S. R. Dick, 17 September 1868, Letterbook, 1866–69, ACUSC.

46. AC to Thomas A. Scott, 19 January 1869, Letterbook, 1866–69, ACUSC.

47. See receipt from AC & Associates to Pacific and Atlantic Telegraph Co., dated 19 January 1872, Letterbook, 1871–72, ACUSC; AC to W. J. Howard, 2 March 1871, Telegraph File, ACUSC.

48. Reid, op. cit. 450.

49. David McCargo to AC, 17 January 1872, Telegraph File, ACUSC.

50. McCargo to AC, 27 January 1872, Telegraph File, ACUSC.

51. See McCargo to AC, 11 April 1873, Telegraph File, ACUSC; Reid, op. cit. 450.

52. Reid, op. cit. 450.

53. See telegrams between AC and A. Q. Casselberry, and Hart, Caughey and Company, 2 May 1873; also letters between AC and William G. Johnston, 8 May 1873; AC and C. B. M. Smith, 9 May 1873, Telegraph File, ACUSC.

54. McCargo to AC, 12 May 1873, Telegraph File, ACUSC.

55. AC to William Orton, 3 June 1873, Letterbook, 1873–74, ACUSC.

56. Johnston to AC, 24 May 1873, Telegraph File, ACUSC.

57. Johnston to AC, 3 June 1873, Telegraph File, ACUSC.

58. Harlow, op. cit. 259; William Chauncy Landon, "Orton, William," *D.A.B.*, Vol. 14, 65–66.

59. See AC's letter to J. W. Weir, 4 September 1873, Telegraph File, ACUSC.

60. See list of stock delivered by AC and exchanged for Western Union stock, 11 May and subsequent days, 1873; also AC to Orton, 3 June 1873, Telegraph File, ACUSC.

61. Reid, op. cit. 450; AC to Weir, 4 December 1873, and Johnston to AC, 27 January 1874, Telegraph File, ACUSC.

62. Reid, op. cit. 595.

63. Quoted in John A. Kouwenhoven, *The Columbia Historical Portrait of New York,* New York, 1953, 277.

64. Statement of Business Holdings, Carnegie Collection, Miscellaneous Papers, MS Division, New York Public Library (hereafter cited as ACNYPL).

65. AC to Thomas A. Scott, 1 January 1865, and Scott to Simon Cameron, undated, 1865, Cameron Papers, Box 17, Library of Congress.

66. Photostatic copy, ACNYPL. Original in the possession of the Carnegie family.

CHAPTER IX

1. *Autobiography,* 122.

2. Hendrick, *Life,* I, 128.

3. Notice, dated 16 May 1865, Early Investment File, ACUSC.

4. AC, on board the *Scotia*, to his mother and brother, 25 May 1865, Travel Letters, 1865–66.

5. AC to Margaret and Tom Carnegie, undated (June 1865), Travel Letters, 1865–66.

6. John Franks, Letterbook, Frankfurt am Main, 18 October 1865, copy in ACLC, Vol. 3.

7. J. Franks, Letterbook, Antwerp, 29 October 1865, ACLC, Vol. 3.

8. J. Franks, Letterbook, Berlin, 12 November 1865, ACLC, Vol. 3.

9. J. Franks, Letterbook, Dresden, 19 November 1865, ACLC, Vol. 3.

10. J. Franks, Letterbook, Vienna, 26 November 1865, ACLC, Vol. 3.

11. AC to Margaret and Tom Carnegie, Amsterdam, 5 November 1865, Travel Letters, 1865–66.

12. AC to Margaret Carnegie, Dunfermline, 2 September 1865, Travel Letters, 1865–66.

13. AC to Margaret and Tom Carnegie, Dresden, 19 November 1865, Travel Letters, 1865–66.

14. AC to Margaret and Tom Carnegie, Mannheim, 16 October 1865, Travel Letters, 1865–66.

15. AC to Margaret Carnegie, Paris, 5 October 1865, Travel Letters, 1865–66.

16. AC to Margaret Carnegie, Dunfermline, 2 September 1865, Travel Letters, 1865–66.

17. AC to Margaret and Tom Carnegie, Dresden, 19 November 1865, Travel Letters, 1865–66.

18. AC to Margaret and Tom Carnegie, Amsterdam, 5 November 1865, Travel Letters, 1865–66.

19. AC to Margaret and Tom Carnegie, 16 October, 31 December 1865, 7 January 1866, Travel Letters, 1865–66.

20. AC to Margaret and Tom Carnegie, London, 26 July 1865, Travel Letters, 1865–66.

21. AC to Tom Carnegie, undated (autumn 1865), Travel Letters, 1865–66.

22. AC to Margaret and Tom Carnegie, Mannheim, 16 October 1865, Travel Letters, 1865–66.

23. AC to Margaret and Tom Carnegie, Amsterdam, 5 November 1865, Travel Letters, 1865–66.

24. Excerpts from AC's letters to Tom Carnegie, summer and fall of 1865, Travel Letters, 1865–66.

25. AC to Margaret and Tom Carnegie, Adlesburg, Austria, 3 December 1865, Travel Letters, 1865–66.

26. AC to Tom Carnegie, Parma, 14 December 1865, Travel Letters, 1865–66.

27. James H. Bridge, *The Inside History of the Carnegie Steel Company*, New York, 1903, 29; see also Hendrick, *Life*, I, 187–88, for an excellent comparison of the two brothers.

28. AC to Margaret Carnegie, Dunfermline, 2 September 1865, Travel Letters, 1865–66.

29. Bridge, op. cit. 1–3.

30. Ibid. 4–5.

31. Articles of Partnership, Kloman and Company, 17 November 1861, quoted in Bridge, op. cit. 5–8.

32. Thomas N. Miller's memorandum to AC, quoted in Bridge, op. cit. 10.

33. Ibid.

34. Quoted by John Walker, interviewed by Burton J. Hendrick. 12 November 1928, ACLC, Vol. 239.

35. Ibid.

36. See Bridge, op. cit. 12, and Winkler, op. cit. 80.

37. Quoted in Bridge, op. cit. 18–19.

38. Quoted in Bridge, op. cit. 17.

39. Ibid. 19.

40. See Miller's letter to AC, 7 April 1903, ACLC, Vol. 95.

41. Miller quotes this remark in a letter recalling the affair, published in the *Pittsburgh Leader*, 25 September 1903, copy in ACLC, Vol. 99.

42. See Miller's letter to AC, 7 April 1903, ACLC, Vol. 95.

43. Hendrick, *Life*, I, 137.

44. Miller's letter in *Pittsburgh Leader*, 25 September 1903, loc. cit.

45. Incident related by John Walker, interviewed by Hendrick, 12 November 1928, loc. cit. See also Miller's letter in *Pittsburgh Leader*, 25 September 1903, loc. cit.

46. AC to Miller, 3 June 1867, Letterbook, 1866–69, ACUSC.

47. AC to Miller, 4 September 1867, quoted in Bridge, op. cit. 23, 29.

48. See Agreement between T. N. Miller and Andrew and Thomas Carnegie, 19 March 1868, Manufacturing Ventures File, ACUSC.

49. Miller to AC, 2 April 1903, ACLC, Vol. 95.

50. Miller's letter in *Pittsburgh Leader*, 25 September 1903, loc. cit.

51. See statement and supplement, 22 November 1869, Manufacturing Ventures File, ACUSC.

52. James Livesey to AC, 9 June 1866, Dodd Patented Rail File, ACUSC.

53. Livesey to AC, 11 August 1866, Dodd Patented Rail File, ACUSC.

54. AC to David Burr, 24 July 1866, Dodd Patented Rail File, ACUSC.

55. AC to Livesey, 18 August 1866, Dodd Patented Rail File, ACUSC.

56. Livesey to AC, 29 December 1866, Dodd Patented Rail File, ACUSC.

57. See letters of AC to various railway executives, 1 July, 1 and 12 September 1866, etc., Letterbook, 1866–69, ACUSC.

58. AC to Henry Bakewell, 4 November 1867, Letterbook, 1866–69, ACUSC.

59. J. Edgar Thomson to AC, 12 and 15 March 1867, Dodd Patented Rail File, ACUSC.

60. AC to W. B. Ogden, 12 March 1867, Letterbook, 1866–69, ACUSC.

61. Livesey to AC, 17 November 1866, Dodd Patented Rail File, ACUSC.

62. AC to Livesey, 2 July 1867, Letterbook, 1866–69, ACUSC.

63. AC to T. A. Scott, 8 March 1869, Letterbook, 2 March to 28 June 1869, ACUSC.

64. See Bridge, op. cit. 74–75, Winkler, op. cit. 123, and numerous articles which have repeated Bridge's fanciful account. Burton Hendrick is one of the few Carnegie biographers who correctly identifies Andrew Carnegie as the original sponsor of the Thomson Steel Works, who had to force his reluctant partners into joining him in the enterprise. But even Hendrick pictures Carnegie's acceptance of Bessemer steel as being a sudden decision made only after visiting a steel plant in England. See Hendrick, *Life*, I, 183ff.

65. John A. Wright to Tom Carnegie, 13 February 1866, Early Investments File, ACUSC.

66. AC to Wright, 6 September 1867, Letterbook, 1866–69, ACUSC.

67. See AC's letter to Livesey, 2 July 1867, Letterbook, 1866–69, ACUSC.

68. AC to Livesey, 21 November 1867, Letterbook, 1866–69, ACUSC.

69. See Herbert Casson, *The Romance of Steel*, New York, 1907; and Hendrick, *Life*, I, chap. IX.

70. Quoted in Hendrick, *Life*, I, 163.

71. AC to H. J. Lombaert, 15 January 1867, Letterbook, 1866–69, ACUSC.

72. Quoted in Hendrick, *Life*, I, 173.

CHAPTER X

1. *Autobiography*, 130.

2. Ibid. 131.

3. Bridge, *Inside History of Carnegie Steel*, 32–33.

4. *Autobiography*, 122.

5. See Calvin M. Woodward, *A History of the St. Louis Bridge*, St. Louis, 1881, 7ff.

6. AC to the President and Directors of the Keystone Bridge Co., 20 January 1868, Letterbook, 1866–69, ACUSC.

7. AC to James B. Eads, 29 October 1867, Letterbook, 1866–69, ACUSC.

8. Calvin Woodward, op. cit. 18ff.

9. AC to Amos Cutting, 7 March 1870, Letterbook, 1869–70, ACUSC.

10. See AC's letters to J. Edgar Thomson, 1 March 1870, and to Thomas A. Scott, 7 March 1870, Letterbook, 1869–70, ACUSC.

11. See Gardner F. McCandless's letter to Tom Carnegie, 25 March 1870, Letterbook, 1869–70, ACUSC.

12. AC to McPherson, Taussig, and Britton, Executive Committee, St. Louis Bridge Company, 2 June 1870, Letterbook, 26 February to 31 October 1870, ACUSC.

13. Carnegie means the St. Louis Bridge Company, not Keokuk.

14. AC to Henry Phipps, 3 June 1870, Letterbook, 26 February to 31 October 1870, ACUSC.

15. See various letters: G. F. McCandless to AC, 21 July and 1 and 3 August 1870, and AC to William McPherson, 20 July 1870, Letterbook, 26 February to 31 October 1870, ACUSC.

16. William Taussig to AC, December 1870, and AC to Taussig, 30 December 1870, quoted in Calvin Woodward, op. cit. 70–71.

17. See AC's letters to Eads, 4 October 1870, and to W. McPherson, 5 October 1870, Letterbook, 26 February to 31 October 1870, ACUSC.

18. AC to W. McPherson, 5 October 1870, Letterbook, 26 February to 31 October 1870, ACUSC.

19. AC to J. E. Thomson, 27 November 1871, Letterbook, 1871–72, ACUSC.

20. Calvin Woodward, op. cit. 129n.

21. Resolution of St. Louis Bridge Company, 5 June 1872, copy in Letterbook, 1872–73, ACUSC.

22. AC to Junius S. Morgan, 5 December 1873, Letterbook, 1873–74, ACUSC.

23. AC to G. F. McCandless, 13 July 1874, St. Louis Bridge File, ACUSC.

24. *Autobiography*, 121; Calvin Woodward, op. cit. 195–96.

25. Calvin Woodward, op. cit. 197.

26. See AC's letters to Edward Smith, 31 October 1870, and to S. M. Shoemaker, 24 December 1870, Letterbooks, 26 February to 31 October 1870 and 1 November 1870 to 14 March 1871, ACUSC.

27. Memorandum listing AC as President of Keokuk and Hamilton Bridge Company, undated, Letterbook, 1875–76, ACUSC.

28. G. F. McCandless to Tom Carnegie, 7 November 1870, Letterbook, 1 November 1870 to 14 March 1871, ACUSC.

29. See letter to AC from E. V. McCandless, 15 July 1871, listing subscribers and officers in the Davenport and St. Paul Construction Company, Letterbook, 1871–72, ACUSC.

30. See a series of letters to AC from W. H. Holmes, 21, 26, 27, February, 8 March, and 24, 29, and 30 June 1871, Davenport and St. Paul File, ACUSC.

31. See Holmes's letter to AC, T. A. Scott, and B. E. Smith, 6 October 1871, Davenport and St. Paul File, ACUSC.

32. B. E. Smith to AC, 1 August 1871, Davenport and St. Paul File, ACUSC.

33. George French to AC, 16 March 1872, Davenport & St. Paul File, ACUSC.

34. Gebruder Sulzbach to Drexel, Morgan and Company, 29 April 1872, Davenport & St. Paul File, ACUSC.

35. A. J. Drexel to AC, 22 July 1872, Davenport and St. Paul File, ACUSC.

36. AC to G. F. McCandless, 12 June 1872, Davenport and St. Paul File, ACUSC.

37. J. P. Morgan to AC, 23 July 1872, Davenport and St. Paul File, ACUSC.

38. See P. P. Sulzbach to AC, 31 July 1872, Davenport and St. Paul File, ACUSC.

39. *Autobiography*, 167–68.

40. Ibid. 169.

41. AC to William Phillips, 27 November 1871, Letterbook, 1871–72, ACUSC.

42. AC to Phillips, 29 November 1871, Letterbook, 1871–72, ACUSC.

43. AC to Baring Brothers & Co., 8 December 1871, Letterbook, 1871–72, ACUSC.

44. *Autobiography*, 170.

45. AC to J. E. Thomson, 8 December 1871, Letterbook, 1871–72, ACUSC.

46. AC to J. E. Thomson, 16 December 1871, Letterbook, 1871–72, ACUSC.

47. *Autobiography*, 170–71; AC to Junius S. Morgan, 9 February 1874, Letterbook, 1873–74, ACUSC.

48. AC to J. E. Thomson, 8 December 1871, Letterbook, 1871–72, ACUSC.

49. *The Railroad Gazette*, 11 February 1871, quoted in Julius Grodinsky, *Jay Gould, 1867–1892*, Philadelphia, 1957, 116.

50. *Autobiography*, 164–65.

51. AC to John Duff, 6 March 1871, Union Pacific File, ACUSC.

52. G. F. McCandless to AC, 15 April 1871, Union Pacific File, ACUSC.

53. AC to George M. Pullman, 8 May 1871, Union Pacific File, ACUSC.

54. Grodinsky, op. cit. 116–17.

55. G. F. McCandless to AC, 9 May 1871, Union Pacific File, ACUSC.

56. AC to L. B. Boomer, 27 January 1871, Letterbook, 1 November 1870 to 14 March 1871, ACUSC.

57. AC to Edward Jay Allen, 14 December 1871, Letterbook, 1871–72, ACUSC.

58. AC to A. G. Eastman, 1 May 1873, Letterbook, 1872–73, ACUSC.

59. AC to J. R. Jones, 26 April 1877, Letterbook, 1877, ACUSC.

60. See AC's letters to Simon Cameron, 3 March 1874, and to J. Lowber Welsh, 22 January 1874, Letterbook, 1873–74, ACUSC; see also E. E. Moore, *Pittsburgh and the Steel Industry*, unpublished MS, 9–10, ACUSC.

61. See AC's letters to Thomas Leighton and John Scott, both dated 29 June 1878, Letterbook, 1878–79, ACUSC.

62. See E. E. Moore, op. cit.

63. AC to J. H. Linville, 26 April 1877, Letterbook, 1877, ACUSC.

64. AC to Linville, 29 June 1878, Letterbook, 1878–79, ACUSC.

65. AC to Allen, 14 December 1871, Letterbook, 1871–72, ACUSC.

66. AC to Linville, 31 July 1871, Letterbook, 1871–72, ACUSC.

67. AC to Linville, 14 August 1871, Letterbook, 1871–72, ACUSC.

68. *Autobiography*, 176–77.

69. AC to Henry Hill, 17 May 1878, Letterbook, 1878–79, ACUSC.

70. G. F. McCandless to French, 18 September 1880, Davenport and St. Paul File, ACUSC.

71. George M. Dallas to AC, 12 February 1884, Davenport and St. Paul File, ACUSC.

72. See Miller's letter to AC, 10 April 1903, ACLC, Vol. 95.

73. *Autobiography*, 152; Winkler, *Incredible Carnegie*, 112.

74. Grodinsky, op. cit. 113ff.

75. *Autobiography*, 152.

76. Ibid. 151.

77. Ibid. 173.

78. J. E. Thomson to AC, 3 October 1873, ACNYPL.

79. Hendrick, *Life*, I, 196–97.

80. *Autobiography*, 174.

81. Andrew Carnegie, "The Road to Business Success," address to students of Curry Commercial College, Pittsburgh, June 23, 1885, reprinted in *The Empire of Business*, 3–6.

82. *Autobiography*, 174.

CHAPTER XI

1. New York *Evening Post*, 12 January 1901, reprinted in *The Empire of Business*, 204.

2. Bridge, *Inside History of Carnegie Steel*, 73.

3. E. E. Moore, unpublished MS, ACUSC; Articles of Co-Partnership, dated 5 November 1872, ACLC, Vol. 4.

4. AC to William P. Shinn, 21 May 1873, Letterbook, 1872–73, ACUSC.

5. AC to J. Edgar Thomson, 30 October 1872, Letterbook, 1872–73, ACUSC.

6. J. E. Thomson to AC, 14 November 1872, Edgar Thomson Operating File, ACUSC.

7. AC to William Phillips, 24 September 1872, Letterbook, 1872–73, ACUSC.

8. See E. E. Moore, *List of Carnegie Associates*, ACUSC.

9. Alexander J. Holley to William Coleman, 18 September 1872, E.T. Operating File, ACUSC.

10. See Tom Carnegie's letter to AC, 24 September 1872, E.T. Operating File, ACUSC.

11. Holley to AC, 8 November 1872, E.T. Operating File, ACUSC.

12. MS on Capt. William R. Jones, undated, unsigned, ACLC, Vol. 243; John Gray

and A. J. Edwards, *Biographical Sketches of Captain W. R. Jones,* Pittsburgh, 1913, 3–6.

13. MS on Capt. William R. Jones, undated, unsigned, ACLC, Vol. 243; Bridge, op. cit. 79.

14. Casson, *The Romance of Steel,* 27.

15. AC to Junius S. Morgan & Co., 5 December 1873, Letterbook, 1873–74, ACUSC.

16. Data sheet on cost of construction of E.T. Works up to 31 October 1875, E.T. Operating File, ACUSC.

17. Quoted by Walter M. Kelley, in testimony given to the Honorable A. O. Stanley, Chairman of the Congressional steel investigating committee, 5 January 1912, excerpt in ACLC, Vol. 202.

18. Tariff Hearings, House of Representatives, 1908, 5797, quoted in Hendrick, *Life,* I, 199.

19. *Autobiography,* 190.

20. See Shinn's letter to Holley, 6 April 1874, E.T. Operating File, ACUSC.

21. Holley to AC, 4 May 1874, E.T. Operating File, ACUSC.

22. AC to Shinn, 10 April 1876, ACLC, Vol. 4.

23. AC to Messrs. Richmond, Potts, and Loring, 30 January 1873, Letterbook, 1872–73, ACUSC.

24. Shinn to Holley, 6 April 1874, E.T. Operating File, ACUSC.

25. Bridge, op. cit. 55–56.

26. Ibid. 56–58.

27. Shinn to AC, 6 August 1875, E.T. S. Rail Orders File, ACUSC.

28. Shinn to AC, 26 November 1875, E.T. Operating File, ACUSC.

29. AC to Shinn, 10 April 1876, ACLC, Vol. 4.

30. AC to Shinn, 28 August 1876, ACLC, Vol. 4.

31. See AC's letter to Shinn, 4 April 1879, ACLC, Vol. 4.

32. *Autobiography,* 142.

33. The last two pages (pp. 284–85) of Letterbook, 1868–69, ACUSC, give a list of AC's accounts in the Union Iron Mills Company. This list shows that Carnegie was receiving a salary of $250 per quarter up to 1 July 1869.

34. Bridge, op. cit. 104–5.

35. AC to Junius S. Morgan, 7 June 1876, Letterbook, 1876, ACUSC.

36. D. J. Morrell to Shinn, 10 June 1875, E.T. Operating File, ACUSC.

37. AC quoted directly by John Walker, partner in Carnegie Steel and Frick Coke Company, in an interview given to Burton J. Hendrick, 16 February 1928, ACLC, Vol. 239; repeated in a paraphrased form in Hendrick, *Life,* I, 211–13.

38. Reported by Baron Alexander Forbes-Leith's grandson, Baron Ian Forbes-Leith, of Fyfvie, Scotland, in an interview with the writer, April 1958. Unfortunately, Baron Alexander Forbes-Leith's personal correspondence, which would offer an invaluable record of his relationship with Carnegie, is not available to scholars, and the writer was not given permission to see this collection at Fyfvie Castle. Baron Alexander Forbes-Leith and Carnegie had similar careers. Like Carnegie, Forbes-Leith emigrated from Scotland as a young man and entered the steel business. He developed the Joliet Steel Company into a very large and profitable business and was instrumental in the formation of Illinois Steel Company in 1890. He also bought a castle in Scotland, but, unlike Carnegie, he resumed his British citizenship and accepted a title after his retirement in 1901. See A. W. W. Stirling, *Fyfvie Castle: Its Lairds*

and Their Times, London, 1928; *Who Was Who,* 1916-28, Vol. II, London, 1941, 621.

39. See various letters in Letterbook, 1866-69; Letterbook, 2 February to 31 October 1870, and Letterbook, 1 November 1870 to 14 March 1871, ACUSC.

40. AC to Samuel Reeves, 29 December 1870, Letterbook, 1 November 1870 to 14 March 1871, ACUSC.

41. AC to Tom Carnegie, 28 March 1872, Letterbook, 1872-73, ACUSC.

42. AC to Cooper & Hewitt Co., 16 December, 1873, Letterbook, 1873-74, ACUSC.

43. AC to Carnegie Bros. & Co., 12 January 1876, Letterbook, 1875-76, ACUSC.

44. AC to E. Y. Townsend, 5 June 1876, Letterbook, 1876, ACUSC.

45. AC to Townsend, 19 April 1877, Letterbook, 1877, ACUSC.

46. AC to Shinn, 30 April 1877, Letterbook, 1877, ACUSC.

47. See AC's letter to Townsend, 5 January 1878; Letterbook, 1877-78, ACUSC.

48. AC to Townsend, 28 December 1877, Letterbook, 1877-78, ACUSC.

49. See AC's letters to Townsend, 19 April, 1877, Letterbook, 1877; to Dr. Linderman, Bethlehem Iron Company, 19 December 1877, Letterbook, 1877-78; mention of similar letters to Scranton and Felton in above letters, ACUSC.

50. AC to John Fritz, 8 December 1877, Letterbook, 1877-78, ACUSC.

51. AC to Carnegie Bros. & Co., 8 December 1877, Letterbook, 1877-78, ACUSC.

52. Charles M. Schwab, quoted in David Brody's excellent chapter, "The Psychology and Method of Steelmaking," in Brody, *Steelworkers in America: The Nonunion Era,* Cambridge, Mass., 1960, 2.

53. Brody, op. cit. 2, 5.

54. AC to Shinn, 10 April 1876, ACLC, Vol. 4.

55. *Autobiography,* 194-96; Hendrick, *Life,* I, 218-19, Bridge, op. cit. 66-69; E. E. Moore, unpublished MS, ACUSC.

56. See William L. Abbott, interviewed by Hendrick, notes, August 1929, ACLC, Vol. 239.

57. Bridge, op. cit. 63-64.

58. Abbott, interviewed by Hendrick, August 1929, ACLC, Vol. 239.

59. AC to Shinn, 27 April 1877, Letterbook, 1877, ACUSC.

60. AC to Tom Carnegie, 28 November 1872, Letterbook, 1872-73, ACUSC.

61. AC to Shinn, 15 January 1876, Letterbook, 1875-76, ACUSC.

62. AC to Shinn, 2 June 1876, Letterbook, 1876, ACUSC.

63. Shinn to AC, 21 October 1876, E.T. Operating File, ACUSC.

64. AC to Carnegie Bros. & Co., 2 April 1878, Letterbook, 1877-78, ACUSC.

65. AC to Capt. William R. Jones, 24 April 1877, Letterbook, 1877, ACUSC.

66. AC to Shinn, 29 December 1876, Letterbook, 1876-77, ACUSC.

67. W. R. Jones to AC, 24 March 1878, William R. Jones Letterfile, ACUSC.

68. W. R. Jones to AC, 31 December 1877, W. R. Jones Letterfile, ACUSC.

69. W. R. Jones to AC, 22 February 1877, W. R. Jones Letterfile, ACUSC.

70. W. R. Jones to AC, 6 May 1878, W. R. Jones Letterfile, ACUSC.

71. W. R. Jones to AC, 5 December 1879, W. R. Jones Letterfile, ACUSC.

72. Quoted in Brody, op. cit. 17.

73. Statement, undated, Letterbook, 1877, ACUSC.

74. Quoted in Hendrick, *Life,* I, 209-10.

75. Memorandum from AC to Editor of *Iron Age,* 30 November 1877, Lucy Furnace File, ACUSC.

76. AC to Shinn, 9 December 1875, Letterbook, 1875–76, ACUSC.

77. AC to Shinn, 15 January 1876, Letterbook, 1875–76, ACUSC.

78. See AC's letters to Townsend, 30 August, 9 October 1878, and AC to D. K. Ferguson, Vulcan Iron Co., St. Louis, 12 October 1878, Letterbook, 1878–79, ACUSC.

79. AC to Townsend, 9 October 1878, Letterbook, 1878–79, ACUSC.

80. Shinn to AC, 13 December 1875, E.T. Operating File, ACUSC.

81. AC to Shinn, 14 December 1875, Letterbook, 1875–76, ACUSC.

82. AC to Shinn 29 November 1875, Letterbook, 1875–76, ACUSC.

83. AC to J. J. Hammer, 10 May 1877, Letterbook, 1877, ACUSC.

84. W. R. McKeen to AC, 19 January 1877, E.T. S. Rail Orders File, ACUSC.

85. See long list of testimonial statements which Carnegie prepared for general distribution, undated, Letterbook, 1877, ACUSC.

86. AC to Bailey, Lang and Co., 8 May 1876, Letterbook, 1876, ACUSC.

87. AC to Shinn, 12 May 1876, Letterbook, 1876, ACUSC.

88. See AC's letter to Shinn, 18 February 1876, discussing the advantages of rolling rather than hammering blooms for rails, as an example of how thoroughly he would study a specialized problem in steel manufacturing. Letterbook, 1875–76, ACUSC.

89. Ibid.

90. AC to Thomas Whitwell, 4 April 1877, Letterbook, 1877, ACUSC.

91. AC to Shinn, 10 April 1876, ACLC, Vol. 4.

92. AC to Shinn, quoted in Bridge, op. cit. 118.

93. Agreement between AC and Coleman, 1 May 1876, E.T. Operating File, ACUSC.

94. AC to Shinn, 1 May 1877, ACLC, Vol. 4.

95. See AC's letter to Carnegie Bros. & Co., 12 March 1875, Letterbook, 1874–75, and Carnegie Bros. & Co. Journal, January 1876; Articles of Partnership File, 1 April 1875, ACUSC.

96. Amendment to Articles of Edgar Thomson Steel Works, Ltd., dated 9 December 1878, ACLC, Vol. 4; List of Net Profits of the Carnegie Association, 1876–99, ACLC, Vol. 73.

97. AC to Shinn, October 1878, ACLC, Vol. 4.

98. AC to Moses Taylor, 25 May 1878, Letterbook, 1878–79, ACUSC.

99. AC to Shinn, 4 April 1879, ACLC, Vol. 4.

100. AC to John Scott, 7 April 1879, William Shinn Suit File, ACUSC.

101. AC's statement to the court, dated 7 and 15 January 1880; see also, in the same testimony, AC's sworn statement that on 1 May 1879, Shinn and his brother, John K. Shinn, set up the Peerless Lime Company, Ltd., in William Shinn Suit File, ACUSC.

102. AC to Shinn, 14 September 1879, William Shinn Suit File, ACUSC.

103. Testimony given by AC, 7 to 15 January 1880; see also sworn testimony of Daniel E. Garrison and O. L. Garrison, of Vulcan Iron Co., undated, but sometime in late spring, 1881, William Shinn Suit File, ACUSC.

104. See Agreement, dated October 1879, and letters from AC to Shinn, regarding the selection of arbitrators, dated 12 and 29 November 1879, William Shinn Suit File, ACUSC.

105. Bridge, op. cit. 129–30.

106. W. R. Jones to AC, 5 November 1880, W. R. Jones Letterfile, ACUSC.

107. AC to W. R. Jones, 8 November 1880, Letterbook, 1880–81, ACUSC.
108. W. R. Jones to AC, 9 November 1880, W. R. Jones Letterfile, ACUSC.
109. *Autobiography*, 203.
110. W. R. Jones to AC, 19 December 1880, W. R. Jones Letterfile, ACUSC.
111. W. R. Jones to AC, 7 May 1881, W. R. Jones Letterfile, ACUSC.
112. List of companies organized by Andrew Carnegie, E. E. Moore's papers, ACUSC.
113. List of Net Profits of the Carnegie Association, 1876–99, ACLC, Vol. 73.

CHAPTER XII

1. Andrew Carnegie, *Round the World*, Garden City, N.Y., 1933, 1 (hereafter cited as *Round the World*).
2. Ibid.
3. Carnegie implies in his autobiography—an implication accepted at face value by Burton Hendrick—that he and his brother Tom came upon Spencer's and Darwin's writings while Carnegie was still living in Pittsburgh. (See *Autobiography*, 339, and Hendrick, *Life*, I, 238.) While this is possible, it is highly unlikely that Carnegie should have known about Spencer, and particularly about Darwin, at this early date, for neither was widely read or accepted in this country until after the Civil War (see Richard Hofstadter, *Social Darwinism in American Thought*, Chaps. 1 and 2, Boston, 1963). Certainly there is no mention of either men or of evolution in Carnegie's correspondence until after his moving to New York in 1867. From 1868 on, there are many such allusions.
4. See Andrew Carnegie, "Characteristics," in *Memoirs of Anne C. L. Botta, Written By Her Friends*, New York, 1894, 167; *D.A.B.*, Mary A. Wyman, "Botta, Anne Charlotte Lynch," 469–70; Hendrick, *Life*, I, 220ff.
5. Carnegie, "Characteristics," loc. cit. 166.
6. Hendrick, *Life*, I 224ff.
7. *Autobiography*, 339.
8. Herbert Spencer, *Autobiography*, II, New York, 1904, 5. Quoted in Hofstadter, op. cit. 220, n. 13.
9. *Round the World*, 25.
10. Ibid. 17.
11. Ibid. 23.
12. Ella J. Newton, Foochow, China, to AC, 15 August 1895, ACLC, Vol. 32, and AC to Miss Newton, 26 November 1895, ACLC, Vol. 34. Carnegie must have sent a copy of this letter to his good friend, Henry Van Dyke, pastor of the Brick Church in New York, for when Van Dyke protested that the American missionaries were not kept in China by American guns, Carnegie hotly reiterated his charge: "You say that no attempt is made to force the Chinese to adopt Christianity. Now that troubles me, because the Chinese Government was forced after a way to allow missionaries in their midst; and if the guns of Britain and America were not behind these missionaries, not one would remain in China twenty-four hours. . . . I have been in China and heard the piteous appeals of good devout religious men whose feelings were outraged by our missionaries. I know if you would go there and have a similar experience that you would think of the Golden Rule—'Do unto others as you would have others do to you'; and it grieves me much to see your great influence thrown into a cause which, in my opinion, violates every principle of your religion." AC to Henry Van Dyke, 7 December 1895, ACLC, Vol. 34.

13. *Round the World,* 67–68.
14. Ibid. 168ff.; AC to Sir James Donaldson, Principal of St. Andrews University, 1 June 1905, ACLC, Vol. 117.
15. *Round the World,* 42.
16. Ibid. 176.
17. Ibid. 187.
18. Ibid. 194.
19. Ibid. 100–101.
20. Ibid. 134–35.
21. Ibid. 289–90.
22. Ibid. 306–11.
23. Ibid. 171.
24. Burton J. Hendrick, *The Age of Big Business,* New Haven, Conn., 1922, 22.
25. Hofstadter, op. cit. 44.
26. This is true not only of monographic studies of the period but also of virtually all of the survey textbooks in American history.
27. See House of Representatives, Committee on Manufactures, Proceedings, 1888, No. 3112; U.S. Industrial Commission Report on Trusts, 1899–1900; John Moody, *The Truth About Trusts,* New York, 1904; Gustavus Myers, *History of the Great American Fortunes,* New York, 1910; Ida Tarbell, *History of the Standard Oil Company,* New York, 1904; Eliot Jones, *The Trust Problem in the United States,* New York, 1921; T. W. Lawson, "Frenzied Finance," *Everybody's Magazine,* October 1904 to February 1906.
28. This is a generous estimate of business success in the late nineteenth century. Carnegie himself stated flatly that nine out of ten men who were engaged in the iron and steel industry in the last three decades of the nineteenth century failed to survive the fierce competition.
29. See esp. Irvin G. Wyllie, "Social Darwinism and the Businessman," *Proceedings of the American Philosophical Society,* Vol. 103, No 5, Philadelphia, 1959. and also his *The Self-made Man in America,* New Brunswick, N.J., 1954. Other economic historians who have raised questions about the significance of Social Darwinism for the American businessman are Thomas C. Cochrane, *Railroad Leaders, 1845–1890,* Cambridge, Mass., 1953, and Edward Chase Kirkland, *Dream and Thought in the Business Community, 1860–1900,* Ithaca, N.Y., 1956.
30. Wyllie, "Social Darwinism and the Businessman," loc. cit. 635.
31. Quoted in Harvey O'Connor, *Mellon's Millions,* New York, 1933, 4.
32. John G. Cawelti, *Apostles of the Self-made Man,* Chicago, 1965, 168. See also Sigmund Diamond, *The Reputation of the American Businessman,* Cambridge, Mass., 1955. Mr. Diamond explores the reaction of the press to several prominent American businessmen at their deaths: Stephen Girard, John Jacob Astor, Cornelius Vanderbilt, J. P. Morgan, John D. Rockefeller, and Henry Ford. This study covers a long period in American history—from 1831 to 1947—and in each case, those newspapers which were laudatory of "the departed great" (a majority of the press *was* laudatory in each period) praised them for their personal character (hard work, sacrifice, religious activity, temperance, family life) or because they had contributed to the common good by providing jobs and by philanthropic works. Those few publications that condemned the wealthy entrepreneurs did so in Marxist terms of class struggle, comparing the life of the oppressed worker with the luxury of the plutocrat. In no instance was there a justification or a condemnation of the man by his contemporary

1071

press in terms of Social Darwinistic tenets—no reference to the natural struggle nor to the survival of the fittest.

33. In addition to the primary and secondary sources already noted, see Freeman Hunt, *Lives of American Merchants*, New York, 1858; Phineas T. Barnum, *How I Made Millions*, Chicago, 1884; Charles Schwab, *Succeeding with What You Have*, New York, 1917; John D. Rockefeller, Jr., *Character, the Foundation of Successful Business*, New York, 1927; Henry Clews, *Twenty-eight Years in Wall Street*, New York, 1887; Thomas Mellon, *Thomas Mellon and His Times*, Pittsburgh, 1885; John D. Rockefeller, *Random Reminiscences of Men and Events*, New York, 1909; and many others, including Andrew Carnegie's own autobiographical writings.

34. Wyllie, "Social Darwinism and the Businessman," loc. cit. 631. See also Wyllie's assessment of Carnegie as "a good Darwinist" in his *The Self-made Man in America*, 92.

35. *Autobiography*, 333.

36. "The sales of Spencer's books in America from their earliest publication in the 1860's to December 1903 came to 368,755 volumes, a figure probably unparalleled for works in such difficult spheres as philosophy and sociology." Hofstadter, op. cit. 34. These sales represent several times the number of sales of his works in Britain. Indeed, sales in Britain for the first volume of *Synthetic Philosophy* were so poor that his American disciple, Edward L. Youmans, had to raise the necessary $7000 to enable Spencer to bring out the later volumes of that work. Ibid. 33.

37. Spencer, *Autobiography*, II, 455.

38. *Autobiography*, 333.

39. Ibid.

40. Spencer, *Autobiography*, II, 424.

41. Ibid. 463.

42. Ibid.

43. Ibid. 465.

44. Hendrick, *Life*, I, 240.

45. Spencer, *Autobiography*, II, 468.

46. Ibid.; William L. Abbott, interviewed by Hendrick, August 1929, ACLC, Vol. 239.

47. Spencer, *Autobiography*, II, 478.

48. *Autobiography*, 336.

49. Spencer, *Autobiography*, II, 478.

50. Ibid.

51. See Hofstadter, op. cit. 48.

52. Ibid. 48–49; *Nation*, Vol. XXXV, (1882), 348–49.

53. Hendrick, *Life*, I, 240.

54. Quoted in Hendrick, *Life*, II, 159.

55. *Mr. Andrew Carnegie on Socialism, Labour and Home Rule—An Interview*, reprinted from *Northern Daily News*, Aberdeen, Scotland, September 23, 24, 26, and 29, 1891, Aberdeen, 1892, 21–23.

56. Andrew Carnegie, "The Advantages of Poverty," *Nineteenth Century*, XXIX, March 1891, reprinted in *The Gospel of Wealth*, edited by Edward C. Kirkland, Cambridge, Mass., 1962, 64 (hereafter cited as *The Gospel of Wealth*). See also "Mr. Carnegie in Praise of Poverty," *Review of Reviews*, June 1896, 741.

57. Andrew Carnegie, "How To Win Fortune," New York *Tribune*, 13 April 1890, reprinted in *The Empire of Business*, 94.

58. Quoted in Hofstadter, op. cit. 129. This parody was not original with James; he took it from Thomas Kirkman, *Philosophy Without Assumptions*, London, 1876, 292.

59. Andrew Carnegie, "Popular Illusions about Trusts," first published in *Century Magazine*, LX, May 1900, reprinted in *The Gospel of Wealth*, 80–81. See Edward Kirkland's footnote, ibid. 81.

60. *Triumphant Democracy*, 32.

61. See numerous letters between Spencer and Carnegie, ACLC.

62. AC to Spencer, 5 January 1897, ACLC, Vol. 41.

CHAPTER XIII

1. For a description of the Carnegies' hotel life, see Hendrick, *Life*, I, 144–45.

2. For information on the early life of Louise Whitfield, I have drawn from Burton J. Hendrick and Daniel Henderson, *Louise Whitfield Carnegie*, New York, 1950, 19ff.

3. Ibid. 48.

4. *Autobiography*, 213.

5. See notes in collection of letters between Carnegie and Louise Whitfield, in the possession of their daughter, Mrs. Margaret Carnegie Miller (hereafter cited as AC-LW Letters). I am greatly indebted to Mrs. Miller for her kindness in permitting me to read this exchange of letters between her father and mother written during the years of their courtship. I have respected Mrs. Miller's wishes that the more personal parts of these letters not be quoted directly. I have, therefore, generally restricted direct quotations to those letters which have already been published in Hendrick and Henderson, op. cit.

6. John Robertson, interviewed by the writer, Dunfermline, November 1957.

7. Hendrick and Henderson, op. cit. 58–59.

8. Ibid. 59.

9. Ibid.

10. Burton Hendrick, interviewed by Allan Nevins, March 1949, Oral History Project, Columbia University.

11. Andrew Carnegie, *Our Coaching Trip: Brighton to Inverness*, New York: Private Circulation, 1882, 9 (hereafter cited as *Our Coaching Trip*). This account was published by Charles Scribner's in 1883, under the title *An American Four-in-Hand in Britain*, and republished by Doubleday, Doran in 1933 under the same title (hereafter cited as *An American Four-in-Hand in Britain*).

12. Ibid. 31.

13. Ibid. 32.

14. See letter from John Kennedy of the Bessemer Steel Association to Edgar Thomson Steel Company, 20 March 1880, and agreement signed by AC, dated 29 May 1880, Bessemer Steel Association File, ACUSC. For a fuller account of the Thomas basic process, see Chapter XIV: "The Two Worlds of Andrew Carnegie."

15. *An American Four-in-Hand in Britain*, 83–87. The account of Carnegie's meeting with Thomas does not appear in *Our Coaching Trip*, but only in the later, commercially published version.

16. Lillian G. Thompson, *Sidney Gilchrist Thomas*, London, 1940, 169.

17. *Our Coaching Trip,* 94.
18. Ibid. 97.
19. Ibid. 108.
20. Ibid. 140.
21. Ibid. 152.
22. Ibid. 183–85.
23. Carnegie quotes at length the details of the Dunfermline reception from the Dunfermline newspapers, *Press* and *Journal,* 30 July 1881, in *Our Coaching Trip,* 186–239.
24. Ibid. 269.
25. Ibid. 273–74.
26. Carnegie to Louise Whitfield, 21 June 1881, quoted in Hendrick and Henderson, op. cit. 60–61.
27. Quoted in *Our Coaching Trip,* 210.
28. *Our Coaching Trip,* 123.
29. For a fuller account of Carnegie's journalistic venture, see Chapter XIV.
30. All of these diary notations are quoted in Hendrick and Henderson, op. cit. 64–65.
31. Ibid. 66.
32. Carnegie to Louise Whitfield, 11 June 1884, AC-LW Letters.
33. Carnegie to Louise Whitfield, 19 July 1884, AC-LW Letters.
34. *An American Four-in-Hand in Britain,* 182.
35. Carnegie to Louise Whitfield, undated, but apparently written 15 November 1884, and Louise Whitfield to Carnegie, 17 November 1884, AC-LW Letters.
36. Louise Whitfield to Carnegie, 20 November 1884, AC-LW Letters.
37. Carnegie to Louise Whitfield, 29 June 1885, AC-LW Letters.
38. Louise Whitfield to Carnegie, 1 July 1885, AC-LW Letters.
39. Carnegie to Louise Whitfield, 23 July 1885, AC-LW Letters.
40. Louise Whitfield to Carnegie, undated, but sometime after 17 September 1885, AC-LW Letters.
41. Carnegie to Louise Whitfield, 22 July 1886, AC-LW Letters.
42. Carnegie to Louise Whitfield, 23 September 1886, AC-LW Letters.
43. Carnegie to Louise Whitfield, 17 October 1885, AC-LW Letters.
44. John Walker, interviewed by Hendrick, 16–18 February 1928, ACLC, Vol. 239.
45. Carnegie to Louise Whitfield, undated, but sometime in October 1886, AC-LW Letters.
46. Carnegie to Louise Whitfield, 21 October 1886, AC-LW Letters.
47. J. H. Bridge to Mrs. Whitfield, 10 November 1886, AC-LW Letters.
48. Dr. F. S. Dennis, interviewed by Hendrick, 17 November 1927, ACLC, Vol. 239.
49. Carnegie to Louise Whitfield, 24 November 1886, AC-LW Letters.
50. Carnegie to Louise Whitfield, 2 December 1886, AC-LW Letters.
51. Carnegie to Louise Whitfield, 4 April 1887, AC-LW Letters.
52. AC to Charles Eaton, 16 April 1887, AC-LW Letters.
53. Newspaper clipping, unspecified source and date, in AC-LW Letters.

CHAPTER XIV

1. Louise Carnegie to her mother, Mrs. Fannie Whitfield, quoted in Hendrick and Henderson, *Louise Whitfield Carnegie*, 105.

2. Carnegie's address on receiving the Freedom of the City of Edinburgh, July 1887, reprinted in Hendrick and Henderson, op. cit. 98–99.

3. Hendrick and Henderson, op. cit. 123.

4. See letter to AC from Lord William Farmer, owner of Coworth Park, 23 June 1892, ACLC, Vol. 16, and letter to AC from Lord Cantelupe, owner of Buckhurst, 27 June 1894, ACLC, Vol. 26.

5. George Lauder to AC, 15 April 1880, George Lauder File, ACUSC.

6. John Walker, interviewed by Hendrick, 16–18 February 1928, ACLC, Vol. 239.

7. Matthew Arnold, *Letters of Matthew Arnold*, Vol. II, New York, 1900, 396.

8. Quoted in Hendrick, *Life*, I, 245. For a full account of Matthew Arnold's visit to the United States, see Ibid., I, Chap. XIII, 242–55.

9. Ibid. 246.

10. J. B. Pond, *Eccentricities of Genius*, New York, 1900, 396–98.

11. Robert Morrison, Carnegie's valet, interviewed by the writer, August 1959.

12. John Morley to AC, 2 October 1898, ACLC, Vol. 55.

13. Morley to AC, 29 October 1907, ACLC, Vol. 145.

14. Morley to AC, 5 October 1913, ACLC, Vol. 218.

15. Numerous letters of such nature, e.g. Henry Fowler to AC, 20 January 1885, and Joseph Chamberlain to AC, 12 May 1884, ACNYPL.

16. William E. Gladstone to AC, 1 July 1887, ACNYPL.

17. AC to Gladstone, 21 July 1887, Gladstone Papers, Vol. 416, 44, 501. fol. 199, British Museum.

18. See numerous letters, e.g. AC to Samuel Storey, 13 February 1883, Letterbook, 1883, ACUSC; AC to Morley, 29 June 1886, Letterbook, 1885, ACUSC; William Digby to AC, 30 May 1892, ACLC, Vol. 16; and I. G. Manen to AC, 22 June 1892, ACLC, Vol. 16.

19. See Robert G. McCloskey, *American Conservatism In the Age of Enterprise*, Cambridge, Mass., 1951, 136.

20. Ibid. 156.

21. "Edwards, John Passmore," *Dictionary of National Biography*, Supplement 1901–11, 612–14; E. H. Burrage, *J. Passmore Edwards, Philanthropist*, London, 1902, 32ff.

22. J. Passmore Edwards, *A Few Footprints*, London, 1906, 37.

23. The newspapers belonging to the Carnegie-Storey syndicate were: *The Midland* (Birmingham) *Echo; Wolverhampton Express and Star; Sunderland Echo; Tyneside* (Newcastle) *Echo; Portsmouth Evening News; Northern Daily Mail* (Hartlepool, Durham); *North Eastern Gazette* (Middlesbrough, Yorkshire), all dailies; and the *Guardian* (Northampton); *North Eastern Gazette Weekly; Stockton Herald; Hampshire Telegraph* (Portsmouth); *Midland Counties Express* (Wolverhampton), *South Durham Herald; Stockton Journal; Free Press* (Walsall, Staffordshire); *Wolverhampton Chronicle;* and *Sunderland Weekly Echo*, all weeklies. This information found in *The Newspaper Press Directory, Published in the United Kingdom and the British Isles*, London, 39th and 40th Annual Issues, 1884, 1885.

24. *Wolverhampton Evening Express and Star*, 16 July and 30 July 1884. See also

files for *London Echo, Tyneside Echo,* and other papers belonging to the syndicate, British Museum, Newspaper Collection at Colindale.

25. *Tyneside Echo* (Newcastle), 16 July 1886, British Museum, Newspaper Collection at Colindale.

26. AC to Storey, 5 November 1884, ACLC, Vol. 8.

27. AC to Morley, 10 December 1883, ACLC, Vol. 8.

28. AC to Storey, 22 April 1884, Letterbook, 1884, ACUSC.

29. AC to Storey, 5 November 1884, Letterbook, 1884–85, ACUSC.

30. For a fuller account of this second coaching trip, see Hendrick, *Life,* I, 251–52.

31. William Black, "A Few Days' More Driving," *Harper's New Monthly Magazine,* Vol. 70, December 1884, 32.

32. AC to Col. Thomas Higginson, 10 December 1884, ACUSC.

33. Interview with AC in *Philadelphia Bulletin,* 27 August 1884, copy in Carnegie scrapbook, ACLC, Vol. 265.

34. AC to J. H. Menzis, 5 January 1885, Letterbook, 1884–85, ACUSC.

35. AC to "My Dear Friend" (name not given), 18 October 1884, ACLC, Vol. 8.

36. AC to J. Stuart Blackie, 22 April 1884, Blackie Letters, 1883–84, MS 2635, National Library of Scotland, Edinburgh.

37. See letter from Charles T. O. Mackie, Carnegie's secretary, to John Peacock, manager of John Burns's campaign, 11 November 1885, Letterbook, 1884–85, ACUSC.

38. George Macaulay Trevelyan, *History of England,* New York, 1926, 688.

39. AC to Gladstone, 25 January 1886, Gladstone Papers, Vol. 409, Add. Ms. 44; 494, fol. 71, British Museum.

40. Ibid.

41. Edwards, op. cit. 37; Burrage, op. cit. 34.

42. Thomas Graham to John Ross, Carnegie's lawyer in Dunfermline, 11 July 1902, from Carnegie Legal Box, Ross-Connell Law Office, Dunfermline. See also correspondence between Storey and AC, and Thomas Graham and AC, for the years 1886–95, in ACLC and in Letterbooks, 1885–87, ACUSC, and correspondence between Graham and Ross, Carnegie Legal Box, Ross-Connell Law Office, Dunfermline.

43. A typical request was from J. Quail, editor of the *Northern Daily News* of Aberdeen, Scotland, to Carnegie, 21 March 1892, asking for his financial support for the *Northern Daily News* "before it folds completely." Quail said it was the only Radical paper in northeast Scotland. Carnegie's answer was a flat no. ACLC, Vol. 15.

44. W. T. Stead to AC, 2 December 1899, and AC to Stead, 12 December 1899, ACLC, Vol. 70.

45. AC to Stead, 25 June 1910, ACLC, Vol. 178.

46. *Triumphant Democracy,* 1.

47. Ibid. vii.

48. Quoted in Hendrick, *Life,* I, 274.

49. *Mr. Andrew Carnegie on Socialism, Labour and Home Rule—An Interview,* loc. cit. 16, 17.

50. *Letters of Matthew Arnold,* Vol. II, 396, quoted in Hendrick, *Life,* I, 277.

51. See Ralph Gabriel, *The Course of American Democratic Thought,* New York, 1956, Chap. II.

52. See Stow Person's excellent statement in *American Minds,* Part IV, "The Naturalistic Mind," New York, 1958.

53. *Triumphant Democracy*, dedicatory page (unnumbered) and v.

54. McCloskey, op. cit. 157–58.

55. "Home Rule in America," address before the Glasgow Junior Liberal Association, Glasgow, 13 September 1887, reprinted in *The Gospel of Wealth*, 201–25.

56. *Andrew Carnegie's Reply to a Radical Address*, Dunfermline, 1887, Carnegie Public Library, Dunfermline. See also his address, "America and the Land Question," delivered to the Glasgow Junior Liberal Association, 24 September 1888, published by the Glasgow Junior Liberal Association, 1888, Carnegie Public Library, Dunfermline.

57. "Men You Know—No. 778: Mr. Andrew Carnegie," *The Bailie*, 14 September 1887, Glasgow, Carnegie Public Library, Dunfermline.

58. See AC's letter to E. L. Godkin, 8 November 1884, Andrew Carnegie letters, Houghton Library, Harvard University.

59. See AC's letter to William McKinley, 18 October 1897, asking that McKinley raise to prohibitive levels the tariff on all Canadian products and forbid the passage under bond of British imports to Canada through the territory of the United States, ACLC, Vol. 46.

60. AC to James M. Swank, 31 August 1895, ACLC, Vol. 32.

61. AC to Senator Arthur Gorman, giving recommendations for changes in the proposed Wilson Tariff bill of 1894, ACLC, Vol. 24; see also his letter to Representative John Dalzell, 6 December 1893, making many of the same recommendations and arguing forcibly against ad valorum duties and in favor of fixed specific duties, ACLC, Vol. 23.

62. Andrew Carnegie, "Summing Up the Tariff Discussion," *North American Review*, Vol. 151, July 1890, 47–48, 50.

63. Ibid. 51.

64. Ibid. 73.

65. Ibid. 74.

66. According to the article on "Wages" by Wladimir Woytinsky in the *Encyclopaedia of Social Sciences*, Vol. XV, New York, 318, "The first systematic and comprehensive investigation [on international comparison of wages] was carried out in 1905–09 by the British Board of Trade." These statistical indices show that on the basis of 100 for Great Britain, the average real wage per day for all workers in the United States was 163.

67. Andrew Carnegie, "The President's Puzzle: The Surplus," *North American Review*, Vol. 146, March 1888, 275, 279.

68. Andrew Carnegie, "What Would I Do with the Tariff If I Were Czar," *Forum*, Vol. 19, March 1895, 18–21.

69. Ibid. 23.

70. Ibid. 24.

71. AC to Grover Cleveland, 14 December 1894, ACLC, Vol. 29.

72. AC to Editor, New York *Tribune*, 3 January 1894, ACLC, Vol. 24.

73. *Triumphant Democracy*, 255, 257.

74. Platform of the People's Party of America, Preamble, Omaha, Nebraska, 4 July 1892 (hereafter cited as Populist Platform), in *A Handbook of Politics for 1892*, edited by E. McPherson, Washington, D.C., 1892, 269–71.

75. See Fred E. Haynes, *Third Party Movements Since the Civil War*, Iowa City, The State Historical Society of Iowa, 1916, 268–69.

76. See AC's letters to J. Donald Cameron, 16 January 1878, and to William A. Wallace, same date, Letterbook, 1877–78, ACUSC.

77. Interview with *Northern Daily News*, Aberdeen, Scotland, loc. cit. 16–17.

78. See AC's letter to Morley, 8 October 1884 (misfiled under 8 October 1894), ACLC, Vol. 27.

79. AC to Godkin, 8 November 1884, Andrew Carnegie letters, Houghton Library, Harvard University.

80. Andrew Carnegie, "The ABC of Money," *North American Review*, Vol. 152, June 1891, 748.

81. Ibid. 723–24.

82. Ibid. 744 *passim*.

83. Ibid. 735–36.

84. Ibid. 750.

85. John Sherman to AC, 29 June 1891, ACNYPL.

86. See AC's letter to Richard Watson Gilder upon the death of Cleveland, 27 July 1908, ACLC, Vol. 155.

87. AC to Col. Daniel S. Lamont, 26 November 1894, Papers of Daniel S. Lamont, Vol. 44, Library of Congress. See also Lamont's letter to AC, undated, reporting on the President's health, Carnegie Collection, ACNYPL, and AC to Lamont, 17 December 1894, Papers of Daniel Lamont, Vol. 45.

88. AC to Wayne MacVeagh, 26 October 1896, ACLC, Vol. 39.

89. Andrew Carnegie, "The Ship of State Adrift," *North American Review*, Vol. 163, October 1896, 497.

90. Mark Hanna to AC, 17 October 1896, ACLC, Vol. 39.

91. AC to Editor, *The* (London) *Times*, 30 September 1896.

92. AC to H. Y. Thompson, 26 September 1896, ACLC, Vol. 39.

93. Andrew Carnegie, "Mr. Bryan, the Conjurer," *North American Review*, Vol. 164, January 1897, 106–18.

94. AC to Professor James Donaldson, St. Andrews University, 23 November 1896, ACLC, Vol. 39.

95. Andrew Carnegie, "Mr. Bryan, the Conjurer," loc. cit. 106.

CHAPTER XV

1. See statement of Carnegie Bros. & Co., Ltd., dated 1 April 1881, and Act of Association of Carnegie Bros. & Co., Ltd., same date, ACLC, Vol. 5.

2. See E. E. Moore, unpublished MS, ACUSC.

3. Ibid.

4. Net Profits Sheet of Carnegie Association, ACLC, Vol. 73.

5. Ibid.

6. Bridge, *Inside History of Carnegie Steel*, 105.

7. Ibid. 152.

8. Ibid.

9. Ibid. 141–42. Bridge gives an excellent brief description of the part that coke plays in the making of steel.

10. Quoted in *Pennsylvania: A Guide to the Keystone State*, 572.

11. George Harvey, *Henry Clay Frick, The Man*, New York (privately printed), 1936, 16.

12. Ibid. 15, 19.

13. Ibid. 29–30.

14. Ibid. 66.

15. Ibid. 72.

16. Hendrick, *Life,* I, 296; Harvey, op. cit. 74–75.

17. Harvey, op. cit. 79.

18. See Henry C. Frick's letter to AC, 13 August 1883, printed in Harvey, op. cit. 79–80.

19. Hendrick, *Life,* I, 295.

20. Ibid.

21. Ibid.

22. Ibid. 301–2; Harvey, op. cit. 153–59.

23. E. E. Moore, unpublished MS, ACUSC.

24. Ibid.

25. Statement of Carnegie Bros. & Company, Ltd., dated 1 April 1881, ACLC, Vol. 5, and Statement of Carnegie, Phipps & Company, Ltd., Articles of Association, dated 1 January 1886, ACLC, Vol. 8.

26. John Walker, interviewed by Hendrick, notes, 16–18 February 1923, ACLC, Vol. 239.

27. Copy of agreement, dated 10 January 1887, between Carnegie Bros. & Company, Ltd., party of the first part, and each individual partner as parties of the second part, ACLC, Vol. 10. An identical agreement, drawn up at the same time, existed between Carnegie, Phipps & Company and the individual partners in that company.

28. Ibid.

29. Articles of Agreement between Carnegie Bros. & Company, Ltd., and Henry C. Frick, dated 31 January 1887, ACLC, Vol. 10.

30. *Autobiography,* 222.

31. Reprinted in Harvey, op. cit. 85–86.

32. Ibid. 90.

33. E. E. Moore, unpublished MS, ACUSC.

34. Bridge, op. cit. 176–77.

35. Ibid. 178–80.

36. Quoted in Harvey, op. cit. 90.

37. "Charlie Schwab's View of Andrew Carnegie," *Literary Digest,* Vol. 64, 21 February 1920, 56.

38. Charles M. Schwab, *Andrew Carnegie: His Methods With His Men,* address, Carnegie Hall, 25 November 1919, New York (privately printed pamphlet), 10.

39. For this information on Thomas's discovery and the first tests of his process, see the long letter from George W. Maynard to AC, 25 February 1909, ACLC, Vol. 163.

40. Ibid.

41. AC to Sidney G. Thomas, 10 February 1880, Letterbook, 1879–80, ACUSC.

42. AC to E. Y. Townsend, 23 April 1880, Letterbook, 1879–80, ACUSC.

43. See AC's letter to John M. Kennedy, 26 April 1881, Letterbook, 1880–81, and Kennedy to AC, 20 January 1882, Bessemer Steel Association File, ACUSC. Carnegie demanded and got a reduced price from the original stipulated price of $300,000 on the ground that Maynard had previously sold a license to use the patent to the Shoenberger Blair Steel Company. See Maynard's letter to AC, 25 February 1909, ACLC, Vol. 163.

44. Kennedy to AC, 20 January 1882, op. cit.

45. See letter from James Bertram to Maynard, 15 March 1909, ACLC, Vol. 164.

46. See AC's letters to Thomas, 23 December 1879 and 16 January 1880, Letter-book, 1879–80, ACUSC; Maynard to AC, 8 April 1892, ACLC, Vol. 15.

47. AC to William Abbott, 28 October 1888, ACLC. Vol. 10.

48. AC to Abbott, 29 December 1888 and 16 January 1889, ACLC, Vol. 10.

49. AC to A. J. Cassatt, 5 March 1881, Letterbook, 1880–81, ACUSC.

50. See AC's letters to Robert Garrett, vice president of the B. & O., 28 December 1881, and to Cassatt, 11 January 1882, Letterbook 1881–83, ACUSC.

51. AC to John S. Wilson, 22 February 1884, ACUSC.

52. AC to Frank Thomson, 23 January 1884, Letterbook, 1884, ACUSC.

53. See George H. Burgess and Miles C. Kennedy, *Centennial History of the Pennsylvania Railroad Company*, Philadelphia, 1949, 408.

54. Ibid. 409–10.

55. Hendrick, *Life*, II, 26–27.

56. AC to W. C. Whitney, 10 November 1884, Letterbook, 1884–85, ACUSC.

57. AC to George B. Roberts, 10 January 1885, Letterbook, 1884–85, ACUSC.

58. Frederick Lewis Allen, *The Great Pierpont Morgan*, New York, 1956, 36–41.

59. *Pennsylvania: A Guide to the Keystone State*, 93.

60. AC to John S. Wilson, 4 April 1887, Letterbook, 1887–88, ACUSC.

61. AC to Wilson, 7 April 1887, Letterbook, 1887–88, ACUSC.

62. Andrew Carnegie, "Pennsylvania's Industrial and Railroad Policy," address delivered before the Pennsylvania Legislature, 8 April 1889, reprinted in *Miscellaneous Writings of Andrew Carnegie*, Vol. 1, Garden City, N.Y., 1933, 271.

63. Ibid. 291.

64. Ibid. 293.

65. Ibid. 280–81.

66. Ibid. 295.

67. Ibid. 303–4.

68. Ibid. 297.

69. Frick to AC, 9 August 1889, published in Harvey, op. cit. 97.

70. Ibid. 96.

71. AC to Carnegie Bros. & Co., 30 November 1883, E.T. Operations File, ACUSC.

72. AC to A. L. Griffin, 21 April 1884, Letterbook, 1884, ACUSC. See also AC's letters to G. B. Linderman of Bethlehem Iron and Steel, 5 November 1884, and to Silas Bent, Superintendent of the Pennsylvania Steel Company's plant in Harrisburg, 26 November 1884, illustrative of AC's requests to get information on labor costs. Letterbook, 1884–85, ACUSC.

73. AC to Capt. W. R. Jones, 1 June 1885, Letterbook, 1884–85, ACUSC.

74. W. R. Jones, address to the British Iron and Steel Institute, London, May 1881, printed in Bridge, op. cit. 110.

75. See W. R. Jones's letter to E. V. McCandless, 25 February 1875, printed in Bridge, op. cit. 81.

76. Andrew Carnegie, "An Employer's View of the Labor Question," *Forum*, Vol. I, April 1886, 114–25.

77. Andrew Carnegie, "Results of the Labor Struggle," *Forum*, Vol. 1, August 1886, 538–51.

78. AC to W. R. Thompson, Corresponding Secretary of the Brotherhood of Locomotive Engineers, April 1887, Letterbook, 1887–88, ACUSC.

79. Told in Bridge, op. cit. 199.

80. See undated letters, AC to Abbott, ACLC. Vol. 10; also Hendrick, *Life*, I, 372–76.

81. J. Bernard Hogg, *The Homestead Strike of 1892*, unpublished Ph.D. thesis, University of Chicago, 1943, 32–34.

82. AC to Abbott, undated, but sometime in early July 1889, ACLC, Vol. 10.

83. Ibid.

84. Hogg, op. cit. 36–37; Bridge, op. cit. 201–2.

85. AC to Abbott, 7 August 1889, ACLC, Vol. 10.

86. These patent papers still exist among the collection of papers of Robert A. Franks, Carnegie's business secretary, deposited in the Home Trust Office, Hoboken, N. J.

87. See letters to AC from D. D. Gage, Jones's son-in-law, 12 May 1905, ACLC, Vol. 116, 30 August 1905, ACLC, Vol. 119, and from George Lauder to D. D. Gage, 31 August 1905, ACLC, Vol. 119.

88. Quoted in Bridge, op. cit. 113.

89. Harvey, op. cit. 101–2.

90. Frick to AC, 10 February 1890, printed in Harvey, op. cit. 102.

91. Listing of profits from 1875–98, ACLC, Vol. 61.

92. Papers creating the Association of Carnegie Steel Company, Limited, notarized 9 April 1892, ACLC, Vol. 17.

93. AC to Frick, 3 September 1889, printed in Winkler, *Incredible Carnegie*, 181.

CHAPTER XVI

1. For a history of the early trades-union movement in the iron and steel industries, see H. E. Hoagland, "Trade Unionism in the Iron Industry: A Decadent Organization," *Quarterly Journal of Economics*, Vol. 31, August 1917, 674–89; John A. Fitch, "Unionism in the Iron and Steel Industry," *Political Science Quarterly*, Vol. 24, March 1909, 57–59; and Carroll D. Wright, "The Amalgamated Association of Iron and Steel Workers," *Quarterly Journal of Economics*, Vol. 7, July 1893, 400–32.

2. Quoted in Brody, *Steelworkers in America*, 57.

3. AC at the Company's Annual Meeting, reported in *Engineering and Mining Journal*, Vol. LIII, 16 April 1892, 439, quoted in Hogg, *Homestead Strike of 1892*, 42. I am much indebted to Mr. Hogg for information and interpretation given in this chapter. His is quite the best study of Homestead I have seen.

4. Brody, op. cit. 51.

5. Ibid. 58.

6. Bridge, *Inside History of Carnegie Steel*, 204–5.

7. Andrew Carnegie, "An Employer's View of the Labor Question," loc. cit. 119.

8. Hendrick, *Life*, I, 384.

9. "Mr. Andrew Carnegie on Socialism, Labour and Home Rule—An Interview," loc. cit. 24.

10. Andrew Carnegie, "An Employer's View of the Labour Question," loc. cit. 124. Italics mine.

11. AC to Henry Frick, 4 May 1892, quoted in Harvey, op. cit. 165–66.

12. W. and A. K. Johnston, *Map of the Railway Systems of Scotland*, Johnston of Edinburgh, Lithographer, 1896, National Library of Scotland, Edinburgh.

13. AC to Frick, 10 June 1892, quoted in Bridge, op. cit. 205.

14. Report of the Committee of the Judiciary on "Employment of Pinkerton Detectives," House Report No. 2447, 52nd Cong., 2nd sess., 1892–93, Vol. 3, 34 (hereafter cited as House Report 2447). See also Edward W. Bemis, "The Homestead Strike," *Journal of Political Economy*, Vol. 2, June 1894, 373.

15. House Report 2447, vii, 33–35; Hogg, op. cit. 74.

16. Stefan Wloszcewski, "The Polish Sociological Group in America," *The American Slavic and East European Review*, Vol. 4, 153–54.

17. See "Pinkerton, Allan," *D.A.B.*, Vol. 14, 622–23. Conversations with Professor George S. Shepperson of the University of Edinburgh, on Pinkerton's Scottish background, also served as a basis for this section.

18. Hogg, op. cit. Chap. VI, "Pinkertonism," 67–75; Populist Platform, 4 July 1892, loc. cit.

19. A. C. Buell to a Mr. Cramp, 8 January 1892, Papers of Secretary of the Navy Benjamin F. Tracy, Library of Congress.

20. Testimony of a strike leader before the Senate investigating committee, quoted in Brody, op. cit. 55.

21. Quoted in Brody, op. cit. 55.

22. Quoted in Bemis, op. cit. 373.

23. Ibid. 373–74.

24. Ibid. 374.

25. AC to Frick, 10 June 1892 and 28 June 1892, quoted in Bridge, op. cit. 205–6.

26. Quoted in Hogg, op. cit. 242.

27. Quoted in Bemis, op. cit. 375.

28. Both Bridge, *Inside History of Carnegie Steel*, and Harvey, *Henry Clay Frick, The Man*, repeat these stories in their accounts of Homestead as if they were actual fact.

29. Bemis, op. cit. 378–79.

30. Hogg, op. cit. 53–55.

31. Hendrick gives this standard interpretation, *Life*, I, 382–88.

32. See William Weihe's testimony, House Report 2447, 73.

33. Frick to Robert A. Pinkerton, 25 June 1892, reprinted in Harvey, op. cit. 114–15.

34. Bridge, op. cit. 212.

35. Hogg, op. cit. 91.

36. Henry Phipps's account of the incident, printed in the New York *Herald*, 31 January 1904, reprinted in Hendrick, *Life*, I, 401.

37. AC to Dod [George Lauder] 17 July 1892, ACLC, Vol. 17. Burton Hendrick, in quoting this letter, omits "such a fiasco trying to send guards by Boat and then leaving space between River and fences for the men to get opposite landing and fire." Yet he does not add the usual notation of ellipsis. The omission, of course, gives quite a different meaning to the letter. Hendrick, *Life*, I, 404.

38. Quoted in Harvey, op. cit. 134.

39. A complete account of the attempted assassination is given in Harvey, op. cit. 136–45.

40. Hogg, op. cit. 121.

41. Hugh O'Donnell to Whitelaw Reid, dated Homestead, 15 July 1892, but actually written in New York on 17 July 1892, quoted at length in Bemis, op. cit. 384–85.

42. Reid to John Foster of State Department, to transmit to John New, 20 July 1892, Whitelaw Reid Papers, Box 146, Library of Congress.

43. AC to Frick, telegram in code, 28 July 1892, ACLC, Vol. 17, decoded message reprinted in Harvey, op. cit. 152.

44. Hendrick, *Life*, I, 408.

45. Ibid. 402.

46. Ibid. 408.

47. Harvey, op. cit. 151.

48. O'Donnell to Edward Bemis, February 1894, quoted in Bemis, op. cit. 386.

49. Paraphrase of Harrison's remarks by Bridge, op. cit. 248.

50. Ibid. 247.

51. AC to Reid, 20 March 1893, ACLC, Vol. 19.

52. Quoted in Bridge, op. cit. 247.

53. Reid to W. E. Chandler, 11 January 1894, Nelson Aldrich Manuscripts, Library of Congress.

54. See New York *Tribune* editorial, 1 January 1895, attacking Carnegie, and Carnegie's reply, printed in the *Tribune*, 7 January 1895; also James M. Swank to AC, 2 January 1895: "While you were in Europe last year several villainous editorials concerning you appeared in the New York Tribune. . . . In the Tribune of Tuesday there appears another editorial article which . . . I think that you ought to reply to. . . . If Mr. Reid at home an inquiry into his own motives in attacking you would be justifiable. . . ."

55. Bernard Hogg has made a careful analysis of the election of 1892 to disprove the claim that the Homestead strike was the decisive issue in that election. Hogg, op. cit. 166–70.

56. Frick to AC and AC to Frick, both letters dated 9 November 1892, reprinted in Harvey, op. cit. 157.

57. Cablegrams: Frick to AC, 18 November and 21 November 1892; AC to Frick, 27 November 1892, reprinted in Harvey, op. cit. 172.

58. AC to Frick, undated, reprinted in Harvey, op. cit. 173.

59. *Autobiography*, 232.

60. *The* (London) *Times*, 12 July 1892.

61. *Edinburgh Dispatch*, 30 July 1892.

62. *Dunfermline Journal*, 30 July 1892.

63. *Sheffield Daily Telegraph*, 1 September 1892.

64. *St. James's Gazette*, 7 July 1892.

65. Quoted in Bridge, op. cit. 233–34.

66. "The Typical American Employer: Mr. Andrew Carnegie," *Blackwood's Edinburgh Magazine*, Vol. 152, No. 924, October 1892, 556–73. *The Star* (London), 12 July 1892.

67. *Cleveland Press*, 19 February 1896.

68. See AC's letter to C. S. Scotell of the Pittsburgh Art Association, published in *The New York Times*, 18 December 1892.

69. William E. Gladstone to AC, 19 September 1892, Gladstone Papers, Vol. 431, Add. Ms. 44,516, fol. 41, British Museum.

70. AC to Gladstone, 24 September 1892, Gladstone Papers, Vol. 437, Adds. Ms. 44,522, fol. 302, British Museum.

71. Lord Rosebery to AC, 10 October 1892, ACLC, Vol. 13 (misfiled in the wrong year).

72. John Morley to AC, 3 April 1893, ACLC, Vol. 19.

73. See letter from John E. Milholland, 12 July 1904, denying any knowledge of

such a telegram: "I never imagined such a thing at the time; I am unable to do so now." ACLC, Vol. 106. See also letter from Alexander Peacock to AC, 25 April and 11 May 1912, ACLC, Vols. 205 and 206.

74. *Autobiography*, 232.

75. Charles B. Spahr, *America's Working People*, New York, 1900, 148.

76. Speech as reported in *The* (London) *Times*, 31 January 1893, and quoted in Harvey, op. cit. 173–74.

77. AC to Morley, 16 April 1893, ACLC, Vol. 20.

78. House Report 2447; see also Select Committee To Investigate the Employment for Private Purpose of Armed Bodies of Men, U.S. Senate Report 1280, 52nd Cong., 2nd sess., Vol. I.

79. Hogg, op. cit. 188–89.

80. Hogg, op. cit. 216; Brody, op. cit. 69; Fitch, "Unionism in the Iron and Steel Industry," loc. cit. 78.

81. See Carnegie's sentimental account of John Van Dyke's finding McLuckie in Mexico, *Autobiography*, 235–38.

82. Bemis, op. cit. 388.

83. Hogg, op. cit. 201–10.

84. Spahr, op. cit. 146–47, 154.

85. John A. Fitch, *The Steel Workers*, Vol. 3 of *The Pittsburgh Survey*, New York, Charities Publication Committee, 1910, 233. See also Margaret F. Byington, *Homestead: The Households of a Mill Town*, Vol. 4 of *The Pittsburgh Survey*.

86. Hamlin Garland, "Homestead and Its Perilous Trades," *McClure's Magazine*, Vol. 3, June 1894, 3–5.

87. Quoted in Hogg, op. cit. 181.

CHAPTER XVII

1. AC to Charles Schwab, 4 June 1900, ACLC, Vol. 171. See also AC's letter to George Lauder: "I do not think the consumption of steel is to be small, on the contrary, it will be great, only the little percentage less than the country wishes to make, but that lowers prices to the point of decreased production by the stoppage of the 'least fit.' " 3 June 1900, ACLC, Vol. 75.

2. AC to William L. Abbott, undated, probably 1888 or 1889, ACLC, Vol. 240. Many instances of this same advice could be quoted.

3. Andrew Carnegie, "Pennsylvania's Industrial and Railroad Policy," *Miscellaneous Writings of Andrew Carnegie*, 267.

4. See Minutes of Board Meeting, 31 August 1897, ACLC, Vol. 44.

5. AC to H. Y. Thompson, 26 September 1896, ACLC, Vol. 39.

6. AC to J. G. A. Leishman, 31 March 1896, ACLC, Vol. 37; Minutes of Board Meeting, 26 October 1897, ACLC, Vol. 46.

7. See AC's letters to Henry Phipps, 18 September 1896, and to J. A. Jamieson, Bank of Scotland, Edinburgh, 19 September 1896, ACLC, Vol. 39.

8. See considerable correspondence and Minutes of Board Meetings regarding Russian trade, ACLC, Vols, 66 and 67, June through August 1899.

9. AC to W. T. Stead, 22 December 1897, ACLC, Vol. 47.

10. AC to Schwab, 4 June 1900, ACLC, Vol. 177.

11. See AC's letter of 25 July 1898, reported in Minutes of Board Meeting, 23 August 1898, ACLC, Vol. 54.

12. Albert H. Chester, "Exploration of the Iron Regions of Northern Minnesota During the Years 1875 to 1880," paper presented to St. Louis County Historical Society, Duluth, Minn., 28 September 1923; Herbert N. Casson, "The Romance of Steel and Iron in America," Part II, *Munsey's Magazine*, Vol. 35, May 1906, 159–61. (Casson's book, *The Romance of Steel*, New York, 1907, was adapted from these articles.)

13. For an excellent series on mining methods, see the articles by C. A. Mitke in the *Engineering and Mining Journal*, 8 October, 10 and 24 December 1917, 10 September 1924, 3 March, 7 April, and 1 May 1928. Also see Robert Strong Lewis, "Mining," *Encyclopaedia Britannica*, Vol. 15, 1951, 548.

14. See Kloman Mine File, ACUSC, including incorporation papers, Kloman Mining Company, dated 10 September 1872, and numerous letters from mine managers to AC, ACUSC, 1873–80.

15. W. G. Swart, "Notes of Work Done in Eastern Mesabi Range," paper presented to St. Louis County Historical Society, Duluth, Minn., 7 August 1923; Vera Jusela, "The Early History of the Ore Industry of Mountain Iron," paper presented to St. Louis County Historical Society, 23 May 1927.

16. James B. Greggie's letter to Dwight E. Woodbridge, 22 October 1904, copy in St. Louis County Historical Society Library.

17. Hendrick, *Life*, II, 9–10; Casson, "Steel and Iron in America," 162; Thomas T. Read, "Merritt, Leonidas," *D.A.B.*, Vol. XII, 571–72.

18. From the Stanley Committee Report, p. 1889, quoted in Hendrick, *Life*, II, 10.

19. Ibid.

20. Ibid.

21. Stanley Committee Report, p. 1892, quoted in Hendrick, *Life*, II, 11

22. Casson, "Steel and Iron in America," loc. cit. 163.

23. "The Discovery of Iron Ore and Development of the Mining Industry at Chisholm, Minnesota," by Willard Bayliss, Superintendent, Oliver Iron Mining Company, unpublished MS, undated, St. Louis County Historical Society Library, Duluth, Minn.; Edmund J. Longyear, *Mesabi Pioneer*, edited by Grace Lee Nute, Minnesota Historical Society, St. Paul, 1951.

24. Bayliss, op. cit.

25. AC to Frick, 29 August 1892, quoted in Bridge, *Inside History of Carnegie Steel*, 259.

26. AC to Board of Managers, Carnegie Steel, 18 April 1894, quoted in Bridge, op. cit. 259.

27. AC to Leishman, 14 November 1895, ACLC, Vol. 34.

28. Various letters from AC to H. M. Curry, 9, 12, and 19 December 1895, ACLC, Vol. 35.

29. AC to the Hon. H. E. Davis, 18 November 1896, ACLC, Vol. 39.

30. AC's testimony before the Stanley Committee, 1912, 2500, 2360–61, quoted in Hendrick, *Life*, II, 14–15.

31. Frederick T. Gates, "The Inside Story of Rockefeller and Missabe Mines," *The New York Times Sunday Magazine*, 21 January 1912, 1–3.

32. Ibid. For a full account of John D. Rockefeller's entry into the iron ore field, see Allan Nevins, *Study in Power, John D. Rockefeller*, New York, 1933, Vol. II, Chap. 32, 245–63.

33. Nevins, *Study in Power*, Vol. II, 255–56.

34. AC to Board of Managers of Carnegie Steel, 16 March 1894, quoted in Harvey, *Henry Clay Frick, The Man*, 190.

35. AC to John D. Rockefeller, 30 October 1896, ACLC, Vol. 39.

36. AC to Lauder, 18 November 1896, ACLC, Vol. 39.

37. Terms given in Bridge, op. cit. 260–61.

38. AC to Curry, 22 December 1896, ACLC, Vol. 40.

39. "The Carnegie-Rockefeller Deal," *Iron Age*, Vol. 58, 17 December 1896, 1217–18.

40. AC to Chairman, President, and Managers of Carnegie Steel, 31 December 1896, ACLC, Vol. 40.

41. Bridge, op. cit. 261.

42. Henry Oliver to Frick, 27 July 1897, ACLC, Vol. 43.

43. AC to Leishman, 18 December 1896, ACLC, Vol. 40.

44. See Oliver to Frick, 29 July 1897, and AC's penciled approval on the bottom of the letter, ACLC, Vol. 43.

45. Oliver to Frick, 30 July 1897, ACLC, Vol. 43.

46. Schwab to Frick, 30 July 1897, ACLC, Vol. 43.

47. Unsigned cablegram to Carnegie Steel, 17 August 1897, ACLC Vol. 43; AC to Board of Managers, memorandum, 18 August 1897, quoted in Minutes of Board Meeting, 31 August 1897, ACLC, Vol. 44.

48. Schwab to AC, 20 August 1897, ACLC, Vol. 44.

49. Frick to Phipps, 31 August 1897, and Frick quoted in Minutes of Board Meeting, 7 September 1897, ACLC, Vol. 44.

50. Frick to AC, 10 September 1897, Vol. 44.

51. AC to Frick, cablegram, 20 September 1897, ACLC, Vol. 45.

52. Oliver to AC, cablegram, 25 August 1897, ACLC, Vol. 45.

53. AC to Oliver, cablegram, 27 September 1897, and AC to Carnegie Steel, same date, ACLC, Vol. 45.

54. Minutes of Board Meeting, 27 September 1897, ACLC, Vol. 45.

55. "The Carnegie-Oliver Party on the Gogebic Range," *Iron Age*, Vol. 60, 7 October 1897, 17.

56. See Minutes of Board Meeting, 9 November 1897, ACLC, Vol. 46.

57. John C. Spooner to John A. Humbird, 14 December 1897, John C. Spooner Letterbooks, Vol. 36, Library of Congress.

58. Spooner to Humbird, 7 July 1898, Spooner Letterbooks, Vol. 43.

59. See Minutes of Board Meeting, 19 July 1898, quoting cablegram from AC authorizing purchases, ACLC, Vol. 53; see also H. C. Reed, Spooner's secretary, to Spooner, 8 August 1898, Spooner Letterbooks, Vol. 43, and Spooner to Oliver, 15 September 1898, Spooner Letterbooks, Vol. 44.

60. Spooner to Capt. Thomas Wilson, 17 February 1899, Spooner Letterbooks, Vol. 47.

61. "The Carnegie-Oliver Ore Interests," *Iron Age*, Vol. 62, 15 September 1898, 19.

62. For a listing of the mines and areas of exploration, see Minutes of Board Meeting, 13 November 1899, ACLC, Vol. 70.

63. See Minutes of Board Meeting, 9 October 1899, ACLC, Vol. 69.

64. Letter from F. T. Gates to Oliver, 26 September 1899, entered into Minutes of Board Meeting, 2 October 1899, ACLC, Vol. 69.

65. Memorandum from James Gayley and Daniel Clemson to Board of Managers, dated 20 February 1900, quoted in Minutes of Board Meeting, same date, ACLC, Vol. 73.

66. See Minutes of Board Meeting, 3 July 1900, for the separate contracts, ACLC, Vol. 76.

1086

67. Oliver to Gayley, 22 February 1900, quoted in Minutes of Board Meeting, 26 February 1900, ACLC, Vol. 73.
68. See Minutes of Board Meeting, 9 October 1899, ACLC, Vol. 69.
69. George E. McCague to Frick, 27 December 1894, ACLC, Vol. 29.
70. Ibid.
71. Frick to AC, note added to McCague's letter to Frick, 28 December 1894, ACLC, Vol. 29.
72. Frick to AC, 28 December 1894, quoted in Hendrick, *Life*, II, 27.
73. Bridge, op. cit. 256–57.
74. Ibid. 269.
75. See numerous letters and telegrams between S. B. Dick and AC, 3 February, 28 February, 1, 6, 7, 9, 10, 17, 24, 28, and 29 March and 6 April 1896, ACLC, Vols. 36 and 37.
76. See the terms of the "understanding" between Dick and Carnegie, dated April 1896, ACLC, Vol. 37.
77. This is a well-known Carnegie story, told to me by several persons who were friends of the Carnegie family.
78. AC to John A. Stewart, 18 April 1896, ACLC, Vol. 37.
79. Stewart to AC, 20 April 1896, ACLC, Vol. 37.
80. AC to Stewart, 21 April 1896, ACLC, Vol. 37.
81. AC to R. A. Franks, 1 May 1896, ACLC, Vol. 37.
82. AC to Frick, 7 February 1896, ACLC, Vol. 36.
83. AC to Frank Thomson, 5 May 1896, ACLC, Vol. 37.
84. Andrew Carnegie, "My Experience with Railway Rates and Rebates," *Century Magazine*, March 1908, reprinted in Andrew Carnegie, *Problems To-Day*, New York, 1908, 196–99.
85. See copy of memorandum outlining the terms of the agreement, dated 16 May 1896. Present were Carnegie and Frick for Carnegie Steel and President Roberts, Vice President Thomson, and the general freight agent, McCrea, for the Pennsylvania Railroad. ACLC, Vol. 38.
86. Judge J. H. Reed to AC, 25 April 1898, ACLC, Vol. 51.
87. W. Frank McClure, "The Carnegie Railroad," *National Magazine*, Vol. 16, June 1902, 308–16.
88. See Minutes of Board Meeting, 26 April 1898, ACLC, Vol. 51; Schwab to AC, 7 July 1898, ACLC, Vol. 53.
89. AC to Frank Thomson, 12 November 1896, ACLC, Vol. 39.
90. Agreement between the Pennsylvania Railroad and the Carnegie Steel Company, undated, but written in July 1898, ACLC, Vol. 40; see Schwab's letter to AC, 6 July 1898, ACLC, Vol. 53.
91. AC to Frank Thomson, undated, but written in July 1898, shortly after the agreement with the Pennsylvania Railroad, ACLC, Vol. 40.
92. M. M. Bosworth to AC, 4 May 1907, ACLC, Vol. 142.
93. Bridge, op. cit. 272–74.
94. Quoted in Hendrick, *Life*, II, 33.
95. AC to Editor of *Outlook*, 11 May 1896, ACLC, Vol. 38.
96. *Pittsburgh Post*, 28 December 1893.
97. Paul H. Douglas, *Real Wages in the United States, 1890–1926*, Boston, 1930, Appendix E, 623.
98. *Pittsburgh Times*, 28 December 1893.

99. Quoted in the *Cleveland World*, 6 January 1894.
100. Schwab to Frick, 11 December 1894, Frick-Leishman Letterfile, ACUSC.
101. Schwab to Frick, 16 November 1894, Frick-Leishman Letterfile, ACUSC.
102. Schwab to Frick, 10 December 1894, Frick-Leishman Letterfile, ACUSC.
103. See *Iron Age*, Vol. 55, 3 January 1895, 18.
104. AC to Carnegie Steel, 16 May 1895, ACLC, Vol. 31.
105. Quoted in *The* (London) *Times*, 16 May 1895.
106. AC to Frick, 15 February 1897, ACLC, Vol. 41.
107. Minutes of Board Meeting, 6 July 1897, ACLC, Vol. 43.
108. Minutes of Board Meeting, 26 July 1897, ACLC, Vol. 43.
109. AC to Carnegie Steel, 17 August 1897, ACLC, Vol. 43.
110. Minutes of Board Meeting, 17 August 1897, ACLC, Vol. 43.
111. Schwab to Frick, undated, but sometime in July or August 1897, ACLC, Vol. 43.
112. Minutes of Board Meeting, 31 January and 7 February 1899, ACLC, Vol. 62.
113. John A. Fitch, *The Steel Workers*, 174–75.
114. For letters to and from the company labor spies, see Bureau of Information, Letters to Operatives File, ACUSC, 1896–1904.
115. J. R. Mack to Scott McCollough, 1 February 1896, Bureau of Information, Letters to Operatives File, ACUSC.
116. See Mack's letters to operatives, 18 December 1902, Letters to Operatives File, ACUSC.
117. Schwab to AC, 26 May 1899, ACLC, Vol. 65.
118. Minutes of Board Meeting, 6 June 1899; Schwab to AC, 12 June 1899, ACLC, Vol. 66.
119. Minutes of Board Meeting, 13 June 1899, ACLC, Vol. 66.
120. Quoted in Minutes of Board Meeting, 27 June 1899, ACLC, Vol. 66.
121. AC to Schwab, 1 July 1899, ACLC, Vol. 66.
122. Minutes of Board Meeting, 5 July 1899, ACLC, Vol. 66.
123. Schwab to AC, 6 July 1899, ACLC, Vol. 67.
124. Phipps to AC, 2 June 1895, ACLC, Vol. 32.
125. Lauder to AC, 12 June 1895, ACLC, Vol. 32.
126. See Frick's letter to AC, 3 September 1894, ACLC, Vol. 27.
127. Quoted in the New York *Herald*, 30 May 1893.
128. Listing of Net Profits of Carnegie Steel, 1892–99, ACLC, Vol. 73.
129. Oliver to Frick, 27 July 1897, ACLC, Vol. 43.
130. Quoted in Brody, *Steelworkers in America*, 17.
131. Sir James Kitson, "The Iron and Steel Industries of America," *Contemporary Review*, Vol. 59, May 1891, 629; see also John Fitch, "Old Age at Forty," *The American Magazine*, Vol. 71, March 1911, 655–64.
132. AC to Schwab, 31 January 1900, ACLC, Vol. 72.
133. Swank to AC, 29 May 1897, ACLC, Vol. 42.
134. AC to Leishman, 1 August 1895, ACLC, Vol. 32.
135. AC to Lauder, 8 January 1897, ACLC, Vol. 41.
136. See various documents: Minutes of Board Meeting, 13 September 1898, ACLC, Vol. 55; AC to Lauder, 31 January 1899, ACLC, Vol. 61; "The Metal Mixer Patent," *Iron Age*, Vol. 64, 23 November 1899, 20; and "The Jones Mixer Patent," *Iron Age*, Vol. 67, 24 January 1901, 10.

137. Frick to AC, 16 December 1896, ACLC, Vol. 40.

138. AC to William McKinley, 17 December 1896, ACLC, Vol. 40.

139. Thomas A. Bailey, *The American Pageant*, Boston, 1956, 671.

140. Carnegie to Louise Whitfield, 2 March 1887, and Louise Whitfield to Carnegie, 7 March 1887, AC-LW Letters.

141. AC to W. C. Whitney, undated, but filed under date of February 1886, Henry Payne Whitney Collection of W. C. Whitney Papers, Vol. 31, Library of Congress.

142. AC to Whitney, 27 December 1886, Henry Payne Whitney Collection of W. C. Whitney Papers, Vol. 39, Library of Congress.

143. AC to Abbott, undated, but sometime in the spring of 1889, ACLC, Vol. 240.

144. See various documents: F. Rey to Abbott, 6 May 1890; Rey to Carnegie, Phipps & Co., 16 June 1890; Rey to AC, 23 June 1890; and AC to Rey, 26 June 1890, ACLC, Vol. 11.

145. W. H. Emory to AC, 30 June 1890, ACLC, Vol. 11.

146. C. A. Stone to Millard Hunsiker, 17 September 1894, ACLC, Vol. 27.

147. AC to James G. Blaine, 9 May 1891, ACLC, Vol. 12, and Blaine to AC, 28 March 1892, ACLC, Vol. 15.

148. AC to Robert P. Linderman, 25 February 1895, ACLC, Vol. 31.

149. See Schwab's letter to AC, 7 March 1898, ACLC, Vol. 49.

150. See AC's letters to Frick, undated, but in the summer of 1890, ACLC, Vol. 11.

151. Schwab to AC, 7 March 1898, ACLC, Vol. 49.

152. AC to Abbott and to Frick, undated, but in the summer of 1890, ACLC, Vol. 11.

153. Cartoon from the New York *Herald,* reprinted in Winkler, *Incredible Carnegie,* opposite page 234.

154. For an account of the armor plate issue highly exculpatory of Carnegie, see Appendix in Hendrick, *Life,* II, 401–6.

155. Ibid. 403.

156. AC to Grover Cleveland, 20 December 1893, McElroy Collection, Library of Congress. Copy also in ACLC, Vol. 23.

157. Copy of Frick's telegram to AC, 26 December 1893, and AC to Cleveland, 27 December 1893, McElroy Collection, Library of Congress. Also in ACLC, Vol. 24.

158. *New York Mail & Express,* 26 March 1894, clipping in scrapbook on Armor Plates, ACLC, Vol. 269.

159. See various documents on reports of tests by Bureau of Ordnance, 3 and 12 April 1894, and Millard Hunsiker to AC, 13 April 1894, ACLC, Vol. 24; "The Carnegie Armor Plate Test," *Iron Age,* Vol. 55, 21 March 1895, 602.

160. Schwab to Leishman, 24 October 1896, Frick-Leishman Letterfile, ACUSC.

161. "The Cost of Armor Plate," *Iron Age,* Vol. 59, 7 January 1897, 19–22, and 6 May 1897, 2.

162. Schwab to AC, 27 July 1897, ACLC, Vol. 43.

163. AC to Schwab, 24 September 1897, ACLC, Vol. 45.

164. Minutes of Board Meeting, 31 May and 14 June 1898, ACLC, Vol. 52.

165. See Schwab's letter to Frick, 30 October 1894, Frick-Leishman Letterfile, ACUSC.

166. Minutes of Board Meeting, 17 May 1898, ACLC, Vol. 51.

167. AC to Carnegie Steel, 25 July 1898, read into Minutes of Board Meeting, 23 August 1898, ACLC, Vol. 54.

168. "Andrew Carnegie on the Trade Situation," *Iron Age*, Vol. 56, 31 October 1895, 898.

169. Extract from a copy of a letter by Edward Atkinson to J. S. Jeans, 7 June 1895, ACLC, Vol. 32.

170. See Minutes of Board Meeting, 29 March 1898, and Frick to AC, 5 April 1898, ACLC, Vol. 50.

171. AC to Schwab, 22 December 1898, ACLC, Vol. 58.

172. Phipps to AC, 16 September 1897, ACLC, Vol. 44.

173. AC to Frick, 15 January 1898, and Frick's reply, reported in Minutes of Board Meeting, 1 February 1898, ACLC, Vol. 48.

174. Schwab to AC, 26 April 1898, and Minutes of Board Meeting, 17 May 1898, ACLC, Vol. 51.

175. See various documents: Schwab to AC, 21 and 23 May 1898, ACLC, Vol. 51; Minutes of Board Meeting, 31 May and 7 June 1898; AC to Carnegie Steel, 6 June 1898, ACLC, Vol. 52; Minutes of Board Meeting, 12 and 26 July 1898, ACLC, Vol. 53; Minutes of Board Meeting, 15 November 1898, ACLC, Vol. 56.

176. Minutes of Board Meeting, 31 January 1899, ACLC, Vol. 31.

177. AC to Lauder, 7 February 1899, ACLC, Vol. 62.

178. Minutes of Board Meeting, 7 February 1899, ACLC, Vol. 62.

179. Terms of Agreement in Minutes of Board Meeting, 14 February 1899, ACLC, Vol. 62.

180. AC to Lauder, 16 February 1899, and AC to Carnegie Steel, reported in Minutes of Board Meeting, 21 February 1899, ACLC, Vol. 62.

181. See various documents: Schwab to AC, 7 March 1898, ACLC, Vol. 49; AC to Carnegie Steel, 25 July 1898, Minutes of Board Meeting, 23 August 1898, ACLC, Vol. 54; AC to Schwab, 22 December 1898, ACLC, Vol. 58; Minutes of Board Meeting, 7 February 1899, ACLC, Vol. 62; AC to Carnegie Steel, in Minutes of Board Meeting, 21 February 1899, ACLC, Vol. 62; Minutes of Board Meeting, 6 November 1899, ACLC, Vol. 70.

182. AC to Carnegie Steel, in Minutes of Board Meeting, 31 January 1899, ACLC, Vol. 61.

183. AC to Francis Lovejoy, 30 December 1898, entered in Minutes of Board Meeting, 3 January 1899, ACLC, Vol. 60.

184. AC to Schwab, 4 June 1900, ACLC, Vol. 171.

185. See "Carnegie Steel Company Changes," *Iron Age*, Vol. 59, 18 February 1897, 7–8.

186. AC to Leishman, 4 January 1896, ACLC, Vol. 35.

187. AC to Leishman, 27 January 1896, ACLC, Vol. 36.

188. AC to Leishman, 28 January 1896, ACLC, Vol. 36.

189. AC to Leishman, 4 February 1896, ACLC, Vol. 36.

190. Leishman to AC, 11 January 1896, ACLC, Vol. 35.

191. "Carnegie Steel Changes," loc. cit.

192. Hendrick, *Life*, II, 297–98.

193. AC to Frick, 30 December 1896, ACLC, Vol. 40.

194. AC to Schwab, 22 December 1898, ACLC, Vol. 58.

195. Quoted in Hendrick, *Life*, II, 5.

196. See John Walker, interviewed by Hendrick, 12 November 1928, copy in ACLC, Vol. 239. It is significant to note that none of Carnegie's associates ever gave any credit to Lauder for contributing to the success of the company.

197. See Alexander Peacock's letter to AC, 7 September 1889, and AC's note to Frick written on the back of Peacock's letter, ACLC, Vol. 10.

198. Frick to AC, 9 May 1898, ACLC, Vol. 51.

199. John Walker, interviewed by Hendrick, notes, 16 February 1928, ACLC, Vol. 239.

200. AC to Lovejoy, 11 February 1895, ACLC, Vol. 30.

201. AC to Lovejoy, 9 December 1895, quoted in Hendrick, *Life*, II, 44.

202. AC to Leishman, 3 April 1896, ACLC, Vol. 37.

203. AC to Leishman, 26 August 1895, ACLC, Vol. 32.

204. William Abbott, interviewed by Hendrick, notes, August 1929, ACLC, Vol. 239.

CHAPTER XVIII

1. AC to James G. Blaine, 14 January 1882, Blaine MSS, 1882, Library of Congress.

2. AC to William E. Gladstone, 28 March 1891, Gladstone Papers, Vol. 427, Add. Ms. 44,512, fol. 199.

3. Andrew Carnegie, "Imperial Federation," *Nineteenth Century*, Vol. 30, September 1891, 492.

4. Ibid. 502.

5. Ibid. 507–8.

6. AC to John Patterson, 13 January 1892, ACLC, Vol. 14.

7. Herbert Spencer to AC, 23 September 1891, ACNYPL.

8. AC to John Morley, 16 April 1893, ACLC, Vol. 20.

9. Andrew Carnegie, *The Reunion of Britain and America: A Look Ahead*, reprinted from *North American Review*, June 1893, Edinburgh, 1893. Collected Pamphlet No. 7, Foreign Colonial Collection, National Library of Scotland, Edinburgh.

10. Henry Cabot Lodge, "England, Venezuela, and the Monroe Doctrine," *North American Review*, Vol. 160, June 1895, 658, quoted in Thomas A. Bailey, *A Diplomatic History of the American People*, New York, 1940, 481. See also P. R. Fossum, "The Anglo-Venezuelan Boundary Controversy," *Hispanic American Historical Review*, Vol. 8, 1928, 299–329.

11. Quoted in Bailey, op. cit. 485.

12. Andrew Carnegie, "The Venezuelan Question," *North American Review*, Vol. 162, February 1896, 136–37.

13. Ibid. 142–44. See also Carnegie's letter to *The* (London) *Times*, 24 December 1895.

14. AC to the Duke of Devonshire, 26 December 1895, ACLC, Vol. 35.

15. AC to Morley, 27 January 1896, ACLC, Vol. 36.

16. William Black to AC, 6 February 1896, ACLC, Vol. 36.

17. Morley to AC, 17 August 1896, ACLC, Vol. 39.

18. AC to Morley, 19 August 1896, ACLC, Vol. 39.

19. Andrew Carnegie, "Does America Hate England?" *Contemporary Review*, Vol. 72, November 1897, 661.

20. Andrew Carnegie, "Some Important Results of the Jubilee," *North American Review*, Vol. 165, October 1897, 506.

21. Ibid. 498–99.

22. See letter from Carnegie to Louise Carnegie, quoted in Hendrick and Henderson, *Louise Whitfield Carnegie*, 144–45.

23. *Autobiography*, 217.

24. See Peter Gray, *Skibo: Its Lairds and History*, Edinburgh, 1906; see also Hendrick, *Life*, II, 147–50.

25. Andrew Carnegie, "The Reunion of Britain and America: A Look Ahead," *North American Review*, Vol. 156, June 1898, 685–710.

26. See Frick's letter to AC, 4 April 1898, ACLC, Vol. 50.

27. Henry Frick to AC, 25 April 1898, ACLC, Vol. 51.

28. AC to President McKinley, 27 April 1898, Papers of William McKinley, Vol. 13, Library of Congress.

29. AC to General Nelson Miles, cablegram, undated, but sometime in July 1898, ACLC, Vol. 53.

30. Nelson A. Miles, *Serving the Republic*, New York, 1911, 274.

31. AC to Dr. Adolf Gurlt, 1 June 1898, misfiled under 1 June 1896, ACLC, Vol. 38.

32. AC to George Lauder, 9 June 1898, ACLC, Vol. 52.

33. Quoted in Margaret Leech, *In the Days of McKinley*, New York, 1959, 345.

34. AC to Editor, New York *World*, 8 December 1898.

35. AC to John Hay, 11 December 1898, ACLC, Vol. 58.

36. See letter from AC to Erving Winslow, Secretary of the League, 11 April 1898, ACLC, Vol. 50.

37. Andrew Carnegie, "Distant Possessions—The Parting of the Ways," *North American Review*, Vol. 167, August 1898, 293 *passim*.

38. Morley to AC, 28 August 1898, ACLC, Vol. 54.

39. AC to Editor, *The* (London) *Times*, 30 August 1898.

40. Newspaper story in New York *World*, 16 May 1902, clipping in Miscellaneous Scrapbook, ACLC, Vol. 275.

41. See AC to Editor, New York *World*, 1 January 1899, misdated as 1 January 1898, providing for the mailing of one of his "Letters To The Editor" to all Representatives and Senators, the President, and the Cabinet. James Wright Brown Collection, New York Historical Society.

42. AC to Hay, 24 November 1898, ACLC, Vol. 57.

43. Hay to Whitelaw Reid, 29 November 1898, quoted in C. Hartley Gratlan, "Saint Andy," *American Mercury*, Vol. 14, July 1928, 367.

44. AC to Reid, 1 December 1899, ACLC, Vol. 70.

45. Charles B. Spahr, op. cit., 160–61.

46. Quoted in William J. Hartford, "Andrew Carnegie," *Successful American*, Vol. 3, March 1901, 124.

47. Andrew Carnegie, "Americanism *versus* Imperialism," Parts 1 and 2, *North American Review*, Vol. 168, January 1899, 1–13, March 1899, 362–72.

48. See letters to AC from Herbert Myrick, editor of farm journals in Springfield, Mass., 12 January 1899, ACLC, Vol. 60; Goldwyn Smith to AC, 7 February 1899, ACLC, Vol. 62; AC to McKinley, 28 November 1898, ACLC, Vol. 57; AC to James Wilson, Secretary of Agriculture, 3 December 1898, ACLC, Vol. 57; AC to Hay, 27 December 1898, ACLC, Vol. 59.

49. AC to Editor, New York *World*, 4 January 1899.

50. Story in *The New York Times*, 22 December 1898.

51. Wilkinson Call to AC, 4 December 1898, ACLC, Vol. 57.

52. William Jennings Bryan to AC, 17 December 1898, ACLC, Vol. 58.

53. Bryan to AC, telegram, 24 December 1898, ACLC, Vol. 59.

54. Bryan to AC, 24 December 1898, ACLC, Vol. 59.

55. Bryan to AC, 30 December 1898, ACLC, Vol. 59.

56. Call to Bryan, copy of telegram, undated, ACLC, Vol. 60.

57. Carnegie to Bryan, 19 January 1899, quoted in Paolo E. Coletta, "Bryan, McKinley and the Treaty of Paris," *Pacific Historical Review*, Vol. XXVI, May 1957, 133.

58. Bryan to AC, 13 January 1899, ACLC, Vol. 60.

59. AC to Editor, New York *World*, 30 January 1899.

60. Bryan to AC, undated, ACLC, Vol. 71.

61. See Richard Pettigrew, *Imperial Washington,* quoted in Coletta, op. cit. 142.

62. Quoted in Coletta, op. cit. 141.

63. Senator W. E. Mason to AC, 6 February 1899 ACLC, Vol. 62.

64. Mason to AC, 8 February 1899, ACLC, Vol. 62.

65. *Congressional Record,* 55th Cong., 3rd sess., Vol. 32, Part 1, 561.

66. *Autobiography,* 364.

67. See Walter Millis, *The Martial Spirit,* New York, 1965; Paxton Hibben, *The Peerless Leader: William Jennings Bryan,* New York, 1929; John A. Garraty, *Henry Cabot Lodge,* New York, 1953; Julius W. Pratt, *Expansionists of 1898,* Chicago, 1964; and *A History of the United States Foreign Policy,* Englewood Cliffs, N.J., 1965; also most standard survey texts.

68. *Autobiography,* 364; George F. Hoar, *Autobiography of Seventy Years,* New York, 1903, Vol. II, 322.

69. Paolo Coletta's article (see above, note 57) is the best statement on Bryan's role in the ratification of the treaty that I have seen. Professor Coletta completely exonerates Bryan from having an ulterior political motive in his support of the treaty.

70. AC to Editor, New York *World,* 18 February, 1899.

71. Edward Atkinson to AC, 22 June 1899, ACLC, Vol. 66.

72. AC to Andrew White, 16 March 1899, ACLC, Vol. 63.

73. Herbert Spencer to AC, 28 October 1899, ACLC, Vol. 70.

74. AC to White, 23 June 1900, ACLC, Vol. 76.

75. *The New York Times,* 22 August 1900, copy of story in Miscellaneous Scrapbook, ACLC, Vol. 275.

76. AC to Morley, 23 September 1900, ACLC, Vol. 78.

77. Andrew Carnegie, "The Presidential Election—Our Duty," *North American Review,* Vol. 172, October 1900, 495–507.

78. Atkinson to AC, 19 November 1900, ACLC, Vol. 79.

79. Benjamin Harrison to AC, 26 December 1900, ACLC, Vol. 80.

80. Andrew Carnegie, "The Presidential Election—Our Duty," loc. cit. 505.

81. George Shiras to AC, 26 December 1900, ACLC, Vol. 80.

82. Finley Peter Dunne, *Mr. Dooley At His Best,* New York, 1938, 73.

83. AC to Editor, New York *World,* 31 December 1900, copy in ACLC, Vol. 80.

84. Morley to AC, 23 July 1900, ACLC, Vol. 76.

CHAPTER XIX

1. AC to John Hay, 26 February 1900, ACLC, Vol. 73.

2. See Minutes of Board Meeting, Carnegie Steel, 23 August 1898, ACLC, Vol. 54.

3. AC to George Lauder, 17 January 1899, ACLC, Vol. 60.

4. Minutes of Board Meeting, Carnegie Steel, 16 January 1899, ACLC, Vol. 60.

5. Hendrick, *Life*, II, 77.

6. AC to Lauder, 17 January 1899, and Lauder to AC, 16 January 1899, ACLC, Vol. 60.

7. AC to Lauder, 17 January 1899, ACLC, Vol. 60.

8. Minutes of Special Board Meeting, Carnegie Steel, 19 January 1899, ACLC, Vol. 60.

9. Lauder to AC, 19 January 1899, ACLC, Vol. 60.

10. Quoted in Hendrick, *Life*, II, 77.

11. Statement of Profits and Distribution, year 1898, ACLC, Vol. 59.

12. AC to Lauder, business memorandum, undated, ACLC, Vol. 59.

13. Henry Frick to AC, 30 December 1898, ACLC, Vol. 59.

14. Undated draft of a prospectus in AC's handwriting, ACLC, Vol. 59.

15. See Agreement between AC, party of the first part, and Frick and Phipps, parties of the second part, dated April 1899, ACLC, Vol. 64.

16. For a full account of these maneuvers in regard to the option, see Francis Lovejoy's letter to AC, 20 April 1908, ACLC, Vol. 152.

17. See copy of Agreement of Option, 19 May 1899, ACLC, Vol. 65. There is considerable mystery about the details of the option. The $10,000,000 stock bonus is clearly part of the agreement and appears as a part of the Minutes of the Board Meeting, 22 May 1899, ACLC, Vol. 64. See also Lovejoy's letter to AC, 20 April 1908, loc. cit. But Schwab and the other members of the Board later told Carnegie they knew nothing of this provision. See also Lawrence Phipps's angry letter to AC, 10 February 1900, denying that his uncle, Henry Phipps, was a party to any such arrangement or had any intention to benefit from his role in the negotiations for the option, ACLC, Vol. 73.

18. Handwritten MS, undated, in possession of the writer.

19. AC to A. I. Findley, 19 April 1899, reprinted in A. I. Findley, "Andrew Carnegie Succeeded by Knowing Men," *Iron Age*, Vol. 104, 14 August 1919, 435.

20. Quoted, Ibid.

21. Quoted in Hendrick, *Life*, II, 82.

22. Frick and Henry Phipps, to AC, cablegram, 20 May 1899, ACLC, Vol. 51.

23. See *Iron Age*, Vol. 63, May 4, 31; May 11, 16; May 25, 42; 1899; "The Carnegie Fortune," *American Monthly Review of Reviews*, Vol. 19, June 1899, 648–50.

24. See Bridge, *Inside History of Carnegie Steel*, 319.

25. Stanley Committee Report, 62nd Cong., 2nd sess., Report No. 1127, p. 2373, quoted in Hendrick, *Life*, II, 82.

26. See Hendrick, *Life*, II, 84.

27. See Frick's letter to AC, 23 May 1899, ACLC, Vol. 65.

28. AC to Lauder, 23 June 1899, ACLC, Vol. 66.

29. Minutes of Board Meeting, Carnegie Steel, 27 June 1899, Vol. 66.

30. See Bridge, op. cit. 320, for a photographic copy of that letter.

31. Quoted in Hendrick, *Life*, II, 88.

32. Harvey, *Henry Clay Frick, The Man*, 216–17.

33. For an account of this dispute, see Hendrick, *Life*, II, 58–64.

34. See Charles Schwab's memorandum of 8 December 1899 in Iron Clad Agreement File, ACUSC, and Thomas Miller's letter to AC, 4 May 1910, ACLC, Vol. 176, for the background on the coke price dispute.

35. AC to Lauder, 17 January 1899, ACLC, Vol. 60.

36. See Thomas Lynch's report to the Board of Managers, Minutes of Henry C. Frick Coke Company, ACLC, Vol. 70.

37. See Schwab's memorandum, 8 December 1899, in Iron Clad Agreement File, ACUSC.

38. Minutes of Board Meeting, Frick Coke Company, 25 October 1899, ACLC, Vol. 70.

39. Minutes of Board Meeting, Carnegie Steel, 6 November 1899, ACLC, Vol. 70.

40. AC to Frick, undated, quoted in Harvey, op. cit. 225.

41. Ibid. 225–26.

42. See Frick's letter to AC, 18 November 1899, and AC's response, 20 November 1899, ACLC, Vol. 70.

43. Minutes of Board Meeting, Carnegie Steel, 20 November 1899, ACLC, Vol. 70.

44. Lauder to AC, 24 November 1899, ACLC, Vol. 70.

45. AC to Lauder, 25 November 1899, ACLC, Vol. 70.

46. Schwab to AC, 27 November 1899, ACLC, Vol. 70.

47. Ibid.

48. Schwab to Frick, 3 December 1899, reprinted in Harvey, op. cit. 231–32.

49. Minutes of Board Meeting, Carnegie Steel, 5 December 1899, reprinted in Bridge, op. cit. 326.

50. Ibid.

51. See J. V. Thompson to E. Queen, 22 November 1899, AC to Lauder, 23 November 1899, and D. M. Clemson to Lauder, 25 November 1899, ACLC, Vol. 70.

52. AC to Lauder, memoranda, both undated, ACLC, Vol. 70.

53. AC to Lauder, 23 December 1899, ACLC, Vol. 70.

54. Lauder to AC, 26 December 1899 and AC to Lauder, 27 December 1899, ACLC, Vol. 71.

55. Schwab to AC, 27 December 1899, ACLC, Vol. 71.

56. Minutes of Board Meeting, Carnegie Steel, 2 January 1900, ACLC, Vol. 72.

57. See Chapter XV: "Enter Mr. Frick."

58. AC to Francis Lovejoy, 20 January 1896, ACLC, Vol. 36.

59. See Minutes of Board Meeting, Carnegie Steel, 1 June 1897, ACLC, Vol. 42.

60. See Minutes of Board Meeting, Carnegie Steel, 15 June, and also 20 July 1897 (containing letter from AC, dated 8 July), ACLC, Vol. 43; see also AC to W. W. Blackburn, Assistant Treasurer, Carnegie Steel, 24 August and AC to Lovejoy, 25 August 1897, ACLC, Vol. 44.

61. See copy of Iron Clad Agreement, dated 1 September 1897, ACLC, Vol. 44.

62. Phipps to AC, 25 September 1897, ACLC, Vol. 45.

63. AC to Frick, 9 October 1897, ACLC, Vol. 45.

64. Minutes of Board Meeting, Carnegie Steel, 19 October 1897, Vol. 46.

65. Ibid.

66. Minutes of Board Meeting, Carnegie Steel, including AC's letter, 3 January 1899, ACLC, Vol. 60.

67. Minutes of Board Meeting, Carnegie Steel, 8 January 1900.

68. Ibid.

69. Minutes of Board Meeting, Frick Coke Company, 9 January 1900, see Hendrick, *Life*, II, 102–3; Harvey, op. cit. 234–35.

70. The most vivid and probably the most accurate account of this meeting was given by John Walker, interviewed by Hendrick, 16 February 1928, ACLC, Vol. 239. It is probably the most accurate inasmuch as Frick reported all of the details to Walker immediately after the incident occurred. But see also Hendrick, *Life*, II, 103–4, who quotes Carnegie directly on the incident; Bridge, op. cit. 332; and Harvey, op. cit. 227–30. The accounts given by both Bridge and Harvey are entirely sympathetic to Frick.

71. See statement of resolution, dated 10/11 June 1900, in Iron Clad Agreement File, ACUSC.

72. See A. M. Moreland's Letter to Alexander Peacock, 3 March 1900, Iron Clad Agreement File, ACUSC.

73. Minutes of Board Meeting, Carnegie Steel, 22 January 1900, ACLC, Vol. 72.

74. Lovejoy to AC, 17 January 1900, ACLC, Vol. 72.

75. Harvey, op. cit. 230–31; John Walker, interviewed by Hendrick, 16 February 1928, ACLC, Vol. 239.

76. See Minutes of Board Meeting, Carnegie Steel, 16 and 24 January 1900, ACLC, Vol. 72.

77. John Walker, interviewed by Hendrick, 16 February 1928, loc. cit.

78. Letter from Frick to Board of Managers, Carnegie Steel, 13 January 1900 and letter from Phipps to Carnegie Steel, 15 January 1900, Iron Clad Agreement File, ACUSC.

79. Phipps and Frick to Carnegie Steel, 29 January 1900, Iron Clad Agreement File, ACUSC.

80. Minutes of Board Meeting, 1 February 1900, ACLC, Vol. 72; official paper signed by Schwab in Iron Clad Agreement File, ACUSC. Harvey is in error throughout his account of the affair in stating that Frick held a one-sixth interest in Carnegie Steel. Harvey, op. cit. 237ff. This is quite a different matter from a 6 per cent interest, which is the amount Frick actually held.

81. See Schwab's letter to AC, 1 February 1900, ACLC, Vol. 72.

82. Gibson D. Packer to AC, 3 February 1900, ACLC, Vol. 72.

83. See letters of protest from John Walker and S. L. Schoonmaker, 1 February 1900, and from John Pontefract, 12 February 1900, Iron Clad Agreement File, ACUSC.

84. Copy of letter from AC to Lynch, undated, but probably early February 1900, ACLC, Vol. 86; see also Schwab's letter to AC regarding this proposal, 10 February 1900, ACLC, Vol. 73. Once again, Bridge allows his antipathy toward Carnegie to warp his presentation of the facts. In his account, (Bridge, op. cit. 328), Bridge claims that Carnegie tried to make a secret deal with John Walker whereby only his interest would be exempt from the contract. There is no evidence to support this.

85. Extracts from the pleadings of Henry C. Frick in the Equity Suit, printed as Appendix in Bridge, op. cit. 365. See also "The Carnegie-Frick Disagreement," *Iron Age*, Vol. 65, 15 February 1900, 23–25.

86. See rough draft in AC's handwriting of his response, ACLC, Vol. 86; see also "Carnegie Answers Frick's Complaint," *Iron Age*, Vol. 65, 18 March 1900,

14–17, and galley proofs of the "Joint and Several Answers of the Carnegie Steel Company, Limited and Andrew Carnegie in response to H. C. Frick–Case in Equity–Court of Common Pleas No. 1 of Allegheny County, Pennsylvania, Term 1900" in Iron Clad Agreement File, ACUSC.

87. AC to Lauder, 4 March 1900, ACLC, Vol. 73.

88. W. H. Singer to AC, 30 January 1900, ACLC, Vol. 72.

89. Schwab to AC, 30 January 1900, ACLC, Vol. 72.

90. *The New York Times*, 15 February 1900; New York *World*, 13 February 1900.

91. "Profits in the Iron Industry," *Iron Age*, Vol. 65, 22 February 1900, 17.

92. George Westinghouse to AC, 8 February 1900, ACLC, Vol. 73.

93. Copy of the charter of the Carnegie Company, 22 March 1900, ACLC, Vol. 73; Bridge, op. cit., 348–57; "The Frick-Carnegie Settlement," *Iron Age*, Vol. 65, 29 March 1900, 16–17.

94. See AC's letter to Schwab, undated, ACLC, Vol. 81; see also Minutes of Board Meeting, Carnegie Steel, 5 February 1900, ACLC, Vol. 72. H. P. Bope, for example, got an increase of one-ninth of 1 per cent, James Gayley, an increase of one-eighteenth of 1 per cent. Robert A. Franks to AC, 23 April 1900, Robert A. Franks Letterbooks, ACLC. Vol. 289.

95. Jane Fleming Lovejoy to AC, 14 September 1908, ACLC, Vol. 156.

96. Peacock to AC, 29 May 1913, ACLC, Vol. 216.

97. This story has been told by many people who knew both Carnegie and Frick. It may be apocryphal, but it is widely accepted as true.

CHAPTER XX

1. John Morley to AC, 25 April 1900, ACLC, Vol. 74.

2. AC to George Lauder, 1 January 1901, ACLC, Vol. 81.

3. Henry C. Frick to AC, cablegram, August 1900, quoted in Harvey, *Henry Clay Frick, The Man*, 257.

4. AC to Lauder, undated, ACLC, Vol. 240.

5. For figures on steel production, see memorandum, undated, ACLC, Vol. 81.

6. AC to Charles Schwab, 20 June 1900, ACLC, Vol. 75.

7. Ibid.

8. Minutes of Board Meeting, Carnegie Steel, 18 April 1899, ACLC, Vol. 64.

9. Almost weekly notes of such advice from Carnegie appear in the Minutes of the Board Meetings. See esp. AC's letter to Schwab, 22 December 1898, ACLC, Vol. 58.

10. AC to Morley, 17 December 1899, ACLC, Vol. 70.

11. Minutes of Board Meeting, Carnegie Company, 16 July 1900, ACLC, Vol. 76.

12. AC to Schwab, 26 June 1900, quoted in Minutes of Board Meeting, 9 July 1900, ACLC, Vol. 76.

13. AC, to Schwab, cablegram, 7 July 1900, quoted in Minutes of Board Meeting, 9 July 1900, ACLC, Vol. 76.

14. AC to Schwab, 11 July 1900, quoted in Minutes of Board Meeting, 31 July 1900, ACLC, Vol. 76.

15. AC to Schwab, 5 July 1900, quoted in Minutes of Board Meeting, 31 July 1900, ACLC, Vol. 76.

16. Lawrence C. Phipps's report to the Board, Minutes of Board Meeting, 20 November 1900, ACLC, Vol. 79.

17. See letter of AC to Frank Thomson, undated, probably 1898, ACLC, Vol. 40.

18. See letter to AC from M. M. Bosworth, former secretary of the Henry C. Frick Coke Company, 4 May 1907, in which he accused Carnegie and Frick of stealing "vast millions" from the stockholders of the PRR through rebates. He revealed that December 1899 was the last full month of rebates that PRR granted Carnegie and Frick. ACLC, Vol. 142.

19. AC to Lauder, 9 June 1898, ACLC, Vol. 52.

20. See Henry Phipps's report to the Board, 20 November 1900, ACLC, Vol. 79; see also AC's letter to Henry B. Hebert, Chairman of the Canal Association of New York, 8 February 1902, regarding his plans for using the Erie Canal had he built his plant at Conneaut. Miscellaneous Carnegie Papers, New York Historical Society.

21. See AC's letter to Schwab, 9 October 1900, telling him to "put McCague on the job." ACLC, Vol. 78. See also George McCague to AC, 4 December 1900, Vol. 80.

22. AC to Schwab, 9 October 1900, ACLC, Vol. 78.

23. Draft of memorandum from AC to Alexander J. Cassatt, 7 December 1900, ACLC, Vol. 80.

24. AC to Cassatt, 31 December 1900, ACLC, Vol. 81.

25. AC to Lauder, 1 January 1901, ACLC, Vol. 81.

26. AC to Schwab, 11 January 1901, ACLC, Vol. 81.

27. AC to Cassatt, 14 January 1901, ACLC, Vol. 81.

28. See J. H. Reed's letter to AC, 19 November 1900, ACLC, Vol. 79.

29. Arthur B. Yates, president of the Buffalo, Rochester and Pittsburgh Railway Co. to AC, 9 October 1900, ACLC, Vol. 78.

30. See J. W. Widgley's letter to AC, 31 December 1900, regarding Gould's plans to build west out of Pittsburgh to St. Louis and Chicago, ACLC, Vol. 81; Hendrick, *Life*, II, 127–28; see also letters regarding the possibility of utilizing the Wheeling & L. E. Railroad Co. by the Gould-Carnegie interests, Charles Blackwell to R. Blickensderfer, president of the W. & L. E. R.R. Co., 17 December 1900, copy in ACLC, Vol. 80; and W. G. Connor to AC, 31 December 1900, ACLC, Vol. 81.

31. Figures given in undated memoranda in ACLC, Vol. 81.

32. Story of Carnegie-Schwab conversation quoted in Frederick Lewis Allen, *The Great Pierpont Morgan*, 133; on seamless tube, see Minutes of Board Meeting, 16 October 1900, ACLC, Vol. 79.

33. Minutes of Board Meeting, 6 November 1900, ACLC, Vol. 79.

34. Wayne McVeagh to AC, 26 January 1901, ACLC, Vol. 81.

35. McVeagh to AC, 31 January 1901, ACLC, Vol. 81.

36. Frederick Lewis Allen, op. cit. 134.

37. See AC's letter to Lauder, bragging about the dinner to be given Schwab, 8 December 1900, ACLC, Vol. 80.

38. Horace White to AC, 14 January 1901, ACLC, Vol. 81.

39. AC to Lauder, 24 January 1901, ACLC, Vol. 81.

40. Schwab to AC, 24 January 1901, ACLC, Vol. 81.

41. See Andrew Carnegie, "Dr. Golf," *Independent*, Vol. 70, 1 June 1911, 1181–92.

42. See Hendrick, *Life*, II, 137–38.

43. This story has been told many times. See Hendrick, *Life*, II, 138–39; see also Frederick Lewis Allen, op. cit. 137.

44. Letter, Board of Carnegie Company to AC, 4 February 1901, ACLC, Vol. 81.

45. AC to Lauder, 5 February 1901, ACLC. Vol. 81.

46. AC to Morley, 3 February 1901, ACLC, Vol. 81.

47. Morley to AC, 16 February 1901, ACLC, Vol. 81.

48. Dr. J. Garmany, interviewed by Hendrick, 29 November 1929, ACLC, Vol. 82.

49. John Walker, interviewed by Hendrick, 16 February 1928, ACLC, Vol. 239.

50. AC to J. P. Morgan & Co., 26 February 1901, J. P. Morgan Papers, 23 Wall Street (courtesy of Russell Leffingwell, Gordon Wasson, and Leonard Keyes).

51. AC to Lauder, 26 February 1901, ACLC, Vol. 82.

52. AC to Lauder, 5 March 1901, ACLC, Vol. 82.

53. AC to Lauder, 6 March 1901, ACLC, Vol. 82.

CHAPTER XXI

1. Memorandum in AC's handwriting, undated, ACLC, Vol. 81.

2. John Brisben Walker, "The World's Greatest Revolution," *The Cosmopolitan*, Vol. 30, April 1901, 677–80.

3. AC to Oswald Garrison Villard, 8 December 1905, Carnegie Collection, Houghton Library, Harvard University.

4. See Schwab's letter to AC, 20 May 1901, ACLC, Vol. 83.

5. AC to Schwab, cablegram, 18 January 1902, quoted in John A. Garraty, "Charlie Schwab Breaks the Bank," *American Heritage*, Vol. VIII, April 1957, 46.

6. Ibid.

7. Schwab to AC, 26 January 1902, ACLC.

8. Schwab to AC, 28 January 1902, ACLC. Vol. 90.

9. Garraty, op. cit. 103.

10. AC to George Lauder, 7 December 1902, ACLC, Vol. 92.

11. AC to Lauder, 3 July 1903, ACLC, Vol. 97.

12. Francis Lynde Stetson to AC, 22 April 1903, ACLC, Vol. 95.

13. AC to E. H. Gary, 1 February 1904, ACLC, Vol. 102; and Gary to AC, 1 February 1904, ACLC, Vol. 102.

14. AC to Gary, 14 March 1904, ACLC, Vol. 104.

15. AC to Lauder, 1 July 1902, ACLC, Vol. 89.

16. See series of letters and reports in ACLC: C.R. Van Hise to AC, 23 July 1905, Vol. 118; AC to Van Hise, 12 August 1905, Vol. 119; AC to Van Hise, 21 August 1905, Vol. 119; Van Hise to AC, 23 August 1905, Vol. 119; AC to Van Hise, 7 September 1905, Vol. 119; Van Hise to AC, 25 September 1905, Vol. 120; Van Hise to AC, 27 January 1906, Vol. 124; Van Hise to AC, 9 January 1907, and AC to Van Hise, 12 January 1907, Vol. 139; Report from Van Hise for 1907, undated, Vol. 147; Report from Van Hise, 29 June 1908, Vol. 154; AC to Van Hise, 18 August 1908, Vol. 155; AC to Van Hise, 9 November 1910, Vol. 182; and R. A. Franks to J. A. Poynton, AC's personal secretary, 17 June 1918, Vol. 237.

17. Morley to AC, 5 April, and AC to Morley, 9 April 1901, ACLC, Vol. 82.

18. Andrew Carnegie, "Wealth," *North American Review*, Vol. CXLVIII, June 1889, 653–64, and Vol. CXLIX, December 1889, 682–98. Reprinted in Andrew Carnegie, *The Gospel of Wealth and Other Timely Essays*, edited by Edward C. Kirkland, Cambridge, Mass., 1962; all page references that follow refer to this edition.

19. Ibid. 20–21.

20. Ibid. 21–22.

21. Ibid. 23.

22. Ibid. 25.

23. Ibid. 31.

24. Ibid. 32ff. The concluding quotation is on pp. 47–48.

25. For these replies to Carnegie's "Wealth," see *Nineteenth Century*, Vol. 28, December 1890, 876–900.

26. "Irresponsible Wealth," Part III, Rev. Hugh Price Hughes, 891, loc. cit.

27. Ibid.

28. Ibid. 895.

29. William Jewett Tucker, " 'The Gospel of Wealth,' " *Andover Review*, Vol. XV, June 1891, 633–34, 645.

30. Ibid. 636–37.

31. Andrew Carnegie, "The Advantages of Poverty," *The Gospel of Wealth and Other Timely Essays*, 73. The quotation from Wesley is here abbreviated and paraphrased.

32. Ibid. 67.

33. See Wall, "Andrew Carnegie: Child of Chartism," loc. cit.

34. For information on these early gifts of Carnegie, see pamphlet by William M. Stevenson, *Carnegie and his Libraries*, n.d., n.p., British Museum; letter of Ray L. Heddaeus, president of Church Council, Bellevue, Pennsylvania, to Carnegie Corporation of New York, 23 October 1935, Carnegie Corporation Files on AC; AC to Carnegie Bros., 17 September 1875, Letterbook, 1874–75, ACUSC.

35. Stevenson, op. cit.; AC to Alan Reid, 11 July 1887, Alan Reid Letters, National Library of Scotland, Edinburgh; AC to W. Gordon, Town Clerk of Aberdeen, 26 June 1892, ACLC, Vol. 16; Craibe Angus, Glasgow to AC, 12 September 1894, ACLC, Vol. 27; Elizabeth Haldane to AC, 6 January 1897, and AC to Elizabeth Haldane, 24 September 1897, Haldane Papers, National Library of Scotland.

36. AC to Rollin J. Wilson, 6 August 1895, ACLC, Vol. 32.

37. Ralph Munn, "Hindsight on the Gifts of Carnegie," *Library Journal*, Vol. 76, 1 December 1951, 1968.

38. See AC's letter to E. S. Douglas, Sec'y, St. Joseph [Mo.] *Herald*, 12 March 1890, Letterbook, 1888–92, ACUSC.

39. AC to W. N. Frew, telegram, 4 November 1895, ACLC, Vol. 34.

40. AC to Frew, 24 October 1894, ACLC, Vol. 28.

41. AC to the President and Trustees of the Carnegie Institute, October 1897, ACLC, Vol. 46.

42. Burton J. Hendrick, *The Benefactions of Andrew Carnegie*, New York, 1935, 14.

43. Munn, op. cit. 1969.

44. AC to E. S. Douglas, Letterbook, 1888–92, ACUSC.

45. For an account of the development of this type of building plan see *A Manual of the Public Benefactions of Andrew Carnegie*, compiled and published by The Carnegie Endowment for International Peace, Washington, D.C., 1919 (hereafter cited as *Public Benefactions*), 298.

46. AC to Frew, 1 October 1894, ACLC, Vol. 27.

47. See AC to Lauder, 4 June 1905, ACLC, Vol. 117.

48. *The* (London) *Times*, 22 May 1906.

49. Morley to AC, 19 April 1902, ACLC, Vol. 88.

50. Addresses by Andrew Carnegie on his Receiving the Freedom of Jedburgh and the Opening of the Public Library, 4 October 1894, Pamphlet #10, National Library of Scotland, Edinburgh.

51. AC to "Dear Friend indeed," 11 July 1912, ACLC, Vol. 207.

52. Poultney Bigelow, *Seventy Summers*, Vol. II, London, 1925, 194.

53. AC to Charles Eliot, 31 December 1904, ACLC, Vol. 110.

54. List of private pensioners in AC Papers, Ross-Connell Law Offices, Dunfermline. There were twenty-four persons in Scotland on his private pension list (five of them descendants of Ailie Fargie, who had loaned the Carnegies money for their emigration to America in 1848). The amounts of the pensions ranged from £80 down to £10 per annum.

55. Lord Acton to William E. Gladstone, 23 May 1890, copy of letter in ACLC, Vol. X.

56. Gladstone, Diary, Vol. VIIIA, copy of notation in ACLC, Vol. 11.

57. AC to Gladstone, 13 June 1890, Gladstone Papers, Vol. 424, British Museum, Add. Mss. 44, 510, fol. 91; see also paper of indenture, 28 August 1890 between George Earl Granville and William James Freshfield, representing Lord Acton's interest, and AC, ACLC, Vol. 11.

58. AC to Morley, 21 June 1902, ACLC, Vol. 89.

59. Morley to AC, 24 October 1902, ACLC, Vol. 92.

60. See AC's letter to John Ross, 29 September 1908, ACLC, Vol. 157.

61. AC to Gladstone, 3 February 1897, ACLC, Vol. 41.

62. Mark Twain to AC, 6 February, no year, ACLC, Vol. 242.

63. See Mark Twain's letter to "Miss Carnegie," which is actually a "begging" letter to AC, asking him to invest in Plasman Syndicate Ltd., a company that made a new kind of food out of skimmed milk, 28 May 1900, ACNYPL.

64. Andrew D. White to AC, 25 January 1904, ACLC, Vol. 102.

65. AC to President and Managers of the Carnegie Company, 12 March 1901, ACLC, Vol. 82.

66. See John Bigelow, Diary, Vol. 1901–1902, for dates 17 March and 13 May 1901, 27–31, 57, NYPL; Preamble and Resolution of the Board of Estimate of the City of New York, 26 December 1901, ACNYPL.

67. *The* (London) *Times,* 5 April 1901.

68. AC to "Dear Friend" (probably Hamilton Holt, Editor of *The Independent*), 26 July 1913, A. W. Anthony Collection, NYPL.

CHAPTER XXII

1. Figures given in *Public Benefactions*, 317. The actual number of libraries which were finally built was 2589, of which 1681 were built in the United States.

2. See James Bertram to Richard R. Bowker, Editor of *Library Journal*, quoting from an editorial in the *Library Journal*, 14 February, 1908, Richard Rogers Bowker Papers, NYPL. This collection has an interesting exchange of letters between Bertram and Bowker from 1899–1925. Bertram constantly criticizes Bowker for misrepresenting the Carnegie Libraries.

3. Arthur Lawrence, "The Beatitudes of Mr. Carnegie," *New Liberal Review*, Vol. V, June 1903, 631.

4. Quoted in Hendrick, *Life*, II, 203.

5. See Robert A. Franks's letters, 1 August 1898 and 17 April 1900, as examples

of his investigations of the financial condition of the church making the application. Robert A. Franks, Letterbooks, ACLC, Vol. 289.

6. AC to Elizabeth Haldane, 4 August 1909, Haldane Papers, National Library of Scotland, Edinburgh.

7. *Public Benefactions*, 320–21. The actual number of organs given was 7629, of which 4032 were in the United States.

8. "The Topic of the Month: The Best Use of Great Wealth," *Review of Reviews* (London), Vol. 23, April 1901, 344.

9. Dr. F. S. Dennis, interviewed by Hendrick, notes, 17 November 1927, ACLC. Vol. 239; also AC to William C. Whitney, 6 December 1883, Harry Payne Whitney Collection of Papers of W. C. Whitney, Vol. 27, Library of Congress.

10. See Clyde Ferguson, *The Political and Social Ideas of John D. Rockefeller and Andrew Carnegie*, unpublished doctoral dissertatation, University of Illinois, 1951, 143.

11. *Public Benefactions*, 311; see numerous letters from Helen Keller to Mrs. Carnegie, 1910 through 1940, ACNYPL.

12. AC to Howard C. Smith, 20 December 1905, ACLC, Vol. 123.

13. Quoted in Robert H. Bremner, *American Philanthropy*, Chicago, 1960, 116–17. This is an excellent short study of the history of American philanthropy.

14. AC to W. N. Frew, 2 December 1895, ACLC, Vol. 34.

15. AC, speech at the opening of the Elder Free Library, reported in *The* (London) *Times*, 8 September 1903.

16. Andrew Carnegie, *Annual Address, Annual Graduating Exercises, Pierce College of Business and Shorthand, American Academy of Music, Philadelphia, 17 December 1891*, Philadelphia.

17. Andrew Carnegie, "How To Win a Fortune," New York *Tribune*, 18 April 1890, reprinted in *The Empire of Business*, 91–93.

18. See New York *Tribune*, 1 February 1892.

19. Edward Atkinson to AC, 3 February 1892, ACLC, Vol. 14.

20. "The Wealth of Mr. Carnegie," *Blackwood's Edinburgh Magazine*, Vol. 171, June 1902, 840–45.

21. See AC's letter to John Morley, 31 May 1901, ACLC, Vol. 83.

22. Deed of Trust, dated 7 June 1901, creating the Carnegie Trust for the Universities of Scotland, reprinted in *Public Benefactions*, 230.

23. Morley to AC, 17 April 1901, ACLC, Vol. 82.

24. AC to Morley, 19 April 1910, ACLC, Vol. 82.

25. AC to Morley, 24 June 1901, ACLC, Vol. 83.

26. All of the foregoing background material on the formation of the Carnegie Trust for the Universities of Scotland was taken from Lord Thomas Shaw of Dunfermline, *Letters to Isabel*, London, 1921, 151–69, letters dated 2 September through 13 September 1919, Signet Library, Edinburgh.

27. AC to the Earl of Elgin, 21 September 1910, ACLC, Vol. 180.

28. W. M. Ramsay, "The Carnegie Trust for the Scottish Universities," *The Contemporary Review*, Vol. 93, June 1908, 715.

29. "Will Mr. Carnegie Corrupt Scotland," *The National Review*, Vol. 42, September 1903, 56–58.

30. Ramsay, op. cit. 713ff.

31. Edinburgh University, Laureation Addresses, 1894–1910, Opening Ceremony, 16 October 1906, Letters and files of the University of Edinburgh.

32. See AC's letter to James Bryce, 30 May 1902, Bryce Papers, Bodleian Library, Oxford University.

33. AC to Col. Edward Jay Allen, 19 June 1905, ACLC, Vol. 118.

34. A familiar story in Dunfermline, told in Hendrick, *Life*, II, 247.

35. See letters from Keith R. Maitland, Hunt's agent, to John Ross, 3 September and 4 September 1900, Andrew Carnegie Papers, Ross-Connell Law Offices, Dunfermline; Ross to AC, 8 September and 20 September 1900, ACLC, Vol. 78.

36. See Maitland's letter to Ross, 2 October 1900, AC Papers, Ross-Connell Law Offices, Dunfermline.

37. See Ross's letter to Col. Hunt, 1 October 1901, and Hunt's answer, 15 October 1901, Maitland to Ross, 26 December 1902, AC Papers, Ross-Connell Law Offices; AC to Ross, 1 April 1906, ACLC, Vol. 82; Ross to AC, 21 September 1901, ACLC, Vol. 84; Ross to AC, 25 December 1902, ACLC, Vol. 93.

38. AC to George Lauder, 16 June 1903, ACLC, Vol. 97.

39. AC to Morley, 18 January 1903, ACLC, Vol. 93.

40. AC to Shaw 10 November 1903, ACLC, Vol. 100.

41. Ross to AC, 22 November 1903, ACLC, Vol. 100.

42. See AC's letters to Provost Macbeth, December 1903, ACLC Vol. 101, and 25 January 1904, ACLC, Vol. 102.

43. Third and final draft of deed creating the Carnegie-Dunfermline Trust, Records of Carnegie-Dunfermline Trust, Abbey House, Dunfermline.

44. First draft of the deed. In all draft copies, the main body of the text is in Ross's handwriting, with marginal addenda and deletions in Carnegie's handwriting. Records of Carnegie-Dunfermline Trust, Dunfermline.

45. AC to the Gentlemen of the Commission, Carnegie-Dunfermline Trust, 2 August 1903, reprinted in *The Carnegie-Dunfermline Trust*, Dunfermline, 1953, 6.

46. Ross to AC, 7 July 1903, ACLC, Vol. 97; AC to Ross, undated memorandum, ACLC, Vol. 98.

47. Deed of the Carnegie-Dunfermline Trust, loc. cit.

48. AC to Ross, 25 February 1911, ACLC, Vol. 188.

49. Ross to AC, 9 March 1911, ACLC, Vol. 189.

50. AC to Ross, 22 March 1911, ACLC, Vol. 189.

51. AC to Ross, 14 January 1913, ACLC, Vol. 212.

52. Sir William Robertson to AC, two letters, both dated 11 January 1913, ACLC, Vol. 212; AC to Robertson, 20 January 1913, ACLC, Vol. 212.

53. J. B. Mackie, op. cit. 102.

54. AC to Lauder, 6 May 1907, ACLC, Vol. 142.

55. AC to Lauder, 20 January 1908, ACLC, Vol. 147.

56. Mackie, op. cit. 130.

57. Samuel Harden Church, "Andrew Carnegie's Endowments at Dunfermline," *Survey*, Vol. 28, 4 May 1912, 211; *The* (London) *Times*, 25 September 1912.

58. AC to Chairman and Members of the Dunfermline Trust, 1 March 1914, Records of the Carnegie-Dunfermline Trust, Dunfermline.

59. AC to Lauder, 9 January 1903, ACLC, Vol. 93.

60. John A. Kouwenhoven, *The Columbia Historical Portrait of New York*, Garden City, N. Y., 1953, 393.

61. Andrew Carnegie, "Wealth," loc. cit. 15.

62. See Edward C. Kirkland's perceptive chapter on "The Big House," in *Dream and Thought in the Business Community*, Ithaca, N. Y., 1956, 29–49.

63. See Edward Ellis, "Mansion Goes Classy," New York *World-Telegram and Sun*, 26 May 1960; "Facts About 2 East 91st Street," pamphlet distributed by The New York School of Social Work, Columbia University, 17 September 1956. I

am also obligated to Mr. Manuel Perez, manager of the house for The New York School of Social Work, who kindly gave me an extended tour of the house.

64. Robert Franks to AC, 30 January 1901, Robert Franks Papers, Home Trust Company, Hoboken, N. J.

65. AC to Andrew White, 26 April 1901, ACLC, Vol. 82.

66. Andrew White to AC, 13 May 1901, ACLC, Vol. 82.

67. AC to Andrew White, 2 May 1901, ACLC, Vol. 82.

68. AC to Theodore Roosevelt, 26 November 1901, ACLC, Vol. 85.

69. Robert M. Lester, *Forty Years of Carnegie Giving*, New York, 1941, 19–20.

70. TR to AC, 31 December 1901, ACLC, Vol. 86.

71. AC to Lauder, 10 January 1902, ACLC, Vol. 87.

72. *Public Benefactions*, 81–2, 88–9.

73. "Carnegie and Nobel Awards," *Independent*, Vol. 56, 14 January 1904, 106–7.

74. Phoned interview, interviewer not identified, 20 January 1911, ACLC, Vol. 187.

75. AC to R. S. Woodward, 28 September 1909, ACLC, Vol. 170.

76. Lester, op. cit. 15–16. See also Arthur W. Tarbell, *The Story of Carnegie Tech, 1900–1935*, Pittsburgh, 1937.

77. William Jay Schieffelin, interviewed by Dean Albertson, February 1949. Oral History Project, Butler Library, Columbia University.

78. AC to David Starr Jordan, ACLC, Vol. 136.

79. AC to Andrew White, 4 May 1906, ACLC, Vol. 129; AC to Charles W. Eliot, 3 February 1910, ACLC, Vol. 173; see letters from H. B. Frissell, Principal, Hampton Institute, to Robert A. Franks, 15 November 1913 and 30 March 1915, indicating that AC gave $15,000 annually to Hampton Institute. Robert Franks, Letterbooks, ACLC, Vol. 281.

80. Woodrow Wilson to AC, 18 May 1914, ACLC, Vol. 223; see also AC to Wilson, 21 May 1914 and Wilson to AC, 22 May 1914, ACLC, Vol. 224.

81. Wilson to AC, 17 April 1903, ACLC, Vol. 95.

82. AC to Eliot, 7 December 1906, ACLC, Vol. 137.

83. See AC's letter to Lauder, 10 January 1902, ACLC, Vol. 87.

84. See Papers of Howard Russell Butler, 1904–1906, Princeton University. Mr. Butler gives a slightly different version of Carnegie's inspiration to give Princeton a lake. According to Butler, it was he who gave Carnegie the idea as the branch train crossed the trestle over Stony Brook on the way back to Princeton Junction.

85. A copy of Wilson's speech, 5 December 1906, in ACLC, Vol. 137; *The* (London) *Times*, 6 December 1906.

86. AC to Eliot, 7 December 1906; Eliot to AC, 8 December 1906, ACLC, Vol. 137.

87. Lester, op. cit. 45.

88. Ibid. 45; AC to Trustees of Carnegie Teachers Pension Fund, 16 April 1905, ACLC, Vol. 114.

89. Ibid.

90. Robert W. Bruère, "Educational Efficiency: The Carnegie Foundation," *The Outlook*, Vol. 85, 16 March 1907, 603–8.

91. Ibid. 606.

92. Quoted in a clipping from the Bloomington *Pantagraph*, undated, sent to AC by Rev. James Shaw of Bloomington, along with a letter pleading the cause of Illinois Wesleyan, and American University in Washington, D.C., 15 February 1906, ACLC, Vol. 125.

93. See the article by Charles F. Thwing, President of Western Reserve, "The Carnegie Foundation for the Advancement of Teaching," *Independent*, Vol. 63. 31 October 1907, 1056–57.

94. AC to Henry S. Pritchett, 3 March 1908, ACLC, Vol. 150; see also article by Joseph Jastrow, Professor of Psychology at the University of Wisconsin, "The Advancement of Teaching," *North American Review*, Vol. 186, September 1907, 213–24, as an example of the kind of pressure that came from the faculty at state universities to be included in the pension fund. Professor Jastrow continued to be a severe and prolific critic of the pension plan, even after he was admitted into its fold. See "Ten Years of the Carnegie Foundation," *School and Society*, Vol. 4, 7 October 1916, 533–51.

95. Abram W. Harris to Pritchett, 16 April 1908, ACLC, Vol. 152; Harris to AC, 22 February 1909, ACLC, Vol. 163.

96. TR to AC, 2 February 1909, ACLC, Vol. 162.

97. AC to TR, 3 February 1909, ACLC, Vol. 162.

98. Pritchett to AC, 13 March 1909, ACLC. Vol. 163.

99. AC to Harris, 16 March 1909, ACLC, Vol. 164.

100. Harris to AC, 25 March 1909, ACLC, Vol. 164.

101. Pritchett to AC, 25 November 1911, ACLC, Vol. 200.

102. Bremner, op. cit. 120, 136; Hendrick, *Life*, II, 265–66.

103. Lester, op. cit. 47; see also excerpts from the Minutes of the Twelfth Meeting of the Executive Committee of the Carnegie Corporation of New York, 31 January 1913, ACLC, Vol. 281.

104. *The* (London) *Times*, 26 December 1911.

105. See Chapter XXIII: "The Quest for Peace," for a discussion of these foundations.

106. Andrew Carnegie, "Wealth," loc. cit. 25.

107. *The* (London) *Times*, 4 January 1904; New York *American*, 21 December 1910, clipping in Carnegie Scrapbook, Vol. I, Carnegie Library, Pittsburgh.

108. See AC's letter to Mrs. Russell Sage, 26 February 1901, ACLC, Vol. 174; see also letter of J. D. Rockefeller, Jr. asking for advice in setting up a trust, 8 May 1909, ACLC, Vol. 166, and a letter thanking AC for that advice on behalf of his father and himself, 23 June 1909, ACLC, Vol. 167.

109. AC to Ross, 11 February 1913, ACLC, Vol. 213.

110. Andrew Carnegie, *William Chambers*, Edinburgh, 1909.

111. "Carnegie as a Socialist," *Independent*, Vol. 58, 12 January 1905, 104–6; "Some Replies to Mr. Carnegie's Article," *Review of Reviews* (London), Vol. 35, March 1907, 312–13.

112. Lester, op. cit. 97, 57.

113. *Public Benefactions*, 206.

114. Lester, op. cit. 65; *The* (London) *Times*, 19 July 1913.

115. AC to Ross, 11 February 1913, ACLC, Vol. 213.

116. "What is Andrew Carnegie Really Worth Now?" feature story, *The New York Times*, *Sunday Magazine*, 14 January 1912, 3.

117. The New York *Herald*, 22 November 1912.

CHAPTER XXIII

1. AC to W. T. Stead, 4 October, 1900, ACLC, Vol. 78.

2. AC to Charles W. Eliot, 15 March 1907, ACLC, Vol. 140.

3. AC to David J. Hill, 21 June 1909, ACLC, Vol. 167.

4. See *Speech by Andrew Carnegie at the Annual Meeting of the Peace Society, Guildhall, London, E.C., 24 May 1910*, London, 1910.

5. See AC to Editor, *Morning Post* (London), 27 May 1910.

6. See AC's letter to James Bryce, 21 October 1912, Bryce Papers, Bodleian Library, Oxford University.

7. See numerous letters in the Gladstone Papers (British Museum) and in ACLC from Carnegie to William E. Gladstone on this subject; see esp. AC to Gladstone, 27 April and 14 July 1885, ACLC, Vol. 8.

8. See *Bulletin of the Pan American Union*, Vol. 70, January 1936. The entire issue is dedicated to Andrew Carnegie in commemoration of the centennial of his birth. There are three articles in this issue on Carnegie, relating to his efforts to achieve hemispheric peace.

9. AC to Arthur J. Balfour, 9 August 1901, ACLC, Vol. 84.

10. See numerous letters and articles, esp. Andrew Carnegie, *Preferential Tariffs*, pamphlet, Edinburgh, 1903; see also AC to Editor, *The* (London) *Times*, 25 July 1903, and letters to Secretary of Agriculture James Wilson, 10 July 1903; to John Hay, 17 July 1903; and to Prime Minister Arthur J. Balfour, 23 July 1903, ACLC, Vol. 97.

11. James Wilson to AC, 24 July 1903, ACLC, Vol. 97.

12. Henry Cabot Lodge to AC, undated, summer 1903, ACLC, Vol. 101.

13. The New York *World*, 11 April 1903; *The* (London) *Times*, 14 December 1903.'

14. *Public Benefactions*, 311.

15. See Melvil Dewey's letter to AC, 1 April 1903, ACLC, Vol. 95.

16. See J. Brander Matthews to AC, 17 June 1905, ACLC, Vol. 118; Statement on signers of the Simplified Spelling Board pledge card, 1 August 1905, Vol. 118.

17. AC to Theodore Roosevelt, 8 August 1906, ACLC, Vol. 132.

18. Quoted in "Andrew Carnegie's 'Spelling Reform' Crusade," *Current Literature*, Vol. 40, May 1906, 497–99.

19. AC to Whitelaw Reid, 11 October 1909, ACLC, Vol. 170.

20. AC to Matthews, 16 January 1915, Brander Matthews Special Manuscript Collection, Columbia University; see also other letters between AC and Matthews in that collection, including a manuscript by AC on "My Views about Improved Spelling," 1906–15.

21. Robert S. Woodward to AC, 18 November 1911, ACLC, Vol. 200.

22. AC to Henry Holt, copy to Robert A. Franks, 25 February 1915, ACLC, Vol. 238.

23. AC to John Ross, 16 March 1911, ACLC, Vol. 189; AC to Stead, 23 November 1908, ACLC, Vol. 158.

24. Inscription on the monument in Townhill, West Fife, Scotland.

25. Quoted in *Public Benefactions*, 110.

26. Finley Peter Dunne, *Mr. Dooley on Mr. Carnegie's Hero Fund*, New York, 1904.

27. AC to John Morley, 29 December 1907, ACLC, Vol. 146.

28. Ibid.

29. AC to Henry White, 2 December 1908, ACLC, Vol. 159.

30. Numerous letters and documents in ACLC from Carnegie to American ambassadors, heads of state of other nations, etc., establishing these Hero Funds. Also summarized in *Public Benefactions*, 124.

31. AC to Ross, undated, sometime in September 1908, ACLC, Vol. 157.

32. AC to Henry White, 19 March 1909, ACLC, Vol. 164.

33. See letter from Mead, Dutton, Holt, et al. to AC, 21 December 1908, Columbiana Collection of Papers of N. M. Butler, Columbia University.

34. AC to Mead, Dutton, et al., 11 January 1909, quoted in N. M. Butler's letter to AC, 6 April 1909, ACLC, Vol. 165.

35. James T. Shotwell, interviewed by both Allan Nevins and Dean Albertson, June 1949, Oral History Project, Columbia University.

36. AC to the Trustees of the Carnegie Fund for Peace, 25 November 1910, ACLC, Vol. 182.

37. *The* (London) *Times,* 15 December 1910.

38. AC to R.A. Franks, 7 December 1910, Robert A. Franks Papers, Home Trust, Hoboken, N. J.

39. Nicholas Murray Butler, "The Carnegie Endowment for International Peace," *Independent,* Vol. 76, 27 November 1913, 396–400.

40. Baron d'Estournelles de Constant to AC, cablegram, 15 December 1910, ACLC, Vol. 184.

41. Paul S. Reinsch, "The Carnegie Peace Fund," *The North American Review,* Vol. 193, February 1911, 180–92.

42. Morley to AC, 15 December 1910, ACLC, Vol. 184.

43. John Bigelow to J. G. Schmidlapp, 22 December 1910, copy in ACLC, Vol. 185.

44. Sir Norman Angell, interviewed by Wendell H. Link, May 1951, Oral History Project, Columbia University.

45. Butler, op. cit. 399–400.

46. Letter dated 10 February 1914, in Lester, *Forty Years of Carnegie Giving,* 177–78.

47. AC to Morley, 25 January 1914, ACLC, Vol. 220.

48. Minutes of the first meeting of the Church Peace Union, 10 February 1914, ACLC. Vol. 221.

49. Frederick Lynch to AC, 9 June 1914, ACLC, Vol. 224.

50. See Frederick W. Holls's letter to AC, 17 November 1899, ACLC, Vol. 70.

51. Andrew D. White to AC, 18 June 1900, ACLC, Vol. 75.

52. AC to Holls, 4 April 1902, Andrew Carnegie Collection, Houghton Library, Harvard University (hereafter cited as ACHL).

53. AC to Holls, 7 August 1902, ACHL.

54. Andrew D. White to Holls, 11 December 1902, copy in Holls's letter to AC, 23 December 1902, ACHL.

55. AC to Andrew D. White, 10 August 1902, ACLC, Vol. 90.

56. Holls to Robert S. McCormick, 21 January 1903, Letters and Papers of Frederick W. Holls, Vol. III, No. 2, in possession of Columbia University. Quoted by permission of the Librarian, Columbia University.

57. See Holls's letters to Baron de Gevers, 24 January, 24 March, 15 April, and 4 May 1903, Letters and Papers of Frederick W. Holls, Vol. I, Nos. 129–33, loc. cit.; AC to Holls, 22 April 1903, ACHL.

58. Copy of the deed in the Bibliotheque du Palais de la Paix, Paris, S.I., 1903.

59. Holls to Baron de Bildt, 15 April 1903, Letters and Papers of Frederick W. Holls, Vol. I, No. 35, Columbia University. Quoted by permission of the Librarian, Columbia University.

60. Andrew D. White to AC, 30 April 1903, ACLC, Vol. 96.

1107

61. *The* (London) *Times,* 20 May 1905.

62. AC to David J. Hill, 18 June 1906, ACLC, Vol. 130.

63. AC to Hill, 20 June 1906, ACLC, Vol. 130.

64. AC to Hill, 10 July 1906, ACLC, Vol. 131.

65. Samuel Harden Church to AC, 18 July 1906, ACLC, Vol. 131.

66. See Hill to AC, 2 August 1906, and AC to Hill, 13 August 1906, ACLC, Vol. 132.

67. AC to Van Karnebeck, 23 August, 27 August, 1906, ACLC, Vol. 132; AC to Van Karnebeck, 29 September 1906, ACLC, Vol. 133.

68. *The* (London) *Times,* 29 August 1913.

69. *The* (London) *Times,* 30 August 1913.

70. Letters of Elihu Root to AC, 4 December 1906 and of AC to Root, 1 January 1907, printed in *Public Benefactions,* 285–87.

71. Several letters in ACLC on the plans for the Pan American Union Building. See also the article by John Barnett, Director General of the Pan American Union, "Mr. Carnegie's Interest in the Pan American Union," *Bulletin of the Pan American Union,* Vol. 49, September 1919, 257–61; Andrew Carnegie, "Speech of Mr. Carnegie," *Bulletin of the International Bureau of the American Republics,* Vol. 26, Part II, May 1908, xxii–xxiv; *The* (London) *Times,* 12 May 1908.

72. AC to Root, 9 June 1908, ACLC. Vol. 154.

73. AC to Joseph H. Choate, 4 July 1907, ACLC, Vol. 143.

74. Choate, to AC, 20 August 1907, ACLC, Vol. 143.

75. AC to Hill, 21 June 1909, ACLC, Vol. 167.

76. AC to Morley, undated, probably June 1909, ACLC, Vol. 167.

77. TR to Reid, 10 January 1907, in *The Letters of Theodore Roosevelt,* edited by Elting E. Morison, Vol. 5, 543, Cambridge, 1952 (hereafter cited as Morison, Letters of TR).

92. AC to TR, 5 February 1905, ACLC, Vol. 111.

93. TR to AC, 6 February 1905, ACLC, Vol. 111.

94. TR to AC, 19 May 1906, ACLC, Vol. 129. Carnegie wrote a marginal note to Morley on this letter, and sent it on to him.

95. AC to TR, 18 November 1907, ACLC, Vol. 145.

96. TR to AC, 19 November 1907, ACLC, Vol. 145.

97. AC to Morley, 28 November 1907, ACLC. Vol. 145.

98. TR to AC, 22 January 1908, ACLC, Vol. 148.

99. *The* (London) *Times,* 16 April 1907.

100. See Andrew Carnegie, "The Cry of 'Wolf,'" *Nineteenth Century and After,* Vol. 60, August 1906, 224–33; Morley to AC, 30 September 1906, ACLC, Vol. 133.

101. Charlemagne Tower to AC, 17 April 1907; AC to Tower, 20 April 1907; Tower to AC, 23 April 1907, ACLC, Vol. 141.

102. AC to Morley, n.d., probably early June 1907; Morley to AC, 14 June 1907, ACLC, Vol. 142.

103. AC to James Donaldson, 3 July 1907, ACLC, Vol. 143.

104. Root to AC, 3 April 1909, ACLC, Vol. 165.

105. Andrew Carnegie, "Kaiser Wilhelm II, Peace Maker," *The New York Times Sunday Magazine,* 8 June 1913.

106. AC to George Lauder, 26 September 1901, ACLC, Vol. 78; AC to Morley, n.d., but probably September 1901, ACLC, Vol. 84.

107. Note on the back of a letter from TR to AC, 13 June 1902, ACLC, Vol. 89.

108. TR to Reid, 13 November 1905, Whitelaw Reid Papers, Vol. 105, No. 11, 157, Library of Congress.

109. TR to AC, 6 August 1906, ACLC, Vol. 132.

110. AC to Sydney Buxton, Inveran, Sutherland, 17 June 1908, ACLC, Vol. 154.

111. AC to TR, 6 October 1909, ACLC, Vol. 170.

112. TR to AC, 1 June 1909, ACLC, Vol. 166; AC to Charles Walcott, 25 June 1909, ACLC, Vol. 167.

113. AC to Robert A. Franks, 14 September 1909, ACLC, Vol. 169.

114. AC to TR, 26 June 1909, ACLC, Vol. 167.

115. Ibid.

116. AC to TR, 3 January 1910, ACLC, Vol. 173.

117. Root to AC, 11 February 1910, ACLC, Vol. 174.

118. AC to Morley, 22 October 1909, ACLC, Vol. 170.

119. AC to TR, 24 November 1909, ACLC, Vol. 171; 6 October 1909, ACLC, Vol. 170; 26 June 1909, ACLC, Vol. 167.

120. TR, on safari, to AC, 22 November 1909, ACLC, Vol. 171; AC to TR, 11 January 1910, ACLC, Vol. 173. Either Carnegie was confused in one of his two letters as to which Scottish university was offering Roosevelt a degree, or he had arranged for both to so honor the former President.

121. TR to AC, 16 October 1909, ACLC, Vol. 170.

122. AC to TR, 24 December 1909, ACLC, Vol. 172.

123. AC to Morley, 17 January 1910, ACLC, Vol. 173.

124. TR, from Gondokoro, to AC, 18 February 1910, ACLC. Vol. 174.

125. AC to Hill, 25 March 1910, ACLC, Vol. 175.

126. AC to Reid, 10 May 1910, ACLC, Vol. 176.

127. AC to Hill, 11 May 1910, ACLC, Vol. 176.

128. Morley to AC, 12 May 1910, ACLC, Vol. 176.

129. See the lengthy letter from TR to the British historian, George Otto Trevelyan, 1 October 1911, giving the full details of his trip, Morison, *Letters of TR*, Vol. 7, 348–99, esp. 390–99.

130. TR, from Paris, to AC, 22 April 1910, ACLC, Vol. 176.

131. For a lively account of Roosevelt's activities at the funeral, see Henry F. Pringle, *Theodore Roosevelt*, New York, 1931, 520–24.

132. AC to Reid, 14 May 1910, ACLC, Vol. 175.

133. TR, on board S.S. *Dampfers*, to AC, 14 June 1910, ACLC, Vol. 177.

CHAPTER XXIV

1. John Morley to AC, 15 January 1909, ACLC, Vol. 161.

2. Quoted in Hendrick, *Life*, II, 154.

3. See the delightful reminiscences of Angus Macpherson, *A Highlander Looks Back,* Oban, Scotland, 1956. Mr. Macpherson was the Skibo piper from 1898 to 1905 and later, as manager of the Inveran Hotel, on the banks of the river Shin, was a tenant of the Carnegies.

4. AC to John Ross, 18 May 1906, ACLC, Vol. 129.

5. The catalogue of books in the library at Skibo Castle consists of 747 pages, with an average of eleven tiles to a page. There are, interestingly enough, 177 books on Scotland, only 23 on the United States. There are very few books on

science, and most of those are on astronomy. There is virtually nothing on steel or metallurgy.

6. AC to Hew Morrison, 18 December 1900, ACLC. Vol. 80.

7. AC to Hew Morrison, 11 March 1902, ACLC, Vol. 88.

8. See Louise Carnegie's letter to Oscar Straus, 28 April 1913, Oscar S. Straus Papers, Box 13, Library of Congress.

9. AC to Morley, 13 October 1907, ACLC, Vol. 145.

10. Morley to Andrew and Louise Carnegie, 29 December 1908, ACLC, Vol. 160.

11. AC to Morley, 5 August 1908, ACLC, Vol. 155.

12. Morley to AC, 8 August 1908, ACLC, 155.

13. There are a few letters from Louise Carnegie to John Ross that indicate how tired and emotionally exhausted she occasionally became. See, for example, her letter of 6 August 1903 to Ross, Andrew Carnegie Papers, Ross-Connell Law Office, Dunfermline.

14. AC to James Donaldson, 20 March 1904, ACLC, Vol. 104.

15. AC to Morley, 29 June 1904, ACLC, Vol. 105.

16. See AC's letter to Whitelaw Reid, 15 July 1910, ACLC, Vol. 178.

17. AC to Morley, 21 November 1905, ACLC, Vol. 122.

18. AC to Morley, 14 January 1906, ACLC, Vol. 124.

19. AC to George Lauder, 20 April 1908, ACLC, Vol. 152.

20. AC to Morley, undated, March 1909, ACLC, Vol. 164.

21. AC to R. W. Gilder, 2 August 1906, ACLC, Vol. 132.

22. Morley to AC, 30 August 1904; and AC to Morley, 3 September 1904, ACLC, Vol. 106.

23. Morley to AC, 6 September 1904, ACLC, Vol. 106.

24. Morley to AC, 6 November 1904, ACLC, Vol. 108.

25. R. W. Gilder to Miss M. H. Lansdale, 25 November 1904, Letters of Richard Watson Gilder, Box 365, Gilder Papers, copy in ACLC, Vol. 109. For another account of the dinner by one of the guests, see John Bigelow, Diary, 6 November 1903 through 30 April 1905, entry dated 24 November 1904, Manuscript Division, NYPL.

26. AC to Morley, 6 December 1904, ACLC, Vol. 109.

27. Morley to AC, 6 February 1905, ACLC, Vol. 111.

28. AC to Lauder, 24 January 1905, ACLC, Vol. 111.

29. AC to Lauder, 1 March 1902, ACLC, Vol. 87.

30. AC to Lauder, 14 February 1907, ACLC, Vol. 139.

31. AC to Editor of *New York Commercial*, 20 December 1901, ACLC, Vol. 86.

32. AC to Moses H. Clapp, 29 March 1906, Moses H. Clapp Papers, Minnesota Historical Society Library; see also AC to TR, 18 March 1906, and TR to AC, 28 March 1906, ACLC, Vol. 126.

33. AC to TR, 12 March 1907, ACLC, Vol. 140.

34. AC to TR, 7 April 1907, ACLC, Vol. 141.

35. Quoted in Sir Charles W. Macara, *Recollections*, London, 1921, 262.

36. Andrew Carnegie, *The Conservation of Ores and Related Minerals*, Washington, D.C., G.P.O., 1908. See also TR's letter to AC, 4 March 1908, inviting him to participate in the Conference on the Conservation of Natural Resources, ACLC, Vol. 149.

37. Andrew Carnegie, "The Worst Banking System in the World," *The Outlook*, Vol. 88, 29 February 1908, 487–88.

38. AC to TR, 28 February 1908, ACLC, Vol. 149.

39. Andrew Carnegie, "The Worst Banking System in the World," loc. cit., 487.

40. AC to Charles F. Rideal, 1 April 1908, ACLC, Vol. 151.

41. AC to C. N. Fowler, 25 February 1908, ACLC, Vol. 149.

42. Andrew Carnegie, "The Worst Banking System in the World," loc. cit. 489.

43. Nicholas Murray Butler to AC, 28 February 1908, Columbiana Collection of Papers of N. M. Butler, Columbia University.

44. See letter to AC from Robert E. Ely, president of the Economic Club of New York, 28 March 1908, ACLC, Vol. 150.

45. R. U. Johnson to TR, 25 August 1908, copy in ACLC, Vol. 155.

46. William Howard Taft to R. U. Johnson, 27 August 1908, Taft Papers, Letter press 19, Vol. 23, Library of Congress.

47. Andrew Carnegie, "My Experience With, and Views Upon, the Tariff," *The Century Magazine*, Vol. 77, December 1908, 197.

48. Ibid. 204.

49. New York *Tribune*, 23 November 1908.

50. *The* (London) *Times*, 25 November 1908.

51. Both men quoted in *The* (London) *Times*, 27 November 1908.

52. New York *World*, 24 November 1908.

53. AC to Seth Low, 22 September 1908, ACLC, Vol. 156.

54. AC to Representative Sereno Payne, 17 December 1908, ACLC, Vol. 159, and Payne's telegram to AC, 18 December 1908, ACLC, Vol. 160.

55. AC to Lauder, 19 December 1908, ACLC, Vol. 160.

56. Story by the New York Correspondent to *The* (London) *Times*, quoted in issue of 22 December 1908.

57. AC to the Chairman of the Tariff Revision Committee, 21 December 1908, MS in ACLC, Vol. 160.

58. AC to Judge Elbert H. Gary, 23 December 1908, ACLC, Vol. 160.

59. Herbert Myrick to AC, 21 December 1908, ACLC, Vol. 160.

60. George P. Hampton to AC, 1 January 1908 (should be dated 1909), ACLC, Vol. 147.

61. AC to Editors of *American Industries*, 11 February 1909, ACLC, Vol. 163.

62. AC to TR, 15 December 1907, ACLC, Vol. 146.

63. AC to Morley, 28 February 1908, ACLC, Vol. 149.

64. AC to Morley, 5 April 1908, ACLC, Vol. 151.

65. See AC's letter to Seth Low, 22 September 1908, ACLC, Vol. 156.

66. AC to Morley, 5 April 1908, ACLC, Vol. 151.

67. "Review of *The Roosevelt Policy*," *Times Literary Supplement* (London), 16 July 1908, 228. The quotations in the review are taken from Carnegie's introduction to the book.

68. AC to Benjamin M. Gemmill, 13 October 1896, ACLC, Vol. 39.

69. AC to President Woodrow Wilson, 23 January 1915, ACLC, Vol. 228.

70. Edward A. Steiner to AC, 23 October 1906, and AC to Steiner, 7 November 1906, ACNYPL.

71. AC to William Archer, 15 August 1910, ACLC, Vol. 179.

72. See numerous memoranda between AC and H. B. Frissell, ACLC, Vol. 140; see also AC to Booker T. Washington, 5 January 1907, ACLC, Vol. 139, and Emmett J. Scott of Tuskegee Institute to AC, 20 May 1907, Vol. 142.

73. Andrew Carnegie, *The Negro in America*, Inverness, Scotland, 1907, 11ff.
74. Ibid. 12.
75. Ibid. 30–40.
76. Ibid. 41–42.
77. Morley to AC, 3 December 1907, ACLC, Vol. 146.
78. Quoted in *The* (London) *Times*, 17 October 1907.
79. *Glasgow Herald*, 18 October 1907.
80. Booker T. Washington to AC, 22 October 1907, ACLC, Vol. 145.
81. AC to Morley, 24 February 1909, ACLC, Vol. 163.
82. AC to Morley, 16 May 1909, ACLC, Vol. 166.
83. AC to TR, 10 April 1907, ACLC, Vol. 141.
84. Speech of President William Howard Taft before the Peace and Arbitration Society in New York, 22 March 1910, quoted by AC in his letter to Taft, 26 March 1910, ACLC, Vol. 175.
85. AC to Taft, 26 March 1910, ACLC, Vol. 175.
86. AC to TR, 27 April 1910, ACLC, Vol. 176.
87. AC to David J. Hill, 11 May 1910, ACLC, Vol. 176.
88. See AC's letter to Morley, 25 April 1909, ACLC, Vol. 166.
89. Andrew Carnegie, "Peace Versus War: The President's Solution," *The Century Magazine*, Vol. 80, June 1910, 307–10.
90. AC to Taft, 22 July 1910, ACLC, Vol. 178.
91. Taft to Philander C. Knox, 7 July 1910, William Howard Taft Papers, the President's Letter press 17, Library of Congress.
92. Taft wrote a note at the top of one letter he received from AC (25 March 1911), and sent it on to Knox: "Respectfully referred to Secretary Knox with the expectation that he will call the Princes of Humbugs into close and intimate conference on this and every other subject. W.H.T." Philander C. Knox Papers, Vol. 14, Library of Congress.
93. Knox to AC, 27 March 1911, Knox Papers, Vol. 14.
94. AC to Knox, 19 May 1911, Knox Papers, Vol. 14.
95. See letters to and from AC: AC to William Jennings Bryan, 30 March 1911, Samuel Baldwin to AC, 31 March 1911, ACLC, Vol. 190; Champ Clark to AC, 3 April 1911, Eugene Foss to AC, 5 April 1911, Bryan to AC, 13 April 1911, AC to Morley, 9 April 1911, ACLC, Vol. 191.
96. Charles D. Hilles to AC, 28 June 1911, ACLC, Vol. 195.
97. Hilles to AC, 18 May 1911, ACLC, Vol. 193.
98. AC to Morley, 29 June 1911, ACLC, Vol. 195; Morley to AC, 30 June 1911, ACLC, Vol. 195.
99. AC to Morley, 2 July 1911, ACLC, Vol. 195.
100. Theodore Roosevelt, "The Arbitration Treaty With Great Britain," *Outlook*, Vol. 98, 20 May 1911, 97–98.
101. Taft to AC, 20 May 1911, ACLC, Vol. 193.
102. TR to AC, 23 May 1911, ACLC, Vol. 193.
103. TR to Henry Cabot Lodge, 12 September 1911, TR to Arthur Hamilton Lee, 29 September 1911, and TR to Cecil Arthur Spring Rice, 22 August 1911, Morison, *Letters of TR*, Vol. 7, 343, 347, 334.
104. James Bryce to AC, 24 June 1911, ACLC, Vol. 194.
105. Edward Grey to AC, 26 June 1911, ACLC, Vol. 195.
106. James Bryce to AC, 30 June 1911, ACLC, Vol. 195.

107. AC to Knox, 7 January 1911, Knox Papers, Vol. 11, Library of Congress.

108. James Bryce to AC, 24 June 1911, ACLC, Vol. 194.

109. Taft to AC, 5 August 1911, ACLC, Vol. 196.

110. See James Bryce's letter to AC, 19 August 1911, ACLC, Vol. 197, and AC's memorandum to Taft, 15 December 1911, ACLC, Vol. 201, listing these various objections offered by Senators to the treaties.

111. Root to AC, 29 August 1911, ACLC, Vol. 197.

112. AC to James Bryce, 2 September 1911, Bryce Papers, Bodleian Library, Oxford University.

113. AC to James Bryce, 28 September 1911, Bryce Papers, Bodleian Library, Oxford University.

114. James Bryce to AC, 16 September 1911, ACLC, Vol. 197.

115. AC to James Bryce, 12 October 1911, ACLC, Vol. 198.

116. See W. H. Short's letter to AC, asking him to speak at Carnegie Hall, 20 November 1911, ACLC, Vol. 200; Francis B. Loomis to AC, 13 December 1911, ACLC, Vol. 201.

117. AC to Dr. S. A. Knopf, 27 December 1911, ACLC, Vol. 202; Henry Watterson to AC, 16 January 1912, ACLC, Vol. 203.

118. Taft to AC, 28 March 1912, ACLC, Vol. 204.

119. AC to Taft, 6 March 1912, ACLC, Vol. 204.

120. Taft to AC, 29 December 1911, ACLC, Vol. 202.

121. AC to Morley, 3 February 1912, ACLC, Vol. 203.

122. Ibid.; AC to Edward Grey, 27 January 1912, ACLC, Vol. 203.

123. AC to Morley, 12 May 1912, ACLC, Vol. 206.

124. AC to TR, 1 March 1912, ACLC, Vol. 204.

125. TR to AC, 5 March 1912, Morison, *Letters of TR*, Vol. 7, 520.

126. AC to TR, 10 March 1912, ACLC, Vol. 204.

127. TR to William D. Foulke, 1 July 1912, Morison, *Letters of TR*, Vol. 7, 568.

128. AC to Morley, 23 March 1912, ACLC, Vol. 204.

129. See Hilles's letter to AC, 1 November 1912, and AC's penciled note at the bottom, "I gave . . . in all 100,000$. Glad I was the largest contributor for Taft." ACLC, Vol. 210. Carnegie's full contribution to McKinley in 1896 is not on record. It could well have exceeded $100,000.

130. AC to James Bryce, 12 November 1912, Bryce Papers, Bodleian Library, Oxford University.

131. James Bryce to AC, 13 November 1912, ACLC, Vol. 210.

132. AC to Taft, 15 December 1912, Knox Papers, Vol. 20, Library of Congress.

133. Knox to William H. Taft, 3 March 1913, Knox Papers, Vol. 20, Library of Congress.

134. AC to Woodrow Wilson, 6 November 1912, ACLC, Vol. 210.

135. Woodrow Wilson to AC, 19 November 1912, ACLC, Vol. 210.

136. AC to Morley, 7 November 1912, ACLC, Vol. 210.

137. Morley to AC, 20 November 1912, ACLC, Vol. 210.

138. William Barnes, Chairman, Republican State Committee, to AC, 4 December 1912, and AC to Barnes, 6 December 1912, ACLC, Vol. 211.

139. Mrs. Jack Beall, quoted in New York *Herald*, 13 January 1912; Henry Watterson to AC, 16 January 1912, ACLC, Vol. 203; see also J. C. Hemphill, Editor of the Charlotte (North Carolina) *Observer*, to AC, 18 January 1912, with editorial enclosed: "It was all wonderfully well done; highly artistic . . . the way

this hard-headed Scotchman played with the Committee and proved that, after all, the genuine Scot has a very saving sense of humor." ACLC, Vol. 203. Contrast with editorial in *The New York Times*, 22 January 1912, criticizing the Stanley Committee for having "allowed Mr. Carnegie to 'get by' without answering the question where 'he got it' . . . The steel investigation is a much more serious affair than the Committee and Mr. Carnegie have made it."

140. For a full account of Carnegie's testimony see *The New York Times*, 11 and 12 January 1912, also United States Steel Corporation Investigation, 62nd Cong., 2nd sess., H.R. Report No. 1127.

141. AC to C. A. Rook, Editor of *Pittsburgh Dispatch*, 18 November 1912, ACLC, Vol. 210.

142. AC to Morley, 30 July 1912, ACLC, Vol. 208.

143. AC to James Bryce, 22 October 1913, Bryce Papers, Bodleian Library, Oxford University.

144. AC to Morley, 12 March 1913, ACLC, Vol. 214.

145. AC to Morley, 12 January 1913, ACLC, Vol. 212.

146. Quoted in Bailey, *A Diplomatic History of the American People*, 594.

147. Ibid.

148. AC to Bryan, 9 February 1914, ACLC, Vol. 221. But see also Carnegie's criticism of these treaties in his letter to Bryan, 6 February 1914, ACLC, Vol. 220.

149. AC to Robert Underwood Johnson, 6 February 1913, ACLC, Vol. 213.

150. AC to Woodrow Wilson, 11 October 1913, ACLC, Vol. 218.

151. AC to Morley, 11 October 1913, ACLC, Vol. 218.

152. AC to Morley, 18 March 1914, ACLC, Vol. 222.

153. AC to Wilson, 13 June 1914, ACLC, Vol. 224.

154. AC to Wilson, 3 November 1913, ACLC, Vol. 218.

155. AC to Wilson, 17 November 1913, ACLC, Vol. 218.

156. AC to Wilson, 21 April 1914, ACLC, Vol. 223.

157. AC to Wilson, 11 May 1914, ACLC, Vol. 223.

158. AC to Morley, 17 July 1914, ACLC, Vol. 225.

159. AC to Wilson, 23 November 1914, ACLC, Vol. 226.

160. Andrew Carnegie, "A Silver Lining to War Clouds," *The World To-Day*, Vol. 21, February 1912, 1792.

161. See AC's letter to Nicholas Murray Butler, 8 March 1913, ACLC, Vol. 214, and a copy of the memorial, undated, ACLC, Vol. 214.

162. AC to Sir Max Waechter, 9 July 1913, ACLC, Vol. 216; *The* (London) *Times*, 14 June 1913.

163. Andrew Carnegie, *Rectorial Address Delivered to Students, University of Aberdeen*, New York, 1912.

164. Baroness Berthe von Suttner to AC, 22 May 1909, ACLC, Vol. 166.

165. Butler to AC, 24 November 1910, ACLC, Vol. 182.

166. See letter to AC from Herbert H. D. Peirce, American Minister to Norway, 26 October 1911, ACLC, Vol. 199.

167. Pamphlet, *Presentation of Pan American Gold Medal to Andrew Carnegie*, London, 1911, copy, autographed by AC to Kaiser Wilhelm II, in British Museum.

168. AC to Morley, 2 July 1911, ACLC, Vol. 195.

169. The Andrew Carnegies' New Year Greetings for 1914, in a collection of the Carnegies' New Year's Greeting cards, Dunfermline, Scotland.

170. See P. H. Coats's letter to AC, 14 January 1902, and AC's note to John Ross at the bottom of this letter, ACLC, Vol. 87.

171. W. T. Stead to AC, 9 April 1910, ACLC, Vol. 175; AC to Stead, 21 April 1910, ACLC, Vol. 176.

172. AC to Ross, 11 February 1913, ACLC, Vol. 213. Italics are Carnegie's.

173. AC to Elizabeth Haldane, 21 November 1913, Haldane Papers, National Library of Scotland, Edinburgh.

174. AC to Morley, 16 July 1911, ACLC, Vol. 196.

175. AC to Morley, 3 May 1914, ACLC, Vol. 223.

176. AC to Morley, 16 July 1914, ACLC, Vol. 225; see also AC's letter to Herbert Asquith, 9 June 1914, ACLC, Vol. 224.

177. AC to Editor, *The* (London) *Times*, 28 July 1914, ACLC, Vol. 225.

178. AC to Morley, 16 July 1914, ACLC, Vol. 225.

179. *Autobiography*, 371.

180. Ibid. 371–72.

181. Ibid. v.

182. AC to J. Allen Baker, 2 August 1914, ACLC, Vol. 225.

183. Morley to AC, 4 August 1914, Vol. 225.

184. AC to Royal Bank of Scotland, telegram, 5 August 1914, ACLC, Vol. 225; see also Frederick Lynch to AC, 5 August, ACLC, Vol. 225.

185. Lynch to AC, 6 August 1914, ACLC, Vol. 225.

186. AC to "Dear Friend" [John Ross], 17 August 1914, misfiled under 17 April 1914, ACLC, Vol. 223.

187. Morley to AC, 28 August 1914, ACLC, Vol. 225.

188. See AC's letter to J. Allen Baker, 15 August 1914, ACLC, Vol. 225. In this letter, Carnegie mentions that they are sailing on the *Campania* on 26 September. They actually sailed at a somewhat earlier date on the *Mauretania*; see Wilson's letter to AC, 29 September 1914, ACLC, Vol. 225.

CHAPTER XXV

1. AC to John Ross, 18 January 1915, ACLC, Vol. 228.

2. Woodrow Wilson to AC, 29 September 1914, ACLC, Vol. 225.

3. John Morley to AC, 30 November 1914, ACLC, Vol. 227.

4. Andrew Carnegie, "A League of Peace—Not 'Preparation for War,'" *Independent*, Vol. 80, 19 October 1914, 89–90.

5. Morley to AC, 16 October 1914, ACLC, Vol. 226.

6. William Jennings Bryan to AC, 7 October 1914, ACLC, Vol. 226.

7. AC to Kaiser Wilhelm II, 16 October 1914, ACLC, Vol. 226.

8. See AC's letter to Josephus Daniels, 27 January 1915, ACLC, Vol. 228.

9. See AC's letter to Senator Benjamin Tillman, praising him, as chairman of the Senate Naval Committee, "for the wisest advice upon the Army and Navy yet given in or out of Congress," 27 January 1915, ACLC, Vol. 228.

10. TR to James Bryce, 31 March 1915, printed in Morison, *Letters of TR*, Vol. 8, 913–18.

11. AC to Editor of *Pittsburgh Dispatch*, 1 January 1915, clipping in files of the Carnegie Corporation of New York.

12. Robert Franks to J. A. Poynton, 3 August 1914, ACLC, Vol. 225.

13. Morley to AC, 13 November 1914, ACLC, Vol. 226.
14. AC to Ross, 18 January 1915, ACLC, Vol. 228.
15. AC to George Lauder, undated, filed under the year 1909, but obviously written in late 1914 or early 1915, ACLC, Vol. 162.
16. *Mr. Carnegie's Testimony Before the United States Commission on Industrial Relations,* 5 February 1915, pamphlet reprint from the New York *Herald,* 6 February 1915, 32 pp.
17. Frederic Harrison to AC, 9 October 1916, Vol. 233.
18. Morley to AC, 6 November 1914, ACLC, Vol. 226.
19. Morley to AC, 12 January 1915, ACLC, Vol. 228.
20. Ross to AC, 5 January 1915, ACLC, Vol. 228.
21. Morley to AC, 30 November 1914, ACLC, Vol. 227.
22. Louise Carnegie to Theodore Marburg, 29 July 1915, ACLC, Vol. 231.
23. Louise Carnegie to Franks, 10 August 1915, ACLC, Vol. 278.
24. Louise Carnegie to Franks, 20 January 1916, Robert Franks Papers, Home Trust, Hoboken, N. J.
25. *The New York Times,* 31 October 1916, clipping in Carnegie scrapbook, ACLC, Vol. 272.
26. Morley to AC, 31 December 1915, ACLC, Vol. 232.
27. AC to Wilson, 14 February 1917, ACLC, Vol. 234.
28. See J. Allen Baker to AC, 12 April 1917, ACLC, Vol. 235, and James Bryce to Louise Carnegie, 27 December 1917, ACLC, Vol. 236, both expressing their joy at the entry of the United States into the war; also *The* (London) *Times,* 15 May 1917.
29. AC to Wilson, 7 April 1917, ACLC, Vol. 235.
30. AC to Franks, 12 June 1917, Robert A. Franks Papers, Home Trust, Hoboken, N.J.
31. Louise Carnegie to Robert Franks, 21 June 1917, Robert A. Franks Papers, Home Trust, Hoboken, N.J.
32. AC to Bryce, 16 October 1917, Bryce Papers, Bodleian Library, Oxford University.
33. See Louise Carnegie's letter to Franks, urging him to come up for a visit, 29 September 1918, Robert A. Franks Papers, Home Trust, Hoboken, N.J.; Hendrick, *Life,* II, 382.
34. AC to Morley, 21 January 1918, ACLC, Vol. 236.
35. Morley to AC, 8 February 1918, ACLC, Vol. 237.
36. Louise Carnegie to Franks, 31 October 1918, Robert A. Franks Papers, Home Trust, Hoboken, N.J.
37. AC to Wilson, 10 November 1918, ACLC, Vol. 237.
38. Wilson to AC, 13 November 1918, ACLC, Vol. 237.
39. Morley to AC, 21 November 1918, ACLC, 238.
40. Louise Carnegie's diary, 22 April 1919, quoted in Hendrick and Henderson, *Louise Whitfield Carnegie,* 212; see also an account of the wedding in *The* (London) *Times,* 23 April 1919.
41. Louise Carnegie to Margaret Carnegie Miller, 2 May 1919, printed in Hendrick and Henderson, op. cit. 213; Robert Morrison, Carnegie's valet, as told to the author in an interview, August 1959.
42. Louise Carnegie, Diary, 4 June 1919, 5 August 1919, quoted in Hendrick and Henderson, op. cit. 215.

43. Louise Carnegie, Diary, 11 August 1919, quoted in Hendrick and Henderson, op. cit. 215.

44. Morley to Louise Carnegie, undated (August 1919), ACLC, Vol. 239.

EPILOGUE

1. New York *Sun*, quoted in Andrew Carnegie, "Pioneer in Two Fields," *Literary Digest*, Vol. 62, 30 August 1919, 42.

2. Andrew Carnegie, "Pioneer in Two Fields," loc. cit. 45.

3. New York *Herald*, 30 August 1919; *The New York Times*, 29 August 1919; *The* (London) *Times*, 29 August 1919.

4. For full text of Andrew Carnegie's will, see *The New York Times*, 29 August 1919.

5. Ibid.

6. Quoted in Andrew Carnegie, "Pioneer in Two Fields," loc. cit.; see also pamphlet, untitled and undated, printed by the National City Bank of New York.

7. See A. C. Murray of Eli Bank, 13 July 1910, ACLC, Vol. 178.

8. Quoted in H. C. F. Bell, *Woodrow Wilson and the People*, Garden City, N.Y.; 1945, 378–79.

9. Quoted in Burton J. Hendrick and Daniel Henderson, *Louise Whitfield Carnegie*, N.Y., 1950, pp. 264–65.

10. Ibid. 288.

11. If a personal note is permitted, I first became interested in the Carnegies when, as a young ensign in the United States Navy, stationed in New York, I was invited to a Christmas party at the Carnegie home in December 1942, along with two hundred other Navy men. There I met Louise Carnegie, sang Christmas carols, and under the rather forbidding stares of ten footmen, ate copiously of the canapés—it being the night before payday and I had the total assets of fifteen cents in my pocket.

12. *Carnegie Quarterly*, Vol. 17, No. 2, Spring 1969, 8.

Index

1119

1120

1130

1134

1136